Fifth Edition

D0479355

Complete Solutions Guide

Chemical Principles

Steven S. Zumdahl

Thomas J. Hummel
Steven S. Zumdahl

University of Illinois at Urbana-Champaign

HOUGHTON MIFFLIN COMPANY   **Boston   New York**

Vice President and Publisher: Charles Hartford
Executive Editor: Richard Stratton
Development Editor: Rebecca Berardy
Editorial Associate: Rosemary Mack
Senior Project Editor: Cathy Labresh Brooks
Senior Production/Design Coordinator: Jill Haber
Senior Manufacturing Coordinator: Marie Barnes
Senior Marketing Manager: Katherine Greig
Marketing Associate: Alexandra Shaw

Cover Image: Karl E. Deckart/Molecular Expressions

Copyright © 2005 by Houghton Mifflin Company. All rights reserved.

No part of this work may be reproduced or transmitted in any form or by any means,
electronic or mechanical, including photocopying and recording, or by any information
storage or retrieval system without the prior written permission of Houghton Mifflin
Company unless such copying is expressly permitted by federal copyright law. Address
inquiries to College Permissions, Houghton Mifflin Company, 222 Berkeley Street,
Boston, MA   02116.

Printed in the U.S.A.

ISBN: 0-618-37209-1

456789-CRS-08 07 06 05

TABLE OF CONTENTS

Page

TO THE STUDENT: HOW TO USE THIS GUIDE

Solutions to all of the end of chapter exercises are in this manual. This "Solutions Guide" can be very valuable if you use it properly. The way <u>NOT</u> to use it is to look at an exercise in the book and then immediately check the solution, often saying to yourself, "That's easy, I can do it." Developing problem solving skills takes practice. Don't look up a solution to a problem until you have tried to work it on your own. If you are completely stuck, see if you can find a similar problem in the Sample Exercises in the chapter. Only look up the solution as a last resort. If you do this for a problem, look for a similar problem in the end of chapter exercises and try working it. The more problems you do, the easier chemistry becomes. It is also in your self interest to try to work as many problems as possible. Most exams that you will take in chemistry will involve a lot of problem solving. If you have worked several problems similar to the ones on an exam, you will do much better than if the exam is the first time you try to solve a particular type of problem. No matter how much you read and study the text, or how well you think you understand the material, you don't really understand it until you have taken the information in the text and applied the principles to problem solving. You will make mistakes, but the good students learn from their mistakes.

In this manual we have worked problems as in the textbook. We have shown intermediate answers to the correct number of significant figures and used the rounded answer in later calculations. Thus, some of your answers may differ slightly from ours. When we have not followed this convention, we have usually noted this in the solution. The most common exception is when working with the natural logarithm (ln) function, where we usually carried extra significant figures in order to reduce round-off error. In addition, we tried to use constants and conversion factors reported to at least one more significant figure as compared to numbers given in the problem. For some problems, this required the use of more precise atomic masses for H, C, N and O as given in Chapter 3. This practice of carrying one extra significant figure in constants helps minimize round-off error.

We are grateful to Claire Szoke for her outstanding effort in preparing the manuscript of this manual. We also thank Linda C. Bush and Jon Booze for their careful and thorough accuracy review of the Solutions Guide. We also are grateful to Don DeCoste for his assistance in creating solutions to some of the problems in this Solutions Guide.

TJH
SSZ

CHAPTER TWO

ATOMS, MOLECULES, AND IONS

Development of the Atomic Theory

18. $\dfrac{1.188}{1.188} = 1.000$; $\dfrac{2.375}{1.188} = 1.999$; $\dfrac{3.563}{1.188} = 2.999$

The masses of fluorine are simple ratios of whole numbers to each other, 1:2:3.

19. From Avogadro's hypothesis, volume ratios are equal to molecule ratios at constant temperature and pressure. Therefore, we can write a balanced equation using the volume data, $Cl_2 + 3 F_2 \rightarrow 2 X$. Two molecules of X contain 6 atoms of F and two atoms of Cl. The formula of X is ClF_3 for a balanced reaction.

20. a. The composition of a substance depends on the numbers of atoms of each element making up the compound (i.e., depends on the formula of the compound) and not on the composition of the mixture from which it was formed.

    b. Avogadro's hypothesis implies that volume ratios are equal to molecule ratios at constant temperature and pressure. $H_2 + Cl_2 \rightarrow 2 HCl$. From the balanced equation, the volume of HCl produced will be twice the volume of H_2 (or Cl_2) reacted.

21. To get the atomic mass of H to be 1.00, we divide the mass that reacts with 1.00 g of oxygen by 0.126, i.e., $\dfrac{0.126}{0.126} = 1.00$. To get Na, Mg, and O on the same scale, we do the same division.

Na: $\dfrac{2.875}{0.126} = 22.8$; Mg: $\dfrac{1.500}{0.126} = 11.9$; O: $\dfrac{1.00}{0.126} = 7.94$

	H	O	Na	Mg
Relative Value	1.00	7.94	22.8	11.9
Accepted Value	1.0079	15.999	22.99	24.31

The atomic masses of O and Mg are incorrect. The atomic masses of H and Na are close. Something must be wrong about the assumed formulas of the compounds. It turns out the correct formulas are H_2O, Na_2O, and MgO. The smaller discrepancies result from the error in the assumed atomic mass of H.

The Nature of the Atom

22.   Deflection of cathode rays by magnetic and electric fields led to the conclusion that they were negatively charged. The cathode ray was produced at the negative electrode and repelled by the negative pole of the applied electric field.

23.   β particles are electrons. A cathode ray is a stream of electrons (β particles).

24.   Density of hydrogen nucleus (contains one proton only):

$$V_{nucleus} = \frac{4}{3} \pi r^3 = \frac{4}{3} (3.14) (5 \times 10^{-14} \text{ cm})^3 = 5 \times 10^{-40} \text{ cm}^3$$

$$d = \text{density} = \frac{1.67 \times 10^{-24} \text{ g}}{5 \times 10^{-40} \text{ cm}^3} = 3 \times 10^{15} \text{ g/cm}^3$$

Density of H-atom (contains one proton and one electron):

$$V_{atom} = \frac{4}{3} (3.14) (1 \times 10^{-8} \text{ cm})^3 = 4 \times 10^{-24} \text{ cm}^3$$

$$d = \frac{1.67 \times 10^{-24} + 9 \times 10^{-28} \text{ g}}{4 \times 10^{-24} \text{ cm}^3} = 0.4 \text{ g/cm}^3$$

Since electrons move about the nucleus at an average distance of about 1×10^{-8} cm, then the diameter of an atom is about 2×10^{-8} cm. Let's set up a ratio:

$$\frac{\text{diameter of nucleus}}{\text{diameter of atom}} = \frac{1 \text{ mm}}{\text{diameter of model}} = \frac{1 \times 10^{-13} \text{ cm}}{2 \times 10^{-8} \text{ cm}}, \text{ Solving:}$$

diameter of model = 2×10^5 mm = 200 m

25.   First, divide all charges by the smallest quantity, 6.40×10^{-13}.

$$\frac{2.56 \times 10^{-12}}{6.40 \times 10^{-13}} = 4.00; \quad \frac{7.68}{0.640} = 12.00; \quad \frac{3.84}{0.640} = 6.00$$

Since all charges are whole number multiples of 6.40×10^{-13} zirkombs then the charge on one electron could be 6.40×10^{-13} zirkombs. However, 6.40×10^{-13} zirkombs could be the charge of two electrons (or three electrons, etc.). All one can conclude is that the charge of an electron is 6.40×10^{-13} zirkombs or an integer fraction of 6.40×10^{-13}.

26.   J. J. Thomson discovered the electrons. Henri Becquerel discovered radioactivity. Lord Rutherford proposed the nuclear model of the atom. Dalton's original model proposed that atoms were indivisible particles (that is, atoms had no internal structure). Thomson and Becquerel discovered subatomic particles and Rutherford's model attempted to describe the internal structure of the atom composed of these subatomic particles. In addition, the existence of isotopes, atoms of the same element but with different mass, had to be included in the model.

27. The proton and neutron have similar mass with the mass of the neutron slightly larger than that of the proton. Each of these particles has a mass approximately 1800 times greater than that of an electron. The combination of the protons and the neutrons in the nucleus makes up the bulk of the mass of an atom, but the electrons make the greatest contribution to the chemical properties of the atom.

28. If the plum pudding model were correct (a diffuse positive charge with electrons scattered throughout), then alpha particles should have traveled through the thin foil with very minor deflections in their path. This was not the case as a few of the alpha particles were deflected at very large angles. Rutherford reasoned that the large deflections of these alpha particles could be caused only by a center of concentrated positive charge that contains most of the atom's mass (the nuclear model of the atom).

Elements and the Periodic Table

29. The atomic number of an element is equal to the number of protons in the nucleus of an atom of that element. The mass number is the sum of the number of protons plus neutrons in the nucleus. The atomic mass is the actual mass of a particular isotope (including electrons). As we will see in chapter three, the average mass of an atom is taken from a measurement made on a large number of atoms. The average atomic mass value is listed in the periodic table.

30. promethium (Pm) and technetium (Tc)

31. a. Eight; Li to Ne   b. Eight; Na to Ar

     c. Eighteen; K to Kr   d. Four; Fe, Ru, Os, Hs

     e. Five; O, S, Se, Te, Po   f. Four; Ni, Pd, Pt, Uun (#110)

32. a. Element #5 is boron. $^{12}_{5}B$ b. $Z = 7$; $A = 7 + 8 = 15$; $^{15}_{7}N$

     c. $Z = 17$; $A = 17 + 18 = 35$; $^{35}_{17}Cl$ d. $A = 92 + 143 = 235$; $^{235}_{92}U$

     e. $Z = 6$; $A = 14$; $^{14}_{6}C$ f. $Z = 15$; $A = 31$; $^{31}_{15}P$

33. a. $^{24}_{12}Mg$: 12 protons, 12 neutrons, 12 electrons

     b. $^{24}_{12}Mg^{2+}$: 12 p, 12 n, 10 e   c. $^{59}_{27}Co^{2+}$: 27 p, 32 n, 25 e

     d. $^{59}_{27}Co^{3+}$: 27 p, 32 n, 24 e   e. $^{59}_{27}Co$: 27 p, 32 n, 27 e

f. $^{79}_{34}$Se: 34 p, 45 n, 34 e   g. $^{79}_{34}$Se^{2-}: 34 p, 45 n, 36 e

h. $^{63}_{28}$Ni: 28 p, 35 n, 28 e   i. $^{59}_{28}$Ni^{2+}: 28 p, 31 n, 26 e

34.

Symbol	Number of protons in nucleus	Number of neutrons in nucleus	Number of electrons	Net charge
$^{238}_{92}$U	92	146	92	0
$^{40}_{20}$Ca^{2+}	20	20	18	2+
$^{51}_{23}$V^{3+}	23	28	20	3+
$^{89}_{39}$Y	39	50	39	0
$^{79}_{35}$Br^{-}	35	44	36	1-
$^{31}_{15}$P^{3-}	15	16	18	3-

35.   Metals lose electrons to form cations in ionic compounds and nonmetals gain electrons to form anions. Group IA, IIA and IIIA metals form stable +1, +2 and +3 charged cations, respectively. Group VA, VIA and VIIA nonmetals form -3, -2 and -1 charged anions, respectively.

    a. Lose one e$^-$ to form Na$^+$.   b. Lose two e$^-$ to form Sr^{2+}.

    c. Lose two e$^-$ to form Ba^{2+}.   d. Gain one e$^-$ to form I$^-$.

    e. Lose three e$^-$ to form Al^{3+}.   f. Gain two e$^-$ to form S^{2-}.

    g. Gain three e$^-$ to form N^{3-}.   h. Lose one e$^-$ to form Cs$^+$.

    i. Gain two e$^-$ to form Se^{2-}.

36.   Carbon is a nonmetal. Silicon and germanium are called metalloids as they exhibit both metallic and nonmetallic properties. Tin and lead are metals. Thus, metallic character increases as one goes down a family in the periodic table. The metallic character decreases from left to right across the periodic table.

Nomenclature

37. a. sulfur difluoride   b. dinitrogen tetroxide
     c. iodine trichloride   d. tetraphosphorus hexoxide

38. a. sodium perchlorate   b. magnesium phosphate
     c. aluminum sulfate   d. sulfur difluoride
     e. sulfur hexafluoride   f. sodium hydrogen phosphate
     g. sodium dihydrogen phosphate   h. lithium nitride
     i. sodium hydroxide   j. magnesium hydroxide
     k. aluminum hydroxide   l. silver chromate

39. a. copper(I) iodide   b. copper(II) iodide   c. cobalt(II) iodide
     d. sodium carbonate   e. sodium hydrogen carbonate or sodium bicarbonate
     f. tetrasulfur tetranitride g. sulfur hexafluoride   h. sodium hypochlorite
     i. barium chromate   j. ammonium nitrate

40. a. acetic acid   b. ammonium nitrite   c. colbalt(III) sulfide
     d. iodine monochloride   e. lead(II) phosphate   f. potassium iodate
     g. sulfuric acid   h. strontium nitride   i. aluminum sulfite
     j. tin(IV) oxide   k. sodium chromate   l. hypochlorous acid

41. a. SO_2 b. SO_3 c. Na_2SO_3 d. $KHSO_3$
     e. Li_3N f. $Cr_2(CO_3)_3$ g. $Cr(C_2H_3O_2)_2$ h. SnF_4
     i. NH_4HSO_4: Composed of NH_4^+ and HSO_4^- ions.
     j. $(NH_4)_2HPO_4$ k. $KClO_4$ l. NaH
     m. HBrO   n. HBr

42. a. Na_2O b. Na_2O_2 c. KCN   d. $Cu(NO_3)_2$
     e. $SiCl_4$ f. PbO   g. PbO_2 h. CuCl
     i. GaAs: We would predict the stable ions to be Ga^{3+} and As^{3-}.
     j. CdSe   k. ZnS   l. Hg_2Cl_2: Mercury(I) exists as Hg_2^{2+}.
     m. HNO_2 n. P_2O_5

43. a. $Pb(C_2H_3O_2)_2$: lead(II) acetate   b. $CuSO_4$: copper(II) sulfate
     c. CaO: calcium oxide   d. $MgSO_4$: magnesium sulfate
     e. $Mg(OH)_2$: magnesium hydroxide   f. $CaSO_4$: calcium sulfate

   g. N_2O: dinitrogen monoxide or nitrous oxide (common name)

Additional Exercises

44.   There should be no difference. The chemical composition of insulin from both sources will be the same and therefore, it will have the same activity regardless of the source. As a practical note, trace contaminants in the two types of insulin may be different. These trace components may be important.

45.   a. nitric acid, HNO_3 b. perchloric acid, $HClO_4$ c. acetic acid, $HC_2H_3O_2$

        d. sulfuric acid, H_2SO_4 e. phosphoric acid, H_3PO_4

46.   a. Fe^{2+}: 26 protons (Fe is element 26.); protons - electrons = charge, 26 -2 = 24 electrons; FeO is the formula since the oxide ion has a -2 charge.

        b. Fe^{3+}: 26 protons; 23 electrons; Fe_2O_3 c. Ba^{2+}: 56 protons; 54 electrons; BaO

        d. Cs^+: 55 protons; 54 electrons; Cs_2O e. S^{2-}: 16 protons; 18 electrons; Al_2S_3

        f. P^{3-}: 15 protons; 18 electrons; AlP   g. Br^-: 35 protons; 36 electrons; $AlBr_3$

        h. N^{3-}: 7 protons; 10 electrons; AlN

47.   From the XBr_2 formula, the charge on element X is +2. Therefore, the element has 88 protons, which identifies it as radium, Ra. 230 - 88 = 142 neutrons

48.   The solid residue must have come from the flask.

49.   In the case of sulfur, SO_4^{2-} is sulfate and SO_3^{2-} is sulfite. By analogy:

       SeO_4^{2-}: selenate; SeO_3^{2-}: selenite; TeO_4^{2-} tellurate; TeO_3^{2-}: tellurite

50.   The PO_4^{3-} ion is phosphate and PO_3^{3-} is phosphite. By analogy:

       $Mg_3(AsO_4)_2$: magnesium arsenate; H_3AsO_4: arsenic acid; Na_3SbO_4: sodium antimonate;

       Na_3AsO_3: sodium asenite; Na_2HAsO_4: sodium hydrogen arsenate

51.   If the formula is InO, then one atomic mass of In would combine with one atomic mass of O, or:

$$\frac{A}{16.00} = \frac{4.784 \text{ g In}}{1.000 \text{ g O}}, \quad A = \text{atomic mass of In} = 76.54$$

       If the formula is In_2O_3, then two times the atomic mass of In will combine with three times the atomic mass of O, or:

$$\frac{2A}{(3)16.00} = \frac{4.784 \text{ g In}}{1.000 \text{ g O}}, \quad A = \text{atomic mass of In} = 114.8$$

The latter number is the atomic mass of In used in the modern periodic table.

52. a. Ca^{2+} and N^{3-}: Ca_3N_2, calcium nitride

    b. K^+ and O^{2-}: K_2O, potassium oxide

    c. Rb^+ and F^-: RbF, rubidium fluoride

    d. Mg^{2+} and S^{2-}: MgS, magnesium sulfide

    e. Ba^{2+} and I^-: BaI_2, barium iodide

    f. Al^{3+} and Se^{2-}: Al_2Se_3, aluminum selenide

    g. Cs^+ and P^{3-}: Cs_3P, cesium phosphide

    h. In^{3+} and Br^-: $InBr_3$, indium(III) bromide; In also forms In^+ ions, but you would predict In^{3+} ions from its position in the periodic table.

53. Hydrazine: 1.44×10^{-1} g H/g N; Ammonia: 2.16×10^{-1} g H/g N

Hydrogen azide: 2.40×10^{-2} g H/g N

Let's try all of the ratios:

$$\frac{0.216}{0.144} = 1.50 = \frac{3}{2}; \quad \frac{0.144}{0.0240} = 6.00; \quad \frac{0.216}{0.0240} = 9.00$$

All the masses of hydrogen in these three compounds can be expressed as simple whole number ratios of each other. The g H/g N in hydrazine, ammonia, and hydrogen azide are in the ratios 6:9:1.

54. a. This is element 52, tellurium. Te forms stable -2 charged ions in ionic compounds (like other oxygen family members).

    b. Rubidium. Rb, element 37, forms stable +1 charged ions.

    c. Argon. Ar is element 18.

    d. Astatine. At is element 85.

55. Yes, 1.0 g H would react with 37.0 g ^{37}Cl and 1.0 g H would react with 35.0 g ^{35}Cl.

No, the mass ratio of H/Cl would always be 1 g H/37 g Cl for ^{37}Cl and 1 g H/35 g Cl for ^{35}Cl. As long as we had pure ^{35}Cl or pure ^{37}Cl, the above ratios will always hold. If we have a mixture (such as the natural abundance of chlorine), the ratio will also be constant as long as the composition of the mixture of the two isotopes does not change.

Challenge Problems

56. Because the gases are at the same temperature and pressure, the volumes are directly related to the number of moles. Let's consider hydrogen and oxygen to be monatomic gases, and that water has the simplest possible formula (HO). We have the equation:

$$H + O \rightarrow HO$$

But, the volume ratios are also the mole ratios, which correspond to coefficients in the equation:

$$2H + O \rightarrow 2HO$$

Since atoms cannot be created nor destroyed in a chemical reaction, this is not possible. To correct this, we can make oxygen a diatomic molecule:

$$2H + O_2 \rightarrow 2HO$$

This does not require hydrogen to be diatomic. Of course, if we know water has the formula H_2O, we get:

$$2H + O_2 \rightarrow 2H_2O.$$

The only was to balance this is to make hydrogen diatomic:

$$2H_2 + O_2 \rightarrow 2H_2O$$

57. a. Both compounds have C_2H_6O as the formula. Since they have the same formula, their mass percent composition will be identical. However, these are different compounds with different properties since the atoms are bonded together differently. These compounds are called isomers of each other.

   b. When wood burns, most of the solid material in wood is converted to gases, which escape. The gases produced are most likely CO_2 and H_2O.

   c. The atom is not an indivisible particle, but is instead composed of other smaller particles, e.g., electrons, neutrons, protons.

   d. The two hydride samples contain different isotopes of either hydrogen and/or lithium. Although the compounds are composed of different isotopes, their properties are similar because different isotopes of the same element have similar properties (except, of course, their mass).

58. For each experiment, divide the larger number by the smaller. In doing so, we get:

expt. 1	x = 1.0	y = 10.5
expt. 2	y = 1.4	z = 1.0
expt. 3	x = 1.0	y = 3.5

   Our assumption about formulas dictate the rest of the solution. For example, if we assume the formula of the compound in expt. 1 is XY and that of expt. 2 is YZ, we get relative masses of:

X = 2.0	Y = 21	Z = 15 (= 21/1.4)

   and a formula of X_3Y for expt. 3 (three times as much X must be present in expt. 3 as compared to expt. 1 (10.5/3.5 = 3).

However, if we assume the formula for expt. 2 is YZ and that of expt. 3 is XZ, then we get:

$$X = 2.0 \qquad Y = 7.0 \qquad Z = 5.0 \; (= 7.0/1.4)$$

and a formula of XY_3 for expt. 1.

Any answer which is consistent with your initial assumptions is correct.

The answer to part d depends on which (if any) of experiments 1 and 3 have a formula of XY in the compound. If the compound in expt. 1 has formula XY, then:

$$21 \text{g XY} \times \frac{4.2 \text{ g Y}}{(4.2 + 0.4 \text{ g}) \text{ XY}} = 19.2 \text{ g Y (and 1.8 g X)}$$

If the compound in expt. 3 has the XY formula, then:

$$21 \text{ g XY} \times \frac{7.0 \text{ g Y}}{(7.0 + 2.0) \text{ g XY}} = 16.3 \text{ g Y (and 4.7 g X)}$$

Note, it could be that neither experiment 1 or 3 have XY as the formula. Therefore, there is no way of knowing an absolute answer here.

59.   Compound I: $\dfrac{14.0 \text{ g R}}{3.00 \text{ g Q}} = \dfrac{4.67 \text{ g R}}{1.00 \text{ g Q}}$; Compound II: $\dfrac{7.00 \text{ g R}}{4.50 \text{ g Q}} = \dfrac{1.56 \text{ g R}}{1.00 \text{ g Q}}$

The ratio of the masses of R that combines with 1.00 g Q is: $\dfrac{4.67}{1.56} = 2.99 \approx 3$

As expected from the law of multiple proportions, this ratio is a small whole number.

Since compound I contains three times the mass of R per gram of Q as compared to compound II (RQ), then the formula of compound I should be R_3Q.

60.   The law of multiple proportions does not involve looking at the ratio of the mass of one element with the total mass of the compounds. We can show this supports the law of multiple proportions by comparing the mass of carbon that combines with 1.0 g of oxygen in each compound:

Compound 1:   27.2 g C and 72.8 g O   (100.0 - 27.2)
Compound 2:   42.9 g C and 57.1 g O   (100.0 - 42.9)

Reduce this ratio so that each is compared to 1.0 g oxygen

Compound 1: $\dfrac{27.2 \text{ g C}}{72.8 \text{ g O}} = 0.374 \text{ g C/g O}$

Compound 2: $\dfrac{42.9 \text{ g C}}{57.1 \text{ g O}} = 0.751 \text{ g C/g O}$

$\dfrac{0.751}{0.374} = \dfrac{2}{1}$,   thus supporting the law of multiple proportions

61.   Avogadro proposed that equal volumes of gases (at constant temperature and pressure) contain equal numbers of molecules. In terms of balanced equations, Avogadro's hypothesis implies that volume ratios will be identical to molecule ratios. Assuming one molecule of octane (C_xH_y) reacting, then 1 molecule of C_xH_y produces 8 molecules of CO_2 and 9 molecules of H_2O. $C_xH_y + n\ O_2 \rightarrow$ $8\ CO_2 + 9\ H_2O$. Since all the carbon in octane ends up as carbon in CO_2, then octane contains 8 atoms of C. Similarly, all hydrogen in octane ends up as hydrogen in H_2O, so one molecule of octane contains $9 \times 2 = 18$ atoms of H. Octane formula = C_8H_{18} and the ratio of C:H = 8:18 or 4:9.

Marathon Problem

62.   a. $\dfrac{0.602}{0.295} = 2.04$ A = 2.04   B = 1.00

         $\dfrac{0.401}{0.172} = 2.33$ B = 1.00   C = 2.33

         $\dfrac{0.374}{0.320} = 1.17$ A = 1.00   C = 1.17

To determine whole numbers, multiply through by 3 first.

         A = 6.1   B = 3.0
         B = 3.0   C = 7.0
         A = 3.0   C = 3.5 or A = 6.0 and C = 7.0

From these numbers, the relative masses would be: A = 6.0,   B = 3.0,   C = 7.0

   b.   There are many consistent solutions. One such solution is:

         $6\ A_2 + B_4 \rightarrow 4\ A_3B$
         $B_4 + 4\ C_3 \rightarrow 4\ BC_3$
         $3\ A_2 + 2\ C_3 \rightarrow 6\ AC$

In any set of reactions, the calculated mass data must match the mass data given initially in the problem. Here, the new table of relative masses would be:

         A = 6.0   B = 9.0   C = 7.0

Any set of balanced reactions that confirms the initial mass data is correct.

CHAPTER THREE

STOICHIOMETRY

Atomic Masses and the Mass Spectrometer

23.   A = atomic mass = 0.7899(23.9850 amu) + 0.1000(24.9858 amu) + 0.1101(25.9826 amu)

A = 18.95 amu + 2.499 amu + 2.861 amu = 24.31 amu

24.   Let x = % of ^{151}Eu and y = % of ^{153}Eu, then $x + y$ = 100 and y = 100 - x.

$$151.96 = \frac{x(150.9196) + (100 - x)(152.9209)}{100}$$

15196 = 150.9196 x + 15292.09 - 152.9209 x, -96 = -2.0013 x

x = 48%; 48% ^{151}Eu and 100 - 48 = 52% ^{153}Eu

25.   186.207 = 0.6260(186.956) + 0.3740(A), 186.207 - 117.0 = 0.3740(A)

$A = \dfrac{69.2}{0.3740}$ = 185 amu (A = 184.95 amu without rounding to proper significant figures.)

26.   A = 0.0140(203.973) + 0.2410(205.9745) + 0.2210(206.9759) + 0.5240(207.9766)

A = 2.86 + 49.64 + 45.74 + 109.0 = 207.2 amu; From the periodic table, the element is Pb.

27.   There are three peaks in the mass spectrum, each 2 mass units apart. This is consistent with two isotopes, differing in mass by two mass units. The peak at 157.84 corresponds to a Br_2 molecule composed of two atoms of the lighter isotope. This isotope has mass equal to 157.84/2 or 78.92. This corresponds to ^{79}Br. The second isotope is ^{81}Br with mass equal to 161.84/2 = 80.92. The peaks in the mass spectrum correspond to $^{79}Br_2$, $^{79}Br^{81}Br$ and $^{81}Br_2$ in order of increasing mass. The intensities of the highest and lowest mass tell us the two isotopes are present at about equal abundance. The actual abundance is 50.68% ^{79}Br and 49.32% ^{81}Br.

28.

Compound	Mass	Intensity	Scaled Intensity Largest Peak = 100
$H_2{}^{120}Te$	121.92	0.09	0.3
$H_2{}^{122}Te$	123.92	2.46	7.1
$H_2{}^{123}Te$	124.92	0.87	2.5
$H_2{}^{124}Te$	125.92	4.61	13.4
$H_2{}^{125}Te$	126.92	6.99	20.3
$H_2{}^{126}Te$	127.92	18.71	54.3
$H_2{}^{128}Te$	129.92	31.79	92.2
$H_2{}^{130}Te$	131.93	34.48	100.0

29.   GaAs can be either $^{69}GaAs$ or $^{71}GaAs$. The mass spectrum for GaAs will have 2 peaks at 144 (= 69 + 75) and 146 (= 71 + 75) with intensities in the ratio of 60:40 or 3:2.

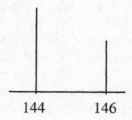

Ga_2As_2 can be $^{69}Ga_2As_2$, $^{69}Ga^{71}GaAs_2$ or $^{71}Ga_2As_2$. The mass spectrum will have 3 peaks at 288, 290, and 292 with intensities in the ratio of 36:48:16 or 9:12:4. We get this ratio from the following probability table:

	^{69}Ga (0.60)	^{71}Ga (0.40)
^{69}Ga (0.60)	0.36	0.24
^{71}Ga (0.40)	0.24	0.16

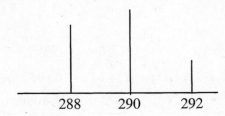

Moles and Molar Masses

30.   a. $1.27 \text{ mmol CO}_2 \times \dfrac{1 \text{ mol}}{1000 \text{ mmol}} \times \dfrac{44.01 \text{ g CO}_2}{\text{mol CO}_2} = 5.59 \times 10^{-2} \text{ g CO}_2$

  b. $2.00 \times 10^{22} \text{ molecules NCl}_3 \times \dfrac{1 \text{ mol NCl}_3}{6.022 \times 10^{23} \text{ molecules}} \times \dfrac{120.36 \text{ g}}{\text{mol NCl}_3} = 4.00 \text{ g NCl}_3$

  c. $0.00451 \text{ mol (NH}_4)_2\text{CO}_3 \times \dfrac{96.09 \text{ g (NH}_4)_2\text{CO}_3}{\text{mol (NH}_4)_2\text{CO}_3} = 0.433 \text{ g (NH}_4)_2\text{CO}_3$

  d. $1 \text{ molecule N}_2 \times \dfrac{1 \text{ mol N}_2}{6.022 \times 10^{23} \text{ molecules N}_2} \times \dfrac{28.02 \text{ g N}_2}{\text{mol N}_2} = 4.653 \times 10^{-23} \text{ g N}_2$

  e. $62.7 \text{ mol CuSO}_4 \times \dfrac{159.62 \text{ g CuSO}_4}{\text{mol CuSO}_4} = 1.00 \times 10^4 \text{ g CuSO}_4$

31.   a. $2.49 \times 10^{20} \text{ molecules CO} \times \dfrac{1 \text{ mol CO}}{6.022 \times 10^{23} \text{ molecules CO}} = 4.13 \times 10^{-4} \text{ mol CO}$

  b. $15.0 \text{ g CuSO}_4 \times \dfrac{1 \text{ mol CuSO}_4}{159.62 \text{ g CuSO}_4} = 9.40 \times 10^{-2} \text{ mol CuSO}_4$

  c. $100 \text{ molecules H}_2\text{SO}_4 \times \dfrac{1 \text{ mol H}_2\text{SO}_4}{6.022 \times 10^{23} \text{ molecules H}_2\text{SO}_4} = 1.661 \times 10^{-22} \text{ mol H}_2\text{SO}_4$

  d. $6.210 \text{ mg K}_2\text{O} \times \dfrac{1 \text{ g}}{1000 \text{ mg}} \times \dfrac{1 \text{ mol K}_2\text{O}}{94.20 \text{ g K}_2\text{O}} = 6.592 \times 10^{-5} \text{ mol K}_2\text{O}$

32.   a.   A chemical formula gives atom ratios as well as mole ratios. We will use both ideas to show how these conversion factors can be used.

Molar mass of $C_2H_5O_2N = 2(12.01) + 5(1.008) + 2(16.00) + 14.01 = 75.07$ g/mol

$$5.00 \text{ g } C_2H_5O_2N \times \frac{1 \text{ mol } C_2H_5O_2N}{75.07 \text{ g } C_2H_5O_2N} \times \frac{6.022 \times 10^{23} \text{ molecules } C_2H_5O_2N}{\text{mol } C_2H_5O_2N}$$

$$\times \frac{1 \text{ atom N}}{\text{molecule } C_2H_5O_2N} = 4.01 \times 10^{22} \text{ atoms N}$$

b.   Molar mass of $Mg_3N_2 = 3(24.31) + 2(14.01) = 100.95$ g/mol

$$5.00 \text{ g } Mg_3N_2 \times \frac{1 \text{ mol } Mg_3N_2}{100.95 \text{ g } Mg_3N_2} \times \frac{6.022 \times 10^{23} \text{ formula units } Mg_3N_2}{\text{mol } Mg_3N_2} \times \frac{2 \text{ atoms N}}{\text{mol } Mg_3N_2}$$

$$= 5.97 \times 10^{22} \text{ atoms N}$$

c.   Molar mass of $Ca(NO_3)_2 = 40.08 + 2(14.01) + 6(16.00) = 164.10$ g/mol

$$5.00 \text{ g } Ca(NO_3)_2 \times \frac{1 \text{ mol } Ca(NO_3)_2}{164.10 \text{ g } Ca(NO_3)_2} \times \frac{2 \text{ mol N}}{\text{mol } Ca(NO_3)_2} \times \frac{6.022 \times 10^{23} \text{ atoms N}}{\text{mol N}}$$

$$= 3.67 \times 10^{22} \text{ atoms N}$$

d.   Molar mass of $N_2O_4 = 2(14.01) + 4(16.00) = 92.02$ g/mol

$$5.00 \text{ g } N_2O_4 \times \frac{1 \text{ mol } N_2O_4}{92.02 \text{ g } N_2O_4} \times \frac{2 \text{ mol N}}{\text{mol } N_2O_4} \times \frac{6.022 \times 10^{23} \text{ atoms N}}{\text{mol N}} = 6.54 \times 10^{22} \text{ atoms N}$$

33. $$4.0 \text{ g } H_2 \times \frac{1 \text{ mol } H_2}{2.016 \text{ g } H_2} \times \frac{2 \text{ mol H}}{1 \text{ mol } H_2} \times \frac{6.02 \times 10^{23} \text{ atoms H}}{1 \text{ mol H}} = 2.4 \times 10^{24} \text{ atoms}$$

$$4.0 \text{ g He} \times \frac{1 \text{ mol He}}{4.003 \text{ g He}} \times \frac{6.02 \times 10^{23} \text{ atoms He}}{1 \text{ mol He}} = 6.0 \times 10^{23} \text{ atoms}$$

$$1.0 \text{ mol } F_2 \times \frac{2 \text{ mol F}}{1 \text{ mol } F_2} \times \frac{6.02 \times 10^{23} \text{ atoms F}}{1 \text{ mol F}} = 1.2 \times 10^{24} \text{ atoms}$$

$$44.0 \text{ g } CO_2 \times \frac{1 \text{ mol } CO_2}{44.01 \text{ g } CO_2} \times \frac{3 \text{ mol atom}(1 \text{ C} + 2 \text{ O})}{1 \text{ mol } CO_2} \times \frac{6.022 \times 10^{23} \text{ atoms}}{1 \text{ mol atoms}} = 1.81 \times 10^{24} \text{ atoms}$$

$$146. \text{ g } SF_6 \times \frac{1 \text{ mol } SF_6}{146.07 \text{ g } SF_6} \times \frac{7 \text{ mol atoms } (1 \text{ S} + 6 \text{ F})}{1 \text{ mol } SF_6} \times \frac{6.022 \times 10^{23} \text{ atoms}}{1 \text{ mol atoms}} = 4.21 \times 10^{24} \text{ atoms}$$

4.0 g He < 1.0 mol F_2 < 44.0 g CO_2 < 4.0 g H_2 < 146 g SF_6

34.   a. $14 \text{ mol C} \times \dfrac{12.011 \text{ g}}{\text{mol C}} + 18 \text{ mol H} \times \dfrac{1.0079 \text{ g}}{\text{mol H}} + 2 \text{ mol N} \times \dfrac{14.007 \text{ g}}{\text{mol N}}$

$+ 5 \text{ mol O} \times \dfrac{15.999 \text{ g}}{\text{mol O}} = 294.305 \text{ g/mol}$

b. $10.0 \text{ g } C_{14}H_{18}N_2O_5 \times \dfrac{1 \text{ mol } C_{14}H_{18}N_2O_5}{294.3 \text{ g } C_{14}H_{18}N_2O_5} = 3.40 \times 10^{-2} \text{ mol } C_{14}H_{18}N_2O_5$

c. $1.56 \text{ mol} \times \dfrac{294.3 \text{ g}}{\text{mol}} = 459 \text{ g } C_{14}H_{18}N_2O_5$

d. $5.0 \text{ mg} \times \dfrac{1 \text{ g}}{1000 \text{ mg}} \times \dfrac{1 \text{ mol}}{294.3 \text{ g}} \times \dfrac{6.02 \times 10^{23} \text{ molecules}}{\text{mol}} = 1.0 \times 10^{19} \text{ molecules } C_{14}H_{18}N_2O_5$

e. $1.2 \text{ g } C_{14}H_{18}N_2O_5 \times \dfrac{1 \text{ mol } C_{14}H_{18}N_2O_5}{294.3 \text{ g } C_{14}H_{18}N_2O_5} \times \dfrac{2 \text{ mol N}}{\text{mol } C_{14}H_{18}N_2O_5} \times \dfrac{6.02 \times 10^{23} \text{ atoms N}}{\text{mol N}}$

$= 4.9 \times 10^{21} \text{ atoms N}$

f. $1.0 \times 10^9 \text{ molecules} \times \dfrac{1 \text{ mol}}{6.02 \times 10^{23} \text{ molecules}} \times \dfrac{294.3 \text{ g}}{\text{mol}} = 4.9 \times 10^{-13} \text{ g or } 490 \text{ fg } C_{14}H_{18}N_2O_5$

g. $1 \text{ molecule} \times \dfrac{1 \text{ mol}}{6.022 \times 10^{23} \text{ molecules}} \times \dfrac{294.305 \text{ g}}{\text{mol}} = 4.887 \times 10^{-22} \text{ g } C_{14}H_{18}N_2O_5$

35.   a. $2(12.01) + 3(1.008) + 3(35.45) + 2(16.00) = 165.39 \text{ g/mol}$

b. $500.0 \text{ g} \times \dfrac{1 \text{ mol}}{165.39 \text{ g}} = 3.023 \text{ mol}$ c. $2.0 \times 10^{-2} \text{ mol} \times \dfrac{165.39 \text{ g}}{\text{mol}} = 3.3 \text{ g}$

d. $5.0 \text{ g } C_2H_3Cl_3O_2 \times \dfrac{1 \text{ mol}}{165.39 \text{ g}} \times \dfrac{6.02 \times 10^{23} \text{ molecules}}{\text{mol}} \times \dfrac{3 \text{ atoms Cl}}{\text{molecule}}$

$= 5.5 \times 10^{22} \text{ atoms of chlorine}$

e. $1.0 \text{ g Cl} \times \dfrac{1 \text{ mol Cl}}{35.45 \text{ g}} \times \dfrac{1 \text{ mol } C_2H_3Cl_3O_2}{3 \text{ mol Cl}} \times \dfrac{165.39 \text{ g } C_2H_3Cl_3O_2}{\text{mol } C_2H_3Cl_3O_2} = 1.6 \text{ g chloral hydrate}$

f. $500 \text{ molecules} \times \dfrac{1 \text{ mol}}{6.022 \times 10^{23} \text{ molecules}} \times \dfrac{165.39 \text{ g}}{\text{mol}} = 1.373 \times 10^{-19} \text{ g}$

36. $1.0 \text{ lb flour} \times \dfrac{454 \text{ g flour}}{\text{lb flour}} \times \dfrac{30.0 \times 10^{-9} \text{ g } C_2H_4Br_2}{\text{g flour}} \times \dfrac{1 \text{ mol } C_2H_4Br_2}{187.9 \text{ g } C_2H_4Br_2} \times \dfrac{6.02 \times 10^{23} \text{ molecules}}{\text{mol } C_2H_4Br_2}$

$= 4.4 \times 10^{16} \text{ molecules } C_2H_4Br_2$

Percent Composition

37.   In 1 mole of $YBa_2Cu_3O_7$ there are 1 mole of Y, 2 moles of Ba, 3 moles of Cu, and 7 moles of O.

$$\text{Molar mass} = 1 \text{ mol Y} \times \frac{88.91 \text{ g Y}}{\text{mol Y}} + 2 \text{ mol Ba} \times \frac{137.3 \text{ g Ba}}{\text{mol Ba}}$$

$$+ 3 \text{ mol Cu} \times \frac{63.55 \text{ g Cu}}{\text{mol Cu}} + 7 \text{ mol O} \times \frac{16.00 \text{ g O}}{\text{mol O}}$$

Molar mass = 88.91 + 274.6 + 190.65 + 112.00 = 666.2 g/mol

$$\% \text{ Y} = \frac{88.91 \text{ g}}{666.2 \text{ g}} \times 100 = 13.35\% \text{ Y}; \quad \% \text{ Ba} = \frac{274.6 \text{ g}}{666.2 \text{ g}} \times 100 = 41.22\% \text{ Ba}$$

$$\% \text{ Cu} = \frac{190.65 \text{ g}}{666.2 \text{ g}} \times 100 = 28.62\% \text{ Cu}; \quad \% \text{ O} = \frac{112.0 \text{ g}}{666.2 \text{ g}} \times 100 = 16.81\% \text{ O}$$

or % O = 100.00 - (13.35 + 41.22 + 28.62) = 100.00 - (83.19) = 16.81% O

38.   a. $C_8H_{10}N_4O_2$: molar mass = 8(12.01) + 10(1.008) + 4(14.01) + 2(16.00) = 194.20 g/mol

$$\text{mass} \% \text{ C} = \frac{8(12.01) \text{ g C}}{194.20 \text{ g } C_8H_{10}N_4O_2} \times 100 = \frac{96.08}{194.20} \times 100 = 49.47\% \text{ C}$$

b. $C_{12}H_{22}O_{11}$: molar mass = 12(12.01) + 22(1.008) + 11(16.00) = 342.30 g/mol

$$\text{mass} \% \text{ C} = \frac{12(12.01) \text{ g C}}{342.30 \text{ g } C_{12}H_{22}O_{11}} \times 100 = 42.10\% \text{ C}$$

c. C_2H_5OH: molar mass = 2(12.01) + 6(1.008) + 1(16.00) = 46.07 g/mol

$$\text{mass} \% \text{ C} = \frac{2(12.01) \text{ g C}}{46.07 \text{ g } C_2H_5OH} \times 100 = 52.14\% \text{ C}$$

The order from lowest to highest mass percentage of carbon is: sucrose ($C_{12}H_{22}O_{11}$) < caffeine ($C_8H_{10}N_4O_2$) < ethanol (C_2H_5OH)

39.   For each compound, determine the mass of one mol of compound then calculate the mass percentage of N in one mole of that compound.

a.   NO: $\% \text{ N} = \dfrac{14.007 \text{ g N}}{30.006 \text{ g NO}} \times 100 = 46.681\% \text{ N}$

b. NO_2: $\% \text{ N} = \dfrac{14.007 \text{ g N}}{46.005 \text{ g } NO_2} \times 100 = 30.447\% \text{ N}$

c. N_2O_4: $\% \text{ N} = \dfrac{28.014 \text{ g N}}{92.010 \text{ g } N_2O_4} \times 100 = 30.447\% \text{ N}$

d. N_2O: $\% N = \dfrac{28.014 \text{ g N}}{44.013 \text{ g } N_2O} \times 100 = 63.649\% \text{ N}$

40.   Assuming 100.00 g cyanocobalamin:

mol cyanocobalamin $= 4.34 \text{ g Co} \times \dfrac{1 \text{ mol Co}}{58.93 \text{ g Co}} \times \dfrac{1 \text{ mol cyanocobalamin}}{\text{mol Co}}$

$$= 7.36 \times 10^{-2} \text{ mol cyanocobalamin}$$

$\dfrac{x \text{ g cyanocobalamin}}{1 \text{ mol cyanocobalamin}} = \dfrac{100.00 \text{ g}}{7.36 \times 10^{-2} \text{ mol}}$, $x =$ molar mass $= 1360$ g/mol

41.   There are 0.390 g Cu for every 100.00 g of fungal laccase. Assuming 100.00 g fungal laccase:

mol fungal laccase $= 0.390 \text{ g Cu} \times \dfrac{1 \text{ mol Cu}}{63.55 \text{ g Cu}} \times \dfrac{1 \text{ mol fungal laccase}}{4 \text{ mol Cu}} = 1.53 \times 10^{-3} \text{ mol}$

$\dfrac{x \text{ g fungal laccase}}{1 \text{ mol fungal laccase}} = \dfrac{100.00 \text{ g}}{1.53 \times 10^{-3} \text{ mol}}$, $x =$ molar mass $= 6.54 \times 10^{4}$ g/mol

42.   If we have 100.0 g of Portland cement, we have 50. g Ca_3SiO_5, 25 g Ca_2SiO_4, 12 g $Ca_3Al_2O_6$, 8.0 g Ca_2AlFeO_5, and 3.5 g $CaSO_4 \cdot 2H_2O$.

Mass percent Ca:

$50. \text{ g } Ca_3SiO_5 \times \dfrac{1 \text{ mol } Ca_3SiO_5}{228.33 \text{ g } Ca_3SiO_5} \times \dfrac{3 \text{ mol Ca}}{1 \text{ mol } Ca_3SiO_5} \times \dfrac{40.08 \text{ g Ca}}{1 \text{ mol Ca}} = 26 \text{ g Ca}$

$25 \text{ g } Ca_2SiO_4 \times \dfrac{80.16 \text{ g Ca}}{172.25 \text{ g } Ca_2SiO_4} = 12 \text{ g Ca}$

$12 \text{ g } Ca_3Al_2O_6 \times \dfrac{120.24 \text{ g Ca}}{270.20 \text{ g } Ca_3Al_2O_6} = 5.3 \text{ g Ca}$

$8.0 \text{ g } Ca_2AlFeO_5 \times \dfrac{80.16 \text{ g Ca}}{242.99 \text{ g } Ca_2AlFeO_5} = 2.6 \text{ g Ca}$

$3.5 \text{ g } CaSO_4 \cdot 2H_2O \times \dfrac{40.08 \text{ g Ca}}{172.18 \text{ g } CaSO_4 \cdot 2H_2O} = 0.81 \text{ g Ca}$

Mass of Ca $= 26 + 12 + 5.3 + 2.6 + 0.81 = 47$ g Ca

$\% \text{ Ca} = \dfrac{47 \text{ g Ca}}{100.0 \text{ g cement}} \times 100 = 47\% \text{ Ca}$

Mass percent Al:

$$12 \text{ g Ca}_3\text{Al}_2\text{O}_6 \times \frac{53.96 \text{ g Al}}{270.20 \text{ g Ca}_3\text{Al}_2\text{O}_6} = 2.4 \text{ g Al}$$

$$8.0 \text{ g Ca}_2\text{AlFeO}_5 \times \frac{26.98 \text{ g Al}}{242.99 \text{ g Ca}_2\text{AlFeO}_5} = 0.89 \text{ g Al}$$

$$\% \text{ Al} = \frac{2.4 \text{ g} + 0.89 \text{ g}}{100.0 \text{ g}} \times 100 = 3.3\% \text{ Al}$$

Mass percent Fe:

$$8.0 \text{ g Ca}_2\text{AlFeO}_5 \times \frac{55.85 \text{ g Fe}}{242.99 \text{ g Ca}_2\text{AlFeO}_5} = 1.8 \text{ g Fe}; \quad \% \text{ Fe} = \frac{1.8 \text{ g}}{100.0 \text{ g}} \times 100 = 1.8\% \text{ Fe}$$

Empirical and Molecular Formulas

43.   a.   Molar mass of $CH_2O = 1 \text{ mol C} \left(\frac{12.011 \text{ g}}{\text{mol C}} \right) + 2 \text{ mol H} \left(\frac{1.0079 \text{ g H}}{\text{mol H}} \right)$

$$+ 1 \text{ mol O} \left(\frac{15.999 \text{ g}}{\text{mol O}} \right) = 30.026 \text{ g/mol}$$

$$\% \text{ C} = \frac{12.011 \text{ g C}}{30.026 \text{ g CH}_2\text{O}} \times 100 = 40.002\% \text{ C}; \quad \% \text{ H} = \frac{2.0158 \text{ g H}}{30.026 \text{ g CH}_2\text{O}} \times 100 = 6.7135\% \text{ H}$$

$$\% \text{ O} = \frac{15.999 \text{ g O}}{30.026 \text{ g CH}_2\text{O}} \times 100 = 53.284\% \text{ O} \text{ or } \% \text{ O} = 100.000 - (40.002 + 6.7135)$$
$$= 53.285\%$$

   b.   Molar Mass of $C_6H_{12}O_6 = 6(12.011) + 12(1.0079) + 6(15.999) = 180.155 \text{ g/mol}$

$$\% \text{ C} = \frac{72.066 \text{ g C}}{180.155 \text{ g C}_6\text{H}_{12}\text{O}_6} \times 100 = 40.002\%; \quad \% \text{ H} = \frac{12(1.0079) \text{ g}}{180.155 \text{ g}} \times 100 = 6.7136\%$$

$$\% \text{ O} = 100.00 - (40.002 + 6.7136) = 53.284\%$$

   c.   Molar mass of $HC_2H_3O_2 = 2(12.011) + 4(1.0079) + 2(15.999) = 60.052 \text{ g/mol}$

$$\% \text{ C} = \frac{24.022 \text{ g}}{60.052 \text{ g}} \times 100 = 40.002\%; \quad \% \text{ H} = \frac{4.0316 \text{ g}}{60.052 \text{ g}} \times 100 = 6.7135\%$$

$$\% \text{ O} = 100.00 - (40.002 + 6.7135) = 53.285\%$$

All three compounds have the same empirical formula, CH_2O, and different molecular formulas. The composition of all three in mass percent is also the same (within rounding differences). Therefore, elemental analysis will give us only the empirical formula.

44.   a.   The molecular formula is N_2O_4.   The smallest whole number ratio of the atoms (the empirical formula) is NO_2.

       b.   Molecular formula: C_3H_6; empirical formula = CH_2

       c.   Molecular formula: P_4O_{10}; empirical formula = P_2O_5

       d.   Molecular formula: $C_6H_{12}O_6$; empirical formula = CH_2O

45.   Compound I: mass O = 0.6498 g Hg_xO_y - 0.6018 g Hg = 0.0480 g O

       $$0.6018 \text{ g Hg} \times \frac{1 \text{ mol Hg}}{200.6 \text{ g Hg}} = 3.000 \times 10^{-3} \text{ mol Hg}$$

       $$0.0480 \text{ g O} \times \frac{1 \text{ mol O}}{16.00 \text{ g O}} = 3.00 \times 10^{-3} \text{ mol O}$$

       The mol ratio between Hg and O is 1:1, so the empirical formula of compound I is HgO.

       Compound II: mass Hg = 0.4172 g Hg_xO_y - 0.016 g O = 0.401 g Hg

       $$0.401 \text{ g Hg} \times \frac{1 \text{ mol Hg}}{200.6 \text{ g Hg}} = 2.00 \times 10^{-3} \text{ mol Hg}; \quad 0.016 \text{ g O} \times \frac{1 \text{ mol O}}{16.00 \text{ g O}} = 1.0 \times 10^{-3} \text{ mol O}$$

       The mol ratio between Hg and O is 2:1, so the empirical formula is Hg_2O.

46.   Out of 100.00 g of adrenaline, there are:

       $$56.79 \text{ g C} \times \frac{1 \text{ mol C}}{12.011 \text{ g C}} = 4.728 \text{ mol C}; \quad 6.56 \text{ g H} \times \frac{1 \text{ mol H}}{1.008 \text{ g H}} = 6.51 \text{ mol H}$$

       $$28.37 \text{ g O} \times \frac{1 \text{ mol O}}{15.999 \text{ g O}} = 1.773 \text{ mol O}; \quad 8.28 \text{ g N} \times \frac{1 \text{ mol N}}{14.01 \text{ g N}} = 0.591 \text{ mol N}$$

       Dividing each mol value by the smallest number:

       $$\frac{4.728}{0.591} = 8.00; \quad \frac{6.51}{0.591} = 11.0; \quad \frac{1.773}{0.591} = 3.00; \quad \frac{0.591}{0.591} = 1.00$$

       This gives adrenaline an empirical formula of $C_8H_{11}O_3N$.

47.   First, we will determine composition in mass percent. We assume all of the carbon in 0.213 g CO_2 came from 0.157 g of the compound and that all of the hydrogen in the 0.0310 g H_2O came from the 0.157 g of the compound.

       $$0.213 \text{ g CO}_2 \times \frac{12.01 \text{ g C}}{44.01 \text{ g CO}_2} = 0.0581 \text{ g C}; \quad \% C = \frac{0.0581 \text{ g C}}{0.157 \text{ g compound}} \times 100 = 37.0\% \text{ C}$$

       $$0.0310 \text{ g H}_2O \times \frac{2.016 \text{ g H}}{18.02 \text{ g H}_2O} = 3.47 \times 10^{-3} \text{ g H}; \quad \% H = \frac{3.47 \times 10^{-3} \text{ g}}{0.157 \text{ g}} = 2.21\% \text{ H}$$

We get the mass % N from the second experiment:

$$0.0230 \text{ g NH}_3 \times \frac{14.01 \text{ g N}}{17.03 \text{ g NH}_3} = 1.89 \times 10^{-2} \text{ g N}$$

$$\% \text{ N} = \frac{1.89 \times 10^{-2} \text{ g}}{0.103 \text{ g}} \times 100 = 18.3\% \text{ N}$$

The mass percent of oxygen is obtained by difference:

$$\% \text{ O} = 100.00 - (37.0 + 2.21 + 18.3) = 42.5\%$$

So out of 100.00 g of compound, there are:

$$37.0 \text{ g C} \times \frac{1 \text{ mol C}}{12.01 \text{ g C}} = 3.08 \text{ mol C}; \quad 2.21 \text{ g H} \times \frac{1 \text{ mol H}}{1.008 \text{ g H}} = 2.19 \text{ mol H}$$

$$18.3 \text{ g N} \times \frac{1 \text{ mol N}}{14.01 \text{ g N}} = 1.31 \text{ mol N}; \quad 42.5 \text{ g O} \times \frac{1 \text{ mol O}}{16.00 \text{ g O}} = 2.66 \text{ mol O}$$

Lastly, and often the hardest part, we need to find simple whole number ratios. Divide all mole values by the smallest number:

$$\frac{3.08}{1.31} = 2.35; \quad \frac{2.19}{1.31} = 1.67; \quad \frac{1.31}{1.31} = 1.00; \quad \frac{2.66}{1.31} = 2.03$$

Multiplying all these ratios by 3 gives an empirical formula of $C_7H_5N_3O_6$.

48.   Assuming 100.00 g of compound (mass oxygen = 100.00 g - 41.39 g C - 3.47 g H = 55.14 g O):

$$41.39 \text{ g C} \times \frac{1 \text{ mol C}}{12.011 \text{ g C}} = 3.446 \text{ mol C}; \quad 3.47 \text{ g H} \times \frac{1 \text{ mol H}}{1.008 \text{ g H}} = 3.44 \text{ mol H}$$

$$55.14 \text{ g O} \times \frac{1 \text{ mol O}}{15.999 \text{ g O}} = 3.446 \text{ mol O}$$

All are the same mol values so the empirical formula is CHO. The empirical formula mass is 12.01 + 1.008 + 16.00 = 29.02 g/mol.

$$\text{molar mass} = \frac{15.0 \text{ g}}{0.129 \text{ mol}} = 116 \text{ g/mol}$$

$$\frac{\text{molar mass}}{\text{empirical mass}} = \frac{116}{29.02} = 4.00; \quad \text{molecular formula} = (CHO)_4 = C_4H_4O_4$$

49.   Assuming 100.00 g of compound (mass hydrogen = 100.00 g - 49.31 g C - 43.79 g O = 6.90 g H):

$$49.31 \text{ g C} \times \frac{1 \text{ mol C}}{12.011 \text{ g C}} = 4.105 \text{ mol C}; \quad 6.90 \text{ g H} \times \frac{1 \text{ mol H}}{1.008 \text{ g H}} = 6.85 \text{ mol H}$$

$$43.79 \text{ g O} \times \frac{1 \text{ mol O}}{15.999 \text{ g O}} = 2.737 \text{ mol O}$$

Dividing all mole values by 2.737 gives:

$$\frac{4.105}{2.737} = 1.500; \quad \frac{6.85}{2.737} = 2.50; \quad \frac{2.737}{2.737} = 1.000$$

Since a whole number ratio is required, then the empirical formula is $C_3H_5O_2$.

Empirical formula mass $\approx$ 3(12.0) + 5(1.0) + 2(16.0) = 73.0 g/mol

$$\frac{molar\ mass}{empirical\ formula\ mass} = \frac{146.1}{73.0} = 2.00; \quad molecular\ formula = (C_3H_5O_2)_2 = C_6H_{10}O_4$$

50. $41.98\ mg\ CO_2 \times \dfrac{12.011\ mg\ C}{44.009\ mg\ CO_2} = 11.46\ mg\ C; \quad \%\ C = \dfrac{11.46\ mg}{19.81\ mg} \times 100 = 57.85\%\ C$

$6.45\ mg\ H_2O \times \dfrac{2.016\ mg\ H}{18.02\ mg\ H_2O} = 0.722\ mg\ H; \quad \%\ H = \dfrac{0.722\ mg}{19.81\ mg} \times 100 = 3.64\%\ H$

% O = 100.00 − (57.85 + 3.64) = 38.51% O

Out of 100.00 g terephthalic acid, there are:

$$57.85\ g\ C \times \frac{1\ mol\ C}{12.011\ g\ C} = 4.816\ mol\ C; \quad 3.64\ g\ H \times \frac{1\ mol\ H}{1.008\ g\ H} = 3.61\ mol\ H$$

$$38.51\ g\ O \times \frac{1\ mol\ O}{15.999\ g\ O} = 2.407\ mol\ O$$

$$\frac{4.816}{2.407} = 2.001; \quad \frac{3.61}{2.407} = 1.50; \quad \frac{2.407}{2.407} = 1.000$$

C:H:O mol ratio is 2:1.5:1 or 4:3:2. Empirical formula = $C_4H_3O_2$

Mass of $C_4H_3O_2 \approx$ 4(12) + 3(1) + 2(16) = 83;

Molar mass = $\dfrac{41.5\ g}{0.250\ mol}$ = 166 g/mol; $\quad \dfrac{166}{83} = 2$; Molecular formula = $C_8H_6O_4$

51.   The combustion data allows determination of the amount of hydrogen in cumene. One way to determine the amount of carbon in cumene is to determine the mass percent of hydrogen in the compound from the data in the problem, then determine the mass percent of carbon by difference (100.0 − mass % H = mass % C).

$$42.8\ mg\ H_2O \times \frac{1\ g}{1000\ mg} \times \frac{2.016\ g\ H}{18.02\ g\ H_2O} \times \frac{1000\ mg}{g} = 4.79\ mg\ H$$

$\%\ H = \dfrac{4.79\ mg\ H}{47.6\ mg\ cumene} \times 100 = 10.1\%\ H; \quad \%\ C = 100.0 - 10.1 = 89.9\%\ C$

Now solve this empirical formula problem. Out of 100.0 g cumene, we have:

$$89.9 \text{ g C} \times \frac{1 \text{ mol C}}{12.01 \text{ g C}} = 7.49 \text{ mol C}; \quad 10.1 \text{ g H} \times \frac{1 \text{ mol H}}{1.008 \text{ g H}} = 10.0 \text{ mol H}$$

$$\frac{10.0}{7.49} = 1.34 \approx \frac{4}{3}, \text{ i.e., mol H to mol C are in a 4:3 ratio. Empirical formula} = C_3H_4$$

Empirical formula mass $\approx 3(12.0) + 4(1.0) = 40.0$ g/mol

The molecular formula is $(C_3H_4)_3$ or C_9H_{12} since the molar mass will be between 115 and 125 g/mol (molar mass $\approx 3 \times 40.0$ g/mol = 120. g/mol).

52.   a.   Only acrylonitrile contains nitrogen. If we have 100.00 g of polymer:

$$8.80 \text{ g N} \times \frac{1 \text{ mol C}_3\text{H}_3\text{N}}{14.01 \text{ g N}} \times \frac{53.06 \text{ g C}_3\text{H}_3\text{N}}{1 \text{ mol C}_3\text{H}_3\text{N}} = 33.3 \text{ g C}_3\text{H}_3\text{N}$$

$$\% \text{ C}_3\text{H}_3\text{N} = \frac{33.3 \text{ g C}_3\text{H}_3\text{N}}{100.00 \text{ g polymer}} = 33.3\% \text{ C}_3\text{H}_3\text{N}$$

Only butadiene in the polymer reacts with Br_2:

$$0.605 \text{ g Br}_2 \times \frac{1 \text{ mol Br}_2}{159.8 \text{ g Br}_2} \times \frac{1 \text{ mol C}_4\text{H}_6}{\text{mol Br}_2} \times \frac{54.09 \text{ g C}_4\text{H}_6}{\text{mol C}_4\text{H}_6} = 0.205 \text{ g C}_4\text{H}_6$$

$$\% \text{ C}_4\text{H}_6 = \frac{0.205 \text{ g}}{1.20 \text{ g}} \times 100 = 17.1\% \text{ C}_4\text{H}_6$$

b.   If we have 100.0 g of polymer:

$$33.3 \text{ g C}_3\text{H}_3\text{N} \times \frac{1 \text{ mol C}_3\text{H}_3\text{N}}{53.06 \text{ g}} = 0.628 \text{ mol C}_3\text{H}_3\text{N}$$

$$17.1 \text{ g C}_4\text{H}_6 \times \frac{1 \text{ mol C}_4\text{H}_6}{54.09 \text{ g C}_4\text{H}_6} = 0.316 \text{ mol C}_4\text{H}_6$$

$$49.6 \text{ g C}_8\text{H}_8 \times \frac{1 \text{ mol C}_8\text{H}_8}{104.14 \text{ g C}_8\text{H}_8} = 0.476 \text{ mol C}_8\text{H}_8$$

Dividing by 0.316: $\dfrac{0.628}{0.316} = 1.99; \quad \dfrac{0.316}{0.316} = 1.00; \quad \dfrac{0.476}{0.316} = 1.51$

This is close to a mol ratio of 4:2:3. Thus, there are 4 acrylonitrile to 2 butadiene to 3 styrene molecules in the polymer or $(A_4B_2S_3)_n$.

Balancing Chemical Equations

53.   Unbalanced equation:

$$CaF_2 \cdot 3Ca_3(PO_4)_2(s) + H_2SO_4(aq) \rightarrow H_3PO_4(aq) + HF(aq) + CaSO_4 \cdot 2H_2O(s)$$

Balancing Ca^{2+}, F^-, and PO_4^{3-}:

$$CaF_2 \cdot 3Ca_3(PO_4)_2(s) + H_2SO_4(aq) \rightarrow 6 \; H_3PO_4(aq) + 2 \; HF(aq) + 10 \; CaSO_4 \cdot 2H_2O(s)$$

On the right hand side there are 20 extra hydrogen atoms, 10 extra sulfates, and 20 extra water molecules. We can balance the hydrogen and sulfate with 10 sulfuric acid molecules. The extra waters came from the water in the sulfuric acid solution. The balanced equation is:

$$CaF_2 \cdot 3Ca_3(PO_4)_2(s) + 10 \; H_2SO_4(aq) + 20 \; H_2O(l) \rightarrow 6 \; H_3PO_4(aq) + 2 \; HF(aq) + 10 \; CaSO_4 \cdot 2H_2O(s)$$

54.   a. $Fe + O_2 \rightarrow Fe_2O_3$; $2 \; Fe(s) + 3/2 \; O_2(g) \rightarrow Fe_2O_3(s)$

Multiply all coefficients by 2 to convert the fraction coefficient of oxygen to a whole number. The balanced equation is: $4 \; Fe(s) + 3 \; O_2(g) \rightarrow 2 \; Fe_2O_3(s)$

b. $C_6H_{12}O_6 + O_2 \rightarrow CO_2 + H_2O$

Balance C-atoms first assuming 1 mol of $C_6H_{12}O_6$, then balance the H-atoms.

$$C_6H_{12}O_6 + O_2 \rightarrow 6 \; CO_2 + 6 \; H_2O$$

Balancing the O-atoms gives the balanced equation:

$$C_6H_{12}O_6(s) + 6 \; O_2(g) \rightarrow 6 \; CO_2(g) + 6 \; H_2O(g)$$

c. $Ca(s) + 2 \; H_2O(l) \rightarrow Ca(OH)_2(aq) + H_2(g)$

d. $Ba(OH)_2(aq) + H_2SO_4(aq) \rightarrow BaSO_4(s) + 2 \; H_2O(l)$

55.   a. $16 \; Cr(s) + 3 \; S_8(s) \rightarrow 8 \; Cr_2S_3(s)$

b. $2 \; NaHCO_3(s) \rightarrow Na_2CO_3(s) + CO_2(g) + H_2O(g)$

c. $2 \; KClO_3(s) \rightarrow 2 \; KCl(s) + 3 \; O_2(g)$

d. $2 \; Eu(s) + 6 \; HF(g) \rightarrow 2 \; EuF_3(s) + 3 \; H_2(g)$

e. $2 \; C_6H_6(l) + 15 \; O_2(g) \rightarrow 12 \; CO_2(g) + 6 \; H_2O(g)$

56. $C_{12}H_{22}O_{11}(aq) + H_2O(l) \rightarrow 4 \; C_2H_5OH(aq) + 4 \; CO_2(g)$

Reaction Stoichiometry

57. $1.000 \text{ kg Al} \times \dfrac{1000 \text{ g Al}}{\text{kg Al}} \times \dfrac{1 \text{ mol Al}}{26.98 \text{ g Al}} \times \dfrac{3 \text{ mol NH}_4\text{ClO}_4}{3 \text{ mol Al}} \times \dfrac{117.49 \text{ g NH}_4\text{ClO}_4}{\text{mol NH}_4\text{ClO}_4} = 4355 \text{ g NH}_4\text{ClO}_4$

58. $1.0 \times 10^6 \text{ kg HNO}_3 \times \dfrac{1000 \text{ g HNO}_3}{\text{kg HNO}_3} \times \dfrac{1 \text{ mol HNO}_3}{63.0 \text{ g HNO}_3} = 1.6 \times 10^7 \text{ mol HNO}_3$

We need to get the relationship between moles of HNO_3 and moles of NH_3. We have to use all 3 equations:

$$\dfrac{2 \text{ mol HNO}_3}{3 \text{ mol NO}_2} \times \dfrac{2 \text{ mol NO}_2}{2 \text{ mol NO}} \times \dfrac{4 \text{ mol NO}}{4 \text{ mol NH}_3} = \dfrac{16 \text{ mol HNO}_3}{24 \text{ mol NH}_3}$$

Thus, we can produce 16 mol HNO_3 for every 24 mol NH_3 that we begin with:

$$1.6 \times 10^7 \text{ mol HNO}_3 \times \dfrac{24 \text{ mol NH}_3}{16 \text{ mol HNO}_3} \times \dfrac{17.0 \text{ g NH}_3}{\text{mol NH}_3} = 4.1 \times 10^8 \text{ g or } 4.1 \times 10^5 \text{ kg NH}_3$$

This is an oversimplified answer. In practice, the NO produced in the third step is recycled back continuously into the process in the second step. If this is taken into consideration, then the conversion factor between mol NH_3 and mol HNO_3 turns out to be 1:1, i.e., 1 mol of NH_3 produces 1 mol of HNO_3. Taking into consideration that NO is recycled back gives an answer of $2.7 \times 10^5 \text{ kg NH}_3$ reacted.

59. $Fe_2O_3(s) + 2 \text{ Al}(s) \rightarrow 2 \text{ Fe}(l) + Al_2O_3(s)$

$15.0 \text{ g Fe} \times \dfrac{1 \text{ mol Fe}}{55.85 \text{ g Fe}} = 0.269 \text{ mol Fe};\ \ 0.269 \text{ mol Fe} \times \dfrac{2 \text{ mol Al}}{2 \text{ mol Fe}} \times \dfrac{26.98 \text{ g Al}}{\text{mol Al}} = 7.26 \text{ g Al}$

$0.269 \text{ mol Fe} \times \dfrac{1 \text{ mol Fe}_2\text{O}_3}{2 \text{ mol Fe}} \times \dfrac{159.70 \text{ g Fe}_2\text{O}_3}{\text{mol Fe}_2\text{O}_3} = 21.5 \text{ g Fe}_2\text{O}_3$

$0.269 \text{ mol Fe} \times \dfrac{1 \text{ mol Al}_2\text{O}_3}{2 \text{ mol Fe}} \times \dfrac{101.96 \text{ g Al}_2\text{O}_3}{\text{mol Al}_2\text{O}_3} = 13.7 \text{ g Al}_2\text{O}_3$

60. $1.0 \times 10^4 \text{ kg waste} \times \dfrac{3.0 \text{ kg NH}_4^+}{100 \text{ kg waste}} \times \dfrac{1000 \text{ g}}{\text{kg}} \times \dfrac{1 \text{ mol NH}_4^+}{18.04 \text{ g NH}_4^+} \times \dfrac{1 \text{ mol C}_5\text{H}_7\text{O}_2\text{N}}{55 \text{ mol NH}_4^+}$

$\times \dfrac{113.1 \text{ g C}_5\text{H}_7\text{O}_2\text{N}}{\text{mol C}_5\text{H}_7\text{O}_2\text{N}} = 3.4 \times 10^4 \text{ g tissue if all NH}_4^+ \text{ converted}$

Since only 95% of the NH_4^+ ions react:

mass of tissue = $(0.95) (3.4 \times 10^4 \text{ g}) = 3.2 \times 10^4 \text{ g or } 32 \text{ kg bacterial tissue}$

61. $100. \text{ g K}_2\text{PtCl}_4 \times \dfrac{1 \text{ mol K}_2\text{PtCl}_4}{415.1 \text{ g K}_2\text{PtCl}_4} \times \dfrac{1 \text{ mol Pt(NH}_3)_2\text{Cl}_2}{\text{mol K}_2\text{PtCl}_4} \times \dfrac{300.1 \text{ g Pt(NH}_3)_2\text{Cl}_2}{\text{mol Pt(NH}_3)_2\text{Cl}_2}$

$$= 72.3 \text{ g Pt(NH}_3)_2\text{Cl}_2$$

$100. \text{ g K}_2\text{PtCl}_4 \times \dfrac{1 \text{ mol K}_2\text{PtCl}_4}{415.1 \text{ g K}_2\text{PtCl}_4} \times \dfrac{2 \text{ mol KCl}}{\text{mol K}_2\text{PtCl}_4} \times \dfrac{74.55 \text{ g KCl}}{\text{mol KCl}} = 35.9 \text{ g KCl}$

62. Total mass of copper used:

$$10,000 \text{ boards} \times \dfrac{(8.0 \text{ cm} \times 16.0 \text{ cm} \times 0.060 \text{ cm})}{\text{board}} \times \dfrac{8.96 \text{ g}}{\text{cm}^3} = 6.9 \times 10^5 \text{ g Cu}$$

Amount of Cu to be recovered = $0.80 \times 6.9 \times 10^5 \text{ g} = 5.5 \times 10^5 \text{ g Cu}$

$5.5 \times 10^5 \text{ g Cu} \times \dfrac{1 \text{ mol Cu}}{63.55 \text{ g Cu}} \times \dfrac{1 \text{ mol Cu(NH}_3)_4\text{Cl}_2}{\text{mol Cu}} \times \dfrac{202.6 \text{ g Cu(NH}_3)_4\text{Cl}_2}{\text{mol Cu(NH}_3)_4\text{Cl}_2}$

$$= 1.8 \times 10^6 \text{ g Cu(NH}_3)_4\text{Cl}_2$$

$5.5 \times 10^5 \text{ g Cu} \times \dfrac{1 \text{ mol Cu}}{63.55 \text{ g Cu}} \times \dfrac{4 \text{ mol NH}_3}{\text{mol Cu}} \times \dfrac{17.03 \text{ g NH}_3}{\text{mol NH}_3} = 5.9 \times 10^5 \text{ g NH}_3$

Limiting Reactants and Percent Yield

63. $1.50 \text{ g BaO}_2 \times \dfrac{1 \text{ mol BaO}_2}{169.3 \text{ g BaO}_2} = 8.86 \times 10^{-3} \text{ mol BaO}_2$

$25.0 \text{ mL} \times \dfrac{0.0272 \text{ g HCl}}{\text{mL}} \times \dfrac{1 \text{ mol HCl}}{36.46 \text{ g HCl}} = 1.87 \times 10^{-2} \text{ mol HCl}$

The required mol ratio from the balanced reaction is 2 mol HCl to 1 mol BaO$_2$. The actual ratio is:

$$\dfrac{1.87 \times 10^{-2} \text{ mol HCl}}{8.86 \times 10^{-3} \text{ mol BaO}_2} = 2.11$$

Since the actual mol ratio is larger than the required mol ratio, the denominator (BaO$_2$) is the limiting reagent.

$8.86 \times 10^{-3} \text{ mol BaO}_2 \times \dfrac{1 \text{ mol H}_2\text{O}_2}{\text{mol BaO}_2} \times \dfrac{34.02 \text{ g H}_2\text{O}_2}{\text{mol H}_2\text{O}_2} = 0.301 \text{ g H}_2\text{O}_2$

The amount of HCl reacted is:

$8.86 \times 10^{-3} \text{ mol BaO}_2 \times \dfrac{2 \text{ mol HCl}}{\text{mol BaO}_2} = 1.77 \times 10^{-2} \text{ mol HCl}$

excess mol HCl = 1.87×10^{-2} mol - 1.77×10^{-2} mol = 1.0×10^{-3} mol HCl

mass of excess HCl = 1.0×10^{-3} mol HCl $\times \dfrac{36.46 \text{ g HCl}}{\text{mol HCl}}$ = 3.6×10^{-2} g HCl

64. $2 \text{ Al(s)} + 3 \text{ Br}_2\text{(l)} \rightarrow 2 \text{ AlBr}_3\text{(s)}$

6.0 g Al $\times \dfrac{1 \text{ mol Al}}{26.98 \text{ mol Al}} \times \dfrac{2 \text{ mol AlBr}_3}{2 \text{ mol Al}} \times \dfrac{266.68 \text{ g AlBr}_3}{\text{mol AlBr}_3}$ = 59 g AlBr$_3$ (theoretical yield)

% yield = $\dfrac{\text{actual}}{\text{theoretical}} \times 100 = \dfrac{50.3 \text{ g}}{59 \text{ g}} \times 100$ = 85%

65.   2.50 metric tons Cu$_3$FeS$_3$ $\times \dfrac{1000 \text{ kg}}{\text{metric ton}} \times \dfrac{1000 \text{ g}}{\text{kg}} \times \dfrac{1 \text{ mol Cu}_3\text{FeS}_3}{342.71 \text{ g}} \times \dfrac{3 \text{ mol Cu}}{1 \text{ mol Cu}_3\text{FeS}_3} \times \dfrac{63.55 \text{ g}}{\text{mol Cu}}$

$$= 1.39 \times 10^6 \text{ g Cu (theoretical)}$$

1.39×10^6 g Cu (theoretical) $\times \dfrac{86.3 \text{ g Cu (actual)}}{100. \text{ g Cu (theoretical)}} = 1.20 \times 10^6$ g Cu = 1.20×10^3 kg Cu

$$= 1.20 \text{ metric tons Cu (actual)}$$

66.   a.   10.0 g Hg $\times \dfrac{1 \text{ mol Hg}}{200.6 \text{ g Hg}} = 4.99 \times 10^{-2}$ mol Hg

9.00 g Br$_2$ $\times \dfrac{1 \text{ mol Br}_2}{159.8 \text{ g Br}_2} = 5.63 \times 10^{-2}$ mol Br$_2$

The required mol ratio from the balanced equation is 1 mol Br$_2$ to 1 mol Hg. The actual mol ratio is:

$$\dfrac{5.63 \times 10^{-2} \text{ mol Br}}{4.99 \times 10^{-2} \text{ mol Hg}} = 1.13$$

This is higher than the required ratio so Hg is the limiting reagent.

4.99×10^{-2} mol Hg $\times \dfrac{1 \text{ mol HgBr}_2}{\text{mol Hg}} \times \dfrac{360.4 \text{ g HgBr}_2}{\text{mol HgBr}_2}$ = 18.0 g HgBr$_2$ produced

4.99×10^{-2} mol Hg $\times \dfrac{1 \text{ mol Br}_2}{1 \text{ mol Hg}} \times \dfrac{159.8 \text{ g Br}_2}{\text{mol Br}_2}$ = 7.97 g Br$_2$ reacted

excess Br$_2$ = 9.00 g Br$_2$ - 7.97 g Br$_2$ = 1.03 g Br$_2$

        b.   5.00 mL Hg $\times \dfrac{13.6 \text{ g Hg}}{\text{mL Hg}} \times \dfrac{1 \text{ mol Hg}}{200.6 \text{ g Hg}}$ = 0.339 mol Hg

5.00 mL Br$_2$ $\times \dfrac{3.10 \text{ g Br}_2}{\text{mL Br}_2} \times \dfrac{1 \text{ mol Br}_2}{159.8 \text{ g Br}_2}$ = 0.0970 mol Br$_2$

Br_2 is limiting since the actual moles of Br_2 present is well below the required 1:1 mol ratio.

$$0.0970 \text{ mol Br}_2 \times \frac{1 \text{ mol HgBr}_2}{\text{mol Br}_2} \times \frac{360.4 \text{ g HgBr}_2}{\text{mol HgBr}_2} = 35.0 \text{ g HgBr}_2 \text{ produced}$$

67. An alternative method to solve limiting reagent problems is to assume each reactant is limiting then calculate how much product could be produced from each reactant. The reactant that produces the smallest amount of product will run out first and is the limiting reagent.

$$5.00 \times 10^6 \text{ g NH}_3 \times \frac{1 \text{ mol NH}_3}{17.03 \text{ g NH}_3} \times \frac{2 \text{ mol HCN}}{2 \text{ mol NH}_3} = 2.94 \times 10^5 \text{ mol HCN}$$

$$5.00 \times 10^6 \text{ g O}_2 \times \frac{1 \text{ mol O}_2}{32.00 \text{ g O}_2} \times \frac{2 \text{ mol HCN}}{3 \text{ mol O}_2} = 1.04 \times 10^5 \text{ mol HCN}$$

$$5.00 \times 10^6 \text{ g CH}_4 \times \frac{1 \text{ mol CH}_4}{16.04 \text{ g CH}_4} \times \frac{2 \text{ mol HCN}}{2 \text{ mol CH}_4} = 3.12 \times 10^5 \text{ mol HCN}$$

O_2 is limiting since it produces the smallest amount of HCN. Although more product could be produced from NH_3 and CH_4, only enough O_2 is present to produce 1.04×10^5 mol HCN. The mass of HCN produced is:

$$1.04 \times 10^5 \text{ mol HCN} \times \frac{27.03 \text{ g HCN}}{\text{mol HCN}} = 2.81 \times 10^6 \text{ g HCN}$$

$$5.00 \times 10^6 \text{ g O}_2 \times \frac{1 \text{ mol O}_2}{32.00 \text{ g O}_2} \times \frac{6 \text{ mol H}_2\text{O}}{3 \text{ mol O}_2} \times \frac{18.02 \text{ g H}_2\text{O}}{1 \text{ mol H}_2\text{O}} = 5.63 \times 10^6 \text{ g H}_2\text{O}$$

68. $2 \text{ C}_3\text{H}_6(g) + 2 \text{ NH}_3(g) + 3 \text{ O}_2(g) \rightarrow 2 \text{ C}_3\text{H}_3\text{N}(g) + 6 \text{ H}_2\text{O}(g)$

a. We will solve this limiting reagent problem using the same method as described in Exercise 3.67.

$$1.00 \times 10^3 \text{ g C}_3\text{H}_6 \times \frac{1 \text{ mol C}_3\text{H}_6}{42.08 \text{ g C}_3\text{H}_6} \times \frac{2 \text{ mol C}_3\text{H}_3\text{N}}{2 \text{ mol C}_3\text{H}_6} = 23.8 \text{ mol C}_3\text{H}_3\text{N}$$

$$1.50 \times 10^3 \text{ g NH}_3 \times \frac{1 \text{ mol NH}_3}{17.03 \text{ g NH}_3} \times \frac{2 \text{ mol C}_3\text{H}_3\text{N}}{2 \text{ mol NH}_3} = 88.1 \text{ mol C}_3\text{H}_3\text{N}$$

$$2.00 \times 10^3 \text{ g O}_2 \times \frac{1 \text{ mol O}_2}{32.00 \text{ g O}_2} \times \frac{2 \text{ mol C}_3\text{H}_3\text{N}}{3 \text{ mol O}_2} = 41.7 \text{ mol C}_3\text{H}_3\text{N}$$

Therefore, C_3H_6 is limiting since it produces the smallest amount of product and the mass of acrylonitrile produced is:

$$23.8 \text{ mol} \times \frac{53.06 \text{ g C}_3\text{H}_3\text{N}}{\text{mol}} = 1.26 \times 10^3 \text{ g C}_3\text{H}_3\text{N}$$

b. $23.8 \text{ mol C}_3\text{H}_3\text{N} \times \dfrac{6 \text{ mol H}_2\text{O}}{2 \text{ mol C}_3\text{H}_3\text{N}} \times \dfrac{18.02 \text{ g H}_2\text{O}}{\text{mol H}_2\text{O}} = 1.29 \times 10^3 \text{ g H}_2\text{O}$

Amount NH_3 needed:

$$23.8 \text{ mol } C_3H_3N \times \frac{2 \text{ mol } NH_3}{2 \text{ mol } C_3H_3N} \times \frac{17.03 \text{ g } NH_3}{\text{mol } NH_3} = 405 \text{ g } NH_3$$

Amount NH_3 in excess $= 1.50 \times 10^3$ g - 405 g $= 1.10 \times 10^3$ g NH_3

Amount O_2 needed:

$$23.8 \text{ mol } C_3H_3N \times \frac{3 \text{ mol } O_2}{2 \text{ mol } C_3H_3N} \times \frac{32.00 \text{ g } O_2}{\text{mol } O_2} = 1.14 \times 10^3 \text{ g } O_2$$

Amount O_2 in excess $= 2.00 \times 10^3$ g - 1.14×10^3 g $= 860$ g O_2

1.10×10^3 g NH_3 and 860 g O_2 are in excess.

69. $P_4(s) + 6 F_2(g) \rightarrow 4 PF_3(g)$; The theoretical yield of PF_3 is:

$$120. \text{ g } PF_3 \text{ (actual)} \times \frac{100.0 \text{ g } PF_3 \text{ (theoretical)}}{78.1 \text{ g } PF_3 \text{ (actual)}} = 154 \text{ g } PF_3 \text{ (theoretical)}$$

$$154 \text{ g } PF_3 \times \frac{1 \text{ mol } PF_3}{87.97 \text{ g } PF_3} \times \frac{6 \text{ mol } F_2}{4 \text{ mol } PF_3} \times \frac{38.00 \text{ g } F_2}{\text{mol } F_2} = 99.8 \text{ g } F_2$$

99.8 g F_2 are needed to produce 120. g of PF_3 if the percent yield is 78.1%.

70.   a.   From the reaction stoichiometry we would expect to produce 4 mol of acetaminophen for every 4 mol of $C_6H_5O_3N$ reacted. The actual yield is 3 moles of acetaminophen compared to a theoretical yield of 4 moles of acetaminophen. Solving for percent yield by mass (where M = molar mass acetaminophen):

$$\% \text{ yield} = \frac{3 \text{ mol} \times M}{4 \text{ mol} \times M} \times 100 = 75\%$$

       b.   The product of the percent yields of the individual steps must equal the overall yield, 75%.

            $(0.87)(0.98)(x) = 0.75$, $x = 0.88$; Step III has a % yield = 88%.

Additional Exercises

71. $17.3 \text{ g H} \times \dfrac{1 \text{ mol H}}{1.008 \text{ g H}} = 17.2 \text{ mol H}$; $82.7 \text{ g C} \times \dfrac{1 \text{ mol C}}{12.01 \text{ g C}} = 6.89 \text{ mol C}$

$\dfrac{17.2}{6.89} = 2.50$; The empirical formula is C_2H_5.

The empirical formula mass is ~29 g, so two times the empirical formula would put the compound in the correct range of the molar mass. Molecular formula = $(C_2H_5)_2 = C_4H_{10}$

$$2.59 \times 10^{23} \text{ atoms H} \times \frac{1 \text{ molecule } C_4H_{10}}{10 \text{ atoms H}} \times \frac{1 \text{ mol } C_4H_{10}}{6.022 \times 10^{23} \text{ molecules}} = 4.30 \times 10^{-2} \text{ mol } C_4H_{10}$$

$$4.30 \times 10^{-2} \text{ mol } C_4H_{10} \times \frac{58.12 \text{ g}}{\text{mol } C_4H_{10}} = 2.50 \text{ g } C_4H_{10}$$

72.   Assuming 100.00 g E_3H_8:

$$\text{mol E} = 8.73 \text{ g H} \times \frac{1 \text{ mol H}}{1.008 \text{ g H}} \times \frac{3 \text{ mol E}}{8 \text{ mol H}} = 3.25 \text{ mol E}$$

$$\frac{x \text{ g E}}{1 \text{ mol E}} = \frac{91.27 \text{ g E}}{3.25 \text{ mol E}}, \ x = \text{molar mass of E} = 28.1 \text{ g/mol}; \text{ atomic mass of E} = 28.1 \text{ amu}$$

73.   If the formula was Be_2O_3, then 2 times the atomic mass of Be would combine with three times the atomic mass of oxygen, or:

$$\frac{2A}{3(16.00)} = \frac{0.5633}{1.000} \quad \text{Solving, A} = \text{atomic mass Be} = 13.52.$$

The accepted value is 9.01 and the discrepancy is due to the assumed formula. The actual formula is BeO.

74.   Empirical formula mass = 12.01 + 1.008 = 13.02 g/mol; Since 104.14/13.02 = 7.998 ≈ 8, then the molecular formula for styrene is $(CH)_8 = C_8H_8$.

$$2.00 \text{ g } C_8H_8 \times \frac{1 \text{ mol } C_8H_8}{104.14 \text{ g } C_8H_8} \times \frac{8 \text{ mol H}}{\text{mol } C_8H_8} \times \frac{6.022 \times 10^{23} \text{ atoms H}}{\text{mol H}} = 9.25 \times 10^{22} \text{ atoms H}$$

75.   Mass of H_2O = 0.755 g $CuSO_4 \cdot xH_2O$ - 0.483 g $CuSO_4$ = 0.272 g H_2O

$$0.483 \text{ g } CuSO_4 \times \frac{1 \text{ mol } CuSO_4}{159.62 \text{ g } CuSO_4} = 0.00303 \text{ mol } CuSO_4$$

$$0.272 \text{ g } H_2O \times \frac{1 \text{ mol } H_2O}{18.02 \text{ g } H_2O} = 0.0151 \text{ mol } H_2O$$

$$\frac{0.0151 \text{ mol } H_2O}{0.00303 \text{ mol } CuSO_4} = \frac{4.98 \text{ mol } H_2O}{1 \text{ mol } CuSO_4}; \text{ Compound formula} = CuSO_4 \cdot 5H_2O, \ x = 5$$

76.   In one hour, the 1000. kg of wet cereal contains 580 kg H_2O and 420 kg of cereal. We want the final product to contain 20.% H_2O. Let x = mass of H_2O in final product.

$$\frac{x}{420 + x} = 0.20, \quad x = 84 + 0.20\,x, \quad x = 105 \approx 110 \text{ kg } H_2O$$

The amount of water to be removed is $580 - 110 = 470$ kg/hr.

77.   Consider the case of aluminum plus oxygen. Aluminum forms Al^{3+} ions; oxygen forms O^{2-} anions. The simplest compound of the two elements is Al_2O_3. Similarly we would expect the formula of any group 6A element with Al to be Al_2X_3. Assuming this, out of 100.00 g of compound there are 18.56 g Al and 81.44 g of the unknown element, X. Let's use this information to determine the molar mass of X which will allow us to identify X from the periodic table.

$$18.56 \text{ g Al} \times \frac{1 \text{ mol Al}}{26.98 \text{ g Al}} \times \frac{3 \text{ mol X}}{2 \text{ mol Al}} = 1.032 \text{ mol X}$$

81.44 g of X must contain 1.032 mol of X.

The molar mass of X $= \dfrac{81.44 \text{ g X}}{1.032 \text{ mol X}} = 78.91$ g/mol

From the periodic table, the unknown element is selenium and the formula is Al_2Se_3.

78.   The reaction is: $BaX_2(aq) + H_2SO_4(aq) \rightarrow BaSO_4(s) + 2\ HX(aq)$

$$0.124 \text{ g } BaSO_4 \times \frac{137.3 \text{ g Ba}}{233.4 \text{ g } BaSO_4} = 0.0729 \text{ g Ba}; \ \% \text{ Ba} = \frac{0.0729 \text{ g Ba}}{0.158 \text{ g } BaX_2} \times 100 = 46.1\%$$

The formula is BaX_2 (from positions of the elements in the periodic table) and 100.0 g of compound contains 46.1 g Ba and 53.9 g of the unknown halogen. There must also be:

$$46.1 \text{ g Ba} \times \frac{1 \text{ mol Ba}}{137.3 \text{ g Ba}} \times \frac{2 \text{ mol X}}{\text{mol Ba}} = 0.672 \text{ mol of the halogen in 53.9 g of halogen}$$

Therefore, the molar mass of the halogen is: $\dfrac{53.9 \text{ g}}{0.672 \text{ mol}} = 80.2$ g/mol

This molar mass is close to that of bromine. Thus, the formula of the compound is $BaBr_2$.

79. $1.20 \text{ g } CO_2 \times \dfrac{1 \text{ mol } CO_2}{44.01 \text{ g}} \times \dfrac{1 \text{ mol C}}{\text{mol } CO_2} \times \dfrac{1 \text{ mol } C_{24}H_{30}N_3O}{24 \text{ mol C}} \times \dfrac{376.51 \text{ g}}{\text{mol } C_{24}H_{30}N_3O} = 0.428 \text{ g } C_{24}H_{30}N_3O$

$$\frac{0.428 \text{ g } C_{24}H_{30}N_3O}{1.00 \text{ g sample}} \times 100 = 42.8\% \ C_{24}H_{30}N_3O$$

80. $Ca_3(PO_4)_2(s) + 3\ H_2SO_4(aq) \rightarrow 3\ CaSO_4(s) + 2\ H_3PO_4(aq)$

$$1.0 \times 10^3 \text{ g } Ca_3(PO_4)_2 \times \frac{1 \text{ mol } Ca_3(PO_4)_2}{310.2 \text{ g } Ca_3(PO_4)_2} = 3.2 \text{ mol } Ca_3(PO_4)_2$$

$$1.0 \times 10^3 \text{ g conc. } H_2SO_4 \times \frac{98 \text{ g } H_2SO_4}{100 \text{ g conc. } H_2SO_4} \times \frac{1 \text{ mol } H_2SO_4}{98.1 \text{ g } H_2SO_4} = 10. \text{ mol } H_2SO_4$$

The required mol ratio from the balanced equation is 3 mol H_2SO_4 to 1 mol $Ca_3(PO_4)_2$. The actual ratio is: $\dfrac{10.\ \text{mol }H_2SO_4}{3.2\ \text{mol }Ca_3(PO_4)_2} = 3.1$

This is higher than the required mol ratio so $Ca_3(PO_4)_2$ is the limiting reagent.

$$3.2\ \text{mol }Ca_3(PO_4)_2 \times \frac{3\ \text{mol }CaSO_4}{\text{mol }Ca_3(PO_4)_2} \times \frac{136.2\ \text{g }CaSO_4}{\text{mol }CaSO_4} = 1300\ \text{g }CaSO_4\ \text{produced}$$

$$3.2\ \text{mol }Ca_3(PO_4)_2 \times \frac{2\ \text{mol }H_3PO_4}{\text{mol }Ca_3(PO_4)_2} \times \frac{98.0\ \text{g }H_3PO_4}{\text{mol }H_3PO_4} = 630\ \text{g }H_3PO_4\ \text{produced}$$

81. $453\ \text{g Fe} \times \dfrac{1\ \text{mol Fe}}{55.85\ \text{g Fe}} \times \dfrac{1\ \text{mol }Fe_2O_3}{2\ \text{mol Fe}} \times \dfrac{159.70\ \text{g }Fe_2O_3}{\text{mol }Fe_2O_3} = 648\ \text{g }Fe_2O_3$

mass % $Fe_2O_3 = \dfrac{648\ \text{g }Fe_2O_3}{752\ \text{g ore}} \times 100 = 86.2\%$

82. $^{12}C_2{}^{1}H_6$: $2(12.000000) + 6(1.007825) = 30.046950$ amu

$^{12}C^{1}H_2{}^{16}O$: $1(12.000000) + 2(1.007825) + 1(15.994915) = 30.010565$ amu

$^{14}N^{16}O$: $1(14.003074) + 1(15.994915) = 29.997989$ amu

The peak results from $^{12}C^{1}H_2{}^{16}O$.

83. $\dfrac{^{85}\text{Rb atoms}}{^{87}\text{Rb atoms}} = 2.591$;   If we had exactly 100 atoms: x = number of ^{85}Rb atoms and $100 - x$ = number of ^{87}Rb atoms

$\dfrac{x}{100 - x} = 2.591$, $x = 259.1 - 2.591\,x$, $x = \dfrac{259.1}{3.591} = 72.15\%$ ^{85}Rb

$0.7215\,(84.9117) + 0.2785\,(A) = 85.4678$, $A = \dfrac{85.4678 - 61.26}{0.2785} = 86.92$ amu

84.   Compound I: Out of 100.00 g sample:

$9.93\ \text{g C} \times \dfrac{1\ \text{mol C}}{12.01\ \text{g C}} = 0.827\ \text{mol C}$; $58.6\ \text{g Cl} \times \dfrac{1\ \text{mol Cl}}{35.45\ \text{g Cl}} = 1.65\ \text{mol Cl}$

$31.4\ \text{g F} \times \dfrac{1\ \text{mol F}}{19.00\ \text{g F}} = 1.65\ \text{mol F}$

Dividing all mol quantities by 0.827 gives a C:Cl:F mol ratio of 1:2:2. The empirical formula is CCl_2F_2.

Compound II: Out of 100.0 g sample:

$$11.5 \text{ g C} \times \frac{1 \text{ mol C}}{12.01 \text{ g C}} = 0.958 \text{ mol C} \; ; \quad 33.9 \text{ g Cl} \times \frac{1 \text{ mol Cl}}{35.45 \text{ g Cl}} = 0.956 \text{ mol Cl}$$

$$54.6 \text{ g F} \times \frac{1 \text{ mol F}}{19.00 \text{ g F}} = 2.87 \text{ mol F}$$

Dividing all mol quantities by 0.956 gives a C:Cl:F mol ratio of 1:1:3. The empirical formula is $CClF_3$.

Let's consider the masses of Cl and F that combine with 1.00 g C:

Compound I: 1.00 g C   5.90 g Cl   3.16 g F
Compound II: 1.00 g C   2.95 g Cl   4.75 g F

Cl ratio: $\dfrac{\text{I}}{\text{II}} = \dfrac{5.90}{2.95} = \dfrac{2}{1}$;   F ratio: $\dfrac{\text{I}}{\text{II}} = \dfrac{3.16}{4.75} \approx \dfrac{2}{3}$

Both are small whole number ratios as predicted by law of multiple proportions.

85.   The volume of a gas is proportional to the number of molecules of gas. Thus the formulas are:

I: NH_3;   II: N_2H_4;   III: HN_3

The mass ratios are:

I: $\dfrac{4.634 \text{ g N}}{\text{g H}}$;   II: $\dfrac{6.949 \text{ g N}}{\text{g H}}$;   III: $\dfrac{41.7 \text{ g N}}{\text{g H}}$;

If we set the atomic mass of H equal to 1.008, then the atomic mass for nitrogen is:

I: 14.01;   II: 14.01;   III. 14.0

For example for Compound I: $\dfrac{A}{3(1.008)} = \dfrac{4.634}{1}$, A = 14.01

86. $PaO_2 + O_2 \rightarrow Pa_xO_y$ (unbalanced)

$$0.200 \text{ g PaO}_2 \times \frac{231 \text{ g Pa}}{263 \text{ g PaO}_2} = 0.1757 \text{ g Pa} \quad \text{(We will carry extra significant figures.)}$$

$$0.2081 \text{ g Pa}_x\text{O}_y - 0.1757 \text{ g Pa} = 0.0324 \text{ g O}; \quad 0.0324 \text{ g O} \times \frac{1 \text{ mol O}}{16.00 \text{ g O}} = 2.025 \times 10^{-3} \text{ mol O}$$

$$0.1757 \text{ g Pa} \times \frac{1 \text{ mol Pa}}{231 \text{ g Pa}} = 7.61 \times 10^{-4} \text{ mol Pa}$$

$$\frac{\text{mol O}}{\text{mol Pa}} = \frac{2.025 \times 10^{-3} \text{ mol O}}{7.61 \times 10^{-4} \text{ mol Pa}} = 2.66 \approx 2\frac{2}{3} = \frac{8 \text{ mol O}}{3 \text{ mol Pa}}; \quad \text{Empirical formula} = Pa_3O_8$$

87. $1.375 \text{ g AgI} \times \dfrac{1 \text{ mol AgI}}{234.8 \text{ g AgI}} = 5.856 \times 10^{-3} \text{ mol AgI} = 5.856 \times 10^{-3} \text{ mol I}$

$1.375 \text{ g AgI} \times \dfrac{126.9 \text{ g I}}{234.8 \text{ g AgI}} = 0.7431 \text{ g I};$ XI_2 contains 0.7431 g I and 0.257 g X.

$5.856 \times 10^{-3} \text{ mol I} \times \dfrac{1 \text{ mol X}}{2 \text{ mol I}} = 2.928 \times 10^{-3} \text{ mol X}$

Molar mass $= \dfrac{0.257 \text{ g X}}{2.928 \times 10^{-3} \text{ mol X}} = \dfrac{87.8 \text{ g}}{\text{mol}};$ atomic mass = 87.8 amu (X is Sr.)

88. $\dfrac{6.05 \text{ g "Il"}}{1.00 \text{ g O}} \times \dfrac{16.00 \text{ g O}}{1 \text{ mol O}} = \dfrac{96.8 \text{ g "Il"}}{\text{mol O}}$

If formula of the oxide is: IlO, then atomic mass = 96.8 amu

$\qquad\qquad\qquad\qquad\quad$ IlO_2, then atomic mass = 193.6 amu

$\qquad\qquad\qquad\qquad\quad$ Il_2O_3, then atomic mass = 145.2 amu

Since A $\approx$ 150 amu, then Il_2O_3 with A = 145.2 amu is the best choice. "Illinium" is really promethium, Pm.

89. X_2Z: 40.0% X and 60.0% Z by mass; $\dfrac{\text{mol X}}{\text{mol Z}} = 2 = \dfrac{40.0/A_x}{60.0/A_z} = \dfrac{40.0 \, A_z}{60.0 \, A_x}$ or $A_z = 3 \, A_x$ where A = molar mass

For XZ_2, molar mass $= A_x + 2 \, A_z = A_x + 2(3 \, A_x) = 7 \, A_x$

% X $= \dfrac{A_x}{7A_x} \times 100 = 14.3\% \text{ X};$ % Z = 100.0 - 14.3 = 85.7% Z

90. A + B $\rightarrow$ AB; 6.56 g AB was 76.2% yield, so theoretical yield is $\dfrac{6.56}{0.762} = 8.61 \text{ g AB}.$

8.61 g AB contains 4.72 g A, g B = 8.61 - 4.72 = 3.89 g B.

91. Assuming one mol of vitamin A (286.4 g Vitamin A):

mol C = $286.4 \text{ g Vitamin A} \times \dfrac{0.8386 \text{ g C}}{\text{g Vitamin A}} \times \dfrac{1 \text{ mol C}}{12.011 \text{ g C}} = 20.00 \text{ mol C}$

mol H = $286.4 \text{ g Vitamin A} \times \dfrac{0.1056 \text{ g H}}{\text{g Vitamin A}} \times \dfrac{1 \text{ mol H}}{1.0079 \text{ g H}} = 30.01 \text{ mol H}$

Since one mol of Vitamin A contains 20 mol C and 30 mol H, then the molecular formula of Vitamin A is $C_{20}H_{30}E$. To determine E, lets calculate the molar mass of E.

286.4 g = 20(12.01) + 30(1.008) + molar mass E, molar mass E = 16.0 g/mol

From the periodic table, E = oxygen and the molecular formula of Vitamin A is $C_{20}H_{30}O$.

92.   We would see the peaks corresponding to:

$^{10}B^{35}Cl_3$ [mass $\approx 10 + 3(35) = 115$ amu], $^{10}B^{35}Cl_2^{37}Cl$ (117), $^{10}B^{35}Cl^{37}Cl_2$ (119), $^{10}B^{37}Cl_3$ (121)

$^{11}B^{35}Cl_3$ (116), $^{11}B^{35}Cl_2^{37}Cl$ (118), $^{11}B^{35}Cl^{37}Cl_2$ (120), $^{11}B^{37}Cl_3$ (122)

We would see a total of 8 peaks at approximate masses of 115, 116, 117, 118, 119, 120, 121 and 122.

Challenge Problems

93.   When the discharge voltage is low, the ions present are in the form of molecules. When the discharge voltage is increased, the bonds in the molecules are broken and the ions present are in the form of individual atoms. Therefore, the high discharge data indicates that the ions $^{16}O^+$, $^{18}O^+$ and $^{40}Ar^+$ are present. The only combination of these individual ions that can explain the mass data at low discharge is $^{16}O^{16}O^+$ (mass = 32), $^{16}O^{18}O^+$ (mass = 34) and $^{40}Ar^+$ (mass = 40). Therefore, the gas mixture contains $^{16}O^{16}O$, $^{16}O^{18}O$ and ^{40}Ar. To determine the percent composi-tion of each isotope, we use the relative intensity data from the high discharge data to determine the percentage that each isotope contributes to the total relative intensity. For ^{40}Ar:

$$\frac{1.0000}{0.7500 + 0.0015 + 1.0000} \times 100 = \frac{1.0000}{1.7515} \times 100 = 57.094\% \ ^{40}Ar$$

For ^{16}O: $\dfrac{0.7500}{1.7515} \times 100 = 42.82\% \ ^{16}O$;   For ^{18}O: $\dfrac{0.0015}{1.7515} \times 100 = 8.6 \times 10^{-2}\% \ ^{18}O$

Note: ^{18}F instead of ^{18}O could also explain the data. However, OF(g) is not a stable compound. This is why ^{18}O is the best choice since O_2(g) does form.

94.   The two relevant equations are:

$4 FeO + O_2 \rightarrow 2 Fe_2O_3$

$4 Fe_3O_4 + O_2 \rightarrow 6 Fe_2O_3$

Let x = mass FeO, 5.430 - x = mass Fe_3O_4

$$\text{moles FeO} = \frac{x}{71.85}; \quad \text{moles } Fe_3O_4 = \frac{5.430 - x}{231.55}$$

Thus, moles Fe_2O_3 is:

$$\left(\frac{x}{71.85}\right)\left(\frac{2 \text{ moles } Fe_2O_3}{4 \text{ moles FeO}}\right) + \left(\frac{5.430 - x}{231.35}\right)\left(\frac{6 \text{ moles } Fe_2O_3}{4 \text{ moles } Fe_3O_4}\right)$$

and mass Fe_2O_3 is:

$$159.7 \text{ g/mol}\left[\frac{x}{71.85}\left(\frac{2}{4}\right) + \left(\frac{5.430 - x}{231.55}\right)\left(\frac{6}{4}\right)\right] = 5.779$$

Solving for x, we get 2.10 g.

Thus, the mixture is $\dfrac{2.10}{5.430} \times 100 = 38.7\%$ FeO.

95.   10.00 g XCl_2 + excess $Cl_2 \rightarrow$ 12.55 g XCl_4; 2.55 g Cl reacted with XCl_2 to form XCl_4. XCl_4 contains 2.55 g Cl and 10.00 g XCl_2. From mol ratios, 10.00 g XCl_2 must also contain 2.55 g Cl with 10.00 - 2.55 = 7.45 g X.

$$2.55 \text{ g Cl} \times \frac{1 \text{ mol Cl}}{35.45 \text{ g Cl}} \times \frac{1 \text{ mol } XCl_2}{2 \text{ mol Cl}} \times \frac{1 \text{ mol X}}{\text{mol } XCl_2} = 3.60 \times 10^{-2} \text{ mol X}$$

So, 3.60×10^{-2} mol X must equal 7.45 g X. The molar mass of X is:

$$\frac{7.45 \text{ g X}}{3.60 \times 10^{-2} \text{ mol X}} = \frac{207 \text{ g}}{\text{mol X}}; \quad \text{atomic mass of X} = 207 \text{ amu}; \text{X is Pb.}$$

96.   The two relevant equations are:

$$Zn + 2 \, HCl \rightarrow ZnCl_2 + H_2$$
$$Mg + 2 \, HCl \rightarrow MgCl_2 + H_2$$

let x = mass Mg, so 10.00 - y = mass Zn.

We can also see that moles H_2 = moles Zn + moles Mg

$$\text{mol } H_2 = 0.5171 \text{ g } H_2 \times \frac{1 \text{ mol } H_2}{2.0158 \text{ g}} = 0.2565 \text{ mol}$$

Thus, $0.2565 = \dfrac{x}{24.31} + \dfrac{10.00 - x}{65.39}$; Solving, x = 4.00 g Mg

$$\frac{4.00 \text{ g}}{10.00 \text{ g}} \times 100 = 40.0\% \text{ Mg}$$

97.   For a gas, density and molar mass are proportional.

Molar mass $XH_n = 2.393(32.00) = \dfrac{76.58 \text{ g}}{\text{mol}}$; $0.803 \text{ g } H_2O \times \dfrac{2 \text{ mol H}}{18.02 \text{ g } H_2O} = 8.91 \times 10^{-2} \text{ mol H}$

$$\frac{8.91 \times 10^{-2} \text{ mol H}}{2.23 \times 10^{-2} \text{ mol } XH_n} = \frac{4 \text{ mol H}}{\text{mol } XH_n}$$

Molar mass X = 76.58 - 4(1.008 g) = 72.55 g/mol;   The element is Ge.

98.   The equation is

$$Sc + HCl \rightarrow ScCl_x + H_2$$

To balance this we get:

$$2 \, Sc + 2x \, HCl \rightarrow 2 \, ScCl_x + x \, H_2$$

Thus, the mol ratio of Sc : H_2 = 2 : x

$$\text{moles Sc} = 2.25 \text{ g Sc} \times \frac{1 \text{ mol Sc}}{44.96 \text{ g Sc}} = 0.0500 \text{ mol Sc}$$

$$\text{mol } H_2 = 0.1502 \text{ g } H_2 \times \frac{1 \text{ mol } H_2}{2.0158 \text{ g } H_2} = 0.07451 \text{ mol } H_2$$

$$\frac{2}{x} = \frac{0.0500}{0.07451} \text{ and } x = 3; \text{ The formula is } ScCl_3.$$

99. $4.000 \text{ g } M_2S_3 \rightarrow 3.723 \text{ g } MO_2$

There must be twice as many mol of MO_2 as mol of M_2S_3 in order to balance M in the reaction. Setting up an equation for 2 mol MO_2 = mol M_2S_3 where A = molar mass M:

$$2\left(\frac{4.000 \text{ g}}{2 \text{ A} + 3(32.07)}\right) = \frac{3.723 \text{ g}}{\text{A} + 2(16.00)}, \quad \frac{8.000}{2 \text{ A} + 96.21} = \frac{3.723}{\text{A} + 32.00}$$

$8.000 \text{ A} + 256.0 = 7.446 \text{ A} + 358.2, 0.554 \text{ A} = 102.2, \text{ A} = 184 \text{ g/mol}$; atomic mass = 184 amu

100.   We know water is a product, so one of the elements in the compound is hydrogen. Thus:

$$X_aH_b + O_2 \rightarrow H_2O + ?$$

Thus, the mole ratio between X_aH_b : $H_2O = \dfrac{2}{b}$.

$$\text{mol compound} = \frac{1.39 \text{ g}}{62.09 \text{ g/mol}} = 0.0224 \text{ mol}; \quad \text{mol } H_2O = \frac{1.21 \text{ g}}{18.02 \text{ g/mol}} = 0.0671$$

$$\frac{2}{b} = \frac{0.0224}{0.0671} \text{ and } b = 6; \quad X_AH_6 \text{ has a molar mass of 62.09 g/mol.}$$

Thus, "a" moles of "X" atoms have a mass of 56.04 g.

Some possible identities for X could be Fe (a = 1), Si (a = 2), N (a = 4), Li (a = 8). N fits the data best so N_4H_6 is the formula.

101.   The balanced equations are:

$$C(s) + 1/2 \ O_2(g) \rightarrow CO(g) \text{ and } C(s) + O_2(g) \rightarrow CO_2(g)$$

If we have 100.0 mol of products, we have 72.0 mol CO_2, 16.0 mol CO, and 12.0 mol O_2. The initial mixture contained 72.0 + 16.0 = 88.0 mol C and 72.0 (from CO_2) + $\dfrac{16.0}{2}$ (from CO) + 12.0 (unreacted) = 92.0 mol O_2. Initial reaction mixture contained:

$$\frac{92.0 \text{ mol } O_2}{88.0 \text{ mol C}} = 1.05 \text{ mol } O_2/\text{mol C}$$

102.   a.   Assuming each reactant is limiting:

$$1500 \text{ kg Ca}_3(\text{PO}_4)_2 \times \frac{1 \text{ kmol Ca}_3(\text{PO}_4)_2}{310.18 \text{ kg Ca}_3(\text{PO}_4)_2} \times \frac{2 \text{ kmol P}}{\text{kmol Ca}_3(\text{PO}_4)_2} \times \frac{30.97 \text{ kg P}}{\text{kmol P}} = 3.0 \times 10^2 \text{ kg P}$$

$$250 \text{ kg C} \times \frac{1 \text{ kmol C}}{12.01 \text{ kg C}} \times \frac{2 \text{ kmol P}}{5 \text{ kmol C}} \times \frac{30.97 \text{ kg P}}{\text{kmol P}} = 260 \text{ kg P}$$

$$1.0 \times 10^3 \text{ kg SiO}_2 \times \frac{1 \text{ kmol SiO}_2}{60.09 \text{ kg SiO}_2} \times \frac{2 \text{ kmol P}}{3 \text{ kmol SiO}_2} \times \frac{30.97 \text{ kg P}}{\text{kmol P}} = 340 \text{ kg P}$$

C is the limiting reagent since it produces the smallest amount of product.

b.   From a, the theoretical yield is 260 kg P.

c.   The total reactant mass we began with was 2750 kg (assuming one extra significant figure). After the reaction, this solid mass will be decreased by the amount of CO(g) and P(l) formed. If we let x = kmol of $Ca_3(PO_4)_2$ that reacted, then the balanced equation is:

$$x \text{ Ca}_3(\text{PO}_4)_2(s) + 5x \text{ C}(s) + 3x \text{ SiO}_2(s) \rightarrow 3x \text{ CaSiO}_3(s) + 5x \text{ CO}(g) + 2x \text{ P}(l)$$

We began with (assuming extra S.F.): $250 \text{ kg C} \times \dfrac{1 \text{ kmol C}}{12.01 \text{ kg C}} = 20.8 \text{ kmol C}$

In the slag, % C $= \dfrac{\text{mass C}}{\text{mass slag}} \times 100$:

$$3.8 = \frac{(20.8 \text{ kmol C} - 5x) \, 12.01 \text{ kg/kmol}}{2750 \text{ kg} - 5x(28.01 \text{ kg/kmol}) - 2x(30.97 \text{ kg/kmol})} \times 100$$

$$0.038 \, [2750 - 5x(28.01) - 2x(30.97)] = (20.8 - 5x) \, 12.01$$

$$104.5 - 5.32 \, x - 2.35 \, x = 249.8 - 60.05 \, x, \;\; 52.38 \, x = 145.3, \;\; x = 2.77 \approx 2.8$$

$x = 2.8, \;\; 5x = 14$ kmol of C reacted

$$14 \text{ kmol C} \times \frac{2 \text{ kmol P}}{5 \text{ kmol C}} \times \frac{30.97 \text{ kg P}}{\text{kmol P}} = 170 \text{ kg P actually produced}$$

% yield $= \dfrac{170 \text{ kg P}}{260 \text{ kg P}} \times 100 = 65\%$

Checking with % P calculation:

1500 kg/310.18 kmol/kg = 4.84 kmol $Ca_3(PO_4)_2$ initially

$$5.8 = \frac{(4.84 - x)\,(2)\,(30.97) \text{ kg P}}{2750 - 5x(28.01) - 2x(30.97) \text{ kg slag}} \times 100$$

$$0.058 [2750 - 5x(28.01) - 2x(30.97)] = (4.84 - x) (2) (30.97)$$

$$159.5 - 8.12\,x - 3.59\,x = 299.8 - 61.94\,x, \; 50.23\,x = 140.3, \; x = 2.79 \approx 2.8 \text{ kmol P}$$

We actually produce $2x = 2(2.8 \text{ kmol})(30.97 \text{ kg/kmol}) = 170 \text{ kg P}$. This agrees with our previous answer.

$$\% \text{ yield} = \frac{170 \text{ kg P}}{260 \text{ kg P}} \times 100 = 65\%$$

103. $LaH_{2.90}$ is the formula. If only La^{3+} is present, LaH_3 would be the formula. If only La^{2+} is present, LaH_2 would be the formula. Let x = mol La^{2+} and y = mol La^{3+}:

$$(La^{2+})_x(La^{3+})_y H_{(2x + 3y)} \text{ where } x + y = 1.00 \text{ and } 2x + 3y = 2.90$$

Solving by simultaneous equations:

$$\begin{aligned} 2x + 3y &= 2.90 \\ \underline{-2x - 2y} &= \underline{-2.00} \\ y &= 0.90 \text{ and } x = 0.10 \end{aligned}$$

$LaH_{2.90}$ contains $\dfrac{1}{10}$ La^{2+} or 10.% La^{2+} and $\dfrac{9}{10}$ La^{3+} or 90.% La^{3+}.

104. $MCO_3(s) + 2 H^+(aq) \rightarrow M^{2+}(aq) + H_2O(l) + CO_2(g)$

$$0.421 \text{ g } CO_2 \times \frac{1 \text{ mol } CO_2}{44.01 \text{ g } CO_2} \times \frac{1 \text{ mol } MCO_2}{1 \text{ mol } CO_2} = 9.57 \times 10^{-3} \text{ mol of } MCO_3 \text{ present}$$

Let x = g $SrCO_3$ and y = g $BaCO_3$:

mass balance: x + y = 1.60 g

mole balance: $\dfrac{x}{147.6} + \dfrac{y}{197.3} = 9.57 \times 10^{-3}$ total mol or $1.337\,x + y = 1.89$

Solving: $\begin{aligned} 1.337\,x + y &= 1.89 \\ \underline{-x - y} &= \underline{-1.60} \\ 0.337\,x &= 0.29, \; x = 0.86 \text{ g } SrCO_3 \text{ and } y = 0.74 \text{ g } BaCO_3 \end{aligned}$

$\% \; SrCO_3 = \dfrac{0.86 \text{ g}}{1.60 \text{ g}} \times 100 = 54\%$ by mass; $\% \; BaCO_3 = 46\%$

Note: with no rounding, $\% \; SrCO_3 = 53.4\%$; $\% \; BaCO_3 = 46.6\%$

105. $NaCl(aq) + Ag^+(aq) \rightarrow AgCl(s)$; $KCl(aq) + Ag^+(aq) \rightarrow AgCl(s)$

$$8.5904 \text{ g } AgCl \times \frac{1 \text{ mol } AgCl}{143.4 \text{ g } AgCl} \times \frac{1 \text{ mol } Cl^-}{1 \text{ mol } AgCl} = 5.991 \times 10^{-2} \text{ mol } Cl^-$$

Let x = g NaCl and y = g KCl:

$$x + y = 4.000 \text{ g and } \frac{x}{58.44} + \frac{y}{74.55} = 5.991 \times 10^{-2} \text{ total mol } Cl^- \text{ or } 1.276\,x + y = 4.466$$

Solving using simultaneous equations:

$$1.276\,x + y = 4.466$$
$$\underline{-x - y = -4.000}$$
$$0.276\,x \quad\quad = 0.466, \quad x = 1.69 \text{ g NaCl and } y = 2.31 \text{ g KCl}$$

$$\% \text{ NaCl} = \frac{1.69 \text{ g}}{4.000 \text{ g}} \times 100 = 42.3\% \text{ NaCl}; \quad \% \text{ KCl} = 57.7\%$$

106. $1.297 \text{ g Cu} \times \dfrac{1 \text{ mol Cu}}{63.55 \text{ g Cu}} = 2.041 \times 10^{-2} \text{ mol Cu}$

Let $x = $ g Cu_2O and $y = $ g CuO: $x + y = 1.500$ and:

$$2\left(\frac{x}{143.1}\right) + \frac{y}{79.55} = 2.041 \times 10^{-2} \text{ total mol Cu or } 1.112\,x + y = 1.624$$

Solving:

$$1.112\,x + y = 1.624$$
$$\underline{-x - y = -1.500}$$
$$0.112\,x \quad\quad = 0.124$$

$x = 1.11$ g Cu_2O; $(1.11 \text{ g}/1.500 \text{ g}) \times 100 = 74.0\% \ Cu_2O$ by mass; 26.0% CuO by mass

107.   The balanced equations are:

$$4\,NH_3(g) + 5\,O_2(g) \rightarrow 4\,NO(g) + 6\,H_2O(g) \text{ and } 4\,NH_3(g) + 7\,O_2(g) \rightarrow 4\,NO_2(g) + 6\,H_2O(g)$$

Let $4x = $ number of mol of NO formed, and let $4y = $ number of mol of NO_2 formed. Then:

$$4x\ NH_3 + 5x\ O_2 \rightarrow 4x\ NO + 6x\ H_2O \text{ and } 4y\ NH_3 + 7y\ O_2 \rightarrow 4y\ NO_2 + 6y\ H_2O$$

All the NH_3 reacted, so $4x + 4y = 2.00$. $10.00 - 6.75 = 3.25$ mol O_2 reacted, so $5x + 7y = 3.25$.

Solving by the method of simultaneous equations:

$$20\,x + 28\,y = 13.0$$
$$\underline{-20\,x - 20\,y = -10.0}$$
$$8\,y = \quad 3.0, \quad y = 0.38; \quad 4x + 4 \times 0.38 = 2.00, \quad x = 0.12$$

mol NO $= 4x = 4 \times 0.12 = 0.48$ mol NO formed

108. $a\ C_8H_{18}(l) + b\ O_2(g) \rightarrow c\ CO_2(g) + d\ CO(g) + e\ CH_4(g) + f\ H_2(g) + g\ H_2O(g)$

Volume ratios are proportional to mole ratios. Volume percent of O_2 reacted is:

$$\frac{21 \text{ mol } \% \ O_2}{78 \text{ mol } \% \ N_2} = \frac{x}{82.1 \text{ vol } \% \ N_2}, \quad x = 22 \text{ vol } \% \ O_2 = \text{volume percent of } O_2 \text{ reacted}$$

Determining mole ratios in balanced equation:

$$\frac{b}{c} = \frac{22}{11.5} = 1.9, \ c = 0.52 \ b; \quad \frac{b}{d} = \frac{22}{4.4} = 5.0, \ d = 0.20 \ b$$

$$\frac{b}{e} = \frac{22}{0.5} = 44 \approx 40, \ e = 0.02 \ b; \quad \frac{b}{f} = \frac{22}{1.5} = 15, \ f = 0.068 \ b$$

Balancing the carbon atoms: $8a = c + d + e$

Let's assume $a = 1$, so 1 mol of gasoline consumed:

$8 = 0.52 \ b + 0.20 \ b + 0.02 \ b = 0.74 \ b, \ b = 11$

Using b to determine c, d, e, and f: $c = 5.7; \ d = 2.2; \ e = 0.2; \ f = 0.75$

Balancing the hydrogen atoms: $18 \ a = 4 \ e + 2 \ f + 2 \ g, \ 18 = 4(0.2) + 2(0.75) + 2 \ g, \ g = 7.9$

$C_8H_{18}(l) + 11 \ O_2(g) \rightarrow 5.7 \ CO_2(g) + 2.2 \ CO(g) + 0.2 \ CH_4(g) + 0.75 \ H_2(g) + 7.9 \ H_2O(g)$

Marathon Problems

109.   To solve the limiting reagent problem, we must determine the formulas of all the compounds so we can get a balanced reaction.

    a.   40 million trillion = $40 \times 10^6 \times 10^{12} = 4.000 \times 10^{19}$ (assuming 4 S.F.)

$$4.000 \times 10^{19} \text{ molecules A} \times \frac{1 \text{ mol A}}{6.022 \times 10^{23} \text{ molecules A}} = 6.642 \times 10^{-5} \text{ mol A}$$

$$\text{Molar mass of A} = \frac{4.26 \times 10^{-3} \text{ g A}}{6.642 \times 10^{-5} \text{ mol A}} = 64.1 \text{ g/mol}$$

Mass of carbon in one mol of A is:

$$64.1 \text{ g A} \times \frac{37.5 \text{ g C}}{100.0 \text{ g A}} = 24.0 \text{ g carbon} = 2 \text{ mol carbon in substance A}$$

The remainder of the molar mass (64.1 g - 24.0 g = 40.1 g) is due to the alkaline earth metal. From the periodic table, calcium has a molar mass of 40.08 g/mol. The formula of substance A is CaC_2.

    b.   5.36 g H + 42.5 g O = 47.9 g; Substance B only contains H and O. Determining the empirical formula of B:

$$5.36 \text{ g H} \times \frac{1 \text{ mol H}}{1.008 \text{ g H}} = 5.32 \text{ mol H}; \quad \frac{5.32}{2.66} = 2.00$$

$$42.5 \text{ g O} \times \frac{1 \text{ mol O}}{16.00 \text{ g O}} = 2.66 \text{ mol O}; \quad \frac{2.66}{2.66} = 1.00$$

Empirical formula = H_2O; The molecular formula of substance B could be H_2O, H_4O_2, H_6O_3, etc. The most reasonable choice is water (H_2O) for substance B.

c.   Substance C + O_2 → CO_2 + H_2O; Substance C must contain carbon and hydrogen, and may contain oxygen. Determining the mass of carbon and hydrogen in substance C:

$$33.8 \text{ g } CO_2 \times \frac{1 \text{ mol } CO_2}{44.01 \text{ g } CO_2} \times \frac{1 \text{ mol C}}{\text{mol } CO_2} \times \frac{12.01 \text{ g C}}{\text{mol C}} = 9.22 \text{ g carbon}$$

$$6.92 \text{ g } H_2O \times \frac{1 \text{ mol } H_2O}{18.02 \text{ g } H_2O} \times \frac{2 \text{ mol H}}{\text{mol } H_2O} \times \frac{1.008 \text{ g H}}{\text{mol H}} = 0.774 \text{ g hydrogen}$$

9.22 g carbon + 0.774 g hydrogen = 9.99 g; Since substance C initially weighed 10.0 g, then there is no oxygen present in substance C. Determining the empirical formula for substance C:

$$9.22 \text{ g} \times \frac{1 \text{ mol C}}{12.01 \text{ g C}} = 0.768 \text{ mol carbon}$$

$$0.774 \text{ g H} \times \frac{1 \text{ mol H}}{1.008 \text{ g H}} = 0.768 \text{ mol hydrogen}$$

mol C/mol H = 1.00; The empirical formula is CH which has an empirical formula mass ≈ 13. Since the mass spectrum data indicates a molar mass of 26 g/mol, then the molecular formula for substance C is C_2H_2.

d.   Substance D is $Ca(OH)_2$.

Now we can answer the question. The balanced equation is:

$$CaC_2(s) + 2 \text{ } H_2O(l) → C_2H_2(g) + Ca(OH)_2(aq)$$

$$45.0 \text{ g } CaC_2 \times \frac{1 \text{ mol } CaC_2}{64.10 \text{ g } CaC_2} = 0.702 \text{ mol } CaC_2$$

$$23.0 \text{ g } H_2O \times \frac{1 \text{ mol } H_2O}{18.02 \text{ g } H_2O} = 1.28 \text{ mol } H_2O$$

$$\frac{\text{mol } H_2O}{\text{mol } CaC_2} = \frac{1.28}{0.702} = 1.82$$

Since the actual mol ratio present is smaller than the required 2:1 mol ratio from the balanced equation, then H_2O is limiting.

$$1.28 \text{ mol } H_2O \times \frac{1 \text{ mol } C_2H_2}{2 \text{ mol } H_2O} \times \frac{26.04 \text{ g } C_2H_2}{\text{mol } C_2H_2} = 16.7 \text{ g } C_2H_2 = \text{mass of substance C produced}$$

110.   a.   i.   If the molar mass of A is greater than the molar mass of B, then we cannot determine the limiting reactant because, while we have a fewer number of moles of A, we also need less moles of A (from the balanced reaction).

       ii. If the molar mass of B is greater than the molar mass of A, then B is the limiting reactant because we have a fewer number of moles of B and we need more B (from the balanced reaction).

   b. $A + 5 B \rightarrow 3 CO_2 + 4 H_2O$

       To conserve mass : $44.01 + 5(B) = 3(44.01) + 4(18.02)$; solving: $B = 32.0$ g/mol

       Since it is diatomic, the best choice for B is O_2.

   c. We can solve this without % mass data simply by balancing the equation:

       $A + 5 O_2 \rightarrow 3 CO_2 + 4 H_2O$

       A must be C_3H_8.

       Note: $\dfrac{3(12.01)}{3(12.01) + 8(1.008)} \times 100 = 81.71\%$. So this checks.

CHAPTER FOUR

TYPES OF CHEMICAL REACTIONS AND SOLUTION STOICHIOMETRY

Aqueous Solutions: Strong and Weak Electrolytes

10. The electrolyte designation refers to what happens to a substance when it dissolves in water, i.e., does it produce a lot of ions or a few ions or no ions when the substance dissolves. A weak electrolyte is a substance that only partially dissociates in water to produce only a few ions. Solubility refers to how much substance can dissolve in a solvent. "Slightly soluble" refers to substances that dissolve only to a small extent, whether it is an electrolyte or a nonelectrolyte. A weak electrolyte may be very soluble in water, or it may be slightly soluble. Acetic acid is an example of a weak electrolyte that is very soluble in water.

    Experimentally measure the electrical conductivity of a solution containing the substance and compare it to the conductivity of a solution of some substance of a known strong electrolyte of equal concentration.

11. $MgSO_4(s) \rightarrow Mg^{2+}(aq) + SO_4^{2-}(aq)$; $NH_4NO_3(s) \rightarrow NH_4^+(aq) + NO_3^-(aq)$

12. a. $Ba(NO_3)_2(aq) \rightarrow Ba^{2+}(aq) + 2\ NO_3^-(aq)$; Picture iv represents the Ba^{2+} and NO_3^- ions present in $Ba(NO_3)_2(aq)$.

    b. $NaCl(aq) \rightarrow Na^+(aq) + Cl^-(aq)$; Picture ii represents $NaCl(aq)$.

    c. $K_2CO_3(aq) \rightarrow 2\ K^+(aq) + CO_3^{2-}(aq)$; Picture iii represents $K_2CO_3(aq)$.

    d. $MgSO_4(aq) \rightarrow Mg^{2+}(aq) + SO_4^{2-}(aq)$; Picture i represents $MgSO_4(aq)$.

Solution Concentration: Molarity

13. a. $2.00\ L \times \dfrac{0.250\ mol\ NaOH}{L} \times \dfrac{40.00\ g\ NaOH}{mol} = 20.0\ g\ NaOH$

    Place 20.0 g NaOH in a 2 L volumetric flask; add water to dissolve the NaOH, and fill to the mark with water, mixing several times along the way.

b. $2.00 \text{ L} \times \dfrac{0.250 \text{ mol NaOH}}{\text{L}} \times \dfrac{1 \text{ L stock}}{1.00 \text{ mol NaOH}} = 0.500 \text{ L}$

Add 500. mL of 1.00 M NaOH stock solution to a 2 L volumetric flask; fill to the mark with water, mixing several times along the way.

c. $2.00 \text{ L} \times \dfrac{0.100 \text{ mol K}_2\text{CrO}_4}{\text{L}} \times \dfrac{194.20 \text{ g K}_2\text{CrO}_4}{\text{mol K}_2\text{CrO}_4} = 38.8 \text{ g K}_2\text{CrO}_4$

Similar to the solution made in part a, instead using 38.8 g K_2CrO_4.

d. $2.00 \text{ L} \times \dfrac{0.100 \text{ mol K}_2\text{CrO}_4}{\text{L}} \times \dfrac{1 \text{ L stock}}{1.75 \text{ mol K}_2\text{CrO}_4} = 0.114 \text{ L}$

Similar to the solution made in part b, instead using 114 mL of the 1.75 M K_2CrO_4 stock solution.

14.   a. $M_{\text{Ca(NO}_3)_2} = \dfrac{0.100 \text{ mol Ca(NO}_3)_2}{0.100 \text{ L}} = 1.00 \ M$

$Ca(NO_3)_2(s) \rightarrow Ca^{2+}(aq) + 2 \ NO_3^-(aq); \ M_{Ca^{2+}} = 1.00 \ M; \ M_{NO_3^-} = 2(1.00) = 2.00 \ M$

b. $M_{\text{Na}_2\text{SO}_4} = \dfrac{2.5 \text{ mol Na}_2\text{SO}_4}{1.25 \text{ L}} = 2.0 \ M$

$Na_2SO_4(s) \rightarrow 2 \ Na^+(aq) + SO_4^{2-}(aq); \ M_{Na^+} = 2(2.0) = 4.0 \ M; \ M_{SO_4^{2-}} = 2.0 \ M$

c. $5.00 \text{ g NH}_4\text{Cl} \times \dfrac{1 \text{ mol NH}_4\text{Cl}}{53.49 \text{ g NH}_4\text{Cl}} = 0.0935 \text{ mol NH}_4\text{Cl}$

$M_{\text{NH}_4\text{Cl}} = \dfrac{0.0935 \text{ mol NH}_4\text{Cl}}{0.5000 \text{ L}} = 0.187 M$

$NH_4Cl(s) \rightarrow NH_4^+(aq) + Cl^-(aq); \ M_{NH_4^+} = M_{Cl^-} = 0.187 \ M$

d. $1.00 \text{ g K}_3\text{PO}_4 \times \dfrac{1 \text{ mol K}_3\text{PO}_4}{212.27 \text{ g}} = 4.71 \times 10^{-3} \text{ mol K}_3\text{PO}_4$

$M_{\text{K}_3\text{PO}_4} = \dfrac{4.71 \times 10^{-3} \text{ mol}}{0.2500 \text{ L}} = 0.0188 \ M$

$K_3PO_4(s) \rightarrow 3 \ K^+(aq) + PO_4^{3-}(aq); \ M_{K^+} = 3(0.0188) = 0.0564 \ M; \ M_{PO_4^{3-}} = 0.0188 \ M$

15.   Molar mass of $NaHCO_3 = 22.99 + 1.008 + 12.01 + 3(16.00) = 84.01$ g/mol

Volume = 0.350 g $NaHCO_3 \times \dfrac{1 \text{ mol } NaHCO_3}{84.01 \text{ g } NaHCO_3} \times \dfrac{1 \text{ L}}{0.100 \text{ mol } NaHCO_3} = 0.0417$ L = 41.7 mL

41.7 mL of 0.100 M $NaHCO_3$ contains 0.350 g $NaHCO_3$.

16.   25.0 g $(NH_4)_2SO_4 \times \dfrac{1 \text{ mol}}{132.15 \text{ g}} = 1.89 \times 10^{-1}$ mol $(NH_4)_2SO_4$

Molarity = $\dfrac{1.89 \times 10^{-1} \text{ mol}}{100.0 \text{ mL}} \times \dfrac{1000 \text{ mL}}{L} = 1.89 \ M \ (NH_4)_2SO_4$

Moles of $(NH_4)_2SO_4$ in final solution = 10.00×10^{-3} L $\times \dfrac{1.89 \text{ mol}}{L} = 1.89 \times 10^{-2}$ mol $(NH_4)_2SO_4$

Molarity of final solution = $\dfrac{1.89 \times 10^{-2} \text{ mol}}{(10.00 + 50.00) \text{ mL}} \times \dfrac{1000 \text{ mL}}{L} = 0.315 \ M \ (NH_4)_2SO_4$

$(NH_4)_2SO_4(s) \rightarrow 2 \ NH_4^+(aq) + SO_4^{2-}(aq);$ $M_{NH_4^+} = 2(0.315) = 0.630 \ M;$ $M_{SO_4^{2-}} = 0.315 \ M$

17.   75.0 mL $\times \dfrac{0.79 \text{ g}}{\text{mL}} \times \dfrac{1 \text{ mol}}{46.1 \text{ g}} = 1.3$ mol $C_2H_5OH;$ Molarity = $\dfrac{1.3 \text{ mol}}{0.250 \text{ L}} = 5.2 \ M \ C_2H_5OH$

18.   Stock solution = $\dfrac{10.0 \text{ mg}}{500.0 \text{ mL}} = \dfrac{10.0 \times 10^{-3} \text{ g}}{500.0 \text{ mL}} = \dfrac{2.00 \times 10^{-5} \text{ g steroid}}{\text{mL}}$

100.0×10^{-6} L stock $\times \dfrac{1000 \text{ mL}}{L} \times \dfrac{2.00 \times 10^{-5} \text{ g steroid}}{\text{mL}} = 2.00 \times 10^{-6}$ g steroid

This is diluted to a final volume of 100.0 mL.

$\dfrac{2.00 \times 10^{-6} \text{ g steroid}}{100.0 \text{ mL}} \times \dfrac{1000 \text{ mL}}{L} \times \dfrac{1 \text{ mol steroid}}{336.4 \text{ g steroid}} = 5.95 \times 10^{-8} \ M \text{ steroid}$

19.   Stock solution:

1.584 g $Mn^{2+} \times \dfrac{1 \text{ mol } Mn^{2+}}{54.94 \text{ g } Mn^{2+}} = 2.883 \times 10^{-2}$ mol $Mn^{2+};$ $M = \dfrac{2.883 \times 10^{-2} \text{ mol}}{1.000 \text{ L}}$

$= 2.883 \times 10^{-2} \ M \ Mn^{2+}$

Solution A contains:

50.00 mL $\times \dfrac{1 \text{ L}}{1000 \text{ mL}} \times \dfrac{2.883 \times 10^{-2} \text{ mol}}{L} = 1.442 \times 10^{-3}$ mol Mn^{2+}

Molarity = $\dfrac{1.442 \times 10^{-3} \text{ mol}}{1000.0 \text{ mL}} \times \dfrac{1000 \text{ mL}}{L} = 1.442 \times 10^{-3} \ M \ Mn^{2+}$

Solution B contains:

$$10.00 \text{ mL} \times \frac{1 \text{ L}}{1000 \text{ mL}} \times \frac{1.442 \times 10^{-3} \text{ mol}}{\text{L}} = 1.442 \times 10^{-5} \text{ mol Mn}^{2+}$$

$$\text{Molarity} = \frac{1.442 \times 10^{-5} \text{ mol}}{0.2500 \text{ L}} = 5.768 \times 10^{-5} \text{ } M \text{ Mn}^{2+}$$

Solution C contains:

$$10.00 \times 10^{-3} \text{ L} \times \frac{5.768 \times 10^{-5} \text{ mol}}{\text{L}} = 5.768 \times 10^{-7} \text{ mol Mn}^{2+}$$

$$\text{Molarity} = \frac{5.768 \times 10^{-7} \text{ mol}}{0.5000 \text{ L}} = 1.154 \times 10^{-6} \text{ } M \text{ Mn}^{2+}$$

20.   a.   Procedure i. The greatest error is in the measurement of the sample using the 10 mL pipet. The

error is $\dfrac{0.01}{10.00} \times 100 = 0.1\%$. Procedure ii: The error in measuring the 0.050 mL sample is

$\dfrac{1 \text{ }\mu L}{0.050 \text{ mL} \times 1000 \text{ }\mu L/mL} \times 100 = 2\%$. Three dilutions with a 0.1% error will be more accurate

than a single dilution with 2% error.

b. $\dfrac{0.200 \text{ mol Fe}^{2+}}{\text{L}} \times \dfrac{55.85 \text{ g Fe}^{2+}}{\text{mol Fe}^{2+}} = 11.2 \text{ g Fe}^{2+}/\text{L} = 11.2 \text{ mg Fe}^{2+}/\text{mL}$

The conversions from g to mg and from L to mL cancel each other.

21. $\text{mol Na}_2\text{CO}_3 = 0.0700 \text{ L} \times \dfrac{3.0 \text{ mol Na}_2\text{CO}_3}{\text{L}} = 0.21 \text{ mol Na}_2\text{CO}_3$

$\text{Na}_2\text{CO}_3(s) \rightarrow 2 \text{ Na}^+(aq) + \text{CO}_3^{2-}(aq); \quad \text{mol Na}^+ = 2(0.21) = 0.42 \text{ mol}$

$\text{mol NaHCO}_3 = 0.0300 \text{ L} \times \dfrac{1.0 \text{ mol NaHCO}_3}{\text{L}} = 0.030 \text{ mol NaHCO}_3$

$\text{NaHCO}_3(s) \rightarrow \text{Na}^+(aq) + \text{HCO}_3^-(aq); \quad \text{mol Na}^+ = 0.030 \text{ mol}$

$M_{\text{Na}^+} = \dfrac{\text{total mol Na}^+}{\text{total volume}} = \dfrac{0.42 \text{ mol} + 0.030 \text{ mol}}{0.0700 \text{ L} + 0.0300 \text{ L}} = \dfrac{0.45 \text{ mol}}{0.1000 \text{ L}} = 4.5 \text{ } M \text{ Na}^+$

22.   a.   5.0 ppb Hg in water $= \dfrac{5.0 \text{ ng Hg}}{\text{mL H}_2\text{O}} = \dfrac{5.0 \times 10^{-9} \text{ g Hg}}{\text{mL H}_2\text{O}}$

$\dfrac{5.0 \times 10^{-9} \text{ g Hg}}{\text{mL}} \times \dfrac{1 \text{ mol Hg}}{200.6 \text{ g Hg}} \times \dfrac{1000 \text{ mL}}{\text{L}} = 2.5 \times 10^{-8} \text{ } M \text{ Hg}$

b. $\dfrac{1.0 \times 10^{-9} \text{ g CHCl}_3}{\text{mL}} \times \dfrac{1 \text{ mol CHCl}_3}{119.4 \text{ g CHCl}_3} \times \dfrac{1000 \text{ mL}}{\text{L}} = 8.4 \times 10^{-9} \, M \, \text{CHCl}_3$

c. $10.0 \text{ ppm As} = \dfrac{10.0 \, \mu\text{g As}}{\text{mL}} = \dfrac{10.0 \times 10^{-6} \text{ g As}}{\text{mL}}$

$\dfrac{10.0 \times 10^{-6} \text{ g As}}{\text{mL}} \times \dfrac{1 \text{ mol As}}{74.92 \text{ g As}} \times \dfrac{1000 \text{ mL}}{\text{L}} = 1.33 \times 10^{-4} \, M \, \text{As}$

d. $\dfrac{0.10 \times 10^{-6} \text{ g DDT}}{\text{mL}} \times \dfrac{1 \text{ mol DDT}}{354.5 \text{ g DDT}} \times \dfrac{1000 \text{ mL}}{\text{L}} = 2.8 \times 10^{-7} \, M \, \text{DDT}$

23. $1 \text{ ppm} = \dfrac{1 \, \mu\text{g}}{\text{mL}} = \dfrac{1 \text{ mg}}{\text{L}} ; \quad \dfrac{1 \times 10^{-3} \text{ g F}^{-}}{\text{L}} \times \dfrac{1 \text{ mol F}^{-}}{19.0 \text{ g F}^{-}} = \dfrac{5 \times 10^{-5} \text{ mol}}{\text{L}} = 5 \times 10^{-5} \, M \, \text{F}^{-}$

$2 \text{ ppm F}^{-} = 1 \times 10^{-4} \, M \, \text{F}^{-}; \quad 3 \text{ ppm F}^{-} = \dfrac{1.6 \times 10^{-4} \text{ mol}}{\text{L}} = 2 \times 10^{-4} \, M \, \text{F}^{-}$

$\dfrac{50. \times 10^{-3} \text{ g F}^{-}}{\text{L}} \times \dfrac{1 \text{ mol F}^{-}}{19.0 \text{ g F}^{-}} = 2.6 \times 10^{-3} \, M \, \text{F}^{-}$

24. We want 100.0 mL of each standard. To make the 100. ppm standard:

$\dfrac{100. \, \mu\text{g Cu}}{\text{mL}} \times 100.0 \text{ mL solution} = 1.00 \times 10^{4} \, \mu\text{g Cu needed}$

$1.00 \times 10^{4} \, \mu\text{g Cu} \times \dfrac{1 \text{ mL stock}}{1000.0 \, \mu\text{g Cu}} = 10.0 \text{ mL of stock solution}$

Therefore, to make 100.0 mL of 100. ppm solution, transfer 10.0 mL of the 1000.0 ppm stock solution to a 100 mL volumetric flask and dilute to the mark.

Similarly:

75.0 ppm standard, dilute 7.50 mL of the 1000.0 ppm stock to 100.0 mL.

50.0 ppm standard, dilute 5.00 mL of the 1000.0 ppm stock to 100.0 mL.

25.0 ppm standard, dilute 2.50 mL of the 1000.0 ppm stock to 100.0 mL.

10.0 ppm standard, dilute 1.00 mL of the 1000.0 ppm stock to 100.0 mL.

Precipitation Reactions

25.   For the following answers, the balanced molecular equation is first, followed by the complete ionic equation, then the net ionic equation.

   a. $(NH_4)_2SO_4(aq) + Ba(NO_3)_2(aq) \rightarrow 2\ NH_4NO_3(aq) + BaSO_4(s)$

        $2\ NH_4^+(aq) + SO_4^{2-}(aq) + Ba^{2+}(aq) + 2\ NO_3^-(aq) \rightarrow 2\ NH_4^+(aq) + 2\ NO_3^-(aq) + BaSO_4(s)$

        $Ba^{2+}(aq) + SO_4^{2-}(aq) \rightarrow BaSO_4(s)$ is the net ionic equation (spectator ions omitted).

   b. $Pb(NO_3)_2(aq) + 2\ NaCl(aq) \rightarrow PbCl_2(s) + 2\ NaNO_3(aq)$

        $Pb^{2+}(aq) + 2\ NO_3^-(aq) + 2\ Na^+(aq) + 2\ Cl^-(aq) \rightarrow PbCl_2(s) + 2\ Na^+(aq) + 2\ NO_3^-(aq)$

        $Pb^{2+}(aq) + 2\ Cl^-(aq) \rightarrow PbCl_2(s)$

   c.   The possible products, potassium phosphate and sodium nitrate, are both soluble in water. Therefore, no reaction occurs.

   d.   No reaction occurs since all possible products are soluble.

   e. $CuCl_2(aq) + 2\ NaOH(aq) \rightarrow Cu(OH)_2(s) + 2\ NaCl(aq)$

        $Cu^{2+}(aq) + 2\ Cl^-(aq) + 2\ Na^+(aq) + 2\ OH^-(aq) \rightarrow Cu(OH)_2(s) + 2\ Na^+(aq) + 2\ Cl^-(aq)$

        $Cu^{2+}(aq) + 2\ OH^-(aq) \rightarrow Cu(OH)_2(s)$

26.   The following schemes show reagents to add in order to precipitate one ion at a time. In each scheme, NaOH can be added to precipitate the last remaining ion.

   a.

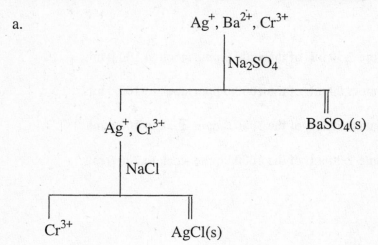

b. 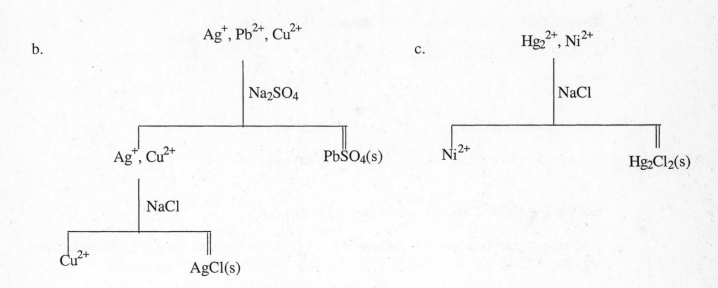 c.

27. a. When $CuSO_4(aq)$ is added to $Na_2S(aq)$, the precipitate that forms is $CuS(s)$. Therefore, Na^+ (the grey spheres) and SO_4^{2-} (the blueish-green spheres) are the spectator ions.

$$CuSO_4(aq) + Na_2S(aq) \rightarrow CuS(s) + Na_2SO_4(aq); \; Cu^{2+}(aq) + S^{2-}(aq) \rightarrow CuS(s)$$

     b. When $CoCl_2(aq)$ is added to $NaOH(aq)$, the precipitate that forms is $Co(OH)_2(s)$. Therefore, Na^+ (the grey spheres) and Cl^- (the green spheres) are the spectator ions.

$$CoCl_2(aq) + 2\,NaOH(aq) \rightarrow Co(OH)_2(s) + 2\,NaCl(aq); \; Co^{2+}(aq) + 2\,OH^-(aq) \rightarrow Co(OH)_2(s)$$

     c. When $AgNO_3(aq)$ is added to $KI(aq)$, the precipitate that forms is $AgI(s)$. Therefore, K^+ (the red spheres) and NO_3^- (the blue spheres) are the spectator ions.

$$AgNO_3(aq) + KI(aq) \rightarrow AgI(s) + KNO_3(aq); \; Ag^+(aq) + I^-(aq) \rightarrow AgI(s)$$

28. There are many acceptable choices for spectator ions. We will generally choose Na^+ and NO_3^- as the spectator ions because sodium salts and nitrate salts are usually soluble in water.

     a. $Fe(NO_3)_3(aq) + 3\,NaOH(aq) \rightarrow Fe(OH)_3(s) + 3\,NaNO_3(aq)$

     b. $Hg_2(NO_3)_2(aq) + 2\,NaCl(aq) \rightarrow Hg_2Cl_2(s) + 2\,NaNO_3(aq)$

     c. $Pb(NO_3)_2(aq) + Na_2SO_4(aq) \rightarrow PbSO_4(s) + 2\,NaNO_3(aq)$

     d. $BaCl_2(aq) + Na_2CrO_4(aq) \rightarrow BaCrO_4(s) + 2\,NaCl(aq)$

29. Since no precipitate formed upon addition of NaCl or Na_2SO_4, we can conclude that Hg_2^{2+} and Ba^{2+} are not present since Hg_2Cl_2 and $BaSO_4$ are insoluble salts. Since a precipitate formed with NaOH, then the solution must contain Mn^{2+} which forms $Mn(OH)_2(s)$.

30. $2\,Na_3PO_4(aq) + 3\,Pb(NO_3)_2(aq) \rightarrow Pb_3(PO_4)_2(s) + 6\,NaNO_3(aq)$

$$0.1500\,L \times \frac{0.250\,mol\,Pb(NO_3)_2}{L} \times \frac{2\,mol\,Na_3PO_4}{3\,mol\,Pb(NO_3)_2} \times \frac{1\,L\,Na_3PO_4}{0.100\,mol\,Na_3PO_4} = 0.250\,L$$

$$= 250.\,mL\,Na_3PO_4$$

31. $2\,AgNO_3(aq) + CaCl_2(aq) \rightarrow 2\,AgCl(s) + Ca(NO_3)_2(aq)$

$$mol\,AgNO_3 = 0.1000\,L \times \frac{0.20\,mol\,AgNO_3}{L} = 0.020\,mol\,AgNO_3$$

$$mol\,CaCl_2 = 0.1000\,L \times \frac{0.15\,mol\,CaCl_2}{L} = 0.015\,mol\,CaCl_2$$

The required mol $AgNO_3$ to mol $CaCl_2$ ratio is 2:1 (from the balanced equation).   The actual mol ratio present is 0.020/0.015 = 1.3 (1.3:1).   Therefore, $AgNO_3$ is the limiting reagent.

$$mass\,AgCl = 0.020\,mol\,AgNO_3 \times \frac{1\,mol\,AgCl}{1\,mol\,AgNO_3} \times \frac{143.4\,g\,AgCl}{mol\,AgCl} = 2.9\,g\,AgCl$$

The net ionic equation is: $Ag^+(aq) + Cl^-(aq) \rightarrow AgCl(s)$.   The ions remaining in solution are the unreacted Cl^- ions and the spectator ions, NO_3^- and Ca^{2+} (all Ag^+ is used up in forming AgCl).   The mol of each ion present initially (before reaction) can be easily determined from the mol of each reactant. 0.020 mol $AgNO_3$ dissolves to form 0.020 mol Ag^+ and 0.020 mol NO_3^-. 0.015 mol $CaCl_2$ dissolves to form 0.015 mol Ca^{2+} and 2(0.015) = 0.030 mol Cl^-.

mol unreacted Cl^- = 0.030 mol Cl^- initially - 0.020 mol Cl^- reacted = 0.010 mol Cl^- unreacted

$$M_{Cl^-} = \frac{0.010\,mol\,Cl^-}{total\,volume} = \frac{0.010\,mol\,Cl^-}{0.1000\,L + 0.1000\,L} = 0.050\,M\,Cl^-$$

The molarity of the spectator ions are:

$$M_{NO_3^-} = \frac{0.020\,mol\,NO_3^-}{0.2000\,L} = 0.10\,M\,NO_3^-; \quad M_{Ca^{2+}} = \frac{0.015\,mol\,Ca^{2+}}{0.2000\,L} = 0.075\,M\,Ca^{2+}$$

32.   a. $Cu(NO_3)_2(aq) + 2\,KOH(aq) \rightarrow Cu(OH)_2(s) + 2\,KNO_3(aq)$

Solution A contains 2.00 L × 2.00 mol/L = 4.00 mol $Cu(NO_3)_2$ and solution B contains 2.00 L × 3.00 mol/L = 6.00 mol KOH. Lets assume in our picture that we have 4 formula units of $Cu(NO_3)_2$ (4 Cu^{2+} ions and 8 NO_3^- ions) and 6 formula units of KOH (6 K^+ ions and 6 OH^- ions). With 4 Cu^{2+} ions and 6 OH^- ions present, then OH^- is limiting. One Cu^{2+} ion remains as 3 $Cu(OH)_2(s)$ formula units form as precipitate. The following drawing summarizes the ions that remain in solution and the relative amount of precipitate that forms. Note that K^+ and NO_3^- ions are spectator ions. In the drawing, V_1 is the volume of solution A or B and V_2 is the volume of the combined solutions with $V_2 = 2\,V_1$. The drawing exaggerates the amount of precipitate that would actually form.

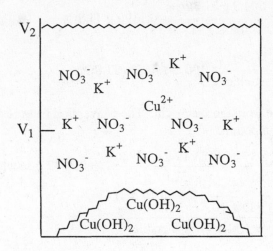

b. The spectator ion concentrations will be one-half of the original spectator ion concentrations in

the individual beakers because the volume was doubled. Or using moles, $M_{K^+} = \dfrac{6.00 \text{ mol K}^+}{4.00 \text{ L}}$

$= 1.50\ M$ and $M_{NO_3^-} = \dfrac{8.00 \text{ mol NO}_3^-}{4.00 \text{ L}} = 2.00\ M$. The concentration of OH⁻ ions will be zero

since OH⁻ is the limiting reagent. From the drawing, the number of Cu^{2+} ions will decrease by

a factor of four as the precipitate forms. Since the volume of solution doubled, the concentration

of Cu^{2+} ions will decrease by a factor of eight after the two beakers are mixed:

$$M_{Cu^{2+}} = 2.00 \left(\frac{1}{8} \right) = 0.250\ M$$

Alternately, one could certainly use moles to solve for $M_{Cu^{2+}}$:

$$\text{mol Cu}^{2+} \text{ reacted} = 2.00 \text{ L} \times \frac{3.00 \text{ mol OH}^-}{L} \times \frac{1 \text{ mol Cu}^{2+}}{2 \text{ mol OH}^-} = 3.00 \text{ mol Cu}^{2+} \text{ reacted}$$

$$\text{mol Cu}^{2+} \text{ present initially} = 2.00 \text{ L} \times \frac{2.00 \text{ mol Cu}^{2+}}{L} = 4.00 \text{ mol Cu}^{2+} \text{ present initially}$$

excess Cu^{2+} present after reaction = 4.00 mol - 3.00 mol = 1.00 mol Cu^{2+} excess

$$M_{Cu^{2+}} = \frac{1.00 \text{ mol Cu}^{2+}}{2.00 \text{ L} + 2.00 \text{ L}} = 0.250\ M$$

$$\text{mass of precipitate} = 6.00 \text{ mol KOH} \times \frac{1 \text{ mol Cu(OH)}_2}{2 \text{ mol KOH}} \times \frac{97.57 \text{ g Cu(OH)}_2}{\text{mol Cu(OH)}_2} = 293 \text{ g Cu(OH)}_2$$

33. $1.00 \text{ L} \times \dfrac{0.200 \text{ mol Na}_2S_2O_3}{L} \times \dfrac{1 \text{ mol AgBr}}{2 \text{ mol Na}_2S_2O_3} \times \dfrac{187.8 \text{ g AgBr}}{\text{mol AgBr}} = 18.8 \text{ g AgBr}$

34. All the Tl in TlI came from Tl in Tl_2SO_4. The conversion from TlI to Tl_2SO_4 utilizes the molar
     masses of each compound.

$$0.1824 \text{ g Tll} \times \frac{204.4 \text{ g Tl}}{331.3 \text{ gTll}} \times \frac{504.9 \text{ g Tl}_2\text{SO}_4}{408.8 \text{ g Tl}} = 0.1390 \text{ g Tl}_2\text{SO}_4$$

$$\text{mass \% Tl}_2\text{SO}_4 = \frac{0.1390 \text{ g Tl}_2\text{SO}_4}{9.486 \text{ g pesticide}} \times 100 = 1.465\% \text{ Tl}_2\text{SO}_4$$

35.   All the sulfur in $BaSO_4$ came from the saccharin. The conversion from $BaSO_4$ to saccharin utilizes the molar masses of each compound.

$$0.5032 \text{ g BaSO}_4 \times \frac{32.07 \text{ g S}}{233.4 \text{ g BaSO}_4} \times \frac{183.19 \text{ g saccharin}}{32.07 \text{ g S}} = 0.3949 \text{ g saccharin}$$

$$\frac{\text{Avg. mass}}{\text{Tablet}} = \frac{0.3949 \text{ g}}{10 \text{ tablets}} = \frac{3.949 \times 10^{-2} \text{ g}}{\text{tablet}} = \frac{39.49 \text{ mg}}{\text{tablet}}$$

$$\text{Avg. mass \%} = \frac{0.3949 \text{ g saccharin}}{0.5894 \text{ g}} \times 100 = 67.00\% \text{ saccharin by mass}$$

36.   Use the silver nitrate data to calculate the mol Cl^- present, then use the formula of douglasite to convert from Cl^- to douglasite. The net ionic reaction is: $Ag^+ + Cl^- \rightarrow AgCl(s)$.

$$0.03720 \text{ L} \times \frac{0.1000 \text{ mol Ag}^+}{\text{L}} \times \frac{1 \text{ mol Cl}^-}{\text{mol Ag}^+} \times \frac{1 \text{ mol douglasite}}{4 \text{ mol Cl}^-} \times \frac{311.88 \text{ g douglasite}}{\text{mol}}$$

$$= 0.2900 \text{ g douglasite}$$

$$\text{Mass \% douglasite} = \frac{0.2900 \text{ g}}{0.4550 \text{ g}} \times 100 = 63.74\%$$

37. $M_2SO_4(aq) + CaCl_2(aq) \rightarrow CaSO_4(s) + 2 \text{ MCl}(aq)$

$$1.36 \text{ g CaSO}_4 \times \frac{1 \text{ mol CaSO}_4}{136.15 \text{ g CaSO}_4} \times \frac{1 \text{ mol M}_2\text{SO}_4}{\text{mol CaSO}_4} = 9.99 \times 10^{-3} \text{ mol M}_2\text{SO}_4$$

From the problem, 1.42 g M_2SO_4 was reacted so:

$$1.42 \text{ g M}_2\text{SO}_4 = 9.99 \times 10^{-3} \text{ mol M}_2\text{SO}_4, \quad \text{molar mass} = \frac{1.42 \text{ g M}_2\text{SO}_4}{9.99 \times 10^{-3} \text{ mol M}_2\text{SO}_4} = 142 \text{ g/mol}$$

142 amu = 2(atomic mass M) + 32.07 + 4(16.00), atomic mass M = 23 amu

From periodic table, M = Na(sodium).

Acid-Base Reactions

38.   a. $NH_3(aq) + HNO_3(aq) \rightarrow NH_4NO_3(aq)$ (molecular equation)

$NH_3(aq) + H^+(aq) + NO_3^-(aq) \rightarrow NH_4^+(aq) + NO_3^-(aq)$ (complete ionic equation)

$NH_3(aq) + H^+(aq) \rightarrow NH_4^+(aq)$ (net ionic equation)

b. $Ba(OH)_2(aq) + 2\ HCl(aq) \rightarrow 2\ H_2O(l) + BaCl_2(aq)$

$Ba^{2+}(aq) + 2\ OH^-(aq) + 2\ H^+(aq) + 2\ Cl^-(aq) \rightarrow Ba^{2+}(aq) + 2\ Cl^-(aq) + 2\ H_2O(l)$

$OH^-(aq) + H^+(aq) \rightarrow H_2O(l)$

c. $3\ HClO_4(aq) + Fe(OH)_3(s) \rightarrow 3\ H_2O(l) + Fe(ClO_4)_3(aq)$

$3\ H^+(aq) + 3\ ClO_4^-(aq) + Fe(OH)_3(s) \rightarrow 3\ H_2O(l) + Fe^{3+}(aq) + 3\ ClO_4^-(aq)$

$3\ H^+(aq) + Fe(OH)_3(s) \rightarrow 3\ H_2O(l) + Fe^{3+}(aq)$

d. $AgOH(s) + HBr(aq) \rightarrow AgBr(s) + H_2O(l)$

$AgOH(s) + H^+(aq) + Br^-(aq) \rightarrow AgBr(s) + H_2O(l)$

$AgOH(s) + H^+(aq) + Br^-(aq) \rightarrow AgBr(s) + H_2O(l)$

39.   a.   Perchloric acid reacted with potassium hydroxide is a possibility.

$HClO_4(aq) + KOH(aq) \rightarrow H_2O(l) + KClO_4(aq)$

b.   Nitric acid reacted with cesium hydroxide is a possibility.

$HNO_3(aq) + CsOH(aq) \rightarrow H_2O(l) + CsNO_3(aq)$

c.   Hydroiodic acid reacted with calcium hydroxide is a possibility.

$2\ HI(aq) + Ca(OH)_2(aq) \rightarrow 2\ H_2O(l) + CaI_2(aq)$

40.   We get the empirical formula from the elemental analysis. Out of 100.00 g carminic acid there are:

$$53.66 \text{ g C} \times \frac{1 \text{ mol C}}{12.011 \text{ g C}} = 4.468 \text{ mol C}; \quad 4.09 \text{ g H} \times \frac{1 \text{ mol H}}{1.008 \text{ g H}} = 4.06 \text{ mol H}$$

$$42.25 \text{ g O} \times \frac{1 \text{ mol O}}{15.999 \text{ g O}} = 2.641 \text{ mol O}$$

Dividing the moles by the smallest number gives:

$$\frac{4.468}{2.641} = 1.692; \quad \frac{4.06}{2.641} = 1.54$$

These numbers don't give obvious mol ratios. Lets determine the mol C to mol H ratio:

$$\frac{4.468}{4.06} = 1.10 = \frac{11}{10}$$

So let's try $\frac{4.06}{10} = 0.406$ as a common factor: $\frac{4.468}{0.406} = 11.0$; $\frac{4.06}{0.406} = 10.0$; $\frac{2.641}{0.406} = 6.50$

Therefore, $C_{22}H_{20}O_{13}$ is the empirical formula.

We can get molar mass from the titration data. The balanced reaction is $HA(aq) + OH^-(aq) \rightarrow H_2O(l) + A^-(aq)$ where HA is an abbreviation for carminic acid, an acid with one acidic H^+.

$$18.02 \times 10^{-3} \text{ L soln} \times \frac{0.0406 \text{ mol NaOH}}{\text{L soln}} \times \frac{1 \text{ mol carminic acid}}{\text{mol NaOH}} = 7.32 \times 10^{-4} \text{ mol carminic acid}$$

$$\text{Molar mass} = \frac{0.3602 \text{ g}}{7.32 \times 10^{-4} \text{ mol}} = \frac{492 \text{ g}}{\text{mol}}$$

The empirical formula mass of $C_{22}H_{20}O_{13} \approx 22(12) + 20(1) + 13(16) = 492$ g.

Therefore, the molecular formula of carminic acid is also $C_{22}H_{20}O_{13}$.

41.   If we begin with 50.00 mL of 0.100 M NaOH, then:

$$50.00 \times 10^{-3} \text{ L} \times \frac{0.100 \text{ mol}}{\text{L}} = 5.00 \times 10^{-3} \text{ mol NaOH to be neutralized.}$$

a. $NaOH(aq) + HCl(aq) \rightarrow NaCl(aq) + H_2O(l)$

$$5.00 \times 10^{-3} \text{ mol NaOH} \times \frac{1 \text{ mol HCl}}{\text{mol NaOH}} \times \frac{1 \text{ L soln}}{0.100 \text{ mol}} = 5.00 \times 10^{-2} \text{ L or 50.0 mL}$$

b. $2 \text{ NaOH}(aq) + H_2SO_3(aq) \rightarrow 2 \text{ H}_2O(l) + Na_2SO_3(aq)$

$$5.00 \times 10^{-3} \text{ mol NaOH} \times \frac{1 \text{ mol H}_2SO_3}{2 \text{ mol NaOH}} \times \frac{1 \text{ L soln}}{0.100 \text{ mol H}_2SO_3} = 2.50 \times 10^{-2} \text{ L or 25.0 mL}$$

c. $3 \text{ NaOH}(aq) + H_3PO_4(aq) \rightarrow Na_3PO_4(aq) + 3 \text{ H}_2O(l)$

$$5.00 \times 10^{-3} \text{ mol NaOH} \times \frac{1 \text{ mol H}_3PO_4}{3 \text{ mol NaOH}} \times \frac{1 \text{ L soln}}{0.200 \text{ mol H}_3PO_4} = 8.33 \times 10^{-3} \text{ L or 8.33 mL}$$

d. $HNO_3(aq) + NaOH(aq) \rightarrow H_2O(l) + NaNO_3(aq)$

$$5.00 \times 10^{-3} \text{ mol NaOH} \times \frac{1 \text{ mol HNO}_3}{\text{mol NaOH}} \times \frac{1 \text{ L soln}}{0.150 \text{ mol HNO}_3} = 3.33 \times 10^{-2} \text{ L or 33.3 mL}$$

e. $HC_2H_3O_2(aq) + NaOH(aq) \rightarrow H_2O(l) + NaC_2H_3O_2(aq)$

$$5.00 \times 10^{-3} \text{ mol NaOH} \times \frac{1 \text{ mol } HC_2H_3O_2}{\text{mol NaOH}} \times \frac{1 \text{ L soln}}{0.200 \text{ mol } HC_2H_3O_2} = 2.50 \times 10^{-2} \text{ L or } 25.0 \text{ mL}$$

f. $H_2SO_4(aq) + 2 \text{ NaOH}(aq) \rightarrow 2 H_2O(l) + Na_2SO_4(aq)$

$$5.00 \times 10^{-3} \text{ mol NaOH} \times \frac{1 \text{ mol } H_2SO_4}{2 \text{ mol NaOH}} \times \frac{1 \text{ L soln}}{0.300 \text{ mol } H_2SO_4} = 8.33 \times 10^{-3} \text{ L or } 8.33 \text{ mL}$$

42.   Since KHP is a monoprotic acid, the reaction is (KHP is an abbreviation for potassium hydrogen phthalate):

$$NaOH(aq) + KHP(aq) \rightarrow NaKP(aq) + H_2O(l)$$

$$0.1082 \text{ g KHP} \times \frac{1 \text{ mol KHP}}{204.22 \text{ g KHP}} \times \frac{1 \text{ mol NaOH}}{\text{mol KHP}} = 5.298 \times 10^{-4} \text{ mol NaOH}.$$

There is 5.298×10^{-4} mol of sodium hydroxide in 34.67 mL of solution. Therefore, the concentration of sodium hydroxide is:

$$\frac{5.298 \times 10^{-4} \text{ mol}}{34.67 \times 10^{-3} \text{ L}} = 1.528 \times 10^{-2} \text{ M NaOH}$$

43.   The pertinent reactions are:

$$2 \text{ NaOH}(aq) + H_2SO_4(aq) \rightarrow Na_2SO_4(aq) + 2 H_2O(l)$$

$$HCl(aq) + NaOH(aq) \rightarrow NaCl(aq) + H_2O(l)$$

Amount of NaOH added $= 0.0500 \text{ L} \times \dfrac{0.213 \text{ mol}}{\text{L}} = 1.07 \times 10^{-2} \text{ mol NaOH}$

Amount of NaOH neutralized by HCl:

$$0.01321 \text{ L HCl} \times \frac{0.103 \text{ mol HCl}}{\text{L HCl}} \times \frac{1 \text{ mol NaOH}}{\text{mol HCl}} = 1.36 \times 10^{-3} \text{ mol NaOH}$$

The difference, 9.3×10^{-3} mol, is the amount of NaOH neutralized by the sulfuric acid.

$$9.3 \times 10^{-3} \text{ mol NaOH} \times \frac{1 \text{ mol } H_2SO_4}{2 \text{ mol NaOH}} = 4.7 \times 10^{-3} \text{ mol } H_2SO_4$$

Concentration of $H_2SO_4 = \dfrac{4.7 \times 10^{-3} \text{ mol}}{0.1000 \text{ L}} = 4.7 \times 10^{-2} \text{ M } H_2SO_4$

44. $2 H_3PO_4(aq) + 3 Ba(OH)_2(aq) \rightarrow 6 H_2O(l) + Ba_3(PO_4)_2(s)$

$$0.01420 \text{ L} \times \frac{0.141 \text{ mol } H_3PO_4}{L} \times \frac{3 \text{ mol } Ba(OH)_2}{2 \text{ mol } H_3PO_4} \times \frac{1 \text{ L } Ba(OH)_2}{0.0521 \text{ mol } Ba(OH)_2} = 0.0576 \text{ L}$$

$$= 57.6 \text{ mL } Ba(OH)_2$$

45. $HC_2H_3O_2(aq) + NaOH(aq) \rightarrow H_2O(l) + NaC_2H_3O_2(aq)$

a. $16.58 \times 10^{-3} \text{ L soln} \times \frac{0.5062 \text{ mol NaOH}}{L \text{ soln}} \times \frac{1 \text{ mol acetic acid}}{\text{mol NaOH}} = 8.393 \times 10^{-3} \text{ mol acetic acid}$

Concentration of acetic acid $= \dfrac{8.393 \times 10^{-3} \text{ mol}}{0.01000 \text{ L}} = 0.8393 \text{ } M \text{ } HC_2H_3O_2$

b.   If we have 1.000 L of solution: total mass $= 1000. \text{ mL} \times \dfrac{1.006 \text{ g}}{\text{mL}} = 1006 \text{ g solution}$

Mass of $HC_2H_3O_2 = 0.8393 \text{ mol} \times \dfrac{60.052 \text{ g}}{\text{mol}} = 50.40 \text{ g } HC_2H_3O_2$

Mass % acetic acid $= \dfrac{50.40 \text{ g}}{1006 \text{ g}} \times 100 = 5.010\%$

46.   Since KHP is a monoprotic acid, the reaction is: $NaOH(aq) + KHP(aq) \rightarrow H_2O(l) + NaKP(aq)$

Mass KHP $= 0.02046 \text{ L NaOH} \times \dfrac{0.1000 \text{ mol NaOH}}{L \text{ NaOH}} \times \dfrac{1 \text{ mol KHP}}{\text{mol NaOH}} \times \dfrac{204.22 \text{ g KHP}}{\text{mol KHP}} = 0.4178 \text{ g KHP}$

47. $HNO_3(aq) + NaOH(aq) \rightarrow NaNO_3(aq) + H_2O(l)$

$$15.0 \text{ g NaOH} \times \frac{1 \text{ mol NaOH}}{40.00 \text{ g}} = 0.375 \text{ mol NaOH}$$

$$0.1500 \text{ L} \times \frac{0.250 \text{ mol } HNO_3}{L} = 0.0375 \text{ mol } HNO_3$$

We have added more moles of NaOH than mol of HNO_3 present. Since NaOH and HNO_3 react in a 1:1 mol ratio, then NaOH is in excess and the solution will be basic. The ions present after reaction will be the excess OH^- ions and the spectator ions, Na^+ and NO_3^-. The moles of ions present initially are:

mol NaOH = mol Na^+ = mol OH^- = 0.375 mol

mol HNO_3 = mol H^+ = mol NO_3^- = 0.0375 mol

The net ionic reaction occurring is: $H^+(aq) + OH^-(aq) \rightarrow H_2O(l)$

The mol of excess OH^- remaining after reaction will be the initial mol of OH^- minus the amount of OH^- neutralized by reaction with H^+:

mol excess OH^- = 0.375 mol - 0.0375 mol = 0.338 mol OH^- excess

The concentration of ions present is:

$$M_{OH^-} = \frac{mol\ OH^-\ excess}{volume} = \frac{0.338\ mol\ OH^-}{0.1500\ L} = 2.25\ M\ OH^-$$

$$M_{NO_3^-} = \frac{0.0375\ mol\ NO_3^-}{0.1500\ L} = 0.250\ M\ NO_3^-;\quad M_{Na^+} = \frac{0.375\ mol}{0.1500\ L} = 2.50\ M\ Na^+$$

48. $39.47 \times 10^{-3}\ L\ HCl \times \dfrac{0.0984\ mol\ HCl}{L} \times \dfrac{1\ mol\ NH_3}{mol\ HCl} = 3.88 \times 10^{-3}\ mol\ NH_3$

Molarity of $NH_3 = \dfrac{3.88 \times 10^{-3}\ mol}{50.00 \times 10^{-3}\ L} = 0.0776\ M\ NH_3$

49. $Ba(OH)_2(aq) + 2\ HCl(aq) \rightarrow BaCl_2(aq) + 2\ H_2O(l);\ H^+(aq) + OH^-(aq) \rightarrow H_2O(l)$

$75.0 \times 10^{-3}\ L \times \dfrac{0.250\ mol\ HCl}{L} = 1.88 \times 10^{-2}\ mol\ HCl = 1.88 \times 10^{-2}\ mol\ H^+ + 1.88 \times 10^{-2}\ mol\ Cl^-$

$225.0 \times 10^{-3}\ L \times \dfrac{0.0550\ mol\ Ba(OH)_2}{L} = 1.24 \times 10^{-2}\ mol\ Ba(OH)_2 = 1.24 \times 10^{-2}\ mol\ Ba^{2+}$
$$+ 2.48 \times 10^{-2}\ mol\ OH^-$$

The net ionic equation requires a 1:1 mol ratio between OH^- and H^+. The actual mol OH^- to mol H^+ ratio is greater than 1:1 so OH^- is in excess.

Since $1.88 \times 10^{-2}\ mol\ OH^-$ will be neutralized by the H^+, then we have $(2.48 - 1.88) \times 10^{-2} = 0.60 \times 10^{-2}\ mol\ OH^-$ remaining in excess.

$$M_{OH^-} = \frac{mol\ OH^-\ excess}{total\ volume} = \frac{6.0 \times 10^{-3}\ mol\ OH^-}{0.0750\ L + 0.2250\ L} = 2.0 \times 10^{-2}\ M\ OH^-$$

50.   Let HA = unknown acid; $HA(aq) + NaOH(aq) \rightarrow NaA(aq) + H_2O(l)$

mol HA present $= 0.0250\ L \times \dfrac{0.500\ mol\ NaOH}{L} \times \dfrac{1\ mol\ HA}{1\ mol\ NaOH} = 0.0125\ mol\ HA$

$\dfrac{x\ g\ HA}{mol\ HA} = \dfrac{2.20\ g\ HA}{0.0125\ mol\ HA}$, x = molar mass of HA = 176 g/mol

Empirical formula weight $\approx 3(12) + 4(1) + 3(16) = 88$ g/mol

Since 176/88 = 2.0, then the molecular formula is $(C_3H_4O_3)_2 = C_6H_8O_6$.

Oxidation-Reduction Reactions

51.   Apply rules in Table 4.3.

   a. $KMnO_4$ is composed of K^+ and MnO_4^- ions. Assign oxygen an oxidation state value of -2 which gives manganese a +7 oxidation state since the sum of oxidation states for all atoms in MnO_4^- must equal the -1 charge on MnO_4^-. K, +1; O, -2; Mn, +7.

b.   Assign O a -2 oxidation state, which gives nickel a +4 oxidation state. Ni, +4; O, -2.

c. $K_4Fe(CN)_6$ is composed of K^+ cations and $Fe(CN)_6^{4-}$ anions. $Fe(CN)_6^{4-}$ is composed of iron and CN^- anions. For an overall anion charge of -4, iron must have a +2 oxidation state.

d. $(NH_4)_2HPO_4$ is made of NH_4^+ cations and HPO_4^{2-} anions. Assign +1 as oxidation state of H and -2 as the oxidation state of O. In NH_4^+, $x + 4(+1) = +1$, $x = -3 =$ oxidation state of N. In HPO_4^{2-}, $+1 + y + 4(-2) = -2$, $y = +5 =$ oxidation state of P.

e.   O, -2; P, +3   f.   O, -2; Fe, + 8/3

g.   O, -2; F, -1; Xe, +6   h.   F, -1; S, +4

i.   O, -2; C, +2   j.   Na, +1; O, -2; C, +3

52. a.   HBr: H, +1; Br, -1

     b.   HOBr: H, +1; O, -2; For Br, $+1 + 1(-2) + x = 0$, $x = +1$

     c. Br_2: Br, 0

     d. $HBrO_4$: H, +1; O, -2; For Br, $+1 + 4(-2) + x = 0$, $x = +7$

     e. BrF_3: F, -1; For Br, $x + 3(-1) = 0$, $x = +3$

53. a.   -3   b.   -3   c. $2(x) + 4(+1) = 0$, $x = -2$

     d.   +2   e.   +1   f.   +4

     g.   +3   h.   +5   i.   0

54. a. UO_2^{2+}: O, -2; For U, $x + 2(-2) = +2$, $x = +6$

     b. As_2O_3: O, -2; For As, $2(x) + 3(-2) = 0$, $x = +3$

     c. $NaBiO_3$: Na, +1; O, -2; For Bi, $+1 + x + 3(-2) = 0$, $x = +5$

     d. As_4: As, 0

     e. $HAsO_2$: assign H = +1 and O = -2; For As, $+1 + x + 2(-2) = 0$; $x = +3$

     f. $Mg_2P_2O_7$: Composed of Mg^{2+} ions and $P_2O_7^{4-}$ ions. Oxidation states are:

          Mg, +2; O, -2; P, +5

     g. $Na_2S_2O_3$: Composed of Na^+ ions and $S_2O_3^{2-}$ ions.   Na, +1; O, -2; S, +2

h. Hg_2Cl_2: Hg, +1; Cl, -1

i. $Ca(NO_3)_2$: Composed of Ca^{2+} ions and NO_3^- ions.   Ca, +2; O, -2; N, +5

55. To determine if the reaction is an oxidation-reduction reaction, assign oxidation states. If the oxidation states change for some elements, then the reaction is a redox reaction. If the oxidation states do not change, then the reaction is not a redox reaction. In redox reactions the species oxidized (called the reducing agent) shows an increase in the oxidation states and the species reduced (called the oxidizing agent) shows a decrease in oxidation states.

	Redox?	Oxidizing Agent	Reducing Agent	Substance Oxidized	Substance Reduced
a.	Yes	O_2	CH_4	CH_4 (C)	O_2 (O)
b.	Yes	HCl	Zn	Zn	HCl (H)
c.	No	-	-	-	-
d.	Yes	O_3	NO	NO (N)	O_3 (O)
e.	Yes	H_2O_2	H_2O_2	H_2O_2 (O)	H_2O_2 (O)
f.	Yes	CuCl	CuCl	CuCl (Cu)	CuCl (Cu)
g.	No	-	-	-	-
h.	No	-	-	-	-
i.	Yes	$SiCl_4$	Mg	Mg	$SiCl_4$ (Si)

In c, g, and h no oxidation states change from reactants to products.

56. a. The first step is to assign oxidation states to all atoms (see numbers above the atoms).

$$\overset{-3 \ +1}{C_2H_6} + \overset{0}{O_2} \rightarrow \overset{+4 \ -2}{CO_2} + \overset{+1 \ -2}{H_2O}$$

Each carbon atom changes from -3 to +4, an increase of seven. Each oxygen atom changes from 0 to -2, a decrease of 2. We need 7/2 O-atoms for every C-atom.

$$C_2H_6 + 7/2 \ O_2 \rightarrow CO_2 + H_2O$$

Balancing the remainder of the equation by inspection:

$$C_2H_6(g) + 7/2 \ O_2(g) \rightarrow 2 \ CO_2(g) + 3 \ H_2O(g)$$
or
$$2 \ C_2H_6(g) + 7 \ O_2(g) \rightarrow 4 \ CO_2(g) + 6 \ H_2O(g)$$

b. The oxidation state of magnesium changes from 0 to +2, an increase of 2. The oxidation state of hydrogen changes from +1 to 0, a decrease of 1. We need 2 H-atoms for every Mg-atom. The balanced equation is:

$$Mg(s) + 2 \ HCl(aq) \rightarrow Mg^{2+}(aq) + 2 \ Cl^-(aq) + H_2(g)$$

c.   The oxidation state of copper increases by 2 (0 to +2) and the oxidation state of silver decreases by 1 (+1 to 0). We need 2 Ag-atoms for every Cu-atom. The balanced equation is:

$$Cu(s) + 2\ Ag^+(aq) \rightarrow Cu^{2+}(aq) + 2\ Ag(s)$$

d.   The equation is balanced. Each hydrogen atom gains one electron (+1 → 0) and each zinc atom loses two electrons (0 → +2). We need 2 H-atoms for every Zn-atom. This is the ratio in the given equation:

$$Zn(s) + H_2SO_4(aq) \rightarrow ZnSO_4(aq) + H_2(g)$$

57.   a.   Review section 4.11 of the text for rules on balancing by the half-reaction method. The first step is to separate the reaction into two half-reactions then balance each half-reaction separately.

$$(Cu \rightarrow Cu^{2+} + 2\ e^-) \times 3 \qquad\qquad NO_3^- \rightarrow NO + 2\ H_2O$$
$$(3\ e^- + 4\ H^+ + NO_3^- \rightarrow NO + 2\ H_2O) \times 2$$

Adding the two balanced half-reactions so electrons cancel:

$$3\ Cu \rightarrow 3\ Cu^{2+} + 6\ e^-$$
$$6\ e^- + 8\ H^+ + 2\ NO_3^- \rightarrow 2\ NO + 4\ H_2O$$
$$\overline{}$$
$$3\ Cu(s) + 8\ H^+(aq) + 2\ NO_3^-(aq) \rightarrow 3\ Cu^{2+}(aq) + 2\ NO(g) + 4\ H_2O(l)$$

b. $(2\ Cl^- \rightarrow Cl_2 + 2\ e^-) \times 3 \qquad\qquad Cr_2O_7^{2-} \rightarrow 2\ Cr^{3+} + 7\ H_2O$
$$6\ e^- + 14\ H^+ + Cr_2O_7^{2-} \rightarrow 2\ Cr^{3+} + 7\ H_2O$$

Add the two balanced half-reactions with six electrons transferred:

$$6\ Cl^- \rightarrow 3\ Cl_2 + 6\ e^-$$
$$6\ e^- + 14\ H^+ + Cr_2O_7^{2-} \rightarrow 2\ Cr^{3+} + 7\ H_2O$$
$$\overline{}$$
$$14\ H^+(aq) + Cr_2O_7^{2-}(aq) + 6\ Cl^-(aq) \rightarrow 3\ Cl_2(g) + 2\ Cr^{3+}(aq) + 7\ H_2O(l)$$

c. $\qquad\qquad Pb \rightarrow PbSO_4 \qquad\qquad\qquad\qquad\qquad PbO_2 \rightarrow PbSO_4$
$Pb + H_2SO_4 \rightarrow PbSO_4 + 2\ H^+ \qquad\qquad PbO_2 + H_2SO_4 \rightarrow PbSO_4 + 2\ H_2O$
$Pb + H_2SO_4 \rightarrow PbSO_4 + 2\ H^+ + 2\ e^- \qquad 2\ e^- + 2\ H^+ + PbO_2 + H_2SO_4 \rightarrow PbSO_4 + 2\ H_2O$

Add the two half-reactions with two electrons transferred:

$$2\ e^- + 2\ H^+ + PbO_2 + H_2SO_4 \rightarrow PbSO_4 + 2\ H_2O$$
$$Pb + H_2SO_4 \rightarrow PbSO_4 + 2\ H^+ + 2\ e^-$$
$$\overline{}$$
$$Pb(s) + 2\ H_2SO_4(aq) + PbO_2(s) \rightarrow 2\ PbSO_4(s) + 2\ H_2O(l)$$

This is the reaction that occurs in an automobile lead storage battery.

d. $\quad\quad\quad\quad\quad\quad Mn^{2+} \rightarrow MnO_4^-$

$\quad\quad (4\ H_2O + Mn^{2+} \rightarrow MnO_4^- + 8\ H^+ + 5\ e^-) \times 2$

$\quad\quad\quad\quad\quad\quad\quad\quad\quad\quad\quad NaBiO_3 \rightarrow Bi^{3+} + Na^+$

$\quad\quad\quad\quad\quad\quad\quad\quad 6\ H^+ + NaBiO_3 \rightarrow Bi^{3+} + Na^+ + 3\ H_2O$

$\quad\quad\quad\quad\quad (2\ e^- + 6\ H^+ + NaBiO_3 \rightarrow Bi^{3+} + Na^+ + 3\ H_2O) \times 5$

$\quad\quad\quad\quad 8\ H_2O + 2\ Mn^{2+} \rightarrow 2\ MnO_4^- + 16\ H^+ + 10\ e^-$

$\quad\quad\quad 10\ e^- + 30\ H^+ + 5\ NaBiO_3 \rightarrow 5\ Bi^{3+} + 5\ Na^+ + 15\ H_2O$

$\rule{12cm}{0.5pt}$

$8\ H_2O + 30\ H^+ + 2\ Mn^{2+} + 5\ NaBiO_3 \rightarrow 2\ MnO_4^- + 5\ Bi^{3+} + 5\ Na^+ + 15\ H_2O + 16\ H^+$

Simplifying:

$14\ H^+(aq) + 2\ Mn^{2+}(aq) + 5\ NaBiO_3(s) \rightarrow 2\ MnO_4^-(aq) + 5\ Bi^{3+}(aq) + 5\ Na^+(aq) + 7\ H_2O(l)$

e. $\quad\quad\quad\quad H_3AsO_4 \rightarrow AsH_3 \quad\quad\quad\quad\quad (Zn \rightarrow Zn^{2+} + 2\ e^-) \times 4$

$\quad\quad\quad\quad\quad H_3AsO_4 \rightarrow AsH_3 + 4\ H_2O$

$\quad\quad 8\ e^- + 8\ H^+ + H_3AsO_4 \rightarrow AsH_3 + 4\ H_2O$

$\quad\quad\quad\quad 8\ e^- + 8\ H^+ + H_3AsO_4 \rightarrow AsH_3 + 4\ H_2O$

$\quad\quad\quad\quad\quad\quad 4\ Zn \rightarrow 4\ Zn^{2+} + 8\ e^-$

$\rule{11cm}{0.5pt}$

$\quad\quad 8\ H^+(aq) + H_3AsO_4(aq) + 4\ Zn(s) \rightarrow 4\ Zn^{2+}(aq) + AsH_3(g) + 4\ H_2O(l)$

f. $\quad As_2O_3 \rightarrow H_3AsO_4$

$\quad As_2O_3 \rightarrow 2\ H_3AsO_4$

$\quad (5\ H_2O + As_2O_3 \rightarrow 2\ H_3AsO_4 + 4\ H^+ + 4\ e^-) \times 3$

$\quad\quad\quad\quad\quad\quad\quad\quad\quad NO_3^- \rightarrow NO + 2\ H_2O$

$\quad\quad\quad\quad\quad\quad\quad 4\ H^+ + NO_3^- \rightarrow NO + 2\ H_2O$

$\quad\quad\quad\quad\quad (3\ e^- + 4\ H^+ + NO_3^- \rightarrow NO + 2\ H_2O) \times 4$

$\quad\quad\quad\quad 12\ e^- + 16\ H^+ + 4\ NO_3^- \rightarrow 4\ NO + 8\ H_2O$

$\quad\quad\quad\quad\quad 15\ H_2O + 3\ As_2O_3 \rightarrow 6\ H_3AsO_4 + 12\ H^+ + 12\ e^-$

$\rule{11cm}{0.5pt}$

$7\ H_2O(l) + 4\ H^+(aq) + 3\ As_2O_3(s) + 4\ NO_3^-(aq) \rightarrow 4\ NO(g) + 6\ H_3AsO_4(aq)$

g. $\quad (2\ Br^- \rightarrow Br_2 + 2\ e^-) \times 5 \quad\quad\quad\quad MnO_4^- \rightarrow Mn^{2+} + 4\ H_2O$

$\quad\quad\quad\quad\quad\quad\quad\quad (5\ e^- + 8\ H^+ + MnO_4^- \rightarrow Mn^{2+} + 4\ H_2O) \times 2$

$\quad\quad\quad\quad\quad\quad 10\ Br^- \rightarrow 5\ Br_2 + 10\ e^-$

$\quad\quad\quad 10\ e^- + 16\ H^+ + 2\ MnO_4^- \rightarrow 2\ Mn^{2+} + 8\ H_2O$

$\rule{11cm}{0.5pt}$

$16\ H^+(aq) + 2\ MnO_4^-(aq) + 10\ Br^-(aq) \rightarrow 5\ Br_2(l) + 2\ Mn^{2+}(aq) + 8\ H_2O(l)$

h. $CH_3OH \rightarrow CH_2O$ $Cr_2O_7^{2-} \rightarrow Cr^{3+}$

$(CH_3OH \rightarrow CH_2O + 2 H^+ + 2 e^-) \times 3$ $14 H^+ + Cr_2O_7^{2-} \rightarrow 2 Cr^{3+} + 7 H_2O$

$6 e^- + 14 H^+ + Cr_2O_7^{2-} \rightarrow 2 Cr^{3+} + 7 H_2O$

$$3 CH_3OH \rightarrow 3 CH_2O + 6 H^+ + 6 e^-$$
$$6 e^- + 14 H^+ + Cr_2O_7^{2-} \rightarrow 2 Cr^{3+} + 7 H_2O$$

$$8 H^+(aq) + 3 CH_3OH(aq) + Cr_2O_7^{2-}(aq) \rightarrow 2 Cr^{3+}(aq) + 3 CH_2O(aq) + 7 H_2O(l)$$

58.   Use the same method as with acidic solutions. After the final balanced equation, then convert H^+ to OH^- as described in section 4.11 of the text. The extra step involves converting H^+ into H_2O by adding equal moles of OH^- to each side of the reaction. This converts the reaction to a basic solution while keeping it balanced.

a. $Al \rightarrow Al(OH)_4^-$ $MnO_4^- \rightarrow MnO_2$

$4 H_2O + Al \rightarrow Al(OH)_4^- + 4 H^+$ $3 e^- + 4 H^+ + MnO_4^- \rightarrow MnO_2 + 2 H_2O$

$4 H_2O + Al \rightarrow Al(OH)_4^- + 4 H^+ + 3 e^-$

$$4 H_2O + Al \rightarrow Al(OH)_4^- + 4 H^+ + 3 e^-$$
$$3 e^- + 4 H^+ + MnO_4^- \rightarrow MnO_2 + 2 H_2O$$

$$2 H_2O(l) + Al(s) + MnO_4^-(aq) \rightarrow Al(OH)_4^-(aq) + MnO_2(s)$$

Since H^+ doesn't appear in the final balanced reaction, we are done.

b. $Cl_2 \rightarrow Cl^-$ $Cl_2 \rightarrow ClO^-$

$2 e^- + Cl_2 \rightarrow 2 Cl^-$ $2 H_2O + Cl_2 \rightarrow 2 ClO^- + 4 H^+ + 2 e^-$

$$2 e^- + Cl_2 \rightarrow 2 Cl^-$$
$$2 H_2O + Cl_2 \rightarrow 2 ClO^- + 4 H^+ + 2 e^-$$

$$2 H_2O + 2 Cl_2 \rightarrow 2 Cl^- + 2 ClO^- + 4 H^+$$

Now convert to a basic solution. Add 4 OH^- to both sides of the equation. The 4 OH^- will react with the 4 H^+ on the product side to give 4 H_2O. After this step, cancel identical species on both sides (2 H_2O). Applying these steps gives: $4 OH^- + 2 Cl_2 \rightarrow 2 Cl^- + 2 ClO^- + 2 H_2O$, which can be further simplified to:

$$2 OH^-(aq) + Cl_2(g) \rightarrow Cl^-(aq) + ClO^-(aq) + H_2O(l)$$

c. $NO_2^- \rightarrow NH_3$ $Al \rightarrow AlO_2^-$

$6 e^- + 7 H^+ + NO_2^- \rightarrow NH_3 + 2 H_2O$ $(2 H_2O + Al \rightarrow AlO_2^- + 4 H^+ + 3 e^-) \times 2$

Common factor is a transfer of 6 e^-.

$$6 e^- + 7 H^+ + NO_2^- \rightarrow NH_3 + 2 H_2O$$
$$4 H_2O + 2 Al \rightarrow 2 AlO_2^- + 8 H^+ + 6 e^-$$

$$OH^- + 2 H_2O + NO_2^- + 2 Al \rightarrow NH_3 + 2 AlO_2^- + H^+ + OH^-$$

Reducing gives: $OH^-(aq) + H_2O(l) + NO_2^-(aq) + 2 Al(s) \rightarrow NH_3(g) + 2 AlO_2^-(aq)$

d. $S^{2-} \rightarrow S$ $\qquad\qquad\qquad\qquad\qquad\qquad\qquad$ $MnO_4^- \rightarrow MnS$
$\qquad$ $(S^{2-} \rightarrow S + 2\ e^-) \times 5$ $\qquad\qquad\qquad\qquad$ $MnO_4^- + S^{2-} \rightarrow MnS$
$\qquad\qquad\qquad\qquad\qquad\qquad\qquad$ $(\ 5\ e^- + 8\ H^+ + MnO_4^- + S^{2-} \rightarrow MnS + 4\ H_2O) \times 2$

Common factor is a transfer of 10 e$^-$.

$$5\ S^{2-} \rightarrow 5\ S + 10\ e^-$$
$$10\ e^- + 16\ H^+ + 2\ MnO_4^- + 2\ S^{2-} \rightarrow 2\ MnS + 8\ H_2O$$

$$\overline{16\ OH^- + 16\ H^+ + 7\ S^{2-} + 2\ MnO_4^- \rightarrow 5\ S + 2\ MnS + 8\ H_2O + 16\ OH^-}$$

$$16\ H_2O + 7\ S^{2-} + 2\ MnO_4^- \rightarrow 5\ S + 2\ MnS + 8\ H_2O + 16\ OH^-$$

Reducing gives: $8\ H_2O(l) + 7\ S^{2-}(aq) + 2\ MnO_4^-(aq) \rightarrow 5\ S(s) + 2\ MnS(s) + 16\ OH^-(aq)$

e. $\qquad\qquad\qquad$ $CN^- \rightarrow CNO^-$
$\qquad\qquad$ $(H_2O + CN^- \rightarrow CNO^- + 2\ H^+ + 2\ e^-) \times 3$

$\qquad\qquad\qquad\qquad\qquad\qquad\qquad\qquad\qquad$ $MnO_4^- \rightarrow MnO_2$
$\qquad\qquad\qquad\qquad\qquad\qquad\qquad$ $(3\ e^- + 4\ H^+ + MnO_4^- \rightarrow MnO_2 + 2\ H_2O) \times 2$

Common factor is a transfer of 6 electrons.

$$3\ H_2O + 3\ CN^- \rightarrow 3\ CNO^- + 6\ H^+ + 6\ e^-$$
$$6\ e^- + 8\ H^+ + 2\ MnO_4^- \rightarrow 2\ MnO_2 + 4\ H_2O$$

$$\overline{2\ OH^- + 2\ H^+ + 3\ CN^- + 2\ MnO_4^- \rightarrow 3\ CNO^- + 2\ MnO_2 + H_2O + 2\ OH^-}$$

Reducing gives:

$$H_2O(l) + 3\ CN^-(aq) + 2\ MnO_4^-(aq) \rightarrow 3\ CNO^-(aq) + 2\ MnO_2(s) + 2\ OH^-(aq)$$

59.   a. HCl(aq) dissociates to $H^+(aq) + Cl^-(aq)$. For simplicity let's use H^+ and Cl^- separately.
$\qquad\qquad$ $H^+ \rightarrow H_2$ $\qquad\qquad\qquad\qquad\qquad\qquad$ $Fe \rightarrow HFeCl_4$
$\qquad$ $(2\ H^+ + 2\ e^- \rightarrow H_2) \times 3$ $\qquad\qquad\qquad$ $(H^+ + 4\ Cl^- + Fe \rightarrow HFeCl_4 + 3\ e^-) \times 2$

$$6\ H^+ + 6\ e^- \rightarrow 3\ H_2$$
$$2\ H^+ + 8\ Cl^- + 2\ Fe \rightarrow 2\ HFeCl_4 + 6\ e^-$$

$$\overline{8\ H^+ + 8\ Cl^- + 2\ Fe \rightarrow 2\ HFeCl_4 + 3\ H_2}$$

or $\qquad$ $8\ HCl(aq) + 2\ Fe(s) \rightarrow 2\ HFeCl_4(aq) + 3\ H_2(g)$

b. $\qquad\qquad\qquad\qquad$ $IO_3^- \rightarrow I_3^-$ $\qquad\qquad\qquad\qquad\qquad\qquad$ $I^- \rightarrow I_3^-$
$\qquad\qquad\qquad\qquad$ $3\ IO_3^- \rightarrow I_3^-$ $\qquad\qquad\qquad\qquad\qquad$ $(3\ I^- \rightarrow I_3^- + 2\ e^-) \times 8$
$\qquad\qquad\qquad\qquad$ $3\ IO_3^- \rightarrow I_3^- + 9\ H_2O$
$\qquad\qquad$ $16\ e^- + 18\ H^+ + 3\ IO_3^- \rightarrow I_3^- + 9\ H_2O$

$$16\ e^- + 18\ H^+ + 3\ IO_3^- \rightarrow I_3^- + 9\ H_2O$$
$$24\ I^- \rightarrow 8\ I_3^- + 16\ e^-$$

$$\overline{18\ H^+ + 24\ I^- + 3\ IO_3^- \rightarrow 9\ I_3^- + 9\ H_2O}$$

Reducing: $6\ H^+(aq) + 8\ I^-(aq) + IO_3^-(aq) \rightarrow 3\ I_3^-(aq) + 3\ H_2O(l)$

c. $(Ce^{4+} + e^- \rightarrow Ce^{3+}) \times 97$

$$Cr(NCS)_6^{4-} \rightarrow Cr^{3+} + NO_3^- + CO_2 + SO_4^{2-}$$
$$54\ H_2O + Cr(NCS)_6^{4-} \rightarrow Cr^{3+} + 6\ NO_3^- + 6\ CO_2 + 6\ SO_4^{2-} + 108\ H^+$$

Charge on left -4. Charge on right $= +3 + 6(-1) + 6(-2) + 108(+1) = +93$. Add 97 e⁻ to the right, then add the two balanced half-reactions with a common factor of 97 e⁻ transferred.

$$54\ H_2O + Cr(NCS)_6^{4-} \rightarrow Cr^{3+} + 6\ NO_3^- + 6\ CO_2 + 6\ SO_4^{2-} + 108\ H^+ + 97\ e^-$$
$$97\ e^- + 97\ Ce^{4+} \rightarrow 97\ Ce^{3+}$$

$$97\ Ce^{4+}(aq) + 54\ H_2O(l) + Cr(NCS)_6^{4-}(aq) \rightarrow 97\ Ce^{3+}(aq) + Cr^{3+}(aq) + 6\ NO_3^-(aq) + 6\ CO_2(g)$$
$$+ 6\ SO_4^{2-}(aq) + 108\ H^+(aq)$$

This is very complicated. A check of the net charge is a good check to see if the equation is balanced. Left: charge $= 97(+4) - 4 = +384$. Right: charge $= 97(+3) + 3 + 6(-1) + 6(-2) + 108(+1) = +384$.

d. $CrI_3 \rightarrow CrO_4^{2-} + IO_4^-$ $Cl_2 \rightarrow Cl^-$
$(16\ H_2O + CrI_3 \rightarrow CrO_4^{2-} + 3\ IO_4^- + 32\ H^+ + 27\ e^-) \times 2$ $(2\ e^- + Cl_2 \rightarrow 2\ Cl^-) \times 27$

Common factor is a transfer of 54 e⁻.

$$54\ e^- + 27\ Cl_2 \rightarrow 54\ Cl^-$$
$$32\ H_2O + 2\ CrI_3 \rightarrow 2\ CrO_4^{2-} + 6\ IO_4^- + 64\ H^+ + 54\ e^-$$

$$32\ H_2O + 2\ CrI_3 + 27\ Cl_2 \rightarrow 54\ Cl^- + 2\ CrO_4^{2-} + 6\ IO_4^- + 64\ H^+$$

Add 64 OH⁻ to both sides and convert 64 H⁺ into 64 H₂O.

$$64\ OH^- + 32\ H_2O + 2\ CrI_3 + 27\ Cl_2 \rightarrow 54\ Cl^- + 2\ CrO_4^{2-} + 6\ IO_4^- + 64\ H_2O$$

Reducing gives:

$$64\ OH^-(aq) + 2\ CrI_3(s) + 27\ Cl_2(g) \rightarrow 54\ Cl^-(aq) + 2\ CrO_4^{2-}(aq) + 6\ IO_4^-(aq) + 32\ H_2O(l)$$

e. $Ce^{4+} \rightarrow Ce(OH)_3$
$(e^- + 3\ H_2O + Ce^{4+} \rightarrow Ce(OH)_3 + 3\ H^+) \times 61$

$$Fe(CN)_6^{4-} \rightarrow Fe(OH)_3 + CO_3^{2-} + NO_3^-$$
$$Fe(CN)_6^{4-} \rightarrow Fe(OH)_3 + 6\ CO_3^{2-} + 6\ NO_3^-$$

There are 39 extra O atoms on right. Add 39 H₂O to left, then add 75 H⁺ to right to balance H⁺.
$$39\ H_2O + Fe(CN)_6^{4-} \rightarrow Fe(OH)_3 + 6\ CO_3^{2-} + 6\ NO_3^- + 75\ H^+$$
net charge = -4   net charge = +57

Add 61 e⁻ to the right then add the two balanced half-reactions with a common factor of 61 e⁻ transferred.

$$39\ H_2O + Fe(CN)_6{}^{4-} \rightarrow Fe(OH)_3 + 6\ CO_3{}^{2-} + 6\ NO_3{}^- + 75\ H^+ + 61\ e^-$$
$$61\ e^- + 183\ H_2O + 61\ Ce^{4+} \rightarrow 61\ Ce(OH)_3 + 183\ H^+$$

$$222\ H_2O + Fe(CN)_6{}^{4-} + 61\ Ce^{4+} \rightarrow 61\ Ce(OH)_3 + Fe(OH)_3 + 6\ CO_3{}^{2-} + 6\ NO_3{}^- + 258\ H^+$$

Adding 258 OH⁻ to each side then reducing gives:

$$258\ OH^-(aq) + Fe(CN)_6{}^{4-}(aq) + 61\ Ce^{4+}(aq) \rightarrow 61\ Ce(OH)_3(s) + Fe(OH)_3(s)$$

$$+ 6\ CO_3{}^{2-}(aq) + 6\ NO_3{}^-(aq) + 36\ H_2O(l)$$

60.   a. $4\ NH_3(g) + 5\ O_2(g) \rightarrow 4\ NO(g) + 6\ H_2O(g)$
       -3 +1   0   +2 -2   +1 -2   oxidation states

$2\ NO(g) + O_2(g) \rightarrow 2\ NO_2(g)$
 +2 -2   0   +4 -2

$3\ NO_2(g) + H_2O(l) \rightarrow 2\ HNO_3(aq) + NO(g)$
 +4 -2   +1 -2   +1 +5 -2   +2 -2

All three reactions are oxidation-reduction reactions. All contain two species which show a change in oxidation states.

   b. $4\ NH_3 + 5\ O_2 \rightarrow 4\ NO + 6\ H_2O$ O_2 is the oxidizing agent. NH_3 is the reducing agent.

       $2\ NO + O_2 \rightarrow 2\ NO_2$ O_2 is the oxidizing agent. NO is the reducing agent.

       $3\ NO_2 + H_2O \rightarrow 2\ HNO_3 + NO$ NO_2 is both the oxidizing and reducing agent.

   c. $5.0 \times 10^6\ g\ NH_3 \times \dfrac{1\ mol\ NH_3}{17.0\ g\ NH_3} = 2.9 \times 10^5\ mol\ NH_3$

       $5.0 \times 10^7\ g\ O_2 \times \dfrac{1\ mol\ O_2}{32.0\ g\ O_2} = 1.6 \times 10^6\ mol\ O_2$

       The actual mol O_2 to mol NH_3 ratio present is:

       $\dfrac{1.6 \times 10^6\ mol\ O_2}{2.9 \times 10^5\ mol\ NH_3} = 5.5$

       The balanced equation requires a 5:4 mol ratio (= 1.25) between O_2 and NH_3. Since the actual mol ratio present is larger than 1.25, then NH_3 is limiting.

       $2.9 \times 10^5\ mol\ NH_3 \times \dfrac{4\ mol\ NO}{4\ mol\ NH_3} \times \dfrac{30.0\ g\ NO}{mol\ NO} = 8.7 \times 10^6\ g\ NO$

61. $Mn \rightarrow Mn^{2+} + 2 e^-$ $HNO_3 \rightarrow NO_2$

$HNO_3 \rightarrow NO_2 + H_2O$

$(e^- + H^+ + HNO_3 \rightarrow NO_2 + H_2O) \times 2$

$Mn \rightarrow Mn^{2+} + 2 e^-$

$2 e^- + 2 H^+ + 2 HNO_3 \rightarrow 2 NO_2 + 2 H_2O$

$2 H^+(aq) + Mn(s) + 2 HNO_3(aq) \rightarrow Mn^{2+}(aq) + 2 NO_2(g) + 2 H_2O(l)$ or

$4 H^+(aq) + Mn(s) + 2 NO_3^-(aq) \rightarrow Mn^{2+}(aq) + 2 NO_2(g) + 2 H_2O(l)$ (HNO_3 is a strong acid.)

$(4 H_2O + Mn^{2+} \rightarrow MnO_4^- + 8 H^+ + 5 e^-) \times 2$ $(2 e^- + 2 H^+ + IO_4^- \rightarrow IO_3^- + H_2O) \times 5$

$8 H_2O + 2 Mn^{2+} \rightarrow 2 MnO_4^- + 16 H^+ + 10 e^-$

$10 e^- + 10 H^+ + 5 IO_4^- \rightarrow 5 IO_3^- + 5 H_2O$

$3 H_2O(l) + 2 Mn^{2+}(aq) + 5 IO_4^-(aq) \rightarrow 2 MnO_4^-(aq) + 5 IO_3^-(aq) + 6 H^+(aq)$

62.   HCl and HNO_3 are strong acids which completely dissociate to H^+ and the anions in solution.

$Au + 4 Cl^- \rightarrow AuCl_4^- + 3 e^-$ $3 e^- + 4 H^+ + NO_3^- \rightarrow NO + 2 H_2O$

Adding the two balanced half-reactions:

$Au(s) + 4 Cl^-(aq) + 4 H^+(aq) + NO_3^-(aq) \rightarrow AuCl_4^-(aq) + NO(g) + 2 H_2O(l)$

63. $(H_2C_2O_4 \rightarrow 2 CO_2 + 2 H^+ + 2 e^-) \times 5$ $(5 e^- + 8 H^+ + MnO_4^- \rightarrow Mn^{2+} + 4 H_2O) \times 2$

$5 H_2C_2O_4 \rightarrow 10 CO_2 + 10 H^+ + 10 e^-$

$10 e^- + 16 H^+ + 2 MnO_4^- \rightarrow 2 Mn^{2+} + 8 H_2O$

$6 H^+(aq) + 5 H_2C_2O_4(aq) + 2 MnO_4^-(aq) \rightarrow 10 CO_2(g) + 2 Mn^{2+}(aq) + 8 H_2O(l)$

$$0.1058 \text{ g } H_2C_2O_4 \times \frac{1 \text{ mol } H_2C_2O_4}{90.034 \text{ g}} \times \frac{2 \text{ mol } MnO_4^-}{5 \text{ mol } H_2C_2O_4} = 4.700 \times 10^{-4} \text{ mol } MnO_4^-$$

$$\text{Molarity} = \frac{4.700 \times 10^{-4} \text{ mol } MnO_4^-}{28.97 \text{ mL}} \times \frac{1000 \text{ mL}}{L} = 1.622 \times 10^{-2} \, M \, MnO_4^-$$

64.   a. $Fe^{2+} \rightarrow Fe^{3+} + e^-$ $5 e^- + 8 H^+ + MnO_4^- \rightarrow Mn^{2+} + 4 H_2O$

The balanced equation is:

$8 H^+(aq) + MnO_4^-(aq) + 5 Fe^{2+}(aq) \rightarrow 5 Fe^{3+}(aq) + Mn^{2+}(aq) + 4 H_2O(l)$

$$20.62 \times 10^{-3} \text{ L soln} \times \frac{0.0216 \text{ mol } MnO_4^-}{\text{L soln}} \times \frac{5 \text{ mol Fe}^{2+}}{\text{mol } MnO_4^-} = 2.23 \times 10^{-3} \text{ mol Fe}^{2+}$$

$$\text{Molarity} = \frac{2.23 \times 10^{-3} \text{ mol Fe}^{2+}}{50.00 \times 10^{-3} \text{ L}} = 4.46 \times 10^{-2} \, M \, Fe^{2+}$$

b. $Fe^{2+} \rightarrow Fe^{3+} + e^-$ $6\ e^- + 14\ H^+ + Cr_2O_7^{2-} \rightarrow 2\ Cr^{3+} + 7\ H_2O$

The balanced equation is:

$$14\ H^+(aq) + Cr_2O_7^{2-}(aq) + 6\ Fe^{2+}(aq) \rightarrow 6\ Fe^{3+}(aq) + 2\ Cr^{3+}(aq) + 7\ H_2O(l)$$

$$50.00 \times 10^{-3}\ L \times \frac{4.46 \times 10^{-2}\ mol\ Fe^{2+}}{L} \times \frac{1\ mol\ Cr_2O_7^{2-}}{6\ mol\ Fe^{2+}} \times \frac{1\ L}{0.0150\ mol\ Cr_2O_7^{2-}}$$

$$= 2.48 \times 10^{-2}\ L\ or\ 24.8\ mL$$

65. $(Fe^{2+} \rightarrow Fe^{3+} + e^-) \times 5$
                             $5\ e^- + 8\ H^+ + MnO_4^- \rightarrow Mn^{2+} + 4\ H_2O$
_____
$$8\ H^+(aq) + MnO_4^-(aq) + 5\ Fe^{2+}(aq) \rightarrow 5\ Fe^{3+}(aq) + Mn^{2+}(aq) + 4\ H_2O(l)$$

From the titration data we can get the number of moles of Fe^{2+}. We then convert this to a mass of iron and calculate the mass percent of iron in the sample.

$$38.37 \times 10^{-3}\ L\ MnO_4^- \times \frac{0.0198\ mol\ MnO_4^-}{L} \times \frac{5\ mol\ Fe^{2+}}{mol\ MnO_4^-} = 3.80 \times 10^{-3}\ mol\ Fe^{2+}$$

$$= 3.80 \times 10^{-3}\ mol\ Fe\ present$$

$$3.80 \times 10^{-3}\ mol\ Fe \times \frac{55.85\ g\ Fe}{mol\ Fe} = 0.212\ g\ Fe$$

$$Mass\ \%\ Fe = \frac{0.212\ g}{0.6128\ g} \times 100 = 34.6\%\ Fe$$

66. $(5\ e^- + 8\ H^+ + MnO_4^- \rightarrow Mn^{2+} + 4\ H_2O) \times 2$
                                     $(C_2O_4^{2-} \rightarrow 2\ CO_2 + 2\ e^-) \times 5$
_____
$$2\ MnO_4^-(aq) + 16\ H^+(aq) + 5\ C_2O_4^{2-}(aq) \rightarrow 10\ CO_2(g) + 2\ Mn^{2+}(aq) + 8\ H_2O(l)$$

Assuming each reactant is limiting:

$$0.250\ g\ Na_2C_2O_4 \times \frac{1\ mol\ Na_2C_2O_4}{134.0\ g\ Na_2C_2O_4} \times \frac{10\ mol\ CO_2}{5\ mol\ Na_2C_2O_4} = 3.73 \times 10^{-3}\ mol\ CO_2$$

$$50.00 \times 10^{-3}\ L\ KMnO_4\ soln \times \frac{0.0200\ mol\ KMnO_4}{L} \times \frac{10\ mol\ CO_2}{2\ mol\ KMnO_4} = 5.00 \times 10^{-3}\ mol\ CO_2$$

The $Na_2C_2O_4$ is the limiting reagent since it produces the smallest amount of product. Amount CO_2 produced is:

$$3.73 \times 10^{-3}\ mol\ CO_2 \times \frac{44.01\ g\ CO_2}{mol\ CO_2} = 0.164\ g\ CO_2$$

67. $Mg(s) + 2\ HCl(aq) \rightarrow MgCl_2(aq) + H_2(g)$

$3.00 \text{ g Mg} \times \dfrac{1 \text{ mol Mg}}{24.31 \text{ g Mg}} \times \dfrac{2 \text{ mol HCl}}{\text{mol Mg}} \times \dfrac{1 \text{ L HCl}}{5.0 \text{ mol HCl}} = 0.0494 \text{ L} = 49.4 \text{ mL HCl}$

68.   a. $16\ e^- + 18\ H^+ + 3\ IO_3^- \rightarrow I_3^- + 9\ H_2O$ $(3\ I^- \rightarrow I_3^- + 2\ e^-) \times 8$

$24\ I^- \rightarrow 8\ I_3^- + 16\ e^-$
$16\ e^- + 18\ H^+ + 3\ IO_3^- \rightarrow I_3^- + 9\ H_2O$

$\overline{}$

$18\ H^+ + 24\ I^- + 3\ IO_3^- \rightarrow 9\ I_3^- + 9\ H_2O$

or $6\ H^+(aq) + 8\ I^-(aq) + IO_3^-(aq) \rightarrow 3\ I_3^-(aq) + 3\ H_2O(l)$

b. $0.6013 \text{ g KIO}_3 \times \dfrac{1 \text{ mol KIO}_3}{214.0 \text{ g KIO}_3} = 2.810 \times 10^{-3} \text{ mol KIO}_3$

$2.810 \times 10^{-3} \text{ mol KIO}_3 \times \dfrac{8 \text{ mol KI}}{\text{mol KIO}_3} \times \dfrac{166.0 \text{ g KI}}{\text{mol KI}} = 3.732 \text{ g KI}$

$2.810 \times 10^{-3} \text{ mol KIO}_3 \times \dfrac{6 \text{ mol HCl}}{\text{mol KIO}_3} \times \dfrac{1 \text{ L}}{3.00 \text{ mol HCl}} = 5.62 \times 10^{-3} \text{ L} = 5.62 \text{ mL HCl}$

c. $I_3^- + 2\ e^- \rightarrow 3\ I^-$ $2\ S_2O_3^{2-} \rightarrow S_4O_6^{2-} + 2\ e^-$

Adding the balanced half-reactions gives:

$2\ S_2O_3^{2-}(aq) + I_3^-(aq) \rightarrow 3\ I^-(aq) + S_4O_6^{2-}(aq)$

d. $25.00 \times 10^{-3} \text{ L KIO}_3 \times \dfrac{0.0100 \text{ mol KIO}_3}{\text{L}} \times \dfrac{3 \text{ mol I}_3^-}{\text{mol KIO}_3} \times \dfrac{2 \text{ mol Na}_2S_2O_3}{\text{mol I}_3^-}$

$= 1.50 \times 10^{-3} \text{ mol Na}_2S_2O_3$

$M_{\text{Na}_2S_2O_3} = \dfrac{1.50 \times 10^{-3} \text{ mol}}{32.04 \times 10^{-3} \text{ L}} = 0.0468\ M \text{ Na}_2S_2O_3$

e. $0.5000 \text{ L} \times \dfrac{0.0100 \text{ mol KIO}_3}{\text{L}} \times \dfrac{214.0 \text{ g KIO}_3}{\text{mol KIO}_3} = 1.07 \text{ g KIO}_3$

Place 1.07 g KIO$_3$ in a 500 mL volumetric flask; add water to dissolve the KIO$_3$; continue adding water to the 500.00 mL mark.

Additional Exercises

69.   mol $CaCl_2$ present $= 0.230$ L $CaCl_2 \times \dfrac{0.275 \text{ mol } CaCl_2}{\text{L } CaCl_2} = 6.33 \times 10^{-2}$ mol $CaCl_2$

The volume of $CaCl_2$ solution after evaporation is:

$$6.33 \times 10^{-2} \text{ mol } CaCl_2 \times \dfrac{1 \text{ L } CaCl_2}{1.10 \text{ mol } CaCl_2} = 5.75 \times 10^{-2} \text{ L} = 57.5 \text{ mL } CaCl_2$$

Volume H_2O evaporated $= 230.$ mL $- 57.5$ mL $= 173$ mL H_2O evaporated

70.   There are other possible correct choices for the following answers. We have listed only three possible reactants in each case.

   a. $AgNO_3$, $Pb(NO_3)_2$, and $Hg_2(NO_3)_2$ would form precipitates with the Cl^- ion.
        $Ag^+(aq) + Cl^-(aq) \rightarrow AgCl(s)$; $Pb^{2+}(aq) + 2\ Cl^-(aq) \rightarrow PbCl_2(s)$;
        $Hg_2^{2+}(aq) + 2\ Cl^-(aq) \rightarrow Hg_2Cl_2(s)$

   b. Na_2SO_4, Na_2CO_3, and Na_3PO_4 would form precipitates with the Ca^{2+} ion.
        $Ca^{2+}(aq) + SO_4^{2-}(aq) \rightarrow CaSO_4(s)$; $Ca^{2+} + CO_3^{2-}(aq) \rightarrow CaCO_3(s)$
        $3\ Ca^{2+}(aq) + 2\ PO_4^{3-}(aq) \rightarrow Ca_3(PO_4)_2(s)$

   c. $NaOH$, Na_2S, and Na_2CO_3 would form precipitates with the Fe^{3+} ion.
        $Fe^{3+}(aq) + 3\ OH^-(aq) \rightarrow Fe(OH)_3(s)$; $2\ Fe^{3+}(aq) + 3\ S^{2-}(aq) \rightarrow Fe_2S_3(s)$;
        $2\ Fe^{3+}(aq) + 3\ CO_3^{2-}(aq) \rightarrow Fe_2(CO_3)_3(s)$

   d. $BaCl_2$, $Pb(NO_3)_2$, and $Ca(NO_3)_2$ would form precipitates with the SO_4^{2-} ion.
        $Ba^{2+}(aq) + SO_4^{2-}(aq) \rightarrow BaSO_4(s)$; $Pb^{2+}(aq) + SO_4^{2-}(aq) \rightarrow PbSO_4(s)$;
        $Ca^{2+}(aq) + SO_4^{2-}(aq) \rightarrow CaSO_4(s)$

   e. Na_2SO_4, $NaCl$, and NaI would form precipitates with the Hg_2^{2+} ion.
        $Hg_2^{2+}(aq) + SO_4^{2-}(aq) \rightarrow Hg_2SO_4(s)$; $Hg_2^{2+}(aq) + 2\ Cl^-(aq) \rightarrow Hg_2Cl_2(s)$;
        $Hg_2^{2+}(aq) + 2\ I^-(aq) \rightarrow Hg_2I_2(s)$

   f. $NaBr$, Na_2CrO_4, and Na_3PO_4 would form precipitates with the Ag^+ ion.
        $Ag^+(aq) + Br^-(aq) \rightarrow AgBr(s)$; $2\ Ag^+(aq) + CrO_4^{2-}(aq) \rightarrow Ag_2CrO_4(s)$;
        $3\ Ag^+(aq) + PO_4^{3-}(aq) \rightarrow Ag_3PO_4(s)$

71.   a. $MgCl_2(aq) + 2\ AgNO_3(aq) \rightarrow 2\ AgCl(s) + Mg(NO_3)_2(aq)$

        $$0.641 \text{ g AgCl} \times \dfrac{1 \text{ mol AgCl}}{143.4 \text{ g AgCl}} \times \dfrac{1 \text{ mol } MgCl_2}{2 \text{ mol AgCl}} \times \dfrac{95.21 \text{ g}}{\text{mol } MgCl_2} = 0.213 \text{ g } MgCl_2$$

        $$\dfrac{0.213 \text{ g } MgCl_2}{1.50 \text{ g mixture}} \times 100 = 14.2\% \text{ } MgCl_2$$

b. $0.213 \text{ g MgCl}_2 \times \dfrac{1 \text{ mol MgCl}_2}{95.21 \text{ g}} \times \dfrac{2 \text{ mol AgNO}_3}{\text{mol MgCl}_2} \times \dfrac{1 \text{ L}}{0.500 \text{ mol AgNO}_3} \times \dfrac{1000 \text{ mL}}{1 \text{ L}}$

$$= 8.95 \text{ mL AgNO}_3$$

72. $\text{Al(NO}_3)_3\text{(aq)} + 3 \text{ KOH(aq)} \rightarrow \text{Al(OH)}_3\text{(s)} + 3 \text{ KNO}_3\text{(aq)}$

$0.0500 \text{ L} \times \dfrac{0.200 \text{ mol Al(NO}_3)_3}{\text{L}} = 0.0100 \text{ mol Al(NO}_3)_3$

$0.2000 \text{ L} \times \dfrac{0.100 \text{ mol KOH}}{\text{L}} = 0.0200 \text{ mol KOH}$

From the balanced equation, 3 mol of KOH are required to react with 1 mol of Al(NO$_3$)$_3$ (3:1 mol ratio). The actual KOH to Al(NO$_3$)$_3$ mol ratio present is 0.0200/0.0100 = 2 (2:1). Since the actual mol ratio present is less than the required mol ratio, then KOH is the limiting reagent.

$0.0200 \text{ mol KOH} \times \dfrac{1 \text{ mol Al(OH)}_3}{3 \text{ mol KOH}} \times \dfrac{78.00 \text{ g Al(OH)}_3}{\text{mol Al(OH)}_3} = 0.520 \text{ g Al(OH)}_3$

73.   a. $0.308 \text{ g AgCl} \times \dfrac{35.45 \text{ g Cl}}{143.4 \text{ g AgCl}} = 0.0761 \text{ g Cl};$ $\%\text{Cl} = \dfrac{0.0761 \text{ g}}{0.256 \text{ g}} \times 100 = 29.7\% \text{ Cl}$

Cobalt(III) oxide, Co$_2$O$_3$: 2(58.93) + 3(16.00) = 165.86 g/mol

$0.145 \text{ g Co}_2\text{O}_3 \times \dfrac{117.86 \text{ g Co}}{165.86 \text{ g Co}_2\text{O}_3} = 0.103 \text{ g Co};$ $\%\text{Co} = \dfrac{0.103 \text{ g}}{0.416 \text{ g}} \times 100 = 24.8\% \text{ Co}$

The remainder, 100.0 - (29.7 + 24.8) = 45.5%, is water.

Assuming 100.0 g of compound:

$45.5 \text{ g H}_2\text{O} \times \dfrac{2.016 \text{ g H}}{18.02 \text{ g H}_2\text{O}} = 5.09 \text{ g H};$ $\%\text{H} = \dfrac{5.09 \text{ g H}}{100.0 \text{ g compound}} \times 100 = 5.09\% \text{ H}$

$45.5 \text{ g H}_2\text{O} \times \dfrac{16.00 \text{ g O}}{18.02 \text{ g H}_2\text{O}} = 40.4 \text{ g O};$ $\%\text{O} = \dfrac{40.4 \text{ g O}}{100.0 \text{ g compound}} \times 100 = 40.4\% \text{ O}$

The mass percent composition is 24.8% Co, 29.7% Cl, 5.09% H and 40.4% O.

b.   Out of 100.0 g of compound, there are:

$24.8 \text{ g Co} \times \dfrac{1 \text{ mol}}{58.93 \text{ g Co}} = 0.421 \text{ mol Co};$ $29.7 \text{ g Cl} \times \dfrac{1 \text{ mol}}{35.45 \text{ g Cl}} = 0.838 \text{ mol Cl}$

$5.09 \text{ g H} \times \dfrac{1 \text{ mol}}{1.008 \text{ g H}} = 5.05 \text{ mol H};$ $40.4 \text{ g O} \times \dfrac{1 \text{ mol}}{16.00 \text{ g O}} = 2.53 \text{ mol O}$

Dividing all results by 0.421, we get CoCl$_2$•6H$_2$O.

c. $CoCl_2 \cdot 6H_2O(aq) + 2\ AgNO_3(aq) \rightarrow 2\ AgCl(s) + Co(NO_3)_2(aq) + 6\ H_2O(l)$

$CoCl_2 \cdot 6H_2O(aq) + 2\ NaOH(aq) \rightarrow Co(OH)_2(s) + 2\ NaCl(aq) + 6\ H_2O(l)$

$Co(OH)_2 \rightarrow Co_2O_3$ This is an oxidation-reduction reaction. Thus, we also need to include an oxidizing agent. The obvious choice is O_2.

$4\ Co(OH)_2(s) + O_2(g) \rightarrow 2\ Co_2O_3(s) + 4\ H_2O(l)$

74.   a. $Fe^{3+}(aq) + 3\ OH^-(aq) \rightarrow Fe(OH)_3(s)$

$Fe(OH)_3$: $55.85 + 3(16.00) + 3(1.008) = 106.87$ g/mol

$$0.107\ g\ Fe(OH)_3 \times \frac{55.85\ g\ Fe}{106.9\ g\ Fe(OH)_3} = 0.0559\ g\ Fe$$

b. $Fe(NO_3)_3$: $55.85 + 3(14.01) + 9(16.00) = 241.86$ g/mol

$$0.0559\ g\ Fe \times \frac{241.9\ g\ Fe(NO_3)_3}{55.85\ g\ Fe} = 0.242\ g\ Fe(NO_3)_3$$

c.   Mass % $Fe(NO_3)_3 = \dfrac{0.242\ g}{0.456\ g} \times 100 = 53.1\%$

75. $Ag^+(aq) + Cl^-(aq) \rightarrow AgCl(s)$; Let x = mol NaCl and y = mol KCl.

$22.90 \times 10^{-3}\ L \times 0.1000\ mol/L = 2.290 \times 10^{-3}\ mol\ Ag^+ = 2.290 \times 10^{-3}\ mol\ Cl^-$ total

$x + y = 2.290 \times 10^{-3}\ mol\ Cl^-$, $x = 2.290 \times 10^{-3} - y$

Since the molar mass of NaCl is 58.44 g/mol and the molar mass of KCl is 74.55 g/mol, then:

$58.44\ x + 74.55\ y = 0.1586$ g

$58.44\ (2.290 \times 10^{-3} - y) + 74.55\ y = 0.1586$, $16.11\ y = 0.0248$, $y = 1.54 \times 10^{-3}\ mol\ KCl$

Mass % KCl $= \dfrac{1.54 \times 10^{-3}\ mol \times 74.55\ g/mol}{0.1586\ g} \times 100 = 72.4\%\ KCl$

% NaCl $= 100.0 - 72.4 = 27.6\%$ NaCl

76.   a. $2\ AgNO_3(aq)\ +\ K_2CrO_4(aq)\ \rightarrow\ Ag_2CrO_4(s) + 2\ KNO_3(aq)$

Molar mass: 169.9 g/mol   194.20 g/mol   331.8 g/mol

The molar mass of Ag_2CrO_4 is 331.8 g/mol, so one mol of precipitate was formed.

We have equal masses of $AgNO_3$ and K_2CrO_4. Since the molar mass of $AgNO_3$ is less than that of K_2CrO_4, then we have more mol of $AgNO_3$ present. However, we will not have twice the mol of $AgNO_3$ present as compared to K_2CrO_4 as required by the balanced reaction; this is because the molar mass of $AgNO_3$ is no where near one-half the molar mass of K_2CrO_4. Therefore, $AgNO_3$ is limiting.

$$\text{mass } AgNO_3 = 1.000 \text{ mol } Ag_2CrO_4 \times \frac{2 \text{ mol } AgNO_3}{\text{mol } Ag_2CrO_4} \times \frac{169.9 \text{ g}}{\text{mol } AgNO_3} = 339.8 \text{ g } AgNO_3$$

Since equal masses of reactants are present, then 339.8 g K_2CrO_4 were present initially.

$$M_{K^+} = \frac{\text{mol } K^+}{\text{total volume}} = \frac{339.8 \text{ g } K_2CrO_4 \times \dfrac{1 \text{ mol } K_2CrO_4}{194.20 \text{ g}} \times \dfrac{2 \text{ mol } K^+}{\text{mol } K_2CrO_4}}{0.5000 \text{ L}} = 7.000 \; M \, K^+$$

b. $\text{mol } CrO_4^{2-}$ present initially $= 339.8 \text{ g } K_2CrO_4 \times \dfrac{1 \text{ mol } K_2CrO_4}{194.20 \text{ g}} \times \dfrac{1 \text{ mol } CrO_4^{2-}}{\text{mol } K_2CrO_4} = 1.750 \text{ mol } CrO_4^{2-}$

$\text{mol } CrO_4^{2-}$ in precipitate $= 1.000 \text{ mol } Ag_2CrO_4 \times \dfrac{1 \text{ mol } CrO_4^{2-}}{1 \text{ mol } Ag_2CrO_4} = 1.000 \text{ mol } CrO_4^{2-}$

$$M_{CrO_4^{2-}} = \frac{\text{excess mol } CrO_4^{2-}}{\text{total volume}} = \frac{1.750 \text{ mol} - 1.000 \text{ mol}}{0.5000 \text{ L} + 0.5000 \text{ L}} = \frac{0.750 \text{ mol}}{1.0000 \text{ L}} = 0.750 \; M$$

77. $Cr(NO_3)_3(aq) + 3 \, NaOH(aq) \rightarrow Cr(OH)_3(s) + 3 \, NaNO_3(aq)$

mol NaOH used to form precipitate $= 2.06 \text{ g } Cr(OH)_3 \times \dfrac{1 \text{ mol } Cr(OH)_3}{103.02 \text{ g}} \times \dfrac{3 \text{ mol NaOH}}{1 \text{ mol } Cr(OH)_3} = 6.00 \times 10^{-2} \text{ mol NaOH}$

$NaOH(aq) + HCl(aq) \rightarrow NaCl(aq) + H_2O(l)$

mol NaOH used to react with HCl $= 0.1000 \text{ L} \times \dfrac{0.400 \text{ mol HCl}}{\text{L}} \times \dfrac{1 \text{ mol NaOH}}{\text{mol HCl}} = 4.00 \times 10^{-2} \text{ mol NaOH}$

$$M_{NaOH} = \frac{\text{mol NaOH}}{\text{volume}} = \frac{6.00 \times 10^{-2} \text{ mol} + 4.00 \times 10^{-2} \text{ mol}}{0.0500 \text{ L}} = 2.00 \; M \, NaOH$$

78.   First we will calculate the molarity of NaCl while ignoring the uncertainty.

$$0.150 \text{ g} \times \frac{1 \text{ mol}}{58.44 \text{ g}} = 2.57 \times 10^{-3} \text{ moles}; \quad \text{Molarity} = \frac{2.57 \times 10^{-3} \text{ mol}}{0.1000 \text{ L}} = \frac{2.57 \times 10^{-2} \text{ mol NaCl}}{\text{L}}$$

The maximum value for the molarity is: $\dfrac{0.153 \text{ g} \times \dfrac{1 \text{ mol}}{58.44 \text{ g}}}{0.0995 \text{ L}} = \dfrac{2.63 \times 10^{-2} \text{ mol NaCl}}{\text{L}}$

The minimum value for the molarity is: $\dfrac{0.147 \text{ g} \times \dfrac{1 \text{ mol}}{58.44 \text{ g}}}{0.1005 \text{ L}} = \dfrac{2.50 \times 10^{-2} \text{ mol NaCl}}{\text{L}}$

The range of the molarity is 0.0250 M to 0.0263 M or we can express this range as 0.0257 ± 0.0007 M.

79.   The amount of KHP used = $0.4016 \text{ g} \times \dfrac{1 \text{ mol}}{204.22 \text{ g}} = 1.967 \times 10^{-3}$ mol KHP

Since one mole of NaOH reacts completely with one mole of KHP, then the NaOH solution contains 1.967×10^{-3} mol NaOH.

Molarity of NaOH = $\dfrac{1.967 \times 10^{-3} \text{ mol}}{25.06 \times 10^{-3} \text{ L}} = \dfrac{7.849 \times 10^{-2} \text{ mol NaOH}}{\text{L}}$

Maximum molarity = $\dfrac{1.967 \times 10^{-3} \text{ mol}}{25.01 \times 10^{-3} \text{ L}} = \dfrac{7.865 \times 10^{-2} \text{ mol NaOH}}{\text{L}}$

Minimum molarity = $\dfrac{1.967 \times 10^{-3} \text{ mol}}{25.11 \times 10^{-3} \text{ L}} = \dfrac{7.834 \times 10^{-2} \text{ mol NaOH}}{\text{L}}$

We can express this as 0.07849 ± 0.00016 M. An alternate way is to express the molarity as 0.0785 ± 0.0002 M. This second way shows the actual number of significant figures in the molarity. The advantage of the first method is that it shows that we made all of our individual measurements to four significant figures.

80.   Desired uncertainty is 1% of 0.02 or ± 0.0002. So we want the solution to be 0.0200 ± 0.0002 M or the concentration should be between 0.0198 and 0.0202 M. We should use a 1-L volumetric flask to make the solution. They are good to ± 0.1%. We want to weigh out between 0.0198 mol and 0.0202 mol of KIO_3.

Molar mass of KIO_3 = 39.10 + 126.9 + 3(16.00) = 214.0 g/mol

$0.0198 \text{ mol} \times \dfrac{214.0 \text{ g}}{\text{mol}} = 4.237 \text{ g}; \quad 0.0202 \text{ mol} \times \dfrac{214.0 \text{ g}}{\text{mol}} = 4.323 \text{ g}$ (carrying extra sig. figs.)

We should weigh out between 4.24 and 4.32 g of KIO_3. We should weigh it to the nearest mg or 0.1 mg. Dissolve the KIO_3 in water and dilute to the mark in a one liter volumetric flask. This will produce a solution whose concentration is within the limits and is known to at least the fourth decimal place.

81.   mol $C_6H_8O_7$ = $0.250 \text{ g } C_6H_8O_7 \times \dfrac{1 \text{ mol } C_6H_8O_7}{192.1 \text{ g } C_6H_8O_7} = 1.30 \times 10^{-3}$ mol $C_6H_8O_7$

Let H_xA represent citric acid where x is the number of acidic hydrogens. The balanced neutralization reaction is:

$$H_xA(aq) + x\ OH^-(aq) \rightarrow x\ H_2O(l) + A^{x-}(aq)$$

$$\text{mol OH}^- \text{ reacted} = 0.0372 \text{ L} \times \frac{0.105 \text{ mol OH}^-}{\text{L}} = 3.91 \times 10^{-3} \text{ mol OH}^-$$

$$x = \frac{\text{mol OH}^-}{\text{mol citric acid}} = \frac{3.91 \times 10^{-3} \text{ mol}}{1.30 \times 10^{-3} \text{ mol}} = 3.01$$

Therefore, the general acid formula for citric acid is H_3A meaning that citric acid has three acidic hydrogens per citric acid molecule (citric acid is a triprotic acid).

Challenge Problems

82. $XCl_2(aq) + 2 \text{ AgNO}_3(aq) \rightarrow 2 \text{ AgCl}(s) + X(NO_3)_2(aq)$

$$1.38 \text{ g AgCl} \times \frac{1 \text{ mol}}{143.4 \text{ g}} \times \frac{1 \text{ mol } XCl_2}{2 \text{ mol AgCl}} = 4.81 \times 10^{-3} \text{ mol } XCl_2$$

$$\frac{1.00 \text{ g}}{4.81 \times 10^{-3} \text{ mol}} = 208 \text{ g/mol}; \quad x + 2(35.45) = 208, \ x = 137 \text{ g/mol}$$

This metal is barium (Ba).

83. $Zn(s) + 2 \text{ AgNO}_2(aq) \rightarrow 2 \text{ Ag}(s) + Zn(NO_2)_2(aq)$

Let x = mass of Ag and y = mass of Zn after the reaction has stopped. Then x + y = 29.0 g. Since the mol of Ag produced will equal two times the mol of Zn reacted, then:

$$(19.0 \text{ - y}) \text{ g Zn} \times \frac{1 \text{ mol Zn}}{65.38 \text{ g Zn}} \times \frac{2 \text{ mol Ag}}{1 \text{ mol Zn}} = x \text{ g Ag} \times \frac{1 \text{ mol Ag}}{107.9 \text{ g Ag}}$$

Simplifying:

$$3.059 \times 10^{-2} (19.0 \text{ - y}) = 9.268 \times 10^{-3} x$$

Substituting x = 29.0 - y into the equation gives:

$$3.059 \times 10^{-2} (19.0 \text{ - y}) = 9.268 \times 10^{-3} (29.0 \text{ - y})$$

Solving:

$$0.581 \text{ - } 3.059 \times 10^{-2} \text{ y} = 0.269 \text{ - } 9.268 \times 10^{-3} \text{ y}, \ 2.132 \times 10^{-2} \text{ y} = 0.312, \ \text{y} = 14.6 \text{ g Zn}$$

14.6 g Zn are present and 29.0 - 14.6 = 14.4 g Ag are present after the reaction is stopped.

84. $275.0 \text{ mL} \times 0.300 \ M = 82.5 \text{ mmol } H^+$;   Let $y = \text{mL}$ delivered by Y and $z = \text{mL}$ delivered by Z.

$$H^+ + OH^- \rightarrow H_2O; \quad \underbrace{y(0.150 \ M) \ + \ z(0.250 \ M) = 82.5}_{\text{mmol } OH^- \qquad \text{mmol } H^+}$$

Note that units of molarity are mol/L but are also equal to mmol/mL.

$275.0 \text{ mL} + y + z = 655 \text{ mL}$, $y + z = 380.$, $z = 380. - y$

$y(0.150) + (380. - y)(0.250) = 82.5$, $y = 125 \text{ mL}$, $z = 255 \text{ mL}$

flow rates: Y $\rightarrow \dfrac{125 \text{ mL}}{60.65 \text{ min}} = 2.06 \text{ mL/min}$ and Z $\rightarrow \dfrac{255 \text{ mL}}{60.65 \text{ min}} = 4.20 \text{ mL/min}$

85.   Molar masses: KCl, $39.10 + 35.45 = 74.55$ g/mol; KBr, $39.10 + 79.90 = 119.00$ g/mol

         AgCl, $107.9 + 35.45 = 143.4$ g/mol; AgBr, $107.9 + 79.90 = 187.8$ g/mol

Let x = number of moles of KCl in mixture and y = number of moles of KBr in mixture. Since $Ag^+ + Cl^- \rightarrow AgCl$ and $Ag^+ + Br^- \rightarrow AgBr$, then x = moles AgCl and y = moles AgBr. Setting up simultaneous equations from the given information:

   $0.1024 \text{ g} = 74.55 \ x + 119.0 \ y$ and $0.1889 \text{ g} = 143.4 \ x + 187.8 \ y$

Multiply the first equation by $\dfrac{187.8}{119.0}$, then subtract from the second.

$\begin{array}{r} 0.1889 = 143.4 \ x + 187.8 \ y \\ \underline{-0.1616 = -117.7 \ x - 187.8 \ y} \\ 0.0273 = 25.7 \ x, \qquad x = 1.06 \times 10^{-3} \text{ mol KCl} \end{array}$

$1.06 \times 10^{-3} \text{ mol KCl} \times \dfrac{74.55 \text{ g KCl}}{\text{mol KCl}} = 0.0790 \text{ g KCl}$

Mass % KCl = $\dfrac{0.0790 \text{ g}}{0.1024 \text{ g}} \times 100 = 77.1\%$, % KBr = $100.0 - 77.1 = 22.9\%$

86. $Pb^{2+} + 2 \ Cl^- \rightarrow PbCl_2$
                     3.407 g

$3.407 \text{ g PbCl}_2 \times \dfrac{1 \text{ mol PbCl}_2}{278.1 \text{ g PbCl}_2} \times \dfrac{1 \text{ mol Pb}^{2+}}{1 \text{ mol PbCl}_2} = 0.01225 \text{ mol Pb}^{2+}$

$\dfrac{0.01225 \text{ mol}}{2.00 \times 10^{-3} \text{ L}} = 6.13 \ M \text{ Pb}^{2+}$ (evaporated concentration)

original concentration = $\dfrac{0.0800 \text{ L} \times 6.13 \text{ mol/L}}{0.100 \text{ L}} = 4.90 \ M$

87.   a. $C_{12}H_{10-n}Cl_n + n\ Ag^+ \rightarrow n\ AgCl$; molar mass (AgCl) = 143.4 g/mol

       molar mass (PCB) = 12(12.01) + (10-n) (1.008) + n(35.45) = 154.20 + 34.44 n

       Since n mol AgCl are produced for every 1 mol PCB reacted, then n(143.4) grams of AgCl will
       be produced for every (154.20 + 34.44 n) grams of PCB reacted.

       $$\frac{\text{mass of AgCl}}{\text{mass of PCB}} = \frac{143.4\ n}{154.20 + 34.44\ n} \quad \text{or} \quad \text{mass}_{\text{AgCl}}\ (154.20 + 34.44\ n) = \text{mass}_{\text{PCB}}\ (143.4\ n)$$

   b.   0.4971 (154.20 + 34.44 n) = 0.1947 (143.4 n), 76.65 + 17.12 n = 27.92 n

       76.65 = 10.80 n, n = 7.097

88.   moles $CuSO_4$ = 87.6 mL $\times \dfrac{1\ L}{1000\ mL} \times \dfrac{0.500\ M}{1\ L} = 0.0439$ mol

       moles Fe = 2.00 g $\times \dfrac{1\ \text{mol Fe}}{55.85\ g} = 0.0358$ mol

       The two possible reactions are:

       I. $CuSO_4(aq) + Fe(s) \rightarrow Cu(s) + FeSO_4(aq)$

       II. $3\ CuSO_4(aq) + 2\ Fe(s) \rightarrow 3\ Cu(s) + Fe_2(SO_4)_3(aq)$

       If reaction I occurs, Fe is limiting and we can produce:

       0.0358 mol Fe $\times \dfrac{1\ \text{mol Cu}}{1\ \text{mol Fe}} \times \dfrac{63.55\ \text{g Cu}}{1\ \text{mol Cu}} = 2.28$ g Cu

       If reaction II occurs, $CuSO_4$ is limiting and we can produce:

       0.0439 mol $CuSO_4 \times \dfrac{3\ \text{mol Cu}}{3\ \text{mol CuSO}_4} \times \dfrac{63.55\ \text{g Cu}}{1\ \text{mol Cu}} = 2.79$ g Cu

       Assuming 100% yield, reaction I occurs since it fits the data best.

89.   a.   Flow rate = 5.00×10^4 L/s + 3.50×10^3 L/s = 5.35×10^4 L/s

   b. $C_{\text{HCl}} = \dfrac{3.50 \times 10^3\ (65.0)}{5.35 \times 10^4} = 4.25$ ppm HCl

   c.   1 ppm = 1 mg/kg H_2O = 1 mg/L   (assuming density = 1.00 g/mL)

       8.00 hr $\times \dfrac{60\ \text{min}}{\text{hr}} \times \dfrac{60\ \text{s}}{\text{min}} \times \dfrac{1.80 \times 10^4\ L}{\text{s}} \times \dfrac{4.25\ \text{mg HCl}}{L} \times \dfrac{1\ g}{1000\ \text{mg}} = 2.20 \times 10^6$ g HCl

       2.20×10^6 g HCl $\times \dfrac{1\ \text{mol HCl}}{36.46\ \text{g HCl}} \times \dfrac{1\ \text{mol CaO}}{2\ \text{mol HCl}} \times \dfrac{56.08\ \text{g CaO}}{\text{mol CaO}} = 1.69 \times 10^6$ g CaO

d.   The concentration of Ca^{2+} going into the second plant was:

$$\frac{5.00 \times 10^4 \,(10.2)}{5.35 \times 10^4} = 9.53 \text{ ppm}$$

The second plant used: 1.80×10^4 L/s $\times (8.00 \times 60 \times 60)$ sec $= 5.18 \times 10^8$ L of water.

$$1.69 \times 10^6 \text{ g CaO} \times \frac{40.08 \text{ g Ca}^{2+}}{56.08 \text{ g CaO}} = 1.21 \times 10^6 \text{ g Ca}^{2+} \text{ was added to this water.}$$

$$C_{Ca^{2+}} \text{ (plant water)} = 9.53 + \frac{1.21 \times 10^9 \text{ mg}}{5.18 \times 10^8 \text{ L}} = 9.53 + 2.34 = 11.87 \text{ ppm}$$

Since 90.0% of this water is returned, $1.80 \times 10^4 \times 0.900 = 1.62 \times 10^4$ L/s of water with 11.87 ppm Ca^{2+} is mixed with $(5.35 - 1.80) \times 10^4 = 3.55 \times 10^4$ L/s of water containing 9.53 ppm Ca^{2+}.

$$C_{Ca^{2+}} \text{ (final)} = \frac{(1.62 \times 10^4 \text{ L/s})(11.87 \text{ ppm}) + (3.55 \times 10^4 \text{ L/s})(9.53 \text{ ppm})}{1.62 \times 10^4 \text{ L/s} + 3.55 \times 10^4 \text{ L/s}} = 10.3 \text{ ppm}$$

90.   a. $7 H_2O + 2 Cr^{3+} \rightarrow Cr_2O_7^{2-} + 14 H^+ + 6 e^-$
                       $(2 e^- + S_2O_8^{2-} \rightarrow 2 SO_4^{2-}) \times 3$
_____

$7 H_2O(l) + 2 Cr^{3+}(aq) + 3 S_2O_8^{2-}(aq) \rightarrow Cr_2O_7^{2-}(aq) + 14 H^+(aq) + 6 SO_4^{2-}(aq)$

$$(Fe^{2+} \rightarrow Fe^{3+} + e^-) \times 6$$
$$6 e^- + 14 H^+ + Cr_2O_7^{2-} \rightarrow 2 Cr^{3+} + 7 H_2O$$
_____

$14 H^+(aq) + 6 Fe^{2+}(aq) + Cr_2O_7^{2-}(aq) \rightarrow 2 Cr^{3+}(aq) + 6 Fe^{3+}(aq) + 7 H_2O(l)$

b. 8.58×10^{-3} L $\times \dfrac{0.0520 \text{ mol Cr}_2O_7^{2-}}{L} \times \dfrac{6 \text{ mol Fe}^{2+}}{\text{mol Cr}_2O_7^{2-}} = 2.68 \times 10^{-3}$ mol of excess Fe^{2+}

Fe^{2+} (total) = 3.000 g $Fe(NH_4)_2(SO_4)_2 \cdot 6H_2O \times \dfrac{1 \text{ mol}}{392.17 \text{ g}} = 7.650 \times 10^{-3}$ mol Fe^{2+}

$7.650 \times 10^{-3} - 2.68 \times 10^{-3} = 4.97 \times 10^{-3}$ mol Fe^{2+} reacted with $Cr_2O_7^{2-}$ generated from the Cr plating.

The Cr plating contained:

$$4.97 \times 10^{-3} \text{ mol Fe}^{2+} \times \frac{1 \text{ mol Cr}_2O_7^{2-}}{6 \text{ mol Fe}^{2+}} \times \frac{2 \text{ mol Cr}^{3+}}{\text{mol Cr}_2O_7^{2-}} = 1.66 \times 10^{-3} \text{ mol Cr}^{3+}$$

$$= 1.66 \times 10^{-3} \text{ mol Cr}$$

$$1.66 \times 10^{-3} \text{ mol Cr} \times \frac{52.00 \text{ g Cr}}{\text{mol Cr}} = 8.63 \times 10^{-2} \text{ g Cr}$$

$$\text{Volume of Cr plating} = 8.63 \times 10^{-2} \text{ g} \times \frac{1 \text{ cm}^3}{7.19 \text{ g}} = 1.20 \times 10^{-2} \text{ cm}^3 = \text{area} \times \text{thickness}$$

$$\text{Thickness of Cr plating} = = \frac{1.20 \times 10^{-2} \text{ cm}^3}{40.0 \text{ cm}^2} = 3.00 \times 10^{-4} \text{ cm} = 300. \; \mu\text{m}$$

91.   a. $YBa_2Cu_3O_{6.5}$:

$$+3 + 2(+2) + 3x + 6.5(-2) = 0$$

$$7 + 3x - 13 = 0, \; 3x = 6, \; x = +2 \qquad \text{Only } Cu^{2+} \text{ present.}$$

$YBa_2Cu_3O_7$:

$$+3 + 2(+2) + 3x + 7(-2) = 0, \; x = +2 \; 1/3 \text{ or } 2.33$$

This corresponds to two Cu^{2+} and one Cu^{3+} present.

$YBa_2Cu_3O_8$:

$$+3 + 2(+2) + 3x + 8(-2) = 0, \; x = +3 \qquad \text{Only } Cu^{3+} \text{ present.}$$

b.

$$(e^- + Cu^{2+} + I^- \rightarrow CuI) \times 2 \qquad\qquad 2 \, e^- + Cu^{3+} + I^- \rightarrow CuI$$
$$3 I^- \rightarrow I_3^- + 2 \, e^- \qquad\qquad\qquad\qquad 3 I^- \rightarrow I_3^- + 2 \, e^-$$
$$\overline{2 \, Cu^{2+}(aq) + 5 \, I^-(aq) \rightarrow 2 \, CuI(s) + I_3^-(aq)} \qquad \overline{Cu^{3+}(aq) + 4 \, I^-(aq) \rightarrow CuI(s) + I_3^-(aq)}$$

$$2 \, S_2O_3^{2-} \rightarrow S_4O_6^{2-} + 2 \, e^-$$
$$2 \, e^- + I_3^- \rightarrow 3 \, I^-$$
$$\overline{2 \, S_2O_3^{2-}(aq) + I_3^-(aq) \rightarrow 3 \, I^-(aq) + S_4O_6^{2-}(aq)}$$

c.   Step II data: All Cu is converted to Cu^{2+}. Note: superconductor abbreviated as "123."

$$22.57 \times 10^{-3} \text{ L} \times \frac{0.1000 \text{ mol } S_2O_3^{2-}}{L} \times \frac{1 \text{ mol } I_3^-}{2 \text{ mol } S_2O_3^{2-}} \times \frac{2 \text{ mol } Cu^{2+}}{\text{mol } I_3^-} = 2.257 \times 10^{-3} \text{ mol } Cu^{2+}$$

$$2.257 \times 10^{-3} \text{ mol Cu} \times \frac{1 \text{ mol "123"}}{3 \text{ mol Cu}} = 7.523 \times 10^{-4} \text{ mol "123"}$$

$$\text{Molar mass of } YBa_2Cu_3O_x = \frac{0.5042 \text{ g}}{7.523 \times 10^{-4} \text{ mol}} = 670.2 \text{ g/mol}$$

$$670.2 = 88.91 + 2(137.3) + 3(63.55) + x(16.00), \; 670.2 = 554.2 + x(16.00)$$

$x = 7.250$; Formula is $YBa_2Cu_3O_{7.25}$.

Check with Step I data: Both Cu^{2+} and Cu^{3+} present.

$$37.77 \times 10^{-3} \text{ L} \times \frac{0.1000 \text{ mol } S_2O_3^{2-}}{L} \times \frac{1 \text{ mol } I_3^-}{2 \text{ mol } S_2O_3^{2-}} = 1.889 \times 10^{-3} \text{ mol } I_3^-$$

We get 1 mol I_3^- per mol Cu^{3+} and 1 mol I_3^- per 2 mol Cu^{2+}. Let $n_{Cu^{3+}}$ = mol Cu^{3+} and $n_{Cu^{2+}}$ = mol Cu^{2+}, then:

$$n_{Cu^{3+}} + \frac{n_{Cu^{2+}}}{2} = 1.889 \times 10^{-3} \text{ mol}$$

In addition: $\dfrac{0.5625 \text{ g}}{670.2 \text{ g/mol}} = 8.393 \times 10^{-4} \text{ mol "123"}$

This amount of "123" contains: $3(8.393 \times 10^{-4}) = 2.518 \times 10^{-3}$ mol Cu total = $n_{Cu^{3+}} + n_{Cu^{2+}}$

Solving by simultaneous equations:

$$n_{Cu^{3+}} + n_{Cu^{2+}} = 2.518 \times 10^{-3}$$

$$-n_{Cu^{3+}} - \frac{n_{Cu^{2+}}}{2} = -1.889 \times 10^{-3}$$

$$\rule{6cm}{0.4pt}$$

$$\frac{n_{Cu^{2+}}}{2} = 6.29 \times 10^{-4}$$

$n_{Cu^{2+}} = 1.26 \times 10^{-3}$ mol Cu^{2+}; $n_{Cu^{3+}} = 2.518 \times 10^{-3} - 1.26 \times 10^{-3} = 1.26 \times 10^{-3}$ mol Cu^{3+}

This sample of superconductor contains equal moles of Cu^{2+} and Cu^{3+}. Therefore, 1 mol of $YBa_2Cu_3O_x$ contains 1.50 mol Cu^{2+} and 1.50 mol Cu^{3+}. Solving for x using oxidation states:

$$+3 + 2(+2) + 1.50(+2) + 1.50(+3) + x(-2) = 0, \quad 14.50 = 2x, \ x = 7.25$$

The two experiments give the same result, $x = 7.25$ with formula $YBa_2Cu_3O_{7.25}$.

Average oxidation state of Cu:

$$+3 + 2(+2) + 3(x) + 7.25(-2) = 0, \quad 3x = 7.50, \ x = +2.50$$

As determined from step I data, this superconductor sample contains equal moles of Cu^{2+} and Cu^{3+}, giving an average oxidation state of +2.50.

92. $0.298 \text{ g BaSO}_4 \times \dfrac{96.07 \text{ g SO}_4^{2-}}{233.4 \text{ g BaSO}_4} = 0.123 \text{ g SO}_4^{2-}$

Mass % SO_4^{2-} = $\dfrac{0.123 \text{ g SO}_4^{2-}}{0.205 \text{ g}} = 60.0\%$

Assume we have 100.0 g of the mixture of Na_2SO_4 and K_2SO_4. There is:

$$60.0 \text{ g SO}_4^{2-} \times \frac{1 \text{ mol}}{96.07 \text{ g}} = 0.625 \text{ mol SO}_4^{2-}$$

There must be $2 \times 0.625 = 1.25$ mol of +1 charged cations to balance the 2- charge of SO_4^{2-}.

Let x = moles of K^+ and y = moles of Na^+. Then, $x + y = 1.25$.

The total mass of Na^+ and K^+ must be 40.0 g in the assumed 100.0 g of mixture, so:

$$x \text{ mol } K^+ \times \frac{39.10 \text{ g}}{\text{mol}} + y \text{ mol } Na^+ \times \frac{22.99 \text{ g}}{\text{mol}} = 40.0 \text{ g}$$

So we have two equations in two unknowns:

$$x + y = 1.25 \text{ and } 39.10\, x + 22.99\, y = 40.0$$

Solving: $x = 1.25 - y,\ \ 39.10(1.25 - y) + 22.99\, y = 40.0$

$$48.9 - 39.10\, y + 22.99\, y = 40.0,\ \ -16.11\, y = -8.9$$

$$y = 0.55 \text{ mol } Na^+ \text{ and } x = 1.25 - 0.55 = 0.70 \text{ mol } K^+$$

Therefore:

$$0.70 \text{ mol } K^+ \times \frac{1 \text{ mol } K_2SO_4}{2 \text{ mol } K^+} = 0.35 \text{ mol } K_2SO_4$$

$$0.35 \text{ mol } K_2SO_4 \times \frac{174.3 \text{ g}}{\text{mol}} = 61 \text{ g } K_2SO_4$$

Since we assumed 100.0 g, then the mixture is 61% K_2SO_4 and 39% Na_2SO_4 by mass.

93.   There are 3 unknowns so we need 3 equations to solve for the unknowns. Let x = mass $AgNO_3$, y = mass $CuCl_2$ and z = mass $FeCl_3$. Then x + y + z = 1.0000 g. The Cl^- in $CuCl_2$ and $FeCl_3$ will react with the excess $AgNO_3$ to form the precipitate AgCl(s). Assuming silver has an atomic mass of 107.90:

$$\text{Mass of Cl in mixture} = 1.7809 \text{ g AgCl} \times \frac{35.45 \text{ g Cl}}{143.35 \text{ g AgCl}} = 0.4404 \text{ g Cl}$$

$$\text{mass of Cl from } CuCl_2 = y \text{ g } CuCl_2 \times \frac{2(35.45) \text{ g Cl}}{134.45 \text{ g } CuCl_2} = 0.5273 \text{ y}$$

$$\text{mass of Cl from } FeCl_3 = z \text{ g } FeCl_3 \times \frac{3(35.45) \text{ g Cl}}{162.20 \text{ g } FeCl_3} = 0.6557 \text{ z}$$

The second equation is: 0.4404 g Cl = 0.5273 y + 0.6557 z

Similarly, let's calculate the mass of metals in each salt.

$$\text{mass of Ag in } AgNO_3 = x \text{ g } AgNO_3 \times \frac{107.9 \text{ g Ag}}{169.91 \text{ g } AgNO_3} = 0.6350 \text{ x}$$

For $CuCl_2$ and $FeCl_3$, we already calculated the amount of Cl in each initial amount of salt; the remainder must be the mass of metal in each salt.

mass of Cu in $CuCl_2$ = y - 0.5273 y = 0.4727 y

mass of Fe in $FeCl_3$ = z - 0.6557 z = 0.3443 z

The third equation is: 0.4684 g metals = 0.6350 x + 0.4727 y + 0.3443 z

We now have three equations with three unknowns. Solving:

$$
\begin{array}{l}
-0.6350\,(1.0000 = \quad\quad x \quad + \quad y \quad + \quad z) \\
\quad\quad\quad 0.4684 = 0.6350\,x + 0.4727\,y + 0.3443\,z \\
\hline
\quad\quad -0.1666 = \quad\quad\quad\quad -0.1623\,y - 0.2907\,z
\end{array}
$$

$$
\begin{array}{l}
\dfrac{0.5273}{0.1623}\,(-0.1666 = -0.1623\,y - 0.2907\,z) \\
\quad\quad\quad 0.4404 = 0.5273\,y + 0.6557\,z \\
\hline
\quad\quad -0.1009 = \quad\quad\quad\quad -0.2888\,z, \quad z = \dfrac{0.1009}{0.2888} = 0.3494 \text{ g FeCl}_3
\end{array}
$$

$0.4404 = 0.5273\,y + 0.6557\,(0.3494), \ y = 0.4007 \text{ g CuCl}_2$

$x = 1.0000 - y - z = 1.0000 - 0.4007 - 0.3494 = 0.2499 \text{ g AgNO}_3$

mass % $AgNO_3 = \dfrac{0.2499 \text{ g}}{1.0000 \text{ g}} \times 100 = 24.99\% \text{ AgNO}_3$

mass % $CuCl_2 = \dfrac{0.4007 \text{ g}}{1.0000 \text{ g}} \times 100 = 40.07\% \text{ CuCl}_2, \ $ mass % $FeCl_3 = 34.94\%$

Marathon Problems

94. $M(CHO_2)_2(aq) + Na_2SO_4(aq) \rightarrow MSO_4(s) + 2\,NaCHO_2(aq)$

From the balanced molecular equation, the moles of $M(CHO_2)_2$ present initially must equal the moles of $MSO_4(s)$ formed. Since moles = mass/molar mass and letting A_M = the atomic mass of M, then:

$$\text{mol } MSO_4 = \frac{\text{mass } MSO_4}{\text{molar mass of } MSO_4} = \frac{9.9392 \text{ g}}{A_M + 96.07}$$

$$\text{mol } M(CHO_2)_2 = \frac{\text{mass } M(CHO_2)_2}{\text{molar mass of } M(CHO_2)_2} = \frac{9.7416 \text{ g}}{A_M + 90.04}$$

Since mol MSO_4 = mol $M(CHO_2)_2$; then:

$$\frac{9.9392}{A_M + 96.07} = \frac{9.7416}{A_M + 90.04}, \ 9.9392\,A_M + 894.9 = 9.7416\,A_M + 935.9$$

$$A_M = \frac{41.0}{0.1976} = 207; \ \text{From the periodic table, the unknown element M is Pb.}$$

From the information in the second paragraph, we can determine the concentration of the $KMnO_4$ solution. Using the half-reaction method, the balanced reaction between MnO_4^- and $C_2O_4^{2-}$ is:

$$5\ C_2O_4^{2-}(aq) + 2\ MnO_4^-(aq) + 16\ H^+(aq) \rightarrow 10\ CO_2(g) + 2\ Mn^{2+}(aq) + 8\ H_2O(l)$$

$$\text{mol } MnO_4^- = 0.9234 \text{ g } Na_2C_2O_4 \times \frac{1 \text{ mol } Na_2C_2O_4}{134.00 \text{ g}} \times \frac{1 \text{ mol } C_2O_4^{2-}}{1 \text{ mol } Na_2C_2O_4} \times \frac{2 \text{ mol } MnO_4^-}{5 \text{ mol } C_2O_4^{2-}}$$

$$= 2.756 \times 10^{-3} \text{ mol } MnO_4^-$$

$$M_{KMnO_4} = M_{MnO_4^-} = \frac{\text{mol } MnO_4^-}{\text{volume}} = \frac{2.756 \times 10^{-3} \text{ mol}}{0.01855 \text{ L}} = 0.1486 \text{ mol/L}$$

From the third paragraph, the standard $KMnO_4$ solution reacts with formate ions from the filtrate. We must determine the moles of CHO_2^- ions present in order to determine volume of $KMnO_4$ solution. The mol of CHO_2^- ions present initially is:

$$9.7416 \text{ g } Pb(CHO_2)_2 \times \frac{\text{mol } Pb(CHO_2)_2}{297.2 \text{ g}} \times \frac{2 \text{ mol } CHO_2^-}{1 \text{ mol } Pb(CHO_2)_2} = 6.556 \times 10^{-2} \text{ mol } CHO_2^-$$

The mol of CHO_2^- present in 10.00 mL of diluted solution is:

$$0.01000 \text{ L} \times \frac{6.556 \times 10^{-2} \text{ mol } CHO_2^-}{0.2500 \text{ L}} = 2.622 \times 10^{-3} \text{ mol } CHO_2^-$$

Using the half-reaction method in basic solution, the balanced reaction between CHO_2^- and MnO_4^- is:

$$3\ CHO_2^-(aq) + 2\ MnO_4^-(aq) + OH^-(aq) \rightarrow 3\ CO_3^{2-}(aq) + 2\ MnO_2(s) + 2\ H_2O(l)$$

Determining the volume of MnO_4^- solution:

$$2.622 \times 10^{-3} \text{ mol } CHO_2^- \times \frac{2 \text{ mol } MnO_4^-}{3 \text{ mol } CHO_2^-} \times \frac{1 \text{ L}}{0.1486 \text{ mol } MnO_4^-} = 1.176 \times 10^{-2} \text{ L} = 11.76 \text{ mL}$$

The titration requires 11.76 mL of the standard $KMnO_4$ solution.

95.   a.   Compound $A = M(NO_3)_x$;   In 100.00 g compound: $8.246 \text{ g N} \times \dfrac{47.997 \text{ g O}}{14.007 \text{ g N}} = 28.26 \text{ g O}$

Thus, the mass of nitrate is: 100.0 g A - 36.51 g if x = 1.

If x = 1, mass of M = 100.00 - 36.51 g = 63.49 g

$$\text{mol M} = \text{mol N} = \frac{8.246 \text{ g}}{14.007 \text{ g/mL}} = 0.5887$$

$$\text{MM of metal M} = \frac{63.49 \text{ g}}{0.5887 \text{ g/mL}} = 107.8 \text{ g/mol (Ag)}$$

If x = 2, 0.5887 mass of M = 100.00 - 2(36.51) = 26.98 g

$$\text{mol M} = 1/2 \text{ mol N} = \frac{0.5887 \text{ mol}}{2} = 0.2944 \text{ mol}$$

$$\text{MM of metal M} = \frac{26.98 \text{ g}}{0.2944 \text{ mol}} = 91.64 \text{ g/mol}$$

This is close to Zr, but Zr does not form stable +2 ions in solution; it forms stable +4 ions. Thus, compound A is $AgNO_3$.

For compound B, the only chromium salt discussed in the solubility rules in Table 4.1 was CrO_4^{2-}. It has Cr in the +6 oxidation state, so let's assume compound B is K_2CrO_4.

b.   The reaction is:

$$2 \text{ AgNO}_3(aq) + \text{K}_2\text{CrO}_4(aq) \rightarrow \text{Ag}_2\text{CrO}_4(s) + 2 \text{ KNO}_3(aq)$$

The blood red precipitate is $Ag_2CrO_4(s)$.

c.   331.8 g Ag_2CrO_4 is formed, which is 1 mol Ag_2CrO_4.

It is important to note that we begin with equal masses of $AgNO_3$ and K_2CrO_4. From the formula for Ag_2CrO_4, we must have at least 2 mol $AgNO_3$ and 1 mol K_2CrO_4.

2.000 mol $AgNO_3$ = 339.8 g $AgNO_3$

1.000 mol K_2CrO_4 = 194.2 g K_2CrO_4

$$\frac{2.000 \text{ mol AgNO}_3}{1.000 \text{ mol K}_2\text{CrO}_4} = \frac{339.8}{194.2} = 1.750; \text{ The balanced equation requires a 2:1 mol ratio, so}$$

$AgNO_3$ is limiting and for equal masses we have 339.8 g $AgNO_3$ and 339.8 g K_2CrO_4.

Initially, solution A = $\dfrac{2.000 \text{ mol Ag}^+}{0.5000 \text{ L}} = 4.000 \ M \text{Ag}^+$ and $\dfrac{2.000 \text{ mol NO}_3^-}{0.5000 \text{ L}} = 4.000 \ M\text{NO}_3^-$.

$$\text{Solution B} = 339.8 \text{ g K}_2\text{CrO}_4 \times \frac{1 \text{ mol}}{194.2 \text{ g}} = 1.750 \text{ mol}$$

$$\frac{2 \times 1.750 \text{ mol K}^+}{0.5000 \text{ L}} = 7.000 \, M \, \text{K}^+ \text{ and } \frac{1.750 \text{ mol CrO}_4^{2-}}{0.5000 \text{ L}} = 3.500 \, M \, \text{CrO}_4^{2-}$$

d. After the reaction, moles of K^+ and moles of NO_3^- remain unchanged since they are spectator ions.

$$2 \text{ Ag}^+ + \text{CrO}_4^{2-} \rightarrow \text{Ag}_2\text{CrO}_4$$

initial   2.000   1.750 mol
after   0   0.750 mol

$$[\text{K}^+] = \frac{2 \times 1.750 \text{ mol}}{1.000 \text{ L}} = 3.500 \, M \, \text{K}^+$$

$$[\text{NO}_3^-] = \frac{2.000 \text{ mol}}{1.000 \text{ L}} = 2.000 \, M \, \text{NO}_3^-$$

$$[\text{CrO}_4^{2-}] = \frac{0.750 \text{ mol}}{1.000 \text{ L}} = 0.750 \, M \, \text{CrO}_4^{2-}; \quad [\text{Ag}^+] = 0 \, M \text{ (the limiting reagent)}$$

CHAPTER FIVE

GASES

Pressure

21. $4.75 \text{ cm} \times \dfrac{10 \text{ mm}}{\text{cm}} = 47.5 \text{ mm Hg or } 47.5 \text{ torr}; \quad 47.5 \text{ torr} \times \dfrac{1 \text{ atm}}{760 \text{ torr}} = 6.25 \times 10^{-2} \text{ atm}$

$6.25 \times 10^{-2} \text{ atm} \times \dfrac{1.013 \times 10^5 \text{ Pa}}{\text{atm}} = 6.33 \times 10^3 \text{ Pa}$

22. If the levels of Hg in each arm of the manometer are equal, then the pressure in the flask is equal to atmospheric pressure. When they are unequal, the difference in height in mm will be equal to the difference in pressure in mm Hg between the flask and the atmosphere. Which level is higher will tell us whether the pressure in the flask is less than or greater than atmospheric.

a. $P_{\text{flask}} < P_{\text{atm}}; \ P_{\text{flask}} = 760. - 118 = 642 \text{ torr}$

$642 \text{ torr} \times \dfrac{1 \text{ atm}}{760 \text{ torr}} = 0.845 \text{ atm}$

$0.845 \text{ atm} \times \dfrac{1.013 \times 10^5 \text{ Pa}}{\text{atm}} = 8.56 \times 10^4 \text{ Pa}$

b. $P_{\text{flask}} > P_{\text{atm}}; \ P_{\text{flask}} = 760. \text{ torr} + 215 \text{ torr} = 975 \text{ torr}$

$975 \text{ torr} \times \dfrac{1 \text{ atm}}{760 \text{ torr}} = 1.28 \text{ atm}$

$1.28 \text{ atm} \times \dfrac{1.013 \times 10^5 \text{ Pa}}{\text{atm}} = 1.30 \times 10^5 \text{ Pa}$

c. $P_{\text{flask}} = 635 - 118 = 517 \text{ torr}; \ P_{\text{flask}} = 635 + 215 = 850. \text{ torr}$

23. Suppose we have a column of Hg $1.00 \text{ cm} \times 1.00 \text{ cm} \times 76.0 \text{ cm} = V = 76.0 \text{ cm}^3$:

$\text{mass} = 76.0 \text{ cm}^3 \times 13.59 \text{ g/cm}^3 = 1.03 \times 10^3 \text{ g} \times \dfrac{1 \text{ kg}}{1000 \text{ g}} = 1.03 \text{ kg}$

$F = mg = 1.03 \text{ kg} \times 9.81 \text{ m/s}^2 = 10.1 \text{ kg m/s}^2 = 10.1 \text{ N}$

$$\frac{\text{Force}}{\text{area}} = \frac{10.1 \, \text{N}}{\text{cm}^2} \times \left(\frac{100 \, \text{cm}}{\text{m}}\right)^2 = 1.01 \times 10^5 \, \frac{\text{N}}{\text{m}^2} \text{ or } 1.01 \times 10^5 \, \text{Pa}$$

(Note: 76.0 cm Hg = 1 atm = 1.01×10^5 Pa.)

To exert the same pressure, a column of water will have to contain the same mass as the 76.0 cm column of Hg. Thus, the column of water will have to be 13.59 times taller or 76.0 cm × 13.59 = 1.03×10^3 cm = 10.3 m.

24.   a. The pressure is proportional to the mass of the fluid. The mass is proportional to the volume of the column of fluid (or to the height of the column assuming the area of the column of fluid is constant).

$$d = \text{density} = \frac{\text{mass}}{\text{volume}}; \quad \text{The volume of silicon oil is the same as the volume of Hg in Exercise 5.22.}$$

$$V = \frac{m}{d}; \quad V_{Hg} = V_{oil}; \quad \frac{m_{Hg}}{d_{Hg}} = \frac{m_{oil}}{d_{oil}}, \quad m_{oil} = \frac{m_{Hg} d_{oil}}{d_{Hg}}$$

Since P is proportional to the mass of liquid:

$$P_{oil} = P_{Hg}\left(\frac{d_{oil}}{d_{Hg}}\right) = P_{Hg}\left(\frac{1.30}{13.6}\right) = 0.0956 \, P_{Hg}$$

This conversion applies only to the column of silicon oil.

a. P_{flask} = 760. torr - (118 × 0.0956) torr = 760. - 11.3 = 749 torr

$$749 \text{ torr} \times \frac{1 \text{ atm}}{760 \text{ torr}} = 0.986 \text{ atm}; \quad 0.986 \text{ atm} \times \frac{1.013 \times 10^5 \text{ Pa}}{\text{atm}} = 9.99 \times 10^4 \text{ Pa}$$

b. P_{flask} = 760. torr + (215 × 0.0956) torr = 760. + 20.6 = 781 torr

$$781 \text{ torr} \times \frac{1 \text{ atm}}{760 \text{ torr}} = 1.03 \text{ atm}; \quad 1.03 \text{ atm} \times \frac{1.013 \times 10^5 \text{ Pa}}{\text{atm}} = 1.04 \times 10^5 \text{ Pa}$$

   b. If we are measuring the same pressure, the height of the silicon oil column would be 13.6 ÷ 1.30 = 10.5 times the height of a mercury column. The advantage of using a less dense fluid than mercury is in measuring small pressures. The height difference measured will be larger for the less dense fluid. Thus, the measurement will be more precise.

25.   a. $4.8 \text{ atm} \times \dfrac{760 \text{ mm Hg}}{\text{atm}} = 3.6 \times 10^3 \text{ mm Hg};$ b. $3.6 \times 10^3 \text{ mm Hg} \times \dfrac{1 \text{ torr}}{\text{mm Hg}} = 3.6 \times 10^3 \text{ torr}$

   c. $4.8 \text{ atm} \times \dfrac{1.013 \times 10^5 \text{ Pa}}{\text{atm}} = 4.9 \times 10^5 \text{ Pa};$ d. $4.8 \text{ atm} \times \dfrac{14.7 \text{ psi}}{\text{atm}} = 71 \text{ psi}$

Gas Laws

26.   a. $PV = nRT$ b. $PV = nRT$ c. $PV = nRT$

        $PV = \text{Constant}$ $P = \left(\dfrac{nR}{V}\right) \times T = \text{Const} \times T$ $T = \left(\dfrac{P}{nR}\right) \times V = \text{Const} \times V$

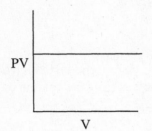

        d. $PV = nRT$ e. $P = \dfrac{nRT}{V} = \dfrac{\text{Constant}}{V}$ f. $PV = nRT$

        $PV = \text{Constant}$ $P = \text{Constant} \times \dfrac{1}{V}$ $\dfrac{PV}{T} = nR = \text{Constant}$

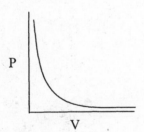
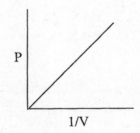
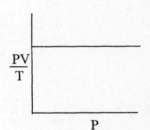

Note: The equation for a straight line is $y = mx + b$ where y is the y-axis and x is the x-axis. Any equation that has this form will produce a straight line with slope equal to m and y-intercept equal to b. Plots b, c, and e have this straight line form.

27.   Treat each gas separately and use the relationship $P_1V_1 = P_2V_2$, since for each gas, n and T are constant.

For H_2: $P_2 = \dfrac{P_1V_1}{V_2} = 475 \text{ torr} \times \dfrac{2.00 \text{ L}}{3.00 \text{ L}} = 317 \text{ torr}$

For N_2: $P_2 = 0.200 \text{ atm} \times \dfrac{1.00 \text{ L}}{3.00 \text{ L}} = 0.0667 \text{ atm}$; $0.0667 \text{ atm} \times \dfrac{760 \text{ torr}}{\text{atm}} = 50.7 \text{ torr}$

$P_{\text{total}} = P_{H_2} + P_{N_2} = 317 + 50.7 = 368 \text{ torr}$

28.   For H_2: $P_2 = \dfrac{P_1 V_1}{V_2} = 360.\text{ torr} \times \dfrac{2.00\text{ L}}{3.00\text{ L}} = 240.\text{ torr}$

$$P_{TOT} = P_{H_2} + P_{N_2}, \quad P_{N_2} = P_{TOT} - P_{H_2} = 320.\text{ torr} - 240.\text{ torr} = 80.\text{ torr}$$

For N_2: $P_1 = \dfrac{P_2 V_2}{V_1} = 80.\text{ torr} \times \dfrac{3.00\text{ L}}{1.00\text{ L}} = 240\text{ torr}$

29. $PV = nRT, \quad \dfrac{nT}{P} = \dfrac{V}{R} = \text{constant}, \quad \dfrac{n_1 T_1}{P_1} = \dfrac{n_2 T_2}{P_2}$; $\text{mol} \times \text{molar mass} = \text{mass}$

$$\dfrac{n_1 \,(\text{molar mass})\, T_1}{P_1} = \dfrac{n_2 \,(\text{molar mass})\, T_2}{P_2}, \quad \dfrac{\text{mass}_1 \times T_1}{P_1} = \dfrac{\text{mass}_2 \times T_2}{P_2}$$

$$\text{mass}_2 = \dfrac{\text{mass}_1 \times T_1 P_2}{T_2 P_1} = \dfrac{1.00 \times 10^3\text{ g} \times 291\text{ K} \times 650.\text{ psi}}{299\text{ K} \times 2050.\text{ psi}} = 309\text{ g}$$

30. $PV = nRT, \quad n \text{ is constant.} \quad \dfrac{PV}{T} = nR = \text{constant}, \quad \dfrac{P_1 V_1}{T_1} = \dfrac{P_2 V_2}{T_2}, \quad V_2 = \dfrac{V_1 P_1 T_2}{P_2 T_1}$

$$V_2 = 1.00\text{ L} \times \dfrac{760.\text{ torr}}{220.\text{ torr}} \times \dfrac{(273-31)\text{ K}}{(273+23)\text{ K}} = 2.82\text{ L}; \quad \Delta V = 2.82 - 1.00 = 1.82\text{ L}$$

31. $P = P_{CO_2} = \dfrac{n_{CO_2} RT}{V} = \dfrac{\left(22.0\text{ g} \times \dfrac{1\text{ mol}}{44.01\text{ g}}\right) \times \dfrac{0.08206\text{ L atm}}{\text{mol K}} \times 300.\text{ K}}{4.00\text{ L}} = 3.08\text{ atm}$

With air present, the partial pressure of CO_2 will still be 3.08 atm. The total pressure will be the sum of the partial pressures.

$$P_{\text{total}} = P_{CO_2} + P_{\text{air}} = 3.08\text{ atm} + \left(740.\text{ torr} \times \dfrac{1\text{ atm}}{760\text{ torr}}\right) = 3.08 + 0.974 = 4.05\text{ atm}$$

32. $\dfrac{PV}{T} = nR = \text{a constant}, \quad \dfrac{P_1 V_1}{T_1} = \dfrac{P_2 V_2}{T_2}$

$$P_2 = \dfrac{P_1 V_1 T_2}{V_2 T_1} = 710\text{ torr} \times \dfrac{5.0 \times 10^2\text{ mL}}{25\text{ mL}} \times \dfrac{(273+820)\text{ K}}{(273+30.)\text{ K}} = 5.1 \times 10^4\text{ torr}$$

33. $n = \dfrac{PV}{RT} = \dfrac{135\text{ atm} \times 200.0\text{ L}}{0.08206\,\dfrac{\text{L atm}}{\text{mol K}} \times (273+24)\text{ K}} = 1.11 \times 10^3\text{ mol}$

For He: $1.11 \times 10^3 \text{ mol} \times \dfrac{4.003 \text{ g He}}{\text{mol}} = 4.44 \times 10^3 \text{ g He}$

For H_2: $1.11 \times 10^3 \text{ mol} \times \dfrac{2.016 \text{ g He}}{\text{mol}} = 2.24 \times 10^3 \text{ g H}_2$

34. $P = \dfrac{nRT}{V} = \dfrac{\left(0.60 \text{ g} \times \dfrac{1 \text{ mol}}{32.00 \text{ g}}\right) \times \dfrac{0.08206 \text{ L atm}}{\text{mol K}} \times (273 + 22) \text{ K}}{5.0 \text{ L}} = 0.091 \text{ atm}$

35. As NO_2 is converted completely into N_2O_4, the moles of gas present will decrease by a factor of one-half (from the 2:1 mol ratio in the balanced equation). Using Avogadro's law,

$\dfrac{V_1}{n_1} = \dfrac{V_2}{n_2}, \ V_2 = V_1 \times \dfrac{n_2}{n_1} = 25.0 \text{ mL} \times \dfrac{1}{2} = 12.5 \text{ mL}$

$N_2O_4(g)$ will occupy one-half the original volume of $NO_2(g)$.

36. $PV = nRT$, n is constant. $\dfrac{PV}{T} = nR = \text{constant}, \ \dfrac{P_1V_1}{T_1} = \dfrac{P_2V_2}{T_2}; \ V_2 = 1.040 \ V_1$, so $\dfrac{V_1}{V_2} = \dfrac{1.000}{1.040}$

$P_2 = \dfrac{P_1V_1T_2}{V_2T_1} = 75. \text{ psi} \times \dfrac{1.000}{1.040} \times \dfrac{(273 + 58) \text{ K}}{(273 + 19) \text{ K}} = 82 \text{ psi}$

37. $PV = nRT$, P is constant. $\dfrac{nT}{V} = \dfrac{P}{R} = \text{constant}, \ \dfrac{n_1T_1}{V_1} = \dfrac{n_2T_2}{V_2}$

$\dfrac{n_2}{n_1} = \dfrac{T_1V_2}{T_2V_1} = \dfrac{294 \text{ K}}{335 \text{ K}} \times \dfrac{4.20 \times 10^3 \text{ m}^3}{4.00 \times 10^3 \text{ m}^3} = 0.921$

38. We can use the ideal gas law to calculate the partial pressure of each gas or to calculate the total pressure. There will be less math if we calculate the total pressure from the ideal gas law.

$n_{O_2} = 1.80 \times 10^2 \text{ mg O}_2 \times \dfrac{1 \text{ g}}{1000 \text{ mg}} \times \dfrac{1 \text{ mol O}_2}{32.00 \text{ g O}_2} = 5.63 \times 10^{-3} \text{ mol O}_2$

$n_{NO} = \dfrac{9.00 \times 10^{18} \text{ molecules NO}}{\text{cm}^3} \times \dfrac{1000 \text{ cm}^3}{\text{L}} \times \dfrac{1 \text{ mol NO}}{6.022 \times 10^{23} \text{ molecules NO}} = 1.49 \times 10^{-2} \text{ mol NO/L}$

$n_{total} = n_{N_2} + n_{O_2} + n_{NO} = 2.00 \times 10^{-2} + 5.63 \times 10^{-3} + 1.49 \times 10^{-2} = 4.05 \times 10^{-2} \text{ mol}$

$P_{total} = \dfrac{n_{total}RT}{V} = \dfrac{4.05 \times 10^{-2} \text{ mol} \times \dfrac{0.08206 \text{ L atm}}{\text{mol K}} \times 273 \text{ K}}{1.00 \text{ L}} = 0.907 \text{ atm}$

$P_{N_2} = \chi_{N_2} P_{total} = \dfrac{2.00 \times 10^{-2} \text{ mol N}_2}{4.05 \times 10^{-2} \text{ mol total}} \times 0.907 \text{ atm} = 0.448 \text{ atm}; \ \chi_{N_2} = \text{mole fraction of N}_2$

$$P_{O_2} = \frac{5.63 \times 10^{-3}}{4.05 \times 10^{-2}} \times 0.907 \text{ atm} = 0.126 \text{ atm}; \quad P_{NO} = \frac{1.49 \times 10^{-2}}{4.05 \times 10^{-2}} \times 0.907 \text{ atm} = 0.334 \text{ atm}$$

39.   At constant T and P, Avogadro's law applies, that is, equal volumes contain equal moles of molecules. In terms of balanced equations, we can say that mol ratios and volume ratios between the various reactants and products will be equal to each other. $Br_2 + 3 F_2 \rightarrow 2 X$; Two moles of X must contain two moles of Br and 6 moles of F; X must have the formula BrF_3.

40. $P_{total} = 1.00 \text{ atm} = 760. \text{ torr} = P_{N_2} + P_{H_2O} = P_{N_2} + 17.5 \text{ torr}, \quad P_{N_2} = 743 \text{ torr}$

$$n_{N_2} = \frac{P_{N_2} \times V}{RT} = \frac{(743 \text{ torr} \times \frac{1 \text{ atm}}{760 \text{ torr}}) \times (2.50 \times 10^2 \text{ mL} \times \frac{1 \text{ L}}{1000 \text{ mL}})}{\frac{0.08206 \text{ L atm}}{\text{mol K}} \times 293 \text{ K}} = 1.02 \times 10^{-2} \text{ mol } N_2$$

$$1.02 \times 10^{-2} \text{ mol } N_2 \times \frac{28.02 \text{ g } N_2}{\text{mol } N_2} = 0.286 \text{ g } N_2$$

41. $P_{He} + P_{H_2O} = 1.00 \text{ atm} = 760. \text{ torr} = P_{He} + 23.8 \text{ torr}, \quad P_{He} = 736 \text{ torr}$

$n_{He} = 0.586 \text{ g} \times \dfrac{1 \text{ mol}}{4.003 \text{ g}} = 0.146 \text{ mol He}$

$$V = \frac{n_{He}RT}{P_{He}} = \frac{0.146 \text{ mol} \times \frac{0.08206 \text{ L atm}}{\text{mol K}} \times 298 \text{ K}}{736 \text{ torr} \times \frac{1 \text{ atm}}{760 \text{ torr}}} = 3.69 \text{ L}$$

42. $1.00 \text{ g } H_2 \times \dfrac{1 \text{ mol } H_2}{2.016 \text{ g } H_2} = 0.496 \text{ mol } H_2; \quad 1.00 \text{ g He} \times \dfrac{1 \text{ mol He}}{4.003 \text{ g He}} = 0.250 \text{ mol He}$

$$P_{H_2} = \chi_{H_2}P_{total} = \frac{0.496 \text{ mol } H_2}{0.250 \text{ mol He} + 0.496 \text{ mol } H_2} \times 0.480 \text{ atm} = 0.319 \text{ atm}$$

$P_{H_2} + P_{He} = 0.480 \text{ atm}, \quad P_{He} = 0.480 - 0.319 = 0.161 \text{ atm}$

43.   a.   mol fraction $CH_4 = \chi_{CH_4} = \dfrac{P_{CH_4}}{P_{total}} = \dfrac{0.175 \text{ atm}}{0.175 \text{ atm} + 0.250 \text{ atm}} = 0.412; \quad \chi_{O_2} = 1.000 - 0.412 = 0.588$

b. $PV = nRT, \quad n_{total} = \dfrac{P_{total} \times V}{RT} = \dfrac{0.425 \text{ atm} \times 10.5 \text{ L}}{\frac{0.08206 \text{ L atm}}{\text{mol K}} \times 338 \text{ K}} = 0.161 \text{ mol}$

c. $\chi_{CH_4} = \dfrac{n_{CH_4}}{n_{total}}$, $n_{CH_4} = \chi_{CH_4} \times n_{total} = 0.412 \times 0.161 \text{ mol} = 6.63 \times 10^{-2} \text{ mol CH}_4$

$6.63 \times 10^{-2} \text{ mol CH}_4 \times \dfrac{16.04 \text{ g CH}_4}{\text{mol CH}_4} = 1.06 \text{ g CH}_4$

$n_{O_2} = 0.588 \times 0.161 \text{ mol} = 9.47 \times 10^{-2} \text{ mol O}_2$; $9.47 \times 10^{-2} \text{ mol O}_2 \times \dfrac{32.00 \text{ g O}_2}{\text{mol O}_2} = 3.03 \text{ g O}_2$

Gas Density, Molar Mass, and Reaction Stoichiometry

44. $P \times (\text{molar mass}) = dRT$, $d = \text{density} = \dfrac{P \times (\text{molar mass})}{RT}$

For $SiCl_4$, molar mass = M = 28.09 + 4(35.45) = 169.89 g/mol

$d = \dfrac{(758 \text{ torr} \times \frac{1 \text{ atm}}{760 \text{ torr}}) \times \frac{169.89 \text{ g}}{\text{mol}}}{\frac{0.08206 \text{ L atm}}{\text{mol K}} \times 358 \text{ K}} = 5.77 \text{ g/L for SiCl}_4$

For $SiHCl_3$, molar mass = M = 28.09 + 1.008 + 3(35.45) = 135.45 g/mol

$d = \dfrac{PM}{RT} = \dfrac{(758 \text{ torr} \times \frac{1 \text{ atm}}{760 \text{ torr}}) \times \frac{135.45 \text{ g}}{\text{mol}}}{\frac{0.08206 \text{ L atm}}{\text{mol K}} \times 358 \text{ K}} = 4.60 \text{ g/L for SiHCl}_3$

45.   Out of 100.0 g of compound, there are:

$87.4 \text{ g N} \times \dfrac{1 \text{ mol N}}{14.01 \text{ g N}} = 6.24 \text{ mol N}$; $\dfrac{6.24}{6.24} = 1.00$

$12.6 \text{ g H} \times \dfrac{1 \text{ mol H}}{1.008 \text{ g H}} = 12.5 \text{ mol H}$; $\dfrac{12.5}{6.24} = 2.00$

Empirical formula is NH_2. $P \times (\text{molar mass}) = dRT$ where d = density.

$\text{Molar mass} = \dfrac{dRT}{P} = \dfrac{\frac{0.977 \text{ g}}{\text{L}} \times \frac{0.08206 \text{ L atm}}{\text{mol K}} \times 373 \text{ K}}{710. \text{ torr} \times \frac{1 \text{ atm}}{760 \text{ torr}}} = 32.0 \text{ g/mol}$

Empirical formula mass of NH_2 = 16.0 g. Therefore, molecular formula is N_2H_4.

46. $P \times$ (molar mass) $= dRT$, $d = \dfrac{mass}{volume}$, $P \times$ (molar mass) $= \dfrac{mass}{V} \times RT$

Molar mass $= M = \dfrac{mass \times RT}{PV} = \dfrac{0.800 \text{ g} \times \dfrac{0.08206 \text{ L atm}}{mol K} \times 373 \text{ K}}{(750. \text{ torr} \times \dfrac{1 \text{ atm}}{760 \text{ torr}}) \times 0.256 \text{ L}} = 96.9 \text{ g/mol}$

Mass of CHCl $\approx 12.0 + 1.0 + 35.5 = 48.5$; $\dfrac{96.9}{48.5} = 2.00$; Molecular formula is $C_2H_2Cl_2$.

47.   If Be^{3+}, the formula is $Be(C_5H_7O_2)_3$ and molar mass $\approx 13.5 + 15(12) + 21(1) + 6(16) = 311$ g/mol.

If Be^{2+}, the formula is $Be(C_5H_7O_2)_2$ and molar mass $\approx 9.0 + 10(12) + 14(1) + 4(16) = 207$ g/mol.

Data Set I (molar mass $= dRT/P$ and $d = mass/V$):

molar mass $= \dfrac{mass \times RT}{PV} = \dfrac{0.2022 \text{ g} \times \dfrac{0.08206 \text{ L atm}}{mol K} \times 286 \text{ K}}{(765.2 \text{ torr} \times \dfrac{1 \text{ atm}}{760 \text{ torr}}) \times 22.6 \times 10^{-3} \text{ L}} = 209 \text{ g/mol}$

Data Set II:

molar mass $= \dfrac{mass \times RT}{PV} = \dfrac{0.2224 \text{ g} \times \dfrac{0.08206 \text{ L atm}}{mol K} \times 290. \text{ K}}{(764.6 \text{ torr} \times \dfrac{1 \text{ atm}}{760 \text{ torr}}) \times 26.0 \times 10^{-3} \text{ L}} = 202 \text{ g/mol}$

These results are close to the expected value of 207 g/mol for $Be(C_5H_7O_2)_2$. Thus, we conclude from these data that beryllium is a divalent element with an atomic weight (mass) of 9.0 g/mol.

48.   We assume that 28.01 g/mol is the true value for the molar mass of N_2. The value of 28.15 g/mol is the average molar mass of the amount of N_2 and Ar in air. Let $x = \%$ of the number of moles that are N_2 molecules. Then $100 - x = \%$ of the number of moles that are Ar atoms. Solving:

$28.15 = \dfrac{x(28.01) + (100 - x)(39.95)}{100}$

$2815 = 28.01 x + 3995 - 39.95 x$, $11.94 x = 1180.$

$x = 98.83\%$ N_2; $\%$ Ar $= 100.00 - x = 1.17\%$ Ar

Ratio of moles of Ar to moles of $N_2 = \dfrac{1.17}{98.83} = 1.18 \times 10^{-2}$.

49.   molar mass $= \dfrac{dRT}{P} = \dfrac{\dfrac{0.70902 \text{ g}}{L} \times \dfrac{0.08206 \text{ L atm}}{mol K} \times 273.2 \text{ K}}{1.000 \text{ atm}} = 15.90 \text{ g/mol}$

15.90 g/mol is the average molar mass of the mixture of methane and helium. Let x = mol % of CH_4. This is also the volume % of CH_4 since T and P are constant.

$$15.90 = \frac{x\,(16.04) + (100 - x)\,(4.003)}{100}, \quad 1590. = 16.04\,x + 400.3 - 4.003\,x, \quad 1190. = 12.04\,x$$

x = 98.84 % CH_4 by volume; % He = 100.00 - x = 1.16 % He by volume

50. 1.00×10^3 kg Mo $\times \dfrac{1000\text{ g}}{\text{kg}} \times \dfrac{1\text{ mol Mo}}{95.94\text{ g Mo}} = 1.04 \times 10^4$ mol Mo

1.04×10^4 mol Mo $\times \dfrac{1\text{ mol } MoO_3}{\text{mol Mo}} \times \dfrac{7/2\text{ mol } O_2}{\text{mol } MoO_3} = 3.64 \times 10^4$ mol O_2

$$V_{O_2} = \frac{n_{O_2}RT}{P} = \frac{3.64 \times 10^4\text{ mol} \times \dfrac{0.08206\text{ L atm}}{\text{mol K}} \times 290.\text{ K}}{1.00\text{ atm}} = 8.66 \times 10^5\text{ L of } O_2$$

8.66×10^5 L $O_2 \times \dfrac{100\text{ L air}}{21\text{ L } O_2} = 4.1 \times 10^6$ L air

1.04×10^4 mol Mo $\times \dfrac{3\text{ mol } H_2}{\text{mol Mo}} = 3.12 \times 10^4$ mol H_2

$$V_{H_2} = \frac{3.12 \times 10^4\text{ mol} \times \dfrac{0.08206\text{ L atm}}{\text{mol K}} \times 290.\text{ K}}{1.00\text{ atm}} = 7.42 \times 10^5\text{ L of } H_2$$

51. $$n_{H_2} = \frac{PV}{RT} = \frac{1.0\text{ atm} \times \left[4800\text{ m}^3 \times \left(\dfrac{100\text{ cm}}{\text{m}} \right)^3 \times \dfrac{1\text{ L}}{1000\text{ cm}^3} \right]}{\dfrac{0.08206\text{ L atm}}{\text{mol K}} \times 273\text{ K}} = 2.1 \times 10^5\text{ mol}$$

2.1×10^5 mol H_2 are in the balloon. This is 80.% of the total amount of H_2 that had to be generated:

0.80 (total mol H_2) = 2.1×10^5, total mol H_2 = 2.6×10^5 mol H_2

2.6×10^5 mol $H_2 \times \dfrac{1\text{ mol Fe}}{\text{mol } H_2} \times \dfrac{55.85\text{ g Fe}}{\text{mol Fe}} = 1.5 \times 10^7$ g Fe

2.6×10^5 mol $H_2 \times \dfrac{1\text{ mol } H_2SO_4}{\text{mol } H_2} \times \dfrac{98.09\text{ g } H_2SO_4}{\text{mol } H_2SO_4} \times \dfrac{100\text{ g reagent}}{98\text{ g } H_2SO_4} = 2.6 \times 10^7$ g of 98% sulfuric acid

52. For ammonia (in one minute):

$$n_{NH_3} = \frac{P_{NH_3} \times V_{NH_3}}{RT} = \frac{90.\text{ atm} \times 500.\text{ L}}{\dfrac{0.08206\text{ L atm}}{\text{mol K}} \times 496\text{ K}} = 1.1 \times 10^3\text{ mol } NH_3$$

NH_3 flows into the reactor at a rate of 1.1×10^3 mol/min.

For CO_2 (in one minute):

$$n_{CO_2} = \frac{P_{CO_2} \times V_{CO_2}}{RT} = \frac{45 \text{ atm} \times 600. \text{ L}}{\dfrac{0.08206 \text{ L atm}}{\text{mol K}} \times 496 \text{ K}} = 6.6 \times 10^2 \text{ mol CO}_2$$

CO_2 flows into the reactor at 6.6×10^2 mol/min.

To react completely with 1.1×10^3 mol NH_3/min, we need:

$$\frac{1.1 \times 10^3 \text{ mol NH}_3}{\text{min}} \times \frac{1 \text{ mol CO}_2}{2 \text{ mol NH}_3} = 5.5 \times 10^2 \text{ mol CO}_2/\text{min}$$

Since 660 mol CO_2/min are present, then ammonia is the limiting reagent.

$$\frac{1.1 \times 10^3 \text{ mol NH}_3}{\text{min}} \times \frac{1 \text{ mol urea}}{2 \text{ mol NH}_3} \times \frac{60.06 \text{ g urea}}{\text{mol urea}} = 3.3 \times 10^4 \text{ g urea/min}$$

53. $C_6H_{12}O_6(s) + 6 \; O_2(g) \rightarrow 6 \; CO_2(g) + 6 \; H_2O(g)$

$$5.00 \text{ g C}_6\text{H}_{12}\text{O}_6 \times \frac{1 \text{ mol C}_6\text{H}_{12}\text{O}_6}{180.16 \text{ g}} \times \frac{6 \text{ mol O}_2}{\text{mol C}_6\text{H}_{12}\text{O}_6} = 0.167 \text{ mol O}_2$$

$$V = \frac{nRT}{P} = \frac{0.167 \text{ mol} \times 0.08206 \dfrac{\text{L atm}}{\text{mol K}} \times 301 \text{ K}}{0.976 \text{ atm}} = 4.23 \text{ L O}_2$$

Since T and P are constant, the volume of each gas will be directly proportional to the mol of gas present. The balanced equation says that equal mol of CO_2 and H_2O will be produced as mol of O_2 reacted. So the volumes of CO_2 and H_2O produced will equal the volume of O_2 reacted.

$$V_{CO_2} = V_{H_2O} = V_{O_2} = 4.23 \text{ L}$$

54. $2 \; NaN_3(s) \rightarrow 2 \; Na(s) + 3 \; N_2(g)$

$$n_{N_2} = \frac{PV}{RT} = \frac{1.00 \text{ atm} \times 70.0 \text{ L}}{\dfrac{0.08206 \text{ L atm}}{\text{mol K}} \times 273 \text{ K}} = 3.12 \text{ mol N}_2 \text{ are needed to fill the air bag.}$$

$$\text{mass NaN}_3 \text{ reacted} = 3.12 \text{ mol N}_2 \times \frac{2 \text{ mol NaN}_3}{3 \text{ mol N}_2} \times \frac{65.02 \text{ g NaN}_3}{\text{mol NaN}_3} = 135 \text{ g NaN}_3$$

55. $2 \; NaClO_3(s) \rightarrow 2 \; NaCl(s) + 3 \; O_2(g)$

$$P_{total} = P_{O_2} + P_{H_2O}, \quad P_{O_2} = P_{total} - P_{H_2O} = 734 \text{ torr} - 19.8 \text{ torr} = 714 \text{ torr}$$

$$n_{O_2} = \frac{P_{O_2} \times V}{RT} = \frac{\left(714 \text{ torr} \times \frac{1 \text{ atm}}{760 \text{ torr}}\right) \times 0.0572 \text{ L}}{\frac{0.08206 \text{ L atm}}{\text{mol K}} \times (273 + 22) \text{ K}} = 2.22 \times 10^{-3} \text{ mol O}_2$$

Mass $NaClO_3$ decomposed $= 2.22 \times 10^{-3} \text{ mol O}_2 \times \dfrac{2 \text{ mol NaClO}_3}{3 \text{ mol O}_2} \times \dfrac{106.44 \text{ g NaClO}_3}{\text{mol NaClO}_3} = 0.158 \text{ g NaClO}_3$

Mass % $NaClO_3 = \dfrac{0.158 \text{ g}}{0.8765 \text{ g}} \times 100 = 18.0\%$

56.   10.10 atm - 7.62 atm = 2.48 atm is the pressure of the amount of F_2 reacted.

PV = nRT, V and T are constant. $\dfrac{P}{n}$ = constant, $\dfrac{P_1}{n_1} = \dfrac{P_2}{n_2}$ or $\dfrac{P_1}{P_2} = \dfrac{n_1}{n_2}$

$\dfrac{\text{moles F}_2 \text{ reacted}}{\text{moles Xe reacted}} = \dfrac{2.48 \text{ atm}}{1.24 \text{ atm}} = 2.00$; So $Xe + 2 F_2 \rightarrow XeF_4$

57. $P_{total} = P_{N_2} + P_{H_2O}$, $P_{N_2} = 726 \text{ torr} - 23.8 \text{ torr} = 702 \text{ torr} \times \dfrac{1 \text{ atm}}{760 \text{ torr}} = 0.924 \text{ atm}$

$$n_{N_2} = \frac{P_{N_2} \times V}{RT} = \frac{0.924 \text{ atm} \times 31.8 \times 10^{-3} \text{ L}}{\frac{0.08206 \text{ L atm}}{\text{mol K}} \times 298 \text{ K}} = 1.20 \times 10^{-3} \text{ mol N}_2$$

Mass of N in compound $= 1.20 \times 10^{-3} \text{ mol N}_2 \times \dfrac{28.02 \text{ g N}_2}{\text{mol}} = 3.36 \times 10^{-2} \text{ g nitrogen}$

Mass % $N = \dfrac{3.36 \times 10^{-2} \text{ g}}{0.253 \text{ g}} \times 100 = 13.3\% \text{ N}$

58. $0.2766 \text{ g CO}_2 \times \dfrac{12.011 \text{ g C}}{44.009 \text{ g CO}_2} = 7.549 \times 10^{-2} \text{ g C}$; % $C = \dfrac{7.549 \times 10^{-2} \text{ g}}{0.1023 \text{ g}} \times 100 = 73.79\% \text{ C}$

$0.0991 \text{ g H}_2O \times \dfrac{2.016 \text{ g H}}{18.02 \text{ g H}_2O} = 1.11 \times 10^{-2} \text{ g H}$; % $H = \dfrac{1.11 \times 10^{-2} \text{ g}}{0.1023 \text{ g}} \times 100 = 10.9\% \text{ H}$

PV = nRT, $n_{N_2} = \dfrac{PV}{RT} = \dfrac{1.00 \text{ atm} \times 27.6 \times 10^{-3} \text{ L}}{\frac{0.08206 \text{ L atm}}{\text{mol K}} \times 273 \text{ K}} = 1.23 \times 10^{-3} \text{ mol N}_2$

$1.23 \times 10^{-3} \text{ mol N}_2 \times \dfrac{28.02 \text{ g N}_2}{\text{mol N}_2} = 3.45 \times 10^{-2} \text{ g nitrogen}$

% $N = \dfrac{3.45 \times 10^{-2} \text{ g}}{0.4831 \text{ g}} \times 100 = 7.14\% \text{ N}$

% O = 100.00 - (73.79 + 10.9 + 7.14) = 8.2% O

Out of 100.00 g of compound, there are:

$$73.79 \text{ g C} \times \frac{1 \text{ mol}}{12.011 \text{ g}} = 6.144 \text{ mol C}; \quad 7.14 \text{ g N} \times \frac{1 \text{ mol}}{14.01 \text{ g}} = 0.510 \text{ mol N}$$

$$10.9 \text{ g H} \times \frac{1 \text{ mol}}{1.008 \text{ g}} = 10.8 \text{ mol H}; \quad 8.2 \text{ g O} \times \frac{1 \text{ mol}}{16.00 \text{ g}} = 0.51 \text{ mol O}$$

Dividing all values by 0.51 gives an empirical formula of $C_{12}H_{21}NO$.

$$\text{Molar mass} = \frac{dRT}{P} = \frac{\dfrac{4.02 \text{ g}}{L} \times \dfrac{0.08206 \text{ L atm}}{\text{mol K}} \times 400. \text{ K}}{256 \text{ torr} \times \dfrac{1 \text{ atm}}{760 \text{ torr}}} = 392 \text{ g/mol}$$

Empirical formula mass of $C_{12}H_{21}NO \approx 195$ g/mol and $\dfrac{392}{195} \approx 2$.

Thus, the molecular formula is $C_{24}H_{42}N_2O_2$.

59.   For NH_3: $P_2 = \dfrac{P_1 V_1}{V_2} = 0.500 \text{ atm} \times \dfrac{2.00 \text{ L}}{3.00 \text{ L}} = 0.333 \text{ atm}$

For O_2: $P_2 = \dfrac{P_1 V_1}{V_2} = 1.50 \text{ atm} \times \dfrac{1.00 \text{ L}}{3.00 \text{ L}} = 0.500 \text{ atm}$

After the stopcock is opened, V and T will be constant, so $P \propto n$. The balanced equation requires:

$$\frac{n_{O_2}}{n_{NH_3}} = \frac{P_{O_2}}{P_{NH_3}} = \frac{5}{4} = 1.25$$

The actual ratio present is: $\dfrac{P_{O_2}}{P_{NH_3}} = \dfrac{0.500 \text{ atm}}{0.333 \text{ atm}} = 1.50$

The actual ratio is larger than the required ratio, so NH_3 in the denominator is limiting. Since equal mol of NO will be produced as NH_3 reacted, the partial pressure of NO produced is 0.333 atm (the same as P_{NH_3} reacted).

60. $PV = nRT$, V and T are constant. $\dfrac{P_1}{n_1} = \dfrac{P_2}{n_2}$ or $\dfrac{P_1}{P_2} = \dfrac{n_1}{n_2}$

When V and T are constant, then pressure is directly proportional to moles of gas present and pressure ratios are identical to mol ratios.

At 25°C: $2 H_2(g) + O_2(g) \rightarrow 2 H_2O(l)$, $H_2O(l)$ is produced.

The balanced equation requires 2 mol H_2 for every mol O_2 reacted. The same ratio (2:1) holds true for pressure units. The actual pressure ratio present is 2 atm H_2 to 3 atm O_2, well below the required 2:1 ratio. Therefore H_2 is the limiting reagent. The only gas present at 25°C after the reaction goes to completion will be the excess O_2.

$$P_{O_2} \text{ (reacted)} = 2.00 \text{ atm } H_2 \times \frac{1 \text{ atm } O_2}{2 \text{ atm } H_2} = 1.00 \text{ atm } O_2$$

$$P_{O_2} \text{ (excess)} = P_{O_2} \text{ (initial)} - P_{O_2} \text{ (reacted)} = 3.00 \text{ atm} - 1.00 \text{ atm} = 2.00 \text{ atm } O_2$$

At $125°C$: $2 H_2(g) + O_2(g) \rightarrow 2 H_2O(g)$, $H_2O(g)$ is produced.

The major difference in the problem is that gaseous water is now a product, which will increase the total pressure.

$$P_{H_2O} \text{ (produced)} = 2.00 \text{ atm } H_2 \times \frac{2 \text{ atm } H_2O}{2 \text{ atm } H_2} = 2.00 \text{ atm } H_2O$$

$$P_{total} = P_{O_2} \text{ (excess)} + P_{H_2O} \text{ (produced)} = 2.00 \text{ atm } O_2 + 2.00 \text{ atm } H_2O = 4.00 \text{ atm}$$

61.   Rigid container (constant volume): As reactants are converted to products, the mol of gas particles present decrease by one-half. As n decreases, the pressure will decrease (by one-half). Density is the mass per unit volume. Mass is conserved in a chemical reaction, so the density of the gas will not change since mass and volume do not change.

Flexible container (constant pressure): Pressure is constant since the container changes volume in order to keep a constant pressure. As the mol of gas particles decrease by a factor of 2, the volume of the container will decrease (by one-half). We have the same mass of gas in a smaller volume, so the gas density will increase (is doubled).

Kinetic Molecular Theory and Real Gases

62.   a.   Containers ii, iv, vi, and viii have volumes twice that of containers i, iii, v, and vii. Containers iii, iv, vii, and viii have twice the number of molecules (mol) present as compared to containers i, ii, v, and vi. The container with the lowest pressure will be the one which has the fewest mol of gas present in the largest volume (containers ii and vi both have the lowest P). The smallest container with the most mol of gas present will have the highest pressure (containers iii and vii both have the highest P). All the other containers (i, iv, v and viii) will have the same pressure between the two extremes. The order is: ii = vi < i = iv = v = viii < iii = vii.

b.   All have the same average kinetic energy since the temperature is the same in each container. Only the temperature determines the average kinetic energy.

c.   The least dense gas will be container ii since it has the fewest of the lighter Ne atoms present in the largest volume. Container vii has the most dense gas since the largest number of the heavier Ar atoms are present in the smallest volume. To figure out the ordering for the other containers, we will calculate the relative density of each. In the following table, m_1 equals the mass of Ne in container i, V_1 equals the volume of container i, and d_1 equals the density of the gas in container i.

Container	i	ii	iii	iv	v	vi	vii	viii
mass, volume	m_1, V_1	$m_1, 2V_1$	$2m_1, V_1$	$2m_1, 2V_1$	$2m_1, V_1$	$2m_1, 2V_1$	$4m_1, V_1$	$4m_1, 2V_1$
density $\left(\dfrac{mass}{volume}\right)$	$\dfrac{m_1}{V_1}=d_1$	$\dfrac{m_1}{2V_1}=\dfrac{1}{2}d_1$	$\dfrac{2m_1}{V_1}=2d_1$	$\dfrac{2m_1}{2V_1}=d_1$	$\dfrac{2m_1}{V_1}=2d_1$	$\dfrac{2m_1}{2V_1}=d_1$	$\dfrac{4m_1}{V_1}=4d_1$	$\dfrac{4m_1}{2V_1}=2d_1$

From the table, the order of gas density is: ii < i = iv = vi < iii = v = viii < vii

d. $u_{rms} = (3\ RT/M)^{1/2}$; the root mean square velocity only depends on the temperature and the molar mass. Since T is constant, the heavier argon molecules will have the slower root mean square velocity as compared to the neon molecules. The order is:

v = vi = vii = viii < i = ii = iii = iv.

63. $(KE)_{avg} = 3/2\ RT$; KE depends only on temperature. At each temperature CH_4 and N_2 will have the same average KE. For energy units of joules (J), use R = 8.3145 J mol^{-1} K^{-1}. To determine average KE per molecule, divide by Avogadro's number, 6.022×10^{23} molecules/mol.

at 273 K: $(KE)_{avg} = \dfrac{3}{2} \times \dfrac{8.3145\ J}{mol\ K} \times 273\ K = 3.40 \times 10^3\ J/mol = 5.65 \times 10^{-21}\ J/molecule$

at 546 K: $(KE)_{avg} = \dfrac{3}{2} \times \dfrac{8.3145\ J}{mol\ K} \times 546\ K = 6.81 \times 10^3\ J/mol = 1.13 \times 10^{-20}\ J/molecule$

64. $u_{rms} = \left(\dfrac{3RT}{M}\right)^{1/2}$, where $R = \dfrac{8.3145\ J}{mol\ K}$ and M = molar mass in kg

For CH_4, M = 1.604×10^{-2} kg and for N_2, M = 2.802×10^{-2} kg.

For CH_4 at 273 K: $u_{rms} = \left(\dfrac{3 \times \dfrac{8.3145\ J}{mol\ K} \times 273\ K}{1.604 \times 10^{-2}\ kg/mol}\right)^{1/2} = 652$ m/s

At 546 K, u_{rms} for CH_4 is 921 m/s.

For N_2, u_{rms} = 493 m/s at 273 K and 697 m/s at 546 K.

65.   No; The numbers calculated in Exercise 5.63 are the average kinetic energies at the various temperatures. At each temperature, there is a distribution of energies. Similarly, the numbers calculated in Exercise 5.64 are a special kind of average velocity. There is a distribution of velocities as shown in Figures 5.15-5.17 of the text. Note that the major reason there is a distribution of kinetic energies is because there is a distribution of velocities for any gas sample at some temperature.

66.   a. All the gases have the same average kinetic energy since they are all at the same temperature $[KE_{ave} = (3/2)RT]$.

b. At constant T, the lighter the gas molecule, the faster the average velocity [$u_{ave} \propto (1/M)^{1/2}$].

Xe (131.3 g/mol) < Cl_2 (70.90 g/mol) < O_2 (32.00 g/mol) < H_2 (2.016 g/mol)
slowest   fastest

c. At constant T, the lighter H_2 molecules have a faster average velocity than the heavier O_2 molecules. As temperature increases, the average velocity of the gas molecules increase. Separate samples of H_2 and O_2 can only have the same average velocities if the temperature of the O_2 sample is greater than the temperature of the H_2 sample.

67.   a. They will all have the same average kinetic energy since they are all at the same temperature. Average kinetic energy depends only on temperature.

b. Flask C; At constant T, $u_{rms} \propto (1/M)^{1/2}$. In general, the lighter the gas molecules the greater the root mean square velocity (at constant T).

c. Flask A: Collision frequency is proportional to average velocity × n/V (as the average velocity doubles, the number of collisions will double and as the number of molecules in the container doubles, the number of collisions again doubles). At constant T and V, n is proportional to P and average velocity is proportional to $(1/M)^{1/2}$. We use these relationships and the data in the problem to determine the following relative values.

	n (relative)	u_{avg} (relative)	Coll. Freq. (relative) = n × u_{avg}
A	1.0	1.0	1.0
B	0.33	1.0	0.33
C	0.13	3.7	0.48

68.

	a	b	c	d
avg. KE ($KE_{avg} \propto T$)	inc	dec	same	same
u_{rms} ($u_{rms}^2 \propto T$)	inc	dec	same	same
coll. freq. gas	inc	dec	inc	inc
coll. freq. wall	inc	dec	inc	inc
impact E (impact E $\propto KE \propto T$)	inc	dec	same	same

Both collision frequencies are proportional to the root mean square velocity (as velocity increases it takes less time to move to the next collision) and the quantity n/V (as molecules per volume increases, collision frequency increases).

69. $\dfrac{Rate_1}{Rate_2} = \left(\dfrac{M_2}{M_1} \right)^{1/2}$ where Rate = rate of effusion and M = molar mass.

$\dfrac{Rate_1}{Rate_2} = \dfrac{31.50}{30.50} = \left(\dfrac{31.998}{M} \right)^{1/2} = 1.033, \ \dfrac{31.998}{M} = 1.067, \ M = 29.99$

Of the choices, the gas with the molar mass closest to 29.99 is NO.

70. $\dfrac{\text{Rate}_1}{\text{Rate}_2} = \left(\dfrac{M_2}{M_1}\right)^{1/2}$, $\dfrac{^{12}C\,^{17}O}{^{12}C\,^{18}O} = \left(\dfrac{30.0}{29.0}\right)^{1/2} = 1.02$; $\dfrac{^{12}C\,^{16}O}{^{12}C\,^{18}O} = \left(\dfrac{30.0}{28.0}\right)^{1/2} = 1.04$

The relative rates of effusion of $^{12}C^{16}O$: $^{12}C^{17}O$: $^{12}C^{18}O$ are 1.04: 1.02: 1.00.

Advantage: CO_2 isn't as toxic as CO.

Major disadvantages of using CO_2 instead of CO:

1. Can get a mixture of oxygen isotopes in CO_2.
2. Some species, e.g., $^{12}C^{16}O^{18}O$ and $^{12}C^{17}O_2$, would effuse (gaseously diffuse) at about the same rate since the masses are about equal. Thus, some species cannot be separated from each other.

71. $\dfrac{\text{Rate}_1}{\text{Rate}_2} = \left(\dfrac{M_2}{M_1}\right)^{1/2}$; $\text{Rate}_1 = \dfrac{24.0 \text{ mL}}{\text{min}}$, $\text{Rate}_2 = \dfrac{47.8 \text{ mL}}{\text{min}}$, $M_2 = \dfrac{16.04 \text{ g}}{\text{mol}}$ and $M_1 = ?$

$\dfrac{24.0}{47.8} = \left(\dfrac{16.04}{M_1}\right)^{1/2} = 0.502$, $16.04 = (0.502)^2 \times M_1$, $M_1 = \dfrac{16.04}{0.252} = \dfrac{63.7 \text{ g}}{\text{mol}}$

72. $\dfrac{\text{Rate}_1}{\text{Rate}_2} = \left(\dfrac{M_2}{M_1}\right)^{1/2}$ where M = molar mass; Let Gas (1) = He, Gas (2) = Cl_2

$\dfrac{\dfrac{1.0 \text{ L}}{4.5 \text{ min}}}{\dfrac{1.0 \text{ L}}{t}} = \left(\dfrac{70.90}{4.003}\right)^{1/2}$, $\dfrac{t}{4.5 \text{ min}} = 4.209$, $t = 19$ min

73. a. PV = nRT

$P = \dfrac{nRT}{V} = \dfrac{0.5000 \text{ mol} \times \dfrac{0.08206 \text{ L atm}}{\text{mol K}} \times (25.0 + 273.2) \text{ K}}{1.0000 \text{ L}} = 12.24$ atm

b. $\left[P + a\left(\dfrac{n}{V}\right)^2\right](V - nb) = nRT$; For N_2: a = 1.39 atm L^2/mol^2 and b = 0.0391 L/mol

$\left[P + 1.39\left(\dfrac{0.5000}{1.0000}\right)^2 \text{atm}\right](1.0000 \text{ L} - 0.5000 \times 0.0391 \text{ L}) = 12.24 \text{ L atm}$

$(P + 0.348 \text{ atm})(0.9805 \text{ L}) = 12.24 \text{ L atm}$

$P = \dfrac{12.24 \text{ L atm}}{0.9805 \text{ L}} - 0.348 \text{ atm} = 12.48 - 0.348 = 12.13$ atm

c.   The ideal gas law is high by 0.11 atm or $\dfrac{0.11}{12.13} \times 100 = 0.91\%$.

74.   a. $PV = nRT$

$$P = \frac{nRT}{V} = \frac{0.5000 \text{ mol} \times \dfrac{0.08206 \text{ L atm}}{\text{mol K}} \times 298.2 \text{ K}}{10.000 \text{ L}} = 1.224 \text{ atm}$$

b. $\left[P + a\left(\dfrac{n}{V}\right)^2 \right] (V - nb) = nRT$;   For N_2: $a = 1.39$ atm L^2/mol^2 and $b = 0.0391$ L/mol

$$\left[P + 1.39 \left(\frac{0.5000}{10.000}\right)^2 \text{atm} \right] (10.000 \text{ L} - 0.5000 \times 0.0391 \text{ L}) = 12.24 \text{ L atm}$$

$$(P + 0.00348 \text{ atm})(10.000 \text{ L} - 0.0196 \text{ L}) = 12.24 \text{ L atm}$$

$$P + 0.00348 \text{ atm} = \frac{12.24 \text{ L atm}}{9.980 \text{ L}} = 1.226 \text{ atm}, \quad P = 1.226 - 0.00348 = 1.223 \text{ atm}$$

c.   The results agree to $\pm$ 0.001 atm (0.08%).

d.   In Exercise 5.73 the pressure is relatively high and there is a significant disagreement. In Exercise 5.74 the pressure is around 1 atm and both gas laws show better agreement. The ideal gas law is valid at relatively low pressures.

75.   The kinetic molecular theory assumes that gas particles do not exert forces on each other and that gas particles are volumeless. Real gas particles do exert attractive forces for each other, and real gas particles do have volumes. A gas behaves most ideally at low pressures and high temperatures. The effect of attractive forces is minimized at high temperatures since the gas particles are moving very rapidly. At low pressure, the container volume is relatively large (P and V are inversely related) so the volume of the container taken up by the gas particles is negligible.

76.   a.   At constant temperature, the average kinetic energy of the He gas sample will equal the average kinetic energy of the Cl_2 gas sample. In order for the average kinetic energy to be the same, the smaller He atoms must move at a faster average velocity as compared to Cl_2. Therefore, plot A, with the slower average velocity, would be for the Cl_2 sample, and plot B would be for the He sample. Note the average velocity in each plot is a little past the top peak.

b.   As temperature increases, the average velocity of a gas will increase. Plot A would be for $O_2(g)$ at 273 K and plot B, with the faster average velocity, would be for $O_2(g)$ at 1273 K.

Since a gas behaves more ideally at higher temperatures, $O_2(g)$ at 1273 K would behave most ideally.

77.   Rearranging the Van der Waals' equation gives: $P = \dfrac{nRT}{V - nb} - a\left(\dfrac{n}{V}\right)^2$

P is the measured pressure and V is the volume of the container.

For NH_3: $a = 4.17$ atm L^2/mol^2 and $b = 0.0371$ L/mol

For the first experiment (assuming four significant figures in all values):

$$P = \frac{nRT}{V - nb} - a\left(\frac{n}{V}\right)^2 = \frac{1.000 \times 0.08206 \times 273.2}{172.1 - 0.0371} - 4.17\left(\frac{1.000}{172.1}\right)^2$$

$P = 0.1303 - 0.0001 = 0.1302$ atm. In Example 5.1, $P_{obs} = 0.1300$ atm. The difference is less than 0.1%. The ideal gas law also gives 0.1302 atm. At low pressures, the van der Waals equation agrees with the ideal gas law.

For experiment 6, the measured pressure is 1.000 atm. The ideal gas law gives $P = 1.015$ atm and the van der Waals equation gives $P = 1.017 - 0.086 = 1.008$ atm. The van der Waals equation accounts for approximately one-half of the deviation from ideal behavior. Note: As pressure increases, deviation from the ideal gas law increases.

78. $\left(P + \dfrac{an^2}{V^2}\right)(V - nb) = nRT,\quad PV + \dfrac{an^2V}{V^2} - nbP - \dfrac{an^3b}{V^2} = nRT;\quad PV + \dfrac{an^2}{V} - nbP - \dfrac{an^3b}{V^2} = nRT$

At low P and high T, the molar volume of a gas will be relatively large. The an^2/V and an^3b/V^2 terms become negligible because V is large. Since nb is the actual volume of the gas molecules themselves, then nb $\ll$ V and -nbP is negligible compared to PV. Thus, PV = nRT.

79.   The corrected (ideal) volume is the volume accessible to the gas molecules. For a real gas, this volume is less than the container volume because of the space occupied by the gas molecules.

80.   The van der Waals constant b is a measure of the size of the molecule. Thus, C_3H_8 should have the largest value of b since it has the largest molar mass (size).

81.   The values of a are: H_2, $\dfrac{0.244 \text{ atm L}^2}{\text{mol}^2}$; CO_2, 3.59; N_2, 1.39; CH_4, 2.25

Since a is a measure of intermolecular attractions, the attractions are greatest for CO_2.

82. $f(u) = 4\pi\left(\dfrac{m}{2\pi k_B T}\right)^{3/2} u^2 e^{(-mu^2/2k_B T)}$

As u → 0, $e^{(-mu^2/2k_B T)}$ → $e^0 = 1$; At small values of u, the u^2 term causes the function to increase. At large values of u, the exponent term, $-mu^2/2k_B T$, is a large negative number and e raised to a large negative number causes the function to decrease. As u → ∞, $e^{-\infty}$ → 0.

83. $u_{rms} = \left(\dfrac{3RT}{M}\right)^{1/2} = \left[\dfrac{3\left(\dfrac{8.3145 \text{ kg m}^2}{\text{s}^2 \text{ mol K}}\right)(227°C + 273)K}{28.02 \times 10^{-3} \text{ kg/mol}}\right]^{1/2} = 667$ m/s

$$u_{mp} = \left(\frac{2RT}{M}\right)^{1/2} = \left[\frac{2\left(\dfrac{8.3145 \text{ kg m}^2}{\text{s}^2 \text{ mol K}}\right)(500.\text{ K})}{28.02 \times 10^{-3} \text{ kg/mol}}\right]^{1/2} = 545 \text{ m/s}$$

$$u_{avg} = \left(\frac{8RT}{\pi M}\right)^{1/2} = \left[\frac{8\left(\dfrac{8.3145 \text{ kg m}^2}{\text{s}^2 \text{ mol K}}\right)(500.\text{ K})}{\pi(28.02 \times 10^{-3} \text{ kg/mol})}\right]^{1/2} = 615 \text{ m/s}$$

84. $KE_{ave} = 3/2 \ RT$ per mol; $KE_{ave} = 3/2 \ k_BT$ per molecule

$KE_{total} = 3/2 \times (1.3807 \times 10^{-23} \text{ J/K}) \times 300.\text{ K} \times (1.00 \times 10^{20} \text{ molecules}) = 0.621$ J

85.   The force per impact is proportional to $\Delta(mu) = 2mu$. Since $m \propto M$, the molar mass, and $u \propto (1/M)^{1/2}$ at constant T, then the force per impact at constant T is proportional to $M \times (1/M)^{1/2} = \sqrt{M}$.

$$\frac{\text{Impact Force (H}_2)}{\text{Impact Force (He)}} = \sqrt{\frac{M_{H_2}}{M_{He}}} = \sqrt{\frac{2.016}{4.003}} = 0.7097$$

86. $\dfrac{\text{diffusion rate } ^{235}UF_6}{\text{diffusion rate } ^{238}UF_6} = 1.0043$ (See Section 5.7 of the text.)

$$\frac{^{235}UF_6}{^{238}UF_6} \times (1.0043)^{100} = \frac{1526}{1.000 \times 10^5 - 1526}, \quad \frac{^{235}UF_6}{^{238}UF_6} \times 1.5358 = \frac{1526}{98500}$$

$$\frac{^{235}UF_6}{^{238}UF_6} = 1.01 \times 10^{-2} = \text{initial } ^{235}U \text{ to } ^{238}U \text{ atom ratio}$$

87. $\Delta(mu) = 2mu$ = change in momentum per impact. Since m is proportional to M, the molar mass, and u is proportional to $(T/M)^{1/2}$, then:

$$\Delta(mu)_{O_2} \propto 2M_{O_2}\left(\frac{T}{M_{O_2}}\right)^{1/2} \quad \text{and} \quad \Delta(mu)_{He} \propto 2M_{He}\left(\frac{T}{M_{He}}\right)^{1/2}$$

$$\frac{\Delta(mu)_{O_2}}{\Delta(mu)_{He}} = \frac{2M_{O_2}\left(\dfrac{T}{M_{O_2}}\right)^{1/2}}{2M_{He}\left(\dfrac{T}{M_{He}}\right)^{1/2}} = \frac{M_{O_2}}{M_{He}}\left(\frac{M_{He}}{M_{O_2}}\right)^{1/2} = \frac{31.998}{4.003}\left(\frac{4.003}{31.998}\right)^{1/2} = 2.827$$

The change in momentum per impact is 2.827 times larger for O_2 molecules than for He atoms.

$$Z = A\frac{N}{V}\left(\frac{RT}{2\pi M}\right)^{1/2} = \text{collision rate}$$

$$\frac{Z_{O_2}}{Z_{He}} = \frac{A\left(\dfrac{N}{V}\right)\left(\dfrac{RT}{2\pi M_{O_2}}\right)^{1/2}}{A\left(\dfrac{N}{V}\right)\left(\dfrac{RT}{2\pi M_{He}}\right)^{1/2}} = \frac{\left(\dfrac{1}{M_{O_2}}\right)^{1/2}}{\left(\dfrac{1}{M_{He}}\right)^{1/2}} = \left(\frac{M_{He}}{M_{O_2}}\right)^{1/2} = 0.3537; \quad \frac{Z_{He}}{Z_{O_2}} = 2.827$$

There are 2.827 times as many impacts per second for He as compared to O_2.

88. $\Delta(mu) = 2mu$ and $u \propto (T/M)^{1/2}$; $\dfrac{\Delta(mu)_{77}}{\Delta(mu)_{27}} = \dfrac{2m\left(\dfrac{350.\ K}{M}\right)^{1/2}}{2m\left(\dfrac{300.\ K}{M}\right)^{1/2}} = \left(\dfrac{350.}{300.}\right)^{1/2} = 1.08$

The change in momentum is 1.08 times greater for Ar at 77°C than for Ar at 27°C.

$$Z = A\frac{N}{V}\left(\frac{RT}{2\pi M}\right)^{1/2}; \quad \frac{Z_{77}}{Z_{27}} = \left(\frac{T_{77}}{T_{27}}\right)^{1/2}, \quad \frac{Z_{77}}{Z_{27}} = \left(\frac{350.}{300.}\right)^{1/2} = 1.08$$

There are 1.08 times as many impacts per second for Ar at 77°C than for Ar at 27°C.

89.   Intermolecular collision frequency $= Z = 4\dfrac{N}{V}d^2\left(\dfrac{\pi RT}{M}\right)^{1/2}$ where d = diameter of He atom

$$\frac{n}{V} = \frac{P}{RT} = \frac{3.0\ atm}{\dfrac{0.08206\ L\ atm}{mol\ K} \times 300.\ K} = 0.12\ mol/L$$

$$\frac{N}{V} = \frac{0.12\ mol}{L} \times \frac{6.022 \times 10^{23}\ molecules}{mol} \times \frac{1000\ L}{m^3} = \frac{7.2 \times 10^{25}\ molecules}{m^3}$$

$$Z = 4 \times \frac{7.2 \times 10^{25}\ molecules}{m^3} \times (50. \times 10^{-12}\ m)^2 \times \left(\frac{\pi(8.3145)\,(300.)}{4.00 \times 10^{-3}}\right)^{1/2} = 1.0 \times 10^9\ collisions/s$$

mean free path $= \lambda = \dfrac{u_{avg}}{Z}$; $u_{avg} = \left(\dfrac{8RT}{\pi M}\right)^{1/2} = 1260\ m/s$; $\lambda = \dfrac{1260\ m/s}{1.0 \times 10^9\ s^{-1}} = 1.3 \times 10^{-6}\ m$

Atmospheric Chemistry

90. $\chi_{NO} = 5 \times 10^{-7}$ from Table 5.4; $P_{NO} = \chi_{NO}P_{total} = 5 \times 10^{-7} \times 1.0\ atm = 5 \times 10^{-7}\ atm$

$$PV = nRT, \quad \frac{n}{V} = \frac{P}{RT} = \frac{5 \times 10^{-7}\ atm}{\dfrac{0.08206\ L\ atm}{mol\ K} \times 273\ K} = \frac{2 \times 10^{-8}\ mol\ NO}{L}$$

$$\frac{2 \times 10^{-8}\ mol}{L} \times \frac{1\ L}{1000\ cm^3} \times \frac{6.02 \times 10^{23}\ molecules}{mol} = \frac{1 \times 10^{13}\ molecules\ NO}{cm^3}$$

91.   a. If we have 1.0×10^6 L of air, then there are 3.0×10^2 L of CO.

$$P_{CO} = \chi_{CO}P_{total}; \quad \chi_{CO} = \frac{V_{CO}}{V_{total}} \text{ since } V \propto n; \quad P_{CO} = \frac{3.0 \times 10^2}{1.0 \times 10^6} \times 628 \text{ torr} = 0.19 \text{ torr}$$

       b. $n_{CO} = \dfrac{P_{CO}V}{RT};$ Assuming 1.0 m^3 air, 1 m^3 = 1000 L:

$$n_{CO} = \frac{\dfrac{0.19}{760} \text{ atm} \times (1.0 \times 10^3 \text{ L})}{\dfrac{0.08206 \text{ L atm}}{\text{mol K}} \times 273 \text{ K}} = 1.1 \times 10^{-2} \text{ mol CO}$$

$$1.1 \times 10^{-2} \text{ mol} \times \frac{6.02 \times 10^{23} \text{ molecules}}{\text{mol}} = 6.6 \times 10^{21} \text{ CO molecules in 1.0 m}^3 \text{ of air}$$

       c. $\dfrac{6.6 \times 10^{21} \text{ molecules}}{\text{m}^3} \times \left(\dfrac{1 \text{ m}}{100 \text{ cm}}\right)^3 = \dfrac{6.6 \times 10^{15} \text{ molecules CO}}{\text{cm}^3}$

92.   A concentration of 1.0 ppbv means there is 1.0 L of CH_2O for every 1.0×10^9 L of air measured at the same temperature and pressure. The molar volume of an ideal gas is 22.42 at STP. Assuming 1.0×10^9 L air:

$$\frac{1.0 \text{ L CH}_2\text{O}}{1.0 \times 10^9 \text{ L}} \times \frac{1 \text{ mol CH}_2\text{O}}{22.42 \text{ L}} \times \frac{6.022 \times 10^{23} \text{ molecules}}{\text{mol}} \times \frac{1 \text{ L}}{1000 \text{ cm}^3} = \frac{2.7 \times 10^{10} \text{ molecules}}{\text{cm}^3}$$

$$V = \left(18.0 \text{ ft} \times \frac{12 \text{ in}}{\text{ft}} \times \frac{2.54 \text{ cm}}{\text{in}}\right) \times \left(24.0 \text{ ft} \times \frac{12 \text{ in}}{\text{ft}} \times \frac{2.54 \text{ cm}}{\text{in}}\right)$$

$$\times \left(8.0 \text{ ft} \times \frac{12 \text{ in}}{\text{ft}} \times \frac{2.54 \text{ cm}}{\text{in}}\right) = 9.8 \times 10^7 \text{ cm}^3$$

$$9.8 \times 10^7 \text{ cm}^3 \times \frac{2.7 \times 10^{10} \text{ molecules}}{\text{cm}^3} \times \frac{1 \text{ mol}}{6.022 \times 10^{23} \text{ molecules}} \times \frac{30.03 \text{ g}}{\text{mol}} = 1.3 \times 10^{-4} \text{ g CH}_2\text{O}$$

93. $N_2(g) + O_2(g) \rightarrow 2 \text{ NO}(g),$ automobile combustion or formed by lightning

      $2 \text{ NO}(g) + O_2(g) \rightarrow 2 \text{ NO}_2(g),$ reaction with atmospheric O_2

      $2 \text{ NO}_2(g) + H_2O(l) \rightarrow HNO_3(aq) + HNO_2(aq),$ reaction with atmospheric H_2O

      $S(s) + O_2(g) \rightarrow SO_2(g),$ combustion of coal

      $2 \text{ SO}_2(g) + O_2(g) \rightarrow 2SO_3(g),$ reaction with atmospheric O_2

      $H_2O(l) + SO_3(g) \rightarrow H_2SO_4(aq),$ reaction with atmospheric H_2O

      $2 \text{ HNO}_3(aq) + CaCO_3(s) \rightarrow Ca(NO_3)_2(aq) + H_2O(l) + CO_2(g)$

      $H_2SO_4(aq) + CaCO_3(s) \rightarrow CaSO_4(aq) + H_2O(l) + CO_2(g)$

94.   For benzene:

$$89.6 \times 10^{-9} \text{ g} \times \frac{1 \text{ mol}}{78.11 \text{ g}} = 1.15 \times 10^{-9} \text{ mol benzene}$$

$$V_{ben} = \frac{n_{ben}RT}{P} = \frac{1.15 \times 10^{-9} \text{ mol} \times \dfrac{0.08206 \text{ L atm}}{\text{mol K}} \times 296 \text{ K}}{748 \text{ torr} \times \dfrac{1 \text{ atm}}{760 \text{ torr}}} = 2.84 \times 10^{-8} \text{ L}$$

$$\text{Mixing ratio} = \frac{2.84 \times 10^{-8} \text{ L}}{3.00 \text{ L}} \times 10^6 = 9.47 \times 10^{-3} \text{ ppmv}$$

$$\text{or ppbv} = \frac{\text{vol. of X} \times 10^9}{\text{total vol.}} = \frac{2.84 \times 10^{-8} \text{ L}}{3.00 \text{ L}} \times 10^9 = 9.47 \text{ ppbv}$$

$$\frac{1.15 \times 10^{-9} \text{ mol benzene}}{3.00 \text{ L}} \times \frac{1 \text{ L}}{1000 \text{ cm}^3} \times \frac{6.022 \times 10^{23} \text{ molecules}}{\text{mol}}$$

$$= 2.31 \times 10^{11} \text{ molecules benzene/cm}^3$$

For toluene:

$$153 \times 10^{-9} \text{ g C}_7\text{H}_8 \times \frac{1 \text{ mol}}{92.13 \text{ g}} = 1.66 \times 10^{-9} \text{ mol toluene}$$

$$V_{tol} = \frac{n_{tol}RT}{P} = \frac{1.66 \times 10^{-9} \text{ mol} \times \dfrac{0.08206 \text{ L atm}}{\text{mol K}} \times 296 \text{ K}}{748 \text{ torr} \times \dfrac{760 \text{ torr}}{\text{atm}}} = 4.10 \times 10^{-8} \text{ L}$$

$$\text{Mixing ratio} = \frac{4.10 \times 10^{-8} \text{ L}}{3.00 \text{ L}} \times 10^6 = 1.37 \times 10^{-2} \text{ ppmv (or 13.7 ppbv)}$$

$$\frac{1.66 \times 10^{-9} \text{ mol toluene}}{3.00 \text{ L}} \times \frac{1 \text{ L}}{1000 \text{ cm}^3} \times \frac{6.022 \times 10^{23} \text{ molecules}}{\text{mol}}$$

$$= 3.33 \times 10^{11} \text{ molecules toluene/cm}^3$$

Additional Exercises

95. $$0.050 \text{ mL} \times \frac{1.149 \text{ g}}{\text{mL}} \times \frac{1 \text{ mol O}_2}{32.0 \text{ g}} = 1.8 \times 10^{-3} \text{ mol O}_2$$

$$V = \frac{nRT}{P} = \frac{1.8 \times 10^{-3} \text{ mol} \times \dfrac{0.08206 \text{ L atm}}{\text{mol K}} \times 310. \text{ K}}{1.0 \text{ atm}} = 4.6 \; 10^{-2} \text{ L} = 46 \text{ mL}$$

96. $$750. \text{ mL juice} \times \frac{12 \text{ mL C}_2\text{H}_5\text{OH}}{100 \text{ mL juice}} = 90. \text{ mL C}_2\text{H}_5\text{OH present}$$

$$90. \text{ mL C}_2\text{H}_5\text{OH} \times \frac{0.79 \text{ g C}_2\text{H}_5\text{OH}}{\text{mL C}_2\text{H}_5\text{OH}} \times \frac{1 \text{ mol C}_2\text{H}_5\text{OH}}{46.07 \text{ g C}_2\text{H}_5\text{OH}} \times \frac{2 \text{ mol CO}_2}{2 \text{ mol C}_2\text{H}_5\text{OH}} = 1.5 \text{ mol CO}_2$$

The CO_2 will occupy (825 - 750. =) 75 mL not occupied by the liquid (headspace).

$$P_{CO_2} = \frac{n_{CO_2} \times RT}{V} = \frac{1.5 \text{ mol} \times \dfrac{0.08206 \text{ L atm}}{\text{mol K}} \times 298 \text{ K}}{75 \times 10^{-3} \text{ L}} = 490 \text{ atm}$$

Actually, enough CO_2 will dissolve in the wine to lower the pressure of CO_2 to a much more reasonable value.

97. $Mn(s) + x \, HCl(g) \rightarrow MnCl_x(s) + \dfrac{x}{2} \, H_2(g)$

$$n_{H_2} = \frac{PV}{RT} = \frac{0.951 \text{ atm} \times 3.22 \text{ L}}{\dfrac{0.08206 \text{ L atm}}{\text{mol K}} \times 373 \text{ K}} = 0.100 \text{ mol } H_2$$

mol Cl in compound = mol HCl = $0.100 \text{ mol } H_2 \times \dfrac{x \text{ mol Cl}}{\dfrac{x}{2} \text{ mol } H_2} = 0.200 \text{ mol Cl}$

$$\frac{\text{mol Cl}}{\text{mol Mn}} = \frac{0.200 \text{ mol Cl}}{2.747 \text{ g Mn} \times \dfrac{1 \text{ mol Mn}}{54.94 \text{ g Mn}}} = \frac{0.200 \text{ mol Cl}}{0.05000 \text{ mol Mn}} = 4.00$$

The formula of compound is $MnCl_4$.

98.   a.   Volume of hot air: $V = \dfrac{4}{3}\pi r^3 = \dfrac{4}{3}\pi(2.50 \text{ m})^3 = 65.4 \text{ m}^3$

(Note: radius = diameter/2 = 5.00/2 = 2.50 m)

$$65.4 \text{ m}^3 \times \left(\frac{10 \text{ dm}}{\text{m}}\right)^3 \times \frac{1 \text{ L}}{\text{dm}^3} = 6.54 \times 10^4 \text{ L}$$

$$n = \frac{PV}{RT} = \frac{\left(745 \text{ torr} \times \dfrac{1 \text{ atm}}{760 \text{ torr}}\right) \times 6.54 \times 10^4 \text{ L}}{\dfrac{0.08206 \text{ L atm}}{\text{mol K}} \times (273 + 65) \text{ K}} = 2.31 \times 10^3 \text{ mol air}$$

Mass of hot air = $2.31 \times 10^3 \text{ mol} \times \dfrac{29.0 \text{ g}}{\text{mol}} = 6.70 \times 10^4 \text{ g}$

Air displaced: $n = \dfrac{PV}{RT} = \dfrac{\dfrac{745}{760} \text{ atm} \times 6.54 \times 10^4 \text{ L}}{\dfrac{0.08206 \text{ L atm}}{\text{mol K}} \times (273 + 21) \text{ K}} = 2.66 \times 10^3 \text{ mol air}$

Mass of air displaced = $2.66 \times 10^3 \text{ mol} \times \dfrac{29.0 \text{ g}}{\text{mol}} = 7.71 \times 10^4 \text{ g}$

Lift = $7.71 \times 10^4 \text{ g} - 6.70 \times 10^4 \text{ g} = 1.01 \times 10^4 \text{ g}$

b. Mass of air displaced is the same, 7.71×10^4 g. Moles of He in balloon will be the same as moles of air displaced, 2.66×10^3 mol, since P, V and T are the same.

$$\text{Mass of He} = 2.66 \times 10^3 \text{ mol} \times \frac{4.003 \text{ g}}{\text{mol}} = 1.06 \times 10^4 \text{ g}$$

$$\text{Lift} = 7.71 \times 10^4 \text{ g} - 1.06 \times 10^4 \text{ g} = 6.65 \times 10^4 \text{ g}$$

c. Hot air: $n = \dfrac{PV}{RT} = \dfrac{\dfrac{630.}{760} \text{ atm} \times 6.54 \times 10^4 \text{ L}}{\dfrac{0.08206 \text{ L atm}}{\text{mol K}} \times 338 \text{ K}} = 1.95 \times 10^3$ mol air

$$1.95 \times 10^3 \text{ mol} \times \frac{29.0 \text{ g}}{\text{mol}} = 5.66 \times 10^4 \text{ g of hot air}$$

Air displaced: $n = \dfrac{PV}{RT} = \dfrac{\dfrac{630.}{760} \text{ atm} \times 6.54 \times 10^4 \text{ L}}{\dfrac{0.08206 \text{ L atm}}{\text{mol K}} \times 294 \text{ K}} = 2.25 \times 10^3$ mol air

$$2.25 \times 10^3 \text{ mol} \times \frac{29.0 \text{ g}}{\text{mol}} = 6.53 \times 10^4 \text{ g of air displaced}$$

Lift = 6.53×10^4 g - 5.66×10^4 g = 8.7×10^3 g

d. mass of hot air = 6.70×10^4 g (from part a)

Air displaced: $n = \dfrac{PV}{RT} = \dfrac{\dfrac{745}{760} \text{ atm} \times 6.54 \times 10^4 \text{ L}}{\dfrac{0.08206 \text{ L atm}}{\text{mol K}} \times 265 \text{ K}} = 2.95 \times 10^3$ mol air

$$2.95 \times 10^3 \text{ mol} \times \frac{29.0 \text{ g}}{\text{mol}} = 8.56 \times 10^4 \text{ g of air displaced}$$

Lift = 8.56×10^4 g - 6.70×10^4 g = 1.86×10^4 g

99.   PV = nRT, V and T are constant. $\dfrac{P_1}{n_1} = \dfrac{P_2}{n_2}, \dfrac{P_2}{P_1} = \dfrac{n_2}{n_1}$

We will do this limiting reagent problem using an alternative method than described in Chapter 3. Let's calculate the partial pressure of C_3H_3N that can be produced from each of the starting materials assuming each reactant is limiting. The reactant that produces the smallest amount of product will run out first and is the limiting reagent.

$$P_{C_3H_3N} = 0.500 \text{ MPa} \times \frac{2 \text{ MPa } C_3H_3N}{2 \text{ MPa } C_3H_6} = 0.500 \text{ MPa if } C_3H_6 \text{ is limiting.}$$

$$P_{C_3H_3N} = 0.800 \text{ MPa} \times \frac{2 \text{ MPa } C_3H_3N}{2 \text{ MPa } NH_3} = 0.800 \text{ MPa if } NH_3 \text{ is limiting.}$$

$$P_{C_3H_3N} = 1.500 \text{ MPa} \times \frac{2 \text{ MPa C}_3\text{H}_3\text{N}}{3 \text{ MPa O}_2} = 1.000 \text{ MPa if O}_2 \text{ is limiting.}$$

Thus, C_3H_6 is limiting. Although more product could be produced from NH_3 and O_2, there is only enough C_3H_6 to produce 0.500 MPa of C_3H_3N. The partial pressure of C_3H_3N in atm after the reaction is:

$$0.500 \times 10^6 \text{ Pa} \times \frac{1 \text{ atm}}{1.013 \times 10^5 \text{ Pa}} = 4.94 \text{ atm}$$

$$n = \frac{PV}{RT} = \frac{4.94 \text{ atm} \times 150. \text{ L}}{\dfrac{0.08206 \text{ L atm}}{\text{mol K}} \times 298 \text{ K}} = 30.3 \text{ mol C}_3\text{H}_3\text{N}$$

$$30.3 \text{ mol} \times \frac{53.06 \text{ g}}{\text{mol}} = 1.61 \times 10^3 \text{ g C}_3\text{H}_3\text{N can be produced.}$$

100.   The partial pressure of CO_2 that reacted is 740. − 390. = 350. torr. Thus, the number of moles of CO_2 that reacts is given by:

$$n = \frac{PV}{RT} = \frac{\dfrac{350.}{760} \text{ atm} \times 3.00 \text{ L}}{\dfrac{0.08206 \text{ L atm}}{\text{mol K}} \times 293 \text{ K}} = 5.75 \times 10^{-2} \text{ mol CO}_2$$

$$5.75 \times 10^{-2} \text{ mol CO}_2 \times \frac{1 \text{ mol MgO}}{1 \text{ mol CO}_2} \times \frac{40.31 \text{ g MgO}}{\text{mol HgO}} = 2.32 \text{ g MgO}$$

$$\text{Mass \% MgO} = \frac{2.32 \text{ g}}{2.85 \text{ g}} \times 100 = 81.4\% \text{ MgO}$$

101. $P_{TOT} = P_{H_2} + P_{H_2O}$, $1.032 \text{ atm} = P_{H_2} + 32 \text{ torr} \times \dfrac{1 \text{ atm}}{760 \text{ torr}}$, $P_{H_2} = 1.032 - 0.042 = 0.990 \text{ atm}$

$$n_{H_2} = \frac{P_{H_2}V}{RT} = \frac{0.990 \text{ atm} \times 0.240 \text{ L}}{0.08206 \dfrac{\text{L atm}}{\text{mol K}} \times 303 \text{ K}} = 9.56 \times 10^{-3} \text{ mol H}_2$$

$$9.56 \times 10^{-3} \text{ mol H}_2 \times \frac{1 \text{ mol Zn}}{\text{mol H}_2} \times \frac{65.38 \text{ g Zn}}{\text{mol Zn}} = 0.625 \text{ g Zn}$$

102.   a.   Initially, $P_{N_2} = P_{H_2} = 1.00$ atm and the total pressure is 2.00 atm ($P_{tot} = P_{N_2} + P_{H_2}$). The total pressure after reaction will also be 2.00 atm since we have a constant pressure container. Since V and T are constant before the reaction takes place, there must be equal moles of N_2 and H_2 present initially. Let x = mol N_2 = mol H_2 that are present initially. From the balanced equation, $N_2(g) + 3 H_2(g) \rightarrow 2 NH_3(g)$, H_2 will be limiting since three times as many mol of H_2 are required to react as compared to mol of N_2.

After the reaction occurs, none of the H_2 remains (it is the limiting reagent).

$$\text{mol NH}_3 \text{ produced} = x \text{ mol H}_2 \times \frac{2 \text{ mol NH}_3}{3 \text{ mol H}_2} = 2x/3$$

$$\text{mol N}_2 \text{ reacted} = x \text{ mol H}_2 \times \frac{1 \text{ mol N}_2}{3 \text{ mol H}_2} = x/3$$

mol N_2 remaining = x mol N_2 present initially - $x/3$ mol N_2 reacted = $2x/3$ mol N_2 remaining

After the reaction goes to completion, equal mol of $N_2(g)$ and $NH_3(g)$ are present ($2x/3$). Since equal mol are present, then the partial pressure of each gas must be equal ($P_{N_2} = P_{NH_3}$).

$P_{tot} = 2.00$ atm $= P_{N_2} + P_{NH_3}$; Solving: $P_{N_2} = 1.00$ atm $= P_{NH_3}$

b. $V \propto n$ since P and T are constant. The mol of gas present initially are:

$$n_{N_2} + n_{H_2} = x + x = 2x \text{ mol}$$

After reaction, the mol of gas present are:

$$n_{N_2} + n_{NH_3} = \frac{2x}{3} + \frac{2x}{3} = 4x/3 \text{ mol}$$

$$\frac{V_{after}}{V_{initial}} = \frac{n_{after}}{n_{initial}} = \frac{4x/3}{2x} = \frac{2}{3}$$

The volume of the container will be two-thirds the original volume so:

$$V = 2/3(15.0 \text{ L}) = 10.0 \text{ L}$$

103. $P_1V_1 = P_2V_2$; The total volume is 1.00 L + 1.00 L + 2.00 L = 4.00 L.

For He: $P_2 = \dfrac{P_1V_1}{V_2} = 200. \text{ torr} \times \dfrac{1.00 \text{ L}}{4.00 \text{ L}} = 50.0$ torr He

For Ne: $P_2 = 0.400$ atm $\times \dfrac{1.00 \text{ L}}{4.00 \text{ L}} = 0.100$ atm; 0.100 atm $\times \dfrac{760 \text{ torr}}{\text{atm}} = 76.0$ torr Ne

For Ar: $P_2 = 24.0$ kPa $\times \dfrac{2.00 \text{ L}}{4.00 \text{ L}} = 12.0$ kPa; 12.0 kPa $\times \dfrac{1 \text{ atm}}{101.3 \text{ kPa}} \times \dfrac{760 \text{ torr}}{\text{atm}} = 90.0$ torr Ar

$P_{total} = 50.0 + 76.0 + 90.0 = 216.0$ torr

104. $2 H_2(g) + O_2(g) \rightarrow 2 H_2O(g)$; Since P and T are constant, then volume ratios will equal mol ratios ($V_f/V_i = n_f/n_i$). Let x = mol H_2 = mol O_2 present initially. H_2 will be limiting since a 2:1 H_2 to O_2 mol ratio is required by the balanced equation, but only a 1:1 mol ratio is present. Therefore, no H_2 will be present after the reaction goes to completion. However, excess $O_2(g)$ will be present as well as the $H_2O(g)$ produced.

$$\text{mol } O_2 \text{ reacted} = x \text{ mol } H_2 \times \frac{1 \text{ mol } O_2}{2 \text{ mol } H_2} = x/2 \text{ mol } O_2$$

$$\text{mol } O_2 \text{ remaining} = x \text{ mol } O_2 \text{ initially} - x/2 \text{ mol } O_2 \text{ reacted} = x/2 \text{ mol } O_2$$

$$\text{mol } H_2O \text{ produced} = x \text{ mol } H_2 \times \frac{2 \text{ mol } H_2O}{2 \text{ mol } H_2} = x \text{ mol } H_2O$$

$$\text{Total mol gas initially} = x \text{ mol } H_2 + x \text{ mol } O_2 = 2x$$

$$\text{Total mol gas after reaction} = x/2 \text{ mol } O_2 + x \text{ mol } H_2O = 1.5x$$

$$\frac{n_f}{n_i} = \frac{V_f}{V_i} = \frac{1.5x}{2x} = \frac{1.5}{2} = 0.75; \quad V_f/V_i = 0.75:1 \text{ or } 3:4$$

105.   Out of 100.00 g compounds, there are:

$$58.51 \text{ g C} \times \frac{1 \text{ mol C}}{12.011 \text{ g C}} = 4.871 \text{ mol C}; \quad \frac{4.871}{2.436} = 2.000$$

$$7.37 \text{ g H} \times \frac{1 \text{ mol H}}{1.008 \text{ g H}} = 7.31 \text{ mol H}; \quad \frac{7.31}{2.436} = 3.00$$

$$34.12 \text{ g N} \times \frac{1 \text{ mol N}}{14.007 \text{ g N}} = 2.436 \text{ mol N}; \quad \frac{2.436}{2.436} = 1.000$$

Empirical formula: C_2H_3N

$$\frac{\text{Rate}_1}{\text{Rate}_2} = \left(\frac{M_2}{M_1}\right)^{1/2}; \quad \text{Let gas (1)} = \text{He}; \quad 3.20 = \left(\frac{M_2}{4.003}\right)^{1/2}, \quad M_2 = 41.0 \text{ g/mol}$$

Empirical formula mass of $C_2H_3N \approx 2(12.0) + 3(1.0) + 1(14.0) = 41.0$. So molecular formula is also C_2H_3N.

106. $$33.5 \text{ mg CO}_2 \times \frac{12.01 \text{ mg C}}{44.01 \text{ mg CO}_2} = 9.14 \text{ mg C}; \quad \% \text{ C} = \frac{9.14 \text{ mg}}{35.0 \text{ mg}} \times 100 = 26.1\% \text{ C}$$

$$41.1 \text{ mg H}_2O \times \frac{2.016 \text{ mg H}}{18.02 \text{ mg H}_2O} = 4.60 \text{ mg H}; \quad \% \text{ H} = \frac{4.60 \text{ mg}}{35.0 \text{ mg}} \times 100 = 13.1\% \text{ H}$$

$$n_{N_2} = \frac{P_{N_2} \times V}{RT} = \frac{\dfrac{740.}{760} \text{ atm} \times 35.6 \times 10^{-3} \text{ L}}{\dfrac{0.08206 \text{ L atm}}{\text{mol K}} \times 298 \text{ K}} = 1.42 \times 10^{-3} \text{ mol N}_2$$

$$1.42 \times 10^{-3} \text{ mol } N_2 \times \frac{28.02 \text{ g } N_2}{\text{mol } N_2} = 3.98 \times 10^{-2} \text{ g nitrogen} = 39.8 \text{ mg nitrogen}$$

$$\% \text{ N} = \frac{39.8 \text{ mg}}{65.2 \text{ mg}} \times 100 = 61.0\% \text{ N}$$

Or we can get % N by difference: % N = 100.0 - (26.1 + 13.1) = 60.8%

Out of 100.0 g:

$$26.1 \text{ g C} \times \frac{1 \text{ mol}}{12.01 \text{ g}} = 2.17 \text{ mol C}; \quad \frac{2.17}{2.17} = 1.00$$

$$13.1 \text{ g H} \times \frac{1 \text{ mol}}{1.008 \text{ g}} = 13.0 \text{ mol H}; \quad \frac{13.0}{2.17} = 5.99$$

$$60.8 \text{ g N} \times \frac{1 \text{ mol}}{14.01 \text{ g}} = 4.34 \text{ mol N}; \quad \frac{4.34}{2.17} = 2.00$$

Empirical formula is CH_6N_2.

$$\frac{\text{Rate}_1}{\text{Rate}_2} = \left(\frac{M}{39.95} \right)^{1/2} = \frac{26.4}{24.6} = 1.07, \quad M = (1.07)^2 \times 39.95 = 45.7 \text{ g/mol}$$

Empirical formula mass of $CH_6N_2 \approx 12 + 6 + 28 = 46$. Thus, molecular formula is also CH_6N_2.

107.   We will apply Boyle's law to solve. $PV = nRT = \text{constant}, \quad P_1V_1 = P_2V_2$

Let condition (1) correspond to He from the tank that can be used to fill balloons. We must leave 1.0 atm of He in the tank, so $P_1 = 200.$ atm - 1.00 = 199 atm and $V_1 = 15.0$ L. Condition (2) will correspond to the filled balloons with $P_2 = 1.00$ atm and $V_2 = N(2.00 \text{ L})$ where N is the number of filled balloons, each at a volume of 2.00 L.

199 atm × 15.0 L = 1.00 atm × N(2.00 L), N = 1492.5; We can't fill 0.5 of a balloon. So N = 1492 balloons or to 3 significant figures, 1490 balloons.

108.   Average velocity $\propto (1/M)^{1/2}$ at constant T; The pressure in container A will increase initially because the lighter H_2 molecules will effuse into container A faster than air will escape. However, the pressures will eventually equalize once the gases have had time to mix thoroughly.

109.   If we had 100.0 g of the gas, we would have 50.0 g He and 50.0 g Xe.

$$\chi_{He} = \frac{n_{He}}{n_{He} + n_{Xe}} = \frac{\dfrac{50.0 \text{ g}}{4.003 \text{ g/mol}}}{\dfrac{50.0 \text{ g}}{4.003 \text{ g/mol}} + \dfrac{50.0 \text{ g}}{131.3 \text{ g/mol}}} = \frac{12.5 \text{ mol He}}{12.5 \text{ mol He} + 0.381 \text{ mol Xe}} = 0.970$$

$$P_{He} = \chi_{He} P_{total} = 0.970 \times 600. \text{ torr} = 582 \text{ torr}; \quad P_{Xe} = 600. - 582 = 18 \text{ torr}$$

110.   a)   Ideal Gas Equation: $PV = nRT$

$$P = \frac{nRT}{V} = \frac{1.00 \text{ mol} \times \dfrac{0.08206 \text{ L atm}}{\text{mol K}} \times 310. \text{ K}}{1.00 \text{ L}} = 25.4 \text{ atm}$$

   b)   Van der Waals Equation: $\left[P + a\left(\dfrac{n}{V} \right)^2 \right](V - nb) = nRT$

$$P = \frac{nRT}{V - nb} - a\left(\frac{n}{V} \right)^2; \quad \text{For } CO_2: \ a = 3.59 \text{ atm L}^2 \text{ mol}^{-2}; \ b = 0.0427 \text{ L/mol}$$

$$P = \frac{1.00 \text{ mol} \times \dfrac{0.08206 \text{ L atm}}{\text{mol K}} \times 310. \text{ K}}{1.00 \text{ L} - 1.00 \text{ mol} \times 0.0427 \text{ L/mol}} - \frac{3.59 \text{ atm L}^2}{\text{mol}^2} \times \frac{(1.00 \text{ mol})^2}{(1.00 \text{ L})^2}$$

   $P = 26.6 \text{ atm} - 3.59 \text{ atm} = 23.0 \text{ atm}$

111. $n_{Ar} = \dfrac{228 \text{ g}}{39.95 \text{ g/mol}} = 5.71 \text{ mol Ar}; \quad \chi_{CH_4} = \dfrac{n_{CH_4}}{n_{CH_4} + n_{Ar}} = 0.650 = \dfrac{n_{CH_4}}{n_{CH_4} + (5.71)}$

   $0.650\,(n_{CH_4} + 5.71) = n_{CH_4}, \ 3.71 = 0.350 \, n_{CH_4}, \ n_{CH_4} = 10.6 \text{ mol CH}_4; \ KE_{avg} = \dfrac{3}{2}RT$ for 1 mol

   So $KE_{total} = (10.6 + 5.71 \text{ mol}) \times 3/2 \times 8.3145 \text{ J mol}^{-1} \text{ K}^{-1} \times 298 \text{ K} = 6.06 \times 10^4 \text{ J} = 60.6 \text{ kJ}$

112.   a) $\dfrac{PV}{n} = \alpha + \beta P$ b) $\dfrac{\Delta(mu)}{\text{impact}} = 2 \, mu \propto M\left(\dfrac{T}{M} \right)^{1/2} = \sqrt{M}$ at constant T

   (straight line, $y = b + mx$)

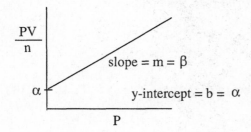

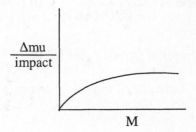

   c) $T_K = T_{°C} + 273; \quad P = \dfrac{nR(T_{°C} + 273)}{V} = \text{constant} \, (T_{°C} + 273)$

   (straight line, $y = mx + b$)

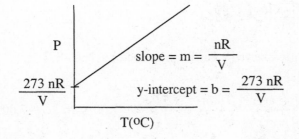

113. $CH_3OH(l) + 3/2 \, O_2(g) \rightarrow CO_2(g) + 2 \, H_2O(g)$ or $2 \, CH_3OH(l) + 3 \, O_2(g) \rightarrow 2 \, CO_2(g) + 4 \, H_2O(g)$

$$50.0 \text{ mL} \times \frac{0.850 \text{ g}}{\text{mL}} \times \frac{1 \text{ mol}}{32.04 \text{ g}} = 1.33 \text{ mol } CH_3OH(l) \text{ available}$$

$$n_{O_2} = \frac{PV}{RT} = \frac{2.00 \text{ atm} \times 22.8 \text{ L}}{\dfrac{0.08206 \text{ L atm}}{\text{mol K}} \times 300. \text{ K}} = 1.85 \text{ mol } O_2 \text{ available}$$

$$1.33 \text{ mol } CH_3OH \times \frac{3 \text{ mol } O_2}{2 \text{ mol } CH_3OH} = 2.00 \text{ mol } O_2 \text{ required for complete reaction}$$

We only have 1.85 mol O_2, so O_2 is limiting. $1.85 \text{ mol } O_2 \times \dfrac{4 \text{ mol } H_2O}{3 \text{ mol } O_2} = 2.47 \text{ mol } H_2O$

114.   Since P and T are constant, then V and n are directly proportional. The balanced equation requires 2 L of H_2 to react with 1 L of CO (2:1 volume ratio due to 2:1 mol ratio in balanced equation). The actual volume ratio present in one minute is 16.0 L/25.0 L = 0.640 (0.640:1). Since the actual volume ratio present is smaller than the required volume ratio, then H_2 is the limiting reactant. The volume of CH_3OH produced at STP will be one-half to the volume of H_2 reacted due to the 1:2 mol ratio in the balanced equation. In one minute 16.0 L/2 = 8.00 L CH_3OH are produced (theoretical yield).

$$n_{CH_3OH} = \frac{PV}{RT} = \frac{1.00 \text{ atm} \times 8.00 \text{ L}}{\dfrac{0.08206 \text{ L atm}}{\text{mol K}} \times 273 \text{ K}} = 0.357 \text{ mol } CH_3OH \text{ in one minute}$$

$$0.357 \text{ mol } CH_3OH \times \frac{32.04 \text{ g } CH_3OH}{\text{mol } CH_3OH} = 11.4 \text{ g } CH_3OH \text{ (theoretical yield per minute)}$$

$$\% \text{ yield} = \frac{\text{actual yield}}{\text{theoretical yield}} \times 100 = \frac{5.30 \text{ g}}{11.4 \text{ g}} \times 100 = 46.5\% \text{ yield}$$

115.   For 1 mol of gas: $KE_{ave} = 3/2 \, RT$

For 1 molecule of gas (N_A = Avogadro's number): $KE_{ave} = \dfrac{3RT}{2N_A} = \dfrac{3}{2} k_B T$, $k_B = 1.3807 \times 10^{-23}$ J/K

$$KE_{ave} = \frac{3}{2}(1.3807 \times 10^{-23} \text{ J/K})(400. \text{ K}) = 8.28 \times 10^{-21} \text{ J/molecule}$$

116.   mol of He removed $= \dfrac{PV}{RT} = \dfrac{1.00 \text{ atm} \times (1.75 \times 10^{-3} \text{ L})}{\dfrac{0.08206 \text{ L atm}}{\text{mol K}} \times 298 \text{ K}} = 7.16 \times 10^{-5} \text{ mol He}$

In the original flask, 7.16×10^{-5} mol of He exerted a partial pressure of 1.960 - 1.710 = 0.250 atm.

$$V = \frac{nRT}{P} = \frac{(7.16 \times 10^{-5} \text{ mol}) \times 0.08206 \text{ L atm K}^{-1} \text{mol}^{-1} \times 298 \text{ K}}{0.250 \text{ atm}} = 7.00 \times 10^{-3} \text{ L} = 7.00 \text{ mL}$$

117.   a.   Out of 100.00 g of Z, we have:

$$34.38 \text{ g Ni} \times \frac{1 \text{ mol}}{58.69 \text{ g}} = 0.5858 \text{ mol Ni}$$

$$28.13 \text{ g C} \times \frac{1 \text{ mol}}{12.011 \text{ g}} = 2.342 \text{ mol C}; \quad \frac{2.342}{0.5858} = 3.998$$

$$37.48 \text{ g O} \times \frac{1 \text{ mol}}{15.999 \text{ g}} = 2.343 \text{ mol O}; \quad \frac{2.343}{0.5858} = 4.000$$

The empirical formula is NiC_4O_4.

b. $\dfrac{\text{rate Z}}{\text{rate Ar}} = \left(\dfrac{M_{Ar}}{M_Z}\right)^{1/2} = \left(\dfrac{39.95}{M_Z}\right)^{1/2}$; Since initial mol Ar = mol Z, then:

$$0.4837 = \left(\frac{39.95}{M_Z}\right)^{1/2}, \quad M_Z = 170.8 \text{ g/mol}$$

c. NiC_4O_4: M = 58.69 + 4(12.01) + 4(16.00) = 170.73 g/mol

Molecular formula is also NiC_4O_4.

d.   Each effusion step changes the concentration of Z in the gas by a factor of 0.4837. The original concentration of Z molecules to Ar atoms is a 1:1 ratio. After 5 stages:

$$n_Z/n_{Ar} = (0.4837)^5 = 2.648 \times 10^{-2}$$

118.   For O_2, n and T are constant, so $P_1V_1 = P_2V_2$.

$$P_1 = \frac{P_2V_2}{V_1} = 785 \text{ torr} \times \frac{1.94 \text{ L}}{2.00 \text{ L}} = 761 \text{ torr} = P_{O_2}; \quad P_{total} = P_{O_2} + P_{H_2O}, \quad P_{H_2O} = 785 - 761 = 24 \text{ torr}$$

119.   a. $2 \text{ CH}_4(g) + 2 \text{ NH}_3(g) + 3 \text{ O}_2(g) \rightarrow 2 \text{ HCN}(g) + 6 \text{ H}_2\text{O}(g)$

b.   Volumes of gases are proportional to moles at constant T and P. Using the balanced equation, methane and ammonia are in stoichiometric amounts and oxygen is in excess. In 1 second:

$$n_{CH_4} = \frac{PV}{RT} = \frac{1.00 \text{ atm} \times 20.0 \text{ L}}{0.08206 \text{ L atm K}^{-1}\text{mol}^{-1} \times 423 \text{ K}} = 0.576 \text{ mol CH}_4$$

$$\frac{0.576 \text{ mol CH}_4}{s} \times \frac{2 \text{ mol HCN}}{2 \text{ mol CH}_4} \times \frac{27.03 \text{ g HCN}}{\text{mol HCN}} = 15.6 \text{ g HCN/s}$$

Challenge Problems

120.   a.   The number of collisions of gas particles with the walls of the container is proportional to:

$$Z_A \propto \frac{N}{V}\sqrt{\frac{T}{M}}$$

Where N = # of gas particles, V = volume of container, T = temperature (Kelvin), and M = molar mass of gas particles in kg.

Since both He samples are in separate containers of the same volume, then V and M are constant. Since pressure and volume are constant, then $P \propto nT$ (also $n \propto N$).

Thus $Z_A \propto N\sqrt{T}$

So, we have: $\dfrac{Z_1}{Z_2} = \dfrac{N_1\sqrt{T_1}}{N_2\sqrt{T_2}} = 2$, and and $N_1T_1 = N_2T_2$

Thus, $\dfrac{N_1}{N_2} = \dfrac{2\sqrt{T_2}}{\sqrt{T_1}} = \dfrac{T_2}{T_1}, \dfrac{2\,T_1}{\sqrt{T_1}} = \dfrac{T_2}{\sqrt{T_2}}, 2\sqrt{T_1} = \sqrt{T_2}$

Solving: $4\,T_1 = T_2$, $T_1 = 1/4\,T_2$; and since $P \propto nT$, then $n_1 = 4\,n_2$

Although the number of collisions in container #1 is twice as high, the temperature is one-fourth that of container #2. This is because there are four times the number of moles of helium gas in container #1.

b.   There are two times the number of collisions, but because the temperature is lower, the gas particles are hitting with less forceful collisions. Overall, the pressure is the same in each container.

121. $Cr(s) + 3\,HCl(aq) \rightarrow CrCl_3(aq) + 3/2\,H_2(g)$; $Zn(s) + 2\,HCl(aq) \rightarrow ZnCl_2(aq) + H_2(g)$

$$\text{mol } H_2 \text{ produced} = n = \frac{PV}{RT} = \frac{\left(750.\text{ torr} \times \dfrac{1\text{ atm}}{760\text{ torr}}\right) \times 0.225\text{ L}}{\dfrac{0.08206\text{ L atm}}{\text{mol K}} \times (273 + 27)\text{ K}} = 9.02 \times 10^{-3}\text{ mol } H_2$$

9.02×10^{-3} mol H_2 = mol H_2 from Cr reaction + mol H_2 from Zn reaction

From the balanced equation: 9.02×10^{-3} mol H_2 = mol Cr × (3/2) + mol Zn × 1

Let x = mass of Cr and y = mass of Zn, then:

$$x + y = 0.362\text{ g and } 9.02 \times 10^{-3} = \frac{1.5\,x}{52.00} + \frac{y}{65.38}$$

We have two equations and two unknowns. Solving by simultaneous equations:

$$9.02 \times 10^{-3} = 0.02885\,x + 0.01530\,y$$
$$\underline{-0.01530 \times 0.362 = -0.01530\,x - 0.01530\,y}$$
$$3.48 \times 10^{-3} = 0.01355\,x$$

$$x = \text{mass of Cr} = \frac{3.48 \times 10^{-3}}{0.01355} = 0.257 \text{ g}$$

$$y = \text{mass of Zn} = 0.362 \text{ g} - 0.257 \text{ g} = 0.105 \text{ g Zn}; \quad \text{mass \% Zn} = \frac{0.105 \text{ g}}{0.362 \text{ g}} \times 100 = 29.0\% \text{ Zn}$$

122. a.   The balloon will float because when it is heated, the balloon will expand (P and n remain constant). The mass of the balloon is the same, and since the volume increases, the density of the argon in the balloon decreases. When the density is less than that of air, the balloon will rise.

b.   Assuming the balloon has no mass, when the density of the argon = the density of air, the balloon will float in air. Above this temperature, the balloon will rise.

$$d_{air} = \frac{mass_{air}}{V} = \frac{n \cdot MM_{air}}{V} = \frac{\frac{PV}{RT} \cdot MM_{air}}{V} = \frac{P \cdot MM_{air}}{RT}$$

$$MM_{air} = (0.79)(28.02 \text{ g/mol}) + (0.21)(32.00 \text{ g/mol}) = 28.86 \text{ g/mol}$$

$$d_{air} = \frac{(1.00 \text{ atm})(28.86 \text{ g/mol})}{(0.08206 \frac{\text{L atm}}{\text{mol K}})(298 \text{ K})} = 1.18 \text{ g/L}$$

$$d_{argon} = \frac{(1.00 \text{ atm})(39.95 \text{ g/mol})}{(0.08206 \frac{\text{L atm}}{\text{mol K}})(T)} = 1.18 \text{ g/L}, \ T = 413 \text{ K}$$

Heat above 413 K or 140.°C so the balloon would float.

123.   molar mass $= \dfrac{dRT}{P}$, P and molar mass are constant; $dT = \dfrac{P \times \text{molar mass}}{R} = \text{constant}$

$d = \text{constant} (1/T)$ or $d_1 T_1 = d_2 T_2$, where T is in kelvin (K).

$T = x + °C; \ 1.2930(x + 0.0) = 0.9460(x + 100.0)$

$1.2930\,x = 0.9460\,x + 94.60, \ 0.3470\,x = 94.60, \ x = 272.6$

From these data absolute zero would be -272.6°C. Actual value is -273.15°C.

124. $BaO(s) + CO_2(g) \rightarrow BaCO_3(s); \ CaO(s) + CO_2(g) \rightarrow CaCO_3(s)$

$$n_i = \frac{P_i V}{RT} = \text{initial moles of } CO_2 = \frac{\frac{750.}{760} \text{ atm} \times 1.50 \text{ L}}{\frac{0.08206 \text{ L atm}}{\text{mol K}} \times 303.2 \text{ K}} = 0.0595 \text{ mol } CO_2$$

$$n_f = \frac{P_f V}{RT} = \text{final moles of } CO_2 = \frac{\frac{230.}{760}\text{ atm} \times 1.50\text{ L}}{\frac{0.08206\text{ L atm}}{\text{mol K}} \times 303.2\text{ K}} = 0.0182\text{ mol } CO_2$$

0.0595 - 0.0182 = 0.0413 mol CO_2 reacted.

Since each metal reacts 1:1 with CO_2, then the mixture contains 0.0413 mol of BaO and CaO. The molar masses of BaO and CaO are 153.3 g/mol and 56.08 g/mol, respectively.

Let x = mass of BaO and y = mass of CaO, so:

$$x + y = 5.14\text{ g and } \frac{x}{153.3} + \frac{y}{56.08} = 0.0413\text{ mol or } x + 2.734\text{ y} = 6.33$$

Solving by simultaneous equations:

$$x + 2.734\text{ y} =\ \ 6.33$$
$$\underline{-x\ \ \ \ \ \ \ \ \ \ -y = -5.14}$$
$$1.734\text{ y} =\ \ 1.19,\ \ y = 1.19/1.734 = 0.686$$

y = 0.686 g CaO and 5.14 - y = x = 4.45 g BaO

$$\text{mass \% BaO} = \frac{4.45\text{ g BaO}}{5.14\text{ g}} \times 100 = 86.6\%\text{ BaO};\ \ \%\text{ CaO} = 100.0 - 86.6 = 13.4\%\text{ CaO}$$

125. $\dfrac{PV}{nRT} = 1 + \beta P$; $\dfrac{n}{V} \times$ molar mass = d

$$\frac{\text{molar mass}}{RT} \times \frac{P}{d} = 1 + \beta P,\ \ \frac{P}{d} = \frac{RT}{\text{molar mass}} + \frac{\beta RTP}{\text{molar mass}}$$

This is in the equation for a straight line: y = b + mx. If we plot P/d vs P and extrapolate to P = 0, we get a y-intercept = b = 1.398 = RT/molar mass.

At 0.00°C, molar mass = $\dfrac{0.08206 \times 273.15}{1.398}$ = 16.03 g/mol

126. $Z = A\left(\dfrac{N}{V}\right)\left(\dfrac{RT}{2\pi M}\right)^{1/2}$; $\dfrac{Z_1}{Z_2} = \dfrac{\left(\dfrac{T_1}{M_1}\right)^{1/2}}{\left(\dfrac{T_2}{M_2}\right)^{1/2}} = \left(\dfrac{M_2 T_1}{M_1 T_2}\right)^{1/2} = 1.00$,   So, $M_1 T_2 = M_2 T_1$

$$\frac{T_2}{T_1} = \frac{M_2}{M_1};\ \ \frac{T_{UF_6}}{T_{He}} = \frac{M_{UF_6}}{M_{He}} = \frac{352.0}{4.003} = 87.93$$

127.   Figure 5.16 shows the effect of temperature on the Maxwell-Boltzmann distribution of velocities of molecules. Note that as temperature increases, the probability that a gas particle has the most probable velocity decreases. Thus, since the probability of the gas particle with the most probable velocity decreased by one-half, then the temperature must be higher than 300. K.

The equation that determines the probability that a gas molecule has a certain velocity is:

$$f(u) = 4\pi \left(\frac{m}{2\pi k_B T} \right)^{3/2} u^2 e^{-mu^2/2k_B T}$$

Let T_x = the unknown temperature, then:

$$\frac{f(u_{mp,x})}{f(u_{mp,300})} = \frac{1}{2} = \frac{4\pi \left(\dfrac{m}{2\pi k_B T_x} \right)^{3/2} u_{mp,x}^2 \, e^{-mu_{mp,x}^2/2k_B T_x}}{4\pi \left(\dfrac{m}{2\pi k_B T_{300}} \right)^{3/2} u_{mp,300}^2 \, e^{-mu_{mp,300}^2/2k_B T_{300}}}$$

Since $u_{mp} = \sqrt{\dfrac{2k_B T}{m}}$, then the equation reduces to:

$$\frac{1}{2} = \frac{\left(\dfrac{1}{T_x} \right)^{3/2} (T_x)}{\left(\dfrac{1}{T_{300}} \right)^{3/2} (T_{300})} = \left(\frac{T_{300}}{T_x} \right)^{1/2}$$

Note that the overall exponent term cancels from the expression when $2k_B T/m$ is substituted for u_{mp}^2 in the exponent term; the temperatures cancel. Solving for T_x:

$$\frac{1}{2} = \left(\frac{300.\,K}{T_x} \right)^{1/2}, \quad T_x = 1.20 \times 10^3 \, K$$

As expected, T_x is higher than 300. K.

128.   Dalton's Law states: $P_{TOT} = P_1 + P_2 + ... + P_k$ for k different types of gas molecules in a mixture. The postulates of the kinetic molecular theory are:

1.   the volume of the individual particles can be assumed to be negligible.
2.   the collisions of the particles with the walls of the container are the cause of the pressure exerted by the gas.
3.   the particles assert no forces on each other.
4.   the average kinetic energy of a collection of gas particles is assumed to be directly proportional to the Kelvin temperature of the gas.

The derivation is very similar to the ideal gas law derivation covered in section 5.6 of the text. For a mixture of gases in a cube, there exist k different types of gas molecules. For each type (i) of gas molecule, the force on the cube = $F_i = (2m_i/L)u_i^2$

Since the gas particles are assumed non-interacting, the total force for all the gas molecules in the mixture is:

$$F_{total} = \sum_{i=1}^{k} \frac{2m_i}{L} (u_i^2)$$

Now we want the average force for each type of gas particle, which is:

$$\overline{F}_{total} = \sum_{i=1}^{k} \frac{2m_i}{L} (\overline{u_i^2})$$

Pressure due to the average particle in this gas mixture of k types is the average total force divided by the total area. The expression for pressure is:

$$P = \frac{\displaystyle\sum_{i=1}^{k} \frac{2m_i}{L}(\overline{u_i^2})}{6L^2} = \frac{\displaystyle\sum_{i=1}^{k} m_i(\overline{u_i^2})}{3V} \text{ where V is the volume of the cube}$$

Total pressure due to the number of mol of different gases is:

$$P_{total} = \frac{\displaystyle\sum_{i=1}^{k} n_i N_A m_i (\overline{u_i^2})}{3V} \text{ where } N_A = \text{Avogadro's number}$$

Since molar $KE_{i,\,avg} = N_A\,(\frac{1}{2} m_i \overline{u_i^2})$, then the expression for total pressure can be written as:

$$P_{total} = \sum_{i=1}^{k} \frac{\frac{2}{3} n_i N_A (\frac{1}{2} m_i \overline{u_i^2})}{V} = \sum_{i=1}^{k} \frac{\frac{2}{3} n_i KE_{i,\,avg}}{V}$$

Assuming molar $KE_{i,\,avg}$ is proportional to T and is equal to $\frac{3}{2}$ RT, then:

$$P_{total} = \sum_{i=1}^{k} \frac{n_i RT}{V} = \sum_{i=1}^{k} P_i, \text{ since } P_i = \frac{n_i RT}{V}$$

This is Dalton's law of partial pressure. Note that no additional assumptions are necessary other than the postulates of the kinetic molecular theory and the conclusions drawn from the ideal gas law derivation.

129. $C_6H_{14}(l) + 19/2\ O_2(g) \rightarrow 6\ CO_2(g) + 7\ H_2O(l)$ or $2\ C_6H_{14}(l) + 19\ O_2(g) \rightarrow 12\ CO_2(g) + 14\ H_2O(l)$

$C_3H_8(l) + 5\ O_2(g) \rightarrow 3\ CO_2(g) + 4\ H_2O(l)$

$0.8339 \text{ g } CO_2 \times \dfrac{1 \text{ mol } CO_2}{44.009 \text{ g } CO_2} = 1.895 \times 10^{-2} \text{ mol } CO_2$

Let x = mass of C_6H_{14} and y = mass of C_3H_8, so x + y = 0.2759 g.

$1.895 \times 10^{-2} \text{ mol } CO_2 = 6 \times \text{mol } C_6H_{14} + 3 \times \text{mol } C_3H_8$

$1.895 \times 10^{-2} = \dfrac{6x}{86.177} + \dfrac{3y}{44.096}$; Rearranging:

$x + \dfrac{3y}{44.096} \times \dfrac{86.177}{6} = 1.895 \times 10^{-2} \times \dfrac{86.177}{6}, \ x + 0.9772\ y = 0.2722$

Solving:

$$x + y = 0.2759$$
$$\underline{-x - 0.9772\,y = -0.2722}$$
$$0.0288\,y = 0.0037, \quad y = 0.16 = \text{mass of } C_3H_8$$

$$\text{mass \% } C_3H_8 = \frac{0.16\text{ g}}{0.2759\text{ g}} \times 100 = 58\% \text{ } C_3H_8; \quad \% \text{ } C_6H_{14} = 42\%$$

130. Assuming 1.000 L of the hydrocarbon (C_xH_y), then the volume of products will be 4.000 L and the mass of products ($H_2O + CO_2$) will be:

$$1.391 \text{ g/L} \times 4.000 \text{ L} = 5.564 \text{ g products}$$

$$\text{moles } C_xH_y = n_{C_xH_y} = \frac{PV}{RT} = 0.0392 \text{ mol}$$

$$\text{moles products} = n_p = \frac{PV}{RT} = 0.196 \text{ mol}$$

$$C_xH_y + O_2 \rightarrow x\,CO_2 + y/2\,H_2O$$

Setting up two equations:

$$0.0392x + 0.0392(y/2) = 0.196$$

$$0.0392x(44.01 \text{ g/mol}) + 0.0392(y/2)(18.02 \text{ g/mol}) = 5.564 \text{ g}$$

Solving: $x = 2$ and $y = 6$, so the formula of the hydrocarbon is C_2H_6.

131. The reactions are:

$$C(s) + 1/2\,O_2(g) \rightarrow CO(g) \text{ and } C(s) + O_2(g) \rightarrow CO_2(g)$$

$$PV = nRT, \quad P = n\left(\frac{RT}{V}\right) = n \text{ (constant)}$$

Since the pressure has increased by 17.0%, then the number of moles of gas has also increased by 17.0%.

$$n_{final} = 1.170 \text{ } n_{initial} = 1.170 \text{ } (5.00) = 5.85 \text{ mol gas} = n_{O_2} + n_{CO} + n_{CO_2}$$

$$n_{CO} + n_{CO_2} = 5.00 \quad \text{(balancing moles of C)}$$

If all C was converted to CO_2, no O_2 would be left. If all C was converted to CO, we would get 5 mol CO and 2.5 mol excess O_2 in the reaction mixture. In the final mixture: $n_{CO} = 2n_{O_2}$

$$n_{O_2} + n_{CO} + n_{CO_2} = 5.85$$
$$\underline{-(n_{CO} + n_{CO_2} = 5.00)}$$
$$n_{O_2} = 0.85$$

$n_{CO} = 2n_{O_2} = 1.70$ mol CO; $1.70 + n_{CO_2} = 5.00$, $n_{CO_2} = 3.30$ mol CO_2

$$\chi_{CO} = \frac{1.70}{5.85} = 0.291; \quad \chi_{CO_2} = \frac{3.30}{5.85} = 0.564; \quad \chi_{O_2} = \frac{0.85}{5.85} = 0.145 \approx 0.15$$

132. nSO_2, nO_2, xHe where $n = mol\ SO_2 = mol\ O_2$ and $x = mol\ He$

a. $$d = \frac{mass}{V} = \frac{n \bullet MM}{V} = \frac{\frac{PV}{RT} \bullet MM}{V} = \frac{P \bullet MM}{RT}$$

$$1.924\ g/L = \frac{(1.000\ atm)(MM)}{(0.08206\ \frac{L\ atm}{mol\ K})(273.15\ K)}, \quad MM_{mixture} = 43.13 g/mol$$

Assume 1.000 total mol of mixture is present, then: $n + n + z = 1.000$

$(64.06\ g/mol)(n) + (32.00\ g/mol)\ (n) + (4.003\ g/mol)\ (z) = 43.13\ g$

$2n + z = 1.000$ and $96.06n + 4.003z = 43.13$

Solving: $n = 0.444$ mol and $z = 0.112$ mol

Thus, $\chi_{He} = 0.112\ mol/1.000\ mol = 0.112$

b. $2\ SO_2 + O_2 \rightarrow 2\ SO_3$

Initially, assume 0.444 mol SO_2, 0.444 mol O_2 and 0.112 mol He

Since SO_2 is limiting, we end with 0.222 mol O_2, 0.444 mol SO_3, and 0.112 mol He

Thus, $n_{init} = 1.000$ mol and $n_{final} = 0.778$ mol

$d = \frac{m}{V}$ but mass is constant.

Thus, $d \propto \frac{1}{V}$ and $V \propto n$, so, $d \propto \frac{1}{n}$.

$$\frac{n_1}{n_2} = \frac{1.000}{0.778} = \frac{d_2}{d_1}, d_2 = \left(\frac{1.000}{0.778}\right)(1.924\ g/L), d_2 = 2.47\ g/L$$

133.   a.   The reaction is: $CH_4(g) + 2\ O_2(g) \rightarrow CO_2(g) + 2\ H_2O(g)$

$$PV = nRT, \quad \frac{PV}{n} = RT = constant, \quad \frac{P_{CH_4}V_{CH_4}}{n_{CH_4}} = \frac{P_{air}V_{air}}{n_{air}}$$

The balanced equation requires 2 mol O_2 for every mol of CH_4 that reacts. For three times as much oxygen, we would need 6 mol O_2 per mol of CH_4 reacted $(n_{O_2} = 6\ n_{CH_4})$. Air is 21%

mol percent O_2, so $n_{O_2} = 0.21\ n_{air}$. Therefore, the mol of air we would need to delivery the excess O_2 is:

$$n_{O_2} = 0.21\ n_{air} = 6\ n_{CH_4}, \quad n_{air} = 29\ n_{CH_4}, \quad \frac{n_{air}}{n_{CH_4}} = 29$$

In one minute:

$$V_{air} = V_{CH_4} \times \frac{n_{air}}{n_{CH_4}} \times \frac{P_{CH_4}}{P_{air}} = 200.\ L \times 29 \times \frac{1.50\ atm}{1.00\ atm} = 8.7 \times 10^3\ L\ air/min$$

b.   If x moles of CH_4 were reacted, then 6 x mol O_2 were added, producing 0.950 x mol CO_2 and 0.050 x mol of CO. In addition, 2 x mol H_2O must be produced to balance the hydrogens.

$$CH_4(g) + 2\ O_2(g) \rightarrow CO_2(g) + 2\ H_2O(g); \quad CH_4(g) + 3/2\ O_2(g) \rightarrow CO(g) + 2\ H_2O(g)$$

Amount O_2 reacted:

$$0.950\ x\ mol\ CO_2 \times \frac{2\ mol\ O_2}{mol\ CO_2} = 1.90\ x\ mol\ O_2$$

$$0.050\ x\ mol\ CO \times \frac{1.5\ mol\ O_2}{mol\ CO} = 0.075\ x\ mol\ O_2$$

Amount of O_2 left in reaction mixture = 6.00 x - 1.90 x - 0.075 x = 4.03 x mol O_2

Amount of $N_2 = 6.00\ x\ mol\ O_2 \times \dfrac{79\ mol\ N_2}{21\ mol\ O_2} = 22.6\ x \approx 23\ x\ mol\ N_2$

The reaction mixture contains:

$$0.950\ x\ mol\ CO_2 + 0.050\ x\ mol\ CO + 4.03\ x\ mol\ O_2 + 2.00\ x\ mol\ H_2$$
$$+\ 23\ x\ mol\ N_2 = 30.\ x\ mol\ of\ gas\ total$$

$$\chi_{CO} = \frac{0.050\ x}{30.\ x} = 0.0017; \quad \chi_{CO_2} = \frac{0.950\ x}{30.\ x} = 0.032; \quad \chi_{O_2} = \frac{4.03\ x}{30.\ x} = 0.13$$

$$\chi_{H_2O} = \frac{2.00\ x}{30.\ x} = 0.067; \quad \chi_{N_2} = \frac{23\ x}{30.\ x} = 0.77$$

c.   The partial pressures are determined by $P = \chi P_{tot}$. Since $P_{tot} = 1.00$ atm, then $P_{CO} = 0.0017$ atm, P_{CO_2} = 0.032 atm, $P_{O_2} = 0.13$ atm, $P_{H_2O} = 0.067$ atm and $P_{N_2} = 0.77$ atm.

134. n_{total} = total number of mol of gas that have effused into the container

$$n_{total} = \frac{PV}{RT} = \frac{1.20 \times 10^{-6}\ atm \times 1.00\ L}{\dfrac{0.08206\ L\ atm}{mol\ K} \times 300.\ K} = 4.87 \times 10^{-8}\ mol$$

This amount has entered over a time span of 24 hours:

$$24 \text{ hr} \times \frac{60 \text{ min}}{1 \text{ hr}} \times \frac{60 \text{ s}}{1 \text{ min}} = 8.64 \times 10^4 \text{ s}$$

So: $\dfrac{4.87 \times 10^{-8} \text{ mol}}{8.64 \times 10^4 \text{ s}} = 5.64 \times 10^{-13}$ mol/s have entered the container.

$$\frac{5.64 \times 10^{-13} \text{ mol}}{\text{s}} \times \frac{6.022 \times 10^{23} \text{ molecules}}{\text{mol}} = 3.40 \times 10^{11} \text{ molecules/s}$$

The frequency of collisions of the gas with a given area is:

$$Z = A \left(\frac{N}{V} \right) \left(\frac{RT}{2\pi M} \right)^{1/2} ; \quad Z_{\text{total}} = \frac{3.40 \times 10^{11} \text{ molecules}}{\text{s}} = Z_{N_2} + Z_{O_2}$$

$$\frac{n}{V} = \frac{P}{RT} = \frac{1.00 \text{ atm}}{\dfrac{0.08206 \text{ L atm}}{\text{mol K}} \times 300. \text{ K}} = 4.06 \times 10^{-2} \text{ mol/L}$$

$$\frac{N}{V} = \frac{4.06 \times 10^{-2} \text{ mol}}{\text{L}} \times \frac{6.022 \times 10^{23} \text{ molecules}}{\text{mol}} \times \frac{1000 \text{ L}}{\text{m}^3} = 2.44 \times 10^{25} \text{ molecules/m}^3$$

For N_2: $\dfrac{N}{V} = (0.78)(2.44 \times 10^{25}) = 1.9 \times 10^{25}$ molecules/m^3

For O_2: $\dfrac{N}{V} = (0.22)(2.44 \times 10^{25}) = 5.4 \times 10^{24}$ molecules/m^3

$$Z_{\text{total}} = 3.40 \times 10^{11} \text{ molecules/s} = Z_{N_2} + Z_{O_2}$$

$$3.40 \times 10^{11} = A \left[1.9 \times 10^{25} \left(\frac{8.3145 \times 300.}{2\pi(28.0 \times 10^{-3})} \right)^{1/2} + 5.4 \times 10^{24} \left(\frac{8.3145 \times 300.}{2\pi(32.0 \times 10^{-3})} \right)^{1/2} \right]$$

$$\frac{3.40 \times 10^{11} \text{ molecules}}{\text{s}} = A \left[\frac{2.3 \times 10^{27} \text{ molecules}}{\text{m}^2 \text{ s}} + \frac{6.0 \times 10^{26} \text{ molecules}}{\text{m}^2 \text{ s}} \right]$$

$$A = \frac{3.40 \times 10^{11}}{2.9 \times 10^{27}} \text{ m}^2 = 1.2 \times 10^{-16} \text{ m}^2 = \pi r^2, \quad r = \left(\frac{1.2 \times 10^{-16} \text{ m}^2}{\pi} \right)^{1/2} = 6.2 \times 10^{-9} \text{ m} = 6.2 \text{ nm}$$

diameter of hole = $2r = 2(6.2 \times 10^{-9} \text{ m}) = 1.2 \times 10^{-8}$ m = 12 nm

135.   Each stage will give an enrichment of:

$$\frac{\text{Diff. Rate } {}^{12}CO_2}{\text{Diff. Rate } {}^{13}CO_2} = \left(\frac{M_{{}^{13}CO_2}}{M_{{}^{12}CO_2}} \right)^{1/2} = \left(\frac{45.001}{43.998} \right)^{1/2} = 1.0113$$

Since ${}^{12}CO_2$ moves slightly faster, each successive stage will have less ${}^{13}CO_2$.

$$\frac{99.90 \ ^{12}CO_2}{0.10 \ ^{13}CO_2} \times 1.0113^N = \frac{99.990 \ ^{12}CO_2}{0.010 \ ^{13}CO_2}$$

$$1.0113^N = \frac{9{,}999.0}{999.00} = 10.009 \quad \text{(carrying extra significant figures)}$$

$$N \log(1.0113) = \log(10.009), \quad N = \frac{1.000391}{4.88 \times 10^{-3}} = 2.05 \times 10^2 \approx 2.1 \times 10^2 \text{ stages are needed.}$$

136.   After the hole develops, assume each He that collides with the hole goes into the Rn side and that each Rn that collides with the hole goes into the He side. Assume no molecules return to the side in which they began. Initial moles of each gas:

$$n = \frac{PV}{RT} = \frac{(2.00 \times 10^{-6} \text{ atm}) \times 1.00 \text{ L}}{\dfrac{0.08206 \text{ L atm}}{\text{mol K}} \times 300. \text{ K}} = 8.12 \times 10^{-8} \text{ mol}$$

$$Z_{He} = A \times \frac{N}{V} \times \left(\frac{RT}{2\pi M} \right)^{1/2}, \quad \frac{N}{V} = \frac{P}{RT} \times N_A \times 1000 \text{ L/m}^3 \text{ and } A = \pi r^2$$

$$Z_{He} = \pi (1.00 \times 10^{-6} \text{ m})^2 \times \frac{2.00 \times 10^{-6}}{0.08206 \times 300.} \times (6.022 \times 10^{23}) \times 1000$$

$$\times \left(\frac{8.3145 \times 300.}{2\pi(4.003 \times 10^{-3})} \right)^{1/2} = 4.84 \times 10^{10} \text{ collisions/s}$$

Therefore, 4.84×10^{10} atoms/s leave He side.

$$10.0 \text{ hr} \times \frac{60 \text{ min}}{1 \text{ hr}} \times \frac{60 \text{ s}}{1 \text{ min}} \times \frac{4.84 \times 10^{10} \text{ atoms}}{\text{s}} = 1.74 \times 10^{15} \text{ atoms}$$

or $\dfrac{1.74 \times 10^{15} \text{ atoms}}{6.022 \times 10^{23} \text{ atoms/mol}} = 2.89 \times 10^{-9} \text{ mol He leave in 10.0 hr.}$

$$Z_{Rn} = \pi (1.00 \times 10^{-6} \text{ m})^2 \times \frac{2.00 \times 10^{-6}}{0.08206 \times 300.} \times (6.022 \times 10^{23}) \times 1000$$

$$\times \left(\frac{8.3145 \times 300.}{2\pi(222 \times 10^{-3})} \right)^{1/2} = 6.50 \times 10^9 \text{ collisions/s}$$

6.50×10^9 atoms/s leave Rn side.

$$3.60 \times 10^4 \text{ s} \times \frac{6.50 \times 10^9 \text{ atoms}}{\text{s}} \times \frac{1 \text{ mol}}{6.022 \times 10^{23} \text{ atoms}} = 3.89 \times 10^{-10} \text{ mol Rn leave in 10.0 hr.}$$

Side that began with He now contains:

$$8.12 \times 10^{-8} - 2.89 \times 10^{-9} = 7.83 \times 10^{-8} \text{ mol He} + 3.89 \times 10^{-10} \text{ mol Rn} = 7.87 \times 10^{-8} \text{ mol total}$$

The pressure in the He side is:

$$P = \frac{nRT}{V} = \frac{(7.87 \times 10^{-8} \text{ mol}) \times 0.08206 \text{ L atm K}^{-1} \text{mol}^{-1} \times 300. \text{ K}}{1.00 \text{ L}} = 1.94 \times 10^{-6} \text{ atm}$$

We can determine the pressure in the Rn chamber two ways. Since no gas has escaped and since the initial pressures were equal and the pressure in one of the sides decreased by 0.06×10^{-6} atm, then P in the second side must increase by 0.06×10^{-6} atm. So the pressure on the side that originally contained Rn is 2.06×10^{-6} atm. Or we can calculate P the same way as with He. The Rn side contains:

$$8.12 \times 10^{-8} - 3.89 \times 10^{-10} = 8.08 \times 10^{-8} \text{ mol Rn} + 2.89 \times 10^{-9} \text{ mol He} = 8.37 \times 10^{-8} \text{ mol total}$$

$$P = \frac{nRT}{V} = \frac{(8.37 \times 10^{-8} \text{ mol}) \times 0.08206 \text{ L atm K}^{-1} \text{mol}^{-1} \times 300. \text{ K}}{1.00 \text{ L}} = 2.06 \times 10^{-6} \text{ atm}$$

Marathon Problems

137.   We must determine the identities of element A and compound B in order to answer the questions. Use the first set of data to determine the identity of element A.

Mass N_2 = 659.452 g - 658.572 g = 0.880 g N_2

$$0.880 \text{ g N}_2 \times \frac{1 \text{ mol N}_2}{28.02 \text{ g N}_2} = 0.0314 \text{ mol N}_2$$

$$V = \frac{nRT}{P} = \frac{0.0314 \text{ mol} \times \dfrac{0.08206 \text{ L atm}}{\text{mol K}} \times 288 \text{ K}}{790. \text{ torr} \times \dfrac{1 \text{ atm}}{760 \text{ torr}}} = 0.714 \text{ L}$$

$$\text{moles of A} = n = \frac{\left(745 \text{ torr} \times \dfrac{1 \text{ atm}}{760 \text{ torr}}\right) \times 0.714 \text{ L}}{0.08206 \text{ L atm K}^{-1} \text{mol}^{-1} \times (273 + 26) \text{ K}} = 0.0285 \text{ mol A}$$

Mass of A = 660.59 - 658.572 g = 2.02 g A

$$\text{Molar mass of A} = \frac{2.02 \text{ g A}}{0.0285 \text{ mol A}} = 70.9 \text{ g/mol}$$

The only element that is a gas at 26°C and 745 torr and has a molar mass close to 70.9 g/mol is chlorine = Cl_2 = element A.

The remainder of the information is used to determine the formula of compound B. Assuming 100.00 g of B:

$$85.6 \text{ g C} \times \frac{1 \text{ mol C}}{12.01 \text{ g C}} = 7.13 \text{ mol C}; \quad \frac{7.13}{7.13} = 1.00$$

$$14.4 \text{ g H} \times \frac{1 \text{ mol H}}{1.008 \text{ g H}} = 14.3 \text{ mol H}; \quad \frac{14.3}{7.13} = 2.01$$

Empirical formula of B = CH_2; Molecular formula = C_xH_{2x} where x is a whole number.

The balanced combustion reaction of C_xH_{2x} with O_2 is:

$$C_xH_{2x}(g) + 3x/2 \ O_2(g) \rightarrow x \ CO_2(g) + x \ H_2O(l)$$

To determine the formula of C_xH_{2x}, we need to determine the actual moles of all species present.

Mass of $CO_2 + H_2O$ produced = 846.7 g - 765.3 g = 81.4 g

Since mol CO_2 = mol H_2O = x (see balanced equation), then:

$$81.4 \text{ g} = x \text{ mol } CO_2 \times \frac{44.01 \text{ g } CO_2}{\text{mol } CO_2} + x \text{ mol } H_2O \times \frac{18.02 \text{ g } H_2O}{\text{mol } H_2O}, \quad x = 1.31 \text{ mol}$$

$$\text{mol } O_2 \text{ reacted} = 1.31 \text{ mol } CO_2 \times \frac{1.5 \text{ mol } O_2}{\text{mol } CO_2} = 1.97 \text{ mol } O_2$$

From the data, we can calculate moles excess O_2 since only $O_2(g)$ remains after the combustion reaction has gone to completion.

$$n_{O_2} = \frac{PV}{RT} = \frac{6.02 \text{ atm} \times 10.68 \text{ L}}{0.08206 \text{ L atm K}^{-1}\text{mol}^{-1} \times (273 + 22) \text{ K}} = 2.66 \text{ mol excess } O_2$$

mol O_2 present initially = 1.97 mol + 2.66 mol = 4.63 mol O_2

$$\text{Total mol gaseous reactants before reaction} = \frac{PV}{RT} = \frac{11.98 \text{ atm} \times 10.68 \text{ L}}{0.08206 \times 295 \text{ K}} = 5.29 \text{ mol total}$$

mol C_xH_{2x} = 5.29 mol total - 4.63 mol O_2 = 0.66 mol C_xH_{2x}

Summarizing:

$$0.66 \text{ mol } C_xH_{2x} + 1.97 \text{ mol } O_2 \rightarrow 1.31 \text{ mol } CO_2 + 1.31 \text{ mol } H_2O$$

Dividing all quantities by 0.66 gives:

$$C_xH_{2x} + 3 \ O_2 \rightarrow 2 \ CO_2 + 2 \ H_2O$$

To balance the equation, C_xH_{2x} must be C_2H_4 = compound B.

a.   Now we can answer the questions. The reaction is:

$$C_2H_4(g) + Cl_2(g) \rightarrow C_2H_4Cl_2(g)$$
$$\quad \text{B} \quad + \quad \text{A} \quad\quad\quad \text{C}$$

$$\text{mol Cl}_2 = n = \frac{PV}{RT} = \frac{1.00 \text{ atm} \times 10.0 \text{ L}}{0.08206 \text{ L atm K}^{-1}\text{mol}^{-1} \times 273 \text{ K}} = 0.446 \text{ mol Cl}_2$$

$$\text{mol C}_2\text{H}_4 = n = \frac{PV}{RT} = \frac{1.00 \text{ atm} \times 8.60 \text{ L}}{0.08206 \text{ L atm K}^{-1}\text{mol}^{-1} \times 273 \text{ K}} = 0.384 \text{ mol C}_2\text{H}_4$$

Since a 1:1 mol ratio is required by the balanced reaction, then C_2H_4 is limiting.

$$\text{Mass C}_2\text{H}_4\text{Cl}_2 \text{ produced} = 0.384 \text{ mol C}_2\text{H}_4 \times \frac{1 \text{ mol C}_2\text{H}_4\text{Cl}_2}{\text{mol C}_2\text{H}_4} \times \frac{98.95 \text{ g}}{\text{mol C}_2\text{H}_4\text{Cl}_2} = 38.0 \text{ g C}_2\text{H}_4\text{Cl}_2$$

b. excess mol Cl_2 = 0.446 mol Cl_2 - 0.384 mol Cl_2 reacted = 0.062 mol Cl_2

$$P_{total} = \frac{n_{total}RT}{V}; \quad n_{total} = 0.384 \text{ mol C}_2\text{H}_4\text{Cl}_2 \text{ produced} + 0.062 \text{ mol Cl}_2 \text{ excess} = 0.446 \text{ mol}$$

$$V = 10.0 \text{ L} + 8.60 \text{ L} = 18.6 \text{ L}$$

$$P_{total} = \frac{0.446 \text{ mol} \times 0.08206 \text{ L atm K}^{-1}\text{mol}^{-1} \times 273 \text{ K}}{18.6 \text{ L}} = 0.537 \text{ atm}$$

138.   a.   Average molar mass of "air" = (0.79)(28.02 g/mol) + (0.21)(32.00 g/mol) = 28.86 g/mol
(carrying extra sig figs)

molar mass of helium = 4.003 g/mol

Thus, a given volume of air at a given set of conditions has a higher density than helium. We need to heat the air to greater than 25°C to lower the air density (by driving air out of the hot air balloon) until the density is the same as that for helium (at 25°C and 1.00 atm).

b.   To provide the same lift as the helium balloon (assume V = 1.00 L), the mass of air in the hot air balloon (V = 1.00 L) must be the same as that in the helium balloon.

$$PV = nRT = \left(\frac{\text{mass}}{\text{MM}}\right)(RT), \quad \text{mass} = \frac{(\text{MM})(PV)}{(RT)}, \quad \text{Solving: mass He} = 0.164 \text{ g}$$

$$\text{mass air} = 0.164 \text{ g} = \frac{(28.86 \text{ g/mol})(1.00 \text{ atm})(1.00 \text{ L})}{(0.08206\frac{\text{L atm}}{\text{mol K}})(T)}, \quad T = 2140 \text{ K}$$

CHAPTER SIX

CHEMICAL EQUILIBRIUM

Characteristics of Chemical Equilibrium

10.   a.   The rates of the forward and reverse reactions are equal.

   b.   There is no net change in the composition (as long as temperature is constant).

11. $2 NOCl(g) \rightleftharpoons 2 NO(g) + Cl_2(g)$ $K = 1.6 \times 10^{-5}$ mol/L

The expression for K is the product concentrations divided by the reactant concentrations. When K has a value much less than one, the product concentrations are relatively small and the reactant concentrations are relatively large.

$2 NO(g) \rightleftharpoons N_2(g) + O_2(g)$ $K = 1 \times 10^{31}$

When K has a value much greater than one, the product concentrations are relatively large and the reactant concentrations are relatively small. In both cases, however, the rate of the forward reaction equals the rate of the reverse reaction at equilibrium (this is a definition of equilibrium).

12.   No, equilibrium is a dynamic process. Both reactions:

   $H_2O + CO \rightarrow H_2 + CO_2$ and $H_2 + CO_2 \rightarrow H_2O + CO$

are occurring, but at equal rates. Thus, ^{14}C atoms will be distributed between CO and CO_2.

13.   No, it doesn't matter which direction the equilibrium position is reached. Both experiments will give the same equilibrium position since both experiments started with stoichiometric amounts of reactants or products.

14. $H_2O(g) + CO(g) \rightleftharpoons H_2(g) + CO_2(g)$ $K = \dfrac{[H_2][CO_2]}{[H_2O][CO]} = 2.0$

K is a unitless number since there is an equal number of moles of product gases as compared to moles of reactant gases in the balanced equation. Therefore, we can use units of molecules per liter instead of moles per liter to determine K.

By trial and error, if 3 molecules of CO react, then 3 molecules of H_2O must react, and 3 molecules each of H_2 and CO_2 are formed. We would have $6 - 3 = 3$ molecules CO, $8 - 3 = 5$ molecules H_2O, $0 + 3 = 3$ molecules H_2, and $0 + 3 = 3$ molecules CO_2 present. This will be an equilibrium mixture if $K = 2.0$:

$$K = \frac{\left(\dfrac{3 \text{ molecules } H_2}{L}\right)\left(\dfrac{3 \text{ molecules } CO_2}{L}\right)}{\left(\dfrac{5 \text{ molecules } H_2O}{L}\right)\left(\dfrac{3 \text{ molecules } CO}{L}\right)} = \frac{3}{5}$$

Since this mixture does not give a value of $K = 2.0$, this is not an equilibrium mixture. Let's try 4 molecules of CO reacting to reach equilibrium.

molecules CO remaining $= 6 - 4 = 2$ molecules CO;
molecules H_2O remaining $= 8 - 4 = 4$ molecules H_2O;
molecules H_2 present $= 0 + 4 = 4$ molecules H_2;
molecules CO_2 present $= 0 + 4 = 4$ molecules CO_2

$$K = \frac{\left(\dfrac{4 \text{ molecules } H_2}{L}\right)\left(\dfrac{4 \text{ molecules } CO_2}{L}\right)}{\left(\dfrac{4 \text{ molecules } H_2O}{L}\right)\left(\dfrac{2 \text{ molecules } CO}{L}\right)} = 2.0$$

Since $K = 2.0$ for this reaction mixture, we are at equilibrium.

15.   When equilibrium is reached, there is no net change in the amount of reactants and products present since the rates of the forward and reverse reactions are equal to each other. The first diagram has 4 A_2B molecules, 2 A_2 molecules and 1 B_2 molecule present. The second diagram has 2 A_2B molecules, 4 A_2 molecules, and 2 B_2 molecules. Therefore, the first diagram cannot represent equilibrium since there was a net change in reactants and products. Is the second diagram the equilibrium mixture? That depends on whether there is a net change between reactants and products when going from the second diagram to the third diagram. The third diagram contains the same number and type of molecules as the second diagram, so the second diagram is the first illustration that represents equilibrium.

The reaction container initially contained only A_2B. From the first diagram, 2 A_2 molecules and 1 B_2 molecule are present (along with 4 A_2B molecules). From the balanced reaction, these 2 A_2 molecules and 1 B_2 molecule were formed when 2 A_2B molecules decomposed. Therefore, the initial number of A_2B molecules present equals $4 + 2 = 6$ molecules A_2B.

The Equilibrium Constant

16. The equilibrium constant is a number that tells us the relative concentrations (pressures) of reactants and products at equilibrium. An equilibrium position is a set of concentrations that satisfy the equilibrium constant expression. More than one equilibrium position can satisfy the same equilibrium constant expression.

   Table 6.1 of the text illustrates this nicely. Each of the three experiments in Table 6.1 have different equilibrium positions; that is, each experiment has different equilibrium concentrations. However, when these equilibrium concentrations are inserted into the equilibrium constant expression, each experiment gives the same value for K. The equilibrium position depends on the initial concentrations one starts with. Since there are an infinite number of initial conditions, there are an infinite number of equilibrium positions. However, each of these infinite equilibrium positions will always give the same value for the equilibrium constant (assuming temperature is constant).

17. For the gas phase reaction a A + b B $\rightleftharpoons$ c C + d D:

   the equilibrium constant expression is: $K = \dfrac{[C]^c [D]^d}{[A]^a [B]^b}$

   and the reaction quotient has the same form: $Q = \dfrac{[C]^c [D]^d}{[A]^a [B]^b}$

   The difference is that in the expression for K we use equilibrium concentrations, i.e., [A], [B], [C] and [D] are all in equilibrium with each other. Any set of concentrations can be plugged into the reaction quotient expression. Typically, we plug in initial concentrations into the Q expression then compare the value of Q to K to see how far we are from equilibrium. If Q = K, then the reaction is at equilibrium with these concentrations. If Q ≠ K, then the reaction will have to shift either to products (Q < K) or to reactants (Q > K) to reach equilibrium.

18. The units for both reactions are: $\dfrac{(\text{molecules/cm}^3)}{(\text{molecules/cm}^3)(\text{molecules/cm}^3)} = \dfrac{\text{cm}^3}{\text{molecules}}$

   a. $K = \dfrac{1.26 \times 10^{-11} \text{ cm}^3}{\text{molecules}} \times \dfrac{1 \text{ L}}{1000 \text{ cm}^3} \times \dfrac{6.022 \times 10^{23} \text{ molecules}}{\text{mol}} = 7.59 \times 10^9 \text{ L/mol}$

   $K_P = K(RT)^{\Delta n}$, where Δn = moles gaseous products - moles gaseous reactants
   $\Delta n = 1 - 2 = -1$

   $K_p = \dfrac{7.59 \times 10^9 \text{ L/mol}}{\left(\dfrac{0.08206 \text{ L atm}}{\text{mol K}}\right) \times 300. \text{ K}} = 3.08 \times 10^8 \text{ atm}^{-1}$

   b. $K = \dfrac{2.09 \times 10^{-12} \text{ cm}^3}{\text{molecules}} \times \dfrac{1 \text{ L}}{1000 \text{ cm}^3} \times \dfrac{6.022 \times 10^{23} \text{ molecules}}{\text{mol}} = 1.26 \times 10^9 \text{ L/mol}$

   $K_P = K(RT)^{\Delta n}, \quad \Delta n = -1; \quad K_p = \dfrac{1.26 \times 10^9 \text{ L/mol}}{\left(\dfrac{0.08206 \text{ L atm}}{\text{mol K}}\right) \times 300. \text{ K}} = 5.12 \times 10^7 \text{ atm}^{-1}$

c. $K^* = \dfrac{[HO_2NO_2]}{[HO_2][NO_2]} = 1.26 \times 10^{-11}$ cm^3/molecules

$[HO_2NO_2] = (1.26 \times 10^{-11})(1.65 \times 10^{10})(6.00 \times 10^{12}) = 1.25 \times 10^{12}$ molecules/cm^3

19. $K_p = K(RT)^{\Delta n}$ where Δn = sum of gaseous product coefficients - sum of gaseous reactant coefficients. For this reaction, $\Delta n = 1 - 2 = -1$.

$K_p = \dfrac{3.7 \times 10^9 \text{ L}}{\text{mol}} \times \left(\dfrac{0.08206 \text{ L atm}}{\text{mol K}} \times 298 \text{ K} \right)^{-1} = 1.5 \times 10^8$ atm^{-1}

20. $H_2(g) + Br_2(g) \rightleftharpoons 2\,HBr(g)$ $K_p = \dfrac{P^2_{HBr}}{(P_{H_2})(P_{Br_2})} = 3.5 \times 10^4$

a. $HBr \rightleftharpoons 1/2\,H_2 + 1/2\,Br_2$ $K_p' = \dfrac{(P_{H_2})^{1/2}(P_{Br_2})^{1/2}}{P_{HBr}} = \left(\dfrac{1}{K_p}\right)^{1/2} = \left(\dfrac{1}{3.5 \times 10^4}\right)^{1/2} = 5.3 \times 10^{-3}$

b. $2\,HBr \rightleftharpoons H_2 + Br_2$ $K_p'' = \dfrac{(P_{H_2})(P_{Br_2})}{P^2_{HBr}} = \dfrac{1}{K_p} = \dfrac{1}{3.5 \times 10^4} = 2.9 \times 10^{-5}$

c. $1/2\,H_2 + 1/2\,Br_2 \rightleftharpoons HBr$ $K_p''' = \dfrac{P_{HBr}}{(P_{H_2})^{1/2}(P_{Br_2})^{1/2}} = (K_p)^{1/2} = 190$

21. $[NO] = \dfrac{4.5 \times 10^{-3} \text{ mol}}{3.0 \text{ L}} = 1.5 \times 10^{-3}\,M;\;\; [Cl_2] = \dfrac{2.4 \text{ mol}}{3.0 \text{ L}} = 0.80\,M$

$[NOCl] = \dfrac{1.0 \text{ mol}}{3.0 \text{ L}} = 0.33\,M;\;\; K = \dfrac{[NO]^2[Cl_2]}{[NOCl]^2} = \dfrac{(1.5 \times 10^{-3})^2(0.80)}{(0.33)^2} = 1.7 \times 10^{-5}\,M$

22. $K_P = \dfrac{P^2_{NOBr}}{P^2_{NO} \times P_{Br_2}},\;\; 109 = \dfrac{(0.0768)^2}{P^2_{NO} \times 0.0159},\;\; P_{NO} = 0.0583$ atm

23. $K_p = \dfrac{P^4_{H_2}}{P^4_{H_2O}};\;\; P_{tot} = P_{H_2O} + P_{H_2},\;\; 36.3 \text{ torr} = 15.0 \text{ torr} + P_{H_2},\;\; P_{H_2} = 21.3$ torr

Since l atm = 760 torr, then: $K_p = \dfrac{\left(21.3 \text{ torr} \times \dfrac{1 \text{ atm}}{760 \text{ torr}} \right)^4}{\left(15.0 \text{ torr} \times \dfrac{1 \text{ atm}}{760 \text{ torr}} \right)^4} = 4.07$

Note: Solids and pure liquids are not included in K expressions.

24. $NH_4Cl(s) \rightleftharpoons NH_3(g) + HCl(g)$ $K_P = P_{NH_3} \times P_{HCl}$

For this system to reach equilibrium, some of the $NH_4Cl(s)$ decomposes to form equal moles of $NH_3(g)$ and $HCl(g)$ at equilibrium. Since mol HCl = mol NH_3, then the partial pressures of each gas must be equal to each other.

At equilibrium: $P_{total} = P_{NH_3} + P_{HCl}$ and $P_{NH_3} = P_{HCl}$.

$P_{total} = 4.4$ atm $= 2P_{NH_3}$, 2.2 atm $= P_{NH_3} = P_{HCl}$; $K_p = (2.2$ atm$)(2.2$ atm$) = 4.8$ atm^2

25. $PCl_5(g) \rightleftharpoons PCl_3(g) + Cl_2(g)$ $K_p = \dfrac{P_{PCl_3} \times P_{Cl_2}}{P_{PCl_5}}$

To determine K_p, we must determine the equilibrium partial pressures of each gas. Initially, $P_{PCl_5} =$ 0.50 atm and $P_{PCl_3} = P_{Cl_2} = 0$ atm. To reach equilibrium some of the PCl_5 reacts to produce some PCl_3 and Cl_2, all in a 1:1 mol ratio. We must determine the change in partial pressures necessary to reach equilibrium. Since moles $\propto$ P at constant V and T, then if we let x = atm of PCl_5 that reacts to reach equilibrium, this will produce x atm of PCl_3 and x atm of Cl_2 at equilibrium. The equilibrium partial pressures of each gas will be the initial partial pressure of each gas plus the change necessary to reach equilibrium. The equilibrium partial pressures are:

$P_{PCl_5} = 0.50$ atm - x, $P_{PCl_3} = P_{Cl_2} = $ x

Now we solve for x using the information in the problem:

$P_{total} = P_{PCl_5} + P_{PCl_3} + P_{Cl_2}$,   0.84 atm $= 0.50 - x + x + x$,   0.84 atm $= 0.50 + x$,   x $= 0.34$ atm

The equilibrium partial pressures are:

$P_{PCl_5} = 0.50 - 0.34 = 0.16$ atm, $P_{PCl_3} = P_{Cl_2} = 0.34$ atm

$K_p = \dfrac{P_{PCl_3} \times P_{Cl_2}}{P_{PCl_5}} = \dfrac{(0.34)\,(0.34)}{(0.16)} = 0.72$ atm

$K = \dfrac{K_p}{(RT)^{\Delta n}}$, $\Delta n = 2 - 1 = 1$; $K_p = \dfrac{0.72}{(0.08206)\,(523)} = 0.017$ mol/L

26. $S_8(g) \rightleftharpoons 4\,S_2(g)$ $K_P = \dfrac{P_{S_2}^4}{P_{S_8}}$

Initially: $P_{S_8} = 1.00$ atm and $P_{S_2} = 0$ atm

Change: Since 0.25 atm of S_8 remain at equilibrium, then 1.00 atm - 0.25 atm = 0.75 atm of S_8 must have reacted in order to reach equilibrium. Since there is a 4:1 mol ratio between S_2 and S_8 (from the balanced reaction), then 4(0.75 atm) = 3.0 atm of S_2 must have been produced when the reaction went to equilibrium (moles and pressure are directly related at constant T and V).

Equilibrium: P_{S_8} = 0.25 atm, P_{S_2} = 0 + 3.0 atm = 3.0 atm; Solving for K_p:

$$K_P = \frac{(3.0)^4}{0.25} = 3.2 \times 10^2$$

27.   When solving equilibrium problems, a common method to summarize all the information in the problem is to set up a table. We commonly call this table the ICE table since it summarizes initial concentrations, changes that must occur to reach equilibrium and equilibrium concentrations (the sum of the initial and change columns). For the change column, we will generally use the variable x which will be defined as the amount of reactant (or product) that must react to reach equilibrium. In this problem, the reaction must shift right to reach equilibrium since there are no products present initially. Therefore, x is defined as the amount of reactant SO_3 that reacts to reach equilibrium and we use the coefficients in the balanced equation to relate the net change in SO_3 to the net change in SO_2 and O_2. The general ICE table for this problem is:

$$2\,SO_3(g) \;\rightleftharpoons\; 2\,SO_2(g) \;+\; O_2(g) \qquad K = \frac{[SO_2]^2[O_2]}{[SO_3]^2}$$

Initial	12.0 mol/3.0 L	0	0
	Let x mol/L of SO_3 react to reach equilibrium		
Change	$-x$ $\rightarrow$	$+x$	$+x/2$
Equil.	$4.0 - x$	x	$x/2$

From the problem, we are told that the equilibrium SO_2 concentration is 3.0 mol/3.0 L = 1.0 M ($[SO_2]_e$ = 1.0 M). From the ICE table set-up, $[SO_2]_e = x$ so x = 1.0. Solving for the other equilibrium concentrations: $[SO_3]_e$ = 4.0 - x = 4.0 - 1.0 = 3.0 M; $[O_2]$ = $x/2$ = 1.0/2 = 0.50 M.

$$K = \frac{[SO_2]^2[O_2]}{[SO_3]^2} = \frac{(1.0\,M)^2\,(0.50\,M)}{(3.0\,M)^2} = 0.056 \text{ mol/L}$$

Alternate Method: Fractions in the change column can be avoided (if you want) be defining x differently. If we were to let $2x$ mol/L of SO_3 react to reach equilibrium then the ICE table set-up is:

$$2\,SO_3(g) \;\rightleftharpoons\; 2\,SO_2(g) \;+\; O_2(g) \qquad K = \frac{[SO_2]^2[O_2]}{[SO_3]^2}$$

Initial	4.0 M	0	0
	Let $2x$ mol/L of SO_3 react to reach equilibrium		
Change	$-2x$ $\rightarrow$	$+2x$	$+x$
Equil.	$4.0 - 2x$	$2x$	x

Solving: $2x = [SO_2]_e$ = 1.0 M, x = 0.50 M; $[SO_3]_e$ = 4.0 - 2(0.50) = 3.0 M; $[O_2]_e = x$ = 0.50 M

These are exactly the same equilibrium concentrations as solved for previously, thus K will be the same (as it must be). The moral of the story is define x in a manner that is most comfortable for you. Your final answer is independent of how you define x initially.

Equilibrium Calculations

28. $2 \, NO(g) \rightleftharpoons N_2(g) + O_2(g)$ $K = \dfrac{[N_2][O_2]}{[NO]^2} = 2.4 \times 10^3$;   Since $\Delta n = 0$, then $K = K_p$.

Use the reaction quotient Q to determine which way the reaction shifts to reach equilibrium. For the reaction quotient, initial concentrations given in a problem are used to calculate the value for Q. If $Q < K$, then the reaction shifts right to reach equilibrium. If $Q > K$, then the reaction shifts left to reach equilibrium. If $Q = K$, then the reaction does not shift in either direction since the reaction is at equilibrium.

a. $[N_2] = \dfrac{2.0 \text{ mol}}{1.0 \text{L}} = 2.0 \, M$; $[O_2] = \dfrac{2.6 \text{ mol}}{1.0 \text{L}} = 2.6 \, M$; $[NO] = \dfrac{0.024 \text{ mol}}{1.0 \text{ L}} = 0.024 \, M$

$$Q = \frac{[N_2]_o[O_2]_o}{[NO]_o^2} = \frac{(2.0 \, M)(2.6 \, M)}{(0.024 \, M)^2} = 9.0 \times 10^3$$

$Q > K$ so the reaction shifts left to produce more reactants in order to reach equilibrium.

b. $[N_2] = \dfrac{0.62 \text{ mol}}{2.0 \text{ L}} = 0.31 \, M$; $[O_2] = \dfrac{4.0 \text{ mol}}{2.0 \text{ L}} = 2.0 \, M$; $[NO] = \dfrac{0.032 \text{ mol}}{2.0 \text{ L}} = 0.016 \, M$

$$Q = \frac{(0.31 \, M)(2.0 \, M)}{(0.016 \, M)^2} = 2.4 \times 10^3 = K; \text{ at equilibrium}$$

c. $[N_2] = \dfrac{2.4 \text{ mol}}{3.0 \text{ L}} = 0.80 \, M$; $[O_2] = \dfrac{1.7 \text{ mol}}{3.0 \text{ L}} = 0.57 \, M$; $[NO] = \dfrac{0.060 \text{ mol}}{3.0 \text{ L}} = 0.020 \, M$

$$Q = \frac{(0.80 \, M)(0.57 \, M)}{(0.020 \, M)^2} = 1.1 \times 10^3 < K; \text{ Reaction shifts right to reach equilibrium.}$$

d. $Q = \dfrac{P_{N_2} \times P_{O_2}}{P_{NO}^2} = \dfrac{(0.11 \text{ atm})(2.0 \text{ atm})}{(0.010 \text{ atm})^2} = 2.2 \times 10^3$

$Q < K_p \, (2.4 \times 10^3)$ so the reaction shifts right to reach equilibrium.

e. $Q = \dfrac{(0.36 \text{ atm})(0.67 \text{ atm})}{(0.0078 \text{ atm})^2} = 4.0 \times 10^3 > K_p$; Reaction shifts left to reach equilibrium.

f. $Q = \dfrac{(0.51 \text{ atm})(0.18 \text{ atm})}{(0.0062 \text{ atm})^2} = 2.4 \times 10^3 = K_p$; at equilbrium

29. $CH_3CO_2H + C_2H_5OH \rightleftharpoons CH_3CO_2C_2H_5 + H_2O$ $K = \dfrac{[CH_3CO_2C_2H_5]\,[H_2O]}{[CH_3CO_2H]\,[C_2H_5OH]} = 2.2$

a. $Q = \dfrac{[CH_3CO_2C_2H_5]_o\,[H_2O]_o}{[CH_3CO_2H]_o\,[C_2H_5OH]_o} = \dfrac{(0.22\ M)\,(0.10\ M)}{(0.010\ M)\,(0.010\ M)} = 220 > K;$

Reaction will shift left to reach equilibrium since Q > K, so the concentration of water will decrease.

b. $Q = \dfrac{(0.22)\,(0.0020)}{(0.0020)\,(0.10)} = 2.2 = K;$ Reaction is at equilibrium since Q = K, so the concentration of water will remain the same.

c. $Q = \dfrac{(0.88)\,(0.12)}{(0.044)\,(6.0)} = 0.40 < K;$ Since Q < K, the concentration of water will increase since the reaction shifts right to reach equilibrium.

d. $Q = \dfrac{(4.4)\,(4.4)}{(0.88)\,(10.0)} = 2.2 = K;$ At equilibrium so the water concentration is unchanged.

e. $K = 2.2 = \dfrac{(2.0\ M)\,[H_2O]}{(0.10\ M)\,(5.0\ M)},$ $[H_2O] = 0.55\ M$

f.   Water is a product of the reaction, but it is not the solvent. Thus, the concentration of water must be included in the equilibrium expression since it is a solute in the reaction. Only when water is the solvent do we not include it in the equilibrium expression.

30. $CaCO_3(s) \rightleftharpoons CaO(s) + CO_2(g)$ $K_P = P_{CO_2} = 1.04$ atm

We only need to calculate the initial partial pressure of CO_2 and compare this value to 1.04 atm. At this temperature, all CO_2 will be in the gas phase.

a. $PV = nRT,\ \ Q = P_{CO_2} = \dfrac{n_{CO_2}RT}{V} = \dfrac{\dfrac{58.4\ g\ CO_2}{44.01\ g/mol} \times \dfrac{0.08206\ L\ atm}{mol\ K} \times 1173\ K}{50.0\ L} = 2.55\ atm > K_p$

Reaction will shift to the left since Q > K_p; the mass of CaO will decrease.

b. $Q = P_{CO_2} = \dfrac{(23.76)\,(0.08206)\,(1173)}{(44.01)\,(50.0)} = 1.04\ atm = K_p$

At equilibrium since Q = K_p; mass of CaO will not change.

c.   Mass of CO_2 is the same as in part b. P = 1.04 atm = K_P. At equilibrium; mass of CaO will not change.

d. $Q = P_{CO_2} = \dfrac{(4.82)\,(0.08206)\,(1173)}{(44.01)\,(50.0)} = 0.211\ atm < K_p$

Reaction will shift to the right since Q < K_p; the mass of CaO will increase.

31. $H_2O(g) + Cl_2O(g) \rightleftharpoons 2 \, HOCl(g)$ $K = 0.090 = \dfrac{[HOCl]^2}{[H_2O] \, [Cl_2O]}$

a.   The initial concentrations of H_2O and Cl_2O are:

$$\dfrac{1.0 \, g \, H_2O}{1.0 \, L} \times \dfrac{1 \, mol}{18.0 \, g} = 5.6 \times 10^{-2} \, mol/L; \quad \dfrac{2.0 \, g \, Cl_2O}{1.0 \, L} \times \dfrac{1 \, mol}{86.9 \, g} = 2.3 \times 10^{-2} \, mol/L$$

Since only reactants are present initially, the reaction must proceed to the right to reach equilibrium. Summarizing the problem in a table:

	$H_2O(g)$	+	$Cl_2O(g)$	$\rightleftharpoons$	$2 \, HOCl(g)$
Initial	$5.6 \times 10^{-2} \, M$		$2.3 \times 10^{-2} \, M$		0
	x mol/L of H_2O reacts to reach equilibrium				
Change	$-x$		$-x$	$\rightarrow$	$+2x$
Equil.	$5.6 \times 10^{-2} - x$		$2.3 \times 10^{-2} - x$		$2x$

$K = 0.090 = \dfrac{(2x)^2}{(5.6 \times 10^{-2} - x)(2.3 \times 10^{-2} - x)}, \quad 1.16 \times 10^{-4} - 7.11 \times 10^{-3} \, x + 0.090 \, x^2 = 4 \, x^2$

$3.91 \, x^2 + 7.11 \times 10^{-3} \, x - 1.16 \times 10^{-4} = 0$ (We carried extra significant figures.)

Solving using the quadratic formula (see Appendix 1.4 of the text):

$$x = \dfrac{-7.11 \times 10^{-3} \pm (5.06 \times 10^{-5} + 1.81 \times 10^{-3})^{1/2}}{7.82} = 4.6 \times 10^{-3} \, M \text{ or } -6.4 \times 10^{-3} \, M$$

A negative answer makes no physical sense; we can't have less than nothing.
So $x = 4.6 \times 10^{-3} \, M$.

$[HOCl] = 2x = 9.2 \times 10^{-3} \, M; \quad [Cl_2O] = 2.3 \times 10^{-2} - x = 0.023 - 0.0046 = 1.8 \times 10^{-2} \, M$

$[H_2O] = 5.6 \times 10^{-2} - x = 0.056 - 0.0046 = 5.1 \times 10^{-2} \, M$

b.

	$H_2O(g)$	+	$Cl_2O(g)$	$\rightleftharpoons$	$2 \, HOCl(g)$
Initial	0		0		$1.0 \, mol/2.0 \, L = 0.50 \, M$
	$2x$ mol/L of HOCl reacts to reach equilibrium				
Change	$+x$		$+x$	$\leftarrow$	$-2x$
Equil.	x		x		$0.50 - 2x$

$K = 0.090 = \dfrac{[HOCl]^2}{[H_2O] \, [Cl_2O]} = \dfrac{(0.50 - 2x)^2}{x^2}$

The expression is a perfect square, so we can take the square root of each side:

$$0.30 = \dfrac{0.50 - 2x}{x}, \quad 0.30 \, x = 0.50 - 2x, \quad 2.30 \, x = 0.50$$

$x = 0.217 \, M$ (We carried extra significant figures.)

$x = [H_2O] = [Cl_2O] = 0.217 = 0.22 \, M; \quad [HOCl] = 0.50 - 2x = 0.50 - 0.434 = 0.07 \, M$

32. $K = \dfrac{[HF]^2}{[H_2][F_2]} = \dfrac{(0.400\ M)^2}{(0.0500\ M)\ (0.0100\ M)} = 320.;\quad 0.200\ mol\ F_2/5.00\ L = 0.0400\ M\ F_2$ added

After F_2 has been added, the concentrations of species present are: $[HF] = 0.400\ M$, $[H_2] = [F_2] =$ $0.0500\ M.$ $Q = (0.400)^2 / (0.0500)^2 = 64.0;$ Since $Q < K$, then the reaction will shift right to reestablish equilibrium.

$$H_2(g) \quad + \quad F_2(g) \quad \rightleftharpoons \quad 2\ HF(g)$$

Initial	0.0500 M	0.0500 M	0.400 M

x mol/L of F_2 reacts to reach equilibrium

Change	$-x$	$-x$	$\rightarrow$	$+2x$
Equil.	0.0500 $-x$	0.0500 $-x$		0.400 $+ 2x$

$K = 320. = \dfrac{(0.400 + 2x)^2}{(0.0500 - x)^2}$; Taking the square root of each side:

$17.9 = \dfrac{0.400 + 2x}{0.0500 - x},$ $0.895 - 17.9\,x = 0.400 + 2x,$ $19.9\,x = 0.495,$ $x = 0.0249$ mol/L

$[HF] = 0.400 + 2(0.0249) = 0.450\ M;$ $[H_2] = [F_2] = 0.0500 - 0.0249 = 0.0251\ M$

33. $2\ SO_2(g) \quad + \quad O_2(g) \quad \rightleftharpoons \quad 2\ SO_3(g) \quad K_p = 0.25$

Initial	0.50 atm	0.50 atm	0

$2x$ atm of SO_2 reacts to reach equilibrium

Change	$-2x$	$-x$	$\rightarrow$	$+2x$
Equil.	0.50 - 2x	0.50 - x		2x

$K_p = 0.25 = \dfrac{P_{SO_3}^2}{P_{SO_2}^2 \times P_{O_2}} = \dfrac{(2x)^2}{(0.50 - 2x)^2(0.50 - x)}$

This will give a cubic equation. Graphing calculators can be used to solve this expression. If you don't have a graphing calculator, an alternative method for solving a cubic equation is to use the method of successive approximations (see Appendix 1.4 of the text). The first step is to guess a value for x. Since the value of K is small (K < 1), then not much of the forward reaction will occur to reach equilibrium. This tells us that x is small. Lets guess that $x = 0.050$ atm. Now we take this estimated value for x and substitute it into the equation everywhere that x appears except for one. For equilibrium problems, we will substitute the estimated value for x into the denominator, then solve for the numerator value of x. We continue this process until the estimated value of x and the calculated value of x converge on the same number. This is the same answer we would get if we were to solve the cubic equation exactly. Applying the method of successive approximations and carrying extra significant figures:

$$\dfrac{4x^2}{[0.50 - 2(0.050)]^2\ [0.50 - (0.050)]} = \dfrac{4x^2}{(0.40)^2(0.45)} = 0.25,\ x = 0.067$$

$$\dfrac{4x^2}{[0.50 - 2(0.067)]^2\ [0.50 - (0.067)]} = \dfrac{4x^2}{(0.366)^2(0.433)} = 0.25,\ x = 0.060$$

$$\frac{4x^2}{(0.38)^2(0.44)} = 0.25, \ x = 0.063; \quad \frac{4x^2}{(0.374)^2(0.437)} = 0.25, \ x = 0.062$$

The next trial gives the same value for $x = 0.062$ atm. We are done except for determining the equilibrium concentrations. They are:

$$P_{SO_2} = 0.50 - 2x = 0.50 - 2(0.062) = 0.376 = 0.38 \text{ atm}$$

$$P_{O_2} = 0.50 - x = 0.438 = 0.44 \text{ atm}; \ P_{SO_3} = 2x = 0.124 = 0.12 \text{ atm}$$

34.   Since only reactants are present initially, the reaction must proceed to the right to reach equilibrium. Summarizing the problem in a table:

$$N_2(g) \quad + \quad O_2(g) \quad \rightleftharpoons \quad 2\ NO(g) \quad K_p = 0.050$$

Initial	0.80 atm	0.20 atm	0
	x atm of N_2 reacts to reach equilibrium		
Change	$-x$	$-x$ $\rightarrow$	$+2x$
Equil.	$0.80 - x$	$0.20 - x$	$2x$

$$K_p = 0.050 = \frac{P_{NO}^2}{P_{N_2} \times P_{O_2}} = \frac{(2x)^2}{(0.80 - x)(0.20 - x)}, \ 0.050(0.16 - 1.00\ x + x^2) = 4\ x^2$$

$$4\ x^2 = 8.0 \times 10^{-3} - 0.050\ x + 0.050\ x^2, \ 3.95\ x^2 + 0.050\ x - 8.0 \times 10^{-3} = 0$$

Solving using the quadratic formula (see Appendix 1.4 of the text):

$$x = \frac{-b \pm (b^2 - 4ac)^{1/2}}{2a} = \frac{-0.050 \pm [(0.050)^2 - 4(3.95)(-8.0 \times 10^{-3})]^{1/2}}{2(3.95)}$$

$x = 3.9 \times 10^{-2}$ atm or $x = -5.2 \times 10^{-2}$ atm; Only $x = 3.9 \times 10^{-2}$ atm makes sense (x cannot be negative), so the equilibrium NO concentration is:

$$P_{NO} = 2x = 2(3.9 \times 10^{-2} \text{ atm}) = 7.8 \times 10^{-2} \text{ atm}$$

35.   a.   The reaction must proceed to products to reach equilibrium since only reactants are present initially. Summarizing the problem in a table:

$$2\ NOCl(g) \quad \rightleftharpoons \quad 2\ NO(g) \quad + \quad Cl_2(g) \quad K = 1.6 \times 10^{-5}$$

Initial	$\dfrac{2.0 \text{ mol}}{2.0 \text{ L}} = 1.0\ M$	0	0
	$2x$ mol/L of NOCl reacts to reach equilibrium		
Change	$-2x$ $\rightarrow$	$+2x$	$+x$
Equil.	$1.0 - 2x$	$2x$	x

$$K = 1.6 \times 10^{-5} = \frac{[NO]^2[Cl_2]}{[NOCl]^2} = \frac{(2x)^2\ (x)}{(1.0 - 2x)^2}$$

If we assume that $1.0 - 2x \approx 1.0$ (from the small size of K, we know that the product concentrations will be small so x will be small), then:

$$1.6 \times 10^{-5} = \frac{4x^3}{1.0^2}, \quad x = 1.6 \times 10^{-2} \ M; \ \text{Now we must check the assumption.}$$

$1.0 - 2x = 1.0 - 2(0.016) = 0.97 = 1.0$ (to proper significant figures)

Our error is about 3%, i.e., $2x$ is 3.2% of 1.0 M. Generally, if the error we introduce by making simplifying assumptions is less than 5%, we go no further, the assumption is said to be valid. We call this the 5% rule. Solving for the equilibrium concentrations:

$$[NO] = 2x = 0.032 \ M; \quad [Cl_2] = x = 0.016 \ M; \quad [NOCl] = 1.0 - 2x = 0.97 \ M \approx 1.0 \ M$$

Note: If we were to solve this cubic equation exactly (a longer process), we get $x = 0.016$. This is the exact same answer we determined by making a simplifying assumption. We saved time and energy. Whenever K is a very small value, always make the assumption that x is small. If the assumption introduces an error of less than 5%, then the answer you calculated making the assumption will be considered the correct answer.

b. There is a little trick we can use to solve this problem in order to avoid solving a cubic equation. Since K for this reaction is very small (K << 1), then the reaction will contain mostly reactants at equilibrium (the equilibrium position lies far to the left). We will let the products react to completion by the reverse reaction, then we will solve the forward equilibrium problem to determine the equilibrium concentrations. Summarizing these steps in a table:

	2 NOCl(g)	$\rightleftharpoons$	2 NO(g)	+	Cl$_2$(g)	$K = 1.6 \times 10^{-5}$
Before	0		2.0 M		1.0 M	
	Let 1.0 mol/L Cl$_2$ react completely.					(K is small, reactants dominate.)
Change	+2.0	$\leftarrow$	-2.0		-1.0	React completely
After	2.0		0		0	New initial conditions
	2x mol/L of NOCl reacts to reach equilibrium					
Change	-2x	$\rightarrow$	+2x		+x	
Equil.	2.0 - 2x		2x		x	

$$K = 1.6 \times 10^{-5} = \frac{(2x)^2 (x)}{(2.0 - 2x)^2} \approx \frac{4x^3}{2.0^2} \ \text{(assuming } 2.0 - 2x \approx 2.0\text{)}$$

$x^3 = 1.6 \times 10^{-5}, \quad x = 2.5 \times 10^{-2} \ M; \ \text{Assumption good by the 5% rule (2x is 2.5% of 2.0).}$

$[NOCl] = 2.0 - 0.050 = 1.95 \ M = 2.0 \ M; \quad [NO] = 0.050 \ M; \quad [Cl_2] = 0.025 \ M$

Note: If we do not break this problem into two parts (a stoichiometric part and an equilibrium part), then we are faced with solving a cubic equation. The set-up would be:

	2 NOCl	$\rightleftharpoons$	2 NO	+	Cl$_2$
Initial	0		2.0 M		1.0 M
Change	+2y	$\leftarrow$	-2y		-y
Equil.	2y		2.0 - 2y		1.0 - y

$1.6 \times 10^{-5} = \dfrac{(2.0 - 2y)^2 \, (1.0 - y)}{(2y)^2}$;   If we say that y is small to simplify the problem, then:

$1.6 \times 10^{-5} = \dfrac{2.0^2}{4y^2}$;   We get $y = 250$.   This is impossible!

To solve this equation, we cannot make any simplifying assumptions; we have to find a way to solve a cubic equation. Or, we can use some chemical common sense and solve the problem the easier way.

c. $2 \, NOCl(g) \;\rightleftharpoons\; 2 \, NO(g) \;+\; Cl_2(g)$

Initial	1.0 M	1.0 M	0

2x mol/L NOCl reacts to reach equilibrium

Change	-2x	$\rightarrow$	+2x	+x
Equil.	1.0 - 2x		1.0 + 2x	x

$1.6 \times 10^{-5} = \dfrac{(1.0 + 2x)^2 \, (x)}{(1.0 - 2x)^2} \approx \dfrac{(1.0)^2(x)}{(1.0)^2}$ (Assuming $2x \ll 1.0$)

$x = 1.6 \times 10^{-5} \, M$; Assumptions are great ($2x$ is 3.2×10^{-3} % of 1.0).

$[Cl_2] = 1.6 \times 10^{-5} \, M$ and $[NOCl] = [NO] = 1.0 \, M$

d. $2 \, NOCl(g) \;\rightleftharpoons\; 2 \, NO(g) \;+\; Cl_2(g)$

Before	0	3.0 M	1.0 M

Let 1.0 mol/L Cl_2 react completely.

Change	+2.0	$\leftarrow$	-2.0	-1.0	React completely
After	2.0		1.0	0	New Initial

2x mol/L NOCl reacts to reach equilibrium

Change	-2x	$\rightarrow$	+2x	+x
Equil.	2.0 - 2x		1.0 + 2x	x

$1.6 \times 10^{-5} = \dfrac{(1.0 + 2x)^2 \, (x)}{(2.0 - 2x)^2} \approx \dfrac{x}{4.0}$; Solving: $x = 6.4 \times 10^{-5} \, M$

Assumptions great ($2x$ is 1.3×10^{-2} % of 1.0).

$[Cl_2] = 6.4 \times 10^{-5} \, M$; $[NOCl] = 2.0 \, M$; $[NO] = 1.0 \, M$

e. $2 \, NOCl(g) \;\rightleftharpoons\; 2 \, NO(g) \;+\; Cl_2(g)$

Before	2.0 M	2.0 M	1.0 M

Let 1.0 mol/L Cl_2 react completely.

Change	+2.0	$\leftarrow$	-2.0	-1.0	React completely
After	4.0		0	0	New Initial

2x mol/L NOCl reacts to reach equilibrium

Change	-2x	$\rightarrow$	+2x	+x
Equil.	4.0 - 2x		2x	x

$$1.6 \times 10^{-5} = \frac{(2x)^2(x)}{(4.0-2x)^2} \approx \frac{4x^3}{16}, \ x = 4.0 \times 10^{-2} \ M; \quad \text{Assumption good (2\% error).}$$

$[Cl_2] = 0.040 \ M; \ [NO] = 0.080 \ M; \ [NOCl] = 4.0 - 2(0.040) = 3.92 \ M \approx 3.9 \ M$

f.

	$2 \ NOCl(g)$	$\rightleftharpoons$	$2 \ NO(g)$	$+$	$Cl_2(g)$	
Before	$1.00 \ M$		$1.00 \ M$		$1.00 \ M$	

Let 1.00 mol/L NO react completely (the limiting reagent).

Change	$+1.00$	$\leftarrow$	-1.00		-0.500	React completely
After	2.00		0		0.50	New Initial

$2x$ mol/L NOCl reacts to reach equilibrium

Change	$-2x$	$\rightarrow$	$+2x$		$+x$
Equil.	$2.00 - 2x$		$2x$		$0.50 + x$

$$K = \frac{(2x)^2(0.50+x)}{(2.00-2x)^2} \approx \frac{4x^2(0.50)}{(2.00)^2} = 1.6 \times 10^{-5}, \ x = 5.7 \times 10^{-3} \ M$$

Assumptions good (x is 1.1% of 0.50).

$[NO] = 2x = 1.1 \times 10^{-2} \ M; \ [Cl_2] = 0.50 + 0.0057 = 0.51 \ M; \ [NOCl] = 2.00 - 2(0.0057) = 1.99 \ M$

36.

	$2 \ CO_2(g)$	$\rightleftharpoons$	$2 \ CO(g)$	$+$	$O_2(g)$	$K = \dfrac{[CO]^2[O_2]}{[CO_2]^2} = 2.0 \times 10^{-6}$
Initial	2.0 mol/5.0 L		0		0	

$2x$ mol/L of CO_2 reacts to reach equilibrium

Change	$-2x$	$\rightarrow$	$+2x$		$+x$
Equil.	$0.40 - 2x$		$2x$		x

$$K = 2.0 \times 10^{-6} = \frac{[CO]^2[O_2]}{[CO_2]^2} = \frac{(2x)^2(x)}{(0.40-2x)^2}; \quad \text{Assuming } 2x \ll 0.40:$$

$$2.0 \times 10^{-6} \approx \frac{4x^3}{(0.40)^2}, \ 2.0 \times 10^{-6} = \frac{4x^3}{0.16}, \ x = 4.3 \times 10^{-3} \ M$$

Checking assumption: $\dfrac{2(4.3 \times 10^{-3})}{0.40} \times 100 = 2.2\%;$ Assumption valid by the 5% rule.

$[CO_2] = 0.40 - 2x = 0.40 - 2(4.3 \times 10^{-3}) = 0.39 \ M$

$[CO] = 2x = 2(4.3 \times 10^{-3}) = 8.6 \times 10^{-3} \ M; \ [O_2] = x = 4.3 \times 10^{-3} \ M$

37.   a.   The reaction must proceed to products to reach equilibrium since no product is present initially. Summarizing the problem in a table where x atm of N_2O_4 reacts to reach equilibrium:

	$N_2O_4(g)$	$\rightleftharpoons$	$2 \ NO_2(g)$	$K_p = 0.25$
Initial	4.5 atm		0	
Change	$-x$	$\rightarrow$	$+2x$	
Equil.	$4.5 - x$		$2x$	

$$K_p = \frac{P_{NO_2}^2}{P_{N_2O_4}} = \frac{(2x)^2}{4.5-x} = 0.25, \ 4x^2 = 1.125 - 0.25 \ x, \ 4x^2 + 0.25 \ x - 1.125 = 0$$

We carried extra significant figures in this expression (as will be typical when we solve an expression using the quadratic formula). Solving using the quadratic formula (see Appendix 1.4 of text):

$$x = \frac{-0.25 \pm [(0.25)^2 - 4(4)(-1.125)]^{1/2}}{2(4)} = \frac{-0.25 \pm 4.25}{8}, \; x = 0.50 \text{ (Other value is negative.)}$$

$P_{NO_2} = 2x = 1.0 \text{ atm}; \; P_{N_2O_4} = 4.5 - x = 4.0 \text{ atm}$

b. The reaction must shift to reactants (shift left) to reach equilibrium.

$$N_2O_4(g) \;\rightleftharpoons\; 2\,NO_2(g)$$

Initial	0		9.0 atm
Change	+x	←	-2x
Equil.	x		9.0 - 2x

$K_p = \dfrac{(9.0 - 2x)^2}{x} = 0.25, \; 4x^2 - 36.25\,x + 81 = 0$ (carrying extra sig. figs.)

Solving using quadratic formula: $x = \dfrac{-(-36.25) \pm [(-36.25)^2 - 4(4)(81)]^{1/2}}{2(4)}, \; x = 4.0 \text{ atm}$

The other value, 5.1, is impossible. $P_{N_2O_4} = x = 4.0 \text{ atm}; \; P_{NO_2} = 9.0 - 2x = 1.0 \text{ atm}$

c. No, we get the same equilibrium position starting with either pure N_2O_4 or pure NO_2 in stoichiometric amounts.

d. From part a, the equilibrium partial pressures are $P_{NO_2} = 1.0 \text{ atm}$ and $P_{N_2O_4} = 4.0 \text{ atm}$. Halving the container volume will increase each of these partial pressures by a factor of 2.

$Q = (2.0)^2 / 8.0 = 0.50$. Since $Q > K_p$, then the reaction will shift left to reestablish equilibrium.

$$N_2O_4(g) \;\rightleftharpoons\; 2\,NO_2(g)$$

Initial	4.0 atm		1.0 atm
New Initial	8.0		2.0
Change	+x	←	-2x
Equil.	8.0 + x		2.0 - 2x

$K_p = \dfrac{(2.0 - 2x)^2}{8.0 + x} = 0.25, \; 4\,x^2 - 8.25\,x + 2.0 = 0$ (carrying extra sig. figs.)

Solving using the quadratic formula: $x = 0.28 \text{ atm}$

$P_{N_2O_4} = 8.0 + x = 8.3 \text{ atm}; \; P_{NO_2} = 2.0 - 2x = 1.4 \text{ atm}$

38. This is a typical equilibrium problem except that the reaction contains a solid. Whenever solids and liquids are present, we basically ignore them in the equilibrium problem.

$$NH_4OCONH_2(s) \rightleftharpoons 2\,NH_3(g) + CO_2(g) \qquad K_p = 2.9 \times 10^{-3}$$

Initial	-	0	0

Some NH_4OCONH_2 decomposes to produce $2x$ atm of NH_3 and x atm of CO_2.

Change	-	$\rightarrow \; +2x$	$+x$
Equil.	-	$2x$	x

$$K_p = 2.9 \times 10^{-3} = P_{NH_3}^2 \times P_{CO_2} = (2x)^2(x) = 4x^3$$

$$x = \left(\frac{2.9 \times 10^{-3}}{4} \right)^{1/3} = 9.0 \times 10^{-2} \text{ atm}; \quad P_{NH_3} = 2x = 0.18 \text{ atm}; \quad P_{CO_2} = x = 9.0 \times 10^{-2} \text{ atm}$$

$$P_{total} = P_{NH_3} + P_{CO_2} = 0.18 \text{ atm} + 0.090 \text{ atm} = 0.27 \text{ atm}$$

39.   a. $K_p = K(RT)^{\Delta n} = \dfrac{4.5 \times 10^9 \text{ L}}{\text{mol}} \left(\dfrac{0.08206 \text{ L atm}}{\text{mol K}} \times 373 \text{ K} \right)^{-1}$ where $\Delta n = 1 - 2 = -1$

          $K_p = 1.5 \times 10^8 \text{ atm}^{-1}$

   b. K_p is so large that at equilibrium we will have almost all $COCl_2$. Assume $P_{total} \approx P_{COCl_2} \approx 5.0$.

$$CO(g) + Cl_2(g) \rightleftharpoons COCl_2(g) \qquad K_p = 1.5 \times 10^8$$

Initial	0	0	5.0 atm

x atm $COCl_2$ reacts to reach equilibrium

Change	$+x$	$+x$	$\leftarrow \quad -x$
Equil.	x	x	$5.0 - x$

$$K_p = 1.5 \times 10^8 = \frac{5.0 - x}{x^2} \approx \frac{5.0}{x^2} \quad \text{(Assuming } 5.0 - x \approx 5.0)$$

Solving: $x = 1.8 \times 10^{-4}$ atm.   Check assumptions: $5.0 - x = 5.0 - 1.8 \times 10^{-4} = 5.0$ atm.
Assumptions are good (well within the 5% rule).

$$P_{CO} = P_{Cl_2} = 1.8 \times 10^{-4} \text{ atm and } P_{COCl_2} = 5.0 \text{ atm}$$

40. $Fe^{3+}(aq) + SCN^-(aq) \rightleftharpoons FeSCN^{2+}(aq) \qquad K = 1.1 \times 10^3$

Before	0.020 M	0.10 M	0

Let 0.020 mol/L Fe^{3+} react completely (K is large, products dominate).

Change	-0.020	-0.020	$\rightarrow \; +0.020$	React completely
After	0	0.08	0.020	New Initial

x mol/L $FeSCN^{2+}$ reacts to reach equilibrium

Change	$+x$	$+x$	$\leftarrow \quad -x$
Equil.	x	$0.08 + x$	$0.020 - x$

$$K = 1.1 \times 10^3 = \frac{[\text{FeSCN}^{2+}]}{[\text{Fe}^{3+}][\text{SCN}^-]} = \frac{0.020 - x}{(x)(0.08 + x)} \approx \frac{0.020}{0.08\,x}$$

$x = 2 \times 10^{-4}\,M$; x is 1% of 0.020. Assumptions good by the 5% rule.

$x = [\text{Fe}^{3+}] = 2 \times 10^{-4}\,M$; $[\text{SCN}^-] = 0.08 + 2 \times 10^{-4} = 0.08\,M$

$[\text{FeSCN}^{2+}] = 0.020 - 2 \times 10^{-4} = 0.020\,M$

Le Chatelier's Principle

41.   For this reaction, we want to maximize the amount of ethyl butyrate produced and minimize the amount of butyric acid present at equilibrium. First, we should avoid water. Any extra water we add from the solvent tends to push the equilibrium to the left. This eliminates water and 95% ethanol as solvent choices. Of the remaining two solvents, acetonitrile will not take part in the reaction, whereas ethanol is a reactant. If we use ethanol as the solvent it will drive the equilibrium to the right, thereby reducing the concentration of the objectionable butyric acid to a minimum while maximizing the yield of ethyl butyrate. Thus, the best solvent is 100% ethanol.

42.   A change in volume will change the partial pressure of all reactants and products by the same factor. The shift in equilibrium depends on the number of gaseous particles on each side. An increase in volume will shift the equilibrium to the side with the greater number of particles in the gas phase. A decrease in volume will favor the side with lesser gas phase particles. If there are the same number of gas phase particles on each side of the reaction, a change in volume will not shift the equilibrium.

   When we change the pressure by adding an unreactive gas, we do not change the partial pressures (or concentrations) of any of the substances in equilibrium with each other since the volume of the container did not change. If the partial pressures (and concentrations) are unchanged, the reaction is still at equilibrium.

43.   a.   No effect; Adding more of a pure solid or pure liquid has no effect on the equilibrium position.

   b.   Shifts left; HF(g) will be removed by reaction with the glass. As HF(g) is removed, the reaction will shift left to produce more HF(g).

   c.   Shifts right; As $H_2O(g)$ is removed, the reaction will shift right to produce more $H_2O(g)$.

44.   a.   Doubling the volume will decrease all concentrations by a factor of one-half.

$$Q = \frac{\frac{1}{2}[\text{FeSCN}^{2+}]_{eq}}{\left(\frac{1}{2}[\text{Fe}^{3+}]_{eq}\right)\left(\frac{1}{2}[\text{SCN}^-]_{eq}\right)} = 2\,K, \quad Q > K$$

   The reaction will shift to the left to reestablish equilibrium.

b. Adding Ag^+ will remove SCN^- through the formation of $AgSCN(s)$. The reaction will shift to the left to produce more SCN^-.

c. Removing Fe^{3+} as $Fe(OH)_3(s)$ will shift the reaction to the left to produce more Fe^{3+}.

d. Reaction shifts to the right as Fe^{3+} is added.

45. $H^+ + OH^- \rightarrow H_2O$; Sodium hydroxide (NaOH) will react with the H^+ on the product side of the reaction. This effectively removes H^+ from the equilibrium, which will shift the reaction to the right to produce more H^+ and CrO_4^{2-}. Since more CrO_4^{2-} is produced, the solution turns yellow.

46. $CoCl_2(s) + 6\,H_2O(g) \rightleftharpoons CoCl_2 \cdot 6\,H_2O(s)$; If rain is imminent, there will be a lot of water vapor in the air. The reaction will shift to the right and the indicator will take on the pink color of $CoCl_2 \cdot 6\,H_2O$.

47.   a. right   b. right   c. no effect; $He(g)$ is neither a reactant nor a product.

d. left; Since the reaction is exothermic, heat is a product:

$$CO(g) + H_2O(g) \rightarrow H_2(g) + CO_2(g) + heat$$

Increasing T will add heat. The equilibrium shifts to the left to use up the added heat.

e. No effect; Since these are equal moles of gaseous reactants as gaseous products (2 mol vs. 2 mol), then a change in volume will have no effect on the equilibrium.

48.   a. shift to left

b. shift to right; Since the reaction is endothermic (heat is a reactant), an increase in temperature will shift the equilibrium to the right.

c. no effect   d. shift to right

e. shift to right; Since there are more gaseous product molecules than gaseous reactant molecules, the equilibrium will shift right with an increase in volume.

49.   a. left   b. right   c. left

d. no effect (reactant and product concentrations are unchanged)

e. no effect; Since there are equal numbers of product and reactant gas molecules, then a change in volume has no effect on the equilibrium position.

f. right; A decrease in temperature will shift the equilibrium to the right since heat is a product in this reaction (as is true in all exothermic reactions).

50.   As temperature increases, the value of K decreases. This is consistent with an exothermic reaction. In an exothermic reaction, heat is a product and an increase in temperature shifts the equilibrium to the reactant side (as well as lowering the value of K).

Additional Exercises

51.   a. $N_2(g) + O_2(g) \rightleftharpoons 2\,NO(g)$ $K_p = 1 \times 10^{-31} = \dfrac{P_{NO}^2}{P_{N_2} \times P_{O_2}} = \dfrac{P_{NO}^2}{(0.8)(0.2)}$, $P_{NO} = 1 \times 10^{-16}$ atm

In 1.0 cm³ of air: $n_{NO} = \dfrac{PV}{RT} = \dfrac{(1 \times 10^{-16}\ \text{atm})\,(1.0 \times 10^{-3}\ \text{L})}{\left(\dfrac{0.08206\ \text{L atm}}{\text{mol K}}\right)(298\ \text{K})} = 4 \times 10^{-21}$ mol NO

$\dfrac{4 \times 10^{-21}\ \text{mol NO}}{\text{cm}^3} \times \dfrac{6.02 \times 10^{23}\ \text{molecules}}{\text{mol NO}} = \dfrac{2 \times 10^3\ \text{molecules NO}}{\text{cm}^3}$

b.   There is more NO in the atmosphere than we would expect from the value of K. The answer must lie in the rates of the reaction. At 25°C the rates of both reactions:

$$N_2 + O_2 \rightarrow 2\,NO \quad \text{and} \quad 2\,NO \rightarrow N_2 + O_2$$

are so slow that they are essentially zero. Very strong bonds must be broken; the activation energy is very high. Therefore, the reaction essentially doesn't occur at low temperatures. Nitric oxide, however, can be produced in high energy or high temperature environments since the production of NO is endothermic. In nature, some NO is produced by lightning and the primary manmade source is from automobiles. At these high temperatures, K will increase and the rates of the reaction will also increase, resulting in a higher production of NO. Once the NO gets into a more normal temperature environment, it doesn't go back to N_2 and O_2 because of the slow rate.

c. $K_p = P_{NO}^2/(P_{N_2} \times P_{O_2})$

To convert from partial pressures to concentrations in molecules/cm³, we will have to do the same conversion to all concentrations. All of these conversions will cancel since there are equal product and reactant moles of gas ($\Delta n = 0$). Therefore, $K^* = K_p = 1 \times 10^{-31}$. The equilibrium constant for this reaction is unitless.

52.   a.
$$
\begin{array}{ll}
Na_2O(s) \rightleftharpoons 2\,Na(l) + 1/2\,O_2(g) & K_1 \\
2\,Na(l) + O_2(g) \rightleftharpoons Na_2O_2(s) & 1/K_3 \\
\hline
Na_2O(s) + 1/2\,O_2(g) \rightleftharpoons Na_2O_2(s) & K = (K_1)(1/K_3)
\end{array}
$$

$K = \dfrac{2 \times 10^{-25}}{5 \times 10^{-29}} = 4 \times 10^3\ \text{L}^{1/2}/\text{mol}^{1/2}$

b.
$$
\begin{array}{ll}
NaO(g) \rightleftharpoons Na(l) + 1/2\,O_2(g) & K_2 \\
Na_2O(s) \rightleftharpoons 2\,Na(l) + 1/2\,O_2(g) & K_1 \\
2\,Na(l) + O_2(g) \rightleftharpoons Na_2O_2(s) & 1/K_3 \\
\hline
NaO(g) + Na_2O(s) \rightleftharpoons Na_2O_2(s) + Na(l) & K = K_2(K_1)(1/K_3) = 8 \times 10^{-2}\ \text{L/mol}
\end{array}
$$

c.
$$2\,NaO(g) \rightleftharpoons 2\,Na(l) + O_2(g) \qquad\qquad K_2^2$$
$$2\,Na(l) + O_2(g) \rightleftharpoons Na_2O_2(s) \qquad\qquad 1/K_3$$

$$2\,NaO(g) \rightleftharpoons Na_2O_2(s) \qquad\qquad K = K_2^2(1/K_3) = 8 \times 10^{18}\ L^2/mol^2$$

53.
$$O(g) + NO(g) \rightleftharpoons NO_2(g) \qquad\qquad K = 1/6.8 \times 10^{-49} = 1.5 \times 10^{48}$$
$$NO_2(g) + O_2(g) \rightleftharpoons NO(g) + O_3(g) \qquad\qquad K = 1/5.8 \times 10^{-34} = 1.7 \times 10^{33}$$

$$O_2(g) + O(g) \rightleftharpoons O_3(g) \qquad\qquad K = (1.5 \times 10^{48})(1.7 \times 10^{33}) = 2.6 \times 10^{81}\ L/mol$$

54.   In an exothermic reaction, heat is a product. To maximize product yield , one would want as low a temperature as possible since high temperatures would shift the reaction left (away from products). Since temperature changes also change the value of K, then at low temperatures the value of K will be largest, which maximizes yield of products.

55.
$$3\,H_2(g) \quad + \quad N_2(g) \quad \rightleftharpoons \quad 2\,NH_3(g)$$

Initial	$[H_2]_o$	$[N_2]_o$	0

x mol/L of N_2 reacts to reach equilibrium

Change	$-3x$	$-x$ $\rightarrow$	$+2x$
Equil	$[H_2]_o - 3x$	$[N_2]_o\ -x$	$2x$

From the problem:

$$[NH_3]_e = 4.0\ M = 2x,\ x = 2.0\ M;\ [H_2]_e = 5.0\ M = [H_2]_o - 3x;\ [N_2]_e = 8.0\ M = [N_2]_o - x$$

$$5.0\ M = [H_2]_o - 3(2.0\ M),\ [H_2]_o = 11.0\ M;\ 8.0\ M = [N_2]_o - 2.0\ M,\ [N_2]_o = 10.0\ M$$

56.
$$N_2(g) \quad + \quad 3\,H_2(g) \quad \rightleftharpoons \quad 2\,NH_3(g) \qquad K_p = 5.3 \times 10^5$$

Initial	0	0	P_0	P_0 = initial pressure of NH_3

$2x$ atm of NH_3 reacts to reach equilibrium

Change	$+x$	$+3x$ $\leftarrow$	$-2x$
Equil.	x	$3x$	$P_0 - 2x$

From problem, $P_0 - 2x = \dfrac{P_0}{2.00}$, so $P_0 = 4.00\,x$

$$K_p = \frac{(4.00\,x - 2x)^2}{(x)(3x)^3} = \frac{(2.00\,x)^2}{(x)(3x)^3} = \frac{4.00\,x^2}{27x^4} = \frac{4.00}{27x^2} = 5.3 \times 10^5,\ x = 5.3 \times 10^{-4}\ atm$$

$$P_0 = 4.00\,x = 4.00 \times (5.3 \times 10^{-4}\ atm) = 2.1 \times 10^{-3}\ atm$$

57.   a.
$$PCl_5(g) \quad \rightleftharpoons \quad PCl_3(g) \quad + \quad Cl_2(g) \qquad K_p = P_{PCl_3} \times P_{Cl_2}/P_{PCl_5}$$

Initial	P_0	0	0	P_0 = initial PCl_5 pressure
Change	$-x$ $\rightarrow$	$+x$	$+x$	
Equil.	$P_0 - x$	x	x	

$$P_{total} = P_0 - x + x + x = P_0 + x = 358.7 \text{ torr}$$

$$P_0 = \frac{n_{PCl_5}RT}{V} = \frac{\dfrac{2.4156 \text{ g}}{208.22 \text{ g mol}^{-1}} \times \dfrac{0.08206 \text{ L atm}}{\text{mol K}} \times 523.2 \text{ K}}{2.000 \text{ L}} = 0.2490 \text{ atm or } 189.2 \text{ torr}$$

$$x = P_{total} - P_0 = 358.7 - 189.2 = 169.5 \text{ torr}$$

$$P_{PCl_3} = P_{Cl_2} = 169.5 \text{ torr} = 0.2230 \text{ atm}$$

$$P_{PCl_5} = 189.2 - 169.5 = 19.7 \text{ torr} = 0.0259 \text{ atm}$$

$$K_p = \frac{(0.2230)^2}{0.0259} = 1.92 \text{ atm}$$

b. $P_{Cl_2} = \dfrac{n_{Cl_2}RT}{V} = \dfrac{0.250 \times 0.08206 \times 523.2}{2.000} = 5.37 \text{ atm } Cl_2 \text{ added}$

	$PCl_5(g)$	$\rightleftharpoons$	$PCl_3(g)$	+	$Cl_2(g)$	
Initial	0.0259 atm		0.2230 atm		0.2230 atm	(from a)
	Adding 0.250 mol Cl_2 increases P_{Cl_2} by 5.37 atm.					
Initial'	0.0259		0.2230		5.59	
Change	+0.2230	$\leftarrow$	-0.2230		-0.2230	React completely
After	0.2489		0		5.37	New initial
Change	-x	$\rightarrow$	+x		+x	
Equil.	0.2489 -x		x		5.37 + x	

$$\frac{(5.37 + x)\,(x)}{(0.2489 - x)} = 1.92, \quad x^2 + 7.29\,x - 0.478 = 0$$

Solving using the quadratic formula: $x = 0.0650 \text{ atm}$

$$P_{PCl_3} = 0.0650 \text{ atm}; \quad P_{PCl_5} = 0.2489 - 0.0650 = 0.1839 \text{ atm}; \quad P_{Cl_2} = 5.37 + 0.0650 = 5.44 \text{ atm}$$

58. $SO_2Cl_2(g) \quad \rightleftharpoons \quad Cl_2(g) \quad + \quad SO_2(g)$

	SO_2Cl_2		Cl_2	SO_2	
Initial	P_0		0	0	P_0 = initial pressure of SO_2Cl_2
Change	-x	$\rightarrow$	+x	+x	
Equil.	P_0 - x		x	x	

$$P_{total} = 0.900 \text{ atm} = P_0 - x + x + x = P_0 + x$$

$$\frac{x}{P_0} \times 100 = 12.5, \quad P_0 = 8.00\,x$$

Solving: $0.900 = P_0 + x = 9.00\,x, \quad x = 0.100 \text{ atm}$

$$x = 0.100 \text{ atm} = P_{Cl_2} = P_{SO_2}; \quad P_0 - x = 0.800 - 0.100 = 0.700 \text{ atm} = P_{SO_2Cl_2}$$

$$K_p = \frac{P_{Cl_2} \times P_{SO_2}}{P_{SO_2Cl_2}} = \frac{(0.100)^2}{0.700} = 1.43 \times 10^{-2} \text{ atm}$$

59. $N_2O_4(g) \rightleftharpoons 2 NO_2(g)$ $K_p = \dfrac{P_{NO_2}^2}{P_{N_2O_4}} = \dfrac{(1.20)^2}{0.34} = 4.2$

Doubling the volume decreases each partial pressure by a factor of 2 ($P = nRT/V$).

$P_{NO_2} = 0.600$ atm and $P_{N_2O_4} = 0.17$ atm are the new partial pressures.

$$Q = \frac{(0.600)^2}{0.17} = 2.1, \ Q < K \qquad \text{Equilibrium will shift to the right.}$$

$$N_2O_4(g) \quad \rightleftharpoons \quad 2 NO_2(g)$$

Initial   0.17 atm   0.600 atm
Equil.   0.17 - x 0.600 + 2x

$K_p = 4.2 = \dfrac{(0.600 + 2x)^2}{(0.17 - x)}$, $\ 4x^2 + 6.6x - 0.354 = 0$ (carrying extra sig. figs.)

Solving using the quadratic formula: $x = 0.052$ atm

$P_{NO_2} = 0.600 + 2(0.052) = 0.704$ atm; $\ P_{N_2O_4} = 0.17 - 0.052 = 0.12$ atm

60.   a. $P_{PCl_5} = \dfrac{n_{PCl_5}RT}{V} = \dfrac{\dfrac{2.450 \text{ g PCl}_5}{208.22 \text{ g/mol}} \times \dfrac{0.08206 \text{ L atm}}{\text{mol K}} \times 600. \text{ K}}{0.500 \text{ L}} = 1.16$ atm

b. $PCl_5(g) \quad \rightleftharpoons \quad PCl_3(g) \ + \ Cl_2(g)$ $K_p = \dfrac{P_{PCl_3} \times P_{Cl_2}}{P_{PCl_5}} = 11.5$

Initial   1.16 atm   0   0
                 x atm of PCl$_5$ reacts to reach equilibrium
Change   -x $\rightarrow$ +x +x
Equil.   1.16 - x x x

$K_p = \dfrac{x^2}{1.16 - x} = 11.5$, $\ x^2 + 11.5x - 13.3 = 0$;   Using the quadratic formula: $x = 1.06$ atm

$P_{PCl_5} = 1.16 - 1.06 = 0.10$ atm

c. $P_{PCl_3} = P_{Cl_2} = 1.06$ atm; $P_{PCl_5} = 0.10$ atm

$P_{total} = P_{PCl_5} + P_{PCl_3} + P_{Cl_2} = 0.10 + 1.06 + 1.06 = 2.22$ atm

d.   Percent dissociation $= \dfrac{x}{1.16} \times 100 = \dfrac{1.06}{1.16} \times 100 = 91.4\%$

61.   a. $2 NaHCO_3(s)$ $\rightleftharpoons$ $Na_2CO_3(s)$ + $CO_2(g)$ + $H_2O(g)$ $K_p = 0.25$

| | Initial | - | | - | | 0 | 0 |

NaHCO₃(s) decomposes to form x atm each of $CO_2(g)$ and $H_2O(g)$ at equilibrium.

Change   - $\rightarrow$ - $+x$ $+x$
Equil.   -   - x x

$K_p = 0.25 = P_{CO_2} \times P_{H_2O},\ 0.25 = x^2,\ x = P_{CO_2} = P_{H_2O} = 0.50$ atm

b. $n_{CO_2} = \dfrac{P_{CO_2} \times V}{RT} = \dfrac{(0.50\ \text{atm})(1.00\ \text{L})}{(0.08206\ \text{L atm mol}^{-1}\ \text{K}^{-1})(398\ \text{K})} = 1.5 \times 10^{-2}$ mol CO_2

Mass of Na_2CO_3 produced:

$$1.5 \times 10^{-2}\ \text{mol}\ CO_2 \times \frac{1\ \text{mol}\ Na_2CO_3}{\text{mol}\ CO_2} \times \frac{106.0\ \text{g}\ Na_2CO_3}{\text{mol}\ Na_2CO_3} = 1.6\ \text{g}\ Na_2CO_3$$

Mass of $NaHCO_3$ reacted:

$$1.5 \times 10^{-2}\ \text{mol}\ CO_2 \times \frac{2\ \text{mol}\ NaHCO_3}{1\ \text{mol}\ CO_2} \times \frac{84.01\ \text{g}\ NaHCO_3}{\text{mol}} = 2.5\ \text{g}\ NaHCO_3$$

Mass of $NaHCO_3$ remaining = 10.0 - 2.5 = 7.5 g

c. $10.0\ \text{g}\ NaHCO_3 \times \dfrac{1\ \text{mol}\ NaHCO_3}{84.01\ \text{g}\ NaHCO_3} \times \dfrac{1\ \text{mol}\ CO_2}{2\ \text{mol}\ NaHCO_3} = 5.95 \times 10^{-2}$ mol CO_2

When all of the $NaHCO_3$ has just been consumed, we will have 5.95×10^{-2} mol CO_2 gas at a pressure of 0.50 atm (from a).

$$V = \frac{nRT}{P} = \frac{(5.95 \times 10^{-2}\ \text{mol})(0.08206\ \text{L atm mol}^{-1}\ \text{K}^{-1})(398\ \text{K})}{0.50\ \text{atm}} = 3.9\ \text{L}$$

62.   a. $2 AsH_3(g)$ $\rightleftharpoons$ $2 As(s)$ + $3 H_2(g)$

Initial   392.0 torr   -   0
Equil.   392.0 - 2x -   3x

$P_{total} = 488.0\ \text{torr} = 392.0 - 2x + 3x,\ x = 96.0$ torr

$P_{H_2} = 3x = 3(96.0) = 288\ \text{torr};\ P_{AsH_3} = 392.0 - 2(96.0) = 200.0$ torr

b. $K_p = \dfrac{(P_{H_2})^3}{(P_{AsH_3})^2} = \dfrac{(288)^3}{(200.0)^2} = 597\ \text{torr} \times \dfrac{1\ \text{atm}}{760\ \text{torr}} = 0.786$ atm

Challenge Problems

63.   a. $2\,NO(g)\ +\ Br_2(g)\ \rightleftharpoons\ 2\,NOBr(g)$

Initial	98.4 torr	41.3 torr	0

2x torr of NO reacts to reach equilibrium

Change	-2x	-x	$\rightarrow$	+2x
Equil.	98.4 - 2x	41.3 - x		2x

$P_{total} = P_{NO} + P_{Br_2} + P_{NOBr} = (98.4 - 2x) + (41.3 - x) + 2x = 139.7 - x$

$P_{total} = 110.5 = 139.7 - x, \ x = 29.2$ torr; $P_{NO} = 98.4 - 2(29.2) = 40.0$ torr $= 0.0526$ atm

$P_{Br_2} = 41.3 - 29.2 = 12.1$ torr $= 0.0159$ atm; $P_{NOBr} = 2(29.2) = 58.4$ torr $= 0.0768$ atm

$$K_p = \frac{P_{NOBr}^2}{P_{NO}^2 \times P_{Br_2}} = \frac{(0.0768\ atm)^2}{(0.0526\ atm)^2\,(0.0159\ atm)} = 134\ atm^{-1}$$

   b. $2\,NO(g)\ +\ Br_2(g)\ \rightleftharpoons\ 2\,NOBr(g)$

Initial	0.30 atm	0.30 atm	0

2x atm of NO reacts to reach equilibrium

Change	-2x	-x	$\rightarrow$	+2x
Equil.	0.30 - 2x	0.30 - x		2x

This would yield a cubic equation which can be difficult to solve unless you have a graphing calculator. Since K_p is pretty large, so let us approach equilibrium in two steps; assume the reaction goes to completion then solve the back equilibrium problem.

                              $2\,NO\ +\ Br_2\ \rightleftharpoons\ 2\,NOBr$

Before	0.30 atm	0.30 atm	0

Let 0.30 atm NO react completely.

Change	-0.30	-0.15	$\rightarrow$	+0.30	React completely
After	0	0.15		0.30	New initial

2y atm of NOBr reacts to reach equilibrium

Change	+2y	+y	$\leftarrow$	-2y
Equil.	2y	0.15 + y		0.30 - 2y

$$K_p = \frac{(0.30 - 2y)^2}{(2y)^2\,(0.15 + y)} = 134, \quad \frac{(0.30 - 2y)^2}{(0.15 + y)} = 134 \times 4\,y^2 = 536\,y^2$$

If $y \ll 0.15$: $\dfrac{(0.30)^2}{0.15} \approx 536\,y^2$ and $y = 0.034$;   Assumptions are poor (y is 23% of 0.15).

Use 0.034 as an approximation for y and solve by successive approximations (Appendix 1.4):

$$\frac{(0.30 - 0.068)^2}{0.15 + 0.034} = 536\,y^2, \ y = 0.023; \quad \frac{(0.30 - 0.046)^2}{0.15 + 0.023} = 536\,y^2, \ y = 0.026$$

$$\frac{(0.30 - 0.052)^2}{0.15 + 0.026} = 536\,y^2, \ y = 0.026 \text{ atm} \quad \text{(We have converged on the correct answer.)}$$

So: $P_{NO} = 2y = 0.052$ atm; $\quad P_{Br_2} = 0.15 + y = 0.18$ atm; $\quad P_{NOBr} = 0.30 - 2y = 0.25$ atm

64. a. If the volume is increased, equilibrium will shift to the right so the mole percent of N_2O_5 decomposed will be greater than 0.50%.

b.

	$2\,N_2O_5$	$\rightleftharpoons$	$4NO_2$	$+$	O_2
Initial	1.000 atm		0		0
Change	-0.0050		+0.010		+0.0025
Equil.	0.995		0.010		0.0025

$$K_p = \frac{(0.010)^4(0.0025)}{(0.995)^2} = 2.5 \times 10^{-11} \text{ atm}^3$$

The new volume is ten times the old volume.

$$P_{N_2O_5} = \frac{1.00}{10.0} = 0.100 \text{ atm}$$

	$2\,N_2O_5$	$\rightleftharpoons$	$4\,NO_2$	$+$	O_2
Initial	0.100 atm		0		0
Change	-2x		+4x		+x
Equil.	0.100-2x		4x		x

$$2.5 \times 10^{-11} = \frac{(4x)^4(x)}{(0.100 - 2x)^2} \approx \frac{(4x)^4(x)}{(0.100)^2}, \ 2x = 2.0 \times 10^{-3} \text{ atm} = P_{N_2O_5} \text{ decomposed}$$

$$\frac{2.0 \times 10^{-3}}{0.100} \times 100 = 2.0\% \ N_2O_5 \text{ decomposed (moles and P are directly related)}$$

65. $P_4(g) \rightleftharpoons 2\,P_2(g)$ $K_p = 0.100 = \dfrac{P_{P_2}^2}{P_{P_4}}$; $P_{P_4} + P_{P_2} = P_{total} = 1.00$ atm, $P_{P_4} = 1.00 - P_{P_2}$

Let $y = P_{P_2}$ at equilibrium, then $K_p = \dfrac{y^2}{1.00 - y} = 0.100$

Solving: $y = 0.270$ atm $= P_{P_2}$; $P_{P_4} = 1.00 - 0.270 = 0.73$ atm

To solve for the fraction dissociated, we need the initial pressure of P_4.

	$P_4(g)$	$\rightleftharpoons$	$2\,P_2(g)$	
Initial	P_0		0	$P_0 = $ initial pressure of P_4
	x atm of P_4 reacts to reach equilibrium			
Change	-x	$\rightarrow$	+2x	
Equil.	$P_0 - x$		2x	

$P_{total} = P_0 - x + 2x = 1.00 \text{ atm} = P_0 + x$

Solving: $0.270 \text{ atm} = P_{P_2} = 2x$, $x = 0.135 \text{ atm}$; $P_0 = 1.00 - 0.135 = 0.87 \text{ atm}$

Fraction dissociation $= \dfrac{x}{P_0} = \dfrac{0.135}{0.87} = 0.16$ or 16% of P_4 is dissociated to reach equilibrium.

66.   Equilibria lies to the right (K_p values are very large). Let them go to completion initially.

$$CH_4 + 2O_2 \rightarrow CO_2 + 2H_2O$$

	CH_4	$2O_2$		CO_2	$+$	$2H_2O$
Before	1.50	15.00		0		0
After	0	12.00		1.50		3.00 atm

$$2C_2H_6 + 7O_2 \rightarrow 4CO_2 + 6H_2O$$

	$2C_2H_6$	$7O_2$		$4CO_2$	$+$	$6H_2O$
Before	2.50	12.00		1.50		3.00
After	0	3.25		6.50		10.50 atm

$$1.0 \times 10^4 = \frac{(P_{CO_2})(P_{H_2O})^2}{(P_{CH_4})(P_{O_2})^2} = \frac{(1.50 - x)(3.00 - 2x)^2}{(x)(12.00 + 2x)^2} \approx \frac{(1.50)(3.00)^2}{(x)(12.0)^2}$$

$x = P_{CH_4} = 9.4 \times 10^{-6} \text{ atm}$

$$1.0 \times 10^8 = \frac{(P_{CO_2})^4(P_{H_2O})^6}{(P_{C_2H_6})^2(P_{O_2})^7} = \frac{(6.50 - 4x)^4(10.50 - 6x)^6}{(2x)^2(3.25 + 7x)^7} \approx \frac{(6.50)^4(10.50)^6}{(2x)^2(3.25)^7}$$

$2x = P_{C_2H_6} = 7.90 \times 10^{-2} \text{ atm}$

67. $d = \text{density} = \dfrac{P \times (\text{molar mass})}{RT} = \dfrac{P_{O_2}(\text{molar mass}_{O_2}) + P_{O_3}(\text{molar mass}_{O_3})}{RT}$

$0.168 \text{ g/L} = \dfrac{P_{O_2}(32.00 \text{ g/mol}) + P_{O_3}(48.00 \text{ g/mol})}{\dfrac{0.08206 \text{ L atm}}{\text{mol K}} \times 448 \text{ K}}$, $32.00\,P_{O_2} + 48.00\,P_{O_3} = 6.18$ (P in atm)

$P_{total} = P_{O_2} + P_{O_3} = 128 \text{ torr} \times \dfrac{1 \text{ atm}}{760 \text{ torr}} = 0.168 \text{ atm}$

We have two equations in two unknowns. Solving using simultaneous equations:

$$
\begin{aligned}
32.00\,P_{O_2} + 48.00\,P_{O_3} &= 6.18 \\
-32.00\,P_{O_2} - 32.00\,P_{O_3} &= -5.38 \\
\hline
16.00\,P_{O_3} &= 0.80
\end{aligned}
$$

$P_{O_3} = \dfrac{0.80}{16.00} = 0.050 \text{ atm}$ and $P_{O_2} = 0.118 \text{ atm}$

$$K_p = \frac{P_{O_3}^2}{P_{O_2}^3} = \frac{(0.050)^2}{(0.118)^3} = 1.5 \text{ atm}^{-1}$$

68. $O_2 \rightleftharpoons 2O$ Assuming 100 O_2 molecules

Initial   100   0
Change   -83   +166
Equil.   17   166

Thus: $\chi_O = \frac{166}{183} = 0.9071$ and $\chi_{O_2} = 0.0929$

Since $P \propto n$, then $P_{O_2} \propto \chi_{O_2}$ and $P_O \propto \chi_O$.

Since $P_{TOTAL} = 1.000$ atm, then $P_{O_2} = 0.0929$ atm and $P_O = 0.9071$ atm.

$$K_p = \frac{(0.9071)^2}{0.0929} = 8.857 \text{ atm}$$

                           $O_2 \rightleftharpoons 2O$
Initial   x   0
Change   -y   +2y
Equil.   x-y   2y

$$\frac{(2y)^2}{x-y} = 8.857; \quad \frac{y}{x} \times 100 = 95.0$$

Solving: x = 0.123 atm and y = 0.117 atm; P_{total} = 0.240 atm

69.   2 NOBr (g) $\rightleftharpoons$ 2 NO(g) + Br_2(g)

Initial P_0 0   0 P_0 = initial pressure of NOBr
Equil. $P_0 - 2x$ 2x   x   Note: $P_{NO} = 2P_{Br_2}$

$P_{total} = 0.0515$ atm $= (P_0 - 2x) + (2x) + (x) = P_0 + x$; 0.0515 atm $= P_{NOBr} + 3 P_{Br_2}$

$$d = \frac{P \times (\text{molar mass})}{RT} = 0.1861 \text{ g/L} = \frac{P_{NOBr}(109.9) + 2P_{Br_2}(30.01) + P_{Br_2}(159.8)}{0.08206 \times 298}$$

$4.55 = 109.9\ P_{NOBr} + 219.8\ P_{Br_2}$

Solving using simultaneous equations:

    $\begin{aligned} 0.0515 &= P_{NOBr} + \quad 3\ P_{Br_2} \\ -0.0414 &= -P_{NOBr} - 2.000\ P_{Br_2} \\ \hline 0.0101 &= \qquad\qquad P_{Br_2} \end{aligned}$

$P_{Br_2} = 1.01 \times 10^{-2}$ atm; $P_{NO} = 2\ P_{Br_2} = 2.02 \times 10^{-2}$ atm

$P_{NOBr} = 0.0515 - 3(1.01 \times 10^{-2}) = 2.12 \times 10^{-2}$ atm

$$K_p = \frac{P_{Br_2} \times P_{NO}^2}{P_{NOBr}^2} = \frac{(1.01 \times 10^{-2})(2.02 \times 10^{-2})^2}{(2.12 \times 10^{-2})^2} = 9.17 \times 10^{-3} \text{ atm}$$

70.   a. $SbCl_5(g) \rightleftharpoons SbCl_3(g) + Cl_2(g)$ 89.7 g $SbCl_5$ = 0.300 mol $SbCl_5$

Initial   0.300 mol   0   0
Change   -(0.292)(0.300)   +0.0876   +0.0876
Equil.   0.212 mol   0.0876 mol   0.0876 mol

$$K = \frac{\left(\dfrac{0.0876 \text{ mol}}{15.0 \text{ L}}\right)\left(\dfrac{0.0876 \text{ mol}}{15.0 \text{ L}}\right)}{\left(\dfrac{0.212 \text{ mol}}{15.0 \text{ L}}\right)} = 2.41 \times 10^{-3} \text{ mol/L}$$

b. Let x = moles Cl_2 added

moles $SbCl_3 = \dfrac{0.0876}{2} = 0.0438$ mol; moles $Cl_2 = x + 0.0438$

moles $SbCl_5 = 0.212 + 0.0438 = 0.256$ mol

$$2.41 \times 10^{-3} = \frac{\left(\dfrac{x + 0.0438}{15.0}\right)\left(\dfrac{0.0438}{15.0}\right)}{\left(\dfrac{0.256}{15.0}\right)}; \quad \text{Solving, x = 0.168 mol } Cl_2 \text{ added}$$

71.   a. $P_{PCl_5} = \dfrac{n_{PCl_5}RT}{V} = \dfrac{0.100 \text{ mol} \times \dfrac{0.08206 \text{ L atm}}{\text{mol K}} \times 480. \text{ K}}{12.0 \text{ L}} = 0.328$ atm

$PCl_5(g) \rightleftharpoons PCl_3(g) + Cl_2(g)$ $K_p = 0.267$ atm

Initial   0.328 atm   0   0
Change   -x $\rightarrow$ +x   +x
Equil.   0.328 -x   x   x

$K_p = \dfrac{x^2}{0.328 - x} = 0.267$, $x^2 + 0.267 x - 0.08758 = 0$ (carrying extra sig. figs.)

Solving using the quadratic formula: $x = 0.191$ atm

$P_{PCl_3} = P_{Cl_2} = 0.191$ atm; $P_{PCl_5} = 0.328 - 0.191 = 0.137$ atm

b. $PCl_5(g) \rightleftharpoons PCl_3(g) + Cl_2(g)$

Initial	P_0	0	0
Change	$-x$	$+x$	$+x$
Equil.	$P_0 - x$	x	x

P_0 = initial pressure of PCl_5

$P_{total} = 2.00 \text{ atm} = (P_0 - x) + x + x = P_0 + x$, $P_0 = 2.00 - x$

$K_p = \dfrac{x^2}{P_0 - x} = 0.267$; $\dfrac{x^2}{2.00 - 2x} = 0.267$, $x^2 = 0.534 - 0.534\,x$

$x^2 + 0.534\,x - 0.534 = 0$;   Solving using the quadratic formula:

$$x = \frac{-0.534 \pm \sqrt{(0.534)^2 + 4(0.534)}}{2} = 0.511 \text{ atm}$$

$P_0 = 2.00 - x = 2.00 - 0.511 = 1.49$ atm; The initial pressure of PCl_5 was 1.49 atm.

$$n_{PCl_5} = \frac{P_{PCl_5} \times V}{RT} = \frac{(1.49 \text{ atm})(5.00 \text{ L})}{(0.08206 \text{ L atm mol}^{-1} \text{ K}^{-1})(480. \text{ K})} = 0.189 \text{ mol } PCl_5$$

0.189 mol PCl_5 × 208.22 g PCl_5/mol = 39.4 g PCl_5 was initially introduced.

72. $P_0(O_2) = n_{O_2} RT/V = (6.400 \text{ g} \times 0.08206 \times 684 \text{ K}) / (32.00 \text{ g/mol} \times 2.50 \text{ L}) = 4.49$ atm

	$CH_4(g)$ +	$2\,O_2(g)$ →	$CO_2(g)$ +	$2\,H_2O(g)$
Change	$-x$	$-2x$ →	$+x$	$+2x$

	$CH_4(g)$ +	$3/2\,O_2(g)$ →	$CO(g)$ +	$2\,H_2O(g)$
Change	$-y$	$-3/2\,y$ →	$+y$	$+2y$

Amount of O_2 reacted = 4.49 atm - 0.326 atm = 4.16 atm O_2

$2\,x + 3/2\,y = 4.16$ atm O_2 and $2\,x + 2\,y = 4.45$ atm H_2O

Solving using simultaneous equations:

$$
\begin{aligned}
2\,x + 2\,y &= 4.45 \\
-2\,x - 3/2\,y &= -4.16 \\
\hline
0.50\,y &= 0.29, \quad y = 0.58 \text{ atm} = P_{CO}
\end{aligned}
$$

$2\,x + 2(0.58) = 4.45$, $x = \dfrac{4.45 - 1.16}{2} = 1.65$ atm $= P_{CO_2}$

73. $N_2(g) + O_2(g) \rightleftharpoons 2\,NO(g)$ Let:

Equil.	3.7 p	p	x

equilibrium $P_{O_2} = p$
equilibrium $P_{N_2} = 78/21\,P_{O_2} = 3.7\,p$
equilibrium $P_{NO} = x$
equilibrium $P_{NO_2} = y$

$$K_p = 1.5 \times 10^{-4} = \frac{P_{NO}^2}{P_{O_2} \times P_{N_2}}$$

$$N_2 \quad + \quad 2\,O_2 \quad \rightleftharpoons \quad 2\,NO_2$$

Equil.   3.7 p   p   y

$$K_p = 1.0 \times 10^{-5} = \frac{P_{NO_2}^2}{P_{O_2}^2 \times P_{N_2}}$$

We want $P_{NO_2} = P_{NO}$ at equilibrium, so $x = y$.

Taking the ratio of the two K_p expressions:

$$\frac{\dfrac{P_{NO}^2}{P_{O_2} \times P_{N_2}}}{\dfrac{P_{NO_2}^2}{P_{O_2}^2 \times P_{N_2}}} = \frac{1.5 \times 10^{-4}}{1.0 \times 10^{-5}} \; ; \; \text{Since } P_{NO} = P_{NO_2}, \; P_{O_2} = \frac{1.5 \times 10^{-4}}{1.0 \times 10^{-5}} = 15 \text{ atm}$$

Air is 21 mol % O_2, so:

$$P_{O_2} = 0.21\,P_{total}, \; P_{total} = \frac{15 \text{ atm}}{0.21} = 71 \text{ atm}$$

To solve for the equilibrium concentrations of all gases (not required to answer the question), solve one of the K_p expressions where $p = P_{O_2} = 15$ atm.

$$1.5 \times 10^{-4} = \frac{x^2}{15[3.7(15)]}, \; x = P_{NO} = P_{NO_2} = 0.35 \text{ atm}$$

Equilibrium pressures:

$$P_{O_2} = 15 \text{ atm}; \quad P_{N_2} = 3.7(15) = 55.5 = 56 \text{ atm}; \quad P_{NO} = P_{NO_2} = 0.35 \text{ atm}$$

74. $CCl_4(g) \quad \rightleftharpoons \quad C(s) \quad + \quad 2\,Cl_2(g) \quad K_p = 0.76$

Initial P_0 -   0 P_0 = initial pressure of CCl_4
Change $-x$ $\rightarrow$ - $+2x$
Equil. $P_0 - x$ - $2x$

$$P_{total} = P_0 - x + 2x = P_0 + x = 1.20 \text{ atm}$$

$$K_p = \frac{(2x)^2}{P_0 - x} = 0.76, \; 4x^2 = 0.76\,P_0 - 0.76\,x, \; P_0 = \frac{4x^2 + 0.76\,x}{0.76}; \; \text{Substituting into } P_0 + x = 1.20:$$

$$\frac{4x^2}{0.76} + x + x = 1.20 \text{ atm}, \; 5.3\,x^2 + 2x - 1.20 = 0; \; \text{Solving using the quadratic formula:}$$

$$x = \frac{-2 \pm (4 + 25.4)^{1/2}}{2(5.3)} = 0.32 \text{ atm}; \; P_0 + 0.32 = 1.20, \; P_0 = 0.88 \text{ atm}$$

75. $SO_3(g)$ $\rightleftharpoons$ $SO_2(g)$ + $1/2\ O_2(g)$

Initial	P_0	0	0	P_0 = initial pressure of SO_3
Change	$-x$	$\rightarrow$ $+x$	$+x/2$	
Equil.	$P_0 - x$	x	$x/2$	

Average molar mass of the mixture is:

$$\text{average molar mass} = \frac{dRT}{P} = \frac{(1.60\ \text{g/L})\ (0.08206\ \text{L atm mol}^{-1}\ \text{K}^{-1})\ (873\ \text{K})}{1.80\ \text{atm}} = 63.7\ \text{g/mol}$$

The average molar mass is determined by:

$$\text{average molar mass} = \frac{n_{SO_3}\ (80.07\ \text{g/mol}) + n_{SO_2}\ (64.07\ \text{g/mol}) + n_{O_2}\ (32.00\ \text{g/mol})}{n_{total}}$$

Since χ_A = mol fraction of component A = $n_A/n_{total} = P_A/P_{total}$, then:

$$63.7\ \text{g/mol} = \frac{P_{SO_3}\ (80.07) + P_{SO_2}\ (64.07) + P_{O_2}\ (32.00)}{P_{total}}$$

$P_{total} = P_0 - x + x + x/2 = P_0 + x/2 = 1.80\ \text{atm},\ \ P_0 = 1.80 - x/2$

$$63.7 = \frac{(P_0 - x)\ (80.07) + x(64.07) + \frac{x}{2}(32.00)}{1.80}$$

$$63.7 = \frac{(1.80 - 3/2x)\ (80.07) + x(64.07) + \frac{x}{2}(32.00)}{1.80}$$

$115 = 144 - 120.1\ x + 64.07\ x + 16.00\ x,\ \ 40.0\ x = 29,\ \ x = 0.73\ \text{atm}$

$P_{SO_3} = P_0 - x = 1.80 - 3/2\ x = 0.71\ \text{atm};\ \ P_{SO_2} = 0.73\ \text{atm};\ \ P_{O_2} = x/2 = 0.37\ \text{atm}$

$$K_p = \frac{P_{SO_2} \times P_{O_2}^{1/2}}{P_{SO_3}} = \frac{(0.73)\ (0.37)^{1/2}}{(0.71)} = 0.63\ \text{atm}^{1/2}$$

76.   The first reaction produces equal amounts of SO_3 and SO_2. Using the second reaction, calculate the SO_3, SO_2 and O_2 partial pressures at equilibrium.

                       $SO_3(g)$ $\rightleftharpoons$ $SO_2(g)$ + $1/2\ O_2(g)$

Initial	P_0	P_0	0	P_0 = initial pressure of SO_3 and SO_2
Change	$-x$	$\rightarrow$ $+x$	$+x/2$	after first reaction occurs.
Equil.	$P_0 - x$	$P_0 + x$	$x/2$	

$P_{total} = P_0 - x + P_0 + x + x/2 = 2\,P_0 + x/2 = 0.836$ atm

$P_{O_2} = x/2 = 0.0275$ atm, $x = 0.0550$ atm

$2\,P_0 + x/2 = 0.836$ atm; $2\,P_0 = 0.836 - 0.0275 = 0.809$ atm, $P_0 = 0.405$ atm

$P_{SO_3} = P_0 - x = 0.405 - 0.0550 = 0.350$ atm; $P_{SO_2} = P_0 + x = 0.405 + 0.0550 = 0.460$ atm

For $2\,FeSO_4(s) \rightleftharpoons Fe_2O_3(s) + SO_3(g) + SO_2(g)$:

$\quad K_p = P_{SO_2} \times P_{SO_3} = (0.460)(0.350) = 0.161$ atm^2

For $SO_3(g) \rightleftharpoons SO_2(g) + 1/2\,O_2(g)$:

$$K_p = \frac{P_{SO_2} \times P_{O_2}^{1/2}}{P_{SO_3}} = \frac{(0.460)\,(0.0275)^{1/2}}{0.350} = 0.218 \text{ atm}^{1/2}$$

77. $N_2(g) + 3\,H_2\,(g) \rightleftharpoons 2\,NH_3(g)$ $K_p = \dfrac{P_{NH_3}^2}{P_{N_2} \times P_{H_2}^3} = 6.5 \times 10^{-3}$

<u>1.0 atm</u>	$N_2(g)$	+	$3\,H_2(g)$	$\rightleftharpoons$	$2\,NH_3(g)$
Initial	0.25 atm		0.75 atm		0
Equil.	0.25 - x		0.75 - 3x		2x

$$\frac{(2x)^2}{(0.75 - 3x)^3\,(0.25 - x)} = 6.5 \times 10^{-3}; \text{ Using successive approximations:}$$

$\quad x = 1.2 \times 10^{-2}$ atm; $P_{NH_3} = 2x = 0.024$ atm

<u>10 atm</u>	$N_2(g)$	+	$3\,H_2(g)$	$\rightleftharpoons$	$2\,NH_3(g)$
Initial	2.5 atm		7.5 atm		0
Equil.	2.5 - x		7.5 - 3x		2x

$$\frac{(2x)^2}{(7.5 - 3x)^3\,(2.5 - x)} = 6.5 \times 10^{-3}; \text{ Using successive approximations:}$$

$\quad x = 0.69$ atm; $P_{NH_3} = 1.4$ atm

<u>100 atm</u>   Using the same setup as above: $\dfrac{4x^2}{(75 - 3x)^3\,(25 - x)} = 6.5 \times 10^{-3}$

Solving by successive approximations: $x = 16$ atm; $P_{NH_3} = 32$ atm

<u>1000 atm</u>

$$N_2(g) \quad + \quad 3\,H_2(g) \quad \rightleftharpoons \quad 2\,NH_3(g)$$

Initial   250 atm   750 atm   0
                 Let 250 atm N_2 react completely.
New Initial   0   0 5.0×10^2
Equil. x $3x$ $5.0 \times 10^2 - 2x$

$$\frac{(5.0 \times 10^2 - 2x)^2}{(3x)^3 x} = 6.5 \times 10^{-3}; \text{ Assume } x \text{ is small, then:}$$

$$\frac{(5.0 \times 10^2)^2}{(3x)^3 x} \approx 6.5 \times 10^{-3}, \ x = 35$$

Assumption is poor (14% error).

Solving by successive approximations:

   $x = 32$ atm

$$P_{NH_3} = 5.0 \times 10^2 - 2x = 440 \text{ atm}$$

The results are plotted as $\log P_{NH_3}$ vs.
$\log P_{total}$. Notice that as P_{total} increases, a
larger fraction of N_2 and H_2 is converted to
NH_3, i.e., as P_{total} increases (V decreases),
the reaction shifts further to the right as
predicted by LeChatelier's Principle.

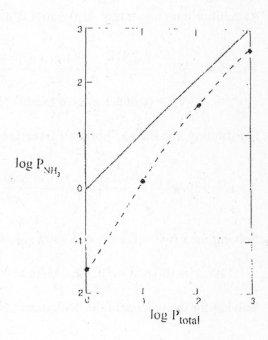

Marathon Problems

78.   Concentration units involve both moles and volume and since both quantities are changing at the
        same time, we have a complicated system. Lets simplify the set-up to the problem initially by only
        worrying about the changes that occur to the moles of each gas.

$$A(g) \quad + \quad B(g) \quad \rightleftharpoons \quad C(g) \qquad K = 130.$$

Initial   0   0   0.406 mol
               Let x mol of C(g) react to reach equilibrium
Change $+x$ $+x$ $\leftarrow$ $-x$
Equil. x x $0.406 - x$

Let V_{eq} = the equilibrium volume of the container, so:

$$[A]_{eq} = [B]_{eq} = \frac{x}{V_{eq}}; \ [C]_{eq} = \frac{0.406 - x}{V_{eq}}$$

$$K = 130. = \frac{[C]}{[A][B]} = \frac{\dfrac{0.406 - x}{V_{eq}}}{\dfrac{x}{V_{eq}} \times \dfrac{x}{V_{eq}}} = \frac{(0.406 - x)V_{eq}}{x^2}$$

From the ideal gas equation: $V = \dfrac{nRT}{P}$

To calculate the equilibrium volume from the ideal gas law, we need the total moles of gas present at equilibrium.

At equilibrium: n_{total} = mol A(g) + mol B(g) + mol C(g) = $x + x + 0.406 - x = 0.406 + x$

Therefore: $V_{eq} = \dfrac{n_{total}RT}{P} = \dfrac{(0.406 + x)(0.08206 \text{ L atm mol}^{-1}\text{ K}^{-1})(300.0 \text{ K})}{1.00 \text{ atm}}$

$V_{eq} = (0.406 + x)\ 24.6 \text{ L/mol}$

Substituting into the equilibrium expression for V_{eq}:

$$K = 130. = \frac{(0.406 - x)(0.406 + x)\ 24.6}{x^2}$$

Solving for x (we will carry one extra significant figure):

$\quad$ 130. $x^2 = (0.1648 - x^2)\ 24.6$, $154.6\ x^2 = 4.054$, $x = 0.162$ mol

Solving for the volume of the container at equilibrium:

$$V_{eq} = \frac{(0.406 + 0.162 \text{ mol})(0.08206)(300.0 \text{ K})}{1.00 \text{ atm}} = 14.0 \text{ L}$$

79.

	N_2O_4	$\rightleftharpoons$	2 NO_2
Initial	x		0
Change	-0.16x		+0.32x
Equil.	0.84x		0.32x

$0.84x + 0.32x = 1.5$ atm, $x = 1.3$ atm

a. $K_p = \dfrac{(0.42)^2}{1.1} = 0.16$ atm

b. $N_2O_4 \;\rightleftharpoons\; 2\,NO_2$

Equil.   x   y

$x + y = 1.0$ atm; $\dfrac{y^2}{x} = 0.16$

Solving, $x = 0.67$ atm ($= P_{N_2O_4}$) and $y = 0.33$ atm ($= P_{NO_2}$)

c. $N_2O_4 \;\rightleftharpoons\; 2\,NO_2$

Initial $P_{N_2O_4}$ 0

Change   -x   +2x

Equil.   0.67   0.33

$x = 0.165$ (using extra sig figs)

$P_{N_2O_4}$ - x = 0.67; Solving: $P_{N_2O_4}$ = 0.84

$\dfrac{0.165}{0.84} \times 100 = 20.\%$ dissociated

CHAPTER SEVEN

ACIDS AND BASES

Nature of Acids and Bases

16. a. $HClO_4(aq) + H_2O(l) \rightarrow H_3O^+(aq) + ClO_4^-(aq)$. Only the forward reaction is indicated since $HClO_4$ is a strong acid and is basically 100% dissociated in water. For acids, the dissociation reaction is commonly written without water as a reactant. The common abbreviation for this reaction is: $HClO_4(aq) \rightarrow H^+(aq) + ClO_4^-(aq)$. This reaction is also called the K_a reaction as the equilibrium constant for this reaction is designated K_a.

   b. Propanoic acid is a weak acid, so it is only partially dissociated in water. The dissociation reaction is: $CH_3CH_2CO_2H(aq) + H_2O(l) \rightleftharpoons H_3O^+(aq) + CH_3CH_2CO_2^-(aq)$ or $CH_3CH_2CO_2H(aq) \rightleftharpoons H^+(aq) + CH_3CH_2CO_2^-(aq)$.

   c. NH_4^+ is a weak acid. Similar to propanoic acid, the dissociation reaction is:

   $$NH_4^+(aq) + H_2O(l) \rightleftharpoons H_3O^+(aq) + NH_3(aq) \text{ or } NH_4^+(aq) \rightleftharpoons H^+(aq) + NH_3(aq)$$

17. The dissociation reaction (the K_a reaction) of an acid in water commonly omits water as a reactant. We will follow this practice. All dissociation reactions produce H^+ and the conjugate base of the acid that is dissociated.

   a. $HC_2H_3O_2(aq) \rightleftharpoons H^+(aq) + C_2H_3O_2^-(aq)$ $\qquad K_a = \dfrac{[H^+][C_2H_3O_2^-]}{[HC_2H_3O_2]}$

   b. $Co(H_2O)_6^{3+}(aq) \rightleftharpoons H^+(aq) + Co(H_2O)_5(OH)^{2+}(aq)$ $\qquad K_a = \dfrac{[H^+][Co(H_2O)_5(OH)^{2+}]}{[Co(H_2O)_6^{3+}]}$

   c. $CH_3NH_3^+(aq) \rightleftharpoons H^+(aq) + CH_3NH_2(aq)$ $\qquad K_a = \dfrac{[H^+][CH_3NH_2]}{[CH_3NH_3^+]}$

18. Strong acids have a $K_a \gg 1$ and weak acids have $K_a < 1$. Table 7.2 in the text lists some K_a values for weak acids. K_a values for strong acids are hard to determine so they are not listed in the text. However, there are only a few common strong acids so if you memorize the strong acids, then all other acids will be weak acids. The strong acids to memorize are HCl, HBr, HI, HNO_3, $HClO_4$ and H_2SO_4.

   a. $HClO_4$ is a strong acid.
   b. HOCl is a weak acid ($K_a = 3.5 \times 10^{-8}$).

c. H_2SO_4 is a strong acid.

d. H_2SO_3 is a weak diprotic acid since the K_{a1} and K_{a2} values are less than one.

19.   The beaker on the left represents a strong acid in solution; the acid, HA, is 100% dissociated into the H^+ and A^- ions. The beaker on the right represents a weak acid in solution; only a little bit of the acid, HB, dissociates into ions, so the acid exists mostly as undissociated HB molecules in water.

a. HNO_2: weak acid beaker

b. HNO_3: strong acid beaker

c. HCl: strong acid beaker

d. HF: weak acid beaker

e. $HC_2H_3O_2$: weak acid beaker

20.   All K_b reactions refer to the base reacting with water to produce the conjugate acid of the base and OH^-.

a. $NH_3(aq) + H_2O(l) \rightleftharpoons NH_4^+(aq) + OH^-(aq)$ $\qquad$ $K_b = \dfrac{[OH^-][NH_4^+]}{[NH_3]}$

b. $CN^-(aq) + H_2O(l) \rightleftharpoons HCN(aq) + OH^-(aq)$ $\qquad$ $K_b = \dfrac{[OH^-][HCN]}{[CN^-]}$

c. $C_5H_5N(aq) + H_2O(l) \rightleftharpoons C_5H_5NH^+(aq) + OH^-(aq)$ $\qquad$ $K_b = \dfrac{[OH^-][C_5H_5NH^+]}{[C_5H_5N]}$

d. $C_6H_5NH_2(aq) + H_2O(l) \rightleftharpoons C_6H_5NH_3^+(aq) + OH^-(aq)$ $\quad$ $K_b = \dfrac{[OH^-][C_6H_5NH_3^+]}{[C_6H_5NH_2]}$

21.   The K_a value is directly related to acid strength. As K_a increases, acid strength increases. For water, use K_w when comparing the acid strength of water to other species. The K_a values are:

$HClO_4$: strong acid ($K_a \gg 1$); $HClO_2$: $K_a = 1.2 \times 10^{-2}$

HOC_6H_5: $K_a = 1.6 \times 10^{-10}$; H_2O: $K_a = K_w = 1.0 \times 10^{-14}$

From the K_a values, the ordering is: $HClO_4 > HClO_2 > HOC_6H_5 > H_2O$.

22.   Except for water, these are the conjugate bases of the acids in the previous exercise. In general, the weaker the acid, the stronger the conjugate base. ClO_4^- is the conjugate base of a strong acid. It is a terrible base (worse than water). The ordering is: $OC_6H_5^- > ClO_2^- > H_2O > ClO_4^-$

23.   a. H_2SO_4 is a strong acid and water is a very weak acid with $K_a = K_w = 1.0 \times 10^{-14}$. H_2SO_4 is a much stronger acid than H_2O.

b. H_2O, $K_a = K_w = 1.0 \times 10^{-14}$; HOCl, $K_a = 3.5 \times 10^{-8}$; HOCl is a stronger acid than H_2O since K_a for HOCl > K_a for H_2O.

c. NH_4^+, $K_a = 5.6 \times 10^{-10}$; $HC_2H_2ClO_2$, $K_a = 1.35 \times 10^{-3}$; $HC_2H_2ClO_2$ is a stronger acid than NH_4^+ since K_a for $HC_2H_2ClO_2 > K_a$ for NH_4^+.

24.   a. H_2O; The conjugate bases of strong acids are terrible bases ($K_b < 10^{-14}$).

      b. OCl^-; The conjugate bases of weak acids are weak bases ($10^{-14} < K_b < 1$); even though they are designated as weak bases, the conjugate bases of weak acids are all better bases than H_2O.

      c. NH_3; For a conjugate acid-base pair, $K_a \times K_b = K_w$. From this relationship, the stronger the acid the weaker the conjugate base (K_b decreases as K_a increases). Since $HC_2H_2ClO_2$ is a stronger acid than NH_4^+ (K_a for $HC_2H_2ClO_2 > K_a$ for NH_4^+), then NH_3 will be a stronger base than $C_2H_2ClO_2^-$.

25.   a. H_2O and $CH_3CO_2^-$

      b.   An acid-base reaction can be thought of as a competition between two opposing bases. Since this equilibrium lies far to the left ($K_a < 1$), then $CH_3CO_2^-$ is a stronger base than H_2O.

      c.   The acetate ion is a better base than water and produces basic solutions in water. When we put acetate ion into solution as the only major basic species, the reaction is:

$$CH_3CO_2^- + H_2O \rightleftharpoons CH_3CO_2H + OH^-$$

      Now the competition is between $CH_3CO_2^-$ and OH^- for the proton. Hydroxide ion is the strongest base possible in water. The above equilibrium lies far to the left resulting in a K_b value less than one. Those species we specifically call weak bases ($10^{-14} < K_b < 1$) lie between H_2O and OH^- in base strength. Weak bases are stronger bases than water but are weaker bases than OH^-.

26.   The NH_4^+ ion is a weak acid because it lies between H_2O and H_3O^+ (H^+) in terms of acid strength. Weak acids are better acids than water, thus their aqueous solutions are acidic. They are weak acids because they are not as strong as H_3O^+ (H^+). Weak acids only partially dissociate in water and have K_a values between 10^{-14} and 1.

27.   In deciding whether a substance is an acid or a base, strong or weak, you should keep in mind a couple ideas:

      1.   There are only a few common strong acids and strong bases all of which should be memorized. Common strong acids = HCl, HBr, HI, HNO_3, $HClO_4$ and H_2SO_4. Common strong bases = LiOH, NaOH, KOH, RbOH, CsOH, $Ca(OH)_2$, $Sr(OH)_2$ and $Ba(OH)_2$.

      2.   All other acids and bases are weak and will have K_a and K_b values less than one but greater than K_w (10^{-14}). Reference Table 7.2 for K_a values for some weak acids and Table 7.3 for K_b values for some weak bases. There are too many weak acids and weak bases to memorize them all. Therefore, use the tables of K_a and K_b values to help you identify weak acids and weak bases. Appendix 5 contains more complete tables of K_a and K_b values.

           a.   weak acid ($K_a = 4.0 \times 10^{-4}$)   b.   strong acid
           c.   weak base ($K_a = 4.38 \times 10^{-4}$)   d.   strong base
           e.   weak base ($K_b = 1.8 \times 10^{-5}$)   f.   weak acid ($K_a = 7.2 \times 10^{-4}$)
           g.   weak acid ($K_a = 1.8 \times 10^{-4}$)   h.   strong base   i.   strong acid

Autoionization of Water and pH Scale

28.   a.   Since the value of the equilibrium constant increases as the temperature increases, then
             the reaction is endothermic. In endothermic reactions, heat is a reactant so an increase
             in temperature (heat) shifts the reaction to produce more products and increases K in the process.

       b. $H_2O(l) \rightleftharpoons H^+(aq) + OH^-(aq)$ $K_w = 5.47 \times 10^{-14} = [H^+][OH^-]$

            In pure water $[H^+] = [OH^-]$, so $5.47 \times 10^{-14} = [H^+]^2$, $[H^+] = 2.34 \times 10^{-7}\ M$

            $pH = - \log [H^+] = - \log (2.34 \times 10^{-7}) = 6.631$

            A neutral solution of water at 50. °C has:

            $[H^+] = [OH^-]$; $[H^+] = 2.34 \times 10^{-7}\ M$; $pH = 6.631$

            Obviously, the condition that $[H^+] = [OH^-]$ is the most general definition of a neutral solution.

       c.

Temp (°C)	Temp (K)	1/T (K^{-1})	K_w	ln K_w
0	273	3.66×10^{-3}	1.14×10^{-15}	-34.408
25	298	3.36×10^{-3}	1.00×10^{-14}	-32.236
35	308	3.25×10^{-3}	2.09×10^{-14}	-31.499
40.	313	3.19×10^{-3}	2.92×10^{-14}	-31.165
50.	323	3.10×10^{-3}	5.47×10^{-14}	-30.537

            From the graph: 37°C = 310. K; 1/T = 3.23×10^{-3} K^{-1}

            ln K_w = -31.38, $K_w = e^{-31.38} = 2.35 \times 10^{-14}$

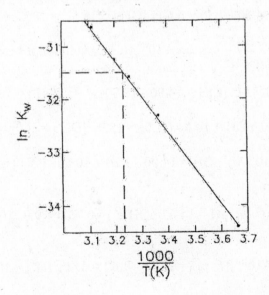

d.   At 37°C, $K_w = 2.35 \times 10^{-14} = [H^+][OH^-] = [H^+]^2$, $[H^+] = 1.53 \times 10^{-7}\,M$

pH = -log $[H^+]$ = -log (1.53×10^{-7}) = 6.815

29.   At 25°C, the relationship: $[H^+]\,[OH^-] = K_w = 1.0 \times 10^{-14}$ always holds for aqueous solutions. When $[H^+]$ is greater than $1.0 \times 10^{-7}\,M$, then the solution is acidic; when $[H^+]$ is less than $1.0 \times 10^{-7}\,M$, then the solution is basic; when $[H^+] = 1.0 \times 10^{-7}\,M$, then the solution is neutral. In terms of $[OH^-]$, an acidic solution has $[OH^-] < 1.0 \times 10^{-7}\,M$, a basic solution has $[OH^-] > 1.0 \times 10^{-7}\,M$ and a neutral solution has $[OH^-] = 1.0 \times 10^{-7}\,M$.

a. $[OH^-] = \dfrac{K_w}{[H^+]} = \dfrac{1.0 \times 10^{-14}}{1.0 \times 10^{-7}} = 1.0 \times 10^{-7}\,M$; The solution is neutral.

pH = -log $[H^+]$; pOH = -log $[OH^-]$; At 25°C, pH + pOH = 14.00

pH = -log $[H^+]$ = -log (1.0×10^{-7}) = 7.00; pOH = 14.00 - pH = 14.00 - 7.00 = 7.00

b. $[OH^-] = \dfrac{1.0 \times 10^{-14}}{6.7 \times 10^{-4}} = 1.5 \times 10^{-11}\,M$; The solution is acidic.

pH = -log (6.7×10^{-4}) = 3.17; pOH = 14.00 - 3.17 = 10.83

c. $[OH^-] = \dfrac{1.0 \times 10^{-14}}{1.9 \times 10^{-11}} = 5.3 \times 10^{-4}\,M$; The solution is basic.

pH = -log (1.9×10^{-11}) = 10.72; pOH = 14.00 - 10.72 = 3.28

d. $[OH^-] = \dfrac{1.0 \times 10^{-14}}{2.3} = 4.3 \times 10^{-15}\,M$; The solution is acidic.

pH = -log (2.3) = -0.36; pOH = 14.00 - (-0.36) = 14.36

30.   a. $[H^+] = 10^{-pH}$, $[H^+] = 10^{-7.40} = 4.0 \times 10^{-8}\,M$

pOH = 14.00 - pH = 14.00 - 7.40 = 6.60; $[OH^-] = 10^{-pOH} = 10^{-6.60} = 2.5 \times 10^{-7}\,M$

or $[OH^-] = \dfrac{K_w}{[H^+]} = \dfrac{1.0 \times 10^{-14}}{4.0 \times 10^{-8}} = 2.5 \times 10^{-7}\,M$; This solution is basic since pH > 7.00.

b. $[H^+] = 10^{-15.3} = 5 \times 10^{-16}\,M$; pOH = 14.00 - 15.3 = -1.3; $[OH^-] = 10^{-(-1.3)} = 20\,M$; basic

c. $[H^+] = 10^{-(-1.0)} = 10\,M$;   pOH = 14.0 - (-1.0) = 15.0; $[OH^-] = 10^{-15.0} = 1 \times 10^{-15}\,M$; acidic

d. $[H^+] = 10^{-3.20} = 6.3 \times 10^{-4}\,M$; pOH = 14.00 - 3.20 = 10.80; $[OH^-] = 10^{-10.80} = 1.6 \times 10^{-11}\,M$; acidic

e. $[OH^-] = 10^{-5.0} = 1 \times 10^{-5}\,M$; pH = 14.0 - pOH = 14.0 - 5.0 = 9.0; $[H^+] = 10^{-9.0} = 1 \times 10^{-9}\,M$; basic

f. $[OH^-] = 10^{-9.60} = 2.5 \times 10^{-10}\,M$; pH = 14.00 - 9.60 = 4.40; $[H^+] = 10^{-4.40} = 4.0 \times 10^{-5}\,M$; acidic

Solutions of Acids

31.   Strong acids are assumed to completely dissociate in water, e.g., $HCl(aq) + H_2O(l) \rightarrow H_3O^+(aq) + Cl^-(aq)$ or $HCl(aq) \rightarrow H^+(aq) + Cl^-(aq)$.

a.   A 0.10 M HCl solution gives 0.10 M H^+ and 0.10 M Cl^- since HCl completely dissociates. The amount of H^+ from H_2O will be insignificant.

pH = -log $[H^+]$ = -log (0.10) = 1.00

b.   5.0 M H^+ is produced when 5.0 M $HClO_4$ completely dissociates. The amount of H^+ from H_2O will be insignificant.   pH = -log (5.0) = -0.70   (Negative pH values just indicate very concentrated acid solutions.)

c. 1.0×10^{-11} M H^+ is produced when 1.0×10^{-11} M HI completely dissociates. If you take the negative log of 1.0×10^{-11} this gives pH = 11.00. This is impossible! We dissolved an acid in water and got a basic pH. What we must consider in this problem is that water by itself donates 1.0×10^{-7} M H^+. We can normally ignore the small amount of H^+ from H_2O except when we have a very dilute solution of an acid (as in the case here). Therefore, the pH is that of neutral water (pH = 7.00) since the amount of HI present is insignificant.

32.   50.0 mL con. HCl soln $\times \dfrac{1.19\text{ g}}{\text{mL}} \times \dfrac{38\text{ g HCl}}{100\text{ g con. HCl soln}} \times \dfrac{1\text{ mol HCl}}{36.5\text{ g}} = 0.62$ mol HCl

20.0 mL con. HNO_3 soln $\times \dfrac{1.42\text{ g}}{\text{mL}} \times \dfrac{70.\text{ g }HNO_3}{100\text{ g soln}} \times \dfrac{1\text{ mol }HNO_3}{63.0\text{ g }HNO_3} = 0.32$ mol HNO_3

$HCl(aq) \rightarrow H^+(aq) + Cl^-(aq)$ and $HNO_3(aq) \rightarrow H^+(aq) + NO_3^-(aq)$ (Both are strong acids.)

So we will have 0.62 + 0.32 = 0.94 mol of H^+ in the final solution.

$[H^+] = \dfrac{0.94\text{ mol}}{1.00\text{ L}} = 0.94\ M;$ pH = -log $[H^+]$ = -log (0.94) = 0.027 = 0.03

$[OH^-] = \dfrac{K_w}{[H^+]} = \dfrac{1.0 \times 10^{-14}}{0.94} = 1.1 \times 10^{-14}\ M$

33.   a.   Major species = $H^+(aq)$, $Cl^-(aq)$ and $H_2O(l)$ (HCl is a strong acid.) $[H^+] = 0.250\ M$

pH = -log $[H^+]$ = -log(0.250) = 0.602

b. $H^+(aq)$, $Br^-(aq)$ and $H_2O(l)$ (HBr is a strong acid.) pH = 0.602

c. $H^+(aq)$, $ClO_4^-(aq)$ and $H_2O(l)$ ($HClO_4$ is a strong acid.) pH = 0.602

d. $H^+(aq)$, $NO_3^-(aq)$ and $H_2O(l)$ (HNO_3 is a strong acid.) pH = 0.602

e. HNO_2 ($K_a = 4.0 \times 10^{-4}$) and H_2O ($K_a = K_w = 1.0 \times 10^{-14}$) are the major species. HNO_2 is much stronger acid than H_2O so it is the major source of H^+. However, HNO_2 is a weak acid ($K_a < 1$) so it only partially dissociates in water. We must solve an equilibrium problem to determine [H^+]. In the Solutions Guide, we will summarize the initial, change and equilibrium concentrations into one table called the ICE table. Solving the weak acid problem:

$$HNO_2(aq) \quad \rightleftharpoons \quad H^+(aq) \quad + \quad NO_2^-(aq)$$

Initial   0.250 M ~0   0
                 x mol/L HNO_2 dissociates to reach equilibrium
Change   -x $\rightarrow$ +x +x
Equil.   0.250 -x x x

$K_a = \dfrac{[H^+][NO_2^-]}{[HNO_2]} = 4.0 \times 10^{-4} = \dfrac{x^2}{0.250 - x}$; If we assume $x \ll 0.250$, then:

$$4.0 \times 10^{-4} \approx \dfrac{x^2}{0.250}, x = \sqrt{4.0 \times 10^{-4}(0.250)} = 0.010\ M$$

We must check the assumption: $\dfrac{x}{0.250} \times 100 = \dfrac{0.010}{0.250} \times 100 = 4.0\%$

All the assumptions are good. The H^+ contribution from water ($10^{-7}\ M$) is negligible and x is small compared to 0.250 (percent error = 4.0%). If the percent error is less than 5% for an assumption, we will consider it a valid assumption (called the 5% rule). Finishing the problem: $x = 0.010\ M = [H^+]$; pH = -log [H^+] = -log(0.010) = 2.00

f. CH_3CO_2H ($K_a = 1.8 \times 10^{-5}$) and H_2O ($K_a = K_w = 1.0 \times 10^{-14}$) are the major species. CH_3CO_2H is the major source of H^+. Solving the weak acid problem:

$$CH_3CO_2H \quad \rightleftharpoons \quad H^+ \quad + \quad CH_3CO_2^-$$

Initial   0.250 M ~0   0
                 x mol/L CH_3CO_2H dissociates to reach equilibrium
Change   -x $\rightarrow$ +x +x
Equil.   0.250 - x x x

$K_a = \dfrac{[H^+][CH_3CO_2^-]}{[CH_3CO_2H]} = 1.8 \times 10^{-5} = \dfrac{x^2}{0.250 - x} \approx \dfrac{x^2}{0.250}$ (assuming $x \ll 0.250$)

$x = 2.1 \times 10^{-3}\ M$; Checking assumption: $\dfrac{2.1 \times 10^{-3}}{0.250} \times 100 = 0.84\%$. Assumptions good.

[H^+] $= x = 2.1 \times 10^{-3}\ M$; pH $= -$log $(2.1 \times 10^{-3}) = 2.68$

g. HCN ($K_a = 6.2 \times 10^{-10}$) and H_2O are the major species. HCN is the major source of H^+.

$$HCN \quad \rightleftharpoons \quad H^+ \quad + \quad CN^-$$

Initial   0.250 M ~0   0
                   x mol/L HCN dissociates to reach equilibrium
Change   -x $\rightarrow$ +x +x
Equil.   0.250 - x x x

$$K_a = 6.2 \times 10^{-10} = \frac{[H^+][CN^-]}{[HCN]} = \frac{x^2}{0.250 - x} \approx \frac{x^2}{0.250} \quad \text{(assuming } x \ll 0.250)$$

$x = [H^+] = 1.2 \times 10^{-5}$ M; Checking assumption: x is 4.8×10^{-3}% of 0.250

Assumptions good. pH = -log (1.2×10^{-5}) = 4.92

34.   At pH = 2.000, $[H^+] = 10^{-2.000} = 1.00 \times 10^{-2}$ M; At pH = 4.000, $[H^+] = 10^{-4.000} = 1.00 \times 10^{-4}$ M

mol H^+ present = 0.0100 L $\times \dfrac{0.0100 \text{ mol } H^+}{L} = 1.00 \times 10^{-4}$ mol H^+

Let V = total volume of solution at pH = 4.000: 1.00×10^{-4} mol/L = $\dfrac{1.00 \times 10^{-4} \text{ mol } H^+}{V}$, V = 1.00 L

Volume of water added = 1.00 L - 0.0100 L = 0.99 L = 990 mL

35.   a. Major species: $HC_2H_3O_2$ ($K_a = 1.8 \times 10^{-5}$) and water; Major source of H^+ = $HC_2H_3O_2$. Since K_a for $HC_2H_3O_2$ is less than one, then $HC_2H_3O_2$ is a weak acid and we must solve an equilibrium problem to determine $[H^+]$. The set-up is:

$$HC_2H_3O_2(aq) \quad \rightleftharpoons \quad H^+(aq) + \quad C_3H_3O_2^-(aq)$$

Initial   0.20 M ~0   0
                   x mol/L $HC_2H_3O_2$ dissociates to reach equilibrium
Change   -x $\rightarrow$ +x +x
Equil.   0.20 - x x x

$$K_a = 1.8 \times 10^{-5} = \frac{[H^+][C_2H_3O_2^-]}{[HC_2H_3O_2]} = \frac{x^2}{0.20 - x} \approx \frac{x^2}{0.20} \quad \text{(assuming } x \ll 0.20)$$

$x = [H^+] = 1.9 \times 10^{-3}$ M

We have made two assumptions which we must check.

1. 0.20 - $x \approx$ 0.20

(x/0.20) $\times$ 100 = (1.9×10^{-3}/0.20) $\times$ 100 = 0.95%. Good assumption (1% error). If the percent error in the assumption is < 5%, then the assumption is valid.

2.   Acetic acid is the major source of H^+, i.e., we can ignore 10^{-7} M H^+ already present in neutral H_2O.

[H^+] from $HC_2H_3O_2 = 1.9 \times 10^{-3} >> 10^{-7}$;   This assumption is valid.

In future problems we will always begin the problem solving process by making these assumptions and we will always check them. However, we may not explicitly state that the assumptions are valid. We will <u>always</u> state when the assumptions are <u>not</u> valid and we have to use other techniques to solve the problem. Remember, anytime we make an assumption, we must check its validity before the solution to the problem is complete. Answering the question:

$$[H^+] = [C_2H_3O_2^-] = 1.9 \times 10^{-3} \ M; \quad [OH^-] = 5.3 \times 10^{-12} \ M$$

$$[HC_2H_3O_2] = 0.20 - x = 0.198 \approx 0.20 \ M; \quad pH = -\log [H^+] = -\log (1.9 \times 10^{-3}) = 2.72$$

b. HNO_2 ($K_a = 4.0 \times 10^{-4}$) is the dominant producer of H^+. Solving the weak acid problem:

$$HNO_2 \quad \rightleftharpoons \quad H^+ \quad + \quad NO_2^- \qquad K_a = 4.0 \times 10^{-4}$$

Initial	1.5 M	~0	0
	x mol/L HNO_2 dissociates to reach equilibrium		
Change	$-x$ $\rightarrow$	$+x$	$+x$
Equil.	1.5 - x	x	x

$$K_a = 4.0 \times 10^{-4} = \frac{[H^+][NO_2^-]}{[HNO_2]} = \frac{x^2}{1.5 - x} \approx \frac{x^2}{1.5} \ \text{(assuming } x << 1.5)$$

$x = [H^+] = 2.4 \times 10^{-2} \ M$; Assumptions good: $10^{-7} << 2.4 \times 10^{-2} << 1.5$

$[H^+] = [NO_2^-] = 2.4 \times 10^{-2} \ M$; $[OH^-] = 4.2 \times 10^{-13} \ M$

$[HNO_2] = 1.5 - x = 1.48 \approx 1.5 \ M$; $pH = -\log (2.4 \times 10^{-2}) = 1.62$

c.   This is a weak acid in water. Solving the weak acid problem:

$$HF \quad \rightleftharpoons \quad H^+ \quad + \quad F^- \qquad K_a = 7.2 \times 10^{-4}$$

Initial	0.020 M	~0	0
	x mol/L HF dissociates to reach equilibrium		
Change	$-x$ $\rightarrow$	$+x$	$+x$
Equil.	0.020 - x	x	x

$$K_a = 7.2 \times 10^{-4} = \frac{[H^+][F^-]}{[HF]} = \frac{x^2}{0.020 - x} \approx \frac{x^2}{0.020} \ \text{(assuming } x << 0.020)$$

$x = [H^+] = 3.8 \times 10^{-3} \ M$; Check assumptions: $\dfrac{x}{0.020} \times 100 = \dfrac{3.8 \times 10^{-3}}{0.020} \times 100 = 19\%$

The assumption $x \ll 0.020$ is not good (x is more than 5% of 0.020). We must solve $x^2/(0.020 - x) = 7.2 \times 10^{-4}$ exactly by using either the quadratic formula or by the method of successive approximations (see Appendix 1.4 of text). Using successive approximations, we let 0.016 M be a new approximation for [HF]. That is, in the denominator try $x = 0.0038$ (the value of x we calculated making the normal assumption), so $0.020 - 0.0038 = 0.016$, then solve for a new value of x in the numerator.

$$\frac{x^2}{0.020 - x} \approx \frac{x^2}{0.016} = 7.2 \times 10^{-4}, \ x = 3.4 \times 10^{-3}$$

We use this new value of x to further refine our estimate of [HF], i.e., $0.020 - x = 0.020 - 0.0034 = 0.0166$ (carrying an extra significant figure).

$$\frac{x^2}{0.020 - x} \approx \frac{x^2}{0.0166} = 7.2 \times 10^{-4}, \ x = 3.5 \times 10^{-3}$$

We repeat, until we get a self-consistent answer. This would be the same answer we would get solving exactly using the quadratic equation. In this case it is: $x = 3.5 \times 10^{-3}$

So: $[H^+] = [F^-] = x = 3.5 \times 10^{-3} \ M$; $[OH^-] = K_w/[H^+] = 2.9 \times 10^{-12} \ M$

$[HF] = 0.020 - x = 0.020 - 0.0035 = 0.017 \ M$; pH = 2.46

Note: When the 5% assumption fails, use whichever method you are most comfortable with to solve exactly. The method of successive approximations is probably fastest when the percent error is less than ~25% (unless you have a graphing calculator).

36.   Major species: $HC_2H_2ClO_2$ ($K_a = 1.35 \times 10^{-3}$) and H_2O; Major source of H^+: $HC_2H_2ClO_2$

$$HC_2H_2ClO_2 \ \rightleftharpoons \ H^+ + C_2H_2ClO_2^-$$

Initial   0.10 M ~0   0
               x mol/L $HC_2H_2ClO_2$ dissociates to reach equilibrium
Change $-x$ $\rightarrow$ $+x$ $+x$
Equil. $0.10 - x$ x x

$$K_a = 1.35 \times 10^{-3} = \frac{x^2}{0.10 - x} \approx \frac{x^2}{0.10}, \ x = 1.2 \times 10^{-2} \ M$$

Checking the assumptions finds that x is 12% of 0.10 which fails the 5% rule. We must solve $1.35 \times 10^{-3} = x^2/(0.10 - x)$ exactly using either the method of successive approximations or the quadratic equation. Using either method gives $x = [H^+] = 1.1 \times 10^{-2} \ M$. pH = $-\log [H^+] = -\log (1.1 \times 10^{-2}) = 1.96$.

37.   Major species: HIO_3, H_2O; Major source of H^+: HIO_3 (a weak acid, $K_a = 0.17$)

$$HIO_3 \ \rightleftharpoons \ H^+ + IO_3^-$$

Initial   0.010 M ~0   0
               x mol/L HIO_3 dissociates to reach equilibrium

Change $-x$ $\rightarrow$ $+x$ $+x$
Equil. $0.010 - x$ x x

$$K_a = 0.17 = \frac{[H^+][IO_3^-]}{[HIO_3]} = \frac{x^2}{0.010 - x} \approx \frac{x^2}{0.010}, \quad x = 0.041; \quad \text{Check assumption.}$$

Assumption is horrible. (x is more than 400% of 0.010). When the assumption is this poor, it is generally quickest to solve exactly using the quadratic formula (see Appendix 1.4 in text). Using the quadratic formula and carrying extra significant figures:

$$0.17 = \frac{x^2}{0.010 - x}, \quad x^2 = 0.17(0.010 - x), \quad x^2 + 0.17\,x - 1.7 \times 10^{-3} = 0$$

$$x = \frac{-0.17 \pm [(0.17)^2 - 4(1)(-1.7 \times 10^{-3})]^{1/2}}{2(1)} = \frac{-0.17 \pm 0.189}{2}, \quad x = 9.5 \times 10^{-3}\,M$$
$$\text{(x must be positive)}$$

$$x = 9.5 \times 10^{-3}\,M = [H^+]; \quad pH = -\log(9.5 \times 10^{-3}) = 2.02$$

38. $HC_3H_5O_2$ ($K_a = 1.3 \times 10^{-5}$) and H_2O ($K_a = K_w = 1.0 \times 10^{-14}$) are the major species present. $HC_3H_5O_2$ will be the dominant producer of H^+ since $HC_3H_5O_2$ is a stronger acid than H_2O. Solving the weak acid problem:

$$HC_3H_5O_2 \quad\rightleftharpoons\quad H^+ \quad + \quad C_3H_5O_2^-$$

Initial	0.100 M	~0	0
	x mol/L $HC_3H_5O_2$ dissociates to reach equilibrium		
Change	$-x$ $\rightarrow$	$+x$	$+x$
Equil.	0.100 $- x$	x	x

$$K_a = 1.3 \times 10^{-5} = \frac{[H^+][C_3H_5O_2^-]}{[HC_3H_5O_2]} = \frac{x^2}{0.100 - x} \approx \frac{x^2}{0.100}$$

$$x = [H^+] = 1.1 \times 10^{-3}\,M; \quad pH = -\log(1.1 \times 10^{-3}) = 2.96$$

Assumption follows the 5% rule (x is 1.1% of 0.100).

$$[H^+] = [C_3H_5O_2^-] = 1.1 \times 10^{-3}\,M; \quad [OH^-] = K_w/[H^+] = 9.1 \times 10^{-12}\,M$$

$$[HC_3H_5O_2] = 0.100 - 1.1 \times 10^{-3} = 0.099\,M$$

$$\text{Percent dissociation} = \frac{[H^+]}{[HC_3H_5O_2]_o} \times 100 = \frac{1.1 \times 10^{-3}}{0.100} \times 100 = 1.1\%$$

39.   This is a weak acid in water. We must solve a weak acid problem. Let $HBz = C_6H_5CO_2H$.

$$0.56\ \text{g HBz} \times \frac{1\ \text{mol HBz}}{122.1\ \text{g}} = 4.6 \times 10^{-3}\ \text{mol}; \quad [HBz]_o = 4.6 \times 10^{-3}\,M$$

$$HBz \quad \rightleftharpoons \quad H^+ + Bz^-$$

Initial	$4.6 \times 10^{-3}\, M$	~0	0

x mol/L HBz dissociates to reach equilibrium

Change	$-x$	$+x$	$+x$
Equil.	$4.6 \times 10^{-3} - x$	x	x

$$K_a = 6.4 \times 10^{-5} = \frac{[H^+][Bz^-]}{[HBz]} = \frac{x^2}{4.6 \times 10^{-3} - x} \approx \frac{x^2}{4.6 \times 10^{-3}}$$

$$x = [H^+] = 5.4 \times 10^{-4}; \quad \text{Check assumptions:} \quad \frac{x}{4.6 \times 10^{-3}} \times 100 = \frac{5.4 \times 10^{-4}}{4.6 \times 10^{-3}} \times 100 = 12\%$$

Assumption is not good (x is 12% of 4.6×10^{-3}). When assumption(s) fail, we must solve exactly using the quadratic formula or the method of successive approximations (see Appendix 1.4 of text). Using successive approximations:

$$\frac{x^2}{(4.6 \times 10^{-4} - 5.4 \times 10^{-4})} = 6.4 \times 10^{-5}, \; x = 5.1 \times 10^{-4}$$

$$\frac{x^2}{(4.6 \times 10^{-3} - 5.1 \times 10^{-4})} = 6.4 \times 10^{-5}, \; x = 5.1 \times 10^{-4}\, M \text{ (consistent answer)}$$

So: $x = [H^+] = [Bz^-] = [C_6H_5CO_2^-] = 5.1 \times 10^{-4}\, M$

$[HBz] = [C_6H_5CO_2H] = 4.6 \times 10^{-3} - x = 4.1 \times 10^{-3}\, M$

$pH = -\log(5.1 \times 10^{-4}) = 3.29; \; pOH = 14.00 - pH = 10.71; \; [OH^-] = 10^{-10.71} = 1.9 \times 10^{-11}\, M$

40.
$$HBz \quad \rightleftharpoons \quad H^+ + Bz^- \qquad HBz = C_6H_5CO_2H$$

Initial	C	~0	0

C = $[HBz]_o$ = concentration of HBz that dissolves to give saturated solution.

x mol/L HBz dissociates to reach equilibrium

Change	$-x$	$+x$	$+x$
Equil.	$C - x$	x	x

$$K_a = \frac{[H^+][Bz^-]}{[HBz]} = 6.4 \times 10^{-5} = \frac{x^2}{C - x}, \text{ where } x = [H^+]$$

$$6.4 \times 10^{-5} = \frac{[H^+]^2}{C - [H^+]}; \; pH = 2.80; \; [H^+] = 10^{-2.80} = 1.6 \times 10^{-3}\, M$$

$$C - 1.6 \times 10^{-3} = \frac{(1.6 \times 10^{-3})^2}{6.4 \times 10^{-5}} = 4.0 \times 10^{-2}, \; C = 4.0 \times 10^{-2} + 1.6 \times 10^{-3} = 4.2 \times 10^{-2}\, M$$

The molar solubility of $C_6H_5CO_2H$ is 4.2×10^{-2} mol/L.

$$\frac{4.2 \times 10^{-2} \text{ mol } C_6H_5CO_2H}{L} \times \frac{122.1 \text{ g } C_6H_5CO_2H}{\text{mol } C_6H_5CO_2H} \times 0.100 \text{ L} = 0.51 \text{ g per 100. mL solution}$$

41.   20.0 mL glacial acetic acid $\times \dfrac{1.05 \text{ g}}{\text{mL}} \times \dfrac{1 \text{ mol}}{60.05 \text{ g}} = 0.350 \text{ mol } HC_2H_3O_2$

Initial concentration of $HC_2H_3O_2 = \dfrac{0.350 \text{ mol}}{0.2500 \text{ L}} = 1.40 \ M$

	$HC_2H_3O_2$	$\rightleftharpoons$	H^+	$+$	$C_2H_3O_2^-$	$K_a = 1.8 \times 10^{-5}$
Initial	1.40 M		~0		0	

x mol/L $HC_2H_3O_2$ dissociates to reach equilibrium

Change	$-x$	$\rightarrow$	$+x$		$+x$
Equil.	$1.40 - x$		x		x

$$K_a = 1.8 \times 10^{-5} = \frac{[H^+][C_2H_3O_2^-]}{[HC_2H_3O_2]} = \frac{x^2}{1.40 - x} \approx \frac{x^2}{1.40}$$

$x = [H^+] = 5.0 \times 10^{-3} \ M; \ \text{pH} = 2.30$ Assumptions good (x is 0.36% of 1.40).

42.   HF and HOC_6H_5 are both weak acids with K_a values of 7.2×10^{-4} and 1.6×10^{-10}, respectively. Since the K_a value for HF is much greater than the K_a value for HOC_6H_5, then HF will be the dominant producer of H^+ (we can ignore the amount of H^+ produced from HOC_6H_5 since it will be insignificant).

	HF	$\rightleftharpoons$	H^+	$+$	F^-
Initial	0.10 M		~0		0

x mol/L HF dissociates to reach equilibrium

Change	$-x$	$\rightarrow$	$+x$	$+x$
Equil.	$0.10 - x$		x	x

$$K_a = 7.2 \times 10^{-4} = \frac{[H^+][F^-]}{[HF]} = \frac{x^2}{1.0 - x} \approx \frac{x^2}{1.0}$$

$x = [H^+] = 2.7 \times 10^{-2} \ M; \ \text{pH} = -\log(2.7 \times 10^{-2}) = 1.57$ Assumptions good.

Solving for $[OC_6H_5^-]$ using $HOC_6H_5 \rightleftharpoons H^+ + OC_6H_5^-$ equilibrium:

$$K_a = 1.6 \times 10^{-10} = \frac{[H^+][OC_6H_5^-]}{[HOC_6H_5]} = \frac{(2.7 \times 10^{-2})[OC_6H_5^-]}{1.0}, \ [OC_6H_5^-] = 5.9 \times 10^{-9} \ M$$

Note that this answer indicates that only $5.9 \times 10^{-9} \ M$ HOC_6H_5 dissociates which indicates that HF is truly the only significant producer of H^+ in this solution.

43.   a.   HCl is a strong acid. It will produce 0.10 M H^+. HOCl is a weak acid. Let's consider the equilibrium:

$$HOCl \quad \rightleftharpoons \quad H^+ \quad + \quad OCl^- \quad K_a = 3.5 \times 10^{-8}$$

Initial	$0.10\ M$	$0.10\ M$	0
	x mol/L HOCl dissociates to reach equilibrium		
Change	$-x$ $\rightarrow$	$+x$	$+x$
Equil.	$0.10 - x$	$0.10 + x$	x

$$K_a = 3.5 \times 10^{-8} = \frac{[H^+][OCl^-]}{[HOCl]} = \frac{(0.10 + x)(x)}{0.10 - x} \approx x, x = 3.5 \times 10^{-8}\ M$$

Assumptions are great (x is 3.5×10^{-5}% of 0.10). We are really assuming that HCl is the only important source of H^+, which it is. The $[H^+]$ contribution from HOCl, x, is negligible. Therefore, $[H^+] = 0.10\ M$; pH = 1.00.

b. HNO_3 is a strong acid, giving an initial concentration of H^+ equal to $0.050\ M$. Consider the equilibrium:

$$HC_2H_3O_2 \quad \rightleftharpoons \quad H^+ \quad + \quad C_2H_3O_2^- \quad K_a = 1.8 \times 10^{-5}$$

Initial	$0.50\ M$	$0.050\ M$	0
	x mol/L $HC_2H_3O_2$ dissociates to reach equilibrium		
Change	$-x$ $\rightarrow$	$+x$	$+x$
Equil.	$0.50 - x$	$0.050 + x$	x

$$K_a = 1.8 \times 10^{-5} = \frac{[H^+][C_2H_3O_2^-]}{[HC_2H_3O_2]} = \frac{(0.050 + x)x}{(0.50 - x)} \approx \frac{0.050\ x}{0.50}$$

$x = 1.8 \times 10^{-4}$; Assumptions are good (well within the 5% rule).

$[H^+] = 0.050 + x = 0.050\ M$ and pH = 1.30

44.   Both are strong acids.

$0.0500\ L \times 0.050\ mol/L = 2.5 \times 10^{-3}\ mol\ HCl = 2.5 \times 10^{-3}\ mol\ H^+ + 2.5 \times 10^{-3}\ mol\ Cl^-$

$0.1500\ L \times 0.10\ mol/L = 1.5 \times 10^{-2}\ mol\ HNO_3 = 1.5 \times 10^{-2}\ mol\ H^+ + 1.5 \times 10^{-2}\ mol\ NO_3^-$

$$[H^+] = \frac{(2.5 \times 10^{-3} + 1.5 \times 10^{-2})\ mol}{0.2000\ L} = 0.088\ M; \quad [OH^-] = \frac{K_w}{[H^+]} = 1.1 \times 10^{-13}\ M$$

$$[Cl^-] = \frac{2.5 \times 10^{-3}\ mol}{0.2000\ L} = 0.013\ M; \quad [NO_3^-] = \frac{1.5 \times 10^{-2}\ mol}{0.2000\ L} = 0.075\ M$$

45. $$HF \quad \rightleftharpoons \quad H^+ \quad + \quad F^-$$

Initial	$0.100\ M$	~ 0	0
	x mol/L HF dissociates to reach equilibrium		
Change	$-x$ $\rightarrow$	$+x$	$+x$
Equil.	$0.100 - x$	x	x

$$K_a = \frac{[H^+][F^-]}{[HF]} = \frac{x^2}{0.100 - x}; \quad x = [H^+] = [F^-] = 0.081 \times (0.100 \ M) = 8.1 \times 10^{-3} \ M$$

$$[HF] = 0.100 - 8.1 \times 10^{-3} = 0.092 \ M; \quad K_a = \frac{(8.1 \times 10^{-3})^2}{0.092} = 7.1 \times 10^{-4}$$

46.   HX $\rightleftharpoons$ H^+ + X^-

Initial	I	~0	0

where I = $[HX]_o$

x mol/L HX dissociates to reach equilibrium

Change	-x	$\rightarrow$ +x	+x
Equil.	I - x	x	x

From the problem, $x = 0.25(I)$ and $I - x = 0.30 \ M$.

$I - 0.25(I) = 0.30 \ M$, $I = 0.40 \ M$ and $x = 0.25 (0.40 \ M) = 0.10 \ M$

$$K_a = \frac{[H^+][X^-]}{[HX]} = \frac{x^2}{I - x} = \frac{(0.10)^2}{0.30} = 0.033$$

47.   In all parts of this problem, acetic acid ($HC_2H_3O_2$) is the best weak acid present. We must solve a weak acid problem.

a. $HC_2H_3O_2$ $\rightleftharpoons$ H^+ + $C_2H_3O_2^-$

Initial	0.50 M	~0	0

x mol/L $HC_2H_3O_2$ dissociates to reach equilibrium

Change	-x	$\rightarrow$ +x	+x
Equil.	0.50 - x	x	x

$$K_a = 1.8 \times 10^{-5} = \frac{[H^+][C_2H_3O_2^-]}{[HC_2H_3O_2]} = \frac{x^2}{0.50 - x} \approx \frac{x^2}{0.50}$$

$x = [H^+] = [C_2H_3O_2^-] = 3.0 \times 10^{-3} \ M$ Assumptions good.

$$\text{Percent dissociation} = \frac{[H^+]}{[HC_2H_3O_2]_o} \times 100 = \frac{3.0 \times 10^{-3}}{0.50} \times 100 = 0.60\%$$

b.   The set-up for solutions b and c are similar to solution a except the final equation is slightly different, reflecting the new concentration of $HC_2H_3O_2$.

$$K_a = 1.8 \times 10^{-5} = \frac{x^2}{0.050 - x} \approx \frac{x^2}{0.050}$$

$x = [H^+] = [C_2H_3O_2^-] = 9.5 \times 10^{-4} \ M$ Assumptions good.

$$\% \text{ dissociation} = \frac{9.5 \times 10^{-4}}{0.050} \times 100 = 1.9\%$$

c. $K_a = 1.8 \times 10^{-5} = \dfrac{x^2}{0.0050 - x} \approx \dfrac{x^2}{0.0050}$

$x = [H^+] = [C_2H_3O_2^-] = 3.0 \times 10^{-4}\ M;$ Check assumptions.

Assumption that x is negligible is borderline (6.0% error). We should solve exactly. Using the method of successive approximations (see Appendix 1.4 of text):

$$1.8 \times 10^{-5} = \dfrac{x^2}{0.0050 - 3.0 \times 10^{-4}} = \dfrac{x^2}{0.0047},\ x = 2.9 \times 10^{-4}$$

Next trial also gives $x = 2.9 \times 10^{-4}$.

% dissociation $= \dfrac{2.9 \times 10^{-4}}{5.0 \times 10^{-3}} \times 100 = 5.8\%$

d.   As we dilute a solution, all concentrations are decreased. Dilution will shift the equilibrium to the side with the greater number of particles. For example, suppose we double the volume of an equilibrium mixture of a weak acid by adding water, then:

$$Q = \dfrac{\left(\dfrac{[H^+]_{eq}}{2}\right)\left(\dfrac{[X^-]_{eq}}{2}\right)}{\left(\dfrac{[HX]_{eq}}{2}\right)} = \dfrac{1}{2} K_a$$

$Q < K_a$, so the equilibrium shifts to the right or towards a greater percent dissociation.

e. $[H^+]$ depends on the initial concentration of weak acid and on how much weak acid dissociates. For solutions a–c the initial concentration of acid decreases more rapidly than the percent dissociation increases. Thus, $[H^+]$ decreases.

48. $HClO_2 \rightleftharpoons H^+ + ClO_2^-$ $K_a = 1.2 \times 10^{-2}$

Initial	0.22 M	~0	0

x mol/L $HClO_2$ dissociates to reach equilibrium

Change	-x	$\rightarrow$	+x	+x
Equil.	0.22 - x		x	x

$K_a = 1.2 \times 10^{-2} = \dfrac{[H^+][ClO_2^-]}{[HClO_2]} = \dfrac{x^2}{0.22 - x} \approx \dfrac{x^2}{0.22},\ x = 5.1 \times 10^{-2}$

The assumption that x is small is not good (x is 23% of 0.22). Using the method of successive approximations and carrying extra significant figures:

$$\dfrac{x^2}{0.22 - 0.051} = \dfrac{x^2}{0.169} = 1.2 \times 10^{-2},\ x = 4.5 \times 10^{-2}$$

$$\dfrac{x^2}{0.175} = 1.2 \times 10^{-2},\ x = 4.6 \times 10^{-2};\ x = 4.6 \times 10^{-2}\ (\text{repeats})$$

$[H^+] = [ClO_2^-] = x = 4.6 \times 10^{-2}\ M;$ % dissociation $= \dfrac{4.6 \times 10^{-2}}{0.22} \times 100 = 21\%$

49.   pH = 2.77, $[H^+] = 10^{-2.77} = 1.7 \times 10^{-3}$ M

$$HOCN \rightleftharpoons H^+ + OCN^-$$

Initial   0.0100   ~0   0
Equil.   0.0100 - x x x

$x = [H^+] = [OCN^-] = 1.7 \times 10^{-3}$ M; $[HOCN] = 0.0100 - x = 0.0100 - 0.0017 = 0.0083$ M

$K_a = \dfrac{[H^+][OCN^-]}{[HOCN]} = \dfrac{(1.7 \times 10^{-3})^2}{8.3 \times 10^{-3}} = 3.5 \times 10^{-4}$

50. $HClO_4$ is a strong acid with $[H^+] = 0.040$ M. This equals the $[H^+]$ in the trichloroacetic acid solution. Set-up the problem using the K_a equilibrium reaction for CCl_3CO_2H.

$$CCl_3CO_2H \rightleftharpoons H^+ + CCl_3CO_2^-$$

Initial   0.050 M ~0   0
Equil.   0.050 - x x x

$K_a = \dfrac{[H^+][CCl_3CO_2^-]}{[CCl_3CO_2H]} = \dfrac{x^2}{0.050 - x}$;   From the problem, $x = [H^+] = 4.0 \times 10^{-2}$ M.

$K_a = \dfrac{(4.0 \times 10^{-2})^2}{0.050 - (4.0 \times 10^{-2})} = 0.16$

51.   Major species: HCOOH and H_2O; Major source of H^+: HCOOH

$$HCOOH \rightleftharpoons H^+ + HCOO^-$$

Initial   C   ~0   0   where C = $[HCOOH]_o$
                 x mol/L HCOOH dissociates to reach equilibrium
Change   -x $\rightarrow$ +x +x
Equil.   C - x x x

$K_a = 1.8 \times 10^{-4} = \dfrac{[H^+][HCOO^-]}{[HCOOH]} = \dfrac{x^2}{C - x}$ where $x = [H^+]$

$1.8 \times 10^{-4} = \dfrac{[H^+]^2}{C - [H^+]}$;   Since pH = 2.70, then: $[H^+] = 10^{-2.70} = 2.0 \times 10^{-3}$ M

$1.8 \times 10^{-4} = \dfrac{(2.0 \times 10^{-3})^2}{C - (2.0 \times 10^{-3})}$, $C - (2.0 \times 10^{-3}) = \dfrac{4.0 \times 10^{-6}}{1.8 \times 10^{-4}}$, $C = 2.4 \times 10^{-2}$ M

A 0.024 M formic acid solution will have pH = 2.70.

52.   When an acid dissociates, ions are produced. The conductivity of the solution is a measure of the number of ions. In addition the colligative properties, which will be discussed in Chapter 17, depend on the number of particles present. So measurements of osmotic pressure, vapor pressure lowering,

freezing point depression or boiling point elevation will also allow us to determine the extent of ionization.

53.   The reactions are:

$$H_3AsO_4 \rightleftharpoons H^+ + H_2AsO_4^- \qquad K_{a_1} = 5 \times 10^{-3}$$

$$H_2AsO_4^- \rightleftharpoons H^+ + HAsO_4^{2-} \qquad K_{a_2} = 8 \times 10^{-8}$$

$$HAsO_4^{2-} \rightleftharpoons H^+ + AsO_4^{3-} \qquad K_{a_3} = 6 \times 10^{-10}$$

We will deal with the reactions in order of importance, beginning with the largest K_a, K_{a_1}.

$$H_3AsO_4 \rightleftharpoons H^+ + H_2AsO_4^- \qquad K_{a_1} = 5 \times 10^{-3} = \frac{[H^+][H_2AsO_4^-]}{[H_3AsO_4]}$$

	H_3AsO_4	H^+	$H_2AsO_4^-$
Initial	0.20 M	~0	0
Equil.	0.20 - x	x	x

$$5 \times 10^{-3} = \frac{x^2}{0.20 - x} \approx \frac{x^2}{0.20}, \quad x = 3 \times 10^{-2} \, M; \text{ Assumption fails the 5\% rule.}$$

Solving by the method of successive approximations:

$$5 \times 10^{-3} = x^2 / (0.20 - 0.03), \quad x = 3 \times 10^{-2} \text{ (consistent answer)}$$

$[H^+] = [H_2AsO_4^-] = 3 \times 10^{-2} \, M; \; [H_3AsO_4] = 0.20 - 0.03 = 0.17 \, M$

Since $K_{a_2} = \dfrac{[H^+][HAsO_4^{2-}]}{[H_2AsO_4^-]} = 8 \times 10^{-8}$ is much smaller than the K_{a_1} value, then very little of $H_2AsO_4^-$ (and $HAsO_4^{2-}$) dissociates as compared to H_3AsO_4. Therefore, $[H^+]$ and $[H_2AsO_4^-]$ will not change significantly by the K_{a_2} reaction. Using the previously calculated concentrations of H^+ and $H_2AsO_4^-$ to calculate the concentration of $HAsO_4^{2-}$:

$$8 \times 10^{-8} = \frac{(3 \times 10^{-2})[HAsO_4^{2-}]}{3 \times 10^{-2}}, \quad [HAsO_4^{2-}] = 8 \times 10^{-8} \, M$$

Assumption that the K_{a_2} reaction does not change $[H^+]$ and $[H_2AsO_4^-]$ is good. We repeat the process using K_{a_3} to get $[AsO_4^{3-}]$.

$$K_{a_3} = 6 \times 10^{-10} = \frac{[H^+][AsO_4^{3-}]}{[HAsO_4^{2-}]} = \frac{(3 \times 10^{-2})[AsO_4^{3-}]}{(8 \times 10^{-8})}$$

$[AsO_4^{3-}] = 1.6 \times 10^{-15} \approx 2 \times 10^{-15} \, M$ Assumption good.

So in 0.20 M analytical concentration of H_3AsO_4:

$[H_3AsO_4] = 0.17 \, M; \; [H^+] = [H_2AsO_4^-] = 3 \times 10^{-2} \, M;$

$[HAsO_4^{2-}] = 8 \times 10^{-8} \, M; \; [AsO_4^{3-}] = 2 \times 10^{-15} \, M; \; [OH^-] = K_w/[H^+] = 3 \times 10^{-13} \, M$

54.   The relevant reactions are:

$$H_2CO_3 \rightleftharpoons H^+ + HCO_3^-   \quad K_{a_1} = 4.3 \times 10^{-7}; \quad HCO_3^- \rightleftharpoons H^+ + CO_3^{2-}   \quad K_{a_2} = 4.8 \times 10^{-11}$$

Initially, we deal only with the first reaction (since $K_{a_1} \gg K_{a_2}$) and then let those results control values of concentrations in the second reaction.

$$H_2CO_3 \quad \rightleftharpoons \quad H^+ \quad + \quad HCO_3^-$$

Initial	0.010 M	~0	0
Equil.	0.010 - x	x	x

$$K_{a_1} = 4.3 \times 10^{-7} = \frac{[H^+][HCO_3^-]}{[H_2CO_3]} = \frac{x^2}{0.010 - x} \approx \frac{x^2}{0.010}$$

$x = 6.6 \times 10^{-5} \, M = [H^+] = [HCO_3^-]$ Assumptions good.

$$HCO_3^- \quad \rightleftharpoons \quad H^+ \quad + \quad CO_3^{2-}$$

Initial	$6.6 \times 10^{-5} \, M$	$6.6 \times 10^{-5} \, M$	0
Equil.	$6.6 \times 10^{-5} - y$	$6.6 \times 10^{-5} + y$	y

If y is small, then $[H^+] = [HCO_3^-]$ and $K_{a_2} = 4.8 \times 10^{-11} = \dfrac{[H^+][CO_3^{2-}]}{[HCO_3^-]} \approx y$

$y = [CO_3^{2-}] = 4.8 \times 10^{-11} \, M$ Assumptions good.

The amount of H^+ from the second dissociation is $4.8 \times 10^{-11} \, M$ or:

$$\frac{4.8 \times 10^{-11}}{6.6 \times 10^{-5}} \times 100 = 7.3 \times 10^{-5} \, \%$$

This result justifies our treating the equilibria separately. If the second dissociation contributed a significant amount of H^+ we would have to treat both equilibria simultaneously.

The reaction that occurs when acid is added to a solution of HCO_3^- is:

$$HCO_3^-(aq) + H^+(aq) \rightarrow H_2CO_3(aq) \rightarrow H_2O(l) + CO_2(g)$$

The bubbles are $CO_2(g)$ and are formed by the breakdown of unstable H_2CO_3 molecules. We should write $H_2O(l) + CO_2(aq)$ or $CO_2(aq)$ for what we call carbonic acid. It is for convenience, however, that we write $H_2CO_3(aq)$.

55.   The dominant H^+ producer is the strong acid H_2SO_4. A 2.0 $M \, H_2SO_4$ solution produces 2.0 $M \, HSO_4^-$ and 2.0 $M \, H^+$. However, HSO_4^- is a weak acid which could also add H^+ to the solution.

$$HSO_4^- \quad \rightleftharpoons \quad H^+ \quad + \quad SO_4^{2-}$$

Initial	2.0 M		2.0 M	0
	x mol/L HSO_4^- dissociates to reach equilibrium			
Change	-x	$\rightarrow$	+x	+x
Equil.	2.0 - x		2.0 + x	x

$$K_{a_2} = 1.2 \times 10^{-2} = \frac{[H^+][SO_4^{2-}]}{[HSO_4^-]} = \frac{(2.0 + x)(x)}{2.0 - x} \approx \frac{2.0(x)}{2.0}, \quad x = 1.2 \times 10^{-2}\,M$$

Since x is 0.60% of 2.0, then the assumption is valid by the 5% rule. The amount of additional H^+ from HSO_4^- is 1.2×10^{-2}. The total amount of H^+ present is:

$$[H^+] = 2.0 + 1.2 \times 10^{-2} = 2.0\,M; \quad pH = -\log(2.0) = -0.30$$

Note: In this problem, H^+ from HSO_4^- could have been ignored. However, this is not usually the case, especially in more dilute solutions of H_2SO_4.

56.   For H_2SO_4, the first dissociation occurs to completion. The hydrogen sulfate ion, HSO_4^-, is a weak acid with $K_{a_2} = 1.2 \times 10^{-2}$. We will consider this equilibrium for additional H^+ production:

	HSO_4^-	$\rightleftharpoons$	H^+	$+$	SO_4^{2-}
Initial	0.0050 M		0.0050 M		0
	x mol/L HSO_4^- dissociates to reach equilibrium				
Change	$-x$	$\rightarrow$	$+x$		$+x$
Equil.	$0.0050 - x$		$0.0050 + x$		x

$$K_{a_2} = 0.012 = \frac{(0.0050 + x)(x)}{(0.0050 - x)} \approx x, \quad x = 0.012; \quad \text{Assumption is horrible (240\% error).}$$

Using the quadratic formula:

$$6.0 \times 10^{-5} - 0.012\,x = x^2 + 0.0050\,x, \quad x^2 + 0.017\,x - 6.0 \times 10^{-5} = 0$$

$$x = \frac{-0.017 \pm (2.9 \times 10^{-4} + 2.4 \times 10^{-4})^{1/2}}{2} = \frac{-0.017 \pm 0.023}{2}, \quad x = 3.0 \times 10^{-3}\,M$$

$$[H^+] = 0.0050 + x = 0.0050 + 0.0030 = 0.0080\,M; \quad pH = 2.10$$

Note: We had to consider both H_2SO_4 and HSO_4^- for H^+ production in this problem.

Solutions of Bases

57. NO_3^-: $K_b \ll K_w$ since HNO_3 is a strong acid. All conjugate bases of strong acids have no base strength in water. H_2O: $K_b = K_w = 1.0 \times 10^{-14}$; NH_3: $K_b = 1.8 \times 10^{-5}$; C_5H_5N: $K_b = 1.7 \times 10^{-9}$

Base strength = $NH_3 > C_5H_5N > H_2O > NO_3^-$ (As K_b increases, base strength increases.)

58.   Excluding water, these are the conjugate acids of the bases in the previous exercise. In general, the stronger the base, the weaker the conjugate acid. Note: Even though NH_4^+ and $C_5H_5NH^+$ are conjugate acids of weak bases, they are still weak acids with K_a values between K_w and 1. Prove this to yourself by calculating the K_a values for NH_4^+ and $C_5H_5NH^+$ ($K_a = K_w/K_b$).

Acid strength = $HNO_3 > C_5H_5NH^+ > NH_4^+ > H_2O$

59.   a. $C_2H_5NH_2$ b. $C_2H_5NH_2$ c. OH^- d. $C_2H_5NH_2$

The base with the largest K_b value is the strongest base (K_b for $C_2H_5NH_2 = 5.6 \times 10^{-4}$ and K_b for $C_6H_5NH_2 = 3.8 \times 10^{-10}$). OH^- is the strongest base possible in water.

60.   a. HNO_3 b. $C_2H_5NH_3^+$ c. $C_6H_5NH_3^+$

The acid with the largest K_a value is the strongest acid. To calculate K_a values for $C_6H_5NH_3^+$ and $C_2H_5NH_3^+$, use $K_a = K_w/K_b$ where K_b refers to the bases $C_6H_5NH_2$ or $C_2H_5NH_2$

61. $NaOH(aq) \rightarrow Na^+(aq) + OH^-(aq)$; NaOH is a strong base which completely dissociates into Na^+ and OH^-. The initial concentration of NaOH will equal the concentration of OH^- donated by NaOH.

   a. $[OH^-] = 0.10\ M$; $pOH = -\log[OH^-] = -\log(0.10) = 1.00$

       $pH = 14.00 - pOH = 14.00 - 1.00 = 13.00$

       Note that H_2O is also present but the amount of OH^- produced by H_2O will be insignificant as compared to 0.10 M OH^- produced from the NaOH.

   b. The $[OH^-]$ concentration donated by the NaOH is $1.0 \times 10^{-10}\ M$. Water by itself donates $1.0 \times 10^{-7}\ M$. In this problem, water is the major OH^- contributor and $[OH^-] = 1.0 \times 10^{-7}\ M$.

       $pOH = -\log(1.0 \times 10^{-7}) = 7.00$; $pH = 14.00 - 7.00 = 7.00$

   c. $[OH^-] = 2.0\ M$; $pOH = -\log(2.0) = -0.30$; $pH = 14.00 - (-0.30) = 14.30$

62.   a. $Ca(OH)_2 \rightarrow Ca^{2+} + 2\ OH^-$; $Ca(OH)_2$ is a strong base and dissociates completely.

       $[OH^-] = 2(0.00040) = 8.0 \times 10^{-4}\ M$; $pOH = -\log[OH^-] = 3.10$; $pH = 14.00 - pOH = 10.90$

   b. $\dfrac{25\ g\ KOH}{L} \times \dfrac{1\ mol\ KOH}{56.1\ g\ KOH} = 0.45\ mol\ KOH/L$

       KOH is a strong base, so $[OH^-] = 0.45\ M$; $pOH = -\log(0.45) = 0.35$; $pH = 13.65$

   c. $\dfrac{150.0\ g\ NaOH}{L} \times \dfrac{1\ mol}{40.00\ g} = 3.750\ M$; NaOH is a strong base, so $[OH^-] = 3.750\ M$.

       $pOH = -\log(3.750) = -0.5740$ and $pH = 14.0000 - (-0.5740) = 14.5740$

       Although we are justified in calculating the answer to four decimal places, in reality the pH can only be measured to $\pm$ 0.01 pH units.

63. $pH = 10.50$; $pOH = 14.00 - 10.50 = 3.50$; $[OH^-] = 10^{-3.50} = 3.2 \times 10^{-4}\ M$

       $Ba(OH)_2(aq) \rightarrow Ba^{2+}(aq) + 2\ OH^-(aq)$; $Ba(OH)_2$ donates two mol OH^- per mol $Ba(OH)_2$.

       $[Ba(OH)_2] = 3.2 \times 10^{-4}\ M\ OH^- \times \left(\dfrac{1\ M\ Ba(OH)_2}{2\ M\ OH^-} \right) = 1.6 \times 10^{-4}\ M\ Ba(OH)_2$

       A $1.6 \times 10^{-4}\ M\ Ba(OH)_2$ solution will produce a pH = 10.50 solution.

64.   Neutrally charged organic compounds containing at least one nitrogen atom generally behave as weak bases. The nitrogen atom has an unshared pair of electrons around it. This lone pair of electrons is used to form a bond to H^+.

65.   a.   These are all solutions of weak bases in water. We must solve the weak base equilibrium problem.

$$C_2H_5NH_2(aq) + H_2O(l) \rightleftharpoons C_2H_5NH_3^+(aq) + OH^-(aq) \quad K_b = 5.6 \times 10^{-4}$$

Initial	0.20 M	0	~0

x mol/L $C_2H_5NH_2$ reacts with H_2O to reach equilibrium

Change	$-x$	$\rightarrow$	$+x$	$+x$
Equil.	0.20 - x		x	x

$$K_b = \frac{[C_2H_5NH_3^+][OH^-]}{[C_2H_5NH_2]} = \frac{x^2}{0.20 - x} \approx \frac{x^2}{0.20} \quad \text{(assuming } x \ll 0.20)$$

$x = 1.1 \times 10^{-2}$;   Checking assumption: $\dfrac{1.1 \times 10^{-2}}{0.20} \times 100 = 5.5\%$

Assumption fails the 5% rule. We must solve exactly using either the quadratic equation or the method of successive approximations (see Appendix 1.4 of the text). Using successive approximations and carrying extra significant figures:

$$\frac{x^2}{0.20 - 0.011} = \frac{x^2}{0.189} = 5.6 \times 10^{-4}, \ x = 1.0 \times 10^{-2} \ M \ \text{(consistent answer)}$$

$x = [OH^-] = 1.0 \times 10^{-2} \ M$; $[H^+] = \dfrac{K_w}{[OH^-]} = \dfrac{1.0 \times 10^{-14}}{1.0 \times 10^{-2}} = 1.0 \times 10^{-12} \ M$;   pH = 12.00

   b. $$(C_2H_5)_2NH + H_2O \rightleftharpoons (C_2H_5)_2NH_2^+ + OH^- \quad K_b = 1.3 \times 10^{-3}$$

Initial	0.20 M	0	~0

x mol/L $(C_2H_5)_2NH$ reacts with H_2O to reach equilibrium

Change	$-x$	$\rightarrow$	$+x$	$+x$
Equil.	0.20 - x		x	x

$$K_b = 1.3 \times 10^{-3} = \frac{[(C_2H_5)_2NH_2^+][OH^-]}{[(C_2H_5)_2NH)]} = \frac{x^2}{0.20 - x} \approx \frac{x^2}{0.20} \quad \text{(assuming } x \ll 0.20)$$

$x = 1.6 \times 10^{-2}$;   Assumption is bad (x is 8.0% of 0.20).

Using successive approximations:

$$\frac{x^2}{0.20 - 0.016} = \frac{x^2}{0.184} = 1.3 \times 10^{-3}, \ x = 1.55 \times 10^{-2} \ \text{(carry extra significant figure)}$$

$$\frac{x^2}{0.185} = 1.3 \times 10^{-3}, \ x = 1.55 \times 10^{-2} \ \text{(consistent answer)}$$

$[OH^-] = x = 1.55 \times 10^{-2} M$; $[H^+] = 6.45 \times 10^{-13} M$; To correct significant figures:

$[OH^-] = 1.6 \times 10^{-2} M$; $[H^+] = 6.5 \times 10^{-13} M$; $pH = -\log [H^+] = 12.19$

c. $\qquad (C_2H_5)_3N + H_2O \rightleftharpoons (C_2H_5)_3NH^+ + OH^- \qquad K_b = 4.0 \times 10^{-4}$

Initial   0.20 M 0   ~0
$\qquad$ x mol/L of $(C_2H_5)_3N$ reacts with H_2O to reach equilibrium
Change $-x$ $\rightarrow$ $+x$ $+x$
Equil.   0.20 - x x x

$K_b = 4.0 \times 10^{-4} = \dfrac{[(C_2H_5)_3NH^+][OH^-]}{[(C_2H_5)_3N]} = \dfrac{x^2}{0.20 - x} \approx \dfrac{x^2}{0.20}$, $x = [OH^-] = 8.9 \times 10^{-3} M$

Assumptions good (x is 4.5% of 0.20). $[OH^-] = 8.9 \times 10^{-3} M$

$[H^+] = \dfrac{K_w}{[OH^-]} = \dfrac{1.0 \times 10^{-14}}{8.9 \times 10^{-3}} = 1.1 \times 10^{-12} M$; $pH = 11.96$

d. $\qquad C_6H_5NH_2 + H_2O \rightleftharpoons C_6H_5NH_3^+ + OH^- \qquad K_b = 3.8 \times 10^{-10}$

Initial   0.20 M 0   ~0
$\qquad$ x mol/L of $C_6H_5NH_2$ reacts with H_2O to reach equilibrium
Change $-x$ $\rightarrow$ $+x$ $+x$
Equil.   0.20 - x x x

$K_b = 3.8 \times 10^{-10} = \dfrac{x^2}{0.20 - x} \approx \dfrac{x^2}{0.20}$, $x = [OH^-] = 8.7 \times 10^{-6} M$; Assumptions good.

$[H^+] = K_w/[OH^-] = 1.1 \times 10^{-9} M$; $pH = 8.96$

e. $\qquad C_5H_5N + H_2O \rightleftharpoons C_5H_5NH^+ + OH^- \qquad K_b = 1.7 \times 10^{-9}$

Initial   0.20 M 0   ~0
Equil.   0.20 - x x x

$K_b = 1.7 \times 10^{-9} = \dfrac{x^2}{0.20 - x} \approx \dfrac{x^2}{0.20}$, $x = 1.8 \times 10^{-5} M$; Assumptions good.

$[OH^-] = 1.8 \times 10^{-5} M$; $[H^+] = 5.6 \times 10^{-10} M$; $pH = 9.25$

f. $\qquad HONH_2 + H_2O \rightleftharpoons HONH_3^+ + OH^- \qquad K_b = 1.1 \times 10^{-8}$

Initial   0.20 M 0   ~0
Equil.   0.20 - x x x

$K_b = 1.1 \times 10^{-8} = \dfrac{x^2}{0.20 - x} \approx \dfrac{x^2}{0.20}$, $x = [OH^-] = 4.7 \times 10^{-5} M$; Assumptions good.

$[H^+] = 2.1 \times 10^{-10} M$; $pH = 9.68$

66.   Major species: H_2NNH_2 ($K_b = 3.0 \times 10^{-6}$) and H_2O ($K_b = K_w = 1.0 \times 10^{-14}$); The weak base H_2NNH_2 will dominate OH^- production. We must perform a weak base equilibrium calculation.

$$H_2NNH_2 + H_2O \rightleftharpoons H_2NNH_3^+ + OH^- \qquad K_b = 3.0 \times 10^{-6}$$

Initial	2.0 M	0	~0

x mol/L H_2NNH_2 reacts with H_2O to reach equilibrium

Change	-x	$\rightarrow$	+x	+x
Equil.	2.0 - x		x	x

$$K_b = 3.0 \times 10^{-6} = \frac{[H_2NNH_3^+][OH^-]}{[H_2NNH_2]} = \frac{x^2}{2.0 - x} \approx \frac{x^2}{2.0} \quad \text{(assuming } x << 2.0\text{)}$$

$x = [OH^-] = 2.4 \times 10^{-3} \ M$; pOH = 2.62; pH = 11.38   Assumptions good (x is 0.12% of 2.0).

67. $\dfrac{5.0 \times 10^{-3} \text{ g}}{0.0100 \text{ L}} \times \dfrac{1 \text{ mol}}{299.4 \text{ g}} = 1.7 \times 10^{-3} \ M = [\text{codeine}]_o$; Let cod = codeine, $C_{18}H_{21}NO_3$

Solving the weak base equilibrium problem:

$$\text{cod} + H_2O \rightleftharpoons \text{codH}^+ + OH^- \qquad K_b = 10^{-6.05} = 8.9 \times 10^{-7}$$

Initial	$1.7 \times 10^{-3} \ M$	0	~0

x mol/L codeine reacts with H_2O to reach equilibrium

Change	-x	$\rightarrow$	+x	+x
Equil.	$1.7 \times 10^{-3} - x$		x	x

$$K_b = 8.9 \times 10^{-7} = \frac{x^2}{1.7 \times 10^{-3} - x} \approx \frac{x^2}{1.7 \times 10^{-3}}, \quad x = 3.9 \times 10^{-5} \qquad \text{Assumptions good.}$$

$[OH^-] = 3.9 \times 10^{-5} \ M$; $[H^+] = K_w/[OH^-] = 2.6 \times 10^{-10} \ M$; pH = -log $[H^+]$ = 9.59

68.   Codeine: $C_{18}H_{21}NO_3$;   Codeine sulfate = $C_{36}H_{44}N_2O_{10}S$

The formula for codeine sulfate works out to (codeine H^+)$_2SO_4^{2-}$ where codeine $H^+ = HC_{18}H_{21}NO_3^+$. Two codeine molecules are protonated by H_2SO_4, forming the conjugate acid of codeine. The SO_4^{2-} then acts as the counter ion to give a neutral compound. Codeine sulfate is an ionic compound which is more soluble in water than codeine, allowing more of the drug into the bloodstream.

69.   To solve for percent ionization, just solve the weak base equilibrium problem.

a. $$NH_3 + H_2O \rightleftharpoons NH_4^+ + OH^- \qquad K_b = 1.8 \times 10^{-5}$$

Initial	0.10 M	0	~0
Equil.	0.10 - x	x	x

$$K_b = 1.8 \times 10^{-5} = \frac{x^2}{0.10 - x} \approx \frac{x^2}{0.10}, \quad x = [OH^-] = 1.3 \times 10^{-3} \ M; \quad \text{Assumptions good.}$$

$$\text{Percent ionization} = \frac{[OH^-]}{[NH_3]_o} \times 100 = \frac{1.3 \times 10^{-3} \ M}{0.10 \ M} \times 100 = 1.3\%$$

b. $NH_3 + H_2O \rightleftharpoons NH_4^+ + OH^-$

Initial   0.010 M 0   ~0
Equil.   0.010 - x x x

$$1.8 \times 10^{-5} = \frac{x^2}{0.010 - x} \approx \frac{x^2}{0.010}, \quad x = [OH^-] = 4.2 \times 10^{-4} \, M; \text{ Assumptions good.}$$

Percent ionization = $\dfrac{4.2 \times 10^{-4}}{0.010} \times 100 = 4.2\%$

Note: For the same base, the percent ionization increases as the initial concentration of base decreases.

c. $CH_3NH_2 + H_2O \rightleftharpoons CH_3NH_3^+ + OH^- \quad K_b = 4.38 \times 10^{-4}$

Initial   0.10 M 0   ~0
Equil.   0.10 - x x x

$$4.38 \times 10^{-4} = \frac{x^2}{0.10 - x} \approx \frac{x^2}{0.10}, \quad x = 6.6 \times 10^{-3}; \text{ Assumption fails the 5\% rule (x is 6.6\%}$$
$$\text{of 0.10).}$$

Using successive approximations and carrying extra significant figures:

$$\frac{x^2}{0.10 - 0.0066} = \frac{x^2}{0.093} = 4.38 \times 10^{-4}, \quad x = 6.4 \times 10^{-3} \quad \text{(consistent answer)}$$

Percent ionization = $\dfrac{6.4 \times 10^{-3}}{0.10} \times 100 = 6.4\%$

70. $\dfrac{1.0 \text{ g quinine}}{1.9000 \text{ L}} \times \dfrac{1 \text{ mol quinine}}{324.4 \text{ g quinine}} = 1.6 \times 10^{-3} \, M \text{ quinine}; \text{ Let Q = quinine} = C_{20}H_{24}N_2O_2$

$$Q + H_2O \rightleftharpoons QH^+ + OH^- \quad K_b = 10^{-5.1} = 8 \times 10^{-6}$$

Initial $1.6 \times 10^{-3} \, M$ 0   ~0
                 x mol/L quinine reacts with H_2O to reach equilibrium
Change   -x $\rightarrow$ +x +x
Equil. 1.6×10^{-3} - x x x

$$K_b = 8 \times 10^{-6} = \frac{[QH^+][OH^-]}{[Q]} = \frac{x^2}{1.6 \times 10^{-3} - x} \approx \frac{x^2}{1.6 \times 10^{-3}}$$

$x = 1 \times 10^{-4}$; Assumption fails 5% rule (x is 6% of 0.0016). Using successive approximations:

$$\frac{x^2}{1.6 \times 10^{-3} - 1 \times 10^{-4}} = 8 \times 10^{-6}, \quad x = 1 \times 10^{-4} \, M \text{ (consistent answer)}$$

$x = [OH^-] = 1 \times 10^{-4} \, M; \text{ pOH} = 4.0; \text{ pH} = 10.0$

71.   Using the K_b reaction to solve where PT = p-toluidine, $CH_3C_6H_4NH_2$:

$$PT \ + \ H_2O \ \rightleftharpoons \ PTH^+ \ + \ OH^-$$

Initial	0.016 M	0	~0

x mol/L of PT reacts with H_2O to reach equilibrium

Change	-x	$\rightarrow$	+x	+x
Equil.	0.016 - x		x	x

$$K_b = \frac{[PTH^+][OH^-]}{[PT]} = \frac{x^2}{0.016 - x}$$

Since pH = 8.60: pOH = 14.00 - 8.60 = 5.40 and $[OH^-] = x = 10^{-5.40} = 4.0 \times 10^{-6} \ M$

$$K_b = \frac{(4.0 \times 10^{-6})^2}{0.016 - 4.0 \times 10^{-6}} = 1.0 \times 10^{-9}$$

72.   Using the K_b reaction to solve where PY = pyrrolidine, C_4H_8NH:

$$PY \ + \ H_2O \ \rightleftharpoons \ PYH^+ \ + \ OH^-$$

Initial	1.00×10^{-3} M	0	~0
Equil.	1.00×10^{-3} - x	x	x

$$K_b = \frac{x^2}{1.00 \times 10^{-3} - x}; \text{ Since pH} = 10.82: \text{ pOH} = 3.18 \text{ and } [OH^-] = x = 10^{-3.18} = 6.6 \times 10^{-4} \ M$$

$$K_b = \frac{(6.6 \times 10^{-4})^2}{1.00 \times 10^{-3} - 6.6 \times 10^{-4}} = 1.3 \times 10^{-3}$$

Acid-Base Properties of Salts

73.   One difficult aspect of acid-base chemistry is recognizing what types of species are present in solution, i.e., whether a species is a strong acid, strong base, weak acid, weak base or a neutral species. Below are some ideas and generalizations to keep in mind that will help in recognizing types of species present.

a.   Memorize the following strong acids: HCl, HBr, HI, HNO_3, $HClO_4$ and H_2SO_4

b.   Memorize the following strong bases: LiOH, NaOH, KOH, RbOH, $Ca(OH)_2$, $Sr(OH)_2$ and $Ba(OH)_2$

c.   Weak acids have a K_a value less than 1 but greater than K_w. Some weak acids are in Table 7.2 of the text. Weak bases have a K_b value less than 1 but greater than K_w. Some weak bases are in Table 7.3 of the text.

d.   Conjugate bases of weak acids are weak bases, i.e., all have a K_b value less than 1 but greater than K_w. Some examples of these are the conjugate bases of the weak acids in Table 7.2 of the text.

e.   Conjugate acids of weak bases are weak acids, i.e., all have a K_a value less than 1 but greater than K_w. Some examples of these are the conjugate acids of the weak bases in Table 7.3 of the text.

f.   Alkali metal ions (Li^+, Na^+, K^+, Rb^+, Cs^+) and some alkaline earth metal ions (Ca^{2+}, Sr^{2+}, Ba^{2+}) have no acidic or basic properties in water.

g.   Conjugate bases of strong acids (Cl^-, Br^-, I^-, NO_3^-, ClO_4^-, HSO_4^-) have no basic properties in water ($K_b \ll K_w$) and only HSO_4^- has any acidic properties in water.

Lets apply these ideas to this problem to see what type of species are present. The letters in parenthesis is/are the generalization(s) above which identifies that species.

KOH: strong base (b)
KCl: neutral; K^+ and Cl^- have no acidic/basic properties (f and g).
KCN: CN^- is a weak base, $K_b = 1.0 \times 10^{-14}/6.2 \times 10^{-10} = 1.6 \times 10^{-5}$ (c and d). Ignore K^+(f).
NH$_4$Cl: NH_4^+ is a weak acid, $K_a = 5.6 \times 10^{-10}$ (c and e). Ignore Cl^-(g).
HCl: strong acid (a)

The most acidic solution will be the strong acid followed by the weak acid. The most basic solution will be the strong base followed by the weak base. The KCl solution will be between the acidic and basic solutions at pH = 7.00.

Most acidic → most basic; HCl > NH$_4$Cl > KCl > KCN > KOH

74.   See the generalizations in Exercise 7.73.

a.   HI: strong acid; HF: weak acid ($K_a = 7.2 \times 10^{-4}$)

NaF: F^- is the conjugate base of the weak acid HF so F^- is a weak base. The K_b value for $F^- = K_w/K_{a,\, HF} = 1.4 \times 10^{-11}$. Na^+ has no acidic or basic properties.

NaI: neutral (pH = 7.0); Na^+ and I^- have no acidic/basic properties.

In order of increasing pH, we place the compounds from most acidic (lowest pH) to most basic (highest pH). Increasing pH: HI < HF < NaI < NaF.

b.   NH$_4$Br: NH_4^+ is a weak acid ($K_a = 5.6 \times 10^{-10}$) and Br^- is a neutral species.
     HBr: strong acid
     KBr: neutral; K^+ and Br^- have no acidic/basic properties
     NH$_3$:   weak base, $K_b = 1.8 \times 10^{-5}$

Increasing pH: HBr < NH$_4$Br < KBr < NH$_3$
                most   most
                acidic   basic

c. $C_6H_5NH_3NO_3$: $C_6H_5NH_3^+$ is a weak acid ($K_w/K_{b,\, C_6H_5NH_2} = 1.0 \times 10^{-14}/3.8 \times 10^{-10} = 2.6 \times 10^{-5}$) and NO_3^- is a neutral species.
     NaNO$_3$:   neutral; Na^+ and NO_3^- have no acidic/basic properties.
     NaOH: strong base
     HOC$_6$H$_5$:   weak acid ($K_a = 1.6 \times 10^{-10}$)
     KOC$_6$H$_5$: $OC_6H_5^-$ is a weak base ($K_b = K_w/K_{a,\, HOC_6H_5} = 6.3 \times 10^{-5}$) and K^+ is a neutral species.
     $C_6H_5NH_2$:   weak base ($K_b = 3.8 \times 10^{-10}$)
     HNO$_3$:   strong acid

This is a little more difficult than the previous parts of this problem because two weak acids and two weak bases are present. Between the weak acids, $C_6H_5NH_3^+$ is a stronger weak acid than HOC_6H_5 since the K_a value for $C_6H_5NH_3^+$ is larger than the K_a value for HOC_6H_5. Between the two weak bases, since the K_b value for $OC_6H_5^-$ is larger than the K_b value for $C_6H_5NH_2$, then $OC_6H_5^-$ is a stronger weak base than $C_6H_5NH_2$.

Increasing pH: $HNO_3 < C_6H_5NH_3NO_3 < HOC_6H_5 < NaNO_3 < C_6H_5NH_2 < KOC_6H_5 < NaOH$
                   most   most
                   acidic   basic

75. Reference Table 7.6 of the text and the solution to Exercise 7.73 for some generalizations on acid-base properties of salts. The letters in parenthesis is/are the generalization(s) listed in Exercise 7.73 which identifies that species.

$CaBr_2$:   neutral; Ca^{2+} and Br^- have no acidic/basic properties (f and g).
KNO_2: NO_2^- is a weak base, $K_b = 1.0 \times 10^{-14}/4.0 \times 10^{-4} = 2.5 \times 10^{-11}$ (c and d). Ignore K^+(f).
$HClO_4$:   strong acid (a)
HNO_2:   weak acid, $K_a = 4.0 \times 10^{-4}$ (c)
NH_4ClO_4: NH_4^+ is a weak acid, $K_a = 5.6 \times 10^{-10}$ (c and e). Ignore ClO_4^- (g).
NH_4NO_2: NH_4^+ is a weak acid, $K_a = 5.6 \times 10^{-10}$ (c and e). NO_2^- is a weak base, $K_b = 2.5 \times 10^{-11}$ (c and d). Since the K_a value for NH_4^+ is a slightly larger than K_b for NO_2^-, then the solution will be slightly acidic with a pH a little lower than 7.0.

Using the information above (identity and K_a or K_b values), the ordering is:

most acidic → most basic: $HClO_4 > HNO_2 > NH_4ClO_4 > NH_4NO_2 > CaBr_2 > KNO_2$

76. Reference Table 7.6 of the text and the solution to Exercise 7.73 for some generalizations on acid-base properties of salts.

a. $KCl \rightarrow K^+ + Cl^-$ neutral; K^+ and Cl^- have no effect on pH.

b. $NaNO_3 \rightarrow Na^+ + NO_3^-$ neutral; Neither species have any acidic/basic properties.

c. $NaNO_2 \rightarrow Na^+ + NO_2^-$ basic; NO_2^- is a weak base and Na^+ has no effect on pH.

$$NO_2^- + H_2O \rightleftharpoons HNO_2 + OH^- \quad K_b = \frac{K_w}{K_{a,\,HNO_2}} = \frac{1.0 \times 10^{-14}}{4.0 \times 10^{-4}} = 2.5 \times 10^{-11}$$

d. $C_2H_5NH_3I \rightarrow C_2H_5NH_3^+ + I^-$ acidic; $C_2H_5NH_3^+$ is a weak acid and I^- has no effect on pH.

$$C_2H_5NH_3^+ \rightleftharpoons C_2H_5NH_2 + H^+ \quad K_a = \frac{K_w}{K_{b,\,C_2H_5NH_2}} = \frac{1.0 \times 10^{-14}}{5.6 \times 10^{-4}} = 1.8 \times 10^{-11}$$

e. $NH_4CN \rightarrow NH_4^+ + CN^-$ basic; NH_4^+ is a weak acid ($K_a = 5.6 \times 10^{-10}$) and CN^- is a weak base ($K_b = K_w/K_{a,\,HCN}, = 1.0 \times 10^{-14}/6.2 \times 10^{-10} = 1.6 \times 10^{-5}$). Since $K_{b,\,CN^-} > K_{a,\,NH_4^+}$, then the solution is basic.

$$NH_4^+ \rightleftharpoons NH_3 + H^+ \quad K_a = 5.6 \times 10^{-10}; \quad CN^- + H_2O \rightleftharpoons HCN + OH^- \quad K_b = 1.6 \times 10^{-5}$$

f. $NaHCO_3 \rightarrow Na^+ + HCO_3^-$ basic; HCO_3^- can be either an acid or a base. Ignore Na^+.

$HCO_3^- \rightleftharpoons H^+ + CO_3^{2-}$ $K_{a_2} = 4.8 \times 10^{-11}$

$HCO_3^- + H_2O \rightleftharpoons H_2CO_3 + OH^-$ $K_b = \dfrac{K_w}{K_{a_1}} = \dfrac{1.0 \times 10^{-14}}{4.3 \times 10^{-7}} = 2.3 \times 10^{-8}$

HCO_3^- is a stronger base than an acid since $K_b > K_a$. Therefore, the solution is basic.

g. $NH_4C_2H_3O_2 \rightarrow NH_4^+ + C_2H_3O_2^-$ neutral; NH_4^+ is a weak acid ($K_a = 5.6 \times 10^{-10}$) and $C_2H_3O_2^-$ is a weak base ($K_b = K_w/K_{a, HC_2H_3O_2} = 1.0 \times 10^{-14}/1.8 \times 10^{-5} = 5.6 \times 10^{-10}$). Since $K_{a, NH_4^+} = K_{b, C_2H_3O_2^-}$, then pH = 7.00.

$NH_4^+ \rightleftharpoons NH_3 + H^+$ $K_a = 5.6 \times 10^{-10}$; $C_2H_3O_2^- + H_2O \rightleftharpoons HC_2H_3O_2 + OH^-$ $K_b = 5.6 \times 10^{-10}$

h. $NaF \rightarrow Na^+ + F^-$ basic; F^- is a weak base and Na^+ has no effect on pH.

$F^- + H_2O \rightleftharpoons HF + OH^-$ $K_b = \dfrac{K_w}{K_{a, HF}} = \dfrac{1.0 \times 10^{-14}}{7.2 \times 10^{-4}} = 1.4 \times 10^{-11}$

77.   From the K_a values, acetic acid is a stronger acid than hypochlorous acid. Conversely, the conjugate base of acetic acid, $C_2H_3O_2^-$, will be a weaker base than the conjugate base of hypochlorous acid, OCl^-. Thus, the hypochlorite ion, OCl^-, is a stronger base than the acetate ion, $C_2H_3O_2^-$. In general, the weaker the acid, the stronger the conjugate base. This statement comes from the relationship $K_w = K_a \times K_b$, which holds for all conjugate acid-base pairs.

78. $K_a \times K_b = K_w$, $-\log (K_a \times K_b) = -\log K_w$

$-\log K_a - \log K_b = -\log K_w$, $pK_a + pK_b = pK_w = 14.00$ (at 25°C since $K_w = 1.0 \times 10^{-14}$ at 25°C)

79.   a. $CH_3NH_3Cl \rightarrow CH_3NH_3^+ + Cl^-$; $CH_3NH_3^+$ is a weak acid since it is the conjugate acid of the weak base CH_3NH_2 ($K_b = 4.38 \times 10^{-4}$). Cl^- is the conjugate base of a strong acid. Cl^- has no basic (or acidic) properties. Solving the weak acid problem:

$CH_3NH_3^+ \rightleftharpoons CH_3NH_2 + H^+$ $K_a = \dfrac{[CH_3NH_2][H^+]}{[CH_3NH_3^+]} = \dfrac{K_w}{K_b} = \dfrac{1.00 \times 10^{-14}}{4.38 \times 10^{-4}} = 2.28 \times 10^{-11}$

	$CH_3NH_3^+$	$\rightleftharpoons$	CH_3NH_2	+	H^+
Initial	0.10 M		0		~0
	x mol/L $CH_3NH_3^+$ dissociates to reach equilibrium				
Change	$-x$	$\rightarrow$	$+x$		$+x$
Equil.	0.10 - x		x		x

$K_a = 2.28 \times 10^{-11} = \dfrac{x^2}{0.10 - x} \approx \dfrac{x^2}{0.10}$ (assuming x << 0.10)

$x = [H^+] = 1.5 \times 10^{-6}\ M$; pH = 5.82   Assumptions good.

b. $NaCN \rightarrow Na^+ + CN^-$ CN^- is a weak base since it is the conjugate base of the weak acid HCN ($K_a = 6.2 \times 10^{-10}$). Na^+ has no acidic (or basic) properties. Solving the weak base problem:

$$\text{CN}^- + \text{H}_2\text{O} \rightleftharpoons \text{HCN} + \text{OH}^- \quad K_b = \frac{K_w}{K_a} = \frac{1.0 \times 10^{-14}}{6.2 \times 10^{-10}} = 1.6 \times 10^{-5}$$

Initial	0.050 M		0	~0

x mol/L CN^- reacts with H_2O to reach equilibrium

Change	$-x$	$\rightarrow$	$+x$	$+x$
Equil.	0.050 - x		x	x

$$K_b = 1.6 \times 10^{-5} = \frac{[\text{HCN}][\text{OH}^-]}{[\text{CN}^-]} = \frac{x^2}{0.050 - x} \approx \frac{x^2}{0.050}$$

$x = [\text{OH}^-] = 8.9 \times 10^{-4} \, M$; pOH = 3.05; pH = 10.95   Assumptions good.

c. $\text{Na}_2\text{CO}_3 \rightarrow 2\,\text{Na}^+ + \text{CO}_3^{2-}$ CO_3^{2-} is a weak base. Ignore Na^+.

$$\text{CO}_3^{2-} + \text{H}_2\text{O} \rightleftharpoons \text{HCO}_3^- + \text{OH}^- \quad K_b = \frac{K_w}{K_{a_2}} = \frac{1.0 \times 10^{-14}}{4.8 \times 10^{-11}} = 2.1 \times 10^{-4}$$

Initial	0.20 M		0	~0
Equil.	0.20 - x		x	x

$$K_b = 2.1 \times 10^{-4} = \frac{[\text{HCO}_3^-][\text{OH}^-]}{[\text{CO}_3^{2-}]} = \frac{x^2}{0.20 - x} \approx \frac{x^2}{0.20}$$

$x = 6.5 \times 10^{-3} \, M = [\text{OH}^-]$; pOH = 2.19; pH = 11.81   Assumptions good.

d. $\text{KNO}_2 \rightarrow \text{K}^+ + \text{NO}_2^-$ NO_2^- is a weak base. Ignore K^+.

$$\text{NO}_2^- + \text{H}_2\text{O} \rightleftharpoons \text{HNO}_2 + \text{OH}^- \quad K_b = \frac{K_w}{K_a} = \frac{1.0 \times 10^{-14}}{4.0 \times 10^{-4}} = 2.5 \times 10^{-11}$$

Initial	0.12 M		0	~0
Equil.	0.12 - x		x	x

$$K_b = 2.5 \times 10^{-11} = \frac{[\text{OH}^-][\text{HNO}_2]}{[\text{NO}_2^-]} = \frac{x^2}{0.12 - x} \approx \frac{x^2}{0.12}$$

$x = [\text{OH}^-] = 1.7 \times 10^{-6} \, M$; pOH = 5.77; pH = 8.23   Assumptions good.

e. $\text{NH}_4\text{Br} \rightarrow \text{NH}_4^+ + \text{Br}^-$: NH_4^+ is a weak acid. Br^- is the conjugate base of a strong acid. Br^- has no basic (or acidic) properties.

$$\text{NH}_4^+ \rightleftharpoons \text{NH}_3 + \text{H}^+ \quad K_a = \frac{K_w}{K_b} = \frac{1.0 \times 10^{-14}}{1.8 \times 10^{-5}} = 5.6 \times 10^{-10}$$

Initial	0.40 M	0	~0
Equil.	0.40 - x	x	x

$$K_a = 5.6 \times 10^{-10} = \frac{[\text{NH}_3][\text{H}^+]}{[\text{NH}_4^+]} = \frac{x^2}{0.40 - x} \approx \frac{x^2}{0.40}$$

$x = [\text{H}^+] = 1.5 \times 10^{-5} \, M$; pH = 4.82;   Assumptions good.

80.   Solution is acidic from $HSO_4^- \rightleftharpoons H^+ + SO_4^{2-}$. Solving the weak acid problem:

$$HSO_4^- \quad\rightleftharpoons\quad H^+ \quad+\quad SO_4^{2-} \qquad K_a = 1.2 \times 10^{-2}$$

Initial	0.10 M	~0	0
Equil.	0.10 - x	x	x

$$K_a = 1.2 \times 10^{-2} = \frac{[H^+][SO_4^{2-}]}{[HSO_4^-]} = \frac{x^2}{0.10 - x} \approx \frac{x^2}{0.10}, \ x = 0.035$$

Assumption is not good (35% error). Using successive approximations:

$$\frac{x^2}{0.10 - x} \approx \frac{x^2}{0.10 - 0.035} = 1.2 \times 10^{-2}, \ x = 0.028$$

$$\frac{x^2}{0.10 - 0.028} = 1.2 \times 10^{-2}, \ x = 0.029 \ M \quad \text{(consistent answer)}$$

$x = [H^+] = 0.029 \ M; \ pH = 1.54$

If we add Na_2CO_3 to a solution of $NaHSO_4$, the base CO_3^{2-} will react with the acid HSO_4^-. Depending on relative amounts, two reactions are possible.

$$CO_3^{2-}(aq) + HSO_4^-(aq) \rightleftharpoons HCO_3^-(aq) + SO_4^{2-}(aq)$$

or

$$CO_3^{2-}(aq) + 2 \ HSO_4^-(aq) \rightleftharpoons 2 \ SO_4^{2-}(aq) + H_2O(l) + CO_2(g)$$

81. $NaN_3 \rightarrow Na^+ + N_3^-$; Azide, N_3^-, is a weak base since it is the conjugate base of a weak acid. All conjugate bases of weak acids are weak bases ($K_w < K_b < 1$). Ignore Na^+.

$$N_3^- + H_2O \quad\rightleftharpoons\quad HN_3 \quad+\quad OH^- \qquad K_b = \frac{K_w}{K_a} = \frac{1.0 \times 10^{-14}}{1.9 \times 10^{-5}} = 5.3 \times 10^{-10}$$

Initial	0.010 M	0	~0
	x mol/L of N_3^- reacts with H_2O to reach equilibrium		
Change	-x $\rightarrow$	+x	+x
Equil.	0.010 - x	x	x

$$K_b = \frac{[HN_3][OH^-]}{[N_3^-]} = 5.3 \times 10^{-10} = \frac{x^2}{0.010 - x} \approx \frac{x^2}{0.010} \quad \text{(assuming } x \ll 0.010)$$

$$x = [OH^-] = 2.3 \times 10^{-6} \ M; \ [H^+] = \frac{1.0 \times 10^{-14}}{2.3 \times 10^{-6}} = 4.3 \times 10^{-9} \ M \quad \text{Assumptions good.}$$

$[HN_3] = [OH^-] = 2.3 \times 10^{-6} \ M; \ [Na^+] = 0.010 \ M; \ [N_3^-] = 0.010 - 2.3 \times 10^{-6} = 0.010 \ M$

82. $C_2H_5NH_3Cl \rightarrow C_2H_5NH_3^+ + Cl^-$; $C_2H_5NH_3^+$ is the conjugate acid of the weak base $C_2H_5NH_2$ ($K_b = 5.6 \times 10^{-4}$). As is true for all conjugate acids of weak bases, $C_2H_5NH_3^+$ is a weak acid. Cl^- has no basic (or acidic) properties. Ignore Cl^-. Solving the weak acid problem:

$$C_2H_5NH_3^+ \quad \rightleftharpoons \quad C_2H_5NH_2 \quad + \quad H^+ \qquad K_a = K_w/5.6 \times 10^{-4} = 1.8 \times 10^{-11}$$

Initial   0.25 M 0   ~0

               x mol/L $C_2H_5NH_3^+$ dissociates to reach equilibrium

Change $-x$ $\rightarrow$ $+x$ $+x$

Equil.   0.25 - x x x

$$K_a = 1.8 \times 10^{-11} = \frac{[C_2H_5NH_2]\,[H^+]}{[C_2H_5NH_3^+]} = \frac{x^2}{0.25 - x} \approx \frac{x^2}{0.25} \quad (\text{assuming } x \ll 0.25)$$

$x = [H^+] = 2.1 \times 10^{-6}\ M;$ pH = 5.68; Assumptions good.

$[C_2H_5NH_2] = [H^+] = 2.1 \times 10^{-6}\ M;$ $[C_2H_5NH_3^+] = 0.25\ M;$ $[Cl^-] = 0.25\ M$

$[OH^-] = K_w/[H^+] = 4.8 \times 10^{-9}\ M$

83.   All these salts contain Na^+ which has no acidic/basic properties and a conjugate base of a weak acid (except for NaCl where Cl^- is a neutral species.). All conjugate bases of weak acids are weak bases since K_b for these species are between K_w and 1. To identify the species, we will use the data given to determine the K_b value for the weak conjugate base. From the K_b value and data in Table 7.2 of the text, we can identify the conjugate base present by calculating the K_a value for the weak acid. We will use A^- as an abbreviation for the weak conjugate base.

$$A^- + H_2O \quad \rightleftharpoons \quad HA \quad + \quad OH^-$$

Initial   0.100 mol/1.00 L   0   ~0

               x mol/L A^- reacts with H_2O to reach equilibrium

Change $-x$ $\rightarrow$ $+x$ $+x$

Equil.   0.100 - x x x

$$K_b = \frac{[HA]\,[OH^-]}{[A^-]} = \frac{x^2}{0.100 - x}; \text{ From the problem, pH = 8.07:}$$

   pOH = 14.00 - 8.07 = 5.93; $[OH^-] = x = 10^{-5.93} = 1.2 \times 10^{-6}\ M$

$$K_b = \frac{(1.2 \times 10^{-6})^2}{0.100 - 1.2 \times 10^{-6}} = 1.4 \times 10^{-11} = K_b \text{ value for the conjugate base of a weak acid.}$$

The K_a value for the weak acid equals K_w/K_b: $K_a = \dfrac{1.0 \times 10^{-14}}{1.4 \times 10^{-11}} = 7.1 \times 10^{-4}$

From Table 7.2 of the text, this K_a value is closest to HF. Therefore, the unknown salt is NaF.

84. $BHCl \rightarrow BH^+ + Cl^-;$ Cl^- is the conjugate base of the strong acid HCl, so Cl^- has no acidic/basic properties. BH^+ is a weak acid since it is the conjugate acid of a weak base, B. Determining the K_a value for BH^+:

$$\text{BH}^+ \quad\rightleftharpoons\quad \text{B} \;+\; \text{H}^+$$

Initial	0.10 M		0	$\sim$0

x mol/L BH^+ dissociates to reach equilibrium

Change	$-x$	$\rightarrow$	$+x$	$+x$
Equil.	0.10 - x		x	x

$$K_a = \frac{[\text{B}]\,[\text{H}^+]}{[\text{BH}^+]} = \frac{x^2}{0.10 - x}; \quad \text{From the problem, pH} = 5.82:$$

$$[\text{H}^+] = x = 10^{-5.82} = 1.5 \times 10^{-6}\,M; \quad K_a = \frac{(1.5 \times 10^{-6})^2}{0.10 - 1.5 \times 10^{-6}} = 2.3 \times 10^{-11}$$

K_b for the base, $\text{B} = K_w \backslash K_a = 1.0 \times 10^{-14}/2.3 \times 10^{-11} = 4.3 \times 10^{-4}$.

From Table 7.3 of the text, this K_b value is closest to CH_3NH_2 so the unknown salt is CH_3NH_3Cl.

85.   Major species: $Co(H_2O)_6{}^{3+}$ ($K_a = 1.0 \times 10^{-5}$), Cl^- (neutral) and H_2O ($K_w = 1.0 \times 10^{-14}$); $Co(H_2O)_6{}^{3+}$ will determine the pH since it is a stronger acid than water. Solving the weak acid problem in the usual manner:

$$Co(H_2O)_6{}^{3+} \quad\rightleftharpoons\quad Co(H_2O)_5(OH)^{2+} \;+\; H^+ \quad K_a = 1.0 \times 10^{-5}$$

Initial	0.10 M	0	$\sim$0
Equil.	0.10 - x	x	x

$$K_a = 1.0 \times 10^{-5} = \frac{x^2}{0.10 - x} \approx \frac{x^2}{0.10}, \quad x = [\text{H}^+] = 1.0 \times 10^{-3}\,M$$

$\text{pH} = -\log(1.0 \times 10^{-3}) = 3.00;$ Assumptions good.

86.   Major species present are H_2O, $C_5H_5NH^+$ ($K_a = K_w/K_b(C_5H_5N) = 1.0 \times 10^{-14}/1.7 \times 10^{-9} = 5.9 \times 10^{-6}$) and F^- ($K_b = K_w/K_a(HF) = 1.0 \times 10^{-14}/7.2 \times 10^{-4} = 1.4 \times 10^{-11}$). The reaction to consider is the best acid present ($C_5H_5NH^+$) reacting with the best base present (F^-). Solving for the equilibrium concentrations:

$$C_5H_5NH^+(aq) \;+\; F^-(aq) \quad\rightleftharpoons\quad C_5H_5N(aq) \;+\; HF(aq)$$

Initial	0.200 M	0.200 M		0	0
Change	$-x$	$-x$	$\rightarrow$	$+x$	$+x$
Equil.	0.200 - x	0.200 - x		x	x

$$K = K_{a,\,C_5H_5NH^+} \times \frac{1}{K_{a,\,HF}} = 5.9 \times 10^{-6}\,(1/7.2 \times 10^{-4}) = 8.2 \times 10^{-3}$$

$$K = \frac{[C_5H_5N]\,[HF]}{[C_5H_5NH^+]\,[F^-]} = 8.2 \times 10^{-3} = \frac{x^2}{(0.200 - x)^2}; \quad \text{Taking the square root of both sides:}$$

$$0.091 = \frac{x}{0.200 - x} \quad x = 0.018 - 0.091\,x, \quad x = 0.016\,M$$

From the set-up to the problem, $x = [C_5H_5N] = [HF] = 0.016 \, M$ and $0.200 - x = 0.200 - 0.016 = 0.184$ $M = [C_5H_5NH^+] = [F^-]$. To solve for the $[H^+]$, we can use either the K_a equilibrium for $C_5H_5NH^+$ or the K_a equilibrium for HF. Using $C_5H_5NH^+$ data:

$$K_{a, C_5H_5NH^+} = 5.9 \times 10^{-6} = \frac{[C_5H_5N][H^+]}{[C_5H_5NH^+]} = \frac{(0.016)[H^+]}{(0.184)}, \quad [H^+] = 6.8 \times 10^{-5} \, M$$

$$pH = -\log(6.8 \times 10^{-5}) = 4.17$$

As one would expect, since the K_a for the weak acid is larger than the K_b for the weak base, then a solution of this salt should be acidic.

Solutions of Dilute Acids and Bases

87. $HBrO \quad \rightleftharpoons \quad H^+ \quad + \quad BrO^- \quad K_a = 2 \times 10^{-9}$

Initial	$1.0 \times 10^{-6} \, M$	~ 0	0

x mol/L HBrO dissociates to reach equilibrium

Change	$-x$	$\rightarrow$ $+x$	$+x$
Equil.	$1.0 \times 10^{-6} - x$	x	x

$$K_a = 2 \times 10^{-9} = \frac{x^2}{1.0 \times 10^{-6} - x} \approx \frac{x^2}{1.0 \times 10^{-6}}; \quad x = [H^+] = 4 \times 10^{-8} \, M; \quad pH = 7.4$$

Lets check the assumptions. This answer is impossible! We can't add a small amount of an acid to a neutral solution and get a basic solution. The highest pH possible for an acid in water is 7.0. In the correct solution, we would have to take into account the autoionization of water.

88. $C_6H_5OH \quad \rightleftharpoons \quad C_6H_5O^- \quad + \quad H^+ \quad C_6H_5OH = phenol$

Initial	$4.0 \times 10^{-5} \, M$	0	~ 0
Equil.	$4.0 \times 10^{-5} - x$	x	x

$$K_a = \frac{x^2}{4.0 \times 10^{-5}} \approx 1.6 \times 10^{-10}, \quad x = [H^+] \approx 8.0 \times 10^{-8} \, M \qquad \text{Check assumptions.}$$

The assumption that the H^+ contribution from water is negligible is poor. Whenever the calculated pH is greater than 6.0 ($[H^+] < 1 \times 10^{-6} \, M$) for an acid solution, the H^+ contribution from water should be considered. From Section 7.9 in text, try $[H^+] = (K_a[HA]_o + K_w)^{1/2}$.

$$[H^+] = [(1.6 \times 10^{-10})(4.0 \times 10^{-5}) + (1.0 \times 10^{-14})]^{1/2} = 1.3 \times 10^{-7} \, M$$

This equation will work if $[HA]_o = 4.0 \times 10^{-5} \gg \dfrac{[H^+]^2 - K_w}{[H^+]} = 5.3 \times 10^{-8}$. Assumption good.

$$[H^+] = 1.3 \times 10^{-7} \, M; \quad pH = 6.89$$

Note: If the assumption that $([H^+]^2 - K_w)/[H^+] \ll K_a$ is bad, then the full equation derived in Section 7.9 of the text should be used.

89.   HCN $\rightleftharpoons$ H^+ + CN^- $K_a = 6.2 \times 10^{-10}$

Initial $5.0 \times 10^{-4}\ M$ ~ 0 0
Equil. $5.0 \times 10^{-4} - x$ x x

$$K_a = \frac{x^2}{5.0 \times 10^{-4} - x} \approx \frac{x^2}{5.0 \times 10^{-4}} = 6.2 \times 10^{-10},\ x = 5.6 \times 10^{-7}\ M \quad \text{Check assumptions.}$$

The assumption that the H^+ contribution from water is negligible is poor. Whenever the calculated pH is greater than 6.0 for a weak acid, water contribution to $[H^+]$ must be considered. From Section 7.9 in text:

if $\dfrac{[H^+]^2 - K_w}{[H^+]} \ll [HCN]_o = 5.0 \times 10^{-4}$ then we can use: $[H^+] = (K_a[HCN]_o + K_w)^{1/2}$.

Using this formula: $[H^+] = [(6.2 \times 10^{-10})(5.0 \times 10^{-4}) + (1.0 \times 10^{-14})]^{1/2}$, $[H^+] = 5.7 \times 10^{-7}\ M$

Checking assumptions: $\dfrac{[H^+]^2 - K_w}{[H^+]} = 5.5 \times 10^{-7} \ll 5.0 \times 10^{-4}$

Assumptions good. $pH = -\log(5.7 \times 10^{-7}) = 6.24$

90.   We can't neglect the $[H^+]$ contribution from H_2O since this is a very dilute solution of the strong acid. Following the strategy developed in Section 7.10 of the text, we first determine the charge balance equation and then manipulate this equation to get into one unknown.

Charge balance: $[H^+] = [NO_3^-] + [OH^-]$, $[H^+] = [NO_3^-] + K_w/[H^+]$

$[H^+]^2 - 1.0 \times 10^{-14} = [H^+](5.0 \times 10^{-8})$, $[H^+]^2 - 5.0 \times 10^{-8}\ [H^+] - 1.0 \times 10^{-14} = 0$

Using the quadratic formula: $[H^+] = 1.3 \times 10^{-7}\ M$; $pH = 6.89$

91.   We can't neglect the $[H^+]$ contribution from H_2O since this is a very dilute solution of the strong acid. Following the strategy developed in Section 7.10 of the text, we first determine the charge balance equation and then manipulate this equation to get into one unknown.

[positive charge] = [negative charge]

$[H^+] = [Cl^-] + [OH^-]$, $[H^+] = 7.0 \times 10^{-7} + \dfrac{K_w}{[H^+]}$ since $[Cl^-] = 7.0 \times 10^{-7}$ and $[OH^-] = \dfrac{K_w}{[H^+]}$

$\dfrac{[H^+]^2 - K_w}{[H^+]} = 7.0 \times 10^{-7}$, $[H^+]^2 - 7.0 \times 10^{-7}\ [H^+] - 1.0 \times 10^{-14} = 0$

Using the quadratic formula to solve:

$$[H^+] = \frac{-(-7.0 \times 10^{-7}) \pm [(-7.0 \times 10^{-7})^2 - 4(1)(-1.0 \times 10^{-14})]^{1/2}}{2(1)}$$

$[H^+] = 7.1 \times 10^{-7}\ M$; $pH = -\log(7.1 \times 10^{-7}) = 6.15$

92.   Since this is a very dilute solution of NaOH, then we must worry about the amount of OH⁻ donated from the autoionization of water.

$$NaOH \rightarrow Na^+ + OH^-$$

$$H_2O \rightleftharpoons H^+ + OH^- \quad K_w = [H^+][OH^-] = 1.0 \times 10^{-14}$$

This solution, like all solutions, must be charged balance, that is [positive charge] = [negative charge]. For this problem, the charge balance equation is:

$$[Na^+] + [H^+] = [OH^-], \text{ where } [Na^+] = 1.0 \times 10^{-7}\ M \text{ and } [H^+] = \frac{K_w}{[OH^-]}$$

Substituting into the charge balance equation:

$$1.0 \times 10^{-7} + \frac{1.0 \times 10^{-14}}{[OH^-]} = [OH^-], \quad [OH^-]^2 - 1.0 \times 10^{-7}\,[OH^-] - 1.0 \times 10^{-14} = 0$$

Using the quadratic formula to solve:

$$[OH^-] = \frac{-(-1.0 \times 10^{-7}) \pm [(-1.0 \times 10^{-7})^2 - 4(1)(-1.0 \times 10^{-14})]^{1/2}}{2(1)}$$

$$[OH^-] = 1.6 \times 10^{-7}\ M; \quad pOH = -\log(1.6 \times 10^{-7}) = 6.80; \quad pH = 7.20$$

Additional Exercises

93.   a. $NH_3 + H_3O^+ \rightleftharpoons NH_4^+ + H_2O$

$$K_{eq} = \frac{[NH_4^+]}{[NH_3][H^+]} = \frac{1}{K_a \text{ for } NH_4^+} = \frac{K_b}{K_w} = \frac{1.8 \times 10^{-5}}{1.0 \times 10^{-14}} = 1.8 \times 10^9$$

b. $NO_2^- + H_3O^+ \rightleftharpoons H_2O + HNO_2 \quad K_{eq} = \dfrac{[HNO_2]}{[NO_2^-][H^+]} = \dfrac{1}{K_a} = \dfrac{1}{4.0 \times 10^{-4}} = 2.5 \times 10^3$

c. $NH_4^+ + CH_3CO_2^- \rightleftharpoons NH_3 + CH_3CO_2H \quad K_{eq} = \dfrac{[NH_3][CH_3CO_2H]}{[NH_4^+][CH_3CO_2^-]} \times \dfrac{[H^+]}{[H^+]}$

$$K_{eq} = \frac{K_a \text{ for } NH_4^+}{K_a \text{ for } HOAc} = \frac{K_w}{(K_b \text{ for } NH_3)(K_a \text{ for } HOAc)} = \frac{1.0 \times 10^{-14}}{(1.8 \times 10^{-5})(1.8 \times 10^{-5})}$$

$$K_{eq} = 3.1 \times 10^{-5}$$

d. $H_3O^+ + OH^- \rightleftharpoons 2\,H_2O \quad K_{eq} = \dfrac{1}{K_w} = 1.0 \times 10^{14}$

e. $NH_4^+ + OH^- \rightleftharpoons NH_3 + H_2O \quad K_{eq} = \dfrac{1}{K_b \text{ for } NH_3} = 5.6 \times 10^4$

f. $HNO_2 + OH^- \rightleftharpoons H_2O + NO_2^-$

$$K_{eq} = \frac{[NO_2^-]}{[HNO_2][OH^-]} \times \frac{[H^+]}{[H^+]} = \frac{K_a \text{ for } HNO_2}{K_w} = \frac{4.0 \times 10^{-4}}{1.0 \times 10^{-14}} = 4.0 \times 10^{10}$$

94. a. In the lungs, there is a lot of O_2 and the equilibrium favors $Hb(O_2)_4$. In the cells there is a deficiency of O_2 and the equilibrium favors HbH_4^{4+}.

b. CO_2 is a weak acid, $CO_2 + H_2O \rightleftharpoons HCO_3^- + H^+$. Removing CO_2 essentially decreases H^+. $Hb(O_2)_4$ is then favored and O_2 is not released by hemoglobin in the cells. Breathing into a paper bag increases CO_2 in the blood, thus increasing $[H^+]$ which shifts the reaction left.

c. CO_2 builds up in the blood and it becomes too acidic, driving the equilibrium to the left. Hemoglobin can't bind O_2 as strongly in the lungs. Bicarbonate ion acts as a base in water and neutralizes the excess acidity.

95. The light bulb is bright because a strong electrolyte is present, i.e., a solute is present that dissolves to produce a lot of ions in solution. The pH meter value of 4.6 indicates that a weak acid is present. (If a strong acid were present, the pH would be close to zero.) Of the possible substances, only HCl (strong acid), NaOH (strong base) and NH_4Cl are strong electrolytes. Of these three substances, only NH_4Cl contains a weak acid (the HCl solution would have a pH close to zero and the NaOH solution would have a pH close to 14.0). NH_4Cl dissociates into NH_4^+ and Cl^- ions when dissolved in water. Cl^- is the conjugate base of a strong acid, so it has no basic (or acidic properties) in water. NH_4^+, however, is the conjugate acid of the weak base NH_3, so NH_4^+ is a weak acid and would produce a solution with a pH = 4.6 when the concentration is ~1.0 M.

96. From the pH, $C_7H_4ClO_2^-$ is a weak base. Use the weak base data to determine K_b for $C_7H_4ClO_2^-$ (which we will abbreviate as CB^-).

	CB^-	+	H_2O	$\rightleftharpoons$	HCB	+	OH^-
Initial	0.20 M				0		~0
Equil.	0.20 - x				x		x

Since pH = 8.65, then pOH = 5.35 and $[OH^-] = 10^{-5.35} = 4.5 \times 10^{-6} M = x$.

$$K_b = \frac{[HCB][OH^-]}{[CB^-]} = \frac{x^2}{0.20 - x} = \frac{(4.5 \times 10^{-6})^2}{0.20 - 4.5 \times 10^{-6}} = 1.0 \times 10^{-10}$$

Since CB^- is a weak base, then HCB, chlorobenzoic acid, is a weak acid. Solving the weak acid problem:

	HCB	$\rightleftharpoons$	H^+	+	CB^-
Initial	0.20 M		~0		0
Equil.	0.20 - x		x		x

$$K_a = \frac{K_w}{K_b} = \frac{1.0 \times 10^{-14}}{1.0 \times 10^{-10}} = 1.0 \times 10^{-4} = \frac{x^2}{0.20 - x} \approx \frac{x^2}{0.20}$$

$x = [H^+] = 4.5 \times 10^{-3} M;$ pH = 2.35   Assumptions good.

97.   For 0.0010% dissociation: $[NH_4^+] = 1.0 \times 10^{-5} (0.050) = 5.0 \times 10^{-7}\ M$

$NH_3 + H_2O \rightleftharpoons NH_4^+ + OH^-$ $K_b = \dfrac{(5.0 \times 10^{-7})[OH^-]}{0.050 - 5.0 \times 10^{-7}} = 1.8 \times 10^{-5}$

Solving: $[OH^-] = 1.8\ M$; Assuming no volume change:

$$1.0\ L \times \frac{1.8\ mol\ NaOH}{L} \times \frac{40.0\ g\ NaOH}{mol\ NaOH} = 72\ g\ of\ NaOH$$

98.   For this problem we will abbreviate $CH_2=CHCO_2H$ as Hacr and $CH_2=CHCO_2^-$ as acr⁻.

a.   Hacr $\rightleftharpoons$ H^+ +   acr⁻

Initial   0.10 M ~0   0
Equil.   0.10 - x x x

$K_a = \dfrac{x^2}{0.10 - x} = 5.6 \times 10^{-5} \approx \dfrac{x^2}{0.10}$, $x = [H^+] = 2.4 \times 10^{-3}\ M$; pH = 2.62

Assumptions good.

b.   % dissociation $= \dfrac{2.4 \times 10^{-3}}{0.10} \times 100 = 2.4\%$

c.   For 0.010% dissociation: $[acr^-] = 1.0 \times 10^{-4} (0.10) = 1.0 \times 10^{-5}\ M$

$K_a = \dfrac{[H^+][acr^-]}{[Hacr]} = 5.6 \times 10^{-5} = \dfrac{[H^+](1.0 \times 10^{-5})}{0.10 - 1.0 \times 10^{-5}}$, $[H^+] = 0.56\ M$

d.   acr⁻ is a weak base and the major source of OH⁻ in this solution.

       acr⁻   + H_2O $\rightleftharpoons$ Hacr   +   OH⁻ $K_b = \dfrac{K_w}{K_a} = \dfrac{1.0 \times 10^{-14}}{5.6 \times 10^{-5}}$

Initial   0.050 M 0   ~0 $K_b = 1.8 \times 10^{-10}$
Equil.   0.050 - x x x

$K_b = \dfrac{[OH^-][Hacr]}{[acr^-]} = 1.8 \times 10^{-10} = \dfrac{x^2}{0.050 - x} \approx \dfrac{x^2}{0.050}$

$x = [OH^-] = 3.0 \times 10^{-6}\ M$; pOH = 5.52; pH = 8.48   Assumptions good.

99.   a. $Fe(H_2O)_6^{3+}$ + H_2O $\rightleftharpoons$ $Fe(H_2O)_5(OH)^{2+}$ + H_3O^+

Initial   0.10 M 0   ~0
Equil.   0.10 - x x x

$K_a = \dfrac{[H_3O^+][Fe(H_2O)_5(OH)^{2+}]}{[Fe(H_2O)_6^{3+}]} = 6.0 \times 10^{-3} = \dfrac{x^2}{0.10 - x} \approx \dfrac{x^2}{0.10}$

$x = 2.4 \times 10^{-2}\ M$; Assumption is poor (24% error).

Using successive approximations:

$$\frac{x^2}{0.10 - 0.024} = 6.0 \times 10^{-3},\ x = 0.021$$

$$\frac{x^2}{0.10 - 0.021} = 6.0 \times 10^{-3},\ x = 0.022; \quad \frac{x^2}{0.10 - 0.022} = 6.0 \times 10^{-3},\ x = 0.022$$

$x = [H^+] = 0.022\ M$; pH = 1.66

b. $\dfrac{[Fe(H_2O)_5(OH)^{2+}]}{[Fe(H_2O)_6^{3+}]} = \dfrac{0.0010}{0.9990}$; $K_a = 6.0 \times 10^{-3} = \dfrac{[H^+](0.0010)}{(0.9990)}$

Solving: $[H^+] = 6.0\ M$; pH = -log (6.0) = -0.78

c.   Because of the lower charge, Fe^{2+}(aq) will not be as strong an acid as Fe^{3+}(aq). A solution of iron(II) nitrate will be less acidic (have a higher pH) than a solution with the same concentration of iron(III) nitrate.

100.   At a pH = 0.00, the $[H^+] = 10^{-0.00} = 1.0\ M$. Begin with 1.0 L $\times$ 2.0 mol/L NaOH = 2.0 mol OH^-. We will need 2.0 mol HCl to neutralize the OH^- plus an additional 1.0 mol excess to reduce to a pH of 0.00. Need 3.0 mol HCl total to achieve pH = 0.00.

101.   0.50 M HA, $K_a = 1.0 \times 10^{-3}$; 0.20 M HB, $K_a = 1.0 \times 10^{-10}$; 0.10 M HC, $K_a = 1.0 \times 10^{-12}$

Major source of H^+ is HA since its K_a value is significantly larger than other K_a values.

	HA	$\rightleftharpoons$	H^+	+	A^-
Initial	0.50 M		~0		0
Equil.	0.50 - x		x		x

$K_a = \dfrac{x^2}{0.50 - x} = 1.0 \times 10^{-3} \approx \dfrac{x^2}{0.50}$, $x \approx 0.022\ M = [H^+]$, $\dfrac{0.022}{0.50} \times 100 = 4.4\ \%$ error

Assumptions good. Let's check out the assumption that only HA is an important source of H^+.

For HB: $1.0 \times 10^{-10} = \dfrac{(0.022)\,[B^-]}{(0.20)}$, $[B^-] = 9.1 \times 10^{-10}\ M$

At most, HB will produce an additional $9.1 \times 10^{-10}\ M$ H^+. Even less will be produced by HC. Thus, our original assumption was good. $[H^+] = 0.022\ M$.

102. $[HA]_o = \dfrac{1.0\ mol}{2.0\ L} = 0.50$ mol/L; Solve using the K_a equilibrium reaction.

$$HA \rightleftharpoons H^+ + A^-$$

Initial	$0.50\ M$	~ 0	0
Equil.	$0.50 - x$	x	x

$K_a = \dfrac{[H^+][A^-]}{[HA]} = \dfrac{x^2}{0.50 - x}$; In this problem, $[HA] = 0.45\ M$ so:

$$[HA] = 0.45\ M = 0.50\ M - x, \quad x = 0.05\ M; \quad K_a = \frac{(0.05)^2}{0.45} = 6 \times 10^{-3}$$

103. Since NH_3 is so concentrated, we need to calculate the OH^- contribution from the weak base NH_3.

$$NH_3 + H_2O \rightleftharpoons NH_4^+ + OH^- \qquad K_b = 1.8 \times 10^{-5}$$

Initial	$15.0\ M$	0	$0.0100\ M$ (Assume no volume change.)
Equil.	$15.0 - x$	x	$0.0100 + x$

$K_b = 1.8 \times 10^{-5} = \dfrac{x(0.0100 + x)}{15.0 - x} \approx \dfrac{x(0.0100)}{15.0}$, $x = 0.027$; Assumption is horrible (x is 270% of 0.0100).

Using the quadratic formula:

$$1.8 \times 10^{-5}(15.0 - x) = 0.0100\ x + x^2, \quad x^2 + 0.0100\ x - 2.7 \times 10^{-4} = 0$$

$$x = 1.2 \times 10^{-2}\ M, \quad [OH^-] = 1.2 \times 10^{-2} + 0.0100 = 0.022\ M$$

104. $[H^+]_o = 1.0 \times 10^{-2} + 1.0 \times 10^{-2} = 2.0 \times 10^{-2}\ M$ from strong acids HCl and H_2SO_4.

HSO_4^- is a good weak acid ($K_a = 0.012$). However, HCN is a poor weak acid ($K_a = 6.2 \times 10^{-10}$) and can be ignored. Calculating the H^+ contribution from HSO_4^-:

$$HSO_4^- \rightleftharpoons H^+ + SO_4^{2-} \qquad K_a = 0.012$$

Initial	$0.010\ M$	$0.020\ M$	0
Equil.	$0.010 - x$	$0.020 + x$	x

$K_a = \dfrac{x(0.020 + x)}{(0.010 - x)} = 0.012 \approx \dfrac{x(0.020)}{(0.010)}$, $x = 0.0060$; Assumption poor (60% error).

Using the quadratic formula: $x^2 + 0.032\ x - 1.2 \times 10^{-4} = 0$, $x = 3.4 \times 10^{-3}\ M$

$[H^+] = 0.020 + x = 0.020 + 3.4 \times 10^{-3} = 0.023\ M$; pH = 1.64

105. a. The initial concentrations are halved since equal volumes of the two solutions are mixed.

$$HC_2H_3O_2 \rightleftharpoons H^+ + C_2H_3O_2^-$$

Initial	$0.100\ M$	$5.00 \times 10^{-4}\ M$	0
Equil.	$0.100 - x$	$5.00 \times 10^{-4} + x$	x

$K_a = 1.8 \times 10^{-5} = \dfrac{x(5.00 \times 10^{-4} + x)}{(0.100 - x)} \approx \dfrac{x(5.00 \times 10^{-4})}{0.100}$

$x = 3.6 \times 10^{-3}$; Assumption is horrible. Using the quadratic formula:

$$x^2 + 5.18 \times 10^{-4}\, x - 1.8 \times 10^{-6} = 0$$

$$x = 1.1 \times 10^{-3}\, M; \quad [H^+] = 5.00 \times 10^{-4} + x = 1.6 \times 10^{-3}\, M; \quad pH = 2.80$$

b. $x = [C_2H_3O_2^-] = 1.1 \times 10^{-3}\, M$

106. a. $NH_4(HCO_3) \rightarrow NH_4^+ + HCO_3^-$

$$K_a(NH_4^+) = \frac{1.0 \times 10^{-14}}{1.8 \times 10^{-5}} = 5.6 \times 10^{-10}; \quad K_b(HCO_3^-) = \frac{K_w}{K_{a_1}} = \frac{1.0 \times 10^{-14}}{4.3 \times 10^{-7}} = 2.3 \times 10^{-8}$$

Solution is basic since HCO_3^- is a stronger base than NH_4^+ is as an acid. The acidic properties of HCO_3^- were ignored since K_{a_2} is small (5.6×10^{-11}).

b. $NaH_2PO_4 \rightarrow Na^+ + H_2PO_4^-$; Ignore Na^+.

$$K_{a_2}(H_2PO_4^-) = 6.2 \times 10^{-8}; \quad K_b(H_2PO_4^-) = \frac{K_w}{K_{a_1}} = \frac{1.0 \times 10^{-14}}{7.5 \times 10^{-3}} = 1.3 \times 10^{-12}$$

Solution is acidic since $K_a > K_b$.

c. $Na_2HPO_4 \rightarrow 2\, Na^+ + HPO_4^{2-}$; Ignore Na^+.

$$K_{a_3}(HPO_4^{2-}) = 4.8 \times 10^{-13}; \quad K_b(HPO_4^{2-}) = \frac{K_w}{K_{a_2}} = \frac{1.0 \times 10^{-14}}{6.2 \times 10^{-8}} = 1.6 \times 10^{-7}$$

Solution is basic since $K_b > K_a$.

d. $NH_4(H_2PO_4) \rightarrow NH_4^+ + H_2PO_4^-$

NH_4^+ is weak acid and $H_2PO_4^-$ is also acidic (see b). Solution with both ions present will be acidic.

e. $NH_4(HCO_2) \rightarrow NH_4^+ + HCO_2^-$; From Appendix 5, $K_a(HCO_2H) = 1.8 \times 10^{-4}$.

$$K_a(NH_4^+) = 5.6 \times 10^{-10}; \quad K_b(HCO_2^-) = \frac{K_w}{K_a} = \frac{1.0 \times 10^{-14}}{1.8 \times 10^{-4}} = 5.6 \times 10^{-11}$$

Solution is acidic since NH_4^+ is a stronger acid than HCO_2^- is as a base.

107. For $H_2C_6H_6O_6$. $K_{a_1} = 7.9 \times 10^{-5}$ and $K_{a_2} = 1.6 \times 10^{-12}$. Since $K_{a_1} >> K_{a_2}$, then the amount of H^+ produced by the K_{a_2} reaction will be negligible.

$$[H_2C_6H_6O_6]_o = \frac{0.500\ g \times \dfrac{1\ mol\ H_2C_6H_6O_6}{176.1\ g}}{0.2000\ L} = 0.0142\ M$$

$$H_2C_6H_6O_6(aq) \quad \rightleftharpoons \quad HC_6H_6O_6^-(aq) \quad + \quad H^+(aq) \quad K_{a_1} = 7.9 \times 10^{-5}$$

Initial   0.0142 M   0   ~0

Equil.   0.0142 - x   x   x

$$K_{a_1} = 7.9 \times 10^{-5} = \frac{x^2}{0.0142 - x} \approx \frac{x^2}{0.0142}, \quad x = 1.1 \times 10^{-3}; \quad \text{Assumption fails the 5\% rule.}$$

Solving by the method of successive approximations:

$$7.9 \times 10^{-5} = \frac{x^2}{0.0142 - 1.1 \times 10^{-3}}, \quad x = 1.0 \times 10^{-3} \, M \text{ (consistent answer)}$$

Since H^+ produced by the K_{a_2} reaction will be negligible, $[H^+] = 1.0 \times 10^{-3}$ and pH = 3.00.

108.   Since the values of K_{a_1} and K_{a_2} are fairly close to each other, then we should consider the amount of H^+ produced by the K_{a_1} and the K_{a_2} reaction.

$$H_3C_6H_5O_7 \quad \rightleftharpoons \quad H_2C_6H_5O_7^- \quad + \quad H^+ \quad K_{a_1} = 8.4 \times 10^{-4}$$

Initial   0.15 M   0   ~0

Equil.   0.15 - x   x   x

$$8.4 \times 10^{-4} = \frac{x^2}{0.15 - x} \approx \frac{x^2}{0.15}, \quad x = 1.1 \times 10^{-2}. \quad \text{Assumption fails the 5\% rule.}$$

Solving more exactly using the method of successive approximations:

$$8.4 \times 10^{-4} = \frac{x^2}{0.15 - 1.1 \times 10^{-2}}, \quad x = 1.1 \times 10^{-2} \, M \text{ (consistent answer)}$$

Now let's solve for the H^+ contribution from the K_{a_2} reaction.

$$H_2C_6H_5O_7^- \quad \rightleftharpoons \quad HC_6H_5O_7^{2-} \quad + \quad H^+ \quad\quad K_{a_2} = 1.8 \times 10^{-5}$$

Initial $1.1 \times 10^{-2} \, M$ 0 $1.1 \times 10^{-2} \, M$

Equil. $1.1 \times 10^{-2} - x$ x $1.1 \times 10^{-2} + x$

$$1.8 \times 10^{-5} = \frac{x(1.1 \times 10^{-2} + x)}{1.1 \times 10^{-2} - x} \approx \frac{x(1.1 \times 10^{-2})}{1.1 \times 10^{-2}}, \quad x = 1.8 \times 10^{-5} \, M; \quad \text{Assumption good, 0.2\% error.}$$

At most, $1.8 \times 10^{-5} \, M \, H^+$ will be added from the K_{a_2} reaction.

$[H^+]_{total} = 1.1 \times 10^{-2} + 1.8 \times 10^{-5} = 1.1 \times 10^{-2} \, M$

Note that the H^+ contribution from the K_{a_2} reaction was negligible as compared to the H^+ contribution from the K_{a_1} reaction even though the two K_a values only differed by a factor of 50. Therefore, the H^+ contribution from the K_{a_3} reaction will also be negligible since $K_{a_3} < K_{a_2}$.

Solving: pH = $-\log(1.1 \times 10^{-2})$ = 1.96

Challenge Problems

109.   a. $HCO_3^- + HCO_3^- \rightleftharpoons H_2CO_3 + CO_3^{2-}$

$$K_{eq} = \frac{[H_2CO_3][CO_3^{2-}]}{[HCO_3^-][HCO_3^-]} \times \frac{[H^+]}{[H^+]} = \frac{K_{a_2}}{K_{a_1}} = \frac{4.8 \times 10^{-11}}{4.3 \times 10^{-7}} = 1.1 \times 10^{-4}$$

      b. $[H_2CO_3] = [CO_3^{2-}]$ since the reaction in part a is the principle equilibrium reaction.

      c. $H_2CO_3 \rightleftharpoons 2 H^+ + CO_3^{2-}$ $K_{eq} = \dfrac{[H^+]^2 [CO_3^{2-}]}{[H_2CO_3]} = K_{a_1} \times K_{a_2}$

         Since $[H_2CO_3] = [CO_3^{2-}]$ from part b, then $[H^+]^2 = K_{a_1} \times K_{a_2}$.

         $[H^+] = (K_{a_1} \times K_{a_2})^{1/2}$ or taking the -log of both sides: $pH = \dfrac{pK_{a_1} + pK_{a_2}}{2}$

      d. $[H^+] = [(4.3 \times 10^{-7}) \times (4.8 \times 10^{-11})]^{1/2}$, $[H^+] = 4.5 \times 10^{-9}\ M$; $pH = 8.35$

110.   Molar mass $= \dfrac{dRT}{P} = \dfrac{5.11\ \text{g/L} \times \dfrac{0.08206\ \text{L atm}}{\text{mol K}} \times 298\ \text{K}}{1.00\ \text{atm}} = 125$ g/mol

$$[HA]_o = \frac{1.50\ \text{g} \times \dfrac{1\ \text{mol}}{125\ \text{g}}}{0.100\ \text{L}} = 0.120\ M;\ \ pH = 1.80,\ [H^+] = 10^{-1.80} = 1.6 \times 10^{-2}\ M$$

                $HA \quad\quad \rightleftharpoons \quad\quad H^+ \ + \ A^-$

Equil. $0.120 - x$ x x $x = [H^+] = 1.6 \times 10^{-2}\ M$

$$K_a = \frac{[H^+][A^-]}{[HA]} = \frac{(1.6 \times 10^{-2})^2}{0.120 - 0.016} = 2.5 \times 10^{-3}$$

111.   Major species: BH^+, X^-, H_2O; Since BH^+ is the best acid and X^- is the best base in solution, then the principal equilibrium is:

                  $BH^+ \ + \quad X^- \quad \rightleftharpoons \quad B \ + \ HX$

        Initial $0.100\ M$ $0.100\ M$ 0 0
        Equil. $0.100 - x$ $0.100 - x$ x x

$$K = \frac{K_{a,\,BH^+}}{K_{a,\,HX}} = \frac{[B][HX]}{[BH^+][X^-]} \quad \text{where } [B] = [HX] \text{ and } [BH^+] = [X^-] \ \text{(See set-up above.)}$$

To solve for the K_a of HX, let's use the equilibrium expression to derive a general expression that relates pH to the pK_a for BH^+ and to the pK_a for HX.

$$\frac{K_{a,\,BH^+}}{K_{a,\,HX}} = \frac{[HX]^2}{[X^-]^2};\ \ K_{a,\,HX} = \frac{[H^+][X^-]}{[HX]},\ \ \frac{[HX]}{[X^-]} = \frac{[H^+]}{K_{a,\,HX}}$$

$$\frac{K_{a,\,BH^+}}{K_{a,\,HX}} = \frac{[HX]^2}{[X^-]^2} = \left(\frac{[H^+]}{K_{a,\,HX}}\right)^2,\ \ [H^+]^2 = K_{a,\,BH^+} \times K_{a,\,HX}$$

Taking the -log of both sides: $pH = \dfrac{pK_{a, BH^+} + pK_{a, HX}}{2}$

This is a general equation that applies to all BHX type salts. Solving the problem:

$$K_b \text{ for } B = 1.0 \times 10^{-3}; \quad K_a \text{ for } BH^+ = \dfrac{K_w}{K_b} = 1.0 \times 10^{-11}$$

$$pH = 8.00 = \dfrac{11.00 + pK_{a, HX}}{2}, \quad pK_{a, HX} = 5.00 \text{ and } K_a \text{ for } HX = 10^{-5.00} = 1.0 \times 10^{-5}$$

112.   0.0500 M HCO$_2$H (HA), $K_a = 1.77 \times 10^{-4}$; 0.150 M CH$_3CH_2CO_2$H (HB), $K_a = 1.34 \times 10^{-5}$

Since two comparable weak acids are present, each contributes to the total pH.

Charge balance: $[H^+] = [A^-] + [B^-] + [OH^-] = [A^-] + [B^-] + K_w/[H^+]$

Mass balance for HA and HB: $0.0500 = [HA] + [A^-]$ and $0.150 = [HB] + [B^-]$

$\dfrac{[H^+][A^-]}{[HA]} = 1.77 \times 10^{-4}; \quad \dfrac{[H^+][B^-]}{[HB]} = 1.34 \times 10^{-5}$

We have 5 equations and 5 unknowns. Manipulate the equations to solve.

$[H^+] = [A^-] + [B^-] + K_w/[H^+]; \quad [H^+]^2 = [H^+][A^-] + [H^+][B^-] + K_w$

$[H^+][A^-] = [HA](1.77 \times 10^{-4}) = (1.77 \times 10^{-4})(0.0500 - [A^-])$

If $[A^-] \ll 0.0500$, then $[H^+][A^-] \approx (1.77 \times 10^{-4})(0.0500) = 8.85 \times 10^{-6}$

Similarly, assume $[H^+][B^-] \approx (1.34 \times 10^{-5})(0.150) = 2.01 \times 10^{-6}$

$[H^+]^2 = 8.85 \times 10^{-6} + 2.01 \times 10^{-6} + 1.00 \times 10^{-14}, \quad [H^+] = 3.30 \times 10^{-3} \text{ mol/L}$

Check assumptions: $[H^+][A^-] \approx 8.85 \times 10^{-6}, \quad [A^-] \approx \dfrac{8.85 \times 10^{-6}}{3.30 \times 10^{-3}} \approx 2.68 \times 10^{-3}$

Assumed $0.0500 - [A^-] \approx 0.0500$. This assumption is borderline (2.68×10^{-3} is 5.4% of 0.0500). The HB assumption is good (0.4% error).

Using successive approximations to refine the $[H^+][A^-]$ value:

   $[H^+] = 3.22 \times 10^{-3} M$, pH = -log $(3.22 \times 10^{-3}) = 2.492$.

Note: If we treat each acid separately:

   H$^+$ from HA = 2.9×10^{-3}
   <u>H$^+$ from HB = 1.4×10^{-3}</u>
                $4.3 \times 10^{-3} M = [H^+]$ total.

This assumes the acids did not suppress each others ionization. They do and we expect the $[H^+]$ to be less than 4.3×10^{-3}. We get such an answer.

113.   HA $\rightleftharpoons$ H^+ + A^- $K_a = 1.00 \times 10^{-6}$

Initial   C   ~0   0   C = $[HA]_o$ for pH = 4.000 solution
Equil.   C - 1.00×10^{-4} 1.00×10^{-4} 1.00×10^{-4} $x = [H^+] = 1.00 \times 10^{-4}$ M

$$K_a = \frac{(1.00 \times 10^{-4})^2}{C - 1.00 \times 10^{-4}} = 1.00 \times 10^{-6};\ \text{Solving:}\ C = 0.0101\ M$$

The solution initially contains 50.0×10^{-3} L $\times$ 0.0101 mol/L = 5.05×10^{-4} mol HA. We then dilute to a total volume V in liters. The resulting pH = 5.000, so $[H^+] = 1.00 \times 10^{-5}$. In the typical weak acid problem, $x = [H^+]$, so:

                       HA $\rightleftharpoons$ H^+ + A^-

Initial 5.05×10^{-4} mol/V   ~0   0
Equil. 5.05×10^{-4}/V - 1.00×10^{-5} 1.00×10^{-5} 1.00×10^{-5}

$$K_a = \frac{(1.00 \times 10^{-5})^2}{5.05 \times 10^{-4}/V - 1.00 \times 10^{-5}} = 1.00 \times 10^{-6},\ 1.00 \times 10^{-4} = 5.05 \times 10^{-4}/V - 1.00 \times 10^{-5}$$

V = 4.59 L; 50.0 mL are present initially, so we need to add 4540 mL of water.

114.   Major species = Na^+, HSO_4^-, NH_3; reaction: $HSO_4^- + NH_3 \rightleftharpoons SO_4^{2-} + NH_4^+$

$$K = \frac{[SO_4^{2-}][NH_4^+]}{[HSO_4^-][NH_3]} = \frac{K_a(HSO_4^-)}{K_a(NH_4^+)} = \frac{1.2 \times 10^{-2}}{5.6 \times 10^{-10}} = 2.1 \times 10^7$$

                $HSO_4^- + NH_3 \rightleftharpoons SO_4^{2-} + NH_4^+$

Before   0.10 M 0.10 M 0   0
After   0   0   0.10   0.10

Allow the reaction to attain equilibrium:

                    $HSO_4^- + NH_3 \rightleftharpoons SO_4^{2-} + NH_4^+$
Initial   0   0   0.10 M 0.10 M
Change   +x   +x   -x   -x
Equil.   x   x   0.10-x   0.10-x

$$\frac{(0.10 - x)^2}{(x)^2} \approx \frac{(0.10)^2}{x^2} = 2.1 \times 10^7,\ x = 2.2 \times 10^{-5}$$

$[HSO_4^-] = 2.2 \times 10^{-5}\ M$ $[SO_4^{2-}] = 0.10\ M$

$[NH_3] = 2.2 \times 10^{-5}\ M$ $[NH_4^+] = 0.10\ M$

$$\frac{[H^+](0.10\ M)}{2.2 \times 10^{-5}\ M} = 1.2 \times 10^{-2}\ \text{or}\ \frac{[H^+](2.2 \times 10^{-5}\ M)}{0.10\ M} = 5.6 \times 10^{-10};\ \text{pH} = 5.58$$

115. $\dfrac{0.135 \, \text{mol} \, CO_2}{2.50 \, \text{L}} = 5.40 \times 10^{-2} \, \text{mol} \, CO_2/\text{L} = 5.40 \times 10^{-2} \, M \, H_2CO_3; \; 0.105 \, M \, CO_3^{2-}$

The best acid (H_2CO_3) reacts with the best base present (CO_3^{2-}) for the principle equilibrium.

$H_2CO_3 + CO_3^{2-} \rightarrow 2 \, HCO_3^{-}$ $\qquad$ $K = \dfrac{1}{1.3 \times 10^{-4}} = 7.7 \times 10^3$ (See Exercise 7.109)

Since $K \gg 1$, assume all CO_2 (H_2CO_3) is converted into HCO_3^-, i.e., 5.40×10^{-2} mol/L CO_3^{2-} is converted into HCO_3^-.

$[HCO_3^-] = 2(5.40 \times 10^{-2}) = 0.108 \, M; \; [CO_3^{2-}] = 0.105 - 0.0540 = 0.051 \, M$

Note: If we solve for the $[H_2CO_3]$ using these concentrations, we get $[H_2CO_3] = 3.0 \times 10^{-5} \, M$; our assumption that the reaction goes to completion is good (3.0×10^{-5} is 0.06% of 0.051). Whenever $K \gg 1$, always assumes the reaction goes to completion.

To solve for the $[H^+]$ in equilibrium with HCO_3^- and CO_3^{2-}, use the K_a expression for HCO_3^-.

$HCO_3^- \rightleftharpoons H^+ + CO_3^{2-}$ $\quad$ $K_{a_2} = 4.8 \times 10^{-11}$

$4.8 \times 10^{-11} = \dfrac{[H^+][CO_3^{2-}]}{[HCO_3^-]} \approx [H^+] \left(\dfrac{0.051}{0.108} \right)$

$[H^+] = 1.0 \times 10^{-10}; \; pH = 10.00$ $\quad$ Assumptions good.

116. $H_2O \rightleftharpoons H^+ + OH^-$

$B + H_2O \rightleftharpoons HB^+ + OH^-$

$K_w = [H^+][OH^-]$ $\qquad$ $K_b = \dfrac{[HB^+][OH^-]}{[B]}$

charge balance: $[H^+] + [HB^+] = [OH^-]$

material balance: $\quad [B]_o = [B] + [HB]^+$

So, $[OH^-] = [H^+] + [HB^+]$

$\qquad [OH^-] = \dfrac{K_w}{[OH^-]} + [HB^+]$ or, $[HB^+] = [OH^-] - \dfrac{K_w}{[OH^-]}$

$\qquad [B] = [B]_o - [HB^+]$

$\qquad [B] = [B]_o - \left([OH^-] - \dfrac{K_w}{[OH^-]} \right)$

$K_b = \dfrac{\left([OH^-] - \dfrac{K_w}{[OH^-]} \right) [OH^-]}{[B]_o - \left([OH^-] - \dfrac{K_w}{[OH^-]} \right)} = \dfrac{[OH^-]^2 - K_w}{[B]_o - \dfrac{[OH^-]^2 - K_w}{[OH^-]}}$

$$K_b \approx \frac{[OH^-]^2 - K_w}{[B]_o} = 6.1 \times 10^{-11} = \frac{[OH^-]^2 - 1.0 \times 10^{-14}}{2.0 \times 10^{-5}} \quad \text{(See Exercise 7.117 for assumption.)}$$

$[OH^-] = 1.1 \times 10^{-7}$; pOH = 6.96; pH = 7.04 (Assumption good.)

117.   Major species: H_2O, Na^+, NO_2^-; NO_2^- is a weak base. $NO_2^- + H_2O \rightleftharpoons HNO_2 + OH^-$

Since this is a very dilute solution of a weak base, the OH^- contribution from H_2O must be considered. The weak base equations for dilute solutions are analogous to the weak acid equations derived in Section 7.9 of the text. They are:

For $A^- + H_2O \rightleftharpoons HA + OH^-$

I. $K_b = \dfrac{[OH^-]^2 - K_w}{[A^-]_o - \dfrac{[OH^-]^2 - K_w}{[OH^-]}}$

II.   When $[A^-]_o \gg \dfrac{[OH^-]^2 - K_w}{[OH^-]}$, then $K_b = \dfrac{[OH^-]^2 - K_w}{[A^-]_o}$ and $[OH^-] = (K_b[A^-]_o + K_w)^{1/2}$

$$\text{Try } [OH^-] = \left(\frac{1.0 \times 10^{-14}}{4.0 \times 10^{-4}} \times (6.0 \times 10^{-4}) + 1.0 \times 10^{-14} \right)^{1/2} = 1.6 \times 10^{-7} \, M$$

Checking assumption: $6.0 \times 10^{-4} \gg \dfrac{(1.6 \times 10^{-7})^2 - 1.0 \times 10^{-14}}{1.6 \times 10^{-7}} = 9.8 \times 10^{-8}$

Assumption good. $[OH^-] = 1.6 \times 10^{-7} \, M$; pOH = 6.80; pH = 7.20

118.   MS = H^+, HSO_4^-, H_2O (water is important!)

charge balance: $[H^+] = [OH^-] + [HSO_4^-] + 2[SO_4^{2-}]$

material balance: $[HSO_4^-]_o = [SO_4^{2-}] + [HSO_4^-] = 1.00 \times 10^{-7} \, M$

$K_w = [H^+][OH^-] = 1.0 \times 10^{-14}$

$K_a = 1.2 \times 10^{-2} = \dfrac{[H^+][SO_4^{2-}]}{[HSO_4^-]}$; $[HSO_4^-] = 1.00 \times 10^{-7} - [SO_4^{2-}]$

$[H^+] = \dfrac{K_w}{[H^+]} + 1.00 \times 10^{-7} - [SO_4^{2-}] + 2[SO_4^{2-}]$; $[SO_4^{2-}] = [H^+] - \dfrac{K_w}{[H^+]} - 1.00 \times 10^{-7}$

$$1.2 \times 10^{-2} = \frac{[H^+][SO_4^{2-}]}{[HSO_4^-]} = \frac{[H^+]\left([H^+] - \dfrac{K_w}{[H^+]} - 1.00 \times 10^{-7} \right)}{\underbrace{1.00 \times 10^{-7} - [H^+] + \dfrac{K_w}{[H^+]} + 1.00 \times 10^{-7}}_{\text{very close to zero}}}$$

Let $[SO_4^{2-}] = 1.00 \times 10^{-7}$ (close approx.):

$$[H^+] = \frac{K_w}{[H^+]} + 1.00 \times 10^{-7} + [SO_4^{2-}] = \frac{K_w}{[H^+]} + 2.00 \times 10^{-7}$$

$[H^+] = 2.4 \times 10^{-7} \ M$

pH = 6.62 (Assumptions good.)

119.   Major species: NH_3, H^+, Cl^-; The H^+ from the strong acid will react with the best base present, NH_3. Since strong acids are great at donating protons, then the reaction between H^+ and NH_3 essentially goes to completion, i.e., until one or both of the reactants runs out. The reaction is:

$$NH_3 + H^+ \rightarrow NH_4^+$$

Since equal volumes of $1.0 \times 10^{-4} \ M \ NH_3$ and $1.0 \times 10^{-4} \ M \ H^+$ are mixed, then both reactants are in stoichiometric amounts and both reactants will run out at the same time. After reaction only NH_4^+ and Cl^- remains. Cl^- has no basic properties since it is the conjugate base of a strong acid. Therefore, the only species with acid-base properties is NH_4^+, a weak acid. The initial concentration of NH_4^+ will be exactly one-half of $1.0 \times 10^{-4} \ M$ since equal volumes of NH_3 and HCl were mixed. Now we must solve the weak acid problem involving $5.0 \times 10^{-5} \ M \ NH_4^+$.

$$NH_4^+ \quad \rightleftharpoons \quad H^+ \quad + \quad NH_3 \qquad K_a = \frac{K_w}{K_b} = 5.6 \times 10^{-10}$$

Initial $5.0 \times 10^{-5} \ M$ ~ 0 0
Equil. $5.0 \times 10^{-5} - x$ x x

$$K_a = \frac{x^2}{5.0 \times 10^{-5} - x} \approx \frac{x^2}{5.0 \times 10^{-5}} = 5.6 \times 10^{-10}, \quad x = 1.7 \times 10^{-7} \ M \quad \text{Check assumptions.}$$

We cannot neglect $[H^+]$ that comes from H_2O. As discussed in Section 7.9 of the text, assume $5.0 \times 10^{-5} \gg ([H^+]^2 - K_w)/[H^+]$. If this is the case, then:

$$[H^+] = (K_a[HA]_o + K_w)^{1/2} = 1.9 \times 10^{-7} \ M: \text{ Checking assumption:}$$

$$\frac{[H^+]^2 - K_w}{[H^+]} = 1.4 \times 10^{-7} \ll 5.0 \times 10^{-5} \quad \text{Assumption good.}$$

So, $[H^+] = 1.9 \times 10^{-7} \ M$; pH = 6.72

120. $Ca(OH)_2 (s) \rightarrow Ca^{2+} (aq) + 2 \ OH^- (aq)$

This is a very dilute solution of $Ca(OH)_2$ so we can't ignore the OH^- contribution from H_2O. From the dissociation of $Ca(OH)_2$ alone, $2[Ca^{2+}] = [OH^-]$. Including H_2O autoionization to H^+ and OH^-, the overall charge balance is:

$$2[Ca^{2+}] + [H^+] = [OH^-]$$

$2(3.0 \times 10^{-7} \ M) + K_w/[OH^-] = [OH^-], \quad [OH^-]^2 = 6.0 \times 10^{-7} [OH^-] + K_w$

$[OH^-]^2 - 6.0 \times 10^{-7} [OH^-] - 1.0 \times 10^{-14} = 0$; Using quadratic formula: $[OH^-] = 6.2 \times 10^{-7} \ M$

Marathon Problems

121.   To determine the pH of solution A, the K_a value for HX must be determined. Use solution B to determine K_b for X^-, which can then be used to calculate K_a for HX ($K_a = K_w/K_b$).

Solution B:

$$X^- \quad + \quad H_2O \quad \rightleftharpoons \quad HX \quad + \quad OH^- \qquad K_b = \frac{[HX]\,[OH^-]}{[X^-]}$$

Initial	0.0500 M		0	~0
Change	$-x$	$\rightarrow$	$+x$	$+x$
Equil.	0.0500 - x		x	x

$K_b = \dfrac{x^2}{0.0500 - x}$; From the problem, pH = 10.02, so pOH = 3.98 and $[OH^-] = x = 10^{-3.98}$

$$K_b = \frac{(10^{-3.98})^2}{0.0500 - 10^{-3.98}} = 2.2 \times 10^{-7}$$

Solution A:

$K_{a,\,HX} = K_w/K_{b,\,X^-} = 1.0 \times 10^{-14}/2.2 \times 10^{-7} = 4.5 \times 10^{-8}$

$$HX \quad \rightleftharpoons \quad H^+ \quad + \quad X^- \qquad K_a = 4.5 \times 10^{-8} = \frac{[H^+]\,[X^-]}{[HX]}$$

Initial	0.100 M		~0	0
Change	$-x$	$\rightarrow$	$+x$	$+x$
Equil.	0.100 - x		x	x

$K_a = 4.5 \times 10^{-8} = \dfrac{x^2}{0.100 - x} \approx \dfrac{x^2}{0.100}$, $x = [H^+] = 6.7 \times 10^{-5}\ M$

Assumptions good (x is 6.7×10^{-2} % of 0.100); pH = 4.17

Solution C:

Major species: HX ($K_a = 4.5 \times 10^{-8}$), Na^+, OH^-; The OH^- from the strong base is exceptional at accepting protons. OH^- will react with the best acid present (HX) and we can assume that OH^- will react to completion with HX, i.e., until one (or both) of the reactants runs out. Since we have added one volume of substance to another, we have diluted both solutions from their initial concentrations. What hasn't changed is the moles of each reactant. So let's work with moles of each reactant initially.

$$\text{mol HX} = 0.0500\ \text{L} \times \frac{0.100\ \text{mol HX}}{\text{L}} = 5.00 \times 10^{-3}\ \text{mol HX}$$

$$\text{mol OH}^- = 0.0150\ \text{L} \times \frac{0.250\ \text{mol NaOH}}{\text{L}} \times \frac{1\ \text{mol OH}^-}{\text{mol NaOH}} = 3.75 \times 10^{-3}\ \text{mol OH}^-$$

Now lets determine what is remaining in solution after OH^- reacts completely with HX. Note that OH^- is the limiting reagent.

	HX	+	OH⁻	→	X⁻	+	H₂O
Initial	5.00×10^{-3} mol		3.75×10^{-3} mol		0		-----
Change	-3.75×10^{-3}		-3.75×10^{-3}	→	$+3.75 \times 10^{-3}$		$+3.75 \times 10^{-3}$
After completion	1.25×10^{-3} mol		0		3.75×10^{-3} mol		-----

After reaction, the solution contains HX, X⁻, Na⁺ and H₂O. The Na⁺ (like most +1 metal ions) has no effect on the pH of water. However, HX is a weak acid and its conjugate base, X⁻, is a weak base. Since both K_a and K_b reactions refer to these species, we could use either reaction to solve for the pH; we will use the K_b reaction. To solve the equilibrium problem using the K_b reaction, we need to convert to concentration units since K_b is in concentration units of mol/L.

$$[HX] = \frac{1.25 \times 10^{-3} \text{ mol}}{(0.0500 + 0.0150) \text{ L}} = 0.0192 \, M; \quad [X^-] = \frac{3.75 \times 10^{-3} \text{ mol}}{0.0650 \text{ L}} = 0.0577 \, M$$

$[OH^-] = 0$ (We reacted all of it to completion.)

	X⁻	+	H₂O	⇌	HX	+	OH⁻	$K_b = 2.2 \times 10^{-7}$
Initial	$0.0577 \, M$				$0.0192 \, M$		0	
	x mol/L of X⁻ reacts to reach equilibrium							
Change	$-x$			→	$+x$		$+x$	
Equil.	$0.0577 - x$				$0.0192 + x$		x	

$$K_b = 2.2 \times 10^{-7} = \frac{(0.0192 + x)(x)}{(0.0577 - x)} \approx \frac{(0.0192)x}{(0.0577)} \quad \text{(assuming } x \text{ is} \ll 0.0192)$$

$$x = [OH^-] = \frac{2.2 \times 10^{-7}(0.0577)}{0.0192} = 6.6 \times 10^{-7} \, M \text{ Assumptions great (}x \text{ is } 3.4 \times 10^{-3} \text{ \% of } 0.0192).$$

$[OH^-] = 6.6 \times 10^{-7} \, M$, pOH = 6.18, pH = 14.00 = 6.18 = 7.82 = pH of solution C

The combination is 4-17-7-82.

122. a. Strongest acid from group I = HCl;   Weakest base from group II = $NaNO_2$

0.20 M HCl + 0.20 M $NaNO_2$; Major species = H⁺, Cl⁻, Na⁺, NO_2^-, H₂O

	H⁺	+	NO₂⁻	→	HNO₂	
Initial	0.10 M		0.10 M		0	(Molarities are halved due to dilution.)
After	0		0		0.10 M	

	HNO₂	⇌	H⁺	+	NO₂⁻
Initial	0.10 M		0		0
Change	$-x$		$+x$		$+x$
Equil.	0.10-x		x		x

$$\frac{x^2}{0.10 - x} = 4.0 \times 10^{-4}; \quad \text{Solving, pH} = 2.20$$

b.   Weakest acid from group I $= (C_2H_5)_3NHCl$; Best base from group II $=$ KOI

$$OI^- + (C_2H_5)_3NH^+ \rightleftharpoons HOI + (C_2H_5)_3N$$

$$K = \frac{K_a [(C_2H_5)_3NH^+)]}{K_a (HOI)} = \frac{1.0 \times 10^{-14}}{4.0 \times 10^{-4}} \times \frac{1}{2.0 \times 10^{-11}} = 1.25 \text{ (carrying extra sig fig)}$$

$$\frac{x^2}{(0.10 - x)^2} = 1.25; \qquad \frac{x}{0.10 - x} = 1.12; \quad x = 0.053$$

$[HOI] = 0.053 \ M$ and $[OI^-] = 0.047 \ M$

$$2.0 \times 10^{-11} = \frac{[H^+](0.047 \ M)}{(0.053 \ M)}$$

$[H^+] = 2.3 \times 10^{-11}$, pH $= 10.64$

c. K_a for $(C_2H_5)_3NH^+ = \dfrac{1.0 \times 10^{-14}}{4.0 \times 10^{-4}} = 2.5 \times 10^{-11}$; K_b for $NO_2^- = \dfrac{1.0 \times 10^{-14}}{4.0 \times 10^{-4}} = 2.5 \times 10^{-11}$

Since $K_a = K_b$, then mixing $(C_2H_5)_3NHCl$ with $NaNO_2$ will result in a solution with pH $= 7.00$.

CHAPTER EIGHT

APPLICATIONS OF AQUEOUS EQUILIBRIA

Buffers

15. A buffered solution must contain both a weak acid and a weak base. Most buffered solutions are prepared using a weak acid plus the conjugate base of the weak acid (which is a weak base). Buffered solutions are useful for controlling the pH of a solution since they resist pH change.

16. When strong acid or strong base is added to a sodium dihydrogen phosphate/sodium hydrogen phosphate buffer mixture, the strong acid/base is neutralized. The reaction goes to completion resulting in the strong acid/base being replaced with a weak acid/base. This results in a new buffer solution. The reactions are:

$$H^+(aq) + HPO_4^-(aq) \rightarrow H_2PO_4^-(aq); \quad OH^-(aq) + H_2PO_4^-(aq) \rightarrow HPO_4^{2-}(aq) + H_2O(l)$$

17. The capacity of a buffer is a measure of how much strong acid or strong base the buffer can neutralize. All the buffers listed have the same pH (= pK_a = 4.74) since they all have a 1:1 concentration ratio between the weak acid and the conjugate base. The 1.0 M buffer has the greatest capacity; the 0.01 M buffer the least capacity. In general, the larger the concentrations of weak acid and conjugate base, the greater the buffer capacity, i.e., the greater the ability to neutralize added strong acid or strong base.

18. $NH_3 + H_2O \rightleftharpoons NH_4^+ + OH^- \quad K_b = \dfrac{[NH_4^+][OH^-]}{[NH_3]}$; Taking the -log of the K_b expression:

$$- \log K_b = - \log [OH^-] - \log \frac{[NH_4^+]}{[NH_3]}, \quad - \log [OH^-] = - \log K_b + \log \frac{[NH_4^+]}{[NH_3]}$$

$$pOH = pK_b + \log \frac{[NH_4^+]}{[NH_3]} \quad \text{or} \quad pOH = pK_b + \log \frac{[Acid]}{[Base]}$$

19. a. This is a weak acid problem. Let $HC_3H_5O_2$ = HOPr and $C_3H_5O_2^-$ = OPr$^-$.

$$HOPr(aq) \rightleftharpoons H^+(aq) + OPr^-(aq) \qquad K_a = 1.3 \times 10^{-5}$$

Initial	0.100 M		~0	0
	x mol/L HOPr dissociates to reach equilibrium			
Change	$-x$	$\rightarrow$	$+x$	$+x$
Equil.	0.100 - x		x	x

215

$$K_a = 1.3 \times 10^{-5} = \frac{[H^+][OPr^-]}{[HOPr]} = \frac{x^2}{0.100 - x} \approx \frac{x^2}{0.100}$$

$x = [H^+] = 1.1 \times 10^{-3}\ M;\ pH = 2.96$ Assumptions good by the 5% rule.

b. This is a weak base problem.

$$OPr^-(aq) \ + \ H_2O(l) \ \rightleftharpoons \ HOPr(aq) \ + \ OH^-(aq) \quad K_b = \frac{K_w}{K_a} = 7.7 \times 10^{-10}$$

Initial	0.100 M		0	~0

x mol/L OPr^- reacts with H_2O to reach equilibrium

Change	-x	$\rightarrow$	+x	+x
Equil.	0.100 - x		x	x

$$K_b = 7.7 \times 10^{-10} = \frac{[HOPr][OH^-]}{[OPr^-]} = \frac{x^2}{0.100 - x} \approx \frac{x^2}{0.100}$$

$x = [OH^-] = 8.8 \times 10^{-6}\ M;\ pOH = 5.06;\ pH = 8.94$ Assumptions good.

c. pure H_2O, $[H^+] = [OH^-] = 1.0 \times 10^{-7}\ M;\ pH = 7.00$

d. This solution contains a weak acid and its conjugate base. This is a buffer solution. We will solve for the pH through the weak acid equilibrium reaction.

$$HOPr(aq) \ \rightleftharpoons \ H^+(aq) \ + \ OPr^-(aq) \qquad K_a = 1.3 \times 10^{-5}$$

Initial	0.100 M	~0	0.100 M

x mol/L HOPr dissociates to reach equilibrium

Change	-x	$\rightarrow$	+x	+x
Equil.	0.100 - x		x	0.100 + x

$$1.3 \times 10^{-5} = \frac{(0.100 + x)(x)}{0.100 - x} \approx \frac{(0.100)(x)}{0.100} = x = [H^+]$$

$[H^+] = 1.3 \times 10^{-5}\ M;\ pH = 4.89$ Assumptions good.

Alternately, we can use the Henderson-Hasselbalch equation to calculate the pH of buffer solutions.

$$pH = pK_a + \log \frac{[Base]}{[Acid]} = pK_a + \log \frac{(0.100)}{(0.100)} = pK_a = -\log (1.3 \times 10^{-5}) = 4.89$$

The Henderson-Hasselbalch equation will be valid when an assumption of the type, $0.1 + x \approx 0.1$, that we just made in this problem is valid. From a practical standpoint, this will almost always be true for useful buffer solutions. If the assumption is not valid, the solution will have such a low buffering capacity it will not be of any use to control the pH. Note: The Henderson-Hasselbalch equation can only be used to solve for the pH of buffer solutions.

20. a. We have a weak acid (HOPr = $HC_3H_5O_2$) and a strong acid (HCl) present. The amount of H^+ donated by the weak acid will be negligible. To prove it lets consider the weak acid equilibrium reaction:

$$HOPr \quad \rightleftharpoons \quad H^+ \quad + \quad OPr^- \qquad K_a = 1.3 \times 10^{-5}$$

Initial   0.100 M 0.020 M 0
             x mol/L HOPr dissociates to reach equilibrium
Change $-x$ $\rightarrow$ $+x$ $+x$
Equil.   0.100 - x 0.020 + x x

$[H^+] = 0.020 + x \approx 0.020\ M$; pH = 1.70   Assumption good ($x = 6.5 \times 10^{-5}$ is $\ll 0.020$).

Note: The H^+ contribution from the weak acid HOPr was negligible. The pH of the solution can be determined by only considering the amount of strong acid present.

b. Added H^+ reacts completely with the best base present, OPr^-.

$$OPr^- \quad + \quad H^+ \quad \rightarrow \quad HOPr$$

Before   0.100 M 0.020 M 0
Change   -0.020   -0.020 $\rightarrow$ +0.020   Reacts completely
After   0.080   0   0.020 M

After reaction, a weak acid, HOPr , and its conjugate base, OPr^-, are present. This is a buffer solution. Using the Henderson-Hasselbalch equation where $pK_a = -\log (1.3 \times 10^{-5}) = 4.89$:

$$pH = pK_a + \log \frac{[Base]}{[Acid]} = 4.89 + \log \frac{(0.080)}{(0.020)} = 5.49 \qquad \text{Assumptions good.}$$

c. This is a strong acid problem. $[H^+] = 0.020\ M$; pH = 1.70

d. Added H^+ reacts completely with the best base present, OPr^-.

$$OPr^- \quad + \quad H^+ \quad \rightarrow \quad HOPr$$

Before   0.100 M 0.020 M 0.100 M
Change   -0.020   -0.020 $\rightarrow$ +0.020   Reacts completely
After   0.080   0   0.120

A buffer solution results (weak acid + conjugate base). Using the Henderson-Hasselbalch equation:

$$pH = pK_a + \log \frac{[Base]}{[Acid]} = 4.89 + \log \frac{(0.080)}{(0.120)} = 4.71$$

21.   a.   OH⁻ will react completely with the best acid present, HOPr.

$$\text{HOPr} \quad + \quad \text{OH}^- \quad \rightarrow \quad \text{OPr}^- \quad + \quad H_2O$$

Before	0.100 M	0.020 M		0
Change	-0.020	-0.020	$\rightarrow$	+0.020	Reacts completely
After	0.080	0		0.020

A buffer solution results after the reaction. Using the Henderson-Hasselbalch equation:

$$pH = pK_a + \log \frac{[\text{Base}]}{[\text{Acid}]} = 4.89 + \log \frac{(0.020)}{(0.080)} = 4.29$$

b.   We have a weak base and a strong base present at the same time. The amount of OH⁻ added by the weak base will be negligible. To prove it, lets consider the weak base equilibrium:

$$\text{OPr}^- \quad + \quad H_2O \quad \rightleftharpoons \quad \text{HOPr} \quad + \quad \text{OH}^- \qquad K_b = 7.7 \times 10^{-10}$$

Initial	0.100 M		0	0.020 M
	x mol/L OPr⁻ reacts with H_2O to reach equilibrium			
Change	-x	$\rightarrow$	+x	+x
Equil.	0.100 - x		x	0.020 + x

$[\text{OH}^-] = 0.020 + x \approx 0.020\ M$; pOH = 1.70; pH = 12.30   Assumption good.

Note: The OH⁻ contribution from the weak base OPr⁻ was negligible ($x = 3.9 \times 10^{-9}\ M$ as compared to 0.020 M OH⁻ from the strong base). The pH can be determined by only considering the amount of strong base present.

c.   This is a strong base in water. $[\text{OH}^-] = 0.020\ M$; pOH = 1.70; pH = 12.30

d.   OH⁻ will react completely with HOPr, the best acid present.

$$\text{HOPr} \quad + \quad \text{OH}^- \quad \rightarrow \quad \text{OPr}^- \quad + \quad H_2O$$

Before	0.100 M	0.020 M		0.100 M
Change	-0.020	-0.020	$\rightarrow$	+0.020	Reacts completely
After	0.080	0		0.120

Using the Henderson-Hasselbalch equation to solve for the pH of the resulting buffer solution:

$$pH = pK_a + \log \frac{[\text{Base}]}{[\text{Acid}]} = 4.89 + \log \frac{(0.120)}{(0.080)} = 5.07$$

22.   Consider all of the results to Exercises 8.19, 8.20, and 8.21:

Solution	Initial pH	after added acid	after added base
a	2.96	1.70	4.29
b	8.94	5.49	12.30
c	7.00	1.70	12.30
d	4.89	4.71	5.07

The solution in Exercise 8.19d is a buffer; it contains both a weak acid ($HC_3H_5O_2$) and a weak base ($C_3H_5O_2^-$). Solution d shows the greatest resistance to changes in pH when either strong acid or strong base is added, which is the primary property of buffers.

23.   Major species: HF, F^- and K^+ (no acidic/basic properties). The appropriate equilibrium reaction to use is the K_a reaction of HF which contains both HF and F^-.

$$HF \quad \rightleftharpoons \quad F^- \quad + \quad H^+$$

Initial   0.60 M 1.00 M ~0
                 x mol/L HF dissociates to reach equilibrium
Change $-x$ $\rightarrow$ $+x$ $+x$
Equil.   0.60 - x 1.00 + x x

$$K_a = 7.2 \times 10^{-4} = \frac{[F^-][H^+]}{[HF]} = \frac{(1.00 + x)(x)}{(0.60 - x)} \approx \frac{1.00(x)}{0.60} \quad \text{(assuming } x \ll 0.60\text{)}$$

$x = [H^+] = 0.60 \times (7.2 \times 10^{-4}) = 4.3 \times 10^{-4} \, M$;   Assumptions good ($x$ is 7.2×10^{-2}% of 0.60).

pH = -log (4.3×10^{-4}) = 3.37

24.   When NaOH is added, the OH^- reacts completely with the best acid present, HF.

$$OH^- \quad + \quad HF \quad \rightarrow \quad F^- \quad + \quad H_2O$$

Before $\dfrac{0.10 \text{ mol}}{1.00 \text{ L}}$ 0.60 M 1.00 M

Change   -0.10 M -0.10 M $\rightarrow$ +0.10 M Reacts completely
After   0   0.50   1.10

We now have a new buffer problem. Solving the equilibrium part of the problem:

$$HF \quad \rightleftharpoons \quad F^- \quad + \quad H^+$$

Initial   0.50 M 1.10 M ~0
Equil.   0.50 - x 1.10 + x x

$$K_a = 7.2 \times 10^{-4} = \frac{(1.10 + x)(x)}{(0.50 - x)} \approx \frac{1.10(x)}{(0.50)}, \quad x = [H^+] = 3.3 \times 10^{-4} \, M$$

pH = 3.48;   Assumptions good.

When HCl is added, H^+ reacts to completion with the best base (F^-) present.

$$H^+ \quad + \quad F^- \quad \rightarrow \quad HF$$

Before	0.20 M	1.00 M	0.60 M
After	0	0.80 M	0.80 M

After reaction, we have a buffer problem:

$$HF \quad \rightleftharpoons \quad F^- \quad + \quad H^+$$

Initial	0.80 M	0.80 M	0
Equil.	0.80 - x	0.80 + x	x

$K_a = 7.2 \times 10^{-4} = \dfrac{(0.80 + x)(x)}{0.80 - x} \approx x$, $x = [H^+] = 7.2 \times 10^{-4}$ M; pH = 3.14; Assumptions good.

25. a. $\quad HC_2H_3O_2 \quad \rightleftharpoons \quad H^+ \quad + \quad C_2H_3O_2^- \qquad\qquad K_a = 1.8 \times 10^{-5}$

Initial	0.10 M	~0	0.25 M

x mol/L $HC_2H_3O_2$ dissociates to reach equilibrium

Change	-x	$\rightarrow$ +x	+x
Equil.	0.10 - x	x	0.25 + x

$1.8 \times 10^{-5} = \dfrac{x(0.25 + x)}{(0.10 - x)} \approx \dfrac{x(0.25)}{0.10}$ (assuming $0.25 + x \approx 0.25$ and $0.10 - x \approx 0.10$)

$x = [H^+] = 7.2 \times 10^{-6}$ M; pH = 5.14   Assumptions good by the 5% rule.

Alternatively, we can use the Henderson-Hasselbalch equation:

$$pH = pK_a + \log \frac{[\text{Base}]}{[\text{Acid}]} \quad \text{where } pK_a = -\log (1.8 \times 10^{-5}) = 4.74$$

$$pH = 4.74 + \log \frac{(0.25)}{(0.10)} = 4.74 + 0.40 = 5.14$$

The Henderson-Hasselbalch equation will be valid when assumptions of the type $0.10 - x \approx 0.10$ that we just made are valid. From a practical standpoint, this will almost always be true for useful buffer solutions. Note: The Henderson-Hasselbalch equation can <u>only</u> be used to solve for the pH of buffer solutions.

b. $pH = 4.74 + \log \dfrac{(0.10)}{(0.25)} = 4.74 + (-0.40) = 4.34$

c. $pH = 4.74 + \log \dfrac{(0.25)}{(0.25)} = 4.74 + 0.00 = 4.74$ (pH = pK_a since [acid] = [base])

d. $pH = pK_a + \log \dfrac{[\text{base}]}{[\text{acid}]}$; [base] = $[C_2H_5NH_2]$ = 0.50 M; [acid] = $[C_2H_5NH_3^+]$ = 0.25 M

$$K_a = \frac{K_w}{K_b} = \frac{1.0 \times 10^{-14}}{5.6 \times 10^{-4}} = 1.8 \times 10^{-11}$$

$$pH = -\log(1.8 \times 10^{-11}) + \log\left(\frac{0.50\,M}{0.25\,M}\right) = 10.74 + 0.30 = 11.04$$

e. $pH = 10.74 + \log\left(\dfrac{0.50\,M}{0.50\,M}\right) = 10.74 + 0.00 = 10.74$

26.   a. $HNO_2 \rightleftharpoons H^+ + NO_2^-$ $K_a = 4.0 \times 10^{-4}$, $pK_a = -\log(4.0 \times 10^{-4}) = 3.40$

This is a buffer solution. Using the Henderson-Hasselbalch equation:

$$pH = pK_a + \log\frac{[Base]}{[Acid]} = 3.40 + \log\frac{(0.15)}{(0.10)} = 3.40 + 0.18 = 3.58$$

b. $25.0\ g\ HC_2H_3O_2 \times \dfrac{1\ mol}{60.05\ g} = 0.416\ mol\ HC_2H_3O_2$; $[HC_2H_3O_2] = \dfrac{0.416\ mol}{0.500\ L} = 0.832\ M$

$40.0\ g\ NaC_2H_3O_2 \times \dfrac{1\ mol}{82.03\ g} = 0.488\ mol\ NaC_2H_3O_2$; $[C_2H_3O_2^-] = \dfrac{0.488\ mol}{0.500\ L} = 0.976\ M$

$$pH = pK_a + \log\frac{[Base]}{[Acid]};\ K_a = 1.8 \times 10^{-5};\ pK_a = -\log(1.8 \times 10^{-5}) = 4.74$$

$$pH = 4.74 + \log\frac{(0.976)}{(0.832)} = 4.74 + 0.0693 = 4.81$$

c.   Let's work with mmol in this problem. This requires the use of mmol/mL for molarity units instead of mol/L (the 10^3 conversion factors cancel).

$$50.0\ mL \times \frac{1.0\ mmol}{mL} = 50.\ mmol\ HOCl;\ 30.0\ mL \times \frac{0.80\ mmol\ NaOH}{mL} = 24\ mmol\ OH^-$$

The strong base reacts with the best acid available, HOCl. The reaction goes to completion. Whenever strong base or strong acid reacts, the reaction is always assumed to go to completion.

	HOCl	+	OH⁻	→	OCl⁻	+	H₂O
Before	50. mmol		24 mmol		0		
	24 mmol OH⁻ reacts completely.						
Change	-24		-24	→	+24		Reacts completely
After	26 mmol		0		24 mmol		

After reaction, the solution contains 26 mmol HOCl and 24 mmol OCl⁻ in 250 mL of solution. This is a buffer solution. Using the Henderson-Hasselbalch equation:

$$pH = pK_a + \log\frac{[Base]}{[Acid]};\ K_a = 3.5 \times 10^{-8};\ pK_a = 7.46$$

$$pH = 7.46 + \log \dfrac{\dfrac{24 \text{ mmol OCl}^-}{250 \text{ mL}}}{\dfrac{26 \text{ mmol HOCl}}{250 \text{ mL}}} = 7.46 + (-0.035) = 7.43$$

d. $26.4 \text{ g NaC}_2\text{H}_3\text{O}_2 \times \dfrac{1 \text{ mol}}{82.03 \text{ g}} = 0.322 \text{ mol NaC}_2\text{H}_3\text{O}_2$

$50.0 \text{ mL HCl} \times \dfrac{1 \text{ L}}{1000 \text{ mL}} \times \dfrac{6.00 \text{ mol HCl}}{\text{L}} = 0.300 \text{ mol HCl}$

H^+ reacts completely with best base present, $C_2H_3O_2^-$. (Strong acids are always assumed to react to completion.)

	H^+	$+$	$C_2H_3O_2^-$	$\rightarrow$	$HC_2H_3O_2$	
Before	0.300 mol		0.322 mol		0	
Change	-0.300		-0.300	$\rightarrow$	+0.300	Reacts completely
After	0		0.022 mol		0.300 mol	

After reaction, a buffer solution results. Using the Henderson-Hasselbalch equation:

$$pH = pK_a + \log \dfrac{[C_2H_3O_2^-]}{[HC_2H_3O_2]} = 4.74 + \log \dfrac{(0.022 \text{ mol}/0.500 \text{ L})}{(0.300 \text{ mol}/0.500 \text{ L})}, \ pH = 4.74 - 1.13 = 3.61$$

27. $C_5H_5NH^+ \rightleftharpoons H^+ + C_5H_5N \quad K_a = \dfrac{K_w}{K_b} = \dfrac{1.0 \times 10^{-14}}{1.7 \times 10^{-9}} = 5.9 \times 10^{-6}; \ pK_a = -\log(5.9 \times 10^{-6}) = 5.23$

We will use the Henderson-Hasselbalch equation to calculate the concentration ratio necessary for each buffer.

$$pH = pK_a + \log \dfrac{[\text{base}]}{[\text{acid}]}, \ pH = 5.23 + \log \dfrac{[C_5H_5N]}{[C_5H_5NH^+]}$$

a. $4.50 = 5.23 + \log \dfrac{[C_5H_5N]}{[C_5H_5NH^+]}$ b. $5.00 = 5.23 + \log \dfrac{[C_5H_5N]}{[C_5H_5NH^+]}$

$\log \dfrac{[C_5H_5N]}{[C_5H_5NH^+]} = -0.73$ $\log \dfrac{[C_5H_5N]}{[C_5H_5NH^+]} = -0.23$

$\dfrac{[C_5H_5N]}{[C_5H_5NH^+]} = 10^{-0.73} = 0.19$ $\dfrac{[C_5H_5N]}{[C_5H_5NH^+]} = 10^{-0.23} = 0.59$

c. $5.23 = 5.23 + \log \dfrac{[C_5H_5N]}{[C_5H_5NH^+]}$ d. $5.50 = 5.23 + \log \dfrac{[C_5H_5N]}{[C_5H_5NH^+]}$

$\dfrac{[C_5H_5N]}{[C_5H_5NH^+]} = 10^{0.0} = 1.0$ $\dfrac{[C_5H_5N]}{[C_5H_5NH^+]} = 10^{0.27} = 1.9$

28.   When OH⁻ is added, it converts $HC_2H_3O_2$ into $C_2H_3O_2^-$: $HC_2H_3O_2 + OH^- \rightarrow C_2H_3O_2^- + H_2O$

From this reaction, the moles of $C_2H_3O_2^-$ produced <u>equals</u> the moles of OH⁻ added. Also, the total concentration of acetic acid plus acetate ion must equal 2.0 M (assuming no volume change on addition of NaOH). Summarizing for each solution:

$[C_2H_3O_2^-] + [HC_2H_3O] = 2.0\ M$ and $[C_2H_3O_2^-]$ produced = [OH⁻] added

a. $pH = pK_a + \log \dfrac{[C_2H_3O_2^-]}{[HC_2H_3O_2]}$; For $pH = pK_a$, $\log \dfrac{[C_2H_3O_2^-]}{[HC_2H_3O_2]} = 0$

Therefore, $\dfrac{[C_2H_3O_2^-]}{[HC_2H_3O_2]} = 1.0$ and $[C_2H_3O_2^-] = [HC_2H_3O_2]$

Since $[C_2H_3O_2^-] + [HC_2H_3O_2] = 2.0\ M$, then $[C_2H_3O_2^-] = [HC_2H_3O_2] = 1.0\ M = $ [OH⁻] added

To produce a 1.0 M $C_2H_3O_2^-$ solution we need to add 1.0 mol of NaOH to 1.0 L of the 2.0 M $HC_2H_3O_2$ solution. The resultant solution will have $pH = pK_a = 4.74$.

b. $4.00 = 4.74 + \log \dfrac{[C_2H_3O_2^-]}{[HC_2H_3O_2]}$, $\dfrac{[C_2H_3O_2^-]}{[HC_2H_3O_2]} = 10^{-0.74} = 0.18$

$[C_2H_3O_2^-] = 0.18\ [HC_2H_3O_2]$ or $[HC_2H_3O_2] = 5.6\ [C_2H_3O_2^-]$; Since $[C_2H_3O_2^-] + [HC_2H_3O_2] = 2.0\ M$, then:

$[C_2H_3O_2^-] + 5.6\ [C_2H_3O_2^-] = 2.0\ M$, $[C_2H_3O_2^-] = \dfrac{2.0}{6.6} = 0.30\ M = $ [OH⁻] added

We need to add 0.30 mol of NaOH to 1.0 L of 2.0 M $HC_2H_3O_2$ solution to produce 0.30 M $C_2H_3O_2^-$. The resultant solution will have $pH = 4.00$.

c. $5.00 = 4.74 + \log \dfrac{[C_2H_3O_2^-]}{[HC_2H_3O_2]}$, $\dfrac{[C_2H_3O_2^-]}{[HC_2H_3O_2]} = 10^{0.26} = 1.8$

$1.8\ [HC_2H_3O_2] = [C_2H_3O_2^-]$ or $[HC_2H_3O_2] = 0.56\ [C_2H_3O_2^-]$; Since $[HC_2H_3O_2] + [C_2H_3O_2^-] = 2.0\ M$, then:

$1.56\ [C_2H_3O_2^-] = 2.0\ M$, $[C_2H_3O_2^-] = 1.3\ M = $ [OH⁻] added

We need to add 1.3 mol of NaOH to 1.0 L of 2.0 M $HC_2H_3O_2$ to produce a solution with $pH = 5.00$.

29. $pH = pK_a + \log \dfrac{[C_2H_3O_2^-]}{[HC_2H_3O_2]}$; $pK_a = -\log(1.8 \times 10^{-5}) = 4.74$

Since the buffer components, $C_2H_3O_2^-$ and $HC_2H_3O_2$, are both in the same volume of water, the concentration ratio of $[C_2H_3O_2^-]/[HC_2H_3O_2]$ will equal the mol ratio of mol $C_2H_3O_2^-$/mol $HC_2H_3O_2$.

$5.00 = 4.74 + \log \dfrac{\text{mol } C_2H_3O_2^-}{\text{mol } HC_2H_3O_2}$; $\text{mol } HC_2H_3O_2 = 0.5000 \text{ L} \times \dfrac{0.200 \text{ mol}}{\text{L}} = 0.100 \text{ mol}$

$0.26 = \log \dfrac{\text{mol } C_2H_3O_2^-}{0.100 \text{ mol}}$, $\dfrac{\text{mol } C_2H_3O_2^-}{0.100} = 10^{0.26} = 1.8$, $\text{mol } C_2H_3O_2^- = 0.18 \text{ mol}$

$\text{mass } NaC_2H_3O_2 = 0.18 \text{ mol } NaC_2H_3O_2 \times \dfrac{82.03 \text{ g}}{\text{mol}} = 15 \text{ g } NaC_2H_3O_2$

30. $[H^+] \text{ added} = \dfrac{0.010 \text{ mol}}{0.2500 \text{ L}} = 0.040 \ M$;   The added H^+ reacts completely with NH_3 to form NH_4^+.

a.
	NH_3	+	H^+	→	NH_4^+	
Before	0.050 M		0.040 M		0.15 M	
Change	-0.040		-0.040	→	+0.040	Reacts completely
After	0.010		0		0.19	

A buffer solution still exists after H^+ reacts completely. Using the Henderson-Hasselbalch equation:

$$pH = pK_a + \log \dfrac{[NH_3]}{[NH_4^+]} = -\log (5.6 \times 10^{-10}) + \log \left(\dfrac{0.010}{0.19} \right) = 9.25 + (-1.28) = 7.97$$

b.
	NH_3	+	H^+	→	NH_4^+	
Before	0.50 M		0.040 M		1.50 M	
Change	-0.040		-0.040	→	+0.040	Reacts completely
After	0.46		0		1.54	

A buffer solution still exists. $pH = pK_a + \log \dfrac{[NH_3]}{[NH_4^+]} = 9.25 + \log \left(\dfrac{0.46}{1.54} \right) = 8.73$

Note: The two buffers differ in their capacity and not the pH (both buffers had an initial pH = 8.77). Solution b has the greatest capacity since it has the largest concentrations of weak acid and conjugate base. Buffers with greater capacities will be able to absorb more H^+ or OH^- added.

31.   a. pK_b for $C_6H_5NH_2 = -\log(3.8 \times 10^{-10}) = 9.42$; pK_a for $C_6H_5NH_3^+ = 14.00 - 9.42 = 4.58$

$pH = pK_a + \log \dfrac{[C_6H_5NH_2]}{[C_6H_5NH_3^+]}$, $4.20 = 4.58 + \log \dfrac{0.50 \ M}{[C_6H_5NH_3^+]}$

$-0.38 = \log \dfrac{0.50 \ M}{[C_6H_5NH_3^+]}$, $[C_6H_5NH_3^+] = [C_6H_5NH_3Cl] = 1.2 \ M$

b. $4.0 \text{ g NaOH} \times \dfrac{1 \text{ mol NaOH}}{40.00 \text{ g}} \times \dfrac{1 \text{ mol OH}^-}{\text{mol NaOH}} = 0.10 \text{ mol OH}^-, \;\; [\text{OH}^-] = \dfrac{0.10 \text{ mol}}{1.0 \text{ L}} = 0.10 \; M$

$$C_6H_5NH_3^+ \quad + \quad OH^- \quad \rightarrow \quad C_6H_5NH_2 \quad + \quad H_2O$$

Before	1.2 M	0.10 M		0.50 M
Change	-0.10	-0.10	$\rightarrow$	+0.10
After	1.1	0		0.60

A buffer solution exists. $\text{pH} = 4.58 + \log\left(\dfrac{0.60}{1.1}\right) = 4.32$

32. $\text{pH} = \text{p}K_a + \log\dfrac{[\text{NO}_2^-]}{[\text{HNO}_2]}, \;\; 3.55 = \log(4.0 \times 10^{-4}) + \log\dfrac{[\text{NO}_2^-]}{[\text{HNO}_2]}$

$3.55 = 3.40 + \log\dfrac{[\text{NO}_2^-]}{[\text{HNO}_2]}, \;\; \dfrac{[\text{NO}_2^-]}{[\text{HNO}_2]} = 10^{0.15} = 1.4$

Let x = volume (L) HNO$_2$ solution needed, then 1.00 - x = volume of NaNO$_2$ solution needed to form this buffer solution.

$$\dfrac{[\text{NO}_2^-]}{[\text{HNO}_2]} = 1.4 = \dfrac{(1.00 - x) \times \dfrac{0.50 \text{ mol NaNO}_2}{\text{L}}}{x \times \dfrac{0.50 \text{ mol HNO}_2}{\text{L}}} = \dfrac{0.50 - 0.50x}{0.50x}$$

$0.70\, x = 0.50 - 0.50\, x, \;\; 1.20\, x = 0.50, \;\; x = 0.42 \text{ L}$

We need 0.42 L of 0.50 M HNO$_2$ and 1.00 - 0.42 = 0.58 L of 0.50 M NaNO$_2$ to form a pH = 3.55 buffer solution.

33.   a. $\text{pH} = \text{p}K_a + \log\dfrac{[\text{Base}]}{[\text{Acid}]}, \;\; 7.40 = -\log(4.3 \times 10^{-7}) + \log\dfrac{[\text{HCO}_3^-]}{[\text{H}_2\text{CO}_3]} = 6.37 + \log\dfrac{[\text{HCO}_3^-]}{[\text{H}_2\text{CO}_3]}$

$\dfrac{[\text{HCO}_3^-]}{[\text{H}_2\text{CO}_3]} = 10^{1.03} = 11; \;\; \dfrac{[\text{H}_2\text{CO}_3]}{[\text{HCO}_3^-]} = \dfrac{[\text{CO}_2]}{[\text{HCO}_3^-]} = \dfrac{1}{11} = 0.091$

b. $7.15 = -\log(6.2 \times 10^{-8}) + \log\dfrac{[\text{HPO}_4^{2-}]}{[\text{H}_2\text{PO}_4^-]}, \;\; 7.15 = 7.21 + \log\dfrac{[\text{HPO}_4^{2-}]}{[\text{H}_2\text{PO}_4^-]}$

$\dfrac{[\text{HPO}_4^{2-}]}{[\text{H}_2\text{PO}_4^-]} = 10^{-0.06} = 0.9, \;\; \dfrac{[\text{H}_2\text{PO}_4^-]}{[\text{HPO}_4^{2-}]} = \dfrac{1}{0.9} = 1.1 \approx 1$

c. A best buffer has approximately equal concentrations of weak acid and conjugate base so that pH $\approx$ pK_a for a best buffer. The pK_a value for a H$_3$PO$_4$/H$_2$PO$_4^-$ buffer is -log (7.5 × 10^{-3}) = 2.12. A pH of 7.1 is too high for a H$_3$PO$_4$/H$_2$PO$_4^-$ buffer to be effective. At this high of pH, there would be so little H$_3$PO$_4$ present that we could hardly consider it a buffer; this solution would not be effective in resisting pH changes, especially when strong base is added.

34.   The reaction $OH^- + CH_3NH_3^+ \rightarrow CH_3NH_2 + H_2O$ goes to completion for solutions a, c and d (no reaction occurs between the species in solution b since both species are bases). After the OH^- reacts completely, there must be both $CH_3NH_3^+$ and CH_3NH_2 in solution for it to be a buffer. The important components of each solution (after the OH^- reacts completely) is/are:

a.   0.05 M CH_3NH_2 (no $CH_3NH_3^+$ remains, no buffer)

b.   0.05 M OH^- and 0.1 M CH_3NH_2 (two bases present, no buffer)

c.   0.05 M OH^- and 0.05 M CH_3NH_2 (too much OH^- added, no $CH_3NH_3^+$ remains, no buffer)

d.   0.05 M CH_3NH_2 and 0.05 M $CH_3NH_3^+$ (a buffer solution results)

Only the combination in mixture d results in a buffer. Note that the concentrations are halved from the initial values. This is because equal volumes of two solutions were added together which halves the concentrations.

35.   When OH^- is added, it converts $HC_2H_3O_2$ into $C_2H_3O_2^-$: $HC_2H_3O_2 + OH^- \rightarrow C_2H_3O_2^- + H_2O$
From this reaction, the moles of $C_2H_3O_2^-$ produced <u>equal</u> the moles of OH^- added. Also, the total concentration of acetic acid plus acetate ion must equal 2.0 M (assuming no volume change on addition of NaOH). Summarizing for each solution:

$[C_2H_3O_2^-] + [HC_2H_3O] = 2.0\ M$ and $[C_2H_3O_2^-]$ produced $= [OH^-]$ added

a. $pH = pK_a + \log \dfrac{[C_2H_3O_2^-]}{[HC_2H_3O_2]}$; For $pH = pK_a$, $\log \dfrac{[C_2H_3O_2^-]}{[HC_2H_3O_2]} = 0$

Therefore, $\dfrac{[C_2H_3O_2^-]}{[HC_2H_3O_2]} = 1.0$ and $[C_2H_3O_2^-] = [HC_2H_3O_2]$

Since $[C_2H_3O_2^-] + [HC_2H_3O_2] = 2.0\ M$, then $[C_2H_3O_2^-] = [HC_2H_3O_2] = 1.0\ M = [OH^-]$ added

To produce a 1.0 M $C_2H_3O_2^-$ solution, we need to add 1.0 mol of NaOH to 1.0 L of the 2.0 M $HC_2H_3O_2$ solution. The resultant solution will have $pH = pK_a = 4.74$.

b. $4.00 = 4.74 + \log \dfrac{[C_2H_3O_2^-]}{[HC_2H_3O_2]}$, $\dfrac{[C_2H_3O_2^-]}{[HC_2H_3O_2]} = 10^{-0.74} = 0.18$

$[C_2H_3O_2^-] = 0.18\ [HC_2H_3O_2]$ or $[HC_2H_3O_2] = 5.6\ [C_2H_3O_2^-]$; Since $[C_2H_3O_2^-] + [HC_2H_3O_2] = 2.0\ M$, then:

$[C_2H_3O_2^-] + 5.6\ [C_2H_3O_2^-] = 2.0\ M$, $[C_2H_3O_2^-] = \dfrac{2.0}{6.6} = 0.30\ M = [OH^-]$ added

We need to add 0.30 mol of NaOH to 1.0 L of 2.0 M $HC_2H_3O_2$ solution to produce 0.30 M $C_2H_3O_2^-$. The resultant solution will have $pH = 4.00$.

c. $5.00 = 4.74 + \log \dfrac{[C_2H_3O_2^-]}{[HC_2H_3O_2]}, \quad \dfrac{[C_2H_3O_2^-]}{[HC_2H_3O_2]} = 10^{0.26} = 1.8$

$1.8\,[HC_2H_3O_2] = [C_2H_3O_2^-]$ or $[HC_2H_3O_2] = 0.56\,[C_2H_3O_2^-]$; Since $[HC_2H_3O_2] + [C_2H_3O_2^-] = 2.0$ *M*, then:

$1.56\,[C_2H_3O_2^-] = 2.0\ M, \quad [C_2H_3O_2^-] = 1.3\ M = [OH^-]$ added

We need to add 1.3 mol of NaOH to 1.0 L of 2.0 *M* $HC_2H_3O_2$ to produce a solution with pH = 5.00.

36.   Since we have added two solutions together, the concentrations of each reagent has changed. What hasn't changed is the mol or mmol of each reagent. Let's determine the mmol of each reagent present by multiplying the volume in mL by the molarity in units of mmol/mL.

100.0 mL × 0.100 *M* = 10.0 mmol NaF;   100.0 mL × 0.025 *M* = 2.5 mmol HCl

$H^+ + F^- \rightarrow HF$;   2.5 mmol H^+ converts 2.5 mmol F^- into 2.5 mmol HF. After the reaction, a buffer solution results containing 2.5 mmol HF and (10.0 - 2.5 =) 7.5 mmol F^- in 200.0 mL of solution.

$pH = pK_a + \log \dfrac{[F^-]}{[HF]} = 3.14 + \log \left(\dfrac{7.5\ \text{mmol/200.0 mL}}{2.5\ \text{mmol/200.0 mL}} \right) = 3.62$ Assumptions good.

37.   A best buffer has large and equal quantities of weak acid and conjugate base. Since [acid] = [base] for a best buffer, then $pH = pK_a + \log \dfrac{[\text{base}]}{[\text{acid}]} = pK_a + 0 = pK_a$.

The best acid choice for a pH = 7.00 buffer would be the weak acid with a pK_a close to 7.0 or $K_a \approx 1 \times 10^{-7}$. HOCl is the best choice in Table 7.2 ($K_a = 3.5 \times 10^{-8}$; $pK_a = 7.46$). To make this buffer, we need to calculate the [base]/[acid] ratio.

$7.00 = 7.46 + \log \dfrac{[\text{base}]}{[\text{acid}]}, \quad \dfrac{[OCl^-]}{[HOCl]} = 10^{-0.46} = 0.35$

Any OCl^-/HOCl buffer in a concentration ratio of 0.35:1 will have a pH = 7.00. One possibility is [NaOCl] = 0.35 *M* and [HOCl] = 1.0 *M*.

38.   For a pH = 5.00 buffer, we want an acid with pK_a close to 5.00. For a conjugate acid-base pair, 14.00 = $pK_a + pK_b$. So for a pH = 5.00 buffer, we want the base to have a pK_b close to (14.0-5.0 =) 9.0 or a K_b close to 1×10^{-9}. The best choice in Table 7.3 is pyridine, C_5H_5N, with $K_b = 1.7 \times 10^{-9}$.

$pH = pK_a + \log \dfrac{[\text{base}]}{[\text{acid}]}; \quad pK_a = \dfrac{K_w}{K_b} = \dfrac{1.0 \times 10^{-14}}{1.7 \times 10^{-9}} = 5.9 \times 10^{-6}$

$5.00 = -\log (5.9 \times 10^{-6}) + \log \dfrac{[\text{base}]}{[\text{acid}]}, \quad \dfrac{[C_5H_5N]}{[C_5H_5NH^+]} = 10^{-0.23} = 0.59$

There are several possibilities to make this buffer. One possibility is a solution of $[C_5H_5N] = 0.59\ M$ and $[C_5H_5NHCl] = 1.0\ M$. The pH of this solution will be 5.00 since the base to acid concentration ratio is 0.59:1.

39. To solve for [KOCl], we need to use the equation derived in Section 8.3 of the text on the Exact Treatment of Buffered Solutions. The equation is:

$$K_a = \frac{[H^+]\left([A^-]_o + \dfrac{[H^+]^2 - K_w}{[H^+]}\right)}{[HA]_o - \dfrac{[H^+]^2 - K_w}{[H^+]}}$$

Since pH = 7.20, then $[H^+] = 10^{-7.20} = 6.3 \times 10^{-8} \, M$.

$$K_a = 3.5 \times 10^{-8} = \frac{6.3 \times 10^{-8}\left([OCl^-] + \dfrac{(6.3 \times 10^{-8})^2 - 1.0 \times 10^{-14}}{6.3 \times 10^{-8}}\right)}{1.0 \times 10^{-6} - \dfrac{(6.3 \times 10^{-8})^2 - 1.0 \times 10^{-14}}{6.3 \times 10^{-8}}}$$

$$3.5 \times 10^{-8} = \frac{6.3 \times 10^{-8}([OCl^-] - 9.57 \times 10^{-8})}{1.0 \times 10^{-6} + 9.57 \times 10^{-8}} \quad \text{(Carrying extra sig. figs.)}$$

$3.83 \times 10^{-14} = 6.3 \times 10^{-8} ([OCl^-] - 9.57 \times 10^{-8})$, $[OCl^-] = [KOCl] = 7.0 \times 10^{-7} \, M$

40. $B + H_2O \rightleftharpoons BH^+ + OH^-$ $\quad K_b = \dfrac{[BH^+][OH^-]}{[B]}$

The equation for the exact treatment of B/BHCl type buffers would be analogous to the equation for HA/NaA type buffers. The equation is:

$$K_b = \frac{[OH^-]\left([BH^+]_o + \dfrac{[OH^-]^2 - K_w}{[OH^-]}\right)}{[B]_o - \dfrac{[OH^-]^2 - K_w}{[OH^-]}}$$

Solving the buffer problem using the regular procedures:

$HONH_2 + H_2O \rightleftharpoons HONH_3^+ + OH^-$ $\quad K_b = 1.1 \times 10^{-8}$

Initial $\quad 1.0 \times 10^{-4} \, M \qquad\qquad 1.0 \times 10^{-5} \, M \quad \sim 0$

x mol/L of $HONH_2$ reacts with H_2O to reach equilibrium

Change $\quad -x \qquad\qquad\qquad\qquad +x \qquad\quad +x$

Equil. $\quad 1.0 \times 10^{-4} - x \qquad\qquad 1.0 \times 10^{-5} + x \quad\quad x$

$$K_b = 1.1 \times 10^{-8} = \frac{[HONH_3^+][OH^-]}{[HONH_2]} = \frac{(1.0 \times 10^{-5} + x)x}{1.0 \times 10^{-4} - x} \approx \frac{(1.0 \times 10^{-5})x}{1.0 \times 10^{-4}}$$

(Assuming $x \ll 1.0 \times 10^{-5}$.)

$x = [OH^-] = 1.1 \times 10^{-7}$ M; Assumption that $x \ll 1.0 \times 10^{-5}$ is good (x is 1.1% of 1.0×10^{-5}).

In the regular procedure to solve the buffer problem, the problem reduced down to the expression:

$$K_b = \frac{[HONH_3^+]_o[OH^-]}{[HONH_2]_o}$$

This expression holds if x is negligible as compared to $[HONH_3^+]_o$ and $[HONH_2]_o$ as it was in this problem. Now we want to know if we need to worry about the contribution of OH⁻ from water. From the equation for the exact treatment of buffers, if $([OH^-]^2 - K_w) / [OH^-]$ is much less than $[HONH_3^+]_o$ and $[HONH_2]_0$, then the exact equation reduces to:

$$K_b = \frac{[OH^-][HONH_3^+]_0}{[HONH_2]_o}$$

This is the same expression we ended up with to solve the problem using the regular procedures. Checking the neglected term using the [OH⁻] calculated above:

$$\frac{[OH^-]^2 - K_w}{[OH^-]} = \frac{(1.1 \times 10^{-7})^2 - 1.0 \times 1.0^{-14}}{1.1 \times 10^{-7}} = 1.9 \times 10^{-8}$$

This is indeed much smaller than $[HONH_3^+]_o$ and $[HONH_2]_o$ (1.9×10^{-8} is 0.19% of 1.0×10^{-5}). So for this problem we would calculate the same [OH⁻] using the exact equation as we calculated using the regular procedures. In general, we only need to use the exact equation when the buffering materials have a concentration of 10^{-6} M or less.

41.   Using regular procedures, pH = pK_a = $-\log(1.6 \times 10^{-7})$ = 6.80 since $[A^-]_o = [HA]_o$ in this buffer solution. However, the pH is very close to that of neutral water so maybe we need to consider the H⁺ contribution from water. Another problem with this answer is that x (= [H⁺]) is not small as compared to $[HA]_o$ and $[A^-]_o$, which was assumed when solving using the regular procedures. Since the concentrations of the buffer components are less than 10^{-6} M, then let us use the expression for the exact treatment of buffers to solve.

$$K_a = 1.6 \times 10^{-7} = \frac{[H^+]\left([A^-]_o + \dfrac{[H^+]^2 - K_w}{[H^+]}\right)}{[HA]_o - \dfrac{[H^+]^2 - K_w}{[H^+]}} = \frac{[H^+]\left(5.0 \times 10^{-7} + \dfrac{[H^+]^2 - 1.0 \times 10^{-14}}{[H^+]}\right)}{5.0 \times 10^{-7} - \dfrac{[H^+]^2 - 1.0 \times 10^{-14}}{[H^+]}}$$

Solving exactly requires solving a cubic equation. Instead, we will use the method of successive approximations where our initial guess for [H⁺] = 1.6×10^{-7} M (the value obtained using the regular procedures).

$$1.6 \times 10^{-7} = \cfrac{[H^+]\left(5.0 \times 10^{-7} + \cfrac{(1.6 \times 10^{-7})^2 - 1.0 \times 10^{-14}}{1.6 \times 10^{-7}}\right)}{5.0 \times 10^{-7} - \cfrac{(1.6 \times 10^{-7})^2 - 1.0 \times 10^{-14}}{1.6 \times 10^{-7}}} \,, \quad [H^+] = 1.1 \times 10^{-7}$$

We continue the process using 1.1×10^{-7} as our estimate for $[H^+]$. This gives $[H^+] = 1.5 \times 10^{-7}$. We continue the process until we get a self consistent answer. After three more iterations, we converge on $[H^+] = 1.3 \times 10^{-7}\ M$. Solving for the pH:

$$pH = -\log(1.3 \times 10^{-7}) = 6.89$$

Note that if we were to solve this problem exactly (using the quadratic formula) while ignoring the H^+ contribution from water, the answer comes out to $[H^+] = 1.0 \times 10^{-7}\ M$. We get a significantly different answer when we consider the H^+ contribution from H_2O.

Acid-Base Titrations

42.

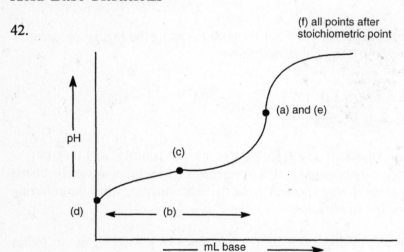

HA + OH$^-$ → A$^-$ + H$_2$O; Added OH$^-$ from the strong base converts the weak acid, HA, into its conjugate base, A$^-$. Initially before any OH$^-$ is added (point d), HA is the dominant species present. After OH$^-$ is added, both HA and A$^-$ are present and a buffer solution results (region b). At the equivalence point (points a and e), exactly enough OH$^-$ has been added to convert all of the weak acid, HA, into its conjugate base, A$^-$. Past the equivalence point (region f), excess OH$^-$ is present. For the answer to part b, we included almost the entire buffer region. The maximum buffer region (or the region which is the best buffer solution) is around the halfway point to equivalence (point c). At this point, enough OH$^-$ has been added to convert exactly one-half of the weak acid present initially into its conjugate base so [HA] = [A$^-$] and pH = pK_a. A best buffer has about equal concentrations of weak acid and conjugate base present.

43.

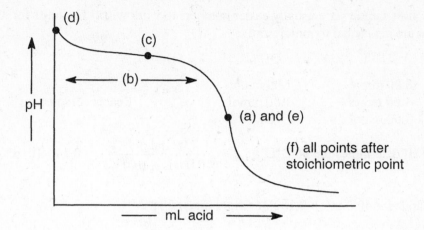

$B + H^+ \rightarrow BH^+$; Added H^+ from the strong acid converts the weak base, B, into its conjugate acid, BH^+. Initially, before any H^+ is added (point d), B is the dominant species present. After H^+ is added, both B and BH^+ are present and a buffered solution results (region b). At the equivalence point (points a and e), exactly enough H^+ has been added to convert all of the weak base present initially into its conjugate acid, BH^+. Past the equivalence point (region f), excess H^+ is present. For the answer to b, we included almost the entire buffer region. The maximum buffer region is around the halfway point to equivalence (point c) where $[B] = [BH^+]$. Here, $pH = pK_a$ which is a characteristic of a best buffer.

44. a. Since all acids are the same initial concentration, the pH curve with the highest pH at 0 mL of NaOH added will correspond to the titration of the weakest acid. This is pH curve f.

b. The pH curve with the lowest pH at 0 mL of NaOH added will correspond to the titration of the strongest acid. This is pH curve a.

The best point to look at to differentiate a strong acid from a weak acid titration (if initial concentrations are not known) is the equivalence point pH. If the pH = 7.00, the acid titrated is a strong acid; if the pH is greater than 7.00, the acid titrated is a weak acid.

c. For a weak acid-strong base titration, the pH at the halfway point to equivalence is equal to the pK_a value. The pH curve, which represents the titration of an acid with $K_a = 1.0 \times 10^{-6}$, will have a $pH = -\log(1 \times 10^{-6}) = 6.0$ at the halfway point. The equivalence point, from the plots, occurs at 50 mL NaOH added, so the halfway point is 25 mL. Plot d has a pH ~6.0 at 25 mL of NaOH added, so the acid titrated in this pH curve (plot d) has $K_a \sim 1 \times 10^{-6}$.

45. This is a strong acid ($HClO_4$) titrated by a strong base (KOH). Added OH^- from the strong base will react completely with the H^+ present from the strong acid to produce H_2O.

a. Only strong acid present. $[H^+] = 0.200\ M$; $pH = 0.699$

b. mmol OH^- added $= 10.0\ mL \times \dfrac{0.100\ mmol\ OH^-}{mL} = 1.00\ mmol\ OH^-$

mmol H^+ present $= 40.0\ mL \times \dfrac{0.200\ mmol\ H^+}{mL} = 8.0\ mmol\ H^+$

Note: The units mmoles are usually easier numbers to work with. The units for molarity are moles/L but are also equal to mmoles/mL.

$$H^+ \quad + \quad OH^- \quad \rightarrow \quad H_2O$$

Before	8.00 mmol	1.00 mmol	
Change	-1.00 mmol	-1.00 mmol	Reacts completely
After	7.00 mmol	0	

The excess H^+ determines the pH. $[H^+]_{excess} = \dfrac{7.00 \text{ mmol } H^+}{40.0 \text{ mL} + 10.0 \text{ mL}} = 0.140 \, M;\ pH = 0.854$

c. mmol OH^- added = 40.0 mL × 0.100 M = 4.00 mmol OH^-

$$H^+ \quad + \quad OH^- \quad \rightarrow \quad H_2O$$

Before	8.00 mmol	4.00 mmol
After	4.00 mmol	0

$[H^+]_{excess} = \dfrac{4.00 \text{ mmol}}{(40.0 + 40.0) \text{ mL}} = 0.0500 \, M;\ pH = 1.301$

d. mmol OH^- added = 80.0 mL × 0.100 M = 8.00 mmol OH^-; This is the equivalence point since we have added just enough OH^- to react with all the acid present. For a strong acid-strong base titration, pH = 7.00 at the equivalence point since only neutral species are present (K^+, ClO_4^-, H_2O).

e. mmol OH^- added = 100.0 mL × 0.100 M = 10.0 mmol OH^-

$$H^+ \quad + \quad OH^- \quad \rightarrow \quad H_2O$$

Before	8.00 mmol	10.0 mmol
After	0	2.0 mmol

Past the equivalence point, the pH is determined by the excess OH^- present.

$[OH^-]_{excess} = \dfrac{2.0 \text{ mmol}}{(40.0 + 100.0) \text{ mL}} = 0.014 \, M;\ pOH = 1.85;\ pH = 12.15$

46. This is a strong base, $Ba(OH)_2$, titrated by a strong acid, HCl. The added strong acid will neutralize the OH^- from the strong base. As is always the case when a strong acid and/or strong base reacts, the reaction is assumed to go to completion.

a. Only a strong base is present, but it breaks up into two mol of OH^- ions for every mol of $Ba(OH)_2$. $[OH^-] = 2 \times 0.100 \, M = 0.200 \, M;\ pOH = 0.699;\ pH = 13.301$

b. mmol OH^- present = 80.0 mL × $\dfrac{0.100 \text{ mmol } Ba(OH)_2}{\text{mL}} \times \dfrac{2 \text{ mmol } OH^-}{\text{mmol } Ba(OH)_2} = 16.0$ mmol OH^-

mmol H^+ added = 20.0 mL × $\dfrac{0.400 \text{ mmol } H^+}{\text{mL}} = 8.00$ mmol H^+

$$OH^- \quad + \quad H^+ \quad \rightarrow \quad H_2O$$

	OH⁻	H⁺	
Before	16.0 mmol	8.00 mmol	
Change	-8.00 mmol	-8.00 mmol	Reacts completely
After	8.0 mmol	0	

$$[OH^-]_{excess} = \frac{8.0 \text{ mmol } OH^-}{80.0 \text{ mL} + 20.0 \text{ mL}} = 0.080 \ M; \quad pOH = 1.10; \quad pH = 12.90$$

c. mmol H^+ added = 30.0 mL $\times$ 0.400 M = 12.0 mmol H^+

$$OH^- \quad + \quad H^+ \quad \rightarrow \quad H_2O$$

	OH⁻	H⁺
Before	16.0 mmol	12.0 mmol
After	4.0 mmol	0

$$[OH^-]_{excess} = \frac{4.0 \text{ mmol } OH^-}{(80.0 + 30.0) \text{ mL}} = 0.036 \ M; \quad pOH = 1.44; \quad pH = 12.56$$

d. mmol H^+ added = 40.0 mL $\times$ 0.400 M = 16.0 mmol H^+; This is the equivalence point. Since the H^+ will exactly neutralize the OH^- from the strong base, then all we have in solution is Ba^{2+}, Cl^- and H_2O. All are neutral species so pH = 7.00.

e. mmol H^+ added = 80.0 mL $\times$ 0.400 M = 32.0 mmol H^+

$$OH^- \quad + \quad H^+ \quad \rightarrow \quad H_2O$$

	OH⁻	H⁺
Before	16.0 mmol	32.0 mmol
After	0	16.0 mmol

$$[H^+]_{excess} = \frac{16.0 \text{ mmol}}{(80.0 + 80.0) \text{ mL}} = 0.100 \ M; \quad pH = 1.000$$

47.   This is a weak acid ($HC_2H_3O_2$) titrated by a strong base (KOH).

a. Only weak acid is present. Solving the weak acid problem:

$$HC_2H_3O_2 \quad \rightleftharpoons \quad H^+ \quad + \quad C_2H_3O_2^-$$

	HC₂H₃O₂	H⁺	C₂H₃O₂⁻
Initial	0.200 M	~0	0
	x mol/L $HC_2H_3O_2$ dissociates to reach equilibrium		
Change	-x $\rightarrow$	+x	+x
Equil.	0.200 - x	x	x

$$K_a = 1.8 \times 10^{-5} = \frac{x^2}{0.200 - x} = \frac{x^2}{0.200}, \quad x = [H^+] = 1.9 \times 10^{-3} \ M$$

pH = 2.72; Assumptions good.

b.   The added OH⁻ will react completely with the best acid present, $HC_2H_3O_2$.

$$\text{mmol } HC_2H_3O_2 \text{ present} = 100.0 \text{ mL} \times \frac{0.200 \text{ mmol } HC_2H_3O_2}{\text{mL}} = 20.0 \text{ mmol } HC_2H_3O_2$$

$$\text{mmol } OH^- \text{ added} = 50.0 \text{ mL} \times \frac{0.100 \text{ mmol } OH^-}{\text{mL}} = 5.00 \text{ mmol } OH^-$$

	$HC_2H_3O_2$	+	OH^-	→	$C_2H_3O_2^-$	+	H_2O	
Before	20.0 mmol		5.00 mmol		0			
Change	-5.00 mmol		-5.00 mmol	→	+5.00 mmol			Reacts completely
After	15.0 mmol		0		5.00 mmol			

After reaction of all the strong base, we have a buffer solution containing a weak acid ($HC_2H_3O_2$) and its conjugate base ($C_2H_3O_2^-$). We will use the Henderson-Hasselbalch equation to solve for the pH.

$$pH = pK_a + \log \frac{[C_2H_3O_2^-]}{[HC_2H_3O_2]} = -\log (1.8 \times 10^{-5}) + \log \left(\frac{5.00 \text{ mmol}/V_T}{15.0 \text{ mmol}/V_T} \right) \text{ where } V_T = \text{total volume}$$

$$pH = 4.74 + \log \left(\frac{5.00}{15.0} \right) = 4.74 + (-0.477) = 4.26$$

Note that the total volume cancels in the Henderson-Hasselbalch equation. For the [base]/[acid] term, the mole ratio equals the concentration ratio since the components of the buffer are always in the same volume of solution.

c.   mmol OH⁻ added = 100.0 mL × 0.100 mmol OH⁻/mL = 10.0 mmol OH⁻; The same amount (20.0 mmol) of $HC_2H_3O_2$ is present as before (it never changes). As before, let the OH⁻ react to completion, then see what is remaining in solution after this reaction.

	$HC_2H_3O_2$	+	OH^-	→	$C_2H_3O_2^-$	+	H_2O
Before	20.0 mmol		10.0 mmol		0		
After	10.0 mmol		0		10.0 mmol		

A buffer solution results after reaction. Since $[C_2H_3O_2^-] = [HC_2H_3O_2] = 10.0$ mmol/total volume, then pH = pK_a. This is always true at the halfway point to equivalence for a weak acid/strong base titration, pH = pK_a.

$$pH = -\log (1.8 \times 10^{-5}) = 4.74$$

d.   mmol OH⁻ added = 150.0 mL × 0.100 M = 15.0 mmol OH⁻. Added OH⁻ reacts completely with the weak acid.

	$HC_2H_3O_2$	+	OH^-	→	$C_2H_3O_2^-$	+	H_2O
Before	20.0 mmol		15.0 mmol		0		
After	5.0 mmol		0		15.0 mmol		

We have a buffer solution after all the OH$^-$ reacts to completion. Using the Henderson-Hasselbalch equation:

$$pH = 4.74 + \log \frac{[C_2H_3O_2^-]}{[HC_2H_3O_2]} = 4.74 + \log\left(\frac{15.0 \text{ mmol}}{5.0 \text{ mmol}}\right) \text{ (Total volume cancels, so we can use mol ratios.)}$$

$$pH = 4.74 + 0.48 = 5.22$$

e.   mmol OH$^-$ added = 200.00 mL × 0.100 M = 20.0 mmol OH$^-$; As before, let the added OH$^-$ react to completion with the weak acid, then see what is in solution after this reaction.

	HC$_2$H$_3$O$_2$	+	OH$^-$	→	C$_2$H$_3$O$_2^-$	+	H$_2$O
Before	20.0 mmol		20.0 mmol		0		
After	0		0		20.0 mmol		

This is the equivalence point. Enough OH$^-$ has been added to exactly neutralize all the weak acid present initially. All that remains that affects the pH at the equivalence point is the conjugate base of the weak acid, C$_2$H$_3$O$_2^-$. This is a weak base equilibrium problem.

$$C_2H_3O_2^- + H_2O \rightleftharpoons HC_2H_3O_2 + OH^- \quad K_b = \frac{K_w}{K_a} = \frac{1.0 \times 10^{-14}}{1.8 \times 10^{-5}} = 5.6 \times 10^{-10}$$

	C$_2$H$_3$O$_2^-$		HC$_2$H$_3$O$_2$	OH$^-$
Initial	20.0 mmol/300.0 mL		0	0
	x mol/L C$_2$H$_3$O$_2^-$ reacts with H$_2$O to reach equilibrium			
Change	$-x$	→	$+x$	$+x$
Equil.	0.0667 − x		x	x

$$K_b = 5.6 \times 10^{-10} = \frac{x^2}{0.0667 - x} \approx \frac{x^2}{0.0667}, \quad x = [OH^-] = 6.1 \times 10^{-6} \, M$$

pOH = 5.21; pH = 8.79; Assumptions good.

f.   mmol OH$^-$ added = 250.0 mL × 0.100 M = 25.0 mmol OH$^-$

	HC$_2$H$_3$O$_2$	+	OH$^-$	→	C$_2$H$_3$O$_2^-$	+	H$_2$O
Before	20.0 mmol		25.0 mmol		0		
After	0		5.0 mmol		20.0 mmol		

After the titration reaction, we have a solution containing excess OH$^-$ and a weak base, C$_2$H$_3$O$_2^-$. When a strong base and a weak base are both present, assume the amount of OH$^-$ added from the weak base will be minimal, i.e., the pH past the equivalence point is determined by the amount of excess base.

$$[OH^-]_{excess} = \frac{5.0 \text{ mmol}}{100.0 \text{ mL} + 250.0 \text{ mL}} = 0.014 \, M; \quad pOH = 1.85; \quad pH = 12.15$$

48.   This is a weak base (H$_2$NNH$_2$) titrated by a strong acid (HNO$_3$). To calculate the pH at the various points, let the strong acid react completely with the weak base present, then see what is in solution.

a. Only a weak base is present. Solve the weak base equilibrium problem.

$$H_2NNH_2 + H_2O \rightleftharpoons H_2NNH_3^+ + OH^-$$

Initial	0.100 M	0	~0
Equil.	0.100 - x	x	x

$$K_b = 3.0 \times 10^{-6} = \frac{x^2}{0.100 - x} \approx \frac{x^2}{0.100}, \quad x = [OH^-] = 5.5 \times 10^{-4} M$$

pOH = 3.26; pH = 10.74; Assumptions good.

b. mmol H_2NNH_2 present = 100.0 mL $\times \dfrac{0.100 \text{ mmol } H_2NNH_2}{mL} = 10.0$ mmol H_2NNH_2

mmol H^+ added = 20.0 mL $\times \dfrac{0.200 \text{ mmol } H^+}{mL} = 4.00$ mmol H^+

	H_2NNH_2	+	H^+	$\rightarrow$	$H_2NNH_3^+$	
Before	10.0 mmol		4.00 mmol		0	
Change	-4.00 mmol		-4.00 mmol	$\rightarrow$	+4.00 mmol	Reacts completely
After	6.0 mmol		0		4.00 mmol	

A buffer solution results after the titration reaction. Solving using the Henderson-Hasselbalch equation:

$$pH = pK_a + \log \frac{[base]}{[acid]}, \quad K_a = \frac{K_w}{K_b} = \frac{1.0 \times 10^{-14}}{3.0 \times 10^{-6}} = 3.3 \times 10^{-9}$$

$$pH = -\log (3.3 \times 10^{-9}) + \log \left(\frac{6.0 \text{ mmol}/V_T}{4.00 \text{ mmol}/V_T} \right) \text{ where } V_T = \text{total volume, which cancels}$$

$$pH = 8.48 + \log (1.5) = 8.48 + 0.18 = 8.66$$

c. mmol H^+ added = 25.0 mL $\times$ 0.200 M = 5.00 mmol H^+

	H_2NNH_2	+	H^+	$\rightarrow$	$H_2NNH_3^+$
Before	10.0 mmol		5.00 mmol		0
After	5.0 mmol		0		5.00 mmol

This is the halfway point to equivalence where $[H_2NNH_3^+] = [H_2NNH_2]$. At this point,   pH = pK_a (which is characteristic of the halfway point for any weak base/strong acid titration).

$$pH = -\log (3.3 \times 10^{-9}) = 8.48$$

d. mmol H^+ added = 40.0 mL $\times$ 0.200 M = 8.00 mmol H^+

	H_2NNH_2	+	H^+	$\rightarrow$	$H_2NNH_3^+$
Before	10.0 mmol		8.00 mmol		0
After	2.0 mmol		0		8.00 mmol

A buffer solution results.

$$pH = pK_a + \log \frac{[base]}{[acid]} = 8.48 + \log\left(\frac{2.0\ mmol/V_T}{8.00\ mmol/V_T}\right) = 8.48 + (-0.60) = 7.88$$

e.   mmol H^+ added = 50.0 mL × 0.200 M = 10.0 mmol H^+

	H_2NNH_2	+	H^+	$\rightarrow$	$H_2NNH_3^+$
Before	10.0 mmol		10.0 mmol		0
After	0		0		10.0 mmol

As is always the case in a weak base/strong acid titration, the pH at the equivalence point is acidic because only a weak acid ($H_2NNH_3^+$) is present. Solving the weak acid equilibrium problem:

	$H_2NNH_3^+$	$\rightleftharpoons$	H^+	+	H_2NNH_2
Initial	10.0 mmol/150.0 mL		0		0
Equil.	0.0667 - x		x		x

$$K_a = 3.3 \times 10^{-9} = \frac{x^2}{0.0667 - x} \approx \frac{x^2}{0.0667}, \quad x = [H^+] = 1.5 \times 10^{-5}\ M$$

pH = 4.82; Assumptions good.

f.   mmol H^+ added = 100.0 mL × 0.200 M = 20.0 mmol H^+

	H_2NNH_2	+	H^+	$\rightarrow$	$H_2NNH_3^+$
Before	10.0 mmol		20.0 mmol		0
After	0		10.0 mmol		10.0 mmol

Two acids are present past the equivalence point, but the excess H^+ will determine the pH of the solution since $H_2NNH_3^+$ is a weak acid.

$$[H^+]_{excess} = \frac{10.0\ mmol}{100.0\ mL + 100.0\ mL} = 0.0500\ M;\ pH = 1.301$$

49.   We will do sample calculations for the various parts of the titration. All results are summarized in Table 8.1 at the end of Exercise 8.52.

At the beginning of the titration, only the weak acid $HC_3H_5O_3$ is present.

$$HLac \quad \rightleftharpoons \quad H^+ \quad + \quad Lac^- \quad K_a = 10^{-3.86} = 1.4 \times 10^{-4} \quad HLac = HC_3H_5O_3$$
$$Lac^- = C_3H_5O_3^-$$

Initial	0.100 M	~0	0
	x mol/L HLac dissociates to reach equilibrium		
Change	$-x$ $\rightarrow$	$+x$	$+x$
Equil.	0.100 - x	x	x

$$1.4 \times 10^{-4} = \frac{x^2}{0.100 - x} = \frac{x^2}{0.100}, \quad x = [H^+] = 3.7 \times 10^{-3} \ M; \quad pH = 2.43 \quad \text{Assumptions good.}$$

Up to the stoichiometric point, we calculate the pH using the Henderson-Hasselbalch equation. This is the buffer region. For example, at 4.0 mL of NaOH added:

$$\text{initial mmol HLac present} = 25.0 \text{ mL} \times \frac{0.100 \text{ mmol}}{\text{mL}} = 2.50 \text{ mmol HLac}$$

$$\text{mmol OH}^- \text{ added} = 4.0 \text{ mL} \times \frac{0.100 \text{ mmol}}{\text{mL}} = 0.40 \text{ mmol OH}^-$$

Note: The units mmol are usually easier numbers to work with. The units for molarity are moles/L but are also equal to mmoles/mL.

The 0.40 mmol added OH$^-$ converts 0.40 mmoles HLac to 0.40 mmoles Lac$^-$ according to the equation:

$$HLac + OH^- \rightarrow Lac^- + H_2O \qquad \text{Reacts completely}$$

mmol HLac remaining = 2.50 - 0.40 = 2.10 mmol; mmol Lac$^-$ produced = 0.40 mmol

We have a buffer solution. Using the Henderson-Hasselbalch equation where pK_a = 3.86:

$$pH = pK_a + \log \frac{[Lac^-]}{[HLac]} = 3.86 + \log \frac{(0.40)}{(2.10)} \qquad \text{(Total volume cancels, so we can use use the ratio of moles or mmoles.)}$$

$$pH = 3.86 - 0.72 = 3.14$$

Other points in the buffer region are calculated in a similar fashion. Perform a stoichiometry problem first, followed by a buffer problem. The buffer region includes all points up to 24.9 mL OH$^-$ added.

At the stoichiometric point (25.0 mL OH$^-$ added), we have added enough OH$^-$ to convert all of the HLac (2.50 mmol) into its conjugate base, Lac$^-$. All that is present is a weak base. To determine the pH, we perform a weak base calculation.

$$[Lac^-]_o = \frac{2.50 \text{ mmol}}{25.0 \text{ mL} + 25.0 \text{ mL}} = 0.0500 \ M$$

$$Lac^- + H_2O \rightleftharpoons HLac + OH^- \qquad K_b = \frac{1.0 \times 10^{-14}}{1.4 \times 10^{-4}} = 7.1 \times 10^{-11}$$

Initial	0.0500 M		0	0

x mol/L Lac^- reacts with H_2O to reach equilibrium

Change	-x	$\rightarrow$	+x	+x
Equil.	0.0500 - x		x	x

$$K_b = \frac{x^2}{0.0500 - x} = \frac{x^2}{0.0500} = 7.1 \times 10^{-11}$$

$x = [OH^-] = 1.9 \times 10^{-6}\,M$; pOH = 5.72; pH = 8.28   Assumptions good.

Past the stoichiometric point, we have added more than 2.50 mmol of NaOH. The pH will be determined by the excess OH^- ion present. An example of this calculation follows.

At 25.1 mL: OH^- added = 25.1 mL $\times \dfrac{0.100\ mmol}{mL}$ = 2.51 mmol OH^-; 2.50 mmol OH^- neutralizes all the weak acid present. The remainder is excess OH^-.

Excess $OH^- = 2.51 - 2.50 = 0.01$ mmol OH^-

$$[OH^-]_{excess} = \frac{0.01\ mmol}{(25.0 + 25.1)\ mL} = 2 \times 10^{-4}\,M; \text{ pOH} = 3.7; \text{ pH} = 10.3$$

All results are listed in Table 8.1 at the end of the solution to Exercise 8.52.

50.   Results for all points are summarized in Table 8.1 at the end of the solution to Exercise 8.52. At the beginning of the titration, we have a weak acid problem:

$$HOPr \rightleftharpoons H^+ + OPr^- \qquad \begin{array}{l} HOPr = HC_3H_5O_2 \\ OPr^- = C_3H_5O_2^- \end{array}$$

Initial	0.100 M		~0	0

x mol/L HOPr acid dissociates to reach equilibrium

Change	-x	$\rightarrow$	+x	+x
Equil.	0.100 - x		x	x

$$K_a = \frac{[H^+][OPr^-]}{[HOPr]} = 1.3 \times 10^{-5} = \frac{x^2}{0.100 - x} \approx \frac{x^2}{0.100}$$

$x = [H^+] = 1.1 \times 10^{-3}\,M$; pH = 2.96   Assumptions good.

The buffer region is from 4.0 - 24.9 mL of OH^- added. We will do a sample calculation at 24.0 mL OH^- added.

initial mmol HOPr present = 25.0 mL $\times \dfrac{0.100\ mmol}{mL}$ = 2.50 mmol HOPr

mmol OH^- added = 24.0 mL $\times \dfrac{0.100\ mmol}{mL}$ = 2.40 mmol OH^-

The added strong base converts HOPr into OPr^-.

	HOPr	+	OH^-	$\rightarrow$	OPr^-	+	H_2O
Before	2.50 mmol		2.40 mmol		0		
Change	-2.40		-2.40	$\rightarrow$	+2.40		Reacts completely
After	0.10 mmol		0		2.40 mmol		

A buffer solution results. Using the Henderson-Hasselbalch equation where $pK_a = -\log(1.3 \times 10^{-5}) = 4.89$:

$$pH = pK_a + \log \frac{[Base]}{[Acid]} = 4.89 + \log \frac{[OPr^-]}{[HOPr]}$$

$$pH = 4.89 + \log\left(\frac{2.40}{0.10}\right) = 4.89 + 1.38 = 6.27 \quad \text{(Volume cancels, so we can use the mmol ratio in the log term.)}$$

All points in the buffer region, 4.0 mL to 24.9 mL, are calculated this way. See Table 8.1 at the end of Exercise 8.52 for all the results.

At the stoichiometric point, only a weak base (OPr^-) is present:

	OPr^-	+	H_2O	$\rightleftharpoons$	OH^-	+	HOPr
Initial	$\dfrac{2.50 \text{ mmol}}{50.0 \text{ mL}} = 0.0500\ M$				0		0

x mol/L OPr^- reacts with H_2O to reach equilibrium

Change	-x			$\rightarrow$	+x		+x
Equil.	0.0500 - x				x		x

$$K_b = \frac{[OH^-][HOPr]}{[OPr^-]} = \frac{K_w}{K_a} = 7.7 \times 10^{-10} = \frac{x^2}{0.0500 - x} \approx \frac{x^2}{0.0500}$$

$x = 6.2 \times 10^{-6}\ M = [OH^-]$, $pOH = 5.21$, $pH = 8.79$ \qquad Assumptions good.

Beyond the stoichiometric point, the pH is determined by the excess strong base added. The results are the same as those in Exercise 8.49 (see Table 8.1).

For example at 26.0 mL NaOH added:

$$[OH^-] = \frac{2.60 \text{ mmol} - 2.50 \text{ mmol}}{(25.0 + 26.0) \text{ mL}} = 2.0 \times 10^{-3}\ M; \quad pOH = 2.70; \quad pH = 11.30$$

51.   At beginning of the titration, only the weak base NH_3 is present. As always, solve for the pH using the K_b reaction for NH_3.

	NH_3	+	H_2O	$\rightleftharpoons$	NH_4^+	+	OH^-	$K_b = 1.8 \times 10^{-5}$
Initial	0.100 M				0		~0	
Equil.	0.100 - x				x		x	

$$K_b = \frac{x^2}{0.100 - x} = \frac{x^2}{0.100} = 1.8 \times 10^{-5}$$

$x = [OH^-] = 1.3 \times 10^{-3} \, M$; pOH = 2.89; pH = 11.11   Assumptions good.

In the buffer region (4.0 - 24.9 mL), we can use the Henderson-Hasselbalch equation:

$$K_a = \frac{1.0 \times 10^{-14}}{1.8 \times 10^{-5}} = 5.6 \times 10^{-10}; \quad pK_a = 9.25; \quad pH = 9.25 + \log \frac{[NH_3]}{[NH_4^+]}$$

We must determine the amounts of NH_3 and NH_4^+ present after the added H^+ reacts completely with the NH_3. For example, after 8.0 mL HCl added:

$$\text{initial mmol } NH_3 \text{ present} = 25.0 \text{ mL} \times \frac{0.100 \text{ mmol}}{\text{mL}} = 2.50 \text{ mmol } NH_3$$

$$\text{mmol } H^+ \text{ added} = 8.0 \text{ mL} \times \frac{0.100 \text{ mmol}}{\text{mL}} = 0.80 \text{ mmol } H^+$$

Added H^+ reacts with NH_3 to completion: $NH_3 + H^+ \rightarrow NH_4^+$

mmol NH_3 remaining = 2.50 - 0.80 = 1.70 mmol; mmol NH_4^+ produced = 0.80 mmol

$$pH = 9.25 + \log \frac{1.70}{0.80} = 9.58 \quad \text{(Mole ratios can be used since the total volume cancels.)}$$

Other points in the buffer region are calculated in similar fashion. Results are summarized in Table 8.1 at the end of Exercise 8.52.

At the stoichiometric point (25.0 mL H^+ added), just enough HCl has been added to convert all of the weak base (NH_3) into its conjugate acid (NH_4^+). Perform a weak acid calculation. $[NH_4^+]_o = 2.50$ mmol/50.0 mL = 0.0500 M

$$NH_4^+ \quad \rightleftharpoons \quad H^+ \; + \; NH_3 \quad K_a = 5.6 \times 10^{-10}$$

Initial	0.0500 M	0	0
Equil.	0.0500 - x	x	x

$$5.6 \times 10^{-10} = \frac{x^2}{0.0500 - x} = \frac{x^2}{0.0500}, \quad x = [H^+] = 5.3 \times 10^{-6} \, M; \quad pH = 5.28 \quad \text{Assumptions good.}$$

Beyond the stoichiometric point, the pH is determined by the excess H^+. For example, at 28.0 mL of H^+ added:

$$H^+ \text{ added} = 28.0 \text{ mL} \times \frac{0.100 \text{ mmol}}{\text{mL}} = 2.80 \text{ mmol } H^+$$

Excess H^+ = 2.80 mmol - 2.50 mmol = 0.30 mmol excess H^+

$$[H^+]_{excess} = \frac{0.30 \text{ mmol}}{(25.0 + 28.0) \text{ mL}} = 5.7 \times 10^{-3} \, M; \quad pH = 2.24$$

All results are summarized in Table 8.1.

52.   Initially, a weak base problem:

$$py \quad + \quad H_2O \quad \rightleftharpoons \quad Hpy^+ \quad + \quad OH^- \qquad \text{py is pyridine}$$

Initial   0.100 M   0   ~0
Equil.   0.100 - x   x   x

$$K_b = \frac{[Hpy^+][OH^-]}{[py]} = \frac{x^2}{0.100 - x} = \frac{x^2}{0.100} = 1.7 \times 10^{-9}$$

$x = [OH^-] = 1.3 \times 10^{-5}\ M;$ pOH = 4.89; pH = 9.11   Assumptions good.

Buffer region (4.0 - 24.5 mL): Added H^+ reacts completely with py: $py + H^+ \rightarrow Hpy^+$. Determine the moles (or mmoles) of py and Hpy^+ after reaction and use the Henderson-Hasselbalch equation to solve for the pH.

$$K_a = \frac{K_w}{K_b} = \frac{1.0 \times 10^{-14}}{1.7 \times 10^{-9}} = 5.9 \times 10^{-6};\ pK_a = 5.23;\ pH = 5.23 + \log \frac{[py]}{[Hpy^+]}$$

Results in the buffer region are summarized in Table 8.1 that follows this problem. See Exercise 8.51 for a similar sample calculation.

At the stoichiometric point (25.0 mL H^+ added), this is a weak acid problem since just enough H^+ has been added to convert all of the weak base into its conjugate acid. The initial concentration of $[Hpy^+] = 0.0500\ M$.

$$Hpy^+ \quad \rightleftharpoons \quad py \quad + \quad H^+ \qquad K_a = 5.9 \times 10^{-6}$$

Initial   0.0500 M   0   0
Equil.   0.0500 - x   x   x

$5.9 \times 10^{-6} = \dfrac{x^2}{0.0500 - x} = \dfrac{x^2}{0.0500}$, $x = [H^+] = 5.4 \times 10^{-4}\ M;$ pH = 3.27   Assumptions good.

Beyond the equivalence point, the pH determination is made by calculating the concentration of excess H^+. See Exercise 8.51 for an example. All results are summarized in Table 8.1 that follows.

Table 8.1: Summary of pH Results for Exercises 8.49 - 8.52   (Graph follows)

titrant mL	Exercise 8.49	Exercise 8.50	Exercise 8.51	Exercise 8.52
0.0	2.43	2.96	11.11	9.11
4.0	3.14	4.17	9.97	5.95
8.0	3.53	4.56	9.58	5.56
12.5	3.86	4.89	9.25	5.23
20.0	4.46	5.49	8.65	4.63
24.0	5.24	6.27	7.87	3.85
24.5	5.6	6.6	7.6	3.5
24.9	6.3	7.3	6.9	-
25.0	8.28	8.79	5.28	3.27
25.1	10.3	10.3	3.7	-
26.0	11.29	11.30	2.71	2.71
28.0	11.75	11.75	2.24	2.25
30.0	11.96	11.96	2.04	2.04

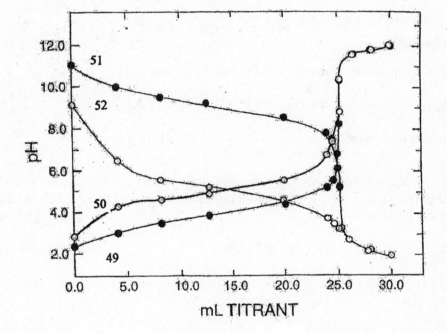

53.   a.   This is a weak acid/strong base titration. At the halfway point to equivalence, [weak acid] = [conjugate base], so pH = pK_a (always for a weak acid/strong base titration).

pH = -log (6.4 × 10^{-5}) = 4.19

mmol HC$_7$H$_5$O$_2$ present = 100. mL × 0.10 M = 10. mmol HC$_7$H$_5$O$_2$. For the equivalence point, 10. mmol of OH$^-$ must be added. The volume of OH$^-$ added to reach the equivalence point is:

$$10. \text{ mmol OH}^- \times \frac{1 \text{ mL}}{0.10 \text{ mmol OH}^-} = 1.0 \times 10^2 \text{ mL OH}^-$$

At the equivalence point, 10. mmol of $HC_7H_5O_2$ is neutralized by 10. mmol of OH^- to produce 10. mmol of $C_7H_5O_2^-$. This is a weak base. The total volume of the solution is $100.0 \text{ mL} + 1.0 \times 10^2 \text{ mL} = 2.0 \times 10^2 \text{ mL}$. Solving the weak base equilibrium problem:

$$C_7H_5O_2^- + H_2O \rightleftharpoons HC_7H_5O_2 + OH^- \quad K_b = \frac{K_w}{K_a} = \frac{1.0 \times 10^{-14}}{6.4 \times 10^{-5}} = 1.6 \times 10^{-10}$$

Initial   10. mmol/2.0×10^2 mL   0   0
Equil. $0.050 - x$ x x

$$K_b = 1.6 \times 10^{-10} = \frac{x^2}{0.050 - x} \approx \frac{x^2}{0.050}, \quad x = [OH^-] = 2.8 \times 10^{-6} \ M$$

pOH = 5.55; pH = 8.45   Assumptions good.

b. At the halfway point to equivalence for a weak base/strong acid titration, $pH = pK_a$ since [weak base] = [conjugate acid].

$$K_a = \frac{K_w}{K_b} = \frac{1.0 \times 10^{-14}}{5.6 \times 10^{-4}} = 1.8 \times 10^{-11}; \quad pH = pK_a = -\log(1.8 \times 10^{-11}) = 10.74$$

For the equivalence point (mmol acid added = mmol base present):

mmol $C_2H_5NH_2$ present = $100.0 \text{ mL} \times 0.10 \ M = 10.$ mmol $C_2H_5NH_2$

mL H^+ added = $10. \text{ mmol } H^+ \times \frac{1 \text{ mL}}{0.20 \text{ mmol } H^+} = 50.$ mL H^+

The strong acid added completely converts the weak base into its conjugate acid. Therefore, at the equivalence point, $[C_2H_5NH_3^+]_o = 10. \text{ mmol}/(100.0 + 50.) \text{ mL} = 0.067 \ M$. Solving the weak acid equilibrium problem:

$$C_2H_5NH_3^+ \rightleftharpoons H^+ + C_2H_5NH_2$$

Initial   0.067 M 0   0
Equil. $0.067 - x$ x x

$$K_a = 1.8 \times 10^{-11} = \frac{x^2}{0.067 - x} \approx \frac{x^2}{0.067}, \quad x = [H^+] = 1.1 \times 10^{-6} \ M$$

pH = 5.96; Assumptions good.

c. In a strong acid/strong base titration, the halfway point has no special significance other than exactly one-half of the original amount of acid present has been neutralized.

mmol H^+ present = $100.0 \text{ mL} \times 0.50 \ M = 50.$ mmol H^+

$$\text{mL OH}^- \text{ added} = 25. \text{ mmol OH}^- \times \frac{1 \text{ mL}}{0.25 \text{ mmol}} = 1.0 \times 10^2 \text{ mL OH}^-$$

$$\text{H}^+ \quad + \quad \text{OH}^- \quad \rightarrow \quad \text{H}_2\text{O}$$

Before	50. mmol	25 mmol
After	25 mmol	0

$$[\text{H}^+]_{excess} = \frac{25 \text{ mmol}}{(100.0 + 1.0 \times 10^2) \text{ mL}} = 0.13 \ M; \ \text{pH} = 0.89$$

At the equivalence point of a strong acid/strong base titration, only neutral species are present $(\text{Na}^+, \text{Cl}^-, \text{H}_2\text{O})$ so the pH = 7.00.

54.   At equivalence point: $16.00 \text{ mL} \times 0.125 \text{ mmol/mL} = 2.00 \text{ mmol OH}^-$ added; There must be 2.00 mmol HX present initially.

2.00 mL NaOH added = $2.00 \text{ mL} \times 0.125 \text{ mmol/mL} = 0.250 \text{ mmol OH}^-$; 0.250 mmol of OH^- added will convert 0.250 mmol HX into 0.250 mmol X^-. Remaining HX = 2.00 - 0.250 = 1.75 mmol HX; This is a buffer solution where $[\text{H}^+] = 10^{-6.912} = 1.22 \times 10^{-7} \ M$. Since total volume cancels:

$$K_a = \frac{[\text{H}^+][\text{X}^-]}{[\text{HX}]} = \frac{1.22 \times 10^{-7} (0.250)}{1.75} = 1.74 \times 10^{-8}$$

Note: We could also solve for K_a using the Henderson-Hasselbalch equation.

55.   a. $1.00 \text{ L} \times 0.100 \text{ mol/L} = 0.100 \text{ mol HCl}$ added to reach stoichiometric point.

The 10.00 g sample must have contained 0.100 mol of NaA. $\dfrac{10.00 \text{ g}}{0.100 \text{ mol}} = 100. \text{ g/mol}$

b.   500.0 mL of HCl added represents the halfway point to equivalence. So, pH = $\text{p}K_a$ = 5.00 and $K_a = 1.0 \times 10^{-5}$. At the equivalence point, enough H^+ has been added to convert all the A^- present initially into HA. The concentration of HA at the equivalence point is:

$$[\text{HA}]_0 = \frac{0.100 \text{ mol}}{1.10 \text{ L}} = 0.0909 \ M$$

	HA	$\rightleftharpoons$	H^+	+	A^-	$K_a = 1.0 \times 10^{-5}$
Initial	0.0909 M		0		0	
Equil.	0.0909 - x		x		x	

$$K_a = 1.0 \times 10^{-5} = \frac{x^2}{0.0909 - x} \approx \frac{x^2}{0.0909}$$

$x = 9.5 \times 10^{-4} \ M = [\text{H}^+];$ pH = 3.02   Assumptions good.

56.   pH > 5 for bromcresol green to be blue. pH < 8 for thymol blue to be yellow. The pH is between 5 and 8.

57.   a. yellow   b. green (Both yellow and blue forms are present.)

c. yellow   d. blue

58.   No, since there are three colored forms, there must be two proton transfer reactions. Thus, there must be at least two acidic protons in the acid (orange) form of thymol blue.

59.   Equivalence point: when enough titrant has been added to react exactly with the substance in solution being titrated. End point: indicator changes color. We want the indicator to tell us when we have reached the equivalence point. We can detect the end point visually and assume it is the equivalence point for doing stoichiometric calculations. They don't have to be as close as 0.01 pH unit since at the equivalence point the pH is changing very rapidly with added titrant. The range over which an indicator changes color only needs to be close to the pH of the equivalence point.

60.   The two forms of an indicator are different colors. The HIn form has one color and the In⁻ form has another color. To see only one color, that form must be in an approximately ten fold excess or greater over the other form. When the ratio of the two forms is less than 10, both colors are present. To go from [HIn]/[In⁻] = 10 to [HIn]/[In⁻] = 0.1 requires a change of 2 pH units (a 100 fold decrease in [H⁺]) as the indicator changes from the HIn color to the In⁻ color.

61.   When choosing an indicator, we want the color change of the indicator to occur approximately at the pH of the equivalence point. Since the pH generally changes very rapidly at the equivalence point, we don't have to be exact. This is especially true for strong acid/strong base titrations. Some choices where color change occurs at about the pH of the equivalence point are:

Exercise	pH at eq. pt.	Indicator
8.45	7.00	bromthymol blue or phenol red
8.47	8.79	o-cresolphthalein or phenolphthalein

62.

Exercise	pH at eq. pt.	Indicator
8.46	7.00	bromthymol blue or phenol red
8.48	4.82	bromcresol green

63.

Exercise	pH at eq. pt.	Indicator
8.49	8.28	o-cresolphthalein or phenolphthalein
8.51	5.28	bromcresol green

64.

Exercise	pH at eq. pt.	Indicator
8.50	8.79	o-cresolphthalein or phenolphthalein
8.52	3.27	2,4-dinitrophenol

The titration in 8.52 is not feasible. The pH break at the equivalence point is too small.

65.   The color of the indicator will change over the approximate range of pH = $pK_a \pm 1 = 5.3 \pm 1$. Therefore, the useful pH range of methyl red where it changes color would be about: 4.3 (red) - 6.3 (yellow). Note that at pH < 4.3, the HIn form of the indicator dominates and the color of the solution

is the color of HIn (red). At pH > 6.3, the In⁻ form of the indicator dominates and the color of the solution is the color of In⁻ (yellow). In titrating a weak acid with base, we start off with an acidic solution with pH < 4.3 so the color would change from red to reddish-orange at pH ~ 4.3. In titrating a weak base with acid, the color change would be from yellow to yellowish-orange at pH ~ 6.3. Only a weak base/strong acid titration would have an acidic pH at the equivalence point so only in this type of titration would the color change of methyl red indicate the approximate endpoint.

66.   For bromcresol green, the resultant green color indicates that both HIn and In⁻ are present in significant amounts. This occurs when pH ~ pK_a of the indicator. From results of the bromcresol green indicator, pH ≈ 5.0. Note that the results of the first two indicators are inconclusive.

$HX \rightleftharpoons H^+ + X^-$; From the typical weak acid setup: $[H^+] = [X^-] \approx 1 \times 10^{-5} M$ and $[HX] \approx 0.01 M$

$$K_a = \frac{[H^+][X^-]}{[HX]} \approx \frac{(1 \times 10^{-5})^2}{0.01} = 1 \times 10^{-8}$$

67. $100.0 \text{ mL} \times 0.0500 M = 5.00 \text{ mmol } H_3X$ initially

   a. Since $K_{a_1} >> K_{a_2} >> K_{a_3}$, pH initially determined by H_3X.

$$H_3X \quad\rightleftharpoons\quad H^+ \quad + \quad H_2X^-$$

Initial	0.0500 M	~0	0
Equil.	0.0500 - x	x	x

$K_{a_1} = 1.0 \times 10^{-3} = \dfrac{x^2}{0.0500 - x} \approx \dfrac{x^2}{0.0500}$, $x = 7.1 \times 10^{-3}$ Assumption poor.

Using the quadratic formula:

$$x^2 + 1.0 \times 10^{-3} x - 5.0 \times 10^{-5} = 0, \quad x = 6.6 \times 10^{-3} M = [H^+]; \quad pH = 2.18$$

   b. 1.00 mmol OH⁻ added converts H_3X into H_2X^-. After this reaction goes to completion, 4.00 mmol H_3X and 1.00 mmol H_2X^- are in a total volume of 110.0 mL. Solving the buffer problem:

$$H_3X \quad\rightleftharpoons\quad H^+ \quad + \quad H_2X^-$$

Initial	0.0364 M	~0	0.00909 M
Equil.	0.0364 - x	x	0.00909 + x

$K_{a_1} = 1.0 \times 10^{-3} = \dfrac{x(0.00909 + x)}{0.0364 - x}$ Assumption that x is small does not work here.

Using the quadratic formula and carrying extra sig. figs: $x^2 + 1.01 \times 10^{-2} x - 3.64 \times 10^{-5} = 0$

$$x = 2.8 \times 10^{-3} M = [H^+]; \quad pH = 2.55$$

   c. 2.50 mmol OH⁻ added, results in 2.50 mmol H_3X and 2.50 mmol H_2X^- after OH⁻ reacts completely with H_3X. This is the first halfway point to equivalence. pH = pK_{a_1} = 3.00; Assumptions good (5% error).

d. 5.00 mmol OH$^-$ added, results in 5.00 mmol H$_2$X$^-$ after OH$^-$ reacts completely with H$_3$X. This is the 1st stoichiometric point.

$$pH = \frac{pK_{a_1} + pK_{a_2}}{2} = \frac{3.00 + 7.00}{2} = 5.00$$

e. 6.0 mmol OH$^-$ added, results in 4.00 mmol H$_2$X$^-$ and 1.00 mmol HX^{2-} after OH$^-$ reacts completely with H$_3$X and then reacts completely with H$_2$X$^-$.

Using the H$_2$X$^- \rightleftharpoons$ H$^+$ + HX^{2-} reaction:

$$pH = pK_{a2} + \log \frac{[HX^{2-}]}{[H_2X^-]} = 7.00 - \log(1.00/4.00) = 6.40 \qquad \text{Assumptions good.}$$

f. 7.50 mmol KOH added, results in 2.50 mmol H$_2$X$^-$ and 2.50 mmol HX^{2-} after OH$^-$ reacts completely. This is the second halfway point to equivalence.

pH = pK$_{a_2}$ = 7.00   Assumptions good.

g. 10.0 mmol OH$^-$ added, results in 5.0 mmol HX^{2-} after OH$^-$ reacts completely. This is the 2nd stoichiometric point.

$$pH = \frac{pK_{a_2} + pK_{a_3}}{2} = \frac{7.00 + 12.00}{2} = 9.50$$

h. 12.5 mmol OH$^-$ added, results in 2.5 mmol HX^{2-} and 2.5 mmol X^{3-} after OH$^-$ reacts completely with H$_3$X first, then H$_2$X$^-$ and finally HX^{2-}. This is the third halfway point to equivalence. Usually pH = pK$_{a_3}$ but normal assumptions don't hold. We must solve for the pH exactly.

[X^{3-}] = [HX^{2-}] = 2.5 mmol/225.0 mL = 1.1 × 10^{-2} M

	X^{3-} + H$_2$O	$\rightleftharpoons$	HX^{2-}	+	OH$^-$	$K_b = \dfrac{K_w}{K_{a_3}} = 1.0 \times 10^{-2}$
Initial	0.011 M		0.011 M		0	
Equil.	0.011 - x		0.011 + x		x	

$$K_b = 1.0 \times 10^{-2} = \frac{x(0.011 + x)}{(0.011 - x)}; \text{ Using the quadratic formula:}$$

$$x^2 + 2.1 \times 10^{-2}\, x - 1.1 \times 10^{-4} = 0, \ \ x = 4.3 \times 10^{-3}\, M = [\text{OH}^-]; \ \ pH = 11.63$$

i. 15.0 mmol OH$^-$ added, results in 5.0 mmol X^{3-} after OH$^-$ reacts completely. This is the 3rd stoichiometric point.

	X^{3-} + H$_2$O	$\rightleftharpoons$	HX^{2-}	+	OH$^-$	$K_b = \dfrac{K_w}{K_{a_3}} = 1.0 \times 10^{-2}$
Initial	$\dfrac{5.0 \text{ mmol}}{250.0 \text{ mL}} = 0.020 \ M$		0		0	
Equil.	0.020 - x		x		x	

$$K_b = \frac{x^2}{0.020 - x} = 1.0 \times 10^{-2} \approx \frac{x^2}{0.020}, \ \ x = 1.4 \times 10^{-2} \quad \text{Assumption poor.}$$

Using the quadratic formula: $x^2 + 1.0 \times 10^{-2} \, x - 2.0 \times 10^{-4} = 0$

$x = [OH^-] = 1.0 \times 10^{-2} \, M; \quad pH = 12.00$

j. 20.0 mmol OH^- added, results in 5.0 mmol X^{3-} and 5.0 mmol OH^- excess after OH^- reacts completely. Since K_b for X^{3-} is fairly large for a weak base, we have to worry about the OH^- contribution from X^{3-}.

$$[X^{3-}] = [OH^-] = \frac{5.0 \text{ mmol}}{300.0 \text{ mL}} = 1.7 \times 10^{-2} \, M$$

$$X^{3-} \quad + \quad H_2O \quad \rightleftharpoons \quad OH^- \quad + \quad HX^{2-}$$

Initial	$1.7 \times 10^{-2} \, M$	$1.7 \times 10^{-2} \, M$	0
Equil.	$1.7 \times 10^{-2} - x$	$1.7 \times 10^{-2} + x$	x

$$K_b = \frac{[OH^-][HX^{2-}]}{[X^{3-}]} = 1.0 \times 10^{-2} = \frac{(1.7 \times 10^{-2} + x)x}{(1.7 \times 10^{-2} - x)}$$

Using the quadratic formula: $x^2 + 2.7 \times 10^{-2} \, x - 1.7 \times 10^{-4} = 0, \quad x = 5.3 \times 10^{-3} \, M$

$[OH^-] = 1.7 \times 10^{-2} + x = 1.7 \times 10^{-2} + 5.3 \times 10^{-3} = 2.2 \times 10^{-2} \, M; \quad pH = 12.34$

68. a. Since $K_{a_1} >> K_{a_2} >> K_{a_3}$, then the initial pH is determined by H_3A. Consider only the first dissociation:

$$H_3A \quad \rightleftharpoons \quad H^+ \quad + \quad H_2A^-$$

Initial	$0.100 \, M$	~0	0
Equil.	$0.100 - x$	x	x

$$K_{a_1} = \frac{[H^+][H_2A^-]}{[H_3A]} = \frac{x^2}{0.100 - x} = 1.5 \times 10^{-4} \approx \frac{x^2}{0.100}, \quad x = 3.9 \times 10^{-3}$$

$[H^+] = 3.9 \times 10^{-3} \, M; \quad pH = 2.41$ Assumptions good.

b. $10.0 \text{ mL} \times 1.00 \, M = 10.0$ mmol NaOH. Began with $100.0 \text{ mL} \times 0.100 \, M = 10.0$ mmol H_3A. Added OH^- converts H_3A into H_2A^-. This takes us to the 1st stoichiometric point where the amphoteric H_2A^- is the major species present.

$$pH = \frac{pK_{a_1} + pK_{a_2}}{2} = \frac{3.82 + 7.52}{2} = 5.67$$

c. $25.0 \text{ mL} \times 1.00 \, M = 25.0$ mmol NaOH added. After OH^- reacts completely, the mixture contains 5.00 mmol HA^{2-} and 5.00 mmol A^{3-}.

$$K_{a_3} = \frac{[H^+][A^{3-}]}{[HA^{2-}]}; \quad \text{Since } [A^{3-}] = [HA^{2-}], \text{ then } [H^+] = K_{a_3}; \quad pH = pK_{a_3} = 11.30$$

Assumptions good.

69. **a.** Na^+ is present in all solutions. The added H^+ from HCl reacts completely with CO_3^{2-} to convert it into HCO_3^-. After all CO_3^{2-} is reacted (after point C, the first equivalence point), then H^+ reacts completely with the next best base present, HCO_3^-. Point E represents the second equivalence point. The major species present at the various points after H^+ reacts completely follow.

A. CO_3^{2-}, H_2O B. CO_3^{2-}, HCO_3^-, H_2O, Cl^-

C. HCO_3^-, H_2O, Cl^- D. HCO_3^-, CO_2 (H_2CO_3), H_2O, Cl^-

E. CO_2 (H_2CO_3), H_2O, Cl^- F. H^+ (excess), CO_2 (H_2CO_3), H_2O, Cl^-

b. <u>Point A</u> (initially):

$$CO_3^{2-} + H_2O \;\rightleftharpoons\; HCO_3^- + OH^- \quad K_b(CO_3^{2-}) = \frac{K_w}{K_{a_2}} = \frac{1.0 \times 10^{-14}}{4.8 \times 10^{-11}} = 2.1 \times 10^{-4}$$

	CO_3^{2-}	HCO_3^-	OH^-
Initial	0.100 M	0	~0
Equil.	0.100 - x	x	x

$$K_b = 2.1 \times 10^{-4} = \frac{[HCO_3^-][OH^-]}{[CO_3^{2-}]} = \frac{x^2}{0.100 - x} \approx \frac{x^2}{0.100}$$

$x = 4.6 \times 10^{-3}\ M = [OH^-]$; pH = 11.66   Assumptions good.

<u>Point B</u>: The first halfway point where $[CO_3^{2-}] = [HCO_3^-]$.

pH = pK_{a_2} = -log (4.8×10^{-11}) = 10.32   Assumptions good.

<u>Point C</u>:   First equivalence point (25.00 mL of 0.100 M HCl added). The amphoteric HCO_3^- is the major acid/base species present.

$$pH = \frac{pK_{a_1} + pK_{a_2}}{2}; \quad pK_{a_1} = \text{-log } (4.3 \times 10^{-7}) = 6.37$$

$$pH = \frac{6.37 + 10.32}{2} = 8.35$$

<u>Point D</u>: The second halfway point where $[HCO_3^-] = [H_2CO_3]$.

pH = pK_{a_1} = 6.37   Assumptions good.

<u>Point E</u>: This is the second equivalence point where all of the CO_3^{2-} present initially has been converted into H_2CO_3 by the added strong acid. 50.0 mL HCl added. $[H_2CO_3]$ = 2.50 mmol/75.0 mL = 0.0333 M

$$H_2CO_3 \;\rightleftharpoons\; H^+ + HCO_3^- \qquad K_{a_1} = 4.3 \times 10^{-7}$$

	H_2CO_3	H^+	HCO_3^-
Initial	0.0333 M	0	0
Equil.	0.0333 - x	x	x

$$K_{a_1} = 4.3 \times 10^{-7} = \frac{x^2}{0.0333 - x} \approx \frac{x^2}{0.0333}$$

$x = [H^+] = 1.2 \times 10^{-4} M; \quad pH = 3.92 \quad$ Assumptions good.

70.   a. $HA^- \rightleftharpoons H^+ + A^{2-} \quad K_a = 1 \times 10^{-8}$; When $[HA^-] = [A^{2-}]$, $pH = pK_{a_2} = 8.00$.

The titration reaction is $A^{2-} + H^+ \rightarrow HA^-$ (goes to completion). Begin with 100.0 mL $\times$ 0.200 mmol/mL = 20.0 mmol A^{2-}. We need to convert 10.0 mmol A^{2-} into HA^- by adding 10.0 mmol H^+. This will produce a solution where $[HA^-] = [A^{2-}]$ and $pH = pK_{a_2} = 8.00$.

10.0 mmol = 1.00 mmol/mL $\times$ V, V = 10.0 mL HCl

b.   At the 2nd stoichiometric point, all A^{2-} is converted into H_2A. This requires 40.0 mmol HCl which is 40.0 mL of 1.00 M HCl.

$[H_2A]_0 = \dfrac{20.0 \text{ mmol}}{140.0 \text{ mL}} = 0.143 M$; Since $K_{a_1} >> K_{a_2}$, H_2A is the major source of H^+.

$$H_2A \quad \rightleftharpoons \quad H^+ \quad + \quad HA^-$$

Initial   0.143 M 0   0
Equil.   0.143 - x x x

$K_{a1} = \dfrac{x^2}{0.143 - x} = 1.0 \times 10^{-3} \approx \dfrac{x^2}{0.143}$, $x = 0.012 M$ Check assumptions:

$\dfrac{0.012}{0.143} \times 100 = 8.4\%$; Can't neglect x. Using successive approximations:

$x = 0.0115$ (carrying extra sig. figs) so $[H^+] = 0.0115 M$ and $pH = 1.94$

Solubility Equilibria

71.   In our set-ups, s = solubility in mol/L. Since solids do not appear in the K_{sp} expression, we do not need to worry about their initial or equilibrium amounts.

a. $Ag_3PO_4(s) \quad \rightleftharpoons \quad 3 Ag^+(aq) \quad + \quad PO_4^{3-}(aq)$

Initial   0   0
          s mol/L of $Ag_3PO_4(s)$ dissolves to reach equilibrium
Change $-s$ $\rightarrow$ $+3s$ $+s$
Equil. $3s$ s

$K_{sp} = 1.8 \times 10^{-18} = [Ag^+]^3 [PO_4^{3-}] = (3s)^3(s) = 27s^4$

$27s^4 = 1.8 \times 10^{-18}$, $s = (6.7 \times 10^{-20})^{1/4} = 1.6 \times 10^{-5}$ mol/L = molar solubility

$$\frac{1.6 \times 10^{-5} \text{ mol } Ag_3PO_4}{L} \times \frac{418.7 \text{ g } Ag_3PO_4}{\text{mol } Ag_3PO_4} = 6.7 \times 10^{-3} \text{ g/L}$$

b. $$CaCO_3(s) \rightleftharpoons Ca^{2+}(aq) + CO_3^{2-}(aq)$$

Initial s = solubility (mol/L)   0   0
Equil. s s

$K_{sp} = 8.7 \times 10^{-9} = [Ca^{2+}][CO_3^{2-}] = s^2$, $s = 9.3 \times 10^{-5}$ mol/L

$$\frac{9.3 \times 10^{-5} \text{ mol}}{L} \times \frac{100.1 \text{ g}}{\text{mol}} = 9.3 \times 10^{-3} \text{ g/L}$$

c. $$Hg_2Cl_2(s) \rightleftharpoons Hg_2^{2+}(aq) + 2 Cl^-(aq)$$

Initial s = solubility (mol/L)   0   0
Equil. s $2s$

$K_{sp} = 1.1 \times 10^{-18} = [Hg_2^{2+}][Cl^-]^2 = (s)(2s)^2 = 4s^3$, $s = 6.5 \times 10^{-7}$ mol/L

$$\frac{6.5 \times 10^{-7} \text{ mol}}{L} \times \frac{472.1 \text{ g}}{\text{mol}} = 3.1 \times 10^{-4} \text{ g/L}$$

72.   a. $$PbI_2(s) \rightleftharpoons Pb^{2+}(aq) + 2 I^-(aq)$$

Initial s = solubility (mol/L)   0   0
Equil. s $2s$

$K_{sp} = 1.4 \times 10^{-8} = [Pb^{2+}][I^-]^2 = s(2s)^2 = 4s^3$

$s = (1.4 \times 10^{-8}/4)^{1/3} = 1.5 \times 10^{-3}$ mol/L = molar solubility

b. $$CdCO_3(s) \rightleftharpoons Cd^{2+}(aq) + CO_3^{2-}(aq)$$
Initial s = solubility (mol/L)   0   0
Equil. s s

$K_{sp} = 5.2 \times 10^{-12} = [Cd^{2+}][CO_3^{2-}] = s^2$, $s = 2.3 \times 10^{-6}$ mol/L

c. $$Sr_3(PO_4)_2(s) \rightleftharpoons 3 Sr^{2+}(aq) + 2 PO_4^{3-}(aq)$$

Initial s = solubility (mol/L)   0   0
Equil. $3s$ $2s$

$K_{sp} = 1 \times 10^{-31} = [Sr^{2+}]^3[PO_4^{3-}]^2 = (3s)^3(2s)^2 = 108 s^5$, $s = 2 \times 10^{-7}$ mol/L

73.   In our set-up, s = solubility of the ionic solid in mol/L. This is defined as the maximum amount of a salt which can dissolve. Since solids do not appear in the K_{sp} expression, we do not need to worry about their initial and equilibrium amounts.

a. $CaC_2O_4(s)$ $\rightleftharpoons$ $Ca^{2+}(aq)$ + $C_2O_4^{2-}(aq)$

Initial   0   0
            s mol/L of $CaC_2O_4(s)$ dissolves to reach equilibrium
Change   -s $\rightarrow$ +s   +s
Equil.   s   s

From the problem, $s = 4.8 \times 10^{-5}$ mol/L.

$K_{sp} = [Ca^{2+}] [C_2O_4^{2-}] = (s)(s) = s^2$, $K_{sp} = (4.8 \times 10^{-5})^2 = 2.3 \times 10^{-9}$

b. $PbBr_2(s)$ $\rightleftharpoons$ $Pb^{2+}(aq)$ + $2 Br^-(aq)$

Initial   0   0
            s mol/L of $PbBr_2(s)$ dissolves to reach equilibrium
Change   -s $\rightarrow$ +s   +2s
Equil.   s   2s

From the problem, $s = [Pb^{2+}] = 2.14 \times 10^{-2} M$. So:

$K_{sp} = [Pb^{2+}] [Br^-]^2 = s(2s)^2 = 4s^3$, $K_{sp} = 4(2.14 \times 10^{-2})^3 = 3.92 \times 10^{-5}$

c. $BiI_3(s)$ $\rightleftharpoons$ $Bi^{3+}(aq)$ + $3 I^-(aq)$

Initial   0   0
            s mol/L of $BiI_3(s)$ dissolves to reach equilibrium
Change   -s $\rightarrow$ +s   +3s
Equil.   s   3s

$K_{sp} = [Bi^{3+}] [I^-]^3 = (s)(3s)^3 = 27 s^4$, $K_{sp} = 27(1.32 \times 10^{-5})^4 = 8.20 \times 10^{-19}$

d. $FeC_2O_4(s)$ $\rightleftharpoons$ Fe^{2+} + $C_2O_4^{2-}$

Initial   s = solubility (mol/L)   0   0
Equil.   s   s

$s = \dfrac{65.9 \times 10^{-3}\text{ g}}{L} \times \dfrac{1\text{ mol}}{143.9\text{ g}} = 4.58 \times 10^{-4}$ mol/L

$[Fe^{2+}] = [C_2O_4^{2-}] = 4.58 \times 10^{-4} M$; $K_{sp} = [Fe^{2+}] [C_2O_4^{2-}] = (4.58 \times 10^{-4})^2 = 2.10 \times 10^{-7}$

e. $Cu(IO_4)_2(s)$ $\rightleftharpoons$ Cu^{2+} + $2 IO_4^-$

Initial   s = solubility (mol/L   0   0
Equil.   s   2s

$s = \dfrac{0.146\text{ g Cu(IO}_4)_2}{0.100\text{ L}} \times \dfrac{1\text{ mol}}{445.4\text{ g}} = 3.28 \times 10^{-3}$ mol/L

$K_{sp} = [Cu^{2+}] [IO_4^-]^2 = (3.28 \times 10^{-3}) (6.56 \times 10^{-3})^2 = 1.41 \times 10^{-7}$

74.   a. $Pb_3(PO_4)_2(s)$ $\rightleftharpoons$ $3\ Pb^{2+}(aq)\ +\ 2\ PO_4^{3-}(aq)$

Initial   0   0

s mol/L of $Pb_3(PO_4)_2(s)$ dissolves to reach equilibrium = molar solubility

Change $-s$ $\rightarrow$ $+3s$ $+2s$
Equil. $3s$ $2s$

$K_{sp} = [Pb^{2+}]^3\ [PO_4^{3-}]^2 = (3s)^3(2s)^2 = 108\ s^5,\ \ K_{sp} = 108(6.2 \times 10^{-12})^5 = 9.9 \times 10^{-55}$

   b. $Li_2CO_3(s)$ $\rightleftharpoons$ $2\ Li^+(aq)\ +\ CO_3^{2-}(aq)$

Initial s = solubility (mol/L)   0   0
Equil. $2s$ s

$K_{sp} = [Li^+]^2\ [CO_3^{2-}] = (2s)^2(s) = 4s^3,\ K_{sp} = 4(7.4 \times 10^{-2})^3 = 1.6 \times 10^{-3}$

75.   a.   Since both solids dissolve to produce 3 ions in solution, then we can compare values of K_{sp} to determine relative solubility. Since the K_{sp} for CaF_2 is the smallest, then $CaF_2(s)$ has the smallest molar solubility.

   b.   We must calculate molar solubilities since each salt yields a different number of ions when it dissolves.

                          $Ca_3(PO_4)_2(s)$ $\rightleftharpoons$ $3\ Ca^{2+}(aq)\ +\ 2\ PO_4^{3-}(aq)$ $K_{sp} = 1.3 \times 10^{-32}$

Initial s = solubility (mol/L)   0   0
Equil. $3s$ $2s$

$K_{sp} = [Ca^{2+}]^3\ [PO_4^{3-}]^2 = (3s)^3(2s)^2 = 108s^5,\ \ s = (1.3 \times 10^{-32}/108)^{1/5} = 1.6 \times 10^{-7}$ mol/L

                          $FePO_4(s)$ $\rightleftharpoons$ $Fe^{3+}(aq)\ +\ PO_4^{3-}(aq)$ $K_{sp} = 1.0 \times 10^{-22}$

Initial s = solubility (mol/L)   0   0
Equil. s s

$K_{sp} = [Fe^{3+}]\ [PO_4^{3-}] = s^2,\ \ s = \sqrt{1.0 \times 10^{-22}} = 1.0 \times 10^{-11}$ mol/L

$FePO_4$ has the smallest molar solubility.

76.   a. $Ag_2SO_4(s)$ $\rightleftharpoons$ $2\ Ag^+(aq)\ +\ SO_4^{2-}(aq)$

Initial s = solubility (mol/L)   0   0
Equil. $2s$ s

$K_{sp} = 1.2 \times 10^{-5} = [Ag^+]^2\ [SO_4^{2-}] = (2s)^2 s = 4s^3,\ \ s = 1.4 \times 10^{-2}$ mol/L

   b. $Ag_2SO_4(s)$ $\rightleftharpoons$ $2\ Ag^+(aq)\ +\ SO_4^{2-}(aq)$

Initial s = solubility (mol/L)   0.10 M 0
Equil.   0.10 + 2s s

$K_{sp} = 1.2 \times 10^{-5} = (0.10 + 2s)^2(s) \approx (0.10)^2(s),\ \ s = 1.2 \times 10^{-3}$ mol/L;   Assumption good.

c. $Ag_2SO_4(s)$ $\rightleftharpoons$ $2 Ag^+(aq)$ + $SO_4^{2-}(aq)$

Initial s = solubility (mol/L)   0   0.20 M
Equil $2s$ $0.20 + s$

$1.2 \times 10^{-5} = (2s)^2(0.20 + s) \approx 4s^2(0.20)$, $s = 3.9 \times 10^{-3}$ mol/L; Assumption good.

Note: Comparing the solubilities in parts b and c to part a illustrates that the solubility of a salt decreases when a common ion is present.

77. a. $Fe(OH)_3(s)$ $\rightleftharpoons$ Fe^{3+} + $3 OH^-$ pH = 7.0 so $[OH^-] = 1 \times 10^{-7}\ M$

Initial   0 $1 \times 10^{-7}\ M$

s mol/L of $Fe(OH)_3(s)$ dissolves to reach equilibrium = molar solubility

Change $-s$ $\rightarrow$ $+s$ $+3s$
Equil. s $3s + 1 \times 10^{-7}$

$K_{sp} = 4 \times 10^{-38} = [Fe^{3+}] [OH^-]^3 = (s)(3s + 1 \times 10^{-7})^3 \approx s(1 \times 10^{-7})^3$

$s = 4 \times 10^{-17}$ mol/L   Assumption good ($3s << 1 \times 10^{-7}$).

b. $Fe(OH)_3(s)$ $\rightleftharpoons$ Fe^{3+} + $3 OH^-$ pH = 5.0 so $[OH^-] = 1 \times 10^{-9}\ M$

Initial   0 $1 \times 10^{-9}\ M$ (buffered)
                    s mol/L dissolves to reach equilibrium
Change $-s$ $\rightarrow$ $+s$ -----   (assume no pH change in
                                                                        buffer)
Equil. s 1×10^{-9}

$K_{sp} = 4 \times 10^{-38} = [Fe^{3+}] [OH^-]^3 = (s)(1 \times 10^{-9})^3$, $s = 4 \times 10^{-11}$ mol/L = molar solubility

c. $Fe(OH)_3(s)$ $\rightleftharpoons$ Fe^{3+} + $3 OH^-$ pH = 11.0 so $[OH^-] = 1 \times 10^{-3}\ M$

Initial   0   0.001 M (buffered)
                    s mol/L dissolves to reach equilibrium
Change $-s$ $\rightarrow$ $+s$ -----   (assume no pH change)
Equil. s 0.001

$K_{sp} = 4 \times 10^{-38} = [Fe^{3+}] [OH^-]^3 = (s)(0.001)^3$, $s = 4 \times 10^{-29}$ mol/L = molar solubility

Note: As $[OH^-]$ increases, solubility decreases. This is the common ion effect.

78. $Ce(IO_3)_3(s)$ $\rightleftharpoons$ $Ce^{3+}(aq)$ + $3 IO_3^-(aq)$

Initial s = solubility (mol/L)   0   0.20 M
Equil. s $0.20 + 3s$

$K_{sp} = [Ce^{3+}] [IO_3^-]^3 = s(0.20 + 3s)^3$

From the problem, $s = 4.4 \times 10^{-8}$ mol/L; Solving for K_{sp}:

$$K_{sp} = (4.4 \times 10^{-8}) \times [0.20 + 3(4.4 \times 10^{-8})]^3 = 3.5 \times 10^{-10}$$

79. If the anion in the salt can act as a base in water, then the solubility of the salt will increase as the solution becomes more acidic. Added H^+ will react with the base forming the conjugate acid. As the basic anion is removed, more of the salt will dissolve to replenish the basic anion. The salts with basic anions are Ag_3PO_4, $CaCO_3$, $CdCO_3$ and $Sr_3(PO_4)_2$. Hg_2Cl_2 and PbI_2 do not have any pH dependence since Cl^- and I^- are terrible bases (the conjugate bases of a strong acids).

$$Ag_3PO_4(s) + H^+(aq) \rightarrow 3\ Ag^+(aq) + HPO_4^{2-}(aq) \xrightarrow{\text{excess } H^+} 3\ Ag^+(aq) + H_3PO_4(aq)$$

$$CaCO_3(s) + H^+ \rightarrow Ca^{2+} + HCO_3^- \xrightarrow{\text{excess } H^+} Ca^{2+} + H_2CO_3\ [H_2O(l) + CO_2(g)]$$

$$CdCO_3(s) + H^+ \rightarrow Cd^{2+} + HCO_3^- \xrightarrow{\text{excess } H^+} Cd^{2+} + H_2CO_3\ [H_2O(l) + CO_2(g)]$$

$$Sr_3(PO_4)_2(s) + 2\ H^+ \rightarrow 3\ Sr^{2+} + 2\ HPO_4^{2-} \xrightarrow{\text{excess } H^+} 3\ Sr^{2+} + 2\ H_3PO_4$$

80.

	$Ca_5(PO_4)_3OH(s)$	$\rightleftharpoons$	$5\ Ca^{2+}$	$+$	$3\ PO_4^{3-}$	$+$	OH^-
Initial	s = solubility (mol/L)		0		0		1.0×10^{-7}
Equil.			$5s$		$3s$		$s + 1.0 \times 10^{-7} \approx s$

$K_{sp} = 6.8 \times 10^{-37} = [Ca^{2+}]^5\ [PO_4^{3-}]^3\ [OH^-] = (5s)^5(3s)^3(s)$

$6.8 \times 10^{-37} = (3125)(27)s^9$, $s = 2.7 \times 10^{-5}$ mol/L   Assumption good.

The solubility of hydroxyapatite will increase as the solution gets more acidic. Both the phosphate and hydroxide ions can react with H^+ since they are bases in water.

	$Ca_5(PO_4)_3F(s)$	$\rightleftharpoons$	$5\ Ca^{2+}$	$+$	$3\ PO_4^{3-}$	$+$	F^-
Initial	s = solubility (mol/L)		0		0		0
Equil.			$5s$		$3s$		s

$K_{sp} = 1 \times 10^{-60} = (5s)^5(3s)^3(s) = (3125)(27)s^9$, $s = 6 \times 10^{-8}$ mol/L

The hydroxyapatite in the tooth enamel is converted to the less soluble fluorapatite by fluoride treated water. The less soluble fluorapatite is more difficult to remove, making teeth less susceptible to decay.

81. The formation of $Mg(OH)_2(s)$ is the only possible precipitate. $Mg(OH)_2(s)$ will form if $Q > K_{sp}$.

$$Mg(OH)_2(s) \rightleftharpoons Mg^{2+}(aq) + 2\ OH^-(aq)\quad K_{sp} = [Mg^{2+}][OH^-]^2 = 8.9 \times 10^{-12}$$

$$[Mg^{2+}]_0 = \frac{100.0 \text{ mL} \times 4.0 \times 10^{-4} \text{ mmol Mg}^{2+}/\text{mL}}{100.0 \text{ mL} + 100.0 \text{ mL}} = 2.0 \times 10^{-4} \, M$$

$$[OH^-]_0 = \frac{100.0 \text{ mL} \times 2.0 \times 10^{-4} \text{ mmol OH}^-/\text{mL}}{200.0 \text{ mL}} = 1.0 \times 10^{-4} \, M$$

$$Q = [Mg^{2+}]_0[OH^-]_0^2 = (2.0 \times 10^{-4} \, M)(1.0 \times 10^{-4})^2 = 2.0 \times 10^{-12}$$

Since $Q < K_{sp}$, then $Mg(OH)_2(s)$ will not precipitate, so no precipitate forms.

82. $$[Ba^{2+}]_0 = \frac{75.0 \text{ mL} \times \dfrac{0.020 \text{ mmol}}{\text{mL}}}{200. \text{ mL}} = 7.5 \times 10^{-3} \, M$$

$$[SO_4^{2-}]_0 = \frac{125 \text{ mL} \times \dfrac{0.040 \text{ mmol}}{\text{mL}}}{200. \text{ mL}} = 2.5 \times 10^{-2} \, M$$

$$Q = [Ba^{2+}]_0[SO_4^{2-}]_0 = (7.5 \times 10^{-3})(2.5 \times 10^{-2}) = 1.9 \times 10^{-4} > K_{sp} (1.5 \times 10^{-9})$$

A precipitate of $BaSO_4(s)$ will form.

	$BaSO_4(s)$	$\rightleftharpoons$	Ba^{2+}	$+$	SO_4^{2-}	
Before			0.0075 M		0.025 M	

Let 0.0075 mol/L Ba^{2+} react with SO_4^{2-} to completion since $K_{sp} << 1$.

Change		$\leftarrow$	-0.0075		-0.0075	Reacts completely
After			0		0.0175	New initial (carry extra S.F.)

s mol/L $BaSO_4$ dissolves to reach equilibrium

Change	-s	$\rightarrow$	+s		+s	
Equil.			s		0.0175 + s	

$$K_{sp} = 1.5 \times 10^{-9} = [Ba^{2+}][SO_4^{2-}] = (s)(0.0175 + s) \approx s(0.0175)$$

$s = 8.6 \times 10^{-8}$ mol/L; $[Ba^{2+}] = 8.6 \times 10^{-8} \, M$; $[SO_4^{2-}] = 0.018 \, M$ Assumption good.

83.   The concentrations of ions are large, so Q will be greater than K_{sp} and $BaC_2O_4(s)$ will form. To solve this problem, we will assume that the precipitation reaction goes to completion; then we will solve an equilibrium problem to get the actual ion concentrations.

$$100. \text{ mL} \times \frac{0.200 \text{ mmol K}_2C_2O_4}{\text{mL}} = 20.0 \text{ mmol K}_2C_2O_4$$

$$150. \text{ mL} \times \frac{0.250 \text{ mmol BaBr}_2}{\text{mL}} = 37.5 \text{ mmol BaBr}_2$$

$$Ba^{2+}(aq) \quad + \quad C_2O_4^{2-}(aq) \quad \rightarrow \quad BaC_2O_4(s) \qquad K = 1/K_{sp} \gg 1$$

Before	37.5 mmol	20.0 mmol		0
Change	-20.0	-20.0	$\rightarrow$	+20.0
After	17.5	0		20.0

Reacts completely (K is large)

New initial concentrations (after complete precipitation) are: $[Ba^{2+}] = \dfrac{17.5 \text{ mmol}}{250. \text{ mL}} = 7.00 \times 10^{-2} \, M$

$[K^+] = \dfrac{2(20.0 \text{ mmol})}{250. \text{ mL}} = 0.160 \, M; \quad [Br^-] = \dfrac{2(37.5 \text{ mmol})}{250. \text{ mL}} = 0.300 \, M$

For K^+ and Br^-, these are also the final concentrations. For Ba^{2+} and $C_2O_4^{2-}$, we need to perform an equilibrium calculation.

$$BaC_2O_4(s) \quad \rightleftharpoons \quad Ba^{2+}(aq) \quad + \quad C_2O_4^{2-}(aq) \qquad K_{sp} = 2.3 \times 10^{-8}$$

Initial	0.0700 M	0

s mol/L of $BaC_2O_4(s)$ dissolves to reach equilibrium

Equil.	0.0700 + s	s

$K_{sp} = 2.3 \times 10^{-8} = [Ba^{2+}] [C_2O_4^{2-}] = (0.0700 + s)(s) \approx 0.0700 \, s$

$s = [C_2O_4^{2-}] = 3.3 \times 10^{-7}$ mol/L; $[Ba^{2+}] = 0.0700 \, M$ Assumption good ($s \ll 0.0700$).

84.   50.0 mL $\times$ 0.10 M = 5.0 mmol Pb^{2+}; 50.0 mL $\times$ 1.0 M = 50. mmol Cl^-. For this solution, $Q > K_{sp}$, so $PbCl_2$ precipitates. Assume precipitation of $PbCl_2(s)$ is complete. 5.0 mmol Pb^{2+} requires 10. mmol of Cl^- for complete precipitation, which leaves 40. mmol Cl^- in excess. Now, let some of the $PbCl_2(s)$ redissolve to establish equilibrium

$$PbCl_2(s) \quad \rightleftharpoons \quad Pb^{2+}(aq) \quad + \quad 2 \, Cl^-(aq)$$

Initial	0	$\dfrac{40. \text{ mmol}}{100.0 \text{ mL}} = 0.40 \, M$

s mol/L of $PbCl_2(s)$ dissolves to reach equilibrium

Equil.	s	0.40 + 2s

$K_{sp} = [Pb^{2+}] [Cl^-]^2, \quad 1.6 \times 10^{-5} = s(0.40 + 2s)^2 \approx s(0.40)^2$

$s = 1.0 \times 10^{-4}$ mol/L;   Assumption good.

At equilibrium: $[Pb^{2+}] = s = 1.0 \times 10^{-4}$ mol/L; $[Cl^-] = 0.40 + 2s, \; 0.40 + 2(1.0 \times 10^{-4}) = 0.40 \, M$

85. $Ag_3PO_4(s) \rightleftharpoons 3 \, Ag^+(aq) + PO_4^{3-}(aq)$; When Q is greater than K_{sp}, then precipitation will occur. We will calculate the $[Ag^+]_o$ necessary for $Q = K_{sp}$. Any $[Ag^+]_o$ greater than this calculated number will cause precipitation of $Ag_3PO_4(s)$. In this problem, $[PO_4^{3-}]_o = [Na_3PO_4]_o = 1.0 \times 10^{-5} \, M$.

$K_{sp} = 1.8 \times 10^{-18};$ $Q = 1.8 \times 10^{-18} = [Ag^+]_o^3 \, [PO_4^{3-}]_o = [Ag^+]_o^3 \, (1.0 \times 10^{-5} \, M)$

$$[Ag^+]_o = \left(\frac{1.8 \times 10^{-18}}{1.0 \times 10^{-5}} \right)^{1/3}, \quad [Ag^+]_o = 5.6 \times 10^{-5} \, M$$

When $[Ag^+]_o = [AgNO_3]_o$ is greater than $5.6 \times 10^{-5} \, M$, then $Ag_3PO_4(s)$ will precipitate.

86.   From Table 8.5, K_{sp} for $NiCO_3 = 1.4 \times 10^{-7}$ and K_{sp} for $CuCO_3 = 2.5 \times 10^{-10}$. From the K_{sp} values $CuCO_3$ will precipitate first since it has the smaller K_{sp} value and will be least soluble. For $CuCO_3(s)$, precipitation begins when:

$$[CO_3^{2-}] = \frac{K_{sp, \, CuCO_3}}{[Cu^{2+}]} = \frac{2.5 \times 10^{-10}}{0.25 \, M} = 1.0 \times 10^{-9} \, M \, CO_3^{2-}$$

For $NiCO_3(s)$ to precipitate:

$$[CO_3^{2-}] = \frac{K_{sp, \, NiCO_3}}{[Ni^{2+}]} = \frac{1.4 \times 10^{-7}}{0.25 \, M} = 5.6 \times 10^{-7} \, M \, CO_3^{2-}$$

Determining the $[Cu^{2+}]$ when $NiCO_3(s)$ begins to precipitate:

$$[Cu^{2+}] = \frac{K_{sp, \, CuCO_3}}{[CO_3^{2-}]} = \frac{2.5 \times 10^{-10}}{5.6 \times 10^{-7} \, M} = 4.5 \times 10^{-4} \, M \, Cu^{2+}$$

For successful separation, 1% Cu^{2+} or less of the initial amount of Cu^{2+} (0.25 M) must be present before $NiCO_3(s)$ begins to precipitate. The percent of Cu^{2+} present when $NiCO_3(s)$ begins to precipitate is:

$$\frac{4.5 \times 10^{-4} \, M}{0.25 \, M} \times 100 = 0.18\% \, Cu^{2+}$$

Since less than 1% Cu^{2+} remains of the initial amount, then the metals can be separated through slow addition of $Na_2CO_3(aq)$.

87.   a.

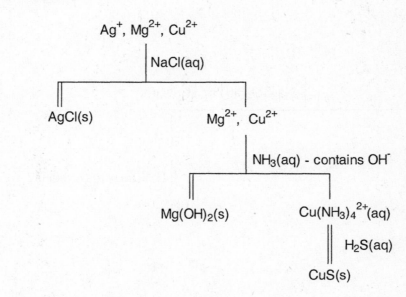

b.

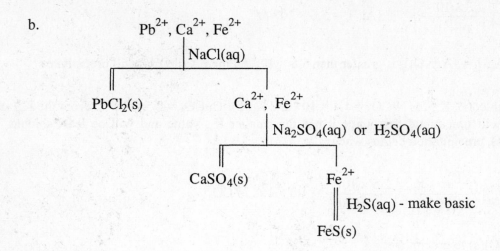

c.

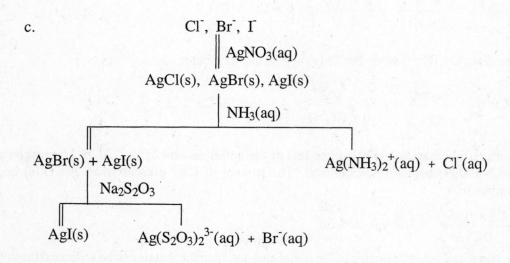

d.

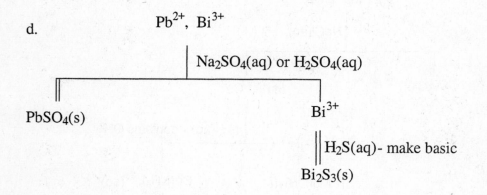

Complex Ion Equilibria

88.
$$Mn^{2+} + C_2O_4^{2-} \rightleftharpoons MnC_2O_4 \qquad K_1 = 7.9 \times 10^3$$
$$MnC_2O_4 + C_2O_4^{2-} \rightleftharpoons Mn(C_2O_4)_2^{2-} \qquad K_2 = 7.9 \times 10^1$$

$$Mn^{2+}(aq) + 2\ C_2O_4^{2-}(aq) \rightleftharpoons Mn(C_2O_4)_2^{2-}(aq) \qquad K_f = K_1K_2 = 6.2 \times 10^5$$

89. $Hg^{2+}(aq) + 2\ I^-(aq) \rightarrow HgI_2(s)$, orange ppt; $HgI_2(s) + 2\ I^-(aq) \rightarrow HgI_4^{2-}(aq)$, soluble complex ion

90. $Ag^+(aq) + Cl^-(aq) \rightleftharpoons AgCl(s)$, white ppt.; $AgCl(s) + 2\ NH_3(aq) \rightleftharpoons Ag(NH_3)_2^+(aq) + Cl^-(aq)$

$Ag(NH_3)_2^+(aq) + Br^-(aq) \rightleftharpoons AgBr(s) + 2\ NH_3(aq)$, pale yellow ppt.

$AgBr(s) + 2\ S_2O_3^{2-}(aq) \rightleftharpoons Ag(S_2O_3)_2^{3-}(aq) + Br^-(aq)$

$Ag(S_2O_3)_2^{3-}(aq) + I^-(aq) \rightleftharpoons AgI(s) + 2\ S_2O_3^{2-}(aq)$, yellow ppt.

The least soluble salt (smallest K_{sp} value) must be AgI since it forms in the presence of Cl^- and Br^-. The most soluble salt (largest K_{sp} value) must be AgCl since it forms initially, but never reforms. The order of K_{sp} values are: K_{sp} (AgCl) > K_{sp} (AgBr) > K_{sp} (AgI)

The order of formation constants is $K_f[Ag(S_2O_3)_2^{3-}] > K_f[Ag(NH_3)_2^+]$ since addition of $S_2O_3^{2-}$ causes the AgBr(s) precipitate to dissolve but the presence of NH_3 was unable to prevent AgBr(s) from forming. This assumes concentrations are about equal.

91. $\dfrac{65\ g\ KI}{0.500\ L} \times \dfrac{1\ mol\ KI}{166.0\ g\ KI} = 0.78\ M\ KI$

The formation constant for HgI_4^{2-} is an extremely large number. Because of this, we will let the Hg^{2+} and I^- ions present initially react to completion, and then solve an equilibrium problem to determine the Hg^{2+} concentration.

	Hg^{2+}	+	$4\ I^-$	$\rightleftharpoons$	HgI_4^{2-}	$K = 1.0 \times 10^{30}$
Before	0.010 M		0.78 M		0	
Change	-0.010		-0.040	$\rightarrow$	+0.010	Reacts completely (K large)
After	0		0.74		0.010	New initial

x mol/L HgI_4^{2-} dissociates to reach equilibrium

Change	+x		+$4x$	$\leftarrow$	-x	
Equil.	x		0.74 + $4x$		0.010 - x	

$$K = 1.0 \times 10^{30} = \frac{[HgI_4^{2-}]}{[Hg^{2+}][I^-]^4} = \frac{(0.010 - x)}{(x)(0.74 + 4x)^4}; \text{ Making normal assumptions:}$$

$$1.0 \times 10^{30} \approx \frac{(0.010)}{(x)(0.74)^4}, \quad x = [Hg^{2+}] = 3.3 \times 10^{-32} \; M \quad \text{Assumptions good.}$$

Note: 3.3×10^{-32} mol/L corresponds to one Hg^{2+} ion per 5×10^7 L. It is very reasonable to approach the equilibrium in two steps. The reaction does essentially go to completion.

92. Fe^{3+} + $6\,CN^-$ $\rightleftharpoons$ $Fe(CN)_6^{3-}$ $K = 1 \times 10^{42}$

Initial	0	2.0 M	0.090 mol/0.60 L = 0.15 M

         x mol/L $Fe(CN)_6^{3-}$ dissociates to reach equilibrium

Change	$+x$	$+6x$ $\leftarrow$	$-x$
Equil.	x	$2.0 + 6x$	$0.15 - x$

$$K = 1 \times 10^{42} = \frac{[Fe(CN)_6^{3-}]}{[Fe^{3+}][CN^-]^6} = \frac{(0.15 - x)}{(x)(2.0 + 6x)^6}, \quad 1 \times 10^{42} \approx \frac{(0.15)}{(x)(2.0)^6}$$

$x = [Fe^{3+}] = 2 \times 10^{-45} \; M; \quad [Fe(CN)_6^{3-}] = 0.15 \; M - x = 0.15 \; M \quad$ Assumptions good.

93.   a. $Cu(OH)_2 \rightleftharpoons Cu^{2+} + 2\,OH^-$ $K_{sp} = 1.6 \times 10^{-19}$

                      $Cu^{2+} + 4\,NH_3 \rightleftharpoons Cu(NH_3)_4^{2+}$ $K_f = 1.0 \times 10^{13}$

                     _____

       $Cu(OH)_2(s) + 4\,NH_3(aq) \rightleftharpoons Cu(NH_3)_4^{2+}(aq) + 2\,OH^-(aq)$ $K = K_{sp}K_f = 1.6 \times 10^{-6}$

   b. $Cu(OH)_2(s)$ + $4\,NH_3$ $\rightleftharpoons$ $Cu(NH_3)_4^{2+}$ + $2\,OH^-$ $K = 1.6 \times 10^{-6}$

Initial	5.0 M	0	0.0095 M

         s mol/L $Cu(OH)_2$ dissolves to reach equilibrium

Equil.	$5.0 - 4s$	s	$0.0095 + 2s$

$$K = 1.6 \times 10^{-6} = \frac{[Cu(NH_3)_4^{2+}][OH^-]^2}{[NH_3]^4} = \frac{s(0.0095 + 2s)^2}{(5.0 - 4s)^4}$$

If s is small: $1.6 \times 10^{-6} = \dfrac{s(0.0095)^2}{(5.0)^4}, \quad s = 11. \text{ mol/L}$

Assumptions are not good. We will solve the problem by successive approximations.

$$s_{calc} = \frac{1.6 \times 10^{-6} (5.0 - 4s_{guess})^4}{(0.0095 + 2s_{guess})^2}, \quad \text{The results from six trials are:}$$

     s_{guess}:   0.10, 0.050, 0.060, 0.055, 0.056

     s_{calc}: 1.6×10^{-2}, 0.071, 0.049, 0.058, 0.056

Thus, the solubility of $Cu(OH)_2$ is 0.056 mol/L in 5.0 M NH_3.

94.   a. $CuCl(s)$ $\rightleftharpoons$ Cu^+ $+$ Cl^-

Initial s = solubility (mol/L)   0   0
Equil. s s

$K_{sp} = 1.2 \times 10^{-6} = [Cu^+][Cl^-] = s^2$, $s = 1.1 \times 10^{-3}$ mol/L

b. Cu^+ forms the complex ion $CuCl_2^-$ in the presence of Cl^-. We will consider both the K_{sp} reaction and the complex ion reaction at the same time.

$$CuCl(s) \rightleftharpoons Cu^+(aq) + Cl^-(aq) \qquad\qquad K_{sp} = 1.2 \times 10^{-6}$$
$$Cu^+(aq) + 2\,Cl^-(aq) \rightleftharpoons CuCl_2^-(aq) \qquad\qquad K_f = 8.7 \times 10^4$$

$$CuCl(s) + Cl^-(aq) \rightleftharpoons CuCl_2^-(aq) \qquad\qquad K = K_{sp} \times K_f = 0.10$$

$$CuCl(s) + Cl^- \rightleftharpoons CuCl_2^-$$

Initial   0.10 M 0
Equil.   0.10 - s s where s = solubility of CuCl(s) in mol/L

$K = 0.10 = \dfrac{[CuCl_2^-]}{[Cl^-]} = \dfrac{s}{0.10 - s}$, $1.0 \times 10^{-2} - 0.10\,s = s$, $1.10\,s = 1.0 \times 10^{-2}$, $s = 9.1 \times 10^{-3}$ mol/L

95. $AgBr(s) \rightleftharpoons Ag^+ + Br^-$ $K_{sp} = 5.0 \times 10^{-13}$
                 $Ag^+ + 2\,S_2O_3^{2-} \rightleftharpoons Ag(S_2O_3)_2^{3-}$ $K_f = 2.9 \times 10^{13}$

$AgBr(s) + 2\,S_2O_3^{2-} \rightleftharpoons Ag(S_2O_3)_2^{3-} + Br^-$ $K = K_{sp} \times K_f = 14.5$ (Carry extra sig. figs.)

$$AgBr(s) + 2\,S_2O_3^{2-} \rightleftharpoons Ag(S_2O_3)_2^{3-} + Br^-$$

Initial   0.500 M 0   0
                 s mol/L AgBr(s) dissolves to reach equilibrium
Change $-s$ $-2s$ $\rightarrow$ $+s$ $+s$
Equil.   0.500 - 2s s s

$K = \dfrac{s^2}{(0.500 - 2s)^2} = 14.5$;   Taking the square root of both sides:

$\dfrac{s}{0.500 - 2s} = 3.81$, $s = 1.91 - 7.62\,s$, $s = 0.222$ mol/L

$1.00\ L \times \dfrac{0.222\ \text{mol AgBr}}{L} \times \dfrac{187.8\ \text{g AgBr}}{\text{mol AgBr}} = 41.7$ g AgBr = 42 g AgBr

96.   a. $AgI(s)$ $\rightleftharpoons$ $Ag^+(aq)$ $+$ $I^-(aq)$ $K_{sp} = [Ag^+][I^-] = 1.5 \times 10^{-16}$

Initial s = solubility (mol/L)   0   0
Equil. s s

$K_{sp} = 1.5 \times 10^{-16} = s^2$, $s = 1.2 \times 10^{-8}$ mol/L

b.
$$AgI(s) \rightleftharpoons Ag^+ + I^- \qquad\qquad K_{sp} = 1.5 \times 10^{-16}$$
$$Ag^+ + 2\,NH_3 \rightleftharpoons Ag(NH_3)_2^+ \qquad K_f = 1.7 \times 10^7$$

$$AgI(s) + 2\,NH_3(aq) \rightleftharpoons Ag(NH_3)_2^+(aq) + I^-(aq) \qquad K = K_{sp} \times K_f = 2.6 \times 10^{-9}$$

	$AgI(s)$	+	$2\,NH_3$	$\rightleftharpoons$	$Ag(NH_3)_2^+$	+	I^-
Initial			$3.0\,M$		0		0

s mol/L of AgI(s) dissolves to reach equilibrium = molar solubility

| Equil. | | | $3.0 - 2s$ | | s | | s |

$$K = \frac{[Ag(NH_3)_2^+][I^-]}{[NH_3]^2} = \frac{s^2}{(3.0 - 2s)^2} = 2.6 \times 10^{-9} \approx \frac{s^2}{(3.0)^2}, \quad s = 1.5 \times 10^{-4} \text{ mol/L}$$

Assumption good.

c.   The presence of NH_3 increases the solubility of AgI. Added NH_3 removes Ag^+ from solution by forming the complex ion, $Ag(NH_3)_2^+$. As Ag^+ is removed, more AgI(s) will dissolve to replenish the Ag^+ concentration.

97.   Test tube 1: added Cl^- reacts with Ag^+ to form a silver chloride precipitate. The net ionic equation is $Ag^+(aq) + Cl^-(aq) \rightarrow AgCl(s)$. Test tube 2: added NH_3 reacts with Ag^+ ions to form a soluble complex ion, $Ag(NH_3)_2^+$. As this complex ion forms, Ag^+ is removed from the solution, which causes the AgCl(s) to dissolve. When enough NH_3 is added, all of the silver chloride precipitate will dissolve. The equation is $AgCl(s) + 2\,NH_3(aq) \rightarrow Ag(NH_3)_2^+(aq) + Cl^-(aq)$. Test tube 3: added H^+ reacts with the weak base, NH_3, to form NH_4^+. As NH_3 is removed from the $Ag(NH_3)_2^+$ complex ion, Ag^+ ions are released to solution and can then react with Cl^- to reform AgCl(s). The equations are $Ag(NH_3)_2^+(aq) + 2\,H^+(aq) \rightarrow Ag^+(aq) + 2\,NH_4^+(aq)$ and $Ag^+(aq) + Cl^-(aq) \rightarrow AgCl(s)$.

Additional Exercises

98. $1.0 \text{ mL} \times \dfrac{1.0 \text{ mmol}}{\text{mL}} = 1.0 \text{ mmol } Cd^{2+}$ added to the ammonia solution

Thus, $[Cd^{2+}]_0 = 1.0 \times 10^{-3}$ mol/L. We will first calculate the equilibrium Cd^{2+} concentration using the complex ion equilibrium, then determine if this Cd^{2+} concentration is large enough to cause precipitation of $Cd(OH)_2(s)$.

	Cd^{2+}	+	$4\,NH_3$	$\rightleftharpoons$	$Cd(NH_3)_4^{2+}$	$K_f = 1.0 \times 10^7$

Before	$1.0 \times 10^{-3}\,M$	$5.0\,M$		0	
Change	-1.0×10^{-3}	-4.0×10^{-3}	$\rightarrow$	$+1.0 \times 10^{-3}$	Reacts completely
After	0	$4.996 \approx 5.0$		1.0×10^{-3}	New initial

x mol/L $Cd(NH_3)_4^{2+}$ dissociates to reach equilibrium

| Change | $+x$ | $+4x$ | $\leftarrow$ | $-x$ | |
| Equil. | x | $5.0 + 4x$ | | $0.0010 - x$ | |

$$K_f = 1.0 \times 10^7 = \frac{(0.0010 - x)}{(x)(5.0 + 4x)^4} \approx \frac{(0.0010)}{(x)(5.0)^4}$$

$x = [Cd^{2+}] = 1.6 \times 10^{-13}$ M; Assumptions good. This is the maximum $[Cd^{2+}]$ possible. Now we will determine if $Cd(OH)_2(s)$ forms at this concentration of Cd^{2+}. In 5.0 M NH_3 we can calculate the pH:

$$NH_3 + H_2O \rightleftharpoons NH_4^+ + OH^- \qquad K_b = 1.8 \times 10^{-5}$$

Initial   5.0 M 0   ~0
Equil.   5.0 - y y y

$$K_b = 1.8 \times 10^{-5} = \frac{[NH_4^+][OH^-]}{[NH_3]} = \frac{y^2}{5.0 - y} \approx \frac{y^2}{5.0}, \quad y = [OH^-] = 9.5 \times 10^{-3} \, M; \quad \text{Assumptions good.}$$

We now calculate the value of the solubility quotient, Q:

$$Q = [Cd^{2+}][OH^-]^2 = (1.6 \times 10^{-13})(9.5 \times 10^{-3})^2$$

$$Q = 1.4 \times 10^{-17} < K_{sp} \, (5.9 \times 10^{-15}); \quad \text{Therefore, no precipitate forms.}$$

99.   a.   The optimum pH for a buffer is when pH = pK_a. At this pH a buffer will have equal neutralization capacity for both added acid and base. As shown below, since the pK_a for TRISH$^+$ is 8.1, then the optimal buffer pH is about 8.1.

$K_b = 1.19 \times 10^{-6}$; $K_a = K_w/K_b = 8.40 \times 10^{-9}$; $pK_a = -\log(8.40 \times 10^{-9}) = 8.076$

b. $pH = pK_a + \log \dfrac{[TRIS]}{[TRISH^+]}$, $\quad 7.00 = 8.076 + \log \dfrac{[TRIS]}{[TRISH^+]}$

$\dfrac{[TRIS]}{[TRISH^+]} = 10^{-1.08} = 0.083$ (at pH = 7.00)

$9.00 = 8.076 + \log \dfrac{[TRIS]}{[TRISH^+]}$, $\quad \dfrac{[TRIS]}{[TRISH^+]} = 10^{0.92} = 8.3$ (at pH = 9.00)

c. $\dfrac{50.0 \text{ g TRIS}}{2.0 \text{ L}} \times \dfrac{1 \text{ mol}}{121.14 \text{ g}} = 0.206 \, M = 0.21 \, M = [TRIS]$

$\dfrac{65.0 \text{ g TRISHCl}}{2.0 \text{ L}} \times \dfrac{1 \text{ mol}}{157.60 \text{ g}} = 0.206 \, M = 0.21 \, M = [TRISHCl] = [TRISH^+]$

$pH = pK_a + \log \dfrac{[TRIS]}{[TRISH^+]} = 8.076 + \log \dfrac{(0.21)}{(0.21)} = 8.08$

The amount of H$^+$ added from HCl is: $0.50 \times 10^{-3} \text{ L} \times \dfrac{12 \text{ mol}}{\text{L}} = 6.0 \times 10^{-3} \text{ mol H}^+$

The H$^+$ from HCl will convert TRIS into TRISH$^+$. The reaction is:

	TRIS	+	H^+	$\rightarrow$	TRISH$^+$
Before	0.21 M		$\dfrac{6.0 \times 10^{-3}}{0.2005} = 0.030\ M$		0.21 M
Change	-0.030		-0.030	$\rightarrow$	+0.030	Reacts completely
After	0.18		0		0.24

Now use the Henderson-Hasselbalch equation to solve the buffer problem.

$$pH = 8.076 + \log\left(\frac{0.18}{0.24}\right) = 7.95$$

100. $pH = pK_a + \log \dfrac{[(CH_3)_2AsO_2^-]}{[(CH_3)_2AsO_2H]}$, $6.60 = 6.19 + \log \dfrac{[(CH_3)_2AsO_2^-]}{[(CH_3)_2AsO_2H]}$

$$\frac{[(CH_3)_2AsO_2^-]}{[(CH_3)_2AsO_2H]} = 10^{0.41} = 2.6, \quad [(CH_3)_2AsO_2^-] = 2.6\,[(CH_3)_2AsO_2H]$$

$[(CH_3)_2AsO_2^-] + [(CH_3)_2AsO_2H] = 0.25;\ \ 3.6\,[(CH_3)_2AsO_2H] = 0.25$

$[(CH_3)_2AsO_2H] = 0.069\ M$ and $[(CH_3)_2AsO_2^-] = 0.18\ M$

$$0.500\ L \times \frac{0.069\ mol\ (CH_3)_2AsO_2H}{L} \times \frac{138.0\ g}{mol} = 4.8\ g\ cacodylic\ acid$$

$$0.500\ L \times \frac{0.18\ mol\ (CH_3)_2AsO_2^-}{L} \times \frac{160.0\ g\ (CH_3)_2AsO_2Na}{mol} = 14\ g\ sodium\ cacodylate$$

101.

Acid	pK$_a$
$(CH_3)_2AsO_2H$	6.19
TRISHCl	8.08
benzoic acid	4.19
acetic acid	4.74
HF	3.14
NH$_4$Cl	9.26

Best buffer is when pH = pK$_a$ which requires equal concentrations of weak acid and conjugate base. Choose combinations that yield a buffer where pH $\approx$ pK$_a$. We will use HCl or NaOH when necessary to convert either weak base into its conjugate acid or weak acid into its conjugate base. Remember that a buffer must have both the weak acid and weak base present at the same time.

a. potassium fluoride + HCl   b. benzoic acid + NaOH

c. sodium acetate + acetic acid

d. $(CH_3)_2AsO_2Na$ + HCl: This is a good choice to produce a conjugate acid/base pair for a pH = 7.0 buffer. Actually the best choice is an equimolar mixture of ammonium chloride and sodium acetate. NH$_4^+$ is a weak acid (K$_a$ = 5.6 × 10^{-10}). C$_2$H$_3$O$_2^-$ is a weak base (K$_b$ = 5.6 × 10^{-10}). A mixture of the two will give a buffer at pH = 7.0 since the weak acid and weak base are the same strengths. $NH_4C_2H_3O_2$ is commercially available and its solutions are used as pH = 7.0 buffers.

    e.   ammonium chloride + NaOH

102. a.   pH = pK_a = -log (6.4 × 10^{-5}) = 4.19 since [HBz] = [Bz$^-$] where HBz = $C_6H_5CO_2H$ and [Bz$^-$] = $C_6H_5CO_2^-$.

    b.   [Bz$^-$] will increase to 0.120 M and [HBz] will decrease to 0.080 M after OH$^-$ reacts completely with HBz.

$$pH = pK_a + \log \frac{[Bz^-]}{[HBz]}, \quad pH = 4.19 + \log \frac{(0.120)}{(0.080)} = 4.37$$

    c.

	Bz$^-$	+	H$_2$O	⇌	HBz	+	OH$^-$
Initial	0.120 M				0.080 M		0
Equil.	0.120 - x				0.080 + x		x

$$K_b = \frac{K_w}{K_a} = \frac{1.0 \times 10^{-14}}{6.4 \times 10^{-5}} = \frac{(0.080 + x)(x)}{(0.120 - x)} \approx \frac{(0.080)(x)}{0.120}$$

x = [OH$^-$] = 2.34 × 10^{-10} M (carrying extra sig. fig.); Assumptions good.

pOH = 9.63; pH = 4.37

    d.   We get the same answer. Both equilibria involve the two major species, benzoic acid and benzoate anion. Both equilibria must hold true. K_b is related to K_a by K_w and [OH$^-$] is related to [H$^+$] by K_w, so all constants are interrelated.

103.   NaOH added = 50.0 mL × $\dfrac{0.500 \text{ mmol}}{\text{mL}}$ = 25.0 mmol NaOH

NaOH left unreacted = 31.92 mL HCl × $\dfrac{0.289 \text{ mmol}}{\text{mL}}$ × $\dfrac{1 \text{ mmol NaOH}}{\text{mmol HCl}}$ = 9.22 mmol NaOH

NaOH reacted with aspirin = 25.0 - 9.22 = 15.8 mmol NaOH

15.8 mmol NaOH × $\dfrac{1 \text{ mmol aspirin}}{2 \text{ mmol NaOH}}$ × $\dfrac{180.2 \text{ mg}}{\text{mmol}}$ = 1420 mg = 1.42 g aspirin

Purity = $\dfrac{1.42 \text{ g}}{1.427 \text{ g}}$ × 100 = 99.5%

Here, a strong base is titrated by a strong acid. The equivalence point will be at pH = 7.0. Bromthymol blue would be the best indicator since it changes color at pH ≈ 7 (from base color to acid color). See Figure 8.8 of the text.

104.   At 4.0 mL NaOH added: $\left|\dfrac{\Delta pH}{\Delta mL}\right| = \left|\dfrac{2.43 - 3.14}{0 - 4.0}\right| = 0.18$

The other points are calculated in a similar fashion. The results are summarized and plotted below. As can be seen from the plot, the advantage of this approach is that it is much easier to accurately determine the location of the equivalence point.

mL	pH	$|\Delta pH/\Delta mL|$
0	2.43	-
4.0	3.14	0.18
8.0	3.53	0.098
12.5	3.86	0.073
20.0	4.46	0.080
24.0	5.24	0.20
24.5	5.6	0.7
24.9	6.3	2
25.0	8.28	20
25.1	10.3	20
26.0	11.29	1
28.0	11.75	0.23
30.0	11.96	0.11

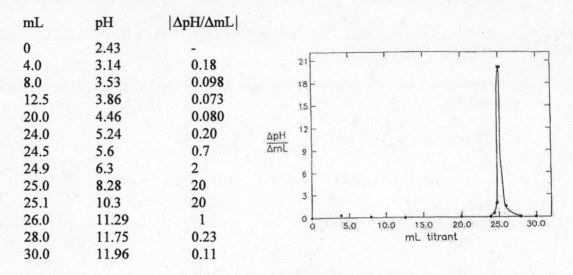

105.   At the equivalence point, P^{2-} is the major species. It is a weak base in water since it is the conjugate base of a weak acid.

$$P^{2-} \quad + \quad H_2O \quad \rightleftharpoons \quad HP^- \quad + \quad OH^-$$

Initial $\dfrac{0.5\ g}{0.1\ L} \times \dfrac{1\ mol}{204.2\ g} = 0.024\ M$ 0   ~0   (carry extra sig. fig.)

Equil. $0.024 - x$ x x

$$K_b = \frac{[HP^-]\,[OH^-]}{[P^{2-}]} = \frac{K_w}{K_a} = \frac{1.0 \times 10^{-14}}{10^{-5.51}} = 3.2 \times 10^{-9} = \frac{x^2}{0.024 - x} \approx \frac{x^2}{0.024}$$

$x = [OH^-] = 8.8 \times 10^{-6}\ M$; pOH = 5.1; pH = 8.9   Assumptions good.

Phenolphthalein would be the best indicator for this titration because it changes color at pH ~ 9.

106. $$Cr^{3+} \quad + \quad H_2EDTA^{2-} \quad \rightleftharpoons \quad CrEDTA^- \quad + \quad 2\,H^+$$

	Cr^{3+}	H_2EDTA^{2-}		$CrEDTA^-$	$2\,H^+$	
Before	0.0010 M	0.050 M		0	$1.0 \times 10^{-6}\ M$	(buffer, $[H^+]$ constant)
Change	-0.0010	-0.0010	$\rightarrow$	+0.0010	No change	Reacts completely
After	0	0.049		0.0010	1.0×10^{-6}	New initial

x mol/L $CrEDTA^-$ dissociates to reach equilibrium

Change	$+x$	$+x$	$\leftarrow$	$-x$	---	
Equil.	x	$0.049 + x$		$0.0010 - x$	1.0×10^{-6}	(buffer)

$$K_f = 1.0 \times 10^{23} = \frac{[CrEDTA^-]\,[H^+]^2}{[Cr^{3+}]\,[H_2EDTA^{2-}]} = \frac{(0.0010 - x)\,(1.0 \times 10^{-6})^2}{(x)\,(0.049 + x)}$$

$$1.0 \times 10^{23} \approx \frac{(0.0010)\,(1.0 \times 10^{-12})}{x\,(0.049)}, \quad x = [Cr^{3+}] = 2.0 \times 10^{-37}\,M \quad \text{Assumptions good.}$$

107. a.

	$Pb(OH)_2(s)$	$\rightleftharpoons$	Pb^{2+}	+	2 OH$^-$
Initial	s = solubility (mol/L)		0		$1.0 \times 10^{-7}\,M$ from water
Equil.			s		$1.0 \times 10^{-7} + 2s$

$$K_{sp} = 1.2 \times 10^{-15} = [Pb^{2+}]\,[OH^-]^2 = s(1.0 \times 10^{-7} + 2s)^2 \approx s(2s^2) = 4s^3$$

$s = [Pb^{2+}] = 6.7 \times 10^{-6}\,M;$ Assumption to ignore OH$^-$ from water is good by the 5% rule.

  b.

	$Pb(OH)_2(s)$	$\rightleftharpoons$	Pb^{2+}	+	2 OH$^-$
Initial			0		0.10 M pH = 13.00, [OH$^-$] = 0.10 M
	s mol/L $Pb(OH)_2(s)$ dissolves to reach equilibrium				
Equil.			s		0.10 (buffered solution)

$$1.2 \times 10^{-15} = (s)(0.10)^2, \quad s = [Pb^{2+}] = 1.2 \times 10^{-13}\,M$$

  c. We need to calculate the Pb^{2+} concentration in equilibrium with EDTA^{4-}. Since K is large for the formation of PbEDTA^{2-}, let the reaction go to completion then solve an equilibrium problem to get the Pb^{2+} concentration.

	Pb^{2+}	+	EDTA^{4-}	$\rightleftharpoons$	PbEDTA^{2-}	K = 1.1×10^{18}
Before	0.010 M		0.050 M		0	
	0.010 mol/L Pb^{2+} reacts completely (large K)					
Change	-0.010		-0.010	$\rightarrow$	$+0.010$	Reacts completely
After	0		0.040		0.010	New initial
	x mol/L PbEDTA^{2-} dissociates to reach equilibrium					
Equil.	x		$0.040 + x$		$0.010 - x$	

$$1.1 \times 10^{18} = \frac{(0.010 - x)}{(x)\,(0.040 + x)} \approx \frac{(0.010)}{x(0.040)}, \quad x = [Pb^{2+}] = 2.3 \times 10^{-19}\,M \quad \text{Assumptions good.}$$

Now calculate the solubility quotient for $Pb(OH)_2$ to see if precipitation occurs. The concentration of OH$^-$ is 0.10 M since we have a solution buffered at pH = 13.00.

$$Q = [Pb^{2+}]_o\,[OH^-]_o^2 = (2.3 \times 10^{-19})(0.10)^2 = 2.3 \times 10^{-21} < K_{sp}\,(1.2 \times 10^{-15})$$

$Pb(OH)_2(s)$ will not form since Q is less than K_{sp}.

108. a. AgF   b. $Pb(OH)_2$ c. $Sr(NO_2)_2$ d. $Ni(CN)_2$

All the above salts have anions that are bases. The anions of the other choices are conjugate bases of strong acids. They have no basic properties in water and, therefore, do not have solubilities which depend on pH.

109. It will be more soluble in base. Addition of OH$^-$ will react with H$^+$ to produce H_2O. This drives the equilibrium $H_4SiO_4 \rightleftharpoons H_3SiO_4^- + H^+$ to the right. This, in turn, drives the solubility reaction $SiO_2(s) + 2\,H_2O \rightleftharpoons H_4SiO_4$ to the right, increasing the solubility of the silica.

110.   The solubility of SiO_2 will equal the sum of the concentrations of H_4SiO_4 and $H_3SiO_4^-$.

$SiO_2(s) + 2 H_2O(l) \rightleftharpoons H_4SiO_4(aq) \quad K = 2 \times 10^{-3} \ M = [H_4SiO_4]$

$H_4SiO_4(aq) \rightleftharpoons H_3SiO_4^-(aq) + H^+(aq) \quad K_a = 10^{-9.46} = 3.5 \times 10^{-10} = \dfrac{[H_3SiO_4^-] [H^+]}{[H_4SiO_4]}$

At pH = 7.0: $3.5 \times 10^{-10} = \dfrac{[H_3SiO_4^-] (1 \times 10^{-7})}{2 \times 10^{-3}}$, $[H_3SiO_4^-] = 7 \times 10^{-6} \ M$

Solubility = $2 \times 10^{-3} + 7 \times 10^{-6} = 2 \times 10^{-3}$ mol/L at pH = 7.0

At pH = 10.0: $3.5 \times 10^{-10} = \dfrac{[H_3SiO_4^-] (1 \times 10^{-10})}{2 \times 10^{-3}}$, $[H_3SiO_4^-] = 7 \times 10^{-3} \ M$

Solubility = $2 \times 10^{-3} + 7 \times 10^{-3} = 9 \times 10^{-3}$ mol/L at pH = 10.0

111. $[BaBr_2]_o = \dfrac{0.150(1.0 \times 10^{-4})}{0.250} = 6.0 \times 10^{-5} \ M$

$[K_2C_2O_4] = \dfrac{0.100(6.0 \times 10^{-4})}{0.250} = 2.4 \times 10^{-4} \ M$

$Q = [Ba^{2+}][C_2O_4^{2-}] = (6.0 \times 10^{-5})(2.4 \times 10^{-4}) = 1.5 \times 10^{-8} \ M$

Since $Q < K_{sp}$, then $BaC_2O_4(s)$ will not precipitate. The final concentration of ions will be:

$[Ba^{2+}] = 6.0 \times 10^{-5} \ M$, $[Br^-] = 1.2 \times 10^{-4} \ M$,

$[K^+] = 4.8 \times 10^{-4} \ M$, $[C_2O_4^{2-}] = 2.4 \times 10^{-4} \ M$

112.   a. $C_2H_5NH_3^+ \rightleftharpoons H^+ + C_2H_5NH_2 \quad K_a = \dfrac{K_w}{K_b} = \dfrac{1.0 \times 10^{-14}}{5.6 \times 10^{-4}} = 1.8 \times 10^{-11}$; $pK_a = 10.74$

$pH = pK_a + \log \dfrac{[C_2H_5NH_2]}{[C_2H_5NH_3^+]} = 10.74 + \log \dfrac{0.10}{0.20} = 10.74 - 0.30 = 10.44$

b. $C_2H_5NH_3^+ + OH^- \rightleftharpoons C_2H_5NH_2$; After 0.050 M OH$^-$ reacts to completion, a buffer solution still exists where $[C_2H_5NH_3^+] = [C_2H_5NH_2] = 0.15 \ M$.

$pH = 10.74 + \log \dfrac{0.15}{0.15} = 10.74$

113. $HC_2H_3O_2 \rightleftharpoons H^+ + C_2H_3O_7^-$; Let C_o = initial concentration of $HC_2H_3O_2$

From normal weak-acid setup: $K_a = 1.8 \times 10^{-5} = \dfrac{[H^+] [C_2H_3O_2^-]}{[HC_2H_3O_2]} = \dfrac{[H^+]^2}{C_o - [H^+]}$

$$[H^+] = 10^{-2.68} = 2.1 \times 10^{-3} \ M; \ \ 1.8 \times 10^{-5} = \frac{(2.1 \times 10^{-3})^2}{C_o - 2.1 \times 10^{-3}}, \ C_o = 0.25 \ M$$

$25.0 \ mL \times 0.25 \ mmol/mL = 6.3 \ mmol \ HC_2H_3O_2$

Need $6.3 \ mmol \ KOH = V_{KOH} \times 0.0975 \ mmol/mL, \ V_{KOH} = 65 \ mL$

114.   In the final solution: $[H^+] = 10^{-2.15} = 7.1 \times 10^{-3} \ M$

Beginning mmol HCl = $500.0 \ mL \times 0.200 \ mmol/mL = 100. \ mmol \ HCl$

Amount of HCl that reacts with NaOH = $1.50 \times 10^{-2} \ mmol/mL \times V$

$$\frac{7.1 \times 10^{-3} \ mmol}{mL} = \frac{final \ mmol \ H^+}{total \ volume} = \frac{100. - 0.0150 \ V}{500.0 + V}$$

$3.6 + 7.1 \times 10^{-3} \ V = 100. - 1.50 \times 10^{-2} \ V, \ 2.21 \times 10^{-2} \ V = 100. - 3.6$

$V = 4.36 \times 10^3 \ mL = 4.36 \ L = 4.4 \ L \ NaOH$

115. $0.400 \ mol/L \times V_{NH_3} = mol \ NH_3 = mol \ NH_4^+$ after reaction with HCl at the equivalence point.

At the equivalence point: $[NH_4^+]_o = \dfrac{mol \ NH_4^+}{total \ volume} = \dfrac{0.400 \times V_{NH_3}}{1.50 \times V_{NH_3}} = 0.267 \ M$

	NH_4^+	$\rightleftharpoons$	H^+	$+$	NH_3
Initial	$0.267 \ M$		0		0
Equil.	$0.267 - x$		x		x

$$K_a = \frac{K_w}{K_b} = \frac{1.0 \times 10^{-14}}{1.8 \times 10^{-5}} = 5.6 \times 10^{-10} = \frac{x^2}{0.267 - x} \approx \frac{x^2}{0.267}$$

$x = [H^+] = 1.2 \times 10^{-5} \ M; \ \ pH = 4.92$ Assumptions good.

116. $50.0 \ mL \times 0.100 \ M = 5.00 \ mmol \ NaOH$ initially

at pH = 10.50, pOH = 3.50, $[OH^-] = 10^{(-3.50)} = 3.2 \times 10^{-4} \ M$

mmol OH^- remaining = $3.2 \times 10^{-4} \ mmol/mL \times 73.75 \ mL = 2.4 \times 10^{-2} \ mmol$
mmol OH^- that reacted = $5.00 - 0.024 = 4.98 \ mmol$

Since the weak acid is monoprotic, then 23.75 mL of the weak acid solution contains 4.98 mmol HA.

$[HA]_o = \dfrac{4.98 \ mmol}{23.75 \ mL} = 0.210 \ M$

117. $HA + OH^- \rightarrow A^- + H_2O$ where HA = acetylsalicylic acid

mmol HA present = $27.36 \ mL \ OH^- \times \dfrac{0.5106 \ mmol \ OH^-}{mL \ OH^-} \times \dfrac{1 \ mmol \ HA}{mmol \ OH^-} = 13.97 \ mmol \ HA$

molar mass of HA = $\dfrac{\text{grams}}{\text{moles}} = \dfrac{2.51 \text{ g HA}}{13.97 \times 10^{-3} \text{ mol HA}}$ = 180. g/mol

To determine the K_a value, use the pH data. After complete neutralization of acetylsalicylic acid by OH^-, we have 13.97 mmol of A^- produced from the neutralization reaction. A^- will react completely with the added H^+ and reform acetylsalicylic acid, HA.

mmol H^+ added = 15.44 mL $\times \dfrac{0.4524 \text{ mmol } H^+}{\text{mL}}$ = 6.985 mmol H^+

$$A^- \quad + \quad H^+ \quad \rightarrow \quad HA$$

Before	13.97 mmol	6.985 mmol		0	
Change	-6.985	-6.985	$\rightarrow$	+6.985	Reacts completely
After	6.985 mmol	0		6.985 mmol	

We have back titrated this solution to the halfway point to equivalence where pH = pK_a (assuming HA is a weak acid). This is true because after H^+ reacts completely, equal mmol of HA and A^- are present which only occurs at the halfway point to equivalence. Assuming acetylsalicylic acid is a weak acid, then pH = pK_a = 3.48. $K_a = 10^{-3.48} = 3.3 \times 10^{-4}$

118.   Since pK_{a_2} = 7.00, an equimolar mixture of H_2A^- and HA^{2-} will produce a solution with pH = pK_{a_2} = 7.00.

20.8 g $Na_3A \times \dfrac{1 \text{ mol}}{208 \text{ g}}$ = 0.100 mol Na_3A = 100. mmol Na_3A

To convert 100. mmol Na_3A to an equimolar solution of H_2A^- and HA^{2-}, we must add 100. mmol H^+ + 50. mmol H^+ = 150. mmol H^+. 100. mmol H^+ converts all A^{3-} into HA^{2-}. The next 50. mmol H^+ converts half of the HA^{2-} into H_2A^-: Only answer c adds 150. mmol H^+ (= 1500 mL $\times$ 0.100 mmol/mL).

119. $[X^-]_0$ = 5.00 M and $[Cu^+]_0 = 1.0 \times 10^{-3}$ M since equal volumes of each reagent are mixed.

Since the K values are large, assume the reaction goes completely to CuX_3^{2-}, then solve an equilibrium problem.

$$Cu^+ \quad + \quad 3 X^- \quad \rightleftharpoons \quad CuX_3^{2-} \quad K = K_1 \times K_2 \times K_3 = 1.0 \times 10^9$$

Before	1.0×10^{-3} M	5.00 M	0
After	0	$5.00 - 3(10^{-3}) \approx 5.00$	1.0×10^{-3}
Equil.	x	$5.00 + 3x$	$1.0 \times 10^{-3} - x$

$K = \dfrac{(1.0 \times 10^{-3} - x)}{x(5.00 + 3x)^3} = 1.0 \times 10^9 \approx \dfrac{1.0 \times 10^{-3}}{x(5.00)^3}$, $x = [Cu^+] = 8.0 \times 10^{-15}$ M Assumptions good.

$[CuX_3^{2-}] = 1.0 \times 10^{-3} - 8.0 \times 10^{-15} = 1.0 \times 10^{-3}$ M

$K_3 = \dfrac{[CuX_3^{2-}]}{[CuX_2^-][X^-]} = 1.0 \times 10^3 = \dfrac{(1.0 \times 10^{-3})}{[CuX_2^-](5.00)}$, $[CuX_2^-] = 2.0 \times 10^{-7}$ M

Summarizing:

$[CuX_3^{2-}] = 1.0 \times 10^{-3}\ M$ (answer a)
$[CuX_2^{-}] = 2.0 \times 10^{-7}\ M$ (answer b)
$[Cu^{2+}] = 8.0 \times 10^{-15}\ M$ (answer c)

120. K_{a_3} is so small (4.8×10^{-13}) that a break is not seen at the third stoichiometric point.

121. $50.0\ \text{mL} \times \dfrac{0.10\ \text{mmol H}_2\text{A}}{\text{mL}} = 5.0\ \text{mmol H}_2\text{A initially}$

To reach the first equivalence point, 5.0 mmol OH⁻ must be added. This occurs after addition of 50.0 mL of 0.10 M NaOH. At the first equivalence point for a diprotic acid, pH = $(pK_{a_1} + pK_{a_2})/2 = 8.00$. Addition of 25.0 mL of 0.10 M NaOH will be the first halfway point to equivalence where $[H_2A] = [HA^-]$ and pH = $pK_{a_1} = 6.70$. Solving for the K_a values:

$pK_{a_1} = 6.70,\ K_{a_1} = 10^{-6.70} = 2.0 \times 10^{-7}$

$\dfrac{pK_{a_1} + pK_{a_2}}{2} = 8.00,\quad \dfrac{6.70 + pK_{a_2}}{2} = 8.00,\ pK_{a_2} = 9.30,\ K_{a_2} = 10^{-9.30} = 5.0 \times 10^{-10}$

122.   We will see only the first stoichiometric point in the titration of salicylic acid because K_{a2} is so small. For adipic acid the K_a's are fairly close to each other. Both protons will be titrated almost simultaneously, giving us only one break. The stoichiometric points will occur when 1 mol of H⁺ is added per mol of salicylic acid present and when 2 mol of H⁺ is added per mol of adipic acid present. Thus, the 25.00 mL volume corresponded to the titration of salicylic acid and the 50.00 mL volume corresponded to the titration of adipic acid.

Challenge Problems

123.   mmol $HC_3H_5O_2$ present initially = $45.0\ \text{mL} \times \dfrac{0.750\ \text{mmol}}{\text{mL}} = 33.8\ \text{mmol HC}_3\text{H}_5\text{O}_2$

mmol $C_3H_5O_2^{-}$ present initially = $55.0\ \text{mL} \times \dfrac{0.700\ \text{mmol}}{\text{mL}} = 38.5\ \text{mmol C}_3\text{H}_5\text{O}_2^{-}$

The initial pH of the buffer is:

$$pH = pK_a + \log \dfrac{[C_3H_5O_2^-]}{[HC_3H_5O_2]} = -\log(1.3 \times 10^{-5}) + \log \dfrac{\dfrac{38.5\ \text{mmol}}{100.0\ \text{mL}}}{\dfrac{33.8\ \text{mmol}}{100.0\ \text{mL}}} = 4.89 + \log \dfrac{38.5}{33.8} = 4.95$$

Note: Since the buffer components are in the same volume of solution, we can use the mol (or mmol) ratio in the Henderson-Hasselbalch equation to solve for pH instead of using the concentration ratio of $[C_3H_5O_2^-]/[HC_3H_5O_2]$. The total volume always cancels for buffer solutions.

When NaOH is added, the pH will increase and the added OH⁻ will convert $HC_3H_5O_2$ into $C_3H_5O_2^{-}$.

The pH after addition OH⁻ increases by 2.5%, so the resulting pH is:

$4.95 + 0.025\,(4.95) = 5.07$

At this pH, a buffer solution still exists and the mmol ratio between $C_3H_5O_2^-$ and $HC_3H_5O_2$ is:

$$pH = pK_a + \log \frac{\text{mmol } C_3H_5O_2^-}{\text{mmol } HC_3H_5O_2}, \quad 5.07 = 4.89 + \log \frac{\text{mmol } C_3H_5O_2^-}{\text{mmol } HC_3H_5O_2}$$

$$\frac{\text{mmol } C_3H_5O_2^-}{\text{mmol } HC_3H_5O_2} = 10^{0.18} = 1.5$$

Let x = mmol OH⁻ added to increase pH to 5.07. Since OH⁻ will essentially react to completion with $HC_3H_5O_2$ then the set-up to the problem using mmol is:

	$HC_3H_5O_2$	+	OH⁻	→	$C_3H_5O_2^-$	
Before	33.8 mmol		x mmol		38.5 mmol	
Change	$-x$		$-x$	→	$+x$	Reacts completely
After	$33.8 - x$		0		$38.5 + x$	

Solving for x:

$$\frac{\text{mmol } C_3H_5O_2^-}{\text{mmol } HC_3H_5O_2} = 1.5 = \frac{38.5 + x}{33.8 - x}, \quad 1.5\,(33.8 - x) = 38.5 + x, \quad x = 4.9 \text{ mmol OH⁻ added}$$

The volume of NaOH necessary to raise the pH by 2.5% is:

$$4.9 \text{ mmol NaOH} \times \frac{1 \text{ mL}}{0.10 \text{ mmol NaOH}} = 49 \text{ mL}$$

49 mL of 0.10 M NaOH must be added to increase the pH by 2.5%.

124. $\dfrac{0.200 \text{ g}}{165.0 \text{ g/mL}} = 1.212 \text{ mmol } H_3A$ (carrying extra sig figs)

a.   At 10.50 mL → $(10.50)(0.0500) = 0.525 \text{ mmol OH⁻}$

$1.212 - 0.525 = 0.687 \text{ mmol } H_3A$ left, 0.525 mmol H_2A^- formed

$$K_{a_1} = \frac{(10^{-3.73})\left(\dfrac{0.525}{60.50} + 10^{-3.73}\right)}{\dfrac{0.687}{60.50} - 10^{-3.73}} = 1.5 \times 10^{-4} \; (pK_{a_1} = 3.82)$$

first stoich. pt.: $pH = \dfrac{pK_{a_1} + pK_{a_2}}{2} = 5.19 = \dfrac{3.82 + pK_{a_2}}{2}$

$pK_{a_2} = 6.56 \; (K_{a_2} = 2.8 \times 10^{-7})$

second stoich. pt.: $pH = \dfrac{pK_{a_2} + pK_{a_3}}{2} = 8.00 = \dfrac{6.56 + pK_{a_3}}{2}$

$pK_{a_3} = 9.44\ (K_{a_3} = 3.6 \times 10^{-10})$

b. Stoich. pt. = 24.24 mL: 1.212 mol $H_3A = (0.0500\ M\ OH^-)(V_{OH^-})$, $V_{OH^-} = 24.2$ mL

Since it will require 60.5 mL to reach the third half-way point to equivalence (where $pH = pK_{a_3}$), then the pH should be a little lower than 9.44.

c. 59.0 mL of 0.0500 M OH$^-$ = 2.95 mmol

$$H_3A\ +\ OH^-\ \rightarrow\ H_2A^-\ +\ H_2O$$

Before	1.212	2.95	0
After	0	1.74	1.212

$$H_2A^-\ +\ OH^-\ \rightarrow\ HA^{2-}\ +\ H_2O$$

Before	1.212	1.74	0
After	0	0.53	1.212

$$HA^2\ +\ OH^-\ \rightarrow\ A^{3-}\ +\ H_2O$$

Before	1.212	0.53	0
After	0.68	0	0.53

$K_{a_3} = 3.6 \times 10^{-10} = \dfrac{\left(\dfrac{0.53\ mmol}{109\ mL}\right)[H^+]}{\left(\dfrac{0.68\ mmol}{109\ mL}\right)}$, $[H^+] = 4.6 \times 10^{-10}\ M$, pH = 9.34

125. a. Best acid will react with the best base present, so the dominate equilibrium is:

$NH_4^+ + X^- \rightleftharpoons NH_3 + HX$ $K_{eq} = \dfrac{[NH_3][HX]}{[NH_4^+][X^-]} = \dfrac{K_a(NH_4^+)}{K_a(HX)}$

Since initially $[NH_4^+]_o = [X^-]_o$ and $[NH_3]_o = [HX]_o = 0$, then at equilibrium $[NH_4^+] = [X^-]$ and $[NH_3] = [HX]$.
Therefore, $K_{eq} = \dfrac{K_a(NH_4^+)}{K_a(HX)} = \dfrac{[HX]^2}{[X^-]^2}$

The K_a expression for HX is: $K_a(HX) = \dfrac{[H^+][X^-]}{[HX]}$, $\dfrac{[HX]}{[X^-]} = \dfrac{[H^+]}{K_a(HX)}$

Substituting into the K_{eq} expression: $K_{eq} = \dfrac{K_a(NH_4^+)}{K_a(HX)} = \dfrac{[HX]^2}{[X^-]^2} = \left(\dfrac{[H^+]}{K_a(HX)}\right)^2$

Rearranging: $[H^+]^2 = K_a(NH_4^+) \times K_a(HX)$ or taking the -log of both sides:

$$pH = \frac{pK_a(NH_4^+) + pK_a(HX)}{2}$$

b. Ammonium formate = $NH_4(HCO_2)$

$$K_a(NH_4^+) = \frac{1.0 \times 10^{-14}}{1.8 \times 10^{-5}} = 5.6 \times 10^{-10}; \quad K_a(HCO_2H) = 1.8 \times 10^{-4}; \quad pK_a = 3.74$$

$$pH = \frac{pK_a(NH_4^+) + pK_a(HCO_2H)}{2} = \frac{9.25 + 3.74}{2} = 6.50$$

Ammonium acetate = $NH_4(C_2H_3O_2)$; $K_a (HC_2H_3O_2) = 1.8 \times 10^{-5}$; $pK_a = 4.74$

$$pH = \frac{9.25 + 4.74}{2} = 7.00$$

Ammonium bicarbonate = $NH_4(HCO_3)$; $K_a(H_2CO_3) = 4.3 \times 10^{-7}$; $pK_a = 6.37$

$$pH = \frac{9.25 + 6.37}{2} = 7.81$$

c. $NH_4^+(aq) + OH^-(aq) \rightarrow NH_3(aq) + H_2O(l); \quad C_2H_3O_2^-(aq) + H^+(aq) \rightarrow HC_2H_3O_2(aq)$

126. a. Major species: H^+, HSO_4^-, $H_2C_6H_6O_6$, H_2O; HSO_4^- is the best acid.

$$HSO_4^- \quad \rightleftharpoons \quad H^+ \quad + \quad SO_4^{2-}$$

Initial	0.050	0.050	0
Change	-x	+x	x
Equil.	0.050-x	0.050+x	x

$$\frac{(0.050 + x)(x)}{(0.050 - x)} = 1.2 \times 10^{-2}$$

Must use the quadratic equation:

$x = 8.5 \times 10^{-3}$, $[H^+] = 5.85 \times 10^{-2} M$, $pH = 1.23$

b. Major species: H^+, $\quad\quad\quad HSO_4^-$, $\quad H_2C_6H_6O_6$, $\quad OH^-$, Na^+, H_2O
$\quad\quad\quad\quad\quad\quad\quad$ 5.0 mmol 5.0 mmol   20. mmol   10. mmol

$$H^+ \quad + \quad OH^- \quad \rightarrow \quad H_2O$$

Before	5.0	10.	–
After	0	5.0	–

$$HSO_4^- \quad + \quad OH^- \quad \rightarrow \quad H_2O \quad + \quad SO_4^{2-}$$

Before	5.0	5.0	–	0
After	0	0	–	5.0

$$H_2C_6H_6O_6 + SO_4^{2-} \rightleftharpoons HC_6H_6O_6^- + HSO_4^-$$

Initial	20./200.	5.0/200.	0	0
Change	-x	-x	+x	+x
Equil.	0.10-x	0.025-x	x	x

$$K = \frac{K_{a_1}(H_2C_6H_6O_6)}{K_{a_2}(H_2SO_4)} = 6.6 \times 10^{-3}$$

$$\frac{x^2}{(0.10-x)(0.025-x)} = 6.6 \times 10^{-3}$$

Using the quadratic, $x = 3.7 \times 10^{-3}$

Use either K_{a_1} for $H_2C_6H_6O_6$ or K_{a_2} for H_2SO_4 to calculate $[H^+]$.

For example, $7.9 \times 10^{-5} = \dfrac{[H^+][HC_6H_6O_6^-]}{[H_2C_6H_6O_6]} = \dfrac{[H^+](0.0037)}{(0.10-0.0037)}$

$[H^+] = 2.1 \times 10^{-3} M$, pH = 2.68

c. Major species: H^+, HSO_4^-, $H_2C_6H_6O_6$, OH^-, Na^+, H_2O
                    5.0 mmol 5.0 mmol   20. mmol   30. mmol

$$H^+ + OH^- \rightarrow H_2O$$

Before	5.0	30.	–
After	0	25	–

$$HSO_4^- + OH^- \rightarrow H_2O + SO_4^{2-}$$

Before	5.0	25	–	0
After	0	20.	–	5.0

$$H_2C_6H_6O_6 + OH^- \rightleftharpoons HC_6H_6O_6^- + H_2O$$

Before	20.	20.	0	–
After	0	0	20.	–

Thus, major species: $HC_6H_6O_6^-$, SO_4^{2-}, H_2O, Na^+ ;
                      20. mmol   5.0 mmol

$HC_6H_6O_6^-$ is the best acid and the best base.

dominant reaction: $HC_6H_6O_6^- + HC_6H_6O_6^- \rightleftharpoons H_2C_6H_6O_6 + C_6H_6O_6^{2-}$ amphoteric!

$$pH = \frac{pK_{a_1} + pK_{a_2}}{2} = \frac{4.10 + 11.80}{2} = 7.95$$

d. Major species: H^+, HSO_4^-, $H_2C_6H_6O_6$, OH^-, Na^+, H_2O
                    5.0 mmol 5.0 mmol   20. mmol   50. mmol

$$H^+ \; + \; OH^- \rightarrow H_2O$$

Before	5.0	50.	–
After	0	45	–

$$HSO_4^- \; + \; OH^- \rightarrow H_2O \; + \; SO_4^{2-}$$

Before	5.0	45	–	0
After	0	40.	–	5.0

$$H_2C_6H_6O_6 \; + \; OH^- \; \rightarrow \; H_2O \; + HC_6H_6O_6^-$$

Before	20.	40.	–	0
After	0	20.	–	20.

$$HC_6H_6O_6^- \; + \; OH^- \; \rightarrow \; C_6H_6O_6^{2-} \; + \; H_2O$$

Before	20.	20.	0	–
After	0	0	20.	–

$$C_6H_6O_6^{2-} \; + \; H_2O \; \rightleftharpoons \; HC_6H_6O_6^- \; + \; OH^-$$

Initial	20./600.	–	0	0
Change	-x	–	+x	+x
Equil.	0.033-x	–	x	x

$$K_b = \frac{K_w}{K_{a_2}} = 6.3 \times 10^{-3}$$

$$\frac{x^2}{0.033 - x} = 6.3 \times 10^{-3}$$

Using the quadratic, $x = [OH^-] = 1.2 \times 10^{-2} \; M$; pOH = 1.92, pH = 12.08

127.   a. $$SrF_2(s) \; \rightleftharpoons \; Sr^{2+}(aq) \; + \; 2\,F^-(aq)$$

Initial	0	0

s mol/L SrF$_2$ dissolves to reach equilibrium

Equil.	s	$2s$

$[Sr^{2+}] \, [F^-]^2 = K_{sp} = 7.9 \times 10^{-10} = 4s^3$, $s = 5.8 \times 10^{-4}$ mol/L

b. Greater, because some of the F^- would react with water:

$$F^- + H_2O \rightleftharpoons HF + OH^- \quad K_b = \frac{K_w}{K_a(HF)} = 1.4 \times 10^{-11}$$

This lowers the concentration of F^-, forcing more SrF$_2$ to dissolve.

c. $SrF_2(s) \rightleftharpoons Sr^{2+} + 2\,F^- \quad K_{sp} = 7.9 \times 10^{-10} = [Sr^{2+}] \, [F^-]^2$

Let s = solubility = $[Sr^{2+}]$, then $2s$ = total F^- concentration.

Since F⁻ is a weak base, some of the F⁻ is converted into HF. Therefore:

total F⁻ concentration $= 2s = [F^-] + [HF]$.

$$HF \rightleftharpoons H^+ + F^- \quad K_a = 7.2 \times 10^{-4} = \frac{[H^+][F^-]}{[HF]} = \frac{1.0 \times 10^{-2}[F^-]}{[HF]} \quad \text{(since pH = 2.00 buffer)}$$

$$7.2 \times 10^{-2} = \frac{[F^-]}{[HF]}, \quad [HF] = 14\,[F^-]; \text{ Solving:}$$

$$[Sr^{2+}] = s; \quad 2s = [F^-] + [HF] = [F^-] + 14\,[F^-], \quad 2s = 15\,[F^-], \quad [F^-] = 2s/15$$

$$7.9 \times 10^{-10} = [Sr^{2+}][F^-]^2 = (s)\left(\frac{2s}{15}\right)^2, \quad s = 3.5 \times 10^{-3}\ \text{mol/L}$$

128. $K_{sp} = [Ni^{2+}][S^{2-}] = 3 \times 10^{-21}$

$$H_2S \rightleftharpoons H^+ + HS^- \qquad K_{a_1} = 1.0 \times 10^{-7}$$
$$HS^- \rightleftharpoons H^+ + S^{2-} \qquad K_{a_2} = 1 \times 10^{-19}$$
$$\rule{5cm}{0.4pt}$$
$$H_2S \rightleftharpoons 2\,H^+ + S^{2-} \qquad K = K_{a_1} \times K_{a_1} = 1 \times 10^{-26}$$

$[H_2S] = 0.10\ M;\ [H^+]^2[S^{2-}] = 1 \times 10^{-27}$

$[H^+] = 1 \times 10^{-3}$, so $[S^{2-}] = 1 \times 10^{-21}\ M$

$$[Ni^{2+}] = \frac{K_{sp}}{[S^{2-}]} = \frac{3.0 \times 10^{-21}}{1 \times 10^{-21}} = 3\ M$$

129.   a. $Al(OH)_3(s) \rightleftharpoons Al^{3+} + 3\,OH^-; \quad Al(OH)_3(s) + OH^- \rightleftharpoons Al(OH)_4^-$

S = solubility = total Al^{3+} concentration $= [Al^{3+}] + [Al(OH)_4^-]$

$$[Al^{3+}] = \frac{K_{sp}}{[OH^-]^3} = K_{sp} \times \frac{[H^+]^3}{K_w^3} \quad \text{since } [OH^-]^3 = (K_w/[H^+])^3$$

$$\frac{[Al(OH)_4^-]}{[OH^-]} = K; \quad [OH^-] = \frac{K_w}{[H^+]}; \quad [Al(OH)_4^-] = K\,[OH^-] = \frac{KK_w}{[H^+]}$$

$S = [Al^{3+}] + [Al(OH)_4^-] = [H^+]^3\,K_{sp}/K_w^3 + KK_w/[H^+]$

b. $K_{sp} = 2 \times 10^{-32}; \quad K_w = 1.0 \times 10^{-14}; \quad K = 40.0$

$$S = \frac{[H^+]^3\,(2 \times 10^{-32})}{(1.0 \times 10^{-14})^3} + \frac{40.0\,(1.0 \times 10^{-14})}{[H^+]} = [H^+]^3\,(2 \times 10^{10}) + \frac{4.0 \times 10^{-13}}{[H^+]}$$

pH	solubility (S, mol/L)	log S
4.0	2×10^{-2}	-1.7
5.0	2×10^{-5}	-4.7
6.0	4.2×10^{-7}	-6.38
7.0	4.0×10^{-6}	-5.40
8.0	4.0×10^{-5}	-4.40
9.0	4.0×10^{-4}	-3.40
10.0	4.0×10^{-3}	-2.40
11.0	4.0×10^{-2}	-1.40
12.0	4.0×10^{-1}	-0.40

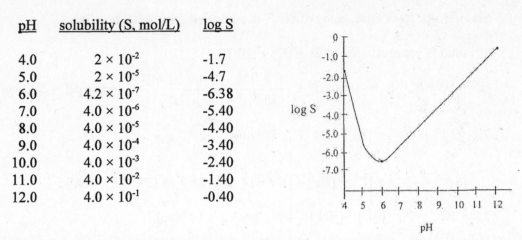

As expected, the solubility of $Al(OH)_3(s)$ is increased by very acidic solutions and by very basic solutions.

130. $MX(s) \rightleftharpoons M^+ + X^-$; $[M^+]$ = solubility = 3.17×10^{-8} mol/L in 1.00 M H^+ solution

$X^- + H_2O \rightleftharpoons HX + OH^-$ $K_b = \dfrac{1.00 \times 10^{-14}}{1.00 \times 10^{-15}} = 10.0$; when $[H^+] = 1.00\ M$, $[OH^-] = 1.00 \times 10^{-14}\ M$

$K_b = 10.0 = \dfrac{1.00 \times 10^{-14}\ [HX]}{[X^-]}$, $[X^-] = 1.00 \times 10^{-15}\ [HX]$

$[M^+]$ = total X^- concentration = $[HX] + [X^-] \approx [HX]$ (since K_b is large)

Thus $[X^-] = 1.00 \times 10^{-15}\ [M^+]$ and $[M^+]$ = solubility = $3.17 \times 10^{-8}\ M$.

$[X^-] = (1.00 \times 10^{-15})(3.17 \times 10^{-8}) = 3.17 \times 10^{-23}\ M$

$K_{sp} = [M^+][X^-] = (3.17 \times 10^{-8})\ (3.17 \times 10^{-23}) = 1.00 \times 10^{-30}$

When MX dissolves in H_2O, the reaction is:

$\quad\quad MX(s) + H_2O \rightleftharpoons M^+ + HX + OH^-$ $K = K_{sp} \times K_b = 1.00 \times 10^{-30}\ (10.) = 1.00 \times 10^{-29}$

Initial s = solubility   0   0 1.00×10^{-7}
Equil. s s $1.00 \times 10^{-7} + s$

$1.00 \times 10^{-29} = [M^+]\ [HX]\ [OH^-] = (s)\ (s)\ (1.00 \times 10^{-7} + s) \approx 1.00 \times 10^{-7}\ s^2$

$s^2 = \dfrac{1.00 \times 10^{-29}}{1.00 \times 10^{-7}} = 1.00 \times 10^{-22}$, $s = 1.00 \times 10^{-11}$ mol/L   Assumption good.

131.   For HOCl, $K_a = 3.5 \times 10^{-8}$ and $pK_a = -\log (3.5 \times 10^{-8}) = 7.46$. This will be a buffer solution since the pH is close to the pK_a value.

$pH = pK_a + \log \dfrac{[OCl^-]}{[HOCl]}$, $8.00 = 7.46 + \log \dfrac{[OCl^-]}{[HOCl]}$, $\dfrac{[OCl^-]}{[HOCl]} = 10^{0.54} = 3.5$

1.00 L $\times$ 0.0500 M = 0.0500 mol HOCl initially. Added OH^- converts HOCl into OCl^-. The total moles of OCl^- and HOCl must equal 0.0500 mol. Solving where n = moles:

$$n_{OCl^-} + n_{HOCl} = 0.0500 \text{ and } n_{OCl^-} = 3.5\ n_{HOCl}$$

$$4.5\ n_{HOCl} = 0.0500, \quad n_{HOCl} = 0.011 \text{ mol}; \quad n_{OCl^-} = 0.039 \text{ mol}$$

Need to add 0.039 mol NaOH to produce 0.039 mol OCl^-.

$$0.039 \text{ mol} = V \times 0.0100\ M, \quad V = 3.9 \text{ L NaOH}$$

Note: Normal buffer assumptions hold.

132. a. $HA \rightleftharpoons H^+ + A^-$ $K_a = 5.0 \times 10^{-10}$; $[HA]_0 = 1.00 \times 10^{-4}\ M$

Since this is a dilute solution of a very weak acid, H_2O cannot be ignored as a source of H^+.

From Section 7.9 of text, try: $[H^+] = (K_a[HA]_0 + K_w)^{1/2} = 2.4 \times 10^{-7}\ M$; pH = 6.62

Check assumption:
$$\frac{[H^+]^2 - K_w}{[H^+]} = 2.0 \times 10^{-7} \ll 1.0 \times 10^{-4} \quad \text{Assumption good. pH = 6.62}$$

b. 100.0 mL $\times$ (1.00×10^{-4} mmol/mL) = 1.00×10^{-2} mmol HA

5.00 mL $\times$ (1.0×10^{-3} mmol/mL) = 5.00×10^{-3} mmol NaOH added; Reacts completely with HA.

After reaction 5.00×10^{-3} mmol HA and 5.00×10^{-3} mmol A^- are in 105.0 mL. $[A^-]_0 = [HA]_0 =$ 5.00×10^{-3} mmol/105.0 mL = $4.76 \times 10^{-5}\ M$

	A^-	+	H_2O	$\rightleftharpoons$	HA	+	OH^-	$K_b = K_w/K_a = 2.0 \times 10^{-5}$
Initial	$4.76 \times 10^{-5}\ M$				$4.76 \times 10^{-5}\ M$		0	
Equil.	$4.76 \times 10^{-5} - x$				$4.76 \times 10^{-5} + x$		x	

$$K_b = 2.0 \times 10^{-5} = \frac{(4.76 \times 10^{-5} + x)x}{(4.76 \times 10^{-5} - x)}; \quad x \text{ will not be small.}$$

Using the quadratic formula and carrying extra sig. figs.: $x^2 + 6.76 \times 10^{-5}\ x - 9.52 \times 10^{-10} = 0$

$$x = [OH^-] = 1.2 \times 10^{-5}\ M; \quad pOH = 4.92; \quad pH = 9.08$$

c. At the stoichiometric point, all the HA is converted into A^-.

	A^-	+	H_2O	$\rightleftharpoons$	HA	+	OH^-	$K_b = 2.0 \times 10^{-5}$
Initial	$\dfrac{0.0100 \text{ mmol}}{110.0 \text{ mL}} = 9.09 \times 10^{-5}\ M$				0		0	
Equil.	$9.09 \times 10^{-5} - x$				x		x	

$$K_b = 2.0 \times 10^{-5} = \frac{x^2}{9.09 \times 10^{-5} - x} \approx \frac{x^2}{9.09 \times 10^{-5}}, \quad x = [OH^-] = 4.3 \times 10^{-5}; \quad \text{Assumption poor.}$$

Using the quadratic formula and carrying extra sig. figs.: $x^2 + 2.0 \times 10^{-5} x - 1.82 \times 10^{-9} = 0$

$$x = 3.4 \times 10^{-5} \, M = [OH^-] \; ; \; pOH = 4.47; \; pH = 9.53$$

Assumption to ignore H_2O contribution to OH^- is good.

133.   a. $200.0 \text{ mL} \times 0.250 \text{ mmol } Na_3PO_4/\text{mL} = 50.0 \text{ mmol } Na_3PO_4$

$135.0 \text{ mL} \times 1.000 \text{ mmol } HCl/\text{mL} = 135.0 \text{ mmol } HCl$

$100.0 \text{ mL} \times 0.100 \text{ mmol } NaCN/\text{mL} = 10.0 \text{ mmol } NaCN$

Let H^+ from the HCl react to completion with the bases in solution. In general, react the strongest base first and so on. Here, 110.0 mmol of HCl reacts to convert all CN^- to HCN and all PO_4^{3-} to $H_2PO_4^-$. At this point 10.0 mmol HCN, 50.0 mmol $H_2PO_4^-$ and 25.0 mmol HCl are in solution. The remaining HCl reacts completely with $H_2PO_4^-$, converting 25.0 mmol to H_3PO_4. Final solution contains: 25.0 mmol H_3PO_4, (50.0 - 25.0 =) 25.0 mmol $H_2PO_4^-$ and 10.0 mmol HCN. HCN ($K_a = 6.2 \times 10^{-10}$) is a much weaker acid than either H_3PO_4 ($K_{a_1} = 7.5 \times 10^{-3}$) or $H_2PO_4^-$ ($K_{a_2} = 6.2 \times 10^{-8}$), so ignore it. Principle equilibrium reaction is:

$$H_3PO_4 \quad \rightleftharpoons \quad H^+ \; + \; H_2PO_4^- \qquad K_{a_1} = 7.5 \times 10^{-3}$$

Initial	25.0 mmol/435.0 mL	0	25.0/435.0
Equil.	0.0575 - x	x	0.0575 + x

$$K_{a_1} = 7.5 \times 10^{-3} = \frac{x(0.0575 + x)}{0.0575 - x}; \quad \text{Normal assumptions don't hold here.}$$

Using the quadratic formula and carrying extra sig. figs.:

$$x^2 + 0.0650 \, x - 4.31 \times 10^{-4} = 0, \quad x = 0.0061 \, M = [H^+]; \; pH = 2.21$$

   b. $[HCN] = \dfrac{10.0 \text{ mmol}}{435.0 \text{ mL}} = 2.30 \times 10^{-2} \, M$; HCN dissociation will be minimal.

134. $50.0 \text{ mL} \times 0.100 \, M = 5.00 \text{ mmol } H_2SO_4$; $30.0 \text{ mL} \times 0.100 \, M = 3.00 \text{ mmol } HOCl$

$25.0 \text{ mL} \times 0.200 \, M = 5.00 \text{ mmol } NaOH$; $10.0 \text{ mL} \times 0.150 \, M = 1.50 \text{ mmol } KOH$

$25.0 \text{ mL} \times 0.100 \, M = 2.50 \text{ mmol } Ba(OH)_2 = 5.00 \text{ mmol } OH^-$; We've added 11.50 mmol OH^- total.

Let OH^- react completely with the best acid present, H_2SO_4

$10.00 \text{ mmol } OH^- + 5.00 \text{ mmol } H_2SO_4 \rightarrow 10.00 \text{ mmol } H_2O + 5.00 \text{ mmol } SO_4^{2-}$

OH^- still remains and it reacts with the next best acid, HOCl. The remaining 1.50 mmol OH^- will convert 1.50 mmol HOCl into 1.50 mmol OCl^-, resulting in a solution with 1.50 mmol OCl^- and

(3.00 - 1.50 =) 1.50 mmol HOCl. Major species at this point: $HOCl$, OCl^-, SO_4^{2-}, H_2O plus cations that don't affect pH. SO_4^{2-} is an extremely weak base ($K_b = 8.3 \times 10^{-13}$). Major equilibrium affecting pH: $HOCl \rightleftharpoons H^+ + OCl^-$. Since $[HOCl] = [OCl^-]$:

$$[H^+] = K_a = 3.5 \times 10^{-8} \, M; \quad pH = 7.46 \quad \text{Assumptions good.}$$

135. H_3A: $pK_{a_1} = 3.00$, $pK_{a_2} = 7.30$, $pK_{a_3} = 11.70$

$$pH = 9.50 = \frac{pK_{a_2} + pK_{a_3}}{2} = \frac{7.30 + 11.70}{2} = pH \text{ at 2nd equivalence point where } HA^{2-} \text{ dominates.}$$

See Section 8.7 of text on calculating the pH of amphoteric species like HA^{2-} or H_2A^-.

100.0 mL $\times$ 0.0500 M = 5.00 mmol H_3A initially. To reach the 2nd stoichiometric point, need 10.0 mmol OH^- = 1.00 mmol/mL $\times V_{NaOH}$. Solving for V_{NaOH}:

$$V_{NaOH} = 10.0 \text{ mL (to reach pH} = 9.50)$$

pH = 4.00 is between the first halfway point to equivalence (pH = pK_{a_1} = 3.00) and the first stoichiometric point (pH = $\dfrac{pK_{a_1} + pK_{a_2}}{2}$ = 5.15).

This is the buffer region controlled by: $H_3A \rightleftharpoons H_2A^- + H^+$

$$pH = pK_{a_1} + \log \frac{[H_2A^-]}{[H_3A]}, \quad 4.00 = 3.00 + \log \frac{[H_2A^-]}{[H_3A]}, \quad \frac{[H_2A^-]}{[H_3A]} = 10.$$

Since both species are in the same volume, the mole ratio also equals 10. Let n = mmol:

$$\frac{n_{H_2A^-}}{n_{H_3A}} = 10. \text{ and } n_{H_2A^-} + n_{H_3A} = 5.00 \text{ mmol (mass balance)}$$

11 n_{H_3A} = 5.00, n_{H_3A} = 0.45 mmol; $n_{H_2A^-}$ = 4.55 mmol

We need to add 4.55 mmol OH^- to get 4.55 mmol H_2A^- from the original H_3A present.

4.55 mmol = 1.00 mmol/mL $\times V_{NaOH}$, V_{NaOH} = 4.55 mL of NaOH (to reach pH = 4.00)

Note: Normal buffer assumptions are good.

136.   100.0 mL $\times$ 0.100 M = 10.0 mmol H_3A initially

a.   100.0 mL $\times$ 0.0500 mmol/mL = 5.00 mmol OH^- added

This is the first halfway point to equivalence where $[H_3A] = [H_2A^-]$ and pH = pK_{a1}.

pH = -log (5.0×10^{-4}) = 3.30   Assumptions good.

b. Since $pK_{a2} = 8.00$, a buffer mixture of H_2A^- and HA^{2-} can produce a $pH = 8.67$ solution.

$$8.67 = 8.00 + \log \frac{[HA^{2-}]}{[H_2A^-]}, \quad \frac{[HA^{2-}]}{[H_2A^-]} = 10^{+0.67} = 4.7$$

Both species are in the same volume, so the mole ratio also equals 4.7. Let n = mmol:

$$\frac{n_{HA^{2-}}}{n_{H_2A^-}} = 4.7, \quad n_{HA^{2-}} = 4.7\, n_{H_2A^-}; \quad n_{HA^{2-}} + n_{H_2A^-} = 10.0 \text{ mmol (mass balance)}$$

$$5.7\, n_{H_2A^-} = 10.0 \text{ mmol}, \quad n_{H_2A^-} = 1.8 \text{ mmol}; \quad n_{HA^{2-}} = 8.2 \text{ mmol}$$

To reach this point, we must add a total of 18.2 mmol NaOH. 10.0 mmol OH^- converts all of the 10.0 mmol H_3A into H_2A^-. The next 8.2 mmol OH^- converts 8.2 mmol H_2A^- into 8.2 mmol HA^{2-}, leaving 1.8 mmol H_2A^-.

$$18.2 \text{ mmol} = 0.0500\, M \times V, \quad V = 364 \text{ mL NaOH}$$

Note: Normal buffer assumptions are good.

137. a. V_1 corresponds to the titration reaction of $CO_3^{2-} + H^+ \rightarrow HCO_3^-$; V_2 corresponds to the titration reaction of $HCO_3^- + H^+ \rightarrow H_2CO_3$.

Here, there are two sources of HCO_3^-: $NaHCO_3$ and the titration of Na_2CO_3. So, $V_2 > V_1$

b. V_1 corresponds to the titration reactions of $OH^- + H^+ \rightarrow H_2O$ and $CO_3^{2-} + H^+ \rightarrow HCO_3^-$. V_2 corresponds to the titration reaction of $HCO_3^- + H^+ \rightarrow H_2CO_3$.

Here, $V_1 > V_2$ due to the presence of OH^- which is titrated in the V_1 region.

c. 0.100 mmol HCl/mL $\times$ 18.9 mL = 1.89 mmol H^+

Since the first stoichiometric point only involves the titration of Na_2CO_3 by H^+, then 1.89 mmol of CO_3^{2-} has been converted into HCO_3^-. The sample contains 1.89 mmol $Na_2CO_3 \times 105.99$ mg/mmol = 2.00×10^2 mg = 0.200 g Na_2CO_3.

The second stoichiometric point involves the titration of HCO_3^- by H^+.

$$\frac{0.100 \text{ mmol } H^+}{\text{mL}} \times 36.7 \text{ mL} = 3.67 \text{ mmol } H^+ = 3.67 \text{ mmol } HCO_3^-$$

1.89 mmol $NaHCO_3$ came from the first stoichiometric point of the Na_2CO_3 titration.
3.67 - 1.89 = 1.78 mmol HCO_3^- came from $NaHCO_3$.

1.78 mmol $NaHCO_3 \times 84.01$ mg $NaHCO_3$/mmol = 1.50×10^2 mg $NaHCO_3$ = 0.150 g $NaHCO_3$

$$\% \, Na_2CO_3 = \frac{0.200 \text{ g}}{(0.200 + 0.150) \text{ g}} \times 100 = 57.1 \, \% \, Na_2CO_3 \text{ by mass}$$

$$\% \, NaHCO_3 = \frac{0.150 \text{ g}}{0.350 \text{ g}} \times 100 = 42.9 \, \% \, NaHCO_3 \text{ by mass}$$

138.   The relevant reactions are:

$$2\,Ag^+(aq) + CrO_4^{2-}(aq) \;\rightleftharpoons\; Ag_2CrO_4(s)$$
$$\text{(red)}$$

$$Ag^+(aq) + Cl^-(aq) \;\rightleftharpoons\; AgCl(s)$$
$$\text{(white)}$$

In the first reaction, solid Ag_2CrO_4 is formed leaving some $Ag^+(aq)$ and $CrO_4^{2-}(aq)$ in solution. As $Cl^-(aq)$ is added, the $AgCl$ solid forms, lowering the concentration of $Ag^+(aq)$. Thus, equilibrium is shifted to the left (1st reaction above) and the red solid disappears. As more $CrO_4^{2-}(aq)$ goes into solution, the solution turns yellow. This means that $Ag_2CrO_4(s)$ is more soluble than $AgCl(s)$, which we can verify using K_{sp} values. The yellow color is due to $CrO_4^{2-}(aq)$.

$$Ag_2CrO_4(s) \;\rightleftharpoons\; 2\,Ag^+ + CrO_4^{2-}$$

Initial	0	0
Change	+2s	+s
Equil.	2s	s

$(2s)^2(s) = K_{sp} = 9.0 \times 10^{-12}, \quad s = 1.3 \times 10^{-4}\,M$

$$AgCl(s) \;\rightleftharpoons\; Ag^+(aq) + Cl^-(aq)$$

Initial	0	0
Change	+s	+s
Equil.	s	s

$s^2 = K_{sp} = 1.6 \times 10^{-10}, \quad s = 1.3 \times 10^{-5}\,M$

Thus, $Ag_2CrO_4(s)$ is more soluble than $AgCl(s)$.

Marathon Problems

139.   a.   Since $K_{a1} \gg K_{a2}$, then the amount of H^+ contributed by the K_{a2} reaction will be negligible. The $[H^+]$ donated by the K_{a1} reaction is $10^{-2.06} = 8.7 \times 10^{-3}\,M\,H^+$.

$$H_2A \quad\rightleftharpoons\quad H^+ \;+\; HA^- \qquad K_{a1} = 5.90 \times 10^{-2}$$

Initial	$[H_2A]_o$	~0	0	$[H_2A]_o$ = initial concentration
Equil.	$[H_2A]_o - x$	x	x	

$$K_{a1} = 5.90 \times 10^{-2} = \frac{x^2}{[H_2A]_o - x} = \frac{(8.7 \times 10^{-3})^2}{[H_2A]_o - 8.7 \times 10^{-3}}, \quad [H_2A]_o = 1.0 \times 10^{-2}\,M$$

$$\text{mol } H_2A \text{ present initially} = 0.250\,L \times \frac{1.0 \times 10^{-2}\,\text{mol } H_2A}{L} = 2.5 \times 10^{-3}\,\text{mol } H_2A$$

$$\text{molar mass } H_2A = \frac{0.225\,g\,H_2A}{2.5 \times 10^{-3}\,\text{mol } H_2A} = 90.\,g/mol$$

b. $H_2A + 2\ OH^- \rightarrow A^{2-} + H_2O$; At the second equivalence point, the added OH^- has converted all the H_2A into A^{2-}, so A^{2-} is the major species present that determines the pH. The mmol of A^{2-} present at the equivalence point equals the mmol of H_2A present initially (2.5 mmol) and the mmol of OH^- added to reach the second equivalence point is $2(2.5\ mmol) = 5.0\ mmol\ OH^-$ added. The only information we need now in order to calculate the K_{a_2} value is the volume of $Ca(OH)_2$ added in order to reach the second equivalent point. We will use the K_{sp} value for $Ca(OH)_2$ to help solve for the volume of $Ca(OH)_2$ added.

$$Ca(OH)_2(s) \quad\rightleftharpoons\quad Ca^{2+} \ + \ 2\ OH^- \quad K_{sp} = 1.3 \times 10^{-6} = [Ca^{2+}]\,[OH^-]^2$$

Initial	s = solubility (mol/L)	0	~0
Equil.		s	$2s$

$K_{sp} = 1.3 \times 10^{-6} = (s)\,(2s)^2 = 4s^3, \ \ s = 6.9 \times 10^{-3}\ M\ Ca(OH)_2$ Assumptions good.

The volume of $Ca(OH)_2$ required to deliver 5.0 mmol OH^- (the amount of OH^- necessary to reach the second equivalence point) is:

$$5.0\ mmol\ OH^- \times \frac{1\ mmol\ Ca(OH)_2}{2\ mmol\ OH^-} \times \frac{1\ mL}{6.9 \times 10^{-3}\ mmol\ Ca(OH)_2}$$

$$= 362\ mL = 360\ mL\ Ca(OH)_2$$

At the second equivalence point, the total volume of solution is:

250. mL + 360 mL = 610 mL

Now we can solve for K_{a_2} using the pH data at the second equivalence point. Since the only species present which has any effect on pH is the weak base, A^{2-}, then the set-up to the problem requires the K_b reaction for A^{2-}.

$$A^{2-} \ + \ H_2O \quad\rightleftharpoons\quad HA^- \ + \ OH^- \qquad K_b = \frac{K_w}{K_{a_2}} = \frac{1.0 \times 10^{-14}}{K_{a_2}}$$

Initial	$\dfrac{2.5\ mmol}{610\ mL}$	0	0
Equil.	$4.1 \times 10^{-3}\ M - x$	x	x

$$K_b = \frac{1.0 \times 10^{-14}}{K_{a_2}} = \frac{x^2}{4.1 \times 10^{-3} - x}$$

From the problem, pH = 7.96 so $[OH^-] = 10^{-6.04} = 9.1 \times 10^{-7}\ M = x$

$$K_b = \frac{1.0 \times 10^{-14}}{K_{a_2}} = \frac{(9.1 \times 10^{-7})^2}{4.1 \times 10^{-3} - 9.1 \times 10^{-7}} = 2.0 \times 10^{-10}, \ \ K_{a_2} = 5.0 \times 10^{-5}$$

Note: The amount of OH^- donated by the weak base HA^- will be negligible since the K_b value for A^{2-} is more than a 1000 times the K_b value for HA^-. In addition, since the pH is less than 8.0 at the second equivalence point, then the amount of OH^- added by H_2O may need to be considered. Using the equation derived in Exercise 7.117, we get the same K_{a_2} value as calculated above by ignoring the OH^- contribution from H_2O.

140.   a.   At the third half-equivalence point, $pH = pK_{a_2} = -\log(4.8 \times 10^{-13}) = 12.32$

   b.   At third equivalence point, the rxn is:

$$PO_4^{3-} + H_2O \rightleftharpoons HPO_4^{2-} + OH^-$$

Initial	$\dfrac{10.\ mmol}{400.\ mL}$	–	0	0
Change	-x		+x	+x
Equil.	0.025-x		x	x

$K_b = \dfrac{K_w}{K_{a_3}} = \dfrac{1.0 \times 10^{-14}}{4.8 \times 10^{-13}}$

$K_b = 2.1 \times 10^{-2}$

$$\dfrac{x^2}{0.025 - x} = 2.1 \times 10^{-2}$$

Using the quadratic equation, $x = 1.5 \times 10^{-2}\ M$; $pOH = 1.82$; $pH = 12.18$

   c.   In part a, we assumed that "x" was negligible:

$$HPO_4^{3-} + H_2O \rightleftharpoons PO_4^{3-} + H_3O^+ \quad K_{a_3} = 4.8 \times 10^{-13}$$

Initial	5.0/350.	–	5.0/350.	0
Change	-x		+x	+x
Equil.	0.014		0.014+x	x

$$\dfrac{(0.14 + x)(x)}{(0.14 - x)} \approx \dfrac{(0.14)(x)}{(0.14)}, \qquad x = 4.8 \times 10^{-13}\ M$$

But, this actually is not the dominant reaction because PO_4^{3-} is such a strong base. We need to use the following reaction and the quadratic equation:

$$PO_4^{3-} + H_2O \rightleftharpoons HPO_4^{2-} + OH^-$$

   d.

$$PO_4^{3-} + H_2O \rightleftharpoons HPO_4^{2-} + OH^- \quad K_b = 2.1 \times 10^{-2}$$

Initial	0.014 M	–	0.014 M	0
Change	-x	–	+x	+x
Equil.	0.014-x	–	0.014+x	x

$$\dfrac{(0.014 + x)(x)}{(0.014 - x)} = 2.1 \times 10^{-2}$$

Using the quadratic equation: $x = [OH^-] = 7.0 \times 10^{-3}\ M$; $pOH = 2.15$, $pH = 11.85$

CHAPTER NINE

ENERGY, ENTHALPY, AND THERMOCHEMISTRY

The Nature of Energy

15.   Ball A: $PE = mgz = 2.00 \text{ kg} \times \dfrac{9.80 \text{ m}}{s^2} \times 10.0 \text{ m} = \dfrac{196 \text{ kg m}^2}{s^2} = 196 \text{ J}$

At Point I: All of this energy is transferred to Ball B. All of B's energy is kinetic energy at this point. $E_{total} = KE = 196 \text{ J}$. At point II, the sum of the total energy will equal 196 J.

At Point II: $PE = mgz = 4.00 \text{ kg} \times \dfrac{9.80 \text{ m}}{s^2} \times 3.00 \text{ m} = 118 \text{ J}$

   $KE = E_{total} - PE = 196 \text{ J} - 118 \text{ J} = 78 \text{ J}$

16.   Plot a represents an exothermic reaction. In an exothermic process, the bonds in the product molecules are stronger (on average) than those in the reactant molecules. The net result is that the quantity of energy $\Delta(PE)$ is transferred to the surroundings as heat when reactants are converted to products.

For an endothermic process (plot b), energy flows into the system as heat to increase the potential energy of the system. In an endothermic process, the products have higher potential energy (weaker bonds on average) than the reactants.

17.   Step 1: $\Delta E_1 = q + w = 72 \text{ J} + 35 \text{ J} = 107 \text{ J}$;   Step 2: $\Delta E_2 = 35 \text{ J} - 72 \text{ J} = -37 \text{ J}$

$\Delta E_{overall} = \Delta E_1 + \Delta E_2 = 107 \text{ J} - 37 \text{ J} = 70. \text{ J}$

18. $KE = \dfrac{1}{2}mv^2 = \dfrac{1}{2} \times 2.0 \text{ kg} \times \left(\dfrac{1.0 \text{ m}}{s}\right)^2 = 1.0 \text{ J}$; $KE = \dfrac{1}{2}mv^2 = \dfrac{1}{2} \times 1.0 \text{ kg} \times \left(\dfrac{2.0 \text{ m}}{s}\right)^2 = 2.0 \text{ J}$

The 1.0 kg object with a velocity of 2.0 m/s has the greater kinetic energy.

19. $q = \text{molar heat capacity} \times \text{mol} \times \Delta T = \dfrac{20.8 \text{ J}}{°\text{C mol}} \times 39.1 \text{ mol} \times (38.0 - 0.0) \, °\text{C} = 30,900 \text{ J} = 30.9 \text{ kJ}$

$w = -P\Delta V = -1.00 \text{ atm} \times (998 \text{ L} - 876 \text{ L}) = -122 \text{ L atm} \times \dfrac{101.3 \text{ J}}{\text{L atm}} = -12,400 \text{ J} = -12.4 \text{ kJ}$

$\Delta E = q + w = 30.9 \text{ kJ} + (-12.4 \text{ kJ}) = 18.5 \text{ kJ}$

20.   In this problem q = w = -950. J

$$-950. \text{ J} \times \frac{1 \text{ L atm}}{101.3 \text{ J}} = -9.38 \text{ L atm of work done by the gases.}$$

$$w = -P\Delta V, \ -9.38 \text{ L atm} = \frac{-650.}{760} \text{ atm} \times (V_f - 0.040 \text{ L}), \ V_f - 0.040 = 11.0 \text{ L}, \ V_f = 11.0 \text{ L}$$

21. $H_2O(g) \rightarrow H_2O(l); \ \Delta E = q + w; \ q = -40.66 \text{ kJ}; \ w = -P\Delta V$

$$\text{Volume of one mol } H_2O(l) = 1.000 \text{ mol } H_2O(l) \times \frac{18.02 \text{ g}}{\text{mol}} \times \frac{1 \text{cm}^3}{0.996 \text{ g}} = 18.1 \text{ cm}^3 = 18.1 \text{ mL}$$

$$w = -P\Delta V = -1.00 \text{ atm} \times (0.0181 \text{ L} - 30.6 \text{ L}) = 30.6 \text{ L atm} \times \frac{101.3 \text{ J}}{\text{L atm}} = 3.10 \times 10^3 \text{ J} = 3.10 \text{ kJ}$$

$$\Delta E = q + w = -40.66 \text{ kJ} + 3.10 \text{ kJ} = -37.56 \text{ kJ}$$

Properties of Enthalpy

22.   A state function is a function whose change depends only on the initial and final states and not on how one got from the initial to the final state. If H and E were not state functions, the law of conservation of energy (first law) would not be true.

23.   One should try to cool the reaction mixture or provide some means of removing heat since the reaction is very exothermic (heat is released). The $H_2SO_4(aq)$ will get very hot and possibly boil, unless cooling is provided.

24.   This is an endothermic reaction so heat must be absorbed in order to convert reactants into products. The high temperature environment of internal combustion engines provides the heat.

25.   a. $1.00 \text{ mol } H_2O \times \dfrac{-572 \text{ kJ}}{2 \text{ mol } H_2O} = -286 \text{ kJ heat released}$

       b. $4.03 \text{ g } H_2 \times \dfrac{1 \text{ mol } H_2}{2.016 \text{ g } H_2} \times \dfrac{-572 \text{ kJ}}{2 \text{ mol } H_2} = -572 \text{ kJ heat released}$

       c. $186 \text{ g } O_2 \times \dfrac{1 \text{ mol } O_2}{32.00 \text{ g } O_2} \times \dfrac{-572 \text{ kJ}}{\text{mol } O_2} = -3320 \text{ kJ heat released}$

       d. $n_{H_2} = \dfrac{PV}{RT} = \dfrac{1.0 \text{ atm} \times 2.0 \times 10^8 \text{ L}}{\dfrac{0.08206 \text{ L atm}}{\text{mol K}} \times 298 \text{ K}} = 8.2 \times 10^6 \text{ mol } H_2$

            $8.2 \times 10^6 \text{ mol } H_2 \times \dfrac{-572 \text{ kJ}}{2 \text{ mol } H_2} = -2.3 \times 10^9 \text{ kJ heat released}$

26.   The combustion of phosphorus is exothermic. Thus the product, P_4O_{10}, is lower in energy than either red or white phosphorus. Since the conversion of white phosphorus to red phosphorus is exothermic, red phosphorus is lower in energy than white phosphorus. Thus, white phosphorus will release more heat when burned in air since there is a larger energy difference between white phosphorus and products.

The Thermodynamics of Ideal Gases

27.   Consider the constant volume process first.

$n = 1.00 \times 10^3 \text{ g} \times \dfrac{1 \text{ mol}}{30.07 \text{ g}} = 33.3 \text{ mol } C_2H_6;\quad C_v = \dfrac{44.60 \text{ J}}{K \text{ mol}} = \dfrac{44.60 \text{ J}}{°C \text{ mol}}$

$\Delta E = nC_v\Delta T = (33.3 \text{ mol}) (44.60 \text{ J }°C^{-1} \text{ mol}^{-1}) (75.0 - 25.0°C) = 74{,}300 \text{ J} = 74.3 \text{ kJ}$

$\Delta E = q + w;\ \text{ Since } \Delta V = 0,\ w = 0;\ \ \Delta E = q_v = 74.3 \text{ kJ}$

$\Delta H = \Delta E + \Delta PV = \Delta E + nR\Delta T$

$\Delta H = 74.3 \text{ kJ} + (33.3 \text{ mol})(8.3145 \text{ J mol}^{-1} \text{ K}^{-1}) (50.0 \text{ K})(1 \text{ kJ}/1000 \text{ J})$

$\Delta H = 74.3 \text{ kJ} + 13.8 \text{ kJ} = 88.1 \text{ kJ}$

Now consider the constant pressure process.

$q_p = \Delta H = nC_p\Delta T = (33.3 \text{ mol}) (52.92 \text{ J mol}^{-1} \text{ K}^{-1}) (50.0 \text{ K})$

$q_p = 88{,}100 \text{ J} = 88.1 \text{ kJ} = \Delta H$

$w = -P\Delta V = -nR\Delta T = -(33.3 \text{ mol}) (8.3145 \text{ J mol}^{-1} \text{ K}^{-1}) (50.0 \text{ K}) = -13{,}800 \text{ J} = -13.8 \text{ kJ}$

$\Delta E = q + w = 88.1 \text{ kJ} - 13.8 \text{ kJ} = 74.3 \text{ kJ}$

Summary:	Constant V	Constant P
q	74.3 kJ	88.1 kJ
ΔE	74.3 kJ	74.3 kJ
ΔH	88.1 kJ	88.1 kJ
w	0	-13.8 kJ

28. $88.0 \text{ g N}_2O \times \dfrac{1 \text{ mol N}_2O}{44.02 \text{ g N}_2O} = 2.00 \text{ mol N}_2O$

At constant pressure, $q_p = \Delta H$

$\Delta H = nC_p\Delta T = (2.00 \text{ mol}) (38.70 \text{ J mol}^{-1} °C^{-1}) (55°C - 165°C)$

$\Delta H = -8510 \text{ J} = -8.51 \text{ kJ} = q_p$

$w = -P\Delta V = -nR\Delta T = -(2.00 \text{ mol}) (8.3145 \text{ J mol}^{-1} \text{ K}^{-1}) (-110. \text{ K}) = 1830 \text{ J} = 1.83 \text{ kJ}$

$\Delta E = q + w = -8.51 \text{ kJ} + 1.83 \text{ kJ} = -6.68 \text{ kJ}$

29.   Pathway I:

Step 1: (5.00 mol, 3.00 atm, 15.0 L) → (5.00 mol, 3.00 atm, 55.0 L)

$w = -P\Delta V = -(3.00 \text{ atm})(55.0 - 15.0 \text{ L}) = -120. \text{ L atm}$

$w = -120. \text{ L atm} \times \dfrac{101.3 \text{ J}}{\text{L atm}} \times \dfrac{1 \text{ kJ}}{1000 \text{ J}} = -12.2 \text{ kJ}$

$\Delta H = q_p = nC_p\Delta T = nC_p \dfrac{\Delta(PV)}{nR} = \dfrac{C_p\Delta(PV)}{R}; \quad \Delta(PV) = (P_2V_2 - P_1V_1)$

For an ideal monatomic gas: $C_p = \dfrac{5}{2} R$

$\Delta H = q_p = \dfrac{5}{2}\Delta(PV) = \dfrac{5}{2}(165 - 45.0) \text{ L atm} = 300. \text{ L atm}$

$\Delta H = q_p = 300. \text{ L atm} \times \dfrac{101.3 \text{ J}}{\text{L atm}} \times \dfrac{1 \text{ kJ}}{1000 \text{ J}} = 30.4 \text{ kJ}$

$\Delta E = q + w = 30.4 \text{ kJ} - 12.2 \text{ kJ} = 18.2 \text{ kJ}$

Step 2: (5.00 mol, 3.00 atm, 55.0 L) → (5.00 mol, 6.00 atm, 20.0 L)

$\Delta E = nC_v\Delta T = n\left(\dfrac{3}{2} R\right)\left(\dfrac{\Delta(PV)}{nR}\right) = \dfrac{3}{2}\Delta PV$

$\Delta E = \dfrac{3}{2}(120. - 165) \text{ L atm} = -67.5 \text{ L atm}$ (Carry extra significant figure.)

$\Delta E = -67.5 \text{ L atm} \times \dfrac{101.3 \text{ J}}{\text{L atm}} \times \dfrac{1 \text{ kJ}}{1000 \text{ J}} = -6.8 \text{ kJ}$

$\Delta H = nC_p\Delta T = n\left(\dfrac{5}{2} R\right)\left(\dfrac{\Delta(PV)}{nR}\right) = \dfrac{5}{2}\Delta(PV)$

$\Delta H = \dfrac{5}{2}(-45 \text{ L atm}) = -113 \text{ L atm}$ (Carry extra significant figure.)

$\Delta H = -113 \text{ L atm} \times \dfrac{101.3 \text{ J}}{\text{L atm}} \times \dfrac{1 \text{ kJ}}{1000 \text{ J}} = -11.4 = -11 \text{ kJ}$

$w = -P_{ext}\Delta V = -(6.00 \text{ atm})(20.0 - 55.0)\text{L} = 210. \text{ L atm}$

$w = 210. \text{ L atm} \times \dfrac{101.3 \text{ J}}{\text{L atm}} \times \dfrac{1 \text{ kJ}}{1000 \text{ J}} = 21.3 \text{ kJ}$

$\Delta E = q + w, \; -6.8 \text{ kJ} = q + 21.3 \text{ kJ}, \; q = -28.1 \text{ kJ}$

Summary: Path I   Step 1   Step 2   Total

q 30.4 kJ   -28.1 kJ   2.3 kJ

w -12.2 kJ   21.3 kJ   9.1 kJ

ΔE 18.2 kJ   -6.8 kJ   11.4 kJ

ΔH 30.4 kJ   -11 kJ   19 kJ

Pathway II:

Step 3: (5.00 mol, 3.00 atm, 15.0 L) $\rightarrow$ (5.00 mol, 6.00 atm, 15.0 L)

$$\Delta E = q_v = \frac{3}{2}\Delta(PV) = \frac{3}{2}(90.0 - 45.0)\text{L atm} = 67.5 \text{ L atm}$$

$$\Delta E = q_v = 67.5 \text{ L atm} \times \frac{101.3 \text{ J}}{\text{L atm}} \times \frac{1 \text{ kJ}}{1000 \text{ J}} = 6.84 \text{ kJ}$$

$w = -P\Delta V = 0$ since $\Delta V = 0$

$\Delta H = \Delta E + \Delta(PV) = 67.5 \text{ L atm} + 45.0 \text{ L atm} = 112.5 \text{ L atm} = 11.40 \text{ kJ}$

Step 4: (5.00 mol, 6.00 atm, 15.0 L) $\rightarrow$ (5.00 mol, 6.00 atm, 20.0 L)

$$\Delta H = q_p = nC_p\Delta T = n\left(\frac{5}{2}R\right)\left(\frac{\Delta(PV)}{nR}\right) = \frac{5}{2}\Delta PV$$

$$\Delta H = \frac{5}{2}(120. - 90.0) \text{ L atm} = 75 \text{ L atm}$$

$$\Delta H = q_p = 75 \text{ L atm} \times \frac{101.3 \text{ J}}{\text{L atm}} \times \frac{1 \text{ kJ}}{1000 \text{ J}} = 7.6 \text{ kJ}$$

$w = -P\Delta V = -(6.00 \text{ atm})(20.0 - 15.0)\text{L} = -30. \text{ L atm}$

$$w = -30. \text{ L atm} \times \frac{101.3 \text{ J}}{\text{L atm}} \times \frac{1 \text{ kJ}}{1000 \text{ J}} = -3.0 \text{ kJ}$$

$\Delta E = q + w = 7.6 \text{ kJ} - 3.0 \text{ kJ} = 4.6 \text{ kJ}$

Summary: Path II   Step 3   Step 4   Total

q 6.84 kJ   7.6 kJ   14.4 kJ

w 0   -3.0 kJ   -3.0 kJ

ΔE 6.84 kJ   4.6 kJ   11.4 kJ

ΔH 11.40 kJ   7.6 kJ   19.0 kJ

State functions are independent of the particular pathway taken between two states; path functions are dependent on the particular pathway. In this problem, the overall values of ΔH and ΔE for the two pathways are the same; hence, ΔH and ΔE are state functions. The overall values of q and w for the two pathways are different; hence, q and w are path functions.

30.   Step 1: (2.00 mol, 10.0 atm, 10.0 L) → (2.00 mol, 10.0 atm, 5.0 L)

$$\Delta H = q_p = nC_p\Delta T = n\left(\frac{5}{2}R\right)\left(\frac{\Delta(PV)}{nR}\right) = \frac{5}{2}\Delta(PV)$$

$$\Delta H = q_p = \frac{5}{2}(50. - 100.) = -125 \text{ L atm} = -12.7 \text{ kJ} \quad \text{(We will carry all calculations to 0.1 kJ.)}$$

$$w = -P\Delta V = -(10.0 \text{ atm})(5.0 - 10.0)L = 50. \text{ L atm} = 5.1 \text{ kJ}$$

$$\Delta E = q + w = -12.7 + 5.1 = -7.6 \text{ kJ}$$

Step 2: (2.00 mol, 10.0 atm, 5.0 L) → (2.00 mol, 20.0 atm, 5.0 L)

$$\Delta E = q_v = \frac{3}{2}\Delta(PV) = \frac{3}{2}(100 - 50.) = 75 \text{ L atm} = 7.6 \text{ kJ}; \quad w = 0 \text{ since } \Delta V = 0$$

$$\Delta H = \Delta E + \Delta(PV) = 75 \text{ L atm} + 50 \text{ L atm} = 125 \text{ L atm} = 12.7 \text{ kJ}$$

Step 3: (2.00 mol, 20.0 atm, 5.0 L) → (2.00 mol, 20.0 atm, 25.0 L)

$$\Delta H = q_p = \frac{5}{2}\Delta(PV) = \frac{5}{2}(500. - 100) = 1.0 \times 10^3 \text{ L atm} = 101.3 \text{ kJ}$$

$$w = -P\Delta V = -(20.0 \text{ atm})(25.0 - 5.0)L = -400. \text{ L atm} = -40.5 \text{ kJ}$$

$$\Delta E = q + w = 101.3 - 40.5 = 60.8 \text{ kJ}$$

Summary:		Step 1	Step 2	Step 3	Total
	q	-12.7 kJ	7.6 kJ	101.3 kJ	96.2 kJ
	w	5.1 kJ	0	-40.5 kJ	-35.4 kJ
	ΔE	-7.6 kJ	7.6 kJ	60.8 kJ	60.8 kJ
	ΔH	-12.7 kJ	12.7 kJ	101.3 kJ	101.3 kJ

Calorimetry and Heat Capacity

31.   A coffee-cup calorimeter is at constant (atmospheric) pressure. The heat released or gained at constant pressure is ΔH. A bomb calorimeter is at constant volume. The heat released or gained at constant volume is ΔE.

32. a. s = specific heat capacity = $\dfrac{0.24\ \text{J}}{\text{g}\ {}^{\circ}\text{C}} = \dfrac{0.24\ \text{J}}{\text{g K}}$ since $\Delta T(K) = \Delta T({}^{\circ}C)$.

energy = $s \times m \times \Delta T = \dfrac{0.24\ \text{J}}{\text{g}\ {}^{\circ}\text{C}} \times 150.0\ \text{g} \times (298\ \text{K} - 273\ \text{K}) = 9.0 \times 10^2\ \text{J}$

b. molar heat capacity = $\dfrac{0.24\ \text{J}}{\text{g}\ {}^{\circ}\text{C}} \times \dfrac{107.9\ \text{g Ag}}{\text{mol Ag}} = \dfrac{26\ \text{J}}{\text{mol}\ {}^{\circ}\text{C}}$

c. $1250\ \text{J} = \dfrac{0.24\ \text{J}}{\text{g}\ {}^{\circ}\text{C}} \times m \times (15.2{}^{\circ}\text{C} - 12.0{}^{\circ}\text{C})$, $m = \dfrac{1250}{0.24 \times 3.2} = 1.6 \times 10^3\ \text{g Ag}$

33. Specific heat capacity is defined as the amount of heat necessary to raise the temperature of one gram of substance by one degree Celsius. Therefore, $H_2O(l)$ with the largest heat capacity value requires the largest amount of heat for this process. The amount of heat for $H_2O(l)$ is:

energy = $s \times m \times \Delta T = \dfrac{4.18\ \text{J}}{\text{g}\ {}^{\circ}\text{C}} \times 25.0\ \text{g} \times (37.0{}^{\circ}\text{C} - 15.0{}^{\circ}\text{C}) = 2.30 \times 10^3\ \text{J}$

The largest temperature change when a certain amount of energy is added to a certain mass of substance will occur for the substance with the smallest specific heat capacity. This is $Hg(l)$, and the temperature change for this process is:

$$\Delta T = \dfrac{\text{energy}}{s \times m} = \dfrac{10.7\ \text{kJ} \times \dfrac{1000\ \text{J}}{\text{kJ}}}{\dfrac{0.14\ \text{J}}{\text{g}\ {}^{\circ}\text{C}} \times 550.\ \text{g}} = 140{}^{\circ}\text{C}$$

34. Heat gain by water = heat loss by Cu; Keeping all quantities positive to avoid sign errors:

$\dfrac{4.18\ \text{J}}{\text{g}\ {}^{\circ}\text{C}} \times m \times (24.9{}^{\circ}\text{C} - 22.3{}^{\circ}\text{C}) = \dfrac{0.20\ \text{J}}{\text{g}\ {}^{\circ}\text{C}} \times 110.\ \text{g Cu} \times (82.4{}^{\circ}\text{C} - 24.9{}^{\circ}\text{C})$

$11\ m = 1300$, $m = 120\ \text{g}\ H_2O$

35. Heat gained by water = Heat lost by copper; Let s = specific capacity of copper.

$\dfrac{4.18\ \text{J}}{\text{g}\ {}^{\circ}\text{C}} \times 75.0\ \text{g} \times 2.2{}^{\circ}\text{C} = s \times 46.2\ \text{g} \times 73.6{}^{\circ}\text{C}$, $s = 0.20\ \text{J}\ {}^{\circ}\text{C}^{-1}\ \text{g}^{-1}$

36. Heat loss by Al + heat loss by Fe = heat gain by water; Keeping all quantities positive to avoid sign error:

$\dfrac{0.89\ \text{J}}{\text{g}\ {}^{\circ}\text{C}} \times 5.00\ \text{g Al} \times (100.0{}^{\circ}\text{C} - T_f) + \dfrac{0.45\ \text{J}}{\text{g}\ {}^{\circ}\text{C}} \times 10.00\ \text{g Fe} \times (100.0 - T_f)$

$= \dfrac{4.18\ \text{J}}{\text{g}\ {}^{\circ}\text{C}} \times 97.3\ \text{g}\ H_2O \times (T_f - 22.0{}^{\circ}\text{C})$

$4.5(100.0 - T_f) + 4.5(100.0 - T_f) = 407(T_f - 22.0)$, $450 - 4.5\ T_f + 450 - 4.5\ T_f = 407\ T_f - 8950$

$416\ T_f = 9850$, $T_f = 23.7{}^{\circ}\text{C}$

37. 50.0×10^{-3} L $\times$ 0.100 mol/L = 5.00×10^{-3} mol of both $AgNO_3$ and HCl are reacted. Thus, 5.00×10^{-3} mol of AgCl will be produced since there is a 1:1 mol ratio between reactants.

Heat lost by chemicals = Heat gained by solution

Heat gain = $\dfrac{4.18 \text{ J}}{\text{g} \, ^\circ\text{C}} \times 100.0$ g $\times$ (23.40 - 22.60)$^\circ$C = 330 J

Heat loss = 330 J; This is the heat evolved (exothermic reaction) when 5.00×10^{-3} mol of AgCl is produced. So q = -330 J and ΔH (heat per mol AgCl formed) is negative with a value of:

$$\Delta H = \dfrac{-330 \text{ J}}{5.00 \times 10^{-3} \text{ mol}} \times \dfrac{1 \text{ kJ}}{1000 \text{ J}} = \text{-66 kJ/mol}$$

Note: Sign errors are common with calorimetry problems. However, the correct sign for ΔH can easily be determined from the ΔT data, i.e., if ΔT of the solution increases, then the reaction is exothermic since heat was released, and if ΔT of the solution decreases, then the reaction is endothermic since the reaction absorbed heat from the water. For calorimetry problems, keep all quantities positive until the end of the calculation, then decide the sign for ΔH. This will help eliminate sign errors.

38. $NH_4NO_3(s) \rightarrow NH_4^+(aq) + NO_3^-(aq)$ ΔH = ?; mass of solution = 75.0 g + 1.60 g = 76.6 g

Heat lost by solution = Heat gained as NH_4NO_3 dissolves. To help eliminate sign errors, we will keep all quantities positive (q and ΔT), then deduce the correct sign for ΔH at the end of the problem. Here, since temperature decreases as NH_4NO_3 dissolves, then heat is absorbed as NH_4NO_3 dissolves so it is an endothermic process (ΔH is positive).

Heat lost by solution = $\dfrac{4.18 \text{ J}}{\text{g} \, ^\circ\text{C}} \times 76.6$ g $\times$ (25.00 - 23.34)$^\circ$C = 532 J = heat gained as NH_4NO_3 dissolves

$$\Delta H = \dfrac{532 \text{ J}}{1.60 \text{ g } NH_4NO_3} \times \dfrac{80.05 \text{ g } NH_4NO_3}{\text{mol } NH_4NO_3} \times \dfrac{1 \text{ kJ}}{1000 \text{ J}} = \text{26.6 kJ/mol } NH_4NO_3 \text{ dissolving}$$

39.   Since ΔH is exothermic, then the temperature of the solution will increase as $CaCl_2(s)$ dissolves. Keeping all quantities positive:

Heat loss as $CaCl_2$ dissolves = 11.0 g $CaCl_2$ $\times \dfrac{1 \text{ mol } CaCl_2}{110.98 \text{ g } CaCl_2} \times \dfrac{81.5 \text{ kJ}}{\text{mol } CaCl_2} = $ **8.08 kJ**

Heat gained by solution = 8.08×10^3 J = $\dfrac{4.18 \text{ J}}{\text{g} \, ^\circ\text{C}} \times (125 + 11.0)$ g $\times$ (T_f - 25.0°C)

T_f - 25.0°C = $\dfrac{8.08 \times 10^3}{4.18 \times 136}$ = 14.2°C, T_f = 14.2°C + 25.0°C = 39.2°C

40. $0.100 \text{ L} \times \dfrac{0.500 \text{ mol HCl}}{\text{L}} = 5.00 \times 10^{-2} \text{ mol HCl}$

$0.300 \text{ L} \times \dfrac{0.100 \text{ mol Ba(OH)}_2}{\text{L}} = 3.00 \times 10^{-2} \text{ mol Ba(OH)}_2$

To react with all the HCl present, $5.00 \times 10^{-2}/2 = 2.50 \times 10^{-2}$ mol Ba(OH)$_2$ is required. Since 0.0300 mol Ba(OH)$_2$ is present, then HCl is the limiting reactant.

$5.00 \times 10^{-2} \text{ mol HCl} \times \dfrac{118 \text{ kJ}}{2 \text{ mol HCl}} = 2.95 \text{ kJ of heat is evolved by reaction.}$

Heat gained by solution = $2.95 \times 10^3 \text{ J} = \dfrac{4.18 \text{ J}}{\text{g }^\circ\text{C}} \times 400.0 \text{ g} \times \Delta T$

$\Delta T = 1.76\,^\circ\text{C} = T_f - T_i = T_f - 25.0\,^\circ\text{C}, \ T_f = 26.8\,^\circ\text{C}$

41.   Heat gain by calorimeter = $\dfrac{1.56 \text{ kJ}}{^\circ\text{C}} \times 3.2\,^\circ\text{C} = 5.0 \text{ kJ} = \text{heat loss by quinone}$

Heat loss = 5.0 kJ, which is the heat evolved (exothermic reaction) by the combustion of 0.1964 g of quinone.

$\Delta E_{comb} = \dfrac{-5.0 \text{ kJ}}{0.1964 \text{ g}} = -25 \text{ kJ/g;} \qquad \Delta E_{comb} = \dfrac{-25 \text{ kJ}}{\text{g}} \times \dfrac{108.09 \text{ g}}{\text{mol}} = -2700 \text{ kJ/mol}$

42.   First, we need to get the heat capacity of the calorimeter from the combustion of benzoic acid.

Heat lost by combustion = Heat gained by calorimeter

Heat loss = $0.1584 \text{ g} \times \dfrac{26.42 \text{ kJ}}{\text{g}} = 4.185 \text{ kJ}$

Heat gain = $4.185 \text{ kJ} = C_{cal} \times \Delta T, \ C_{cal} = \dfrac{4.185 \text{ kJ}}{2.54\,^\circ\text{C}} = 1.65 \text{ kJ/}^\circ\text{C}$

Now we can calculate the heat of combustion of vanillin. Heat loss = Heat gain

Heat gain by calorimeter = $\dfrac{1.65 \text{ kJ}}{^\circ\text{C}} \times 3.25\,^\circ\text{C} = 5.36 \text{ kJ}$

Heat loss = 5.36 kJ which is the heat evolved by the combustion of the vanillin.

$\Delta E_{comb} = \dfrac{-5.36 \text{ kJ}}{0.2130 \text{ g}} = -25.2 \text{ kJ/g;} \ \Delta E_{comb} = \dfrac{-25.2 \text{ kJ}}{\text{g}} \times \dfrac{152.14 \text{ g}}{\text{mol}} = -3830 \text{ kJ/mol}$

43.   a. $C_{12}H_{22}O_{11}(s) + 12 \ O_2(g) \rightarrow 12 \ CO_2(g) + 11 \ H_2O(l)$

b.   A bomb calorimeter is at constant volume, so heat released = $q_v = \Delta E$:

$\Delta E = \dfrac{-24.00 \text{ kJ}}{1.46 \text{ g}} \times \dfrac{342.30 \text{ g}}{\text{mol}} = -5630 \text{ kJ/mol } C_{12}H_{22}O_{11}$

c. $\Delta H = \Delta E + \Delta(PV) = \Delta E + \Delta(nRT) = \Delta E + \Delta nRT$ where Δn = mol gaseous products - mol gaseous reactants.

For this reaction $\Delta n = 12 - 12 = 0$, so $\Delta H = \Delta E = -5630$ kJ/mol.

44. $A(l) \rightarrow A(g)$ $\Delta H_{vap} = 30.7$ kJ

$w = -P\Delta V = -\Delta nRT$ where $\Delta n = n_{prod} - n_{react} = 1-0 = 1$

$w = -(1 \text{ mol}) (8.3145 \text{ J mol}^{-1} \text{ K}^{-1}) (80. + 273 \text{ K}) = -2940$ J; Since at constant P:

$\Delta E = q_p + w = \Delta H + w = 30.7 \text{ kJ} + (-2.94 \text{ kJ}) = 27.8$ kJ

Hess's Law

45. $2 \text{ C} + 2 \text{ O}_2 \rightarrow 2 \text{ CO}_2$ $\Delta H = 2(-394 \text{ kJ})$
           $\text{H}_2 + 1/2 \text{ O}_2 \rightarrow \text{H}_2\text{O}$ $\Delta H = -286$ kJ
           $2 \text{ CO}_2 + \text{H}_2\text{O} \rightarrow \text{C}_2\text{H}_2 + 5/2 \text{ O}_2$ $\Delta H = -(-1300.\text{kJ})$
           _____

           $2 \text{ C(s)} + \text{H}_2\text{(g)} \rightarrow \text{C}_2\text{H}_2\text{(g)}$ $\Delta H = 226$ kJ

Note: The enthalpy change for a reaction that is reversed is the negative quantity of the enthalpy change for the original reaction. If the coefficients in a balanced reaction are multiplied by an integer, then the value of ΔH is multiplied by the same integer.

46. $2 \text{ NO}_2 \rightarrow \text{N}_2 + 2 \text{ O}_2$ $\Delta H = -(67.7 \text{ kJ})$
           $\text{N}_2 + 2 \text{ O}_2 \rightarrow \text{N}_2\text{O}_4$ $\Delta H = 9.7$ kJ
           _____

           $2 \text{ NO}_2\text{(g)} \rightarrow \text{N}_2\text{O}_4\text{(g)}$ $\Delta H = -58.0$ kJ

47. $4 \text{ HNO}_3 \rightarrow 2 \text{ N}_2\text{O}_5 + 2 \text{ H}_2\text{O}$ $\Delta H = -2(-76.6 \text{ kJ})$
           $2 \text{ N}_2 + 6 \text{ O}_2 + 2 \text{ H}_2 \rightarrow 4 \text{ HNO}_3$ $\Delta H = 4(-174.1 \text{ kJ})$
                   $2 \text{ H}_2\text{O} \rightarrow 2 \text{ H}_2 + \text{O}_2$ $\Delta H = -2(-285.8 \text{ kJ})$
           _____

           $2 \text{ N}_2\text{(g)} + 5 \text{ O}_2\text{(g)} \rightarrow 2 \text{ N}_2\text{O}_5\text{(g)}$ $\Delta H = 28.4$ kJ

48.   To avoid fractions, let's first calculate ΔH for the reaction:

$6 \text{ FeO(s)} + 6 \text{ CO(g)} \rightarrow 6 \text{ Fe(s)} + 6 \text{ CO}_2\text{(g)}$

           $6 \text{ FeO} + 2 \text{ CO}_2 \rightarrow 2 \text{ Fe}_3\text{O}_4 + 2 \text{ CO}$ $\Delta H = -2(18 \text{ kJ})$
           $2 \text{ Fe}_3\text{O}_4 + \text{CO}_2 \rightarrow 3 \text{ Fe}_2\text{O}_3 + \text{CO}$ $\Delta H = -(-39 \text{ kJ})$
           $3 \text{ Fe}_2\text{O}_3 + 9 \text{ CO} \rightarrow 6 \text{ Fe} + 9 \text{ CO}_2$ $\Delta H = 3(-23 \text{ kJ})$
           _____

           $6 \text{ FeO(s)} + 6 \text{ CO(g)} \rightarrow 6 \text{ Fe(s)} + 6 \text{ CO}_2\text{(g)}$ $\Delta H = -66$ kJ

So for: $\text{FeO(s)} + \text{CO(g)} \rightarrow \text{Fe(s)} + \text{CO}_2\text{(g)}$ $\Delta H = \dfrac{-66 \text{ kJ}}{6} = -11$ kJ

49.
$$C_4H_4(g) + 5\ O_2(g) \rightarrow 4\ CO_2(g) + 2\ H_2O(l) \qquad \Delta H_{comb} = -2341\ kJ$$
$$C_4H_8(g) + 6\ O_2(g) \rightarrow 4\ CO_2(g) + 4\ H_2O(l) \qquad \Delta H_{comb} = -2755\ kJ$$
$$H_2(g) + 1/2\ O_2(g) \rightarrow H_2O(l) \qquad \Delta H_{comb} = -286\ kJ$$

By convention, $H_2O(l)$ is produced when enthalpies of combustion are given and, since per mol quantities are given, the combustion reaction refers to 1 mol of that quantity reacting with $O_2(g)$.

Using Hess's Law to solve:

$$C_4H_4(g) + 5\ O_2(g) \rightarrow 4\ CO_2(g) + 2\ H_2O(l) \qquad \Delta H_1 = -2341\ kJ$$
$$4\ CO_2(g) + 4\ H_2O(l) \rightarrow C_4H_8(g) + 6\ O_2(g) \qquad \Delta H_2 = -(-2755\ kJ)$$
$$2\ H_2(g) + O_2(g) \rightarrow 2\ H_2O(l) \qquad \Delta H_3 = 2(-286\ kJ)$$
_____
$$C_4H_4(g) + 2\ H_2(g) \rightarrow C_4H_8(g) \qquad \Delta H = \Delta H_1 + \Delta H_2 + \Delta H_3 = -158\ kJ$$

50.
$$NO + O_3 \rightarrow NO_2 + O_2 \qquad \Delta H = -199\ kJ$$
$$3/2\ O_2 \rightarrow O_3 \qquad \Delta H = -1/2(-427\ kJ)$$
$$O \rightarrow 1/2\ O_2 \qquad \Delta H = -1/2(495\ kJ)$$
_____
$$NO(g) + O(g) \rightarrow NO_2(g) \qquad \Delta H = -233\ kJ$$

51.
$$C_6H_4(OH)_2 \rightarrow C_6H_4O_2 + H_2 \qquad \Delta H = 177.4\ kJ$$
$$H_2O_2 \rightarrow H_2 + O_2 \qquad \Delta H = -(-191.2\ kJ)$$
$$2\ H_2 + O_2 \rightarrow 2\ H_2O(g) \qquad \Delta H = 2(-241.8\ kJ)$$
$$2\ H_2O(g) \rightarrow 2\ H_2O(l) \qquad \Delta H = 2(-43.8\ kJ)$$
_____
$$C_6H_4(OH)_2(aq) + H_2O_2(aq) \rightarrow C_6H_4O_2(aq) + 2\ H_2O(l) \qquad \Delta H = -202.6\ kJ$$

52.
$$P_4O_{10} \rightarrow P_4 + 5\ O_2 \qquad \Delta H = -(-2967.3\ kJ)$$
$$10\ PCl_3 + 5\ O_2 \rightarrow 10\ Cl_3PO \qquad \Delta H = 10(-285.7\ kJ)$$
$$6\ PCl_5 \rightarrow 6\ PCl_3 + 6\ Cl_2 \qquad \Delta H = -6(-84.2\ kJ)$$
$$P_4 + 6\ Cl_2 \rightarrow 4\ PCl_3 \qquad \Delta H = -1225.6\ kJ$$
_____
$$P_4O_{10}(s) + 6\ PCl_5(g) \rightarrow 10\ Cl_3PO(g) \qquad \Delta H = -610.1\ kJ$$

53.
$$2\ N_2(g) + 6\ H_2(g) \rightarrow 4\ NH_3(g) \qquad \Delta H = -4(46\ kJ)$$
$$6\ H_2O(g) \rightarrow 6\ H_2(g) + 3\ O_2(g) \qquad \Delta H = -3(-484\ kJ)$$
_____
$$2\ N_2(g) + 6\ H_2O(g) \rightarrow 3\ O_2(g) + 4\ NH_3(g) \qquad \Delta H = 1268\ kJ$$

No, since the reaction is very endothermic (requires a lot of heat), it would not be a practical way of making ammonia due to the high energy costs required.

Standard Enthalpies of Formation

54.   The change in enthalpy that accompanies the formation of one mole of a compound from its elements, with all substances in their standard states is the standard enthalpy of formation for a compound. The reactions that refer to ΔH_f° are:

$Na(s) + 1/2\ Cl_2(g) \rightarrow NaCl(s);\ \ H_2(g) + 1/2\ O_2(g) \rightarrow H_2O(l)$

$6\ C(graphite,\ s) + 6\ H_2(g) + 3\ O_2(g) \rightarrow C_6H_{12}O_6(s);\ \ Pb(s) + S(s) + 2\ O_2(g) \rightarrow PbSO_4(s)$

55.   In general: $\Delta H^\circ = \Sigma n_p \Delta H^\circ_{f,\ products} - \Sigma n_r \Delta H^\circ_{f,\ reactants}$ and all elements in their standard state have $\Delta H^\circ_f = 0$ by definition.

a.   The balanced equation is: $2\ NH_3(g) + 3\ O_2(g) + 2\ CH_4(g) \rightarrow 2\ HCN(g) + 6\ H_2O(g)$

$$\Delta H^\circ = [2\ mol\ HCN \times \Delta H^\circ_{f,\ HCN} + 6\ mol\ H_2O(g) \times \Delta H^\circ_{f,\ H_2O}]$$

$$- [2\ mol\ NH_3 \times \Delta H^\circ_{f,\ NH_3} + 2\ mol\ CH_4 \times \Delta H^\circ_{f,\ CH_4}]$$

$$\Delta H^\circ = [2(135.1) + 6(-242)] - [2(-46) + 2(-75)] = -940.\ kJ$$

b. $Ca_3(PO_4)_2(s) + 3\ H_2SO_4(l) \rightarrow 3\ CaSO_4(s) + 2\ H_3PO_4(l)$

$$\Delta H^\circ = \left[3\ mol\ CaSO_4 \left(\frac{-1433\ kJ}{mol} \right) + 2\ mol\ H_3PO_4(l) \left(\frac{-1267\ kJ}{mol} \right) \right]$$

$$- \left[1\ mol\ Ca_3(PO_4)_2 \left(\frac{-4126\ kJ}{mol} \right) + 3\ mol\ H_2SO_4(l) \left(\frac{-814\ kJ}{mol} \right) \right]$$

$$\Delta H^\circ = -6833\ kJ - (-6568\ kJ) = -265\ kJ$$

c. $NH_3(g) + HCl(g) \rightarrow NH_4Cl(s)$

$$\Delta H^\circ = [1\ mol\ NH_4Cl \times \Delta H^\circ_{f,\ NH_4Cl}] - [1\ mol\ NH_3 \times \Delta H^\circ_{f,\ NH_3} + 1\ mol\ HCl \times \Delta H^\circ_{f,\ HCl}]$$

$$\Delta H^\circ = \left[1\ mol \left(\frac{-314\ kJ}{mol} \right) \right] - \left[1\ mol \left(\frac{-46\ kJ}{mol} \right) + 1\ mol \left(\frac{-92\ kJ}{mol} \right) \right]$$

$$\Delta H^\circ = -314\ kJ + 138\ kJ = -176\ kJ$$

d.   The balanced equation is: $C_2H_5OH(l) + 3\ O_2(g) \rightarrow 2\ CO_2(g) + 3\ H_2O(g)$

$$\Delta H^\circ = \left[2\ mol \left(\frac{-393.5\ kJ}{mol} \right) + 3\ mol \left(\frac{-242\ kJ}{mol} \right) \right] - \left[1\ mol \left(\frac{-278\ kJ}{mol} \right) \right]$$

$$= -1513\ kJ - (-278\ kJ) = -1235\ kJ$$

e. $SiCl_4(l) + 2\ H_2O(l) \rightarrow SiO_2(s) + 4\ HCl(aq)$

Since $HCl(aq)$ is $H^+(aq) + Cl^-(aq)$, then $\Delta H^\circ_f = 0 - 167 = -167\ kJ/mol$.

$$\Delta H^\circ = \left[4\ mol \left(\frac{-167\ kJ}{mol} \right) + 1\ mol \left(\frac{-911\ kJ}{mol} \right) \right] - \left[1\ mol \left(\frac{-687\ kJ}{mol} \right) + 2\ mol \left(\frac{-286\ kJ}{mol} \right) \right]$$

$$\Delta H^\circ = -1579\ kJ - (-1259\ kJ) = -320.\ kJ$$

f. $MgO(s) + H_2O(l) \rightarrow Mg(OH)_2(s)$

$$\Delta H° = \left[1 \text{ mol}\left(\frac{-925 \text{ kJ}}{\text{mol}} \right) \right] - \left[1 \text{ mol}\left(\frac{-602 \text{ kJ}}{\text{mol}} \right) + 1 \text{ mol}\left(\frac{-286 \text{ kJ}}{\text{mol}} \right) \right]$$

$\Delta H° = -925 \text{ kJ} - (-888 \text{ kJ}) = -37 \text{ kJ}$

56.   a. $4 \text{ NH}_3(g) + 5 \text{ O}_2(g) \rightarrow 4 \text{ NO}(g) + 6 \text{ H}_2O(g);$ $\Delta H° = \Sigma n_p \Delta H°_{f, \text{ products}} - \Sigma n_r \Delta H°_{f, \text{ reactants}}$

$$\Delta H° = \left[4 \text{ mol}\left(\frac{90. \text{ kJ}}{\text{mol}} \right) + 6 \text{ mol}\left(\frac{-242 \text{ kJ}}{\text{mol}} \right) \right] - \left[4 \text{ mol}\left(\frac{-46 \text{ kJ}}{\text{mol}} \right) \right] = \textbf{-908 kJ}$$

$2 \text{ NO}(g) + \text{O}_2(g) \rightarrow 2 \text{ NO}_2(g)$

$$\Delta H° = \left[2 \text{ mol}\left(\frac{34 \text{ kJ}}{\text{mol}} \right) \right] - \left[2 \text{ mol}\left(\frac{90. \text{ kJ}}{\text{mol}} \right) \right] = \textbf{-112 kJ}$$

$3 \text{ NO}_2(g) + \text{H}_2O(l) \rightarrow 2 \text{ HNO}_3(aq) + \text{NO}(g)$

$$\Delta H° = \left[2 \text{ mol}\left(\frac{-207 \text{ kJ}}{\text{mol}} \right) + 1 \text{ mol}\left(\frac{90. \text{ kJ}}{\text{mol}} \right) \right]$$

$$- \left[3 \text{ mol}\left(\frac{34 \text{ kJ}}{\text{mol}} \right) + 1 \text{ mol}\left(\frac{-286 \text{ kJ}}{\text{mol}} \right) \right] = \textbf{-140. kJ}$$

Note: All $\Delta H°_f$ values are assumed ± 1 kJ.

b. $12 \text{ NH}_3(g) + 15 \text{ O}_2(g) \rightarrow 12 \text{ NO}(g) + 18 \text{ H}_2O(g)$
     $12 \text{ NO}(g) + 6 \text{ O}_2(g) \rightarrow 12 \text{ NO}_2(g)$
     $12 \text{ NO}_2(g) + 4 \text{ H}_2O(l) \rightarrow 8 \text{ HNO}_3(aq) + 4 \text{ NO}(g)$
     $4 \text{ H}_2O(g) \rightarrow 4 \text{ H}_2O(l)$

     _____

     $12 \text{ NH}_3(g) + 21 \text{ O}_2(g) \rightarrow 8 \text{ HNO}_3(aq) + 4 \text{ NO}(g) + 14 \text{ H}_2O(g)$

The overall reaction is exothermic since each step is exothermic.

57. $4 \text{ Na}(s) + \text{O}_2(g) \rightarrow 2 \text{ Na}_2O(s),$ $\Delta H° = 2 \text{ mol}\left(\frac{-416 \text{ kJ}}{\text{mol}} \right) = \textbf{-832 kJ}$

$2 \text{ Na}(s) + 2 \text{ H}_2O(l) \rightarrow 2 \text{ NaOH}(aq) + \text{H}_2(g)$

$$\Delta H° = \left[2 \text{ mol}\left(\frac{-470. \text{ kJ}}{\text{mol}} \right) \right] - \left[2 \text{ mol}\left(\frac{-286 \text{ kJ}}{\text{mol}} \right) \right] = \textbf{-368 kJ}$$

$$2Na(s) + CO_2(g) \rightarrow Na_2O(s) + CO(g)$$

$$\Delta H° = \left[1\ mol\left(\frac{-416\ kJ}{mol}\right) + 1\ mol\left(\frac{-110.5\ kJ}{mol}\right)\right] - \left[1\ mol\left(\frac{-393.5\ kJ}{mol}\right)\right] = -133\ kJ$$

In reactions 2 and 3, sodium metal reacts with the "extinguishing agent." Both reactions are exothermic and each reaction produces a flammable gas, H_2 and CO, respectively.

58. $3\ Al(s) + 3\ NH_4ClO_4(s) \rightarrow Al_2O_3(s) + AlCl_3(s) + 3\ NO(g) + 6\ H_2O(g)$

$$\Delta H° = \left[6\ mol\left(\frac{-242\ kJ}{mol}\right) + 3\ mol\left(\frac{90.\ kJ}{mol}\right) + 1\ mol\left(\frac{-704\ kJ}{mol}\right) + 1\ mol\left(\frac{-1676\ kJ}{mol}\right)\right]$$

$$- \left[3\ mol\left(\frac{-295\ kJ}{mol}\right)\right] = -2677\ kJ$$

59. $5\ N_2O_4(l) + 4\ N_2H_3CH_3(l) \rightarrow 12\ H_2O(g) + 9\ N_2(g) + 4\ CO_2(g)$

$$\Delta H° = \left[12\ mol\left(\frac{-242\ kJ}{mol}\right) + 4\ mol\left(\frac{-393.5\ kJ}{mol}\right)\right]$$

$$- \left[5\ mol\left(\frac{-20.\ kJ}{mol}\right) + 4\ mol\left(\frac{54\ kJ}{mol}\right)\right] = -4594\ kJ$$

60.   For Exercise 58 a mixture of 3 mol Al and 3 mol NH_4ClO_4 yields 2677 kJ of energy. The mass of the stoichiometric reactant mixture is:

$$\left(3\ mol \times \frac{26.98\ g}{mol}\right) + \left(3\ mol \times \frac{117.49\ g}{mol}\right) = 433.41\ g$$

For 1.000 kg of fuel: $1.000 \times 10^3\ g \times \dfrac{-2677\ kJ}{433.41\ g} = -6177\ kJ$

In Exercise 59 we get 4594 kJ of energy from 5 mol of N_2O_4 and 4 mol of $N_2H_3CH_3$. The mass is: $\left(5\ mol \times \dfrac{92.02\ g}{mol}\right) + \left(4\ mol \times \dfrac{46.08\ g}{mol}\right) = 644.42\ kJ$

For 1.000 kg of fuel: $1.000 \times 10^3\ g \times \dfrac{-4594\ kJ}{644.42\ g} = -7129\ kJ$

Thus, we get more energy per kg from the $N_2O_4/N_2H_3CH_3$ mixture.

61.   a. $\Delta H° = 3\ mol\ (227\ kJ/mol) - 1\ mol\ (49\ kJ/mol) = 632\ kJ$

        b.   Since 3 $C_2H_2(g)$ is higher in energy than $C_6H_6(l)$, then acetylene will release more energy per gram when burned in air.

62. a. $C_2H_4(g) + O_3(g) \rightarrow CH_3CHO(g) + O_2(g)$, $\Delta H° = -166 \text{ kJ} - [143 \text{ kJ} + 52 \text{ kJ}] = -361 \text{ kJ}$

  b. $O_3(g) + NO(g) \rightarrow NO_2(g) + O_2(g)$, $\Delta H° = 34 \text{ kJ} - [90. \text{ kJ} + 143 \text{ kJ}] = -199 \text{ kJ}$

  c. $SO_3(g) + H_2O(l) \rightarrow H_2SO_4(aq)$, $\Delta H° = -909 \text{ kJ} - [-396 \text{ kJ} + (-286 \text{ kJ})] = -227 \text{ kJ}$

  d. $2 NO(g) + O_2(g) \rightarrow 2 NO_2(g)$, $\Delta H° = 2(34) \text{ kJ} - 2(90.) \text{ kJ} = -112 \text{ kJ}$

63. $2 ClF_3(g) + 2 NH_3(g) \rightarrow N_2(g) + 6 HF(g) + Cl_2(g)$ $\Delta H° = -1196 \text{ kJ}$

  $\Delta H° = [6 \Delta H°_{f, HF}] - [2 \Delta H°_{f, ClF_3} + 2 \Delta H°_{f, NH_3}]$

  $-1196 \text{ kJ} = 6 \text{ mol} \left(\dfrac{-271 \text{ kJ}}{\text{mol}} \right) - 2 \Delta H°_{f, ClF_3} - 2 \text{ mol} \left(\dfrac{-46 \text{ kJ}}{\text{mol}} \right)$

  $-1196 \text{ kJ} = -1626 \text{ kJ} - 2 \Delta H°_{f, ClF_3} + 92 \text{ kJ}, \ \Delta H°_{f, ClF_3} = \dfrac{(-1626 + 92 + 1196) \text{ kJ}}{2 \text{ mol}} = \dfrac{-169 \text{ kJ}}{\text{mol}}$

64. $C_2H_4(g) + 3 O_2(g) \rightarrow 2 CO_2(g) + 2 H_2O(l)$ $\Delta H° = -1411 \text{ kJ}$

  $\Delta H° = -1411.1 \text{ kJ} = 2(-393.5) \text{ kJ} + 2(-285.8) \text{ kJ} - \Delta H°_{f, C_2H_4}$

  $-1411.1 \text{ kJ} = -1358.6 \text{ kJ} - \Delta H°_{f, C_2H_4}, \ \Delta H°_{f, C_2H_4} = 52.5 \text{ kJ/mol}$

Energy Consumption and Sources

65. Mass of H_2O = $1.00 \text{ gal} \times \dfrac{3.785 \text{ L}}{\text{gal}} \times \dfrac{1000 \text{ mL}}{\text{L}} \times \dfrac{1.00 \text{ g}}{\text{mL}} = 3790 \text{ g } H_2O$

  Energy required (theoretical) = $s \times m \times \Delta T = \dfrac{4.18 \text{ J}}{\text{g °C}} \times 3790 \text{ g} \times 10.0 \text{ °C} = 1.58 \times 10^5 \text{ J}$

  For an actual (80.0% efficient) process, more than this quantity of energy is needed since heat is always lost in any transfer of energy. The energy required is:

  $1.58 \times 10^5 \text{ J} \times \dfrac{100. \text{ J}}{80.0 \text{ J}} = 1.98 \times 10^5 \text{ J}$

  Mass of C_2H_2 = $1.98 \times 10^5 \text{ J} \times \dfrac{1 \text{ mol } C_2H_2}{1300. \times 10^3 \text{ J}} \times \dfrac{26.04 \text{ g } C_2H_2}{\text{mol } C_2H_2} = 3.97 \text{ g } C_2H_2$

66. $C_2H_5OH(l) + 3 O_2(g) \rightarrow 2 CO_2(g) + 3 H_2O(l)$

  $\Delta H° = [2 (-393.5 \text{ kJ}) + 3(-286 \text{ kJ})] - (-278 \text{ kJ}) = -1367 \text{ kJ/mol ethanol}$

  $\dfrac{-1367 \text{ kJ}}{\text{mol}} \times \dfrac{1 \text{ mol}}{46.068 \text{ g}} = -29.67 \text{ kJ/g}$

67. $CO(g) + 2 H_2(g) \rightarrow CH_3OH(l)$ $\Delta H° = (-239 \text{ kJ}) - (-110.5 \text{ kJ}) = -129 \text{ kJ}$

68. $C_3H_8(g) + 5 O_2(g) \rightarrow 3 CO_2(g) + 4 H_2O(l)$

$\Delta H° = [3(-393.5 \text{ kJ}) + 4(-286 \text{ kJ})] - (-104 \text{ kJ}) = -2221 \text{ kJ/mol } C_3H_8$

$\dfrac{-2221 \text{ kJ}}{\text{mol}} \times \dfrac{1 \text{ mol}}{44.096 \text{ g}} = \dfrac{-50.37 \text{ kJ}}{\text{g}}$ vs. -47.7 kJ/g for octane (Example 9.8)

The fuel values of the fuels are very close. An advantage of propane is that it burns more cleanly. The boiling point of propane is -42 °C. Thus, it is more difficult to store propane and there are extra safety hazards associated with using high pressure compressed gas tanks.

Additional Exercises

69. $\Delta E_{overall} = \Delta E_{step\ 1} + \Delta E_{step\ 2}$; This is a cyclic process which means that the overall initial state and final state are the same. Since ΔE is a state function, then $\Delta E_{overall} = 0$ and $\Delta E_{step\ 1} = -\Delta E_{step\ 2}$.

$\Delta E_{step\ 1} = q + w = 45 \text{ J} + (-10. \text{ J}) = 35 \text{ J}$

$\Delta E_{step\ 2} = -\Delta E_{step\ 1} = -35 \text{ J} = q + w,\ -35 \text{ J} = -60 \text{ J} + w,\ w = 25 \text{ J}$

70. $w = -P\Delta V$; We need the final volume of the gas. Since T and n are constant, then $P_1V_1 = P_2V_2$.

$V_2 = \dfrac{V_1P_1}{P_2} = \dfrac{10.0 \text{ L } (15.0 \text{ atm})}{2.00 \text{ atm}} = 75.0 \text{ L}$

$w = -P\Delta V = -2.00 \text{ atm } (75.0 \text{ L} - 10.0 \text{ L}) = -130. \text{ L atm} \times \dfrac{101.3 \text{ J}}{\text{L atm}} \times \dfrac{1 \text{ kJ}}{1000 \text{ J}} = -13.2 \text{ kJ} = \text{work}$

71. $H_2(g) + 1/2\ O_2(g) \rightarrow H_2O(l)$ $\Delta H° = \Delta H°_{f,\ H_2O(l)} = -285.8 \text{ kJ}$

$H_2O(l) \rightarrow H_2(g) + 1/2\ O_2(g)$ $\Delta H° = 285.8 \text{ kJ}$

$\Delta E° = \Delta H° - P\Delta V = \Delta H° - \Delta nRT = 285.8 \text{ kJ} - (1.50 - 0 \text{ mol}) (8.3145 \text{ J mol}^{-1} \text{ K}^{-1}) (298 \text{ K}) \left(\dfrac{1 \text{ kJ}}{1000 \text{ J}} \right)$

$\Delta E° = 285.8 \text{ kJ} - 3.72 \text{ kJ} = 282.1 \text{ kJ}$

72. $400 \text{ kcal} \times \dfrac{4.18 \text{ kJ}}{\text{kcal}} = 1.67 \times 10^3 \text{ kJ} \approx 2 \times 10^3 \text{ kJ}$

$PE = mgz = \left(180 \text{ lb} \times \dfrac{1 \text{ kg}}{2.205 \text{ lb}} \right) \times \dfrac{9.80 \text{ m}}{\text{s}^2} \times \left(8 \text{ in} \times \dfrac{2.54 \text{ cm}}{\text{in}} \times \dfrac{1 \text{ m}}{100 \text{ cm}} \right) = 160 \text{ J} \approx 200 \text{ J}$

200 J of energy are needed to climb one step. The total number of steps to climb are:

$$2 \times 10^6 \text{ J} \times \frac{1 \text{ step}}{200 \text{ J}} = 1 \times 10^4 \text{ steps}$$

73.   The specific heat of water is 4.18 J $°C^{-1}$ g^{-1}, which is equal to 4.18 kJ $°C^{-1}$ kg^{-1}

We have 1.00 kg of H_2O, so: $1.00 \text{ kg} \times \frac{4.18 \text{ kJ}}{\text{kg } °C} = 4.18 \text{ kJ/}°C$

This is the portion of the heat capacity that can be attributed to H_2O.

Total heat capacity = $C_{cal} + C_{H_2O}$, $C_{cal} = 10.84 - 4.18 = 6.66 \text{ kJ/}°C$

74.   Heat released = 1.056 g $\times$ 26.42 kJ/g = 27.90 kJ = Heat gain by water and calorimeter

$$\text{Heat gain} = 27.90 \text{ kJ} = \left(\frac{4.18 \text{ kJ}}{\text{kg } °C} \times 0.987 \text{ kg} \times \Delta T \right) + \left(\frac{6.66 \text{ kJ}}{°C} \times \Delta T \right)$$

27.90 = (4.13 + 6.66) ΔT = 10.79 ΔT, ΔT = 2.586°C

2.586°C = T_f - 23.32°C, T_f = 25.91°C

75. $N_2H_4(l) + O_2(g) \rightarrow N_2(g) + 2 H_2O(g)$ $\Delta H° = 2(-242 \text{ kJ}) - (51 \text{ kJ}) = -535 \text{ kJ}$

$2 N_2H_4(l) + N_2O_4(l) \rightarrow 3 N_2(g) + 4 H_2O(g)$ $\Delta H° = 4(-242 \text{ kJ}) - [2(51 \text{ kJ}) + (-20. \text{ kJ})] = -1050. \text{ kJ}$

For hydrazine plus oxygen the stoichiometric reactant mixture contains 1 mol N_2H_4 for every mol O_2. This is a total mass of 64.05 g or 0.06405 kg.

$$\Delta H = \frac{-535 \text{ kJ}}{0.06405 \text{ kg}} = -8.35 \times 10^3 \text{ kJ/kg for } N_2H_4(l) + O_2(g)$$

For hydrazine plus N_2O_4 the optimum mixture contains 2 mol of N_2H_4 for every mol N_2O_4. This is a total mass of 156.12 g or 0.15612 kg.

$$\Delta H = \frac{-1050. \text{ kJ}}{0.15612 \text{ kg}} = -6.726 \times 10^3 \text{ kJ/kg for } 2 N_2H_4(l) + N_2O_4(l)$$

From Exercise 60, the most efficient fuel was methyl hydrazine ($N_2H_3CH_3$) plus N_2O_4, with a fuel value of -7129 kJ/kg . Therefore, the hydrazine plus oxygen combination is the most efficient fuel.

76.   a. $2 SO_2(g) + O_2(g) \rightarrow 2 SO_3(g)$ (w = -PΔV); Since the volume of the piston apparatus decreased as reactants were converted to products, w is positive (w > 0).

b. $COCl_2(g) \rightarrow CO(g) + Cl_2(g)$; Since the volume increased, w is negative (w < 0).

c. $N_2(g) + O_2(g) \rightarrow 2 NO(g)$; Since the volume did not change, no PV work is done ($w = 0$).

In order to predict the sign of w for a reaction, compare the coefficients of all the product gases in the balanced equation to the coefficients of all the reactant gases. When a balanced reaction has more mol of product gases than mol of reactant gases (as in b), the reaction will expand in volume (ΔV positive), and the system does work on the surroundings. When a balanced reaction has a decrease in the mol of gas from reactants to products (as in a), the reaction will contract in volume (ΔV negative), and the surroundings will do compression work on the system. When there is no change in the mol of gas from reactants to products (as in c), $\Delta V = 0$ and $w = 0$.

77. $w = -P\Delta V$; Δn = mol gaseous products - mol gaseous reactants. Only gases can do PV work (we ignore solids and liquids). When a balanced reaction has more mol of product gases than mol of reactant gases (Δn positive), the reaction will expand in volume (ΔV positive) and the system will do work on the surroundings. For example, in reaction c, $\Delta n = 2 - 0 = 2$ mol, and this reaction would do expansion work against the surroundings. When a balanced reaction has a decrease in the mol of gas from reactants to products (Δn negative), the reaction will contract in volume (ΔV negative) and the surroundings will do compression work on the system, e.g., reaction a where $\Delta n = 0 - 1 = -1$. When there is no change in the mol of gas from reactants to products, $\Delta V = 0$ and $w = 0$, e.g., reaction b where $\Delta n = 2 - 2 = 0$.

When $\Delta V > 0$ ($\Delta n > 0$), then $w < 0$ and system does work on the surroundings (c and e).

When $\Delta V < 0$ ($\Delta n < 0$), then $w > 0$ and the surroundings do work on the system (a and d).

When $\Delta V = 0$ ($\Delta n = 0$), then $w = 0$ (b).

78.   The specific heat capacities are: 0.89 J $°C^{-1}$ g^{-1} (Al) and 0.45 J $°C^{-1}$ g^{-1} (Fe). Al would be the better choice. It has a higher heat capacity and a lower density than Fe. Using Al, the same amount of heat could be dissipated by a smaller mass, keeping the mass of the amplifier down.

79.   a.   aluminum oxide = Al_2O_3; $2 Al(s) + 3/2 O_2(g) \rightarrow Al_2O_3(s)$

      b. $C_2H_5OH(l) + 3 O_2(g) \rightarrow 2 CO_2(g) + 3 H_2O(l)$

      c. $Ba(OH)_2(aq) + 2 HCl(aq) \rightarrow 2 H_2O(l) + BaCl_2(aq)$

      d. $2 C \text{ (graphite, s)} + 3/2 H_2(g) + 1/2 Cl_2(g) \rightarrow C_2H_3Cl(g)$

      e. $C_6H_6(l) + 15/2 O_2(g) \rightarrow 6 CO_2(g) + 3 H_2O(l)$

           Note: ΔH_{comb} values assume one mol of compound combusted.

      f. $NH_4Br(s) \rightarrow NH_4^+(aq) + Br^-(aq)$

Challenge Problems

80. $H = E + PV$, $\Delta H = \Delta E + \Delta(PV)$, $\Delta E = \Delta H - \Delta(PV)$

Assume $H_2O(g)$ is ideal.

We go from $n = 0$ to $n = 1$, thus $\Delta n = 1$. [$H_2O(l)$ is a liquid].

$\Delta(PV) = \Delta(nRT) = RT\Delta n$

$\Delta E = \Delta H - (8.3145 \text{ J/Kmol})(373 \text{ K})\,(1 \text{ mol})$

$\Delta H = -242 \text{ kJ/mol} - (-286 \text{ kJ/mol}) = 44 \text{ kJ/mol}$

$\Delta E = (44 - 3.1) \text{ kJ}$, $\Delta E = 41 \text{ kJ}$

81.   If the gas is monoatomic, then $C_v = \dfrac{3}{2}R = 12.47 \text{ J mol}^{-1}\text{ K}^{-1}$ and $C_p = \dfrac{5}{2}R = 20.79 \text{ J mol}^{-1}\text{ K}^{-1}$. If the gas is behaving ideally, then $C_p - C_v = R = 8.3145 \text{ J mol}^{-1}\text{ K}^{-1}$.

At constant volume: $q_v = 2079 \text{ J} = nC_v\Delta T$

$C_v = \dfrac{2079 \text{ J}}{n\Delta T} = \dfrac{2079 \text{ J}}{(1 \text{ mol})\,(400.0 - 300.0 \text{ K})} = 20.79 \text{ J mol}^{-1}\text{ K}^{-1}$

Since $C_v \neq 3/2\ R = 12.47 \text{ J}$, then the gas is not a monoatomic gas.

At constant pressure: $q_p = nC_p\Delta T$

$q_p = \Delta E - w = 1305 \text{ J} - (-150.\text{ J}) = 1455 \text{ J}$ (Gas expansion so system does work or surroundings.)

$C_p = \dfrac{q_p}{n\Delta T} = \dfrac{1455 \text{ J}}{(1 \text{ mol})\,(600.0 - 550.0 \text{ K})} = 29.1 \text{ J mol}^{-1}\text{ K}^{-1}$

$C_p - C_v = 29.1 - 20.79 = 8.31 \text{ J mol}^{-1}\text{ K}^{-1} = R$

The gas is behaving ideally since $C_p - C_v = R$.

82.   You need to reference a CRC Handbook (or other reference) to find ΔH_f° for H_2CO_3 (= -698.7 kJ/mol).

$$H_2O(l) + CO_2(aq) \xrightarrow{\ \Delta H_2\ =\ 0\ } H_2CO_3(aq)$$

$\Delta H_1 \uparrow$

$H_2O(l) + CO_2(g) \qquad\qquad \Delta H_3 = (-698.7) - (-285.8) - (-393.5) = -19.4 \text{ kJ}$

$\Delta H_1 + \Delta H_2 = \Delta H_3$, $\Delta H_1 + 0 = -19.4 \text{ kJ/mol}$, $\Delta H_1 = -19.4 \text{ kJ/mol}$

83. $H_2O(s) \rightarrow H_2O(l)$ $\Delta H = \Delta H_{fus}$; For 1 mol of supercooled water at -15.0°C (or 258.2 K),
$\Delta H_{fus, 258.2 K} = 10.9$ kJ/2 = 5.45 kJ/mol. Using Hess's Law and the equation $\Delta H = nC_p\Delta T$:

H_2O (s, 273.2 K) $\rightarrow$ H_2O (s, 258.2 K) $\Delta H_1 = 1$ mol (37.5 J K^{-1} mol^{-1}) (-15.0 K)
$\qquad\qquad\qquad\qquad\qquad\qquad\qquad\qquad\qquad\quad = -563$ J = -0.563 kJ

H_2O (s, 258.2 K) $\rightarrow$ H_2O (l, 258.2 K) $\Delta H_2 = 1$ mol (5.45 kJ/mol) = 5.45 kJ

H_2O (l, 258.2 K) $\rightarrow$ H_2O (l, 273.2 K) $\Delta H_3 = 1$ mol (75.3 J K^{-1} mol^{-1}) (15.0 K)
$\qquad\qquad\qquad\qquad\qquad\qquad\qquad\qquad\qquad\quad = 1130$ J = 1.13 kJ

H_2O (s, 273. 2 K) $\rightarrow$ H_2O (l, 273.2 K) $\Delta H_{fus, 273.2} = \Delta H_1 + \Delta H_2 + \Delta H_3$

$\Delta H_{fus, 273.2} = -0.563$ kJ + 5.45 kJ + 1.13 kJ = 6.02 kJ; $\Delta H_{fus, 273.2} = 6.02$ kJ/mol

84.   Energy needed = $\dfrac{20. \times 10^3 \text{ g } C_{12}H_{22}O_{11}}{\text{hr}} \times \dfrac{1 \text{ mol } C_{12}H_{22}O_{11}}{342.3 \text{ g } C_{12}H_{22}O_{11}} \times \dfrac{5640 \text{ kJ}}{\text{mol}} = 3.3 \times 10^5$ kJ/hr

Energy from sun = 1.0 KW/m^2 = 1000 W/m^2 = $\dfrac{1000 \text{ J}}{\text{s m}^2} = \dfrac{1.0 \text{ kJ}}{\text{s m}^2}$

10,000 m^2 $\times$ $\dfrac{1.0 \text{ kJ}}{\text{s m}^2}$ $\times$ $\dfrac{60 \text{ s}}{\text{min}}$ $\times$ $\dfrac{60 \text{ min}}{\text{hr}}$ = 3.6×10^7 kJ/hr

% efficiency = $\dfrac{\text{Energy used per hour}}{\text{Total energy per hour}} \times 100 = \dfrac{3.3 \times 10^5 \text{ kJ}}{3.6 \times 10^7 \text{ kJ}} \times 100 = 0.92\%$

85.   Molar heat capacity of $H_2O(l)$ = 4.184 J K^{-1} g^{-1} (18.015 g/mol) = 75.37 J K^{-1} mol^{-1}

Molar heat capacity of $H_2O(g)$ = 2.02 J K^{-1} g^{-1} (18.015 g/mol) = 36.4 J K^{-1} mol^{-1}

Using Hess's Law and the equation $\Delta H = nC_p\Delta T$:

H_2O (l, 340.2 K) $\rightarrow$ H_2O (l, 373.2 K) $\Delta H_1 = 1$ mol (75.37 J K^{-1} mol^{-1})(33.0 K)(1 kJ/1000 J)
$\qquad\qquad\qquad\qquad\qquad\qquad\qquad\qquad\qquad\quad = 2.49$ kJ

H_2O (l, 373.2 K) $\rightarrow$ H_2O (g, 373.2 K) $\Delta H_2 = 1$ mol (40.66 kJ/mol) = 40.66 kJ

H_2O (g, 373.2 K) $\rightarrow$ H_2O (g, 340.2 K) $\Delta H_3 = 1$ mol (36.4 J K^{-1} mol^{-1})(-33.0 K)(1 kJ/1000 J)
$\qquad\qquad\qquad\qquad\qquad\qquad\qquad\qquad\qquad\quad = -1.20$ kJ

H_2O (l, 340.2 K) $\rightarrow$ H_2O (g, 340.2 K) $\Delta H_{vap, 340.2 K} = \Delta H_1 + \Delta H_2 + \Delta H_3 = 41.95$ kJ/mol

86.   a.   Using Hess's Law and the equation $\Delta H = nC_p\Delta T$:

$CH_3Cl(248°C) + H_2(248°C) \rightarrow CH_4(248°C) + HCl(248°C)$ $\Delta H_1 = -83.3$ kJ
$CH_3Cl(25°C) \rightarrow CH_3Cl(248°C)$ $\Delta H_2 = 1$ mol (48.5 J °C^{-1} mol^{-1}) (223°C)
$\qquad\qquad\qquad\qquad\qquad\qquad\qquad\qquad\qquad\quad = 10,800$ J = 10.8 kJ

$H_2(25°C) \rightarrow H_2(248°C)$ $\Delta H_3 = 1(28.9) (223) (1$ kJ/1000 J) = 6.44 kJ
$CH_4(248°C) \rightarrow CH_4(25°C)$ $\Delta H_4 = 1(41.3) (-223) (1/1000) = -9.21$ kJ
$HCl(248°C) \rightarrow HCl(25°C)$ $\Delta H_5 = 1(29.1) (-223) (1/1000) = -6.49$ kJ

$CH_3Cl(25°C) + H_2(25°C) \rightarrow CH_4(25°C) + HCl(25°C)$ $\Delta H° = \Delta H_1 + \Delta H_2 + \Delta H_3 + \Delta H_4 + \Delta H_5$

$\Delta H° = -83.3$ kJ + 10.8 kJ + 6.44 kJ - 9.21 kJ - 6.49 kJ = -81.8 kJ

b. $\Delta H° = [\Delta H_f° (CH_4) + \Delta H_f° (HCl)] - [\Delta H_f° (CH_3Cl) + \Delta H_f° (H_2)]$

-81.8 kJ = -75 kJ - 92 kJ - $[\Delta H_f° (CH_3Cl) + 0]$, $\Delta H_f° (CH_3Cl) = -85$ kJ/mol

87.   Energy used in 8.0 hours = 40. kWh = $\dfrac{40.\ kJ\ h}{s} \times \dfrac{3600\ s}{h} = 1.4 \times 10^5$ kJ

Energy from the sun in 8.0 hours = $\dfrac{1.0\ kJ}{s\ m^2} \times \dfrac{60\ s}{min} \times \dfrac{60\ min}{h} \times 8.0\ h = 2.9 \times 10^4$ kJ/m^2

Only 13% of the sunlight is converted into electricity:

0.13 × (2.9 × 10^4 kJ/m^2) × Area = 1.4 × 10^5 kJ,   Area = 37 m^2

88.   a.   The gas will flow from the 4.0 L bulb to the 20.0 L bulb. Eventually, the gas will be evenly dispersed throughout.

n = constant, V = constant, T = constant,

P changes (P$_{init}$ = 15 atm; P$_{final}$ = 2.5 atm from P = nRT/V)

b.   Free expansion (isothermal)

Thus, $\Delta H = 0$, $\Delta E = 0$, q = 0, w = 0

c.   Although not discussed until Chapter 10, entropy is the driving force for this process.

Marathon Problems

89. $X \rightarrow CO_2(g) + H_2O(l) + O_2(g) + A(g)$ $\Delta H = -1893$ kJ/mol   (unbalanced)

To determine X we must determine the mol of X reacted, the identity of A and the mol of A produced. For the reaction at constant P ($\Delta H = q$):

$-q_{H_2O} = q_{rxn} = -4.184$ J °C^{-1} g^{-1} (1.000 × 10^4 g) (29.52 - 25.00 °C) (1 kJ/1000 J)

q_{rxn} = -189.1 kJ (carrying extra sig. figs.)

Since $\Delta H = -1893$ kJ/mol for the decomposition reaction and since only -189.1 kJ of heat were released for this reaction, then 189.1 kJ × (1 mol X/1893 kJ) = 0.100 mol X were reacted.

Molar mass of X = $\dfrac{22.7\ g\ X}{0.100\ mol\ X}$ = 227 g/mol

From the problem, 0.100 mol X produced 0.300 mol CO$_2$, 0.250 mol H$_2$O and 0.025 mol O$_2$. Therefore, 1.00 mol X contains 3.00 mol CO$_2$, 2.50 mol H$_2$O and 0.25 mol O$_2$.

$$1.00 \text{ mol X} = 227 \text{ g} = 3.00 \text{ mol CO}_2 \left(\frac{44.0 \text{ g}}{\text{mol}} \right) + 2.50 \text{ mol H}_2\text{O} \left(\frac{18.0 \text{ g}}{\text{mol}} \right)$$

$$+ 0.25 \text{ mol O}_2 \left(\frac{32.0 \text{ g}}{\text{mol}} \right) + (\text{mass of A})$$

mass of A in 1.00 mol X = 227 g - 132 g - 45.0 g - 8.0 g = 42 g A

To determine A, we need the mol of A produced. The total mol of gases produced can be determined from the gas law data provided in the problem. Since $H_2O(l)$ is a product, we need to subtract P_{H_2O} from the total pressure.

$$n_{total} = \frac{PV}{RT}; \quad P_{total} = P_{gases} + P_{H_2O}, \quad P_{gases} = 778 \text{ torr} - 31 \text{ torr} = 747 \text{ torr}$$

$$V = \text{height} \times \text{area}; \text{ area} = \pi r^2; \quad V = 59.8 \text{ cm } (\pi) (8.00 \text{ cm})^2 \left(\frac{1 \text{ L}}{1000 \text{ cm}^3} \right) = 12.0 \text{ L}$$

$$T = 273.15 + 29.52 = 302.67 \text{ K}$$

$$n_{total} = \frac{PV}{RT} = \frac{747 \text{ torr} \left(\dfrac{1 \text{ atm}}{760 \text{ torr}} \right) (12.0 \text{ L})}{\dfrac{0.08206 \text{ L atm}}{\text{K mol}} (302.67 \text{ K})} = 0.475 \text{ mol} = \text{mol CO}_2 + \text{mol O}_2 + \text{mol A}$$

mol A = 0.475 mol - 0.300 mol CO_2 - 0.025 mol O_2 = 0.150 mol A

Since 0.100 mol X reacted, then 1.00 mol X would contain 1.50 mol A which from a previous calculation represents 42 g A.

$$\text{Molar mass of A} = \frac{42 \text{ g A}}{1.50 \text{ mol A}} = 28 \text{ g/mol}$$

Since A is a gaseous element, the only element that is a gas and has this molar mass is $N_2(g)$. Thus, A = $N_2(g)$

a. Now we can determine the formula of X.

X → 3 $CO_2(g)$ + 2.5 $H_2O(l)$ + 0.25 $O_2(g)$ + 1.5 $N_2(g)$. For a balanced reaction, X = $C_3H_5N_3O_9$, which, for your information, is nitroglycerine.

b. $w = -P\Delta V = -778 \text{ torr} \left(\dfrac{1 \text{ atm}}{760 \text{ torr}} \right) (12.0 \text{ L} - 0) = -12.3 \text{ L atm}$

$$-12.3 \text{ L atm} \left(\frac{8.3145 \text{ J mol}^{-1} \text{ K}^{-1}}{0.08206 \text{ L atm mol}^{-1} \text{ K}^{-1}} \right) = -1250 \text{ J} = -1.25 \text{ kJ}, \ w = -1.25 \text{ kJ}$$

c. $\Delta E = q + w$, where $q = \Delta H$ since at constant pressure. For 1 mol of X decomposed:

w = -1.25 kJ/0.100 mol = -12.5 kJ/mol

$\Delta E = \Delta H + w = -1893 \text{ kJ/mol} + (-12.5 \text{ kJ/mol}) = -1906 \text{ kJ/mol}$

ΔH_f° for $C_3H_5N_3O_9$ can be estimated from standard enthalpies of formation data and assuming $\Delta H_{rxn} = \Delta H_{rxn}^{\circ}$. For the balanced reaction given in part a:

$\Delta H_{rxn}^{\circ} = -1893 \text{ kJ} = [3 \, \Delta H_{f, CO_2}^{\circ} + 2.5 \, \Delta H_{f, H_2O} + 0.25 \, \Delta H_{f, O_2} + 1.5 \, \Delta H_{f, N_2}] - [\Delta H_{f, C_3H_5N_3O_9}^{\circ}]$

$-1893 \text{ kJ} = [3 \, (-393.5) \text{ kJ} + 2.5 \, (-286) \text{ kJ} + 0 + 0] - \Delta H_{f, C_3H_5N_3O_9}, \quad \Delta H_{f, C_3H_5N_3O_9} = -2.5 \text{ kJ/mol}$

90. $C_xH_y + \left(\dfrac{2x + y/2}{2} \right) O_2 \rightarrow x \, CO_2 + y/2 \, H_2O$

$-393.5x + y/2 \, (-242) - \Delta H_{C_xH_y}^{\circ} = -2044.5, \quad -393.5x - 121y - \Delta H_{C_xH_y} = -2044.5$

$d_{gas} = \dfrac{mass}{V} = \dfrac{n \cdot MM}{nRT/P} = \dfrac{P \cdot MM}{RT}$

$0.751 \text{ g/L} = \dfrac{(1.00 \text{ atm})(MM)}{\left(0.08206 \dfrac{L \text{ atm}}{mol \cdot K} \right)(473 \text{ K})}$, MM of CO_2/H_2O mixture = 29.1 g/mol

Let a = mol CO_2 and 1.00 - a = mol H_2O (assuming 1.00 total mol of mixture)

$44.01 \, a + (1.00 - a)(18.016) = 29.1$

$a = 0.426$ mol CO_2, mol $H_2O = 0.574$; Thus, $\dfrac{0.574}{0.426} = \dfrac{\frac{y}{2}}{x}$

$\dfrac{y}{x} = 2.69, \quad y = 2.69x$

For whole numbers, multiplying by three which gives y = 8, x = 3. Note that y = 16, x = 6 is possible, along with other combinations. Since the hydrocarbon has a lower density than Kr, then the molar mass of C_xH_y must be less than the molar mass of Kr(83.80). Only C_3H_8 works.

$-2044.5 = -393.5(3) - 121(8) - \Delta H_{C_3H_8}^{\circ}, \quad \Delta H_{C_3H_8}^{\circ} = -104 \text{ kJ/mol}$

CHAPTER TEN

SPONTANEITY, ENTROPY, AND FREE ENERGY

Spontaneity and Entropy

12.   A spontaneous process is one that occurs without any outside intervention and entropy is a measure of disorder or randomness (positional probability). The quantity $T\Delta S$ has units of energy.

13.   We draw all of the possible arrangements of the two particles in the three levels.

2 kJ			x		x	xx
1 kJ		x		xx	x	
0 kJ	xx	x	x			

Total E =	0 kJ	1 kJ	2 kJ	2 kJ	3 kJ	4 kJ

The most likely total energy is 2 kJ.

14.

2 kJ			AB			B	A	B	A
1 kJ		AB		B	A			A	B
0 kJ	AB			A	B	A	B		

$E_T =$	0 kJ	2 kJ	4 kJ	1 kJ	1 kJ	2 kJ	2 kJ	3 kJ	3 kJ

The most likely total energy is 2 kJ.

15.   Processes a, b, d, and g are spontaneous. Processes c, e, and f require an external source of energy in order to occur since they are nonspontaneous.

16.   Of the three phases, solids are most ordered and gases are most disordered. Thus, a, b, c, e, and g involve an increase in entropy. All increase disorder.

17.   a. Positional probability increases; there is a greater volume accessible to the randomly moving gas molecules which increases disorder.

       b. The positional probability doesn't change. There is no change in volume and thus, no change in the numbers of positions of the molecules.

       c. Positional probability decreases because the volume decreases (P and V are inversely related).

18.   a. N_2O; It is the more complex molecule, i.e., more parts, more positional probability.

       b. H_2 at $100\,°C$ and 0.5 atm; Higher temperature and lower pressure means greater volume and hence, greater positional probability.

       c. N_2; N_2 at STP has the greater volume.

       d. $H_2O(l)$ has more positional probability than $H_2O(s)$.

19.   There are more ways to roll a seven. We can consider all of the possible throws by constructing a table.

one die	1	2	3	4	5	6	
1	2	3	4	5	6	7	
2	3	4	5	6	7	8	
3	4	5	6	7	8	9	sum of the two dice
4	5	6	7	8	9	10	
5	6	7	8	9	10	11	
6	7	8	9	10	11	12	

There are six ways to get a seven, more than any other number. The seven is not favored by energy; rather it is favored by probability. To change the probability we would have to expend energy (do work).

20.   Arrangement I: $S = k \ln \Omega$; $\Omega = 1$; $S = k \ln 1 = 0$

       Arrangement II: $\Omega = 4$; $S = k \ln 4 = 1.38 \times 10^{-23}$ J/K ln 4, $S = 1.91 \times 10^{-23}$ J/K

       Arrangement III: $\Omega = 6$; $S = k \ln 6 = 2.47 \times 10^{-23}$ J/K

Energy, Enthalpy, and Entropy Changes Involving Ideal Gases and Physical Changes

21.   15.0 g He $\times \dfrac{1\ \text{mol}}{4.003\ \text{g}} = 3.75$ mol He

       $q_v = \Delta E = nC_v\Delta T = 3.75$ mol $(12.47\ \text{J K}^{-1}\ \text{mol}^{-1})\,(56.5\ \text{K}) = 2640$ J $= 2.64$ kJ

22. 1.00×10^3 g $C_2H_6 \times \dfrac{1 \text{ mol}}{30.07 \text{ g}} = 33.3$ mol

$q_v = \Delta E = nC_v\Delta T = 33.3$ mol $(44.60 \text{ J mol}^{-1} \text{ K}^{-1})$ $(48.4 \text{ K}) = 7.19 \times 10^4 \text{ J} = 71.9$ kJ

At constant volume, 71.9 kJ of energy are required and $\Delta E = 71.9$ kJ.

At constant pressure (assuming ethane acts as an ideal gas):

   $C_p = C_v + R = 44.60 + 8.31 = 52.91$ J mol^{-1} K^{-1}

Energy required $= q_p = \Delta H = nC_p\Delta T = 33.3$ mol $(52.91 \text{ J mol}^{-1} \text{ K}^{-1})$ $(48.4 \text{ K}) = 8.53 \times 10^4 \text{ J} = 85.3$ kJ

For the constant pressure process, $\Delta E = 71.9$ kJ as calculated previously (ΔE is unchanged).

23.   It takes $nC_p\Delta T$ amount of energy to carry out this process. The internal energy of the system increases by $nC_v\Delta T$. So the fraction that goes into raising the internal energy is:

   $\dfrac{nC_v\Delta T}{nC_p\Delta T} = \dfrac{C_v}{C_p} = \dfrac{20.8}{29.1} = 0.715$

The remainder of the energy ($nR\Delta T$) goes into expanding the gas against the constant pressure.

100.0 g $N_2 \times \dfrac{1 \text{ mol}}{28.014 \text{ g}} = 3.570$ mol

$q_v = \Delta E = nC_v\Delta T = 3.570$ mol $(20.8 \text{ J mol}^{-1} \text{ K}^{-1})$ $(60.0 \text{ K}) = 4.46 \times 10^3 \text{ J} = 4.46$ kJ

24.   Heat gain by He = Heat loss by N_2; Since ΔT in °C = ΔT in K, then the units on the heat capacities could also be J °C^{-1} mol^{-1}.

$(0.400 \text{ mol})(12.5 \text{ J °C}^{-1} \text{ mol}^{-1})(T_f - 20.0 \text{ °C}) = (0.600 \text{ mol})(20.7 \text{ J °C}^{-1} \text{ mol}^{-1})(100.0 \text{ °C} - T_f)$

$5.00 \, T_f - 100. = 1240 - 12.4 \, T_f$, $T_f = \dfrac{1340}{17.4} = 77.0$ °C

25.   The volumes for each step are:

   a. $P_1 = 5.00$ atm, $n = 1.00$ mol, $T = 350.$ K; $V_1 = \dfrac{nRT}{P_1} = 5.74$ L

   b. $P_2 = 2.24$ atm, $V_2 = \dfrac{nRT}{P_2} = 12.8$ L   c. $P_3 = 1.00$ atm, $V_3 = 28.7$ L

The process can be carried out in the following steps:

   $(P_1, V_1) \rightarrow (P_2, V_1)$ $w = -P\Delta V = 0$ (constant volume process)

   $(P_2, V_1) \rightarrow (P_2, V_2)$ $w = -(2.24 \text{ atm})(12.8 - 5.74 \text{ L}) = -16$ L atm

   $(P_2, V_2) \rightarrow (P_3, V_2)$ $w = 0$

   $(P_3, V_2) \rightarrow (P_3, V_3)$ $w = -(1.00 \text{ atm})(28.7 - 12.8 \text{ L}) = -15.9$ L atm

$$w_{tot} = -16 - 15.9 = -32 \text{ L atm}; \quad -32 \text{ L atm} \times \frac{101.3 \text{ J}}{1 \text{ L atm}} = -3200 \text{ J} = \text{total work}$$

$$w_{rev} = -nRT \ln (P_1/P_2) = -(1.00 \text{ mol}) (8.3145 \text{ J mol}^{-1} \text{ K}^{-1}) (350. \text{ K}) \ln (5.00/1.00) = -4680 \text{ J}$$

26. $P_1V_1 = P_2V_2$ since n and T are constant; $P_2 = \dfrac{P_1V_1}{V_2} = \dfrac{(5.0)(1.0)}{(2.0)} = 2.5 \text{ atm}$

Gas expands isothermally against no pressure, so $\Delta E = 0$, $w = 0$ and $q = 0$.

$\Delta E = 0$, so $q_{rev} = -w_{rev} = nRT \ln (V_2/V_1)$; $T = \dfrac{PV}{nR} = 61 \text{ K}$

$q_{rev} = (1.0 \text{ mol}) (8.3145 \text{ J mol}^{-1} \text{ K}^{-1}) (61 \text{ K}) \ln (2.0/1.0) = 350 \text{ J}$

27. a. $q_v = \Delta E = nC_v\Delta T = (1.000 \text{ mol}) (28.95 \text{ J mol}^{-1} \text{ K}^{-1}) (350.0 - 298.0 \text{ K})$

$q_v = 1.51 \times 10^3 \text{ J} = 1.51 \text{ kJ}$

$q_p = \Delta H = nC_p\Delta T = 1.000 (37.27) (350.0 - 298.0) = 1.94 \times 10^3 \text{ J} = 1.94 \text{ kJ}$

b. $\Delta S = S_{350} - S_{298} = nC_p \ln (T_2/T_1)$

$S_{350} - 213.64 \text{ J/K} = (1.000 \text{ mol}) (37.27 \text{ J mol}^{-1} \text{ K}^{-1}) \ln (350.0/298.0)$

$S_{350} = 213.64 \text{ J/K} + 5.994 \text{ J/K} = 219.63 \text{ J/K} = \text{molar entropy at 350.0 K and 1.000 atm}$

c. $\Delta S = nR \ln (V_2/V_1)$, $V = nRT/P$, $\Delta S = nR \ln (P_1/P_2) = S_{(350, 1.174)} - S_{(350, 1.000)}$

$\Delta S = S_{(350, 1.174)} - 219.63 \text{ J/K} = (1.000 \text{ mol}) (8.3145 \text{ J mol}^{-1} \text{ K}^{-1}) \ln (1.000 \text{ atm}/1.174 \text{ atm})$

$\Delta S = -1.334 \text{ J/K} = S_{(350, 1.174)} - 219.63$, $S_{(350, 1.174)} = 218.30 \text{ J mol}^{-1} \text{ K}^{-1}$

28. a. $He(g, 0.100 \text{ mol}, 25°C, 1.00 \text{ atm}) \rightarrow He(g, 0.100 \text{ mol}, 25°C, 5.00 \text{ L})$

$\Delta S = nR \ln (V_2/V_1) = S_{final} - S_{initial}$; $S_i = 0.100 \text{ mol} (126.1 \text{ J mol}^{-1} \text{ K}^{-1}) = 12.6 \text{ J/K}$

$$V_1 = \frac{nRT}{P_1} = \frac{0.100 \text{ mol} \times \dfrac{0.08206 \text{ L atm}}{\text{mol K}} \times 298 \text{ K}}{1.00 \text{ atm}} = 2.45 \text{ L}$$

$S_f - 12.6 \text{ J/K} = (0.100 \text{ mol}) (8.3145 \text{ J mol}^{-1} \text{ K}^{-1}) \ln (5.00 \text{ L}/2.45 \text{ L})$

$S_f = 12.6 \text{ J/K} + 0.593 \text{ J/K} = 13.2 \text{ J/K}$

b. $He (3.00 \text{ mol}, 25°C, 1.00 \text{ atm}) \rightarrow He (3.00 \text{ mol}, 25°C, 3000.0 \text{ L})$

$\Delta S = nR \ln (V_2/V_1) = S_{final} - S_{initial}$; $S_i = 3.00 \text{ mol} (126.1 \text{ J mol}^{-1} \text{ K}^{-1}) = 378 \text{ J/K}$

$$V_1 = \frac{nRT}{P_1} = \frac{3.00 \text{ mol} \times \dfrac{0.08206 \text{ L atm}}{\text{mol K}} \times 298 \text{ K}}{1.00 \text{ atm}} = 73.4 \text{ L}$$

$$S_f - 378 \text{ J/K} = (3.00 \text{ mol})(8.3145 \text{ J mol}^{-1}\text{ K}^{-1}) \ln\left(\frac{3000.0 \text{ L}}{73.4 \text{ L}}\right) = 92.6 \text{ J/K}$$

$$S_f = 378 + 92.6 = 471 \text{ J/K}$$

29.   For A(l, 125°C) → A(l, 75°C):

$$\Delta S = nC_p \ln (T_2/T_1) = 1.00 \text{ mol } (75.0 \text{ J K}^{-1}\text{ mol}^{-1}) \ln (348 \text{ K}/398 \text{ K}) = -10.1 \text{ J/K}$$

For A(l, 75°C) → A(g, 155°C): $\Delta S = 75.0 \text{ J K}^{-1}\text{ mol}^{-1}$

For A(g, 155°C) → A(g, 125°C):

$$\Delta S = nC_p \ln (T_2/T_1) = 1.00 \text{ mol } (29.0 \text{ J K}^{-1}\text{ mol}^{-1}) \ln (398 \text{ K}/428 \text{ K}) = -2.11 \text{ J/K}$$

The sum of the three step gives A(l, 125°C) → A(g, 125°C). ΔS for this process is the sum of ΔS for each of the three steps.

$$\Delta S = -10.1 + 75.0 - 2.11 = 62.8 \text{ J/K}$$

For a phase change, $\Delta S = \Delta H/T$. At 125°C: $\Delta H_{vap} = T\Delta S = 398 \text{ K } (62.8 \text{ J/K}) = 2.50 \times 10^4 \text{ J}$

30.   Calculate q by breaking up the total process into several steps and use the formulas $q = nC\Delta T$ or the ΔH values to calculate q for each step.

$$q = (1.000 \text{ mol})(37.5 \text{ J mol}^{-1}\text{ K}^{-1})(30.0 \text{ K}) + 6010 \text{ J} + (1.000 \text{ mol})(75.3 \text{ J mol}^{-1}\text{ K}^{-1})(100.0 \text{ K})$$

$$+ 40,700 \text{ J} + (1.000 \text{ mol})(36.4 \text{ J mol}^{-1}\text{ K}^{-1})(40.0 \text{ K})$$

$$q = 1130 \text{ J} + 6010 \text{ J} + 7530 \text{ J} + 40,700 \text{ J} + 1460 \text{ J} = 56,800 \text{ J} = 56.8 \text{ kJ}$$

At constant pressure: $q_p = \Delta H = 56.8 \text{ kJ}$

at 100.0°C: $V = \dfrac{nRT}{P} = \dfrac{1.000 \text{ mol} \times \dfrac{0.08206 \text{ L atm}}{\text{mol K}} \times 373.2 \text{ K}}{1.00 \text{ atm}} = 30.6 \text{ L}$

at 140.0°C: $V = \dfrac{nR(413.2 \text{ K})}{P} = 33.9 \text{ L}$

Work is only done when vaporization occurs and when the vapor expands as T is increased from 100.0°C to 140.0°C.

$$w = -P\Delta V = -1.00 \text{ atm } (30.6 \text{ L} - 0.018 \text{ L}) - 1.00 \text{ atm } (33.9 - 30.6 \text{ L})$$

$$w = -30.6 \text{ L atm} - 3.3 \text{ L atm} = -33.9 \text{ L atm}; -33.9 \text{ L atm} \times \frac{101.3 \text{ J}}{\text{L atm}} = -3430 \text{ J} = -3.43 \text{ kJ}$$

$\Delta E = q + w = 56.8 \text{ kJ} - 3.43 \text{ kJ} = 53.4 \text{ kJ}$

Calculate ΔS by breaking up the total process into several steps and using the formulas $\Delta S = nC_p \ln(T_2/T_1)$ or $\Delta S = \Delta H/T$ (for phase changes) to calculate ΔS for each step.

$$\Delta S = (1.000 \text{ mol})(37.5 \text{ J mol}^{-1} \text{ K}^{-1}) \ln\left(\frac{273.2 \text{ K}}{243.2 \text{ K}}\right) + \frac{6010 \text{ J}}{273.2 \text{ K}}$$

$$+ (1.000 \text{ mol})(75.3 \text{ J mol}^{-1} \text{ K}^{-1}) \ln\left(\frac{373.2}{273.2}\right) + \frac{40{,}700 \text{ J}}{373.2 \text{ K}}$$

$$+ (1.000 \text{ mol})(36.4 \text{ J mol}^{-1} \text{ K}^{-1}) \ln\left(\frac{413.2}{373.2}\right)$$

$\Delta S = 4.36 \text{ J/K} + 22.0 \text{ J/K} + 23.5 \text{ J/K} + 109 \text{ J/K} + 3.71 \text{ J/K} = 163 \text{ J/K}$

Summary: $q = 56.8 \text{ kJ}$; $\Delta H = 56.8 \text{ kJ}$; $w = -3.43 \text{ kJ}$; $\Delta E = 53.4 \text{ kJ}$; $\Delta S = 163 \text{ J/K}$

31.   Calculate the final temperature by equating heat loss to heat gain.

$(3.00 \text{ mol})(75.3 \text{ J mol}^{-1} \, {}^{\circ}\text{C}^{-1})(T_f - 0 \, {}^{\circ}\text{C}) = (1.00 \text{ mol})(75.3 \text{ J mol}^{-1} \, {}^{\circ}\text{C}^{-1})(100. \, {}^{\circ}\text{C} - T_f)$

Solving: $T_f = 25 \, {}^{\circ}\text{C} = 298 \text{ K}$

Now we can calculate ΔS for the various changes using $\Delta S = nC_p \ln(T_2/T_1)$.

Heat 3 mol H_2O: $\Delta S_1 = (3.00 \text{ mol})(75.3 \text{ J mol}^{-1} \text{ K}^{-1}) \ln(298 \text{ K}/273 \text{ K}) = 19.8 \text{ J/K}$

Cool 1 mol H_2O: $\Delta S_2 = (1.00 \text{ mol})(75.3 \text{ J mol}^{-1} \text{ K}^{-1}) \ln(298/373) = -16.9 \text{ J/K}$

$\Delta S_{tot} = \Delta S_{heat} + \Delta S_{cool} = 19.8 - 16.9 = 2.9 \text{ J/K}$

32.   18.02 g ice = 1.000 mol ice; 54.05 g H_2O = 3.000 mol H_2O

Heat gained by the ice:

$(1.000 \text{ mol})(37.5 \text{ J mol}^{-1} \, {}^{\circ}\text{C}^{-1})(10.0 \, {}^{\circ}\text{C}) + 6.01 \times 10^3 \text{ J} + (1.000 \text{ mol})(75.3 \text{ J mol}^{-1} \, {}^{\circ}\text{C}^{-1})(T_f - 0.0)$

Heat lost by $H_2O(l)$ = 3.000 mol $(75.3 \text{ J mol}^{-1} \, {}^{\circ}\text{C}^{-1})(100.0 \, {}^{\circ}\text{C} - T_f)$

Heat gain by ice = Heat lost by H_2O; $375 \text{ J} + 6010 \text{ J} + 75.3 \, T_f = 22{,}600 \text{ J} - 226 \, T_f$

Solving: $T_f = 53.8 \, {}^{\circ}\text{C}$

Now calculate ΔS for the various changes using $\Delta S = nC_p \ln(T_2/T_1)$ or for a phase change, $\Delta S = \Delta H/T$.

$$\Delta S_{ice} = (1.000 \text{ mol}) (37.5 \text{ J mol}^{-1} \text{ K}^{-1}) \ln\left(\frac{273.2 \text{ K}}{263.2 \text{ K}}\right) + \frac{6010 \text{ J}}{273.2 \text{ K}}$$

$$+ (1.000 \text{ mol}) (75.3 \text{ J mol}^{-1} \text{ K}^{-1}) \ln\left(\frac{327.0}{273.2}\right)$$

$\Delta S_{ice} = 1.40 \text{ J/K} + 22.0 \text{ J/K} + 13.5 \text{ J/K} = 36.9 \text{ J/K}$

$\Delta S_{water} = (3.000 \text{ mol})(75.3 \text{ J mol}^{-1} \text{ K}^{-1}) \ln (327.0/373.2) = -29.9 \text{ J/K}$

$\Delta S_{tot} = \Delta S_{ice} + \Delta S_{water} = 36.9 - 29.9 = 7.0 \text{ J/K}$

Entropy and the Second Law of Thermodynamics: Free Energy

33. a.   The system is the portion of the universe in which we are interested.

  b.   The surroundings are everything else in the universe besides the system.

  c.   A closed system can only exchange energy with its surroundings. Matter is not exchanged.

  d.   An open system can exchange both matter and energy with its surroundings.

34. Living organisms need an external source of energy to carry out these processes. Green plants use the energy from sunlight to produce glucose from carbon dioxide and water by photosynthesis. In the human body, the energy released from the metabolism of glucose helps drive the synthesis of proteins. For all processes combined, ΔS_{univ} must be greater than zero (2nd law).

35. No, living organisms need an outside source of matter (food) to survive.

36. It appears that the sum of the two processes has no net change. This is not so. By the second law of thermodynamics, ΔS_{univ} must have increased even though it looks as if we have gone through a cyclic process.

37. a.   To boil a liquid requires heat. Hence, this is an endothermic process. All endothermic processes decrease the entropy of the surroundings (ΔS_{surr} is negative).

  b.   This is an exothermic process. Heat is released when gas molecules slow down enough to form the solid. In exothermic processes, the entropy of the surroundings increases (ΔS_{surr} is positive).

38. a. $\Delta S_{surr} = \dfrac{-\Delta H}{T} = \dfrac{-(-2221 \text{ kJ})}{298 \text{ K}} = 7.45 \text{ kJ/K} = 7.45 \times 10^3 \text{ J/K}$

  b. $\Delta S_{surr} = \dfrac{-\Delta H}{T} = \dfrac{-112 \text{ kJ}}{298 \text{ K}} = -0.376 \text{ kJ/K} = -376 \text{ J/K}$

39. a. $C_{graphite}(s)$; Diamond is a more ordered structure than graphite.

  b. $C_2H_5OH(g)$; The gaseous state is more disordered than the liquid state.

  c. $CO_2(g)$; The gaseous state is more disordered than the solid state.

d. $N_2O(g)$; More complicated molecule with more parts.

e. HCl(g); Larger molecule, more parts (electrons), more disorder.

40. a. Decrease in disorder; $\Delta S°(-)$

b. Increase in disorder; $\Delta S°(+)$

c. Decrease in disorder $(\Delta n < 0)$; $\Delta S°(-)$

d. Decrease in disorder $(\Delta n < 0)$; $\Delta S°(-)$

e. HCl(g) is more disordered than two mol of ions in solution; $\Delta S°(-)$.

f. Increase in disorder; $\Delta S°(+)$

For c, d and e, concentrate on the gaseous products and reactants. When there are more gaseous product molecules than gaseous reactant molecules $(\Delta n > 0)$, then $\Delta S°$ will be positive (disorder increases). When Δn is negative then $\Delta S°$ is negative (disorder decreases).

41. a. $2 H_2S(g) + SO_2(g) \rightarrow 3 S_{rhombic}(s) + 2 H_2O(g)$; Since there are more molecules of reactant gases as compared to product molecules of gas $(\Delta n = 2 - 3 < 0)$, then $\Delta S°$ will be negative.

$$\Delta S° = \Sigma n_p S°_{products} - \Sigma n_r S°_{reactants}$$

$$\Delta S° = [3 \text{ mol } S_{rhombic}(s) (32 \text{ J K}^{-1} \text{ mol}^{-1}) + 2 \text{ mol } H_2O(g) (189 \text{ J K}^{-1} \text{ mol}^{-1})]$$

$$- [2 \text{ mol } H_2S(g) (206 \text{ J K}^{-1} \text{ mol}^{-1}) + 1 \text{ mol } SO_2(g) (248 \text{ J K}^{-1} \text{ mol}^{-1})]$$

$$\Delta S° = 474 \text{ J/K} - 660. \text{ J/K} = -186 \text{ J/K}$$

b. $2 SO_3(g) \rightarrow 2 SO_2(g) + O_2(g)$; Since Δn of gases is positive $(\Delta n = 3-2)$, then $\Delta S°$ will be positive.

$$\Delta S = 2 \text{ mol}(248 \text{ J K}^{-1} \text{ mol}^{-1}) + 1 \text{ mol}(205 \text{ J K}^{-1} \text{ mol}^{-1}) - [2 \text{ mol}(257 \text{ J K}^{-1} \text{ mol}^{-1})] = 187 \text{ J/K}$$

c. $Fe_2O_3(s) + 3 H_2(g) \rightarrow 2 Fe(s) + 3 H_2O(g)$; Since Δn of gases $= 0$ $(\Delta n = 3 - 3)$, then we can't easily predict if $\Delta S°$ will be positive of negative.

$$\Delta S = 2 \text{ mol}(27 \text{ J K}^{-1} \text{ mol}^{-1}) + 3 \text{ mol}(189 \text{ J K}^{-1} \text{ mol}^{-1}) - [1 \text{ mol}(90. \text{ J K}^{-1} \text{ mol}^{-1})$$
$$+ 3 \text{ mol}(131 \text{ J K}^{-1} \text{ mol}^{-1})]$$

$$\Delta S = 138 \text{ J/K}$$

42. $C_2H_2(g) + 4 F_2(g) \rightarrow 2 CF_4(g) + H_2(g)$; $\Delta S° = 2 S°_{CF_4} + S°_{H_2} - [S°_{C_2H_2} + 4 S°_{F_2}]$

$-358 \text{ J/K} = (2 \text{ mol}) S°_{CF_4} + 131 \text{ J/K} - [201 \text{ J/K} + 4(203 \text{ J/K})]$, $S°_{CF_4} = 262 \text{ J K}^{-1} \text{ mol}^{-1}$

43. $-144 \text{ J/K} = (2 \text{ mol}) S°_{AlBr_3} - [2(28 \text{ J/K}) + 3(152 \text{ J/K})]$, $S°_{AlBr_3} = 184 \text{ J K}^{-1} \text{ mol}^{-1}$

44. At the boiling point, $\Delta G = 0$ so $\Delta H = T\Delta S$.

$$\Delta S = \frac{\Delta H}{T} = \frac{27.5 \text{ kJ/mol}}{(273 + 35) \text{ K}} = 8.93 \times 10^{-2} \text{ kJ K}^{-1} \text{ mol}^{-1} = 89.3 \text{ J K}^{-1} \text{ mol}^{-1}$$

45.   At the boiling point, $\Delta G = 0$ so $\Delta H = T\Delta S$. $T = \dfrac{\Delta H}{\Delta S} = \dfrac{58.51 \times 10^3 \text{ J/mol}}{92.92 \text{ J K}^{-1} \text{ mol}^{-1}} = 629.7 \text{ K}$

46.   At the melting point, $\Delta G = 0$ so $\Delta H = T\Delta S$. $\Delta S = \dfrac{\Delta H}{T} = \dfrac{35.2 \times 10^3 \text{ J/mol}}{3680 \text{ K}} = 9.57 \text{ J K}^{-1} \text{ mol}^{-1}$

47.   a. $NH_3(s) \rightarrow NH_3(l)$; $\Delta G = \Delta H - T\Delta S = 5650 \text{ J/mol} - 200. \text{ K } (28.9 \text{ J K}^{-1} \text{ mol}^{-1})$

       $\Delta G = 5650 \text{ J/mol} - 5780 \text{ J/mol} = -130 \text{ J/mol}$

       Yes, NH_3 will melt since $\Delta G < 0$ at this temperature.

       b.   At the melting point, $\Delta G = 0$ so $T = \dfrac{\Delta H}{\Delta S} = \dfrac{5650 \text{ J/mol}}{28.9 \text{ J K}^{-1} \text{ mol}^{-1}} = 196 \text{ K}.$

48.   a. $S_{rhombic} \rightarrow S_{monoclinic}$; This phase transition is spontaneous ($\Delta G < 0$) at temperatures above 95°C. $\Delta G = \Delta H - T\Delta S$; For ΔG to be negative only above a certain temperature, then ΔH is positive and ΔS is positive (see Table 10.6 of text).

       b.   Since ΔS is positive, then $S_{rhombic}$ is the more ordered crystalline structure.

Free Energy and Chemical Reactions

49.   a.

	$CH_4(g)$	$+$	$2\,O_2(g)$	$\rightarrow$	$CO_2(g)$	$+$	$2\,H_2O(g)$
ΔH_f°	-75 kJ/mol		0		-393.5		-242
ΔG_f°	-51 kJ/mol		0		-394		-229 Data from Appendix 4
S°	186 J K^{-1} mol^{-1}		205		214		189

$\Delta H^\circ = \Sigma n_p \Delta H^\circ_{f, products} - \Sigma n_r \Delta H^\circ_{f, reactants}$; $\Delta S^\circ = \Sigma n_p S^\circ_{products} - \Sigma n_r S^\circ_{reactants}$

$\Delta H^\circ = 2 \text{ mol}(-242 \text{ kJ/mol}) + 1 \text{ mol}(-393.5 \text{ kJ/mol}) - [1 \text{ mol}(-75 \text{ kJ/mol})] = -803 \text{ kJ}$

$\Delta S^\circ = 2 \text{ mol}(189 \text{ J K}^{-1} \text{ mol}^{-1}) + 1 \text{ mol}(214 \text{ J K}^{-1} \text{ mol}^{-1})$

$\qquad\qquad\qquad - [1 \text{ mol}(186 \text{ J K}^{-1} \text{ mol}^{-1}) + 2 \text{ mol}(205 \text{ J K}^{-1} \text{ mol}^{-1})] = -4 \text{ J/K}$

There are two ways to get ΔG°. We can use $\Delta G^\circ = \Delta H^\circ - T\Delta S^\circ$ (be careful of units):

$\qquad \Delta G^\circ = \Delta H^\circ - T\Delta S^\circ = -803 \times 10^3 \text{ J} - (298 \text{ K})(-4 \text{ J/K}) = -8.018 \times 10^5 \text{ J} = -802 \text{ kJ}$

or we can use ΔG_f° values where $\Delta G^\circ = \Sigma n_p \Delta G^\circ_{f, products} - \Sigma n_r \Delta G^\circ_{f, reactants}$:

$\Delta G° = 2 \text{ mol}(-229 \text{ kJ/mol}) + 1 \text{ mol}(-394 \text{ kJ/mol}) - [1 \text{ mol}(-51 \text{ kJ/mol})]$

$\Delta G° = -801 \text{ kJ}$ (Answers are the same within round off error.)

b. $6 \text{ CO}_2(g)$ + $6 \text{ H}_2\text{O}(l)$ → $\text{C}_6\text{H}_{12}\text{O}_6(s)$ + $6 \text{ O}_2(g)$

$\Delta H_f°$	-393.5 kJ/mol	-286	-1275	0
$S°$	214 J K^{-1} mol^{-1}	70.	212	205

$\Delta H° = -1275 - [6(-286) + 6(-393.5)] = 2802 \text{ kJ}$

$\Delta S° = 6(205) + 212 - [6(214) + 6(70.)] = -262 \text{ J/K}$

$\Delta G° = 2802 \text{ kJ} - (298 \text{ K})(-0.262 \text{ kJ/K}) = 2880. \text{ kJ}$

c. $\text{P}_4\text{O}_{10}(s)$ + $6 \text{ H}_2\text{O}(l)$ → $4 \text{ H}_3\text{PO}_4(s)$

$\Delta H_f°$ (kJ/mol)	-2984	-286	-1279
$S°$ (J K^{-1} mol^{-1})	229	70.	110.

$\Delta H° = 4 \text{ mol}(-1279 \text{ kJ/mol}) - [1 \text{ mol}(-2984 \text{ kJ/mol}) + 6 \text{ mol}(-286 \text{ kJ/mol})] = -416 \text{ kJ}$

$\Delta S° = 4(110.) - [229 + 6(70.)] = -209 \text{ J/K}$

$\Delta G° = \Delta H° - T\Delta S° = -416 \text{ kJ} - (298 \text{ K})(-0.209 \text{ kJ/K}) = -354 \text{ kJ}$

d. $\text{HCl}(g)$ + $\text{NH}_3(g)$ → $\text{NH}_4\text{Cl}(s)$

$\Delta H_f°$ (kJ/mol)	-92	-46	-314
$S°$ (J K^{-1} mol^{-1})	187	193	96

$\Delta H° = -314 - [-92 - 46] = -176 \text{ kJ}$; $\Delta S° = 96 - [187 + 193] = -284 \text{ J/K}$

$\Delta G° = \Delta H° - T\Delta S° = -176 \text{ kJ} - (298 \text{ K})(-0.284 \text{ kJ/K}) = -91 \text{ kJ}$

50. $-5490. \text{ kJ} = 8(-394 \text{ kJ}) + 10(-237 \text{ kJ}) - 2 \Delta G°_{f, C_4H_{10}}$, $\Delta G°_{f, C_4H_{10}} = -16 \text{ kJ/mol}$

51. $\Delta G° = -58.03$ kJ - (298 K)(-0.1766 kJ/K) = -5.40 kJ

$$\Delta G° = 0 = \Delta H° - T\Delta S°, \quad T = \frac{\Delta H°}{\Delta S°} = \frac{-58.03 \text{ kJ}}{-0.1766 \text{ kJ/K}} = 328.6 \text{ K}$$

$\Delta G°$ is negative below 328.6 K where the favorable $\Delta H°$ term dominates.

52.   a. CH_2—CH_2(g) + HCN(g) $\longrightarrow$ CH_2=CHCN(g) + H_2O(l)
              \\   /
               O

$\Delta H° = 185.0 - 286 - (-53 + 135.1) = -183$ kJ; $\Delta S° = 274 + 70. - (242 + 202) = -100.$ J/K

$\Delta G° = \Delta H° - T\Delta S° = -183$ kJ - 298 K(-0.100 kJ/K) = -153 kJ

b.   HC≡CH(g) + HCN(g) → CH_2=CHCN(g)

$\Delta H° = 185.0 - [135.1 + 227] = -177$ kJ; $\Delta S° = 274 - [202 + 201] = -129$ J/K

$T = 70.°C = 343$ K; $\Delta G°_{343} = \Delta H° - T\Delta S° = -177$ kJ - 343 K (-0.129 kJ/K)

$\Delta G°_{343} = -177$ kJ + 44 kJ = -133 kJ

c.   4 CH_2=$CHCH_3$(g) + 6 NO(g) → 4 CH_2=CHCN(g) + 6 H_2O(g) + N_2(g)

$\Delta H° = 6(-242) + 4(185.0) - [4(20.9) + 6(90.)] = -1336$ kJ

$\Delta S° = 192 + 6(189) + 4(274) - [6(211) + 4(266.9)] = 88$ J/K

$T = 700.°C = 973$ K; $\Delta G°_{973} = \Delta H° - T\Delta S° = -1336$ kJ - 973 K(0.088 kJ/K)

$\Delta G°_{973} = -1336$ kJ - 86 kJ = -1422 kJ

53.   a. $\Delta G° = 2(-270.$ kJ) - 2(-502 kJ) = 464 kJ

b.   Since $\Delta G°$ is positive, then this reaction is not spontaneous at standard conditions at 298 K.

c. $\Delta G° = \Delta H° - T\Delta S°$, $\Delta H° = \Delta G° + T\Delta S° = 464$ kJ + 298 K(0.179 kJ/K) = 517 kJ

We need to solve for the temperature when $\Delta G° = 0$:

$$\Delta G° = 0 = \Delta H° - T\Delta S°, \quad T = \frac{\Delta H°}{\Delta S°} = \frac{517 \text{ kJ}}{0.179 \text{ kJ/K}} = 2890 \text{ K}$$

This reaction will be spontaneous at standard conditions ($\Delta G° < 0$) when T > 2890 K. At these temperatures the favorable entropy term will dominate.

54. $C_2H_4(g) + H_2O(g) \rightarrow CH_3CH_2OH(l)$

$\Delta H° = -278 - (52 - 242) = -88$ kJ; $\Delta S° = 161 - (219 + 189) = -247$ J/K

When $\Delta G° = 0$, $\Delta H° = T\Delta S°$, $T = \dfrac{\Delta H°}{\Delta S°} = \dfrac{-88 \times 10^3 \text{ J}}{-247 \text{ J/K}} = 360$ K

At standard concentrations, $\Delta G = \Delta G°$, so the reaction will be spontaneous when $\Delta G° < 0$.   Since the signs of $\Delta H°$ and $\Delta S°$ are both negative, this reaction will be spontaneous at temperatures below 360 K (where the favorable $\Delta H°$ term will dominate).

$C_2H_6(g) + H_2O(g) \rightarrow CH_3CH_2OH(l) + H_2(g)$

$\Delta H° = -278 - (-84.7 - 242) = 49$ kJ; $\Delta S° = 131 + 161 - (229.5 + 189) = -127$ J/K

This reaction can never be spontaneous at standard conditions because of the signs of $\Delta H°$ and $\Delta S°$.

Thus the reaction $C_2H_4(g) + H_2O(g) \rightarrow C_2H_5OH(l)$ would be preferred at standard conditions.

55. $CH_4(g) + CO_2(g) \rightarrow CH_3CO_2H(l)$

$\Delta H° = -484 - [-75 + (-393.5)] = -16$ kJ; $\Delta S° = 160. - [186 + 214] = -240.$ J/K

$\Delta G° = \Delta H° - T\Delta S° = -16$ kJ $- (298$ K$)(-0.240$ kJ/K$) = 56$ kJ

At standard concentrations where $\Delta G = \Delta G°$, this reaction is spontaneous only at temperatures below T = $\Delta H°/\Delta S° = 67$ K (where the favorable $\Delta H°$ term will dominate, giving a negative $\Delta G°$ value). This is not practical. Substances will be in condensed phases and rates will be very slow at this extremely low temperature.

$CH_3OH(g) + CO(g) \rightarrow CH_3CO_2H(l)$

$\Delta H° = -484 - [-110.5 + (-201)] = -173$ kJ; $\Delta S° = 160. - [198 + 240.] = -278$ J/K

$\Delta G° = -173$ kJ $- (298$ K$)(-0.278$ kJ/K$) = -90.$ kJ

This reaction also has a favorable enthalpy and an unfavorable entropy term. This reaction is spontaneous at temperatures below T = $\Delta H°/\Delta S° = 622$ K (assuming standard concentrations). The reaction of CH_3OH and CO will be preferred at standard conditions. It is spontaneous at high enough temperatures that the rates of reaction should be reasonable.

56. $6 \text{ C(s)} + 6 \text{ O}_2(g) \rightarrow 6 \text{ CO}_2(g)$ $\Delta G° = 6(-394$ kJ$)$
     $3 \text{ H}_2(g) + 3/2 \text{ O}_2(g) \rightarrow 3 \text{ H}_2O(l)$ $\Delta G° = 3(-237$ kJ$)$
   $6 \text{ CO}_2(g) + 3 \text{ H}_2O(l) \rightarrow C_6H_6(l) + 15/2 \text{ O}_2(g)$ $\Delta G° = -1/2 \,(-6399$ kJ$)$

   _____

        $6 \text{ C(s)} + 3 \text{ H}_2(g) \rightarrow C_6H_6(l)$ $\Delta G° = 125$ kJ

57. Enthalpy is not favorable, so ΔS must provide the driving force for the change. Thus, ΔS is positive. There is an increase in disorder, so the original enzyme has the more ordered structure.

58.   a.   When a bond is formed, energy is released so ΔH is negative. Since there are more reactant molecules of gas than product molecules of gas ($\Delta n < 0$), then ΔS will be negative.

        b. $\Delta G = \Delta H - T\Delta S$; For this reaction to be spontaneous ($\Delta G < 0$), the favorable enthalpy term must dominate. The reaction will be spontaneous at low temperatures where the ΔH term dominates.

59.   Since there are more product gas molecules than reactant gas molecules ($\Delta n > 0$), then ΔS will be positive. From the signs of ΔH and ΔS, this reaction is spontaneous at all temperatures. It will cost money to heat the reaction mixture. Since there is no thermodynamic reason to do this, then the purpose of the elevated temperature must be to increase the rate of the reaction, i.e., kinetic reasons.

Free Energy: Pressure Dependence and Equilibrium

60. $\Delta G° = \Sigma n_p \Delta G°_{f,\,products} - \Sigma n_r \Delta G°_{f,\,reactants}$, $\Delta G° = 2(-371) - [2(-300.)] = -142$ kJ

$$\Delta G = \Delta G° + RT \ln Q = -142 \text{ kJ} + RT \ln \left(\frac{P_{SO_3}^2}{P_{SO_2}^2 \times P_{O_2}} \right); \quad \text{Note: } \Delta G = \Delta G° \text{ when all gases are at } 1.00 \text{ atm.}$$

At 10.0 atm: $\Delta G = -142 \text{ kJ} + \dfrac{(8.3145 \text{ J mol}^{-1} \text{ K}^{-1})}{1000 \text{ J/kJ}} (298 \text{ K}) \ln \left(\dfrac{(10.0)^2}{(10.0)^2(10.0)} \right) = -148 \text{ kJ}$

61. $\Delta G = \Delta G° + RT \ln Q = \Delta G° + RT \ln \dfrac{P_{N_2O_4}}{P_{NO_2}^2}$

        $\Delta G° = 1 \text{ mol}(98 \text{ kJ/mol}) - 2 \text{ mol}(52 \text{ kJ/mol}) = -6$ kJ

        a.   These are standard conditions, so $\Delta G = \Delta G°$ since $Q = 1$ and $\ln Q = 0$. Since $\Delta G°$ is negative, then the forward reaction is spontaneous. The reaction shifts right to reach equilibrium.

        b. $\Delta G = -6 \times 10^3 \text{ J} + 8.3145 \text{ J K}^{-1} \text{ mol}^{-1} (298 \text{ K}) \ln \dfrac{0.50}{(0.21)^2}$

             $\Delta G = -6 \times 10^3 \text{ J} + 6.0 \times 10^3 \text{ J} = 0$

             Since $\Delta G = 0$, this reaction is at equilibrium (no shift).

        c. $\Delta G = -6 \times 10^3 \text{ J} + 8.3145 \text{ J K}^{-1} \text{ mol}^{-1} (298 \text{ K}) \ln \dfrac{1.6}{(0.29)^2}$

             $\Delta G = -6 \times 10^3 \text{ J} + 7.3 \times 10^3 \text{ J} = 1.3 \times 10^3 \text{ J} = 1 \times 10^3 \text{ J}$

             Since ΔG is positive, the reverse reaction is spontaneous, so the reaction shifts to the left to reach equilibrium.

62. $\Delta G° = 3(0) + 2(-229) - [2(-34) + 1(-300.)] = -90.$ kJ

$\Delta G = \Delta G° + RT \ln \dfrac{P_{H_2O}^2}{P_{H_2S}^2 \times P_{SO_2}} = -90.$ kJ $+ \dfrac{(8.3145)(298)}{1000}$ kJ $\left[\ln \dfrac{(0.030)^2}{(1.0 \times 10^{-4})^2 (0.010)}\right]$

$\Delta G = -90.$ kJ $+ 39.7$ kJ $= -50.$ kJ

63. $\Delta H° = 2\ \Delta H_{f, NH_3}° = 2(-46) = -92$ kJ; $\Delta G° = 2\ \Delta G_{f, NH_3}° = 2(-17) = -34$ kJ

$\Delta S° = 2(193\ \text{J/K}) - [192\ \text{J/K} + 3(131\ \text{J/K})] = -199\ \text{J/K}$; $\Delta G° = -RT \ln K$

$K = \exp \dfrac{-\Delta G°}{RT} = \exp\left(\dfrac{-(-34,000\ \text{J})}{(8.3145\ \text{J K}^{-1}\ \text{mol}^{-1})(298\ \text{K})}\right) = e^{13.72} = 9.1 \times 10^5$

Note: When determining exponents, we will round off after the calculation is complete. This helps eliminate excessive round off error.

a. $\Delta G = \Delta G° + RT \ln \dfrac{P_{NH_3}^2}{P_{N_2} \times P_{H_2}^3} = -34$ kJ $+ \dfrac{(8.3145\ \text{J K}^{-1}\ \text{mol}^{-1})(298\ \text{K})}{1000\ \text{J/kJ}} \ln \dfrac{(50.)^2}{(200.)(200.)^3}$

$\Delta G = -34$ kJ $- 33$ kJ $= -67$ kJ

b. $\Delta G = -34$ kJ $+ \dfrac{(8.3145\ \text{J K}^{-1}\ \text{mol}^{-1})(298\ \text{K})}{1000\ \text{J/kJ}} \ln \dfrac{(200.)^2}{(200.)(600.)^3}$

$\Delta G = -34$ kJ $- 34.4$ kJ $= -68$ kJ

c.   Assume $\Delta H°$ and $\Delta S°$ are temperature independent.

$\Delta G_{100}° = \Delta H° - T\Delta S°$, $\Delta G_{100}° = -92$ kJ $- (100.\ \text{K})(-0.199\ \text{kJ/K}) = -72$ kJ

$\Delta G_{100} = \Delta G_{100}° + RT \ln Q = -72$ kJ $+ \dfrac{(8.3145\ \text{J K}^{-1}\ \text{mol}^{-1})(100.\ \text{K})}{1000\ \text{J/kJ}} \ln \dfrac{(10.)^2}{(50.)(200.)^3}$

$\Delta G_{100} = -72$ kJ $- 13$ kJ $= -85$ kJ

d. $\Delta G_{700}° = -92$ kJ $- (700.\ \text{K})(-0.199\ \text{kJ/K}) = 47$ kJ

$\Delta G_{700} = 47$ kJ $+ \dfrac{(8.3145\ \text{J K}^{-1}\ \text{mol}^{-1})(700.\ \text{K})}{1000\ \text{J/kJ}} \ln \dfrac{(10.)^2}{(50.)(200.)^3} = 47$ kJ $- 88$ kJ $= -41$ kJ

64.   a. $\Delta G° = -RT \ln K = -\dfrac{8.3145\ \text{J}}{\text{K mol}} (298\ \text{K}) \ln (1.00 \times 10^{-14}) = 7.99 \times 10^4\ \text{J} = 79.9\ \text{kJ/mol}$

b. $\Delta G_{313}° = -RT \ln K = -\dfrac{8.3145\ \text{J}}{\text{K mol}} (313\ \text{K}) \ln (2.92 \times 10^{-14}) = 8.11 \times 10^4\ \text{J} = 81.1\ \text{kJ/mol}$

65.   a.

	ΔH_f° (kJ/mol)	S° (J K^{-1} mol^{-1})
$NH_3(g)$	-46	193
$O_2(g)$	0	205
$NO(g)$	90.	211
$H_2O(g)$	-242	189
$NO_2(g)$	34	240.
$HNO_3(l)$	-174	156
$H_2O(l)$	-286	70.

$4 NH_3(g) + 5 O_2(g) \rightarrow 4 NO(g) + 6 H_2O(g)$

$\Delta H^\circ = 6(-242) + 4(90.) - [4(-46)] = -908$ kJ

$\Delta S^\circ = 4(211) + 6(189) - [4(193) + 5(205)] = 181$ J/K

$\Delta G^\circ = -908$ kJ $- 298$ K $(0.181$ kJ/K$) = -962$ kJ

$\Delta G^\circ = - RT \ln K, \ \ln K = \dfrac{-\Delta G^\circ}{RT} = \left(\dfrac{-(-962 \times 10^3 \text{ J})}{8.3145 \text{ J K}^{-1} \text{ mol}^{-1} \times 298 \text{ K}} \right) = 388$

$\ln K = 2.303 \log K, \ \log K = 168, \ K = 10^{168}$ (an extremely large value)

$2 NO(g) + O_2(g) \rightarrow 2 NO_2(g)$

$\Delta H^\circ = 2(34) - [2(90.)] = -112$ kJ; $\ \Delta S^\circ = 2(240.) - [2(211) + (205)] = -147$ J/K

$\Delta G^\circ = -112$ kJ $- (298$ K$)(-0.147$ kJ/K$) = -68$ kJ

$K = \exp \dfrac{-\Delta G^\circ}{RT} = \exp \left(\dfrac{-(-68,000 \text{ J})}{8.3145 \text{ J K}^{-1} \text{ mol}^{-1} (298 \text{ K})} \right) = e^{27.44} = 8.3 \times 10^{11}$

Note: When determining exponents, we will round off after the calculation is complete.

$3 NO_2(g) + H_2O(l) \rightarrow 2 HNO_3(l) + NO(g)$

$\Delta H^\circ = 2(-174) + (90.) - [3(34) + (-286)] = -74$ kJ

$\Delta S^\circ = 2(156) + (211) - [3(240.) + (70.)] = -267$ J/K

$\Delta G^\circ = -74$ kJ $- (298$ K$)(-0.267$ kJ/K$) = 6$ kJ

$K = \exp \dfrac{-\Delta G^\circ}{RT} = \exp \left(\dfrac{-6000 \text{ J}}{8.3145 \text{ J K}^{-1} \text{ mol}^{-1} (298 \text{ K})} \right) = e^{-2.4} = 9 \times 10^{-2}$

b. $\Delta G° = -RT \ln K$; $T = 825 + 273 = 1098$ K; We must determine $\Delta G°$ at 1098 K.

$$\Delta G°_{1098} = \Delta H° - T\Delta S° = -908 \text{ kJ} - (1098 \text{ K})(0.181 \text{ kJ/K}) = -1107 \text{ kJ}$$

$$K = \exp \frac{-\Delta G°_{1098}}{RT} = \exp\left(\frac{-(-1.107 \times 10^6 \text{ J})}{8.3145 \text{ J K}^{-1} \text{ mol}^{-1} (1098 \text{ K})} \right) = e^{121.258} = 4.589 \times 10^{52}$$

c.   There is no thermodynamic reason for the elevated temperature since $\Delta H°$ is negative and $\Delta S°$ is positive. Thus, the purpose for the high temperature must be to increase the rate of the reaction.

66. $K = \dfrac{P_{NF_3}^2}{P_{N_2} \times P_{F_2}^3} = \dfrac{(0.48)^2}{0.021(0.063)^3} = 4.4 \times 10^4$

$$\Delta G°_{800} = -RT \ln K = -8.3145 \text{ J K}^{-1} \text{ mol}^{-1} (800. \text{ K}) \ln (4.4 \times 10^4) = -7.1 \times 10^4 \text{ J/mol} = -71 \text{ kJ/mol}$$

67. $2 SO_2(g) + O_2(g) \rightarrow 2 SO_3(g)$; $\Delta G° = 2(-371 \text{ kJ}) - [2(-300. \text{ kJ})] = -142 \text{ kJ}$

$$\Delta G° = -RT \ln K, \ln K = \frac{-\Delta G°}{RT} = \frac{-(-142,000 \text{ J})}{8.3145 \text{ J K}^{-1} \text{mol}^{-1} (298 \text{ K})} = 57.311, K = e^{57.311} = 7.76 \times 10^{24}$$

$$K = 7.76 \times 10^{24} = \frac{P_{SO_3}^2}{P_{SO_2}^2 \times P_{O_2}} = \frac{(2.0)^2}{P_{SO_2}^2 \times (0.50)}, \quad P_{SO_2} = 1.0 \times 10^{-12} \text{ atm}$$

From the negative value of $\Delta G°$, this reaction is spontaneous at standard conditions. Since there are more molecules of reactant gases than product gases, then $\Delta S°$ will be negative (unfavorable). Therefore, this reaction must be exothermic ($\Delta H° < 0$). When $\Delta H°$ and $\Delta S°$ are both negative, the reaction will be spontaneous at relatively low temperatures where the favorable $\Delta H°$ term dominates.

68.   a. $\Delta G° = -RT \ln K$, $K = \exp (-\Delta G°/RT) = \exp\left(\dfrac{-(-30,500 \text{ J})}{8.3145 \text{ J K}^{-1} \text{ mol}^{-1} \times 298 \text{ K}} \right) = 2.22 \times 10^5$

b. $C_6H_{12}O_6(s) + 6 O_2(g) \rightarrow 6 CO_2(g) + 6 H_2O(l)$

$$\Delta G° = 6 \text{ mol}(-394 \text{ kJ/mol}) + 6 \text{ mol}(-237 \text{ kJ/mol}) - 1 \text{ mol}(-911 \text{ kJ/mol}) = -2875 \text{ kJ}$$

$$\frac{2875 \text{ kJ}}{\text{mol glucose}} \times \frac{1 \text{ mol ATP}}{30.5 \text{ kJ}} = 94.3 \text{ mol ATP}; \quad 94.3 \text{ molecules ATP/molecule glucose}$$

This is an overstatement. The assumption that all of the free energy goes into this reaction is false. Actually only 38 moles of ATP are produced by metabolism of one mole of glucose.

69. $HgbO_2 \qquad \rightarrow Hgb + O_2 \qquad \Delta G° = -(-70 \text{ kJ})$

$Hgb + CO \rightarrow HgbCO \qquad \Delta G° = -80 \text{ kJ}$

$\overline{HgbO_2 + CO \rightarrow HgbCO + O_2 \quad \Delta G° = -10 \text{ kJ}}$

$$\Delta G° = -RT \ln K, \quad K = \exp\left(\frac{-\Delta G°}{RT} \right) = \exp\left(\frac{-(-10 \times 10^3 \text{ J})}{(8.3145 \text{ J K}^{-1} \text{ mol}^{-1})(298 \text{ K})} \right) = 60$$

70.   a. $\Delta G° = -RT \ln K$

$$\ln K = \frac{-\Delta G°}{RT} = \frac{-14,000 \text{ J}}{(8.3145 \text{ J K}^{-1} \text{ mol}^{-1})(298 \text{ K})} = -5.65, \quad K = e^{-5.65} = 3.5 \times 10^{-3}$$

   b. $\qquad$ Glutamic acid + $NH_3 \rightarrow$ Glutamine + $H_2O \qquad\qquad \Delta G° = 14 \text{ kJ}$

$\qquad\qquad\qquad$ ATP + $H_2O \rightarrow$ ADP + $H_2PO_4^- \qquad\qquad\qquad \Delta G° = -30.5 \text{ kJ}$

$\overline{\qquad\qquad\qquad\qquad\qquad\qquad\qquad\qquad\qquad\qquad\qquad\qquad\qquad\qquad\qquad\qquad}$

$\qquad$ Glutamic acid + ATP + $NH_3 \rightarrow$ Glutamine + ADP + $H_2PO_4^- \qquad \Delta G° = 14 - 30.5 = -17 \text{ kJ}$

$$\ln K = \frac{-\Delta G°}{RT} = \frac{-(-17,000 \text{ J})}{8.3145 \text{ J K}^{-1} \text{ mol}^{-1} (298 \text{ K})} = 6.86, \quad K = e^{6.86} = 9.5 \times 10^2$$

71.   At 25.0°C: $\Delta G° = \Delta H° - T\Delta S° = -58.03 \times 10^3 \text{ J/mol} - (298.2 \text{ K})(-176.6 \text{ J K}^{-1} \text{ mol}^{-1})$

$$= -5.37 \times 10^3 \text{ J/mol}$$

$$\Delta G° = -RT \ln K, \ln K = \frac{-\Delta G°}{RT} = \frac{-(-5.37 \times 10^3 \text{ J/mol})}{(8.3145 \text{ J K}^{-1} \text{mol}^{-1})(298.2 \text{ K})} = 2.166; \quad K = e^{2.166} = 8.72$$

At 100.0°C: $\Delta G° = -58.03 \times 10^3 \text{ J/mol} - (373.2 \text{ K})(-176.6 \text{ J K}^{-1} \text{ mol}^{-1}) = 7.88 \times 10^3 \text{ J/mol}$

$$\ln K = \frac{-(7.88 \times 10^3 \text{ J/mol})}{(8.3145 \text{ J K}^{-1} \text{mol}^{-1})(373.2 \text{ K})} = -2.540, \quad K = e^{-2.540} = 0.0789$$

72.   The equation $\ln K = \frac{-\Delta H°}{R}\left(\frac{1}{T}\right) + \frac{\Delta S°}{R}$ is in the form of a straight line equation ($y = mx + b$).

A graph of ln K vs. 1/T will yield a straight line with slope = $m = -\Delta H°/R$ and a y-intercept = $b = \Delta S°/R$.

From the plot:

$$\text{slope} = \frac{\Delta y}{\Delta x} = \frac{0 - 40.}{3.0 \times 10^{-3} \text{ K}^{-1} - 0} = -1.3 \times 10^4 \text{ K}$$

$-1.3 \times 10^4 \text{ K} = -\Delta H°/R, \quad \Delta H° = 1.3 \times 10^4 \text{ K} \times 8.3145 \text{ J K}^{-1} \text{ mol}^{-1} = 1.1 \times 10^5 \text{ J/mol}$

y-intercept = 40. = $\Delta S°/R$, $\Delta S° = 40. \times 8.3145 \text{ J K}^{-1} \text{ mol}^{-1} = 330 \text{ J K}^{-1} \text{ mol}^{-1}$

As seen here, when $\Delta H°$ is positive, the slope of the ln K vs. 1/T plot is negative. When $\Delta H°$ is negative, as in an exothermic process, the slope of the ln K vs. 1/T plot will be positive (slope = $-\Delta H°/R$).

73.   A graph of ln K vs. 1/T will yield a straight line with slope equal to $-\Delta H°/R$ and y-intercept equal to $\Delta S°/R$ (see Exercise 10.72).

a.

Temp (°C)	T(K)	1000/T (K^{-1})	K_w	ln K_w
0	273	3.66	1.14×10^{-15}	-34.408
25	298	3.36	1.00×10^{-14}	-32.236
35	308	3.25	2.09×10^{-14}	-31.499
40.	313	3.19	2.92×10^{-14}	-31.165
50.	323	3.10	5.47×10^{-14}	-30.537

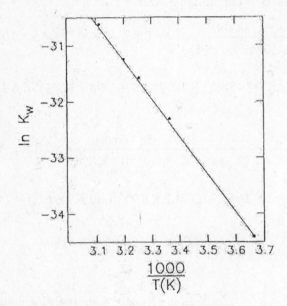

The straight line equation (from a calculator) is: $\ln K = -6.91 \times 10^3 \left(\dfrac{1}{T} \right) - 9.09$

Slope = -6.91×10^3 K = $\dfrac{-\Delta H°}{R}$

$\Delta H° = -(-6.91 \times 10^3 \text{ K} \times 8.3145 \text{ J K}^{-1} \text{ mol}^{-1}) = 5.75 \times 10^4 \text{ J/mol} = 57.5 \text{ kJ/mol}$

y-intercept = $-9.09 = \dfrac{\Delta S°}{R}$, $\Delta S° = -9.09 \times 8.3145 \text{ J K}^{-1} \text{ mol}^{-1} = -75.6 \text{ J K}^{-1} \text{ mol}^{-1}$

b.   From part a, $\Delta H° = 57.5 \text{ kJ/mol}$ and $\Delta S° = -75.6 \text{ J K}^{-1} \text{ mol}^{-1}$. Assuming $\Delta H°$ and $\Delta S°$ are temperature independent:

$$\Delta G° = 57,500 \text{ J/mol} - 647 \text{ K} (-75.6 \text{ J K}^{-1} \text{ mol}^{-1}) = 106,400 \text{ J/mol} = 106.4 \text{ kJ/mol}$$

74.   From Exercise 10.72, $\ln K = \dfrac{-\Delta H°}{RT} + \dfrac{\Delta S°}{R}$, $R = 8.3145 \text{ J K}^{-1} \text{ mol}^{-1}$

For two sets of K and T:

$$\ln K_1 = \frac{-\Delta H°}{R} \left(\frac{1}{T_1} \right) + \frac{\Delta S°}{R}; \ \ \ln K_2 = \frac{-\Delta H°}{R} \left(\frac{1}{T_2} \right) + \frac{\Delta S°}{R}$$

Subtracting the first expression from the second:

$$\ln K_2 - \ln K_1 = \frac{\Delta H^\circ}{R}\left(\frac{1}{T_1} - \frac{1}{T_2}\right) \ \text{ or } \ \ln\frac{K_2}{K_1} = \frac{\Delta H^\circ}{R}\left(\frac{1}{T_1} - \frac{1}{T_2}\right)$$

$$\ln\left(\frac{3.25 \times 10^{-2}}{8.84}\right) = \frac{\Delta H^\circ}{8.3145 \text{ J K}^{-1}\text{mol}^{-1}}\left(\frac{1}{298 \text{ K}} - \frac{1}{348 \text{ K}}\right)$$

$-5.61 = (5.8 \times 10^{-5} \text{ mol/J}) (\Delta H^\circ)$, $\Delta H^\circ = -9.7 \times 10^4$ J/mol

For K = 8.84 at T = 25°C:

$$\ln 8.84 = \frac{-(-9.7 \times 10^4 \text{ J/mol})}{(8.3145 \text{ J K}^{-1}\text{mol}^{-1})(298 \text{ K})} + \frac{\Delta S^\circ}{8.3145 \text{ J K}^{-1}\text{mol}^{-1}}, \ \frac{\Delta S^\circ}{8.3145} = -37$$

$\Delta S^\circ = -310$ J K^{-1} mol^{-1}

We get the same value for ΔS° using K = 3.25×10^{-2} at T = 348 K data. $\Delta G^\circ = -RT \ln K$. When K = 1.00 then $\Delta G^\circ = 0$ since ln 1.00 = 0. $\Delta G^\circ = 0 = \Delta H^\circ - T\Delta S^\circ$. Assuming ΔH° and ΔS° do not depend on temperature:

$$\Delta H^\circ = T\Delta S^\circ, \ T = \frac{\Delta H^\circ}{\Delta S^\circ} = \frac{-9.7 \times 10^4 \text{ J/mol}}{-310 \text{ J K}^{-1}\text{mol}^{-1}} = 310 \text{ K}$$

Additional Exercises

75.   No; When using ΔG_f° values in Appendix 4, we have generally specified a temperature of 25°C. Further, if gases or solutions are involved, we have specified partial pressures of 1 atm and solute concentrations of 1 molar. At other temperatures and compositions, the reaction may not be spontaneous. A negative ΔG° value means the reaction is spontaneous under standard conditions.

76.   When an ionic solid dissolves, one would expect the disorder of the system to increase, so ΔS_{sys} is positive. Since temperature increased as the solid dissolved, this is an exothermic process and ΔS_{surr} is positive ($\Delta S_{surr} = -\Delta H/T$). Since the solid did dissolve, the dissolving process is spontaneous, so ΔS_{univ} is positive (as it must be when ΔS_{sys} and ΔS_{surr} are both positive).

77.   As any process occurs, ΔS_{univ} will increase; ΔS_{univ} cannot decrease. Time also goes in one direction, just as ΔS_{univ} goes in one direction.

78. $w_{max} = \Delta G$; When ΔG is negative, the magnitude of ΔG is equal to the maximum possible useful work obtainable from the process (at constant T and P). When ΔG is positive, the magnitude of ΔG is equal to the minimum amount of work that must be expended to make the process spon-taneous. Due to waste energy (heat) in any real process, the amount of useful work obtainable from a spontaneous process is always less than w_{max} and for a nonspontaneous reaction, an amount of work greater than w_{max} must be applied to make the process spontaneous.

79.   The introduction of mistakes is an effect of entropy. The purpose of redundant information is to provide a control to check the "correctness" of the transmitted information.

80. $\Delta G° = -RT \ln K$; When $K = 1.00$, $\Delta G° = 0$ since $\ln 1.00 = 0$. $\Delta G° = 0 = \Delta H° - T\Delta S°$, so $\Delta H° = T\Delta S°$.

$\Delta H° = 3(-242 \text{ kJ}) - [-826 \text{ kJ}] = 100. \text{ kJ}$; $\Delta S° = 2(27 \text{ J/K}) + 3(189 \text{ J/K}) - [90. \text{ J/K} + 3(131 \text{ J/K})]$
$$= 138 \text{ J/K}$$

$\Delta H° = T\Delta S°$, $T = \dfrac{\Delta H°}{\Delta S°} = \dfrac{100. \text{ kJ}}{0.138 \text{ kJ/K}} = 725 \text{ K}$

81. $HF(aq) \rightleftharpoons H^+(aq) + F^-(aq)$; $\Delta G = \Delta G° + RT \ln \dfrac{[H^+][F^-]}{[HF]}$

$\Delta G° = -RT \ln K = -(8.3145 \text{ J K}^{-1} \text{ mol}^{-1})(298 \text{ K}) \ln(7.2 \times 10^{-4}) = 1.8 \times 10^4 \text{ J/mol}$

a.   The concentrations are all at standard conditions so $\Delta G = \Delta G° = 1.8 \times 10^4 \text{ J/mol}$ (since $Q = 1.0$ and $\ln Q = 0$). Since $\Delta G°$ is positive, then the reaction shifts left to reach equilibrium.

b. $\Delta G = 1.8 \times 10^4 \text{ J/mol} + (8.3145 \text{ J K}^{-1} \text{ mol}^{-1})(298 \text{ K}) \ln \dfrac{(2.7 \times 10^{-2})^2}{0.98}$

$\Delta G = 1.8 \times 10^4 \text{ J/mol} - 1.8 \times 10^4 \text{ J/mol} = 0$

Since $\Delta G = 0$, then the reaction is at equilibrium (no shift).

c. $\Delta G = 1.8 \times 10^4 + 8.3145 (298) \ln \dfrac{(1.0 \times 10^{-5})^2}{1.0 \times 10^{-5}} = -1.1 \times 10^4 \text{ J/mol}$; shifts right

d. $\Delta G = 1.8 \times 10^4 + 8.3145 (298) \ln \dfrac{7.2 \times 10^{-4}(0.27)}{0.27} = 1.8 \times 10^4 - 1.8 \times 10^4 = 0$; at equilibrium

e. $\Delta G = 1.8 \times 10^4 + 8.3145 (298) \ln \dfrac{1.0 \times 10^{-3}(0.67)}{0.52} = 2 \times 10^3 \text{ J/mol}$; shifts left

82. $K^+ (\text{blood}) \rightleftharpoons K^+ (\text{muscle})$ $\Delta G° = 0$; $\Delta G = RT \ln \left(\dfrac{[K^+]_m}{[K^+]_b} \right)$; $\Delta G = w_{max}$

$\Delta G = \dfrac{8.3145 \text{ J}}{K \text{ mol}} (310. \text{ K}) \ln \left(\dfrac{0.15}{0.0050} \right)$, $\Delta G = 8.8 \times 10^3 \text{ J/mol} = 8.8 \text{ kJ/mol}$

At least 8.8 kJ of work must be applied to transport 1 mol K^+.

Other ions will have to be transported in order to maintain electroneutrality. Either anions must be transported into the cells, or cations (Na^+) in the cell must be transported to the blood. The latter is what happens: [Na^+] in blood is greater than [Na^+] in cells as a result of this pumping.

$\dfrac{8.8 \text{ kJ}}{\text{mol } K^+} \times \dfrac{1 \text{ mol ATP}}{30.5 \text{ kJ}} = 0.29 \text{ mol ATP}$

83.   S (monoclinic) → S (rhombic); $\Delta H° = 0 - 0.30 = -0.30$ kJ; $\Delta S° = 31.73 - 32.55 = -0.82$ J/K

At the conversion temperature: $\Delta G° = 0$ so $\Delta H° = T\Delta S°$; $T = \dfrac{\Delta H°}{\Delta S°} = \dfrac{-3.0 \times 10^2 \text{ J}}{-0.82 \text{ J/K}} = 370$ K

84.   At equilibrium:

$$P_{H_2} = \frac{nRT}{V} = \frac{\left(\dfrac{1.10 \times 10^{13} \text{ molecules}}{6.022 \times 10^{23} \text{ molecules/mol}}\right)\left(\dfrac{0.08206 \text{ L atm}}{\text{mol K}}\right)(298 \text{ K})}{1.00 \text{ L}} = 4.47 \times 10^{-10} \text{ atm}$$

The pressure of H_2 decreased from 1.00 atm to 4.47×10^{-10} atm. Essentially all of the H_2 and Br_2 has reacted. Therefore, $P_{HBr} = 2.00$ atm since there is a 2:1 mol ratio between HBr and H_2 in the balanced equation. Since we began with equal moles of H_2 and Br_2, then we will have equal moles of H_2 and Br_2 at equilibrium. Therefore, $P_{H_2} = P_{Br_2} = 4.47 \times 10^{-10}$ atm.

$$K = \frac{P_{HBr}^2}{P_{H_2} \times P_{Br_2}} = \frac{(2.00)^2}{(4.47 \times 10^{-10})^2} = 2.00 \times 10^{19} \quad \text{Assumptions good.}$$

$\Delta G° = -RT \ln K = -(8.3145 \text{ J K}^{-1} \text{ mol}^{-1})(298 \text{ K}) \ln (2.00 \times 10^{19}) = -1.10 \times 10^5$ J/mol

$$\Delta S° = \frac{\Delta H° - \Delta G°}{T} = \frac{-103,800 \text{ J} - (-1.10 \times 10^5 \text{ J})}{298 \text{ K}} = 20 \text{ J/K}$$

85. $1.00 \, M$ HCl → $0.100 \, M$ HCl $\Delta G° = 0$; $\Delta G = \Delta G° + RT \ln Q = RT \ln \dfrac{[H^+][Cl^-]}{[H^+][Cl^-]}$

$$\Delta G = (8.3145 \text{ J mol}^{-1} \text{ K}^{-1})(298 \text{ K}) \ln \left(\frac{(0.100)^2}{(1.00)^2}\right) = -11,400 \text{ J} = -11.4 \text{ kJ}$$

The $0.100 \, M$ HCl is lower in free energy by 11.4 kJ.

86.   Using Le Chatelier's principle: A decrease in pressure (volume increases) will favor the side with the greater number of particles. Thus, 2 I(g) will be favored at low pressure.

Looking at ΔG: $\Delta G = \Delta G° + RT \ln (P_I^2/P_{I_2})$; $\ln (P_I^2/P_{I_2}) > 0$ for $P_I = P_{I_2} = 10$ atm and ΔG is positive (not spontaneous). But at $P_I = P_{I_2} = 0.10$ atm, the logarithm term is negative. If $|RT \ln Q| > \Delta G°$, then ΔG becomes negative and the reaction is spontaneous.

87. $Ba(NO_3)_2(s) \rightleftharpoons Ba^{2+}(aq) + 2 NO_3^-(aq)$ $K = K_{sp}$; $\Delta G° = -561 + 2(-109) - (-797) = 18$ kJ

$$\Delta G° = -RT \ln K_{sp}, \quad \ln K_{sp} = \frac{-\Delta G°}{RT} = \frac{-18,000 \text{ J}}{8.3145 \text{ J K}^{-1} \text{ mol}^{-1}(298 \text{ K})} = -7.26, \quad K_{sp} = e^{-7.26} = 7.0 \times 10^{-4}$$

88.   We would expect the solubility to increase for salts with an endothermic heat of solution. $\Delta H°$ refers to a solution with one molar concentration. Solubility deals with a saturated solution. In a saturated solution the concentrations are not one molar and the sign for ΔH_{sol} may be different.

89. ΔS is more favorable for reaction two than for reaction one, resulting in $K_2 > K_1$. In reaction one, seven particles in solution are forming one particle in solution. In reaction two, four particles are forming one which results in a smaller decrease in disorder than for reaction one.

90.   The hydration of the dissociated ions results in a more ordered "structure" in solution. The smallest ion (F^-) has the largest charge density and should show the most ordering.

91.   Because of hydrogen bonding interactions, there is greater "structure" (or order) in liquid water than in most other liquids. Thus, there is a greater increase in disorder, or a greater increase in entropy when water evaporates.

92. $\Delta S = \dfrac{q_{rev}}{T} = \dfrac{\Delta H_{vap}}{T}$; For methane: $\Delta S = \dfrac{8.20 \times 10^3 \text{ J/mol}}{112 \text{ K}} = 73.2 \text{ J mol}^{-1} \text{ K}^{-1}$

For hexane: $\Delta S = \dfrac{28.9 \times 10^3 \text{ J/mol}}{342 \text{ K}} = 84.5 \text{ J mol}^{-1} \text{ K}^{-1}$

$V_{met} = \dfrac{nRT}{P} = \dfrac{1.00 \text{ mol} (0.08206)(112 \text{ K})}{1.00 \text{ atm}} = 9.19 \text{ L}$; $V_{hex} = \dfrac{nRT}{P} = R(342 \text{ K}) = 28.1 \text{ L}$

$\Delta S_{hex} - \Delta S_{met} = 84.5 - 73.2 = 11.3 \text{ J mol}^{-1} \text{ K}^{-1}$; $R \ln (V_{hex}/V_{met}) = 9.29 \text{ J mol}^{-1} \text{ K}^{-1}$

As the molar volume of a gas increases, ΔS_{vap} also increases. In the case of hexane and methane, the difference in molar volume accounts for 82% of the difference in the entropies.

93. $S = k \ln \Omega$; S has units of $\text{J K}^{-1} \text{ mol}^{-1}$ and k has units of J/K ($k = 1.38 \times 10^{-23}$ J/K)

To make units match: $S (\text{J K}^{-1} \text{ mol}^{-1}) = N_A k \ln \Omega$ when N_A = Avogadro's number

$189 \text{ J K}^{-1} \text{ mol}^{-1} = 8.31 \text{ J K}^{-1} \text{ mol}^{-1} \ln \Omega_g$
$70. \text{ J K}^{-1} \text{ mol}^{-1} = 8.31 \text{ J K}^{-1} \text{ mol}^{-1} \ln \Omega_l$

Subtracting: $119 \text{ J K}^{-1} \text{ mol}^{-1} = 8.31 \text{ J K}^{-1} \text{ mol}^{-1} (\ln \Omega_g - \ln \Omega_l)$

$14.3 = \ln(\Omega_g/\Omega_l)$, $\dfrac{\Omega_g}{\Omega_l} = e^{14.3} = 1.6 \times 10^6$

94. $1000 \text{ gal } H_2O \times \dfrac{4 \text{ qt}}{1 \text{ gal}} \times \dfrac{1 \text{ L}}{1.06 \text{ qt}} \times \dfrac{1000 \text{ g}}{1 \text{ L}} \times \dfrac{1 \text{ mol}}{18.0 \text{ g}} = 2 \times 10^5 \text{ mol } H_2O$

There is such an excess of water, let's assume the final temperature is very close to $0\,°C$. Therefore, $\Delta S_{H_2O} \approx 0$.

$\Delta S = nC_p \ln \dfrac{T_2}{T_1}$, $\Delta S_{Fe} = \left(\dfrac{111.7 \text{ g Fe}}{55.85 \text{ g/mol}} \right) (25.1 \text{ J mol}^{-1} \text{ K}^{-1}) \ln \left(\dfrac{273 \text{ K}}{373 \text{ K}} \right) = -15.7 \text{ J/K}$

95. H_2O (l, 298 K) $\rightarrow$ H_2O (g, V = 1000. L/mol); Break process into 2 steps:

Step 1: H_2O (l, 298 K) $\rightarrow$ H_2O (g, 298 K, V $= \dfrac{nR(298)}{1.00 \text{ atm}} = 24.5$ L)

$$\Delta S = S^\circ_{H_2O(g)} - S^\circ_{H_2O(l)} = 189 \text{ J/K} - 70. \text{ J/K} = 119 \text{ J/K}$$

Step 2: H_2O (g, 298 K, 24.5 L) $\rightarrow$ H_2O (g, 298 K, 1000. L)

$$\Delta S = nR \ln \frac{V_2}{V_1} = (1.00 \text{ mol})(8.3145 \text{ J mol}^{-1} \text{ K}^{-1}) \ln \left(\frac{1000. \text{ L}}{24.5 \text{ L}} \right) = 30.8 \text{ J/K}$$

$$\Delta S_{tot} = 119 + 30.8 = 150. \text{ J/K}$$

$$\Delta G = 44.02 \times 10^3 \text{ J} - 298 \text{ K} (150. \text{ J/K}) = -700 \text{ J}; \quad \text{Spontaneous}$$

For H_2O (l, 298 K) $\rightarrow$ H_2O (g, 298 K, V = 100. L/mol):

$$\Delta S = 119 \text{ J/K} + (8.3145 \text{ J/K}) \ln \left(\frac{100. \text{ L}}{24.5 \text{ L}} \right) = 131 \text{ J/K}$$

$$\Delta G = 44.02 \times 10^3 \text{ J} - 298 \text{ K}(131 \text{ J/K}) = 5.0 \times 10^3 \text{ J}; \quad \text{Not spontaneous}$$

96. Isothermal: $\Delta H = 0$ (assume ideal gas)

$$\Delta S = nR \ln \left(\frac{V_2}{V_1} \right) = (1.00 \text{ mol})(8.3145 \text{ J mol}^{-1} \text{ K}^{-1}) \ln \left(\frac{1.00 \text{ L}}{100.0 \text{ L}} \right) = -38.3 \text{ J/K}$$

$$\Delta G = \Delta H - T\Delta S = 0 - (300. \text{ K})(-38.3 \text{ J/K}) = +11,500 \text{ J} = 11.5 \text{ kJ}$$

97. a. free expansion

w = 0 since $P_{ext} = 0$; $\Delta E = nC_v \Delta T$, since $\Delta T = 0$, $\Delta E = 0$

$\Delta E = q + w$, q = 0; $\Delta H = nC_p \Delta T$, since $\Delta T = 0$, $\Delta H = 0$

$$\Delta S = nR \ln \left(\frac{V_2}{V_1} \right) = (1.00 \text{ mol}) (8.3145 \text{ J mol}^{-1} \text{ K}^{-1}) \ln \left(\frac{40.0 \text{ L}}{30.0 \text{ L}} \right) = 2.39 \text{ J/K}$$

$$\Delta G = \Delta H - T\Delta S = 0 - 300. \text{ K} (2.39 \text{ J/K}) = -717 \text{ J}$$

b. reversible expansion

$\Delta E = 0$; $\Delta H = 0$; $\Delta S = 2.39$ J/K; $\Delta G = -717$ J; These are state functions.

$$w_{rev} = -nRT \ln \left(\frac{V_2}{V_1} \right) = -(1.00 \text{ mol})(8.3145 \text{ J mol}^{-1} \text{ K}^{-1}) (300. \text{ K}) \ln \left(\frac{40.0 \text{ L}}{30.0 \text{ L}} \right) = -718 \text{ J}$$

$\Delta E = 0 = q + w$, $q_{rev} = -w_{rev} = 718$ J

Summary: a) free expansion   b) reversible

	a) free expansion	b) reversible
q	0	718 J
w	0	-718 J
ΔE	0	0
ΔH	0	0
ΔS	2.39 J/K	2.39 J/K
ΔG	-717 J	-717 J

98.   a. $w_{rev} = -nRT \ln (V_2/V_1) = -(1.00 \text{ mol}) (8.3145 \text{ J mol}^{-1} \text{ K}^{-1}) (298 \text{ K}) \ln \left(\dfrac{20.0 \text{ L}}{10.0 \text{ L}} \right) = -1720 \text{ J}$

For isothermal expansion: $\Delta E = 0$, so $q_{rev} = -w_{rev} = 1720$ J

b. $w = -P\Delta V = -1.23 \text{ atm} (20.0 \text{ L} - 10.0 \text{ L}) = -12.3$ L atm

-12.3 L atm $\times 101.3$ J L^{-1} atm^{-1} = -1250 J

$\Delta E = 0$ for isothermal expansion, so q = 1250 J.

99.   a.   Isothermal: $\Delta E = 0$ and $\Delta H = 0$ if gas is ideal.

$\Delta S = nR \ln (P_1/P_2) = (1.00 \text{ mol})(8.3145 \text{ J mol}^{-1} \text{ K}^{-1}) \ln (5.00 \text{ atm}/2.00 \text{ atm}) = 7.62$ J/K

$T = \dfrac{PV}{nR} = \dfrac{5.00 \text{ atm} \times 5.00 \text{ L}}{1.00 \text{ mol} \times 0.08206 \text{ L atm K}^{-1} \text{ mol}^{-1}} = 305$ K

$\Delta G = \Delta H - T\Delta S = 0 - (305 \text{ K})(7.62 \text{ J/K}) = -2320$ J

$w = -P\Delta V = -(2.00 \text{ atm})\Delta V$ where $V_f = \dfrac{nRT}{2.00 \text{ atm}} = 12.5$ L

$w = -2.00 \text{ atm} (12.5 - 5.00 \text{ L}) \times (101.3 \text{ J L}^{-1} \text{ atm}^{-1}) = -1500$ J

$\Delta E = 0 = q + w$, q = 1500 J

b.   Second law, $\Delta S_{univ} > 0$ for spontaneous processes; $\Delta S_{univ} = \Delta S_{sys} + \Delta S_{surr} = \Delta S_{sys} - \dfrac{q_{actual}}{T}$

$\Delta S_{univ} = 7.62 \text{ J/K} - \dfrac{1500 \text{ J}}{305 \text{ K}} = 7.62 - 4.9 = 2.7$ J/K; Thus, the process is spontaneous.

100.   Isothermal: $\Delta E = 0$, $\Delta H = 0$; $V_f = nRT/5.00 \text{ atm} = 2.00$ L

$\Delta S = nR \ln (P_1/P_2) = (1.00 \text{ mol})(8.3145 \text{ J mol}^{-1} \text{ K}^{-1}) \ln (1.50/5.00) = -10.0$ J/K

$w = -5.00 \text{ atm}(2.00 \text{ L} - 6.67 \text{ L})(101.3 \text{ J L}^{-1} \text{ atm}^{-1}) = 2370$ J

$\Delta E = 0 = q + w$, q = -2370 J; $\Delta S_{surr} = \dfrac{-q}{T} = \dfrac{2370 \text{ J}}{122 \text{ K}} = 19.4$ J/K

$\Delta S_{univ} = \Delta S_{sys} + \Delta S_{surr} = -10.0 \text{ J/K} + 19.4 \text{ J/K} = 9.4$ J/K

$\Delta G = \Delta H - T\Delta S = 0 - (122 \text{ K})(-10.0 \text{ J/K}) = 1220$ J

101.   To calculate ΔE and ΔH, we need to determine the molar heat capacity of the ideal gas. As derived

in section 10.14 of the text, for a reversible, adiabatic change (q = 0): $\left(\dfrac{T_2}{T_1}\right)^{C_v} = \left(\dfrac{V_1}{V_2}\right)^{R}$

$$C_v \ln\left(\frac{T_2}{T_1}\right) = R \ln\left(\frac{V_1}{V_2}\right), \quad \frac{C_v}{R} = \frac{\ln\left(\dfrac{V_1}{V_2}\right)}{\ln\left(\dfrac{T_2}{T_1}\right)}$$

Since $V_2 = 2V_1$: $\dfrac{C_v}{R} = \dfrac{\ln(1/2)}{\ln(239\text{ K}/296\text{ K})} = 3.24$

$C_v = 3.24\ (8.3145\text{ J K}^{-1}\text{ mol}^{-1}) = 26.9\text{ J K}^{-1}\text{ mol}^{-1}$

$\Delta E = nC_v\Delta T = 1.50\text{ mol }(26.9\text{ J K}^{-1}\text{ mol}^{-1})(239\text{ K} - 296\text{ K}) = -2,300\text{ J} = -2.3\text{ kJ}$

$\Delta H = \Delta E + nR\Delta T = -2300\text{ J} + 1.50\text{ mol }(8.3145\text{ J K}^{-1}\text{ mol}^{-1})(239\text{ K} - 296\text{ K}) = -3.0 \times 10^3\text{ J}$

$$= -3.0\text{ kJ}$$

102.   Two equations derived in section 10.14 for reversible, adiabatic processes are $T_1V_1^{\gamma-1} = T_2V_2^{\gamma-1}$ and $P_1V_1^{\gamma} = P_2V_2^{\gamma}$ where $\gamma = C_p/C_v$. For a monoatomic ideal gas, $C_p = (5/2)R$ and $C_v = (3/2)R$ so $\gamma = 5/3$ and $\gamma - 1 = 2/3$.

$$T_2 = T_1\left(\frac{V_1}{V_2}\right)^{\gamma-1} = 298\text{ K}\left(\frac{5.00\text{ L}}{12.5\text{ L}}\right)^{2/3} = 162\text{ K}$$

$$P_2 = P_1\left(\frac{V_1}{V_2}\right)^{\gamma} = 1.00\text{ atm}\left(\frac{5.00\text{ L}}{12.5\text{ L}}\right)^{5/3} = 0.217\text{ atm}$$

Since we have an adiabatic process, then q = 0 and $\Delta E = w = nC_v\Delta T$. We need to calculate n.

$$n = \frac{PV}{RT} = \frac{1.00\text{ atm} \times 5.00\text{ L}}{0.08206\text{ L atm K}^{-1}\text{mol}^{-1} \times 298\text{ K}} = 0.204\text{ mol}$$

$\Delta E = w = 0.204\text{ mol }(3/2)(8.3145\text{ J K}^{-1}\text{ mol}^{-1})(162\text{ K} - 298\text{ K}) = -346\text{ J}$

Challenge Problems

103.   a. $V_1 = \dfrac{nRT_1}{P_1} = \dfrac{2.00\text{ mol} \times 0.08206\text{ L atm K}^{-1}\text{mol}^{-1} \times 298\text{ K}}{2.00\text{ atm}} = 24.5\text{ L}$

For an adiabatic, reversible process, $P_1V_1^\gamma = P_2V_2^\gamma$ and $T_1V_1^{\gamma-1} = T_2V_2^{\gamma-1}$ where $\gamma = C_p/C_v$. Since argon is a monoatomic gas, then $C_p = (5/2)R$ and $C_v = (3/2)R$ so $\gamma = 5/3$.

$$V_2^\gamma = \frac{P_1V_1^\gamma}{P_2} = \frac{2.00 \text{ atm}(24.5 \text{ L})^{5/3}}{1.00 \text{ atm}} = 413, \ V_2 = (413)^{3/5} = 37.1 \text{ L}$$

We can either use the ideal gas law or the $T_1V^{\gamma-1} = T_2V_2^{\gamma-1}$ equation to calculate the final temperature. Using the ideal gas law:

$$T_2 = \frac{P_2V_2}{nR} = \frac{1.00 \text{ atm} \times 37.1 \text{ L}}{2.00 \text{ mol} \times 0.08206 \text{ L atm K}^{-1}\text{mol}^{-1}} = 226 \text{ K}$$

b. For an adiabatic process $(q = 0)$, $\Delta E = w = nC_v\Delta T$. For an expansion against a fixed external pressure, $w = -P\Delta V$. From the ideal gas equation (see part a), $V_1 = 24.5 \text{ L}$.

$$w = -P\Delta V = nC_v\Delta T$$

$$-1.00 \text{ atm} (V_2 - 24.5 \text{ L})\left(\frac{101.3 \text{ J}}{\text{L atm}}\right) = 2.00 \text{ mol} (3/2)\left(\frac{8.3145 \text{ J}}{\text{mol K}}\right)(T_2 - 298 \text{ K})$$

We will ignore units from here. Note that both sides of the equation are in units of J.

$$-101 V_2 + 2480 = 24.9 T_2 - 7430$$

To solve for T_2, we need to find an expression for V_2. Using the ideal gas equation:

$$V_2 = \frac{nRT_2}{P_2} = \frac{2.00 (0.08206) T_2}{1.00} = 0.164 T_2; \quad \text{Substituting:}$$

$$-101(0.164 T_2) + 2480 = 24.9 T_2 - 7430, \ 41.5 T_2 = 9910, \ T_2 = 239 \text{ K}$$

104.   For the processes to be spontaneous, $\Delta S_{univ} > 0$, and $\Delta S_{univ} = \Delta S + \Delta S_{surr}$.

$$\Delta S = \frac{q_{rev}}{T}, \ \Delta S_{surr} = \frac{-q}{T}, \ \Delta S_{univ} = \frac{q_{rev} - q}{T}$$

Since the processes are isothermal, $\Delta H = 0$, $\Delta E = 0$, $q = -w$; $n = 1.0$, $V_1 = 5.0 \text{ L}$, $P_1 = 5.0 \text{ atm}$, thus $T = 305 \text{ K}$ from the ideal gas equation.

a. If $P_2 = 2.0 \text{ atm}$, then $V_2 = 12.5 \text{ L}$.

$$q_{rev} = nRT \ln\left(\frac{V_2}{V_1}\right) = 1.0 (8.3145)(305) \ln\left(\frac{12.5}{5.0}\right) = 2320 \text{ J}$$

$$w = -P(\Delta V) = -2.0 \text{ atm} (12.5 \text{ L} - 5.0 \text{ L}) = -15 \text{ L} \cdot \text{atm} = -1520 \text{ J/mol}$$

$$q = 1520 \text{ J/mol}; \ \Delta S_{univ} = \frac{2320 - 1520}{305} = 2.6 \text{ J K}^{-1} \text{ mol}^{-1}$$

Since $\Delta S_{univ} > 0$, then the process is spontaneous.

b. $q_{rev} = nRT \ln\left(\dfrac{V_2}{V_1}\right) = (1.0)(8.3145)(305)\ln\left(\dfrac{5.0}{12.5}\right) = -2320$ J

   $w = -P(\Delta V) = 37.5$ L•atm $= 3800$ J/kmol, $q = -3800$ J

   $\Delta S_{univ} = \dfrac{-2320 - (-3800)}{305} = 4.9$ J K^{-1} mol^{-1} ($\Delta S_{univ} > 0$)

c. $\Delta G = \Delta H - T\Delta S$; $\Delta H = 0$ for both; $\Delta S = \dfrac{q_{rev}}{T}$ so $T\Delta S = q_{rev}$

   For the expansion, $\Delta G = -2320$ J/mol; for the compression, $\Delta G = +2320$ J/mol

   Because pressure is not constant, ΔG cannot be used to predict spontaneity.

105. $K_p = P_{CO_2}$; To insure Ag_2CO_3 from decomposing, P_{CO_2} should be greater than K_p.

   From Exercise 10.72, $\ln K = \dfrac{-\Delta H°}{RT} + \dfrac{\Delta S°}{R}$. For two conditions of K and T, the equation is:

   $\ln\dfrac{K_2}{K_1} = \dfrac{\Delta H°}{R}\left(\dfrac{1}{T_1} - \dfrac{1}{T_2}\right)$

   Let $T_1 = 25°C = 298$ K, $K_1 = 6.23 \times 10^{-3}$ torr; $T_2 = 110.°C = 383$ K, $K_2 = ?$

   $\ln\dfrac{K_2}{6.23 \times 10^{-3} \text{ torr}} = \dfrac{79.14 \times 10^3 \text{ J/mol}}{8.3145 \text{ J K}^{-1} \text{ mol}^{-1}}\left(\dfrac{1}{298 \text{ K}} - \dfrac{1}{383 \text{ K}}\right)$

   $\ln\dfrac{K_2}{6.23 \times 10^{-3}} = 7.1$, $\dfrac{K_2}{6.23 \times 10^{-3}} = e^{7.1} = 1.2 \times 10^3$, $K_2 = 7.5$ torr

   To prevent decomposition of Ag_2CO_3, the partial pressure of CO_2 should be greater than 7.5 torr.

106. $\Delta G = \Delta H - T\Delta S$; We are given that ΔG is negative.

   We can predict that ΔS is also negative because 2 moles of gaseous reactant forms 1 mol gaseous product. For ΔG to be negative, ΔH must also be negative. In other words, the reaction is exothermic. So if the temperature is raised, equilibrium is shifted to the left. So the ratio of the partial pressure of PCl_5 to the partial pressure of PCl_3 will decrease.

107. $3 O_2(g) \rightleftharpoons 2 O_3(g)$; $\Delta H° = 2(143) = 286$ kJ; $\Delta G° = 2(163) = 326$ kJ

   $\ln K = \dfrac{-\Delta G°}{RT} = \dfrac{-326 \times 10^3 \text{ J}}{(8.3145 \text{ J K}^{-1} \text{ mol}^{-1})(298 \text{ K})} = -131.573$, $K = e^{-131.573} = 7.22 \times 10^{-58}$

   We need the value of K at 230. K. From Exercise 10.72: $\ln K = \dfrac{-\Delta H°}{RT} + \dfrac{\Delta S°}{R}$

For two sets of K and T:

$$\ln K_1 = \frac{-\Delta H°}{R}\left(\frac{1}{T_1}\right) + \frac{\Delta S°}{R}; \quad \ln K_2 = \frac{-\Delta H°}{R}\left(\frac{1}{T_2}\right) + \frac{\Delta S°}{R}$$

Subtracting the first expression from the second:

$$\ln K_2 - \ln K_1 = \frac{\Delta H°}{R}\left(\frac{1}{T_1} - \frac{1}{T_2}\right) \text{ or } \ln\frac{K_2}{K_1} = \frac{\Delta H°}{R}\left(\frac{1}{T_1} - \frac{1}{T_2}\right)$$

Let $K_2 = 7.22 \times 10^{-58}$, $T_2 = 298$; $K_1 = K_{230}$, $T_1 = 230.$ K; $\Delta H° = 286 \times 10^3$ J

$$\ln\frac{7.22 \times 10^{-58}}{K_{230}} = \frac{286 \times 10^3}{8.3145}\left(\frac{1}{230.} - \frac{1}{298}\right) = 34.13$$

$$\frac{7.22 \times 10^{-58}}{K_{230}} = e^{34.13} = 6.6 \times 10^{14}, \quad K_{230} = 1.1 \times 10^{-72}$$

$$K_{230} = 1.1 \times 10^{-72} = \frac{P_{O_3}^2}{P_{O_2}^3} = \frac{P_{O_3}^2}{(1.0 \times 10^{-3} \text{ atm})^3}, \quad P_{O_3} = 3.3 \times 10^{-41} \text{ atm}$$

The volume occupied by one molecule of ozone is:

$$V = \frac{nRT}{P} = \frac{(1/6.022 \times 10^{23} \text{ mol})(0.08206 \text{ L atm mol}^{-1} \text{ K}^{-1})(230. \text{ K})}{(3.3 \times 10^{-41} \text{ atm})}, \quad V = 9.5 \times 10^{17} \text{ L}$$

Equilibrium is probably not maintained under these conditions. When only two ozone molecules are in a volume of 9.5×10^{17} L, the reaction is not at equilibrium. Under these conditions, $Q > K$ and the reaction shifts left. But with only 2 ozone molecules in this huge volume, it is extremely unlikely that they will collide with each other. At these conditions, the concentration of ozone is not large enough to maintain equilibrium.

108. $\Delta H = 5/2 \ R(\Delta T) = 5/2 \ (8.3145)(300. - 200.) = 2080$ J/mol

$\Delta E = 3/2 \ R(\Delta T) = 3/2(8.3145)(300. - 200.) = 1250$ J/mol

$w = -P(\Delta V) = -(nR)(\Delta T) = 1.00$ mol $(8.3145)(100. \text{ K}) = 831$ J

$q = C_P \Delta T = 5/2 \ R\Delta T = \Delta H = 2080$ J/mol

$$\Delta S = nC_P \ln\frac{V_2}{V_1} = nC_P \ln\left(\frac{T_2}{T_1}\right) = (1.00)\left(\frac{5}{2}R\right) \ln\left(\frac{300.}{200.}\right) = 8.43 \text{ J/K}$$

$$\Delta S \text{ due to } \Delta V = nR \ln\frac{V_2}{V_1} = nR \ln\left(\frac{T_2}{T_1}\right) = 3.37 \text{ J/K}$$

$$\Delta S \text{ due to } \Delta T = n \ C_V \ln\left(\frac{V_2}{V_1}\right) = n\left(\frac{3}{2}R\right) \ln\left(\frac{T_2}{T_1}\right) = 5.06 \text{ J/K}$$

$G = H - TS, \Delta G = \Delta H - \Delta(TS) = \Delta H - (T_2S_2 - T_1S_1)$

Since $\Delta S = 8.43$ J/K: $S°_1 = 8.00$ J/K so $S°_2 = 16.43$ J/K

$\Delta G = 2080$ J/mol $- [(300.)(16.43) - (200.)(8.00)] = -1250$ J/mol

109.   a. $\Delta G° = G°_B - G°_A = 11{,}718 - 8996 = 2722$ J

$$K = \exp\left(\frac{-\Delta G°}{RT}\right) = \exp\left(\frac{-2722 \text{ J}}{(8.3145 \text{ J K}^{-1} \text{ mol}^{-1})(298 \text{ K})}\right) = 0.333$$

b.   Since $Q = 1.00 > K$, reaction shifts left. Let x = atm of B(g) which reacts to reach equilibrium.

$$A(g) \quad \rightleftharpoons \quad B(g) \qquad\qquad K = P_B/P_A$$

Initial   1.00 atm   1.00 atm
Equil. $1.00 + x$ $1.00 - x$

$$K = \frac{1.00 - x}{1.00 + x} = 0.333, \quad 1.00 - x = 0.333 + 0.333\,x, \quad x = 0.50 \text{ atm}$$

$P_B = 1.00 - 0.50 = 0.50$ atm; $P_A = 1.00 + 0.50 = 1.50$ atm

c. $\Delta G = \Delta G° + RT \ln Q = \Delta G° + RT \ln (P_B/P_A)$

$\Delta G = 2722$ J $+ (8.3145)(298) \ln (0.50/1.50) = 2722$ J $- 2722$ J $= 0$ (carrying extra sig. figs.)

110.   The liquid water will evaporate at first and eventually an equilibrium will be reached (physical equilibrium).

*   Since evaporation is an endothermic, process, ΔH is positive.
*   Since $H_2O(g)$ is more disordered (greater positional probability), ΔS is positive.
*   Since we don't know the relative magnitudes of ΔH and ΔS, we cannot identify the sign for ΔG (since it is not a constant pressure problem, ΔG does not tell us about spontaneity).
*   The water will become cooler (the higher energy water molecules leave), thus ΔT_{water} will be negative.
*   Since the vessel is insulated, $q = 0$, so $\Delta S_{surr} = 0$.
*   Because the process occurs, it is spontaneous, so ΔS_{univ} is positive.

111.   Step 1: $\Delta E = 0$ and $\Delta H = 0$ since $\Delta T = 0$

$$w = -P\Delta V = -(9.87 \times 10^{-3} \text{ atm})\,\Delta V; \quad V = \frac{nRT}{P}, \quad R = 0.08206 \text{ L atm mol}^{-1} \text{ K}^{-1}$$

$$\Delta V = V_f - V_i = nRT \left(\frac{1}{P_f} - \frac{1}{P_i}\right)$$

$$\Delta V = 1.00 \text{ mol } (0.08206)(298 \text{ K}) \left(\frac{1}{9.87 \times 10^{-3} \text{ atm}} - \frac{1}{2.45 \times 10^{-2} \text{ atm}}\right)$$

$\Delta V = 1480$ L (we will carry all values to three sig. figs.)

$$w = -(9.87 \times 10^{-3} \text{ atm})(1480 \text{ L}) = -14.6 \text{ L atm } (101.3 \text{ J L}^{-1} \text{ atm}^{-1}) = -1480 \text{ J}$$

$$\Delta E = q + w = 0, \quad q = -w = +1480 \text{ J}; \quad \Delta S = nR \ln\left(\frac{P_1}{P_2}\right)$$

$$\Delta S = 1.00 \text{ mol } (8.3145 \text{ J mol}^{-1} \text{ K}^{-1}) \ln\left(\frac{2.45 \times 10^{-2} \text{ atm}}{9.87 \times 10^{-3} \text{ atm}}\right), \quad \Delta S = 7.56 \text{ J/K}$$

$$\Delta G = \Delta H - T\Delta S = 0 - 298 \text{ K}(7.56 \text{ J/K}) = -2250 \text{ J}$$

Step 2: $\Delta E = 0, \quad \Delta H = 0$

$$w = -(4.93 \times 10^{-3} \text{ atm})\left(\frac{nRT}{4.93 \times 10^{-3}} - \frac{nRT}{9.87 \times 10^{-3}}\right) \text{L} \times \frac{101.3 \text{ J}}{\text{L atm}} = -1240 \text{ J}$$

$$q = -w = 1240 \text{ J}; \quad \Delta S = nR \ln\left(\frac{9.87 \times 10^{-3} \text{ atm}}{4.93 \times 10^{-3} \text{ atm}}\right) = 5.77 \text{ J/K}$$

$$\Delta G = 0 - 298 \text{ K}(5.77 \text{ J/K}) = -1720 \text{ J}$$

Step 3: $\Delta E = 0, \quad \Delta H = 0$

$$w = -(2.45 \times 10^{-3} \text{ atm})\left(\frac{nRT}{2.45 \times 10^{-3}} - \frac{nRT}{4.93 \times 10^{-3}}\right) \text{L} \times \frac{101.3 \text{ J}}{\text{L atm}} = -1250 \text{ J}$$

$$q = -w = 1250 \text{ J}; \quad \Delta S = nR \ln\left(\frac{4.93 \times 10^{-3} \text{ atm}}{2.45 \times 10^{-3} \text{ atm}}\right) = 5.81 \text{ J/K}$$

$$\Delta G = 0 - 298 \text{ K } (5.81 \text{ J/K}) = -1730 \text{ J}$$

	q	w	ΔE	ΔS	ΔH	ΔG
Step 1	1480 J	-1480 J	0	7.56 J/K	0	-2250 J
Step 2	1240 J	-1240 J	0	5.77 J/K	0	-1720 J
Step 3	1250 J	-1250 J	0	5.81 J/K	0	-1730 J
Total	3970 J	-3970 J	0	19.14 J/K	0	-5.70×10^3 J

112. a. Isothermal: $\Delta E = 0, \Delta H = 0$; $PV = nRT$, $R = 0.08206 \text{ L atm K}^{-1} \text{ mol}^{-1}$

$$w = -P\Delta V = -2.45 \times 10^{-3} \text{ atm}\left(\frac{nRT}{2.45 \times 10^{-3}} - \frac{nRT}{2.45 \times 10^{-2}}\right) \text{L} \times \frac{101.3 \text{ J}}{\text{L atm}} = -2230 \text{ J}$$

$$q = -w = 2230 \text{ J}$$

$$\Delta S = nR \ln \left(\frac{P_1}{P_2} \right) = (1.00 \text{ mol}) (8.3145 \text{ J mol}^{-1} \text{ K}^{-1}) \ln \left(\frac{2.45 \times 10^{-2} \text{ atm}}{2.45 \times 10^{-3} \text{ atm}} \right) = 19.1 \text{ J/K}$$

$$\Delta G = \Delta H - T\Delta S = 0 - (298 \text{ K}) (19.1 \text{ J/K}) = -5.69 \times 10^3 \text{ J} = -5.69 \text{ kJ}$$

b. $\Delta E = 0$; $\Delta H = 0$; $\Delta S = 19.1 \text{ J/K}$; $\Delta G = -5.69 \times 10^3 \text{ J}$; Same as in part a since these are all state functions.

$$\Delta S = \frac{q_{rev}}{T}, \quad q_{rev} = T\Delta S = 298 \text{ K} (19.1 \text{ J/K}) = 5.69 \times 10^3 \text{ J} = 5.69 \text{ kJ}$$

$$\Delta E = 0 = q + w, \quad w_{rev} = -q_{rev} = -5.69 \times 10^3 \text{ J} = -5.69 \text{ kJ}$$

c. $\Delta E = 0$; $\Delta H = 0$; $\Delta S = -19.1 \text{ J/K}$; $\Delta G = 5690 \text{ J}$ (The signs are opposite those in part a.)

$$w = -2.45 \times 10^{-2} \text{ atm} \left(\frac{nRT}{2.45 \times 10^{-2}} - \frac{nRT}{2.45 \times 10^{-3}} \right) \text{L} \times \frac{101.3 \text{ J}}{\text{L atm}} = 22{,}300 \text{ J} = 22.3 \text{ kJ}$$

$$\Delta E = q + w = 0, \quad q = -22.3 \text{ kJ}$$

d.

e. $\Delta S_{surr} = \dfrac{-q_{actual}}{T}$; $\Delta S_{surr, a} = \dfrac{-2230 \text{ J}}{298 \text{ K}} = -7.48 \text{ J/K}$

$\Delta S_{surr, b} = -\Delta S = -19.1 \text{ J/K}$ (reversible process); $\Delta S_{surr, c} = \dfrac{22{,}300 \text{ J}}{298 \text{ K}} = 74.8 \text{ J/K}$

113.   a. $\Delta G° = 2 \text{ mol} (-394 \text{ kJ/mol}) - 2 \text{ mol} (-137 \text{ kJ/mol}) = -514 \text{ kJ}$

$$K = \exp \left(\frac{-\Delta G°}{RT} \right) = \exp \left(\frac{-(-514{,}000 \text{ J})}{(8.3145 \text{ J mol}^{-1} \text{ K}^{-1}) (298 \text{ K})} \right) = 1.24 \times 10^{90}$$

b. $\Delta S° = 2(214 \text{ J/K}) - [2(198 \text{ J/K}) + 205 \text{ J/K}] = -173 \text{ J/K}$

$2 \text{ CO} (1.00 \text{ atm}) + O_2 (1.00 \text{ atm}) \rightarrow 2 \text{ CO}_2 (1.00 \text{ atm})$	$\Delta S° = -173 \text{ J/K}$
$2 \text{ CO}_2 (1.00 \text{ atm}) \rightarrow 2 \text{ CO}_2 (10.0 \text{ atm})$	$\Delta S = nR \ln (P_1/P_2) = -38.3 \text{ J/K}$
$2 \text{ CO} (10.0 \text{ atm}) \rightarrow 2 \text{ CO} (1.00 \text{ atm})$	$\Delta S = nR \ln (P_1/P_2) = 38.3 \text{ J/K}$
$O_2 (10.0 \text{ atm}) \rightarrow O_2 (1.00 \text{ atm})$	$\Delta S = nR \ln (P_1/P_2) = 19.1 \text{ J/K}$

$2 \text{ CO} (10.0 \text{ atm}) + O_2 (10.0 \text{ atm}) \rightarrow CO_2 (10.0 \text{ atm})$	$\Delta S = -173 + 19.1 = -154 \text{ J/K}$

114. $2 \, SO_2(g) \; + \; O_2(g) \; \rightarrow \; 2 \, SO_3(g)$

ΔH_f° -297 kJ/mol   0   -396

S° 248 J K^{-1} mol^{-1} 205   257

$\Delta H_{298}^\circ = 2(-396) - 2(-297) = -198 \text{ kJ}$; $\Delta S_{298}^\circ = 2(257) - [205 + 2(248)] = -187 \text{ J/K}$

Set up a thermochemical cycle to convert to T = 227°C = 500. K.

$2 \, SO_2 \, (g, 227°C) \rightarrow 2 \, SO_2 \, (g, 25°C)$ $\Delta H_1 = nC_p\Delta T$
  $O_2 \, (g, 227°C) \rightarrow O_2 \, (g, 25°C)$ $\Delta H_2 = nC_p\Delta T$
$2 \, SO_2 \, (g, 25°C) + O_2 \, (g, 25°C) \rightarrow 2 \, SO_3 \, (g, 25°C)$ $\Delta H_3 = \Delta H_{298}^\circ = -198 \text{ kJ}$
$2 \, SO_3 \, (g, 25°C) \rightarrow 2 \, SO_3 \, (g, 227°C)$ $\Delta H_4 = nC_p\Delta T$

$2 \, SO_2 \, (g, 227°C) + O_2 \, (g, 227°C) \rightarrow 2 \, SO_3 \, (g, 227°C)$ $\Delta H_{500}^\circ = \Delta H_1 + \Delta H_2 + \Delta H_3 + \Delta H_4$

$\Delta H_{500}^\circ = 2 \text{ mol} \times \dfrac{39.9 \text{ J K}^{-1} \text{ mol}^{-1}}{1000 \text{ J/kJ}} \times (-202 \text{ K}) + 1 \times \dfrac{29.4}{1000} \times (-202) - 198 \text{ kJ} + 2 \times \dfrac{50.7}{1000} \times 202$

$\Delta H_{500}^\circ = -16.1 \text{ kJ} - 5.94 \text{ kJ} - 198 \text{ kJ} + 20.5 \text{ kJ} = -199.5 \text{ kJ} = -200. \text{ kJ}$

For the same cycle but using the equation $\Delta S = nC_p \ln (T_2/T_1)$ and ΔS_{298}°:

$\Delta S_{500}^\circ = 2(39.9) \ln (298 \text{ K}/500. \text{ K}) + 1(29.4) \ln (298/500.) - 187 + 2(50.7) \ln (500./298)$

$\Delta S_{500}^\circ = -41.3 \text{ J/K} - 15.2 \text{ J/K} - 187 \text{ J/K} + 52.5 \text{ J/K} = -191 \text{ J/K}$

115.

T(°C)	T(K)	C$_p$(J K^{-1} mol^{-1})	C$_p$/T (J K^{-2} mol^{-1})
-200.	73	12	0.16
-180.	93	15	0.16
-160.	113	17	0.15
-140.	133	19	0.14
-100.	173	24	0.14
-60.	213	29	0.14
-30.	243	33	0.14
-10.	263	36	0.14
0	273	37	0.14

Total area of C$_p$/T vs T plot = ΔS = I + II + III   (See following plot.)

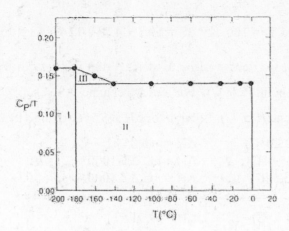

$\Delta S = (0.16 \text{ J K}^{-2} \text{ mol}^{-1})(20. \text{ K}) + (0.14 \text{ J K}^{-2} \text{ mol}^{-1})(180. \text{ K}) + 1/2(0.02 \text{ J K}^{-2} \text{ mol}^{-1})(40. \text{ K})$

$\Delta S = 3.2 + 25 + 0.4 = 29 \text{ J K}^{-1} \text{ mol}^{-1}$

116.   We can set up 3 equations in 3 unknowns:

$28.7262 = a + 300.0 \, b + (300.0)^2 \, c$

$29.2937 = a + 400.0 \, b + (400.0)^2 \, c$

$29.8545 = a + 500.0 \, b + (500.0)^2 \, c$

These can be solved by several methods. One way involves setting up a matrix and solving with a calculator such as:

$$\begin{pmatrix} 1 & 300.0 & 90,000 \\ 1 & 400.0 & 160,000 \\ 1 & 500.0 & 250,000 \end{pmatrix} \begin{pmatrix} a \\ b \\ c \end{pmatrix} = \begin{pmatrix} 28.7262 \\ 29.2937 \\ 29.8545 \end{pmatrix}$$

The solution is: $a = 26.98$; $b = 5.91 \times 10^{-3}$; $c = -3.4 \times 10^{-7}$

At 900. K: $C_p = 26.98 + 5.91 \times 10^{-3}(900.) - 3.4 \times 10^{-7}(900.)^2 = 32.02 \text{ J K}^{-1} \text{ mol}^{-1}$

$$\Delta S = n \int_{T_1}^{T_2} \frac{C_p dT}{T} = n \int_{T_1}^{T_2} \frac{(a + bT + cT^2)}{T} dT, \quad n = 1.00 \text{ mol}$$

$$\Delta S = a \int_{T_1}^{T_2} \frac{dT}{T} + b \int_{T_1}^{T_2} dT + c \int_{T_1}^{T_2} T dT = a \ln\left(\frac{T_2}{T_1}\right) + b\,(T_2 - T_1) + \frac{c(T_2^2 - T_1^2)}{2}$$

Solving using $T_2 = 900.$ K and $T_1 = 100.$ K: $\Delta S = 59.3 + 4.73 - 0.14 = 63.9$ J/K

117.   To calculate ΔS_{sys} at $10.0\,°C$, we need a place to start. From the data in the problem, we can calculate ΔS_{sys} at the melting point $(5.5\,°C)$. For a phase change, $\Delta S_{sys} = q_{rev}/T = \Delta H/T$ where ΔH is determined at the melting point $(5.5\,°C)$. Solving for ΔH at $5.5\,°C$ (using a thermochemical cycle):

C_6H_6 (l, $25.0\,°C$) → C_6H_6 (s, $25.0\,°C$)	$\Delta H = -10.04$ kJ
C_6H_6 (l, $5.5\,°C$) → C_6H_6 (l, $25.0\,°C$)	$\Delta H = nC_p\Delta T/1000 = 2.59$ kJ
C_6H_6 (s, $25.0\,°C$) → C_6H_6 (s, $5.5\,°C$)	$\Delta H = nC_p\Delta T/1000 = -1.96$ kJ

C_6H_6 (l, $5.5\,°C$) → C_6H_6 (s, $5.5\,°C$)	$\Delta H = -9.41$ kJ

At the melting point, $\Delta S_{sys} = \dfrac{\Delta H}{T} = \dfrac{-9.41 \times 10^3\ J}{278.7\ K} = -33.8$ J/K

For the phase change at $10.0\,°C$ $(283.2$ K$)$:

C_6H_6 (l, 278.7 K) → C_6H_6 (s, 278.7 K)	$\Delta S = -33.8$ J/K
C_6H_6 (l, 283.2 K) → C_6H_6 (l, 278.7 K)	$\Delta S = nC_p \ln (T_2/T_1) = -2.130$ J/K
C_6H_6 (s, 278.7 K) → C_6H_6 (s, 283.2 K)	$\Delta S = nC_p \ln (T_2/T_1) = 1.608$ J/K

C_6H_6 (l, 283.2 K) → C_6H_6 (s, 283.2 K)	$\Delta S_{sys} = -34.3$ J/K

To calculate ΔS_{surr}, we need ΔH at $10.0\,°C$ ($\Delta S_{surr} = \dfrac{-\Delta H}{T}$).

C_6H_6 (l, $25.0\,°C$) → C_6H_6 (s, $25.0\,°C$)	$\Delta H = -10.04$ kJ
C_6H_6 (l, $10.0\,°C$) → C_6H_6 (l, $25.0\,°C$)	$\Delta H = nC_p\Delta T/1000 = 2.00$ kJ
C_6H_6 (s, $25.0\,°C$) → C_6H_6 (s, $10.0\,°C$)	$\Delta H = nC_p\Delta T/1000 = -1.51$ kJ

C_6H_6 (l, $10.0\,°C$) → C_6H_6 (s, $10.0\,°C$)	$\Delta H = -9.55$ kJ

$$\Delta S_{surr} = \frac{-\Delta H}{T} = \frac{-(-9.55 \times 10^3\ J)}{283.2\ K} = 33.7\ J/K$$

Marathon Problems

118.   a. $\Delta S°$ will be negative since there is a decrease in the number of moles of gas.

b.   Since $\Delta S°$ is negative, $\Delta H°$ must be negative for the reaction to be spontaneous at some temperatures. Therefore, ΔS_{surr} is positive.

c. $Ni(s) + 4 CO(g) \rightleftharpoons Ni(CO)_4(g)$

$\Delta H° = -607 - [4(-110.5)] = -165$ kJ; $\Delta S° = 417 - [4(198) + (30.)] = -405$ J/K

d. $\Delta G° = 0 = \Delta H° - T\Delta S°$; $T = \dfrac{\Delta H°}{\Delta S°} = \dfrac{-165 \times 10^3 \text{ J}}{-405 \text{ J/K}} = 407$ K or $134°C$

e. $T = 50.°C + 273 = 323$ K

$\Delta G°_{323} = -165$ kJ $- (323$ K$)(-0.405$ kJ/K$) = -34$ kJ

$\ln K = \dfrac{-\Delta G°}{RT} = \dfrac{-(-34,000 \text{ J})}{(8.3145 \text{ J K}^{-1} \text{ mol}^{-1})(323 \text{ K})} = 12.66$, $K = e^{12.66} = 3.1 \times 10^5$

f. $T = 227°C + 273 = 500.$ K

$\Delta G°_{500} = -165$ kJ $- (500.$ K$)(-0.405$ kJ/K$) = 38$ kJ

$\ln K = \dfrac{-38,000}{(8.3145)(500.)} = -9.14$, $K = e^{-9.14} = 1.1 \times 10^{-4}$

g. The temperature change causes the value of the equilibrium constant to change from a large value favoring formation of $Ni(CO)_4$ to a small value favoring the decomposition of $Ni(CO)_4$ into pure Ni and CO. This is exactly what is wanted in order to purify a nickel sample.

h. $Ni(CO)_4(l) \rightleftharpoons Ni(CO)_4(g)$ $K_p = P_{Ni(CO)_4}$

At $42°C$ (the boiling point): $\Delta G° = 0 = \Delta H° - T\Delta S°$

$\Delta S° = \dfrac{\Delta H°}{T} = \dfrac{29.0 \times 10^3 \text{ J}}{315 \text{ K}} = 92.1$ J/K

At $152°C$: $\Delta G°_{152} = \Delta H° - T\Delta S° = 29.0 \times 10^3$ J $- 425$ K $(92.1$ J/K$) = -10,100$ J

$\Delta G° = -RT \ln K_p$, $\ln K_p = \dfrac{10,100 \text{ J}}{8.3145(425 \text{ K})} = 2.86$, $K_p = e^{2.86} = 17$ atm

A maximum pressure of 17 atm can be attained before $Ni(CO)_4(g)$ will liquify.

119.   a. $w = 0, q = 0, \ \Delta E = 0, \ \Delta H = 0$

b. $w = -(1.00 \text{ atm})(2.00 \text{ L}) = (101.3 \text{ J L}^{-1} \text{ atm}^{-1}) = -203$ J; $\Delta E = \Delta H = 0, q = 203$ J

c. $w = -[(1.33 \text{ atm})(1.00 \text{ L}) + (1.00 \text{ atm})(1.00 \text{ L})] \times \dfrac{101.3 \text{ J}}{\text{L atm}} = -236$ J

$q = 236$ J; $\Delta E = \Delta H = 0$

d. $w = -nRT \ln \dfrac{V_2}{V_1} = \left[PV \ln\left(\dfrac{V_2}{V_1} \right) \right] \dfrac{101.3 \text{ J}}{\text{L atm}} = -281 \text{ J}$

$q = 281 \text{ J}; \quad \Delta E = \Delta H = 0$

e. $w = -(2.00 \text{ atm})(-2.00 \text{ L}) \times \left(\dfrac{101.3 \text{ J}}{\text{L atm}} \right) = 405 \text{ J}$

$q = -405 \text{ J}; \quad \Delta E = \Delta H = 0$

f. $w = -[(1.33 \text{ atm})(-1.00 \text{ L}) + 2.00 \text{ atm } (-1.00 \text{ L})] \times \left(\dfrac{101.3 \text{ J}}{\text{L atm}} \right) = 337 \text{ J}$

$q = -337 \text{ J}; \quad \Delta E = \Delta H = 0$

g. $w = 281 \text{ J}$ from $\left(w = -nRT \ln\left(\dfrac{V_2}{V_1} \right) \right)$, $q = -281 \text{ J}$

Note: overall work for the 1 step process = -203 + 405 = 202 J (q = -202 J)

overall work for the 2 step process = -236 + 337 = 101 J (q = -101 J)

for the reversible process = w = -281 + 281 = 0, (q = 0)

Thus, in an overall reversible process (expan + comp), system and surroundings are unchanged.

CHAPTER ELEVEN

ELECTROCHEMISTRY

Galvanic Cells, Cell Potentials, and Standard Reduction Potentials

15. In a galvanic cell, a spontaneous reaction occurs, producing an electric current. In an electrolytic cell, electricity is used to force a reaction to occur that is not spontaneous.

16. The salt bridge completes the electrical circuit and allows counter ions to flow into the two cell compartments to maintain electrical neutrality. It also separates the cathode and anode compartments such that electrical energy can be extracted. If the cathode and anode compartments are not separated the cell would rapidly go to equilibrium without any useful work being done.

17. A typical galvanic cell diagram is:

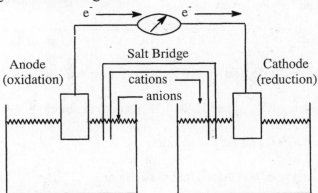

The diagram for all cells will look like this. The contents of each half-cell will be identified for each reaction, with all concentrations at $1.0\ M$ and partial pressures at 1.0 atm. Note that cations always flow into the cathode compartment and anions always flow into the anode compartment. This is required to keep each compartment electrically neutral.

a. Reference Table 11.1 for standard reduction potentials. Remember that $E^\circ_{cell} = E^\circ(\text{cathode}) - E^\circ(\text{anode})$; in the Solutions Guide, we will represent $E^\circ(\text{cathode})$ as E°_c and represent $-E^\circ(\text{anode})$ as $-E^\circ_a$. Also remember that standard potentials are <u>not</u> multiplied by the integer used to obtain the overall balanced equation.

$$(Cl_2 + 2\ e^- \rightarrow 2\ Cl^-) \times 3 \qquad\qquad E^\circ_c = 1.36\ V$$
$$7\ H_2O + 2\ Cr^{3+} \rightarrow Cr_2O_7^{2-} + 14\ H^+ + 6\ e^- \qquad -E^\circ_a = -1.33\ V$$

$$\overline{7\ H_2O(l) + 2\ Cr^{3+}(aq) + 3\ Cl_2(g) \rightarrow Cr_2O_7^{2-}(aq) + 6\ Cl^-(aq) + 14\ H^+(aq) \qquad E^\circ_{cell} = 0.03\ V}$$

The contents of each compartment is:

Cathode: Pt electrode; Cl_2 bubbled into solution, Cl^- in solution

Anode: Pt electrode; Cr^{3+}, H^+, and $Cr_2O_7^{2-}$ in solution

We need a nonreactive metal to use as the electrode in each case, since all of the reactants and products are in solution. Pt is the most common choice. Another possibility is graphite.

b. $\qquad Cu^{2+} + 2\ e^- \rightarrow Cu \qquad\qquad\qquad E_c^\circ = 0.34\ V$

$\qquad\qquad Mg \rightarrow Mg^{2+} + 2\ e^- \qquad\qquad -E_a^\circ = 2.37\ V$

$\overline{\qquad\qquad\qquad\qquad\qquad\qquad\qquad\qquad\qquad\qquad\qquad\qquad}$

$\ Cu^{2+}(aq) + Mg(s) \rightarrow Cu(s) + Mg^{2+}(aq) \qquad E_{cell}^\circ = 2.71\ V$

Cathode: Cu electrode; Cu^{2+} in solution

Anode: Mg electrode; Mg^{2+} in solution

c. $\qquad 5\ e^- + 6\ H^+ + IO_3^- \rightarrow 1/2\ I_2 + 3\ H_2O \qquad\qquad E_c^\circ = 1.20\ V$

$\qquad\qquad (Fe^{2+} \rightarrow Fe^{3+} + e^-) \times 5 \qquad\qquad\qquad -E_a^\circ = -0.77\ V$

$\overline{\qquad\qquad\qquad\qquad\qquad\qquad\qquad\qquad\qquad\qquad\qquad\qquad}$

$\quad 6\ H^+ + IO_3^- + 5\ Fe^{2+} \rightarrow 5\ Fe^{3+} + 1/2\ I_2 + 3\ H_2O \qquad E_{cell}^\circ = 0.43\ V$

or $12\ H^+(aq) + 2\ IO_3^-(aq) + 10\ Fe^{2+}(aq) \rightarrow 10\ Fe^{3+}(aq) + I_2(s) + 6\ H_2O(l) \qquad E_{cell}^\circ = 0.43\ V$

Cathode: Pt electrode; IO_3^-, I_2 and H_2SO_4 (H^+ source) in solution.

Anode: Pt electrode; Fe^{2+} and Fe^{3+} in solution

Note: $I_2(s)$ would make a poor electrode since it sublimes.

d. $\qquad (Ag^+ + e^- \rightarrow Ag) \times 2 \qquad\qquad\qquad E_c^\circ = 0.80\ V$

$\qquad\qquad Zn \rightarrow Zn^{2+} + 2\ e^- \qquad\qquad\qquad -E_a^\circ = 0.76\ V$

$\overline{\qquad\qquad\qquad\qquad\qquad\qquad\qquad\qquad\qquad\qquad\qquad\qquad}$

$\ Zn(s) + 2\ Ag^+(aq) \rightarrow 2\ Ag(s) + Zn^{2+}(aq) \qquad E_{cell}^\circ = 1.56\ V$

Cathode: Ag electrode; Ag^+ in solution

Anode: Zn electrode; Zn^{2+} in solution

18. a. $\qquad 2\ Ag^+ + 2\ e^- \rightarrow 2\ Ag \qquad\qquad\qquad E_c^\circ = 0.80\ V$

$\qquad\qquad Cu \rightarrow Cu^{2+} + 2\ e^- \qquad\qquad\qquad -E_a^\circ = -0.34\ V$

$\overline{\qquad\qquad\qquad\qquad\qquad\qquad\qquad\qquad\qquad\qquad\qquad\qquad}$

$\ 2\ Ag^+(aq) + Cu(s) \rightarrow Cu^{2+}(aq) + 2\ Ag(s) \qquad E_{cell}^\circ = 0.46\ V$ Spontaneous at standard conditions ($E_{cell}^\circ > 0$).

b. $Zn^{2+} + 2\ e^- \rightarrow Zn$ $E_c^\circ = -0.76$ V

               $Ni \rightarrow Ni^{2+} + 2\ e^-$ $-E_a^\circ = 0.23$ V

$Zn^{2+}(aq) + Ni(s) \rightarrow Zn(s) + Ni^{2+}(aq)$ $E_{cell}^\circ = -0.53$ V   Not spontaneous at standard conditions ($E_{cell}^\circ < 0$).

c. $(5\ e^- + 8\ H^+ + MnO_4^- \rightarrow Mn^{2+} + 4\ H_2O) \times 2$ $E_c^\circ = 1.51$ V

               $(2\ I^- \rightarrow I_2 + 2\ e^-) \times 5$ $-E_a^\circ = -0.54$ V

$16\ H^+(aq) + 2\ MnO_4^-(aq) + 10\ I^-(aq) \rightarrow 5\ I_2(s) + 2\ Mn^{2+}(aq) + 8\ H_2O(l)$ $E_{cell}^\circ = 0.97$ V

Spontaneous since $E_{cell}^\circ > 0$.

d. $(5\ e^- + 8\ H^+ + MnO_4^- \rightarrow Mn^{2+} + 4\ H_2O) \times 2$ $E_c^\circ = 1.51$ V

               $(2\ F^- \rightarrow F_2 + 2\ e^-) \times 5$ $-E_a^\circ = -2.87$ V

$16\ H^+(aq) + 2\ MnO_4^-(aq) + 10\ F^-(aq) \rightarrow 5\ F_2(g) + 2\ Mn^{2+}(aq) + 8\ H_2O(l)$ $E_{cell}^\circ = -1.36$ V

Not spontaneous since $E_{cell}^\circ < 0$.

19.   Reference Exercise 11.17 for a typical galvanic cell design. The contents of each half-cell compartment is identified below with all solute concentrations at 1.0 M and all gases at 1.0 atm. For each pair of half-reactions, the half-reaction with the largest standard reduction potential will be the cathode reaction and the half-reaction with the smallest reduction potential will be reversed to become the anode reaction. Only this combination gives a spontaneous overall reaction, i.e., a reaction with a positive overall standard cell potential.

a. $Cl_2 + 2\ e^- \rightarrow 2\ Cl^-$ $E_c^\circ = 1.36$ V

            $2\ Br^- \rightarrow Br_2 + 2\ e^-$ $-E_a^\circ = -1.09$ V

$Cl_2(g) + 2\ Br^-(aq) \rightarrow Br_2(aq) + 2\ Cl^-(aq)$ $E_{cell}^\circ = 0.27$ V

The contents of each compartment is:

     Cathode: Pt electrode; $Cl_2(g)$ bubbled in, Cl^- in solution

     Anode: Pt electrode; Br_2 and Br^- in solution

b. $(2\ e^- + 2\ H^+ + IO_4^- \rightarrow IO_3^- + H_2O) \times 5$ $E_c^\circ = 1.60$ V

            $(4\ H_2O + Mn^{2+} \rightarrow MnO_4^- + 8\ H^+ + 5\ e^-) \times 2$ $-E_a^\circ = -1.51$ V

$10\ H^+ + 5\ IO_4^- + 8\ H_2O + 2\ Mn^{2+} \rightarrow 5\ IO_3^- + 5\ H_2O + 2\ MnO_4^- + 16\ H^+$ $E_{cell}^\circ = 0.09$ V

This simplifies to:

$$3 H_2O(l) + 5 IO_4^-(aq) + 2 Mn^{2+}(aq) \rightarrow 5 IO_3^-(aq) + 2 MnO_4^-(aq) + 6 H^+(aq) \quad E_{cell}^\circ = 0.09 \text{ V}$$

Cathode: Pt electrode; IO_4^-, IO_3^-, and H_2SO_4 (as a source of H^+) in solution

Anode: Pt electrode; Mn^{2+}, MnO_4^- and H_2SO_4 in solution

c. $H_2O_2 + 2 H^+ + 2 e^- \rightarrow 2 H_2O$ $\qquad\qquad E_c^\circ = 1.78 \text{ V}$

$\qquad\qquad H_2O_2 \rightarrow O_2 + 2 H^+ + 2 e^-$ $\qquad -E_a^\circ = -0.68 \text{ V}$

$\overline{\qquad\qquad 2 H_2O_2(aq) \rightarrow 2 H_2O(l) + O_2(g) \qquad\qquad E_{cell}^\circ = 1.10 \text{ V}}$

Cathode: Pt electrode; H_2O_2 and H^+ in solution

Anode: Pt electrode; $O_2(g)$ bubbled in, H_2O_2 and H^+ in solution

d. $\qquad (Fe^{3+} + 3 e^- \rightarrow Fe) \times 2$ $\qquad\qquad E_c^\circ = -0.036 \text{ V}$

$\qquad\qquad (Mn \rightarrow Mn^{2+} + 2 e^-) \times 3$ $\qquad -E_a^\circ = 1.18 \text{ V}$

$\overline{2 Fe^{3+}(aq) + 3 Mn(s) \rightarrow 2 Fe(s) + 3 Mn^{2+}(aq) \qquad E_{cell}^\circ = 1.14 \text{ V}}$

Cathode: Fe electrode; Fe^{3+} in solution; Anode: Mn electrode; Mn^{2+} in solution

20.   Locate the pertinent half-reactions in Table 11.1, and then figure which combination will give a positive standard cell potential. In all cases, the anode compartment contains the species with the smallest standard reduction potential. For part a, the copper compartment is the anode, and in part b, the cadmium compartment is the anode.

a. $\qquad Au^{3+} + 3 e^- \rightarrow Au$ $\qquad\qquad E_c^\circ = 1.50 \text{ V}$

$\qquad\qquad (Cu^+ \rightarrow Cu^{2+} + e^-) \times 3$ $\qquad -E_a^\circ = -0.16 \text{ V}$

$\overline{Au^{3+}(aq) + 3 Cu^+(aq) \rightarrow Au(s) + 3 Cu^{2+}(aq) \qquad E_{cell}^\circ = 1.34 \text{ V}}$

b. $\qquad (VO_2^+ + 2 H^+ + e^- \rightarrow VO^{2+} + H_2O) \times 2$ $\qquad\qquad E_c^\circ = 1.00 \text{ V}$

$\qquad\qquad Cd \rightarrow Cd^{2+} + 2 e^-$ $\qquad\qquad -E_a^\circ = 0.40 \text{ V}$

$\overline{2 VO_2^+(aq) + 4 H^+(aq) + Cd(s) \rightarrow 2 VO^{2+}(aq) + 2 H_2O(l) + Cd^{2+}(aq) \quad E_{cell}^\circ = 1.40 \text{ V}}$

21.   In standard line notation, the anode is listed first and the cathode is listed last. A double line separates the two compartments. By convention, the electrodes are on the ends with all solutes and gases towards the middle. A single line is used to indicate a phase change. We also included all concentrations.

19a.   Pt | Br^- (1.0 M), Br_2 (1.0 M) || Cl_2 (1.0 atm) | Cl^- (1.0 M) | Pt

19b. $Pt \mid Mn^{2+}$ (1.0 M), MnO_4^- (1.0 M), H^+ (1.0 M) $\mid\mid$ IO_4^- (1.0 M), IO_3^- (1.0 M), H^+ (1.0 M) $\mid Pt$

19c. $Pt \mid H_2O_2$ (1.0 M), H^+ (1.0 M) $\mid O_2$ (1.0 atm) $\mid\mid$ H_2O_2 (1.0 M), H^+ (1.0 M) $\mid Pt$

19d. $Mn \mid Mn^{2+}$ (1.0 M) $\mid\mid$ Fe^{3+} (1.0 M) $\mid Fe$

22.   The reduction half-reaction for the SCE is:

$$Hg_2Cl_2 + 2 \; e^- \rightarrow 2 \; Hg + 2 \; Cl^- \qquad E_{SCE} = 0.242 \; V$$

For a spontaneous reaction to occur, E_{cell} must be positive. Using the standard reduction potentials in Table 11.1 and the given SCE potential, deduce which combination will produce a positive overall cell potential.

a. $Cu^{2+} + 2 \; e^- \rightarrow Cu \qquad E° = 0.34 \; V$

   $E_{cell} = 0.34 - 0.242 = 0.10 \; V$; SCE is the anode.

b. $Fe^{3+} + e^- \rightarrow Fe^{2+} \qquad E° = 0.77 \; V$

   $E_{cell} = 0.77 - 0.242 = 0.53 \; V$; SCE is the anode.

c. $AgCl + e^- \rightarrow Ag + Cl^- \qquad E° = 0.22 \; V$

   $E_{cell} = 0.242 - 0.22 = 0.02 \; V$; SCE is the cathode.

d. $Al^{3+} + 3 \; e^- \rightarrow Al \qquad E° = -1.66 \; V$

   $E_{cell} = 0.242 + 1.66 = 1.90 \; V$; SCE is the cathode.

e. $Ni^{2+} + 2 \; e^- \rightarrow Ni \qquad E° = -0.23 \; V$

   $E_{cell} = 0.242 + 0.23 = 0.47 \; V$; SCE is the cathode.

23.   a. $2 \; H^+ + 2 \; e^- \rightarrow H_2 \quad E° = 0.00 \; V$; $Cu \rightarrow Cu^{2+} + 2 \; e^- \quad -E° = -0.34 \; V$

   $E°_{cell} = -0.34 \; V$; No, H^+ cannot oxidize Cu to Cu^{2+} at standard conditions ($E°_{cell} < 0$).

b. $Fe^{3+} + e^- \rightarrow Fe^{2+} \quad E° = 0.77 \; V$; $2 \; I^- \rightarrow I_2 + 2 \; e^- \quad -E° = -0.54 \; V$

   $E°_{cell} = 0.77 - 0.54 = 0.23 \; V$; Yes, Fe^{3+} can oxidize I^- to I_2.

c. $H_2 \rightarrow 2 \; H^+ + 2 \; e^- \quad -E° = 0.00 \; V$; $Ag^+ + e^- \rightarrow Ag \quad E° = 0.80 \; V$

   $E°_{cell} = 0.80 \; V$; Yes, H_2 can reduce Ag^+ to Ag at standard conditions ($E°_{cell} > 0$).

d. $Fe^{2+} \rightarrow Fe^{3+} + e^-$ $-E^\circ = -0.77$ V; $Cr^{3+} + e^- \rightarrow Cr^{2+}$ $E^\circ = -0.50$ V

$E^\circ_{cell} = -0.50 - 0.77 = -1.27$ V; No, Fe^{2+} cannot reduce Cr^{3+} to Cr^{2+} at standard conditions.

24.   Good oxidizing agents are easily reduced. Oxidizing agents are on the left side of the reduction half-reactions listed in Table 11.1. We look for the largest, most positive standard reduction potentials to correspond to the best oxidizing agents. The ordering from worst to best oxidizing agents is:

	K^+	<	H_2O	<	Cd^{2+}	<	I_2	<	$AuCl_4^-$	<	IO_3^-
E°(V)	-2.92		-0.83		-0.40		0.54		0.99		1.20

25.   Good reducing agents are easily oxidized. The reducing agents are on the right side of the reduction half-reactions listed in Table 11.1. The best reducing agents have the most negative standard reduction potentials (E°), i.e., the best reducing agents have the most positive $-E^\circ$ value.

	F^-	<	Cr^{3+}	<	Fe^{2+}	<	H_2	<	Zn	<	Li
$-E^\circ$(V)	-2.87		-1.33		-0.77		0.00		0.76		3.05

26. $Cl_2 + 2 e^- \rightarrow 2 Cl^-$ $E^\circ = 1.36$ V $Ag^+ + e^- \rightarrow Ag$ $E^\circ = 0.80$ V
       $Pb^{2+} + 2 e^- \rightarrow Pb$ $E^\circ = -0.13$ V $Zn^{2+} + 2 e^- \rightarrow Zn$ $E^\circ = -0.76$ V
       $Na^+ + e^- \rightarrow Na$ $E^\circ = -2.71$ V

a.   Oxidizing agents (species reduced) are on the left side of the above reduction half-reactions. Of the species available, Ag^+ would be the best oxidizing agent since it has the most positive E° value.

b.   Reducing agents (species oxidized) are on the right side of the reduction half-reactions. Of the species available, Zn would be the best reducing agent since it has the most positive $-E^\circ$ value.

c. $SO_4^{2-} + 4 H^+ + 2 e^- \rightarrow H_2SO_3 + H_2O$ $E^\circ_c = 0.20$ V; SO_4^{2-} can oxidize Pb and Zn at standard conditions. When SO_4^{2-} is coupled with these reagents, E°_{cell} is positive.

d. $Al \rightarrow Al^{3+} + 3 e^-$ $-E^\circ_a = 1.66$ V; Al can oxidize Ag^+ and Zn^{2+} at standard conditions since $E^\circ_{cell} > 0$.

27.   a. $2 Br^- \rightarrow Br_2 + 2 e^-$ $-E^\circ_a = -1.09$ V; $2 Cl^- \rightarrow Cl_2 + 2 e^-$ $-E^\circ_a = -1.36$ V; $E^\circ_c > 1.09$ V to oxidize Br^-; $E^\circ_c < 1.36$ V to not oxidize Cl^-; $Cr_2O_7^{2-}$, O_2, MnO_2, and IO_3^- are all possible since when all of these oxidizing agents are coupled with Br^- give $E^\circ_{cell} > 0$ and when coupled with Cl^- give $E^\circ_{cell} < 0$ (assuming standard conditions).

b. $Mn \rightarrow Mn^{2+} + 2 e^-$ $-E^\circ_a = 1.18$; $Ni \rightarrow Ni^{2+} + 2 e^-$ $-E^\circ_a = 0.23$ V; Any oxidizing agent with -0.23 V $> E^\circ_c > -1.18$ V will work. $PbSO_4$, Cd^{2+}, Fe^{2+}, Cr^{3+}, Zn^{2+} and H_2O will be able to oxidize Mn but not oxidize Ni (assuming standard conditions).

28. a. $Cu^{2+} + 2\ e^- \rightarrow Cu$ $E_c^\circ = 0.34$ V; $Cu^{2+} + e^- \rightarrow Cu^+$ $E_c^\circ = 0.16$ V; To reduce Cu^{2+} to Cu but
         not reduce Cu^{2+} to Cu^+, the reducing agent must have a $- E_a^\circ$ value between -0.34 V and -0.16
         V (so E_{cell}° is positive only for the Cu^{2+} to Cu reduction). The reducing agents (species oxidized)
         are on the right side of the half-reactions in Table 11.1. The reagents at standard conditions
         which have a $- E_a^\circ$ value between -0.34 V and -0.16 V are Ag (in 1.0 M Cl^-) and H_2SO_3.

     b. $Br_2 + 2\ e^- \rightarrow 2\ Br^-$ $E_c^\circ = 1.09$ V; $I_2 + 2\ e^- \rightarrow 2\ I^-$ $E_c^\circ = 0.54$ V; From Table 11.1, VO^{2+}, Au (in
         1.0 M Cl^-), NO, ClO_2^-, Hg_2^{2+}, Ag, Hg, Fe^{2+}, H_2O_2 and MnO_4^- are all capable at standard
         conditions of reducing Br_2 to Br^- but not reducing I_2 to I^-. When these reagents are coupled with
         Br_2, $E_{cell}^\circ > 0$, and when coupled with I_2, $E_{cell}^\circ < 0$.

29. $ClO^- + H_2O + 2\ e^- \rightarrow 2\ OH^- + Cl^-$ $E^\circ = 0.90$ V
         $2\ NH_3 + 2\ OH^- \rightarrow N_2H_4 + 2\ H_2O + 2\ e^-$ $-E^\circ = 0.10$ V
         _____
         $ClO^-(aq) + 2\ NH_3(aq) \rightarrow Cl^-(aq) + N_2H_4(aq) + H_2O(l)$ $E_{cell}^\circ = 1.00$ V

     Since E_{cell}° is positive for this reaction, then at standard conditions ClO^- can spontaneously oxidize
     NH_3 to the somewhat toxic N_2H_4.

30. $Tl^{3+} + 2\ e^- \rightarrow Tl^+$ $E^\circ = 1.25$ V
         $3\ I^- \rightarrow I_3^- + 2\ e^-$ $-E^\circ = -0.55$ V
         _____
         $Tl^{3+} + 3\ I^- \rightarrow Tl^+ + I_3^-$ $E_{cell}^\circ = 0.70$ V

     In solution, Tl^{3+} can oxidize I^- to I_3^-. Thus, we expect TlI_3 to be thallium(I) triiodide.

31. $H_2O_2 + 2\ H^+ + 2\ e^- \rightarrow 2\ H_2O$ $E_c^\circ = 1.78$ V; H_2O_2 is the oxidizing agent.
         $H_2O_2 \rightarrow O_2 + 2\ H^+ + 2\ e^-$ $- E_a^\circ = -0.68$ V; H_2O_2 is the reducing agent.

         $H_2O_2 + 2\ H^+ + 2\ e^- \rightarrow 2\ H_2O$ $E_c^\circ = 1.78$ V
         $H_2O_2 \rightarrow O_2 + 2\ H^+ + 2\ e^-$ $- E_a^\circ = -0.68$ V
         _____
         $2\ H_2O_2(aq) \rightarrow 2\ H_2O(l) + O_2(g)$ $E_{cell}^\circ = 1.10$ V

32. Consider the strongest oxidizing agent combined with the strongest reducing agent from
     Table 11.1:

         $F_2 + 2\ e^- \rightarrow 2\ F^-$ $E_c^\circ = 2.87$ V
         $(Li \rightarrow Li^+ + e^-) \times 2$ $- E_a^\circ = 3.05$ V
         _____
         $F_2(g) + 2\ Li(s) \rightarrow 2\ Li^+(aq) + 2\ F^-(aq)$ $E_{cell}^\circ = 5.92$ V

     The claim is impossible. The strongest oxidizing agent and reducing agent when combined only give
     E_{cell}° of about 6 V.

Cell Potential, Free Energy, and Equilibrium

33.   Since the cells are at standard conditions, $w_{max} = \Delta G = \Delta G° = -nFE°_{cell}$. See Exercise 17.33 for the balanced overall equations and for $E°_{cell}$.

20a. $w_{max} = -(3 \text{ mol e}^-)(96,485 \text{ C/mol e}^-)(1.34 \text{ J/C}) = -3.88 \times 10^5 \text{ J} = -388 \text{ kJ}$

20b. $w_{max} = -(2 \text{ mol e}^-)(96,485 \text{ C/mol e}^-)(1.40 \text{ J/C}) = -2.70 \times 10^5 \text{ J} = -270. \text{ kJ}$

34.   a.   Possible reaction: $I_2(s) + 2 \text{ Cl}^-(aq) \rightarrow 2 \text{ I}^-(aq) + Cl_2(g)$ $E°_{cell} = 0.54 \text{ V} - 1.36 \text{ V} = -0.82 \text{ V}$
This reaction is not spontaneous at standard conditions since $E°_{cell} < 0$. No reaction occurs.

b.   Possible reaction: $Cl_2(g) + 2 \text{ I}^-(aq) \rightarrow I_2(s) + 2 \text{ Cl}^-(aq)$ $E°_{cell} = 0.82 \text{ V}$; This reaction is spontaneous at standard conditions since $E°_{cell} > 0$. The reaction will occur.

$Cl_2(g) + 2 \text{ I}^-(aq) \rightarrow I_2(s) + 2 \text{ Cl}^-(aq)$ $E°_{cell} = 0.82 \text{ V} = 0.82 \text{ J/C}$

$\Delta G° = -nFE°_{cell} = -(2 \text{ mol e}^-)(96,485 \text{ C/mol e}^-)(0.82 \text{ J/C}) = -1.6 \times 10^5 \text{ J} = -160 \text{ kJ}$

$E° = \dfrac{0.0591}{n} \log K$, $\log K = \dfrac{nE°}{0.0591} = \dfrac{2(0.82)}{0.0591} = 27.75$, $K = 10^{27.75} = 5.6 \times 10^{27}$

c.   Possible reaction: $2 \text{ Ag}(s) + Cu^{2+}(aq) \rightarrow Cu(s) + 2 \text{ Ag}^+(aq)$ $E°_{cell} = -0.46 \text{ V}$; No reaction occurs.

d. Fe^{2+} can be oxidized or reduced. The other species present are H^+, SO_4^{2-}, H_2O, and O_2 from air. Only O_2 in the presence of H^+ has a large enough standard reduction potential to oxidize Fe^{2+} to Fe^{3+} (resulting in $E°_{cell} > 0$). All other combinations, including the possible reduction of Fe^{2+}, give negative cell potentials. The spontaneous reaction is:

$4 \text{ Fe}^{2+}(aq) + 4 \text{ H}^+(aq) + O_2(g) \rightarrow 4 \text{ Fe}^{3+}(aq) + 2 \text{ H}_2O(l)$ $E°_{cell} = 1.23 - 0.77 = 0.46 \text{ V}$

$\Delta G° = -nFE°_{cell} = -(4 \text{ mol e}^-)(96,485 \text{ C/mol e}^-)(0.46 \text{ J/C})(1 \text{ kJ}/1000 \text{ J}) = -180 \text{ kJ}$

$\log K = \dfrac{4(0.46)}{0.0591} = 31.13$, $K = 1.3 \times 10^{31}$

35.   Reference Exercise 11.19 for the balanced reactions and standard cell potentials. The balanced reactions are necessary to determine n, the moles of electrons transferred.

19a. $Cl_2(aq) + 2 \text{ Br}^-(aq) \rightarrow Br_2(aq) + 2 \text{ Cl}^-(aq)$ $E°_{cell} = 0.27 \text{ V} = 0.27 \text{ J/C}$, $n = 2 \text{ mol e}^-$

$\Delta G° = -nFE°_{cell} = -(2 \text{ mol e}^-)(96,485 \text{ C/mol e}^-)(0.27 \text{ J/C}) = -5.2 \times 10^4 \text{ J} = -52 \text{ kJ}$

$E°_{cell} = \dfrac{0.0591}{n} \log K$, $\log K = \dfrac{nE°}{0.0591} = \dfrac{2(0.27)}{0.0591} = 9.14$, $K = 10^{9.14} = 1.4 \times 10^9$

19b. $\Delta G° = -(10 \text{ mol e}^-)(96,485 \text{ C/mol e}^-)(0.09 \text{ J/C}) = -9 \times 10^4 \text{ J} = -90 \text{ kJ}$

$\log K = \dfrac{10(0.09)}{0.0591} = 15.2$, $K = 10^{15.2} = 2 \times 10^{15}$

19c. $\Delta G° = -(2 \text{ mol e}^-)(96{,}485 \text{ C/mol e}^-)(1.10 \text{ J/C}) = -2.12 \times 10^5 \text{ J} = -212 \text{ kJ}$

$\log K = \dfrac{2(1.10)}{0.0591} = 37.225, \; K = 1.68 \times 10^{37}$

19d. $\Delta G° = -(6 \text{ mol e}^-)(96{,}485 \text{ C/mol e}^-)(1.14 \text{ J/C}) = -6.60 \times 10^5 \text{ J} = -660. \text{ kJ}$

$\log K = \dfrac{(6)(1.14)}{0.0591} = 115.736, \; K = 5.45 \times 10^{115}$

36.   a.

$$Cl_2 + 2 \text{ e}^- \rightarrow 2 \text{ Cl}^- \qquad\qquad\qquad E_c° = 1.36 \text{ V}$$
$$(ClO_2^- \rightarrow ClO_2 + \text{e}^-) \times 2 \qquad\qquad -E_a° = -0.954 \text{ V}$$

$$\overline{2 \, ClO_2^-(aq) + Cl_2(g) \rightarrow 2 \, ClO_2(aq) + 2 \, Cl^-(aq) \qquad E_{cell}° = 0.41 \text{ V} = 0.41 \text{ J/C}}$$

$\Delta G° = -nFE_{cell}° = -(2 \text{ mol e}^-)(96{,}485 \text{ C/mol e}^-)(0.41 \text{ J/C}) = -7.91 \times 10^4 \text{ J} = -79 \text{ kJ}$

$\Delta G° = -RT \ln K$ so $K = \exp(-\Delta G°/RT)$

$K = \exp[(7.9 \times 10^4 \text{ J})/(8.3145 \text{ J mol}^{-1} \text{ K}^{-1})(298 \text{ K})] = 7.0 \times 10^{13}$

or $\log K = \dfrac{nE°}{0.0591} = \dfrac{2(0.41)}{0.0591} = 13.87, \; K = 10^{13.87} = 7.4 \times 10^{13}$

b.

$$(H_2O + ClO_2 \rightarrow ClO_3^- + 2 \text{ H}^+ + \text{e}^-) \times 5$$
$$5 \text{ e}^- + 4 \text{ H}^+ + ClO_2 \rightarrow Cl^- + 2 \text{ H}_2O$$

$$\overline{3 \, H_2O(l) + 6 \, ClO_2(g) \rightarrow 5 \, ClO_3^-(aq) + \; Cl^-(aq) + 6 \, H^+(aq)}$$

37.   a.

$$(4 \text{ H}^+ + NO_3^- + 3 \text{ e}^- \rightarrow NO + 2 \text{ H}_2O) \times 2 \qquad\qquad E_c° = 0.96 \text{ V}$$
$$(Mn \rightarrow Mn^{2+} + 2 \text{ e}^-) \times 3 \qquad\qquad\qquad -E_a° = 1.18 \text{ V}$$

$$\overline{3 \, Mn(s) + 8 \, H^+(aq) + 2 \, NO_3^-(aq) \rightarrow 2 \, NO(g) + 4 \, H_2O(l) + 3 \, Mn^{2+}(aq) \qquad E_{cell}° = 2.14 \text{ V}}$$

$$5 \times (2 \text{ e}^- + 2 \text{ H}^+ + IO_4^- \rightarrow IO_3^- + H_2O) \qquad\qquad E_a° = 1.60 \text{ V}$$
$$2 \times (Mn^{2+} + 4 \text{ H}_2O \rightarrow MnO_4^- + 8 \text{ H}^+ + 5 \text{ e}^-) \qquad -E_a° = -1.51 \text{ V}$$

$$\overline{5 \, IO_4^-(aq) + 2 \, Mn^{2+}(aq) + 3 \, H_2O(l) \rightarrow 5 \, IO_3^-(aq) + 2 \, MnO_4^-(aq) + 6 \, H^+(aq) \qquad E_{cell}° = 0.09 \text{ V}}$$

b.   Nitric acid oxidation (see part a for $E_{cell}°$):

$\Delta G° = -nFE_{cell}° = -(6 \text{ mol e}^-)(96{,}485 \text{ C/mol e}^-)(2.14 \text{ J/C}) = -1.24 \times 10^6 \text{ J} = -1240 \text{ kJ}$

$\log K = \dfrac{nE°}{0.0591} = \dfrac{6(2.14)}{0.0591} = 217, \; K \approx 10^{217}$

Periodate oxidation (see part a for E°_{cell}):

$$\Delta G^\circ = -(10 \text{ mol } e^-)(96,485 \text{ C/mol } e^-)(0.09 \text{ J/C})(1 \text{ kJ}/1000 \text{ J}) = -90 \text{ kJ}$$

$$\log K = \frac{10(0.09)}{0.0591} = 15.2, \ K = 10^{15.2} = 2 \times 10^{15}$$

38. $2 \text{ H}_2(g) + \text{O}_2(g) \rightarrow 2 \text{ H}_2\text{O}(l)$; Oxygen goes from the zero oxidation state to the -2 oxidation state in H_2O. Since two mol O appears in the balanced reaction, then n = 4 mol electrons transferred.

a. $E^\circ_{cell} = \dfrac{0.0591}{n} \log K = \dfrac{0.0591}{4} \log (1.28 \times 10^{83}), \ E^\circ_{cell} = 1.23 \text{ V}$

$$\Delta G^\circ = -nFE^\circ_{cell} = -(4 \text{ mol } e^-)(96,485 \text{ C/mol } e^-)(1.23 \text{ J/C}) = -4.75 \times 10^5 \text{ J} = -475 \text{ kJ}$$

b. Since mol of gas decrease as reactants are converted into products, then ΔS° will be negative (unfavorable). Since the value of ΔG° is negative, then ΔH° must be negative ($\Delta G^\circ = \Delta H^\circ - T\Delta S^\circ$).

c. $\Delta G = w_{max} = \Delta H - T\Delta S$. Since ΔS is negative, then as T increases, ΔG becomes more positive (closer to zero). Therefore, w_{max} will decrease as T increases.

39. $\Delta G^\circ = -nFE^\circ = \Delta H^\circ - T\Delta S^\circ, \ E^\circ = \dfrac{T\Delta S^\circ}{nF} - \dfrac{\Delta H^\circ}{nF}$

If we graph E° vs. T we should get a straight line (y = mx + b). The slope of the line (m) is equal to $\Delta S^\circ/nF$ and the y-intercept (b) is equal to $-\Delta H^\circ/nF$.

40. E° will have small temperature dependence for cell reactions with ΔS° close to zero. (See Exercise 11.39.)

41. $\text{CH}_3\text{OH}(l) + 3/2 \ \text{O}_2(g) \rightarrow \text{CO}_2(g) + 2 \ \text{H}_2\text{O}(l)$

$$\Delta G^\circ = \Sigma n_p \Delta G^\circ_{f, \text{ products}} - \Sigma n_r \Delta G^\circ_{f, \text{ reactants}} = 2(-237) + (-394) - [-166] = -702 \text{ kJ}$$

The balanced half-reactions are:

$$\text{H}_2\text{O} + \text{CH}_3\text{OH} \rightarrow \text{CO}_2 + 6 \text{ H}^+ + 6 \text{ e}^- \text{ and } \text{O}_2 + 4 \text{ H}^+ + 4 \text{ e}^- \rightarrow 2 \text{ H}_2\text{O}$$

For 3/2 mol O_2, 6 moles of electrons will be transferred (n = 6).

$$\Delta G^\circ = -nFE^\circ, \ E^\circ = \frac{-\Delta G^\circ}{nF} = \frac{-(-702,000 \text{ J})}{(6 \text{ mol } e^-)(96,485 \text{ C/mol } e^-)} = 1.21 \text{ J/C} = 1.21 \text{ V}$$

For this reaction: $\Delta S^\circ = 2(70.) + 214 - [127 + 3/2(205)] = -81 \text{ J/K}$

From Exercise 11.39, $E^\circ = \dfrac{T\Delta S^\circ}{nF} - \dfrac{\Delta H^\circ}{nF}$.

Since ΔS° is negative, E° will decrease with an increase in temperature.

42. $Fe^{2+} + 2 e^- \rightarrow Fe$ $E° = -0.44$ V $= -0.44$ J/C

$\Delta G° = -nFE° = -(2 \text{ mol } e^-)(96,485 \text{ C/mol } e^-)(-0.44 \text{ J/C})(1 \text{ kJ}/1000 \text{ J}) = 85$ kJ

85 kJ $= 0 - [\Delta G°_{f, Fe^{2+}} + 0]$, $\Delta G°_{f, Fe^{2+}} = -85$ kJ/mol

We can get $\Delta G°_{f, Fe^{3+}}$ two ways. Consider: $Fe^{3+} + e^- \rightarrow Fe^{2+}$ $E° = 0.77$ V

$\Delta G° = -(1 \text{ mol } e^-)(96,485 \text{ C/mol } e^-)(0.77 \text{ J/C}) = -74,300$ J $= -74$ kJ

$Fe^{2+} \rightarrow Fe^{3+} + e^-$ $\Delta G° = 74$ kJ
$Fe \rightarrow Fe^{2+} + 2 e^-$ $\Delta G° = -85$ kJ

_____

$Fe \rightarrow Fe^{3+} + 3 e^-$ $\Delta G° = -11$ kJ, $\Delta G°_{f, Fe^{3+}} = -11$ kJ/mol

or   consider: $Fe^{3+} + 3 e^- \rightarrow Fe$ $E° = -0.036$ V

$\Delta G° = -(3 \text{ mol } e^-)(96,485 \text{ C/mol } e^-)(-0.036 \text{ J/C}) = 10,400$ J $\approx 10.$ kJ

$10.$ kJ $= 0 - [\Delta G°_{f, Fe^{3+}} + 0]$, $\Delta G°_{f, Fe^{3+}} = -10.$ kJ/mol; Round off error explains the 1 kJ
discrepancy.

43.   a. $Cu^+ + e^- \rightarrow Cu$ $E°_c = 0.52$ V
$Cu^+ \rightarrow Cu^{2+} + e^-$ $-E°_a = -0.16$ V

_____

$2 Cu^+(aq) \rightarrow Cu^{2+}(aq) + Cu(s)$ $E°_{cell} = 0.36$ V; Spontaneous

       b. $Fe^{2+} + 2 e^- \rightarrow Fe$ $E°_c = -0.44$ V
$(Fe^{2+} \rightarrow Fe^{3+} + e^-) \times 2$ $-E°_a = -0.77$ V

_____

$3 Fe^{2+}(aq) \rightarrow 2 Fe^{3+}(aq) + Fe(s)$ $E°_{cell} = -1.21$ V; Not spontaneous

       c. $HClO_2 + 2 H^+ + 2 e^- \rightarrow HClO + H_2O$ $E°_c = 1.65$ V
$HClO_2 + H_2O \rightarrow ClO_3^- + 3 H^+ + 2 e^-$ $-E°_a = -1.21$ V

_____

$2 HClO_2(aq) \rightarrow ClO_3^-(aq) + H^+(aq) + HClO(aq)$ $E°_{cell} = 0.44$ V; Spontaneous

44.   43a. $2 Cu^+(aq) \rightarrow Cu^{2+}(aq) + Cu(s)$ $E°_{cell} = 0.36$ V $= 0.36$ J/C, n = 1 mol e^-

$\Delta G° = -nFE°_{cell} = -(1 \text{ mol } e^-)(96,485 \text{ C/mol } e)(0.36 \text{ J/C}) = -34,700$ J $= -35$ kJ

$E°_{cell} = \dfrac{0.0591}{n} \log K$, $\log K = \dfrac{nE°}{0.0591} = \dfrac{1(0.36)}{0.0591} = 6.09$, $K = 10^{6.09} = 1.2 \times 10^6$

43c. $2 HClO_2(aq) \rightarrow ClO_3^-(aq) + H^+(aq) + HClO(aq)$ $E^{\circ}_{cell} = 0.44$ V, n = 2 mol e$^-$

$\Delta G^{\circ} = -nFE^{\circ}_{cell} = -(2 \text{ mol e}^-)(96,485 \text{ C/mol e}^-)(0.44 \text{ J/C}) = -84,900 \text{ J} = -85 \text{ kJ}$

$\log K = \dfrac{nE^{\circ}}{0.0591} = \dfrac{2(0.44)}{0.0591} = 14.89, \ K = 7.8 \times 10^{14}$

45. $Al^{3+} + 3 e^- \rightarrow Al$ $E^{\circ}_c = -1.66$ V
                  $Al + 6 F^- \rightarrow AlF_6^{3-} + 3 e^-$ $E^{\circ}_a = 2.07$ V
_____

$Al^{3+}(aq) + 6 F^-(aq) \rightarrow AlF_6^{3-}(aq)$ $E^{\circ}_{cell} = 0.41$ V   K = ?

$\log K = \dfrac{nE^{\circ}}{0.0591} = \dfrac{3(0.41)}{0.0591} = 20.81, \ K = 10^{20.81} = 6.5 \times 10^{20}$

46. $Ag^+ + e^- \rightarrow Ag$ $E^{\circ}_c = 0.80$ V
              $Ag + 2 S_2O_3^{2-} \rightarrow Ag(S_2O_3)_2^{3-} + e^-$ $- E^{\circ}_a = -0.017$ V
_____

$Ag^+(aq) + 2 S_2O_3^{2-}(aq) \rightarrow Ag(S_2O_3)_2^{3-}(aq)$ $E^{\circ}_{cell} = 0.78$ V   K = ?

For this overall reaction, $E^{\circ}_{cell} = \dfrac{0.0591}{n} \log K$

$\log K = \dfrac{nE^{\circ}}{0.0591} = \dfrac{(1)(0.78)}{0.0591} = 13.20, \ K = 10^{13.20} = 1.6 \times 10^{13}$

47. $CdS + 2 e^- \rightarrow Cd + S^{2-}$ $E^{\circ}_c = -1.21$ V
                  $Cd \rightarrow Cd^{2+} + 2 e^-$ $- E^{\circ}_a = 0.402$ V
_____

$CdS(s) \rightarrow Cd^{2+}(aq) + S^{2-}(aq)$ $E^{\circ}_{cell} = -0.81$ V $K = K_{sp} = ?$

For this overall reaction, $E^{\circ}_{cell} = \dfrac{0.0591}{n} \log K_{sp}$

$\log K_{sp} = \dfrac{nE^{\circ}}{0.0591} = \dfrac{2(-0.81)}{0.0591} = -27.41, \ K_{sp} = 10^{-27.41} = 3.9 \times 10^{-28}$

48. $CuI + e^- \rightarrow Cu + I^-$ $E^{\circ}_{CuI} = ?$
                  $Cu \rightarrow Cu^+ + e^-$ $-E^{\circ}_a = -0.52$ V
_____

$CuI(s) \rightarrow Cu^+(aq) + I^-(aq)$ $E^{\circ}_{cell} = E^{\circ}_{CuI} - 0.52$ V

For this overall reaction, $K = K_{sp} = 1.1 \times 10^{-12}$:

$E^{\circ}_{cell} = \dfrac{0.0591}{n} \log K_{sp} = \dfrac{0.0591}{1} \log (1.1 \times 10^{-12}) = -0.71 \text{ V}$

$E^{\circ}_{cell} = -0.71 \text{ V} = E^{\circ}_{CuI} - 0.52, \ E^{\circ}_{CuI} = -0.19 \text{ V}$

Galvanic Cells: Concentration Dependence

49.   a.
$$Au^{3+} + 3\ e^- \rightarrow Au \qquad\qquad E_c^\circ = 1.50\ V$$
$$(Tl \rightarrow Tl^+ + e^-) \times 3 \qquad -E_a^\circ = 0.34\ V$$

$$\overline{Au^{3+}(aq) + 3\ Tl(s) \rightarrow Au(s) + 3\ Tl^+(aq) \qquad E_{cell}^\circ = 1.84\ V}$$

b. $\Delta G^\circ = -nFE_{cell}^\circ = -(3\ mol\ e^-)(96{,}485\ C/mol\ e^-)(1.84\ J/C) = -5.33 \times 10^5\ J = -533\ kJ$

$$\log K = \frac{nE^\circ}{0.0591} = \frac{3(1.84)}{0.0591} = 93.401, \quad K = 10^{93.401} = 2.52 \times 10^{93}$$

c.   At 25°C, $E_{cell} = E_{cell}^\circ - \dfrac{0.0591}{n} \log Q$ where $Q = \dfrac{[Tl^+]^3}{[Au^{3+}]}$

$$E_{cell} = 1.84\ V - \frac{0.0591}{3} \log \frac{[Tl^+]^3}{[Au^{3+}]} = 1.84 - \frac{0.0591}{3} \log \frac{(1.0 \times 10^{-4})^3}{1.0 \times 10^{-2}}$$

$$E_{cell} = 1.84 - (-0.20) = 2.04\ V$$

50.
$$(Cr^{2+} \rightarrow Cr^{3+} + e^-) \times 2$$
$$Co^{2+} + 2\ e^- \rightarrow Co$$

$$\overline{2\ Cr^{2+}(aq) + Co^{2+}(aq) \rightarrow 2\ Cr^{3+}(aq) + Co(s)}$$

$$E_{cell}^\circ = \frac{0.0591}{n} \log K = \frac{0.0591}{2} \log (2.79 \times 10^7) = 0.220\ V$$

$$E = E^\circ - \frac{0.0591}{n} \log \frac{[Cr^{3+}]^2}{[Cr^{2+}]^2[Co^{2+}]} = 0.220\ V - \frac{0.0591}{2} \log \frac{(2.0)^2}{(0.30)^2(0.20)} = 0.151\ V$$

$$\Delta G = -nFE = -(2\ mol\ e^-)(96{,}485\ C/mol\ e^-)(0.151\ J/C) = -2.91 \times 10^4\ J = -29.1\ kJ$$

51.
$$(Pb^{2+} + 2\ e^- \rightarrow Pb) \times 3 \qquad\qquad E_c^\circ = -0.13\ V$$
$$(Al \rightarrow Al^{3+} + 3\ e^-) \times 2 \qquad -E_a^\circ = 1.66\ V$$

$$\overline{3\ Pb^{2+}(aq) + 2\ Al(s) \rightarrow 3\ Pb(s) + 2\ Al^{3+}(aq) \qquad E_{cell}^\circ = 1.53\ V}$$

From the balanced reaction, when the $[Al^{3+}]$ has increased by 0.60 mol/L (Al^{3+} is a product in the spontaneous reaction), then the Pb^{2+} concentration has decreased by 3/2 (0.60 mol/L) = 0.90 *M*.

$$E_{cell} = 1.53\ V - \frac{0.0591}{6} \log \frac{[Al^{3+}]^2}{[Pb^{2+}]^3} = 1.53 - \frac{0.0591}{6} \log \frac{(1.60)^2}{(0.10)^3}$$

$$E_{cell} = 1.53\ V - 0.034\ V = 1.50\ V$$

52.   a. $E = E° - \dfrac{RT}{nF} \ln Q$ or at 25°C, $E = E° - \dfrac{0.0591}{n} \log Q$

For $Cu^{2+}(aq) + 2\,e^- \rightarrow Cu(s)$ $E° = 0.34$ V; $E = E° - \dfrac{0.0591}{n} \log (1/[Cu^{2+}])$

$E = 0.34\ V - \dfrac{0.0591}{2} \log (1/0.10) = 0.34\ V - 0.030\ V = 0.31\ V$

b. $E = 0.34 - \dfrac{0.0591}{2} \log (1/2.0) = 0.34\ V - (-8.9 \times 10^{-3}\ V) = 0.35\ V$

c. $E = 0.34 - \dfrac{0.0591}{2} \log (1/1.0 \times 10^{-4}) = 0.34 - 0.12 = 0.22\ V$

d. $5\,e^- + 8\,H^+(aq) + MnO_4^-(aq) \rightarrow Mn^{2+}(aq) + 4\,H_2O(l)$ $E° = 1.51\ V$

$E = E° - \dfrac{0.0591}{5} \log \dfrac{[Mn^{2+}]}{[MnO_4^-][H^+]^8} = 1.51\ V - \dfrac{0.0591}{5} \log \dfrac{(0.010)}{(0.10)(1.0 \times 10^{-3})^8}$

$E = 1.51 - \dfrac{0.0591}{5}(23) = 1.51\ V - 0.27\ V = 1.24\ V$

e. $E = 1.51 - \dfrac{0.0591}{5} \log \left[\dfrac{(0.010)}{(0.10)(0.10)^8} \right] = 1.51 - 0.083 = 1.43\ V$

53.   a. $n = 2$ for this reaction (lead goes from $Pb \rightarrow Pb^{2+}$ in $PbSO_4$).

$E_{cell} = E_{cell}° - \dfrac{0.0591}{2} \log \left(\dfrac{1}{[H^+]^2[HSO_4^-]^2} \right) = 2.04\ V - \dfrac{0.0591}{2} \log \dfrac{1}{(4.5)^2(4.5)^2}$

$2.04\ V - (-0.077\ V) = 2.12\ V$

b.   We can calculate $\Delta G°$ from $\Delta G° = \Delta H° - T\Delta S°$ and then $E°$ from $\Delta G° = -nFE°$; or we can use the equation derived in Exercise 11.39.

$E_{-20}° = \dfrac{T\Delta S° - \Delta H°}{nF} = \dfrac{(253\ K)(263.5\ J/K) + 315.9 \times 10^3\ J}{(2\ mol\ e^-)(96{,}485\ C/mol\ e^-)} = 1.98\ J/C = 1.98\ V$

c. $E_{-20} = E_{-20}° - \dfrac{RT}{nF} \ln Q = 1.98\ V - \dfrac{RT}{nF} \ln \dfrac{1}{[H^+]^2[HSO_4^-]^2}$

$E_{-20} = 1.98\ V - \dfrac{(8.3145\ J\ K^{-1}\ mol^{-1})(253\ K)}{(2\ mol\ e^-)(96{,}485\ C/mol\ e^-)} \ln \dfrac{1}{(4.5)^2(4.5)^2} = 1.98\ V - (-0.066\ V) = 2.05\ V$

d.   As the temperature decreases, the cell potential decreases. Also, oil becomes more viscous at lower temperatures, which adds to the difficulty of starting an engine on a cold day. The combination of these two factors results in batteries failing more often on cold days than on warm days.

54.   a. $Ag_2CrO_4(s) + 2 e^- \rightarrow 2 Ag(s) + CrO_4^{2-}(aq)$ $E° = 0.446$ V

$Hg_2Cl_2 + 2 e^- \rightarrow 2 Hg + 2 Cl^-$ $E_{SCE} = 0.242$ V

SCE will be the oxidation half-reaction with $E_{cell} = 0.446 - 0.242 = 0.204$ V.

$\Delta G = -nFE_{cell} = -2(96,485)(0.204)J = -3.94 \times 10^4$ J $= -39.4$ kJ

b.   In SCE, we assume all concentrations are constant. Therefore, only CrO_4^{2-} appears in the Q expression and it will appear in the numerator since CrO_4^{2-} is produced in the reduction half-reaction. To calculate E_{cell} at nonstandard CrO_4^{2-} concentrations, we use the following equation.

$$E_{cell} = E_{cell}° - \frac{0.0591}{2} \log [CrO_4^{2-}] = 0.204 \text{ V} - \frac{0.0591}{2} \log [CrO_4^{2-}]$$

c. $E_{cell} = 0.204 - \dfrac{0.0591}{2} \log (1.00 \times 10^{-5}) = 0.204$ V $- (-0.148$ V$) = 0.352$ V

d. 0.504 V $= 0.204$ V $- (0.0591/2) \log [CrO_4^{2-}]$

$\log [CrO_4^{2-}] = -10.152, \quad [CrO_4^{2-}] = 10^{-10.152} = 7.05 \times 10^{-11}$ M

e. $Ag_2CrO_4 + 2 e^- \rightarrow 2 Ag + CrO_4^{2-}$ $E_c° = 0.446$ V

$(Ag \rightarrow Ag^+ + e^-) \times 2$ $-E_a° = -0.80$ V

_____

$Ag_2CrO_4(s) \rightarrow 2 Ag^+(aq) + CrO_4^{2-}(aq)$ $E_{cell}° = -0.35$ V $K = K_{sp} = ?$

$E_{cell}° = \dfrac{0.0591}{n} \log K_{sp}, \quad \log K_{sp} = \dfrac{(-0.35 \text{ V})(2)}{0.0591} = -11.84, \quad K_{sp} = 10^{-11.84} = 1.4 \times 10^{-12}$

55.   As is the case for all concentration cells, $E_{cell}° = 0$, and the smaller ion concentration is always in the anode compartment. The general Nernst equation for the Ni | Ni^{2+} (x M) || Ni^{2+}(y M) | Ni concentration cell is:

$$E_{cell} = E_{cell}° - \frac{0.0591}{n} \log Q = \frac{-0.0591}{2} \log \frac{[Ni^{2+}]_{anode}}{[Ni^{2+}]_{cathode}}$$

a.   Since both compartments are at standard conditions ($[Ni^{2+}] = 1.0$ M), then $E_{cell} = E_{cell}° = 0$ V. No electron flow occurs.

b.   Cathode $= 2.0$ M Ni^{2+}; Anode $= 1.0$ M Ni^{2+}; Electron flow is always from the anode to the cathode, so electrons flow to the right in the diagram.

$$E_{cell} = \frac{-0.0591}{2} \log \frac{[Ni^{2+}]_{anode}}{[Ni^{2+}]_{cathode}} = \frac{-0.0591}{2} \log \frac{1.0}{2.0} = 8.9 \times 10^{-3} \text{ V}$$

c.   Cathode $= 1.0$ M Ni^{2+}; Anode $= 0.10$ M Ni^{2+}; Electrons flow to the left in the diagram.

$$E_{cell} = \frac{-0.0591}{2} \log \frac{0.10}{1.0} = 0.030 \text{ V}$$

d.   Cathode = 1.0 M Ni^{2+}; Anode = 4.0×10^{-5} M Ni^{2+}; Electrons flow to the left in the diagram.

$$E_{cell} = \frac{-0.0591}{2} \log \frac{4.0 \times 10^{-5}}{1.0} = 0.13 \text{ V}$$

e.   Since both concentrations are equal, $\log (2.5/2.5) = \log 1.0 = 0$ and $E_{cell} = 0$. No electron flow occurs.

56.   Cathode: $M^{2+} + 2e^- \rightarrow M(s)$ $E_c^\circ = 0.80$ V

       Anode: $M(s) \rightarrow M^{2+} + 2e^-$ $-E_a^\circ = -0.80$ V
       _____

                 M^{2+} (cathode) $\rightarrow$ M^{2+} (anode) $E_{cell}^\circ = 0.00$ V

$$E_{cell} = 0.44 \text{ V} = 0.00 \text{ V} - \frac{0.0591}{2} \log \frac{[M^{2+}]_{anode}}{[M^{2+}]_{cathode}}, \quad 0.44 = -\frac{0.0591}{2} \log \frac{[M^{2+}]_{anode}}{1.0}$$

$$\log [M^{2+}]_{anode} = -\frac{2(0.44)}{0.0591} = -14.89, \quad [M^{2+}]_{anode} = 1.3 \times 10^{-15} \text{ M}$$

Since we started with equal numbers of moles of SO_4^{2-} and M^{2+}, then $[M^{2+}] = [SO_4^{2-}]$ at equilibrium.

$$K_{sp} = [M^{2+}][SO_4^{2-}] = (1.3 \times 10^{-15})^2 = 1.7 \times 10^{-30}$$

57. $Cu^{2+}(aq) + H_2(g) \rightarrow 2 H^+(aq) + Cu(s)$ $E_{cell}^\circ = 0.34$ V $- 0.00$V $= 0.34$ V and $n = 2$

Since $P_{H_2} = 1.0$ atm and $[H^+] = 1.0$ M: $E_{cell} = E_{cell}^\circ - \frac{0.0591}{2} \log \frac{1}{[Cu^{2+}]}$

a. $E_{cell} = 0.34 \text{ V} - \frac{0.0591}{2} \log \frac{1}{2.5 \times 10^{-4}} = 0.34 \text{ V} - 0.11 \text{ V} = 0.23 \text{ V}$

b.   Use the K_{sp} expression to calculate the Cu^{2+} concentration in the cell.

$Cu(OH)_2(s) \rightleftharpoons Cu^{2+}(aq) + 2 OH^-(aq)$ $K_{sp} = 1.6 \times 10^{-19} = [Cu^{2+}] [OH^-]^2$

From the problem, $[OH^-] = 0.10$ M, so: $[Cu^{2+}] = \frac{1.6 \times 10^{-19}}{(0.10)^2} = 1.6 \times 10^{-17}$ M

$$E_{cell} = E_{cell}^\circ - \frac{0.0591}{2} \log \frac{1}{[Cu^{2+}]} = 0.34 \text{ V} - \frac{0.0591}{2} \log \frac{1}{1.6 \times 10^{-17}} = 0.34 - 0.50 = -0.16 \text{ V}$$

Since $E_{cell} < 0$, then the forward reaction is not spontaneous, but the reverse reaction is spontaneous. The Cu electrode becomes the anode and $E_{cell} = 0.16$ V for the reverse reaction. The cell reaction is: $2 H^+(aq) + Cu(s) \rightarrow Cu^{2+}(aq) + H_2(g)$.

c. $0.195 \text{ V} = 0.34 \text{ V} - \frac{0.0591}{2} \log \frac{1}{[Cu^{2+}]}, \quad \log \frac{1}{[Cu^{2+}]} = 4.91, \quad [Cu^{2+}] = 10^{-4.91} = 1.2 \times 10^{-5}$ M

Note: When determining exponents, we will carry extra significant figures.

d. $E_{cell} = E^\circ_{cell} - (0.0591/2) \log (1/[Cu^{2+}]) = E^\circ_{cell} + 0.0296 \log [Cu^{2+}]$; This equation is in the form of a straight line equation, $y = mx + b$. A graph of E_{cell} vs. $\log [Cu^{2+}]$ will yield a straight line with slope equal to 0.0296 V or 29.6 mV.

58. $3 Ni^{2+}(aq) + 2 Al(s) \rightarrow 2 Al^{3+}(aq) + 3 Ni(s)$ $E^\circ_{cell} = -0.23 V + 1.66 V = 1.43 V$; $n = 6$

$$E_{cell} = E^\circ_{cell} - \frac{0.0591}{n} \log \frac{[Al^{3+}]^2}{[Ni^{2+}]^3}, \quad 1.82 V = 1.43 V - \frac{0.0591}{6} \log \frac{[Al^{3+}]^2}{(1.0)^3}$$

$\log [Al^{3+}]^2 = -39.59$, $[Al^{3+}]^2 = 10^{-39.59}$, $[Al^{3+}] = 1.6 \times 10^{-20} M$

$Al(OH)_3(s) \rightleftharpoons Al^{3+}(aq) + 3 OH^-(aq)$ $K_{sp} = [Al^{3+}] [OH^-]^3$; From the problem, $[OH^-] = 1.0 \times 10^{-4} M$.

$K_{sp} = (1.6 \times 10^{-20}) (1.0 \times 10^{-4})^3 = 1.6 \times 10^{-32}$

59.   From Exercise 11.17a: $3 Cl_2(g) + 2 Cr^{3+}(aq) + 7 H_2O(l) \rightleftharpoons 14 H^+(aq) + Cr_2O_7^{2-}(aq) + 6 Cl^-(aq)$
$E^\circ_{cell} = 0.03 V$

$$E_{cell} = E^\circ_{cell} - \frac{0.0591}{6} \log \frac{[Cr_2O_7^{2-}] [H^+]^{14} [Cl^-]^6}{[Cr^{3+}]^2 P_{Cl_2}^3}$$

When $K_2Cr_2O_7$ and Cl^- are added to concentrated H_2SO_4, Q becomes a large number due to $[H^+]^{14}$ term. The log of a large number is positive. E_{cell} becomes negative, which means the reverse reaction becomes spontaneous. The pungent fumes were $Cl_2(g)$.

Electrolysis

60.   a. $Al^{3+} + 3 e^- \rightarrow Al$; 3 mol e^- are needed to produce 1 mol Al from Al^{3+}.

$$1.0 \times 10^3 \text{ g} \times \frac{1 \text{ mol Al}}{27.0 \text{ g}} \times \frac{3 \text{ mol } e^-}{\text{mol Al}} \times \frac{96,485 \text{ C}}{\text{mol } e^-} \times \frac{1 \text{ s}}{100.0 \text{ C}} = 1.07 \times 10^5 \text{ s} = 3.0 \times 10^1 \text{ hours}$$

b. $1.0 \text{ g Ni} \times \frac{1 \text{ mol}}{58.7 \text{ g}} \times \frac{2 \text{ mol } e^-}{\text{mol Ni}} \times \frac{96,485 \text{ C}}{\text{mol } e^-} \times \frac{1 \text{ s}}{100.0 \text{ C}} = 33 \text{ s}$

c. $5.0 \text{ mol Ag} \times \frac{1 \text{ mol } e^-}{\text{mol Ag}} \times \frac{96,485 \text{ C}}{\text{mol } e^-} \times \frac{1 \text{ s}}{100.0 \text{ C}} = 4.8 \times 10^3 \text{ s} = 1.3 \text{ hours}$

61. $15A = \frac{15 \text{ C}}{\text{s}} \times \frac{60 \text{ s}}{\text{min}} \times \frac{60 \text{ min}}{\text{h}} = 5.4 \times 10^4 \text{ C of charge passed in 1 hour}$

a. $5.4 \times 10^4 \text{ C} \times \frac{1 \text{ mol } e^-}{96,485 \text{ C}} \times \frac{1 \text{ mol Co}}{2 \text{ mol } e^-} \times \frac{58.9 \text{ g}}{\text{mol}} = 16 \text{ g Co}$

b. $5.4 \times 10^4 \text{ C} \times \frac{1 \text{ mol } e^-}{96,485 \text{ C}} \times \frac{1 \text{ mol Hf}}{4 \text{ mol } e^-} \times \frac{178.5 \text{ g}}{\text{mol}} = 25 \text{ g Hf}$

c. $2 I^- \rightarrow I_2 + 2e^-$; $5.4 \times 10^4 \text{ C} \times \dfrac{1 \text{ mole}^-}{96,485 \text{ C}} \times \dfrac{1 \text{ mol } I_2}{2 \text{ mole}^-} \times \dfrac{253.8 \text{ g } I_2}{\text{mol } I_2} = 71 \text{ g } I_2$

d. Cr is in the +6 oxidation state in CrO_3. Six mol of e^- are needed to produce 1 mol Cr from molten CrO_3.

$5.4 \times 10^4 \text{ C} \times \dfrac{1 \text{ mole}^-}{96,485 \text{ C}} \times \dfrac{1 \text{ mol Cr}}{6 \text{ mole}^-} \times \dfrac{52.0 \text{ g Cr}}{\text{mol Cr}} = 4.9 \text{ g Cr}$

62. $2.30 \text{ min} \times \dfrac{60 \text{ s}}{\text{min}} = 138 \text{ s}$; $138 \text{ s} \times \dfrac{2.00 \text{ C}}{\text{s}} \times \dfrac{1 \text{ mole}^-}{96,485 \text{ C}} \times \dfrac{1 \text{ mol Ag}}{\text{mole}^-} = 2.86 \times 10^{-3} \text{ mol Ag}$

$[Ag^+] = 2.86 \times 10^{-3} \text{ mol Ag}^+/0.250 \text{ L} = 1.14 \times 10^{-2} \text{ } M$

63. First determine the species present, then reference Table 11.1 to help you identify each species as a possible oxidizing agent (species reduced) or as a possible reducing agent (species oxidized). Of all the possible oxidizing agents, the species that will be reduced at the cathode will have the most positive E_c° value; the species that will be oxidized at the anode will be the reducing agent with the most positive $- E_a^\circ$ value.

a. Species present: Ni^{2+} and Br^-; Ni^{2+} can be reduced to Ni and Br^- can be oxidized to Br_2 (from Table 11.1). The reactions are:

Cathode: $Ni^{2+} + 2e^- \rightarrow Ni$ $E_c^\circ = -0.23 \text{ V}$
Anode: $2 Br^- \rightarrow Br_2 + 2 e^-$ $- E_a^\circ = -1.09 \text{ V}$

b. Species present: Al^{3+} and F^-; Al^{3+} can be reduced and F^- can be oxidized. The reactions are:

Cathode: $Al^{3+} + 3 e^- \rightarrow Al$ $E_c^\circ = -1.66 \text{ V}$
Anode: $2 F^- \rightarrow F_2 + 2 e^-$ $- E_a^\circ = -2.87 \text{ V}$

c. Species present: Mn^{2+} and I^-; Mn^{2+} can be reduced and I^- can be oxidized. The reactions are:

Cathode: $Mn^{2+} + 2 e^- \rightarrow Mn$ $E_c^\circ = -1.18 \text{ V}$
Anode: $2 I^- \rightarrow I_2 + 2 e^-$ $- E_a^\circ = -0.54 \text{ V}$

d. For aqueous solutions, we must now consider H_2O as a possible oxidizing agent and a possible reducing agent. Species present: Ni^{2+}, Br^- and H_2O. Possible cathode reactions are:

$Ni^{2+} + 2e^- \rightarrow Ni$ $E_c^\circ = -0.23 \text{ V}$
$2 H_2O + 2 e^- \rightarrow H_2 + 2 OH^-$ $E_c^\circ = -0.83 \text{ V}$

Since it is easier to reduce Ni^{2+} than H_2O (assuming standard conditions), then Ni^{2+} will be reduced by the above cathode reaction.

Possible anode reactions are:

$$2 \text{ Br}^- \rightarrow \text{Br}_2 + 2 \text{ e}^- \qquad\qquad - E_a^\circ = -1.09 \text{ V}$$
$$2 \text{ H}_2\text{O} \rightarrow \text{O}_2 + 4 \text{ H}^+ + 4 \text{ e}^- \qquad - E_a^\circ = -1.23 \text{ V}$$

Since Br^- is easier to oxidize than H_2O (assuming standard conditions), then Br^- will be oxidized by the above anode reaction.

e. Species present: Al^{3+}, F^- and H_2O; Al^{3+} and H_2O can be reduced. The reduction potentials are $E_c^\circ = -1.66 \text{ V}$ for Al^{3+} and $E_c^\circ = -0.83 \text{ V}$ for H_2O (assuming standard conditions). H_2O should be reduced at the cathode ($2 \text{ H}_2\text{O} + 2 \text{ e}^- \rightarrow \text{H}_2 + 2 \text{ OH}^-$).

F^- and H_2O can be oxidized. The oxidation potentials are $- E_a^\circ = -2.87 \text{ V}$ for F^- and $- E_a^\circ = -1.23 \text{ V}$ for H_2O (assuming standard conditions). From the potentials, we would predict H_2O to be oxidized at the anode ($2 \text{ H}_2\text{O} \rightarrow \text{O}_2 + 4 \text{ H}^+ + 4 \text{ e}^-$).

f. Species present: Mn^{2+}, I^- and H_2O; Mn^{2+} and H_2O can be reduced. The possible cathode reactions are:

$$\text{Mn}^{2+} + 2 \text{ e}^- \rightarrow \text{Mn} \qquad\qquad E_c^\circ = -1.18 \text{ V}$$
$$2 \text{ H}_2\text{O} + 2 \text{ e}^- \rightarrow \text{H}_2 + 2 \text{ OH}^- \qquad E_c^\circ = -0.83 \text{ V}$$

Reduction of H_2O should occur at the cathode since $E_{\text{H}_2\text{O}}^\circ$ is most positive.

I^- and H_2O can be oxidized. The possible anode reactions are:

$$2 \text{ I}^- \rightarrow \text{I}_2 + 2 \text{ e}^- \qquad\qquad - E_a^\circ = -0.54 \text{ V}$$
$$2 \text{ H}_2\text{O} \rightarrow \text{O}_2 + 4 \text{ H}^+ + 4 \text{ e}^- \qquad - E_a^\circ = -1.23 \text{ V}$$

Oxidation of I^- will occur at the anode since $- E_{\text{I}^-}^\circ$ is most positive.

64. a. Species present: Na^+, SO_4^{2-} and H_2O. From the potentials, H_2O is the most easily oxidized and the most easily reduced species present. The reactions are:

Cathode: $2 \text{ H}_2\text{O} + 2 \text{ e}^- \rightarrow \text{H}_2(g) + 2 \text{ OH}^-$; Anode: $2 \text{ H}_2\text{O} \rightarrow \text{O}_2(g) + 4 \text{ H}^+ + 4 \text{ e}^-$

b. When water is electrolyzed a significantly higher voltage than predicted is necessary to produce the chemical change (called overvoltage). This higher voltage is probably great enough to cause some SO_4^{2-} to be oxidized instead of H_2O. Thus, the volume of O_2 generated would be less than expected and the measured volume ratio would be greater than 2:1.

65. $\text{Au}^{3+} + 3 \text{ e}^- \rightarrow \text{Au} \qquad E^\circ = 1.50 \text{ V} \qquad\qquad \text{Ni}^{2+} + 2 \text{ e}^- \rightarrow \text{Ni} \qquad E^\circ = -0.23 \text{ V}$
      $\text{Ag}^+ + \text{e}^- \rightarrow \text{Ag} \qquad E^\circ = 0.80 \text{ V} \qquad\qquad \text{Cd}^{2+} + 2 \text{ e}^- \rightarrow \text{Cd} \qquad E^\circ = -0.40 \text{ V}$

      $2 \text{ H}_2\text{O} + 2\text{e}^- \rightarrow \text{H}_2 + 2 \text{ OH}^- \quad E^\circ = -0.83 \text{ V}$

Au(s) will plate out first since it has the most positive reduction potential, followed by Ag(s), which is followed by Ni(s), and finally Cd(s) will plate out last since it has the most negative reduction potential of the metals listed.

66. $\text{mol e}^- = 50.0 \text{ min} \times \dfrac{60 \text{ s}}{\text{min}} \times \dfrac{2.50 \text{ C}}{\text{s}} \times \dfrac{1 \text{ mol e}^-}{96,485 \text{ C}} = 7.77 \times 10^{-2} \text{ mol e}^-$

$\text{mol Ru} = 2.618 \text{ g Ru} \times \dfrac{1 \text{ mol Ru}}{101.1 \text{ g Ru}} = 2.590 \times 10^{-2} \text{ mol Ru}$

$\dfrac{\text{mol e}^-}{\text{mol Ru}} = \dfrac{7.77 \times 10^{-2} \text{ mol e}^-}{2.590 \times 10^{-2} \text{ mol Ru}} = 3.00;$ The charge on the ruthenium ions is +3 ($Ru^{3+} + 3 \text{ e}^- \rightarrow Ru$).

67.   To begin plating out Pd: $E_c = 0.62 \text{ V} - \dfrac{0.0591}{2} \log \dfrac{[Cl^-]^4}{[PdCl_4^{2-}]} = 0.62 - \dfrac{0.0591}{2} \log \dfrac{(1.0)^4}{0.020}$

$E_c = 0.62 \text{ V} - 0.050 \text{ V} = 0.57 \text{ V}$

When 99% of Pd has plated out, $[PdCl_4^-] = \dfrac{1}{100} (0.020) = 0.00020 \text{ } M.$

$E_c = 0.62 - \dfrac{0.0591}{2} \log \dfrac{(1.0)^4}{2.0 \times 10^{-4}} = 0.62 \text{ V} - 0.11 \text{V} = 0.51 \text{ V}$

To begin Pt plating: $E_c = 0.73 \text{ V} - \dfrac{0.0591}{2} \log \dfrac{(1.0)^4}{0.020} = 0.73 - 0.050 = 0.68 \text{ V}$

When 99% of Pt plated: $E_c = 0.73 - \dfrac{0.0591}{2} \log \dfrac{(1.0)^4}{2.0 \times 10^{-4}} = 0.083 - 0.11 = 0.62 \text{ V}$

To begin Ir plating: $E_c = 0.77 \text{ V} - \dfrac{0.0591}{3} \log \dfrac{(1.0)^4}{0.020} = 0.77 - 0.033 = 0.74 \text{ V}$

When 99% of Ir plated: $E_c = 0.77 - \dfrac{0.0591}{3} \log \dfrac{(1.0)^4}{2.0 \times 10^{-4}} = 0.77 - 0.073 = 0.70 \text{ V}$

Yes, since the range of potentials for plating out each metal do not overlap, we should be able to separate the three metals. The exact potential to apply depends on the oxidation reaction. The order of plating will be Ir(s) first, followed by Pt(s) and finally Pd(s) as the potential is gradually increased.

68. $1397 \text{ s} \times \dfrac{6.50 \text{ C}}{\text{s}} \times \dfrac{1 \text{ mol e}^-}{96,485 \text{ C}} \times \dfrac{1 \text{ mol M}}{3 \text{ mol e}^-} = 3.14 \times 10^{-2} \text{ mol M}$ where M = unknown metal

$\text{Molar mass} = \dfrac{1.41 \text{ g M}}{3.14 \times 10^{-2} \text{ mol M}} = \dfrac{44.9 \text{ g}}{\text{mol}};$ The element is scandium. Sc forms 3+ ions.

69.   Alkaline earth metals form +2 ions, so 2 mol of e^- are transferred to form the metal, M.

$$\text{mol M} = 748 \text{ s} \times \frac{5.00 \text{ C}}{\text{s}} \times \frac{1 \text{ mol } e^-}{96,485 \text{ C}} \times \frac{1 \text{ mol M}}{2 \text{ mol } e^-} = 1.94 \times 10^{-2} \text{ mol M}$$

$$\text{molar mass of M} = \frac{0.471 \text{ g M}}{1.94 \times 10^{-2} \text{ mol M}} = 24.3 \text{ g/mol}; \text{MgCl}_2 \text{ was electrolyzed.}$$

70.
$$\frac{150. \times 10^3 \text{ g C}_6\text{H}_8\text{N}_2}{\text{h}} \times \frac{1 \text{ h}}{60 \text{ min}} \times \frac{1 \text{ min}}{60 \text{ s}} \times \frac{1 \text{ mol C}_6\text{H}_8\text{N}_2}{108.14 \text{ g C}_6\text{H}_8\text{N}_2} \times \frac{2 \text{ mol } e^-}{\text{mol C}_6\text{H}_8\text{N}_2} \times \frac{96,485 \text{ C}}{\text{mol } e^-}$$

$$= 7.44 \times 10^4 \text{ C/s or a current of } 7.44 \times 10^4 \text{ A}$$

71. F_2 is produced at the anode: $2 \text{ F}^- \rightarrow \text{F}_2 + 2 \text{ } e^-$

$$2.00 \text{ h} \times \frac{60 \text{ min}}{\text{h}} \times \frac{60 \text{ s}}{\text{min}} \times \frac{10.0 \text{ C}}{\text{s}} \times \frac{1 \text{ mol } e^-}{96,485 \text{ C}} = 0.746 \text{ mol } e^-$$

$$0.746 \text{ mol } e^- \times \frac{1 \text{ mol F}_2}{2 \text{ mol } e^-} = 0.373 \text{ mol F}_2; PV = nRT, V = \frac{nRT}{P}$$

$$V = \frac{(0.373 \text{ mol}) (0.08206 \text{ L atm K}^{-1} \text{mol}^{-1}) (298 \text{ K})}{1.00 \text{ atm}} = 9.12 \text{ L F}_2$$

K is produced at the cathode: $\text{K}^+ + e^- \rightarrow \text{K}$

$$0.746 \text{ mol } e^- \times \frac{1 \text{ mol K}}{\text{mol } e^-} \times \frac{39.10 \text{ g K}}{\text{mol K}} = 29.2 \text{ g K}$$

72. $15 \text{ kWh} = \dfrac{15000 \text{ J h}}{\text{s}} \times \dfrac{60 \text{ s}}{\text{min}} \times \dfrac{60 \text{ min}}{\text{h}} = 5.4 \times 10^7 \text{ J or } 5.4 \times 10^4 \text{ kJ}$ (Hall process)

To melt 1.0 kg Al requires: $1.0 \times 10^3 \text{ g Al} \times \dfrac{1 \text{ mol Al}}{26.98 \text{ g}} \times \dfrac{10.7 \text{ kJ}}{\text{mol Al}} = 4.0 \times 10^2 \text{ kJ}$

It is feasible to recycle Al by melting the metal because in theory, it takes less than 1% of the energy required to produce the same amount of Al by the Hall process.

73.   In the electrolysis of aqueous sodium chloride, H_2O is reduced in preference to Na^+ and Cl^- is oxidized in preference to H_2O. The anode reaction is $2 \text{ Cl}^- \rightarrow \text{Cl}_2 + 2 \text{ } e^-$ and the cathode reaction is $2 \text{ H}_2\text{O} + 2 \text{ } e^- \rightarrow \text{H}_2 + 2 \text{ OH}^-$. The overall reaction is $2 \text{ H}_2\text{O(l)} + 2 \text{ Cl}^-\text{(aq)} \rightarrow \text{Cl}_2\text{(g)} + \text{H}_2\text{(g)} + 2 \text{ OH}^-\text{(aq)}$.

From the 1:1 mol ratio between Cl_2 and H_2 in the overall balanced reaction, if 6.00 L of H_2(g) are produced, then 6.00 L of Cl_2(g) will also be produced since moles and volume of gas are directly proportional at constant T and P (see Chapter 5 of text).

74.   The half-reactions for the electrolysis of water are:

$$(2 \ e^- + 2 \ H_2O \rightarrow H_2 + 2 \ OH^-) \times 2$$
$$2 \ H_2O \rightarrow 4 \ H^+ + O_2 + 4 \ e^-$$

$$2 \ H_2O(l) \rightarrow 2 \ H_2(g) + O_2(g)$$

Note: $4 \ H^+ + 4 \ OH^- \rightarrow 4 \ H_2O$ and $n = 4$ for this reaction as it is written.

$$15.0 \ min \times \frac{60 \ s}{min} \times \frac{2.50 \ C}{s} \times \frac{1 \ mol \ e^-}{96,485 \ C} \times \frac{2 \ mol \ H_2}{4 \ mol \ e^-} = 1.17 \times 10^{-2} \ mol \ H_2$$

At STP, 1 mole of an ideal gas occupies a volume of 22.42 L (see Chapter 5 of the text).

$$1.17 \times 10^{-2} \ mol \ H_2 \times \frac{22.42 \ L}{mol \ H_2} = 0.262 \ L = 262 \ mL \ H_2$$

$$1.17 \times 10^{-2} \ mol \ H_2 \times \frac{1 \ mol \ O_2}{2 \ mol \ H_2} \times \frac{22.42 \ L}{mol \ O_2} = 0.131 \ L = 131 \ mL \ O_2$$

Additional Exercises

75. $$(CO + O^{2-} \rightarrow CO_2 + 2 \ e^-) \times 2$$
$$O_2 + 4 \ e^- \rightarrow 2 \ O^{2-}$$

$$2 \ CO + O_2 \rightarrow 2 \ CO_2$$

$$\Delta G = -nFE, \quad E = \frac{-\Delta G}{nF} = \frac{-(-380 \times 10^3 \ J)}{(4 \ mol \ e^-)(96,485 \ C/mol \ e^-)} = 0.98 \ V$$

76.   a.   Purification by electrolysis is called electrorefining. See the text for a discussion of the electrorefining of copper. Electrorefining is possible because of the selectivity of the electrode reactions. The anode is made up of the impure metal. A potential is applied so just the metal of interest and all more easily oxidized metals are oxidized at the anode. The metal of interest is the only metal plated at the cathode due to the careful control of the potential applied. The metal ions that could plate out at the cathode in preference to the metal we are purifying will not be in solution, since these metals were not oxidized at the anode.

b.   A more easily oxidized metal is placed in electrical contact with the metal we are trying to protect. It is oxidized in preference to the protected metal. The protected metal becomes the cathode electrode, thus, cathodic protection.

77. $Zn \rightarrow Zn^{2+} + 2 \ e^- \quad -E_a^\circ = 0.76 \ V; \quad Fe \rightarrow Fe^{2+} + 2 \ e^- \quad -E_a^\circ = 0.44 \ V$

It is easier to oxidize Zn than Fe, so the Zn will be oxidized, protecting the iron of the *Monitor's* hull.

78.   Moisture must be present to act as a medium for ion flow between the anodic and cathodic regions. Salt provides ions necessary to complete the electrical circuit in the corrosion process. Together, salt and water make up the salt bridge in this spontaneous electrochemical process.

Three methods discussed in the text to prevent corrosion are galvanizing, alloying and cathodic protection. Galvanizing coats the metal of interest (usually iron) with zinc which is an easily oxidized metal. Alloying mixes in metals which form durable, effective oxide coatings over the metal of interest. Cathodic protection connects, via a wire, a more easily oxidized metal to the metal we are trying to protect. The more active metal is preferentially oxidized, thus protecting our metal object from corrosion.

79.   As a battery discharges, E_{cell} decreases, eventually reaching zero. A charged battery is not at equilibrium. At equilibrium $E_{cell} = 0$ and $\Delta G = 0$. We get no work out of an equilibrium system. A battery is useful to us because it can do work as it approaches equilibrium.

80.   Fuel cells are more efficient in converting chemical energy to electrical energy; they are also less massive. The major disadvantage is that they are expensive. In addition, $H_2(g)$ and $O_2(g)$ are an explosive mixture if ignited.

81.
$$O_2 + 2\,H_2O + 4\,e^- \rightarrow 4\,OH^- \qquad\qquad E_c^\circ = 0.40\ V$$
$$(H_2 + 2\,OH^- \rightarrow 2\,H_2O + 2\,e^-) \times 2 \qquad -E_a^\circ = 0.83\ V$$

$$2\,H_2(g) + O_2(g) \rightarrow 2\,H_2O(l) \qquad\qquad E_{cell}^\circ = 1.23\ V = 1.23\ J/C$$

Since standard conditions are assumed, then $w_{max} = \Delta G^\circ$ for 2 mol H_2O produced.

$$\Delta G^\circ = -nFE_{cell}^\circ = -(4\ mol\ e^-)(96,485\ C/mol\ e^-)(1.23\ J/C) = -475,000\ J = -475\ kJ$$

For 1.00×10^3 g H_2O produced, w_{max} is:

$$1.00 \times 10^3\ g\ H_2O \times \frac{1\ mol\ H_2O}{18.02\ g\ H_2O} \times \frac{-475\ kJ}{2\ mol\ H_2O} = -13,200\ kJ = w_{max}$$

The work done can be no larger than the free energy change. The best that could happen is that all of the free energy released goes into doing work, but this does not occur in any real process since there is always waste energy in any real process.

82.   Cadmium goes from the zero oxidation state to the +2 oxidation state in $Cd(OH)_2$. Since one mol of Cd appears in the balanced reaction, then $n = 2$ mol electrons transferred. At standard condi-tions:

$$w_{max} = \Delta G^\circ = -nFE^\circ, \quad w_{max} = -(2\ mol\ e^-)(96,485\ C/mol\ e^-)(1.10\ J/C) = -2.12 \times 10^5\ J = -212\ kJ$$

83.
$$(Al^{3+} + 3\,e^- \rightarrow Al) \times 2 \qquad\qquad E_c^\circ = -1.66\ V$$
$$(M \rightarrow M^{2+} + 2\,e^-) \times 3 \qquad\qquad -E_a^\circ = ?$$

$$3\,M(s) + 2\,Al^{3+}(aq) \rightarrow 2\,Al(s) + 3\,M^{2+}(aq) \qquad E_{cell}^\circ = -E_a^\circ - 1.66\ V$$

$$\Delta G^\circ = -nFE_{cell}^\circ, \quad -411 \times 10^3\ J = -(6\ mol\ e^-)(96,485\ C/mol\ e^-)(E_{cell}^\circ), \quad E_{cell}^\circ = 0.71\ V$$

$$E_{cell}^\circ = -E_a^\circ - 1.66\ V = 0.71\ V, \quad -E_a^\circ = 2.37\ \text{or}\ E_c^\circ = -2.37$$

From Table 11.1, the reduction potential for $Mg^{2+} + 2 e^- \rightarrow Mg$ is -2.37 V which fits the data. Hence, the metal is magnesium.

84.   The potential oxidizing agents are NO_3^- and H^+. Hydrogen ion cannot oxidize Pt under either condition. Nitrate cannot oxidize Pt unless there is Cl^- in the solution. Aqua regia has both Cl^- and NO_3^-. The overall reaction is:

$$(NO_3^- + 4 H^+ + 3 e^- \rightarrow NO + 2 H_2O) \times 2 \qquad\qquad E_c^\circ = 0.96 \text{ V}$$
$$(4 Cl^- + Pt \rightarrow PtCl_4^{2-} + 2 e^-) \times 3 \qquad\qquad -E_a^\circ = -0.755 \text{ V}$$

$$12 Cl^-(aq) + 3 Pt(s) + 2 NO_3^-(aq) + 8 H^+(aq) \rightarrow 3 PtCl_4^{2-}(aq) + 2 NO(g) + 4 H_2O(l) \qquad E_{cell}^\circ = 0.21 \text{ V}$$

85.   a. $3 e^- + 4 H^+ + NO_3^- \rightarrow NO + 2 H_2O \qquad E^\circ = 0.96 \text{ V}$

Nitric acid can oxidize Co to Co^{2+} ($E_{cell}^\circ > 0$), but is not strong enough to oxidize Co to Co^{3+} ($E_{cell}^\circ < 0$). Co^{2+} is the primary product assuming standard conditions.

b.   Concentrated nitric acid is about 16 mol/L. $[H^+] = [NO_3^-] = 16 \; M$; Assume $P_{NO} = 1$ atm

$$E = 0.96 \text{ V} - \frac{0.0591}{3} \log \frac{P_{NO}}{[H^+]^4 [NO_3^-]} = 0.96 - \frac{0.0591}{3} \log \frac{1}{(16)^5} = 0.96 - (-0.12) = 1.08 \text{ V}$$

No, concentrated nitric acid will still only be able to oxidize Co to Co^{2+}.

86.   a. $$Hg_2Cl_2 + 2e^- \rightarrow 2 Hg + 2 Cl^- \qquad\qquad E_{SCE} = 0.242 \text{ V}$$
$$H_2 \rightarrow 2 H^+ + 2 e^- \qquad\qquad -E_a^\circ = 0.000 \text{ V}$$

$$HgCl_2 + H_2(g) \rightarrow 2 H^+(aq) + 2 Cl^- + 2 Hg \qquad E_{cell} = 0.242 \text{ V} = E_{cell}^\circ$$

Note: The concentrations in the SCE reduction half-reaction are not necessarily standard concentrations, but are assumed constant. Therefore, the 0.242 V cell potential can be assumed to be the standard cell potential when writing the Nernst equation.

b.   The hydrogen half-cell is the oxidation half-reaction, thus the hydrogen electrode is the anode.

c.   Ignoring concentrations from the SCE (they are constant):

$$E_{cell} = E_{cell}^\circ - \frac{0.0591}{n} \log Q = 0.242 \text{ V} - \frac{0.0591}{2} \log \frac{[H^+]^2}{P_{H_2}}$$

If we keep $P_{H_2} = 1.0$ atm: $E = 0.241 \text{ V} - \dfrac{0.0591}{2} \log [H^+]^2$

Since, $\log [H^+]^2 = 2 \log [H^+] = -2 \text{ pH}$, $E = 0.242 - 0.0591 \log [H^+]$ or:

$$E_{cell} = 0.242 \text{ V} + 0.0591 \text{ pH}$$

d.   i) $E_{cell} = 0.242 - 0.0591 \log [H^+] = 0.242 - 0.0591 \log (1.0 \times 10^{-3}) = 0.42 \text{ V}$

ii) $E_{cell} = 0.242 - 0.0591 \log (2.5) = 0.242 - 0.024 = 0.218$ V

iii) $E_{cell} = 0.242 - 0.0591 \log (1.0 \times 10^{-9}) = 0.242 - (-0.53) = 0.77$ V

e. $E = 0.242$ V $+ 0.0591$ pH   (from part c)

$0.285 = 0.242 + 0.0591$ pH, pH $= 0.73$

f. Primarily the reason is convenience. It is inconvenient to deal with H_2 gas and particularly to keep P_{H_2} constant. Gas cylinders are bulky and $H_2(g)$ presents a fire and explosion hazard.

87. a. $E_{cell} = E_{ref} + 0.05916$ pH, 0.480 V $= 0.250$ V $+ 0.05916$ pH

pH $= \dfrac{0.480 - 0.250}{0.05916} = 3.888$; Uncertainty $= \pm 1$ mV $= \pm 0.001$ V

$pH_{max} = \dfrac{0.481 - 0.250}{0.05916} = 3.905$; $pH_{min} = \dfrac{0.479 - 0.250}{0.05916} = 3.871$

So if the uncertainty in potential is ± 0.001 V, then the uncertainty in pH is ± 0.017 or about ± 0.02 pH units. For this measurement, $[H^+] = 10^{-3.888} = 1.29 \times 10^{-4}$ M. For an error of $+1$ mV, $[H^+] = 10^{-3.905} = 1.24 \times 10^{-4}$ M. For an error of -1 mV, $[H^+] = 10^{-3.871} = 1.35 \times 10^{-4}$ M. So the uncertainty in $[H^+]$ is $\pm 0.06 \times 10^{-4}$ M $= \pm 6 \times 10^{-6}$ M.

b. From part a, we will be within ± 0.02 pH units if we measure the potential to the nearest ± 0.001 V (1 mV).

88. a. $\Delta G° = \Sigma n_p \Delta G°_{f, products} - \Sigma n_r \Delta G°_{f, reactants} = 2(-480.) + 3(86) - [3(-40.)] = -582$ kJ

From oxidation numbers, n = 6. $\Delta G° = -nFE°$, $E° = \dfrac{-\Delta G°}{nF} = \dfrac{-(-582,000 \text{ J})}{6(96,485) \text{ C}} = 1.01$ V

$\log K = \dfrac{nE°}{0.0591} = \dfrac{6(1.01)}{0.0591} = 102.538$, K $= 10^{102.538} = 3.45 \times 10^{102}$

b.
$$3 \times (2 \text{ e}^- + Ag_2S \rightarrow 2 \text{ Ag} + S^{2-}) \qquad\qquad E°_{Ag_2S} = ?$$
$$2 \times (Al \rightarrow Al^{3+} + 3 \text{ e}^-) \qquad\qquad\qquad -E°_a = 1.66 \text{ V}$$

$$3 \text{ Ag}_2S(s) + 2 \text{ Al}(s) \rightarrow 6 \text{ Ag}(s) + 3 \text{ S}^{2-}(aq) + 2 \text{ Al}^{3+}(aq) \qquad E°_{cell} = 1.01 \text{ V} = E°_{Ag_2S} + 1.66$$

$E°_{Ag_2S} = 1.01 - 1.66 = -0.65$ V

89. $2 \text{ Ag}^+(aq) + \text{Cu}(s) \rightarrow \text{Cu}^{2+}(aq) + 2 \text{ Ag}(s)$ $E°_{cell} = 0.80 - 0.34$ V $= 0.46$ V; A galvanic cell produces a voltage as the forward reaction occurs. Any stress that increases the tendency of the forward reaction to occur will increase the cell potential, while a stress that decreases the tendency of the forward reaction to occur will decrease the cell potential.

a. Added Cu^{2+} (a product ion) will decrease the tendency of the forward reaction to occur which will decrease the cell potential.

b. Added NH_3 removes Cu^{2+} in the form of $Cu(NH_3)_4{}^{2+}$. As a product ion is removed, this will increase the tendency of the forward reaction to occur which will increase the cell potential.

c. Added Cl^- removes Ag^+ in the form of $AgCl(s)$. As a reactant ion is removed, this will decrease the tendency of the forward reaction to occur which will decrease the cell potential.

d. $Q_1 = \dfrac{[Cu^{2+}]_o}{[Ag^+]_o^2}$; As the volume of solution is doubled, each concentration is halved.

$$Q_2 = \frac{1/2\,[Cu^{2+}]_o}{(1/2\,[Ag^+]_o)^2} = \frac{2[Cu^{2+}]_o}{[Ag^+]_o^2} = 2\,Q_1$$

The reaction quotient is doubled as the concentrations are halved. Since reactions are spontaneous when $Q < K$ and since Q increases when the solution volume doubles, then the reaction is closer to equilibrium which will decrease the cell potential.

e. Since $Ag(s)$ is not a reactant in this spontaneous reaction and since solids do not appear in the reaction quotient expressions, then replacing the silver electrode with a platinum electrode will have no effect on the cell potential.

90.   a.

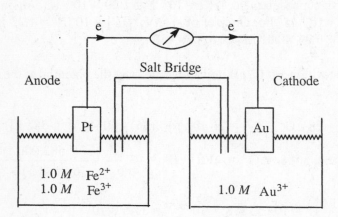

b. $Au^{3+}(aq) + 3\,Fe^{2+}(aq) \rightarrow 3\,Fe^{3+}(aq) + Au(s)$ $E^\circ_{cell} = 1.50 - 0.77 = 0.73\ V$

$$E_{cell} = E^\circ_{cell} - \frac{0.0591}{n}\ \log Q = 0.73\ V - \frac{0.0591}{3}\ \log \frac{[Fe^{3+}]^3}{[Au^{3+}]\,[Fe^{2+}]^3}$$

Since $[Fe^{3+}] = [Fe^{2+}] = 1.0\ M$: $0.31\ V = 0.73\ V - \dfrac{0.0591}{3}\ \log \dfrac{1}{[Au^{3+}]}$

$$\frac{3(-0.42)}{0.0591} = -\log \frac{1}{[Au^{3+}]}, \quad \log [Au^{3+}] = -21.32, \quad [Au^{3+}] = 10^{-21.32} = 4.8 \times 10^{-22}\ M$$

$Au^{3+} + 4\,Cl^- \rightleftharpoons AuCl_4{}^-$; Since the equilibrium Au^{3+} concentration is so small, assume $[AuCl_4{}^-]$ $\approx [Au^{3+}]_o \approx 1.0\ M$, i.e., assume K is large so that the reaction essentially goes to completion.

$$K = \frac{[AuCl_4^-]}{[Au^{3+}]\,[Cl^-]^4} = \frac{1.0}{(4.8 \times 10^{-22})\,(0.10)^4} = 2.1 \times 10^{25};\ \text{Assumption good (K is large).}$$

Challenge Problems

91.   a. $Zn(s) + Cu^{2+}(aq) \rightarrow Zn^{2+}(aq) + Cu(s)$ $E^{\circ}_{cell} = 1.10$ V; $E_{cell} = 1.10$ V $- \dfrac{0.0591}{2} \log \dfrac{[Zn^{2+}]}{[Cu^{2+}]}$

$E_{cell} = 1.10$ V $- \dfrac{0.0591}{2} \log \dfrac{0.10}{2.50} = 1.10$ V $- (-0.041$ V$) = 1.14$ V

   b. 10.0 h $\times \dfrac{60 \text{ min}}{h} \times \dfrac{60 \text{ s}}{\text{min}} \times \dfrac{10.0 \text{ C}}{s} \times \dfrac{1 \text{ mol e}^-}{96{,}485 \text{ C}} \times \dfrac{1 \text{ mol Cu}}{2 \text{ mol e}^-} = 1.87$ mol Cu produced

The Cu^{2+} concentration decreases by 1.87 mol/L and the Zn^{2+} concentration will increase by 1.87 mol/L.

$[Cu^{2+}] = 2.50 - 1.87 = 0.63$ M; $[Zn^{2+}] = 0.10 + 1.87 = 1.97$ M

$E_{cell} = 1.10$ V $- \dfrac{0.0591}{2} \log \dfrac{1.97}{0.63} = 1.10$ V $- 0.015$ V $= 1.09$ V

   c. 1.87 mol Zn consumed $\times \dfrac{65.38 \text{ g Zn}}{\text{mol Zn}} = 122$ g Zn; Mass of electrode $= 200. - 122 = 78$ g Zn

1.87 mol Cu formed $\times \dfrac{63.55 \text{ g Cu}}{\text{mol Cu}} = 119$ g Cu; Mass of electrode $= 200. + 119 = 319$ g Cu

   d.   Three things could possibly cause this battery to go dead:

1. All of the Zn is consumed.
2. All of the Cu^{2+} is consumed.
3. Equilibrium is reached ($E_{cell} = 0$).

We began with 2.50 mol Cu^{2+} and 200. g Zn $\times$ 1 mol Zn/65.38 g Zn = 3.06 mol Zn. Cu^{2+} is the limiting reagent and will run out first. To react all the Cu^{2+} requires:

2.50 mol $Cu^{2+} \times \dfrac{2 \text{ mol e}^-}{\text{mol Cu}^{2+}} \times \dfrac{96{,}485 \text{ C}}{\text{mol e}^-} \times \dfrac{1 \text{ s}}{10.0 \text{ C}} \times \dfrac{1 \text{ h}}{3600 \text{ s}} = 13.4$ h

For equilibrium to be reached: $E = 0 = 1.10$ V $- \dfrac{0.0591}{2} \log \dfrac{[Zn^{2+}]}{[Cu^{2+}]}$

$\dfrac{[Zn^{2+}]}{[Cu^{2+}]} = K = 10^{2(1.10)/0.0591} = 1.68 \times 10^{37}$

This is such a large equilibrium constant that virtually all of the Cu^{2+} must react to reach equilibrium. So, the battery will go dead in 13.4 hours.

92.

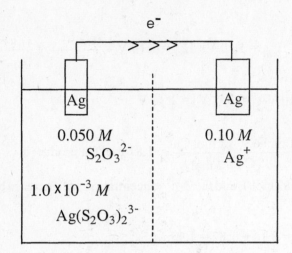

$E° = 0$ (concentration cell)

$$E = E° - \frac{0.0591}{1} \log \frac{(Ag^+)_{anode}}{0.10\ M} = 0.76\ V$$

$[Ag^+]_{anode} = 1.4 \times 10^{-14}\ M$

Anode   Cathode

$$K = \frac{[Ag(S_2O_3)_2^{3-}]}{[Ag^+][S_2O_3^{2-}]^2} = \frac{(1.0 \times 10^{-3})}{(1.4 \times 10^{-14})(0.050)^2} = 2.9 \times 10^{13}$$

93.   a. $E_{meas} = E_{ref} - 0.05916 \log [F^-]$, $0.4462 = 0.2420 - 0.05916 \log [F^-]$

$\log [F^-] = -3.4517$, $[F^-] = 3.534 \times 10^{-4}\ M$

b.   pH = 9.00; pOH = 5.00; $[OH^-] = 1.0 \times 10^{-5}\ M$

$0.4462 = 0.2420 - 0.05916 \log [[F^-] + 10.0(1.0 \times 10^{-5})]$

$\log ([F^-] + 1.0 \times 10^{-4}) = -3.452$, $[F^-] + 1.0 \times 10^{-4} = 3.532 \times 10^{-4}$, $[F^-] = 2.5 \times 10^{-4}\ M$

True value is 2.5×10^{-4} and by ignoring the $[OH^-]$ we would say $[F^-]$ was 3.5×10^{-4}, so:

$$\% \text{ Error} = \frac{1.0 \times 10^{-4}}{2.5 \times 10^{-4}} \times 100 = 40.\ \%$$

c. $[F^-] = 2.5 \times 10^{-4}\ M$; $\dfrac{[F^-]}{k[OH^-]} = 50. = \dfrac{2.5 \times 10^{-4}}{10.0[OH^-]}$

$[OH^-] = \dfrac{2.5 \times 10^{-4}}{10. \times 50.} = 5.0 \times 10^{-7}\ M$; pOH = 6.30; pH = 7.70

d. $HF \rightleftharpoons H^+ + F^-$ $K_a = \dfrac{[H^+][F^-]}{[HF]} = 7.2 \times 10^{-4}$; If 99% is F^-, then $[F^-]/[HF] = 99$.

$99[H^+] = 7.2 \times 10^{-4}$, $[H^+] = 7.3 \times 10^{-6}\ M$; pH = 5.14

e.   The buffer controls the pH so that there is little HF present and that there is little response to OH^-. Typically a buffer of pH = 6.0 is used.

94. $Zn + 2 Ag^+ \rightarrow Zn^{2+} + 2 Ag$

$E° = 1.56$ V (from Table 11.1) $Zn \rightarrow Zn^{2+} + 2 e^-$ $E° = 0.76$ V
$Ag^+ + e^- \rightarrow Ag$ $E° = 0.80$ V

$E = E° - \dfrac{0.0591}{2} \log K$; $\log K = \dfrac{2 E°}{0.0591}$, $K = 6.2 \times 10^{52}$

95.   a. $3 \times (e^- + 2 H^+ + NO_3^- \rightarrow NO_2 + H_2O)$ $E_c° = 0.775$ V
$2 H_2O + NO \rightarrow NO_3^- + 4 H^+ + 3 e^-$ $-E_a° = -0.957$ V

$2 H^+(aq) + 2 NO_3^-(aq) + NO(g) \rightarrow 3 NO_2(g) + H_2O(l)$ $E_{cell}° = -0.182$ V $K = ?$

$\log K = \dfrac{nE°}{0.0591} = \dfrac{3(-0.182)}{0.0591} = -9.239$, $K = 10^{-9.239} = 5.77 \times 10^{-10}$

b.   Let C = concentration of HNO_3 = $[H^+]$ = $[NO_3^-]$

$5.77 \times 10^{-10} = \dfrac{P_{NO_2}^3}{P_{NO} \times [H^+]^2 \times [NO_3^-]^2} = \dfrac{P_{NO_2}^3}{P_{NO} \times C^4}$

If 0.20 mol % NO_2 and $P_{tot} = 1.00$ atm:

$P_{NO_2} = \dfrac{0.20 \text{ mol } NO_2}{100. \text{ mol total}} \times 1.00 \text{ atm} = 2.0 \times 10^{-3}$ atm; $P_{NO} = 1.00 - 0.0020 = 1.00$ atm

$5.77 \times 10^{-10} = \dfrac{(2.0 \times 10^{-3})^3}{(1.00) C^4}$, $C = 1.9$ M HNO_3

96. $2 Ag^+ + Ni \rightarrow Ni^{2+} + Ag$;   The cell is dead at equilibrium.

$E° = 1.03$ V: from Table 11.1 $Ag^+ + e^- \rightarrow Ag$ $E° = 0.80$ V
$Ni \rightarrow Ni^{2+} + 2 e^-$ $E° = 0.23$ V

$0 = 1.03 \text{ V} - \dfrac{0.0591}{2} \log K$, $K = 7.2 \times 10^{34}$

K is very large. Push reaction to the right.

$2Ag^+ + Ni \rightarrow Ni^{2+} + Ag$

Before   1.0 M 1.0 M
After   0 M 1.5 M

Now allow to reach equilibrium.

$2Ag^+ + Ni \rightleftharpoons Ni^{2+} + Ag$

Initial   0   1.5 M
Change   +2x   -x
Equil.   2x   1.5 - x

$$\frac{1.5 - x}{(2x)^2} = 7.2 \times 10^{34} \approx \frac{1.5}{(2x)^2}$$

$$x = 2.3 \times 10^{-18} M \quad [Ag^+] = 2x = 4.6 \times 10^{-18} M$$

$$[Ni^{2+}] = 1.5 M$$

97. $2 H^+ + 2 e^- \rightarrow H_2$ $E_c^\circ = 0.000 V$

      $Fe \rightarrow Fe^{2+} + 2e^-$ $-E_a^\circ = -(-0.440V)$

___

$2 H^+(aq) + Fe(s) \rightarrow H_2(g) + Fe^{3+}(aq)$ $E_{cell}^\circ = 0.440 V$

$$E_{cell} = E_{cell}^\circ - \frac{0.0591}{n} \log Q, \text{ where } n = 2 \text{ and } Q = \frac{P_{H_2} \times [Fe^{3+}]}{[H^+]^2}$$

To determine K_a for the weak acid, first use the electrochemical data to determine the H^+ concentration in the half-cell containing the weak acid.

$$0.333V = 0.440 V - \frac{0.0591}{2} \log \frac{1.00 \text{ atm} (1.00 \times 10^{-3} M)}{[H^+]^2}$$

$$\frac{0.107(2)}{0.0591} = \log \frac{1.00 \times 10^{-3}}{[H^+]^2}, \quad \frac{1.00 \times 10^{-3}}{[H^+]^2} = 10^{3.621} = 4.18 \times 10^3, \quad [H^+] = 4.89 \times 10^{-4} M$$

Now we can solve for the K_a value of the weak acid HA through the normal set-up for a weak acid problem.

	HA	$\rightleftharpoons$	H^+	+	A^-	$K_a = \dfrac{[H^+][A^-]}{[HA]}$
Initial	1.00 M		~0		0	
Equil.	1.00 $- x$		x		x	

$$K_a = \frac{x^2}{1.00 - x} \text{ where } x = [H^+] = 4.89 \times 10^{-4} M, \quad K_a = \frac{(4.89 \times 10^{-4})^2}{1.00 - 4.89 \times 10^{-4}} = 2.39 \times 10^{-7}$$

98.

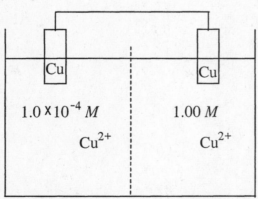

a. $E^\circ = 0$ (concentration cell), $E = 0 - \dfrac{0.0591}{2} \log \left(\dfrac{1.0 \times 10^{-4}}{1.00} \right)$, $E = 0.12 V$

b. $Cu^{2+} + 4 NH_3 \rightleftharpoons Cu(NH_3)_4^{2+}$; Since $[Cu^{2+}] \ll [NH_3]$, then $[NH_3]_0 = 2.0 \, M \, (= [NH_3]_{eq.})$

Also, overall $K = K_1 \cdot K_2 \cdot K_3 \cdot K_4 = 1.0 \times 10^{13}$, so reaction lies heavily to the right.

$$Cu^{2+} \quad + \quad 4 NH_3 \quad \rightarrow \quad Cu(NH_3)_4^{2+}$$

Before $1.0 \times 10^{-4} \, M$ $2.0 \, M$ 0
After 0 2.0 1.0×10^{-4}

Now allow to reach equilibrium.

$$Cu^{2+} \quad + \quad 4 NH_3 \quad \rightarrow \quad Cu(NH_3)_4^{2+}$$

Initial 0 $2.0 \, M$ $1.0 \times 10^{-4} \, M$
Equil. $+x$ $2.0 + 4x$ $-x$

$$\frac{(1.0 \times 10^{-4} - x)}{x \, (2.0 + 4x)^4} \approx \frac{1.0 \times 10^{-4}}{x \, (2.0)^4} = 1.0 \times 10^{13}, \quad x = [Cu^{2+}] = 6.3 \times 10^{-19} \, M$$

Thus, $E = 0 - \dfrac{0.0591}{2} \log \left(\dfrac{6.3 \times 10^{-19}}{1.00} \right)$, $E = 0.54 \, V$

99.   a. $(Ag^+ + e^- \rightarrow Ag) \times 2$ $\qquad\qquad E_c^\circ = 0.80 \, V$
$\qquad\qquad\qquad Cu \rightarrow Cu^{2+} + 2 e^- \qquad\qquad -E_a^\circ = -0.34 \, V$

$$\overline{2 \, Ag^+(aq) + Cu(s) \rightarrow 2 \, Ag(s) + Cu^{2+}(aq) \qquad E_{cell}^\circ = 0.46 \, V}$$

$$E_{cell} = E_{cell}^\circ - \frac{0.0591}{n} \log Q \text{ where } n = 2 \text{ and } Q = \frac{[Cu^{2+}]}{[Ag^+]^2}$$

To calculate E_{cell}, we need to use the K_{sp} data to determine $[Ag^+]$.

$$AgCl(s) \quad \rightleftharpoons \quad Ag^+(aq) \quad + \quad Cl^-(aq) \quad K_{sp} = 1.6 \times 10^{-10} = [Ag^+][Cl^-]$$

Initial s = solubility (mol/L) 0 0
Equil. s s

$K_{sp} = 1.6 \times 10^{-10} = s^2$, $s = [Ag^+] = 1.3 \times 10^{-5}$ mol/L

$$E_{cell} = 0.46 \, V - \frac{0.0591}{2} \log \frac{2.0}{(1.3 \times 10^{-5})^2} = 0.46 \, V - 0.30 = 0.16 \, V$$

b. $Cu^{2+}(aq) + 4 \, NH_3(aq) \rightleftharpoons Cu(NH_4)_4^{2+}(aq) \qquad K = 1.0 \times 10^{13} = \dfrac{[Cu(NH_3)_4^{2+}]}{[Cu^{2+}][NH_3]^4}$

Since K is very large for the formation of $Cu(NH_3)_4^{2+}$, then the forward reaction is dominant. At equilibrium, essentially all of the 2.0 M Cu^{2+} will react to form 2.0 M $Cu(NH_3)_4^{2+}$. This reaction requires 8.0 M NH_3 to react with all of the Cu^{2+} in the balanced equation. Therefore, the mol of NH_3 added to 1.0 L solution will be larger than 8.0 mol since some NH_3 must be present at equilibrium. In order to calculate how much NH_3 is present at equilibrium, we need to use the electrochemical data to determine the Cu^{2+} concentration.

$$E_{cell} = E_{cell}^{\circ} - \frac{0.0591}{n} \log Q, \quad 0.52 \text{ V} = 0.46 \text{ V} - \frac{0.0591}{2} \log \frac{[Cu^{2+}]}{(1.3 \times 10^{-5})^2}$$

$$\log \frac{[Cu^{2+}]}{(1.3 \times 10^{-5})^2} = \frac{-0.06(2)}{0.0591} = -2.03, \quad \frac{[Cu^{2+}]}{(1.3 \times 10^{-5})^2} = 10^{-2.03} = 9.3 \times 10^{-3}$$

$[Cu^{2+}] = 1.6 \times 10^{-12} = 2 \times 10^{-12} \ M$ (We carried extra significant figures in the calculation.)

Note: Our assumption that the 2.0 M Cu^{2+} essentially reacts to completion is excellent as only $2 \times 10^{-12} \ M$ Cu^{2+} remains after this reaction. Now we can solve for the equilibrium $[NH_3]$.

$$K = 1.0 \times 10^{13} = \frac{[Cu(NH_3)_4^{2+}]}{[Cu^{2+}][NH_3]^4} = \frac{(2.0)}{(2 \times 10^{-12})[NH_3]^4}, \quad [NH_3] = 0.6 \ M$$

Since 1.0 L of solution is present, then 0.6 mol NH_3 remains at equilibrium. The total mol of NH_3 added is 0.6 mol plus the 8.0 mol NH_3 necessary to form 2.0 M $Cu(NH_3)_4^{2+}$. Therefore, 8.0 + 0.6 = 8.6 mol NH_3 were added.

100. $(Ag^+ + e^- \rightarrow Ag) \times 2 \qquad\qquad E^{\circ} = 0.80 \text{ V}$

   $Pb \rightarrow Pb^{2+} + 2 e^- \qquad -E^{\circ} = -(-0.13)$

$2 Ag^+ + Pb \rightarrow 2 Ag + Pb^{2+} \quad E_{cell}^{\circ} = 0.93 \text{ V}$

$$E = E^{\circ} - \frac{0.0591}{n} \log \frac{[Pb^{2+}]}{[Ag^+]^2}, \quad 0.83 \text{ V} = 0.93 \text{ V} - \frac{0.0591}{2} \log \frac{(1.8)}{[Ag^+]^2}$$

$$\log \frac{(1.8)}{[Ag^+]^2} = \frac{0.10(2)}{0.0591} = 3.4, \quad \frac{(1.8)}{[Ag^+]^2} = 10^{3.4}, \quad [Ag^+] = 0.027 \ M$$

$$Ag_2SO_4(s) \quad \rightleftharpoons \quad 2 Ag^+(aq) \ + \ SO_4^{2-}(aq) \ \ K_{sp} = [Ag^+]^2[SO_4^{2-}]$$

Initial s = solubility (mol/L)   0   0

Equil. $2s$ s

From problem: $2s = 0.027 \ M$, $s = 0.027/2$

$K_{sp} = (2s)^2(s) = (0.027)^2(0.027/2) = 9.8 \times 10^{-6}$

101.   a. From Table 11.1: $2 H_2O + 2 e^- \rightarrow H_2 + 2 OH^-$ $E° = -0.83$ V

$$E°_{cell} = E°_{H_2O} - E°_{Zr} = -0.83 \text{ V} + 2.36 \text{ V} = 1.53 \text{ V}$$

Yes, the reduction of H_2O to H_2 by Zr is spontaneous at standard conditions since $E°_{cell} > 0$.

     b. $(2 H_2O + 2 e^- \rightarrow H_2 + 2 OH^-) \times 2$
             $Zr + 4 OH^- \rightarrow ZrO_2 \cdot H_2O + H_2O + 4 e^-$

          $3 H_2O(l) + Zr(s) \rightarrow 2 H_2(g) + ZrO_2 \cdot H_2O(s)$

     c. $\Delta G° = -nFE° = -(4 \text{ mol } e^-)(96,485 \text{ C/mol } e^-)(1.53 \text{ J/C}) = -5.90 \times 10^5 \text{ J} = -590. \text{ kJ}$

$$E = E° - \frac{0.0591}{n} \log Q; \text{ At equilibrium, } E = 0 \text{ and } Q = K.$$

$$E° = \frac{0.0591}{n} \log K, \ \log K = \frac{4(1.53)}{0.0591} = 104, \ K \approx 10^{104}$$

     d. $1.00 \times 10^3 \text{ kg Zr} \times \dfrac{1000 \text{ g}}{\text{kg}} \times \dfrac{1 \text{ mol Zr}}{91.22 \text{ g Zr}} \times \dfrac{2 \text{ mol } H_2}{\text{mol Zr}} = 2.19 \times 10^4 \text{ mol } H_2$

$$2.19 \times 10^4 \text{ mol } H_2 \times \frac{2.016 \text{ g } H_2}{\text{mol } H_2} = 4.42 \times 10^4 \text{ g } H_2$$

$$V = \frac{nRT}{P} = \frac{(2.19 \times 10^4 \text{ mol}) (0.08206 \text{ L atm mol}^{-1}\text{K}^{-1}) (1273 \text{ K})}{1.0 \text{ atm}} = 2.3 \times 10^6 \text{ L } H_2$$

     e.   Probably yes; Less radioactivity overall was released by venting the H_2 than what would have been released if the H_2 had exploded inside the reactor (as happened at Chernobyl). Neither alternative is pleasant, but venting the radioactive hydrogen is the less unpleasant of the two alternatives.

Marathon Problems

102   a. $Cu^{2+} + 2 e^- \rightarrow Cu$ $E°_c = 0.34$ V
                     $V \rightarrow V^{2+} + 2 e^-$ $-E°_a = 1.20$ V

          $Cu^{2+}(aq) + V(s) \rightarrow Cu(s) + V^{2+}(aq)$ $E°_{cell} = 1.54$ V

$$E_{cell} = E°_{cell} - \frac{0.0591}{n} \log Q \text{ where } n = 2 \text{ and } Q = \frac{[V^{2+}]}{[Cu^{2+}]} = \frac{[V^{2+}]}{1.00 \ M}$$

To determine E_{cell}, we must know the initial $[V^{2+}]$, which can be determined from the stoichiometric point data. At the stoichiometric point, mol H_2EDTA^{2-} added = mol V^{2+} present initially.

$$\text{mol } V^{2+} \text{ present initially} = 0.5000 \text{ L} \times \frac{0.0800 \text{ mol } H_2EDTA^{2-}}{L} \times \frac{1 \text{ mol } V^{2+}}{\text{mol } H_2EDTA^{2-}}$$

$$= 0.0400 \text{ mol } V^{2+}$$

$$[V^{2+}]_o = \frac{0.0400 \text{ mol } V^{2+}}{1.00 \text{ L}} = 0.0400 \ M$$

$$E_{cell} = 1.54 \text{ V} - \frac{0.0591}{2} \log \frac{0.0400}{1.00} = 1.54 \text{ V} - (-0.0413) = 1.58 \text{ V}$$

b. Use the electrochemical data to solve for the equilibrium $[V^{2+}]$.

$$E_{cell} = E^\circ_{cell} - \frac{0.0591}{n} \log \frac{[V^{2+}]}{[Cu^{2+}]}, \quad 1.98 \text{ V} = 1.54 \text{ V} - \frac{0.0591}{2} \log \frac{[V^{2+}]}{1.00 \ M}$$

$$[V^{2+}] = 10^{-(0.44)(2)/0.0591} = 1.3 \times 10^{-15} \ M$$

$$H_2EDTA^{2-}(aq) + V^{2+}(aq) \rightleftharpoons VEDTA^{2-}(aq) + 2 H^+(aq) \quad K = \frac{[VEDTA^{2-}][H^+]^2}{[H_2EDTA^{2-}][V^{2+}]}$$

In this titration reaction, equal mol of V^{2+} and H_2EDTA^{2-} are reacted at the stoichiometric point. Therefore, equal mol of both reactants must be present at equilibrium, so $[H_2EDTA^{2-}] = [V^{2+}]$ $= 1.3 \times 10^{-15} \ M$. In addition, since $[V^{2+}]$ at equilibrium is very small as compared to the initial $0.0400 \ M$ concentration, then the reaction essentially goes to completion. The mol of $VEDTA^{2-}$ produced will equal the mol of V^{2+} reacted ($= 0.0400$ mol). At equilibrium, $[VEDTA^{2-}] = 0.0400$ mol/(1.00 L + 0.5000 L) $= 0.0267 \ M$. Finally, since we have a buffer solution, then the pH is assumed not to change so $[H^+] = 10^{-10.00} = 1.0 \times 10^{-10} \ M$. Calculating K for the reaction:

$$K = \frac{[VEDTA^{2-}][H^+]^2}{[H_2EDTA^{2-}][V^{2+}]} = \frac{(0.0267)(1.0 \times 10^{-10})^2}{(1.3 \times 10^{-15})(1.3 \times 10^{-15})} = 1.6 \times 10^8$$

c. At the halfway point, 250.0 mL of H_2EDTA^{2-} has been added to 1.00 L of $0.0400 \ M \ V^{2+}$. Exactly one-half of the 0.0400 mol of V^{2+} present initially has been converted into $VEDTA^{2-}$. Therefore, 0.0200 mol of V^{2+} remains in 1.00 + 0.2500 = 1.25 L solution.

$$E_{cell} = 1.54 \text{ V} - \frac{0.0591}{2} \log \frac{[V^{2+}]}{[Cu^{2+}]} = 1.54 - \frac{0.0591}{2} \log \frac{(0.0200/1.25)}{1.00}$$

$$E_{cell} = 1.54 - (-0.0531) = 1.59 \text{ V}$$

103. Begin by choosing any reduction potential as 0.00 V. For example, let's assume

$$B^{2+} + 2 \text{ e-} \rightarrow B \quad E^\circ = 0.00 \text{ V}$$

Now, since, for example, when B/B^{2+}; E/E^{2+} are together as a cell, E = 0.81 V.

$$E^{2+} + 2 \text{ e}^- \rightarrow E \text{ must have a potential of -0.81 V or 0.81 V.}$$

Using this type of reasoning, we can get the table:

$$B^{2+} + 2\ e^- \rightarrow B \qquad 0.00\ V$$
$$E^{2+} + 2\ e^- \rightarrow E \qquad -0.81\ V$$
$$D^{2+} + 2\ e^- \rightarrow D \qquad 0.19\ V$$
$$C^{2+} + 2\ e^- \rightarrow C \qquad -0.94\ V$$
$$A^{2+} + 2\ e^- \rightarrow A \qquad -0.53\ V$$

Arrange this from largest to smallest:

$$D^{2+} + 2\ e^- \rightarrow D \qquad 0.19\ V$$
$$B^{2+} + 2\ e^- \rightarrow B \qquad 0.00\ V$$
$$A^{2+} + 2\ e^- \rightarrow A \qquad -0.53\ V$$
$$E^{2+} + 2\ e^- \rightarrow E \qquad -0.81\ V$$
$$C^{2+} + 2\ e^- \rightarrow C \qquad -0.94\ V$$

So, $A^{2+} + 2\ e^- \rightarrow A$ is in the middle. Let's call this 0.00 V. We get:

$$D^{2+} + 2\ e^- \rightarrow D \qquad 0.72\ V$$
$$B^{2+} + 2\ e^- \rightarrow B \qquad 0.53\ V$$
$$A^{2+} + 2\ e^- \rightarrow A \qquad 0.00\ V$$
$$E^{2+} + 2\ e^- \rightarrow E \qquad -0.28\ V$$
$$C^{2+} + 2\ e^- \rightarrow C \qquad -0.41\ V$$

Of course, we can also get:

$$C^{2+} + 2\ e^- \rightarrow C \qquad 0.41\ V$$
$$E^{2+} + 2\ e^- \rightarrow E \qquad 0.28\ V$$
$$A^{2+} + 2\ e^- \rightarrow A \qquad 0.00\ V$$
$$B^{2+} + 2\ e^- \rightarrow B \qquad -0.53\ V$$
$$D^{2+} + 2\ e^- \rightarrow D \qquad -0.72\ V$$

One way to determine which table is correct is to add metal C to a solution with D^{2+} and metal D to a solution with C^{2+}. If D comes out of solution, the first table is correct. If C comes out of solution, the second table is correct.

CHAPTER TWELVE

QUANTUM MECHANICS AND ATOMIC THEORY

Light and Matter

21. Planck found that heated bodies only give off certain frequencies of light. Einstein's analysis of the photoelectric effect used Planck's concepts suggesting that electromagnetic radiation is "quantized".

22. $\nu = \dfrac{c}{\lambda} = \dfrac{2.998 \times 10^8 \text{ m/s}}{780. \times 10^{-9} \text{ m}} = 3.84 \times 10^{14} \text{ s}^{-1}$; $E = h\nu = 2.54 \times 10^{-19}$ J where h = 6.626×10^{-34} J s

23. $\nu = \dfrac{c}{\lambda} = \dfrac{3.00 \times 10^8 \text{ m/s}}{1.0 \times 10^{-2} \text{ m}} = 3.0 \times 10^{10} \text{ s}^{-1}$

    $E = h\nu = 6.63 \times 10^{-34} \text{ J s} \times 3.0 \times 10^{10} \text{ s}^{-1} = 2.0 \times 10^{-23}$ J/photon

    $\dfrac{2.0 \times 10^{-23} \text{ J}}{\text{photon}} \times \dfrac{6.02 \times 10^{23} \text{ photons}}{\text{mol}} = 12$ J/mol

24. The wavelength is the distance between consecutive wave peaks. Wave a shows 4 wavelengths and wave b shows 8 wavelengths.

    Wave a: $\lambda = \dfrac{1.6 \times 10^{-3} \text{ m}}{4} = 4.0 \times 10^{-4}$ m

    Wave b: $\lambda = \dfrac{1.6 \times 10^{-3} \text{ m}}{8} = 2.0 \times 10^{-4}$ m

    Wave a has the longer wavelength. Since frequency and photon energy are both inversely proportional to wavelength, then wave b will have the higher frequency and larger photon energy since it has the shorter wavelength.

    $\nu = \dfrac{c}{\lambda} = \dfrac{3.00 \times 10^8 \text{ m/s}}{2.0 \times 10^{-4} \text{ m}} = 1.5 \times 10^{12} \text{ s}^{-1}$

    $E = \dfrac{hc}{\lambda} = \dfrac{6.63 \times 10^{-34} \text{ J s} \times 3.00 \times 10^8 \text{ m/s}}{2.0 \times 10^{-4} \text{ m}} = 9.9 \times 10^{-22}$ J

    Since both waves are examples of electromagnetic radiation, then both waves travel at the same speed, c, the speed of light. From Figure 12.3 of the text, both of these waves represent infrared electromagnetic radiation.

25. 99.5 MHz = 99.5×10^6 Hz = 99.5×10^6 s^{-1}; $\lambda = \dfrac{c}{\nu} = \dfrac{2.998 \times 10^8 \text{ m/s}}{99.5 \times 10^6 \text{ s}^{-1}} = 3.01$ m

26. $E = h\nu = \dfrac{hc}{\lambda} = \dfrac{6.63 \times 10^{-34} \text{ J s} \times 3.00 \times 10^8 \text{ m/s}}{25 \text{ nm} \times \dfrac{1 \text{ m}}{1 \times 10^9 \text{ nm}}} = 8.0 \times 10^{-18}$ J/photon

$\dfrac{8.0 \times 10^{-18} \text{ J}}{\text{photon}} \times \dfrac{6.02 \times 10^{23} \text{ photons}}{\text{mol}} = 4.8 \times 10^6$ J/mol

27.   The energy needed to remove a single electron is:

$\dfrac{279.7 \text{ kJ}}{\text{mol}} \times \dfrac{1 \text{ mol}}{6.0221 \times 10^{23}} = 4.645 \times 10^{-22} \text{ kJ} = 4.645 \times 10^{-19}$ J

$E = \dfrac{hc}{\lambda}, \ \lambda = \dfrac{hc}{E} = \dfrac{6.6261 \times 10^{-34} \text{ J s} \times 2.9979 \times 10^8 \text{ m/s}}{4.645 \times 10^{-19} \text{ J}} = 4.277 \times 10^{-7} \text{ m} = 427.7$ nm

28.   Referencing figure 12.3 of the text, 2.12×10^{-10} m electromagnetic radiation is X-rays.

$\lambda = \dfrac{c}{\nu} = \dfrac{2.9979 \times 10^8 \text{ m/s}}{107.1 \times 10^6 \text{ s}^{-1}} = 2.799$ m

From the wavelength calculated above, 107.1 MHz electromagnetic radiation is FM radiowaves.

$\lambda = \dfrac{hc}{E} = \dfrac{6.626 \times 10^{-34} \text{ J s} \times 2.998 \times 10^8 \text{ m/s}}{3.97 \times 10^{-19} \text{ J}} = 5.00 \times 10^{-7}$ m

The 3.97×10^{-19} J/photon electromagnetic radiation is visible (green) light.

The photon energy and frequency order will be the exact opposite of the wavelength ordering because E and ν are both inversely related to λ. From the calculated wavelengths above, the order of photon energy and frequency is:

    FM radiowaves < visible (green) light < X-rays
    longest λ   shortest λ
    lowest ν   highest ν
    smallest E   largest E

29.   The energy to remove a single electron is:

$\dfrac{208.4 \text{ kJ}}{\text{mol}} \times \dfrac{1 \text{ mol}}{6.022 \times 10^{23}} = 3.461 \times 10^{-22} \text{ kJ} = 3.461 \times 10^{-19} \text{ J} = E_w$

Energy of 254 nm light is:

$E = \dfrac{hc}{\lambda} = \dfrac{(6.626 \times 10^{-34} \text{ J s})\,(2.998 \times 10^8 \text{ m/s})}{254 \times 10^{-9} \text{ m}} = 7.82 \times 10^{-19}$ J

$E_{photon} = E_K + E_w, \ E_K = 7.82 \times 10^{-19} \text{ J} - 3.461 \times 10^{-19} \text{ J} = 4.36 \times 10^{-19} \text{ J} = \text{maximum KE}$

Hydrogen Atom: The Bohr Model

30.   When something is quantized, it can only have certain discrete values. In the Bohr model of the H-atom, the energy of the electron is quantized.

31.   For the H-atom (Z = 1): $E_n = -2.178 \times 10^{-18}$ J/n^2; For a spectral transition, $\Delta E = E_f - E_i$:

$$\Delta E = -2.178 \times 10^{-18} \text{ J} \left(\frac{1}{n_f^2} - \frac{1}{n_i^2} \right)$$

where n_i and n_f are the levels of the initial and final states, respectively. A positive value of ΔE always corresponds to an absorption of light and a negative value of ΔE always corresponds to an emission of light.

a. $\Delta E = -2.178 \times 10^{-18} \text{ J} \left(\frac{1}{2^2} - \frac{1}{3^2} \right) = -2.178 \times 10^{-18} \text{ J} \left(\frac{1}{4} - \frac{1}{9} \right)$

$\Delta E = -2.178 \times 10^{-18} \text{ J} \times (0.2500 - 0.1111) = -3.025 \times 10^{-19}$ J

The photon of light must have precisely this energy (3.025×10^{-19} J).

$$|\Delta E| = E_{photon} = h\nu = \frac{hc}{\lambda} \text{ or } \lambda = \frac{hc}{|\Delta E|} = \frac{6.6261 \times 10^{-34} \text{ J s} \times 2.9979 \times 10^8 \text{ m/s}}{3.025 \times 10^{-19} \text{ J}}$$

$$= 6.567 \times 10^{-7} \text{ m} = 656.7 \text{ nm}$$

From Figure 12.3, this is visible electromagnetic radiation (red light).

b. $\Delta E = -2.178 \times 10^{-18} \text{ J} \left(\frac{1}{2^2} - \frac{1}{4^2} \right) = -4.084 \times 10^{-19}$ J

$$\lambda = \frac{hc}{|\Delta E|} = \frac{6.6261 \times 10^{-34} \text{ J s} \times 2.9979 \times 10^8 \text{ m/s}}{4.084 \times 10^{-19} \text{ J}} = 4.864 \times 10^{-7} \text{ m} = 486.4 \text{ nm}$$

This is visible electromagnetic radiation (green-blue light).

c. $\Delta E = -2.178 \times 10^{-18} \text{ J} \left(\frac{1}{1^2} - \frac{1}{2^2} \right) = -1.634 \times 10^{-18}$ J

$$\lambda = \frac{6.6261 \times 10^{-34} \text{ J s} \times 2.9979 \times 10^8 \text{ m/s}}{1.634 \times 10^{-18} \text{ J}} = 1.216 \times 10^{-7} \text{ m} = 121.6 \text{ nm}$$

This is ultraviolet electromagnetic radiation.

d. $\Delta E = -2.178 \times 10^{-18} \text{ J} \left(\dfrac{1}{3^2} - \dfrac{1}{4^2} \right) = -1.059 \times 10^{-19} \text{ J}$

$$\lambda = \frac{hc}{|\Delta E|} = \frac{6.6261 \times 10^{-34} \text{ J s} \times 2.9979 \times 10^8 \text{ m/s}}{1.059 \times 10^{-19} \text{ J}} = 1.876 \times 10^{-6} \text{ m or } 1876 \text{ nm}$$

This is infrared electromagnetic radiation.

32.   Ionization from n = 1 corresponds to the transition $n_i = 1 \rightarrow n_f = \infty$ where $E_\infty = 0$.

$\Delta E = E_\infty - E_1 = -E_1 = R_H \left(\dfrac{1}{1^2} \right) = R_H, \ \ \Delta E = 2.178 \times 10^{-18} \text{ J} = E_{photon}$

$\lambda = \dfrac{hc}{E} = \dfrac{(6.6261 \times 10^{-34} \text{ J s}) (2.9979 \times 10^8 \text{ m/s})}{2.178 \times 10^{-18} \text{ J}} = 9.120 \times 10^{-8} \text{ m} = 91.20 \text{ nm}$

To ionize from n = 3, $\Delta E = 0 - E_3 = R_H \left(\dfrac{1}{3^2} \right) = 2.178 \times 10^{-18} \text{ J} \left(\dfrac{1}{9} \right)$

$\Delta E = 2.420 \times 10^{-19} \text{ J}; \ \lambda = \dfrac{hc}{\Delta E} = 8.208 \times 10^{-7} \text{ m} = 820.8 \text{ nm}$

33.   a.   False;   It takes less energy to ionize an electron from n = 3 than from the ground state.

b.   True

c.   False;   The energy difference between n = 3 and n = 2 is smaller than the energy difference between n = 3 and n = 1. Thus, the wavelength of light emitted is longer for the n = 3 to n = 2 electronic transition than for the n = 3 to n = 1 transition. E and λ are inversely proportional to each other (E = hc/λ).

d.   True

e.   False;   The ground state in hydrogen is n = 1 and all other allowed energy states are called excited states; n = 2 is the first excited state and n = 3 is the second excited state.

34. $\Delta E = -2.178 \times 10^{-18} \text{ J} \left(\dfrac{1}{n_f^2} - \dfrac{1}{n_i^2} \right) = -2.178 \, 10^{-18} \text{ J} \left(\dfrac{1}{5^2} - \dfrac{1}{1^2} \right) = 2.091 \times 10^{-18} \text{ J} = E_{photon}$

$\lambda = \dfrac{hc}{E} = \dfrac{6.6261 \times 10^{-34} \text{ J s} \times 2.9979 \times 10^8 \text{ m/s}}{2.091 \times 10^{-18} \text{ J}} = 9.500 \times 10^{-8} \text{ m} = 95.00 \text{ nm}$

Since wavelength and energy are inversely related, then visible light ($\lambda \approx$ 400 - 700 nm) is not energetic enough to excite an electron in hydrogen from n = 1 to n = 5.

$\Delta E = -2.178 \times 10^{-18} \text{ J} \left(\dfrac{1}{6^2} - \dfrac{1}{2^2} \right) = 4.840 \times 10^{-19} \text{ J}$

$$\lambda = \frac{hc}{E} = \frac{6.6261 \times 10^{-34}\ J\ s \times 2.9979 \times 10^8\ m/s}{4.840 \times 10^{-19}\ J} = 4.104 \times 10^{-7}\ m = 410.4\ nm$$

Visible light with $\lambda = 410.4$ nm will excite an electron from the $n = 2$ to the $n = 6$ energy level.

35. $$|\Delta E| = E_{photon} = \frac{hc}{\lambda} = \frac{6.6261 \times 10^{-34}\ J\ s \times 2.9979 \times 10^8\ m/s}{397.2 \times 10^{-9}\ m} = 5.001 \times 10^{-19}\ J$$

$\Delta E = -5.001 \times 10^{-19}$ J since we have an emission.

$$-5.001 \times 10^{-19}\ J = E_2 - E_n = -2.178 \times 10^{-18}\ J \left(\frac{1}{2^2} - \frac{1}{n^2} \right)$$

$$0.2296 = \frac{1}{4} - \frac{1}{n^2}, \quad \frac{1}{n^2} = 0.0204, \quad n = 7$$

Wave Mechanics and Particle in a Box

36. $\lambda = \dfrac{h}{mv}$ = wavelength of particle

a.   15% of speed of light $= 0.15 \times 3.00 \times 10^8\ m/s = 4.5 \times 10^7\ m/s = v$

$$\lambda = \frac{6.63 \times 10^{-34}\ J\ s}{1.67 \times 10^{-27}\ kg \times (4.5 \times 10^7\ m/s)} = 8.8 \times 10^{-15}\ m = 8.8 \times 10^{-6}\ nm$$

Note: For units to come out, the mass must be in kg since $1\ J = \dfrac{1\ kg\ m^2}{s^2}$.

b. $$\lambda = \frac{6.63 \times 10^{-34}\ J\ s}{9.11 \times 10^{-31}\ kg \times (0.15 \times 3.00 \times 10^8\ m/s)} = 1.6 \times 10^{-11}\ m = 1.6 \times 10^{-2}\ nm$$

c. $$\lambda = \frac{h}{mv} = \frac{6.63 \times 10^{-34}\ J\ s}{0.15\ kg \times 10.0\ m/s} = 4.4 \times 10^{-34}\ m = 4.4 \times 10^{-25}\ nm$$

This number is so small that it is essentially zero. We cannot detect a wavelength this small. The meaning of this number is that we do not have to consider the wave properties of large objects.

37.   a. $$\lambda = \frac{h}{mv} = \frac{6.626 \times 10^{-34}\ J\ s}{(1.675 \times 10^{-27}\ kg)(0.0100 \times 2.998 \times 10^8\ m/s)} = 1.32 \times 10^{-13}\ m$$

b. $$\lambda = \frac{h}{mv}, \quad v = \frac{h}{\lambda m} = \frac{6.626 \times 10^{-34}\ J\ s}{(75 \times 10^{-12}\ m)(1.675 \times 10^{-27}\ kg)} = 5.3 \times 10^3\ m/s$$

38. $\lambda = \dfrac{h}{mv}$, $v = \dfrac{h}{\lambda m}$; For $\lambda = 1.0 \times 10^2$ nm $= 1.0 \times 10^{-7}$ m:

$$v = \frac{6.63 \times 10^{-34} \text{ J s}}{(9.11 \times 10^{-31} \text{ kg}) (1.0 \times 10^{-7} \text{ m})} = 7.3 \times 10^3 \text{ m/s}$$

For $\lambda = 1.0$ nm $= 1.0 \times 10^{-9}$ m: $v = \dfrac{6.63 \times 10^{-34} \text{ J s}}{(9.11 \times 10^{-31} \text{ kg}) (1.0 \times 10^{-9} \text{ m})} = 7.3 \times 10^5 \text{ m/s}$

39.   Only very small particles with a tiny mass exhibit wave and particle properties, e.g., an electron. Some evidence supporting the wave properties of matter are:

1) Electrons can be diffracted like light.

2) The electron microscope uses electrons in a fashion similar to the way in which light is used in a light microscope.

40.   Units of $\Delta E \times \Delta t = J \times s$, the same as the units of Planck's constant. Linear momentum, p, is equal to mass times velocity, $p = mv$.

Units of $\Delta p \Delta x = kg \times \dfrac{m}{s} \times m = \dfrac{kg\ m^2}{s} = \dfrac{kg\ m^2}{s^2} \times s = J \times s$

41.   a. $\Delta p = m \Delta v = 9.11 \times 10^{-31} \text{ kg} \times 0.100 \text{ m/s} = \dfrac{9.11 \times 10^{-32} \text{ kg m}}{s}$

$\Delta p \Delta x \geq \dfrac{h}{4\pi}$, $\Delta x = \dfrac{h}{4\pi \Delta p} = \dfrac{6.626 \times 10^{-34} \text{ J s}}{4 \times 3.142 \times (9.11 \times 10^{-32} \text{ kg m/s})} = 5.79 \times 10^{-4} \text{ m}$

b. $\Delta x = \dfrac{h}{4\pi \Delta p} = \dfrac{6.626 \times 10^{-34} \text{ J s}}{4 \times 3.142 \times 0.145 \text{ kg} \times 0.100 \text{ m/s}} = 3.64 \times 10^{-33} \text{ m}$

c.   The diameter of an H atom is roughly 1.0×10^{-8} cm. The uncertainty in position is much larger than the size of the atom.

d.   The uncertainty is insignificant compared to the size of a baseball.

42. $E_n = \dfrac{n^2 h^2}{8\ mL^2}$; $\Delta E = E_5 - E_1 = \dfrac{h^2}{8\ mL^2} (5^2 - 1^2) = \dfrac{24\ h^2}{8\ mL^2}$

$\Delta E = \dfrac{24(6.626 \times 10^{-34} \text{ J s})^2}{8(9.109 \times 10^{-31} \text{ kg}) (40.0 \times 10^{-12} \text{ m})^2} = 9.04 \times 10^{-16} \text{ J}$

$\Delta E = \dfrac{hc}{\lambda}$, $\lambda = \dfrac{hc}{\Delta E} = \dfrac{(6.626 \times 10^{-34} \text{ J s}) (2.998 \times 10^8 \text{ m/s})}{9.04 \times 10^{-16} \text{ J}} = 2.20 \times 10^{-10} \text{ m} = 0.220 \text{ nm}$

43. $E_n = \dfrac{n^2 h^2}{8\,mL^2}$; $\Delta E = E_3 - E_2 = \dfrac{9\,h^2}{8\,mL^2} - \dfrac{4\,h^2}{8\,mL^2} = \dfrac{5\,h^2}{8\,mL^2}$

$\Delta E = \dfrac{hc}{\lambda} = \dfrac{(6.626 \times 10^{-34}\ J\ s)\,(2.998 \times 10^8\ m/s)}{8080 \times 10^{-9}\ m} = 2.46 \times 10^{-20}\ J$

$\Delta E = 2.46 \times 10^{-20}\ J = \dfrac{5\,h^2}{8\,mL^2} = \dfrac{5(6.626 \times 10^{-34}\ J\ s)^2}{8(9.109 \times 10^{-31}\ kg)\,L^2}$, $L = 3.50 \times 10^{-9}\ m = 3.50\ nm$

44. $\Delta E = E_n - E_1 = \dfrac{n^2 h^2}{8\,mL^2} - \dfrac{1^2 h^2}{8\,mL^2}$

$\Delta E = \dfrac{hc}{\lambda} = \dfrac{(6.6261 \times 10^{-34}\ J\ s)\,(2.9979 \times 10^8\ m/s)}{1.374 \times 10^{-5}\ m} = 1.446 \times 10^{-20}\ J$

$\Delta E = 1.446 \times 10^{-20}\ J = \dfrac{n^2\,(6.626 \times 10^{-34}\ J\ s)^2}{8(9.109 \times 10^{-31}\ kg)\,(10.0 \times 10^{-9}\ m)^2} - \dfrac{(6.626 \times 10^{-34}\ J\ s)^2}{8(9.109 \times 10^{-31}\ kg)\,(10.0 \times 10^{-9}\ m)^2}$

$1.446 \times 10^{-20} = 6.02 \times 10^{-22}\,n^2 - 6.02 \times 10^{-22}$, $n^2 = \dfrac{1.506 \times 10^{-20}}{6.02 \times 10^{-22}} = 25.0$, $n = 5$

45. $E_n = \dfrac{n^2 h^2}{8\,mL^2}$;   As L increases, E_n will decrease and the spacing between energy levels will also decrease.

46.

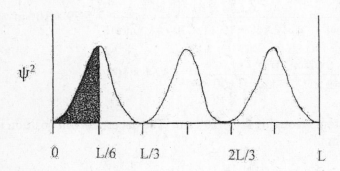

Total Area = 1;   Area of one hump = 1/3

Shaded area = 1/6 = probability of finding the electron between x = 0 and x = L/6 in a one dimensional box with n = 3.

47. $E_n = \dfrac{n^2 h^2}{8\,mL^2}$, n = 1 for ground state;   From equation, as L increases, E_n decreases.

Using numbers: 10^{-6} m box: $E_1 = \dfrac{h^2}{8\,m}\ (10^{12}\ m^{-2})$; 10^{-10} m box: $E_1 = \dfrac{h^2}{8\,m}\ (10^{20}\ m^{-2})$

As expected, the electron in the 10^{-6} m box has the lowest ground state energy.

Orbitals and Quantum Numbers

48.   n: gives the energy (it completely specifies the energy only for the H-atom or ions with one electron) and the relative size of the orbitals.

ℓ: gives the type (shape) of orbital.

m_ℓ: gives information about the direction in which the orbital is pointing in space.

49.   The possible values for n, ℓ and m_ℓ are: n = 1, 2, 3, ... ; ℓ = 0, 1, 2, ... (n - 1); m_ℓ = -ℓ ... -2, -1, 0, 1, 2, ...+ℓ;

1p: n = 1, ℓ = 1 is not possible; 3f: n = 3, ℓ = 3 is not possible; 2d: n = 2, ℓ = 2 is not possible; In all three incorrect cases, n = ℓ. The maximum value ℓ can have is n - 1, not n.

50.   b. ℓ must be smaller than n.   d.   For ℓ = 0, m_ℓ = 0 only allowed value.

f.   For ℓ = 3, m_ℓ can range from -3 to +3; thus +4 is not allowed.

g.   n cannot equal zero.   h. ℓ cannot be a negative number.

51.   No, for n = 2, the allowed values of ℓ are 0 and 1; for n = 3 the allowed values of ℓ are 0, 1, and 2.

52.   5p: three orbitals $3d_{z^2}$: one orbital   4d: five orbitals

n = 5: ℓ = 0 (1 orbital), ℓ = 1 (3 orbitals), ℓ = 2 (5 orbitals), ℓ = 3 (7 orbitals), ℓ = 4 (9 orbitals)

Total for n = 5 is 25 orbitals.

n = 4: ℓ = 0 (1), ℓ = 1 (3), ℓ = 2 (5), ℓ = 3 (7); Total for n = 4 is 16 orbitals.

53.   1p, 0 electrons ($\ell \neq$ 1 when n = 1); $6d_{x^2-y^2}$, 2 electrons (specifies one atomic orbital); 4f, 14 electrons (7 orbitals have 4f designation); $7p_y$, 2 electrons (specifies one atomic orbital); 2s, 2 electrons (specifies one atomic orbital); n = 3, 18 electrons (3s, 3p and 3d orbitals are possible; there are one 3s orbital, three 3p orbitals and five 3d orbitals).

54.   The 2p orbitals differ from each other in the direction in which they point in space. The 2p and 3p orbitals differ from each other in their size, energy and number of nodes.

55.   The diagrams of the orbitals in the text only give 90% probabilities of where the electron may reside. We can never be 100% certain of the path of the electrons due to Heisenburg's uncertainty principle.

56.

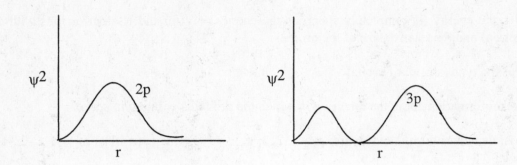

57. A nodal surface in an atomic orbital is a surface in which the probability of finding an electron is zero.

58. ψ^2 gives the probability of finding the electron in a small volume at that point.

59. For $r = a_o$ and $\theta = 0°$ ($Z = 1$ for H):

$$\psi_{2p_z} = \frac{1}{4(2\pi)^{1/2}} \left(\frac{1}{5.29 \times 10^{-11}} \right)^{3/2} (1)\, e^{-1/2} \cos 0 = 1.57 \times 10^{14}; \quad \psi^2 = 2.46 \times 10^{28}$$

For $r = a_o$ and $\theta = 90°$: $\psi_{2p_z} = 0$ since $\cos 90° = 0$; $\psi^2 = 0$

60. A node occurs when $\psi = 0$. $\psi_{300} = 0$ when $27 - 18\sigma + 2\sigma^2 = 0$.

Solving using the quadratic formula: $\sigma = \dfrac{18 \pm \sqrt{(18)^2 - 4(2)\,(27)}}{4} = \dfrac{18 \pm \sqrt{108}}{4}$

$\sigma = 7.10$ or $\sigma = 1.90$; Since $\sigma = r/a_o$, the nodes occur at $r = 7.10\, a_o = 3.76 \times 10^{-10}$ m and at $r = 1.90\, a_o = 1.01 \times 10^{-10}$ m where r is the distance from the nucleus.

Polyelectronic Atoms

61. The electrostatic energy of repulsion from Coulomb's Law will be of the form Q^2/r where Q is the charge of the electron and r is the distance between the two electrons. From the Heisenberg uncertainty principle, we cannot know precisely the path of each electron. Thus, we cannot precisely know the distance between the electrons nor the value of the electrostatic repulsions.

62. For one electron species, $E_n = \dfrac{-R_H Z^2}{n^2}$, $R_H = 2.178 \times 10^{-18}$ J and Z = atomic number (nuclear charge)

The electronic transition is $n = 1 \rightarrow n = \infty$ ($E_\infty = 0$). This is called the ionization energy (IE). Since, $E_\infty = 0$, then the IE is given by the energy of state $n = 1$ ($\Delta E = E_\infty - E_1 = -E_1 = R_H Z^2/1^2 = R_H Z^2$).

a. $IE = 2.178 \times 10^{-18} J (1)^2 = 2.178 \times 10^{-18} J/atom$

$$IE = \frac{2.178 \times 10^{-18} J}{atom} \times \frac{1 \, kJ}{1000 \, J} \times \frac{6.022 \times 10^{23} \, atoms}{mol} = 1311.6 \, kJ/mol \approx 1312 \, kJ/mol$$

The IE of heavier one electron species can be given as:

$$IE = \frac{1311.6 \, kJ}{mol} (Z^2) \quad \text{(We will carry an extra significant figure.)}$$

We get this by combining $IE = 2.178 \times 10^{-18} J (Z^2)$ and

$$\frac{2.178 \times 10^{-18} J}{atom} \times \frac{6.022 \times 10^{23} \, atoms}{mol} \times \frac{1 \, kJ}{1000 \, J} = \frac{1311.6 \, kJ}{mol}.$$

b. He^+: $Z = 2$; $IE = 1311.6 \, kJ/mol \times 2^2 = 5246 \, kJ/mol$ (Assume n = 1 for all.)

c. Li^{2+}: $Z = 3$; $IE = 1311.6 \, kJ/mol \times 3^2 = 1.180 \times 10^4 \, kJ/mol$

d. C^{5+}: $Z = 6$; $IE = 1311.6 \, kJ/mol \times 6^2 = 4.722 \times 10^4 \, kJ/mol$

e. Fe^{25+}: $Z = 26$; $IE = 1311.6 \, kJ/mol \times (26)^2 = 8.866 \times 10^5 \, kJ/mol$

63.   The size of the 1s orbitals would be proportional to 1/Z, that is, as Z increases, the electrons are more strongly attracted to the nucleus and will be drawn in closer. Thus the relative sizes would be:

$$H : He^+ : Li^{2+} : C^{5+} : Fe^{25+} \rightarrow 1 : \frac{1}{2} : \frac{1}{3} : \frac{1}{6} : \frac{1}{26}$$

64. $E_{photon} = \dfrac{hc}{\lambda} = \dfrac{6.626 \times 10^{-34} \, J \, s \, (2.9979 \times 10^8 \, m/s)}{253.4 \times 10^{-9} \, m} = 7.839 \times 10^{-19} \, J$, $\Delta E = -7.839 \times 10^{-19} \, J$

$$\Delta E = -2.178 \times 10^{-18} \, J \, (Z)^2 \left(\frac{1}{n_f^2} - \frac{1}{n_i^2} \right) \text{ where } Z = 4 \text{ for } Be^{3+}$$

$$-7.839 \times 10^{-19} \, J = -2.178 \times 10^{-18} \, (4)^2 \left(\frac{1}{n_f^2} - \frac{1}{5^2} \right)$$

$$\frac{7.839 \times 10^{-19}}{2.178 \times 10^{-18} \, (16)} + \frac{1}{25} = \frac{1}{n_f^2}, \quad \frac{1}{n_f^2} = 0.06249, \quad n_f = 4$$

This emission line corresponds to the n = 5 → n = 4 electronic transition.

65.   No, the spin is a convenient model. Since we cannot know the exact path of the electron, we cannot determine if it is spinning.

66.   a. $n = 4$: ℓ can be 0, 1, 2, or 3. Thus we have s (2 e$^-$), p (6 e$^-$), d (10 e$^-$) and f (14 e$^-$) orbitals present. Total number of electrons to fill these orbitals is 32.

b. $n = 5$, $m_\ell = +1$: For $n = 5$, $\ell = 0, 1, 2, 3, 4$. For $\ell = 1, 2, 3, 4$, all can have $m_\ell = +1$. Four distinct orbitals, thus 8 electrons.

c. $n = 5$, $m_s = +1/2$: For $n = 5$, $\ell = 0, 1, 2, 3, 4$. Number of orbitals = 1, 3, 5, 7, 9 for each value of ℓ, respectively. There are 25 orbitals with $n = 5$. They can hold 50 electrons and 25 of these electrons can have $m_s = +1/2$.

d. $n = 3$, $\ell = 2$: These quantum numbers define a set of 3d orbitals. There are 5 degenerate 3d orbitals which can hold a total of 10 electrons.

e. $n = 2$, $\ell = 1$; These define a set of 2p orbitals. There are 3 degenerate 2p orbitals which can hold a total of 6 electrons.

f.   It is impossible for $n = 0$. Thus, no electrons can have this set of quantum numbers.

g.   The four quantum numbers completely specify a single electron.

h. $n = 3$: 3s, 3p and 3d orbitals all have $n = 3$. These orbitals can hold up to 18 electrons.

i. $n = 2$, $\ell = 2$: This combination is not possible ($\ell \neq 2$ for $n = 2$). Zero electrons in an atom can have these quantum numbers.

j. $n = 1$, $\ell = 0$, $m_\ell = 0$: These define a 1s orbital which can hold 2 electrons.

67.   Si: $1s^2 2s^2 2p^6 3s^2 3p^2$ or $[Ne]3s^2 3p^2$; Ga: $1s^2 2s^2 2p^6 3s^2 3p^6 4s^2 3d^{10} 4p^1$ or $[Ar]4s^2 3d^{10} 4p^1$

As: $[Ar]4s^2 3d^{10} 4p^3$; Ge: $[Ar]4s^2 3d^{10} 4p^2$; Al: $[Ne]3s^2 3p^1$; Cd: $[Kr]5s^2 4d^{10}$

S: $[Ne]3s^2 3p^4$; Se: $[Ar]4s^2 3d^{10} 4p^4$

68.   Cu: $[Ar]4s^2 3d^9$ (using periodic table), $[Ar]4s^1 3d^{10}$ (actual)

O: $1s^2 2s^2 2p^4$; La: $[Xe]6s^2 5d^1$; Y: $[Kr]5s^2 4d^1$; Ba: $[Xe]6s^2$

Tl: $[Xe]6s^2 4f^{14} 5d^{10} 6p^1$; Bi: $[Xe]6s^2 4f^{14} 5d^{10} 6p^3$

69.   The following are complete electron configurations. Noble gas shorthand notation could also be used.

Sc: $1s^2 2s^2 2p^6 3s^2 3p^6 4s^2 3d^1$; Fe: $1s^2 2s^2 2p^6 3s^2 3p^6 4s^2 3d^6$

P: $1s^2 2s^2 2p^6 3s^2 3p^3$; Cs: $1s^2 2s^2 2p^6 3s^2 3p^6 4s^2 3d^{10} 4p^6 5s^2 4d^{10} 5p^6 6s^1$

Eu: $1s^2 2s^2 2p^6 3s^2 3p^6 4s^2 3d^{10} 4p^6 5s^2 4d^{10} 5p^6 6s^2 4f^6 5d^1$*

Pt: $1s^2 2s^2 2p^6 3s^2 3p^6 4s^2 3d^{10} 4p^6 5s^2 4d^{10} 5p^6 6s^2 4f^{14} 5d^8$*

Xe: $1s^2 2s^2 2p^6 3s^2 3p^6 4s^2 3d^{10} 4p^6 5s^2 4d^{10} 5p^6$;   Br: $1s^2 2s^2 2p^6 3s^2 3p^6 4s^2 3d^{10} 4p^5$

*Note: These electron configurations were written down using only the periodic table.

Actual electron configurations are: Eu: $[Xe]6s^2 4f^7$ and Pt: $[Xe]6s^1 4f^{14} 5d^9$

70.   Cl: $1s^2 2s^2 2p^6 3s^2 3p^5$ or $[Ne]3s^2 3p^5$ As: $1s^2 2s^2 2p^6 3s^2 3p^6 4s^2 3d^{10} 4p^3$ or $[Ar]4s^2 3d^{10} 4p^3$

Sr: $1s^2 2s^2 2p^6 3s^2 3p^6 4s^2 3d^{10} 4p^6 5s^2$ or $[Kr]5s^2$ W: $[Xe]6s^2 4f^{14} 5d^4$

Pb: $[Xe]6s^2 4f^{14} 5d^{10} 6p^2$ Cf: $[Rn]7s^2 5f^{10}$*

*Note: Predicting electron configurations for lanthanide and actinide elements is difficult since they have 0, 1 or 2 electrons in d orbitals. This is the actual Cf configuration.

71.   Exceptions: Cr, Cu, Nb, Mo, Tc, Ru, Rh, Pd, Ag, Pt, Au; Tc, Ru, Rh, Pd and Pt do not correspond to the supposed extra stability of half-filled and filled subshells.

72.   a.   Both In and I have one unpaired 5p electron, but only the nonmetal I would be expected to form a covalent compound with the nonmetal F. One would predict an ionic compound to form between the metal In and the nonmetal F.

I: $[Kr]5s^2 4d^{10} 5p^5$ ↿⇂ ↿⇂ ↿
                               5p

b.   From the periodic table, this will be element 120.   Element 120: $[Rn]7s^2 5f^{14} 6d^{10} 7p^6 8s^2$

c.   Rn: $[Xe]6s^2 4f^{14} 5d^{10} 6p^6$; Note that the next discovered noble gas will also have 4f electrons (as well as 5f electrons).

d.   This is chromium, which is an exception to the predicted filling order. Cr has 6 unpaired electrons and the next most is 5 unpaired electrons for Mn.

Cr: $[Ar]4s^1 3d^5$ ↿   ↿ ↿ ↿ ↿ ↿
                     4s   3d

73.   There is a higher probability of finding the 4s electron very close to the nucleus than that for the 3d electron.

74.   Ti : $[Ar]4s^2 3d^2$

	n	ℓ	m_ℓ	m_s
4s	4	0	0	+1/2
4s	4	0	0	-1/2
3d	3	2	-2	+1/2
3d	3	2	-1	+1/2

3d 3 2 -2 +1/2   Only one of 10 possible combinations of m_ℓ and m_s for the first d electron. For the ground state, the second d electron should be in a different orbital with spin parallel; 4 possibilities.

75.   We get the number of unpaired electrons by examining the incompletely filled subshells. The paramagnetic substances have unpaired electrons, and the ones with no unpaired electrons are not paramagnetic (they are called diamagnetic).

Li: $1s^2 2s^1$ ↑ ; Paramagnetic with 1 unpaired electron.
2s

N: $1s^2 2s^2 2p^3$ ↑ ↑ ↑ ; Paramagnetic with 3 unpaired electrons.
2p

Ni: $[Ar]4s^2 3d^8$ ↑↓ ↑↓ ↑↓ ↑ ↑ ; Paramagnetic with 2 unpaired electrons.
3d

Te: $[Kr]5s^2 4d^{10} 5p^4$ ↑↓ ↑ ↑ ; Paramagnetic with 2 unpaired electrons.
5p

Ba: $[Xe]6s^2$ ↑↓ ; Not paramagnetic since no unpaired electrons.
6s

Hg: $[Xe]6s^2 4f^{14} 5d^{10}$ ↑↓ ↑↓ ↑↓ ↑↓ ↑↓ ; Not paramagnetic since no unpaired electrons.

76.   O: $1s^2 2s^2 2p_x^2 2p_y^2$ (↑↓ ↑↓ __); There are no unpaired electrons in this oxygen atom. This configuration would be an excited state and in going to the more stable ground state (↑↓ ↑ ↑), energy would be released.

77.   We get the number of unpaired electrons by examining the incompletely filled subshells.

O:	$[He]2s^2 2p^4$	$2p^4$: ↑↓ ↑ ↑	two unpaired e⁻
O⁺:	$[He]2s^2 2p^3$	$2p^3$: ↑ ↑ ↑	three unpaired e⁻
O⁻:	$[He]2s^2 2p^5$	$2p^5$: ↑↓ ↑↓ ↑	one unpaired e⁻
Os:	$[Xe]6s^2 4f^{14} 5d^6$	$5d^6$: ↑↓ ↑ ↑ ↑ ↑	four unpaired e⁻
Zr:	$[Kr]5s^2 4d^2$	$4d^2$: ↑ ↑ __ __ __	two unpaired e⁻
S:	$[Ne]3s^2 3p^4$	$3p^4$: ↑↓ ↑ ↑	two unpaired e⁻

F: $[He]2s^22p^5$ $2p^5$:   ↑↓ ↑↓ ↑   one unpaired e⁻

Ar: $[Ne]3s^23p^6$ $3p^6$ ↑↓ ↑↓ ↑↓   zero unpaired e⁻

78.   a. excited state of boron   b. ground state of neon

B ground state: $1s^22s^22p^1$

c. excited state of fluorine   d. excited state of iron

F ground state: $1s^22s^22p^5$ Fe ground state: $[Ar]4s^23d^6$

The Periodic Table and Periodic Properties

79.   In general, size decreases from left to right across a period and size increases in going down a group.

a. Be < Mg < Ca   b. Xe < I < Te   c. Ge < Ga < In

d. Be < Na < Rb   e. Ne < Se < Sr

80.   The general ionization energy trend is the opposite of the general radii trend (see Exercise 12.79).

a. Ca < Mg < Be   b. Te < I < Xe   c. In < Ga < Ge

d. Rb < Na < Be   e. Sr < Se < Ne

81.   a. Ba   b. K

c. O; In general, group 6A elements have a lower ionization energy than neighboring group 5A elements. This is an exception to the general ionization energy trend across the periodic table.

d. S^{2-}; This ion has the most electrons as compared to the other sulfur species present. S^{2-} has the largest amount of electron-electron repulsions which leads to S^{2-} having the largest size and smallest ionization energy.

e. Cs; This follows the general ionization energy trend.

82.   a. Li   b. P

c. O^+. This ion has the fewest electrons as compared to the other oxygen species present. O^+ has the smallest amount of electron-electron repulsions which makes it the smallest ion with the largest ionization energy.

d. From the radii trend, Ar < Cl < S and Kr > Ar. Since variation in size down a family is greater than the variation across a period, we would predict Cl to be the smallest of the three.

e. Cu

83.   The outermost electrons are the valence electrons. When atoms interact with each other, it will be the outermost electrons that are involved in these interactions. In addition, how tightly the nucleus holds these outermost electrons determines atomic size, ionization energy and other properties of atoms.

Elements in the same group have similar valence electron configurations and, as a result, have similar chemical properties.

84.   Size decreases from left to right and increases going down the periodic table. So, going one element right and one element down would result in a similar size for the two elements diagonal to each other. The ionization energies will be similar for the diagonal elements since the periodic trends also oppose each other. Electron affinities are harder to predict, but atoms with similar size and ionization energy should also have similar electron affinities.

85.   As: $[Ar]4s^2 3d^{10} 4p^3$; Se: $[Ar]4s^2 3d^{10} 4p^4$; The general ionization energy trend predicts that Se should have a higher ionization energy than As. Se is an exception to the general ionization energy trend. There are extra electron-electron repulsions in Se because two electrons are in the same 4p orbital, resulting in a lower ionization energy for Se than predicted.

86.   If one more electron is added to a half-filled subshell, electron-electron repulsions will increase.

87.   Size also decreases going across a period. Sc and Ti along with Y and Zr are adjacent elements. There are 14 elements (the lanthanides) between La and Hf, making Hf considerably smaller.

88.   a.   Sg: $[Rn]7s^2 5f^{14} 6d^4$ b.   W

c. SgO_3, Sg_2O_3, SgO_4^{2-}, and $Sg_2O_7^{2-}$ are some possibilities

89.   a.   Uus will have 117 electrons. $[Rn]7s^2 5f^{14} 6d^{10} 7p^5$

b.   It will be in the halogen family and will be most similar to astatine, At.

c.   Like the other halogens: $NaUus$, $Mg(Uus)_2$, $C(Uus)_4$, $O(Uus)_2$

d.   Like the other halogens: $UusO^-$, $UusO_2^-$, $UusO_3^-$, $UusO_4^-$

90.   The electron affinity trend is very erratic. In general, EA becomes more positive in going down a group and EA becomes more negative from left to right across a period (with many exceptions).

a. $I < Br < F < Cl$; Cl is most exothermic (F is an exception).

b. $N < O < F$, F is most exothermic.

91.   Electron-electron repulsions become important when we try to add electrons to an atom. From the standpoint of electron-electron repulsions, larger atoms would have more favorable (more exothermic) electron affinities. Considering only electron-nucleus attractions, smaller atoms would be expected to have the more favorable (more exothermic) EA values. These two factors are the opposite of each other. Thus, the overall variation in EA is not as great as ionization energy in which attractions to the nucleus dominate.

92.   Yes; Since Na has an exothermic EA, there are conditions in which we might expect Na$^-$ to exist. Such compounds were first synthesized by James L. Dye at Michigan State University.

93.   O; The electron-electron repulsions will be much more severe for O$^-$ + e$^-$ → O^{2-} than for O + e$^-$ → O$^-$.

94.   Al (-44), Si(-120), P (-74), S (-200.4), Cl (-348.7); Based on the increasing nuclear charge, we would expect the EA to become more exothermic as we go from left to right in the period. Phosphorus is out of line. The reaction for the EA of P is:

$$P(g) + e^- \rightarrow P^-(g)$$

$$[Ne]3s^23p^3 \qquad [Ne]3s^23p^4$$

The additional electron in P$^-$ will have to go into an orbital that already has one electron. There will be greater repulsions between the paired electrons in P$^-$, causing the EA of P to be less favorable than predicted based solely on attractions to the nucleus.

95.   a. P(g) → P$^+$(g) + e$^-$; IE refers to atoms in the gas phase.   b. P(g) + e$^-$ → P$^-$(g)

96.   a. The electron affinity of Mg^{2+} is ΔH for: Mg^{2+}(g) + e$^-$ → Mg$^+$(g); This is just the reverse of the second ionization energy for Mg: EA(Mg^{2+}) = -IE$_2$(Mg) = -1445 kJ/mol (Table 12.6)

       b. EA of Al$^+$ is ΔH for: Al$^+$(g) + e$^-$ → Al(g); EA(Al$^+$) = -IE$_1$(Al) = -580 kJ/mol (Table 12.6)

       c. IE of Cl$^-$ is ΔH for: Cl$^-$(g) → Cl(g) + e$^-$; IE(Cl$^-$) = -EA(Cl) = +348.7 kJ/mol (Table 12.8)

       d. Cl(g) → Cl$^+$(g) + e$^-$ ΔH = IE$_1$(Cl) = 1255 kJ/mol (Table 12.6)

       e. Cl$^+$(g) + e$^-$ → Cl(g)   ΔH = -IE$_1$(Cl) = -1255 kJ/mol = EA(Cl$^+$)

97.   As successive electrons are removed, the net positive charge on the resultant ion increases. This increase in positive charge binds the remaining electrons more firmly, and the ionization energy increases.

       The electron configuration for Si is $1s^22s^22p^63s^23p^2$. There is a large jump in ionization energy when going from the removal of valence electrons to the removal of core electrons. For silicon, this occurs when the fifth electron is removed since we go from the valence electrons in $n = 3$ to the core electrons in $n = 2$. There should be another big jump when the thirteenth electron is removed, i.e., when the 1s electrons are removed.

98.   a. More favorable EA: C, Br, K and Cl; The electron affinity trend is very erratic. Both N, Ar and Mg have positive EA values (unfavorable) due to their electron configurations (see text for detailed explanation). F has a more positive EA value than expected from its position in the periodic table.

       b. Higher IE: N, Ar, Mg, and F (follows the IE trend)

       c. Larger size: C , Br, K, and Cl (follows the radii trend)

The Alkali Metals

99.   Yes; the ionization energy general trend is to decrease down a group, and the atomic radius trend is to increase down a group. The data in Table 12.9 confirm both of these general trends.

100. It should be potassium peroxide, K_2O_2, since K^+ ions are stable in ionic compounds. K^{2+} ions are not stable; the second ionization energy of K is very large as compared to the first.

101. a. $4 Li(s) + O_2(g) \rightarrow 2 Li_2O(s)$ b. $2 K(s) + S(s) \rightarrow K_2S(s)$

      c. $2 Cs(s) + 2 H_2O(l) \rightarrow 2 CsOH(aq) + H_2(g)$ d. $2 Na(s) + Cl_2(g) \rightarrow 2 NaCl(s)$

102. $\nu = \dfrac{c}{\lambda} = \dfrac{2.9979 \times 10^8 \text{ m/s}}{455.5 \times 10^{-9} \text{ m}} = 6.582 \times 10^{14} \text{ s}^{-1}$

      $E = h\nu = (6.626 \times 10^{-34} \text{ J s})(6.582 \times 10^{14} \text{ s}^{-1}) = 4.361 \times 10^{-19} \text{ J}$

103. a.   Carbonate ion is CO_3^{2-}. Lithium form Li^+ ions. Thus, lithium carbonate is Li_2CO_3.

      b. $\dfrac{1 \times 10^{-3} \text{ mol Li}}{\text{L blood}} \times \dfrac{6.9 \text{ g Li}}{\text{mol Li}} = \dfrac{7 \times 10^{-3} \text{ g Li}}{\text{L blood}}$

104. a. Li_3N;   lithium nitride   b.   NaBr;   sodium bromide

      c. K_2S;   potassium sulfide   d. Li_3P;   lithium phosphide

      e.   RbH;   rubidium hydride   f.   NaH;   sodium hydride

105. It should be element #119 with ground state electron configuration: $[Rn] \, 7s^2 5f^{14} 6d^{10} 7p^6 8s^1$

Additional Exercises

106. Each element has a characteristic spectrum. Thus, the presence of the characteristic spectral lines of an element confirms its presence in any particular sample.

107. a.   n   b.   n and ℓ

108. The valence electrons are strongly attracted to the nucleus for elements with large ionization energies. One would expect these species to readily accept another electron and have very exothermic electron affinities. The noble gases are an exception. The noble gases have a large IE but have an endothermic EA. Noble gases have a stable arrangement of electrons. Adding an electron disrupts this stable arrangement, resulting in unfavorable electron affinities.

109.   Ionization energy is for removal of the electron from the atom in the gas phase. The work function is for the removal of an electron from a solid.

$$M(g) \rightarrow M^+(g) + e^- \quad \Delta H = IE; \quad M(s) \rightarrow M^+(s) + e^- \quad \Delta H = \text{work function}$$

110.   The electron is no longer part of that atom. The proton and electron are completely separated.

111.   Yes, the maximum number of unpaired electrons in any configuration corresponds to a minimum in electron-electron repulsions.

112.   Electron-electron repulsions are much greater in O^- than in S^- because the electron goes into a smaller 2p orbital vs. the larger 3p orbital in sulfur. This results in a more favorable (more exothermic) EA for sulfur.

113.   Expected order from IE trend: Li < Be < B < C < N < O < F < Ne

B and O are out of order. The IE of O is lower because of the extra electron-electron repulsions present when two electrons are paired in the same orbital. B is out of order because of the smaller penetrating ability of the 2p electron in B as compared to the 2s electrons in Be.

114.   Energy to make water boil $= s \times m \times \Delta T = \dfrac{4.18\ J}{g\ °C} \times 50.0\ g \times 75.0\ °C = 1.57 \times 10^4\ J$

$$E_{photon} = \frac{hc}{\lambda} = \frac{6.626 \times 10^{-34}\ J\ s \times 2.998 \times 10^8\ m/s}{9.75 \times 10^{-2}\ m} = 2.04 \times 10^{-24}\ J$$

$$1.57 \times 10^4\ J \times \frac{1\ sec}{750.\ J} = 20.9\ sec; \quad 1.57 \times 10^4\ J \times \frac{1\ photon}{2.04 \times 10^{-24}\ J} = 7.70 \times 10^{27}\ photons$$

115. $60 \times 10^6\ km \times \dfrac{1000\ m}{km} \times \dfrac{1\ s}{3.00 \times 10^8\ m} = 200\ s$ (about 3 minutes)

116. $E = \dfrac{310.\ kJ}{mol} \times \dfrac{1\ mol}{6.022 \times 10^{23}} = 5.15 \times 10^{-22}\ kJ = 5.15 \times 10^{-19}\ J$

$$\lambda = \frac{hc}{E} = \frac{6.626 \times 10^{-34}\ J\ s \times (2.998 \times 10^8\ m/s)}{5.15 \times 10^{-19}\ J} = 3.86 \times 10^{-7}\ m = 386\ nm$$

117.   n = 5; m_ℓ = -4, -3, -2, -1, 0, 1, 2, 3, 4; 18 electrons since there are 9 degenerate g orbitals.

118.   The general ionization energy trend says that ionization energy increases going left to right across the periodic table. However, one of the exceptions to this trend occurs between groups 2A and 3A. Between these two groups, group 3A elements usually have a lower ionization energy than group 2A elements. Therefore, Al should have the lowest first ionization energy value, followed by Mg, with Si having the largest ionization energy. Looking at the values for the first ionization energy in the graph, the green plot is Al, the blue plot is Mg, and the red plot is Si.

Mg (the blue plot) is the element with the huge jump between I_2 and I_3. Mg has two valence electrons, so the third electron removed is an inner core electron. Inner core electrons are always much more difficult to remove compared to valence electrons since they are closer to the nucleus, on average, than the valence electrons.

119. a. $Cu^+(g) + e^- \rightarrow Cu(g)$ $-I_1 = -746$ kJ
          $Cu^+(g) \rightarrow Cu^{2+}(g) + e^-$ $I_2 = 1958$ kJ

          _____

          $2\ Cu^+(g) \rightarrow Cu(g) + Cu^{2+}(g)$ $\Delta H = 1212$ kJ

      b. $Na^-(g) \rightarrow Na(g) + e^-$ $-EA = 52$ kJ
              $Na^+(g) + e^- \rightarrow Na(g)$ $-I_1 = -495$ kJ

          _____

          $Na^-(g) + Na^+(g) \rightarrow 2\ Na(g)$ $\Delta H = -443$ kJ

      c. $Mg^{2+}(g) + e^- \rightarrow Mg^+(g)$ $-I_2 = -1445$ kJ
              $K(g) \rightarrow K^+(g) + e^-$ $I_1 = 419$ kJ

          _____

          $Mg^{2+}(g) + K(g) \rightarrow Mg^+(g) + K^+(g)$ $\Delta H = -1026$ kJ

      d. $Na(g) \rightarrow Na^+(g) + e^-$ $I_1 = 495$ kJ
              $Cl(g) + e^- \rightarrow Cl^-(g)$ $EA = -348.7$ kJ

          _____

          $Na(g) + Cl(g) \rightarrow Na^+(g) + Cl^-(g)$ $\Delta H = 146$ kJ

      e. $Mg(g) \rightarrow Mg^+(g) + e^-$ $I_1 = 735$ kJ
              $F(g) + e^- \rightarrow F^-(g)$ $EA = -327.8$ kJ

          _____

          $Mg(g) + F(g) \rightarrow Mg^+(g) + F^-(g)$ $\Delta H = 407$ kJ

      f. $Mg^+(g) \rightarrow Mg^{2+}(g) + e^-$ $I_2 = 1445$ kJ
              $F(g) + e^- \rightarrow F^-(g)$ $EA = -327.8$ kJ

          _____

          $Mg^+(g) + F(g) \rightarrow Mg^{2+}(g) + F^-(g)$ $\Delta H = 1117$ kJ

      g. From parts e and f we get:

          $Mg(g) + F(g) \rightarrow Mg^+(g) + F^-(g)$ $\Delta H = 407$ kJ
          $Mg^+(g) + F(g) \rightarrow Mg^{2+}(g) + F^-(g)$ $\Delta H = 1117$ kJ

          _____

          $Mg(g) + 2\ F(g) \rightarrow Mg^{2+}(g) + 2\ F^-(g)$ $\Delta H = 1524$ kJ

120. a. $Se^{3+}(g) \rightarrow Se^{4+}(g) + e^-$ b. $S^-(g) + e^- \rightarrow S^{2-}(g)$ c. $Fe^{3+}(g) + e^- \rightarrow Fe^{2+}(g)$

      d. $Mg(g) \rightarrow Mg^+(g) + e^-$ e. $Mg(s) \rightarrow Mg^+(s) + e^-$

121.   Valence electrons are easier to remove than inner core electrons. The large difference in energy
between I_2 and I_3 indicates that this element has two valence electrons. This element is most likely
an alkaline earth metal since alkaline earth metal elements all have two valence electrons.

122.   Cd: $1s^2 2s^2 2p^6 3s^2 3p^6 4s^2 3d^{10} 4p^6 5s^2 4d^{10}$

   a. $\ell = 2$ are d orbitals. There are 20 electrons in d orbitals ($3d^{10}$ and $4d^{10}$).

   b.   For n = 4, there are 4s, 4p, 4d and 4f orbitals. Cd only uses the 4s, 4p and 4d orbitals in the
ground state. Since all are filled with electrons, then Cd has 2 + 6 + 10 = 18 electrons with
n = 4.

   c.   All p, d and f orbitals have one orbital which has $m_\ell = -1$. So each of the 2p, 3p, 4p, 3d and 4d
orbitals (which are filled) have an orbital with $m_\ell = -1$; 5(2) = 10 electrons with $m_\ell = -1$.

123.   a.   The 4+ ion contains 20 electrons. Thus, the electrically neutral atom will contain 24 electrons.
The atomic number is 24.

   b.   The ground state electron configuration of the ion must be: $1s^2 2s^2 2p^6 3s^2 3p^6 4s^0 3d^2$; There are
6 electrons in s orbitals.

   c.   12   d.   2

   e.   This is the isotope $^{50}_{24}Cr$. There are 26 neutrons in the nucleus.

   f. 3.01×10^{23} atoms $\times \dfrac{1 \text{ mol}}{6.022 \times 10^{23} \text{ atoms}} \times \dfrac{49.9 \text{ g}}{\text{mol}} = 24.9$ g

   g. $1s^2 2s^2 2p^6 3s^2 3p^6 4s^1 3d^5$ is the ground state electron configuration for Cr. Cr is an exception to the
normal filling order.

124.   a.   As we remove succeeding electrons, the electron being removed is closer to the nucleus and
there are fewer electrons left repelling it. The remaining electrons are more strongly attracted
to the nucleus and it takes more energy to remove these electrons.

   b.   Al: $1s^2 2s^2 2p^6 3s^2 3p^1$; For I_4, we begin removing an electron with n = 2. For I_3, we remove an
electron with n = 3 (the last valence electron). In going from n = 3 to n = 2 there is a big jump
in ionization energy because the n = 2 electrons are much closer to the nucleus on the average
than n = 3 electrons. Since the n = 2 electrons are closer to the nucleus, then they are held more
tightly and require a much larger amount of energy to remove them as com-pared to the n = 3
electrons. In general, valence electrons are much easier to remove as compared to inner core
electrons.

   c. Al^{4+}; The electron affinity for Al^{4+} is ΔH for the reaction:

   $Al^{4+}(g) + e^- \rightarrow Al^{3+}(g)$ $\Delta H = -I_4 = -11{,}600$ kJ/mol

d. The greater the number of electrons, the greater the size.

Size trend: $Al^{4+} < Al^{3+} < Al^{2+} < Al^+ < Al$

125. a. True for H only.   b. True for all atoms.   c. True for all atoms.

d. This is false for all atoms. In the presence of a magnetic field, the d orbitals are no longer degenerate.

126. a. Each orbital could hold 4 electrons.

b. The first period corresponds to n = 1 which can only have 1s orbitals. The 1s orbital could hold 4 electrons hence the first period would have four elements. The second period corresponds to n = 2 which has 2s and 2p orbitals. These four orbitals can each hold four electrons. A total of 16 elements would be in the second period.

c. 20   d. 28

127. None of the noble gases and no subatomic particles had been discovered when Mendeleev published his periodic table. Thus, there was no element out of place in terms of reactivity. There was no reason to predict an entire family of elements. Mendeleev ordered his table by mass; he had no way of knowing there were gaps in atomic numbers (they hadn't been invented yet).

128. $\psi_{2p_z} = \dfrac{1}{4\sqrt{2\pi}} \left(\dfrac{Z}{a_0}\right)^{3/2} \sigma\, (e^{-\sigma/2}) \cos\theta, \quad \sigma = \dfrac{Zr}{a_0}$

z-axis: $\theta = 0°$, $\cos\theta = 1$ which is the maximum value of the $\cos\theta$ part of ψ_{2p_z} function.

xy plane: $\theta = 90°$, $\cos\theta = 0$ so $\psi_{2p_z} = 0$ (a node).

129. At x = 0, the value of the square of the wave function must be zero. The particle must be inside the box. For $\psi = A\cos(Lx)$, at x = 0, $\cos(0) = 1$ and $\psi^2 = A^2$. This violates the boundary condition.

130. Since two electrons can occupy each energy level, then the n = 1 and n = 2 energy levels are filled and the first excited state is n = 3.

$$E_n = \dfrac{n^2h^2}{8mL^2}; \quad \Delta E = E_3 - E_2 = \dfrac{9h^2}{8mL^2} - \dfrac{4h^2}{8mL^2} = \dfrac{5h^2}{8mL^2}$$

$$\Delta E = \dfrac{5(6.626\times10^{-34}\,\text{J s})^2}{8(9.109\times10^{-31}\,\text{kg})(5.64\times10^{-10}\,\text{m})^2} = 9.47\times10^{-19}\,\text{J}$$

$$\lambda = \dfrac{hc}{\Delta E} = \dfrac{6.626\times10^{-34}(2.998\times10^8\,\text{m/s})}{9.47\times10^{-19}\,\text{J}} = 2.10\times10^{-7}\,\text{m} = 210.\,\text{nm}$$

131. a. Since wavelength is inversely proportional to energy, then the spectral line to the right of B (at a larger wavelength) represents the lowest possible energy transition; this is $n = 4$ to $n = 3$. The B line represents the next lowest energy transition which is $n = 5$ to $n = 3$ and the A line corresponds to the $n = 6$ to $n = 3$ electronic transition.

   b. Since this spectrum is for a one electron ion, then $E_n = -2.178 \times 10^{-18}$ J (Z^2/n^2). To determine ΔE and, in turn, the wavelength of spectral line A, we must determine Z, the atomic number of the one electron species. Use spectral line B data to determine Z.

$$\Delta E_{5 \to 3} = -2.178 \times 10^{-18} \text{ J} \left(\frac{Z^2}{3^2} - \frac{Z^2}{5^2} \right) = -2.178 \times 10^{-18} \left(\frac{16 Z^2}{9 \times 25} \right)$$

$$E = \frac{hc}{\lambda} = \frac{6.6261 \times 10^{-34} \text{ J s} (2.9979 \times 10^8 \text{ m/s})}{142.5 \times 10^{-9} \text{ m}} = 1.394 \times 10^{-18} \text{ J}$$

Since an emission occurs, $\Delta E_{5 \to 3} = -1.394 \times 10^{-18}$ J.

$$\Delta E = -1.394 \times 10^{-18} \text{ J} = -2.178 \times 10^{-18} \text{ J} \left(\frac{16 Z^2}{9 \times 25} \right), \quad Z^2 = 9.001, \quad Z = 3; \text{ The ion is Li}^{2+}.$$

Solving for the wavelength of line A:

$$\Delta E_{6 \to 3} = -2.178 \times 10^{-18} \text{ (3)}^2 \left(\frac{1}{3^2} - \frac{1}{6^2} \right) = -1.634 \times 10^{-18} \text{ J}$$

$$\lambda = \frac{hc}{|\Delta E|} = \frac{6.6261 \times 10^{-34} \text{ J s} (2.9979 \times 10^8 \text{ m/s})}{1.634 \times 10^{-18} \text{ J}} = 1.216 \times 10^{-7} \text{ m} = 121.6 \text{ nm}$$

Challenge Problems

132. $$m = \frac{h}{\lambda v} = \frac{6.626 \times 10^{-34} \text{ kg m}^2/\text{s}}{(3.31 \times 10^{-15} \text{ m})(\frac{1}{100} \cdot 2.998 \times 10^8 \text{ m/s})}$$

$m = 6.68 \times 10^{-26}$ kg/atom

$$6.68 \times 10^{-26} \frac{\text{kg}}{\text{atom}} \times \frac{6.022 \times 10^{23} \text{ atoms}}{1 \text{ mol}} \times \frac{1000 \text{ g}}{1 \text{ kg}} = 40.2 \text{ g/mol}$$

The element is calcium.

133. a. Since the energy levels, E_{xy}, are inversely proportional to L^2, then the $n_x = 2$, $n_y = 1$ energy level will be lower in energy than the $n_x = 1$, $n_y = 2$ energy level since $L_x > L_y$. The first three energy levels, E_{xy}, in order of increasing energy are:

$$E_{11} < E_{21} < E_{12}$$

The quantum numbers are:

ground state (E_{11}) $\rightarrow$ $n_x = 1, n_y = 1$

first excited state (E_{21}) $\rightarrow$ $n_x = 2, n_y = 1$

second excited state (E_{12}) $\rightarrow$ $n_x = 1, n_y = 2$

b. $E_{21} \rightarrow E_{12}$ is the transition. $E_{xy} = \dfrac{h^2}{8m}\left(\dfrac{n_x^2}{L_x^2} + \dfrac{n_y^2}{L_y^2} \right)$

$$E_{12} = \dfrac{h^2}{8m}\left[\dfrac{1^2}{(8.00 \times 10^{-9}\,\text{m})^2} + \dfrac{2^2}{(5.00 \times 10^{-9}\,\text{m})^2} \right] = \dfrac{1.76 \times 10^{17}\,h^2}{8m}$$

$$E_{21} = \dfrac{h^2}{8m}\left[\dfrac{2^2}{(8.00 \times 10^{-9}\,\text{m})^2} + \dfrac{1^2}{(5.00 \times 10^{-9})^2} \right] = \dfrac{1.03 \times 10^{17}\,h^2}{8m}$$

$$\Delta E = E_{12} - E_{21} = \dfrac{1.76 \times 10^{17}\,h^2}{8m} - \dfrac{1.03 \times 10^{17}\,h^2}{8m} = \dfrac{7.3 \times 10^{16}\,h^2}{8m}$$

$$\Delta E = \dfrac{(7.3 \times 10^{16}\,\text{m}^{-2})(6.626 \times 10^{-34}\,\text{J s})^2}{8(9.11 \times 10^{-31}\,\text{kg})} = 4.4 \times 10^{-21}\,\text{J}$$

$$\lambda = \dfrac{hc}{\Delta E} = \dfrac{6.626 \times 10^{-34}\,\text{J s}\,(2.998 \times 10^8\,\text{m/s})}{4.4 \times 10^{-21}\,\text{J}} = 4.5 \times 10^{-5}\,\text{m}$$

134.   The ratios for Mg, Si, P, Cl, Ar are about the same. However, the ratios for Na, Al, S are higher. For Na, the second IE is extremely high since the electron is taken from $n = 2$ (the first electron is taken from $n = 3$). For Al, the first electron requires a bit less energy than expected by the trend due to the fact it is a 3p electron. For S, the first electron requires a bit less energy than expected by the trend due to electrons being paired in one of the p orbitals.

135. $\psi_{1s} = \dfrac{1}{\sqrt{\pi}}\left(\dfrac{Z}{a_0} \right)^{3/2} e^{-\sigma};\ \ Z = 1$ for H, $\ \sigma = \dfrac{Zr}{a_0} = \dfrac{r}{a_0},\ \ a_0 = 5.29 \times 10^{-11}\,\text{m}$

$$\psi_{1s} = \dfrac{1}{\sqrt{\pi}}\left(\dfrac{1}{a_0} \right)^{3/2} \exp\left(\dfrac{-r}{a_0} \right)$$

Probability is proportional to ψ^2: $\psi_{1s}^2 = \dfrac{1}{\pi}\left(\dfrac{1}{a_0} \right)^3 \exp\left(\dfrac{-2r}{a_0} \right)$ (units of $\psi^2 = \text{m}^{-3}$)

a. ψ_{1s}^2 (at nucleus) $= \dfrac{1}{\pi}\left(\dfrac{1}{a_0} \right)^3 \exp\left[\dfrac{-2\,(0)}{a_0} \right] = 2.15 \times 10^{30}\,\text{m}^{-3}$

If we assume this probability is constant throughout the 1.0×10^{-3} pm^3 volume then the total probability, p, is $\psi_{1s}^2 \times V$.

$$1.0 \times 10^{-3} \text{ pm}^3 = (1.0 \times 10^{-3} \text{ pm}) \times (10^{-12} \text{ m/pm})^3 = 1.0 \times 10^{-39} \text{ m}^3$$

total probability = p = $(2.15 \times 10^{30} \text{ m}^{-3}) \times (1.0 \times 10^{-39} \text{ m}^3) = 2.2 \times 10^{-9}$

b. For an electron that is 1.0×10^{-11} m from the nucleus:

$$\psi_{1s}^2 = \frac{1}{\pi}\left(\frac{1}{5.29 \times 10^{-11}}\right)^3 \exp\left[\frac{-2(1.0 \times 10^{-11})}{(5.29 \times 10^{-11})}\right] = 1.5 \times 10^{30} \text{ m}^{-3}$$

$V = 1.0 \times 10^{-39} \text{ m}^3; \quad p = \psi_{1s}^2 \times V = 1.5 \times 10^{-9}$

c. $\psi_{1s}^2 = 2.15 \times 10^{30} \text{ m}^{-3} \exp\left[\dfrac{-2(53 \times 10^{-12})}{(5.29 \times 10^{-11})}\right] = 2.9 \times 10^{29}; \quad V = 1.0 \times 10^{-39} \text{ m}^3$

$p = \psi_{1s}^2 \times V = 2.9 \times 10^{-10}$

d. $V = \dfrac{4}{3}\pi[(10.05 \times 10^{-12} \text{ m})^3 - (9.95 \times 10^{-12} \text{ m})^3] = 1.3 \times 10^{-34} \text{ m}^3$

We shall evaluate ψ_{1s}^2 at the middle of the shell, r = 10.00 pm, and assume ψ_{1s}^2 is constant from r = 9.95 to 10.05 pm. The concentric spheres are assumed centered about the nucleus.

$$\psi_{1s}^2 = 2.15 \times 10^{30} \text{ m}^{-3} \exp\left[\frac{-2(10.0 \times 10^{-12} \text{ m})}{(5.29 \times 10^{-11} \text{ m})}\right] = 1.47 \times 10^{30} \text{ m}^{-3}$$

$p = (1.47 \times 10^{30} \text{ m}^{-3})(1.3 \times 10^{-34} \text{ m}^3) = 1.9 \times 10^{-4}$

e. $V = \dfrac{4}{3}\pi[(52.95 \times 10^{-12} \text{ m})^3 - (52.85 \times 10^{-12} \text{ m})^3] = 4 \times 10^{-33} \text{ m}^3$

Evaluate ψ_{1s}^2 at r = 52.90 pm: $\psi_{1s}^2 = 2.15 \times 10^{30} \text{ m}^{-3} (e^{-2}) = 2.91 \times 10^{29} \text{ m}^{-3}; \quad p = 1 \times 10^{-3}$

136. a. $L_x = L_y = L_z; \quad E_{xyz} = \dfrac{h^2(n_x^2 + n_y^2 + n_z^2)}{8\, mL^2}$

$E_{111} = \dfrac{3\,h^2}{8\, mL^2}; \quad E_{112} = \dfrac{h^2}{8\, mL^2}\,(1^2 + 1^2 + 2^2) = \dfrac{6\,h^2}{8\, mL^2}$

$E_{122} = \dfrac{h^2}{8\, mL^2}\,(1^2 + 2^2 + 2^2) = \dfrac{9\,h^2}{8\, mL^2}$

b. E_{111}: only a single state; E_{112}: triple degenerate, either n_x, n_y or n_z can equal 2; E_{122}: triple degenerate, either n_x, n_y or n_z can equal 1; E_{222}: single state

	Cubic Box	Rectangular box
E_{222}	—————	—————
E_{122}	————— ————— —————	————— These are no longer degenerate. ————— —————
E_{112}	————— ————— —————	————— These are no longer degenerate. ————— —————
E_{111}	—————	—————

137. $E = \dfrac{h^2(n_x^2 + n_y^2 + n_z^2)}{8\,mL^2}$; $E_{111} = \dfrac{3\,h^2}{8\,mL^2}$; $E_{112} = \dfrac{6\,h^2}{8\,mL^2}$; $\Delta E = E_{112} - E_{111} = \dfrac{3\,h^2}{8\,mL^2}$

$\Delta E = \dfrac{hc}{\lambda} = \dfrac{(6.626 \times 10^{-34}\,\text{J sec})\,(2.998 \times 10^8\,\text{m/s})}{9.50 \times 10^{-9}\,\text{m}} = 2.09 \times 10^{-17}\,\text{J}$

$L^2 = \dfrac{3\,h^2}{8\,m\Delta E}$, $L = \left(\dfrac{3\,h^2}{8\,m\Delta E} \right)^{1/2} = \left[\dfrac{3(6.626 \times 10^{-34}\,\text{J sec})^2}{8(9.109 \times 10^{-31}\,\text{kg})\,(2.09 \times 10^{-17}\,\text{J})} \right]^{1/2}$

$L = 9.30 \times 10^{-11}\,\text{m} = 93.0\,\text{pm}$

The sphere that fits in this cube will touch the cube at the center of each face. The diameter of the sphere will equal the length of the cube. So:

$2\,r = L$ and $r = 46.5\,\text{pm}$

138. $E_{xyz} = \dfrac{h^2\,(n_x^2 + n_y^2 + n_z^2)}{8\,mL^2}$ where $L = L_x = L_y = L_z$

The first four energy levels will be filled with the 8 electrons. The first four energy levels are:

$E_{111} = \dfrac{h^2\,(1^2 + 1^2 + 1^2)}{8\,mL^2} = \dfrac{3\,h^2}{8\,mL^2}$

$E_{211} = E_{121} = E_{112} = \dfrac{6\,h^2}{8\,mL^2}$ (These three energy levels are degenerate.)

The next energy levels correspond to the first excited state. The energy for these levels are:

$$E_{221} = E_{212} = E_{122} = \frac{9\,h^2}{8\,mL^2} \quad \text{(These three energy levels are degenerate.)}$$

The electronic transition in question is from one of the degenerate E_{211}, E_{121} or E_{112} levels to one of the degenerate E_{221}, E_{212} or E_{122} levels.

$$\Delta E = \frac{9\,h^2}{8\,mL^2} - \frac{6\,h^2}{8\,mL^2} = \frac{3\,h^2}{8\,mL^2}$$

$$\Delta E = \frac{3(6.626 \times 10^{-34}\,J\,s)^2}{8\,(9.109 \times 10^{-31}\,kg)(1.50 \times 10^{-9}\,m)^2} = 8.03 \times 10^{-20}\,J$$

$$\lambda = \frac{hc}{\Delta E} = \frac{6.626 \times 10^{-34}\,J\,s\,(2.998 \times 10^8\,m/s)}{8.03 \times 10^{-20}\,J} = 2.47 \times 10^{-6}\,m = 2470\,nm$$

139. a.   1st period: $p = 1$, $q = 1$, $r = 0$, $s = \pm 1/2$ (2 elements)

2nd period: $p = 2$, $q = 1$, $r = 0$, $s = \pm 1/2$ (2 elements)

3rd period: $p = 3$, $q = 1$, $r = 0$, $s = \pm 1/2$ (2 elements)

$p = 3$, $q = 3$, $r = -2$, $s = \pm 1/2$ (2 elements)

$p = 3$, $q = 3$, $r = 0$, $s = \pm 1/2$ (2 elements)

$p = 3$, $q = 3$, $r = +2$, $s = \pm 1/2$ (2 elements)

4th period: $p = 4$; q and r values are the same as with $p = 3$ (8 total elements)

1							2
3							4
5	6	7	8	9	10	11	12
13	14	15	16	17	18	19	20

b.   Elements 2, 4, 12 and 20 all have filled shells and will be least reactive.

c.   Draw similarities to the modern periodic table.

XY could be X^+Y^-, $X^{2+}Y^{2-}$ or $X^{3+}Y^{3-}$. Possible ions for each are:

X^+ could be elements 1, 3, 5 or 13; Y^- could be 11 or 19.

X^{2+} could be 6 or 14; Y^{2-} could be 10 or 18.

X^{3+} could be 7 or 15; Y^{3-} could be 9 or 17.

Note: X^{4+} and Y^{4-} ions probably won't form.

XY_2 will be $X^{2+}(Y^-)_2$; See above for possible ions.

X_2Y will be $(X^+)_2Y^{2-}$; See above for possible ions.

XY_3 will be $X^{3+}(Y^-)_3$; See above for possible ions.

X_2Y_3 will be $(X^{3+})_2(Y^{2-})_3$; See above for possible ions.

d. From (a), we can see that eight electrons can have p = 3.

e. p = 4, q = 3, r = 2, s = $\pm$ 1/2 (2 electrons)

f. p = 4, q = 3, r = -2 , s = $\pm$ 1/2 (2)

p = 4, q = 3, r = 0, s = $\pm$ 1/2 (2)

p = 4, q = 3, r = +2, s = $\pm$ 1/2 (2)

A total of 6 electrons can have p = 4 and q = 3.

g. p = 3, q = 0, r = 0: This is not allowed; q must be odd. Zero electrons can have these quantum numbers.

h. p = 5, q = 1, r = 0

p = 5, q = 3, r = -2, 0, +2

p = 5, q = 5, r = -4, -2, 0, +2, +4

i. p = 6, q = 1, r = 0, s = $\pm$ 1/2 (2 electrons)

p = 6, q = 3, r = -2, 0, +2; s = $\pm$ 1/2 (6)

p = 6, q = 5, r = -4, -2, 0, +2, +4; s = $\pm$ 1/2 (10)

Eighteen electrons can have p = 6.

140. For hydrogen:

$$\Delta E = -2.178 \times 10^{-18} \text{ J } \left(\frac{1}{2^2} - \frac{1}{5^2} \right)$$

$$\Delta E = -4.57 \times 10^{-19}$$

For helium:

$$\Delta E = -4.57 \times 10^{-19} = -2.178 \times 10^{-18} \left(\frac{2^2}{n_f^2} - \frac{2^2}{4^2} \right)$$

$$0.210 = \frac{4}{n_f^2} - \frac{4}{16}, \quad 0.460 = \frac{4}{n_f^2}, \quad n_f \approx 2.95, \quad n_f = 3$$

Marathon Problem

136. a. Let λ = wavelength corresponding to the energy difference between the excited state, n = ?, and the ground state, n = 1. Use the information in part a to first solve for the energy difference, $\Delta E_{1 \to n}$, and then solve for the value of n. From the problem, $\lambda = (\lambda_{radio}/3.00 \times 10^7)$.

$$\Delta E_{1 \to n} = \frac{hc}{\lambda} = \frac{hc}{(\lambda_{radio}/3.00 \times 10^7)}, \quad \lambda_{radio} = \frac{hc(3.00 \times 10^7)}{\Delta E_{1 \to n}}$$

$$\lambda_{radio} = \frac{c}{\nu_{radio}} = \frac{c}{97.1 \times 10^6 \text{ s}^{-1}}; \text{ Equating the two } \lambda_{radio} \text{ expressions gives:}$$

$$\frac{c}{97.1 \times 10^6} = \frac{hc(3.00 \times 10^7)}{\Delta E_{1 \to n}}, \quad \Delta E_{1 \to n} = h(3.00 \times 10^7)(97.1 \times 10^6)$$

$$\Delta E_{1 \to n} = 6.626 \times 10^{-34} \text{ J s} (3.00 \times 10^7)(97.1 \times 10^6 \text{ s}^{-1}) = 1.93 \times 10^{-18} \text{ J}$$

Now we can solve for the n value of the excited state.

$$\Delta E_{1 \to n} = 1.93 \times 10^{-18} \text{ J} = -2.178 \times 10^{-18} \left(\frac{1}{n^2} - \frac{1}{1^2} \right)$$

$$\frac{1}{n^2} = \frac{-1.93 \times 10^{-18} + 2.178 \times 10^{-18}}{2.178 \times 10^{-18}} = 0.11, \quad n = 3 = \text{ energy level of the excited state}$$

b. From de Broglie's equation:

$$\lambda = \frac{h}{mv} = \frac{6.626 \times 10^{-34} \text{ J s}}{9.109 \times 10^{-31} \text{ kg} (570. \text{ m/s})} = 1.28 \times 10^{-6} \text{ m}$$

Let n = V = principal quantum number of the valence shell of element X. The electronic transition in question will be from n = V to n = 3 (as determined in part a).

$$\Delta E_{n \to 3} = -2.178 \times 10^{-18} \text{ J} \left(\frac{1}{3^2} - \frac{1}{n^2} \right)$$

$$|\Delta E_{n \to 3}| = \frac{hc}{\lambda} = \frac{6.626 \times 10^{-34} \text{ J s} (2.998 \times 10^8 \text{ m/s})}{1.28 \times 10^{-6} \text{ m}} = 1.55 \times 10^{-19} \text{ J}$$

$$\Delta E_{n \to 3} = -1.55 \times 10^{-19} \text{ J} = -2.178 \times 10^{-18} \text{ J} \left(\frac{1}{9} - \frac{1}{n^2} \right)$$

$$\frac{1}{n^2} = \frac{-1.55 \times 10^{-19} + 2.178 \times 10^{-18} \left(\frac{1}{9} \right)}{2.178 \times 10^{-18}} = 0.040, \ n = 5$$

Thus, $V = 5 =$ the principal quantum for the valence shell of element X, that is, element X is in the fifth period (row) of the periodic table (element X = Rb - Xe).

c.   For $n = 2$, we can have 2s and 2p orbitals. None of the 2s orbitals have $m_\ell = -1$ and only one of the 2p orbitals has $m_\ell = -1$. In this one 2p atomic orbital, only one electron can have $m_s = -1/2$. Thus, only one unpaired electron exists in the ground state for element X. From period 5 elements, X could be Rb, Y, Ag, In or I since all of these elements only have one unpaired electron in the ground state.

d.   For a one electron ion, $E_n = -2.178 \times 10^{-18} \text{ J} \left(\frac{Z^2}{n^2} \right)$ where Z = atomic number. For He$^+$, Z = 2. The ground state ($n = 1$) energy for hydrogen is -2.178×10^{-18} J. Equating the two energy level values:

$$-2.178 \times 10^{-18} \text{ J} \left(\frac{2^2}{n^2} \right) = -2.178 \times 10^{-18} \text{ J}, \ n = 2$$

Thus, the azimuthal quantum number (ℓ) for the subshell of X which contains the unpaired electron is 2, which means the unpaired electron is in the d subshell. Although Y and Ag are both d-block elements, only Y has one unpaired electron in the d-block. Silver is an exception to the normal filling order; Ag has the unpaired electron in the 5s orbital. The ground state electron configurations are:

Y: [Kr] $5s^2 4d^1$ and Ag: [Kr] $5s^1 4d^{10}$

Element X is yttrium (Y).

CHAPTER THIRTEEN

BONDING: GENERAL CONCEPTS

Chemical Bonds and Electronegativity

11. a. Electronegativity: The ability of an atom <u>in a molecule</u> to attract electrons to itself.

Electron affinity: The energy change for $M(g) + e^- \rightarrow M^-(g)$. EA deals with isolated atoms in the gas phase.

b. Covalent bond: Sharing of electron pair(s); Polar covalent bond: Unequal sharing of electron pair(s).

c. Ionic bond: Electrons are no longer shared, i.e., complete transfer of electron(s) from one atom to another.

12. a. There are two attractions of the form $\dfrac{(+1)(-1)}{r}$, where $r = 1 \times 10^{-10}$ m $= 0.1$ nm.

$$V = 2 \times (2.31 \times 10^{-19} \text{ J nm}) \left[\frac{(+1)(-1)}{0.1 \text{ nm}} \right] = -4.62 \times 10^{-18} \text{ J}$$

b. There are 4 attractions of +1 and -1 charges at a distance of 0.1 nm from each other. The two negative charges and the two positive charges repel each other across the diagonal of the square. This is at a distance of $\sqrt{2} \times 0.1$ nm.

$$V = 4 \times (2.31 \times 10^{-19}) \left[\frac{(+1)(-1)}{0.1} \right] + 2.31 \times 10^{-19} \left[\frac{(+1)(+1)}{\sqrt{2}(0.1)} \right] + 2.31 \times 10^{-19} \left[\frac{(-1)(-1)}{\sqrt{2}(0.1)} \right]$$

$$V = -9.24 \times 10^{-18} \text{ J} + 1.63 \times 10^{-18} \text{ J} + 1.63 \times 10^{-18} \text{ J} = -5.98 \times 10^{-18} \text{ J}$$

Note: There is a greater net attraction in arrangement b than in a.

13. Using the periodic table we expect the general trend for electronegativity to be:
    1) increase as we go from left to right across a period
    2) decrease as we go down a group

a. $C < N < O$ b. $Se < S < Cl$ c. $Sn < Ge < Si$

d. $Tl < Ge < S$ e. $Rb < K < Na$ f. $Ga < B < O$

14.   The most polar bond will have the greatest difference in electronegativity between the two atoms. From positions in the periodic table, we would predict:

   a. Ge-F   b. P-Cl   c. S-F   d. Ti-Cl   e. Sn-H   f. Tl-Br

15.   The general trends in electronegativity used on Exercises 13.13 and 13.14 are only rules of thumb. In this exercise we use experimental values of electronegativities and can begin to see several exceptions. The order of EN using Figure 13.3 is:

   a. C (2.6) < N (3.0) < O (3.4)   same as predicted

   b. Se (2.6) = S (2.6) < Cl (3.2)   different

   c. Si (1.9) < Ge (2.0) = Sn (2.0) different   d. Tl (2.0) = Ge (2.0) < S (2.6) different

   e. Rb (0.8) = K (0.8) < Na (0.9) different   f. Ga (1.8) < B (2.0) < O (3.4) same

Most polar bonds using actual EN values:

   a. Si-F (Ge-F predicted)   b. P-Cl (same as predicted)

   c. S-F (same as predicted)   d. Ti-Cl (same as predicted)

   e. C-H (Sn-H predicted)   f. Al-Br (Tl-Br predicted)

16.   (IE - EA)   (IE - EA)/502   EN (text)   2006/502 = 4.0

	(IE - EA)	(IE - EA)/502	EN (text)
F	2006 kJ/mol	4.0	4.0
Cl	1604	3.2	3.2
Br	1463	2.9	3.0
I	1302	2.6	2.7

The values calculated from IE and EA show the same trend (and agree fairly closely) to the values given in the text.

Ionic Compounds

17.   a. $Cu > Cu^+ > Cu^{2+}$ b. $Pt^{2+} > Pd^{2+} > Ni^{2+}$ c. $O^{2-} > O^- > O$

   d. $La^{3+} > Eu^{3+} > Gd^{3+} > Yb^{3+}$ e. $Te^{2-} > I^- > Cs^+ > Ba^{2+} > La^{3+}$

For answer a, as electrons are removed from an atom, size decreases. Answers b and d follow the radii trend. For answer c, as electrons are added to an atom, size increases. Answer e follows the trend for an isoelectronic series, i.e., the smallest ion has the most protons.

18. a. Mg^{2+}: $1s^22s^22p^6$ Sn^{2+}: $[Kr]5s^24d^{10}$

      K^+: $1s^22s^22p^63s^23p^6$ Al^{3+}: $1s^22s^22p^6$

      Tl^+: $[Xe]6s^24f^{14}5d^{10}$ As^{3+}: $[Ar]4s^23d^{10}$

   b. N^{3-}, O^{2-} and F^-: $1s^22s^22p^6$ Te^{2-}: $[Kr]5s^24d^{10}5p^6$

   c. Be^{2+}: $1s^2$ Rb^+: $[Ar]4s^23d^{10}4p^6$

      Ba^{2+}: $[Kr]5s^24d^{10}5p^6$ Se^{2-}: $[Ar]4s^23d^{10}4p^6$

      I^-: $[Kr]5s^24d^{10}5p^6$

19. a. Cs_2S is composed of Cs^+ and S^{2-}. Cs^+ has the same electron configuration as Xe, and S^{2-} has the same configuration as Ar.

   b. SrF_2; Sr^{2+} has the Kr electron configuration and F^- has the Ne configuration.

   c. Ca_3N_2; Ca^{2+} has the Ar electron configuration and N^{3-} has the Ne configuration.

   d. $AlBr_3$; Al^{3+} has the Ne electron configuration and Br^- has the Kr configuration.

20. a. Sc^{3+} b. Te^{2-} c. Ce^{4+} and Ti^{4+} d. Ba^{2+}

All of these have the number of electrons of a noble gas.

21. Isoelectronic: Same number of electrons. There are two variables, number of protons and number of electrons, that will determine the size of an ion. Keeping the number of electrons constant, we only have to consider the number of protons to predict trends in size. The smallest ion has the most protons.

Se^{2-}, Br^-, Rb^+, Sr^{2+}, Y^{3+}, Zr^{4+} are some ions which are isoelectronic with Kr (36 electrons). In terms of size, the ion with the most protons will hold the electrons tightest and will be the smallest. The size trend is:

$$Zr^{4+} < Y^{3+} < Sr^{2+} < Rb^+ < Br^- < Se^{2-}$$
smallest   largest

22. Lattice energy is proportional to Q_1Q_2/r where Q is the charge of the ions and r is the distance between the ions. In general, charge effects on lattice energy are greater than size effects.

   a. LiF; Li^+ is smaller than Cs^+.   b. NaBr; Br^- is smaller than I^-.

   c. BaO; O^{2-} has a greater charge than Cl^-.   d. $CaSO_4$; Ca^{2+} has a greater charge than Na^+.

   e. K_2O; O^{2-} has a greater charge than F^-.   f. Li_2O; The ions are smaller in Li_2O.

23.   a. Al^{3+} and Cl^-; $AlCl_3$, aluminum chloride   b. Na^+ and O^{2-}; Na_2O, sodium oxide

       c. Sr^{2+} and F^-; SrF_2, strontium fluoride   d. Ca^{2+} and P^{3-}; Ca_3P_2, calcium phosphide

24.   Ionic solids can be characterized as being held together by strong omnidirectional forces.

       i.   For electrical conductivity, charged species must be free to move. In ionic solids the charged ions are held rigidly in place. Once the forces are disrupted (melting or dissolution), the ions can move about (conduct).

       ii.   Melting and boiling disrupts the attractions of the ions for each other. If the forces are strong, it will take a lot of energy (high temp.) to accomplish this.

       iii. If we try to bend a piece of material, the atoms/ions must slide across each other. For an ionic solid the following might happen:

              strong attraction   strong repulsion

              Just as the layers begin to slide, there will be very strong repulsions causing the solid to snap across a fairly clean plane.

       These properties and their correlation to chemical forces will be discussed in detail in Chapter 16.

25. $Na(s) \rightarrow Na(g)$ $\Delta H = 109$ kJ   (sublimation)
                 $Na(g) \rightarrow Na^+(g) + e^-$ $\Delta H = 495$ kJ   (ionization energy)
                 $1/2\ Cl_2(g) \rightarrow Cl(g)$ $\Delta H = 239/2$ kJ (bond energy)
                 $Cl(g) + e^- \rightarrow Cl^-(g)$ $\Delta H = -349$ kJ (electron affinity)
                 $Na^+(g) + Cl^-(g) \rightarrow NaCl(s)$ $\Delta H = -786$ kJ (lattice energy)

       _____

       $Na(s) + 1/2\ Cl_2(g) \rightarrow NaCl(s)$ $\Delta H_f^\circ = -412$ kJ/mol

26. $Mg(s) \rightarrow Mg(g)$ $\Delta H = 150.$ kJ   (sublimation)
                 $Mg(g) \rightarrow Mg^+(g) + e^-$ $\Delta H = 735$ kJ (IE_1)
                 $Mg^+(g) \rightarrow Mg^{2+}(g) + e^-$ $\Delta H = 1445$ kJ (IE_2)
                 $F_2(g) \rightarrow 2\ F(g)$ $\Delta H = 154$ kJ   (BE)
                 $2\ F(g) + 2\ e^- \rightarrow 2\ F^-(g)$ $\Delta H = 2(-328)$ kJ   (EA)
                 $Mg^{2+}(g) + 2\ F^-(g) \rightarrow MgF_2(s)$ $\Delta H = -3916$ kJ   (LE)

       _____

       $Mg(s) + F_2(g) \rightarrow MgF_2(s)$ $\Delta H_f^\circ = -2088$ kJ/mol

27.   a.   From the data given, less energy is required to produce $Mg^+(g) + O^-(g)$ than to produce $Mg^{2+}(g) + O^{2-}(g)$. However, the lattice energy for $Mg^{2+}O^{2-}$ will be much more exothermic than for Mg^+O^- (due to the greater charges in $Mg^{2+}O^{2-}$). The favorable lattice energy term will dominate and $Mg^{2+}O^{2-}$ forms.

b. Mg^+ and O^- both have unpaired electrons. In Mg^{2+} and O^{2-}, there are no unpaired electrons. Hence, Mg^+O^- would be paramagnetic; $Mg^{2+}O^{2-}$ would be diamagnetic. Paramagnetism can be detected by measuring the mass of a sample in the presence and absence of a magnetic field. The apparent mass of a paramagnetic substance will be larger in a magnetic field because of the force between the unpaired electrons and the field.

28.   Let us look at the complete cycle for Li_2S.

$$2 \, Li(s) \rightarrow 2 \, Li(g) \qquad\qquad 2 \, \Delta H_{sub, \, Li} = 2(161) \text{ kJ}$$
$$2 \, Li(g) \rightarrow 2 \, Li^+(g) + 2 \, e^- \qquad\qquad 2 \, IE = 2(520.) \text{ kJ}$$
$$S(s) \rightarrow S(g) \qquad\qquad \Delta H_{sub, \, S} = 277 \text{ kJ}$$
$$S(g) + e^- \rightarrow S^-(g) \qquad\qquad EA_1 = -200. \text{ kJ}$$
$$S^-(g) + e^- \rightarrow S^{2-}(g) \qquad\qquad EA_2 = ?$$
$$2 \, Li^+(g) + S^{2-}(g) \rightarrow Li_2S \qquad\qquad LE = -2472 \text{ kJ}$$

_____

$$2 \, Li(s) + S(s) \rightarrow Li_2S(s) \qquad\qquad \Delta H_f^{\circ} = -500. \text{ kJ}$$

$\Delta H_f^{\circ} = 2 \, \Delta H_{sub, \, Li} + 2 \, IE + \Delta H_{sub, \, S} + EA_1 + EA_2 + LE$, $-500. = -1033 + EA_2$, $EA_2 = 533 \text{ kJ}$

For each salt: $\Delta H_f^{\circ} = 2 \, \Delta H_{sub, \, M} + 2 \, IE + 277 - 200. + LE + EA_2$

Na_2S: $-365 = 2(109) + 2(495) + 277 - 200. - 2203 + EA_2$; $EA_2 = 553 \text{ kJ}$

K_2S: $-381 = 2(90.) + 2(419) + 277 - 200. - 2052 + EA_2$; $EA_2 = 576 \text{ kJ}$

Rb_2S: $-361 = 2(82) + 2(409) + 277 - 200. - 1949 + EA_2$; $EA_2 = 529 \text{ kJ}$

Cs_2S: $-360. = 2(78) + 2(382) + 277 - 200. - 1850. + EA_2$; $EA_2 = 493 \text{ kJ}$

We get values from 493 to 576 kJ.

The mean value is: $\dfrac{533 + 553 + 576 + 529 + 493}{5} = 537 \text{ kJ}$

We can represent the results as $EA_2 = 540 \pm 50 \text{ kJ}$.

29. Ca^{2+} has a greater charge than Na^+, and Se^{2-} is smaller than Te^{2-}. The effect of charge on the lattice energy is greater than the effect of size. We expect the trend from most exothermic to least exothermic to be:

$$CaSe \; > \; CaTe \; > \; Na_2Se \; > \; Na_2Te$$

(-2862)   (-2721)   (-2130)   (-2095 kJ/mol)   This is what we observe.

30.   Lattice energy is proportional to the charge of the cation times the charge of the anion, Q_1Q_2.

Compound	Q_1Q_2	Lattice Energy
$FeCl_2$	$(+2)(-1) = -2$	-2631 kJ/mol
$FeCl_3$	$(+3)(-1) = -3$	-5339 kJ/mol
Fe_2O_3	$(+3)(-2) = -6$	-14,744 kJ/mol

Bond Energies

31.   a. $H - H + Cl - Cl \rightarrow 2\ H - Cl$

Bonds broken: Bonds formed:

    1 H – H (432 kJ/mol)   2 H – Cl (427 kJ/mol)
    1 Cl – Cl (239 kJ/mol)

$\Delta H = \Sigma D_{broken} - \Sigma D_{formed}$, $\Delta H = 432\ kJ + 239\ kJ - 2(427)\ kJ = -183\ kJ$

b. 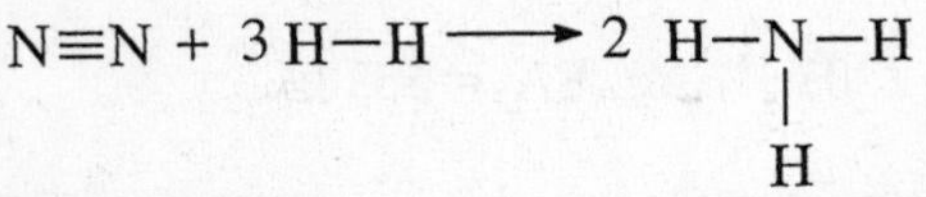 $N \equiv N + 3\ H - H \longrightarrow 2\ H - \underset{\underset{H}{|}}{N} - H$

Bonds broken: Bonds formed:

    1 N $\equiv$ N (941 kJ/mol)   6 N – H (391 kJ/mol)
    3 H – H (432 kJ/mol)

$\Delta H = 941\ kJ + 3(432)\ kJ - 6(391)\ kJ = -109\ kJ$

c.   Sometimes some of the bonds remain the same between reactants and products. To save time, only break and form bonds that are involved in the reaction.

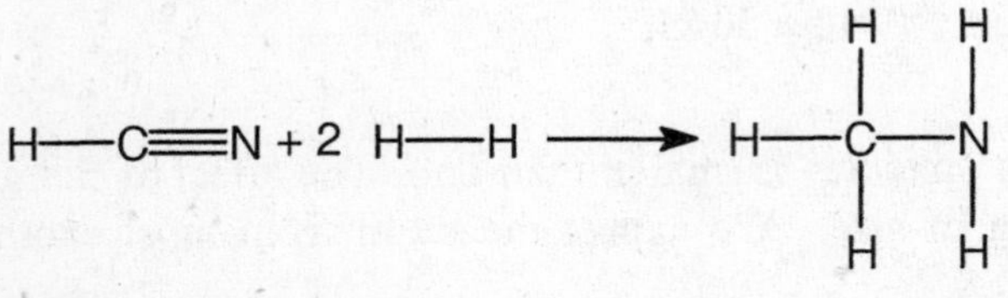

$$H - C \equiv N + 2\ H - H \longrightarrow H - \underset{\underset{H}{|}}{\overset{\overset{H}{|}}{C}} - \underset{\underset{H}{|}}{\overset{\overset{H}{|}}{N}}$$

Bonds broken: Bonds formed:

    1 C $\equiv$ N (891 kJ/mol)   1 C – N (305 kJ/mol)
    2 H – H (432 kJ/mol)   2 C – H (413 kJ/mol)
                                                         2 N – H (391 kJ/mol)

$\Delta H = 891\ kJ + 2(432\ kJ) - [305\ kJ + 2(413\ kJ) + 2(391\ kJ)] = -158\ kJ$

d.

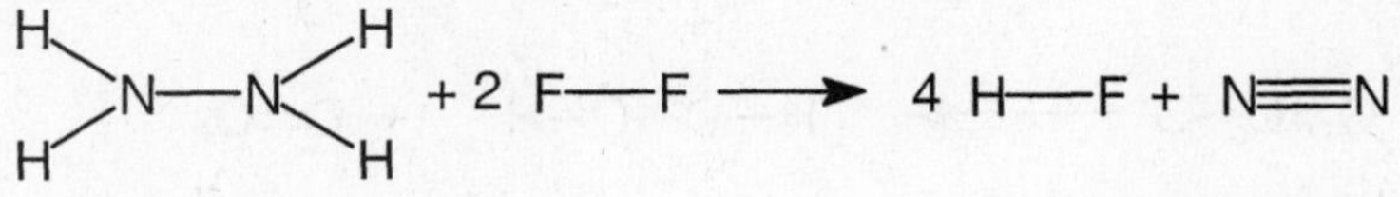

Bonds broken: Bonds formed:

1 N – N (160. kJ/mol)   4 H – F (565 kJ/mol)
4 N – H (391 kJ/mol)   1 N ≡ N (941 kJ/mol)
2 F – F (154 kJ/mol)

ΔH = 160. kJ + 4(391 kJ) + 2(154 kJ) - [4(565 kJ) + 941 kJ] = -1169 kJ

32.   a. $\Delta H = 2\ \Delta H^\circ_{f,\ HCl}$ = 2 mol(-92 kJ/mol) = -184 kJ (-183 kJ from bond energies)

b. $\Delta H = 2\ \Delta H^\circ_{f,\ NH_3}$ = 2 mol(-46 kJ/mol) = -92 kJ (-109 kJ from bond energies)

Comparing the values for each reaction, bond energies seem to give a reasonably good estimate for the enthalpy change of a reaction. The estimate is especially good for gas phase reactions.

33.

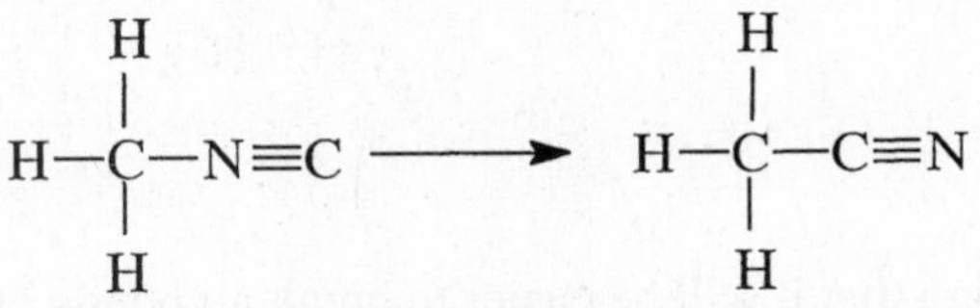

Bonds broken: 1 C – N (305 kJ/mol)   Bonds formed: 1 C – C (347 kJ/mol)

$\Delta H = \Sigma D_{broken} - \Sigma D_{formed}$, ΔH = 305 - 347 = -42 kJ

Note: Some bonds usually remain the same between reactants and products. To save time, only break and form bonds that are involved in the reaction.

34.

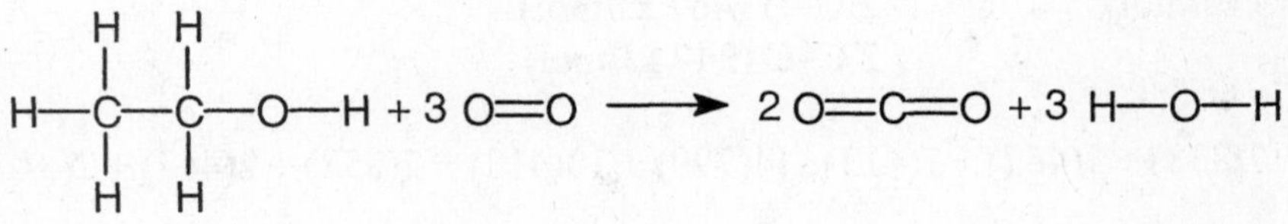

Bonds broken: Bonds formed:

5 C – H (413 kJ/mol)   2 × 2 C = O (799 kJ/mol)
1 C – C (347 kJ/mol)   3 × 2 O – H (467 kJ/mol)
1 C – O (358 kJ/mol)
1 O – H (467 kJ/mol)
3 O = O (495 kJ/mol)

ΔH = 5(413 kJ) + 347 kJ + 358 kJ + 467 kJ + 3(495 kJ) – [4(799 kJ) + 6(467 kJ)]

= -1276 kJ

35.

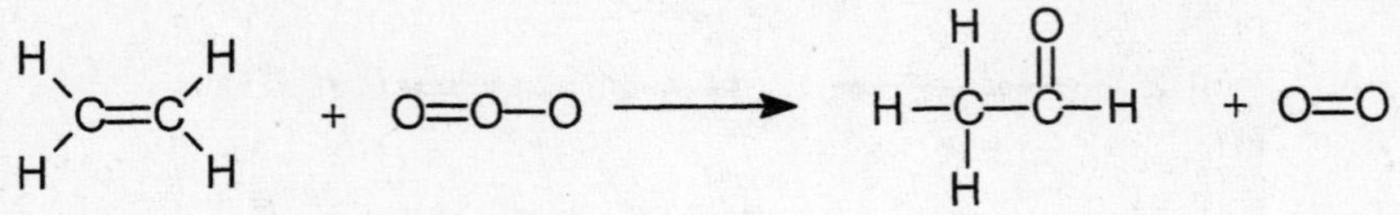

$$H_2C=CH_2 + O=O-O \longrightarrow CH_3-CHO + O=O$$

Bonds broken:

1 C=C (614 kJ/mol)
1 O–O (146 kJ/mol)
1 C–H (413 kJ/mol)

Bonds formed:

1 C–C (347 kJ/mol)
1 C=O (745 kJ/mol)
1 C–H (413 kJ/mol)

$$\Delta H = 614 + 146 + 413 - (347 + 745 + 413) = -332 \text{ kJ}$$

36.

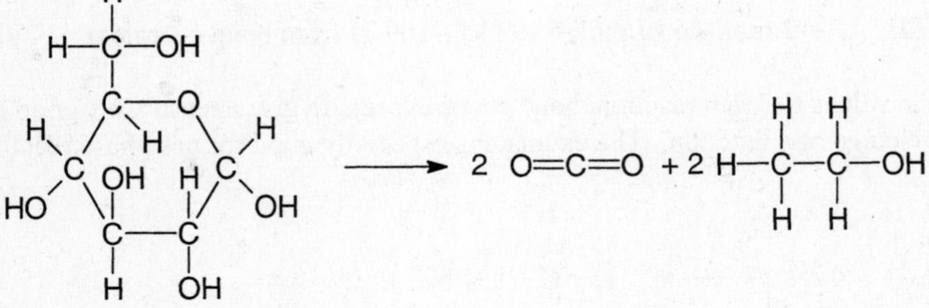

$$\text{glucose} \longrightarrow 2\,O=C=O + 2\,CH_3-CH_2-OH$$

The molecules are complicated enough that it will be easier to break all bonds in glucose and make all the bonds in CO_2 and CH_3CH_2OH.

Bonds broken:

5 C–C (347 kJ/mol)
7 C–O (358 kJ/mol)
5 O–H (467 kJ/mol)
7 C–H (413 kJ/mol)

Bonds formed:

2 × 2 C=O (799 kJ/mol)
2 × 5 C–H (413 kJ/mol)
2 C–O (358 kJ/mol)
2 O–H (467 kJ/mol)
2 C–C (347 kJ/mol)

$$\Delta H = 5(347) + 7(358) + 5(467) + 7(413) - [4(799) + 10(413) + 2(358) + 2(467) + 2(347)] = -203 \text{ kJ}$$

37.

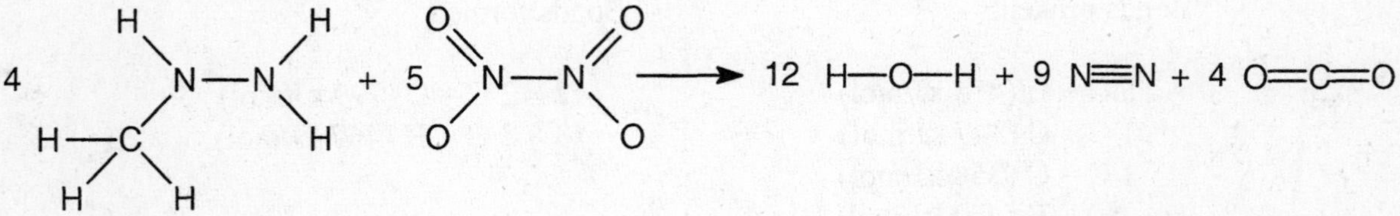

$$4\,(CH_3)N_2H_3 + 5\,N_2O_4 \longrightarrow 12\,H-O-H + 9\,N\equiv N + 4\,O=C=O$$

Bonds broken:

$$9\ N-N\ (160.\ kJ/mol)$$
$$4\ N-C\ (305\ kJ/mol)$$
$$12\ C-H\ (413\ kJ/mol)$$
$$12\ N-H\ (391\ kJ/mol)$$
$$10\ N=O\ (607\ kJ/mol)$$
$$10\ N-O\ (201\ kJ/mol)$$

Bonds made:

$$24\ O-H\ (467\ kJ/mol)$$
$$9\ N\equiv N\ (941\ kJ/mol)$$
$$8\ C=O\ (799\ kJ/mol)$$

$$\Delta H = 9(160.) + 4(305) + 12(413) + 12(391) + 10(607) + 10(201)$$
$$- [24(467) + 9(941) + 8(799)]$$

$$\Delta H = 20{,}388\ kJ - 26{,}069\ kJ = -5681\ kJ$$

38.   a.   I.

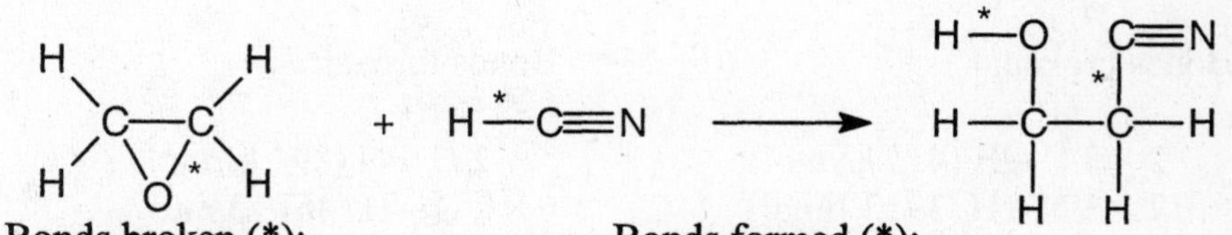

Bonds broken (*):

$$1\ C-O\ (358\ kJ)$$
$$1\ C-H\ (413\ kJ)$$

Bonds formed (*):

$$1\ O-H\ (467\ kJ)$$
$$1\ C-C\ (347\ kJ)$$

$$\Delta H_I = 358\ kJ + 413\ kJ - [467\ kJ + 347\ kJ] = -43\ kJ$$

II.

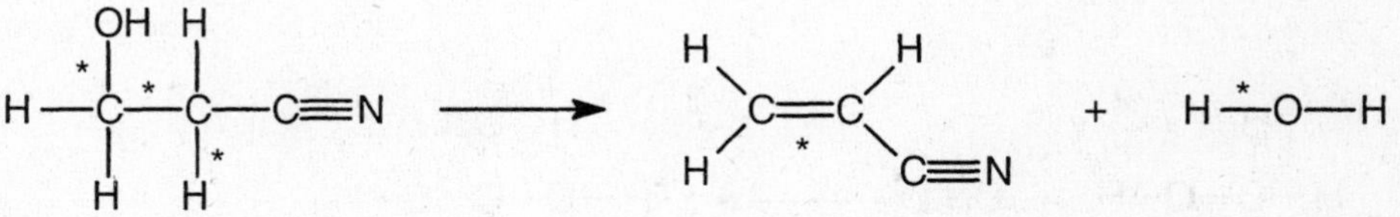

Bonds broken (*):

$$1\ C-O\ (358\ kJ/mol)$$
$$1\ C-H\ (413\ kJ/mol)$$
$$1\ C-C\ (347\ kJ/mol)$$

Bonds formed (*):

$$1\ H-O\ (467\ kJ/mol)$$
$$1\ C=C\ (614\ kJ/mol)$$

$$\Delta H_{II} = 358\ kJ + 413\ kJ + 347\ kJ - [467\ kJ + 614\ kJ] = +37\ kJ$$

$$\Delta H_{overall} = \Delta H_I + \Delta H_{II} = -43\ kJ + 37\ kJ = -6\ kJ$$

b.

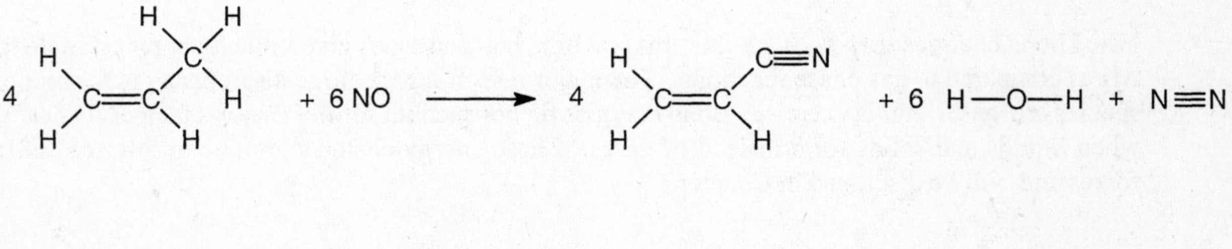

Bonds broken: Bonds formed:

4×3 C – H (413 kJ/mol)   4 C ≡ N (891 kJ/mol)
6 N = O (630. kJ/mol) 6×2 H – O (467 kJ/mol)
                                                1 N ≡ N (941 kJ/mol)

$\Delta H = 12(413) + 6(630.) - [4(891) + 12(467) + 941] = -1373$ kJ

c.

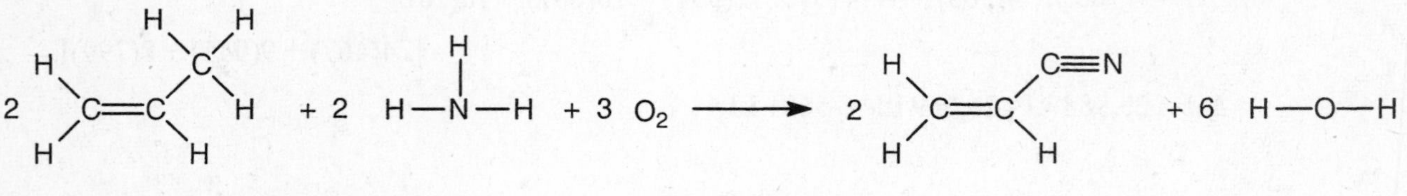

Bonds broken: Bonds formed:

2×3 C – H (413 kJ/mol)   2 C ≡ N (891 kJ/mol)
2×3 N – H (391 kJ/mol) 6×2 O – H (467 kJ/mol)
3 O = O (495 kJ/mol)

$\Delta H = 6(413) + 6(391) + 3(495) - [2(891) + 12(467)] = -1077$ kJ

39.   Since both reactions are highly exothermic, the high temperature is not needed to provide energy. It must be necessary for some other reason. The reason is to increase the speed of the reaction. This will be discussed in Chapter 15 on kinetics.

40.

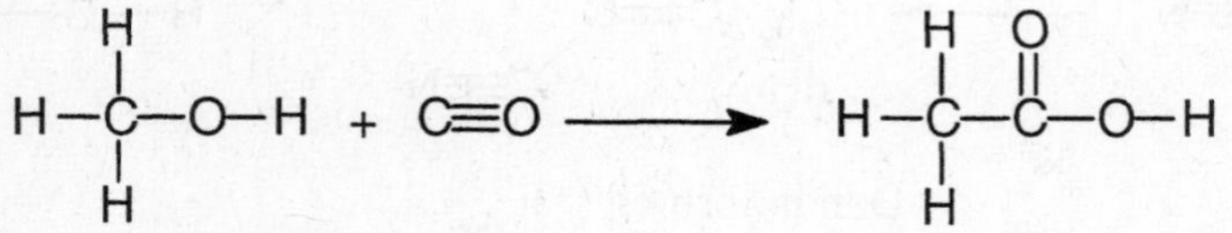

Bonds broken: Bonds formed:

1 C ≡ O (1072 kJ/mol)   1 C – C (347 kJ/mol)
1 C – O (358 kJ/mol)   1 C = O (745 kJ/mol)
                                        1 C – O (358 kJ/mol)

$\Delta H = 1072 + 358 - [347 + 745 + 358] = -20.$ kJ

$CH_3OH(g) + CO(g) \rightarrow CH_3COOH(l)$ $\Delta H° = -484$ kJ - [(-201 kJ) + (-110.5 kJ)] = -173 kJ

Using bond energies, $\Delta H = -20.$ kJ. For this reaction, bond energies give a much poorer estimate for ΔH as compared to gas phase reactions. The major reason for the large discrepancy is that not all species are gases in this exercise. Bond energies do not account for the energy changes that occur when liquids and solids form instead of gases. These energy changes are due to intermolecular forces and will be discussed in Chapter 16.

41.   a. $HF(g) \rightarrow H(g) + F(g)$ $\Delta H = 565$ kJ
                   $H(g) \rightarrow H^+(g) + e^-$ $\Delta H = 1312$ kJ
          $F(g) + e^- \rightarrow F^-(g)$ $\Delta H = -327.8$ kJ

              $HF(g) \rightarrow H^+(g) + F^-(g)$ $\Delta H = 1549$ kJ

   b. $HCl(g) \rightarrow H(g) + Cl(g)$ $\Delta H = 427$ kJ
                   $H(g) \rightarrow H^+(g) + e^-$ $\Delta H = 1312$ kJ
       $Cl(g) + e^- \rightarrow Cl^-(g)$ $\Delta H = -348.7$ kJ

             $HCl(g) \rightarrow H^+(g) + Cl^-(g)$ $\Delta H = 1390.$ kJ

   c. $HI(g) \rightarrow H(g) + I(g)$ $\Delta H = 295$ kJ
                   $H(g) \rightarrow H^+(g) + e^-$ $\Delta H = 1312$ kJ
         $I(g) + e^- \rightarrow I^-(g)$ $\Delta H = -295.2$ kJ

              $HI(g) \rightarrow H^+(g) + I^-(g)$ $\Delta H = 1312$ kJ

   d. $H_2O(g) \rightarrow OH(g) + H(g)$ $\Delta H = 467$ kJ
                   $H(g) \rightarrow H^+(g) + e^-$ $\Delta H = 1312$ kJ
     $OH(g) + e^- \rightarrow OH^-(g)$ $\Delta H = -180.$ kJ

            $H_2O(g) \rightarrow H^+(g) + OH^-(g)$ $\Delta H = 1599$ kJ

42.   a.   Using SF_4 data: $SF_4(g) \rightarrow S(g) + 4\ F(g)$

$$\Delta H° = 4\ D_{SF} = 278.8 \text{ kJ} + 4(79.0 \text{ kJ}) - (-775 \text{ kJ}) = 1370. \text{ kJ}$$

$$D_{SF} = \frac{1370. \text{ kJ}}{4 \text{ mol SF bonds}} = 342.5 \text{ kJ/mol}$$

Using SF_6 data: $SF_6(g) \rightarrow S(g) + 6\ F(g)$

$$\Delta H° = 6\ D_{SF} = 278.8 \text{ kJ} + 6(79.0 \text{ kJ}) - (-1209 \text{ kJ}) = 1962 \text{ kJ}$$

$$D_{SF} = \frac{1962 \text{ kJ}}{6} = 327.0 \text{ kJ/mol}$$

   b.   The S – F bond energy in Table 13.6 is 327 kJ/mol. The value in the table was based on the S – F bond in SF_6.

   c.   S(g) and F(g) are not the most stable form of the element at 25°C and 1 atm. The most stable forms are $S_8(s)$ and $F_2(g)$; $\Delta H_f° = 0$ for these two species.

43. $NH_3(g) \rightarrow N(g) + 3\ H(g)$

$$\Delta H° = 3\ D_{NH} = 472.7 \text{ kJ} + 3(216.0 \text{ kJ}) - (-46.1 \text{ kJ}) = 1166.8 \text{ kJ}$$

$$D_{NH} = \frac{1166.8 \text{ kJ}}{3 \text{ mol NH bonds}} = 388.93 \text{ kJ/mol}$$

$D_{calc} = 389$ kJ/mol as compared to 391 kJ/mol in the table. There is good agreement.

44. $N_2 + 3 H_2 \rightarrow 2 NH_3$; $\Delta H = D_{N_2} + 3 D_{H_2} - 6 D_{NH}$; $\Delta H° = 2(-46 \text{ kJ}) = -92$ kJ

        -92 kJ $= 941$ kJ $+ 3(432 \text{ kJ}) - (6 D_{NH})$, $6 D_{NH} = 2329$ kJ, $D_{NH} = 388.2$ kJ/mol

        Exercise 13.43: 389 kJ/mol; Table in text: 391 kJ/mol; There is good agreement between all three values.

45.   From Exercise 13.43, the N–H bond energy is 388.9 kJ/mol.

        $2 N(g) + 4 H(g)$ $\Delta H = D_{N-N} + 4 D_{N-H} = D_{N-N} + 4(388.9)$

        $\Delta H° = 2 \Delta H°_{f, N} + 4 \Delta H°_{f, H} - \Delta H°_{f, N_2H_4} = 2(472.7 \text{ kJ}) + 4(216.0 \text{ kJ}) - 95.4$ kJ

        $\Delta H° = 1714.0$ kJ $= D_{N-N} + 4(388.9)$, $D_{N-N} = 158.4$ kJ/mol   (160. kJ/mol in Table 13.6)

46. $\Delta H°_f$ for $H(g)$ is $\Delta H°$ for the reaction: $1/2 H_2(g) \rightarrow H(g)$; $\Delta H°_f$ for $H(g)$ equals one-half the H–H bond energy.

Lewis Structures and Resonance

47.   Drawing Lewis structures is mostly trial and error. However, the first two steps are always the same. These steps are 1) count the valence electrons available in the molecule or ion and 2) attach all atoms to each other with single bonds (called the skeletal structure). Generally, the atom listed first is assumed to be the atom in the middle (called the central atom) and all other atoms in the formulas are attached to this atom. The most notable exceptions to the rule are formulas which begin with H, e.g., H_2O, H_2CO, etc. Hydrogen can never be a central atom since this would require H to have more than two electrons.

        After counting valence electrons and drawing the skeletal structure, the rest is trial and error. We place the remaining electrons around the various atoms in an attempt to satisfy the octet rule (or duet rule for H). Keep in mind that practice makes perfect. After practicing you can (and will) become very adept at drawing Lewis structures.

a. HCN has 1 + 4 + 5 = 10 valence electrons.

$$H—C—N \qquad H—C≡N:$$

Skeletal   Lewis
structure   structure

Skeletal structure uses 4 e⁻; 6 e⁻ remain

b. PH₃ has 5 + 3(1) = 8 valence electrons.

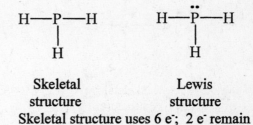

Skeletal   Lewis
structure   structure

Skeletal structure uses 6 e⁻; 2 e⁻ remain

c. CHCl₃ has 4 + 1 + 3(7) = 26 valence electrons.

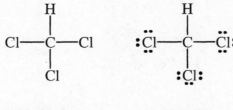

Skeletal   Lewis
structure   structure

Skeletal structure uses 8 e⁻; 18 e⁻ remain

d. NH₄⁺ has 5 + 4(1) - 1 = 8 valence electrons.

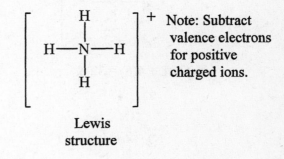

Lewis
structure

Note: Subtract valence electrons for positive charged ions.

e. H₂CO has 2(1) + 4 + 6 = 12 valence electrons.

$$:\overset{\cdot\cdot}{O}:$$
$$\underset{H \qquad H}{C}$$

f. SeF₂ has 6 + 2(7) = 20 valence electrons.

$$:\overset{\cdot\cdot}{\underset{\cdot\cdot}{F}}—\overset{\cdot\cdot}{Se}—\overset{\cdot\cdot}{\underset{\cdot\cdot}{F}}:$$

g. CO₂ has 4 + 2(6) = 16 valence electrons.

$$\overset{\cdot\cdot}{\underset{\cdot\cdot}{O}}=C=\overset{\cdot\cdot}{\underset{\cdot\cdot}{O}}$$

h. O₂ has 2(6) = 12 valence electrons.

$$\overset{\cdot\cdot}{\underset{\cdot\cdot}{O}}=\overset{\cdot\cdot}{\underset{\cdot\cdot}{O}}$$

i. HBr has 1 + 7 = 8 valence electrons.

$$H—\overset{\cdot\cdot}{\underset{\cdot\cdot}{Br}}:$$

48.   a. $POCl_3$ has $5 + 6 + 3(7) = 32$ valence electrons.

Skeletal   Lewis
structure   structure

This structure uses all 32 e⁻ while satisfying the octet rule for all atoms. This is a valid Lewis structure.

SO_4^{2-} has $6 + 4(6) + 2 = 32$ valence electrons.

Note: A negatively charged ion will have additional electrons to those that come from the valence shell of the atoms.

XeO_4, $8 + 4(6) = 32$ e⁻ PO_4^{3-}, $5 + 4(6) + 3 = 32$ e⁻

ClO_4^- has $7 + 4(6) + 1 = 32$ valence electrons.

Note: All of these species have the same number of atoms and the same number of valence electrons. They also have the same Lewis structure.

b. NF_3 has $5 + 3(7) = 26$ valence electrons. SO_3^{2-}, $6 + 3(6) + 2 = 26$ e⁻

Skeletal   Lewis
structure   structure

PO_3^{3-}, $5 + 3(6) + 3 = 26$ e⁻ ClO_3^-, $7 + 3(6) + 1 = 26$ e⁻

$$\left[\begin{array}{c} :\ddot{O}-\overset{\displaystyle ..}{\underset{\displaystyle :\ddot{O}:}{P}}-\ddot{O}: \end{array}\right]^{3-} \qquad\qquad \left[\begin{array}{c} :\ddot{O}-\overset{\displaystyle ..}{\underset{\displaystyle :\ddot{O}:}{Cl}}-\ddot{O}: \end{array}\right]^{-}$$

Note: Species with the same number of atoms and valence electrons have similar Lewis structures.

c. ClO_2^- has $7 + 2(6) + 1 = 20$ valence electrons.

$$O-Cl-O \qquad\qquad \left[:\ddot{O}-\ddot{Cl}-\ddot{O}: \right]^{-}$$

Skeletal   Lewis
structure   structure

SCl_2, $6 + 2(7) = 20$ e⁻ PCl_2^-, $5 + 2(7) + 1 = 20$ e⁻

$$:\ddot{Cl}-\ddot{S}-\ddot{Cl}: \qquad\qquad \left[:\ddot{Cl}-\ddot{P}-\ddot{Cl}: \right]^{-}$$

Note: Species with the same number of atoms and valence electrons have similar Lewis structures.

49.   Molecules/ions that have the same number of valence electrons and the same number of atoms will have similar Lewis structures.

50.   a. NO_2^- has $5 + 2(6) + 1 = 18$ valence electrons. The skeletal structure is: $O-N-O$

To get an octet about the nitrogen and only use 18 e⁻, we must form a double bond to one of the oxygen atoms.

$$\left[\ddot{O}=\ddot{N}-\ddot{O}: \right]^{-} \longleftrightarrow \left[:\ddot{O}-\ddot{N}=\ddot{O} \right]^{-}$$

Since there is no reason to have the double bond to a particular oxygen atom, we can draw two resonance structures. Each Lewis structure uses the correct number of electrons and satisfies the octet rules so each is a valid Lewis structure. Resonance structures occur when you have multiple bonds that can be in various positions. We say the actual structure is an average of these two resonance structures.

NO_3^- has $5 + 3(6) + 1 = 24$ valence electrons. We can draw three resonance structures for NO_3^-, with the double bond rotating between the three oxygen atoms.

N_2O_4 has $2(5) + 4(6) = 34$ valence electrons. We can draw four resonance structures for N_2O_4.

b. OCN^- has $6 + 4 + 5 + 1 = 16$ valence electrons. We can draw three resonance structures for OCN^-.

SCN^- has $6 + 4 + 5 + 1 = 16$ valence electrons. Three resonance structures can be drawn.

N_3^- has $3(5) + 1 = 16$ valence electrons. As with OCN^- and SCN^-, three different resonance structures can be drawn.

51.   Ozone: O_3 has $3(6) = 18$ valence electrons. Two resonance structures can be drawn.

Sulfur dioxide: SO_2 has $6 + 2(6) = 18$ valence electrons. Two resonance structures are possible.

Sulfur trioxide: SO_3 has $6 + 3(6) = 24$ valence electrons. Three resonance structures are possible.

52.   PAN ($H_3C_2NO_5$) has $3(1) + 2(4) + 5 + 5(6) = 46$ valence electrons.

Skeletal structure with complete octets about oxygen atoms (46 electrons used).

This structure has used all 46 electrons, but there are only six electrons around one of the carbon atoms and the nitrogen atom. Two unshared pairs must become shared, that is we form two double bonds.

(last form not important)

53. CH_3NCO has $4 + 3(1) + 5 + 4 + 6 = 22$ valence electrons. The order of the elements in the formula give the skeletal structure.

54. S_2Cl_2 has $2(6) + 2(7) = 26$ valence electrons.

SCl_2 has $6 + 2(7) = 20$ valence electrons.

55.   Benzene has $6(4) + 6(1) = 30$ valence electrons. Two resonance structures can be drawn for benzene. The actual structure of benzene is an average of these two resonance structures, that is, all carbon-carbon bonds are equivalent with a bond length and bond strength somewhere between a single and a double bond.

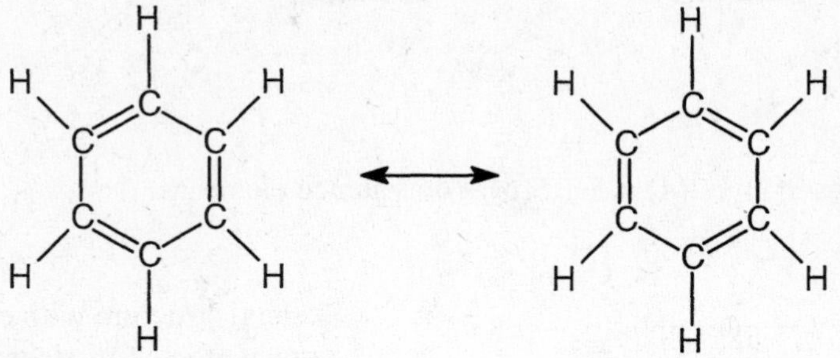

56.   We will use a hexagon to represent the six-membered carbon ring and we will omit the 4 hydrogen atoms and the three lone pairs of electrons on each chlorine. If no resonance exists, we could draw 4 different molecules:

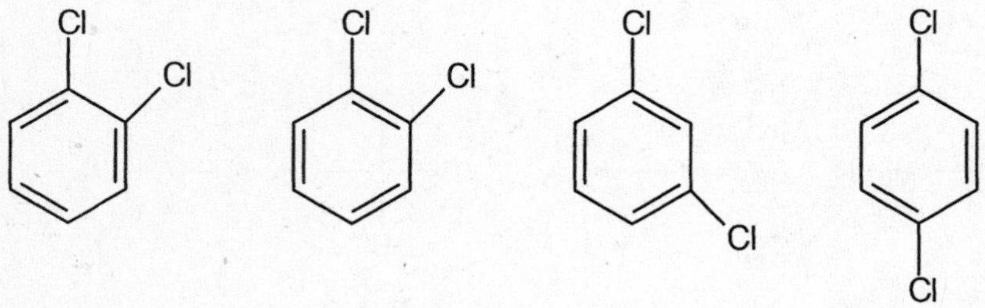

If the double bonds in the benzene ring exhibit resonance, then we can draw only three different dichlorobenzenes. The circle in the hexagon represents the delocalization of the three double bonds in the benzene ring (see Exercise 13.55).

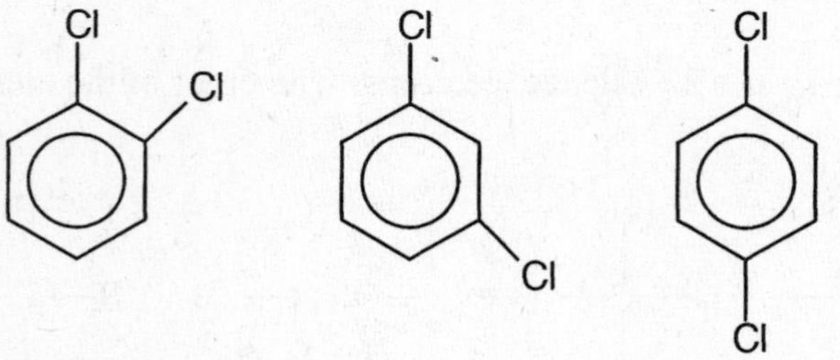

With resonance, all carbon-carbon bonds are equivalent. We can't distinguish between a single and double bond between adjacent carbons that have a chlorine attached. That only 3 isomers are observed provides evidence for the existence of resonance.

57.   Borazine ($B_3N_3H_6$) has $3(3) + 3(5) + 6(1) = 30$ valence electrons. The possible resonance structures are similar to those of benzene in Exercise 13.55.

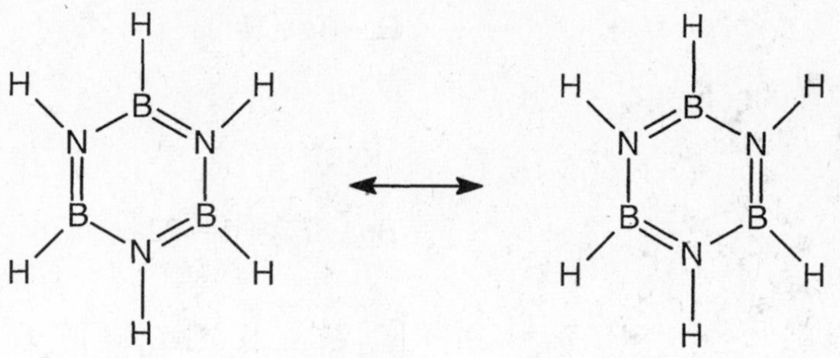

58.

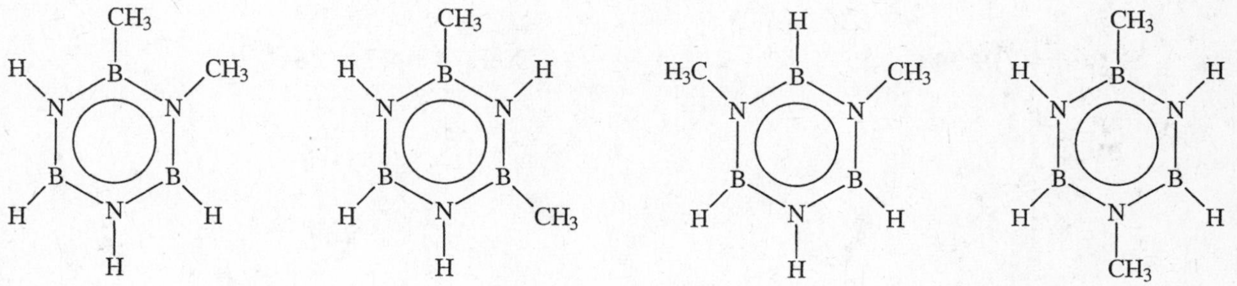

There are four different dimethylborazines. The circle in the above structures represents the ability of borazine to form resonance structures (see Exercise 13.57) and CH_3 is shorthand for three hydrogen atoms singly bonded to a carbon atom.

There would be 5 structures if there were no resonance. All of the structures drawn above plus an additional one related to the first Lewis structure above.

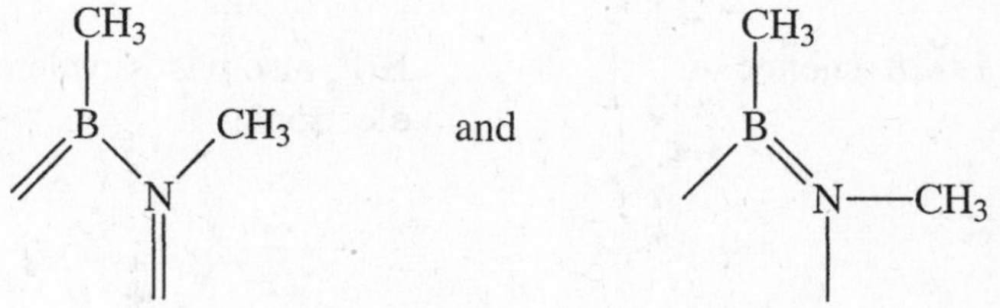

59.   In each case in this problem, the octet rule cannot be satisfied for the central atom. BeH_2 and BH_3 have too few electrons around the central atom and all the others have to many electrons around the central atom. Always try to satisfy the octet rule for every atom, but when it is impossible, the central atom is the species assumed to disobey the octet rule.

PF_5, $5 + 5(7) = 40$ e⁻

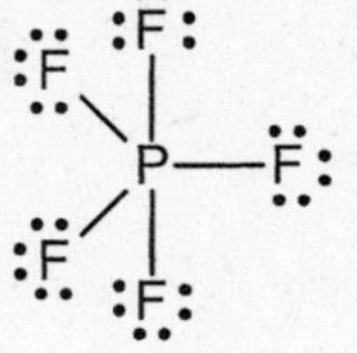

BeH_2, $2 + 2(1) = 4$ e⁻

H – Be – H

BH_3, $3 + 3(1) = 6$ e⁻

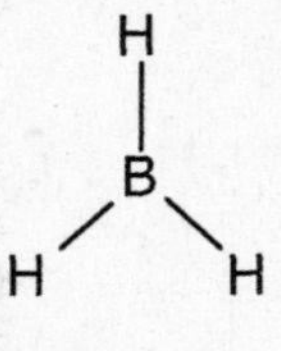

Br_3^-, $3(7) + 1 = 22$ e⁻

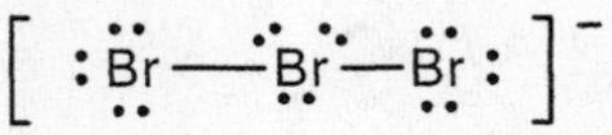

SF_4, $6 + 4(7) = 34$ e⁻

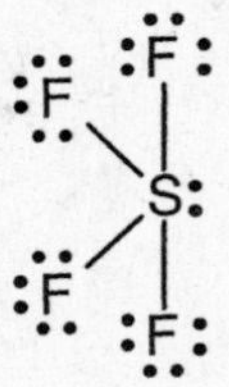

XeF_4, $8 + 4(7) = 36$ e⁻

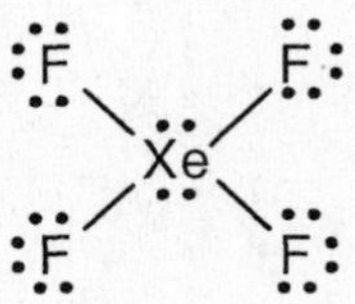

ClF_5, $7 + 5(7) = 42$ e⁻

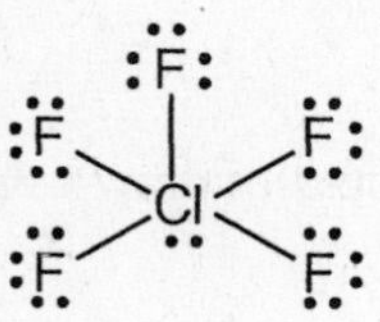

SF_6, $6 + 6(7) = 48$ e⁻

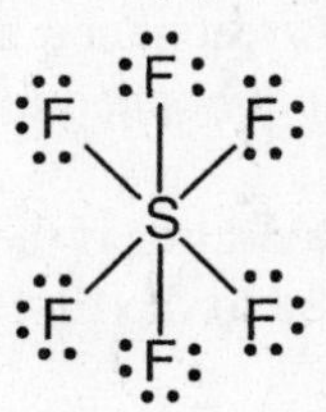

60. ClF_3 has $7 + 3(7) = 28$ valence electrons.

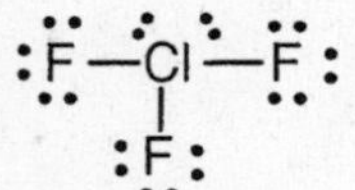

BrF₃ also has 28 valence electrons.

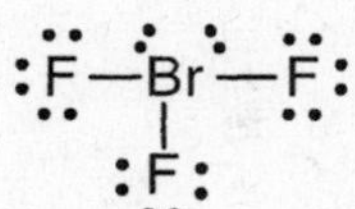

We expand the octet of the central Cl atom in ClF_3 and the central Br atom in BrF_3.

61. CO_3^{2-} has $4 + 3(6) + 2 = 24$ valence electrons.

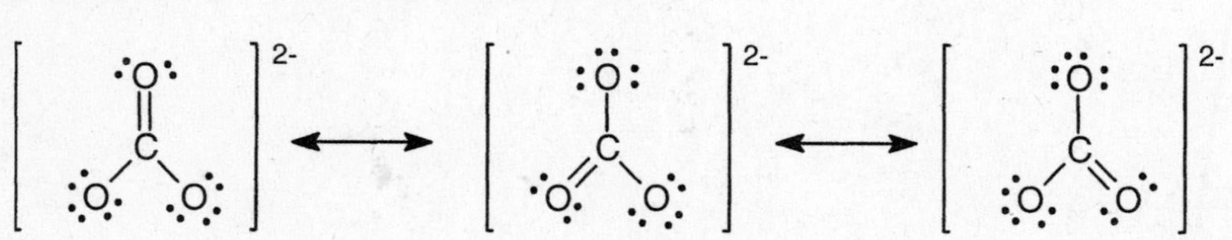

HCO_3^- has $1 + 4 + 3(6) + 1 = 24$ valence electrons.

H_2CO_3 has $2(1) + 4 + 3(6) = 24$ valence electrons.

The Lewis structures for the reactants and products are:

Bonds broken:	Bonds formed:
2 C – O (358 kJ/mol)	1 C = O (799 kJ/mol)
1 O – H (467 kJ/mol)	1 O – H (467 kJ/mol)

$\Delta H = 2(358) + 467 - [799 + 467] = -83$ kJ; The carbon-oxygen double bond is stronger than two carbon-oxygen single bonds, hence CO_2 and H_2O are more stable than H_2CO_3.

62.   The nitrogen-nitrogen bond length of 112 pm is between a double (120 pm) and a triple (110 pm) bond. The nitrogen-oxygen bond length of 119 pm is between a single (147 pm) and a double bond (115 pm). The last resonance structure doesn't appear to be as important as the other two since there is no evidence from bond lengths for a nitrogen-nitrogen single bond or a nitrogen-oxygen triple bond as in the third resonance form. We can adequately describe the structure of N_2O using the resonance forms:

63. CO_3^{2-} has $4 + 3(6) + 2 = 24$ valence electrons.

Three resonance structures can be drawn for CO_3^{2-}. The actual structure for CO_3^{2-} is an average of these three resonance structures. That is, the three C – O bond lengths are all equivalent, with a length somewhere between a single and a double bond. The actual bond length of 136 pm is consistent with this resonance view of CO_3^{2-}.

64.   The Lewis structures for the various species are below:

CO (10 e⁻):   Triple bond between C and O

CO_2 (16 e⁻):   Double bond between C and O

CO_3^{2-} (24 e⁻):

Average of 1 1/3 bond between C and O

CH_3OH (14 e⁻):   Single bond between C and O

As the number of bonds increase between two atoms, bond length decreases and bond strength increases. With this in mind, then:

longest → shortest C – O bond: $CH_3OH > CO_3^{2-} > CO_2 > CO$

weakest → strongest C – O bond: $CH_3OH < CO_3^{2-} < CO_2 < CO$

65. N_2 (10 e⁻):   : N≡N :   Triple bond between N and N.

N_2F_4 (38 e⁻):   Single bond between N and N.

N_2F_2 (24 e⁻):   Double bond between N and N.

As the number of bonds increase between two atoms, bond strength increases and bond length decreases. From the Lewis structure, the shortest to longest N-N bonds is: $N_2 < N_2F_2 < N_2F_4$.

Formal Charge

66. Formal charge = number of valence electrons on free atom - number of lone pair electrons on atom - 1/2 (number of shared electrons of atom). The formal charges for the atoms in the three resonance structures are:

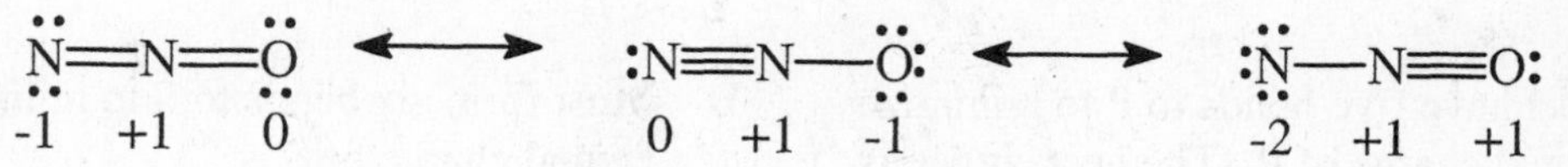

For:

, FC = 5 - 4 - 1/2(4) = -1

, FC = 5 - 1/2(8) = +1, Same for (≡N—) and (—N≡)

, FC = 5 - 6 - 1/2(2) = -2; , FC = 5 - 2 - 1/2(6) = 0

, FC = 6 - 4 - 1/2(4) = 0; , FC = 6 - 6 - 1/2(2) = -1

, FC = 6 - 2 - 1/2(6) = +1

We should eliminate N – N ≡ O since it has a formal charge of +1 on the most electronegative element (O). This is consistent with the observation that the N – N bond is between a double and triple bond and that the N – O bond is between a single and double bond.

67. See Exercise 13.48a for the Lewis structures of $POCl_3$, SO_4^{2-}, ClO_4^- and PO_4^{3-}. All of these compounds/ions have similar Lewis structures to those of SO_2Cl_2 and XeO_4 shown below.

a. $POCl_3$: P, FC = 5 - 1/2(8) = +1   b. SO_4^{2-}: S, FC = 6 - 1/2(8) = +2

c. ClO_4^-: Cl, FC = 7 - 1/2(8) = +3   d. PO_4^{3-}: P, FC = 5 - 1/2(8) = +1

e. SO_2Cl_2, 6 + 2(6) + 2(7) = 32 e⁻   f. XeO_4, 8 + 4(6) = 32 e⁻

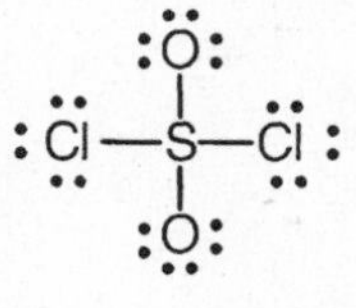

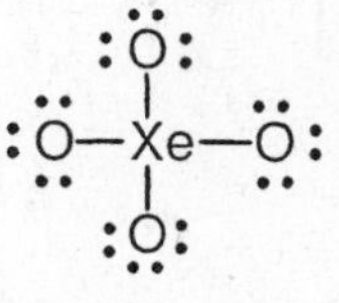

S, FC = 6 - 1/2(8) = +2   Xe, FC = 8 - 1/2(8) = +4

g. ClO_3^-, $7 + 3(6) + 1 = 26$ e$^-$ h. NO_4^{3-}, $5 + 4(6) + 3 = 32$ e$^-$

$$\left[\; :\ddot{O}-\ddot{Cl}-\ddot{O}: \atop \qquad :\ddot{O}: \right]^-$$

$$\left[\; :\ddot{O}-N-\ddot{O}: \atop \qquad :\ddot{O}: \right]^{3-}$$

Cl, FC = 7 - 2 - 1/2(6) = +2   N, FC = 5 - 1/2(8) = +1

68.   For SO_4^{2-}, ClO_4^-, PO_4^{3-} and ClO_3^-, only one of the possible resonance structures is drawn.

a. Must have five bonds to P to minimize   b. Must form six bonds to S to minimize
formal charge of P. The best choice is   formal charge of S.
to form a double bond to O since this
will give O a formal charge of zero
and single bonds to Cl for the same
reason.

$$:\ddot{Cl}-P-\ddot{Cl}: \qquad P, FC = 0$$

$$\left[\; :\ddot{O}-S-\ddot{O}: \right]^{2-} \qquad S, FC = 0$$

c. Must form seven bonds to Cl   d. Must form five bonds to P to
to minimize formal charge.   to minimize formal charge.

$$\left[\; \ddot{O}=Cl-\ddot{O}: \right]^- \qquad Cl, FC = 0$$

$$\left[\; :\ddot{O}-P-\ddot{O}: \right]^{3-} \qquad P, FC = 0$$

e.   f.

$$:\ddot{Cl}-S-\ddot{Cl}: \qquad S, FC = 0$$

$$\ddot{O}=Xe=\ddot{O} \qquad Xe, FC = 0$$

g.

$$\left[\; \ddot{O}=\ddot{Cl}=\ddot{O} \atop \qquad :\ddot{O}: \right]^- \qquad Cl, FC = 0$$

h.   We can't . The following structure has a zero formal charge for N:

$$\begin{bmatrix} & :\overset{..}{O}: & \\ :\overset{..}{O}-N-\overset{..}{O}: & \\ & :\overset{..}{O}: & \end{bmatrix}^{3-}$$

but N does not expand its octet. We wouldn't expect this resonance form to exist.

69. O_2F_2 has $2(6) + 2(7) = 26$ valence e⁻.   The formal charge and oxidation number of each atom is below the Lewis structure of O_2F_2.

$$:\overset{..}{\underset{..}{F}}-\overset{..}{\underset{..}{O}}-\overset{..}{\underset{..}{O}}-\overset{..}{\underset{..}{F}}:$$

Formal Charge	0	0	0	0
Oxid. Number	-1	+1	+1	-1

Oxidation numbers are more useful when accounting for the reactivity of O_2F_2. We are forced to assign +1 as the oxidation number for oxygen. Oxygen is very electronegative, and +1 is not a stable oxidation state for this element.

70.   OCN⁻ has $6 + 4 + 5 + 1 = 16$ valence electrons.

$$\begin{bmatrix} :\overset{..}{O}=C=\overset{..}{N}: \end{bmatrix}^{-} \longleftrightarrow \begin{bmatrix} :\overset{..}{\underset{..}{O}}-C\equiv N: \end{bmatrix}^{-} \longleftrightarrow \begin{bmatrix} :O\equiv C-\overset{..}{\underset{..}{N}}: \end{bmatrix}^{-}$$

Formal charge	0	0	-1		-1	0	0		+1	0	-2

Only the first two resonance structures should be important. The third places a positive formal charge on the most electronegative atom in the ion and a -2 formal charge on N.

CNO⁻:

$$\begin{bmatrix} :\overset{..}{C}=N=\overset{..}{O}: \end{bmatrix}^{-} \longleftrightarrow \begin{bmatrix} :C\equiv N-\overset{..}{\underset{..}{O}}: \end{bmatrix}^{-} \longleftrightarrow \begin{bmatrix} :\overset{..}{\underset{..}{C}}-N\equiv O: \end{bmatrix}^{-}$$

Formal charge	-2	+1	0		-1	+1	-1		-3	+1	+1

All of the resonance structures for fulminate (CNO⁻) involve greater formal charges than in cyanate (OCN⁻), making fulminate more reactive (less stable).

Molecular Structure and Polarity

71.   The first step always is to draw a valid Lewis structure when predicting molecular structure. When resonance is possible, only one of the possible resonance structures is necessary to predict the correct structure since all resonance structures give the same structure. The Lewis structures are in

Exercises 13.47, 13.48 and 13.50. The structures and bond angles for each follow.

13.47   a.   HCN: linear, 180°   b. PH_3: trigonal pyramid, < 109.5°

c. $CHCl_3$: tetrahedral, 109.5°   d. NH_4^+: tetrahedral, 109.5°

e. H_2CO: trigonal planar, 120°   f. SeF_2: V-shaped or bent, < 109.5°

g. CO_2: linear, 180°   h and i. O_2 and HBr are both linear, but there is
                                                     no bond angle in either.

Note: PH_3 and SeF_2 both have lone pairs of electrons on the central atom which result in bond angles that are something less than predicted from a tetrahedral arrangement (109.5°). However, we cannot predict the exact number. For these cases, we will just insert a less than sign to show this phenomenon.

13.48   a.   All are tetrahedral; 109.5°

b.   All are trigonal pyramid; < 109.5°

c.   All are V-shaped; < 109.5°

13.50   a. NO_2^-: V-shaped, ≈ 120°; NO_3^-: trigonal planar, 120°

N_2O_4: trigonal planar, 120° about both N atoms

b. OCN^-, SCN^- and N_3^- are all linear with 180° bond angles.

72.   a. SeO_3, $6 + 3(6) = 24$ e$^-$

SeO_3 has a trigonal planar molecular structure with all bond angles equal to 120°. Note that any one of the resonance structures could be used to predict molecular structure and bond angles.

b. SeO_2, $6 + 2(6) = 18$ e$^-$

SeO_2 has a V-shaped molecular structure. We would expect the bond angle to be approximately 120° as expected for trigonal planar geometry.

Note: Both SeO_3 and SeO_2 structures have three effective pairs of electrons about the central atom. All of the structures are based on a trigonal planar geometry, but only SeO_3 is described as having a trigonal planar structure. Molecular structure always describes the relative positions of the atoms.

c. PCl_3 has $5 + 3(7) =$ 26 valence electrons.

d. SCl_2 has $6 + 2(7) =$ 20 valence electrons

Trigonal pyramid; all angles are $< 109.5°$.

V-shaped; angle is $< 109.5°$.

e. SiF_4 has $4 + 4(7) = 32$ valence electrons.

Tetrahedral; all angles are $109.5°$.

Note: In PCl_3, SCl_2, and SiF_4, there are 4 pairs of electrons about the central atom in each case. All of the structures are based on a tetrahedral geometry, but only SiF_4 has a tetrahedral structure. We consider only the relative positions of the atoms when describing the molecular structure.

73. From the Lewis structures (see Exercises 13.59 and 13.60), Br_3^- would have a linear molecular structure, ClF_3 and BrF_3 would have a T-shaped molecular structure and SF_4 would have a see-saw molecular structure. For example, consider ClF_3 (28 valence electrons):

The central Cl atom is surrounded by 5 electron pairs, which requires a trigonal bipyramid geometry. Since there are 3 bonded atoms and 2 lone pairs of electrons about Cl, we describe the molecular structure of ClF_3 as T-shaped with predicted bond angles of about $90°$. The actual bond angles will be slightly less than $90°$ due to the stronger repulsive effect of the lone pair electrons as compared to the bonding electrons.

74. From the Lewis structures (see Exercise 13.59), XeF_4 would have a square planar molecular structure and ClF_5 would have a square pyramid molecular structure.

75. a. $XeCl_2$ has $8 + 2(7) = 22$ valence electrons.

$180°$

There are 5 pairs of electrons about the central Xe atom. The structure will be based on a trigonal bipyramid geometry. The most stable arrangement of the atoms in $XeCl_2$ is a linear molecular structure with a $180°$ bond angle.

b. ICl_3 has $7 + 3(7) = 28$ valence electrons.

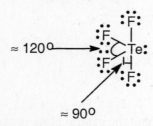

T-shaped; The ClICl angles are $\approx 90°$. Since the lone pairs will take up more space, the ClICl bond angles will probably be slightly less than 90°.

c. TeF_4 has $6 + 4(7) = 34$ valence electrons.

d. PCl_5 has $5 + 5(7) = 40$ valence electrons.

See-saw or teeter-totter or distorted tetrahedron

Trigonal bipyramid

All of the species in this exercise have 5 pairs of electrons around the central atom. All of the structures are based on a trigonal bipyramid geometry, but only in PCl_5 are all of the pairs bonding pairs. Thus, PCl_5 is the only one we describe the molecular structure as trigonal bipyramid. Still, we had to begin with the trigonal bipyramid geometry to get to the structures (and bond angles) of the others.

76. a. ICl_5, $7 + 5(7) = 42$ e⁻

b. $XeCl_4$, $8 + 4(7) = 36$ e⁻

Square pyramid, $\approx 90°$ bond angles

Square planar, 90° bond angles

c. $SeCl_6$ has $6 + 6(7) = 48$ valence electrons.

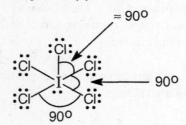

Octahedral, 90° bond angles

Note: All these species have 6 pairs of electrons around the central atom. All three structures are based on the octahedron, but only $SeCl_6$ has an octahedral molecular structure.

77.   Let us consider the molecules with three pairs of electrons around the central atom first; these molecules are SeO_3 and SeO_2 and both have a trigonal planar arrangement of electron pairs. Both these molecules have polar bonds but only SeO_2 has a dipole moment. The three bond dipoles from the three polar $Se - O$ bonds in SeO_3 will all cancel when summed together. Hence, SeO_3 is nonpolar since the overall molecule has no resulting dipole moment. In SeO_2, the two $Se - O$ bond dipoles do not cancel when summed together, hence SeO_2 has a dipole moment (is polar). Since O is more electronegative than Se, the negative end of the dipole moment is between the two O atoms and the positive end is around the Se atom. The arrow in the following illustration represents the overall dipole moment in SeO_2. Note that to predict polarity for SeO_2, either of the two resonance structures can be used.

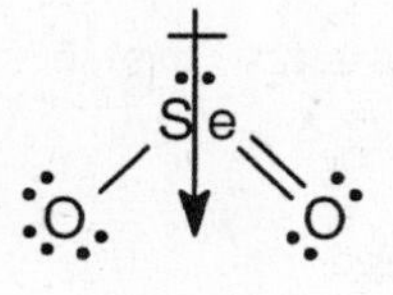

The other molecules in Exercise 13.72 (PCl_3, SCl_2, and SiF_4) have a tetrahedral arrangement of electron pairs. All have polar bonds; in SiF_4 the individual bond dipoles cancel when summed together, and in PCl_3 and SCl_2 the individual bond dipoles do not cancel. Therefore, SiF_4 has no dipole moment (is nonpolar) and PCl_3 and SCl_2 have dipole moments (are polar). For PCl_3, the negative end of the dipole moment is between the more electronegative chlorine atoms and the positive end is around P. For SCl_2, the negative end is between the more electronegative Cl atoms and the positive end of the dipole moment is around S.

78.   The molecules in Exercise 13.75 ($XeCl_2$, ICl_3, TeF_4, and PCl_5) all have a trigonal bipyramid arrangement of electron pairs. All of these molecules have polar bonds, but only TeF_4 and ICl_3 have dipole moments. The bond dipoles from the five P–Cl bonds in PCl_5 cancel each other when summed together so PCl_5 has no dipole moment. The bond dipoles in $XeCl_2$ also cancel:

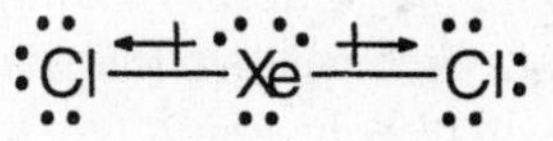

Since the bond dipoles from the two $Xe - Cl$ bonds are equal in magnitude but point in opposite directions, then they cancel each other and $XeCl_2$ has no dipole moment (is nonpolar). For TeF_4 and ICl_3, the arrangement of these molecules are such that the individual bond dipoles do <u>not</u> all cancel so each has an overall dipole moment.

The molecules in Exercise 13.76 (ICl_5, $XeCl_4$, and $SeCl_6$) all have an octahedral arrangement of electron pairs. All of these molecules have polar bonds, but only ICl_5 has an overall dipole moment. The six bond dipoles in $SeCl_6$ all cancel each other so $SeCl_6$ has no dipole moment. The same is true for $XeCl_4$:

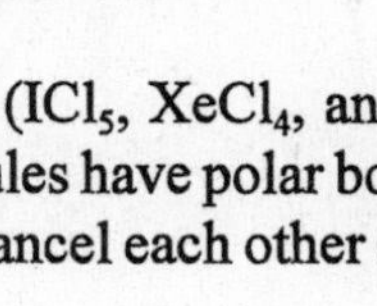

When the four bond dipoles are added together, they all cancel each other and $XeCl_4$ has no overall dipole moment. ICl_5 has a structure where the individual bond dipoles do <u>not</u> all cancel, hence ICl_5 has a dipole moment.

79.   The two usual requirements for a polar molecule are:
       1. polar bonds (bond dipoles)
       2. a structure such that the dipoles due to the polar bonds do not cancel.

       In addition, some molecules that have no polar bonds, but contain unsymmetrical lone pairs are polar. For example, PH_3 is slightly polar even though it contains only nonpolar bonds.

80. EO_3^- is the formula of the ion. The Lewis structure has 26 valence electrons. Let x = number of valence electrons of element E.

       $$26 = x + 3(6) + 1, \ x = 7 \text{ valence electrons}$$

       Element E is a halogen because halogens have 7 valence electrons. Some possible identities are F, Cl, Br and I. The EO_3^- ion has a trigonal pyramid molecular structure with bond angles < 109.5°.

81.   The formula is EF_2O^{2-} and the Lewis structure has 28 valence electrons.

       $$28 = x + 2(7) + 6 + 2, \ x = 6 \text{ valence electrons for element E}$$

       Element E must belong to the group 6A elements since E has 6 valence electrons. E must also be a row 3 or heavier element since this ion has more than 8 electrons around the central E atom (row 2 elements never have more than 8 electrons around them). Some possible identities for E are S, Se and Te. The ion has a T-shaped molecular structure (see Exercise 13.73) with bond angles of ≈90°.

82. H_2O and NH_3 have lone pair electrons on the central atoms. These lone pair electrons require more room than the bonding electrons which tends to compress the angles between the bonding pairs. The bond angle for H_2O is the smallest since oxygen has two lone pairs on the central atom and the bond angle is compressed more than in NH_3 where N has only one lone pair.

83.   Molecules which have an overall dipole moment are called polar molecules and molecules which do not have an overall dipole moment are called nonpolar molecules.

       a. OCl_2, $6 + 2(7) = 20 \ e^-$ KrF_2, $8 + 2(7) = 22 \ e^-$

       V-shaped, polar; OCl_2 is polar because   Linear, nonpolar; The molecule is
       the two O – Cl bond dipoles don't cancel   nonpolar because the two Kr – F
       each other. The resultant dipole moment   bond dipoles cancel each other.
       is shown in the drawing.

BeH_2, $2 + 2(1) = 4$ e$^-$

Linear, nonpolar; Be – H bond dipoles
are equal and point in opposite directions.
They cancel each other. BeH_2 is nonpolar.

SO_2, $6 + 2(6) = 18$ e$^-$

V-shaped, polar; The S – O bond dipoles
do not cancel so SO_2 is polar (has a dipole
moment). Only one resonance structure
is shown.

Note: All four species contain three atoms. They have different structures because the number
of lone pairs of electrons around the central atom are different in each case.

b. SO_3, $6 + 3(6) = 24$ e$^-$

Trigonal planar, nonpolar;
Bond dipoles cancel. Only one
resonance structure is shown.

NF_3, $5 + 3(7) = 26$ e$^-$

Trigonal pyramid, polar;
Bond dipoles do not cancel.

IF_3 has $7 + 3(7) = 28$ valence electrons.

T-shaped, polar; Bond dipoles do not cancel.

Note: Each molecule has the same number of atoms, but the structures are different because of
differing numbers of lone pairs around each central atom.

c. CF_4, $4 + 4(7) = 32$ e$^-$

Tetrahedral, nonpolar;
Bond dipoles cancel.

SeF_4, $6 + 4(7) = 34$ e$^-$

See-saw, polar;
Bond dipoles do not cancel.

KrF_4, $8 + 4(7) = 36$ valence electrons

Square planar, nonpolar;
Bond dipoles cancel.

Again, each molecule has the same number of atoms, but a different structure because of differing numbers of lone pairs around the central atom.

d. IF_5, $7 + 5(7) = 42$ e$^-$ AsF_5, $5 + 5(7) = 40$ e$^-$

Square pyramid, polar;   Trigonal bipyramid, nonpolar;
Bond dipoles do not cancel.   Bond dipoles cancel.

Yet again, the molecules have the same number of atoms, but different structures because of the presence of differing numbers of lone pairs.

84.   a.

The C–H bonds are assumed nonpolar since the electronegativities of C and H are about equal.

$\delta+$ $\delta-$
C – Cl is the charge distribution for each C – Cl bond. The two individual C – Cl bond dipoles add together to give an overall dipole moment for the molecule. The overall dipole will point from C (positive end) to the midpoint of the two Cl atoms (negative end).

δ^+ δ^-
C – Cl

The C – H bond is essentially nonpolar. The three C – Cl bond dipoles in $CHCl_3$ add together to give an overall dipole moment for the molecule. The overall dipole will have the negative end at the midpoint of the three chlorines and the positive end around the carbon.

CCl_4 is nonpolar. CCl_4 is a tetrahedral molecule where all four C – Cl bond dipoles cancel when added together. Let's consider just the C and two of the Cl atoms. There will be a net dipole pointing in the direction of the middle of the two Cl atoms.

There will be an equal and opposite dipole arising from the other two Cl atoms. Combining:

The two dipoles will cancel and CCl_4 is nonpolar.

b. CO_2 is nonpolar. CO_2 is a linear molecule with two equivalence bond dipoles that cancel.

N_2O is polar since the bond dipoles do not cancel.

c. NH_3 is polar. The 3 N – H bond dipoles add together to give a net dipole in the direction of the lone pair. We would predict PH_3 to be nonpolar on the basis of electronegativitity, i.e., P – H bonds are nonpolar. However, the presence of the lone pair makes the PH_3 molecule slightly polar. The net dipole is in the direction of the lone pair and has a magnitude about one third that of the NH_3 dipole.

85.   All these molecules have polar bonds that are symmetrically arranged about the central atoms. In each molecule, the individual bond dipoles cancel to give no net overall dipole moment. All these molecules are nonpolar even though they all contain polar bonds.

86.   a.

Angles a and b are both ≈ 120°.   Angles c and d are both ≈120°.

b.   The N – F bond dipoles cancel in the first structure so it is nonpolar. The N – F bond dipoles do not cancel in the second structure so it is polar.

87.　a.

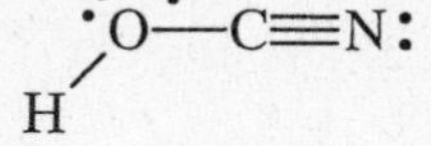

Polar; The bond dipoles do
not cancel.

b.

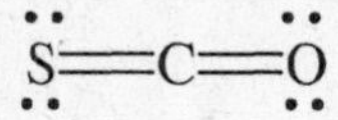

Polar; The C – O bond is a more
polar bond than the C – S bond. So
the two bond dipoles do not cancel
each other.

c.

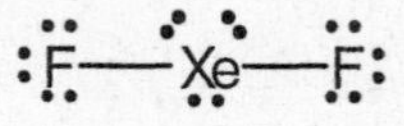

Nonpolar; The two Xe–F bond
dipoles cancel each other.

d.

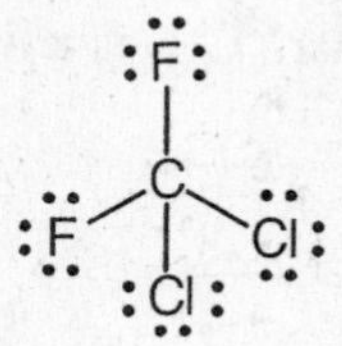

Polar; All the bond dipoles are not
equivalent, so they don't cancel each
other.

e.

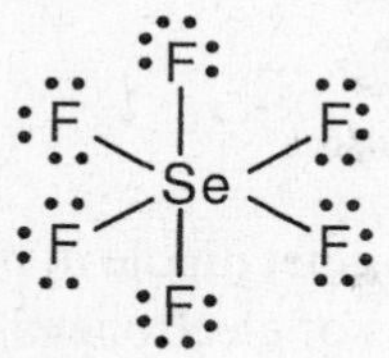

Nonpolar; The six Se – F bond dipoles
cancel each other.

f.

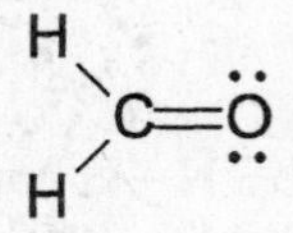

Polar; Bond dipoles are not equivalent
so they don't cancel each other.

Additional Exercises

88.　The general structure of the trihalide ions is:

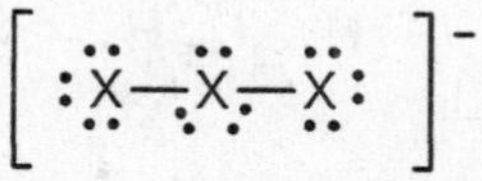

Bromine and iodine are large enough and have low energy, empty d-orbitals to accommodate the
expanded octet. Fluorine is small and its valence shell contains only 2s and 2p orbitals (4 orbitals)
and cannot expand its octet. The lowest energy d orbitals in F are 3d; they are too high in energy
compared to 2s and 2p to be used in bonding.

89.　CS_2 has $4 + 2(6) = 16$ valence electrons. C_3S_2 has $3(4) + 2(6) = 24$ valence electrons.

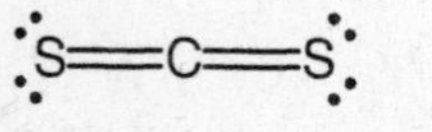

　　linear; 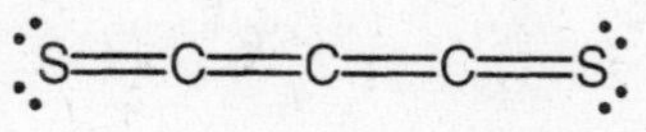　　　　linear

90.　TeF_5^- has $6 + 5(7) + 1 = 42$ valence electrons.

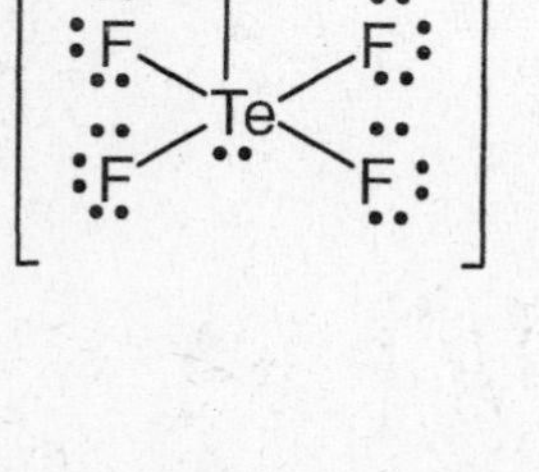

The lone pair of electrons around Te exerts a stronger repulsion than the bonding pairs, pushing the four square planar F's away from the lone pair and thus reducing the bond angles between the axial F atom and the square planar F atoms.

91. As the halogen atoms get larger, it becomes more difficult to fit three halogen atoms around the small nitrogen atom, and the NX_3 molecule becomes less stable.

92. XeF_2Cl_2, $8 + 2(7) + 2(7) = 36$ e⁻

The two possible structures for XeF_2Cl_2 are above. In the first structure, the F atoms are 90° apart from each other and the Cl atoms are also 90° apart. The individual bond dipoles would not cancel in this molecule, so this molecule is polar. In the second possible structure, the F atoms are 180° apart as are the Cl atoms. Here, the bond dipoles are symmetrically arranged so they do cancel out each other, and this molecule is nonpolar. Therefore, measurement of the dipole moment would differentiate between the two compounds.

93. The stable species are:

a. NaBr: In $NaBr_2$, the sodium ion would have a +2 charge assuming each bromine has a -1 charge. Sodium doesn't form stable Na^{2+} compounds.

b. ClO_4^-: ClO_4 has 31 valence electrons so it is impossible to satisfy the octet rule for all atoms in ClO_4. The extra electron from the -1 charge in ClO_4^- allows for complete octets for all atoms.

c. XeO_4: We can't draw a Lewis structure that obeys the octet rule for SO_4 (30 electrons), unlike with XeO_4 (32 electrons).

d. SeF_4: Both compounds require the central atom to expand its octet. O is too small and doesn't have low energy d orbitals to expand its octet (which is true for all row 2 elements).

94. If we can draw resonance forms for the anion after loss of H⁺, we can argue that the extra stability of the anion causes the proton to be more readily lost, i.e., makes the compound a better acid.

a.

b.

c.

In all 3 cases, extra resonance forms can be drawn for the anion that are not possible when the H^+ is present, which leads to enhanced stability.

95.   a.   Radius: $N^+ < N < N^-$;   IE: $N^- < N < N^+$

N$^+$ has the fewest electrons held by the 7 protons in the nucleus while N$^-$ has the most electrons held by the 7 protons. The 7 protons in the nucleus will hold the electrons most tightly in N$^+$ and least tightly in N$^-$. Therefore, N$^+$ has the smallest radius with the largest ionization energy (IE) and N$^-$ is the largest species with the smallest IE.

b.   Radius: $Cl^+ < Cl < Se < Se^-$;   IE: $Se^- < Se < Cl < Cl^+$

The general trends tell us that Cl has a smaller radius than Se and a larger IE than Se. Cl$^+$, with fewer electron-electron repulsions than Cl, will be smaller than Cl and have a larger IE. Se$^-$, with more electron-electron repulsions than Se, will be larger than Se and have a smaller IE.

c.   Radius: $Sr^{2+} < Rb^+ < Br^-$;   IE: $Br^- < Rb^+ < Sr^{2+}$

These ions are isoelectronic. The species with the most protons (Sr^{2+}) will hold the electrons most tightly and will have the smallest radius and largest IE. The ion with the fewest protons (Br$^-$) will hold the electrons least tightly and will have the largest radius and smallest IE.

96.   a. NO_2, $5 + 2(6) = 17$ e⁻ N_2O_4, $2(5) + 4(6) = 34$ e⁻

plus other resonance structures   plus other resonance structures

b. BF_3, $3 + 3(7) = 24$ e⁻ NH_3, $5 + 3(1) = 8$ e⁻

BF_3NH_3, $24 + 8 = 32$ e⁻

In reaction a, NO_2 has an odd number of electrons so it is impossible to satisfy the octet rule. By dimerizing to form N_2O_4, the odd electron on two NO_2 molecules can pair up giving a species whose Lewis structure can satisfy the octet rule. In general odd electron species are very reactive. In reaction b, BF_3 can be considered electron deficient. Boron only has six electrons around it. By forming BF_3NH_3, the boron atom satisfies the octet rule by accepting a lone pair of electrons from NH_3 to form a fourth bond.

97.   Nonmetals form covalent compounds. Nonmetals have valence electrons in the s and p orbitals. Since there are 4 total s and p orbitals, then there is room for only eight electrons (the octet rule).

98.   This molecule has 30 valence electrons. The only C–N bond that can possibly have double bond character is the N bound to the C with O attached. Double bonds to the other two C–N bonds would require carbon in each case to have 10 valence electrons (which carbon never does).

99. S_2N_2 has $2(6) + 2(5) = 22$ valence electrons.

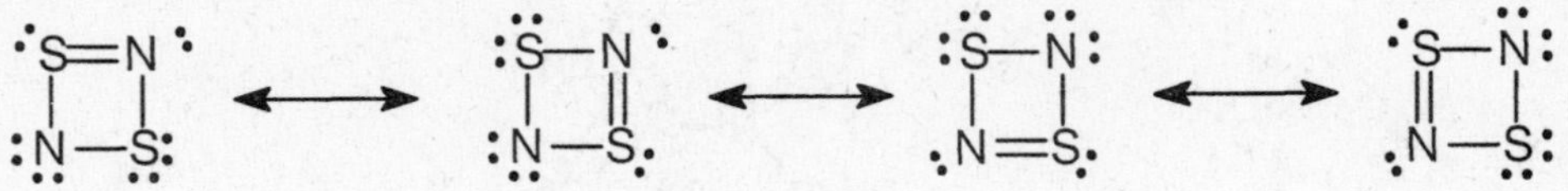

100.   a. $Na^+(g) + Cl^-(g) \rightarrow NaCl(s)$ b. $NH_4^+(g) + Br^-(g) \rightarrow NH_4Br(s)$

        c. $Mg^{2+}(g) + S^{2-}(g) \rightarrow MgS(s)$ d. $1/2\ O_2(g) \rightarrow O(g)$

        e. $O_2(g) \rightarrow 2\ O(g)$

101.   a. Al_2Cl_6 has $2(3) + 6(7) = 48$ valence electrons.

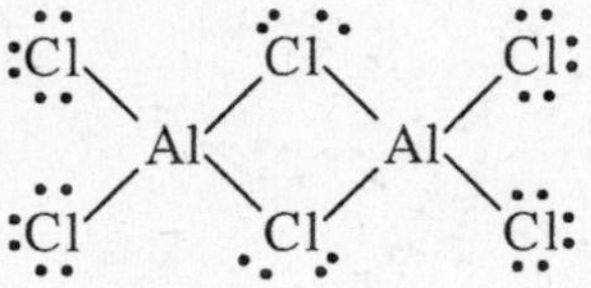

        b.   There are 4 pairs of electrons about each Al, we would predict the bond angles to be close to a tetrahedral angle of $109.5°$.

        c.   nonpolar; The individual bond dipoles will cancel.

102.   For carbon atoms to have a formal charge of zero, each C atom must satisfy the octet rule by forming four bonds (with no lone pairs). For nitrogen atoms to have a formal charge of zero, each N atom must satisfy the octet rule by forming three bonds and have one lone pair of electrons. For oxygen atoms to have a formal charge of zero, each O atom must satisfy the octet rule by forming two bonds and have two lone pairs of electrons. With these bonding requirements in mind, then the Lewis structure of histidine, where all atoms have a formal charge of zero, is:

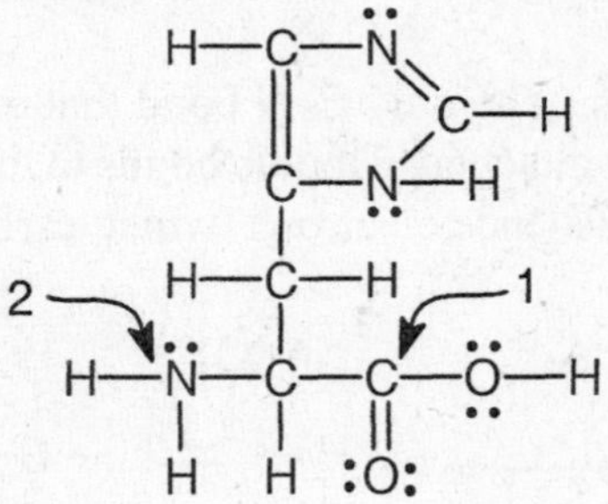

        We would expect $120°$ bond angles about the carbon atom labeled 1 and ~$109.5°$ bond angles about the nitrogen atom labeled 2. The nitrogen bond angles should be slightly smaller than $109.5°$ due to the lone pair of electrons on nitrogen.

103.   Yes, each structure has the same number of effective pairs around the central atom, giving the same predicted molecular structure for each compound/ion. (A multiple bond is counted as a single group of electrons.)

104.   a. $BrFI_2$, $7 + 7 + 2(7) = 28$ e⁻; Two possible structures exist; each has a T-shaped molecular structure.

         90° bond angles between I atoms   180° bond angle between I atoms

       b. XeO_2F_2, $8 + 2(6) + 2(7) = 34$ e⁻; Three possible structures exist; each has a see-saw molecular structure.

       90° bond angle   180° bond angle   120° bond angle
       between O atoms   between O atoms   between O atoms

       c. $TeF_2Cl_3^-$, $6 + 2(7) + 3(7) + 1 = 42$ e⁻; Three possible structures exist; each has a square pyramid molecular structure.

       One F is 180° from   Both F atoms are 90° from   Both F atoms are 90° from
       lone pair.   lone pair and 90° from   lone pair and 180° from
                                   each other.   each other.

Challenge Problems

105. KrF_2, $8 + 2(7) = 22$ e⁻; From the Lewis structure, we have a trigonal bipyramid arrangement of electron pairs with a linear molecular structure.

Hyperconjugation assumes that the overall bonding in KrF_2 is a combination of covalent and ionic contributions (see Section 13.13 of the text for discussion of hyperconjugation). Using hyperconjugation, two resonance structures are possible which keep the linear structure.

106.   See Figure 13.10 to see the data supporting MgO as an ionic compound. Note that the lattice energy is large enough to overcome all of the other processes (removing 2 electrons from Mg, etc.). The bond energy for O_2 (247 kJ/mol) and electron affinity (737 kJ/mol) are the same when making CO. However, ionizing carbon to form a C^{2+} ion must be too large. See Figure 12.35 to see that the first ionization energy for carbon is about 400 kJ/mol greater than the first IE for magnesium. If all other numbers were equal, the overall energy change would be down to ~200 kJ/mol (see Figure 13.10). It is not unreasonable that the second ionization energy for carbon is more than 200 kJ/mol greater than the second ionization energy of magnesium.

107.   a. $N(NO_2)_2^-$ contains $5 + 2(5) + 4(6) + 1 = 40$ valence electrons.

        The most likely structures are:

        There are other possible resonance structures, but these are most likely.

        b.   The NNN and all ONN and ONO bond angles should be about 120°.

c. $NH_4N(NO_2)_2 \rightarrow 2\ N_2 + 2\ H_2O + O_2$; Break and form all bonds.

Bonds broken: Bonds formed:

    4 N – H (391 kJ/mol)   2 N ≡ N (941 kJ/mol)
    1 N – N (160. kJ/mol)   4 H – O (467 kJ/mol)
    1 N = N (418 kJ/mol)   1 O = O (495 kJ/mol)
    3 N – O (201 kJ/mol)
    1 N = O (607 kJ/mol) ΣD_{formed} = 4245 kJ

    ΣD_{broken} = 3352 kJ

    $\Delta H = \Sigma D_{broken} - \Sigma D_{formed}$ = 3352 kJ - 4245 kJ = -893 kJ

d.   To estimate ΔH, we completely ignored the ionic interactions between NH_4^+ and $N(NO_2)_2^-$. In addition, we assumed the bond energies in Table 13.5 applied to the $N(NO_2)^-$ bonds in any one of the resonance structures above. This is a bad assumption since molecules that exhibit resonance generally have stronger overall bonds than predicted. All of these assumptions give an estimated ΔH value which is too negative.

108.   Use Figure 13.10 as a template for this problem:

    Li(s) → Li(g) ΔH_{sub} = ?

    Li(g) → Li$^+$(g) + e$^-$ ΔH = 520 kJ

    1/2 I_2(g) → I(g) ΔH = 151/2 kJ

    I(g) + e$^-$ → I$^-$(g) ΔH = -295 kJ

    Li$^+$(g) + I$^-$(g) → LiI(s) ΔH = -753 kJ

    Li(s) + 1/2 I_2(g) → LiI(s) ΔH = -272 kJ

ΔH_{sub} + 520 + 151/2 - 295 - 753 = -272, ΔH_{sub} -181 kJ

109.   a.   i. $C_6H_6N_{12}O_{12} \rightarrow 6\,CO + 6\,N_2 + 3\,H_2O + 3/2\,O_2$

The NO_2 groups have one $N - O$ single bond and one $N = O$ double bond and each carbon atom has one $C - H$ single bond. We must break and form all bonds.

Bonds broken: Bonds formed:

$3\ C-C$ (347 kJ/mol) $6\ C \equiv O$ (1072 kJ/mol)
$6\ C-H$ (413 kJ/mol) $6\ N \equiv N$ (941 kJ/mol)
$12\ C-N$ (305 kJ/mol) $6\ H-O$ (467 kJ/mol)
$6\ N-N$ (160. kJ/mol) $3/2\ O=O$ (495 kJ/mol)
$6\ N-O$ (201 kJ/mol)
$6\ N=O$ (607 kJ/mol) $\Sigma D_{formed} = 15{,}623$ kJ

$\Sigma D_{broken} = 12{,}987$ kJ

$\Delta H = \Sigma D_{broken} - \Sigma D_{formed} = 12{,}987$ kJ $- 15{,}623$ kJ $= -2636$ kJ

      ii. $C_6H_6N_{12}O_{12} \rightarrow 3\,CO + 3\,CO_2 + 6\,N_2 + 3\,H_2O$

Note: The bonds broken will be the same for all three reactions.

Bonds formed:

$3\ C \equiv O$ (1072 kJ/mol)
$6\ C = O$ (799 kJ/mol)
$6\ N \equiv N$ (941 kJ/mol)
$6\ H-O$ (467 kJ/mol)

$\Sigma D_{formed} = 16{,}458$ kJ

$\Delta H = 12{,}987$ kJ $- 16{,}458$ kJ $= -3471$ kJ

      iii. $C_6H_6N_{12}O_{12} \rightarrow 6\,CO_2 + 6\,N_2 + 3\,H_2$

Bonds formed:

$12\ C = O$ (799 kJ/mol)
$6\ N \equiv N$ (941 kJ/mol)
$3\ H-H$ (432 kJ/mol)

$\Sigma D_{formed} = 16{,}530.$ kJ

$\Delta H = 12{,}987$ kJ $- 16{,}530.$ kJ $= -3543$ kJ

   b.   Reaction iii yields the most energy per mole of CL-20 so it will yield the most energy per kg.

$$\frac{-3543\ \text{kJ}}{\text{mol}} \times \frac{1\ \text{mol}}{438.23\ \text{g}} \times \frac{1000\ \text{g}}{\text{kg}} = \textbf{-8085 kJ/kg}$$

110.   The reaction in question is:

$$1/2\ I_2(g) + 1/2\ Cl_2(g) \rightarrow ICl(g)$$

We can get the relevant numbers using the following:

$1/2\ I_2(s)\ \rightarrow 1/2\ I_2(g)$	$1/2\ (62\ \text{kJ/mol})$	[Appendix 4]
$1/2\ I_2(g)\ \rightarrow I(g)$	$1/2\ (149\ \text{kJ/mol})$	[Table 13.6]
$1/2\ Cl_2(g) \rightarrow Cl(g)$	$1/2\ (239\ \text{kJ/mol})$	[Table 13.6]
$I(g) + Cl(g)\ \rightarrow ICl(g)$	$-208\ \text{kJ/mol}$	[Table 13.6]

$1/2\ I_2(s) + 1/2\ Cl_2(g) \rightarrow ICl(g)\quad 17\ \text{kJ/mol}$

Marathon Problems

111.   Compound A: This compound is a strong acid (part g). HNO_3 is a strong acid and is available in concentrated solutions of 16 M (part c). The highest possible oxidation state of nitrogen is +5, and in HNO_3, the oxidation state of nitrogen is +5 (part b). Therefore, compound A is most likely HNO_3. The Lewis structures for HNO_3 are:

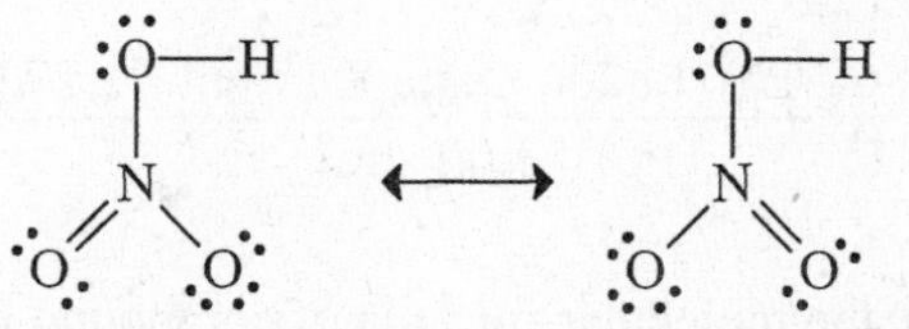

Compound B: This compound is basic (part g) and has one nitrogen (part b). The formal charge of zero (part b) tells us that there are three bonds to the nitrogen and the nitrogen has one lone pair. Assuming compound B is monobasic, then the data in part g tells us that the molar mass of B is 33.0 g/mol (21.98 mL of 1.000 M HCl = 0.02198 mol HCl, thus there are 0.02198 mol of B; 0.726 g/0.02198 mol = 33.0 g/mol). Because this number is rather small, it limits the possibilities. That is, there is one nitrogen, and the remainder of the atoms are O and H. Since the molar mass of B is 33.0 g/mol, then only one O oxygen atom can be present. The N and O atoms have a combined molar mass of 30.0 g/mol; the rest is made up of hydrogens (3 H atoms), giving the formula NH_3O. From the list of K_b values for weak bases in Appendix 5.3 of the text, compound B is most likely NH_2OH. The Lewis structure is:

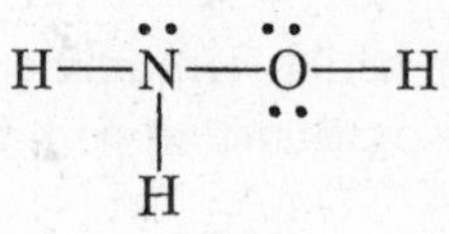

Compound C: From parts a and f and assuming compound A is HNO_3 , then compound C contains the nitrate ion, NO_3^-. Because part b tells us that there are two nitrogens, the other ion needs to have one N and some H's. In addition, compound C must be a weak acid (part g), which must be due to the other ion since NO_3^- has no acidic properties. Also, the nitrogen atom in the other ion must have an oxidation state of -3 (part b) and a formal charge of +1. The ammonium ion fits the data. Thus, compound C is most likely NH_4NO_3. A Lewis structure is:

Note: Two more resonance structures can be drawn for NO_3^-.

Compound D: From part f, this compound has one less oxygen atom than compound C, thus NH_4NO_2 is a likely formula. Data from part e confirms this. Assuming 100.0 g of compound, we have:

43.7 g N × 1 mol/14.01 g = 3.12 mol N
50.0 g O × 1 mol/16.00 g = 3.12 mol O
6.3 g H × 1 mol/1.008 g = 6.25 mol H

There is a 1:1:2 mole ratio of N:O:H, The empirical formula is NOH_2, which has an empirical formula mass of 32.0 g/mol.

$$\text{Molar mass} = \frac{dRT}{P} = \frac{2.86 \text{ g/L} (0.08206 \text{ L atm K}^{-1} \text{ mol}^{-1})(273 \text{ K})}{1.00 \text{ atm}} = 64.1 \text{ g/mol}$$

For a correct molar mass, the molecular formula of compound D is $N_2O_2H_4$ or NH_4NO_2. A Lewis structure is:

Note: One more resonance structure for NO_2^- can be drawn.

Compound E: A basic solution (part g) which is commercially available at 15 M (part c) is ammonium hydroxide, NH_4OH. This is also consistent with the information given in parts b and d. The Lewis structure for NH_4OH is:

112.   a.   1)   removing an electron from the metal: IE, positive (> 0)
            2)   adding an electron to the nonmetal: EA, often negative (< 0)
            3)   allowing the metal : nonmetal to come together: LE, negative (< 0)

       b.   Often, the sign of the sum of the first two processes is positive (or unfavorable). This is especially true due to the fact that we must also vaporize the metal and often break a bond on a diatomic gas.

            For example, the ionization energy for Na is +495 kJ/mol and the electron affinity for F is -328 kJ/mol. Overall, the change is +167 kJ/mol (unfavorable).

       c.   For an ionic compound to form, the sum must be negative (exothermic).

       d.   The lattice energy must be large enough to overcome the endothermic process of forming the ions.

       e.   While Na_2Cl would have a greater lattice energy than NaCl, for example, the energy to make a Cl^{2-} ion must be larger than would be gained by this larger lattice energy. The same argument can be made for MgO compared to MgO_2 or Mg_2O. The energy to make the ions is too unfavorable or the lattice energy is not favorable enough and the compounds do not form.

CHAPTER FOURTEEN

COVALENT BONDING: ORBITALS

The Localized Electron Model and Hybrid Orbitals

9. H_2O has $2(1) + 6 = 8$ valence electrons.

H₂O has a tetrahedral arrangement of the electron pairs about the O atom which requires sp^3 hybridization. Two of the four sp^3 hybrid orbitals are used to form bonds to the two hydrogen atoms and the other two sp^3 hybrid orbitals hold the two lone pairs on oxygen. The two $O - H$ bonds are formed from overlap of the sp^3 hybrid orbitals from oxygen with the 1s atomic orbitals from the hydrogen atoms. Each O–H covalent bond is called a sigma (σ) bond since the shared electron pair in each bond is centered in an area on a line running between the two atoms.

10. H_2CO has $2(1) + 4 + 6 = 12$ valence electrons.

The central carbon atom has a trigonal planar arrangement of the electron pairs which requires sp^2 hybridization. The two $C - H$ sigma bonds are formed from overlap of the sp^2 hybrid orbitals from carbon with the hydrogen 1s atomic orbitals. The double bond between carbon and oxygen consists of one σ and one π bond. The oxygen atom, like the carbon atom, also has a trigonal planar arrangement of the electrons which requires sp^2 hybridization. The σ bond in the double bond is formed from overlap of a carbon sp^2 hybrid orbital with an oxygen sp^2 hybrid orbital. The π bond in the double bond is formed from overlap of the unhybridized p atomic orbitals. Carbon and oxygen each have one unhybridized p atomic orbital which are parallel to each other. When two parallel p atomic orbitals overlap, a π bond results where the shared electron pair occupies the space above and below a line joining the atoms in the bond.

C_2H_2 has $2(4) + 2(1) = 10$ valence electrons.

$$H —— C ≡≡≡ C —— H$$

Each carbon atom in C_2H_2 is sp hybridized since each carbon atom is surrounded by two effective pairs of electrons, i.e., each carbon atom has a linear arrangement of the electrons. Since each carbon atom is sp hybridized, then each carbon atom has two unhybridized p atomic orbitals. The two C – H sigma bonds are formed from overlap of carbon sp hybrid orbitals with hydrogen 1s atomic orbitals. The triple bond is composed of one σ bond and two π bonds. The sigma bond between to the carbon atoms is formed from overlap of sp hybrid orbitals from each carbon atom. The two π bonds of the triple bond are formed from parallel overlap of the two unhybridized p atomic orbitals from each carbon.

11.   See Exercises 13.47. 13.48 and 13.50 for the Lewis structures. To predict the hybridization, first determine the arrangement of electron pairs about each central atom using the VSEPR model, then utilize the information in Figure 14.24 of the text to deduce the hybridization required for that arrangement of electron pairs.

13.47   a.   HCN; C is sp hybridized.   b. PH_3; P is sp^3 hybridized.

         c. $CHCl_3$; C is sp^3 hybridized.   d. NH_4^+; N is sp^3 hybridized.

         e. H_2CO; C is sp^2 hybridized.   f. SeF_2; Se is sp^3 hybridized.

         g. CO_2; C is sp hybridized.   h. O_2; Each O atom is sp^2 hybridized.

         i.   HBr; Br is sp^3 hybridized.

13.48   a.   All the central atoms are sp^3 hybridized.

         b.   All the central atoms are sp^3 hybridized.

         c.   All the central atoms are sp^3 hybridized.

13.50   a.   In NO_2^-, N is sp^2 hybridized in NO_3^-, N is sp^2 hybridized, and in N_2O_4, both central N atoms are also sp^2 hybridized.

         b.   In OCN^- and SCN^-, the central carbon atoms in each ion are sp hybridized and in N_3^-, the central N atom is also sp hybridized.

12.   For the molecules/ion in Exercise 13.75, all have central atoms with dsp^3 hybridization since all are based on the trigonal bipyramid arrangement of electron pairs. See Exercise 13.75 for the Lewis structures.

       For the molecules/ion in Exercise 13.76, all have central atoms with d^2sp^3 hybridization since all are based on the octahedral arrangement of electron pairs. See Exercise 13.76 for the Lewis structures.

13.   a.

b.

tetrahedral   sp³
109.5°   nonpolar

trigonal pyramid   sp³
< 109.5°   polar

The angles in NF₃ should be slightly less than 109.5° because the lone pair requires more room than the bonding pairs.

c.

d.

V-shaped   sp³
< 109.5°   polar

trigonal planar   sp²
120°   nonpolar

e.

f.

linear   sp
180°   nonpolar

see-saw   dsp³
a. ≈ 120°, b. ≈ 90°   polar

g.

h.

trigonal bipyramid   dsp³
a. 90°, b. 120°   nonpolar

linear   dsp³
180°   nonpolar

i.

square planar d^2sp^3
90°   nonpolar

j.

octahedral d^2sp^3
90°   nonpolar

k.

square pyramid d^2sp^3
≈ 90°   polar

l.

T-shaped dsp^3
≈ 90°   polar

14.   a.

V-shaped
120°
sp^2

Only one resonance form is shown. Resonance does not change the position of the atoms. We can predict the geometry and hybridization from any one of the resonance structures.

b.   c.

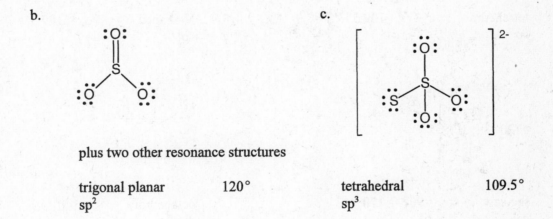

plus two other resonance structures

trigonal planar   120°   tetrahedral   109.5°
sp^2 sp^3

d.

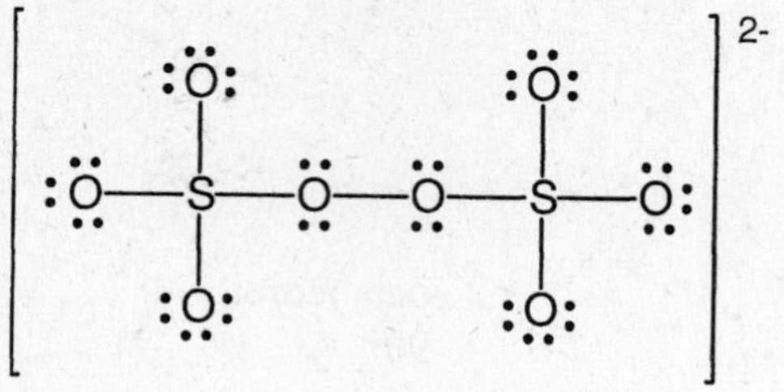

Tetrahedral geometry about each S, 109.5°, sp³ hybrids; V-shaped arrangement about peroxide O's, ≈109.5°, sp³ hybrids

e.

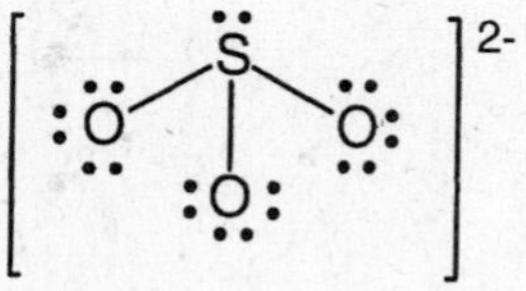

trigonal pyramid
< 109.5°
sp³

f.

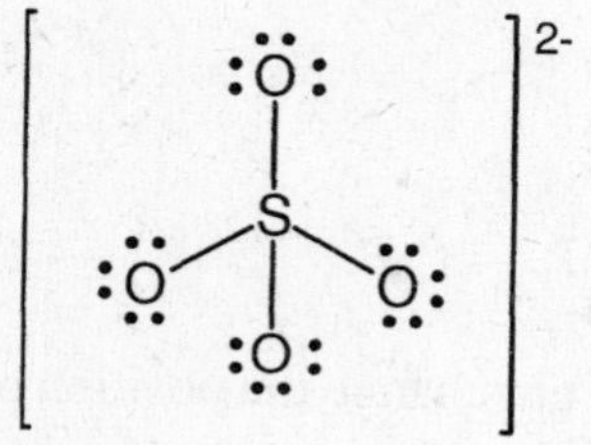

g.

tetrahedral   109.5°
sp³

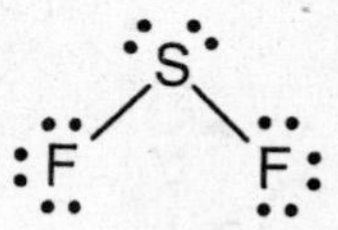

V-shaped   < 109.5°
sp³

h.   ≈90°

≈120°

i.

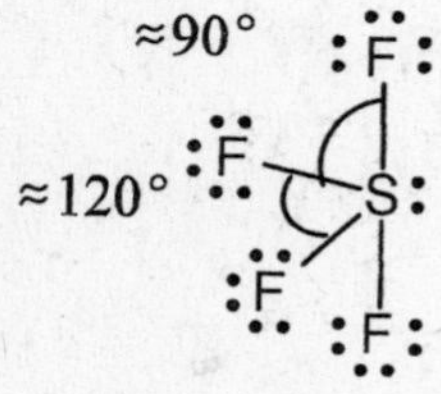

see-saw   ≈90°, ≈120°
dsp³

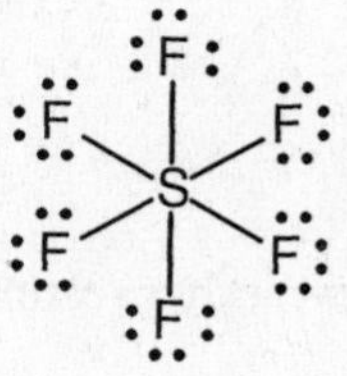

octahedral   90°
d²sp³

j.

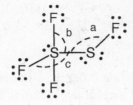

a) ≈ 109.5°   b) ≈ 90°   c) ≈ 120°

See-saw about S atom with one lone pair (dsp³);
bent about S atom with two lone pairs (sp³)

15.

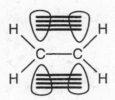

For the p-orbitals to properly line up to form the π bond, all six atoms are forced into the same plane. If the atoms are not in the same plane, then the π bond could not form since the p-orbitals would no longer be parallel to each other.

16.   No, the CH_2 planes are mutually perpendicular to each other. The center C atom is sp hybridized and is involved in two π-bonds. The p-orbitals used to form each π bond must be perpendicular to each other. This forces the two CH_2 planes to be perpendicular.

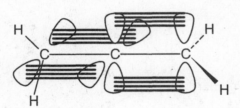

17.   To complete the Lewis structures, just add lone pairs of electrons to satisfy the octet rule for the atoms with fewer than eight electrons.

Biacetyl ($C_4H_6O_2$) has 4(4) + 6(1) + 2(6) = 34 valence electrons.

All CCO angles are 120°. The six atoms are not in the same plane because of free rotation about the carbon-carbon single (sigma) bonds. There are 11 σ and 2 π bonds in biacetyl.

Acetoin ($C_4H_8O_2$) has 4(4) + 8(1) + 2(6) = 36 valence electrons.

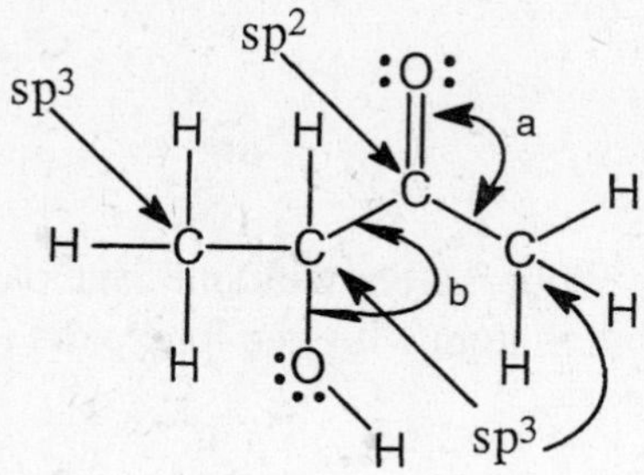

The carbon with the doubly bonded O is sp^2 hybridized. The other 3 C atoms are sp^3 hybridized. Angle a = 120°and angle b = 109.5°. There are 13 σ and 1 π bond in acetoin.

Note: All single bonds are σ bonds, all double bonds are one σ and one π bond and all triple bonds are one σ and two π bonds.

18.   Acrylonitrile: C_3H_3N has $3(4) + 3(1) + 5 = 20$ valence electrons.

a.   120°
b.   120°
c.   180°

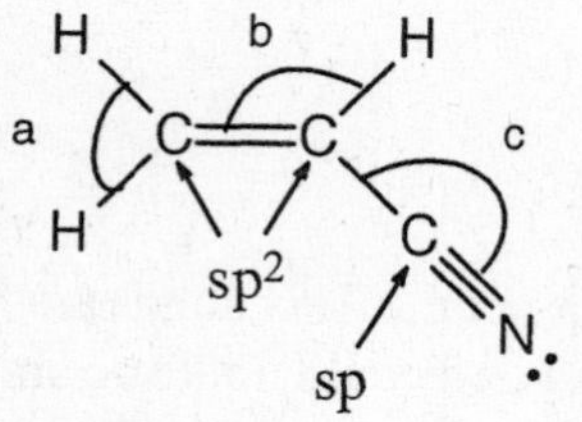

6 σ and 3 π bonds

All atoms of acrylonitrile lie in the same plane. The π bond in the double bond dictates that the C and H atoms are all in the same plane and the triple bond dictates that N is in the same plane with the other atoms.

Methyl methacrylate ($C_5H_8O_2$) has $5(4) + 8(1) + 2(6) = 40$ valence electrons.

d.   120°
e.   120°
f.   ≈ 109.5°

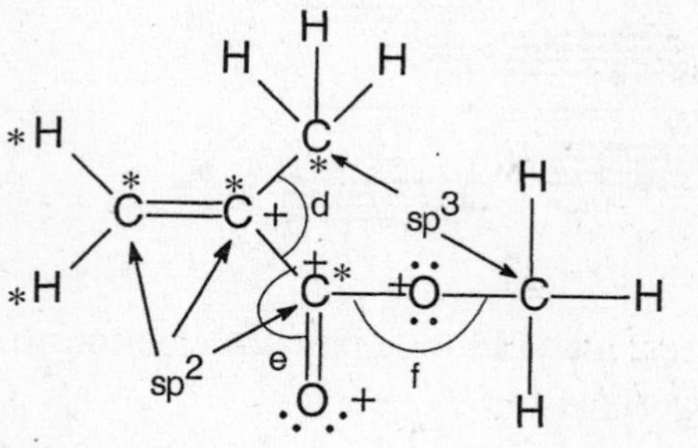

14 σ and 2 π bonds

The atoms marked with an * are coplanar with each other, as well as the atoms marked with a +. The two planes, however, do not have to coincide with each other due to the rotations about sigma (single) bonds.

19.   To complete the Lewis structure, just add lone pairs of electrons to satisfy the octet rule for the
       atoms that have fewer than eight electrons.

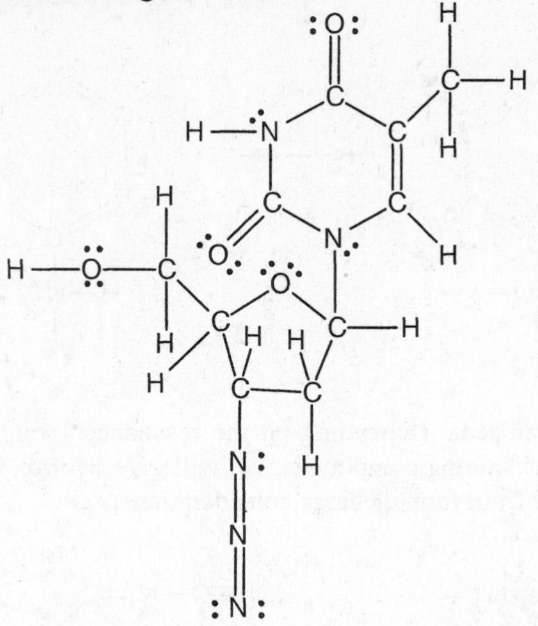

       a. 6   b. 4   c.   The center N in $-N=N=N$ group

       d. 33 σ   e. 5 π   f.   180°

       g. ≈ 109.5°   h. sp³

20.   a. NCN^{2-} has $5 + 4 + 5 + 2 = 16$ valence electrons.

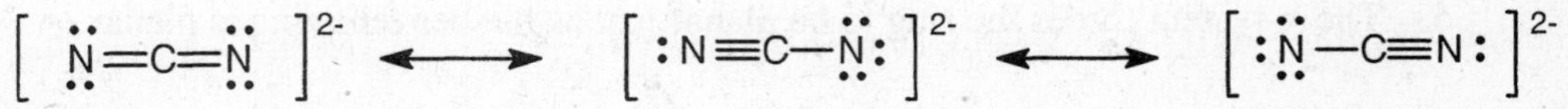

           H_2NCN has $2(1) + 5 + 4 + 5 = 16$ valence electrons.

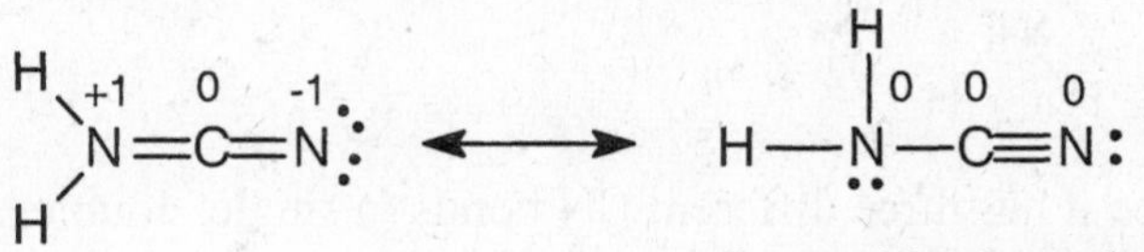

                             favored by formal charge

           $NCNC(NH_2)_2$ has $5 + 4 + 5 + 4 + 2(5) + 4(1) = 32$ valence electrons.

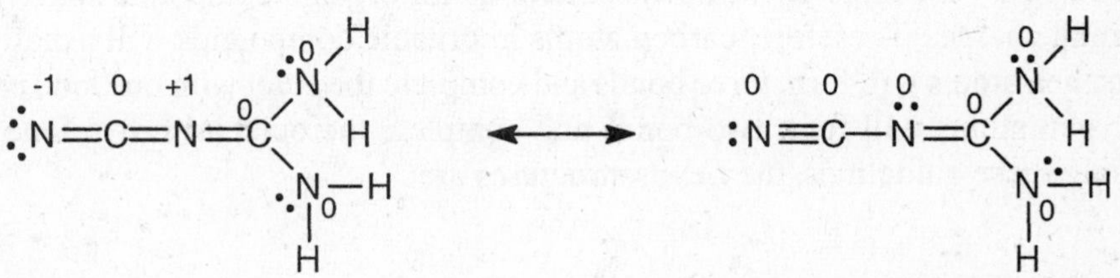

                                               favored by formal charge

Melamine ($C_3N_6H_6$) has $3(4) + 6(5) + 6(1) = 48$ valence electrons.

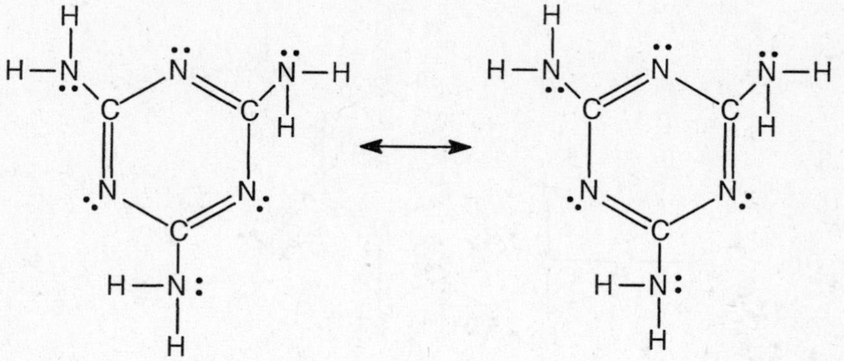

b. NCN^{2-}:   C is sp hybridized. Depending on the resonance form, N can be sp, sp^2, or sp^3 hybridized. For the remaining compounds, we will give hybrids for the favored resonance structures as predicted from formal charge considerations.

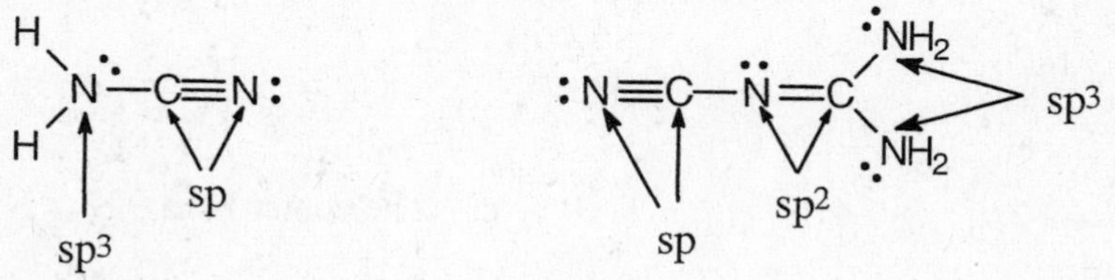

Melamine: N in NH_2 groups are all sp^3 hybridized. Atoms in ring are all sp^2 hybridized.

c. NCN^{2-}: 2 σ and 2 π bonds; H_2NCN: 4 σ and 2 π bonds;   dicyandiamide: 9 σ and 3 π bonds; melamine: 15 σ and 3 π bonds

d.   The π-system forces the ring to be planar just as the benzene ring is planar.

e.   The structure:

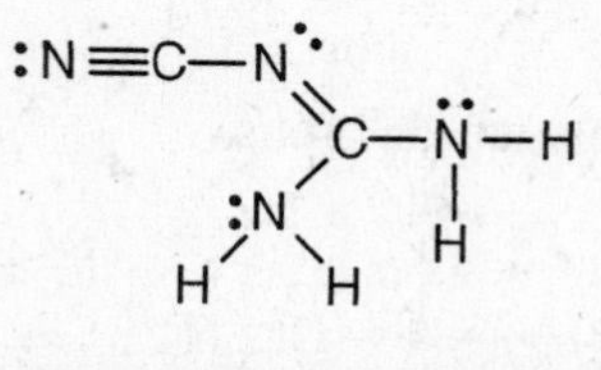

is the most important since it has three different CN bonds (a single, double, and triple bond). This structure is also favored on the basis of formal charge.

21.   a.   Piperine and capsaicin are molecules classified as organic compounds, i.e., compounds based on carbon. The majority of Lewis structures for organic compounds have all atoms with zero formal charge. Therefore, carbon atoms in organic compounds will usually form four bonds, nitrogen atoms will form three bonds and complete the octet with one lone pair of electrons, and oxygen atoms will form two bonds and complete the octet with two lone pairs of electrons. Using these guidelines, the Lewis structures are:

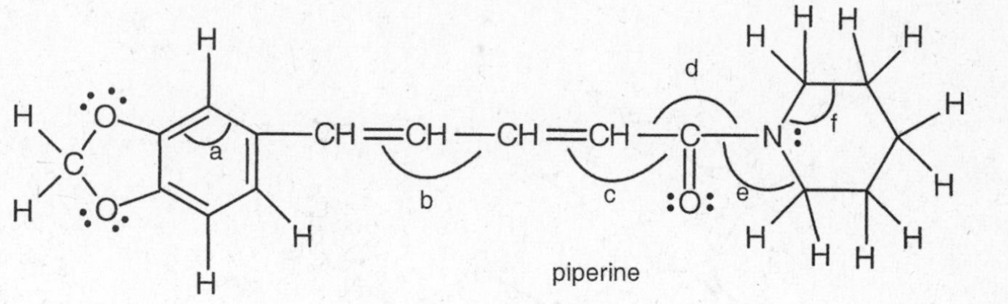

piperine

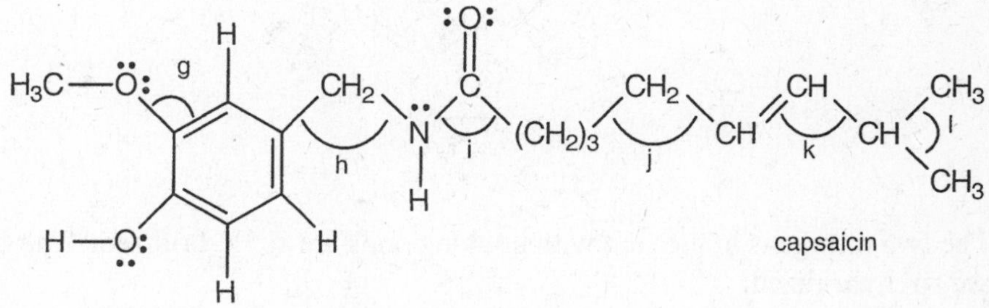

capsaicin

Note: The ring structures are all shorthand notation for rings of carbon atoms. In piperine, the first ring contains 6 carbon atoms and the second ring contains 5 carbon atoms (plus nitrogen). Also notice that CH_3, CH_2 and CH are shorthand for a carbon atoms singly bonded to hydrogen atoms.

b. piperine: 0 sp, 11 sp^2 and 6 sp^3 carbons; capsaicin: 0 sp, 9 sp^2 and 9 sp^3 carbons

c. The nitrogens are sp^3 hybridized in each molecule.

d. a. 120°   e. ≈ 109.5°   i. 120°
   b. 120°   f. 109.5°   j. 109.5°
   c. 120°   g. 120°   k. 120°
   d. 120°   h. 109.5°   l. 109.5°

22.   CO, 4 + 6 = 10 e⁻; CO_2, 4 + 2(6) = 16 e⁻; C_3O_2, 3(4) + 2(6) = 24 e⁻

:C≡O: Ö=C=Ö   Ö=C=C=C=Ö

There is no molecular structure for the diatomic CO molecule. The carbon in CO is sp hybridized. CO_2 is a linear molecule, and the central carbon atom is sp hybridized. C_3O_2 is a linear molecule with all of the central carbon atoms exhibiting sp hybridization.

23.   To complete the Lewis structure, just add lone pairs of electrons to satisfy the octet rule for the atoms with fewer than eight electrons.

a. The two nitrogens in the ring with double bonds are sp^2 hybridized. The other three nitrogens are sp^3 hybridized.

b. The five carbon atoms in the ring with one nitrogen are all sp^3 hybridized. The four carbon atoms in the other ring with double bonds are all sp^2 hybridized.

c. Angles a and b: $\approx 109.5°$; angles c, d, and e: $\approx 120°$

d. 31 sigma bonds

e. 3 pi bonds (Each double bond consists of one sigma and one pi bond.)

The Molecular Orbital (MO) Model

24. Bonding molecular orbitals have maximum electron density between the bonded atoms and are lower in energy than the atomic orbitals from which they are formed. Antibonding molecular orbitals have minimal electron density between the bonded atoms and are higher in energy than the atomic orbitals from which they are formed.

25. Bond energy is directly proportional to bond order. Bond length is inversely proportional to bond order. Bond energy and bond length can be measured.

26. If we calculate a non-zero bond order for a molecule, we predict that it can exist (is stable).

a. H_2^+: $(\sigma_{1s})^1$ B.O. $= (1-0)/2 = 1/2$, stable

    H_2: $(\sigma_{1s})^2$ B.O. $= (2-0)/2 = 1$, stable

    H_2^-: $(\sigma_{1s})^2(\sigma_{1s}*)^1$ B.O. $= (2-1)/2 = 1/2$, stable

    H_2^{2-}: $(\sigma_{1s})^2(\sigma_{1s}*)^2$ B.O. $= (2-2)/2 = 0$, not stable

b. He_2^{2+}: $(\sigma_{1s})^2$ B.O. = (2-0)/2 = 1, stable

   He_2^+ $(\sigma_{1s})^2(\sigma_{1s}*)^1$ B.O. = (2-1)/2 = 1/2, stable

   He_2: $(\sigma_{1s})^2(\sigma_{1s}*)^2$ B.O. = (2-2)/2 = 0, not stable

c. Be_2: $(\sigma_{2s})^2(\sigma_{2s}*)^2$ B.O. = (2-2)/2 = 0, not stable

   B_2: $(\sigma_{2s})^2(\sigma_{2s}*)^2(\pi_{2p})^2$ B.O. = (4-2)/2 = 1, stable

   Li_2: $(\sigma_{2s})^2$ B.O. = (2-0)/2 = 1, stable

27.   Paramagnetic: Unpaired electrons are present. Measure the mass of a substance in the presence and absence of a magnetic field. A substance with unpaired electrons will be attracted by the magnetic field, giving an apparent increase in mass in the presence of the field. Greater number of unpaired electrons will give greater attraction and greater observed mass increase.

28.   The two types of overlap that result in bond formation for p orbitals are side to side overlap (π bond) and head to head overlap (σ bond). Reference Figure 14.36 for representations of the σ_{2p} and π_{2p} bonding orbitals.

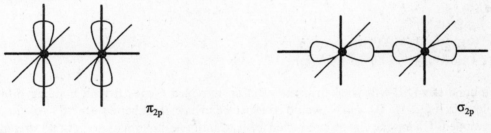

π_{2p} σ_{2p}

29.

σ^*

σ

These molecular orbitals are sigma MOs since the electron density is cylindrically symmetric about the internuclear axis.

30.   The MO energy level diagram for O_2 is:

σ p*

π 2p*

π 2p

σ 2p

σ 2s*

σ 2s

The bond order is 2. In order to make the bond order greater (to 2.5) we need to take away a nonbonding electron. Thus, the charges would be 1+. So O_2^+ would have a bond order of 2.5. (We could also take away 3 electrons, which is much less likely, to have 5 bonding and 0 nonbonding 2p electrons, so O_2^{3+} would work as well).

31.   a. H_2: $(\sigma_{1s})^2$ B.O. = (2-0)/2 = 1, diamagetic (0 unpaired e^-)

       b. B_2: $(\sigma_{2s})^2(\sigma_{2s}^*)^2(\pi_{2p})^2$ B.O. = (4-2)/2 = 1, paramagnetic (2 unpaired e^-)

       c.   NO: $(\sigma_{2s})^2(\sigma_{2s}^*)^2(\pi_{2p})^4(\sigma_{2p})^2(\pi_{2p}^*)^1$ B.O. = (8-3)/2 = 2.5, paramagnetic (1 unpaired e^-)

       d. CN^+: $(\sigma_{2s})^2(\sigma_{2s}^*)^2(\pi_{2p})^4$ B.O. = (6-2)/2 = 2, diamagnetic

       e.   CN: $(\sigma_{2s})^2(\sigma_{2s}^*)^2(\pi_{2p})^4(\sigma_{2p})^1$ B.O. = (7-2)/2 = 2.5, paramagnetic (1 unpaired e^-)

       f. CN^-: $(\sigma_{2s})^2(\sigma_{2s}^*)^2(\pi_{2p})^4(\sigma_{2p})^2$ B.O. = 3, diamagnetic

       g. N_2: $(\sigma_{2s})^2(\sigma_{2s}^*)^2(\pi_{2p})^4(\sigma_{2p})^2$ B.O. = 3, diamagnetic

       h. N_2^+: $(\sigma_{2s})^2(\sigma_{2s}^*)^2(\pi_{2p})^4(\sigma_{2p})^1$ B.O. = 2.5, paramagnetic (1 unpaired e^-)

       i. N_2^-: $(\sigma_{2s})^2(\sigma_{2s}^*)^2(\pi_{2p})^4(\sigma_{2p})^2(\pi_{2p}^*)^1$ B.O. = 2.5, paramagnetic (1 unpaired e^-)

32. H_2: $(\sigma_{1s})^2$
       B_2: $(\sigma_{2s})^2(\sigma_{2s}^*)^2(\pi_{2p})^2$
       N_2: $(\sigma_{2s})^2(\sigma_{2s}^*)^2(\pi_{2p})^4(\sigma_{2p})^2$
       OF: $(\sigma_{2s})^2(\sigma_{2s}^*)^2(\sigma_{2p})^2(\pi_{2p})^4(\pi_{2p}^*)^3$

The bond strength will weaken if the electron removed comes from a bonding orbital. Of the molecules listed, H_2, B_2, and N_2 would be expected to have their bond strength weaken as an electron is removed. OF has the electron removed from an antibonding orbital, so its bond strength increases.

33.   CN: $(\sigma_{2s})^2(\sigma_{2s}^*)^2(\pi_{2p})^4(\sigma_{2p})^1$
       NO: $(\sigma_{2s})^2(\sigma_{2s}^*)^2(\pi_{2p})^4(\pi_{2p})^2(\pi_{2p}^*)^1$
       O_2^{2+}: $(\sigma_{2s})^2(\sigma_{2s}^*)^2(\sigma_{2p})^2(\pi_{2p})^4$
       N_2^{2+}: $(\sigma_{2s})^2(\sigma_{2s}^*)^2(\pi_{2p})^4$

If the added electron goes into a bonding orbital, the bond order would increase, making the species more stable and more likely to form. Between CN and NO, CN would most likely form CN^- since the bond order increases (unlike NO^- where the added electron goes into an antibonding orbital). Between O_2^{2+} and N_2^{2+}, N_2^+ would most likely form since the bond order increases (unlike O_2^+).

34.   The electron configurations are:

       F_2^+: $(\sigma_{2s})^2(\sigma_{2s}^*)^2(\sigma_{2p})^2(\pi_{2p})^4(\pi_{2p}^*)^3$ B.O. = (8-5)/2 = 1.5; 1 unpaired e^-

       F_2: $(\sigma_{2s})^2(\sigma_{2s}^*)^2(\sigma_{2p})^2(\pi_{2p})^4(\pi_{2p}^*)^4$ B.O. = (8-6)/2 = 1;   0 unpaired e^-

       F_2^-: $(\sigma_{2s})^2(\sigma_{2s}^*)^2(\sigma_{2p})^2(\pi_{2p})^4(\pi_{2p}^*)^4(\sigma_{2p}^*)^1$ B.O. = (8-7)/2 = 0.5; 1 unpaired e^-

Since bond order is directly related to bond energy and, in turn, inversely related to bond length, then the bond length order should be: $F_2^+ < F_2 < F_2^-$.

35. The electron configurations are (assuming the same orbital order as that for N_2):

CO: $(\sigma_{2s})^2(\sigma_{2s}*)^2(\pi_{2p})^4(\sigma_{2p})^2$ B.O. = (8-2)/2 = 3; 0 unpaired e$^-$

CO^+: $(\sigma_{2s})^2(\sigma_{2s}*)^2(\pi_{2p})^4(\sigma_{2p})^1$ B.O. = (7-2)/2 = 2.5; 1 unpaired e$^-$

CO^{2+}: $(\sigma_{2s})^2(\sigma_{2s}*)^2(\pi_{2p})^4$ B.O. = (6-2)/2 = 2; 0 unpaired e$^-$

Since bond order is directly related to bond energy and, in turn, inversely related to bond length, then the bond length order should be: $CO < CO^+ < CO^{2+}$.

36. N_2: The π and $\pi*$ orbitals are symmetrical.

CO: The π orbitals would place more electron density nearer the more electronegative oxygen atom and the $\pi*$ orbitals would place more electron density nearer the carbon atom.

37. The π bonds between S atoms and between C and S atoms are not as strong. The atomic orbitals do not overlap with each other as well as the smaller atomic orbitals of C and O overlap.

38.

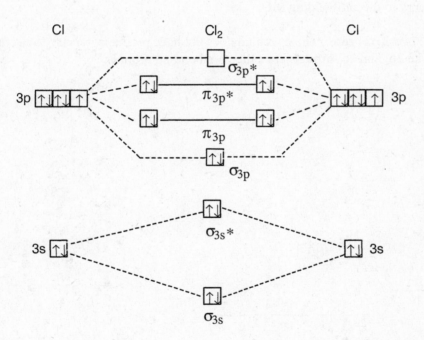

The bond order for Cl_2 is 1 and since all electrons are paired, we would expect Cl_2 to be diamagnetic.

39. Side to side overlap of these d-orbitals would produce a π molecular orbital. There would be no probability of finding an electron on the axis joining the two nuclei, which is characteristic of π MOs.

40. O_2: $(\sigma_{2s})^2(\sigma_{2s}*)^2(\sigma_{2p})^2(\pi_{2p})^4(\pi_{2p}*)^2$; O_2 should have a lower ionization energy than O. The electron removed from O_2 is in a $\pi_{2p}*$ antibonding molecular orbital which is higher in energy than the 2p atomic orbitals from which the electron in atomic oxygen is removed. Since the electron removed from O_2 is higher in energy than the electron removed from O, then it should be easier to remove an electron from O_2 than from O.

41.   a.   The electron density would be closer to F on the average. The F atom is more electronegative than the H atom and the 2p orbital of F is lower in energy than the 1s orbital of H.

       b.   The bonding MO would have more fluorine 2p character since it is closer in energy to the fluorine 2p atomic orbital.

       c.   The antibonding MO would place more electron density closer to H and would have a greater contribution from the higher energy hydrogen 1s atomic orbital.

42.   a.   See the illustrations in Exercise 14.29 for the bonding and antibonding MOs in OH.

       b.   The antibonding MO will have more hydrogen 1s character since the hydrogen 1s atomic orbital is closer in energy to the antibonding MO.

       c.   No, the overall overlap is zero. The p_x orbital does not have proper symmetry to overlap with a 1s orbital. The $2p_x$ and $2p_y$ orbitals are called nonbonding orbitals.

       d.

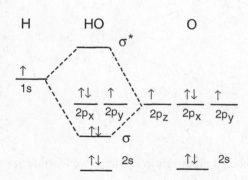

       e.   Bond order $= \dfrac{2-0}{2} = 1$; Note: The 2s, $2p_x$, and $2p_y$ electrons have no effect on the bond order.

       f.   To form OH^+ a nonbonding electron is removed from OH. Since the number of bonding electrons and antibonding electrons are unchanged, then the bond order is still equal to one.

Spectroscopy

43.   reduced mass = $\mu = \dfrac{m_1 m_2}{m_1 + m_2} = \dfrac{(1.0078)(78.918)}{1.0078 + 78.918}$ amu $\times \dfrac{1.66054 \times 10^{-27} \text{ kg}}{\text{amu}} = 1.6524 \times 10^{-27} \text{ kg}$

$\nu_o = \dfrac{1}{2\pi} \sqrt{\dfrac{k}{\mu}} = \dfrac{c}{\lambda} = 2.9979 \times 10^{10} \text{ cm s}^{-1} \times 2650. \text{ cm}^{-1} = 7.944 \times 10^{13} \text{ s}^{-1}$

$7.944 \times 10^{13} \text{ s}^{-1} = \dfrac{1}{2\pi} \sqrt{\dfrac{k}{\mu}} = \dfrac{1}{2\pi} \sqrt{\dfrac{k}{1.6524 \times 10^{-27} \text{ kg}}}$

Solving for k, the force constant: $k = 411.7 \text{ kg s}^{-2} = 411.7 \text{ N m}^{-1}$

Note: 1 newton = 1 N = 1 kg m s^{-2}

44. $\nu_o = \dfrac{1}{2\pi} \sqrt{\dfrac{k}{\mu}}$, $\mu = \dfrac{(14.003)(15.995)}{14.003 + 15.995}$ amu $\times \dfrac{1.66054 \times 10^{-27} \text{ kg}}{\text{amu}} = 1.2398 \times 10^{-26} \text{ kg}$

$\nu_o = \dfrac{1}{2\pi} \sqrt{\dfrac{1550. \text{ N m}^{-1}}{1.2398 \times 10^{-26} \text{ kg}} \times \dfrac{1 \text{ kg m s}^{-2}}{\text{N}}} = 5.627 \times 10^{13} \text{ s}^{-1}$

$\lambda = \dfrac{c}{\nu} = \dfrac{2.9979 \times 10^{10} \text{ cm s}^{-1}}{5.627 \times 10^{13} \text{ s}^{-1}} = 5.328 \times 10^{-4} \text{ cm}$

wave number $= \dfrac{1}{\lambda} = \dfrac{1}{5.328 \times 10^{-4} \text{ cm}} = 1877 \text{ cm}^{-1}$

45.   a. $\Delta E = 2hB (J_i + 1) = h\nu = \dfrac{hc}{\lambda}$, $\dfrac{c}{\lambda} = 2B (J_i + 1)$

$\dfrac{c}{\lambda} = 2B (0 + 1) = 2B = \dfrac{2.998 \times 10^8 \text{ m s}^{-1}}{2.60 \times 10^{-3} \text{ m}} = 1.15 \times 10^{11} \text{ s}^{-1}$

$B = \dfrac{1.15 \times 10^{-11} \text{ s}^{-1}}{2} = 5.75 \times 10^{10} \text{ s}^{-1}$

$I = \dfrac{h}{8\pi^2 B} = \dfrac{6.626 \times 10^{-34} \text{ J s}}{8\pi^2 (5.75 \times 10^{10} \text{ s}^{-1})} = 1.46 \times 10^{-46} \text{ kg m}^2$

$I = \mu R_e^2$, $\mu = \dfrac{m_1 m_2}{m_1 + m_2} = \dfrac{12.000 (15.995)}{12.000 + 15.995}$ amu $\times \dfrac{1.66054 \times 10^{-27} \text{ kg}}{\text{amu}} = 1.1385 \times 10^{-26} \text{ kg}$

$R_e^2 = \dfrac{I}{\mu} = \dfrac{1.46 \times 10^{-46} \text{ kg m}^2}{1.1385 \times 10^{-26} \text{ kg}} = 1.28 \times 10^{-20} \text{ m}^2$, $R_e = $ bond length $= 1.13 \times 10^{-10} \text{ m} = 113 \text{ pm}$

b. $\nu = \dfrac{\Delta E}{h} = 2B\,(J_i + 1) = 2B\,(2 + 1) = 6B$

From part a, B = 5.75×10^{10} s^{-1}, so: $\nu = 6(5.75 \times 10^{10}$ s$^{-1}) = 3.45 \times 10^{11}$ s^{-1}

46.   a.   There are three sets of magnetically equivalent hydrogens (marked a, b, and c in the following structure). We are assuming that all the benzene ring hydrogens (marked c) are equivalent and do not exhibit spin-spin coupling.

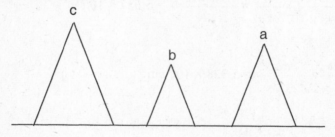

Since the hydrogens marked by a and the hydrogens marked by b are separated by more than three sigma bonds, then they will also not exhibit spin-spin coupling. Thus we will have three singlet peaks (following our assumptions). Predicting the relative loctions of the peaks was not discussed in the text, but they should be in a 3:2:5 relative area ratio (a:b:c). A sketch of the idealized NMR spectrum is:

b.

The different groups of equivalent hydrogen atoms are labeled a and b. Since all H-atoms are separated by more than 3 sigma bonds, then we should have no spin-spin coupling. Again, you do not have the information to predict where the two peaks should be in the idealized NMR spectrum, but they should have relative areas of 9:3 (or 3:1).

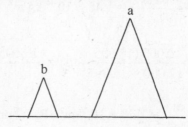

c.

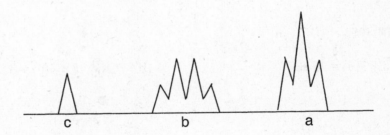

The three different groups of equivalent hydrogen atoms are labeled a, b, and c.. The H-atoms marked c will not exhibit spin-spin coupling, but the H-atoms marked a and b will. Since the H-atoms marked a in the $-CH_3$ groups neighbor $-CH_2$ groups, then a triplet line pattern will result with intensities of 1:2:1. The H-atoms marked b in the $-CH_2$ groups neighbor $-CH_3$ groups, so a quartet peak should result with intensities of 1:3:3:1. The relative area ratios of the three different H-atoms (a:b:c) should be 9:6:3 (or 3:2:1).

47. a. The $-CH_2$ group neighbors a $-CH_3$ group so a quartet of peaks should result (iv).

b. The $-CH_3$ H-atoms are separated by more than three sigma bonds from other H-atoms, so no spin-spin coupling should occur. A singlet peak should result (i).

c. The $-CH_2$ H-atoms neighbor two H-atoms, so a triplet peak should result (iii).

d. The 2 H-atoms in the $-CH_2F$ group neighbor one H-atom, so a doublet peak should result (ii).

48. C_6H_{12} NMR spectrum:

Since only one peak is present, then all of the hydrogen atoms are equivalent in their environment. Knowing this, then the process is trial and error to come up with the correct structure for C_6H_{12}. Following the "organic rules" in Exercise 14.60 and knowing a double bond is present, the only possibility to explain the NMR pattern is:

$$CH_3-\underset{\underset{CH_3}{|}}{C}=\underset{\overset{CH_3}{|}}{C}-CH_3$$

Here, all of the H-atoms have equivalent neighboring atoms and there would be no spin-spin coupling since all H-atoms are separated by more than three sigma bonds.

$C_4H_{10}O$ spectrum:

We have a quartet peak and a triplet peak in the spectrum. The quartet peak indicates hydrogen atom(s) which neighbor three H-atoms; the triplet peak indicates hydrogen atom(s) that neighbor two H-atoms. Again, following the "organic rules" in Exercise 14.60, the only possibility to explain this NMR pattern is:

$$CH_3CH_2-O-CH_2CH_3$$

This compound has two different "types" of hydrogen atoms ($-CH_3$ and $-CH_2$). The $-CH_3$ hydrogen atoms neighbor the $-CH_2$ group which would produce the triplet peak and the $-CH_2$ H-atoms neighbor the $-CH_3$ group which would produce the quartet peak. From inspection, the relative areas of the two different patterns seem to confirm a 6:4 (or 3:2) ratio as it should be.

Additional Exercises

49.   a. XeO_3, $8 + 3(6) = 26$ e[-]   b. XeO_4, $8 + 4(6) = 32$ e[-]

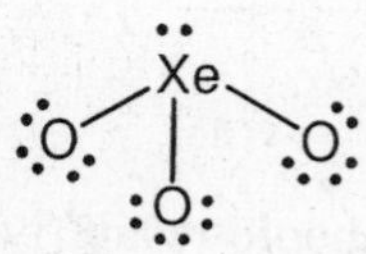

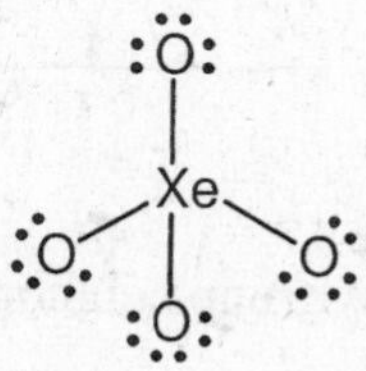

trigonal pyramid; sp^3 tetrahedral; sp^3

c. $XeOF_4$, $8 + 6 + 4(7) = 42$ e[-]   d. $XeOF_2$, $8 + 6 + 2(7) = 28$ e[-]

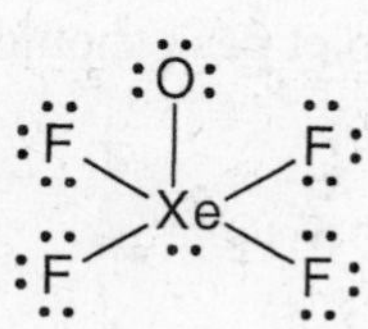

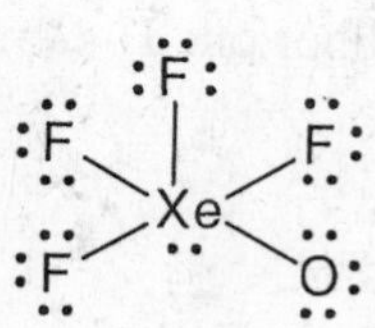

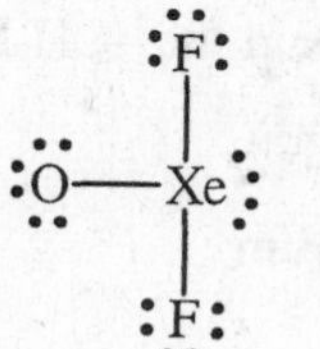

square pyramid; d^2sp^3 T-shaped; dsp^3

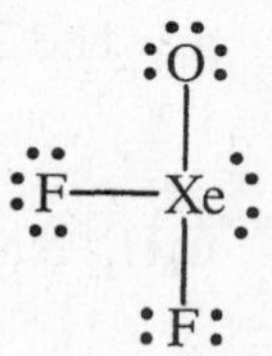

e. XeO_3F_2 has $8 + 3(6) + 2(7) = 40$ valence electrons.

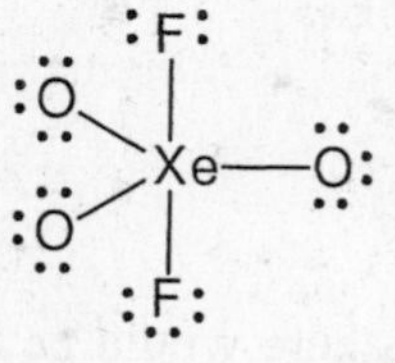

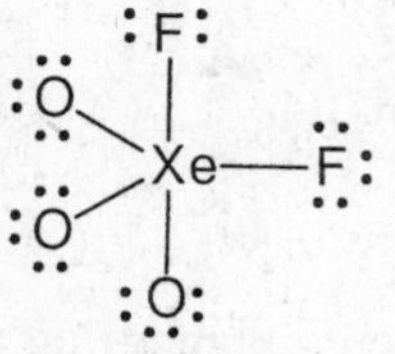

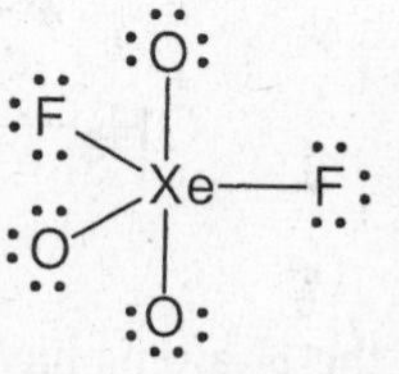

trigonal bipyramid; dsp^3

50. $FClO_2 + F^- \rightarrow F_2ClO_2^-$ $F_3ClO + F^- \rightarrow F_4ClO^-$
        $F_2ClO_2^-$, $2(7) + 7 + 2(6) + 1 = 34$ e⁻ F_4ClO^-, $4(7) + 7 + 6 + 1 = 42$ e⁻

              dsp³ hybridization   d²sp³ hybridization

Note: Similar to Exercise 14.49 c, d and e, $F_2ClO_2^-$ has two additional Lewis structures that are possible and F_4ClO^- has one additional Lewis structure that is possible, depending on the relative placement of the O and F atoms. The predicted hybridization is unaffected.

$F_3ClO \rightarrow F^- + F_2ClO^+$ $F_3ClO_2 \rightarrow F^- + F_2ClO_2^+$
F_2ClO^+, $2(7) + 7 + 6 - 1 = 26$ e⁻ $F_2ClO_2^+$, $2(7) + 7 + 2(6) - 1 = 32$ e⁻

              sp³ hybridization   sp³ hybridization

51.   a. No, some atoms are in different places. Thus, these are not resonance structures; they are different compounds.

        b. For the first Lewis structure, all nitrogens are sp³ hybridized and all carbons are sp² hybridized. In the second Lewis structure, all nitrogens and carbons are sp² hybridized.

        c. For the reaction:

Bonds broken: Bonds formed:

$$3\ C=O\ (745\ kJ/mol)$$ $$3\ C=N\ (615\ kJ/mol)$$
$$3\ C-N\ (305\ kJ/mol)$$ $$3\ C-O\ (358\ kJ/mol)$$
$$3\ N-H\ (391\ kJ/mol)$$ $$3\ O-H\ (467\ kJ/mol)$$

$$\Delta H = 3(745) + 3(305) + 3(391) - [3(615) + 3(358) + 3(467)]$$

$$\Delta H = 4323\ kJ - 4320\ kJ = 3\ kJ$$

The bonds are slightly stronger in the first structure with the carbon-oxygen double bonds since ΔH for the reaction is positive. However, the value of ΔH is so small that the best conclusion is that the bond strengths are comparable in the two structures.

52.

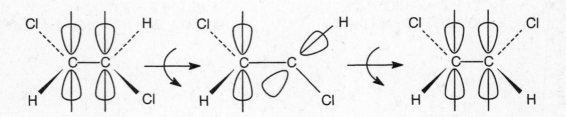

In order to rotate about the double bond, the molecule must go through an intermediate stage where the π bond is broken while the sigma bond remains intact. Bond energies are 347 kJ/mol for a C – C bond and 614 kJ/mol for a C = C bond. If we take the single bond as the strength of the σ bond, then the strength of the π bond is (614 - 347 =) 267 kJ/mol. Thus, 267 kJ/mol must be supplied to rotate about a carbon-carbon double bond.

53. O_3 and NO_2^- are isoelectronic, so we only need to consider one of them since the same bonding ideas apply to both. The Lewis structures for O_3 are:

For each of the two resonance forms, the central O atom is sp^2 hybridized with one unhybridized p atomic orbital. The sp^2 hybrid orbitals are used to form the two sigma bonds to the central atom. The localized electron view of the π bond utilizes unhybridized p atomic orbitals. The π bond resonates between the two positions in the Lewis structures:

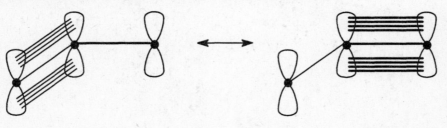

In the MO picture of the π bond, all three unhybridized p-orbitals overlap at the same time, resulting in π electrons that are delocalized over the entire surface of the molecule. This is represented as:

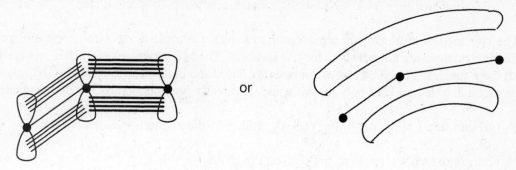

or

54.   The Lewis structures for CO_3^{2-} (24 e⁻) are:

$$\left[\begin{array}{c} :O: \\ \| \\ C \\ :O: \quad :O: \end{array} \right]^{2-} \longleftrightarrow \left[\begin{array}{c} :O: \\ \\ C \\ :O: \quad :O: \end{array} \right]^{2-} \longleftrightarrow \left[\begin{array}{c} :O: \\ \\ C \\ :O: \quad :O: \end{array} \right]^{2-}$$

In the localized electron view, the orbitals on the central carbon atom are sp^2 hybridized and are used to form the three sigma bonds in CO_3^{2-}. The central C atom also has one unhybridized p atomic orbital which overlaps with another p atomic orbital from one of the oxygen atoms to form the π bond in each resonance structure. This localized π bond moves (resonates) from one position to another. In the molecular orbital model for CO_3^{2-}, all four atoms in CO_3^{2-} have a p atomic orbital which is perpendicular to the plane of the ion. All four of these p orbitals overlap at the same time to form a delocalized π bonding system where the π electrons can roam over the entire surface of the ion. The π molecular orbital system for CO_3^{2-} is analogous to that for NO_3^- which is shown in Figure 14.51 of the text.

55.   Lewis structures:

NO⁺: $\left[:N \equiv O: \right]^+$

NO: $N = O \longleftrightarrow N = O \longleftrightarrow N = O$

NO⁻: $\left[N = O \right]^-$

M.O. model (assuming the same orbital order as that for N_2):

NO⁺: $(\sigma_{2s})^2(\sigma_{2s}^*)^2(\pi_{2p})^4(\sigma_{2p})^2$, B.O. = 3, 0 unpaired e⁻ (diamagnetic)

NO: $(\sigma_{2s})^2(\sigma_{2s}^*)^2(\pi_{2p})^4(\sigma_{2p})^2(\pi_{2p}^*)^1$, B.O. = 2.5, 1 unpaired e⁻ (paramagnetic)

NO⁻: $(\sigma_{2s})^2(\sigma_{2s}^*)^2(\pi_{2p})^4(\sigma_{2p})^2(\pi_{2p}^*)^2$ B.O. = 2, 2 unpaired e⁻ (paramagnetic)

From the bond orders:

bond energies: $NO^- < NO < NO^+$; bond lengths: $NO^+ < NO < NO^-$

The two models only give the same results for NO^+ (a triple bond with no unpaired electrons). Lewis structures are not adequate for NO and NO^-. The MO model gives a better representation for all three species. For NO, Lewis structures are poor for odd electron species. For NO^-, both models predict a double bond but only the MO model correctly predicts that NO^- is paramagnetic.

56. N_2 (ground state): $(\sigma_{2s})^2(\sigma_{2s}*)^2(\pi_{2p})^4(\sigma_{2p})^2$, B.O. = 3, diamagnetic (0 unpaired e^-)

   N_2 (1st excited state): $(\sigma_{2s})^2(\sigma_{2s}*)^2(\pi_{2p})^4(\sigma_{2p})^1(\pi_{2p}*)^1$

   B.O. = (7-3)/2 = 2, paramagnetic (2 unpaired e^-)

The first excited state of N_2 should have a weaker bond and should be paramagnetic.

57.   Considering only the twelve valence electrons in O_2, the MO models would be:

| | O₂ ground state | | Arrangement of electrons consistent with the Lewis structure (double bond and no unpaired electrons). |

It takes energy to pair electrons in the same orbital. Thus, the structure with no unpaired electrons is at a higher energy; it is an excited state.

58.   a.   Yes, both have 4 sets of electrons about the P. We would predict a tetrahedral structure for both. See part d for the Lewis structures.

   b.   The hybridization is sp^3 for P in each structure since both structures exhibit a tetrahedral arrangement of electron pairs.

c. P has to use one of its d orbitals to form the π bond since the p orbitals are all used to form the hybrid orbitals.

d. Formal charge = number of valence electrons of an atom - [(number of lone pair electrons) + 1/2 (number of shared electrons)]. The formal charges calculated for the O and P atoms are next to the atoms in the following Lewis structures.

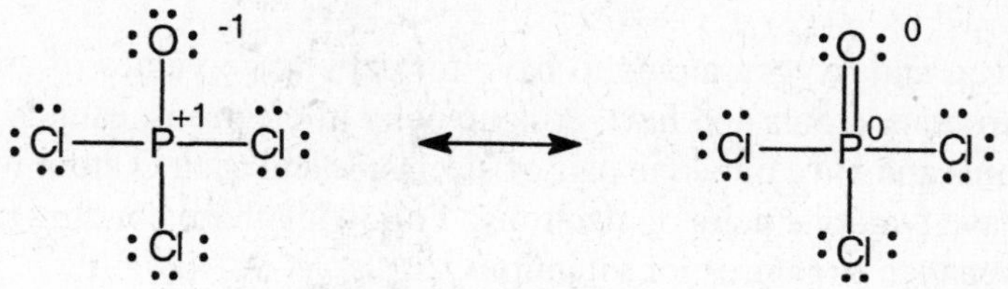

In both structures, the formal charges of the Cl atoms are all zeros. The structure with the P = O bond is favored on the basis of formal charge since it has a zero formal charge for all atoms.

59.　a.　$COCl_2$ has $4 + 6 + 2(7) = 24$ valence electrons.

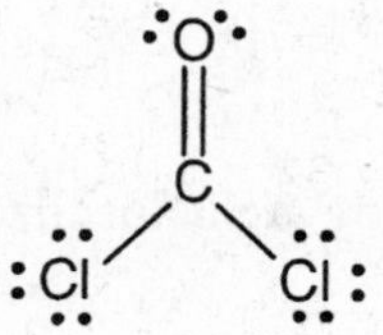

trigonal planar
polar
120°
sp^2

b.　N_2F_2 has $2(5) + 2(7) = 24$ valence electrons.

Can also be:

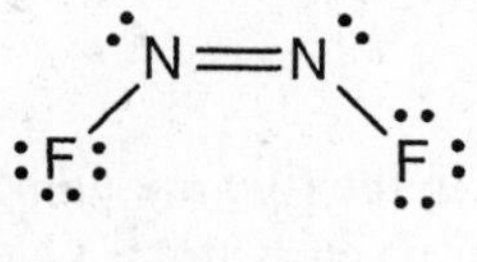

V-shaped about both Ns;
≈ 120° about both Ns;
Both Ns: sp^2

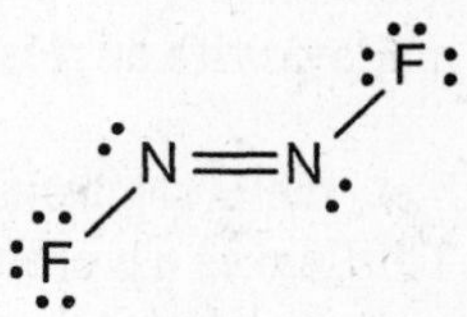

polar

nonpolar

These are distinctly different molecules.

c.　COS has $4 + 6 + 6 = 16$ valence electrons.

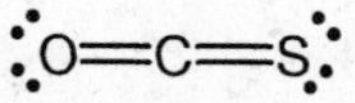

　linear, polar, 180°, sp

d. ICl_3 has $7 + 3(7) = 28$ valence electrons.

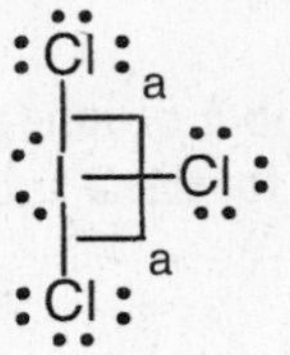

T-shaped
polar
a. $\approx 90°$
dsp^3

60. For carbon, nitrogen and oxygen atoms to have formal charge values of zero, each C atom will form four bonds to other atoms and have no lone pairs of electrons, each N atom will form three bonds to other atoms and have one lone pair of electrons, and each O atom will form two bonds to other atoms and have two lone pairs of electrons. Following these bonding requirements gives the following two resonance structures for vitamin B_6:

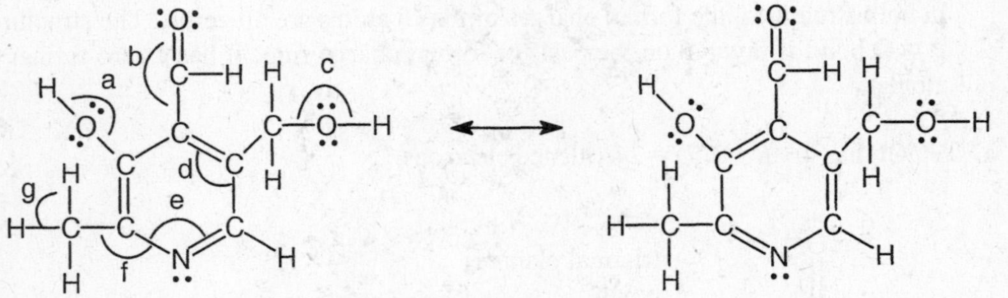

a.   21 σ bonds; 4 π bonds (The electrons in the 3 π bonds in the ring are delocalized.)

b.   angles a, c, and g: $\approx 109.5°$; angles b, d, e and f: $\approx 120°$

c.   6 sp^2 carbons; the 5 carbon atoms in the ring are sp^2 hybridized as is the carbon with the double bond to oxygen.

d.   4 sp^3 atoms; the 2 carbons which are not sp^2 hybridized are sp^3 hybridized and the oxygens marked with angles a and c are sp^3 hybridized.

e.   Yes, the π electrons in the ring are delocalized. The atoms in the ring are all sp^2 hybridized. This leaves a p orbital perpendicular to the plane of the ring from each atom. Overlap of all six of these p orbitals results in a π molecular orbital system where the electrons are delocalized above and below the plane of the ring (similar to benzene in Figure 14.50 of the text).

61. a.   The Lewis structures for NNO and NON are:

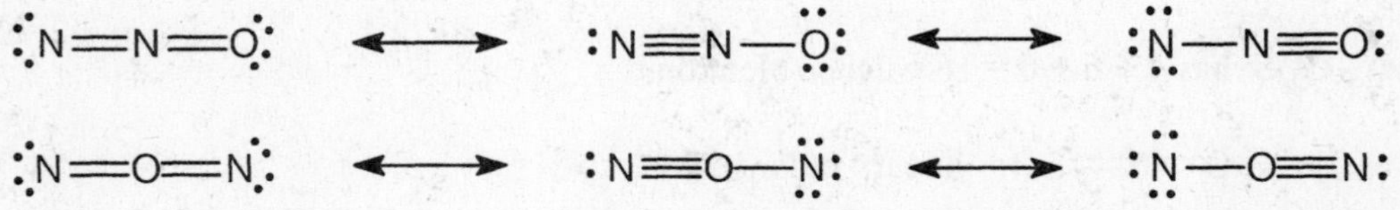

The NNO structure is correct. From the Lewis structures we would predict both NNO and NON to be linear. However, we would predict NNO to be polar and NON to be nonpolar. Since experiments show N_2O to be polar, then NNO is the correct structure.

b. Formal charge = number of valence electrons of atoms - [(number of lone pair electrons) + 1/2 (number of shared electrons)].

The formal charges for the atoms in the various resonance structures are below each atom. The central N is sp hybridized in all of the resonance structures. We can probably ignore the 3rd resonance structure on the basis of the relatively large formal charges as compared to the first two resonance structures.

c. The sp hybrid orbitals from the center N overlap with atomic orbitals (or appropriate hybrid orbitals) from the other two atoms to form the two sigma bonds. The remaining two unhybridized p orbitals from the center N overlap with two p orbitals from the peripheral N to form the two π bonds.

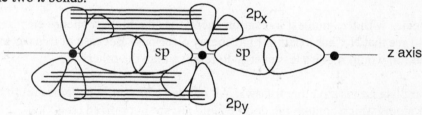

62. O=N–Cl: The bond order of the NO bond in NOCl is 2 (a double bond).

NO: The bond order of this NO bond is 2.5 (see Exercise 14.55).

Both reactions apparently only involve the breaking of the N–Cl bond. However, in the reaction: ONCl → NO + Cl some energy is released in forming the stronger NO bond, lowering the value of ΔH. Therefore, the apparent N–Cl bond energy is artificially low for this reaction. The first reaction only involves the breaking of the N–Cl bond.

Challenge Problems

63. a. $E = \dfrac{hc}{\lambda} = \dfrac{(6.626 \times 10^{-34} \text{ J s}) (2.998 \times 10^{8} \text{ m/s})}{25 \times 10^{-9} \text{ m}} = 7.9 \times 10^{-18} \text{ J}$

$7.9 \times 10^{-18} \text{ J} \times \dfrac{6.022 \times 10^{23}}{\text{mol}} \times \dfrac{1 \text{ kJ}}{1000 \text{ J}} = 4800 \text{ kJ/mol}$

Using ΔH values from the various reactions, 25 nm light has sufficient energy to ionize N_2 and N, and to break the triple bond. Thus, N_2, N_2^+, N, and N^+ will all be present, assuming excess N_2.

b. To produce atomic nitrogen but no ions, the range of energies of the light must be from 941 kJ/mol to just below 1402 kJ/mol.

$\dfrac{941 \text{ kJ}}{\text{mol}} \times \dfrac{1 \text{ mol}}{6.022 \times 10^{23}} \times \dfrac{1000 \text{ J}}{\text{kJ}} = 1.56 \times 10^{-18} \text{ J/photon}$

$$\lambda = \frac{hc}{E} = \frac{(6.626 \times 10^{-34}\ \text{J s})\ (2.998 \times 10^{8}\ \text{m/s})}{1.56 \times 10^{-18}\ \text{J}} = 1.27 \times 10^{-7}\ \text{m} = 127\ \text{nm}$$

$$\frac{1402\ \text{kJ}}{\text{mol}} \times \frac{1\ \text{mol}}{6.0221 \times 10^{23}} \times \frac{1000\ \text{J}}{\text{kJ}} = 2.328 \times 10^{-18}\ \text{J/photon}$$

$$\lambda = \frac{hc}{E} = \frac{(6.6261 \times 10^{-34}\ \text{J s})\ (2.9979 \times 10^{8}\ \text{m/s})}{2.328 \times 10^{-18}\ \text{J}} = 8.533 \times 10^{-8}\ \text{m} = 85.33\ \text{nm}$$

Light with wavelengths in the range of $85.33\ \text{nm} < \lambda \le 127\ \text{nm}$ will produce N but no ions.

c. N_2: $(\sigma_{2s})^2(\sigma_{2s}^*)^2(\pi_{2p})^4(\sigma_{2p})^2$; The electron removed from N_2 is in the σ_{2p} molecular orbital which is lower in energy than the 2p atomic orbital from which the electron in atomic nitrogen is removed. Since the electron removed from N_2 is lower in energy than the electron removed from N, then the ionization energy of N_2 is greater than that for N.

64.   The species with the smallest ionization energy has the highest energy electron. Reference Figure 14.41 to see that N_2^{2-} has a pair of high energy electrons. Because of this pairing (and high energy) the electron would require less energy to remove than the others.

65.   The complete Lewis structure follows. All but two of the carbon atoms are sp³ hybridized. The two carbon atoms which contain the double bond are sp² hybridized (see *).

No; most of the carbons are not in the same plane since a majority of carbon atoms exhibit a tetrahedral structure. Note: CH, CH_2 and CH_3 are shorthand for carbon atoms singly bonded to hydrogen atoms.

66.

$$O_2 \qquad O_2^- \qquad O_2^+ \qquad O$$

lowest IE   highest IE

$$O_2^- \; < \; O_2 \; < \; O_2^+ \; < \; O$$

The electrons for O_2^-, O_2; O_2^+ that are highest in energy are in the π 2p* MO. But for O_2^-, these electrons are paired. The species O_2^+ has an overall positive charge (making it harder to remove an electron from O_2^+ than O_2). The highest energy electrons for O are lower than those for the others.

67.   a.   The CO bond is polar with the negative end around the more electronegative oxygen atom. We would expect metal cations to be attracted to and to bond to the oxygen end of CO on the basis of electronegativity.

      b.

$$FC \text{ (carbon)} = 4 - 2 - 1/2(6) = -1$$

$$:C\equiv O:$$

$$FC \text{ (oxygen)} = 6 - 2 - 1/2(6) = +1$$

From formal charge, we would expect metal cations to bond to the carbon (with the negative formal charge).

      c.   In molecular orbital theory, only orbitals with proper symmetry overlap to form bonding orbitals. The metals that form bonds to CO are usually transition metals, all of which have outer electrons in the d orbitals. The only molecular orbitals of CO that have proper symmetry to overlap with d orbitals are the $\pi_{2p}*$ orbitals, whose shape is similar to the d orbitals (see Figure 14.36). Since the antibonding molecular orbitals have more carbon character, one would expect the bond to form through carbon.

68.   The molecular orbitals for BeH_2 are formed from the two hydrogen 1s orbitals and the 2s and one of the 2p orbitals from beryllium. One of the sigma bonding orbitals forms from overlap of the hydrogen 1s orbitals with a 2s orbital from beryllium. Assuming the z-axis is the internuclear axis in the linear BeH_2 molecule, then the $2p_z$ orbital from beryllium has proper symmetry to overlap with the 1s orbitals from hydrogen; the $2p_x$ and $2p_y$ orbitals are nonbonding orbitals since they don't have proper symmetry necessary to overlap with 1s orbitals. The type of bond formed from the $2p_z$ and 1s orbitals is a sigma bond since the orbitals overlap head to head. The MO diagram for BeH_2 is:

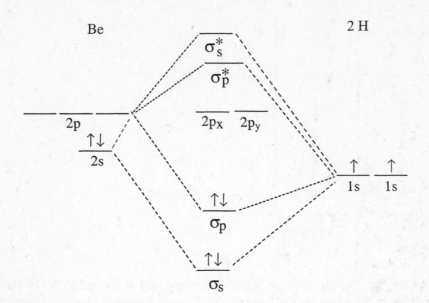

Bond Order = (4 - 0)/2 = 2; The MO diagram predicts BeH_2 to be a stable species and also predicts that BeH_2 is diamagnetic. Note: The σ_s MO is a mixture of the two hydrogen 1s orbitals with the 2s orbital from beryllium and the σ_p MO is a mixture of the two hydrogen 1s orbitals with the $2p_z$ orbital from beryllium. The MOs are not localized between any two atoms; instead, they extend over the entire surface of the three atoms.

69.   One of the resonance structures
       for benzene is:

To break $C_6H_6(g)$ into C(g) and H(g) requires the breaking of 6 C–H bonds, 3 C=C bonds and 3 C–C bonds:

$$C_6H_6(g) \rightarrow 6\ C(g) + 6\ H(g)   \quad \Delta H = 6\ D_{C-H} + 3\ D_{C=C} + 3\ D_{C-C}$$

$$\Delta H = 6(413\ kJ) + 3(614\ kJ) + 3(347\ kJ) = 5361\ kJ$$

The question wants ΔH_f° for $C_6H_6(g)$ which is ΔH for the reaction:

$$6\ C(s) + 3\ H_2(g) \rightarrow C_6H_6(g)   \quad \Delta H = \Delta H_{f,\ C_6H_6(g)}^\circ$$

To calculate ΔH for this reaction, we will use Hess's law along with the ΔH_f° value for C(g) and the bond energy value for H_2 (D_{H_2} = 432 kJ/mol).

$$6\ C(g) + 6\ H(g) \rightarrow C_6H_6(g) \qquad \Delta H_1 = -5361\ kJ$$
$$6\ C(s) \rightarrow 6\ C(g) \qquad \Delta H_2 = 6(717\ kJ)$$
$$3\ H_2(g) \rightarrow 6\ H(g) \qquad \Delta H_3 = 3(432\ kJ)$$

$$6\ C(s) + 3\ H_2(g) \rightarrow C_6H_6(g) \qquad \Delta H = \Delta H_1 + \Delta H_2 + \Delta H_3 = 237\ kJ; \quad \Delta H^\circ_{f,\,C_6H_6(g)} = 237\ kJ/mol$$

The experimental ΔH°_f for $C_6H_6(g)$ is more stable (lower in energy) by 154 kJ as compared to ΔH°_f calculated from bond energies (83 - 237 = -154 kJ). This extra stability is related to benzene's ability to exhibit resonance. Two equivalent Lewis structures can be drawn for benzene. The π bonding system implied by each Lewis structure consists of three localized π bonds. This is not correct as all C–C bonds in benzene are equivalent. We say the π electrons in benzene are delocalized over the entire surface of C_6H_6 (see Section 14.5 of the text). The large discrepancy between ΔH°_f values is due to the delocalized π electrons, whose effect was not accounted for in the calculated ΔH°_f value. The extra stability associated with benzene can be called resonance stabilization. In general, molecules that exhibit resonance are usually more stable than predicted using bond energies.

Marathon Problem

70. φ_1, φ_2, and φ_3 all must be normalized.

$$\int \varphi_1^2\ d_T = 1 = \frac{1}{3}\int \varphi_s^2\ d_T + 4A^2\int \varphi_{px}^2\ d_T + 2\sqrt{\frac{1}{3}}\,2A\int \varphi_s\,\varphi_{px}\ d_T$$

$$= \frac{1}{3} + 4(A^2)(1) + 0$$

$$4A^2 = 1 - \frac{1}{3} = \frac{2}{3};\ A^2 = \frac{1}{6};\ A = \sqrt{\frac{1}{6}}$$

$$\int \varphi_2^2\ d_T = 1 = \frac{1}{3}\int \varphi_s^2\ d_T + A^2\int \varphi_{px}^2\ d_T + B^2\int \varphi_{py}^2\ d_T + 2\sqrt{\frac{1}{3}}\,(-A)\int \varphi_s\,\varphi_{px}\ d_T$$

$$+ 2\sqrt{\frac{1}{3}}\,(B)\int \varphi_s\,\varphi_{py}\ d_T - 2\,AB\int \varphi_{px}\,\varphi_{py}\ d_T$$

$$= \frac{1}{3} + A^2 + B^2 + 0 + 0 + 0$$

$$1 = \frac{1}{3} + \frac{1}{6} + B^2 \qquad \frac{1}{2} = B^2 \qquad B = \sqrt{\frac{1}{2}}$$

CHAPTER FIFTEEN

CHEMICAL KINETICS

Reaction Rates

10. The coefficients in the balanced reaction relate the rate of disappearance of reactants to the rate of production of products. From the balanced reaction, the rate of production of P_4 will be 1/4 the rate of disappearance of PH_3 and the rate of production of H_2 will be 6/4 the rate of disappearance of PH_3. By convention, all rates are given as positive values.

$$\text{Rate} = -\frac{\Delta[PH_3]}{\Delta t} = \frac{-(-0.0048 \text{ mol}/2.0 \text{ L})}{s} = 2.4 \times 10^{-3} \text{ mol L}^{-1} \text{ s}^{-1}$$

$$\frac{\Delta[P_4]}{\Delta t} = -\frac{1}{4}\frac{\Delta[PH_3]}{\Delta t} = 2.4 \times 10^{-3}/4 = 6.0 \times 10^{-4} \text{ mol L}^{-1} \text{ s}^{-1}$$

$$\frac{\Delta[H_2]}{\Delta t} = -\frac{6}{4}\frac{\Delta[PH_3]}{\Delta t} = 6(2.4 \times 10^{-3})/4 = 3.6 \times 10^{-3} \text{ mol L}^{-1} \text{ s}^{-1}$$

11. Using the coefficients in the balanced equation to relate the rates:

$$\frac{d[H_2]}{dt} = 3\frac{d[N_2]}{dt} \text{ and } \frac{d[NH_3]}{dt} = -2\frac{d[N_2]}{dt}; \text{ So, } \frac{1}{3}\frac{d[H_2]}{dt} = -\frac{1}{2}\frac{d[NH_3]}{dt} \text{ or } \frac{d[NH_3]}{dt} = -\frac{2}{3}\frac{d[H_2]}{dt}$$

Ammonia is produced at a rate equal to 2/3 of the rate of consumption of hydrogen.

12. a. The units for rate are always mol L^{-1} s^{-1}. b. Rate = k; k has units of mol L^{-1} s^{-1}.

c. Rate = k[A], $\dfrac{\text{mol}}{\text{L s}} = k\left(\dfrac{\text{mol}}{\text{L}}\right)$ d. Rate = k[A]^2, $\dfrac{\text{mol}}{\text{L s}} = k\left(\dfrac{\text{mol}}{\text{L}}\right)^2$

   k must have units of s^{-1}.   k must have units L mol^{-1} s^{-1}.

e. L^2 mol^{-2} s^{-1}

13. Rate = k[Cl]$^{1/2}$[CHCl$_3$], $\dfrac{\text{mol}}{\text{L s}} = k\left(\dfrac{\text{mol}}{\text{L}}\right)^{1/2}\left(\dfrac{\text{mol}}{\text{L}}\right)$; k must have units of L$^{1/2}$ mol$^{-1/2}$ s^{-1}.

14. $\dfrac{1.24 \times 10^{-12} \text{ cm}^3}{\text{molecules s}} \times \dfrac{1 \text{ L}}{1000 \text{ cm}^3} \times \dfrac{6.022 \times 10^{23} \text{ molecules}}{\text{mol}} = 7.47 \times 10^8 \text{ L mol}^{-1} \text{ s}^{-1}$

Rate Laws from Experimental Data: Initial Rates Method

15.   a.   In the first two experiments, [NO] is held constant and $[Cl_2]$ is doubled. The rate also
            doubled. Thus, the reaction is first order with respect to Cl_2. Or mathematically: Rate =
            $k[NO]^x[Cl_2]^y$

$$\frac{0.36}{0.18} = \frac{k(0.10)^x(0.20)^y}{k(0.10)^x(0.10)^y} = \frac{(0.20)^y}{(0.10)^y}, \ \ 2.0 = 2.0^y, \ y = 1$$

We can get the dependence on NO from the second and third experiments. Here, as the NO
concentration doubles (Cl_2 concentration is constant), the rate increases by a factor of four.
Thus, the reaction is second order with respect to NO. Or mathematically:

$$\frac{1.45}{0.36} = \frac{k(0.20)^x(0.20)}{k(0.10)^x(0.20)} = \frac{(0.20)^x}{(0.10)^x}, \ \ 4.0 = 2.0^x, \ x = 2; \ \text{ So, } \ \text{Rate} = k[NO]^2[Cl_2]$$

Try to examine experiments where only one concentration changes at a time. The more
variables that change, the harder it is to determine the orders. Also, these types of problems
can usually be solved by inspection. In general, we will solve using a mathematical
approach, but keep in mind, you probably can solve for the orders by simple inspection of the
data.

    b.   The rate constant k can be determined from the experiments. From experiment 1:

$$\frac{0.18 \text{ mol}}{\text{L min}} = k \left(\frac{0.10 \text{ mol}}{\text{L}} \right)^2 \left(\frac{0.10 \text{ mol}}{\text{L}} \right), \ \ k = 180 \text{ L}^2 \text{ mol}^{-2} \text{ min}^{-1}$$

From the other experiments:

   $k = 180 \text{ L}^2 \text{ mol}^{-2} \text{ min}^{-1}$ (2nd exp.); $k = 180 \text{ L}^2 \text{ mol}^{-2} \text{ min}^{-1}$ (3rd exp.)

The average rate constant is $k_{mean} = 1.8 \times 10^2 \text{ L}^2 \text{ mol}^{-2} \text{ min}^{-1}$

16.   a.   Rate = $k[I^-]^x[S_2O_8^{2-}]^y$; $\dfrac{12.5 \times 10^{-6}}{6.25 \times 10^{-6}} = \dfrac{k(0.080)^x(0.040)^y}{k(0.040)^x(0.040)^y}$, $2.00 = 2.0^x, \ x = 1$

$\dfrac{12.5 \times 10^{-6}}{6.25 \times 10^{-6}} = \dfrac{k(0.080)^x(0.040)^y}{k(0.080)^x(0.020)^y}$, $2.00 = 2.0^y, y = 1$; Rate = $k[I^-][S_2O_8^{2-}]$

b. For the first experiment:

$$\frac{12.5 \times 10^{-6} \text{ mol}}{\text{L s}} = k\left(\frac{0.080 \text{ mol}}{\text{L}}\right)\left(\frac{0.040 \text{ mol}}{\text{L}}\right), \quad k = 3.9 \times 10^{-3} \text{ L mol}^{-1} \text{ s}^{-1}$$

The other values are:

Initial Rate $(\text{mol L}^{-1} \text{ s}^{-1})$	k $(\text{L mol}^{-1} \text{ s}^{-1})$
12.5×10^{-6}	3.9×10^{-3}
6.25×10^{-6}	3.9×10^{-3}
6.25×10^{-6}	3.9×10^{-3}
5.00×10^{-6}	3.9×10^{-3}
7.00×10^{-6}	3.9×10^{-3}

$k_{mean} = 3.9 \times 10^{-3} \text{ L mol}^{-1} \text{ s}^{-1}$

17. a. Rate = $k[NOCl]^n$; Using experiments two and three:

$$\frac{2.66 \times 10^4}{6.64 \times 10^3} = \frac{k(2.0 \times 10^{16})^n}{k(1.0 \times 10^{16})^n}, \quad 4.01 = 2.0^n, \quad n = 2; \quad \text{Rate} = k[NOCl]^2$$

b. $$\frac{5.98 \times 10^4 \text{ molecules}}{\text{cm}^3 \text{ s}} = k\left(\frac{3.0 \times 10^{16} \text{ molecules}}{\text{cm}^3}\right)^2, \quad k = 6.6 \times 10^{-29} \text{ cm}^3/\text{molecules}^{-1}\text{s}^{-1}$$

The other three experiments give $(6.7, 6.6 \text{ and } 6.6) \times 10^{-29} \text{ cm}^3 \text{ molecules}^{-1}\text{s}^{-1}$, respectively.

The mean value for k is $6.6 \times 10^{-29} \text{ cm}^3 \text{ molecules}^{-1}\text{s}^{-1}$.

c. $$\frac{6.6 \times 10^{-29} \text{ cm}^3}{\text{molecules s}} \times \frac{1 \text{ L}}{1000 \text{ cm}^3} \times \frac{6.022 \times 10^{23} \text{molecules}}{\text{mol}} = \frac{4.0 \times 10^{-8} \text{ L}}{\text{mol s}}$$

18. a. Rate = $k[Hb]^x[CO]^y$

Comparing the first two experiments, [CO] is unchanged, [Hb] doubles, and the rate doubles. Therefore, $x = 1$ and the reaction is first order in Hb. Comparing the second and third experiments, [Hb] is unchanged, [CO] triples and the rate triples. Therefore, $y = 1$ and the reaction is first order in CO.

b. Rate = $k[Hb][CO]$

c. From the first experiment:

$0.619 \text{ } \mu\text{mol L}^{-1} \text{ s}^{-1} = k (2.21 \text{ } \mu\text{mol/L})(1.00 \text{ } \mu\text{mol/L}), \quad k = 0.280 \text{ L } \mu\text{mol}^{-1} \text{ s}^{-1}$

The second and third experiments give similar k values, so $k_{mean} = 0.280 \text{ L } \mu\text{mol}^{-1} \text{ s}^{-1}$.

d.   Rate = k[Hb][CO] = $\dfrac{0.280\ L}{\mu mol\ s} \times \dfrac{3.36\ \mu mol}{L} \times \dfrac{2.40\ \mu mol}{L} = 2.26\ \mu mol\ L^{-1}\ s^{-1}$

19.   a.   Rate = $k[ClO_2]^x[OH^-]^y$; From the first two experiments:

$2.30 \times 10^{-1} = k(0.100)^x(0.100)^y$ and $5.75 \times 10^{-2} = k(0.0500)^x(0.100)^y$

Dividing the two rate laws: $4.00 = \dfrac{(0.100)^x}{(0.0500)^x} = 2.00^x,\ x = 2$

Comparing the second and third experiments:

$2.30 \times 10^{-1} = k(0.100)(0.100)^y$ and $1.15 \times 10^{-1} = k(0.100)(0.0500)^y$

Dividing: $2.00 = \dfrac{(0.100)^y}{(0.050)^y} = 2.0^y,\ y = 1$

The rate law is: Rate = $k[ClO_2]^2[OH^-]$

2.30×10^{-1} mol L^{-1} s^{-1} = $k(0.100$ mol$/L)^2(0.100$ mol$/L)$, $k = 2.30 \times 10^2\ L^2\ mol^{-2}\ s^{-1} = k_{mean}$

b.   Rate = $\dfrac{2.30 \times 10^2\ L^2}{mol^2\ s} \times \left(\dfrac{0.175\ mol}{L}\right)^2 \times \dfrac{0.0844\ mol}{L} = 0.594$ mol L^{-1} s^{-1}

20.   Rate = $k[NO]^x[O_2]^y$; Comparing the first two experiments, $[O_2]$ is unchanged, [NO] is tripled, and the rate increases by a factor of nine. Therefore, the reaction is second order in NO ($3^2 = 9$). The order of O_2 is more difficult to determine. Comparing the second and third experiments;

$\dfrac{3.13 \times 10^{17}}{1.80 \times 10^{17}} = \dfrac{k\,(2.50 \times 10^{18})^2(2.50 \times 10^{18})^y}{k\,(3.00 \times 10^{18})^2(1.00 \times 10^{18})^y}$, $1.74 = 0.694\,(2.50)^y$, $2.51 = 2.50^y$, $y = 1$

Rate = $k[NO]^2[O_2]$; From experiment 1:

2.00×10^{16} molecules cm^{-3} s^{-1} = $k\,(1.00 \times 10^{18}$ molecules/cm$^3)^2\,(1.00 \times 10^{18}$ molecules/cm$^3)$

$k = 2.00 \times 10^{-38}$ cm^6 molecules^{-2} s$^{-1} = k_{mean}$

Rate = $\dfrac{2.00 \times 10^{-38}\ cm^6}{molecules^2\ s} \times \left(\dfrac{6.21 \times 10^{18}\ molecules}{cm^3}\right)^2 \times \dfrac{7.36 \times 10^{18}\ molecules}{cm^3}$

$= 5.68 \times 10^{18}$ molecules cm^{-3} s^{-1}

21.   Rate = $k[N_2O_5]^x$; The rate laws for the first two experiments are:

$2.26 \times 10^{-3} = k(0.190)^x$ and $8.90 \times 10^{-4} = k(0.0750)^x$

Dividing: $2.54 = \dfrac{(0.190)^x}{(0.0750)^x} = (2.53)^x$, $x = 1$; Rate $= k[N_2O_5]$

$k = \dfrac{\text{Rate}}{[N_2O_5]} = \dfrac{8.90 \times 10^{-4} \text{ mol L}^{-1} \text{ s}^{-1}}{0.0750 \text{ mol/L}} = 1.19 \times 10^{-2} \text{ s}^{-1}$; $k_{mean} = 1.19 \times 10^{-2} \text{ s}^{-1}$

Integrated Rate Laws

22. a. Since the 1/[A] vs time plot was linear, then the reaction is second order in A. The slope of the 1/[A] vs. time plot equals the rate constant k. Therefore, the rate law, the integrated rate law and the rate constant value are:

$$\text{Rate} = k[A]^2; \quad \dfrac{1}{[A]} = kt + \dfrac{1}{[A]_o}; \quad k = 3.60 \times 10^{-2} \text{ L mol}^{-1} \text{ s}^{-1}$$

b. The half-life expression for a second order reaction is: $t_{1/2} = \dfrac{1}{k[A]_o}$

For this reaction: $t_{1/2} = \dfrac{1}{3.60 \times 10^{-2} \text{ L mol}^{-1} \text{ s}^{-1} \times 2.80 \times 10^{-3} \text{ mol/L}} = 9.92 \times 10^3 \text{ s}$

Note: We could have used the integrated rate law to solve for $t_{1/2}$ where $[A] = (2.80 \times 10^{-3} / 2)$ mol/L.

c. Since the half-life for a second order reaction depends on concentration, then we must use the integrated rate law to solve.

$$\dfrac{1}{[A]} = kt + \dfrac{1}{[A]_o}, \quad \dfrac{1}{7.00 \times 10^{-4} \, M} = \dfrac{3.60 \times 10^{-2} \text{ L}}{\text{mol s}} \times t + \dfrac{1}{2.80 \times 10^{-3} \, M}$$

$1.43 \times 10^3 - 357 = 3.60 \times 10^{-2} \, t$, $t = 2.98 \times 10^4 \text{ s}$

23. a. Since the ln[A] vs time plot was linear, then the reaction is first order in A. The slope of the ln[A] vs time plot equals -k. Therefore, the rate law, the integrated rate law and the rate constant value are:

$$\text{Rate} = k[A]; \quad \ln[A] = -kt + \ln[A]_o; \quad k = 2.97 \times 10^{-2} \text{ min}^{-1}$$

b. The half-life expression for a first order rate law is:

$$t_{1/2} = \dfrac{\ln 2}{k} = \dfrac{0.6931}{k}, \quad t_{1/2} = \dfrac{0.6931}{2.97 \times 10^{-2} \text{ min}^{-1}} = 23.3 \text{ min}$$

c. $2.50 \times 10^{-3} \, M$ is 1/8 of the original amount of A present initially, so the reaction is 87.5% complete. When a first order reaction is 87.5% complete (or 12.5% remains), then the reaction has gone through 3 half-lives:

$$100\% \xrightarrow[t_{1/2}]{} 50.0\% \xrightarrow[t_{1/2}]{} 25.0\% \xrightarrow[t_{1/2}]{} 12.5\%; \quad t = 3 \times t_{1/2} = 3 \times 23.3 \text{ min} = 69.9 \text{ min}$$

Or we can use the integrated rate law:

$$\ln\left(\frac{[A]}{[A]_o}\right) = -kt, \quad \ln\left(\frac{2.50 \times 10^{-3}\,M}{2.00 \times 10^{-2}\,M}\right) = -(2.97 \times 10^{-2}\,\text{min}^{-1})\,t, \quad t = \frac{\ln(0.125)}{-2.97 \times 10^{-2}\,\text{min}^{-1}}$$

$$= 70.0 \text{ min}$$

24.   a.   Since the $[C_2H_5OH]$ vs time plot was linear, then the reaction is zero order in C_2H_5OH. The slope of the $[C_2H_5OH]$ vs time plot equals -k. Therefore, the rate law, the integrated rate law and the rate constant value are: Rate $= k[C_2H_5OH]^0 = k$; $[C_2H_5OH] = -kt + [C_2H_5OH]_o$; $k = 4.00 \times 10^{-5}$ mol L^{-1} s^{-1}

b.   The half-life expression for a zero order reaction is: $t_{1/2} = [A]_o/2k$.

$$t_{1/2} = \frac{[C_2H_5OH]_o}{2k} = \frac{1.25 \times 10^{-2}\,\text{mol/L}}{2 \times 4.00 \times 10^{-5}\,\text{mol L}^{-1}\,\text{s}^{-1}} = 156 \text{ s}$$

Note: we could have used the integrated rate law to solve for $t_{1/2}$ where $[C_2H_5OH] = (1.25 \times 10^{-2}/2)$ mol/L.

c. $[C_2H_5OH] = -kt + [C_2H_5OH]_o$,   0 mol/L $= -(4.00 \times 10^{-5}$ mol L^{-1} $s^{-1})\,t + 1.25 \times 10^{-2}$ mol/L

$$t = \frac{1.25 \times 10^{-2}\,\text{mol/L}}{4.00 \times 10^{-5}\,\text{mol L}^{-1}\,\text{s}^{-1}} = 313 \text{ s}$$

25.   The first assumption to make is that the reaction is first order. For a first order reaction, a graph of $\ln[H_2O_2]$ vs time will yield a straight line. If this plot is not linear, then the reaction is not first order and we make another assumption.

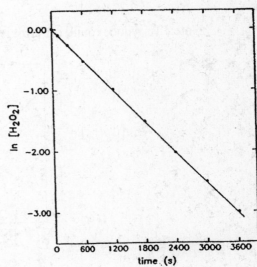

Time (s)	$[H_2O_2]$ (mol/L)	$\ln[H_2O_2]$
0	1.00	0.000
120.	0.91	-0.094
300.	0.78	-0.25
600.	0.59	-0.53
1200.	0.37	-0.99
1800.	0.22	-1.51
2400.	0.13	-2.04
3000.	0.082	-2.50
3600.	0.050	-3.00

Note: We carried extra significant figures in some of the ln values in order to reduce round off error. For the plots, we will do this most of the time when the ln function is involved.

The plot of ln [H$_2$O$_2$] vs. time is linear. Thus, the reaction is first order. The differential rate law and integrated rate law are: Rate = $\dfrac{-d[H_2O_2]}{dt}$ = k[H$_2$O$_2$] and ln [H$_2$O$_2$] = -kt + ln [H$_2$O$_2$]$_o$.

We determine the rate constant k by determining the slope of the ln [H$_2$O$_2$] vs time plot (slope = -k). Using two points on the curve gives:

$$\text{slope} = -k = \frac{\Delta y}{\Delta x} = \frac{0 - (3.00)}{0 - 3600.} = -8.3 \times 10^{-4} \text{ s}^{-1}, \ \ k = 8.3 \times 10^{-4} \text{ s}^{-1}$$

To determine [H$_2$O$_2$] at 4000. s, use the integrated rate law where at t = 0, [H$_2$O$_2$]$_o$ = 1.00 M.

$$\ln [H_2O_2] = -kt + \ln [H_2O_2]_o \ \ \text{or} \ \ \ln\left(\frac{[H_2O_2]}{[H_2O_2]_o}\right) = -kt$$

$$\ln\left(\frac{[H_2O_2]}{1.00}\right) = -8.3 \times 10^{-4} \text{ s}^{-1} \times 4000. \text{ s}, \ \ \ln [H_2O_2] = -3.3, \ \ [H_2O_2] = e^{-3.3} = 0.037 \ M$$

26.   The first assumption to make is that the reaction is first order. For a first order reaction, a graph of ln [C$_4$H$_6$] vs. t should yield a straight line. If this isn't linear, then try the second order plot of 1/[C$_4$H$_6$] vs. t. The data and the plots follow.

Time	195	604	1246	2180	6210 s
[C$_4$H$_6$]	1.6×10^{-2}	1.5×10^{-2}	1.3×10^{-2}	1.1×10^{-2}	0.68×10^{-2} M
ln [C$_4$H$_6$]	-4.14	-4.20	-4.34	-4.51	-4.99
1/[C$_4$H$_6$]	62.5	66.7	76.9	90.9	147 M^{-1}

Note: To reduce round off error, we carried extra sig. figs. in the data points.

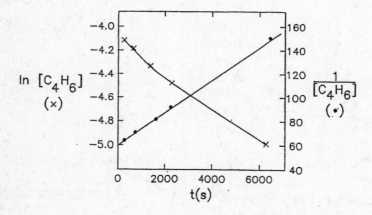

The natural log plot is not linear, so the reaction is not first order. Since the second order plot of 1/[C$_4$H$_6$] vs. t is linear, then we can conclude that the reaction is second order in butadiene. The differential rate law is:

Rate = k[C$_4$H$_6$]^2

For a second order reaction, the integrated rate law is: $\dfrac{1}{[C_4H_6]} = kt + \dfrac{1}{[C_4H_6]_o}$

The slope of the straight line equals the value of the rate constant. Using the points on the line at 1000. and 6000. s:

$$k = slope = \frac{144 \text{ L/mol} - 73 \text{ L/mol}}{6000. \text{ s} - 1000. \text{ s}} = 1.4 \times 10^{-2} \text{ L mol}^{-1} \text{ s}^{-1}$$

27.   Assume the reaction is first order and see if the plot of ln [NO$_2$] vs. time is linear. If this isn't linear, try the second order plot of 1/[NO$_2$] vs. time. The data and plots follow.

Time (s)	[NO$_2$] (M)	ln [NO$_2$]	1/[NO$_2$] (M^{-1})
0	0.500	-0.693	2.00
1.20×10^3	0.444	-0.812	2.25
3.00×10^3	0.381	-0.965	2.62
4.50×10^3	0.340	-1.079	2.94
9.00×10^3	0.250	-1.386	4.00
1.80×10^4	0.174	-1.749	5.75

The plot of 1/[NO$_2$] vs. time is linear. The reaction is second order in NO$_2$. The differential rate law and integrated rate law are: Rate = k[NO$_2$]^2 and $\dfrac{1}{[NO_2]} = kt + \dfrac{1}{[NO_2]_o}$.

The slope of the plot 1/[NO$_2$] vs. t gives the value of k. Using a couple points on the plot:

$$slope = k = \frac{\Delta y}{\Delta x} = \frac{(5.75 - 2.00)\ M^{-1}}{(1.80 \times 10^4 - 0)\ s} = 2.08 \times 10^{-4} \text{ L mol}^{-1} \text{ s}^{-1}$$

To determine [NO$_2$] at 2.70×10^4 s, use the integrated rate law where 1/[NO$_2$]$_o$ = 1/0.500 M = 2.00 M^{-1}.

$$\frac{1}{[NO_2]} = kt + \frac{1}{[NO_2]_o}, \quad \frac{1}{[NO_2]} = \frac{2.08 \times 10^{-4} \, L}{mol \, s} \times 2.70 \times 10^4 \, s + 2.00 \, M^{-1}$$

$$\frac{1}{[NO_2]} = 7.62, \quad [NO_2] = 0.131 \, M$$

28. a. First, assume the reaction to be first order with respect to O. Hence, a graph of ln [O] vs. t should be linear if the reaction is first order.

t (s)	[O] (atoms/cm^3)	ln [O]
0	5.0×10^9	22.33
$10. \times 10^{-3}$	1.9×10^9	21.37
$20. \times 10^{-3}$	6.8×10^8	20.34
$30. \times 10^{-3}$	2.5×10^8	19.34

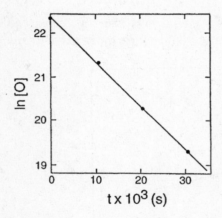

Since the graph is linear, we can conclude the reaction is first order with respect to O.

b. The overall rate law is: Rate = $k[NO_2][O]$

Since NO_2 was in excess, its concentration is constant. So for this experiment, the rate law is: Rate: $k'[O]$ where $k' = k[NO_2]$. In a typical first order plot, the slope equals -k. For this experiment, the slope equals $-k' = -k[NO_2]$. From the graph:

$$\text{slope} = \frac{19.34 - 22.33}{(30. \times 10^{-3} - 0) \, s} = -1.0 \times 10^2 \, s^{-1}, \quad k' = -\text{slope} = 1.0 \times 10^2 \, s^{-1}$$

To determine k, the actual rate constant:

$$k' = k[NO_2], \quad 1.0 \times 10^2 \, s^{-1} = k(1.0 \times 10^{13} \, \text{molecules/cm}^3), \quad k = 1.0 \times 10^{-11} \, cm^3 \, \text{molecules}^{-1} \, s^{-1}$$

29.   From the data, the pressure of C_2H_5OH decreases at a constant rate of 13 torr for every 100. s. Since the rate of disappearance of C_2H_5OH is not dependent on concentration, the reaction is zero order in C_2H_5OH.

$$k = \frac{13 \text{ torr}}{100. \text{ s}} \times \frac{1 \text{ atm}}{760 \text{ torr}} = 1.7 \times 10^{-4} \text{ atm/s}$$

The rate law and integrated rate law are:

$$\text{Rate} = k = 1.7 \times 10^{-4} \text{ atm/s}; \quad P_{C_2H_5OH} = -kt + 250. \text{ torr}\left(\frac{1 \text{ atm}}{760 \text{ torr}}\right) = -kt + 0.329 \text{ atm}$$

At 900. s: $P_{C_2H_5OH} = -1.7 \times 10^{-4} \text{ atm/s} \times 900. \text{ s} + 0.329 \text{ atm} = 0.176 \text{ atm} = 0.18 \text{ atm} = 130 \text{ torr}$

30.   a.   Since the 1/[A] vs. time plot is linear with a positive slope, the reaction is second order with respect to A. The y-intercept in the plot will equal $1/[A]_o$. Extending the plot, the y-intercept will be about 10, so $1/10 = 0.1 \ M = [A]_o$.

       b.   The slope of the 1/[A] vs time plot will equal k.

$$\text{slope} = k = \frac{(60 - 20) \text{ L/mol}}{(5 - 1) \text{ s}} = 10 \text{ L/mol·s}$$

$$\frac{1}{[A]} = kt + \frac{1}{[A]_o} = \frac{10 \text{ L}}{\text{mol s}} \times 9 \text{ s} + \frac{1}{0.1 \text{ M}} = 100, \ [A] = 0.01 \ M$$

       c.   For a second-order reaction, the half-life does depend on concentration: $t_{1/2} = \frac{1}{k[A]_0}$.

             First half-life: $t_{1/2} = \dfrac{1}{\dfrac{10 \text{ L}}{\text{mol s}} \times \dfrac{0.1 \text{ mol}}{\text{L}}} = 1 \text{ s}$

             Second half-life ($[A]_o$ is now 0.05 M): $t_{1/2} = 1/(10 \times 0.05) = 2 \text{ s}$

             Third half-life ($[A]_o$ is now 0.025 M): $t_{1/2} = 1/(10 \times 0.025) = 4 \text{ s}$

31.   a.   We check for first order dependence by graphing ln [concentration] vs. time for each set of data. The rate dependence on NO is determined from the first set of data since the ozone concentration is relatively large compared to the NO concentration, so it is effectively constant.

time (ms)	[NO] (molecules/cm³)	ln [NO]
0	6.0×10^8	20.21
100.	5.0×10^8	20.03
500.	2.4×10^8	19.30
700.	1.7×10^8	18.95
1000.	9.9×10^7	18.41

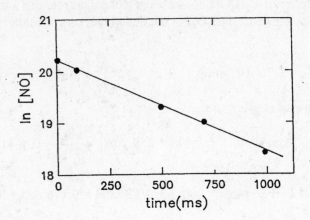

Since ln [NO] vs. t is linear, the reaction is first order with respect to NO.

We follow the same procedure for ozone using the second set of data. The data and plot are:

time (ms)	$[O_3]$ (molecules/cm^3)	ln $[O_3]$
0	1.0×10^{10}	23.03
50.	8.4×10^9	22.85
100.	7.0×10^9	22.67
200.	4.9×10^9	22.31
300.	3.4×10^9	21.95

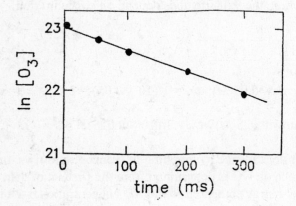

The plot of ln $[O_3]$ vs. t is linear. Hence, the reaction is first order with respect to ozone.

b.   Rate = $k[NO][O_3]$ is the overall rate law.

c.   For NO experiment, Rate = $k'[NO]$ and k' = -(slope from graph of ln [NO] vs. t).

$$k' = \text{-slope} = -\frac{18.41 - 20.21}{(1000. - 0) \times 10^{-3}\text{ s}} = 1.8\text{ s}^{-1}$$

For ozone experiment, Rate = k''[O$_3$] and k'' = -(slope from ln [O$_3$] vs. t).

$$k'' = \text{-slope} = -\frac{(21.95 - 23.03)}{(300. - 0) \times 10^{-3}\ s} = 3.6\ s^{-1}$$

d.   From NO experiment, Rate = k[NO][O$_3$] = k'[NO] where k' = k[O$_3$].

k' = 1.8 s^{-1} = k(1.0 × 10^{14} molecules/cm^3), k = 1.8 × 10^{-14} cm^3 molecules^{-1} s^{-1}

We can check this from the ozone data. Rate = k''[O$_3$] = k[NO][O$_3$] where k'' = k[NO].

k'' = 3.6 s^{-1} = k(2.0 × 10^{14} molecules/cm^3), k = 1.8 × 10^{-14} cm^3 molecules^{-1} s^{-1}

Both values of k agree.

32.   This problem differs in two ways from the previous problems:

1.   a product is measured instead of a reactant and

2.   only the volume of a gas is given and not the concentration.

We can find the initial concentration of C$_6$H$_5$N$_2$Cl from the amount of N$_2$ evolved after infinite time when all the C$_6$H$_5$N$_2$Cl has decomposed (assuming the reaction goes to completion).

$$n = \frac{PV}{RT} = \frac{1.00\ atm \times (58.3 \times 10^{-3}\ L)}{\dfrac{0.08206\ L\ atm}{mol\ K} \times 323\ K} = 2.20 \times 10^{-3}\ mol\ N_2$$

Since each mole of C$_6$H$_5$N$_2$Cl that decomposes produces one mole of N$_2$, then the initial concentration (t = 0) of C$_6$H$_5$N$_2$Cl was:

$$\frac{2.20 \times 10^{-3}\ mol}{40.0 \times 10^{-3}\ L} = 0.0550\ M$$

We can similarly calculate the moles of N$_2$ evolved at each point of the experiment, subtract that from 2.20 × 10^{-3} mol to get the moles of C$_6$H$_5$N$_2$Cl remaining, and then calculate [C$_6$H$_5$N$_2$Cl] at each time. We would then use these results to make the appropriate graph to determine the order of the reaction. Since the rate constant is related to the slope of the straight line, we would favor this approach to get a value for the rate constant.

There is a simpler way to check for the order of the reaction that saves doing a lot of math. The quantity (V$_\infty$ - V$_t$) where V$_\infty$ = 58.3 mL N$_2$ evolved and V$_t$ = mL of N$_2$ evolved at time t will be proportional to the moles of C$_6$H$_5$N$_2$Cl remaining; (V$_\infty$ - V$_t$) will also be proportional to the concentration of C$_6$H$_5$N$_2$Cl. Thus, we can get the same information by using (V$_\infty$ - V$_t$) as our measure of [C$_6$H$_5$N$_2$Cl]. If the reaction is first order, a graph of ln (V$_\infty$ - V$_t$) vs. t would be linear. The data for such a graph are:

t (s)	V_t (mL)	$(V_\infty - V_t)$	ln $(V_\infty - V_t)$
0	0	58.3	4.066
6	19.3	39.0	3.664
9	26.0	32.3	3.475
14	36.0	22.3	3.105
22	45.0	13.3	2.588
30.	50.4	7.9	2.07

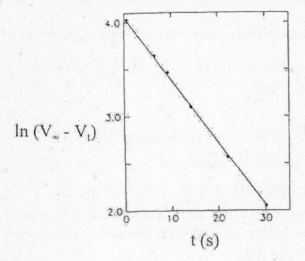

We can see from the graph that this plot is linear, so the reaction is first order. The differential rate law is: $-d[C_6H_5N_2Cl]/dt = \text{rate} = k[C_6H_5N_2Cl]$ and the integrated rate law is: $\ln[C_6H_5N_2Cl] = -kt + \ln[C_6H_5N_2Cl]_o$. From separate data, k was determined to be 6.9×10^{-2} s^{-1}.

33. For a first order reaction, the integrated rate law is: $\ln([A]/[A]_o) = -kt$. Solving for k:

$$\ln\left(\frac{0.250 \text{ mol/L}}{1.00 \text{ mol/L}}\right) = -k \times 120. \text{ s}, \ k = 0.0116 \text{ s}^{-1}$$

$$\ln\left(\frac{0.350 \text{ mol/L}}{2.00 \text{ mol/L}}\right) = -0.0116 \text{ s}^{-1} \times t, \ t = 150. \text{ s}$$

34. $\ln\left(\dfrac{[A]}{[A]_o}\right) = -kt; \quad k = \dfrac{\ln 2}{t_{1/2}} = \dfrac{0.6931}{14.3 \text{ d}} = 4.85 \times 10^{-2} \text{ d}^{-1}$

If $[A]_o = 100.0$, then after 95.0% completion, $[A] = 5.0$.

$$\ln\left(\frac{5.0}{100.0}\right) = -4.85 \times 10^{-2} \text{ d}^{-1} \times t, \ t = 62 \text{ days}$$

35. For a second order reaction: $t_{1/2} = \dfrac{1}{k[A]_o}$ or $k = \dfrac{1}{t_{1/2}[A]_o}$

$k = \dfrac{1}{143 \text{ s}(0.060 \text{ mol/L})} = 0.12 \text{ L mol}^{-1} \text{ s}^{-1}$

36.   a.   The integrated rate law for a second order reaction is: $1/[A] = kt + 1/[A]_o$, and the half-life expression is: $t_{1/2} = 1/k[A]_o$. We could use either to solve for $t_{1/2}$. Using the integrated rate law:

$$\frac{1}{(0.900/2)\ \text{mol/L}} = k \times 2.00\ \text{s} + \frac{1}{0.900\ \text{mol/L}}, \quad k = \frac{1.11\ \text{L/mol}}{2.00\ \text{s}} = 0.555\ \text{L mol}^{-1}\ \text{s}^{-1}$$

   b. $$\frac{1}{0.100\ \text{mol/L}} = 0.555\ \text{L mol}^{-1}\ \text{s}^{-1} \times \text{t} + \frac{1}{0.900\ \text{mol/L}}, \quad \text{t} = \frac{8.9\ \text{L/mol}}{0.555\ \text{L mol}^{-1}\ \text{s}^{-1}} = 16\ \text{s}$$

37.   a.   If the reaction is 38.5% complete, then 38.5% of the original concentration is consumed, leaving 61.5%.

$$[A] = 61.5\%\ \text{of}\ [A]_o\ \text{or}\ [A] = 0.615\ [A]_o; \quad \ln\left(\frac{[A]}{[A]_o}\right) = -kt, \quad \ln\left(\frac{0.615\ [A]_o}{[A]_o}\right) = -k(480.\ \text{s})$$

$$\ln(0.615) = -k(480.\ \text{s}), \quad -0.486 = -k(480.\ \text{s}), \quad k = 1.01 \times 10^{-3}\ \text{s}^{-1}$$

   b. $t_{1/2} = (\ln 2)/k = 0.6931/1.01 \times 10^{-3}\ \text{s}^{-1} = 686\ \text{s}$

   c.   25% complete: $[A] = 0.75\ [A]_o; \quad \ln(0.75) = -1.01 \times 10^{-3}\ (\text{t}), \quad \text{t} = 280\ \text{s}$

   75% complete: $[A] = 0.25\ [A]_o; \quad \ln(0.25) = -1.01 \times 10^{-3}\ (\text{t}), \quad \text{t} = 1.4 \times 10^3\ \text{s}$

   Or, we know it takes $2 \times t_{1/2}$ for reaction to be 75% complete. $\text{t} = 2 \times 686\ \text{s} = 1370\ \text{s}$

   95% complete: $[A] = 0.05\ [A]_o; \quad \ln(0.05) = -1.01 \times 10^{-3}\ (\text{t}), \quad \text{t} = 3 \times 10^3\ \text{s}$

38.   Successive half-lives increase in time for a second order reaction. Therefore, assume reaction is second order in A.

$$t_{1/2} = \frac{1}{k[A]_o}, \quad k = \frac{1}{t_{1/2}[A]_o} = \frac{1}{10.0\ \text{min}\ (0.10\ M)} = 1.0\ \text{L mol}^{-1}\ \text{min}^{-1}$$

   a. $$\frac{1}{[A]} = kt + \frac{1}{[A]_o} = \frac{1.0\ \text{L}}{\text{mol min}} \times 80.0\ \text{min} + \frac{1}{0.10\ M} = 90.\ M^{-1}, \quad [A] = 1.1 \times 10^{-2}\ M$$

   b.   30.0 min = 2 half-lives, so 25% of original A is remaining.

   $[A] = 0.25(0.10\ M) = 0.025\ M$

39.   a. $[A] = -kt + [A]_o;$ If $k = 5.0 \times 10^{-2}\ \text{mol L}^{-1}\ \text{s}^{-1}$ and $[A]_o = 1.00 \times 10^{-3}\ M$, then:

   $[A] = -(5.0 \times 10^{-2}\ \text{mol L}^{-1}\ \text{s}^{-1})\ \text{t} + 1.00 \times 10^{-3}\ \text{mol/L}$

   b. $\dfrac{[A]_o}{2} = -(5.0 \times 10^{-2})\ t_{1/2} + [A]_o$ since at $t = t_{1/2}, [A] = [A]_o/2.$

   $-0.50[A]_o = -(5.0 \times 10^{-2})\ t_{1/2}, \quad t_{1/2} = \dfrac{0.50(1.00 \times 10^{-3})}{5.0 \times 10^{-2}} = 1.0 \times 10^{-2}\ \text{s}; \quad$ Or we can use $t_{1/2} = \dfrac{[A]_o}{2\ k}.$

c. $[A] = -kt + [A]_o = -(5.0 \times 10^{-2} \text{ mol L}^{-1} \text{ s}^{-1})(5.0 \times 10^{-3} \text{ s}) + 1.00 \times 10^{-3} \text{ mol/L} = 7.5 \times 10^{-4} \text{ mol/L}$

$[A]_{reacted} = 1.00 \times 10^{-3} \text{ mol/L} - 7.5 \times 10^{-4} \text{ mol/L} = 2.5 \times 10^{-4} \text{ mol/L}$

$[B]_{produced} = [A]_{reacted} = 2.5 \times 10^{-4} M$

40. $100\% \rightarrow 50\% \rightarrow 25\% \rightarrow 12.5\%$; This process is 3 half-lives = 3(14 h) = 42 hours.

41.   a.   Since $[A]_o << [B]_o$ or $[C]_o$, then the B and C concentrations remain constant at 1.00 M for this experiment. So: rate $= k[A]^2[B][C] = k'[A]^2$ where $k' = k[B][C]$

For this pseudo second order reaction:

$$\frac{1}{[A]} = k't + \frac{1}{[A]_o}, \quad \frac{1}{3.26 \times 10^{-5} M} = k'(3.00 \text{ min}) + \frac{1}{1.00 \times 10^{-4} M}$$

$k' = 6890 \text{ L mol}^{-1} \text{ min}^{-1} = 115 \text{ L mol}^{-1} \text{ s}^{-1}$

$k' = k[B][C], k = \dfrac{k'}{[B][C]} = \dfrac{115 \text{ L mol}^{-1} \text{ s}^{-1}}{(1.00 M)(1.00 M)} = 115 \text{ L}^3 \text{ mol}^{-3} \text{ s}^{-1}$

b.   For this pseudo second order reaction:

$$\text{rate} = k'[A]^2, \quad t_{1/2} = \frac{1}{k'[A]_o} = \frac{1}{115 \text{ L mol}^{-1} \text{s}^{-1}(1.00 \times 10^{-4} \frac{\text{mol}}{\text{L}})} = 87.0 \text{ s}$$

c. $\dfrac{1}{[A]} = k't + \dfrac{1}{[A]_o} = 115 \text{ L mol}^{-1} \text{ s}^{-1} \times 600. \text{ s} + \dfrac{1}{1.00 \times 10^{-4} \frac{\text{mol}}{\text{L}}} = 7.90 \times 10^4 \text{ L/mol,}$

$$[A] = \frac{1}{7.90 \times 10^4 \text{ L/mol}} = 1.27 \times 10^{-5} \frac{\text{mol}}{\text{L}}$$

From the stoichiometry in the balanced reaction, 1 mol of B reacts with every 3 mol of A.

amount A reacted $= 1.00 \times 10^{-4} M - 1.27 \times 10^{-5} M = 8.7 \times 10^{-5} M$

amount B reacted $= 8.7 \times 10^{-5} \text{ mol/L} \times \dfrac{1 \text{ mol B}}{3 \text{ mol A}} = 2.9 \times 10^{-5} M$

$[B] = 1.00 M - 2.9 \times 10^{-5} M = 1.00 M$

As we mentioned in part a, the concentration of B (and C) remain constant since the A concentration is so small.

Reaction Mechanisms

42.   a.   An elementary step (reaction) is one in which the rate law can be written from the molecularity, i.e., from the coefficients in the balanced equation.

b.   The mechanism of a reaction is the series of elementary reactions that occur to give the overall reaction. The sum of all the steps in the mechanism gives the balanced chemical reaction.

c.   The rate determining step is the slowest elementary reaction in any given mechanism.

43.   For elementary reactions, the rate law can be written using the coefficients in the balanced equation to determine the orders.

a.   Rate = $k[CH_3NC]$

b.   Rate = $k[O_3][NO]$

c.   Rate = $k[O_3]$

d.   Rate = $k[O_3][O]$

e.   Rate = $k[{}^{14}_{6}C]$ or Rate = kN where N = the number of ${}^{14}_{6}C$ atoms (convention)

44.   Since the rate of the slowest elementary step equals the rate of a reaction, then:

Rate = rate of step 1 = $k[NO_2]^2$

The sum of all steps in a plausible mechanism must give the overall balanced reaction. Summing all steps gives:

$$NO_2 + NO_2 \rightarrow NO_3 + NO$$
$$NO_3 + CO \rightarrow NO_2 + CO_2$$
$$\overline{}$$
$$NO_2 + CO \rightarrow NO + CO_2$$

45.   A mechanism consists of a series of elementary reactions where the rate law for each step can be determined using the coefficients in the balanced equations. For a plausible mechanism, the rate law derived from a mechanism must agree with the rate law determined from experiment. To derive the rate law from the mechanism, the rate of the reaction is assumed to equal the rate of the slowest step in the mechanism.

Since step 1 is the rate determining step, then the rate law for this mechanism is:
Rate = $k[C_4H_9Br]$. To get the overall reaction, we sum all the individual steps of the mechanism. Summing all steps gives:

$$C_4H_9Br \rightarrow C_4H_9^+ + Br^-$$
$$C_4H_9^+ + H_2O \rightarrow C_4H_9OH_2^+$$
$$C_4H_9OH_2^+ + H_2O \rightarrow C_4H_9OH + H_3O^+$$
$$\overline{}$$
$$C_4H_9Br + 2\ H_2O \rightarrow C_4H_9OH + Br^- + H_3O^+$$

Intermediates in a mechanism are species that are neither reactants nor products, but that are formed and consumed during the reaction sequence. The intermediates for this mechanism are $C_4H_9^+$ and $C_4H_9OH_2^+$.

46.   The rate law is: Rate $= k[NO]^2[Cl_2]$. If we assume the first step is rate determining, we would expect the rate law to be: Rate $= k_1[NO][Cl_2]$. This isn't correct. However, if we assume the second step to be rate determining: Rate $= k_2[NOCl_2][NO]$. To see if this agrees with experiment, we must substitute for the intermediate $NOCl_2$ concentration. Assuming a fast equilibrium first step (rate reverse = rate forward):

$$k_{-1}[NOCl_2] = k_1[NO][Cl_2], \quad [NOCl_2] = \frac{k_1}{k_{-1}}[NO][Cl_2]; \text{ Substituting into the rate equation:}$$

$$\text{Rate} = \frac{k_2 k_1}{k_{-1}}[NO]^2[Cl_2] = k[NO]^2[Cl_2] \text{ where } k = \frac{k_2 k_1}{k_{-1}}$$

This is a possible mechanism with the second step the rate determining step since the derived rate law agrees with experiment.

47.   Let's determine the rate law for each mechanism. If the rate law derived from the mechanism is the same as the experimental rate law, then the mechanism is possible. When deriving rate laws from a mechanism, we must substitute for all intermediate concentrations.

   a.   Rate $= k[NO][O_2]$ not possible

   b.   Rate $= k[NO_3][NO]$ and $\dfrac{[NO_3]}{[NO][O_2]} = K_{eq} = k_1/k_{-1}$ or $[NO_3] = K_{eq}[NO][O_2]$

        Rate $= kK_{eq}[NO]^2[O_2]$ possible

   c.   Rate $= k[NO]^2$ not possible

   d.   Rate $= k[N_2O_2]$ and $[N_2O_2] = K_{eq}[NO]^2$ where $K_{eq} = k_1/k_{-1}$, Rate $= kK_{eq}[NO]^2$ not possible

48.   a.   This rate law occurs when the first step is rate determining.

        Rate $= k_1[Br_2] = k'[Br_2]$

      b.   This rate law occurs when the second step is rate determining and the first step is a fast equilibrium step.

        Rate $= k_2[Br][H_2]$; From the fast equilibrium first step (rate forward = rate reverse):

           $k_1[Br_2] = k_{-1}[Br]^2, \quad [Br] = (k_1/k_{-1})^{1/2}[Br_2]^{1/2}$

        Substituting into the rate equation:

           Rate $= k_2(k_1/k_{-1})^{1/2}[Br_2]^{1/2}[H_2] = k''[H_2][Br_2]^{1/2}$

c.   From a, $k' = k_1$;   From b, $k'' = k_2(k_1/k_{-1})^{1/2}$

49.   Rate $= k_3[Br^-][H_2BrO_3^+]$;   We must substitute for the intermediate concentrations. Since steps 1 and 2 are fast equilibrium steps, then rate forward reaction = rate reverse reaction.

$k_2[HBrO_3][H^+] = k_{-2}[H_2BrO_3^+]$; $k_1[BrO_3^-][H^+] = k_{-1}[HBrO_3]$

$[HBrO_3] = \dfrac{k_1}{k_{-1}}[BrO_3^-][H^+]$; $[H_2BrO_3^+] = \dfrac{k_2}{k_{-2}}[HBrO_3][H^+] = \dfrac{k_2 k_1}{k_{-2} k_{-1}}[BrO_3^-][H^+]^2$

Rate $= \dfrac{k_3 k_2 k_1}{k_{-2} k_{-1}}[Br^-][BrO_3^-][H^+]^2 = k[Br^-][BrO_3^-][H^+]^2$

50.   a.   Rate $= k_3[COCl][Cl_2]$;   From the fast equilibrium reactions 1 and 2:

$\dfrac{[COCl]}{[Cl][CO]} = \dfrac{k_2}{k_{-2}}$, $[COCl] = \dfrac{k_2}{k_{-2}}[CO][Cl]$

$\dfrac{[Cl]^2}{[Cl_2]} = \dfrac{k_1}{k_{-1}}$, $[Cl] = \left(\dfrac{k_1}{k_{-1}}[Cl_2]\right)^{1/2}$

Thus, $[COCl] = \dfrac{k_2}{k_{-2}}\left(\dfrac{k_1}{k_{-1}}\right)^{1/2}[CO][Cl_2]^{1/2}$;   Substituting into rate law:

Rate $= k_3 \dfrac{k_2}{k_{-2}}\left(\dfrac{k_1}{k_{-1}}\right)^{1/2}[CO][Cl_2]^{3/2} = k[CO][Cl_2]^{3/2}$

b.   Cl and COCl are intermediates.

51.   a. $MoCl_5^-$

b.   Rate $= \dfrac{d[NO_2^-]}{dt} = k_2[NO_3^-][MoCl_5^-]$ (Only the last step contains NO_2^-.)

We use the steady-state assumption to substitute for the intermediate concentration in the rate law. The steady-state approximation assumes that the concentration of an intermediate remains constant, i.e., d[intermediate]/dt = 0. To apply the steady-state assumption, we write rate laws for all steps where the intermediate is produced and equate the sum of these rate laws to the sum of the rate laws where the intermediate is consumed. Applying the steady-state approximation to $MoCl_5^-$:

$\dfrac{d[MoCl_5^-]}{dt} = 0$, so $k_1[MoCl_6^{2-}] = k_{-1}[MoCl_5^-][Cl^-] + k_2[NO_3^-][MoCl_5^-]$

$[MoCl_5^-] = \dfrac{k_1[MoCl_6^{2-}]}{k_{-1}[Cl^-] + k_2[NO_3^-]}$;   Rate $= \dfrac{d[NO_2^-]}{dt} = \dfrac{k_1 k_2[NO_3^-][MoCl_6^{2-}]}{k_{-1}[Cl^-] + k_2[NO_3^-]}$

52.   Rate = $\dfrac{-d[O_3]}{dt}$ = $k_1[M][O_3] + k_2[O][O_3] - k_{-1}[M][O_2][O]$; Apply steady-state approx. to O:

$\dfrac{d[O]}{dt} = 0$, so $k_1[M][O_3] = k_{-1}[M][O_2][O] + k_2[O][O_3]$, $k_1[M][O_3] - k_{-1}[M][O_2][O] = k_2[O][O_3]$

Substitute this expression into the rate law: Rate = $\dfrac{-d[O_3]}{dt} = 2\,k_2[O][O_3]$

Rearranging the steady-state approx. for [O]: $[O] = \dfrac{k_1[O_3][M]}{k_{-1}[M][O_2] + k_2[O_3]}$

Substituting into the rate law: Rate = $\dfrac{-d[O_3]}{dt} = \dfrac{2\,k_2 k_1[O_3]^2[M]}{k_{-1}[M][O_2] + k_2[O_3]}$

53.   a.   rate = $\dfrac{d[E]}{dt} = k_2[B^*]$; Assume $\dfrac{d[B^*]}{dt} = 0$, then $k_1[B]^2 = k_{-1}[B][B^*] + k_2[B^*]$

$[B^*] = \dfrac{k_1[B]^2}{k_{-1}[B] + k_2}$; The rate law is: Rate = $\dfrac{d[E]}{dt} = \dfrac{k_1 k_2[B]^2}{k_{-1}[B] + k_2}$

b.   When $k_2 \ll k_{-1}[B]$, then Rate = $\dfrac{d[E]}{dt} = \dfrac{k_1 k_2[B]^2}{k_{-1}[B]} = \dfrac{k_1 k_2}{k_{-1}}[B]$

Reaction is first order when the rate of the second step is very slow (when k_2 is very small).

c.   Collisions between B molecules only transfer energy from one B to another. This occurs at a much faster rate than the decomposition of an energetic B molecule (B*).

Temperature Dependence of Rate Constants and the Collision Model

54.   a.   The greater the frequency of collisions, the greater the opportunities for molecules to react, and, hence, the greater the rate.

b.   Chemical reactions involve the making and breaking of chemical bonds. The kinetic energy of the collision can be used to break bonds. So, as the kinetic energy of the collisions increase, the rate increases.

c.   For a reaction to occur, it is the reactive portion of each molecule that must be involved in a collision. Only some of all the possible collisions have the correct orientation to convert from reactants to products..

55.   In a unimolecular reaction, a single reactant molecule decomposes to product(s). In a bimolecular reaction, two molecules collide to give product(s). The probability of the simultaneous collision of three molecules with enough energy and correct orientation is very small, making termolecular steps very unlikely.

56. $H_3O^+(aq) + OH^-(aq) \rightarrow 2 H_2O(l)$ should have the faster rate. H_3O^+ and OH^- will be electrostatically attracted to each other; Ce^{4+} and Hg_2^{2+} will repel each other (so E_a is much larger).

57. $k = A \exp(-E_a/RT)$ or $\ln k = \dfrac{-E_a}{RT} + \ln A$ (the Arrhenius equation)

For two conditions: $\ln\left(\dfrac{k_2}{k_1}\right) = \dfrac{E_a}{R}\left(\dfrac{1}{T_1} - \dfrac{1}{T_2}\right)$ (Assuming A is temperature independent.)

Let $k_1 = 2.0 \times 10^3 \text{ s}^{-1}$, $T_1 = 298$ K; $k_2 = ?$, $T_2 = 348$ K; $E_a = 15.0 \times 10^3$ J/mol

$$\ln\left(\dfrac{k_2}{2.0 \times 10^3 \text{ s}^{-1}}\right) = \dfrac{15.0 \times 10^3 \text{ J/mol}}{8.3145 \text{ J K}^{-1}\text{mol}^{-1}}\left(\dfrac{1}{298 \text{ K}} - \dfrac{1}{348 \text{ K}}\right) = 0.87$$

$$\ln\left(\dfrac{k_2}{2.0 \times 10^3}\right) = 0.87, \quad \dfrac{k_2}{2.0 \times 10^3} = e^{0.87} = 2.4, \quad k_2 = 2.4(2.0 \times 10^3) = 4.8 \times 10^3 \text{ s}^{-1}$$

58.   For two conditions: $\ln\left(\dfrac{k_2}{k_1}\right) = \dfrac{E_a}{R}\left(\dfrac{1}{T_1} - \dfrac{1}{T_2}\right)$ (Assuming A factor is T independent.)

$$\ln\left(\dfrac{8.1 \times 10^{-2} \text{ s}^{-1}}{4.6 \times 10^{-2} \text{ s}^{-1}}\right) = \dfrac{E_a}{8.3145 \text{ J K}^{-1}\text{mol}^{-1}}\left(\dfrac{1}{273 \text{ K}} - \dfrac{1}{293 \text{ K}}\right)$$

$$0.57 = \dfrac{E_a}{8.3145}(2.5 \times 10^{-4}), \quad E_a = 1.9 \times 10^4 \text{ J/mol} = 19 \text{ kJ/mol}$$

59. $\ln\left(\dfrac{k_2}{k_1}\right) = \dfrac{E_a}{R}\left(\dfrac{1}{T_1} - \dfrac{1}{T_2}\right)$; $\dfrac{k_2}{k_1} = 7.00$, $T_1 = 295$ K, $E_a = 54.0 \times 10^3$ J/mol

$$\ln(7.00) = \dfrac{54.0 \times 10^3 \text{ J/mol}}{8.3145 \text{ J K}^{-1}\text{mol}^{-1}}\left(\dfrac{1}{295 \text{ K}} - \dfrac{1}{T_2}\right), \quad \dfrac{1}{295} - \dfrac{1}{T_2} = 3.00 \times 10^{-4}$$

$$\dfrac{1}{T_2} = 3.09 \times 10^{-3}, \quad T_2 = 324 \text{ K} = 51°C$$

60. $\ln\left(\dfrac{k_2}{k_1}\right) = \dfrac{E_a}{R}\left(\dfrac{1}{T_1} - \dfrac{1}{T_2}\right)$;   Since the rate doubles, then $k_2 = 2 k_1$.

$$\ln 2.00 = \dfrac{E_a}{8.3145 \text{ J K}^{-1}\text{mol}^{-1}}\left(\dfrac{1}{298 \text{ K}} - \dfrac{1}{308 \text{ K}}\right), \quad E_a = 5.3 \times 10^4 \text{ J/mol} = 53 \text{ kJ/mol}$$

61.   From the Arrhenius equation in logarithmic form ($\ln k = -E_a/RT + \ln A$), a graph of $\ln k$ vs. $1/T$ should yield a straight line with a slope equal to $-E_a/R$ and a y-intercept equal to $\ln A$.

   a.   slope $= -E_a/R$, $E_a = 1.10 \times 10^4$ K $\times \dfrac{8.3145 \text{ J}}{\text{K mol}} = 9.15 \times 10^4$ J/mol $= 91.5$ kJ/mol

   b.   The units for A are the same as the units for k (s^{-1}).

   y-intercept $= \ln A$, $A = e^{33.5} = 3.54 \times 10^{14} \text{ s}^{-1}$

   c. $\ln k = -E_a/RT + \ln A$ or $k = A \exp(-E_a/RT)$

   $$k = 3.54 \times 10^{14} \text{ s}^{-1} \times \exp\left(\dfrac{-9.15 \times 10^4 \text{ J/mol}}{8.3145 \text{ J K}^{-1}\text{mol}^{-1} \times 298 \text{ K}}\right) = 3.24 \times 10^{-2} \text{ s}^{-1}$$

62.   A graph of $\ln k$ vs. $1/T$ should be linear with slope $= -E_a/R$.

T (K)	$1/T$ (K^{-1})	k (s^{-1})	ln k
338	2.96×10^{-3}	4.9×10^{-3}	-5.32
318	3.14×10^{-3}	5.0×10^{-4}	-7.60
298	3.36×10^{-3}	3.5×10^{-5}	-10.26

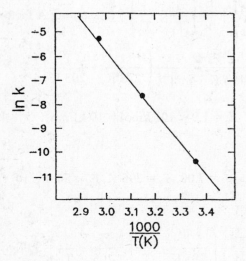

Slope $= \dfrac{-10.76 - (-5.85)}{3.40 \times 10^{-3} - 3.00 \times 10^{-3}} = -1.2 \times 10^4$ K $= -E_a/R$

$E_a = -\text{slope} \times R = 1.2 \times 10^4$ K $\times 8.3145$ J K^{-1} mol^{-1}, $E_a = 1.0 \times 10^5$ J/mol $= 1.0 \times 10^2$ kJ/mol

63.   The Arrhenius equation is: $k = A \exp(-E_a/RT)$ or in logarithmic form, $\ln k = -E_a/RT + \ln A$. Hence, a graph of $\ln k$ vs. $1/T$ should yield a straight line with a slope equal to $-E_a/R$ since the logarithmic form of the Arrhenius equation is in the form of a straight line equation, $y = mx + b$.

   Note: We carried one extra significant figure in the following $\ln k$ values in order to reduce round off error.

T (K)	1/T (K^{-1})	k (L mol^{-1} s^{-1})	ln k
195	5.13×10^{-3}	1.08×10^9	20.80
230.	4.35×10^{-3}	2.95×10^9	21.81
260.	3.85×10^{-3}	5.42×10^9	22.41
298	3.36×10^{-3}	12.0×10^9	23.21
369	2.71×10^{-3}	35.5×10^9	24.29

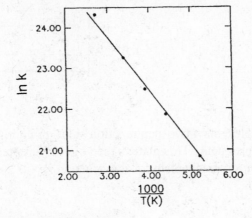

From the "eyeball" line on the graph:

$$\text{slope} = \frac{20.95 - 23.65}{5.00 \times 10^{-3} - 3.00 \times 10^{-3}} = \frac{-2.70}{2.00 \times 10^{-3}} = -1.35 \times 10^3 \text{ K} = \frac{-E_a}{R}$$

$E_a = 1.35 \times 10^3 \text{ K} \times 8.3145 \text{ J K}^{-1} \text{ mol}^{-1} = 1.12 \times 10^4 \text{ J/mol} = 11.2 \text{ kJ/mol}$

From the best straight line (by calculator): slope = -1.43×10^3 K and E_a = 11.9 kJ/mol

64.   When ΔE is positive, the products are at a higher energy relative to reactants and when ΔE is negative, the products are at a lower energy relative to reactants.

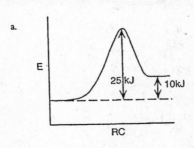

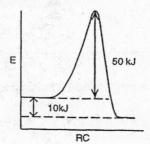

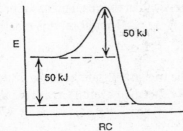

The reaction in part a will have the greatest rate since it has the smallest activation energy.

65. In the following reaction profiles, R = reactants, P = products, E_a = activation energy, ΔE = overall energy change for the reaction and RC = reaction coordinate which is the same as reaction progress.

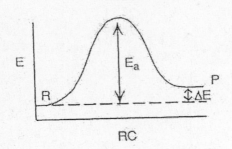   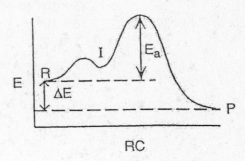

The second reaction profile represents a two step reaction since an intermediate plateau appears between the reactants and the products. This plateau (see I in plot) represents the energy of the intermediate. The general reaction mechanism for this reaction is:

$$R \rightarrow I$$
$$\underline{I \rightarrow P}$$
$$R \rightarrow P$$

In a mechanism, the rate of the slowest step determines the rate of the reaction. The activation energy for the slowest step will be the largest energy barrier that the reaction must overcome. Since the second hump in the diagram is at the highest energy, then the second step has the largest activation energy and will be the rate determining step (the slow step).

66.

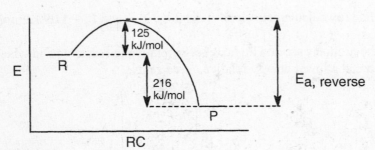

The activation energy for the reverse reaction is:

$$E_{a, reverse} = 216 \text{ kJ/mol} + 125 \text{ kJ/mol} = 341 \text{ kJ/mol}$$

67. When ΔE is positive, (the products have higher energy than the reactants as represented in the energy profile for Exercise 15.65), then $E_{a, forward} > E_{a, reverse}$. Therefore, this reaction has a positive ΔE value.

68. Carbon cannot form the fifth bond necessary for the transition state because of the small atomic size of carbon and because carbon doesn't have low energy d orbitals available to expand the octet.

Catalysis

69.   A catalyst increases the rate of a reaction by providing reactants with an alternate pathway (mechanism) to convert to products. This alternate pathway has a lower activation energy, thus increasing the rate of the reaction.

A heterogeneous catalyst is in a different phase than the reactants. The catalyst is usually a solid, although a catalyst in a liquid phase can act as a heterogeneous catalyst for some gas phase reactions. Since the catalyzed reaction has a different mechanism than the uncatalyzed reaction, the catalyzed reaction most likely will have a different rate law.

70.   a.   NO is the catalyst. NO is present in the first step of the mechanism on the reactant side, but it is not a reactant since it is regenerated in the second step and does not appear in the overall balanced equation.

b. NO_2 is an intermediate. Intermediates also never appear in the overall balanced equation. In a mechanism, intermediates always appear first on the product side while catalysts always appear first on the reactant side.

c. $k = A \exp(-E_a/RT)$; $\dfrac{k_{cat}}{k_{un}} = \dfrac{A \exp[-E_a(cat)/RT]}{A \exp[-E_a(un)/RT]} = \exp\left(\dfrac{E_a(un) - E_a(cat)}{RT}\right)$

$$\frac{k_{cat}}{k_{un}} = \exp\left(\frac{2100 \text{ J/mol}}{8.3145 \text{ J K}^{-1} \text{ mol}^{-1} \times 298 \text{ K}}\right) = e^{0.85} = 2.3$$

The catalyzed reaction is approximately 2.3 times faster than the uncatalyzed reaction at 25°C.

71.   The mechanism for the chlorine catalyzed destruction of ozone is:

$$O_3 + Cl \rightarrow O_2 + ClO \quad \text{(slow)}$$
$$ClO + O \rightarrow O_2 + Cl \quad \text{(fast)}$$
$$\overline{}$$
$$O_3 + O \rightarrow 2 O_2$$

Since the chlorine atom catalyzed reaction has a lower activation energy, then the Cl catalyzed rate is faster. Hence, Cl is a more effective catalyst. Using the activation energy, we can estimate the efficiency that Cl atoms destroy ozone as compared to NO molecules (see Exercise 15.70 c).

At 25°C: $\dfrac{k_{Cl}}{k_{NO}} = \exp\left(\dfrac{-E_a(Cl)}{RT} + \dfrac{E_a(NO)}{RT}\right) = \exp\left(\dfrac{(-2100 + 11{,}900) \text{ J/mol}}{(8.3145 \times 298) \text{ J/mol}}\right) = e^{3.96} = 52$

At 25°C, the Cl catalyzed reaction is roughly 52 times faster than the NO catalyzed reaction, assuming the frequency factor A is the same for each reaction.

72.   The reaction at the surface of the catalyst follows the steps:

metal surface

Thus, CH_2D-CH_2D should be the product.

73.   At high [S], the enzyme is completely saturated with substrate. Once the enzyme is completely saturated, the rate of decomposition of ES can no longer increase and the overall rate remains constant.

Additional Exercises

74.   Comparing the last two experiments, doubling the [B] (keeping [A] constant) doubles the rate. The order with respect to B is 1. We can't get the order with respect to A by inspection. Comparing the 2nd and 3rd experiments:

$$11.8 \text{ mol L}^{-1} \text{ s}^{-1} = (0.5 \text{ } M)^x (1.0 \text{ } M), \quad 33.5 \text{ mol L}^{-1} \text{ s}^{-1} = (1.0 \text{ } M)^x (1.0 \text{ } M)$$

Dividing: $\dfrac{33.5}{11.8} = \dfrac{(1.0)^x}{(0.5)^x} = 2.84 = 2^x$, $\ln 2.84 = x \ln 2$, $x = \dfrac{\ln 2.84}{\ln 2} = 1.5$

The order with respect to A is 1.5.

75.   Rate $= k[I^-]^x[OCl^-]^y[OH^-]^z$; Comparing the first and second experiments:

$$\frac{18.7 \times 10^{-3}}{9.4 \times 10^{-3}} = \frac{k(0.0026)^x (0.012)^y (0.10)^z}{k(0.0013)^x (0.012)^y (0.10)^z}, \quad 2.0 = 2.0^x, \quad x = 1$$

Comparing the first and third experiments:

$$\frac{9.4 \times 10^{-3}}{4.7 \times 10^{-3}} = \frac{k(0.0013) (0.012)^y (0.10)^z}{k(0.0013) (0.0060)^y (0.10)^z}, \quad 2.0 = 2.0^y, \quad y = 1$$

Comparing the first and sixth experiments:

$$\frac{4.7 \times 10^{-3}}{9.4 \times 10^{-3}} = \frac{k(0.0013) (0.012) (0.20)^z}{k(0.0013) (0.012) (0.10)^z}, \quad 1/2 = 2.0^z, \quad z = -1$$

Rate $= \dfrac{k[I^-][OCl^-]}{[OH^-]}$; The presence of OH$^-$ decreases the rate of the reaction.

For the first experiment:

$$\frac{9.4 \times 10^{-3} \text{ mol}}{\text{L s}} = k \frac{(0.0013 \text{ mol/L}) (0.012 \text{ mol/L})}{(0.10 \text{ mol/L})}, \quad k = 60.3 \text{ s}^{-1} = 60. \text{ s}^{-1}$$

For all experiments, $k_{mean} = 60. \text{ s}^{-1}$.

76.   For second order kinetics: $\dfrac{1}{[A]} - \dfrac{1}{[A]_o} = kt$

a. $\dfrac{1}{[A]} = (0.250 \text{ L mol}^{-1}\text{ s}^{-1})\,t + \dfrac{1}{[A]_o}$, $\dfrac{1}{[A]} = (0.250)\,(180.\text{ s}) + \dfrac{1}{1.00 \times 10^{-2}\ M}$

$\dfrac{1}{[A]} = 145\ M^{-1}$, $[A] = 6.90 \times 10^{-3}\ M$

Amount of A that reacted = $0.0100 - 0.00690 = 0.0031\ M$

$[A_2] = \dfrac{1}{2}(3.1 \times 10^{-3}\ M) = 1.6 \times 10^{-3}\ M$

b.   After 3 minutes (180. s): $[A] = 3.00\,[B]$, $6.90 \times 10^{-3}\ M = 3.00\,[B]$, $[B] = 2.30 \times 10^{-3}\ M$

$\dfrac{1}{[B]} = k_2 t + \dfrac{1}{[B]_o}$; $\dfrac{1}{2.30 \times 10^{-3}\ M} = k_2(180.\text{ s}) + \dfrac{1}{2.50 \times 10^{-2}\ M}$, $k_2 = 2.19\text{ L mol}^{-1}\text{ s}^{-1}$

c. $[A]_o = 1.00 \times 10^{-2}\ M$;   At $t = t_{1/2}$, $[A] = 5.00 \times 10^{-3}\ M$

$\dfrac{1}{5.00 \times 10^{-3}} = 0.250\,t + \dfrac{1}{1.00 \times 10^{-2}}$, $t_{1/2} = 4.00 \times 10^2$ s;   Or we can use $t_{1/2} = \dfrac{1}{k[A]_o}$.

77.

Heating Time	Untreated		Deacidifying		Antioxidant	
(days)	s	ln s	s	ln s	s	ln s
0.00	100.0	4.605	100.1	4.606	114.6	4.741
1.00	67.9	4.218	60.8	4.108	65.2	4.177
2.00	38.9	3.661	26.8	3.288	28.1	3.336
3.00	16.1	2.779	-	-	11.3	2.425
6.00	6.8	1.92	-	-	-	-

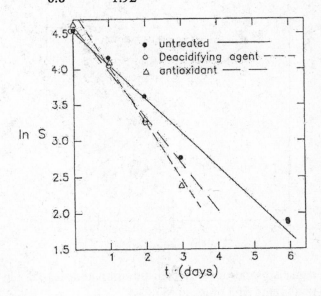

a. We used a calculator to fit the data by least squares. The results follow.

Untreated: $\ln s = -0.465\, t + 4.55$, $k = 0.465$ day^{-1}

Deacidifying agent: $\ln s = -0.659\, t + 4.66$, $k = 0.659$ day^{-1}

Antioxidant: $\ln s = -0.779\, t + 4.84$, $k = 0.779$ day^{-1}

b. No, the silk degrades more rapidly with the additives since k increases.

c. $t_{1/2} = (\ln 2)/k$

Untreated: $t_{1/2} = 1.49$ day; Deacidifying agent: $t_{1/2} = 1.05$ day; Antioxidant: $t_{1/2} = 0.890$ day.

78. The pressure of a gas is directly proportional to concentration. Therefore, we can use the pressure data to solve the problem since $-d[SO_2Cl_2]/dt \propto -d\, P_{SO_2Cl_2}/dt$.

$SO_2Cl_2(g) \rightarrow SO_2(g) + Cl_2(g)$; Let P_O = initial partial pressure of SO_2Cl_2.

If $x = P_{SO_2}$ at some time, then $x = P_{SO_2} = P_{Cl_2}$ and $P_{SO_2Cl_2} = P_O - x$.

$P_{tot} = P_{SO_2Cl_2} + P_{SO_2} + P_{Cl_2} = P_O - x + x + x$, $P_{tot} = P_O + x$, $P_{tot} - P_O = x$

At time = 0 hour, $P_{tot} = P_O = 4.93$ atm. The data for other times are:

Time (hour)	0.00	1.00	2.00	4.00	8.00	16.00
P_{tot} (atm)	4.93	5.60	6.34	7.33	8.56	9.52
$P_{SO_2Cl_2}$ (atm)	4.93	4.26	3.52	2.53	1.30	0.34
$\ln P_{SO_2Cl_2}$		1.595	1.449	1.258	0.928	0.262	-1.08

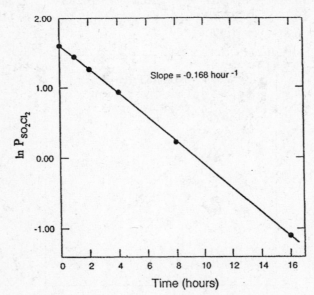

Since pressure of a gas is proportional to concentration and since the $\ln P_{SO_2Cl_2}$ vs. time plot is linear, then the reaction is first order in SO_2Cl_2.

a.   Slope of $\ln(P)$ vs. t plot is -0.168 hour^{-1} = $-k$, $k = 0.168$ hour^{-1} = 4.67×10^{-5} s^{-1};   Since concentration units don't appear in first order rate constants, then this value of k determined from pressure data will be the same as if concentration data in molarity units were used.

b. $t_{1/2} = \dfrac{\ln 2}{k} = \dfrac{0.6931}{k} = \dfrac{0.6931}{0.168 \text{ h}^{-1}} = 4.13$ hour

c.   After 0.500 hr: $\ln P_{SO_2Cl_2} = -kt + \ln P_o = -(0.168 \text{ h}^{-1})(0.500 \text{ h}) + \ln 4.93$

$\ln P_{SO_2Cl_2} = -0.0840 + 1.595 = 1.511$, $P_{SO_2Cl_2} = e^{1.511} = 4.53$ atm

$P_{Cl_2} = P_{SO_2} = 4.93$ atm $- 4.53$ atm $= 0.40$ atm

$P_{tot} = P_{SO_2Cl_2} + P_{Cl_2} + P_{SO_2} = 4.53 + 0.40 + 0.40 = 5.33$ atm

After 12.0 hours: $\ln P_{SO_2Cl_2} = -(0.168 \text{ h}^{-1})(12.0 \text{ h}) + \ln 4.93 = -0.42$

$P_{SO_2Cl_2} = e^{-0.42} = 0.66$ atm, $P_{SO_2} = 4.93 - 0.66 = 4.27$ atm, $P_{Cl_2} = 4.27$ atm

$P_{tot} = 0.66 + 4.27 + 4.27 = 9.20$ atm

d. $\ln\left(\dfrac{P_{SO_2Cl_2}}{P_O}\right) = -0.168 \text{ h}^{-1} (20.0 \text{ hr}) = -3.36$, $\left(\dfrac{P_{SO_2Cl_2}}{P_O}\right) = e^{-3.36} = 3.47 \times 10^{-2}$

Fraction left $= 0.0347 = 3.47\%$

79.   The rate depends on the number of reactant molecules adsorbed on the surface of the catalyst. This quantity is proportional to the concentration of reactant. However, when all of the surface sites of the catalyst are occupied, the rate becomes independent of the concentration of reactant.

80.   a.   W since it has a lower activation energy than the Os catalyst.

b. $k_w = A_w \exp[-E_a(W)/RT]$; $k_{uncat} = A_{uncat} \exp[-E_a(uncat)/RT]$;   Assume $A_w = A_{uncat}$

$$\frac{k_w}{k_{uncat}} = \exp\left(\frac{-E_a(W)}{RT} + \frac{E_a(uncat)}{RT}\right)$$

$$\frac{k_w}{k_{uncat}} = \exp\left(\frac{-163,000 \text{ J/mol} + 335,000 \text{ J/mol}}{(8.3145 \text{ J mol}^{-1} \text{ K}^{-1})(298 \text{ K})}\right) = 1.41 \times 10^{30}$$

The W catalyzed reaction is approximately 10^{30} times faster than the uncatalyzed reaction.

c.   From the rate law, the presence of H_2 decreases the rate of the reaction. For the decomposition to occur, NH_3 molecules must be adsorbed on the surface of the catalyst. If H_2 is also adsorbed on the catalyst, then there are fewer sites for NH_3 molecules to be adsorbed and the rate decreases.

81.   Rate $= k_2[I^-][HOCl]$;   From the fast equilibrium first step:

$$k_1[OCl^-] = k_{-1}[HOCl][OH^-], \quad [HOCl] = \frac{k_1[OCl^-]}{k_{-1}[OH^-]}; \quad \text{Substituting into the rate equation:}$$

$$\text{Rate} = \frac{k_2 k_1 [I^-][OCl^-]}{k_{-1}[OH^-]} = \frac{k[I^-][OCl^-]}{[OH^-]}$$

82.   Rate $= k[BrO_3^-][SO_3^{2-}][H^+]$;   First step: $SO_3^{2-} + H^+ \rightarrow HSO_3^-$ (fast)

The rate law contains BrO_3^-, SO_3^{2-} and H^+. In order to incorporate all of these ions into the rate law, the rate determining step could contain BrO_3^- and HSO_3^-, the intermediate produced in the first step from SO_3^{2-} and H^+. A possible second step is:

$BrO_3^- + HSO_3^- \rightarrow$ Products   (slow)

A likely choice is: $BrO_3^- + HSO_3^- \rightarrow SO_4^{2-} + HBrO_2$ (slow)

Followed by: $HBrO_2 + SO_3^{2-} \rightarrow HBrO + SO_4^{2-}$ (fast);
$\qquad\qquad\quad HBrO + SO_3^{2-} \rightarrow SO_4^{2-} + H^+ + Br^-$ (fast)

All species in this mechanism (HSO_3^-, $HBrO_2$, $HBrO$) are known substances. This mechanism also gives the correct experimentally determined rate law.

Rate $= k_2[BrO_3^-][HSO_3^-]$; Assuming reaction one is a fast equilibrium step:

$$k_1[SO_3^{2-}][H^+] = k_{-1}[HSO_3^-], \quad [HSO_3^-] = \frac{k_1}{k_{-1}}[SO_3^{2-}][H^+]$$

$$\text{Rate} = \frac{k_2 k_1}{k_{-1}}[BrO_3^-][SO_3^{2-}][H^+] = k[BrO_3^-][SO_3^{2-}][H^+]$$

83.   The yellow (rhombic crystals) form is kinetically stable. The orange (tetragonal cyrstals) form is thermodynamically stable.

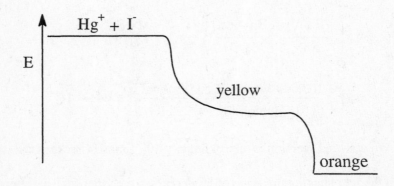

84.   a.   Let P_o = initial partial pressure of C_2H_5OH = 250. torr. If x torr of C_2H_5OH reacts, then at anytime:

$$P_{C_2H_5OH} = 250. - x, \; P_{C_2H_4} = P_{H_2O} = x; \; P_{tot} = 250. - x + x + x = 250. + x$$

Therefore, $P_{C_2H_5OH}$ at any time can be calculated from the data by determining x (= P_{tot} - 250.) and then subtracting from 250. torr. Using the $P_{C_2H_5OH}$ data, a plot of $P_{C_2H_5OH}$ vs. t is linear (plot not included). The reaction is zero order in $P_{C_2H_5OH}$. One could also use the P_{tot} vs. t data since P_{tot} increases at the same rate that $P_{C_2H_5OH}$ decreases. Note: The ln P vs. t plot is also linear. The reaction hasn't been followed for enough time for curvature to be seen. However, since $P_{C_2H_5OH}$ decreases at steady increments of 15 torr for every 10. s of reaction, then we can conclude that the reaction is zero order in C_2H_5OH.

From the data, the integrated rate equation involving P_{tot} is: $P_{tot} = \dfrac{15}{10.}t + 250.$
At t = 80. s, $P_{tot} = \dfrac{15}{10.}(80.) + 250. = 370$ torr

   b.   slope = -k = -15 torr/10. s = 1.5 torr/s (from $P_{C_2H_5OH}$ vs. t plot), k = 1.5 torr/s; The P_{tot} vs. t plot would give the same rate constant since P_{tot} increases at the same rate that $P_{C_2H_5OH}$ decreases.

   c.   zero order

   d. $P_{tot} = \dfrac{15}{10.}(300.) + 250. = 7.0 \times 10^2$ torr   This is an impossible answer!

Since only 250. torr of C_2H_5OH are present initially, the maximum pressure can only be 500. torr when all of the C_2H_5OH is consumed, i.e., $P_{tot} = P_{C_2H_4} + P_{H_2O} = 250. + 250. = 500.$ torr. Therefore, at 300. s, $P_{tot} = 500.$ torr.

85.   a.

t (s)	$[C_4H_6]$ (M)	$\ln[C_4H_6]$	$1/[C_4H_6]$ (M^{-1})
0	0.01000	-4.6052	1.000×10^2
1000.	0.00629	-5.069	1.59×10^2
2000.	0.00459	-5.384	2.18×10^2
3000.	0.00361	-5.624	2.77×10^2

The plot of $1/[C_4H_6]$ vs. t is linear, thus the reaction is second order in butadiene. From the plot (not included), the integrated rate law is:

$$\frac{1}{[C_4H_6]} = (5.90 \times 10^{-2} \text{ L mol}^{-1} \text{ s}^{-1})\,t + 100.0 \; M^{-1}$$

   b.   When dimerization is 1.0% complete, 99.0% of C_4H_6 is left.

$[C_4H_6] = 0.990(0.01000) = 0.00990 \; M$; $\dfrac{1}{0.00990} = 5.90 \times 10^{-2}\,t + 100.0$, t = 17.1 s $\approx$ 20 s

   c.   2.0% complete, $[C_4H_6] = 0.00980 \; M$; $\dfrac{1}{0.00980} = 5.90 \times 10^{-2}\,t + 100.0$, t = 34.6 s $\approx$ 30 s

d. $\dfrac{1}{[C_4H_6]} = kt + \dfrac{1}{[C_4H_6]_o}$; $[C_4H_6]_o = 0.0200\ M$; At $t = t_{1/2}$, $[C_4H_6] = 0.0100\ M$

$\dfrac{1}{0.0100} = (5.90 \times 10^{-2})\ t_{1/2} + \dfrac{1}{0.0200}$, $t_{1/2} = 847\ s = 850\ s$

Or, $t_{1/2} = \dfrac{1}{k[A]_o} = \dfrac{1}{(5.90 \times 10^{-2}\ L\ mol^{-1}\ s^{-1})\ (2.00 \times 10^{-2}\ M)} = 847\ s$

e. From Exercise 15.26, $k = 1.4 \times 10^{-2}\ L\ mol^{-1}\ s^{-1}$ at 500. K. From this problem, $k = 5.90 \times 10^{-2}\ L$ $mol^{-1}\ s^{-1}$ at 620. K.

$\ln\left(\dfrac{k_2}{k_1}\right) = \dfrac{E_a}{R}\left(\dfrac{1}{T_1} - \dfrac{1}{T_2}\right)$, $\ln\left(\dfrac{5.90 \times 10^{-2}}{1.4 \times 10^{-2}}\right) = \dfrac{E_a}{8.3145\ J\ K^{-1}\ mol^{-1}}\left(\dfrac{1}{500.\ K} - \dfrac{1}{620.\ K}\right)$

$12 = E_a\ (3.9 \times 10^{-4})$, $E_a = 3.1 \times 10^4\ J/mol = 31\ kJ/mol$

86. We need the value of k at 500. K. $\ln\left(\dfrac{k_2}{k_1}\right) = \dfrac{E_a}{R}\left(\dfrac{1}{T_1} - \dfrac{1}{T_2}\right)$

$\ln\left(\dfrac{k_2}{2.3 \times 10^{-12}\ L\ mol^{-1}\ s^{-1}}\right) = \dfrac{1.11 \times 10^5\ J/mol}{8.3145\ J\ K^{-1}\ mol^{-1}}\left(\dfrac{1}{273\ K} - \dfrac{1}{500.\ K}\right) = 22.2$

$\dfrac{k_2}{2.3 \times 10^{-12}} = e^{22.2}$, $k_2 = 1.0 \times 10^{-2}\ L\ mol^{-1}\ s^{-1}$

Since the decomposition reaction is an elementary reaction, then the rate law can be written using the coefficients in the balanced equation. For this reaction: Rate = $k[NO_2]^2$. To solve for the time, we must use the integrated rate law for 2nd order kinetics. The major problem now is converting units so they match. Rearranging the ideal gas law gives n/V = P/RT. Substituting P/RT for concentration units in the 2nd order integrated rate equation:

$\dfrac{1}{[NO_2]} = kt + \dfrac{1}{[NO_2]_o}$, $\dfrac{1}{P/RT} = kt + \dfrac{1}{P_o/RT}$, $\dfrac{RT}{P} - \dfrac{RT}{P_o} = kt$, $t = \dfrac{RT}{k}\left(\dfrac{P_o - P}{P \times P_o}\right)$

$t = \dfrac{(0.08206\ L\ atm\ K^{-1}\ mol^{-1})\ (500.\ K)}{1.0 \times 10^{-2}\ mol^{-1}\ s^{-1}} \times \left(\dfrac{2.5\ atm - 1.5\ atm}{1.5\ atm \times 2.5\ atm}\right) = 1.1 \times 10^3\ s$

87. $k = A\ exp\ (-E_a/RT)$; $\dfrac{k_{cat}}{k_{uncat}} = \dfrac{A_{cat}\ exp\ (-E_{a,cat}/RT)}{A_{uncat}\ exp\ (-E_{a,uncat}/RT)} = exp\left(\dfrac{-E_{a,cat} + E_{a,uncat}}{RT}\right)$

$2.50 \times 10^3 = \dfrac{k_{cat}}{k_{uncat}} = exp\left(\dfrac{-E_{a,cat} + 5.00 \times 10^4\ J/mol}{8.3145\ J\ K^{-1}\ mol^{-1} \times 310.\ K}\right)$

$\ln\ (2.50 \times 10^3)\ \times 2.58\ \times 10^3\ J/mol = -E_{a,cat}\ + 5.00 \times 10^4\ J/mol$

$E_{a,cat} = 5.00 \times 10^4\ J/mol - 2.02 \times 10^4\ J/mol = 2.98 \times 10^4\ J/mol = 29.8\ kJ/mol$

88.   From 338 K data, a plot of $\ln[N_2O_5]$ vs. t is linear (plot not included). The integrated rate law is:

$$\ln[N_2O_5] = -4.86 \times 10^{-3}\, t - 2.30; \quad k = 4.86 \times 10^{-3}\ s^{-1} \text{ at } 338 \text{ K}$$

From 318 K data: $\ln[N_2O_5] = -4.98 \times 10^{-4}\, t - 2.30; \quad k = 4.98 \times 10^{-4}\ s^{-1} \text{ at } 318 \text{ K}$

$$\ln\left(\frac{k_2}{k_1}\right) = \frac{E_a}{R}\left(\frac{1}{T_1} - \frac{1}{T_2}\right), \ \ln\left(\frac{4.86 \times 10^{-3}}{4.98 \times 10^{-4}}\right) = \frac{E_a}{8.3145\ \text{J K}^{-1}\ \text{mol}^{-1}}\left(\frac{1}{318\ \text{K}} - \frac{1}{338\ \text{K}}\right)$$

$E_a = 1.0 \times 10^5$ J/mol $= 1.0 \times 10^2$ kJ/mol

89.   a.

T (K)	1/T (K^{-1})	k (min^{-1})	ln k
298.2	3.353×10^{-3}	178	5.182
293.5	3.407×10^{-3}	126	4.836
290.5	3.442×10^{-3}	100.	4.605

A plot of ln k vs. 1/T gives a straight line (plot not included). The equation for the straight line is:

$$\ln k = -6.48 \times 10^3\, (1/T) + 26.9$$

For a ln k vs. 1/T plot, the slope $= -E_a/R = -6.48 \times 10^3$ K.

-6.48×10^3 K $= -E_a/8.3145$ J mol^{-1} K^{-1}, $E_a = 5.39 \times 10^4$ J/mol $= 53.9$ kJ/mol

b. $\ln k = -6.48 \times 10^3(1/288.2) + 26.9 = 4.42,\ k = e^{4.42} = 83$ min^{-1}

About 83 chirps per minute per insect. Note: We carried extra sig. figs.

c.   k gives the number of chirps per minute. The number or chirps in 15 sec is k/4.

T (°C)	T (°F)	k (min^{-1})	42 + 0.80 (k/4)
25.0	77.0	178	78° F
20.3	68.5	126	67°F
17.3	63.1	100.	62°F
15.0	59.0	83	59°F

The rule of thumb appears to be fairly accurate, almost ± 1°F.

90.   a.   If the interval between flashes is 16.3 sec, then the rate is:

1 flash/16.3 s $= 6.13 \times 10^{-2}$ s$^{-1} = k$

Interval	k	T
16.3 s	6.13×10^{-2} s^{-1}	21.0°C (294.2 K)
13.0 s	7.69×10^{-2} s^{-1}	27.8°C (301.0 K)

$$\ln\left(\frac{k_2}{k_1}\right) = \frac{E_a}{R}\left(\frac{1}{T_1} - \frac{1}{T_2}\right); \text{ Solving: } E_a = 2.5 \times 10^4 \text{ J/mol} = 25 \text{ kJ/mol}$$

b. $$\ln\left(\frac{k}{6.13 \times 10^{-2}}\right) = \frac{2.5 \times 10^4 \text{ J/mol}}{8.3145 \text{ J K}^{-1}\text{ mol}^{-1}}\left(\frac{1}{294.2 \text{ K}} - \frac{1}{303.2 \text{ K}}\right) = 0.30$$

$k = e^{-0.30} \times 6.13 \times 10^{-2} = 8.3 \times 10^{-2} \text{ s}^{-1}; \text{ Interval} = 1/k = 12 \text{ seconds}$

c.

T	Interval	54-2(Intervals)
21.0 °C	16.3 s	21 °C
27.8 °C	13.0 s	28 °C
30.0 °C	12 s	30. °C

This rule of thumb gives excellent agreement to two significant figures.

91.   Rate $= \dfrac{d[Cl_2]}{dt} = k_2[NO_2Cl][Cl]$; Assume $\dfrac{d[Cl]}{dt} = 0$, then:

$$k_1[NO_2Cl] = k_{-1}[NO_2][Cl] + k_2[NO_2Cl][Cl], \quad [Cl] = \frac{k_1[NO_2Cl]}{k_{-1}[NO_2] + k_2[NO_2Cl]}$$

Rate $= \dfrac{d[Cl_2]}{dt} = \dfrac{k_1k_2[NO_2Cl]^2}{k_{-1}[NO_2] + k_2[NO_2Cl]}$

92.   Rate $= \dfrac{d[P]}{dt} = k_2[ES]$; Apply the steady-state approximation to ES, $\dfrac{d[ES]}{dt} = 0$.

$k_1[E][S] = k_{-1}[ES] + k_2[ES]; \quad [E]_T = [E] + [ES], \text{ so } [E] = [E]_T - [ES]$

Substituting: $k_1[S]([E]_T - [ES]) = (k_{-1} + k_2)[ES], \quad k_1[E]_T[S] = (k_{-1} + k_2 + k_1[S])\,[ES]$

$[ES] = \dfrac{k_1[E]_T[S]}{k_{-1} + k_2 + k_1[S]}$; Substituting into the rate equation, Rate $= k_2[ES]$:

Rate $= \dfrac{d[P]}{dt} = \dfrac{k_1k_2[E]_T[S]}{k_{-1} + k_2 + k_1[S]}$

Challenge Problems

93.   a.   Rate $= k[CH_3X]^x[Y]^y$; For experiment 1, [Y] is constant so Rate $= k'[CH_3X]^x$ where $k' = k(3.0\ M)^y$.

A plot (not included) of $\ln[CH_3X]$ vs t is linear (x = 1). The integrated rate law is:

$\ln[CH_3X] = -0.93\ t - 3.99; \quad k' = 0.93\ h^{-1}$

For Experiment 2, [Y] is again constant with Rate = $k''[CH_3X]^x$ where $k'' = k(4.5\ M)^y$. The ln plot is linear again with an integrated rate law:

$$\ln[CH_3X] = -0.93\ t - 5.40;\ \ k'' = 0.93\ h^{-1}$$

Dividing the rate constant values: $\dfrac{k'}{k''} = \dfrac{0.93}{0.93} = \dfrac{k(3.0)^y}{k(4.5)^y},\ \ 1.0 = (0.67)^y,\ \ y = 0$

Reaction is first order in CH_3X and zero order in Y. The overall rate law is:

$$\text{Rate} = k[CH_3X]\ \text{where}\ k = 0.93\ h^{-1}\ \text{at}\ 25\,^\circ C.$$

b. $t_{1/2} = (\ln 2)/k = 0.6931/(7.88 \times 10^8\ h^{-1}) = 8.80 \times 10^{-10}$ hour

c. $\ln \dfrac{k_2}{k_1} = \dfrac{E_a}{R}\left(\dfrac{1}{T_1} - \dfrac{1}{T_2}\right),\ \ \ln\left(\dfrac{7.88 \times 10^8}{0.93}\right) = \dfrac{E_a}{8.3145\ J\ K^{-1}\ mol^{-1}}\left(\dfrac{1}{298\ K} - \dfrac{1}{358\ K}\right)$

$E_a = 3.0 \times 10^5$ J/mol $= 3.0 \times 10^2$ kJ/mol

d. From part a, the reaction is first order in CH_3X and zero order in Y. From part c, the activation energy is close to the C-X bond energy. A plausible mechanism that explains the results in parts a and c is:

$$CH_3X \rightarrow CH_3 + X\quad \text{(slow)}$$

$$CH_3 + Y \rightarrow CH_3Y\quad \text{(fast)}$$

Note: This is a possible mechanism since the derived rate law is the same as the experimental rate law.

94.   a. rate $= k_2[A][M]$

$$k_1[A][B] = k_{-1}[M]$$

$$[M] = \frac{k_1[A][B]}{k_{-1}}$$

$$\text{rate} = \frac{k_2 k_1}{k_{-1}}[A]^2[B]$$

b. $k^2[A][M] = $ rate

$$k_1[A][B] = k_{-1}[M] + k_2[A][M]$$

$$[M] = \frac{k_1[A][B]}{k_{-1} + k_2[A]}$$

$$rate = \frac{k_2 k_1 [A]^2 [B]}{k_{-1} + k_2 [A]}$$

c.   If [A] <<< [B], rate from part b $= \dfrac{k_2 k_1}{k_{-1}}$ $[A]^2 [B]$, the same as part a.

95.   Rate $= k[A]^x [B]^y [C]^z$; During the course of experiment 1, [A] and [C] are essentially constant, and Rate $= k'[B]^y$ where $k' = k[A]_o^x [C]_o^z$.

[B] (M)	time (s)	ln[B]	1/[B] (M^{-1})
1.0×10^{-3}	0	-6.91	1.0×10^3
2.7×10^{-4}	1.0×10^5	-8.22	3.7×10^3
1.6×10^{-4}	2.0×10^5	-8.74	6.3×10^3
1.1×10^{-4}	3.0×10^5	-9.12	9.1×10^3
8.5×10^{-5}	4.0×10^5	-9.37	12×10^3
6.9×10^{-5}	5.0×10^5	-9.58	14×10^3
5.8×10^{-5}	6.0×10^5	-9.76	17×10^3

A plot of 1/[B] vs. t is linear (plot not included). The reaction is second order in B and the integrated rate equation is:

$$1/[B] = (2.7 \times 10^{-2} \text{ L mol}^{-1} \text{ s}^{-1}) \, t + 1.0 \times 10^3 \, M^{-1}; \quad k' = 2.7 \times 10^{-2} \text{ L mol}^{-1} \text{ s}^{-1}$$

For experiment 2, [B] and [C] are essentially constant and Rate $= k''[A]^x$ where $k'' = k[B]_o^y [C]_o^z = k[B]_o^2 [C]_o^z$.

[A] (M)	time (s)	ln[A]	1/[A] (M^{-1})
1.0×10^{-2}	0	-4.61	1.0×10^2
8.9×10^{-3}	1.0	-4.72	110
7.1×10^{-3}	3.0	-4.95	140
5.5×10^{-3}	5.0	-5.20	180
3.8×10^{-3}	8.0	-5.57	260
2.9×10^{-3}	10.0	-5.84	340
2.0×10^{-3}	13.0	-6.21	5.0×10^2

A plot of ln[A] vs. t is linear. The reaction is first order in A and the integrated rate law is:

$$\ln[A] = -(0.123 \text{ s}^{-1}) \, t - 4.61; \quad k'' = 0.123 \text{ s}^{-1}$$

Note: We will carry an extra significant figure in k''.

Experiment 3:   [A] and [B] are constant; Rate $= k'''[C]^z$

The plot of [C] vs. t is linear. Thus, $z = 0$.

The overall rate law is: Rate $= k[A][B]^2$

From Experiment 1 (to determine k):

$$k' = 2.7 \times 10^{-2} \text{ L mol}^{-1} \text{ s}^{-1} = k[A]_0^x [C]_0^z = k[A]_0 = k(2.0 \text{ } M),\ k = 1.4 \times 10^{-2} \text{ L}^2 \text{ mol}^{-2} \text{ s}^{-1}$$

From Experiment 2: $k'' = 0.123 \text{ s}^{-1} = k[B]_0^2,\ k = \dfrac{0.123 \text{ s}^{-1}}{(3.0 \text{ } M)^2} = 1.4 \times 10^{-2} \text{ L}^2 \text{ mol}^{-2} \text{ s}^{-1}$

Thus, Rate $= k[A][B]^2$ and $k = 1.4 \times 10^{-2} \text{ L}^2 \text{ mol}^{-2} \text{ s}^{-1}$.

96.   First we need to convert total pressure to pressure of O_2

	$3 O_2$	$\rightarrow$	$2 O_5$
Before	1.000 atm		0
Change	-3x		+2x
After	1.000-3x		2x

Total P $= 1.000-3x + 2x = 1.000-x$

So, at t $= 46.89$, $1.000-x = 0.9500$, x $= 0.0500$ (carrying extra sig fig)

So, $P_{O_2} = 1.000 - 3(.0500) = 0.850$.   The table contains the other values.

Time	P_{O_2}
0	1.000 atm
46.89	0.850 atm
98.82	0.710 atm
137.9	0.620 atm
200.0	0.500 atm
286.9	0.370 atm
337.9	0.310 atm
511.3	0.170 atm

A graph of $\ln(O_2)$ vs. t gives a straight line with a slope of -0.00347.

a.   rate $= k[O_2]$
b. $k = 0.00347 \text{ sec}^{-1}$
c. $P_{O_2} = 0.140$ atm

$\ln(0.140) = -kt + \ln[1.000]$, t $= 567$ sec

97.   Rate $= \dfrac{-d[N_2O_5]}{dt} = k_1[M][N_2O_5] - k_{-1}[NO_3][NO_2][M]$

Assume $d[NO_3]/dt = 0$, so $k_1[N_2O_5][M] = k_{-1}[NO_3][NO_2][M] + k_2[NO_3][NO_2] + k_3[NO_3][NO]$

$$[NO_3] = \dfrac{k_1[N_2O_5][M]}{k_{-1}[NO_2][M] + k_2[NO_2] + k_3[NO]}$$

Assume $\dfrac{d[NO]}{dt} = 0$, so $k_2[NO_3][NO_2] = k_3[NO_3][NO]$, $[NO] = \dfrac{k_2}{k_3}[NO_2]$

Substituting: $[NO_3] = \dfrac{k_1[N_2O_5][M]}{k_{-1}[NO_2][M] + k_2[NO_2] + \dfrac{k_3 k_2}{k_3}[NO_2]} = \dfrac{k_1[N_2O_5][M]}{[NO_2](k_{-1}[M] + 2\,k_2)}$

Solving for the rate law:

$$\text{Rate} = \dfrac{-d[N_2O_5]}{dt} = k_1[N_2O_5][M] - \dfrac{k_{-1}k_1[NO_2][N_2O_5][M]^2}{[NO_2](k_{-1}[M] + 2\,k_2)} = k_1[N_2O_5][M] - \dfrac{k_{-1}k_1[M]^2[N_2O_5]}{k_{-1}[M] + 2\,k_2}$$

$$\text{Rate} = \dfrac{-d[N_2O_5]}{dt} = \left(k_1 - \dfrac{k_{-1}k_1[M]}{k_{-1}[M] + 2\,k_2} \right)[N_2O_5][M]; \ \text{Simplifying:}$$

$$\text{Rate} = \dfrac{-d[N_2O_5]}{dt} = \dfrac{2\,k_1 k_2[M][N_2O_5]}{k_{-1}[M] + 2\,k_2}$$

98.   a.   Rate $= (k_1 + k_2[H^+])[I^-]^m[H_2O_2]^n$

In all the experiments, the concentration of H_2O_2 is small compared to the concentrations of I^- and H^+. Therefore, the concentrations of I^- and H^+ are effectively constant and the rate law reduces to:

Rate $= k_{obs}[H_2O_2]^n$ where $k_{obs} = (k_1 + k_2[H^+])[I^-]^m$

Since all plots of $\ln[H_2O_2]$ vs. time are linear, the reaction is first order with respect to H_2O_2 ($n = 1$). The slopes of the $\ln[H_2O_2]$ vs. time plots equal $-k_{obs}$ which equals $-(k_1 + k_2[H^+])[I^-]^m$. To determine the order of I^-, compare the slopes of two experiments where I^- changes and H^+ is constant. Comparing the first two experiments:

$$\dfrac{\text{slope (exp. 2)}}{\text{slope (exp. 1)}} = \dfrac{-0.360}{-0.120} = \dfrac{-[k_1 + k_2\,(0.0400\ M)]\,(0.3000\ M)^m}{-[k_1 + k_2\,(0.0400\ M)]\,(0.1000\ M)^m},$$

$$3.00 = \left(\dfrac{0.3000}{0.1000} \right)^m = (3.000)^m, \ m = 1$$

The reaction is also first order with respect to I^-.

b.   The slope equation has two unknowns, k_1 and k_2. To solve for k_1 and k_2, we must have two equations. We need to take one of the first set of three experiments and one of the 2nd set of three experiments to generate the two equations in k_1 and k_2.

Experiment 1: slope $= -(k_1 + k_2[H^+])[I^-]$

$-0.120\ \text{min}^{-1} = -[k_1 + k_2\,(0.0400\ M)]\,0.1000\ M$ or $1.20 = k_1 + k_2\,(0.0400)$

Experiment 4:

$-0.0760 \text{ min}^{-1} = -[k_1 + k_2 (0.0200 \ M)] \ 0.0750 \ M$ or $1.01 = k_1 + k_2 (0.0200)$

Subtracting 4 from 1:

$$1.20 = k_1 + k_2 (0.0400)$$
$$-1.01 = -k_1 - k_2 (0.0200)$$
$$\overline{0.19 = \qquad k_2 (0.0200)}, \ k_2 = 9.5 \ L^2 \ mol^{-2} \ min^{-1}$$

$1.20 = k_1 + 9.5(0.0400), \ k_1 = 0.82 \ L \ mol^{-1} \ min^{-1}$

c. There are two pathways, one involving H^+ with rate $= k_2[H^+][I^-][H_2O_2]$ and another pathway not involving H^+ with rate $= k_1[I^-][H_2O_2]$. The overall rate of reaction depends on which of these two pathways dominates, and this depends on the H^+ concentration.

99. a. $[B] >> [A]$ so that $[B]$ can be considered constant over the experiments. (This gives us a pseudo-order rate law equation.)

b. Note in each case the 1/2 life doubles (in expt. 1 the first half life is 40 sec, the second is 80 sec; in expt. 2 the first half life is 20 sec, the second is 40 sec). Thus the reaction is second order in $[A]$. Between expt. 1 and expt. 2 we double $[B]$ and the reaction rate doubles, thus it is first order in $[B]$. The overall rate law equation is rate $= k[A]^2[B]$.

Using $t_{1/2} = \dfrac{1}{k[A]_o}$, we get $k = \dfrac{1}{(40.)(10 \times 10^{-2})} = 0.25$. But this is actually k^1 where rate $= k^1[A]^2$ and $k^1 = k[B]$.

$$k = \frac{k^1}{[B]} = \frac{0.25}{5.0} = 0.050 \ L^2 \ mol^{-2} \ s^{-1}$$

c. i. wrong stoichiometry

ii. rate $= k[E][A]$

$k_1[A][B] = k_{-1}[E]; \ [E] = \dfrac{k_1[A][B]}{k_{-1}}$

rate $= \dfrac{k \, k_1}{k_{-1}}[A]^2[B]$ could be!

iii. rate $= k[A]^2$ (no)

So only mechanism ii is possible.

CHAPTER SIXTEEN

LIQUIDS AND SOLIDS

Intermolecular Forces and Physical Properties

11. Dipole forces are the forces that act between polar molecules. The electrostatic attraction between the positive end of one polar molecule and the negative end of another is the dipole force. Dipole forces are generally weaker than hydrogen bonding. Both of these forces are due to dipole moments in molecules. Hydrogen bonding is given a separate name from dipole forces because hydrogen bonding is a particularly strong dipole force.

London dispersion forces can be referred to as instantaneous-induced dipole forces. As the size of the molecule increases, the strength of the London dispersion forces increases. This is because, as the electron cloud about a molecule gets larger, it is easier for the electrons to be drawn away from the nucleus. The molecule is said to be more polarizable.

12. London dispersion (LD) < dipole-dipole < hydrogen bonding < metallic bonding, covalent network, ionic.

Yes, there is considerable overlap. Consider some of the examples in Exercise 16.20. Benzene (only LD forces) has a higher boiling point than acetone (dipole-dipole). Also, there is even more overlap of the stronger forces (metallic, covalent, and ionic).

13. Fusion refers to a solid converting to a liquid and vaporization refers to a liquid converting to a gas. Only a fraction of the hydrogen bonds are broken in going from the solid phase to the liquid phase. Most of the hydrogen bonds are still present in the liquid phase and must be broken during the liquid to gas phase transition. Thus, the enthalpy of vaporization is much larger than the enthalpy of fusion since more intermolecular forces are broken during the vaporization process.

14. a. Polarizability of an atom refers to the ease of distorting the electron cloud. It can also refer to distorting the electron clouds in molecules or ions. Polarity refers to the presence of a permanent dipole moment in a molecule.

    b. London dispersion (LD) forces are present in all substances. LD forces can be referred to as accidental dipole - induced dipole forces. Dipole - dipole forces involve the attraction of molecules with permanent dipoles for each other.

c.   inter: between; intra: within; For example, in Br_2 the covalent bond is an intramolecular force, holding the two Br-atoms together in the molecule. The much weaker London dispersion forces are the intermolecular forces of attraction which hold different molecules of Br_2 together in the liquid phase.

15.   Ionic compounds have ionic forces. Covalent compounds all have London Dispersion (LD) forces, while polar covalent compounds have dipole forces and/or hydrogen bonding forces. For hydrogen bonding (H-bonding) forces, the covalent compound must have either a N–H, O–H or F–H bond in the molecule.

   a.   LD only   b.   dipole, LD   c.   H–bonding, LD

   d.   ionic   e.   LD only (CH_4 in a nonpolar covalent compound.)

   f.   dipole, LD   g.   ionic   h.   ionic

   i.   LD mostly; C – F bonds are polar, but polymers like teflon are so large that LD forces are the predominant intermolecular forces.

   j.   LD   k.   dipole, LD   l.   H-bonding, LD

   m.   dipole, LD   n.   LD only

16.   a.   OCS; OCS is polar and has dipole-dipole forces in addition to London dispersion (LD) forces. All polar molecules have dipole forces. CO_2 is nonpolar and only has LD forces. To predict polarity, draw the Lewis structure and deduce if the individual bond dipoles cancel.

   b. PF_3; PF_3 is polar (PF_5 is nonpolar).   c. SF_2; SF_2 is polar (SF_6 is nonpolar).

   d. SeO_2; SeO_2 has a larger molar mass than SO_2, so it will have stronger London dispersion forces.

17.   a. $H_2NCH_2CH_2NH_2$; More extensive hydrogen bonding (H-bonding) is possible since two NH_2 groups are present.

   b. H_2CO; H_2CO is polar while CH_3CH_3 is nonpolar. H_2CO_3 has dipole forces in addition to LD forces. CH_3CH_3 only has LD forces.

   c. CH_3OH; CH_3OH can form relatively strong H-bonding interactions, unlike H_2CO.

   d.   HF; HF is capable of forming H-bonding interactions, HBr is not.

18.   As the strengths of the interparticle forces increase, boiling point, freezing point, viscosity, ΔH_{vap} and ΔH_{fus} increases while vapor pressure decreases.

   a.   HCl; HCl is polar while Ar and F_2 are nonpolar. HCl has dipole forces unlike Ar and F_2.

   b.   NaCl; Ionic forces are much stronger than the intermolecular forces for molecular solids.

   c. I_2; All are nonpolar so the largest molecule (I_2) will have the strongest LD forces and the lowest vapor pressure.

d. N_2; Nonpolar and smallest, so it has weakest intermolecular forces.

e. H_2O_2; H–O–O–H structure produces stronger H-bonding interactions than H–F so H_2O_2 has the greatest viscosity.

f. CH_3CH_2OH; Can form H-bonding interactions unlike the other covalent compounds.

g. I_2; I_2 has only LD forces while CsBr and CaO have much stronger ionic forces. I_2 has the weakest intermolecular forces so it has the smallest ΔH_{fusion}.

19.   a. Neopentane is more compact than n-pentane. There is less surface area contact between neopentane molecules. This leads to weaker LD forces and a lower boiling point.

b. Ethanol is capable of hydrogen bonding (H-bonding), dimethyl ether is not.

c. HF is capable of H-bonding, HCl is not.

d. LiCl is ionic and HCl is a molecular solid with only dipole forces and LD forces. Ionic forces are much stronger than the intermolecular forces for molecular solids.

e. n-pentane is a larger molecule so it has stronger LD forces.

f. Dimethyl ether is polar. Dimethyl ether has dipole forces, in addition to LD forces, unlike n-propane, which only has LD forces.

20.   Benzene

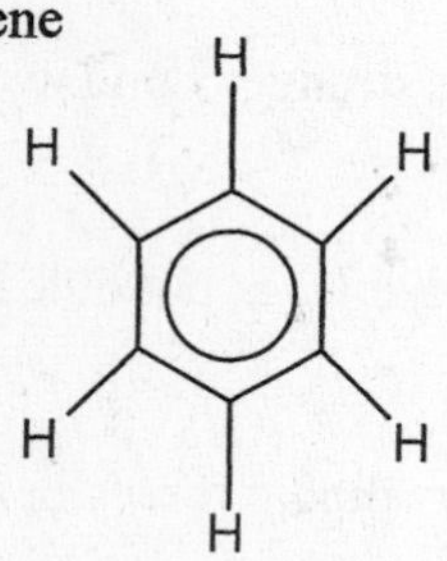

LD forces only

Naphthalene

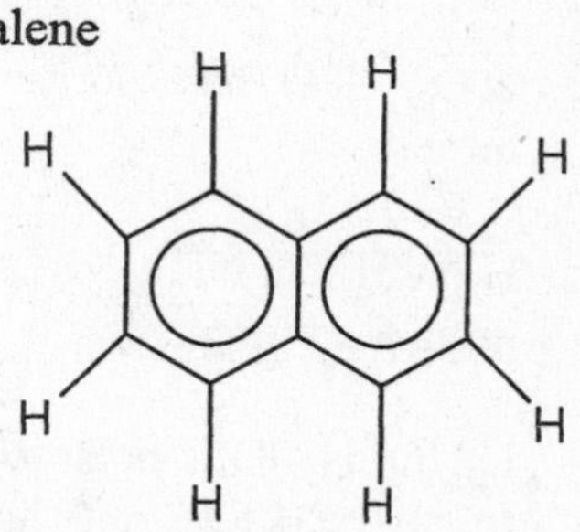

LD forces only

Note: London dispersion forces in molecules like benzene and naphthalene are fairly large. The molecules are flat and there is efficient surface area contact between molecules. Large surface area contact leads to stronger London dispersion forces.

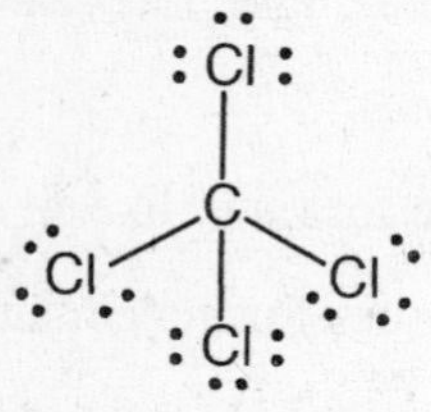

Carbon tetrachloride (CCl_4) has polar bonds but is a nonpolar molecule. CCl_4 only has LD forces.

In terms of size and shape: $CCl_4 < C_6H_6 < C_{10}H_8$

The strengths of the LD forces are proportional to size and are related to shape. Although the size of CCl_4 is fairly large, the overall spherical shape gives rise to relatively weak LD forces as compared to flat molecules like benzene and naphthalene. The physical properties given in the problem are consistent with the order listed previously. Each of the physical properties will increase with an increase in intermolecular forces.

Acetone   Acetic Acid

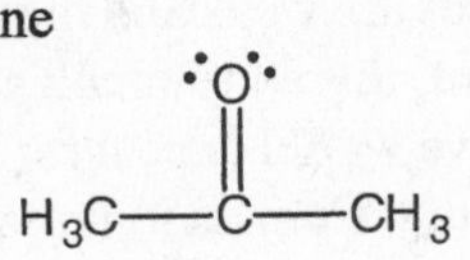

LD, dipole   LD, dipole, H-bonding

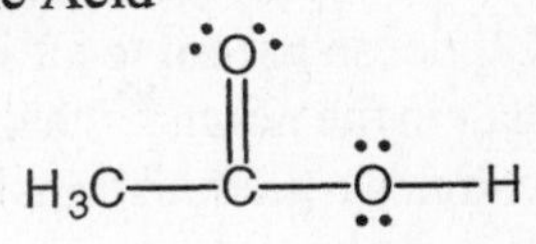

Benzoic Acid

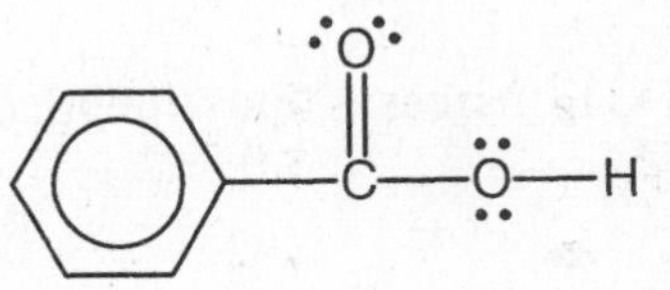

LD, dipole, H-bonding

We would predict the strength of interparticle forces of the last three molecules to be:

    acetone < acetic acid < benzoic acid

    polar   H-bonding   H-bonding, but large LD forces because of greater size and shape.

This ordering is consistent with the values given for bp, mp, and ΔH_{vap}.

The overall order of the strengths of intermolecular forces based on physical properties are:

    acetone < CCl_4 < C_6H_6 < acetic acid < naphthalene < benzoic acid

The order seems reasonable except for acetone and naphthalene. Since acetone is polar, we would not expect it to boil at the lowest temperature. However, in terms of size and shape, acetone is the smallest molecule and the LD forces in acetone must be very small compared to the other molecules. Naphthalene must have very strong LD forces because of its size and flat shape.

21.   Both molecules are capable of H-bonding. However, in oil of wintergreen the hydrogen bonding is <u>intramolecular</u>.

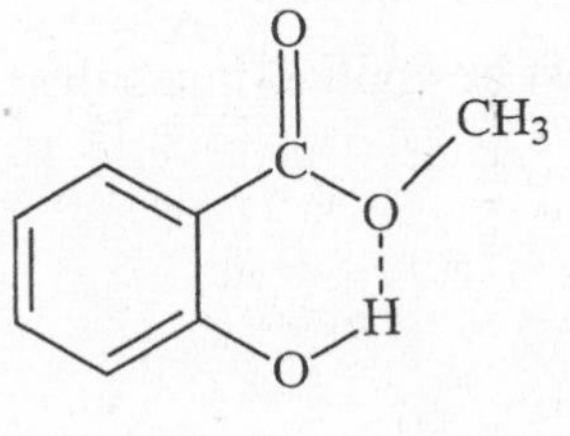

------- = H-bonding

In methyl-4-hydroxybenzoate, the H-bonding is <u>intermolecular</u>, resulting in stronger intermolecular forces and a higher melting point.

22.   NaCl, $MgCl_2$, NaF, MgF_2 AlF_3 all have very high melting points indicative of strong intermolecular forces. They are all ionic solids. $SiCl_4$, SiF_4, F_2, Cl_2, PF_5 and SF_6 are nonpolar covalent molecules. Only LD forces are present. PCl_3 and SCl_2 are polar molecules. LD forces and dipole forces are present. In these 8 molecular substances, the intermolecular forces are weak and the melting points low. $AlCl_3$ doesn't seem to fit in as well. From the melting point, there are much stronger forces present than in the nonmetal halides, but they aren't as strong as we would expect for an ionic solid. $AlCl_3$ illustrates a gradual transition from ionic to covalent bonding; from an ionic solid to discrete molecules.

23. $C_{25}H_{52}$ has the stronger intermolecular forces because it has the higher boiling point. Even though $C_{25}H_{52}$ is nonpolar, it is so large that its London dispersion forces are much stronger than the sum of the hydrogen bonding and London dispersion interactions found in H_2O.

24.   As the electronegativity of the atoms covalently bonded to H increases, the strength of the hydrogen bonding interaction increases.

$$N \cdots H - N < N \cdots H - O < O \cdots H - O < O \cdots H - F < F \cdots H - F$$

weakest   strongest

25.   A single hydrogen bond in H_2O has a strength of 21 kJ/mol. Each H_2O molecule forms two H-bonds. Thus, it should take 42 kJ/mol of energy to break all of the H-bonds in water. Consider the phase transitions:

$$\text{solid} \xrightarrow{6.0\,kJ} \text{liquid} \xrightarrow{40.7\,kJ} \text{vapor} \qquad \Delta H_{sub} = \Delta H_{fus} + \Delta H_{vap}$$

It takes a total of 46.7 kJ/mol to convert solid H_2O to vapor (ΔH_{sub}). This would be the amount of energy necessary to disrupt all of the intermolecular forces in ice. Thus, $(42 \div 46.7) \times 100 = 90.\%$ of the attraction in ice can be attributed to H-bonding.

Properties of Liquids

26.   Liquids and solids both have characteristic volume and are not very compressible. Liquids and gases flow and assume the shape of their container.

27.   Critical temperature: The temperature above which a liquid cannot exist, i.e., the gas cannot be liquefied by increased pressure.

Critical pressure: The pressure that must be applied to a substance at its critical temperature to produce a liquid.

As the strength of the intermolecular forces increases, the critical temperature increases.

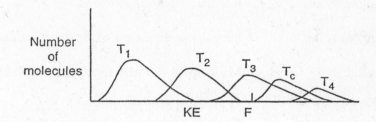

The kinetic energy distribution changes as one raises the temperature ($T_4 > T_c > T_3 > T_2 > T_1$). At the critical temperature, T_c, all molecules have kinetic energies greater than the intermolecular forces, F, and a liquid can't form. Note: The distributions above are not to scale.

28.   The attraction of H_2O for glass is stronger than the $H_2O - H_2O$ attraction. The meniscus is concave to increase the area of contact between glass and H_2O. The $Hg - Hg$ attraction is greater than the $Hg -$ glass attraction. The meniscus is convex to minimize the $Hg -$ glass contact.

29.   As the strengths of intermolecular forces increase, surface tension, viscosity, and boiling point increase, while the vapor pressure decreases.

30. $C_2H_5OH(l) \rightarrow C_2H_5OH(g)$ is an endothermic process. Heat is absorbed when liquid ethanol vaporizes; the internal heat from the body provides this heat which results in the cooling of the body.

31.   Water is a polar substance and wax is a nonpolar substance; they are not attracted to each other. A molecule at the surface of a drop of water is subject to attractions only by water molecules below it and to each side. The effect of this uneven pull on the surface water molecules tends to draw them into the body of the water and causes the droplet to assume the shape that has the minimum surface area, a sphere.

32.   The intermolecular forces are slightly stronger in D_2O than in H_2O.

33.   The structure of H_2O_2 is $H - O - O - H$, which produces greater hydrogen bonding than in water. Thus, the intermolecular forces are stronger in H_2O_2 than in H_2O resulting in a higher normal boiling point for H_2O_2 and a lower vapor pressure.

34. CO_2 is a gas at room temperature. As mp and bp increase, the strength of the intermolecular forces also increases. Therefore, the strength of forces is $CO_2 < CS_2 < CSe_2$. From a structural standpoint this is expected. All three are linear, nonpolar molecules. Thus, only London dispersion forces are present. Since the molecules increase in size from $CO_2 < CS_2 < CSe_2$, then the strength of the intermolecular forces will increase in the same order.

Structures and Properties of Solids

35.   a.   Crystalline solid: Regular, repeating structure

            Amorphous solid: Irregular arrangement of atoms or molecules

       b.   Ionic solid: Made up of ions held together by ionic bonding.

            Molecular solid: Made up of discrete covalently bonded molecules held together in the solid phase by weaker forces (LD, dipole or hydrogen bonds).

       c.   Molecular solid: Discrete, individual molecules

            Covalent network solid: No discrete molecules; A covalent network solid is one large molecule. The interparticle forces are the covalent bonds between atoms.

       d.   Metallic solid: Completely delocalized electrons, conductor of electricity (ions in a sea of electrons)

            Covalent network solid: Localized electrons; Insulator or semiconductor

36.   A crystalline solid because a regular, repeating arrangement is necessary to produce planes of atoms that will diffract the x-rays in regular patterns. An amorphous solid does not have a regular repeating arrangement and will produce a complicated diffraction pattern.

37.   No, an example is common glass, which is primarily amorphous SiO_2 (a covalent network solid) as compared to ice (a crystalline solid held together by weaker H-bonds). The interparticle forces in the amorphous solid in this case are stronger than those in the crystalline solid. Whether a solid is amorphous or crystalline depends on the long range order in the solid and not on the strengths of the interparticle forces.

38.   a. CO_2: molecular   b. SiO_2: covalent network   c.   Si: atomic, covalent network

       d. CH_4: molecular   e.   Ru: atomic, metallic   f. I_2: molecular

       g.   KBr: ionic   h. H_2O: molecular   i.   NaOH: ionic

       j.   U: atomic, metallic   k. $CaCO_3$: ionic   l. PH_3: molecular

       m.   GaAs: covalent network   n.   BaO: ionic   o.   NO: molecular

       p. GeO_2: ionic

39. $n\lambda = 2d \sin \theta$, $\lambda = \dfrac{2d \sin \theta}{n} = \dfrac{2 \times (201 \times 10^{-12} \text{ m}) \sin 34.68°}{1}$, $\lambda = 2.29 \times 10^{-10}$ m $= 229$ pm

40. $n\lambda = 2d \sin \theta$, $d = \dfrac{n\lambda}{2 \sin \theta} = \dfrac{1 \times 2.63 \text{ Å}}{2 \times \sin 15.55°} = 4.91 \text{ Å} = 4.91 \times 10^{-10} \text{ m} = 491 \text{ pm}$

$\sin \theta = \dfrac{n\lambda}{2d} = \dfrac{2 \times 2.63 \text{ Å}}{2 \times 4.91 \text{ Å}} = 0.536$, $\theta = 32.4°$

41. $n\lambda = 2d \sin \theta$, $d = \dfrac{n\lambda}{2 \sin \theta} = \dfrac{1 \times 1.54 \text{ Å}}{2 \times \sin 14.22°} = 3.13 \text{ Å} = 3.13 \times 10^{-10} \text{ m} = 313 \text{ pm}$

42.   Mn at 8 corners × (1/8) + 1 Mn at body center = 2 Mn; There are 2 Mn atoms in each unit cell. The coordination number of Mn is 8.

For Mn at center: coordination number is from 8 Mn at corners.

For Mn at corner: coordination number is from 8 Mn at the center of 8 different cubes that touch each corner Mn.

43.   A cubic closest packed structure has a face-centered cubic unit cell. In a face-centered cubic unit, there are:

$$8 \text{ corners} \times \dfrac{1/8 \text{ atom}}{\text{corner}} + 6 \text{ faces} \times \dfrac{1/2 \text{ atom}}{\text{face}} = 4 \text{ atoms}$$

The atoms in a face-centered cubic unit cell touch along the face diagonal of the cubic unit cell. Using the Pythagorean formula where l = length of the face diagonal and r = radius of the atom:

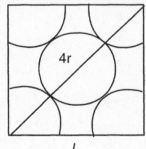

$$l^2 + l^2 = (4r)^2$$

$$2\, l^2 = 16\, r^2$$

$$l = r \sqrt{8}$$

$l = r \sqrt{8} = 197 \times 10^{-12} \text{ m} \times \sqrt{8} = 5.57 \times 10^{-10} \text{ m} = 5.57 \times 10^{-8} \text{ cm}$

Volume of a unit cell = l^3 = $(5.57 \times 10^{-8} \text{ cm})^3 = 1.73 \times 10^{-22} \text{ cm}^3$

Mass of a unit cell = $4 \text{ Ca atoms} \times \dfrac{1 \text{ mol Ca}}{6.022 \times 10^{23} \text{ atoms}} \times \dfrac{40.08 \text{ g Ca}}{\text{mol Ca}} = 2.662 \times 10^{-22} \text{ g Ca}$

density = $\dfrac{\text{mass}}{\text{volume}} = \dfrac{2.662 \times 10^{-22} \text{ g}}{1.73 \times 10^{-22} \text{ cm}^3} = 1.54 \text{ g/cm}^3$

44.   The volume of a unit cell is:

$$V = l^3 = (383.3 \times 10^{-10} \text{ cm})^3 = 5.631 \times 10^{-23} \text{ cm}^3$$

There are 4 Ir atoms in the unit cell as is the case for all face-centered cubic unit cells. The mass of atoms in a unit cell is:

$$\text{mass} = 4 \text{ Ir atoms} \times \frac{1 \text{ mol Ir}}{6.022 \times 10^{23} \text{ atoms}} \times \frac{192.2 \text{ g Ir}}{\text{mol Ir}} = 1.277 \times 10^{-21} \text{ g}$$

$$\text{density} = \frac{\text{mass}}{\text{volume}} = \frac{1.277 \times 10^{-21} \text{ g}}{5.631 \times 10^{-23} \text{ cm}^3} = 22.68 \text{ g/cm}^3$$

45.   There are 4 Ni atoms in each unit cell: For a unit cell:

$$\text{density} = \frac{\text{mass}}{\text{volume}} = 6.84 \text{ g/cm}^3 = \frac{4 \text{ Ni atoms} \times \dfrac{1 \text{ mol Ni}}{6.022 \times 10^{23} \text{ atoms}} \times \dfrac{58.69 \text{ g Ni}}{\text{mol Ni}}}{l^3}$$

Solving: $l = 3.85 \times 10^{-8}$ cm = cube edge length

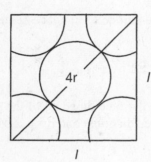

For a face centered cube:

$$(4r)^2 = l^2 + l^2 = 2\, l^2$$

$$r\sqrt{8} = l, \ r = l/\sqrt{8}$$

$$r = 3.85 \times 10^{-8} \text{ cm}/\sqrt{8}$$

$$r = 1.36 \times 10^{-8} \text{ cm} = 136 \text{ pm}$$

46.   A face-centered cubic unit cell contains 4 atoms. For a unit cell:

$$\text{mass of X} = \text{volume} \times \text{density} = (4.09 \times 10^{-8} \text{ cm})^3 \times 10.5 \text{ g/cm}^3 = 7.18 \times 10^{-22} \text{ g}$$

$$\text{mol X} = 4 \text{ atoms X} \times \frac{1 \text{ mol X}}{6.022 \times 10^{23} \text{ atoms}} = 6.642 \times 10^{-24} \text{ mol X}$$

$$\text{Molar mass} = \frac{7.18 \times 10^{-22} \text{ g X}}{6.642 \times 10^{-24} \text{ mol X}} = 108 \text{ g/mol}; \ \text{The metal is silver (Ag).}$$

47.   For a body-centered unit cell: $8 \text{ corners} \times \dfrac{1/8 \text{ Ti}}{\text{corner}} + \text{Ti at body center} = 2 \text{ Ti atoms}$

All body-centered unit cells have 2 atoms per unit cell. For a unit cell:

$$\text{density} = 4.50 \text{ g/cm}^3 = \frac{2 \text{ atoms Ti} \times \dfrac{1 \text{ mol Ti}}{6.022 \times 10^{23} \text{ atoms}} \times \dfrac{47.88 \text{ g Ti}}{\text{mol Ti}}}{l^3}, \ l = \text{cube edge length}$$

Solving: l = edge length of unit cell = 3.28×10^{-8} cm = 328 pm

Assume Ti atoms just touch along the body diagonal of the cube, so body diagonal = 4 × radius of atoms = 4r.

The triangle we need to solve is:

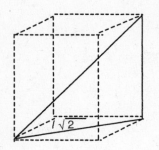

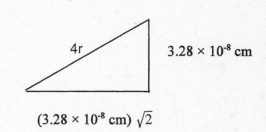

$(4r)^2 = (3.28 \times 10^{-8} \text{ cm})^2 + [(3.28 \times 10^{-8} \text{ cm}) \sqrt{2}\,]^2$, r = 1.42×10^{-8} cm = 142 pm

For a body-centered unit cell, the radius of the atom is related to the cube edge length by $4r = l\sqrt{3}$ or $l = 4r/\sqrt{3}$.

48.   From Exercise 16.47:

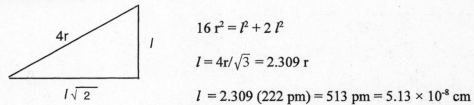

$16\,r^2 = l^2 + 2\,l^2$

$l = 4r/\sqrt{3} = 2.309\,r$

$l = 2.309\,(222 \text{ pm}) = 513 \text{ pm} = 5.13 \times 10^{-8}$ cm

In bcc, there are 2 atoms/unit cell. For a unit cell:

$$\text{density} = \frac{\text{mass}}{\text{volume}} = \frac{2 \text{ atoms Ba} \times \dfrac{1 \text{ mol Ba}}{6.022 \times 10^{23} \text{ atoms}} \times \dfrac{137.3 \text{ g Ba}}{\text{mol Ba}}}{(5.13 \times 10^{-8} \text{ cm})^3} = \frac{3.38 \text{ g}}{\text{cm}^3}$$

49.   If a face-centered cubic structure, then 4 atoms/unit cell and from Exercise 16.43:

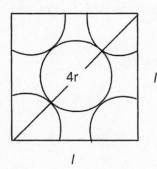

$2\,l^2 = 16\,r^2$

$l = r\sqrt{8} = 144 \text{ pm } \sqrt{8} = 407 \text{ pm}$

$l = 407 \times 10^{-12} \text{ m} = 407 \times 10^{-10}$ cm

$$\text{density} = \frac{4 \text{ atoms Au} \times \dfrac{1 \text{ mol Au}}{6.022 \times 10^{23} \text{ atoms}} \times \dfrac{197.0 \text{ g Au}}{\text{mol Au}}}{(4.07 \times 10^{-8} \text{ cm})^3} = 19.4 \text{ g/cm}^3$$

If a body-centered cubic structure, then 2 atoms/unit cell and from Exercise 16.47:

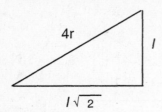

$$16 \, r^2 = l^2 + 2 \, l^2$$

$$l = 4r/\sqrt{3} = 333 \text{ pm} = 333 \times 10^{-12} \text{ m}$$

$$l = 333 \times 10^{-10} \text{ cm} = 3.33 \times 10^{-8} \text{ cm}$$

$$\text{density} = \frac{2 \text{ atoms Au} \times \dfrac{1 \text{ mol Au}}{6.022 \times 10^{23} \text{ atoms}} \times \dfrac{197.0 \text{ g Au}}{\text{mol Au}}}{(3.33 \times 10^{-8} \text{ cm})^3} = 17.7 \text{ g/cm}^3$$

The measured density is consistent with a face-centered cubic unit cell.

50.   In a face-centered unit cell (ccp structure), the atoms touch along the face diagonal:

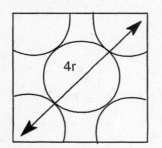

$$(4r)^2 = l^2 + l^2$$

$$l = r\sqrt{8}$$

$$V_{cube} = l^3 = (r\sqrt{8})^3 = 22.63 \, r^3$$

There are four atoms in a face-centered cubic cell (see Exercise 16.43). Each atom has a volume of $4/3 \, \pi r^3$.

$$V_{atoms} = 4 \times \frac{4}{3} \, \pi r^3 = 16.76 \, r^3$$

So, $\dfrac{V_{atom}}{V_{cube}} = \dfrac{16.76 \, r^3}{22.63 \, r^3} = 0.7406$ or 74.06% of the volume of each unit cell is occupied by atoms.

In a simple cubic unit cell, the atoms touch along the cube edge (l):

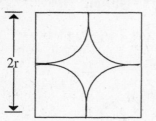

$$2(\text{radius}) = 2r = l$$

$$V_{cube} = l^3 = (2r)^3 = 8 \, r^3$$

There is one atom per simple cubic cell (8 corner atoms × 1/8 atom per corner = 1 atom/unit cell). Each atom has an assumed volume of 4/3 πr^3 = volume of a sphere.

$$V_{atom} = \frac{4}{3}\ \pi r^3 = 4.189\ r^3$$

So, $\dfrac{V_{atom}}{V_{cube}} = \dfrac{4.189\ r^3}{8\ r^3} = 0.5236$ or 52.36% of the volume of each unit cell is occupied by atoms.

A cubic closest packed structure packs the atoms much more efficiently than a simple cubic structure.

51.   Conductor: The energy difference between the filled and unfilled molecular orbitals is minimal. We call this energy difference the band gap. Since the band gap is minimal, electrons can easily move into the conduction bands (the unfilled molecular orbitals).

        Insulator: Large band gap; Electrons do not move from the filled molecular orbitals to the conduction bands since the energy difference is large.

        Semiconductor: Small band gap; Since the energy difference between the filled and unfilled molecular orbitals is smaller than in insulators, some electrons can jump into the conduction bands. The band gap, however, is not as small as with conductors, so semiconductors have intermediate conductivity.

52.   a. As the temperature is increased, more electrons in the filled molecular orbitals have sufficient kinetic energy to jump into the conduction bands (the unfilled molecular orbitals).

        b. A photon of light is absorbed by an electron which then has sufficient energy to jump into the conduction bands.

        c. An impurity either adds electrons at an energy near that of the conduction bands (n-type) or creates holes (empty energy levels) at energies in the previously filled molecular orbitals (p-type).

53.   To produce an n-type semiconductor, dope Ge with a substance that has more than 4 valence electrons, e.g., a group 5A element. Phosphorus or arsenic are two substances which will produce n-type semiconductors when they are doped into germanium. To produce a p-type semiconductor, dope Ge with a substance that has fewer than 4 valence electrons, e.g., a group 3A element. Gallium or indium are two substances which will produce p-type semiconductors when they are doped into germanium.

54.   An alloy is a substance that contains a mixture of elements and has metallic properties. In a substitutional alloy, some of the host metal atoms are replaced by other metal atoms of similar size, e.g., brass, pewter, plumber's solder. An interstitial alloy is formed when some of the interstices (holes) in the closest packed metal structure are occupied by smaller atoms, e.g., carbon steels.

55.   In has fewer valence electrons than Se; thus Se doped with In would be a p-type semiconductor.

56.   To make a p-type semiconductor we need to dope the material with atoms that have fewer valence electrons. The average number of valence electrons is four when 50-50 mixtures of group 3A and group 5A elements are considered. We could dope with more of the Group 3A element or with atoms of Zn or Cd. Cadmium is the most common impurity used to produce p-type GaAs semiconductors. To make a n-type GaAs semiconductor, dope with an excess group 5A element or dope with a Group 6A element such as sulfur.

57. $E_{gap} = 2.5 \text{ eV} \times 1.6 \times 10^{-19} \text{ J/eV} = 4.0 \times 10^{-19} \text{ J};$ We want $E_{gap} = E_{light}$, so:

$$E_{light} = \frac{hc}{\lambda}, \quad \lambda = \frac{hc}{E} = \frac{(6.63 \times 10^{-34} \text{ J s}) (3.00 \times 10^8 \text{ m/s})}{4.0 \times 10^{-19} \text{ J}} = 5.0 \times 10^{-7} \text{ m} = 5.0 \times 10^2 \text{ nm}$$

58. $$E = \frac{hc}{\lambda} = \frac{(6.626 \times 10^{-34} \text{ J s}) (2.998 \times 10^8 \text{ m/s})}{730. \times 10^{-9} \text{ m}} = 2.72 \times 10^{-19} \text{ J} = \text{energy of band gap}$$

59.   There is one octahedral hole per closest packed anion in a closest packed structure. If one-half of the octahedral holes are filled, then there is a 2:1 ratio of fluoride ions to cobalt ions in the crystal. The formula is CoF_2.

60.   There are 2 tetrahedral holes per closest packed anion. Let f = fraction of tetrahedral holes filled by the cations.

Na_2O: cation to anion ratio $= \dfrac{2}{1} = \dfrac{2f}{1}$, $f = 1$; All of the tetrahedral holes are filled by Na^+ cations.

CdS: cation to anion ratio $= \dfrac{1}{1} = \dfrac{2f}{1}$, $f = \dfrac{1}{2}$; $\dfrac{1}{2}$ of the tetrahedral holes are filled by Cd^{2+} cations.

ZrI_4: cation to anion ratio $= \dfrac{1}{4} = \dfrac{2f}{1}$, $f = \dfrac{1}{8}$; $\dfrac{1}{8}$ of the tetrahedral holes are filled by Zr^{4+} cations.

61.   Mn ions at 8 corners: 8(1/8) = 1 Mn ion; F ions at 12 edges: 12(1/4) = 3 F ions

Formula is MnF_3. Assuming fluoride is -1 charged, then the charge on Mn is +3.

62.   Since magnesium oxide has the same structure as NaCl, each unit cell contains 4 Mg^{2+} ions and 4 O^{2-} ions. The mass of a unit cell is:

$$4 \text{ MgO molecules} \left(\frac{1 \text{ mol MgO}}{6.022 \times 10^{23} \text{ molecules}} \right) \left(\frac{40.31 \text{ g MgO}}{1 \text{ mol MgO}} \right) = 2.678 \times 10^{-22} \text{ g MgO}$$

Volume of unit cell $= 2.678 \times 10^{-22} \text{ g MgO} \left(\dfrac{1 \text{ cm}^3}{3.58 \text{ g}} \right) = 7.48 \times 10^{-23} \text{ cm}^3$

Volume of unit cell = l^3, l = cube edge length; $l = (7.48 \times 10^{-23} \text{ cm}^3)^{1/3} = 4.21 \times 10^{-8}$ cm = 421 pm

From the NaCl structure in Figure 16.42 of the text, Mg^{2+} and O^{2-} ions should touch along the cube edge, l:

$$l = 2\,r_{Mg^{2+}} + 2\,r_{O^{2-}} = 2\,(65 \text{ pm}) + 2\,(140.\text{ pm}) = 410.\text{ pm}$$

The two values agree within 3%. In the actual crystals the Mg^{2+} and O^{2-} ions may not touch which is assumed in calculating the 410. pm value.

63.   CsCl is a simple cubic array of Cl^- ions with Cs^+ in the middle of each unit cell. There is one Cs^+ and one Cl^- ion in each unit cell. Cs^+ and Cl^- touch along the body diagonal.

body diagonal = $2r_{Cs^+} + 2r_{Cl^-} = \sqrt{3}\,l$, l = length of cube edge

In each unit cell:

mass = 1 CsCl molecule (1 mol/6.022×10^{23} molecules) (168.4 g/mol) = 2.796×10^{-22} g

volume = l^3 = mass/density = 2.796×10^{-22} g/3.97 g cm^{-3} = 7.04×10^{-23} cm^3

$l^3 = 7.04 \times 10^{-23}$ cm^3, $l = 4.13 \times 10^{-8}$ cm = 413 pm = length of cube edge

$2r_{Cs^+} + 2r_{Cl^-} = \sqrt{3}\,l = \sqrt{3}(413 \text{ pm}) = 715$ pm

The distance between ion centers = $r_{Cs^+} + r_{Cl^-} = 715$ pm/2 = 358 pm

From ionic radius: $r_{Cs^+} = 169$ pm and $r_{Cl^-} = 181$ pm; $r_{Cs^+} + r_{Cl^-} = 169 + 181 = 350.$ pm

The distance calculated from the density is 8 pm (2.3%) greater than that calculated from tables of ionic radii.

64.   Total charge of all iron ions present in a formula unit is +2 to balance the -2 charge from the one O atom. The sum of iron ions in a formula unit is 0.950. Let x = fraction Fe^{2+} ions in a formula unit and y = fraction of Fe^{3+} ions present in a formula unit.

Setting up two equations: x + y = 0.950 and 2x + 3y = 2.000

Solving: 2x + 3(0.950 - x) = 2.000, x = 0.85 and y = 0.10

$$\frac{0.10}{0.95} = 0.11 = \text{fraction of Fe as } Fe^{3+}$$

If all Fe^{2+}, then 1.000 Fe^{2+} ion/O^{2-} ion; 1.000 - 0.950 = 0.050 = vacant sites

5.0% of the Fe^{2+} sites are vacant.

65.   For a cubic hole to be filled, the cation to anion radius ratio is between $0.732 < r_+/r_- < 1.00$.

     CsBr: Cs^+ radius = 169 pm, Br^- radius = 195 pm; $r_+/r_- = 169/195 = 0.867$

            From the radius ratio, Cs^+ should occupy cubic holes. The structure should be the CsCl structure. The actual structure is the CsCl structure.

     KF: K^+ radius = 133 pm, F^- radius = 136 pm; $r_+/r_- = 133/136 = 0.978$

            Again, we would predict a structure similar to CsCl, i.e., cations in the middle of a simple cubic array of anions. The actual structure is the NaCl structure.

     The radius ratio rules fail for KF. Exceptions are common for crystal structures.

66.   a.   The NaCl unit cell has a face centered cubic arrangement of the anions with cations in the octahedral holes. There are 4 NaCl formula units per unit cell and since there is a 1:1 ratio of cations to anions in MnO, then there would be 4 MnO formula units per unit cell assuming an NaCl type structure. The CsCl unit cell has a simple cubic structure of anions with the cations in the cubic holes. There is one CsCl formula unit per unit cell so there would be one MnO formula unit per unit cell if a CsCl structure is observed.

$$\frac{\text{molecules MnO}}{\text{unit cell}} = (4.47 \times 10^{-8} \text{ cm})^3 \times \frac{5.28 \text{ g MnO}}{\text{cm}^3} \times \frac{1 \text{ mol MnO}}{70.94 \text{ g MnO}}$$

$$\times \frac{6.022 \times 10^{23} \text{ molecules MnO}}{\text{mol MnO}_4} = 4.00 \text{ molecules MnO}$$

     From the calculation, MnO crystallizes in the NaCl type structure.

   b.   From the NaCl structure and assuming the ions touch each other, then ℓ = cube edge length = $2r_{Mn^{2+}} + 2r_{O^{2-}}$

     $\ell = 4.47 \times 10^{-8}$ cm $= 2_{Mn^{2+}} + 2(1.40 \times 10^{-8}$ cm$)$, $r_{Mn^{2+}} = 8.35 \times 10^{-8}$ cm $= \textbf{84 pm}$

   c. $\dfrac{r_{Mn^{2+}}}{r_{O^{2-}}} = \dfrac{84 \text{ pm}}{140. \text{ pm}} = 0.60$

     From Table 16.6 of the text, octahedral holes should be filled when: $0.414 < r_+/r_- < 0.732$. Since the calculated radius ratio falls within the prescribed limits, then we would expect Mn^{2+} to occupy the octahedral holes formed by the cubic closest packed array of O^{2-} ions (as predicted in part a).

67.   a.   8 corners $\times \dfrac{1/8 \text{ Xe}}{\text{corner}} + 1$ Xe inside cell = 2 Xe;   8 edges $\times \dfrac{1/4 \text{ F}}{\text{edge}} + 2$ F inside cell = 4 F

     Empirical formula is XeF_2. This is also the molecular formula.

b.   For a unit cell:

$$\text{mass} = 2 \text{ XeF}_2 \text{ molecules} \times \frac{1 \text{ mol XeF}_2}{6.022 \times 10^{23} \text{ molecules}} \times \frac{169.3 \text{ g XeF}_2}{\text{mol XeF}_2} = 5.62 \times 10^{-22} \text{ g}$$

$$\text{volume} = (7.02 \times 10^{-8} \text{ cm})(4.32 \times 10^{-8} \text{ cm})(4.32 \times 10^{-8} \text{ cm}) = 1.31 \times 10^{-22} \text{ cm}^3$$

$$\text{density} = d = \frac{\text{mass}}{\text{volume}} = \frac{5.62 \times 10^{-22} \text{ g}}{1.31 \times 10^{-22} \text{ cm}^3} = 4.29 \text{ g/cm}^3$$

68.   a.   The unit cell consists of Ni at the cube corners and Ti at the body center, or Ti at the cube corners and Ni at the body center.

b. $8 \times 1/8 = 1$ atom from corners + 1 atom at body center; Empirical formula = NiTi

c.   Both have coordination numbers of 8 (both are surrounded by 8 atoms).

69.   There are four sulfur ions per unit cell since the sulfur ions are cubic closest packed (face-centered cubic unit cell). Since there are one octahedral hole and two tetrahedral holes per closest packed ion, then each unit cell has 4 octahedral holes and 8 tetrahedral holes. This gives $4 (1/2) = 2$ Al ions per unit cell and $8 (1/8) = 1$ Zn ion per unit cell. The formula of the mineral is Al_2ZnS_4.

70.   a.   1 Ti at body center; $8 \text{ corners} \times \dfrac{1/8 \text{ Ca}}{\text{corner}} = 1 \text{ Ca atom}$

$6 \text{ face centers} \times \dfrac{1/2 \text{ oxygen}}{\text{face center}} = 3 \text{ O atoms};$ Formula = $CaTiO_3$

b.   The Ti atoms are at the corners of each unit cell and the oxygen atoms are at the center of each edge in the unit cell.

Since each of the 12 cube edges is shared by 4 unit cells:

$12 \times 1/4 = 3$ O atoms; $8 \times 1/8 = 1$ Ti atom; 1 Ca at center; Formula = $CaTiO_3$

c.   Six oxygen atoms surround each Ti atom in the extended lattice of both representations.

71.   a.   Y: 1 Y in center; Ba: 2 Ba in center

Cu: $8 \text{ corners} \times \dfrac{1/8 \text{ Cu}}{\text{corner}} = 1 \text{ Cu},$ $8 \text{ edges} \times \dfrac{1/4 \text{ Cu}}{\text{edge}} = 2 \text{ Cu},$ total = 3 Cu atoms

O: $20 \text{ edges} \times \dfrac{1/4 \text{ O}}{\text{edge}} = 5 \text{ oxygen},$ $8 \text{ faces} \times \dfrac{1/2 \text{ O}}{\text{face}} = 4 \text{ oxygen},$ total = 9 O atoms

Formula: $YBa_2Cu_3O_9$

b.   The structure of this superconductor material follows the alternative perovskite structure described in Exercise 16.70 b. The $YBa_2Cu_3O_9$ structure is three of these cubic perovskite unit cells stacked on top of each other. The oxygen atoms are in the same places, Cu takes the place of Ti, two of the calcium atoms are replaced by two barium atoms, and one Ca is replaced by Y.

c.   Y, Ba, and Cu are the same. Some oxygen atoms are missing.

$$12 \text{ edges} \times \frac{1/4 \text{ O}}{\text{edge}} = 3 \text{ O}, \quad 8 \text{ faces} \times \frac{1/2 \text{ O}}{\text{face}} = 4 \text{ O}, \quad \text{total} = 7 \text{ O atoms}$$

Superconductor formula is $YBa_2Cu_3O_7$.

Phase Changes and Phase Diagrams

72.   a.   Condensation: vapor → liquid   b.   Evaporation: liquid → vapor

c.   Sublimation: solid → vapor

d.   A supercooled liquid is a liquid which is at a temperature below its freezing point.

73.   Equilibrium: There is no change in composition; the vapor pressure is constant.

Dynamic: Two processes, vapor → liquid and liquid → vapor, are both occurring but with equal rates so the composition of the vapor is constant.

74.   a.   As the intermolecular forces increase, the rate of evaporation decreases.

b.   As temperature increases, the rate of evaporation increases.

c.   As surface area increases, the rate of evaporation increases.

75.   At 100.°C (373 K), the vapor pressure of H_2O is 1.00 atm = 760. torr.
For water, $\Delta H_{vap} = 40.7$ kJ/mol.

$$\ln\left(\frac{P_1}{P_2}\right) = \frac{\Delta H_{vap}}{R}\left(\frac{1}{T_2} - \frac{1}{T_1}\right) \text{ or } \ln\left(\frac{P_2}{P_1}\right) = \frac{\Delta H_{vap}}{R}\left(\frac{1}{T_1} - \frac{1}{T_2}\right)$$

$$\ln\left(\frac{520. \text{ torr}}{760. \text{ torr}}\right) = \frac{40.7 \times 10^3 \text{ J/mol}}{8.3145 \text{ J K}^{-1}\text{mol}^{-1}}\left(\frac{1}{373 \text{ K}} - \frac{1}{T_2}\right), \quad -7.75 \times 10^{-5} = \left(\frac{1}{373} - \frac{1}{T_2}\right)$$

$$-7.75 \times 10^{-5} = 2.68 \times 10^{-3} - \frac{1}{T_2}, \quad \frac{1}{T_2} = 2.76 \times 10^{-3}, \quad T_2 = \frac{1}{2.76 \times 10^{-3}} = 362 \text{ K or } 89°C$$

$$\ln\left(\frac{P_2}{1.00}\right) = \frac{40.7 \times 10^3 \text{ J/mol}}{8.3145 \text{ J K}^{-1}\text{mol}^{-1}}\left(\frac{1}{373 \text{ K}} - \frac{1}{623 \text{ K}}\right), \quad \ln P_2 = 5.27, \quad P_2 = e^{5.27} = 194 \text{ atm}$$

76. $\ln\left(\dfrac{P_1}{P_2}\right) = \dfrac{\Delta H_{vap}}{R}\left(\dfrac{1}{T_2} - \dfrac{1}{T_1}\right)$; $P_1 = 760.$ torr, $T_1 = 630.$ K; $P_2 = ?$, $T_2 = 298$ K

$\ln\left(\dfrac{760.}{P_2}\right) = \dfrac{59.1 \times 10^3 \text{ J/mol}}{8.3145 \text{ J K}^{-1}\text{mol}^{-1}}\left(\dfrac{1}{298\text{ K}} - \dfrac{1}{630.\text{ K}}\right) = 12.6$

$760./P_2 = e^{12.6}$, $P_2 = 760./(2.97 \times 10^5) = 2.56 \times 10^{-3}$ torr

77. $\ln\left(\dfrac{P_1}{P_2}\right) = \dfrac{\Delta H_{vap}}{R}\left(\dfrac{1}{T_2} - \dfrac{1}{T_1}\right)$

$P_1 = 760.$ torr, $T_1 = 56.5°C + 273.2 = 329.7$ K; $P_2 = 630.$ torr, $T_2 = ?$

$\ln\left(\dfrac{760.}{630.}\right) = \dfrac{32.0 \times 10^3 \text{ J/mol}}{8.3145 \text{ J K}^{-1}\text{mol}^{-1}}\left(\dfrac{1}{T_2} - \dfrac{1}{329.7}\right)$, $0.188 = 3.85 \times 10^3\left(\dfrac{1}{T_2} - 3.033 \times 10^{-3}\right)$

$\dfrac{1}{T_2} - 3.033 \times 10^{-3} = 4.88 \times 10^{-5}$, $\dfrac{1}{T_2} = 3.082 \times 10^{-3}$, $T_2 = 324.5$ K $= 51.3°C$

$\ln\left(\dfrac{630.\text{ torr}}{P_2}\right) = \dfrac{32.0 \times 10^3 \text{ J/mol}}{8.3145 \text{ J K}^{-1}\text{mol}^{-1}}\left(\dfrac{1}{298.2} - \dfrac{1}{324.5}\right)$, $\ln 630. - \ln P_2 = 1.05$

$\ln P_2 = 5.40$, $P_2 = e^{5.40} = 221$ torr

78. The phase change, $H_2O(g) \rightarrow H_2O(l)$, releases heat that can cause additional damage. Also steam can be at a temperature greater than $100°C$.

79. If we graph $\ln P_{vap}$ vs $1/T$, the slope of the resulting straight line will be $-\Delta H_{vap}/R$.

P_{vap}	$\ln P_{vap}$	T (Li)	1/T	T (Mg)	1/T
1 torr	0	1023 K	9.775×10^{-4} K^{-1}	893 K	11.2×10^{-4} K^{-1}
10.	2.3	1163	8.598×10^{-4}	1013	9.872×10^{-4}
100.	4.61	1353	7.391×10^{-4}	1173	8.525×10^{-4}
400.	5.99	1513	6.609×10^{-4}	1313	7.616×10^{-4}
760.	6.63	1583	6.317×10^{-4}	1383	7.231×10^{-4}

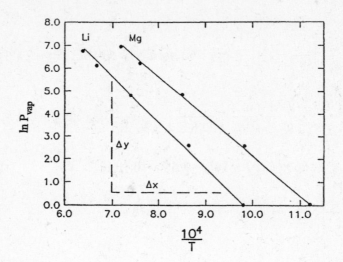

For Li:

We get the slope by taking two points (x, y) that are on the line we draw. For a line:

$$\text{slope} = \frac{\Delta y}{\Delta x} = \frac{y_2 - y_1}{x_2 - x_1}$$

or we can determine the straight line equation using a computer or calculator. The general straight line equation is $y = mx + b$ where m = slope and b = y-intercept.

The equation of the Li line is: $\ln P_{vap} = -1.90 \times 10^4 (1/T) + 18.6$, slope $= -1.90 \times 10^4$ K

Slope $= -\Delta H_{vap}/R$, $\Delta H_{vap} = -\text{slope} \times R = 1.90 \times 10^4$ K $\times$ 8.3145 J K^{-1} mol^{-1}

$\Delta H_{vap} = 1.58 \times 10^5$ J/mol $= 158$ kJ/mol

For Mg:

The equation of the line is: $\ln P_{vap} = -1.67 \times 10^4 (1/T) + 18.7$, slope $= -1.67 \times 10^4$ K

$\Delta H_{vap} = -\text{slope} \times R = 1.67 \times 10^4$ K $\times$ 8.3145 J K^{-1} mol^{-1}, $\Delta H_{vap} = 1.39 \times 10^5$ J/mol $= 139$ kJ/mol

The bonding is stronger in Li since ΔH_{vap} is larger for Li.

80.   Again we graph $\ln P_{vap}$ vs $1/T$. The slope of the line equals $-\Delta H_{vap}/R$.

T(K)	$10^3/T$ (K^{-1})	P_{vap} (torr)	$\ln P_{vap}$
273	3.66	14.4	2.67
283	3.53	26.6	3.28
293	3.41	47.9	3.87
303	3.30	81.3	4.40
313	3.19	133	4.89
323	3.10	208	5.34
353	2.83	670.	6.51

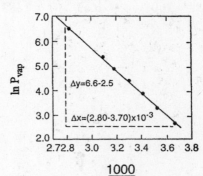

The slope of the line is -4600 K.

$$-4600 \text{ K} = \frac{-\Delta H_{vap}}{R} = \frac{-\Delta H_{vap}}{8.3145 \text{ J K}^{-1} \text{ mol}^{-1}}, \quad \Delta H_{vap} = 38 \text{ kJ/mol}$$

To determine the normal boiling point, we can use the following formula:

$$\ln\left(\frac{P_1}{P_2}\right) = \frac{\Delta H_{vap}}{R}\left(\frac{1}{T_2} - \frac{1}{T_1}\right)$$

At the normal boiling point, the vapor pressure equals 1.00 atm or 760. torr. At 273 K, the vapor pressure is 14.4. torr (from data in the problem).

$$\ln\left(\frac{14.4}{760.}\right) = \frac{38,000 \text{ J/mol}}{8.3145 \text{ J K}^{-1} \text{ mol}^{-1}}\left(\frac{1}{T_2} - \frac{1}{273 \text{ K}}\right), \quad -3.97 = 4.6 \times 10^3 \, (1/T_2 - 3.66 \times 10^{-3})$$

$$-8.6 \times 10^{-4} + 3.66 \times 10^{-3} = 1/T_2 = 2.80 \times 10^{-3}, \quad T_2 = 357 \text{ K} = \text{normal boiling point}$$

81

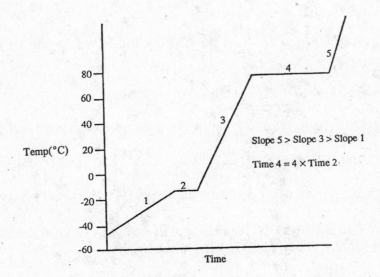

Slope 5 > Slope 3 > Slope 1

Time 4 = 4 × Time 2

82. $X(g, 100.°C) \rightarrow X(g, 75°C), \quad \Delta T = -25°C$

$$q_1 = s_{gas} \times m \times \Delta T = \frac{1.0 \text{ J}}{\text{g °C}} \times 250. \text{ g} \times (-25°C) = -6300 \text{ J} = -6.3 \text{ kJ}$$

$$X(g, 75°C) \rightarrow X(l, 75°C), \quad q_2 = 250. \text{ g} \times \frac{1 \text{ mol}}{75.0 \text{ g}} \times \frac{-20. \text{ kJ}}{\text{mol}} = -67 \text{ kJ}$$

$$X(l, 75°C) \rightarrow X(l, -15°C), \quad q_3 = \frac{2.5 \text{ J}}{\text{g °C}} \times 250. \text{ g} \times (-90.°C) = -56,000 \text{ J} = -56 \text{ kJ}$$

$$X(l, -15°C) \rightarrow X(s, -15°C), \quad q_4 = 250. \text{ g} \times \frac{1 \text{ mol}}{75.0 \text{ g}} \times \frac{-5.0 \text{ kJ}}{\text{mol}} = -17 \text{ kJ}$$

$X(s, -15°C) \rightarrow X(s, -50.°C)$, $q_5 = \dfrac{3.0 \text{ J}}{\text{g °C}} \times 250. \text{ g} \times (-35°C) = -26,000 \text{ J} = -26 \text{ kJ}$

$q_{total} = q_1 + q_2 + q_3 + q_4 + q_5 = -6.3 - 67 - 56 - 17 - 26 = -172 \text{ kJ}$

83.   To calculate q_{total}, break up the heating process into five steps.

$H_2O(s, -20.°C) \rightarrow H_2O(s, 0°C)$, $\Delta T = 20.°C$ and specific heat capacity of ice $= s_{ice} = 2.1 \text{ J °C}^{-1} \text{ g}^{-1}$

$q_1 = s_{ice} \times m \times \Delta T = \dfrac{2.1 \text{ J}}{\text{g °C}} \times 5.00 \times 10^2 \text{ g} \times 20.°C = 2.1 \times 10^4 \text{ J} = 21 \text{ kJ}$

$H_2O(s, 0°C) \rightarrow H_2O(l, 0°C)$, $q_2 = 5.00 \times 10^2 \text{ g } H_2O \times \dfrac{1 \text{ mol}}{18.02 \text{ g}} \times \dfrac{6.01 \text{ kJ}}{\text{mol}} = 167 \text{ kJ}$

$H_2O(l, 0°C) \rightarrow H_2O(l, 100.°C)$, $q_3 = \dfrac{4.2 \text{ J}}{\text{g °C}} \times 5.00 \times 10^2 \text{ g} \times 100.°C = 2.1 \times 10^5 \text{ J} = 210 \text{ kJ}$

$H_2O(l, 100.°C) \rightarrow H_2O(g, 100.°C)$, $q_4 = 5.00 \times 10^2 \text{ g} \times \dfrac{1 \text{ mol}}{18.02 \text{ g}} \times \dfrac{40.7 \text{ kJ}}{\text{mol}} = 1130 \text{ kJ}$

$H_2O(g, 100.°C) \rightarrow H_2O(g, 250.°C)$, $q_5 = \dfrac{2.0 \text{ J}}{\text{g °C}} \times 5.00 \times 10^2 \text{ g} \times 150.°C = 1.5 \times 10^5 \text{ J} = 150 \text{ kJ}$

$q_{total} = q_1 + q_2 + q_3 + q_4 + q_5 = 21 + 167 + 210 + 1130 + 150 = 1680 \text{ kJ}$

84. $H_2O(g, 125°C) \rightarrow H_2O(g, 100.°C)$, $q_1 = 2.0 \text{ J °C}^{-1} \text{ g}^{-1} \times 75.0 \text{ g} \times (-25°C) = -3800 \text{ J} = -3.8 \text{ kJ}$

$H_2O(g, 100.°C) \rightarrow H_2O(l, 100.°C)$, $q_2 = 75.0 \text{ g} \times \dfrac{1 \text{ mol}}{18.02 \text{ g}} \times \dfrac{-40.7 \text{ kJ}}{\text{mol}} = -169 \text{ kJ}$

$H_2O(l, 100.°C) \rightarrow H_2O(l, 0°C)$, $q_3 = 4.2 \text{ J °C}^{-1} \text{ g}^{-1} \times 75.0 \text{ g} \times (-100.°C) = -32,000 \text{ J} = -32 \text{ kJ}$

To convert $H_2O(g)$ at 125°C to $H_2O(l)$ at 0°C requires (-3.8 kJ - 169 kJ - 32 kJ =) -205 kJ of heat removed. To convert from $H_2O(l)$ at 0°C to $H_2O(s)$ at 0°C requires:

$q_4 = 75.0 \text{ g} \times \dfrac{1 \text{ mol}}{18.02 \text{ g}} \times \dfrac{-6.01 \text{ kJ}}{\text{mol}} = -25.0 \text{ kJ}$

This amount of energy puts us over the -215 kJ limit (-205 kJ - 25.0 kJ = -230. kJ). Therefore, a mixture of $H_2O(s)$ and $H_2O(l)$ will be present at 0°C when 215 kJ of heat are removed from the gas sample.

85.   Heat released $= 0.250 \text{ g Na} \times \dfrac{1 \text{ mol}}{22.99 \text{ g}} \times \dfrac{368 \text{ kJ}}{2 \text{ mol}} = 2.00 \text{ kJ}$

To melt 50.0 g of ice requires: $50.0 \text{ g ice} \times \dfrac{1 \text{ mol } H_2O}{18.02 \text{ g}} \times \dfrac{6.01 \text{ kJ}}{\text{mol}} = 16.7 \text{ kJ}$

The reaction doesn't release enough heat to melt all of the ice. The temperature will remain at 0°C.

86.   In order to set-up an equation, we need to know what phase exists at the final temperature. To heat 20.0 g of ice from -10.0°C to 0.0°C requires:

$$q = \frac{2.08 \text{ J}}{\text{g °C}} \times 20.0 \text{ g} \times 10.0°C = 416 \text{ J}$$

To convert ice to water at 0.0°C requires:

$$q = 20.0 \text{ g} \times \frac{1 \text{ mol}}{18.02} \times \frac{6.01 \text{ kJ}}{\text{mol}} = 6.67 \text{ kJ} = 6670 \text{ J}$$

To chill 100.0 g of water from 80.0°C to 0.0° requires:

$$q = \frac{4.18 \text{ J}}{\text{g °C}} \times 100.0 \text{ g} \times 80.0°C = 33{,}400 \text{ J}$$

From the heat values above, the liquid phase exists once the final temperature is reached (a lot more heat is lost when the 80.0 g of water is cooled to 0.0°C than the heat required to convert the ice into water). To calculate the final temperature, we will equate the heat gain by the ice to the heat loss by the water. We will keep all quantities positive in order to avoid sign errors. The heat gain by ice will be the 416 J required to convert the ice to 0.0°C plus the 6670 J required to convert ice at 0.0°C into water at 0.0°C plus the heat required to raise the temperature from 0.0°C to the final temperature.

$$\text{heat gain by ice} = 416 \text{ J} + 6670 \text{ J} + \frac{4.18 \text{ J}}{\text{g °C}} \times 20.0 \text{ g} \times (T_f - 0.0°C) = 7.09 \times 10^3 + 83.6 \, T_f$$

$$\text{heat loss by water} = \frac{4.18 \text{ J}}{\text{g °C}} \times 100.0 \text{ g} \times (80.0°C - T_f) = 3.34 \times 10^4 - 418 \, T_f$$

Solving for the final temperature:

$$7.09 \times 10^3 + 83.6 \, T_f = 3.34 \times 10^4 - 418 \, T_f, \; 502 \, T_f = 2.63 \times 10^4, \; T_f = 52.4°C$$

87.   Total mass H_2O = 18 cubes $\times \dfrac{30.0 \text{ g}}{\text{cube}}$ = 540. g; 540. g $H_2O \times \dfrac{1 \text{ mol } H_2O}{18.02 \text{ g}}$ = 30.0 mol H_2O

Heat removed to produce ice at -5.0°C:

$$\left(\frac{4.18 \text{ J}}{\text{g °C}} \times 540. \text{ g} \times 22.0 \text{ °C} \right) + \left(\frac{6.01 \times 10^3 \text{ J}}{\text{mol}} \times 30.0 \text{ mol} \right) + \left(\frac{2.08 \text{ J}}{\text{g °C}} \times 540. \text{ g} \times 5.0 \text{ °C} \right)$$

$$= 4.97 \times 10^4 \text{ J} + 1.80 \times 10^5 \text{ J} + 5.6 \times 10^3 \text{ J} = 2.35 \times 10^5 \text{ J}$$

$2.35 \times 10^5 \text{ J} \times \dfrac{1 \text{ g } CF_2Cl_2}{158 \text{ J}} = 1.49 \times 10^3 \text{ g } CF_2Cl_2$ must be vaporized.

88. $1.00 \text{ lb} \times \dfrac{454 \text{ g}}{\text{lb}} = 454 \text{ g } H_2O$; A change of 1.00°F is equal to a change of 5/9°C.

The amount of heat in J in 1 Btu is: $\dfrac{4.18 \text{ J}}{\text{g °C}} \times 454 \text{ g} \times \dfrac{5}{9}°C = 1.05 \times 10^3 \text{ J}$ or 1.05 kJ

It takes 40.7 kJ to vaporize 1 mol H_2O (ΔH_{vap}). Combining these:

$$\frac{1.00 \times 10^4 \text{ Btu}}{\text{hr}} \times \frac{1.05 \text{ kJ}}{\text{Btu}} \times \frac{1 \text{ mol H}_2\text{O}}{40.7 \text{ kJ}} = 258 \text{ mol/hr}$$

or: $\dfrac{258 \text{ mol}}{\text{hr}} \times \dfrac{18.02 \text{ g H}_2\text{O}}{\text{mol}} = 4650 \text{ g/hr} = 4.65 \text{ kg/hr}$

89. At any temperature, the plot tells us that substance A has a higher vapor pressure than substance B, with substance C having the lowest vapor pressure. Therefore, the substance with the weakest intermolecular forces is A, and the substance with the strongest intermolecular forces is C.

    NH_3 can form hydrogen bonding interactions while the others cannot. Substance C is NH_3. The other two are nonpolar compounds with only London dispersion forces. Since CH_4 is smaller than SiH_4, CH_4 will have weaker LD forces and is substance A. Therefore, substance B is SiH_4.

90. The following sketch of the Br_2 phase diagram is not to scale. Since the triple point of Br_2 is at a temperature below the freezing point of Br_2, the slope of the solid-liquid line is positive.

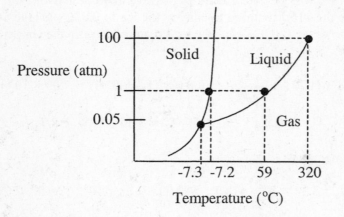

The positive slopes of all the lines indicate that $Br_2(s)$ is more dense than $Br_2(l)$ which is more dense than $Br_2(g)$. At room temperature ($\sim 22\,^\circ$C) and 1 atm, $Br_2(l)$ is the stable phase. $Br_2(l)$ cannot exist at a temperature below the triple point temperature of -7.3 $^\circ$C and at a temperature above the critical point temperature of 320 $^\circ$C. The phase changes that occur as temperature is increased at 0.10 atm are solid → liquid → gas.

91.   A: solid;   B: liquid;   C: vapor

        D: solid + vapor;   E: solid + liquid + vapor

        F: liquid + vapor;   G: liquid + vapor;   H: vapor

        triple point: E;   critical point: G

        normal freezing point: temperature at which solid - liquid line is at 1.0 atm (see following plot).

        normal boiling point: temperature at which liquid - vapor line is at 1.0 atm (see following plot).

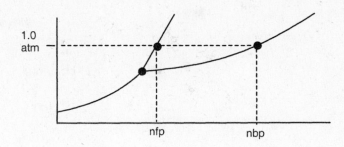

Since the solid-liquid equilibrium line has a positive slope, then the solid phase is denser than the liquid phase.

92.   a.   3

       b.   Triple point at 95.31°C: rhombic, monoclinic, gas
            Triple point at 115.18°C: monoclinic, liquid, gas
            Triple point at 153°C: rhombic, monoclinic, liquid

       c.   From the phase diagram, the rhombic phase is stable at T ≈ 20°C and P = 1.0 atm.

       d.   Yes, monoclinic sulfur and vapor (gas) share a common boundary line in the phase diagram.

       e.   Normal melting point = 115.21°C; normal boiling point = 444.6°C; The normal melting and boiling points occur at P = 1.0 atm.

       f.   Rhombic, since the rhombic-monoclinic equilibrium line has a positive slope.

93.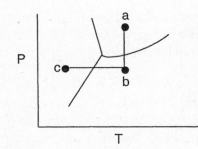

As P is lowered, we go from a to b on the phase diagram. The water boils. The evaporation of the water is endothermic and the water is cooled (b → c), forming some ice. If the pump is left on, the ice will sublime until none is left. This is the basis of freeze drying.

Additional Exercises

94.   One B atom and one N atom together have the same number of electrons as two C atoms. The description of physical properties sound a lot like the properties of graphite and diamond, the two solid forms of carbon. The two forms of BN have structures similar to graphite and diamond.

95.   If TiO_2 conducts electricity as a liquid then it is an ionic solid; if not then TiO_2 is a network solid.

96.   Sublimation will occur allowing water to escape as $H_2O(g)$.

97.

··· = H-bonding

98. CH_3CO_2H: H-bonding + dipole forces + LD forces

   CH_2ClCO_2H: H-bonding + larger electronegative atom replacing H (greater dipole) + LD forces

   $CH_3CO_2CH_3$:   dipole forces (no H-bonding) + LD forces

   From the intermolecular forces listed above, we predict $CH_3CO_2CH_3$ to have the weakest intermolecular forces and CH_2ClCO_2H to have the strongest. The boiling points are consistent with this view.

99. B_2H_6:   This compound contains only nonmetals so it is probably a molecular solid with covalent bonding. The low boiling point confirms this.

   SiO_2:   This is the empirical formula for quartz, which is a network solid.

   CsI: This is a metal bonded to a nonmetal, which generally form ionic solids. The electrical conductivity in aqueous solution confirms this.

   W: Tungsten is a metallic solid as the conductivity data confirms.

100.   The critical temperature is the temperature above which the vapor cannot be liquefied no matter what pressure is applied. Since N_2 has a critical temperature below room temperature (~22°C), it cannot be liquefied at room temperature. NH_3, with a critical temperature above room temperature, can be liquefied at room temperature.

101.   If we extend the liquid-vapor line of the water phase diagram to below the freezing point, we find that supercooled water will have a higher vapor pressure than ice at -10°C (see Figure 16.51 of the text). To achieve equilibrium there must be a constant vapor pressure. Over time super-cooled water will be transformed through the vapor into ice in an attempt to equilibrate the vapor pressure. Eventually there will only be ice at -10°C and its vapor at the vapor pressure given by the solid-vapor line in the phase diagram.

102.   a.   two

   b.   Higher pressure triple point: graphite, diamond and liquid; Lower pressure triple point: graphite, liquid and vapor

   c.   It is converted to diamond (the more dense solid form).

d. Diamond is more dense which is why graphite can be converted to diamond by applying pressure.

103.

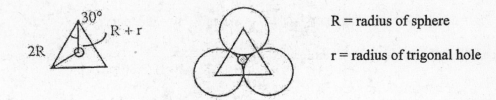

R = radius of sphere

r = radius of trigonal hole

For a right angle triangle (opposite side not drawn in):

$$\cos 30° = \frac{\text{adjacent}}{\text{hypotenuse}} = \frac{R}{R + r}, \quad 0.866 = \frac{R}{R + r}$$

$$0.866\,r = R - 0.866\,R, \quad r = \left(\frac{0.134}{0.866}\right) \times R = 0.155\,R$$

The cation must have a radius which is 0.155 times the radius of the spheres to just fit into the trigonal hole.

104. The unit cell is a parallelpiped. There are three parallelpiped unit cells in a hexagon. In each parallelpiped, there are atoms at each of the 8 corners (shared by eight unit cells) plus one atom inside the unit cell: 2/3 of one atom plus 1/6 from each of two others. Thus, there are two atoms in the unit cell.

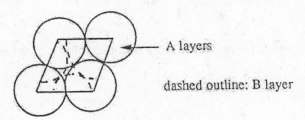

A layers

dashed outline: B layer

105. Ar is cubic closest packed. There are 4 Ar atoms per unit cell and with a face-centered unit cell, the atoms touch along the face diagonal.

face diagonal = $4r = \sqrt{2}\,l$, l = length of cube edge; $l = 4(190.\text{ pm})/\sqrt{2} = 537$ pm $= 5.37 \times 10^{-8}$ cm

$$\text{density} = \frac{\text{mass}}{\text{volume}} = \frac{4 \text{ atoms} \times \dfrac{1 \text{ mol}}{6.022 \times 10^{23} \text{ atoms}} \times \dfrac{39.95 \text{ g}}{\text{mol}}}{(5.37 \times 10^{-8} \text{ cm})^3} = 1.71 \text{ g/cm}^3$$

106. The ionic radius is 148 pm for Rb^+ and 181 pm for Cl^-. Using these values, lets calculate the density of the two structures.

Normal pressure: Rb^+Cl^- touch along cube edge (forms NaCl structure).

cube edge = $l = 2(148 + 181) = 658$ pm $= 6.58 \times 10^{-8}$ cm; There are 4 RbCl molecules/unit cell.

$$\text{density} = d = \frac{4(85.47) + 4(35.45)}{6.022 \times 10^{23} \, (6.58 \times 10^{-8})^3} = 2.82 \text{ g/cm}^3$$

High pressure: Rb^+Cl^- touch along body diagonal (forms CsCl structure).

$$2r_- + 2r_+ = 658 \text{ pm} = \text{body diagonal} = \sqrt{3} \, l, \; l = 658 \text{ pm}/\sqrt{3} = 380. \text{ pm}$$

Since each unit cell contains 1 RbCl molecule: $d = \dfrac{85.47 + 35.45}{(6.022 \times 10^{23}) \, (3.80 \times 10^{-8})^3} = 3.66 \text{ g/cm}^3$

The high pressure form has the higher density. The density ratio is 3.66/2.82 = 1.30. We would expect this since the effect of pressure is to push things closer together and thus, increase density.

107.   Out of 100.00 g: $28.31 \text{ g O} \times \dfrac{1 \text{ mol}}{15.999 \text{ g}} = 1.769 \text{ mol O}$; $71.69 \text{ g Ti} \times \dfrac{1 \text{ mol}}{47.88 \text{ g}} = 1.497 \text{ mol Ti}$

Formula is $TiO_{1.182}$ or $Ti_{0.8462}O$.

For $Ti_{0.8462}O$, let $x = Ti^{2+}$ per mol O^{2-} and $y = Ti^{3+}$ per mol O^{2-}. Setting up two equations and solving:

$$x + y = 0.8462 \text{ and } 2x + 3y = 2; \; 2x + 3(0.8462 - x) = 2$$

$$x = 0.539 \text{ mol } Ti^{2+}/\text{mol } O^{2-} \text{ and } y = 0.307 \text{ mol } Ti^{3+}/\text{mol } O^{2-}$$

$$\frac{0.539}{0.8462} \times 100 = 63.7\% \text{ of the titanium is } Ti^{2+} \text{ and } 36.3\% \text{ is } Ti^{3+}.$$

108.   First we need to get the empirical formula of spinel. Assume 100.0 g of spinel:

$$37.9 \text{ g Al} \times \frac{1 \text{ mol Al}}{26.98 \text{ g Al}} = 1.40 \text{ mol Al}$$

The mole ratios are 2:1:4.

$$17.1 \text{ g Mg} \times \frac{1 \text{ mol Mg}}{24.31 \text{ g Mg}} = 0.703 \text{ mol Mg}$$

Empirical Formula = Al_2MgO_4

$$45.0 \text{ g O} \times \frac{1 \text{ mol O}}{16.00 \text{ g O}} = 2.81 \text{ mol O}$$

Assume each unit cell contains an integral value (n) of Al_2MgO_4 formula units. Each Al_2MgO_4 formula unit has a mass of: $24.31 + 2(26.98) + 4(16.00) = 142.27$ g/mol

$$\text{density} = \frac{n \text{ formula units} \times \dfrac{1 \text{ mol}}{6.022 \times 10^{23} \text{ formula units}} \times \dfrac{142.27 \text{ g}}{\text{mol}}}{(8.09 \times 10^{-8} \text{ cm})^3} = \frac{3.57 \text{ g}}{\text{cm}^3}$$

Solving: n = 8.00

Each unit cell has 8 formula units of Al_2MgO_4 or 16 Al, 8 Mg and 32 O atoms.

109. $24.7 \text{ g C}_6\text{H}_6 \times \dfrac{1 \text{ mol}}{78.11 \text{ g}} = 0.316 \text{ mol C}_6\text{H}_6$

$P_{C_6H_6} = \dfrac{nRT}{V} = \dfrac{0.316 \text{ mol} \times \dfrac{0.08206 \text{ L atm}}{\text{mol K}} \times 293.2 \text{ K}}{100.0 \text{ L}} = 0.0760 \text{ atm or } 57.8 \text{ torr}$

110. $100.0 \text{ g N}_2 \times \dfrac{1 \text{ mol N}_2}{28.014 \text{ g N}_2} = 3.570 \text{ mol N}_2; \quad P_{H_2O} = \chi_{H_2O}P_{tot}, \; \chi_{H_2O} = \dfrac{23.8 \text{ torr}}{700. \text{ torr}} = 0.0340$

$\chi_{H_2O} = 0.0340 = \dfrac{n_{H_2O}}{n_{N_2} + n_{H_2O}} = \dfrac{n_{H_2O}}{3.570 + n_{H_2O}}, \quad n_{H_2O} = 0.121 + 0.0340 \, n_{H_2O}$

$n_{H_2O} = 0.125 \text{ mol}; \quad 0.125 \text{ mol} \times 18.02 \text{ g/mol} = 2.25 \text{ g H}_2\text{O}$

111. $w = -P\Delta V; \quad$ Assume const P of 1 atm.

$V_{373} = \dfrac{nRT}{P} = \dfrac{1.00 \, (0.08206) \, (373)}{1.00} = 30.6 \text{ L for one mol of water vapor}$

Since the density of $H_2O(l)$ is 1.00 g/cm^3, 1.00 mol of $H_2O(l)$ occupies 18.0 cm^3 or 0.0180 L.

$w = -1.00 \text{ atm} \, (30.6 \text{ L} - 0.0180 \text{ L}) = -30.6 \text{ L atm}$

$w = -30.6 \text{ L atm} \times 101.3 \text{ J L}^{-1} \text{ atm}^{-1} = -3.10 \times 10^3 \text{ J} = -3.10 \text{ kJ}$

$\Delta E = q + w = 41.16 \text{ kJ} - 3.10 \text{ kJ} = 38.06 \text{ kJ}$

$\dfrac{38.06}{41.16} \times 100 = 92.47\%$ of the energy goes to increase the internal energy of the water.

The remainder of the energy (7.53%) goes to do work against the atmosphere.

112.   a.   The arrangement of the layers are:

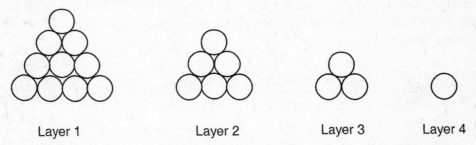

Layer 1   Layer 2   Layer 3   Layer 4

A total of 20 cannon balls will be needed.

b.   The layering alternates abcabc which is cubic closest packing.

c.   tetrahedron

113.   The three sheets of B's form a cube. In this cubic unit cell there are B atoms at every face, B atoms at every edge, B atoms at every corner and one B atom in the center. A representation of this cube is:

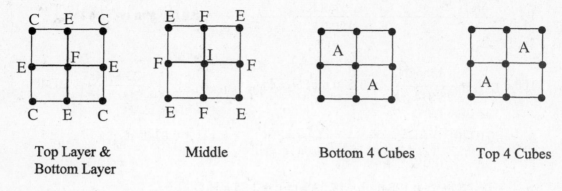

| Top Layer & Bottom Layer | Middle | Bottom 4 Cubes | Top 4 Cubes |

C = corner;   E = edge;   F = face;   I = inside

Each unit cell of B atoms contains 4 A atoms. The number of B atoms in each unit cell is:

(8 corners × 1/8) + (6 faces × 1/2) + (12 edges × 1/4) + (1 middle B) = 8 B atoms

The empirical formula is AB_2.

Each A atom is in a cubic hole of B atoms so 8 B atoms surround each A atom. This will also be true in the extended lattice. The structure of B atoms in the unit cell is a cubic arrangement with B atoms at every face, edge, corner and center of the cube.

114. $$\frac{\text{density}_{Mn}}{\text{density}_{Cu}} = \frac{\text{mass}_{Mn} \times \text{volume}_{Cu}}{\text{volume}_{Mn} \times \text{mass}_{Cu}} = \frac{\text{mass}_{Mn}}{\text{mass}_{Cu}} \times \frac{\text{volume}_{Cu}}{\text{volume}_{Mn}}$$

The type of cubic cell formed is not important; only that Cu and Mn crystallizes in the <u>same</u> type of cubic unit cell is important. Each cubic unit cell has a specific relationship between the cube edge length, ℓ, and the radius, r. In all cases $\ell \propto r$. Therefore, $V \propto \ell^3 \propto r^3$. For the mass ratio, we can use the molar masses of Mn and Cu since each unit cell must contain the same number of Mn and Cu atoms. Solving:

$$\frac{\text{density}_{Mn}}{\text{density}_{Cu}} = \frac{\text{mass}_{Mn}}{\text{mass}_{Cu}} \times \frac{\text{volume}_{Cu}}{\text{volume}_{Mn}} = \frac{54.94 \text{ g/mol}}{63.55 \text{ g/mol}} \times \frac{(r_{Cu})^3}{(1.056\, r_{Cu})^3}$$

$$\frac{\text{density}_{Mn}}{\text{density}_{Cu}} = 0.8645 \times \left(\frac{1}{1.056}\right)^3 = 0.7341$$

$\text{density}_{Mn} = 0.7341 \times \text{density}_{Cu} = 0.7341 \times 8.96 \text{ g/cm}^3 = 6.58 \text{ g/cm}^3$

Challenge Problems

115.   For water vapor at 30.0°C and 31.824 torr:

$$\text{density} = \frac{P(\text{molar mass})}{RT} = \frac{\left(\dfrac{31.824 \text{ atm}}{760}\right)\left(\dfrac{18.015 \text{ g}}{\text{mol}}\right)}{\dfrac{0.08206 \text{ L atm}}{\text{mol K}} \times 303.2 \text{ K}} = 0.03032 \text{ g/L}$$

The volume of one molecule is proportional to d^3 where d is the average distance between molecules. For a large sample of molecules, the volume is still proportional to d^3. So:

$$\frac{V_{gas}}{V_{liq}} = \frac{d_{gas}^3}{d_{liq}^3}$$

If we have 0.99567 g H_2O, then $V_{liq} = 1.0000 \text{ cm}^3 = 1.0000 \times 10^{-3}$ L.

$V_{gas} = 0.99567 \text{ g} \times 1 \text{ L}/0.03032 \text{ g} = 32.84$ L

$$\frac{d_{gas}^3}{d_{liq}^3} = \frac{32.84 \text{ L}}{1.0000 \times 10^{-3} \text{ L}} = 3.284 \times 10^4, \quad \frac{d_{gas}}{d_{liq}} = (3.284 \times 10^4)^{1/3} = 32.02, \quad \frac{d_{liq}}{d_{gas}} = 0.03123$$

116. $(\text{body diagonal})^2 = (\text{face diagonal})^2 + (\text{cube edge length})^2$

In a simple cubic structure, the atoms touch on cube edge so the cube edge = 2R.

face diagonal $= \sqrt{(2R)^2 + (2R)^2} = \sqrt{4R^2 + 4R^2} = R\sqrt{8} = 2\sqrt{2}\,R$

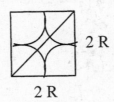

2 R

2 R

body diagonal $= \sqrt{(2\sqrt{2}\,R)^2 + 2R^2} = \sqrt{12R^2} = 2\sqrt{3}\,R$

The diameter of the hole = body diagonal - 2 radius of atoms at corners.

$2\sqrt{3}\,R - 2R$, thus the radius of the hole is $\dfrac{2\sqrt{3}\,R - 2R}{2} = \left(\dfrac{2\sqrt{3} - 2}{2}\right)(R)$

The volume of the hole is: $\dfrac{4}{3}\pi\left[\left(\dfrac{2\sqrt{3} - 2}{2}\right)R\right]^3$

117.   a.   Structure a:

Ba: 2 Ba inside unit cell;   Tl: 8 corners $\times \dfrac{1/8 \text{ Tl}}{\text{corner}} = 1$ Tl;   Cu: 4 edges $\times \dfrac{1/4 \text{ Cu}}{\text{edge}} = 1$ Cu

O: 6 faces $\times \dfrac{1/2 \text{ O}}{\text{face}} + 8$ edges $\times \dfrac{1/4 \text{ O}}{\text{edge}} = 5$ O

Formula = $TlBa_2CuO_5$

Structure b:

Tl and Ba are the same as in structure a.

Ca: 1 Ca inside unit cell;   Cu: 8 edges $\times \dfrac{1/4 \text{ Cu}}{\text{edge}} = 2$ Cu

O: 10 faces $\times \dfrac{1/2 \text{ O}}{\text{face}} + 8$ edges $\times \dfrac{1/4 \text{ O}}{\text{edge}} = 7$ O

Formula = $TlBa_2CaCu_2O_7$

Structure c:

Tl and Ba are the same and two Ca atoms are located inside the unit cell.

Cu: 12 edges $\times \dfrac{1/4 \text{ Cu}}{\text{edge}} = 3$ Cu;   O: 14 faces $\times \dfrac{1/2 \text{ O}}{\text{face}} + 8$ edges $\times \dfrac{1/4 \text{ O}}{\text{edge}} = 9$ O

Formula: $TlBa_2Ca_2Cu_3O_9$

Structure d: Following similar calculations, formula = $TlBa_2Ca_3Cu_4O_{11}$

b.   Structure a has one planar sheet of Cu and O atoms and the number increases by one for each of the remaining structures. The order of superconductivity temperature from lowest to highest temperature is: a < b < c < d.

c. $TlBa_2CuO_5$: $3 + 2(2) + x + 5(-2) = 0$, $x = +3$
Only Cu^{3+} is present in each formula unit.

$TlBa_2CaCu_2O_7$: $3 + 2(2) + 2 + 2(x) + 7(-2) = 0$, $x = +5/2$
Each formula unit contains 1 Cu^{2+} and 1 Cu^{3+}.

$TlBa_2Ca_2Cu_3O_9$: $3 + 2(2) + 2(2) + 3(x) + 9(-2) = 0$, $x = +7/3$
Each formula unit contains 2 Cu^{2+} and 1 Cu^{3+}.

$TlBa_2Ca_3Cu_4O_{11}$: $3 + 2(2) + 3(2) + 4(x) + 11(-2) = 0$, $x = +9/4$
Each formula unit contains 3 Cu^{2+} and 1 Cu^{3+}.

d.   This superconductor material achieves variable copper oxidation states by varying the numbers of Ca, Cu and O in each unit cell. The mixtures of copper oxidation states is discussed in part c. The superconductor material in Exercise 16.71 achieves variable copper oxidation states by omitting oxygen at various sites in the lattice.

118.   The liquid compound must have stronger IM forces.

$$
\begin{array}{ccc}
\text{H} & \text{H} & \\
| & | & \\
\text{H}-\text{C}-\text{C}-\ddot{\text{O}}-\text{H} & & \text{exhibits hydrogen bonding while} \\
| & | & \\
\text{H} & \text{H} &
\end{array}
$$

$$
\begin{array}{ccc}
\text{H} & & \text{H} \\
| & & | \\
\text{H}-\text{C}-\text{O}-\text{C}-\text{H} & & \text{does not} \\
| & & | \\
\text{H} & & \text{H}
\end{array}
$$

Thus, the first compound (ethyl alcohol) is a liquid while the second (dimethyl ether) is a gas.

119.   For an octahedral hole; the geometry is:

2R + 2r $\diagup$ 45°

2R

R = Cl⁻ radius

r = Li⁺ radius

From the diagram: $\cos 45° = \dfrac{\text{adjacent}}{\text{hypotenuse}} = \dfrac{2R}{2R + 2r} = \dfrac{R}{R + r}$, $0.707 = \dfrac{R}{R + r}$

R = 0.707 (R + r), r = 0.414 R

LiCl unit cell:

length of cube edge = 2R + 2r = 514 pm

2R + 2(0.414 R) = 514 pm, R = 182 pm = Cl⁻ radius

2(182 pm) + 2r = 514 pm, r = 75 pm = Li⁺ radius

From Figure 13.7, the Li⁺ radius is 60 pm and the Cl⁻ radius is 181 pm. The Li⁺ ion is much smaller than calculated. This probably means that the ions are not actually in contact with each other. The octahedral holes are larger than the Li⁺ ion.

120. See Exercise 16.50 for the face-centered calculation and the simple cubic calculation. The packing efficiency of the face-centered cubic closest packing is 74.06% while simple cubic is 52.36%. For the body-centered calculation:

Let ℓ = cube edge length

$\sqrt{2}\,\ell$ = face diagonal

$(\text{body diagonal})^2 = \ell^2 + (\sqrt{2}\,\ell)^2$, body diagonal $= \ell\sqrt{3}$

The atoms touch along the body diagonal.

body diagonal $= 4\,r = \ell\sqrt{3}, \ell = \dfrac{4\,r}{\sqrt{3}}$

BCC contains two net atoms.

packing efficiency $= \dfrac{2(4/3\,\pi\,r^3)}{\left(\dfrac{4\,r}{\sqrt{3}}\right)^3} = \dfrac{\sqrt{3}\,\pi}{8} = 0.6802$ or 68.02%

The fcc provides the most efficient cubic packing.

121. Use radius ratios and the information in Table 16.6 of the text to determine the type of structure. In the NaCl type cubic unit cell, the cations occupy octahedral holes; in the CsCl type cubic unit cell, the cations occupy cubic holes; in the Zn S type cubic unit cell, the cations occupy the tetrahedral holes. To determine the fraction of holes filled, the stoichiometry given in the formula will determine this. And finally, to determine the density, use the geometry relationships unique to each structure to determine the edge length (assuming the cations and anions touch); then go on to estimate the density.

For SnO_2: $\dfrac{r_+}{r_-} = \dfrac{71\text{ pm}}{140.\text{ pm}} = 0.51$

Radius ratios predict that octahedral holes will be filled. Therefore, we predict the NaCl type unit cell for SnO_2. Since there is 1 octahedral hole per closest packed anion (O^{2-}), then one-half of the octahedral holes will be filled by the Sn^{4+} cations. This is required by the 1:2 mol ratio of cations to anions in the SnO_2 formula.

To estimate the density in an NaCl type unit cell, the cations and anions are assumed to touch along the cube edge. Since the unit cell contains four O^{2-} ions, then two SnO_2 formula units are contained per unit cell.

ℓ = cube edge length $= 2r_{Sn^{4+}} + 2r_{O^{2-}} = 2(71\text{ pm}) + 2(140.\text{ pm}) = 422\text{ pm}$

density $= \dfrac{\text{mass}}{\text{volume}} = \dfrac{2\text{ SnO}_2\text{ units} \times \dfrac{1\text{ mol SnO}_2}{6.022\times10^{23}\text{ units}} \times \dfrac{150.7\text{ g SnO}_2}{\text{mol SnO}_2}}{(4.22\times10^{-8}\text{ cm})^3} = 6.66\text{ g/cm}^3$

For AlP: $\dfrac{r_+}{r_-} = \dfrac{50.\ \text{pm}}{212\ \text{pm}} = 0.24$

Radius ratios predict tetrahedral holes for the Al^{3+} cations, which occurs in a ZnS type unit cell. Since there are two tetrahedral holes per closest packed anion (P^{3-}), then Al^{3+} ions occupy one-half of the tetrahedral holes. This is required to give the 1:1 formula stoichiometry in AlP.

In a ZnS type unit cell, it is the body diagonal of the unit cell that allows determination of the cube edge length (ℓ). From Figures 16.38 and 16.39 of the text, the body diagonal of a cube that encloses each tetrahedral hole has a length equal to $2r_+ + 2r_-$. From Figure 16.41a, each AlP unit cell consists of eight of these smaller cubes. The length of the body diagonal of the unit cell is equal to $4r_+ + 4r_-$. This relationship, along with realizing that each unit cell contains four P^{3-} ions so four AlP formula units are contained per unit cell, allows determination of the density.

body diagonal $= \sqrt{3}\,\ell = 4r_{Al^{3+}} + 4r_{P^{3-}}$, $\ell = \dfrac{4(50.\ \text{pm}) + 4(212\ \text{pm})}{\sqrt{3}} = 605\ \text{pm}$

density $= \dfrac{\text{mass}}{\text{volume}} = \dfrac{4\ \text{AlP units} \times \dfrac{1\ \text{mol AlP}}{6.022 \times 10^{23}\ \text{units}} \times \dfrac{57.95\ \text{g AlP}}{1\ \text{mol AlP}}}{(6.05 \times 10^{-8}\ \text{cm})^3} = 1.74\ \text{g/cm}^3$

For BaO: $\dfrac{r_+}{r_-} = \dfrac{135\ \text{pm}}{140.\ \text{pm}} = 0.964$

Radius ratios predicts that Ba^{2+} ions occupy cubic holes. This is seen in CsCl type unit cells. Since there is one cubic hole per simple cubic packing of anions (O^{2-}), then all the cubic holes will be filled by Ba^{2+} ions. This is required to give the required 1:1 formula stoichiometry in BaO.

To estimate the density, the ions in a CsCl type unit cell are assumed to just touch along the body diagonal of the unit cell so that body diagonal $= 2r_+ + 2r_-$. Since the unit cell contains one O^{2-} ion, then one BaO formula unit is contained per unit cell.

body diagonal $= \sqrt{3}\,\ell = 2r_{Ba^{2+}} + 2r_{O^{2-}}$, $\ell = \dfrac{2(135\ \text{pm}) + 2(140.\ \text{pm})}{\sqrt{3}} = 318\ \text{pm}$

density $= \dfrac{\text{mass}}{\text{volume}} = \dfrac{1\ \text{BaO unit} \times \dfrac{1\ \text{mol BaO}}{6.022 \times 10^{23}\ \text{units}} \times \dfrac{153.3\ \text{g BaO}}{1\ \text{mol BaO}}}{(3.18 \times 10^{-8}\ \text{cm})^3} = 7.92\ \text{g/cm}^3$

CHAPTER SEVENTEEN

PROPERTIES OF SOLUTIONS

12. $125 \text{ g sucrose} \times \dfrac{1 \text{ mol}}{342.3 \text{ g}} = 0.365 \text{ mol}; \quad M = \dfrac{0.365 \text{ mol}}{1.00 \text{ L}} = \dfrac{0.365 \text{ mol sucrose}}{\text{L}}$

13. $0.250 \text{ L} \times \dfrac{0.100 \text{ mol}}{\text{L}} \times \dfrac{134.0 \text{ g}}{\text{mol}} = 3.35 \text{ g Na}_2\text{C}_2\text{O}_4$

14. $25.00 \times 10^{-3} \text{ L} \times \dfrac{0.308 \text{ mol}}{\text{L}} = 7.70 \times 10^{-3} \text{ mol}; \quad \dfrac{7.70 \times 10^{-3} \text{ mol}}{0.500 \text{ L}} = \dfrac{1.54 \times 10^{-2} \text{ mol NiCl}_2}{\text{L}}$

   $\text{NiCl}_2(s) \rightarrow \text{Ni}^{2+}(aq) + 2 \text{ Cl}^-(aq); \quad M_{\text{Ni}^{2+}} = \dfrac{1.54 \times 10^{-2} \text{ mol}}{\text{L}}; \quad M_{\text{Cl}^-} = \dfrac{3.08 \times 10^{-2} \text{ mol}}{\text{L}}$

15. a. $\text{Ca(NO}_3)_2(s) \rightarrow \text{Ca}^{2+}(aq) + 2 \text{ NO}_3^-(aq); \quad M_{\text{Ca}^{2+}} = \dfrac{1.06 \times 10^{-3} \text{ mol}}{\text{L}}; \quad M_{\text{NO}_3^-} = \dfrac{2.12 \times 10^{-3} \text{ mol}}{\text{L}}$

   b. $1.0 \times 10^{-3} \text{ L} \times \dfrac{1.06 \times 10^{-3} \text{ mol Ca}^{2+}}{\text{L}} \times \dfrac{40.08 \text{ g Ca}^{2+}}{\text{mol}} = 4.2 \times 10^{-5} \text{ g Ca}^{2+}$

   c. $1.0 \times 10^{-6} \text{ L} \times \dfrac{2.12 \times 10^{-3} \text{ mol NO}_3^-}{\text{L}} \times \dfrac{6.02 \times 10^{23} \text{ NO}_3^- \text{ ions}}{\text{mol NO}_3^-} = 1.3 \times 10^{15} \text{ NO}_3^- \text{ ions}$

16. $1.00 \text{ L} \times \dfrac{0.040 \text{ mol HCl}}{\text{L}} = 0.040 \text{ mol HCl}; \quad 0.040 \text{ mol HCl} \times \dfrac{1 \text{ L}}{0.25 \text{ mol HCl}} = 0.16 \text{ L} = 160 \text{ mL}$

17. a. $\text{HNO}_3(l) \rightarrow \text{H}^+(aq) + \text{NO}_3^-(aq)$ b. $\text{Na}_2\text{SO}_4(s) \rightarrow 2 \text{ Na}^+(aq) + \text{SO}_4^{2-}(aq)$

   c. $\text{Al(NO}_3)_3(s) \rightarrow \text{Al}^{3+}(aq) + 3 \text{ NO}_3^-(aq)$ d. $\text{SrBr}_2(s) \rightarrow \text{Sr}^{2+}(aq) + 2 \text{ Br}^-(aq)$

   e. $\text{KClO}_4(s) \rightarrow \text{K}^+(aq) + \text{ClO}_4^-(aq)$ f. $\text{NH}_4\text{Br}(s) \rightarrow \text{NH}_4^+(aq) + \text{Br}^-(aq)$

   g. $\text{NH}_4\text{NO}_3(s) \rightarrow \text{NH}_4^+(aq) + \text{NO}_3^-(aq)$ h. $\text{CuSO}_4(s) \rightarrow \text{Cu}^{2+}(aq) + \text{SO}_4^{2-}(aq)$

   i. $\text{NaOH}(s) \rightarrow \text{Na}^+(aq) + \text{OH}^-(aq)$

Concentration of Solutions

18. $\text{mass \% CsCl} = \dfrac{\text{mass CsCl}}{\text{mass solution}} \times 100 = \dfrac{50.0 \text{ g CsCl}}{100.0 \text{ g solution}} \times 100 = 50.0\% \text{ CsCl by mass}$

$\text{molarity} = M = \dfrac{\text{mol solute}}{\text{L solution}} = \dfrac{50.0 \text{ g}}{63.3 \text{ mL}} \times \dfrac{1000 \text{ mL}}{\text{L}} \times \dfrac{1 \text{ mol}}{168.4 \text{ g}} = 4.69 \text{ mol/L}$

$\text{molality} = m = \dfrac{\text{mol solute}}{\text{kg solvent}} = \dfrac{50.0 \text{ g CsCl}}{50.0 \text{ g solvent}} \times \dfrac{1000 \text{ g}}{\text{kg}} \times \dfrac{1 \text{ mol CsCl}}{168.4 \text{ g}} = 5.94 \text{ mol/kg}$

$50.0 \text{ g CsCl} \times \dfrac{1 \text{ mol}}{168.4 \text{ g}} = 0.297 \text{ mol CsCl}; \quad 50.0 \text{ g H}_2\text{O} \times \dfrac{1 \text{ mol}}{18.02 \text{ g}} = 2.77 \text{ mol H}_2\text{O}$

$\text{mole fraction CsCl} = \chi_{\text{CsCl}} = \dfrac{\text{mol CsCl}}{\text{total mol}} = \dfrac{0.297}{0.297 + 2.77} = 9.68 \times 10^{-2}$

19. $\text{molality} = \dfrac{40.0 \text{ g EG}}{60.0 \text{ g H}_2\text{O}} \times \dfrac{1000 \text{ g}}{\text{kg}} \times \dfrac{1 \text{ mol EG}}{62.07 \text{ g}} = 10.7 \text{ mol/kg}$

$\text{molarity} = \dfrac{40.0 \text{ g EG}}{100.0 \text{ g solution}} \times \dfrac{1.05 \text{ g}}{\text{cm}^3} \times \dfrac{1000 \text{ cm}^3}{\text{L}} \times \dfrac{1 \text{ mol}}{62.07 \text{ g}} = 6.77 \text{ mol/L}$

$40.0 \text{ g EG} \times \dfrac{1 \text{ mol}}{62.07 \text{ g}} = 0.644 \text{ mol EG}; \quad 60.0 \text{ g H}_2\text{O} \times \dfrac{1 \text{ mol}}{18.02 \text{ g}} = 3.33 \text{ mol H}_2\text{O}$

$\chi_{\text{EG}} = \dfrac{0.644}{3.33 + 0.644} = 0.162 = \text{mole fraction ethylene glycol}$

20.   Hydrochloric acid (HCl):

$\text{molarity} = \dfrac{38 \text{ g HCl}}{100. \text{ g soln}} \times \dfrac{1.19 \text{ g soln}}{\text{cm}^3 \text{ soln}} \times \dfrac{1000 \text{ cm}^3}{\text{L}} \times \dfrac{1 \text{ mol HCl}}{36.5 \text{ g}} = 12 \text{ mol/L}$

$\text{molality} = \dfrac{38 \text{ g HCl}}{62 \text{ g solvent}} \times \dfrac{1000 \text{ g}}{\text{kg}} \times \dfrac{1 \text{ mol HCl}}{36.5 \text{ g}} = 17 \text{ mol/kg}$

$38 \text{ g HCl} \times \dfrac{1 \text{ mol}}{36.5 \text{ g}} = 1.0 \text{ mol HCl}; \quad 62 \text{ g H}_2\text{O} \times \dfrac{1 \text{ mol}}{18.0 \text{ g}} = 3.4 \text{ mol H}_2\text{O}$

$\text{mole fraction of HCl} = \chi_{\text{HCl}} = \dfrac{1.0}{3.4 + 1.0} = 0.23$

Nitric acid (HNO_3):

$$\frac{70. \text{ g } HNO_3}{100. \text{ g soln}} \times \frac{1.42 \text{ g soln}}{cm^3 \text{ soln}} \times \frac{1000 \text{ cm}^3}{L} \times \frac{1 \text{ mol } HNO_3}{63.0 \text{ g}} = 16 \text{ mol/L}$$

$$\frac{70. \text{ g } HNO_3}{30. \text{ g solvent}} \times \frac{1000 \text{ g}}{kg} \times \frac{1 \text{ mol } HNO_3}{63.0 \text{ g}} = 37 \text{ mol/kg}$$

$$70. \text{ g } HNO_3 \times \frac{1 \text{ mol}}{63.0 \text{ g}} = 1.1 \text{ mol } HNO_3; \quad 30. \text{ g } H_2O \times \frac{1 \text{ mol}}{18.0 \text{ g}} = 1.7 \text{ mol } H_2O$$

$$\chi_{HNO_3} = \frac{1.1}{1.7 + 1.1} = 0.39$$

Sulfuric acid (H_2SO_4):

$$\frac{95 \text{ g } H_2SO_4}{100. \text{ g soln}} \times \frac{1.84 \text{ g soln}}{cm^3 \text{ soln}} \times \frac{1000 \text{ cm}^3}{L} \times \frac{1 \text{ mol } H_2SO_4}{98.1 \text{ g } H_2SO_4} = 18 \text{ mol/L}$$

$$\frac{95 \text{ g } H_2SO_4}{5 \text{ g } H_2O} \times \frac{1000 \text{ g}}{kg} \times \frac{1 \text{ mol}}{98.1 \text{ g}} = 194 \text{ mol/kg} \approx 200 \text{ mol/kg}$$

$$95 \text{ g } H_2SO_4 \times \frac{1 \text{ mol}}{98.1 \text{ g}} = 0.97 \text{ mol } H_2SO_4; \quad 5 \text{ g } H_2O \times \frac{1 \text{ mol}}{18.0 \text{ g}} = 0.3 \text{ mol } H_2O$$

$$\chi_{H_2SO_4} = \frac{0.97}{0.97 + 0.3} = 0.76$$

Acetic Acid (CH_3CO_2H):

$$\frac{99 \text{ g } CH_3CO_2H}{100. \text{ g soln}} \times \frac{1.05 \text{ g soln}}{cm^3 \text{ soln}} \times \frac{1000 \text{ cm}^3}{L} \times \frac{1 \text{ mol}}{60.05 \text{ g}} = 17 \text{ mol/L}$$

$$\frac{99 \text{ g } CH_3CO_2H}{1 \text{ g } H_2O} \times \frac{1000 \text{ g}}{kg} \times \frac{1 \text{ mol}}{60.05 \text{ g}} = 1600 \text{ mol/kg} \approx 2000 \text{ mol/kg}$$

$$99 \text{ g } CH_3CO_2H \times \frac{1 \text{ mol}}{60.05 \text{ g}} = 1.6 \text{ mol } CH_3CO_2H; \quad 1 \text{ g } H_2O \times \frac{1 \text{ mol}}{18.0 \text{ g}} = 0.06 \text{ mol } H_2O$$

$$\chi_{CH_3CO_2H} = \frac{1.6}{1.6 + 0.06} = 0.96$$

Ammonia (NH_3):

$$\frac{28 \text{ g } NH_3}{100. \text{ g soln}} \times \frac{0.90 \text{ g}}{cm^3} \times \frac{1000 \text{ cm}^3}{L} \times \frac{1 \text{ mol}}{17.0 \text{ g}} = 15 \text{ mol/L}$$

$$\frac{28 \text{ g NH}_3}{72 \text{ g H}_2\text{O}} \times \frac{1000 \text{ g}}{\text{kg}} \times \frac{1 \text{ mol}}{17.0 \text{ g}} = 23 \text{ mol/kg}$$

$$28 \text{ g NH}_3 \times \frac{1 \text{ mol}}{17.0 \text{ g}} = 1.6 \text{ mol NH}_3; \ \ 72 \text{ g H}_2\text{O} \times \frac{1 \text{ mol}}{18.0 \text{ g}} = 4.0 \text{ mol H}_2\text{O}$$

$$\chi_{\text{NH}_3} = \frac{1.6}{4.0 + 1.6} = 0.29$$

21. $$25 \text{ mL C}_5\text{H}_{12} \times \frac{0.63 \text{ g}}{\text{mL}} = 16 \text{ g C}_5\text{H}_{12}; \ \ 25 \text{ mL} \times \frac{0.63}{\text{mL}} \times \frac{1 \text{ mol}}{72.15 \text{ g}} = 0.22 \text{ mol C}_5\text{H}_{12}$$

$$45 \text{ mL C}_6\text{H}_{14} \times \frac{0.66 \text{ g}}{\text{mL}} = 30. \text{ g C}_6\text{H}_{14}; \ \ 45 \text{ mL} \times \frac{0.66 \text{ g}}{\text{mL}} \times \frac{1 \text{ mol}}{86.17 \text{ g}} = 0.34 \text{ mol C}_6\text{H}_{14}$$

$$\text{mass \% pentane} = \frac{\text{mass pentane}}{\text{total mass}} \times 100 = \frac{16 \text{ g}}{16 \text{ g} + 30. \text{ g}} \times 100 = 35\%$$

$$\chi_{\text{pentane}} = \frac{\text{mol pentane}}{\text{total mol}} = \frac{0.22 \text{ mol}}{0.22 \text{ mol} + 0.34 \text{ mol}} = 0.39$$

$$\text{molality} = \frac{\text{mol pentane}}{\text{kg hexane}} = \frac{0.22 \text{ mol}}{0.030 \text{ kg}} = 7.3 \text{ mol/kg}$$

$$\text{molarity} = \frac{\text{mol pentane}}{\text{L solution}} = \frac{0.22 \text{ mol}}{25 \text{ mL} + 45 \text{ mL}} \times \frac{1000 \text{ mL}}{1 \text{ L}} = 3.1 \text{ mol/L}$$

22.   If there are 100.0 mL of wine:

$$12.5 \text{ mL C}_2\text{H}_5\text{OH} \times \frac{0.789 \text{ g}}{\text{mL}} = 9.86 \text{ g C}_2\text{H}_5\text{OH and } 87.5 \text{ mL H}_2\text{O} \times \frac{1.00 \text{ g}}{\text{mL}} = 87.5 \text{ g H}_2\text{O}$$

$$\text{mass \% ethanol} = \frac{9.86}{87.5 + 9.86} \times 100 = 10.1\% \text{ by mass}$$

$$\text{molality} = \frac{9.86 \text{ g C}_2\text{H}_5\text{OH}}{0.0875 \text{ kg H}_2\text{O}} \times \frac{1 \text{ mol}}{46.07 \text{ g}} = 2.45 \text{ mol/kg}$$

23.   If we have 1.00 L of solution:

$$1.37 \text{ mol citric acid} \times \frac{192.1 \text{ g}}{\text{mol}} = 263 \text{ g citric acid}$$

$$1.00 \times 10^3 \text{ mL solution} \times \frac{1.10 \text{ g}}{\text{mL}} = 1.10 \times 10^3 \text{ g solution}$$

$$\text{mass \% of citric acid} = \frac{263 \text{ g}}{1.10 \times 10^3 \text{ g}} \times 100 = 23.9\%$$

In 1.00 L of solution, we have 263 g citric acid and $(1.10 \times 10^3 - 263) = 840$ g of H_2O.

$$\text{molality} = \frac{1.37 \text{ mol citric acid}}{0.84 \text{ kg } H_2O} = 1.6 \text{ mol/kg}$$

$$840 \text{ g } H_2O \times \frac{1 \text{ mol}}{18.0 \text{ g}} = 47 \text{ mol } H_2O; \quad \chi_{\text{citric acid}} = \frac{1.37}{47 + 1.37} = 0.028$$

24. $\dfrac{1.00 \text{ mol acetone}}{1.00 \text{ kg ethanol}} = 1.00 \text{ molal}; \quad 1.00 \times 10^3 \text{ g } C_2H_5OH \times \dfrac{1 \text{ mol}}{46.07 \text{ g}} = 21.7 \text{ mol } C_2H_5OH$

$$\chi_{\text{acetone}} = \frac{1.00}{1.00 + 21.7} = 0.0441$$

$$1 \text{ mol } CH_3COCH_3 \times \frac{58.08 \text{ g } CH_3COCH_3}{\text{mol } CH_3COCH_3} \times \frac{1 \text{ mL}}{0.788 \text{ g}} = 73.7 \text{ mL } CH_3COCH_3$$

$$1.00 \times 10^3 \text{ g ethanol} \times \frac{1 \text{ mL}}{0.789 \text{ g}} = 1270 \text{ mL}; \quad \text{Total volume} = 1270 + 73.7 = 1340 \text{ mL}$$

$$\text{molarity} = \frac{1.00 \text{ mol}}{1.34 \text{ L}} = 0.746 \, M$$

25. $0.40 \text{ mol } CH_3COCH_3 \times \dfrac{58.1 \text{ g}}{\text{mol}} = 23 \text{ g acetone}; \quad 0.60 \text{ mol } C_2H_5OH \times \dfrac{46.1 \text{ g}}{\text{mol}} = 28 \text{ g ethanol}$

$$\text{mass \% acetone} = \frac{23 \text{ g}}{23 \text{ g} + 28 \text{ g}} \times 100 = 45\%$$

26.   a.   If we use 100. mL (100. g) of H_2O, we need:

$$0.100 \text{ kg } H_2O \times \frac{2.0 \text{ mol KCl}}{\text{kg}} \times \frac{74.55 \text{ g}}{\text{mol KCl}} = 14.9 \text{ g} = 15 \text{ g KCl}$$

Dissolve 15 g KCl in 100. mL H_2O to prepare a 2.0 m KCl solution. This will give us slightly more than 100 mL, but this will be the easiest way to make the solution. Since we don't know the density of the solution, we can't calculate the molarity and use a volumetric flask to make exactly 100 mL of solution.

b.   If we took 15 g NaOH and 85 g H_2O, the volume would probably be less than 100 mL. To make sure we have enough solution, lets use 100. mL H_2O (100. g). Let x = mass of NaCl.

$$\text{mass \%} = 15 = \frac{x}{100. + x} \times 100, \quad 1500 + 15 x = 100. \, x, \quad x = 17.6 \text{ g} \approx 18 \text{ g}$$

Dissolve 18 g NaOH in 100. mL H_2O to make a 15% NaOH solution by mass.

c.   In a fashion similar to part b, let's use 100. mL CH_3OH. Let x = mass of NaOH.

$$100. \text{ mL CH}_3\text{OH} \times \frac{0.79 \text{ g}}{\text{mL}} = 79 \text{ g CH}_3\text{OH}$$

$$\text{mass \%} = 25 = \frac{x}{79 + x} \times 100, \quad 25(79) + 25\,x = 100.\,x, \quad x = 26.3 \text{ g} \approx 26 \text{ g}$$

Dissolve 26 g NaOH in 100. mL CH$_3$OH.

d. To make sure we have enough solution, lets use 100. mL (100. g) of H$_2$O. Let x = mol C$_6$H$_{12}$O$_6$.

$$100. \text{ g H}_2\text{O} \times \frac{1 \text{ mol H}_2\text{O}}{18.02 \text{ g}} = 5.55 \text{ mol H}_2\text{O}$$

$$\chi_{C_6H_{12}O_6} = 0.10 = \frac{x}{x + 5.55}, \quad 0.10\,x + 0.56 = x, \, x = 0.62 \text{ mol C}_6\text{H}_{12}\text{O}_6$$

$$0.62 \text{ mol C}_6\text{H}_{12}\text{O}_6 \times \frac{180.2 \text{ g}}{\text{mol}} = 110 \text{ g C}_6\text{H}_{12}\text{O}_6$$

Dissolve 110 g C$_6$H$_{12}$O$_6$ in 100. mL of H$_2$O to prepare a solution with $\chi_{C_6H_{12}O_6} = 0.10$.

Thermodynamics of Solutions and Solubility

27. The nature of the interparticle forces. Polar solutes and ionic solutes dissolve in polar solvents and nonpolar solutes dissolve in nonpolar solvents.

28. The dissolving of an ionic solute in water can be thought of as taking place in two steps. The first step, called the lattice energy term, refers to breaking apart the ionic compound into gaseous ions. This step, as indicated in the problem requires a lot of energy and is unfavorable. The second step, called the hydration energy term, refers to the energy released when the separated gaseous ions are stabilized as water molecules surround the ions. Since the interactions between water molecules and ions are strong, then a lot of energy is released when ions are hydrated. Thus, the dissolution process for ionic compounds can be thought of as consisting of an unfavorable and a favorable energy term. These two processes basically cancel each other out; so when ionic solids dissolve in water, the heat released or gained is minimal and the temperature change is minimal.

29. Using Hess's law:

$$\text{NaI(s)} \rightarrow \text{Na}^+\text{(g)} + \text{I}^-\text{(g)} \qquad \Delta H = -\Delta H_{LE} = -(-686 \text{ kJ/mol})$$
$$\text{Na}^+\text{(g)} + \text{I}^-\text{(g)} \rightarrow \text{Na}^+\text{(aq)} + \text{I}^-\text{(aq)} \qquad \Delta H = \Delta H_{hyd} = -694 \text{ kJ/mol}$$

$$\text{NaI(s)} \rightarrow \text{Na}^+\text{(aq)} + \text{I}^-\text{(aq)} \qquad \Delta H_{soln} = -8 \text{ kJ/mol}$$

ΔH_{soln} refers to the heat released or gained when a solute dissolves in a solvent. Here, an ionic compound dissolves in water.

30.   a. $CaCl_2(s) \rightarrow Ca^{2+}(g) + 2\ Cl^-(g)$ $\Delta H = -\Delta H_{LE} = -(-2247\ kJ)$
             $Ca^{2+}(g) + 2\ Cl^-(g) \rightarrow Ca^{2+}(aq) + 2\ Cl^-(aq)$ $\Delta H = \Delta H_{hyd}$

             $CaCl_2(s) \rightarrow Ca^{2+}(aq) + 2\ Cl^-(aq)$ $\Delta H_{soln} = -46\ kJ$

       $-46\ kJ = 2247\ kJ + \Delta H_{hyd},\ \ \Delta H_{hyd} = -2293\ kJ$

             $CaI_2(s) \rightarrow Ca^{2+}(g) + 2\ I^-(g)$ $\Delta H = -\Delta H_{LE} = -(-2059\ kJ)$
             $Ca^{2+}(g) + 2\ I^-(g) \rightarrow Ca^{2+}(aq) + 2\ I^-(aq)$ $\Delta H = \Delta H_{hyd}$

             $CaI_2(s) \rightarrow Ca^{2+}(aq) + 2\ I^-(aq)$ $\Delta H_{soln} = -104\ kJ$

       $-104\ kJ = 2059\ kJ + \Delta H_{hyd},\ \ \Delta H_{hyd} = -2163\ kJ$

       b.   The enthalpy of hydration for $CaCl_2$ is more exothermic than for CaI_2. Any differences must be due to differences in hydrations between Cl^- and I^-. Thus, the chloride ion is more strongly hydrated as compared to the iodide ion.

31.   Both $Al(OH)_3$ and $NaOH$ are ionic compounds. Since the lattice energy is proportional to the charge of the ions, then the lattice energy of aluminum hydroxide is greater than that of sodium hydroxide. The attraction of water molecules for Al^{3+} and OH^- cannot overcome the larger lattice energy and $Al(OH)_3$ is insoluble. For $NaOH$, the favorable hydration energy is large enough to overcome the smaller lattice energy and $NaOH$ is soluble.

32.   a. Mg^{2+}; smaller, higher charge   b. Be^{2+}; smaller

       c. Fe^{3+}; smaller size, higher charge   d. F^-; smaller

       e. Cl^-; smaller   f. SO_4^{2-}; higher charge

33.   Water is a polar molecule capable of hydrogen bonding. Polar molecules, especially molecules capable of hydrogen bonding, and ions can be hydrated. For covalent compounds, as polarity increases, the attraction to water (hydration) increases. For ionic compounds, as the charge of the ions increase and/or the size of the ions decrease, the attraction to water (hydration) increases.

       a. CH_3CH_2OH; CH_3CH_2OH is polar while $CH_3CH_2CH_3$ is nonpolar.

       b. $CHCl_3$; $CHCl_3$ is polar while CCl_4 is nonpolar.

       c. CH_3CH_2OH; CH_3CH_2OH is much more polar than $CH_3(CH_2)_{14}CH_2OH$.

34.   Water is a polar solvent and dissolves polar solutes and ionic solutes. Carbon tetrachloride (CCl_4) is a nonpolar solvent and dissolves nonpolar solutes (like dissolves like).

       a. CCl_4; CO_2 is a nonpolar molecule.   b.   Water; NH_4NO_3 is an ionic solid.

       c.   Water; CH_3COCH_3 is polar molecule.   d.   Water; $HC_2H_3O_2$ (acetic acid) is a polar molecule.

       e. CCl_4; $CH_3CH_2CH_2CH_2CH_3$ is a nonpolar molecule.

35.   As the length of the hydrocarbon chain increases, the solubility decreases. The –OH end of the alcohols can hydrogen bond with water. The hydrocarbon chain, however, is basically nonpolar and interacts poorly with water. As the hydrocarbon chain gets longer, a greater portion of the molecule cannot interact with the water molecules and the solubility decreases, i.e., the effect of the –OH group decreases as the alcohols get larger.

36.   The main intermolecular forces are:

hexane (C_6H_{14}): London dispersion; chloroform, ($CHCl_3$): dipole-dipole, London dispersion; methanol (CH_3OH): H-bonding; H_2O: H-bonding (two places)

There is a gradual change in the nature of the intermolecular forces (weaker to stronger). Each preceding solvent is miscible in its predecessor because there is not a great change in the strengths of the intermolecular forces from one solvent to the next.

37.   hydrophobic: water hating; hydrophilic: water loving

38. $CO_2 + OH^- \rightarrow HCO_3^-$; No, the reaction of CO_2 with OH^- greatly increases the solubility of CO_2 in basic solution by formation of the soluble bicarbonate anion.

39. $P_{gas} = kC$, $0.790 \text{ atm} = k \times \dfrac{8.21 \times 10^{-4} \text{ mol}}{L}$, $k = 962$ L atm/mol

$P_{gas} = kC$, $1.10 \text{ atm} = \dfrac{962 \text{ L atm}}{mol} \times C$, $C = 1.14 \times 10^{-3}$ mol/L

40. $750. \text{ mL grape juice} \times \dfrac{12 \text{ mL } C_2H_5OH}{100. \text{ mL juice}} \times \dfrac{0.79 \text{ g } C_2H_5OH}{mL} \times \dfrac{1 \text{ mol } C_2H_5OH}{46.07 \text{ g}} \times \dfrac{2 \text{ mol } CO_2}{2 \text{ mol } C_2H_5OH}$

$= 1.54 \text{ mol } CO_2$ (carry extra significant figure)

$1.54 \text{ mol } CO_2 = \text{total mol } CO_2 = \text{mol } CO_2(g) + \text{mol } CO_2(aq) = n_g + n_{aq}$

$$P_{CO_2} = \dfrac{n_g RT}{V} = \dfrac{n_g\left(\dfrac{0.08206 \text{ L atm}}{\text{mol K}}\right)(298 \text{ K})}{75 \times 10^{-3} \text{ L}} = 326\, n_g$$

$$P_{CO_2} = kC = \dfrac{32 \text{ L atm}}{mol} \times \dfrac{n_{aq}}{0.750 \text{ L}} = 42.7\, n_{aq}$$

$P_{CO_2} = 326\, n_g = 42.7\, n_{aq}$ and from above $n_{aq} = 1.54 - n_g$; Solving:

$326\, n_g = 42.7(1.54 - n_g)$, $369\, n_g = 65.8$, $n_g = 0.18$ mol

$P_{CO_2} = 326(0.18) = 59 \text{ atm in gas phase};$ $59 \text{ atm} = \dfrac{32 \text{ L atm}}{mol} \times C$, $C = 1.8 \text{ mol } CO_2/\text{L in wine}$

41.   As the temperature increases the gas molecules will have a greater average kinetic energy. A greater fraction of the gas molecules in solution will have a kinetic energy greater than the attractive forces between the gas molecules and the solvent molecules. More gas molecules are able to escape to the vapor phase and the solubility of the gas decreases.

Vapor Pressures of Solution

42. $P_{H_2O} = \chi_{H_2O} \, P^\circ_{H_2O}$; $\chi_{H_2O} = \dfrac{\text{mol } H_2O \text{ in solution}}{\text{total mol in solution}}$

$50.0 \text{ g } C_6H_{12}O_6 \times \dfrac{1 \text{ mol } C_2H_{12}O_6}{180.16 \text{ g } C_6H_{12}O_6} = 0.278 \text{ mol glucose}$

$600.0 \text{ g } H_2O \times \dfrac{1 \text{ mol}}{18.02 \text{ g}} = 33.30 \text{ mol } H_2O$; Total mol = 0.278 + 33.30 = 33.58 mol

$\chi_{H_2O} = \dfrac{33.30}{33.58} = 0.9917$; $P_{H_2O} = \chi_{H_2O} \, P^\circ_{H_2O} = 0.9917 \times 23.8 \text{ torr} = 23.6 \text{ torr}$

43. $P_{C_2H_5OH} = \chi_{C_2H_5OH} \, P^\circ_{C_2H_5OH}$; $\chi_{C_2H_5OH} = \dfrac{\text{mol } C_2H_5OH \text{ solution}}{\text{total mol in solution}}$

$53.6 \text{ g } C_3H_8O_3 \times \dfrac{1 \text{ mol } C_3H_8O_3}{92.09 \text{ g}} = 0.582 \text{ mol } C_3H_8O_3$

$133.7 \text{ g } C_2H_5OH \times \dfrac{1 \text{ mol } C_2H_5OH}{46.07 \text{ g}} = 2.90 \text{ mol } C_2H_5OH$; total mol = 0.582 + 2.90 = 3.48 mol

$113 \text{ torr} = \dfrac{2.90 \text{ mol}}{3.48 \text{ mol}} \times P^\circ_{C_2H_5OH}$, $P^\circ_{C_2H_5OH} = 136 \text{ torr}$

44.   Compared to H_2O, solution d (methanol/water) will have the highest vapor pressure since methanol is more volatile than water ($P^\circ_{H_2O} = 23.8$ torr at 25°C). Both solution b (glucose/water) and solution c (NaCl/water) will have a lower vapor pressure than water by Raoult's law. NaCl dissolves to give Na^+ ions and Cl^- ions; glucose is a nonelectrolyte. Since there are more solute particles in solution c, the vapor pressure of solution c will be the lowest.

45.   Solution d (methanol/water); Methanol is more volatile than water, which will increase the total vapor pressure to a value greater than the vapor pressure of pure water at this temperature.

46. $P_{total} = P_{CH_2Cl_2} + P_{CH_2Br_2}$; $P = \chi^L P^\circ$; $\chi^L_{CH_2Cl_2} = \dfrac{0.0300 \text{ mol } CH_2Cl_2}{0.0800 \text{ mol total}} = 0.375$

$P_{total} = 0.375 \,(133 \text{ torr}) + (1.000 - 0.375)(11.4 \text{ torr}) = 49.9 + 7.13 = 57.0 \text{ torr}$

In the vapor: $\chi^V_{CH_2Cl_2} = \dfrac{P_{CH_2Cl_2}}{P_{total}} = \dfrac{49.9 \text{ torr}}{57.0 \text{ torr}} = 0.875$; $\chi^V_{CH_2Br_2} = 1.000 - 0.875 = 0.125$

47. $P_B = \chi_B P_B^\circ$, $\chi_B = P_B/P_B^\circ = 0.900$ atm/0.930 atm $= 0.968$

$0.968 = \dfrac{\text{mol benzene}}{\text{total mol}}$; mol benzene $= 78.11$ g $C_6H_6 \times \dfrac{1 \text{ mol}}{78.11} = 1.000$ mol

Let $x =$ mol solute, then: $\chi_B = 0.968 = \dfrac{1.000 \text{ mol}}{1.000 + x}$, $0.968 + 0.968\,x = 1.000$, $x = 0.033$ mol

molar mass $= \dfrac{10.0 \text{ g}}{0.033 \text{ mol}} = 303$ g/mol $\approx 3.0 \times 10^2$ g/mol

48. $P_{CS_2} = \chi_{CS_2}^V P_{tot} = 0.855\,(263 \text{ torr}) = 225$ torr

$P_{CS_2} = \chi_{CS_2}^L P_{CS_2}^\circ$, $\chi_{CS_2}^L = \dfrac{P_{CS_2}}{P_{CS_2}^\circ} = \dfrac{225 \text{ torr}}{375 \text{ torr}} = 0.600$

49. a. 25 mL $C_5H_{12} \times \dfrac{0.63 \text{ g}}{\text{mL}} \times \dfrac{1 \text{ mol}}{72.15 \text{ g}} = 0.22$ mol C_5H_{12}

45 mL $C_6H_{14} \times \dfrac{0.66 \text{ g}}{\text{mL}} \times \dfrac{1 \text{ mol}}{86.17 \text{ g}} = 0.34$ mol C_6H_{14}; total mol $= 0.22 + 0.34 = 0.56$ mol

$\chi_{pen}^L = \dfrac{\text{mol pentane in solution}}{\text{total mol in solution}} = \dfrac{0.22 \text{ mol}}{0.56 \text{ mol}} = 0.39$, $\chi_{hex}^L = 1.00 - 0.39 = 0.61$

$P_{pen} = \chi_{pen}^L P_{pen}^\circ = 0.39(511 \text{ torr}) = 2.0 \times 10^2$ torr; $P_{hex} = 0.61(150. \text{ torr}) = 92$ torr

$P_{total} = P_{pen} + P_{hex} = 2.0 \times 10^2 + 92 = 292$ torr $= 290$ torr

b. From Chapter 5 on gases, the partial pressure of a gas is proportional to the number of moles of gas present. For the vapor phase:

$\chi_{pen}^V = \dfrac{\text{mol pentane in vapor}}{\text{total mol vapor}} = \dfrac{P_{pen}}{P_{total}} = \dfrac{2.0 \times 10^2 \text{ torr}}{290 \text{ torr}} = 0.69$

Note: In the Solutions Guide, we added V or L to the mole fraction symbol to emphasize which value we are solving. If the L or V is omitted, then the liquid phase is assumed.

50. $P_{tol} = \chi_{tol}^L P_{tol}^\circ$; $P_{ben} = \chi_{ben}^L P_{ben}^\circ$; For the vapor, $\chi_A^V = P_A/P_{total}$. Since the mole fractions of benzene and toluene are equal in the vapor phase, then $P_{tol} = P_{ben}$.

$\chi_{tol}^L P_{tol}^\circ = \chi_{ben}^L P_{ben}^\circ = (1.00 - \chi_{tol}^L)P_{ben}^\circ$, $\chi_{tol}^L(28 \text{ torr}) = (1.00 - \chi_{tol}^L)\,95 \text{ torr}$

$123\,\chi_{tol}^L = 95$, $\chi_{tol}^L = 0.77$; $\chi_{ben}^L = 1.00 - 0.77 = 0.23$

51. $P_{total} = P_{meth} + P_{prop}$, 174 torr $= \chi_{meth}^L(303 \text{ torr}) + \chi_{prop}^L(44.6 \text{ torr})$; $\chi_{prop}^L = 1.000 - \chi_{meth}^L$

$174 = 303\,\chi_{meth}^L + (1.000 - \chi_{meth}^L)\,44.6$, $\dfrac{129}{258} = \chi_{meth}^L = 0.500$; $\chi_{prop}^L = 1.000 - 0.500 = 0.500$

52.   If solute-solvent attractions are stronger than the solvent-solvent and solute-solute attractions, then there is a negative deviation from Raoult's law. If solute-solvent attractions are weaker than the solvent-solvent and solute-solute attractions, then there is a positive deviation from Raoult's law.

53. $50.0 \text{ g CH}_3\text{COCH}_3 \times \dfrac{1 \text{ mol}}{58.08 \text{ g}} = 0.861 \text{ mol acetone}$

       $50.0 \text{ g CH}_3\text{OH} \times \dfrac{1 \text{ mol}}{32.04 \text{ g}} = 1.56 \text{ mol methanol}$

       $\chi^{L}_{acetone} = \dfrac{0.861}{0.861 + 1.56} = 0.356; \quad \chi^{L}_{methanol} = 1.000 - \chi^{L}_{acetone} = 0.644$

       $P_{total} = P_{methanol} + P_{acetone} = 0.644(143 \text{ torr}) + 0.356(271 \text{ torr}) = 92.1 \text{ torr} + 96.5 \text{ torr} = 188.6 \text{ torr}$

       Since partial pressures are proportional to the moles of gas present, then in the vapor phase:

       $\chi^{V}_{acetone} = \dfrac{P_{acetone}}{P_{total}} = \dfrac{96.5 \text{ torr}}{188.6 \text{ torr}} = 0.512; \quad \chi^{V}_{methanol} = 1.000 - 0.512 = 0.488$

       The actual vapor pressure of the solution (161 torr) is less than the calculated pressure assuming ideal behavior (188.6 torr). Therefore, the solution exhibits negative deviations from Raoult's law. This occurs when the solute-solvent interactions are stronger than in pure solute and pure solvent.

54.   a.   An ideal solution would have a vapor pressure at any mole fraction of H_2O between that of pure propanol and pure water (between 74.0 torr and 71.9 torr). The vapor pressures of the various solutions are not between these limits so water and propanol do not form ideal solutions.

       b.   From the data, the vapor pressures of the various solutions are greater than if the solutions behaved ideally (positive deviation from Raoult's law). This occurs when the intermolecular forces in solution are weaker than the intermolecular forces in pure solvent and pure solute. This gives rise to endothermic (positive) ΔH_{soln} values.

       c.   The interactions between propanol and water molecules are weaker than between the pure substances since the solutions exhibit a positive deviation from Raoult's law.

       d.   At $\chi_{H_2O} = 0.54$ the vapor pressure is highest as compared to the other solutions. Since a solution boils when the vapor pressure of the solution equals the external pressure, then the $\chi_{H_2O} = 0.54$ solution should have the lowest normal boiling point; this solution will have a vapor pressure equal to 1 atm at a lower temperature as compared to the other solutions.

55.   No, the solution is not ideal. For an ideal solution, the strength of intermolecular forces in the solution are the same as in pure solute and pure solvent. This results in $\Delta H_{soln} = 0$ for an ideal solution. ΔH_{soln} for methanol/water is not zero. Since $\Delta H_{soln} < 0$, then this solution exhibits negative deviation from Raoult's law.

56.   Since the solute is volatile, then both the water and solute will transfer back and forth between the two beakers. The volume in each beaker will become constant when the concentrations of solute in the beakers are equal to each other. Since the solute is less volatile than water, one would expect there to be a larger net transfer of water molecules into the right beaker than the net transfer of solute

molecules into the left beaker. This results in a larger solution volume in the right beaker when equilibrium is reached, i.e., when the solute concentration is identical in each beaker.

57.   Solutions of A and B have vapor pressures less than ideal (see Figure 17.11 of the text), so this plot shows negative deviations from Rault's law. Negative deviations occur when the intermolecular forces are stronger in solution than in pure solvent and solute. This results in an exothermic enthalpy of solution. The only statement that is false is e. A substance boils when the vapor pressure equals the external pressure. Since $X_b = 0.6$ has a lower vapor pressure at the temperature of the plot than either pure A or pure B, then one would expect this solution to require the highest temperature in order for the vapor pressure to reach the external pressure. Therefore, the solution with $X_B = 0.6$ will have a higher boiling point than either pure A or pure B. (Note that since $P°_B > P°_A$, then B is more volatile than A.)

Colligative Properties

58. $\text{molality} = m = \dfrac{4.9 \text{ g sucrose}}{175 \text{ g solvent}} \times \dfrac{1000 \text{ g}}{\text{kg}} \times \dfrac{1 \text{ mol } C_{12}H_{22}O_{11}}{342.3 \text{ g } C_{12}H_{22}O_{11}} = 0.082 \text{ molal}$

$\Delta T_b = K_b m = \dfrac{0.51°C}{\text{molal}} \times 0.082 \text{ molal} = 0.042°C$

The boiling point is raised from $100.000°C$ to $100.042°C$. We assumed $P = 1$ atm and ample significant figures in the boiling point of pure water.

$\Delta T_f = K_f m = \dfrac{1.86°C}{\text{molal}} \times 0.082 \text{ molal} = 0.15°C; \quad T_f = 0.00°C - 0.15°C = -0.15°C$

$\pi = MRT$; In dilute aqueous solutions the density of the solution is about 1.0 g/mL, thus we can assume that molarity $= M =$ molality $= 0.082$.

$\pi = \dfrac{0.082 \text{ mol}}{L} \times \dfrac{0.08206 \text{ L atm}}{\text{mol K}} \times 298 \text{ K} = 2.0 \text{ atm}$

59. $\text{molality} = m = \dfrac{50.0 \text{ g } C_2H_6O_2}{50.0 \text{ g } H_2O} \times \dfrac{1000 \text{ g}}{\text{kg}} \times \dfrac{1 \text{ mol}}{62.07 \text{ g}} = 16.1 \text{ mol/kg}$

$\Delta T_f = K_f m = 1.86°C/\text{molal} \times 16.1 \text{ molal} = 29.9°C; \quad T_f = 0.0°C - 29.9°C = -29.9°C$

$\Delta T_b = K_b m = 0.51°C/\text{molal} \times 16.1 \text{ molal} = 8.2°C; \quad T_b = 100.0°C + 8.2°C = 108.2°C$

60. $\Delta T = 25.50°C - 24.59°C = 0.91°C = K_f m, \quad m = \dfrac{0.91°C}{9.1°C/\text{molal}} = 0.10 \text{ mol/kg}$

$\text{mass } H_2O = 0.0100 \text{ kg t-butanol} \left(\dfrac{0.10 \text{ mol } H_2O}{\text{kg t-butanol}}\right)\left(\dfrac{18.02 \text{ g } H_2O}{\text{mol } H_2O}\right) = 0.018 \text{ g } H_2O$

61. $m = \dfrac{24.0 \text{ g} \times \dfrac{1 \text{ mol}}{58.0 \text{ g}}}{0.600 \text{ kg}} = 0.690 \text{ mol/kg}; \quad \Delta T_b = K_b m = 0.51°C \text{ kg/mol} \times 0.690 \text{ mol/kg} = 0.35°C$

$T_b = 99.725°C + 0.35°C = 100.08°C$

62. $\pi = MRT$, $M = \dfrac{\pi}{RT} = \dfrac{8.00 \text{ atm}}{0.08206 \text{ L atm mol}^{-1}\text{K}^{-1} \times 298 \text{ K}} = 0.327 \text{ mol/L}$

63. $\Delta T_b = 77.85°C - 76.50°C = 1.35°C$; $m = \dfrac{\Delta T_b}{K_b} = \dfrac{1.35°C}{5.03°C \text{ kg/mol}} = 0.268 \text{ mol/kg}$

mol biomolecule $= 0.0150 \text{ kg solvent} \times \dfrac{0.268 \text{ mol hydrocarbon}}{\text{kg solvent}} = 4.02 \times 10^{-3} \text{ mol}$

From the problem, 2.00 g biomolecule was used which must contain 4.02×10^{-3} mol biomolecule. The molar mass of the biomolecule is:

$$\dfrac{2.00 \text{ g}}{4.02 \times 10^{-3} \text{ mol}} = 498 \text{ g/mol}$$

64. $M = \dfrac{\pi}{RT} = \dfrac{0.745 \text{ torr} \times \dfrac{1 \text{ atm}}{760 \text{ torr}}}{\dfrac{0.08206 \text{ L atm}}{\text{mol K}} \times 300. \text{ K}} = 3.98 \times 10^{-5} \text{ mol/L}$

$1.00 \text{ L} \times \dfrac{3.98 \times 10^{-5} \text{ mol}}{\text{L}} = 3.98 \times 10^{-5} \text{ mol catalase}$

molar mass $= \dfrac{10.00 \text{ g}}{3.98 \times 10^{-5} \text{ mol}} = 2.51 \times 10^{5} \text{ g/mol}$

65. $\Delta T_f = K_f m$, $m = \dfrac{\Delta T_f}{K_f} = \dfrac{0.240°C}{4.70°C \text{ kg/mol}} = \dfrac{5.11 \times 10^{-2} \text{ mol biomolecule}}{\text{kg solvent}}$

The mol of biomolecule present is:

$0.0150 \text{ kg solvent} \times \dfrac{5.11 \times 10^{-2} \text{ mol biomolecule}}{\text{kg solvent}} = 7.67 \times 10^{-4} \text{ mol biomolecule}$

From the problem, 0.350 g biomolecule was used which must contain 7.67×10^{-4} mol biomolecule. The molar mass of the biomolecule is:

molar mass $= \dfrac{0.350 \text{ g}}{7.67 \times 10^{-4} \text{ mol}} = 456 \text{ g/mol}$

66. $m = \dfrac{\Delta T_f}{K_f} = \dfrac{30.0°C}{1.86°C \text{ kg/mol}} = 16.1 \text{ mol C}_2\text{H}_6\text{O}_2\text{/kg}$

Since the density of water is 1.00 g/cm^3, the moles of $C_2H_6O_2$ needed are:

$15.0 \text{ L H}_2\text{O} \times \dfrac{1.00 \text{ kg H}_2\text{O}}{\text{L H}_2\text{O}} \times \dfrac{16.1 \text{ mol C}_2\text{H}_6\text{O}_2}{\text{kg H}_2\text{O}} = 242 \text{ mol C}_2\text{H}_6\text{O}_2$

$$\text{Volume } C_2H_6O_2 = 242 \text{ mol } C_2H_6O_2 \times \frac{62.07 \text{ g}}{\text{mol } C_2H_6O_2} \times \frac{1 \text{ cm}^3}{1.11 \text{ g}} = 13,500 \text{ cm}^3 = 13.5 \text{ L}$$

$$\Delta T_b = K_b m = \frac{0.51°C}{\text{molal}} \times 16.1 \text{ molal} = 8.2°C; \quad T_b = 100.0°C + 8.2°C = 108.2°C$$

67. $$M = \frac{1.0 \text{ g}}{\text{L}} \times \frac{1 \text{ mol}}{9.0 \times 10^4 \text{ g}} = 1.1 \times 10^{-5} \text{ mol/L}; \quad \pi = MRT$$

At 298 K: $$\pi = \frac{1.1 \times 10^{-5} \text{ mol}}{\text{L}} \times \frac{0.08206 \text{ L atm}}{\text{mol K}} \times 298 \text{ K} \times \frac{760 \text{ torr}}{\text{atm}}, \quad \pi = 0.20 \text{ torr}$$

Since $d = 1.0 \text{ g/cm}^3$, then 1.0 L solution has a mass of 1.0 kg. Since only 1.0 g of protein is present per liter solution, then 1.0 kg of H_2O is present and molality equals molarity.

$$\Delta T_f = K_f m = \frac{1.86°C}{\text{molal}} \times 1.1 \times 10^{-5} \text{ molal} = 2.0 \times 10^{-5}°C$$

68. Osmotic pressure is better for determining the molar mass of large molecules. A temperature change of $10^{-5}°C$ is very difficult to measure. A change in height of a column of mercury by 0.2 mm (0.2 torr) is not as hard to measure precisely.

69. $$\pi = MRT = \frac{0.1 \text{ mol}}{\text{L}} \times \frac{0.08206 \text{ L atm}}{\text{mol K}} \times 298 \text{ K} = 2.45 \text{ atm} \approx 2 \text{ atm}$$

$$\pi = 2 \text{ atm} \times \frac{760 \text{ mm Hg}}{\text{atm}} \approx 2000 \text{ mm} \approx 2 \text{ m}$$

The osmotic pressure would support a mercury column of ≈ 2 m. The height of a fluid column in a tree will be higher because Hg is more dense than the fluid in a tree. If we assume the fluid in a tree is mostly H_2O, then the fluid has a density of 1.0 g/cm^3. The density of Hg is 13.6 g/cm^3.

Height of fluid $\approx 2 \text{ m} \times 13.6 \approx 30 \text{ m}$

70. $\Delta T_f = 5.51 - 2.81 = 2.70°C; \quad m = \dfrac{\Delta T_f}{K_f} = \dfrac{2.70°C}{5.12°C/\text{molal}} = 0.527 \text{ molal}$

Let x = mass of naphthalene (molar mass = 128.2 g/mol). Then $1.60 - x$ = mass of anthracene (molar mass = 178.2 g/mol).

$$\frac{x}{128.2} = \text{moles naphthalene and } \frac{1.60 - x}{178.2} = \text{moles anthracene}$$

$$\frac{0.527 \text{ moles solute}}{\text{kg solvent}} = \frac{\dfrac{x}{128.2} + \dfrac{1.60 - x}{178.2}}{0.0200 \text{ kg solvent}}, \quad 1.05 \times 10^{-2} = \frac{178.2 x + 1.60(128.2) - 128.2 x}{128.2(178.2)}$$

$50.0 \, x + 205 = 240., \quad 50.0 \, x = 240. - 205, \quad 50.0 \, x = 35, \quad x = 0.70 \text{ g naphthalene}$

So the mixture is:

$$\frac{0.70\ g}{1.60\ g} \times 100 = 44\%\ \text{naphthalene by mass and 56\% anthracene by mass}$$

71.   With addition of salt or sugar, the osmotic pressure inside the fruit cells (and bacteria) is less than outside the cell. Water will leave the cells which will dehydrate any bacteria present, causing them to die.

Properties of Electrolyte Solutions

72.   A strong electrolyte dissociates completely into ions in solution. A weak electrolyte dissociates only partially into ions in solution. Colligative properties depend on the total number of particles in solution. By measuring a property such as freezing point depression, boiling point elevation or osmotic pressure, we can calculate the van't Hoff factor (i) to see if an electrolyte is strong or weak.

73. $19.6\ \text{torr} = \chi_{H_2O}\ (23.8\ \text{torr})$, $\chi_{H_2O} = 0.824$; $\chi_{solute} = 1.000 - 0.824 = 0.176$

0.176 is the mol fraction of all the solute particles present. Since NaCl dissolves to produce two ions in solution (Na^+ and Cl^-), 0.176 is the mole fraction of Na^+ and Cl^- ions present. The mole fraction of NaCl is 1/2 (0.176) = 0.0880 = χ_{NaCl}.

At 45°C, $P_{H_2O} = 0.824\ (71.9\ \text{torr}) = 59.2\ \text{torr}$

74.   If ideal, NaCl dissociates completely and i = 2.00. $\Delta T_f = iK_f m$; Assuming water freezes at 0.00°C:

$$1.28°C = 2 \times 1.86°C\ \text{kg/mol} \times m, \quad m = 0.344\ \text{mol NaCl/kg}\ H_2O$$

Assume an amount of solution which contains 1.00 kg of water (solvent).

$$0.344\ \text{mol NaCl} \times \frac{58.44\ g}{mol} = 20.1\ g\ \text{NaCl};\quad \text{mass \% NaCl} = \frac{20.1\ g}{1.00 \times 10^3\ g + 20.1\ g} \times 100 = 1.97\%$$

75. $Na_3PO_4(s) \rightarrow 3\ Na^+(aq) + PO_4^{3-}(aq)$, i = 4.0; $CaBr_2(s) \rightarrow Ca^{2+}(aq) + 2\ Br^-(aq)$, i = 3.0

$KCl(s) \rightarrow K^+(aq) + Cl^-(aq)$, i = 2.0.

The effective particle concentrations of the solutions are:

4.0(0.010 molal) = 0.040 molal for Na_3PO_4 solution; 3.0(0.020 molal) = 0.060 molal for $CaBr_2$ solution; 2.0(0.020 molal) = 0.040 molal for KCl solution; slightly greater than 0.020 molal for HF solution since HF only partially dissociates in water (it is a weak acid).

a.   The 0.010 m Na_3PO_4 solution and the 0.020 m KCl solution both have effective particle concentrations of 0.040 m (assuming complete dissociation), so both of these solutions should have the same boiling point as the 0.040 m $C_6H_{12}O_6$ solution (a nonelectrolyte).

b. $P = \chi P°$; As the solute concentration decreases, the solvent's vapor pressure increases since χ increases. Therefore, the 0.020 m HF solution will have the highest vapor pressure since it has the smallest effective particle concentration.

c. $\Delta T = K_f m$; The 0.020 m $CaBr_2$ solution has the largest effective particle concentration so it will have the largest freezing point depression (largest ΔT).

76. The solutions of glucose, NaCl and $CaCl_2$ will all have lower freezing points, higher boiling points and higher osmotic pressures than pure water. The solution with the largest particle concentration will have the lowest freezing point, the highest boiling point and the highest osmotic pressure. The $CaCl_2$ solution will have the largest effective particle concentration since it produces three ions per 1 mol of compound.

    a.   pure water   b. $CaCl_2$ solution   c. $CaCl_2$ solution

    d.   pure water   e. $CaCl_2$ solution

77. Ion pairing can occur, resulting in fewer particles than expected. This results in smaller freezing point depressions and smaller boiling point elevations ($\Delta T = K m$). Ion pairing will increase as the concentration of electrolyte increases.

78.   a.   As discussed in Figure 17.16 of the text, the water would migrate from right to left. Initially, the level of liquid in the right arm would go down and the level in the left arm would go up. At some point, the rate of solvent transfer will be the same in both directions and the levels of the liquids in the two arms will stabilize. The height difference between the two arms will be a measure of the osmotic pressure of the NaCl solution.

    b.   Initially, H_2O molecules will have a net migration into the NaCl side. However, NaCl molecules can now migrate into the H_2O side. Because solute and solvent transfer are both possible, the levels of the liquids will be equal once the rate of solute and solvent transfer is equal in both directions. At this point, the concentration of NaCl will be equal in both chambers and the levels of liquid will be equal.

79. $NaCl(s) \rightarrow Na^+(aq) + Cl^-(aq)$, i = 2.0

$$\pi = iMRT = 2.0 \times \frac{0.10 \text{ mol}}{\text{L}} \times \frac{0.08206 \text{ L atm}}{\text{mol K}} \times 293 \text{ K} = 4.8 \text{ atm}$$

A pressure greater than 4.8 atm should be applied to insure purification by reverse osmosis.

80.   a. $MgCl_2(s) \rightarrow Mg^{2+}(aq) + 2 Cl^-(aq)$, i = 3.0 mol ions/mol solute

$\Delta T_f = iK_f m = 3.0 \times 1.86°C/\text{molal} \times 0.050 \text{ molal} = 0.28°C$; $T_f = -0.28°C$ (Assuming water freezes at 0.00°C.)

$\Delta T_b = iK_b m = 3.0 \times 0.51°C/\text{molal} \times 0.050 \text{ molal} = 0.077°C$; $T_b = 100.077°C$ (Assuming water boils at 100.000°C.)

b. $FeCl_3(s) \rightarrow Fe^{3+}(aq) + 3\ Cl^-(aq)$, $i = 4.0$ mol ions/mol solute

$\Delta T_f = iK_f m = 4.0 \times 1.86°C/molal \times 0.050$ molal $= 0.37°C$; $T_f = -0.37°C$

$\Delta T_b = iK_b m = 4.0 \times 0.51°C/molal \times 0.050$ molal $= 0.10°C$; $T_b = 100.10°C$

81.   a. $MgCl_2$, i(observed) $= 2.7$

$\Delta T_f = iK_f m = 2.7 \times 1.86°C/molal \times 0.050$ molal $= 0.25°C$; $T_f = -0.25°C$

$\Delta T_b = iK_b m = 2.7 \times 0.51°C/molal \times 0.050$ molal $= 0.069°C$; $T_b = 100.069°C$

b. $FeCl_3$, i(observed) $= 3.4$

$\Delta T_f = iK_f m = 3.4 \times 1.86\ °C/molal \times 0.050$ molal $= 0.32°C$; $T_f = -0.32°C$

$\Delta T_b = iK_b m = 3.4 \times 0.51°C/molal \times 0.050$ molal $= 0.087°C$; $T_b = 100.087°C$

82. $\Delta T_f = iK_f m$, $i = \dfrac{\Delta T_f}{K_f m} = \dfrac{0.110°C}{1.86°\ C/molal \times 0.0225\ molal} = 2.63$ for $0.0225\ m$ $CaCl_2$

$i = \dfrac{0.440}{1.86 \times 0.0910} = 2.60$ for $0.0910\ m$ $CaCl_2$; $i = \dfrac{1.330}{1.86 \times 0.278} = 2.57$ for $0.278\ m$ $CaCl_2$

Note that i is less than the ideal value of 3.0 for $CaCl_2$. This is due to ion pairing in solution.

83. $\pi = iMRT = 3.0 \times 0.50$ mol/L $\times 0.08206$ L atm K^{-1} mol^{-1} $\times 298$ K $= 37$ atm

Because of ion pairing in solution, we would expect i to be less than 3.0 which results in fewer solute particles in solution which results in a lower osmotic pressure than calculated above.

84.   a. $T_C = (T_F - 32)/9 = 5(-29 - 32)/9 = -34°C$

Assuming the solubility of $CaCl_2$ is temperature independent, the molality of a saturated $CaCl_2$ solution is:

$$\dfrac{74.5\ g\ CaCl_2}{100.0\ g\ H_2O} \times \dfrac{1000\ g}{kg} \times \dfrac{1\ mol\ CaCl_2}{110.98\ g\ CaCl_2} = \dfrac{6.71\ mol\ CaCl_2}{kg\ H_2O}$$

$\Delta T_f = iK_f m = 3.00 \times 1.86°C$ kg/mol $\times 6.71$ mol/kg $= 37.4°C$

Assuming $i = 3.00$, a saturated solution of $CaCl_2$ can lower the freezing point of water to $-37.4°C$. Assuming these conditions, a saturated $CaCl_2$ solution should melt ice at $-34°C$ $(-29°F)$.

b.   From Exercise 17.82, $i \approx 2.6$; $\Delta T_f = iK_f m = 2.6 \times 1.86 \times 6.71 = 32°C$; $T_f = -32°C$

Assuming $i = 2.6$, a saturated $CaCl_2$ solution will not melt ice at $-34°C(-29°F)$.

Additional Exercises

85.   Both solutions and colloids have suspended particles in some medium. The major difference between the two is the size of the particles. A colloid is a suspension of relatively large particles as compared to a solution. Because of this, colloids will scatter light while solutions will not. The scattering of light by a colloidal suspension is called the Tyndall effect.

86.   The micelles form so the ionic ends of the detergent molecules, the SO_4^- ends, are exposed to the polar water molecules on the outside, while the nonpolar hydrocarbon chains from the detergent molecules are hidden from the water by pointing toward the inside of the micelle. Dirt, which is basically nonpolar, is stabilized in the nonpolar interior of the micelle and is washed away.

87.

Benzoic acid is capable of hydrogen bonding, but a significant part of benzoic acid is the nonpolar benzene ring. In benzene, a hydrogen bonded dimer forms.

The dimer is relatively nonpolar and thus more soluble in benzene than in water. Since benzoic acid forms dimers in benzene, the effective solute particle concentration will be less than 1.0 molal. Therefore, the freezing point depression would be less than 5.12 °C ($\Delta T_f = K_f m$).

88.   Benzoic acid would be more soluble in a basic solution because of the reaction:

$$C_6H_5CO_2H + OH^- \rightarrow C_6H_5CO_2^- + H_2O$$

By removing the proton from benzoic acid, an anion forms; and like all anions, the species becomes more soluble in water.

89.   a. $NH_4NO_3(s) \rightarrow NH_4^+(aq) + NO_3^-(aq)$ $\Delta H_{soln} = ?$

Heat gain by dissolution process = heat loss by solution; We will keep all quantities positive in order to avoid sign errors. Since the temperature of the water decreased, then the dissolution of NH_4NO_3 is endothermic (ΔH is positive). Mass of solution = 1.60 + 75.0 = 76.6 g

$$\text{heat loss by solution} = \frac{4.18 \text{ J}}{\text{g} \,^\circ\text{C}} \times 76.6 \text{ g} \times (25.00 \,^\circ\text{C} - 23.34 \,^\circ\text{C}) = 532 \text{ J}$$

$$\Delta H_{soln} = \frac{532 \text{ J}}{1.60 \text{ g NH}_4\text{NO}_3} \times \frac{80.05 \text{ g NH}_4\text{NO}_3}{\text{mol NH}_4\text{NO}_3} = 2.66 \times 10^4 \text{ J/mol} = 26.6 \text{ kJ/mol}$$

b.   We will use Hess's law to solve for the lattice energy. The lattice energy equation is:

$NH_4^+(g) + NO_3^-(g) \rightarrow NH_4NO_3(s)$ ΔH = lattice energy

$NH_4^+(g) + NO_3^-(g) \rightarrow NH_4^+(aq) + NO_3^-(aq)$ $\Delta H = \Delta H_{hyd} = -630.$ kJ/mol
$NH_4^+(aq) + NO_3^-(aq) \rightarrow NH_4NO_3(s)$ $\Delta H = -\Delta H_{soln} = -26.6$ kJ/mol
_____
$NH_4^+(g) + NO_3^-(g) \rightarrow NH_4NO_3(s)$ $\Delta H = \Delta H_{hyd} - \Delta H_{soln} = -657$ kJ/mol

90.   a.   The average values for each ion are:

300. mg Na^+; 15.7 mg K^+; 5.45 mg Ca^{2+}; 388 mg Cl^-; 246 mg lactate, $C_3H_5O_3^-$

Note: Since we can precisely weigh to ± 0.1 mg on an analytical balance, we'll carry extra significant figures and calculate results to ± 0.1 mg.

The only source of lactate is $NaC_3H_5O_3$.

$$246 \text{ mg lactate} \times \frac{112.06 \text{ mg NaC}_3\text{H}_5\text{O}_3}{89.07 \text{ mg C}_3\text{H}_5\text{O}_3^-} = 309.5 \text{ mg sodium lactate}$$

The only source of Ca^{2+} is $CaCl_2 \cdot 2H_2O$.

$$5.45 \text{ mg Ca}^{2+} \times \frac{147.0 \text{ mg CaCl}_2 \cdot 2\text{H}_2\text{O}}{40.08 \text{ mg Ca}^{2+}} = 19.99 \text{ or } 20.0 \text{ mg CaCl}_2 \cdot 2\text{H}_2\text{O}$$

The only source of K^+ is KCl.

$$15.7 \text{ mg K}^+ \times \frac{74.55 \text{ mg KCl}}{39.10 \text{ mg K}^+} = 29.9 \text{ mg KCl}$$

From what we have used already, let's calculate the mass of Na^+ and Cl^- added.

$$309.5 \text{ mg sodium lactate} = 246.0 \text{ mg lactate} + 63.5 \text{ mg Na}^+$$

Thus, we need to add an additional 236.5 mg Na^+ to get the desired 300. mg.

$$236.5 \text{ mg Na}^+ \times \frac{58.44 \text{ mg NaCl}}{22.99 \text{ mg Na}^+} = 601.2 \text{ mg NaCl}$$

Let's check the mass of Cl^- added:

$$20.0 \text{ mg CaCl}_2 \cdot 2H_2O \times \frac{70.90 \text{ mg Cl}^-}{147.0 \text{ mg CaCl}_2 \cdot 2H_2O} = 9.6 \text{ mg Cl}^-$$

$$20.0 \text{ mg CaCl}_2 \cdot 2H_2O = 9.6 \text{ mg Cl}^-$$

$$29.9 \text{ mg KCl} - 15.7 \text{ mg K}^+ = 14.2 \text{ mg Cl}^-$$

$$\underline{601.2 \text{ mg NaCl} - 236.5 \text{ mg Na}^+ = 364.7 \text{ mg Cl}^-}$$

$$\text{Total Cl}^- = 388.5 \text{ mg Cl}^-$$

This is the quantity of Cl^- we want (the average amount of Cl^-).

An analytical balance can weigh to the nearest 0.1 mg. We would use 309.5 mg sodium lactate, 20.0 mg $CaCl_2 \cdot 2H_2O$, 29.9 mg KCl and 601.2 mg NaCl.

b. To get the range of osmotic pressure, we need to calculate the molar concentration of each ion at its minimum and maximum values. At minimum concentrations, we have:

$$\frac{285 \text{ mg Na}^+}{100. \text{ mL}} \times \frac{1 \text{ mmol}}{22.99 \text{ mg}} = 0.124 \text{ } M; \quad \frac{14.1 \text{ mg K}^+}{100. \text{ mL}} \times \frac{1 \text{ mmol}}{39.10 \text{ mg}} = 0.00361 \text{ } M$$

$$\frac{4.9 \text{ mg Ca}^{2+}}{100. \text{ mL}} \times \frac{1 \text{ mmol}}{40.08 \text{ mg}} = 0.0012 \text{ } M; \quad \frac{368 \text{ mg Cl}^-}{100. \text{ mL}} \times \frac{1 \text{ mmol}}{35.45 \text{ mg}} = 0.104 \text{ } M$$

$$\frac{231 \text{ mg C}_3H_5O_3^-}{100. \text{ mL}} \times \frac{1 \text{ mmol}}{89.07 \text{ mg}} = 0.0259 \text{ } M$$

Total = 0.124 + 0.00361 + 0.0012 + 0.104 + 0.0259 = 0.259 M

$$\pi = MRT = \frac{0.259 \text{ mol}}{L} \times \frac{0.08206 \text{ L atm}}{\text{mol K}} \times 310. \text{ K} = 6.59 \text{ atm}$$

Similarly at maximum concentrations, the concentration of each ion is:

Na^+: 0.137 M; K^+: 0.00442 M; Ca^{2+}: 0.0015 M; Cl^-: 0.115 M; $C_3H_5O_3^-$: 0.0293 M

The total concentration of all ions is the sum, 0.287 M.

$$\pi = \frac{0.287 \text{ mol}}{\text{L}} \times \frac{0.08206 \text{ L atm}}{\text{mol K}} \times 310. \text{ K} = 7.30 \text{ atm}$$

Osmotic pressure ranges from 6.59 atm to 7.30 atm.

91. $\chi_{pen}^{V} = 0.15 = \dfrac{P_{pen}}{P_{total}}$; $P_{pen} = \chi_{pen}^{L} P_{pen}^{\circ} = \chi_{pen}^{L}(511 \text{ torr})$; $P_{total} = P_{pen} + P_{hex} = \chi_{pen}^{L}(511) + \chi_{hex}^{L}(150.)$

Since $\chi_{hex}^{L} = 1.000 - \chi_{pen}^{L}$, then: $P_{total} = \chi_{pen}^{L}(511) + (1.000 - \chi_{pen}^{L})(150.) = 150. + 361 \chi_{pen}^{L}$

$\chi_{pen}^{V} = \dfrac{P_{pen}}{P_{total}}$, $0.15 = \dfrac{\chi_{pen}^{L}(511)}{150. + 361 \chi_{pen}^{L}}$, $0.15 (150. + 361 \chi_{pen}^{L}) = 511 \chi_{pen}^{L}$

$23 + 54 \chi_{pen}^{L} = 511 \chi_{pen}^{L}$, $\chi_{pen}^{L} = \dfrac{23}{457} = 0.050$

92.   a.   Water boils when the vapor pressure equals the pressure above the water. In an open pan $P_{atm} \approx 1.0$ atm. In a pressure cooker, $P_{inside} > 1.0$ atm and water boils at a higher temperature. The higher the cooking temperature, the faster the cooking time.

b.   Salt dissolves in water forming a solution with a melting point lower than that of pure water ($\Delta T_f = K_f m$). This happens in water on the surface of ice. If it is not too cold, the ice melts. This won't work if the ambient temperature is lower than the depressed freezing point of the salt solution.

c.   When water freezes from a solution, it freezes as pure water, leaving behind a more concentrated salt solution.

d.   On the CO_2 phase diagram, the triple point is above 1 atm and $CO_2(g)$ is the stable phase at 1 atm and room temperature. $CO_2(l)$ can't exist at normal atmospheric pressures. Therefore, dry ice sublimes instead of boils. In a fire extinguisher, $P > 1$ atm and $CO_2(l)$ can exist. When CO_2 is released from the fire extinguisher, $CO_2(g)$ forms as predicted from the phase diagram.

93. $14.22 \text{ mg } CO_2 \times \dfrac{12.011 \text{ mg C}}{44.009 \text{ mg } CO_2} = 3.881 \text{ mg C}$; $\% \text{ C} = \dfrac{3.881 \text{ mg}}{4.80 \text{ mg}} \times 100 = 80.9\% \text{ C}$

$1.66 \text{ mg } H_2O \times \dfrac{2.016 \text{ mg H}}{18.02 \text{ mg } H_2O} = 0.186 \text{ mg H}$; $\% \text{ H} = \dfrac{0.186 \text{ mg}}{4.80 \text{ mg}} \times 100 = 3.88\% \text{ H}$

$\% \text{ O} = 100.00 - (80.9 + 3.88) = 15.2\% \text{ O}$

Out of 100.00 g:

$80.9 \text{ g C} \times \dfrac{1 \text{ mol}}{12.01 \text{ g}} = 6.74 \text{ mol C}$; $\dfrac{6.74}{0.950} = 7.09 \approx 7$

$3.88 \text{ g H} \times \dfrac{1 \text{ mol}}{1.008 \text{ g}} = 3.85 \text{ mol H}$; $\dfrac{3.85}{0.950} = 4.05 \approx 4$

$15.2 \text{ g O} \times \dfrac{1 \text{ mol}}{16.00 \text{ g}} = 0.950 \text{ mol O}$; $\dfrac{0.950}{0.950} = 1.00$

Therefore, the empirical formula is C_7H_4O.

$$\Delta T_f = K_f m, \quad m = \frac{\Delta T_f}{K_f} = \frac{22.3\,°C}{40.\,°C/molal} = 0.56 \text{ molal}$$

$$\text{mol anthraquinone} = 0.0114 \text{ kg camphor} \times \frac{0.56 \text{ mol anthraquinone}}{\text{kg camphor}} = 6.4 \times 10^{-3} \text{ mol}$$

$$\text{molar mass} = \frac{1.32 \text{ g}}{6.4 \times 10^{-3} \text{ mol}} = 210 \text{ g/mol}$$

The empirical mass of C_7H_4O is: $7(12) + 4(1) + 16 \approx 104$ g/mol. Since the molar mass is twice the empirical mass, then the molecular formula is $C_{14}H_8O_2$.

94.   Out of 100.00 g, there are:

$$31.57 \text{ g C} \times \frac{1 \text{ mol C}}{12.011 \text{ g}} = 2.628 \text{ mol C}; \quad \frac{2.628}{2.628} = 1.000$$

$$5.30 \text{ g H} \times \frac{1 \text{ mol H}}{1.008 \text{ g}} = 5.26 \text{ mol H}; \quad \frac{5.26}{2.628} = 2.00$$

$$63.13 \text{ g O} \times \frac{1 \text{ mol O}}{15.999 \text{ g}} = 3.946 \text{ mol O}; \quad \frac{3.946}{2.628} = 1.502$$

empirical formula: $C_2H_4O_3$; Use the freezing point data to determine the molar mass.

$$m = \frac{\Delta T_f}{K_f} = \frac{5.20\,°C}{1.86\,°C/molal} = 2.80 \text{ molal}$$

$$\text{mol solute} = 0.0250 \text{ kg} \times \frac{2.80 \text{ mol solute}}{\text{kg}} = 0.0700 \text{ mol solute}$$

$$\text{molar mass} = \frac{10.56 \text{ g}}{0.0700 \text{ mol}} = 151 \text{ g/mol}$$

The empirical formula mass of $C_2H_4O_3 = 76.051$ g/mol. Since the molar mass is about twice the empirical mass, then the molecular formula is $C_4H_8O_6$ which has a molar mass of 152.101 g/mol.

Note: We use the experimental molar mass to determine the molecular formula. Knowing this, we calculate the molar mass precisely from the molecular formula using atomic masses.

95.   a. $m = \dfrac{\Delta T_f}{K_f} = \dfrac{1.32\,°C}{5.12\,°C \text{ kg/mol}} = 0.258 \text{ mol/kg}$

$$\text{mol unknown} = 0.01560 \text{ kg} \times \frac{0.258 \text{ mol unknown}}{\text{kg}} = 4.02 \times 10^{-3} \text{ mol}$$

$$\text{molar mass of unknown} = \frac{1.22 \text{ g}}{4.02 \times 10^{-3} \text{ mol}} = 303 \text{ g/mol}$$

Uncertainty in temperature $= \dfrac{0.04}{1.32} \times 100 = 3\%$; A 3% uncertainty in 303 g/mol = 9 g/mol.

So, molar mass $= 303 \pm 9$ g/mol.

b.   No, codeine could not be eliminated since its molar mass is in the possible range including the uncertainty.

c.   We would like the uncertainty to be ± 1 g/mol. We need the freezing point depression to be about 10 times what it was in this problem. Two possibilities are:

1.   make the solution ten times more concentrated (may be solubility problem) or
2.   use a solvent with a larger K_f value, e.g., camphor

96. $MX \rightleftharpoons M^+ + X^-$ $\Delta T = K_f m$ $m = \dfrac{\Delta T}{K_f} = \dfrac{0.028}{1.86} = 0.015$ mol/kg

$\dfrac{0.015 \text{ mol}}{\text{kg}} \times \dfrac{1 \text{ kg}}{1000 \text{ g}} \times 250 \text{ g} = 0.00375$ mol total solute particles (carrying extra sig fig)

Assume a density of 1.00 g/mL.

$[M^+] = \dfrac{(0.00375/2)}{0.250 \text{ L}} = 7.5 \times 10^{-3}\, M$, $[X^-] = \dfrac{(0.00375/2)}{0.250 \text{ L}} = 7.5 \times 10^{-3}\, M$

$K_{sp} = [M^+][X^-] = 5.6 \times 10^{-5}$

97. $M_3X_2(s)$ $\rightarrow$ $3\, M^{2+}(aq)$ + $2\, X^{3-}(aq)$ $K_{sp} = [M^{2+}]^3[X^{3-}]^2$

Initial   s = solubility (mol/L)   0   0
Equil.   3s   2s

$K_{sp} = (3s)^3(2s)^2 = 108\, s^5$; Total ion concentration $= 3s + 2s = 5s$

$\pi = iMRT$, $iM =$ total ion concentration $= \dfrac{\pi}{RT} = \dfrac{2.64 \times 10^{-2} \text{ atm}}{0.08206 \text{ L atm K}^{-1} \text{ mol}^{-1} \times 298 \text{ K}}$

$= 1.08 \times 10^{-3}$ mol/L

$5s = 1.08 \times 10^{-3}$ mol/L, s $= 2.16 \times 10^{-4}$ mol/L; $K_{sp} = 108\, s^5 = 108(2.16 \times 10^{-4})^5 = 5.08 \times 10^{-17}$

98. $\Delta T = K_f m$

$m = \dfrac{\Delta T}{K_f} = \dfrac{0.426\ {}^\circ C}{1.86\ {}^\circ C/m} = 0.229$ m

Assume a density $= 1.00$ g/mL, then 1.00 L contains 0.229 mol solute.

$NaCl \rightarrow Na^+ + Cl^-$ (ideal); So, 2 (moles NaCl) + mol $C_{12}H_{22}O_{11}$ = 0.229 mol

mass NaCl + mass $C_{12}H_{22}O_{11}$ = 20.0 g

$2n_{NaCl} + n_{C_{12}H_{22}O_{11}}$ = 0.229 and 58.44 (n_{NaCl}) + 342.3 $(n_{C_{12}H_{22}O_{11}})$ = 20.0

Solving, we get $n_{C_{12}H_{22}O_{11}}$ = 0.0425 mol = 14.5 g and n_{NaCl} = 0.0932 mol = 5.5 g

% $C_{12}H_{22}O_{11} = \dfrac{14.5}{20.0} \times 100$ = 72.5 % and 27.5% by mass NaCl.

$\chi_{C_{12}H_{22}O_{11}} = \dfrac{0.0425}{0.0425 + 0.0932} = 0.313$

99. $m = \dfrac{0.100 \text{ g} \times \dfrac{1 \text{ mol}}{100.0 \text{ g}}}{0.5000 \text{ kg}}$ = 2.00 × 10⁻³ mol/kg ≈ 2.00 × 10⁻³ mol/L   (dilute solution)

$\Delta T_f = iK_f m$, 0.0056°C = i(1.86°C/molal) (2.00 × 10⁻³ molal), i = 1.5

If i = 1.0, % dissociation = 0% and if i = 2.0, % dissociation = 100%. Since i = 1.5, then the weak acid is 50.% dissociated.

$HA \rightleftharpoons H^+ + A^-$ $K_a = \dfrac{[H^+][A^-]}{[HA]}$

Since the weak acid is 50.% dissociated, then:

$[H^+] = [A^-] = [HA]_o \times 0.50 = 2.00 \times 10^{-3} M \times 0.50 = 1.0 \times 10^{-3} M$

$[HA] = [HA]_o$ - amount HA reacted = $2.00 \times 10^{-3} M$ - $1.0 \times 10^{-3} M = 1.0 \times 10^{-3} M$

$K_a = \dfrac{[H^+][A^-]}{[HA]} = \dfrac{(1.0 \times 10^{-3})(1.0 \times 10^{-3})}{1.0 \times 10^{-3}} = 1.0 \times 10^{-3}$

100. $\Delta T_f = K_f m$, $m = \dfrac{\Delta T}{K_f} = \dfrac{5.40°C}{1.86°C/\text{molal}}$ = 2.90 molal

$\dfrac{2.90 \text{ mol solute}}{\text{kg solvent}} = \dfrac{n}{0.0500 \text{ kg}}$, n = 0.145 mol of ions in solution

Since $NaNO_3$ and $Mg(NO_3)_2$ are strong electrolytes:

n = 2(x mol of $NaNO_3$) + 3[y mol $Mg(NO_3)_2$] = 0.145 mol ions

In addition: 6.50 g = x mol $NaNO_3 \left(\dfrac{85.00 \text{ g}}{\text{mol}} \right)$ + y mol $Mg(NO_3)_2 \left(\dfrac{148.3 \text{ g}}{\text{mol}} \right)$

We have two equations: 2 x + 3 y = 0.145 and 85.00 x + 148.3 y = 6.50

Solving by simultaneous equations:

$$-85.00\,x - 127.5\,y = -6.16$$
$$85.00\,x + 148.3\,y = 6.50$$

_____

$$20.8\,y = 0.34, \quad y = 0.016 \text{ mol } Mg(NO_3)_2$$

mass of $Mg(NO_3)_2$ = 0.016 mol × 148.3 g/mol = 2.4 g $Mg(NO_3)_2$, or 37% $Mg(NO_3)_2$ by mass

mass of $NaNO_3$ = 6.50 g - 2.4 g = 4.1 g $NaNO_3$, or 63% $NaNO_3$ by mass

101. $iM = \dfrac{\pi}{RT} = \dfrac{0.3950 \text{ atm}}{0.08206 \text{ L atm mol}^{-1}\text{K}^{-1}(298.2 \text{ K})} = 0.01614 \text{ mol/L}$ = total ion concentration

$0.01614 \text{ mol/L} = M_{Mg^{2+}} + M_{Na^+} + M_{Cl^-}; \quad M_{Cl^-} = 2\,M_{Mg^{2+}} + M_{Na^+}$ (charge balance)

Combining: $0.01614 = 3\,M_{Mg^{2+}} + 2\,M_{Na^+}$

Let x = mass $MgCl_2$ and y = mass NaCl, then $x + y = 0.5000$ g.

$M_{Mg^{2+}} = \dfrac{x}{95.218}$ and $M_{Na^+} = \dfrac{y}{58.443}$ (Since V = 1.000 L.)

Total ion concentration = $\dfrac{3\,x}{95.218} + \dfrac{2\,y}{58.443} = 0.01614 \text{ mol/L}$; Rearranging: $3\,x + 3.2585\,y = 1.537$

Solving by simultaneous equations:

$$3\,x + 3.2585\,y = 1.537$$
$$-3\,(x + y) = -3(0.5000)$$

_____

$$0.2585\,y = 0.037, \quad y = 0.14 \text{ g NaCl}$$

mass $MgCl_2$ = 0.5000 g - 0.14 g = 0.36 g; mass % $MgCl_2$ = $\dfrac{0.36 \text{ g}}{0.5000 \text{ g}} \times 100 = 72\%$

102.   Use the thermodynamic data to calculate the boiling point of the solvent.

At boiling point, $\Delta G = 0 = \Delta H - T\Delta S$, $\Delta H = T\Delta S$, $T = \dfrac{\Delta H}{\Delta S} = \dfrac{33.90 \times 10^3 \text{ J/mol}}{95.95 \text{ J K}^{-1}\text{mol}^{-1}} = 353.3 \text{ K}$

$\Delta T = K_b m$, (355.4 K - 353.3 K) = 2.5 K kg/mol (m), $m = \dfrac{2.1}{2.5} = 0.84 \text{ mol/kg}$

mass solvent = 150. mL × $\dfrac{0.879 \text{ g}}{\text{mL}} \times \dfrac{1 \text{ kg}}{1000 \text{ g}} = 0.132 \text{ kg}$

mass solute = 0.132 kg solvent × $\dfrac{0.84 \text{ mol solute}}{\text{kg solvent}} \times \dfrac{142 \text{ g}}{\text{mol}} = 15.7 \text{ g} = 16 \text{ g solute}$

Challenge Problems

103.   From the problem, $\chi^L_{C_6H_6} = \chi^L_{CCl_4} = 0.500$. We need the pure vapor pressures (P°) in order to calculate the vapor pressure of the solution. Using the thermodynamic data:

$$C_6H_6(l) \; \rightleftharpoons \; C_6H_6(g) \quad K = P_{C_6H_6} = P^\circ_{C_6H_6} \text{ at } 25\,^\circ C$$

$$\Delta G^\circ_{rxn} = \Delta G^\circ_{f, C_6H_6(g)} - \Delta G^\circ_{f, C_6H_6(l)} = 129.66 \text{ kJ/mol} - 124.50 \text{ kJ/mol} = 5.16 \text{ kJ/mol}$$

$$\Delta G^\circ = -RT\ln K, \; \ln K = \frac{-\Delta G^\circ}{RT} = \frac{-5.16 \times 10^3 \text{ J/mol}}{(8.3145 \text{ J K}^{-1}\text{ mol}^{-1})(298 \text{ K})} = -2.08$$

$$K = P^\circ_{C_6H_6} = e^{-2.08} = 0.125 \text{ atm}$$

For CCl_4: $\Delta G^\circ_{rxn} = \Delta G^\circ_{f, CCl_4(g)} - \Delta G^\circ_{f, CCl_4(l)} = -60.59 \text{ kJ/mol} - (-65.21 \text{ kJ/mol}) = 4.62 \text{ kJ/mol}$

$$K = P^\circ_{CCl_4} = \exp\left(\frac{-\Delta G^\circ}{RT}\right) = \exp\left(\frac{-4620 \text{ J/mol}}{8.3145 \text{ J K}^{-1}\text{ mol}^{-1} \times 298 \text{ K}}\right) = 0.155 \text{ atm}$$

$$P_{C_6H_6} = X^L_{C_6H_6} P^\circ_{C_6H_6} = 0.500 (0.125 \text{ atm}) = 0.0625 \text{ atm}; \quad P_{CCl_4} = 0.500 (0.155 \text{ atm}) = 0.0775 \text{ atm}$$

$$X^V_{C_6H_6} = \frac{P_{C_6H_6}}{P_{tot}} = \frac{0.0625 \text{ atm}}{0.0625 \text{ atm} + 0.0775 \text{ atm}} = \frac{0.0625}{0.1400} = 0.446; \quad X^V_{CCl_4} = 1.000 - 0.446 = 0.554$$

104. $\Delta T = K_f m, \quad m = \dfrac{\Delta T}{K_f} = \dfrac{2.79}{1.86} = 1.50 \text{ mol/kg}$

   a. $\Delta T = K_b \, m, \; \Delta T = (0.51)(1.5) = 0.765\,^\circ C, \; \text{b.p.} = 100.765\,^\circ C$

   b. $P_{water} = \chi_{water} P^\circ_{water}, \; \chi_{water} = \dfrac{\text{mol H}_2\text{O}}{\text{mol H}_2\text{O} + \text{mol solute}}$

        1.00 kg water = 55.5 mol H_2O; 1.50 mol solute are also present.

        $$\chi_{water} = \frac{55.5 \text{ mol}}{1.50 + 55.5} = 0.974$$

        $$P_{water} = (0.974)(23.76) = 23.1 \text{ mm Hg}$$

   c.   Assume ideality and assume i = 1 (no ions form)

105.   a.   Assuming $MgCO_3(s)$ does not dissociate, the solute concentration in water is:

        $$\frac{560 \; \mu g \; MgCO_3(s)}{mL} = \frac{560 \text{ mg}}{L} = \frac{560 \times 10^{-3} \text{ g}}{L} \times \frac{1 \text{ mol MgCO}_3}{84.32 \text{ g}} = 6.6 \times 10^{-3} \text{ mol MgCO}_3/\text{L}$$

An applied pressure of 8.0 atm will purify water up to a solute concentration of:

$$M = \frac{\pi}{RT} = \frac{8.0 \text{ atm}}{0.08206 \text{ L atm K}^{-1} \text{ mol}^{-1} \times 300. \text{ K}} = \frac{0.32 \text{ mol}}{L}$$

When the concentration of $MgCO_3(s)$ reaches 0.32 mol/L, the reverse osmosis unit can no longer purify the water. Let V = volume (L) of water remaining after purifying 45 L of H_2O. When V + 45 L of water has been processed, the moles of solute particles will equal:

6.6×10^{-3} mol/L $\times$ (45 L + V) = 0.32 mol/L $\times$ V

Solving: 0.30 = (0.32 - 0.0066) $\times$ V, V = 0.96 L

The minimum total volume of water that must be processed is 45 L + 0.96 L = 46 L.

Note: If $MgCO_3$ does dissociate into Mg^{2+} and CO_3^{2-} ions, then the solute concentration increases to 1.3×10^{-2} M and at least 47 L of water must be processed.

b. No; A reverse osmosis system that applies 8.0 atm can only purify water with a solute concentration less than 0.32 mol/L. Salt water has a solute concentration of 2(0.60 M) = 1.2 mol/L ions. The solute concentration of salt water is much too high for this reverse osmosis unit to work.

106. $\Delta T = K_f m$

$$m = \frac{0.406}{1.86} = 0.218 \text{ mol/kg}$$

$\pi = MRT$ where M = mol/L

We must assume a density of 1.00 g/mL for the solution so that molarity = molality. This is a reasonable assumption at 25°C for dilute solutions..

$\pi = (0.218 \ M)(0.08206)(298) = 5.33$ atm

107.   a. Assuming no ion association between $SO_4^{2-}(aq)$ and $Fe^{3+}(aq)$, then i = 5 for $Fe_2(SO_4)_3$.

$\pi = iMRT = 5(0.0500 \text{ mol/L})(0.08206 \text{ L atm K}^{-1} \text{ mol}^{-1})(298 \text{ K}) = 6.11$ atm

b. $Fe_2(SO_4)_3(aq) \rightarrow 2 \ Fe^{3+}(aq) + 3 \ SO_4^{2-}(aq)$

Under ideal circumstances, 2/5 of π calculated above results from Fe^{3+} and 3/5 results from SO_4^{2-}. The contribution to π from SO_4^{2-} is 3/5 $\times$ 6.11 atm = 3.67 atm. Since SO_4^{2-} is assumed unchanged in solution, then the SO_4^{2-} contribution in the actual solution will also be 3.67 atm. The contribution to the actual π from the $Fe(H_2O)_6^{3+}$ dissociation reaction is 6.73 - 3.67 = 3.06 atm.

The initial concentration of $Fe(H_2O)_6^{2+}$ is $2(0.0500) = 0.100\ M$. The set-up for the weak acid problem is:

$$Fe(H_2O)_6^{3+} \rightleftharpoons H^+ + Fe(OH)(H_2O)_5^{2+} \qquad K_a = \frac{[H^+][Fe(OH)(H_2O)_5^{2+}]}{[Fe(H_2O)_6^{3+}]}$$

Initial   0.100 M   ~0   0

x mol/L of $Fe(H_2O)_6^{3+}$ reacts to reach equilibrium

Equil.   0.100 - x x x

$$\pi = iMRT;\ \text{Total ion concentration} = iM = \frac{\pi}{RT} = \frac{3.06\ \text{atm}}{0.08206\ \text{L atm K}^{-1}\ \text{mol}^{-1}\ (298\ \text{K})} = 0.125\ M$$

$$0.125\ M = 0.100 - x + x + x = 0.100 + x,\ x = 0.025\ M$$

$$K_a = \frac{[H^+][Fe(OH)(H_2O)_5^{2+}]}{[Fe(H_2O)_6^{3+}]} = \frac{x^2}{0.100 - x} = \frac{(0.025)^2}{(0.100 - 0.025)} = \frac{(0.025)^2}{0.075},\ K_a = 8.3 \times 10^{-3}$$

108.   Initial moles VCl_4 = 6.6834 g VCl_4 × 1 mol VCl_4/192.74 g VCl_4 = 3.4676×10^{-2} mol VCl_4

$$\text{Total molality of solute particles} = im = \frac{\Delta T_f}{K_f} = \frac{5.97°C}{29.8°C\ \text{kg/mol}} = 0.200\ \text{mol/kg}$$

Since we have 0.1000 kg CCl_4, the total moles of solute particles present is:

$$0.200\ \text{mol/kg}\ (0.1000\ \text{kg}) = 0.0200\ \text{mol}$$

$$2\ VCl_4 \rightleftharpoons V_2Cl_8 \qquad K = \frac{[V_2Cl_8]}{[VCl_4]^2}$$

Initial 3.4676×10^{-2} mol   0

$2x$ mol VCl_4 reacts to reach equilibrium

Equil. 3.4676×10^{-2} - $2x$ x

Total moles solute particles = 0.0200 mol = mol VCl_4 + mol V_2Cl_8 = 3.4676×10^{-2} -$2x + x$

$$0.0200 = 3.4676 \times 10^{-2} - x,\ x = 0.0147\ \text{mol}$$

At equilibrium we have 0.0147 mol V_2Cl_8 and 0.0200 - 0.0147 = 0.0053 mol VCl_4. To determine the equilibrium constant, we need the total volume of solution in order to calculate equilibrium concentrations. The total mass of solution is 100.0 g + 6.6834 g = 106.7 g.

Total volume = 106.7 g × 1 cm³/1.696 g = 62.91 cm³ = 0.06291 L

The equilibrium concentrations are:

$$[V_2Cl_8] = \frac{0.0147\ \text{mol}}{0.06291\ \text{L}} = 0.234\ \text{mol/L};\ \ [VCl_4] = \frac{0.0053\ \text{mol}}{0.06291\ \text{L}} = 0.084\ \text{mol/L}$$

$$K = \frac{[V_2Cl_8]}{[VCl_4]^2} = \frac{0.234}{(0.084)^2} = 33$$

109. a. $\pi = iMRT$, $iM = \dfrac{\pi}{RT} = \dfrac{7.83 \text{ atm}}{0.08206 \text{ L atm K}^{-1} \text{ mol}^{-1} \times 298 \text{ K}} = 0.320 \text{ mol/L}$

Assuming 1.000 L of solution:

total mol solute particles = mol Na$^+$ + mol Cl$^-$ + mol NaCl = 0.320 mol

mass solution = 1000. mL $\times \dfrac{1.071 \text{ g}}{\text{mL}} = 1071$ g solution

mass NaCl in solution = 0.0100 $\times$ 1071 g = 10.7 g NaCl

mol NaCl added to solution = 10.7 g $\times \dfrac{1 \text{ mol}}{58.44 \text{ g}} = 0.183$ mol NaCl

Some of this NaCl dissociates into Na$^+$ and Cl$^-$ (two mol ions per mol NaCl) and some remains undissociated. Let x = mol undissociated NaCl = mol ion pairs.

mol solute particles = 0.320 mol = 2(0.183 - x) + x

0.320 = 0.366 - x, x = 0.046 mol ion pairs

fraction of ion pairs = $\dfrac{0.046}{0.183} = 0.25$, or 25%

b. $\Delta T = K_f m$ where $K_f = 1.86$ °C kg/mol; From part a, 1.000 L of solution contains 0.320 mol of solute particles. To calculate the molality of the solution, we need the kg of solvent present in 1.000 L solution.

mass of 1.000 L solution = 1071 g; mass of NaCl = 10.7 g

mass of solvent in 1.000 L solution = 1071 g - 10.7 g = 1060. g

$\Delta T = 1.86$ °C kg/mol $\times \dfrac{0.320 \text{ mol}}{1.060 \text{ kg}} = 0.562$ °C

Assuming water freezes at 0.000 °C, then $T_f = -0.562$ °C.

110. For 30.% A by moles in the vapor:

$\dfrac{\chi_A x}{\chi_A x + \chi_B y} = \dfrac{\chi_A x}{\chi_A x + (1 - \chi_A)y} \times 100 = 30.$

$\dfrac{\chi_A x}{\chi_A x + (1 - \chi_A)y} = 0.30$

$\chi_A x = 0.30(\chi_A x) + 0.30 y - 0.30 \chi_A y$, $\chi_A x - 0.30 \chi_A x + 0.30 \chi_A y = 0.30 y$

$\chi_A(x - 0.30 x + 0.30 y) = 0.30 y$

$$\chi_A = \frac{0.30\,y}{0.70\,x - 0.30\,y} ; \quad \chi_B = 1 - \chi_A$$

Similarly, if vapor above = 50. % A: $\quad \chi_A = \dfrac{y}{x - y} \quad \chi_B = 1 - \dfrac{y}{x - y}$

For vapor above = 80%: $\quad \chi_A = \dfrac{0.80\,y}{0.20\,x - 0.80\,y} ; \quad \chi_B = 1 - \chi_A$

If liquid mixture = 30.% A by moles, $\chi_A = 0.30$.

Thus, $\chi_A{}^V = \dfrac{0.30\,x}{0.30\,x + 0.70\,y} \quad \chi_B = 1 - \dfrac{0.30\,x}{0.30\,x + 0.70\,y}$

If 50.% A, $\chi_A{}^V = \dfrac{x}{x + y} \quad \chi_B = 1 - \chi_A$

If 80.% A, $\chi_A{}^V = \dfrac{0.80\,x}{0.80\,x + 0.20\,y} \quad \chi_B = 1 - \chi_A$

Marathon Problem

111.   a.   From part a information we can calculate the molar mass of Na_nA and deduce the formula.

$$mol\ Na_nA = mol\ reducing\ agent = 0.01526\ L \times \frac{0.02313\ mol}{L} = 3.530 \times 10^{-4}\ mol\ Na_nA$$

$$molar\ mass\ of\ Na_nA = \frac{30.0 \times 10^{-3}\ g}{3.530 \times 10^{-4}\ mol} = 85.0\ g/mol$$

To deduce the formula, we will assume various charges and numbers of oxygens present in the oxyanion, then use the periodic table to see if an element fits the molar mass data.

Assuming n = 1 so the formula is NaA. The molar mass of the oxyanion, A^-, is 85.0 - 23.0 = 62.0 g/mol. The oxyanion part of the formula could be EO^- or $EO_2{}^-$ or $EO_3{}^-$ where E is some element. If EO^-, then the molar mass of E is 62.0 - 16.0 = 46.0 g/mol; no element has this molar mass. If $EO_2{}^-$, molar mass of E = 62.0 - 32.0 = 30.0 g/mol. Phosphorus is close, but $PO_2{}^-$ anions are not common. If $EO_3{}^-$, molar mass of E = 62.0 - 48.0 = 14.0. Nitrogen has this molar mass and $NO_3{}^-$ anions are very common. Therefore, $NO_3{}^-$ is a possible formula for A^-.

Next, we assume Na_2A and Na_3A formulas and go through the same procedure as above. In all cases, no element in the periodic table fits the data. Therefore, we assume the oxyanion is $NO_3{}^-$ = A^-.

b.   The crystal data in part b allows determination of the metal, M, in the formula. See Exercise 16.47 for a review of relationships in body-centered cubic cells. In a bcc unit cell, there are 2 atoms per unit cell and the body diagonal of the cubic cell is related to the radius of the metal by the equation $4r = \sqrt{3}\,\ell$ where ℓ = cubic edge length.

$$\ell = \frac{4r}{\sqrt{3}} = \frac{4(1.984 \times 10^{-8}\ cm)}{\sqrt{3}} = 4.582 \times 10^{-8}\ cm$$

volume of unit cell = $\ell^3 = (4.582 \times 10^{-8})^3 = 9.620 \times 10^{-23}$ cm^3

mass of M in a unit cell = 9.620×10^{-23} cm$^3 \times \dfrac{5.243 \text{ g}}{\text{cm}^3} = 5.044 \times 10^{-22}$ g M

mol M in a unit cell = 2 atoms $\times \dfrac{1 \text{ mol}}{6.022 \times 10^{23}} = 3.321 \times 10^{-24}$ mol M

molar mass of M = $\dfrac{5.044 \times 10^{-22} \text{ g M}}{3.321 \times 10^{-24} \text{ mol M}} = 151.9$ g/mol

From the periodic table, M is europium, Eu. Given the charge of Eu is +3, then the formula of the salt is $Eu(NO_3)_3 \cdot zH_2O$.

c. Part c data allows determination of the molar mass of $Eu(NO_3)_3 \cdot zH_2O$, from which we can determine z, the number of waters of hydration.

$$\pi = iMRT, \quad iM = \dfrac{\pi}{RT} = \dfrac{558 \text{ torr}\left(\dfrac{1 \text{ atm}}{760 \text{ torr}}\right)}{0.08206 \text{ L atm K}^{-1} \text{ mol}^{-1}(298 \text{ K})} = 0.0300 \text{ mol/L}$$

The total molarity of solute particles present is 0.0300 M. The solute particles are Eu^{3+} and NO_3^- ions (the waters of hydration are not solute particles). Since each mol of $Eu(NO_3)_3 \cdot zH_2O$ dissolves to form 4 ions (Eu^{3+} + 3 NO_3^-), then the molarity of $Eu(NO_3)_3 \cdot zH_2O$ is 0.0300/4 = 0.00750 M.

mol $Eu(NO_3)_3 \cdot zH_2O$ = 0.01000 L $\times \dfrac{0.00750 \text{ mol}}{\text{L}} = 7.50 \times 10^{-5}$ mol

molar mass of $Eu(NO_3)_3 \cdot zH_2O$ = $\dfrac{33.45 \times 10^{-3} \text{ g}}{7.50 \times 10^{-5} \text{ mol}} = 446$ g/mol

446 g/mol = 152.0 + 3(62.0) + z(18.0), z(18.0) = 108, z = 6.00

The formula for the strong electrolyte is $Eu(NO_3)_3 \cdot 6H_2O$.

CHAPTER EIGHTEEN

THE REPRESENTATIVE ELEMENTS: GROUPS 1A THROUGH 4A

Group 1A Elements

1. The gravity of the earth is not strong enough to keep the light H_2 molecules in the atmosphere.

2. a. $\Delta H° = -110.5 - [-242 - 75] = 207$ kJ; $\Delta S° = 198 + 3(131) - [186 + 189] = 216$ J/K

   b. $\Delta G° = \Delta H° - T\Delta S°$; $\Delta G° = 0$ when $T = \dfrac{\Delta H°}{\Delta S°} = \dfrac{207 \times 10^3 \text{ J}}{216 \text{ J/K}} = 958$ K

   At $T > 958$ K and standard pressures, the favorable $\Delta S°$ term dominates and the reaction is spontaneous ($\Delta G° < 0$).

3. a. $\Delta H° = 2(-46$ kJ$) = -92$ kJ; $\Delta S° = 2(193$ J/K$) - [3(131$ J/K$) + 192$ J/K$] = -199$ J/K;

   $\Delta G° = \Delta H° - T\Delta S° = -92$ kJ $- 298$ K$(-0.199$ kJ/K$) = -33$ kJ

   b. Since $\Delta G°$ is negative, then this reaction is spontaneous at standard conditions.

   c. $\Delta G° = 0$ when $T = \dfrac{\Delta H°}{\Delta S°} = \dfrac{-92 \text{ kJ}}{-0.199 \text{ kJ/K}} = 460$ K

   At $T < 460$ K and standard pressures, the favorable $\Delta H°$ term dominates and the reaction is spontaneous ($\Delta G° < 0$).

4. 1. Ammonia production and 2. Hydrogenation of vegetable oils

5. Ionic, covalent, and metallic (or interstitial); The ionic and covalent hydrides are true compounds obeying the law of definite proportions and differ from each other in the type of bonding. The interstitial hydrides are more like solid solutions of hydrogen with a transition metal, and do not obey the law of definite proportions.

6. The small size of the Li^+ cation results in a much greater attraction to water. The attraction to water is not so great for the other alkali metal ions. Thus, lithium salts tend to absorb water.

7. a. $2\text{ Rb}(s) + 2\text{ H}_2\text{O}(l) \rightarrow 2\text{ RbOH}(aq) + \text{H}_2(g)$
   b. $\text{Na}_2\text{O}_2(s) + 2\text{ H}_2\text{O}(l) \rightarrow 2\text{ NaOH}(aq) + \text{H}_2\text{O}_2(aq)$
   c. $\text{LiH}(s) + \text{H}_2\text{O}(l) \rightarrow \text{H}_2(g) + \text{LiOH}(aq)$
   d. $2\text{ KO}_2(s) + 2\text{H}_2\text{O}(l) \rightarrow 2\text{ KOH}(aq) + \text{O}_2(g) + \text{H}_2\text{O}_2(aq)$

8. $2 \text{ Li(s)} + 2 \text{ C}_2\text{H}_2\text{(g)} \rightarrow 2 \text{ LiC}_2\text{H(s)} + \text{H}_2\text{(g)}$; This is an oxidation-reduction reaction.

9.   Hydrogen forms many compounds in which the oxidation state is +1, as do the Group 1A elements. For example, H_2SO_4 and HCl as compared to Na_2SO_4 and NaCl. On the other hand, hydrogen forms diatomic H_2 molecules and is a nonmetal, while the Group 1A elements are metals. Hydrogen also forms compounds with a -1 oxidation state, which is not characteristic of Group 1A metals, e.g., NaH.

10.   We need another reactant beside NaCl(aq) since oxygen and hydrogen are in some of the products. The obvious choice is H_2O.

$$2 \text{ NaCl(aq)} + 2 \text{ H}_2\text{O(l)} \rightarrow \text{Cl}_2\text{(g)} + \text{H}_2\text{(g)} + 2 \text{ NaOH(aq)}$$

Note that hydrogen is reduced and chlorine is oxidized in this electrolysis process.

11. $4 \text{ Li(s)} + \text{O}_2\text{(g)} \rightarrow 2 \text{ Li}_2\text{O(s)}$

$16 \text{ Li(s)} + \text{S}_8\text{(s)} \rightarrow 8 \text{ Li}_2\text{S(s)}$; $2 \text{ Li(s)} + \text{Cl}_2\text{(g)} \rightarrow 2 \text{ LiCl(s)}$

$12 \text{ Li(s)} + \text{P}_4\text{(s)} \rightarrow 4 \text{ Li}_3\text{P(s)}$; $2 \text{ Li(s)} + \text{H}_2\text{(g)} \rightarrow 2 \text{ LiH(s)}$

$2 \text{ Li(s)} + 2 \text{ H}_2\text{O(l)} \rightarrow 2 \text{ LiOH(aq)} + \text{H}_2\text{(g)}$; $2 \text{ Li(s)} + 2 \text{ HCl(aq)} \rightarrow 2 \text{ LiCl(aq)} + \text{H}_2\text{(g)}$

12.   a. lithium oxide;   b. potassium superoxide;   c. sodium peroxide

13. $4 \text{ KO}_2\text{(s)} + 2 \text{ CO}_2\text{(g)} \rightarrow 2 \text{ K}_2\text{CO}_3\text{(s)} + 3 \text{ O}_2\text{(g)}$; Potassium superoxide can react with exhaled CO_2 to produce O_2, which then can be inhaled.

14.

	Li	Na	K	Rb	Cs	Fr
Atomic number	3	11	19	37	55	87
MP (°C)	180	98	63	39	29	≈22

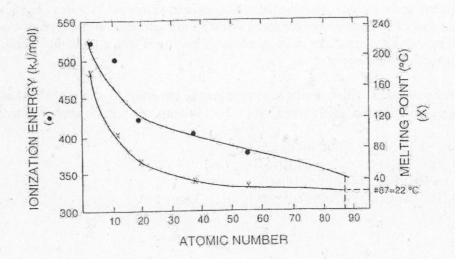

From the plot, we would estimate the melting point of Fr to be around 20°C. Thus, it would be a liquid at room temperature. Note: Ignore the ionization energy plot.

Group 2A Elements

15.   Group IA and IIA metals are all easily oxidized. They must be produced in the absence of materials (H_2O, O_2) that are capable of oxidizing them.

16.   Alkaline earth metals form +2 ions so 2 mol of e^- are transferred to form the metal, M.

$$\text{mol M} = 748\ s \times \frac{5.00\ C}{s} \times \frac{1\ \text{mol } e^-}{96{,}485\ C} \times \frac{1\ \text{mol M}}{2\ \text{mol } e^-} = 1.94 \times 10^{-2}\ \text{mol M}$$

$$\text{molar mass of M} = \frac{0.471\ g\ M}{1.94 \times 10^{-2}\ \text{mol M}} = 24.3\ \text{g/mol};\ \ \text{MgCl}_2\ \text{was electrolyzed.}$$

17.   The acidity decreases. Solutions of Be^{2+} are acidic, while solutions of the other M^{2+} ions are neutral.

18. $BeCl_2NH_3$ has $2 + 2(7) + 5 + 3(1) = 24$ valence electrons.

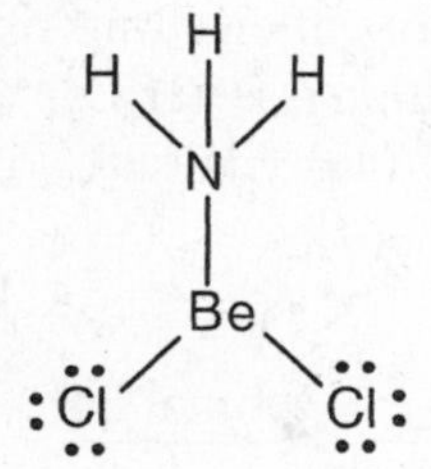

Geometry is trigonal planar about Be.

Be uses sp^2 hybrid orbitals.

N uses sp^3 hybrid orbitals.

$BeCl_2$ is a Lewis acid.

Although we could draw a Lewis structure that obeys the octet for Be, the above structure is best from a formal charge point of view. All atoms but Be and N have a zero formal charge in this structure.

19.   One would predict that $BeCl_2(NH_3)_2$ would form in excess ammonia. $BeCl_2(NH_3)_2$ has $2 + 2(7) + 2(5) + 6(1) = 32$ valence electrons. A structure for this molecule can be drawn that obeys the octet rule for all atoms and has zero formal charge on all atoms except for Be and the N atoms. This is not the case for $BeCl_2NH_3$ (see Exercise 18.18). In $BeCl_2NH_3$, the "best" Lewis structure has only 6 electrons around Be.

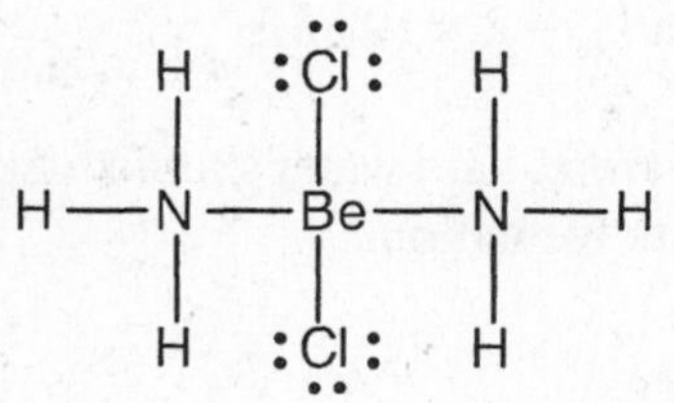

20.   In the gas phase, linear molecules would exist.

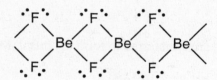

In the solid state, BeF_2 would exist as a polymeric solid with a structure:

21. $2 Sr(s) + O_2(g) \rightarrow 2 SrO(s); \quad 8 Sr(s) + S_8(s) \rightarrow 8 SrS(s)$

$Sr(s) + Cl_2(g) \rightarrow SrCl_2(s); \quad 6 Sr(s) + P_4(s) \rightarrow 2 Sr_3P_2(s)$

$Sr(s) + H_2(g) \rightarrow SrH_2(s); \quad Sr(s) + 2 H_2O(l) \rightarrow Sr(OH)_2(aq) + H_2(g)$

$Sr(s) + 2 HCl(aq) \rightarrow SrCl_2(aq) + H_2(g)$

22.   The Be^{2+} ion is a Lewis acid and has a strong affinity for the lone pairs of electrons on oxygen in water. Thus, the compound is not dehydrated easily. The ion in solution is $Be(H_2O)_4^{2+}$. The acidic solution results from the reaction: $Be(H_2O)_4^{2+}(aq) \rightleftharpoons Be(H_2O)_3(OH)^+(aq) + H^+(aq)$

23. $CaCO_3(s) + H_2SO_4(aq) \rightarrow CaSO_4(aq) + H_2O(l) + CO_2(g)$

24. $Ba^{2+} + 2 e^- \rightarrow Ba; \quad 6.00 \text{ hr} \times \dfrac{60 \text{ min}}{\text{hr}} \times \dfrac{60 \text{ s}}{\text{min}} \times \dfrac{2.50 \times 10^5 \text{ C}}{\text{s}} \times \dfrac{1 \text{ mole } e^-}{96,485 \text{ C}} \times \dfrac{1 \text{ mol Ba}}{2 \text{ mol } e^-}$

$$\times \dfrac{137.3 \text{ g Ba}}{\text{mol Ba}} = 3.84 \times 10^6 \text{ g Ba}$$

25. $\dfrac{1 \text{ mg } F^-}{L} \times \dfrac{1 \text{ g}}{1000 \text{ mg}} \times \dfrac{1 \text{ mol } F^-}{19.0 \text{ g } F^-} = 5.3 \times 10^{-5} \, M F^- = 5 \times 10^{-5} \, M F^-$

$CaF_2(s) \rightleftharpoons Ca^{2+}(aq) + 2 F^-(aq) \quad K_{sp} = [Ca^{2+}][F^-]^2 = 4.0 \times 10^{-11}$; Precipitation will occur when $Q > K_{sp}$. Lets calculate $[Ca^{2+}]$ so that $Q = K_{sp}$.

$Q = 4.0 \times 10^{-11} = [Ca^{2+}]_o[F^-]_o^2 = [Ca^{2+}]_o(5 \times 10^{-5})^2, \quad [Ca^{2+}]_o = 2 \times 10^{-2} \, M$

$CaF_2(s)$ will precipitate when $[Ca^{2+}]_o > 2 \times 10^{-2} \, M$. Therefore, hard water should have a calcium ion concentration of less than $2 \times 10^{-2} \, M$ to avoid precipitate formation.

Group 3A Elements

26. $B_2H_6(g) + 3 O_2(g) \rightarrow 2 B(OH)_3(s)$

27.   a.   AlN   b. GaF_3 c. Ga_2S_3

28.   Assuming $AlCl_3$ is covalent, then the Lewis structure for $AlCl_3$ that has zero formal charge for all atoms is:

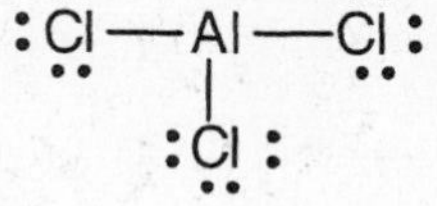

$$:\overset{\cdot\cdot}{\underset{\cdot\cdot}{Cl}} - Al - \overset{\cdot\cdot}{\underset{\cdot\cdot}{Cl}}:$$
$$\overset{|}{:\underset{\cdot\cdot}{Cl}:}$$

Al has room for a pair of electrons. It can act as a Lewis acid. The only lone pairs are on Cl, so the dimer structure is:

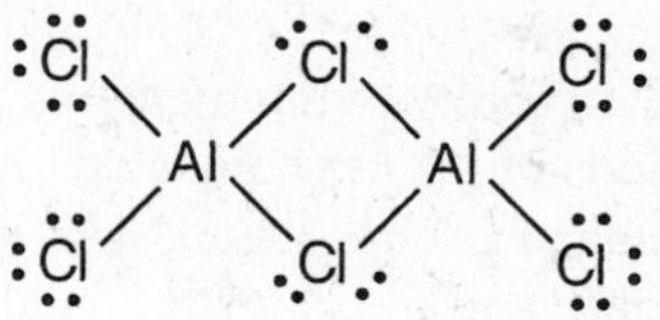

29.   Element 113: $[Rn]\ 7s^25f^{14}6d^{10}7p^1$; Element 113 would fall below Tl in the periodic table. Like Tl, we would expect element 113 to form +1 and +3 oxidation states in its compounds.

30. $B_2O_3(s) + 3\ Mg(s) \rightarrow 3\ MgO(s) + 2\ B(s)$

31. $Ga_2O_3(s) + 6\ H^+(aq) \rightarrow 2\ Ga^{3+}(aq) + 3\ H_2O(l)$

      $Ga_2O_3(s) + 2\ OH^-(aq) + 3\ H_2O(l) \rightarrow 2\ Ga(OH)_4^-(aq)$

      $In_2O_3(s) + 6\ H^+(aq) \rightarrow 2\ In^{3+}(aq) + 3\ H_2O(l)$; $In_2O_3(s) + OH^-(aq) \rightarrow$ no reaction

32. $Al_2O_3(s) + 6\ H^+(aq) \rightarrow 2\ Al^{3+}(aq) + 3\ H_2O(l)$; $Al_2O_3(s) + 3\ H_2O(l) + 2\ OH^-(aq) \rightarrow 2\ Al(OH)_4^-(aq)$

33.   Group 3A elements have one fewer valence electron than Si or Ge. A p-type semiconductor would form.

34.   a.   Out of 100.0 g of compound there are:

$$44.4\ g\ Ca \times \frac{1\ mol}{40.08\ g} = 1.11\ mol\ Ca;\ \ 20.0\ g\ Al \times \frac{1\ mol}{26.98\ g} = 0.741\ mol\ Al$$

$$35.6\ g\ O \times \frac{1\ mol}{16.00\ g} = 2.23\ mol\ O$$

$$\frac{1.11}{0.741} = 1.50;\ \ \frac{0.741}{0.741} = 1.00;\ \ \frac{2.23}{0.741} = 3.01;\ \ \text{Empirical formula is } Ca_3Al_2O_6.$$

      b. $Ca_9Al_6O_{18}$

      c.   There are covalent bonds between Al and O atoms in the $Al_6O_{18}^{18-}$ anion; sp^3 hybrid orbitals on aluminum overlap with sp^3 hybrid orbitals on oxygen to form the sigma bonds.

35. $2 Ga(s) + 3 F_2(g) \rightarrow 2 GaF_3(s); \ 4 Ga(s) + 3 O_2(g) \rightarrow 2 Ga_2O_3(s)$

$16 Ga(s) + 3 S_8(s) \rightarrow 8 Ga_2S_3(s)$

$2 Ga(s) + 6 HCl(aq) \rightarrow 2 GaCl_3(aq) + 3 H_2(g)$

36. $2 Al(s) + 2 NaOH(aq) + 6 H_2O(l) \rightarrow 2 Al(OH)_4^-(aq) + 2 Na^+(aq) + 3 H_2(g)$

37. Tl_2O_3, thallium(III) oxide; Tl_2O, thallium(I) oxide; $InCl_3$, indium(III) chloride; $InCl$, indium(I) chloride

38.   The "inert pair effect" refers to the difficulty of removing the pair of s electrons from some of the elements in the fifth and sixth periods of the periodic table. As a result, multiple oxidation states are exhibited for the heavier elements of Groups 3A and 4A. In^+, In^{3+}, Tl^+ and Tl^{3+} oxidation states are all important to the chemistry of In and Tl.

Group 4A Elements

39.   Compounds containing Si – Si single and multiple bonds are rare, unlike compounds of carbon. The bond strengths of the Si – Si and C – C single bonds are similar. The difference in bonding properties must be for other reasons. One reason is that silicon does not form strong π bonds, unlike carbon. Another reason is that silicon forms particularly strong sigma bonds to oxygen, resulting in compounds with Si – O bonds instead of Si – Si bonds.

40. CF_4, $4 + 4(7) = 32 \ e^-$ GeF_4, $4 + 4(7) = 32 \ e^-$ GeF_6^{2-}, $4 + 6(7) + 2 = 48 \ e^-$

tetrahedral; 109.5°; sp^3 tetrahedral; 109.5°; sp^3 octahedral; 90°; d^2sp^3

In order to form CF_6^{2-}, carbon would have to expand its octet of electrons. Carbon compounds do not expand their octet because of the small atomic size of carbon and because no low energy d-orbitals are available for carbon to accommodate the extra electrons.

41. CS_2 has $4 + 2(6) = 16$ valence electrons. C_3S_2 has $3(4) + 2(6) = 24$ valence electrons.

linear;   linear

42.   The bonds in SnX_4 compounds have a large covalent character. SnX_4 acts as discrete molecules held together by weak London dispersion forces. SnX_2 compounds are ionic and are held in the solid state by strong ionic forces. Since the intermolecular forces are weaker for SnX_4 compounds, then they are more volatile.

43. White tin is stable at normal temperatures. Gray tin is stable at temperatures below 13.2°C. Thus for the phase change: Sn(gray) → Sn(white), ΔG is negative at T > 13.2°C and ΔG is positive at T < 13.2°C. This is only possible if ΔH is positive and ΔS is positive. Thus, gray tin has the more ordered structure.

44. a. $SiO_2(s) + 2\ C(s) \rightarrow Si(s) + 2\ CO(g)$

  b. $SiCl_4(l) + 2\ Mg(s) \rightarrow Si(s) + 2\ MgCl_2(s)$

  c. $Na_2SiF_6(s) + 4\ Na(s) \rightarrow Si(s) + 6\ NaF(s)$

45. $Sn(s) + 2F_2(g) \rightarrow SnF_4(s)$, tin(IV) fluoride; $Sn(s) + F_2(g) \rightarrow SnF_2(s)$, tin(II) fluoride

46. SiC would have a covalent network structure similar to diamond.

47. In graphite planes of carbon atoms slide easily along each other. In addition, graphite is not volatile. The lubricant will not be lost when used in a high vacuum environment.

48. $Sn(s) + 2\ Cl_2(g) \rightarrow SnCl_4(s)$; $Sn(s) + O_2(g) \rightarrow SnO_2(s)$

  $Sn(s) + 2\ HCl(aq) \rightarrow SnCl_2(aq) + H_2(g)$

49. Pb_3O_4: We assign -2 for the oxidation state of O. The sum of the oxidation states of Pb must be +8. We get this if two of the lead atoms are Pb(II) and one is Pb(IV). Therefore, the mole ratio of lead(II) to lead(IV) is 2:1.

50. $$Pb(OH)_2(s) \rightleftharpoons Pb^{2+} + 2\ OH^- \quad K_{sp} = 1.2 \times 10^{-15} = [Pb^{2+}][OH^-]^2$$

Initial	s = solubility (mol/L)	0	$1.0 \times 10^{-7}\ M$
Equil.		s	$1.0 \times 10^{-7} + 2s \approx 2s$

  $K_{sp} = (s)(2s)^2 = 1.2 \times 10^{-15}$, $4s^3 = 1.2 \times 10^{-15}$, $s = 6.7 \times 10^{-6}$ mol/L; Assumption good.

  $Pb(OH)_2(s)$ is more soluble in acidic solutions. Added H^+ reacts with OH^- to form H_2O. As OH^- is removed through this reaction, more $Pb(OH)_2(s)$ will dissolve.

51. Lead is very toxic. As the temperature of the water increases, the solubility of lead will increase. Drinking hot tap water from pipes containing lead solder could result in higher lead concentrations in the body.

52. 750. mL grape juice $\times \dfrac{12\ \text{mL}\ C_2H_5OH}{100.\ \text{mL juice}} \times \dfrac{0.79\ \text{g}\ C_2H_5OH}{\text{mL}} \times \dfrac{1\ \text{mol}\ C_2H_5OH}{46.07\ \text{g}} \times \dfrac{2\ \text{mol}\ CO_2}{2\ \text{mol}\ C_2H_5OH}$

  $= 1.54$ mol CO_2 (carry extra significant figure)

  1.54 mol CO_2 = total mol CO_2 = mol $CO_2(g)$ + mol $CO_2(aq)$ = $n_g + n_{aq}$

$$P_{CO_2} = \frac{n_g RT}{V} = \frac{n_g\left(\dfrac{0.08206\ \text{L atm}}{\text{mol K}}\right)(298\ \text{K})}{75 \times 10^{-3}\ \text{L}} = 326\ n_g; \quad P_{CO_2} = \frac{C}{k} = \frac{\dfrac{n_{aq}}{0.750\ \text{L}}}{\dfrac{3.1 \times 10^{-2}\ \text{mol}}{\text{L atm}}} = 43.0\ n_{aq}$$

$P_{CO_2} = 326\ n_g = 43.0\ n_{aq}$ and from above $n_{aq} = 1.54 - n_g$; Solving:

$326\ n_g = 43.0(1.54 - n_g),\ \ 369\ n_g = 66.2,\ \ n_g = 0.18\ \text{mol}$

$P_{CO_2} = 326(0.18) = 59\ \text{atm in gas phase}$

$C = kP_{CO_2} = \dfrac{3.1 \times 10^{-2}\ \text{mol}}{\text{L atm}} \times 59\ \text{atm},\ \ C = 1.8\ \text{mol CO}_2/\text{L in wine}$

53. $Pb(NO_3)_2(aq) + H_3AsO_4(aq) \rightarrow PbHAsO_4(s) + 2\ HNO_3(aq)$

Note: The insecticide used is $PbHAsO_4$ and is commonly called lead arsenate. This is not the correct name, however. Correctly, lead arsenate would be $Pb_3(AsO_4)_2$ and $PbHAsO_4$ should be named lead hydrogen arsenate.

54. $C_6H_{12}O_6(aq) \rightarrow 2\ C_2H_5OH(aq) + 2\ CO_2(g)$

Additional Exercises

55. Na^+ can oxidize Na^- to Na. The purpose of the cryptand is to encapsulate the Na^+ ion so that it does not come in contact with the Na^- ion and oxidize it to sodium metal.

56.   The crown ether surrounds the cation. The ion pair:

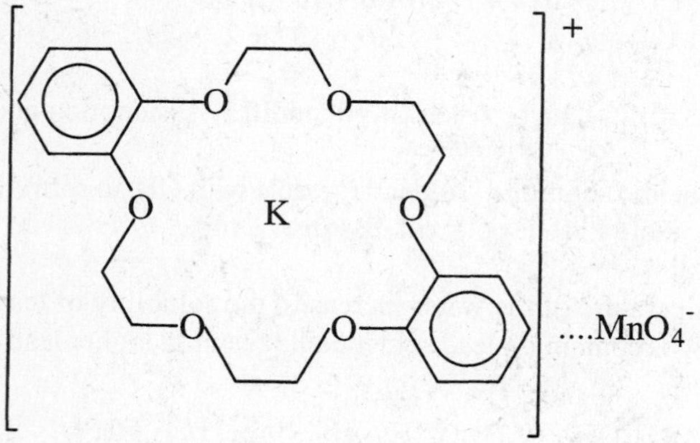

is soluble in nonpolar solvents because the solvent interacts well with the nonpolar hydrocarbon parts of the crown ether. Note: In the shorthand structure above, each point where lines meet represents a carbon atom, and the H atoms are not shown.

57.   a. $2\ Na + 2\ NH_3 \rightarrow 2\ NaNH_2 + H_2$

b.   mass percent = $\dfrac{251.4\ g}{1000.\ g + 251.4\ g} \times 100 = 20.09\ \%$

mol Na = $251.4 \times \dfrac{1\ mol}{22.99\ g} = 10.94$ mol Na;   mol NH_3 = 1000. g $\times \dfrac{1\ mol}{17.031\ g} = 58.72$ mol NH_3

mole fraction = $\chi_{Na} = \dfrac{10.94\ mol}{10.94\ mol + 58.72\ mol} = 0.1570$

molality = $\dfrac{251.4\ g\ Na}{kg} \times \dfrac{1\ mol\ Na}{22.99\ g\ Na} = 10.94$ mol/kg

58. $2\ K(s) + 2\ H_2O(l) \rightarrow 2\ KOH(aq) + H_2(g)$, $\Delta H° = 2(-481\ kJ) - 2(-286\ kJ) = -390.\ kJ$

5.00 g K $\times \dfrac{1\ mol\ K}{39.10\ g\ K} \times \dfrac{-390.\ kJ}{2\ mol\ K} = -24.9$ kJ of heat released upon reaction of 5.00 g of potassium.

24,900 J = $\dfrac{4.18\ J}{g\ °C} \times (1.00 \times 10^3\ g) \times \Delta T$, $\Delta T = \dfrac{24,900}{4.18 \times 1.00 \times 10^3} = 5.96\ °C$

Final temperature = $24.0 + 5.96 = 30.0\ °C$

59. $2\ H_2O + 2\ e^- \rightarrow H_2 + 2\ OH^-$
                $Be + 4\ OH^- \rightarrow Be(OH)_4^{2-} + 2\ e^-$

$\overline{}$

$Be(s) + 2\ H_2O(l) + 2\ OH^-(aq) \rightarrow Be(OH)_4^{2-}(aq) + H_2(g)$

H_2O is the oxidizing agent. Be is the reducing agent.

60.   Size decreases from left to right and increases going down the periodic table. So going one element right and one element down would result in a similar size for the two elements diagonal to each other. The ionization energies will be similar for the diagonal elements since the periodic trends also oppose each other. Electron affinities are harder to predict, but atoms with similar size and ionization energy should also have similar electron affinities.

61.   Strontium and calcium are both alkaline earth metals so both have similar chemical properties. Since milk is a good source of calcium, strontium could replace some calcium in milk without much difficulty.

62.   Major species present: $Al(H_2O)_6^{3+}$ ($K_a = 1.4 \times 10^{-5}$), NO_3^- (neutral) and H_2O ($K_w = 1.0 \times 10^{-14}$); $Al(H_2O)_6^{3+}$ is a stronger acid than water so it will be the dominant H^+ producer.

	$Al(H_2O)_6^{3+}$	$\rightleftharpoons$	$Al(H_2O)_5(OH)^{2+}$	+	H^+
Initial	0.050 M		0		~0
	x mol/L $Al(H_2O)_6^{3+}$ dissociates to reach equilibrium				
Change	$-x$	$\rightarrow$	$+x$		$+x$
Equil.	$0.050 - x$		x		x

$$K_a = 1.4 \times 10^{-5} = \frac{[Al(H_2O)_5(OH)^{2+}][H^+]}{[Al(H_2O)_6^{3+}]} = \frac{x^2}{0.050-x} \approx \frac{x^2}{0.050}$$

$x = 8.4 \times 10^{-4}\ M = [H^+];\ \ pH = -\log(8.4 \times 10^{-4}) = 3.08;\ $ Assumptions good.

63. $Tl^{3+} + 2\ e^- \rightarrow Tl^+$ $\qquad\qquad E_c^\circ = 1.25$ V

$\qquad\ \ 3\ I^- \rightarrow I_3^- + 2\ e^-$ $\qquad\ \ -E_a^\circ = -0.55$ V

$\overline{Tl^{3+} + 3\ I^- \rightarrow Tl^+ + I_3^-}$ $\qquad E_{cell}^\circ = 0.70$ V $\qquad$ (Spontaneous since $E_{cell}^\circ > 0$.)

In solution, Tl^{3+} can oxidize I^- to I_3^-. Thus, we expect TlI_3 to be thallium(I) triiodide.

64.   Ga(I): $[Ar]4s^2 3d^{10}$, no unpaired e^-; Ga(III): $[Ar]3d^{10}$, no unpaired e^-

Ga(II): $[Ar]4s^1 3d^{10}$, 1 unpaired e^-; Note: s electrons are lost before the d electrons.

If the compound contained Ga(II), it would be paramagnetic and if the compound contained Ga(I) and Ga(III), it would be diamagnetic. This can easily be determined by measuring the mass of a sample in the presence and in the absence of a magnetic field. Paramagnetic compounds will have an apparent greater mass in a magnetic field.

65.   The π electrons are free to move in graphite, thus giving it a greater conductivity (lower resistance). The electrons have the greatest mobility within sheets of carbon atoms, resulting in a lower resistance in the basal plane. Electrons in diamond are not mobile (high resistance). The structure of diamond is uniform in all directions; thus, there is no directional dependence of the resistivity.

66.

The compound is held together by covalent bonds. The structure is tetrahedral about the central Sn.

67.   Carbon cannot form the fifth bond necessary for the transition state since carbon doesn't have low energy d orbitals available to expand its octet of valence electrons.

68.   Quartz: Crystalline, long range order; The structure is an ordered arrangement of 12 membered rings, each containing 6 Si and 6 O atoms.

Amorphous SiO_2:   No long range order; Irregular arrangement that contains many different ring sizes. See Section 16.5.

69.   For 589.0 nm: $v = \dfrac{c}{\lambda} = \dfrac{2.9979 \times 10^8 \text{ m/s}}{589.0 \times 10^{-9} \text{ m}} = 5.090 \times 10^{14} \text{ s}^{-1}$

$E = hv = 6.6261 \times 10^{-34} \text{ J s} \times 5.090 \times 10^{14} \text{ s}^{-1} = 3.373 \times 10^{-19} \text{ J}$

For 589.6 nm: $v = c/\lambda = 5.085 \times 10^{14} \text{ s}^{-1}$; $E = hv = 3.369 \times 10^{-19} \text{ J}$

The energies in kJ/mol are:

$3.373 \times 10^{-19} \text{ J} \times \dfrac{1 \text{ kJ}}{1000 \text{ J}} \times \dfrac{6.0221 \times 10^{23}}{\text{mol}} = 203.1 \text{ kJ/mol}$

$3.369 \times 10^{-19} \text{ J} \times \dfrac{1 \text{ kJ}}{1000 \text{ J}} \times \dfrac{6.0221 \times 10^{23}}{\text{mol}} = 202.9 \text{ kJ/mol}$

70.   The answer to the clues are: (1) BeO is amphoteric; (2) NaN$_3$ is the compound used in airbags; (3) Fr is radioactive; (4) Na has the least negative E° value (the symbol in reverse is an); (5) K$_2$O is potash; (6) Only Li forms Li$_3$N; (7) In is the first group 3A element to form stable +1 and +3 ions in its compounds (the second letter of the symbol is n).

Inserting the symbols into the blanks, the name of the American scientist is Ben Franklin.

Challenge Problems

71. Pb^{2+} + H_2EDTA^{2-} $\rightleftharpoons$ $PbEDTA^{2-}$ + $2 H^+$

Before	0.0010 M	0.050 M		0	1.0×10^{-6} M (buffer, [H$^+$] constant)
Change	-0.0010	-0.0010	$\rightarrow$	+0.0010	No change Reacts completely
After	0	0.049		0.0010	1.0×10^{-6} New initial

x mol/L PbEDTA^{2-} dissociates to reach equilibrium

Change	+x	+x	$\leftarrow$	-x	---
Equil.	x	0.049 + x		0.0010 - x	1.0×10^{-6} (buffer)

$K = 1.0 \times 10^{23} = \dfrac{[PbEDTA^{2-}][H^+]^2}{[Pb^{2+}][H_2EDTA^{2-}]} = \dfrac{(0.0010 - x)(1.0 \times 10^{-6})^2}{(x)(0.049 + x)}$

$1.0 \times 10^{23} \approx \dfrac{(0.0010)(1.0 \times 10^{-12})}{x(0.049)}$, $x = [Pb^{2+}] = 2.0 \times 10^{-37}$ M Assumptions good.

72. CO_2 in H_2O reacts to give H_2CO_3(aq), (That is, $CO_2 + H_2O \rightleftharpoons H_2CO_3$)

Thus, we have 0.50 M H_2CO_3 where $K_{a_1} = 4.3 \times 10^{-7}$ and $K_{a_2} = 4.8 \times 10^{-11}$

H_2CO_3 $\rightleftharpoons$ H^+ + HCO_3^-

Initial	0.50	0	0
Change	-x	x	x
Equil.	0.50-x	x	x

$$\frac{x^2}{0.50-x} = 4.3 \times 10^{-7} \approx \frac{x^2}{0.50}, \quad x = [H^+] = 4.6 \times 10^{-4} \, M, \quad pH = 3.34$$

	HCO_3^-	+	HCO_3^-	$\rightleftharpoons$	H_2CO_3	+	CO_3^{2-}
Initial	4.6×10^{-4}		4.6×10^{-4}		0.50		0
Change	-x		-x		+x		+x
Equil.	4.6×10^{-4}-x		4.6×10^{-4} -x		0.50+x		x

$$K = \frac{K_{a_2}}{K_{a_1}} = 1.1 \times 10^{-4}, \quad \frac{(0.50 + x)(x)}{(4.6 \times 10^{-4} - x)(4.6 \times 10^{-4} - x)} = 1.1 \times 10^{-4}$$

$$1.1 \times 10^{-4} \approx \frac{(0.50)(x)}{(4.6 \times 10^{-4})(4.6 \, 10^{-4})}, \quad x = [CO_3^{2-}] = 4.7 \times 10^{-11} \, M$$

73. $SiCl_4(l) + 2 \, H_2O(l) \rightarrow SiO_2(s) + 4 \, H^+(aq) + 4 \, Cl^-(aq)$

$\Delta H° = -911 + 4(0) + 4(-167) - [-687 + 2(-286)] = -320. \, kJ$

$\Delta S° = 42 + 4(0) + 4(57) - [240. + 2(70.)] = -110. \, J/K; \quad \Delta G° = \Delta H° - T\Delta S°$

$\Delta G° = 0$ when $T = \Delta H°/\Delta S° = -320. \times 10^3 \, J/(-110. \, J/K) = 2910 \, K$

Due to the favorable $\Delta H°$ term, this reaction at standard conditions is spontaneous at temperatures below 2910 K.

The corresponding reaction for CCl_4 is:

$CCl_4(l) + 2 \, H_2O(l) \rightarrow CO_2(g) + 4 \, H^+(aq) + 4 \, Cl^-(aq)$

$\Delta H° = -393.5 + 4(0) + 4(-167) - [-135 + 2(-286)] = -355 \, kJ$

$\Delta S° = 214 + 4(0) + 4(57) - [216 + 2(70.)] = 86 \, J/K$

Thermodynamics predicts that this reaction (at standard conditions) would be spontaneous at any temperature.

The answer for the reactivity difference must lie with kinetics. $SiCl_4$ reacts because an activated complex can form by a water molecule attaching to silicon in $SiCl_4$. The activated complex requires silicon to form a fifth bond (See Exercise 18.67). Silicon has low energy 3d orbitals available to expand the octet. Carbon will not break the octet rule, therefore, CCl_4 does not form this activated complex. CCl_4 and H_2O require a different pathway to get to products. The different pathway has a much higher activation energy and, in turn, the reaction is much slower.

74.   The relevant reaction is

$$X + 2\,H_2O \rightarrow H_2 + X(OH)_2$$
10.0 g

6.10 L
1.00 atm
298 K

$PV = nRT$, solving for $n = 0.249$ mol

mol H_2 = mol X, $\dfrac{10.0\,g\,X}{0.249\,mol} = 40.2$ g/mol, X is Ca.

$Ca + 2\,H_2O \rightarrow H_2 + Ca(OH)_2$; $Ca(OH)_2$ is a strong base. $\dfrac{10.0\,g}{40.08} = 0.250$ mol

Thus, 0.250 mol $Ca(OH)_2 \rightarrow 0.500$ mol OH^-

$\dfrac{0.500\,mol\,OH^-}{10.0\,L} = 0.050\,M\,OH$,   pOH = 1.30,   pH = 12.7

75.   a. K^+ (blood) $\rightleftharpoons K^+$ (muscle) $\Delta G^\circ = 0$; $\Delta G = RT \ln\left(\dfrac{[K^+]_m}{[K^+]_b}\right)$; $\Delta G = w_{max}$

$$\Delta G = \dfrac{8.3145\,J}{K\,mol}\,(310.\,K)\ln\left(\dfrac{0.15}{0.0050}\right), \quad \Delta G = 8.8 \times 10^3 \text{ J/mol} = 8.8 \text{ kJ/mol}$$

At least 8.8 kJ of work must be applied to transport 1 mol K^+.

b.   Other ions will have to be transported to maintain electroneutrality. Either anions must be transported into the cells, or cations (Na^+) in the cell must be transported to the blood. The latter is what happens: [Na^+] in blood is greater than [Na^+] in cells as a result of this pumping.

c. $\Delta G^\circ = -RT \ln K = -(8.3145 \text{ J } K^{-1}\,mol^{-1})(310.\,K)\ln 1.7 \times 10^5 = -3.1 \times 10^4$ J/mol = -31 kJ/mol

The hydrolysis of ATP (at standard conditions) provides 31 kJ/mol of energy to do work. We must add 8.8 kJ of work to transport 1.0 mol of K^+.

8.8 kJ $\times \dfrac{1\,mol\,ATP}{31\,kJ} = 0.28$ mol ATP must be hydrolyzed.

76. $PbX_4 \rightarrow PbX_2 + X_2$; 1 mol $PbX_4 \rightarrow$ 1 mol PbX_2
2.00 g   16.12 g

$\dfrac{25.00}{207.2 + 4x} = \dfrac{16.12}{207.2 + 2x}$, $x = 127.1$; $X = I$ (iodine)

CHAPTER NINETEEN

THE REPRESENTATIVE ELEMENTS: GROUPS 5A THROUGH 8A

Group 5A Elements

1. NO_4^{3-}

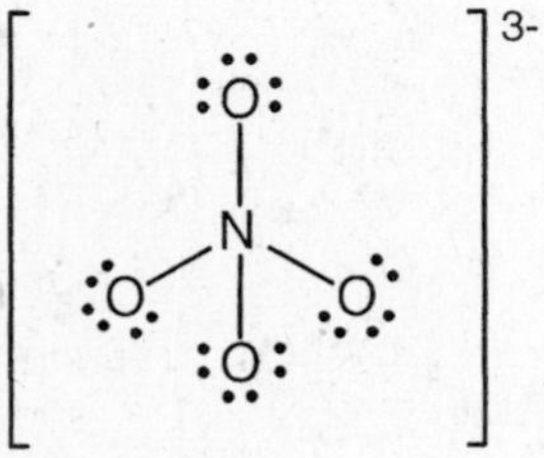

Both NO_4^{3-} and PO_4^{3-} have 32 valence electrons so both have similar Lewis structures. From the Lewis structure for NO_4^{3-}, the central N atom has a tetrahedral arrangement of electron pairs. N is small. There is probably not enough room for all 4 oxygen atoms around N. P is larger, thus, PO_4^{3-} is stable.

PO_3^-

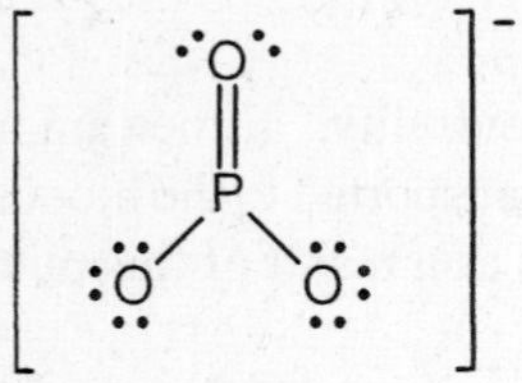

PO_3^- and NO_3^- both have 24 valence electrons so both have similar Lewis structures. From the Lewis structure, PO_3^- has a trigonal arrangement of electron pairs about the central P atom (two single bonds and one double bond). $P = O$ bonds are not particularly stable, while $N = O$ bonds are stable. Thus, NO_3^- is stable.

2. $\Delta H° = 2(90. \text{ kJ}) - [0 + 0] = 180. \text{ kJ};$ $\Delta S° = 2(211 \text{ J/K}) - [192 + 205] = 25 \text{ J/K}$

$\Delta G° = 2(87 \text{ kJ}) - [0] = 174 \text{ kJ}$

At the high temperatures in automobile engines, the reaction $N_2 + O_2 \rightarrow 2 NO$ becomes spontaneous since the favorable $\Delta S°$ term will become dominate. In the atmosphere, even though $2 NO \rightarrow N_2 + O_2$ is spontaneous at the cooler temperatures of the atmosphere, it doesn't occur because the rate is slow. Therefore, higher concentrations of NO are present in the atmosphere as compared to what is predicted by thermodynamics.

3. $2 \, NaN_3(s) \rightarrow 2 \, Na(s) + 3 \, N_2(g)$

$$n_{N_2} = \frac{PV}{RT} = \frac{1.00 \, atm \times 70.0 \, L}{\dfrac{0.08206 \, L \, atm}{mol \, K} \times 273 \, K} = 3.12 \, mol \, N_2 \text{ needed to fill air bag.}$$

mass NaN_3 reacted $= 3.12 \, mol \, N_2 \times \dfrac{2 \, mol \, NaN_3}{3 \, mol \, N_2} \times \dfrac{65.02 \, g \, NaN_3}{mol \, NaN_3} = 135 \, g \, NaN_3$

4.   As the halogen atoms get larger, it becomes more difficult to fit three halogen atoms around the small nitrogen atom, and the NX_3 molecule becomes less stable.

5.   a. NO_2, $5 + 2(6) = 17 \, e^-$ N_2O_4, $2(5) + 4(6) = 34 \, e^-$

plus other resonance structures   plus other resonance structures

         b. BF_3, $3 + 3(7) = 24 \, e^-$ NH_3, $5 + 3(1) = 8 \, e^-$

BF_3NH_3, $24 + 8 = 32 \, e^-$

In reaction a, NO_2 has an odd number of electrons so it is impossible to satisfy the octet rule. By dimerizing to form N_2O_4, the odd electron on two NO_2 molecules can pair up giving a species whose Lewis structure can satisfy the octet rule. In general odd electron species are very reactive.   In reaction b, BF_3 can be considered electron deficient; boron has only six electrons around it. By forming BF_3NH_3, the boron atom satisfies the octet rule by accepting a lone pair of electrons from NH_3 to form a fourth bond.

6.   For the reaction:

$\longrightarrow \quad NO_2 + NO$

the activation energy must in some way involve the breaking of a nitrogen-nitrogen single bond.

For the reaction:

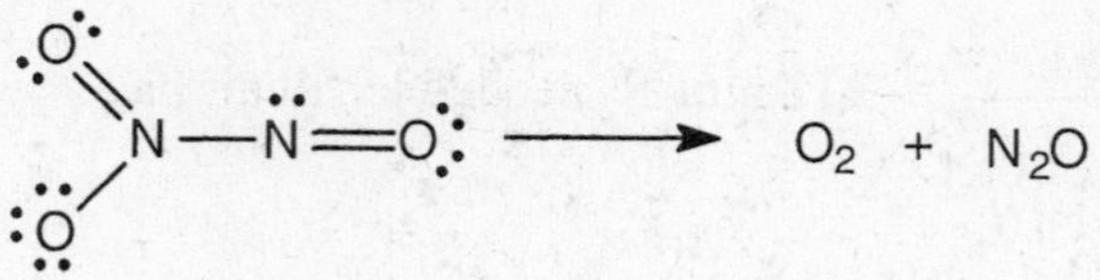

at some point nitrogen-oxygen bonds must be broken. $N-N$ single bonds (160. kJ/mol) are weaker than $N-O$ single bonds (201 kJ/mol). In addition, resonance structures indicate that there is more double bond character in the $N-O$ bonds than in the $N-N$ bond. Thus, NO_2 and NO are preferred by kinetics because of the lower activation energy.

7.   Unbalanced equation:

$$CaF_2 \cdot 3Ca_3(PO_4)_2(s) + H_2SO_4(aq) \rightarrow H_3PO_4(aq) + HF(aq) + CaSO_4 \cdot 2H_2O(s)$$

Balancing Ca^{2+}, F^-, and PO_4^{3-}:

$$CaF_2 \cdot 3Ca_3(PO_4)_2(s) + H_2SO_4(aq) \rightarrow 6\ H_3PO_4(aq) + 2\ HF(aq) + 10\ CaSO_4 \cdot 2H_2O(s)$$

On the righthand side, there are 20 extra hydrogen atoms, 10 extra sulfates, and 20 extra water molecules. We can balance the hydrogen and sulfate with 10 sulfuric acid molecules. The extra waters came from the water in the sulfuric acid solution. The balanced equation is:

$$CaF_2 \cdot 3Ca_3(PO_4)_2(s) + 10\ H_2SO_4(aq) + 20\ H_2O(l) \rightarrow 6\ H_3PO_4(aq) + 2\ HF(aq) + 10\ CaSO_4 \cdot 2H_2O(s)$$

8. $N_2(g) + 3\ H_2(g) \rightleftharpoons 2\ NH_3(g) + heat$

a.   This reaction is exothermic, so an increase in temperature will decrease the value of K (see Table 6.3 of text.) This has the effect of lowering the amount of $NH_3(g)$ produced at equilibrium. The temperature increase, therefore, must be for kinetics reasons. When the temperature increases, the reaction reaches equilibrium much faster. At low temperatures, this reaction is very slow, too slow to be of any use.

b.   As $NH_3(g)$ is removed, the reaction shifts right to produce more $NH_3(g)$.

c.   A catalyst has no effect on the equilibrium position. The purpose of a catalyst is to speed up a reaction so it reaches equilibrium more quickly.

d.   When the pressure of reactants and products is high, the reaction shifts to the side that has fewer gas molecules. Since the product side contains 2 molecules of gas compared to 4 molecules of gas on the reactant side, the reaction shifts right to products at high pressures of reactants and products.

9.   OCN⁻ has $6 + 4 + 5 + 1 = 16$ valence electrons.

$$\left[\ddot{\overset{..}{O}}=C=\ddot{N}: \right]^{-} \longleftrightarrow \left[:\ddot{\overset{..}{O}}-C\equiv N: \right]^{-} \longleftrightarrow \left[:O\equiv C-\ddot{\overset{..}{N}}: \right]^{-}$$

Formal
charge   0   0   -1   -1   0   0   +1   0   -2

Only the first two resonance structures should be important. The third places a positive formal charge on the most electronegative atom in the ion and a -2 formal charge on N.

CNO⁻:

$$\left[:\ddot{C}=N=\ddot{\overset{..}{O}}: \right]^{-} \longleftrightarrow \left[:C\equiv N-\ddot{\overset{..}{O}}: \right]^{-} \longleftrightarrow \left[:\ddot{C}-N\equiv O: \right]^{-}$$

Formal
charge   -2   +1   0   -1   +1   -1   -3   +1   +1

All of the resonance structures for fulminate (CNO⁻) involve greater formal charges than in cynate (OCN⁻), making fulminate more reactive (less stable).

10.

$$\begin{array}{c} H \\ \diagdown \\ \quad \\ H \end{array} N-N \begin{array}{c} H \\ \diagup \\ \quad \\ H \end{array} (l) \ + \ 2 \ F\!-\!F \ (g) \ \longrightarrow \ 4 \ H\!-\!F(g) \ + \ N\!\equiv\!N \ (g)$$

Bonds broken: Bonds formed:

   1 N − N (160. kJ/mol)   4 H − F (565 kJ/mol)
   4 N − H (391 kJ/mol)   1 N≡ N (941 kJ/mol)
   2 F − F (154 kJ/mol)

$\Delta H = 160. + 4(391) + 2(154) - [4(565) + 941] = 2032 \text{ kJ} - 3201 \text{ kJ} = -1169 \text{ kJ}$

11.   a. $NH_4NO_3(s) \xrightarrow{heat} N_2O(g) + 2 H_2O(g)$

        b. $2 N_2O_5(g) \rightarrow 4 NO_2(g) + O_2(g)$

        c. $2 K_3P(s) + 6 H_2O(l) \rightarrow 2 PH_3(g) + 6 KOH(aq)$

        d. $PBr_3(l) + 3 H_2O(l) \rightarrow H_3PO_3(aq) + 3 HBr(aq)$

        e. $2 NH_3(aq) + NaOCl(aq) \rightarrow N_2H_4(aq) + NaCl(aq) + H_2O(l)$

12.   a. PF_5;   N is too small and doesn't have low energy d-orbitals to expand its octet to form NF_5.

        b. AsF_5;   I is too large to fit 5 atoms of I around As.

c. NF_3;   N is too small for three large bromine atoms to fit around it.

13.   Production of bismuth:

$$2 Bi_2S_3(s) + 9 O_2(g) \rightarrow 2 Bi_2O_3(s) + 6 SO_2(g);   2 Bi_2O_3(s) + 3 C(s) \rightarrow 4 Bi(s) + 3 CO_2(g)$$

Production of antimony:

$$2 Sb_2S_3(s) + 9 O_2(g) \rightarrow 2 Sb_2O_3(s) + 6 SO_2(g);   2 Sb_2O_3(s) + 3 C(s) \rightarrow 4 Sb(s) + 3 CO_2(g)$$

14.   a. $H_3PO_4 > H_3PO_3$; The strongest acid has the most oxygen atoms.

b. $H_3PO_4 > H_2PO_4^- > HPO_4^{2-}$; Acid strength decreases as protons are removed.

15.   TSP = Na_3PO_4; PO_4^{3-} is the conjugate base of the weak acid HPO_4^{2-} ($K_a = 4.8 \times 10^{-13}$). All conjugate bases of weak acids are effective bases ($K_b = K_w/K_a = 1.0 \times 10^{-14}/4.8 \times 10^{-13} = 2.1 \times 10^{-2}$). The weak base reaction of PO_4^{3-} with H_2O is: $PO_4^{3-}(aq) + H_2O(l) \rightleftharpoons HPO_4^{2-}(aq) + OH^-(aq)$

16.   The acidic protons are attached to oxygen.

$H_4P_2O_6$ (50 valence e^-): $H_4P_2O_5$ (44 valence e^-):

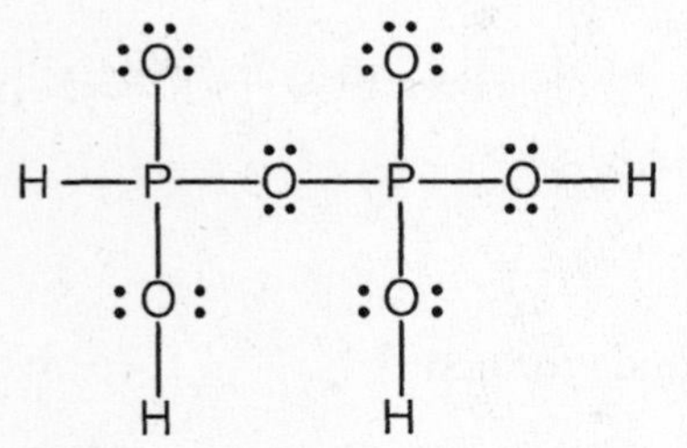

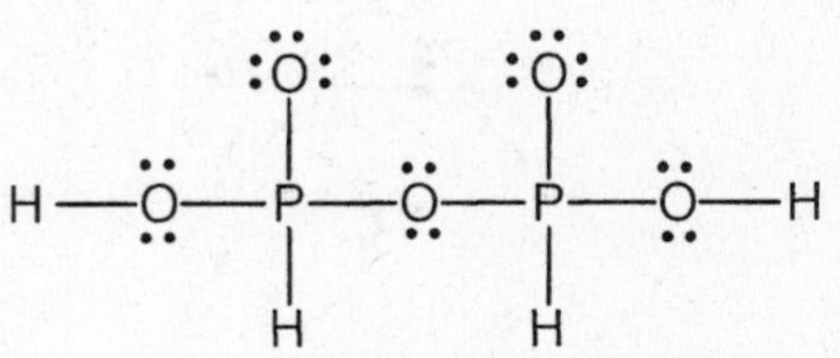

17.   White phosphorus consists of discrete tetrahedral P_4 molecules. The bond angles in the P_4 tetrahedrons are only $60°$, which makes P_4 very reactive especially towards oxygen. Red and black phosphorus are covalent network solids. In red phosphorus the P_4 tetrahedra are bonded to each other in chains making them less reactive than white phosphorus. They need a source of energy to react with oxygen, such as when one strikes a match. Black phosphorus is crystalline with the P atoms tightly bonded to each other in the crystal and are fairly unreactive towards oxygen.

18.   Hypochlorite can act as an oxidizing agent. For example, it is capable of oxidizing I^- to I_2. If a solution containing I^- turns brown when BiOCl is added, then BiOCl is bismuth(I) hypochlorite. The brown color indicates production of I_2. If the solution doesn't change color, then it is bismuthyl chloride.

19. $4 As(s) + 3 O_2(g) \rightarrow As_4O_6(s)$; $4 As(s) + 5 O_2(g) \rightarrow As_4O_{10}(s)$

$As_4O_6(s) + 6 H_2O(l) \rightarrow 4 H_3AsO_3(aq)$; $As_4O_{10}(s) + 6 H_2O(l) \rightarrow 4 H_3AsO_4(aq)$

20.   M.O model:

NO^+: $(\sigma_{2s})^2(\sigma_{2s}{}^*)^2(\pi_{2p})^4(\sigma_{2p})^2$, Bond order = (8 - 2)/2 = 3, 0 unpaired e$^-$ (diamagnetic)

NO: $(\sigma_{2s})^2(\sigma_{2s}{}^*)^2(\pi_{2p})^4(\sigma_{2p})^2(\pi_{2p}{}^*)^1$, B.O. = 2.5, 1 unpaired e$^-$ (paramagnetic)

NO^-: $(\sigma_{2s})^2(\sigma_{2s}{}^*)^2(\pi_{2p})^4(\sigma_{2p})^2(\pi_{2p}{}^*)^2$, B.O. = 2, 2 unpaired e$^-$ (paramagnetic)

Lewis structures: NO^+: $\left[:N\equiv O: \right]^+$

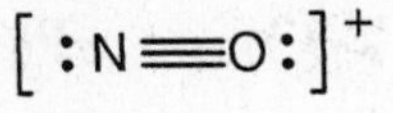

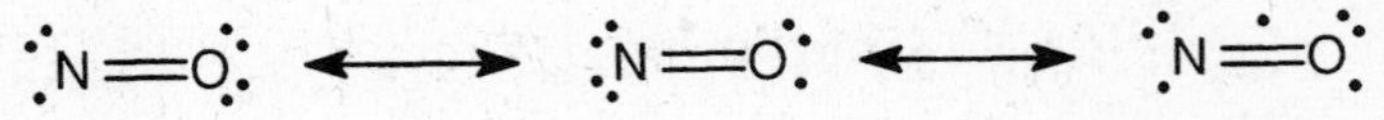

NO: $\ddot{N}=\ddot{O}: \longleftrightarrow :\ddot{N}=\ddot{O}: \longleftrightarrow :\ddot{N}=\ddot{O}$

NO^-: $\left[:\ddot{N}=\ddot{O}: \right]^-$

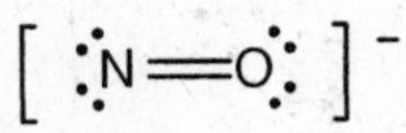

The two models only give the same results for NO^+ (a triple bond with no unpaired electrons). Lewis structure are not adequate for NO and NO^-. The M.O. model gives a better representation for all three species. For NO, Lewis structures are poor for odd electron species. For NO^-, both models predict a double bond but only the MO model correctly predicts that NO^- is paramagnetic.

21.   1/2 N_2(g) + 1/2 O_2(g) → NO(g) $\Delta G° = \Delta G°_{f, NO}$ = 87 kJ/mol; By definition, $\Delta G°_f$ for a compound equals the free energy change that would accompany the formation of 1 mol of that compound from its elements in their standard states. NO (and some other oxides of nitrogen) have weaker bonds as compared to the triple bond of N_2 and the double bond of O_2. Because of this, NO (and some other oxides of nitrogen) have higher (positive) standard free energies of formation as compared to the relatively stable N_2 and O_2 molecules.

22.   a.

$$(2e^- + NaBiO_3 \rightarrow BiO_3{}^{3-} + Na^+) \times 5$$
$$(4\ H_2O + Mn^{2+} \rightarrow MnO_4{}^- + 8\ H^+ + 5e^-) \times 2$$

$$8\ H_2O(l) + 2\ Mn^{2+}(aq) + 5\ NaBiO_3(s) \rightarrow 2\ MnO_4{}^-(aq) + 16\ H^+(aq) + 5\ BiO_3{}^{3-}(aq) + 5\ Na^+(aq)$$

b.   Bismuthate exists as a covalent network solid: $(BiO_3{}^-)_x$.

23. $AsCl_4{}^+$, 5 + 4(7) - 1 = 32 e$^-$ $AsCl_6{}^-$, 5 + 6(7) + 1 = 48 e$^-$

The reaction is a Lewis acid-base reaction. A chloride ion acts as a Lewis base when it is transferred from one $AsCl_5$ to another. Arsenic is the Lewis acid (electron pair acceptor).

24.   a. SbF_5, 40 valence e⁻ HSO_3F, 32 valence e⁻ $H_2SO_3F^+$, 32 valence e⁻

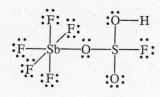   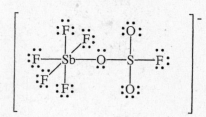

F_5SbOSO_2FH, 72 valence e⁻ $F_5SbOSO_2F^-$, 72 valence e⁻

b.   The active protonating species is $H_2SO_3F^+$.

25.   The pollution provides nitrogen and phosphorus nutrients so the algae can grow. The algae consume oxygen, causing fish to die.

26.   For ammonia (in one minute):

$$n_{NH_3} = \frac{PV}{RT} = \frac{90.\ atm \times 500.\ L}{\frac{0.08206\ L\ atm}{mol\ K} \times 496\ K} = 1.1 \times 10^3\ mol\ NH_3$$

NH_3 flows into the reactor at a rate of 1.1×10^3 mol/min.

For CO_2 (in one minute):

$$n_{CO_2} = \frac{PV}{RT} = \frac{45\ atm \times 600.\ L}{\frac{0.08206\ L\ atm}{mol\ K} \times 496\ K} = 6.6 \times 10^2\ mol\ CO_2$$

CO_2 flows into the reactor at 6.6×10^2 mol/min.

To react completely with 1.1×10^3 mol NH_3/min, we need:

$$\frac{1.1 \times 10^3\ mol\ NH_3}{min} \times \frac{1\ mol\ CO_2}{2\ mol\ NH_3} = 5.5 \times 10^2\ mol\ CO_2/min$$

Since 660 mol CO_2/min are present, ammonia is the limiting reagent.

$$\frac{1.1 \times 10^3\ mol\ NH_3}{min} \times \frac{1\ mol\ urea}{2\ mol\ NH_3} \times \frac{60.06\ g\ urea}{mol\ urea} = 3.3 \times 10^4\ g\ urea/min$$

27. $5 N_2O_4(l) + 4 N_2H_3CH_3(l) \rightarrow 12 H_2O(g) + 9 N_2(g) + 4 CO_2(g)$

$$\Delta H° = \left[12 \text{ mol} \left(\frac{-242 \text{ kJ}}{\text{mol}} \right) + 4 \text{ mol} \left(\frac{-393.5 \text{ kJ}}{\text{mol}} \right) \right]$$

$$- \left[5 \text{ mol} \left(\frac{-20. \text{ kJ}}{\text{mol}} \right) + 4 \text{ mol} \left(\frac{54 \text{ kJ}}{\text{mol}} \right) \right] = -4594 \text{ kJ}$$

Group 6A Elements

28. $O=O-O \rightarrow O=O + O$ (We will ignore resonance stabilization in O_3 bonds.)

Break $O - O$ bond: $\Delta H = 146 \text{ kJ/mol} \times \dfrac{1 \text{ mol}}{6.022 \times 10^{23}} = 2.42 \times 10^{-22} \text{ kJ} = 2.42 \times 10^{-19} \text{ J}$

A photon of light must contain at least 2.42×10^{-19} J to break one $O - O$ bond.

$E_{photon} = \dfrac{hc}{\lambda}, \ \lambda = \dfrac{hc}{E} = \dfrac{(6.626 \times 10^{-34} \text{ J s}) (2.998 \times 10^8 \text{ m/s})}{2.42 \times 10^{-19} \text{ J}} = 8.21 \times 10^{-7} \text{ m} = 821 \text{ nm}$

29.   In the upper atmosphere, O_3 acts as a filter for UV radiation:

$$O_3 \overset{h\nu}{\rightarrow} O_2 + O \quad \text{(See Exercise 19.28.)}$$

O_3 is also a powerful oxidizing agent. It irritates the lungs and eyes, and at high concentration it is toxic. The smell of a "fresh spring day" is O_3 formed during lightning discharges. Toxic materials don't necessarily smell bad. For example, HCN smells like almonds.

30. S_2N_2 has $2(6) + 2(5) = 22$ valence electrons.

31.   a.   As we go down the family, K_a increases. This is consistent with the bond to hydrogen getting weaker.

       b.   Po is below Te, so the K_a should be larger. The K_a for H_2Po should be on the order of 10^{-2}.

32. TeF_5^- has $6 + 5(7) + 1 = 42$ valence electrons.

The lone pair of electrons around Te exerts a stronger repulsion than the bonding pairs, pushing the four square planar F's away from the lone pair and thus reducing the bond angles between the axial F atom and the square planar F atoms.

33.   In the presence of S^{2-}, sulfur forms polysulfide ions, S_n^{2-}, which are soluble like most species with charges, e.g., $S_8 + S^{2-} \rightleftharpoons S_9^{2-}$. Nitric acid oxidizes S^{2-} to S, which then causes sulfur to precipitate out of solution.

34.   Plastic sulfur consists of long S_n chains of sulfur atoms. Plastic sulfur becomes brittle as the long chains break down into S_8 rings.

35.   a. $2 SO_2(g) + O_2(g) \rightarrow 2 SO_3(g)$

      b. $SO_3(g) + H_2O(l) \rightarrow H_2SO_4(aq)$

      c. $2 Na_2S_2O_3(aq) + I_2(aq) \rightarrow Na_2S_4O_6(aq) + 2 NaI(aq)$

      d. $Cu(s) + 2 H_2SO_4(aq) \rightarrow CuSO_4(aq) + 2 H_2O(l) + SO_2(aq)$

36.   a. SO_3^{2-}, $6 + 3(6) + 2 = 26 \ e^-$ b. O_3, $3(6) = 18 \ e^-$

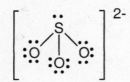

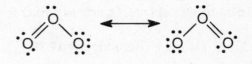

  trigonal pyramid; $\approx 109.5°$; sp^3 V-shaped; $\approx 120°$; sp^2

      c. SCl_2, $6 + 2(7) = 20 \ e^-$ d. $SeBr_4$, $6 + 4(7) = 34 \ e^-$

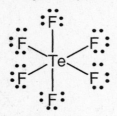

  V-shaped; $\approx 109.5°$; sp^3 see-saw; $a \approx 120°$, $b \approx 90°$; dsp^3

      e. TeF_6, $6 + 6(7) = 48 \ e^-$

  octahedral; $90°$; d^2sp^3

37. $H_2SeO_4(aq) + 3\ SO_2(g) \rightarrow Se(s) + 3\ SO_3(g) + H_2O(l)$

38.   Light from violet to green will work since these have wavelengths between 400 and 500 nm.

39.   This element is in the oxygen family as all oxygen family members have ns^2np^4 valence electron configurations.

   a.   As with all elements of the oxygen family, this element has 6 valence electrons.

   b.   The nonmetals in the oxygen family are O, S, Se and Te, which are all possible identities for the element.

   c.   Ions in the oxygen family are -2 charged in ionic compounds. Li_2X would be the formula between Li^+ and X^{2-} ions.

   d.   In general, radii increases from right to left across the periodic table and increases going down a family. From this trend, the radius of the unknown element must be smaller than the Ba radius.

   e.   The ionization energy trend is the opposite of the radii trend indicated in the previous answer. From this trend, the unknown element will have a smaller ionization energy than fluorine.

Group 7A Elements

40.   a. CCl_2F_2, $4 + 2(7) + 2(7) = 32\ e^-$ b. $HClO_4$, $1 + 7 + 4(6) = 32\ e^-$

   tetrahedral; 109.5°; sp^3 About Cl: tetrahedral; 109.5°; sp^3
                                                            About O: V-shaped; $\approx$ 109.5°; sp^3

   c. ICl_3, $7 + 3(7) = 28\ e^-$ d. BrF_5, $7 + 5(7) = 42\ e^-$

   T-shaped; $\approx$ 90°; dsp^3 square pyramid; $\approx$ 90°; d^2sp^3

41. O_2F_2 has $2(6) + 2(7) = 26$ valence e^-.

$$:\overset{..}{\underset{..}{F}}—\overset{..}{\underset{..}{O}}—\overset{..}{\underset{..}{O}}—\overset{..}{\underset{..}{F}}:$$

Formal Charge   0   0   0   0
Oxidation State   -1   +1   +1   -1

Oxidation states are more useful. We are forced to assign +1 as the oxidation state for oxygen. Oxygen is very electronegative and +1 is not a stable oxidation state for this element.

42.   a. $F_2 + H_2O \rightarrow HOF + HF$; $2 HOF \rightarrow 2 HF + O_2$; $3 HOF + H_2O \rightarrow 3 HF + H_2O_2 + O_2$

In dilute acid, $HOF + H_2O \rightarrow HF + H_2O_2$

In dilute base, HOF exists as OF^- and HF exists as F^-. The balanced reaction is:

$$(2e^- + H_2O + OF^- \rightarrow F^- + 2 OH^-) \times 2$$
$$\underline{4 OH^- \rightarrow O_2 + 2 H_2O + 4e^-}$$
$$2 OF^- \rightarrow O_2 + 2 F^-$$

   b. HOF: Assign +1 to H and -1 to F. The oxidation state of oxygen is then zero. Oxygen is very electronegative. A zero oxidation state is not very stable since oxygen is a very good oxidizing agent.

43.   Fluorine is the most reactive of the halogens because it is the most electronegative atom and the bond in the F_2 molecule is very weak.

44.   One reason is that the $H - F$ bond is stronger than the other hydrohalides, making it more difficult to form H^+ and F^-. The main reason HF is a weak acid is entropy. When $F^-(aq)$ forms from the dissociation of HF, there is a high degree of ordering that takes place as water molecules hydrate this small ion. Entropy is considerably more unfavorable for the formation of hydrated F^- than for the formation of the other hydrated halides. The result of the more unfavorable $\Delta S°$ term is a positive $\Delta G°$ value which leads to a K_a value less than one.

45. $ClO^- + H_2O + 2 e^- \rightarrow 2 OH^- + Cl^-$ $E_c° = 0.90$ V
       $\underline{2 NH_3 + 2 OH^- \rightarrow N_2H_4 + 2 H_2O + 2 e^-}$ $\underline{-E_a° = 0.10 \text{ V}}$

$ClO^-(aq) + 2 NH_3(aq) \rightarrow Cl^-(aq) + N_2H_4(aq) + H_2O(l)$ $E_{cell}° = 1.00$ V

Since $E_{cell}°$ is positive for this reaction, then at standard conditions ClO^- can spontaneously oxidize NH_3 to the somewhat toxic N_2H_4.

46.   A disproportionation reaction is an oxidation-reduction reaction in which one species will act as both an oxidizing agent and reducing agent. The species reacts with itself forming products with higher and lower oxidation states. For example, $2 Cu^+ \rightarrow Cu + Cu^{2+}$ is a disproportionation reaction.

$HClO_2$ will disproportionate at standard conditions since $E_{cell}° > 0$:

$$HClO_2 + 2 H^+ + 2 e^- \rightarrow HClO + H_2O \qquad\qquad E_c^\circ = 1.65 \text{ V}$$

$$HClO_2 + H_2O \rightarrow ClO_3^- + 3 H^+ + 2 e^- \qquad\qquad -E_a^\circ = -1.21 \text{ V}$$

$$2 HClO_2(aq) \rightarrow HClO(aq) + ClO_3^-(aq) + H^+(aq) \qquad E_{cell}^\circ = 0.44 \text{ V}$$

47.   a. $BaCl_2(s) + H_2SO_4(aq) \rightarrow BaSO_4(s) + 2 HCl(g)$

       b. $BrF(s) + H_2O(l) \rightarrow HF(aq) + HOBr(aq)$

       c. $SiO_2(s) + 4 HF(aq) \rightarrow SiF_4(g) + 2 H_2O(l)$

48.   a. $AgCl(s) \xrightarrow{h\nu} Ag(s) + Cl$; The reactive chlorine atom is trapped in the crystal. When light is removed, Cl reacts with silver atoms to reform AgCl, i.e., the reverse reaction occurs. In pure AgCl, the Cl atoms escape, making the reverse reaction impossible.

       b.   Over time chlorine is lost and the presence of the dark silver metal is permanent.

Group 8A Elements

49.   Helium is unreactive and doesn't combine with any other elements. It is a very light gas and would easily escape the earth's gravitational pull as the planet was formed.

50.   In Mendeleev's time none of the noble gases were known. Since an entire family was missing, no gaps seemed to appear in the periodic arrangement. Mendeleev had no evidence to predict the existence of such a family. The heavier members of the noble gases are not really inert. Xe and Kr have been shown to react and form compounds with other elements.

51. $10.0 \text{ m} \times 10.0 \text{ m} \times 10.0 \text{ m} = 1.00 \times 10^3 \text{ m}^3$; From Table 19.12, volume % Ar = 0.9%.

$$1.00 \times 10^3 \text{ m}^3 \times \left(\frac{10 \text{ dm}}{\text{m}}\right)^3 \times \frac{1 \text{ L}}{\text{dm}^3} \times \frac{0.9 \text{ L Ar}}{100 \text{ L air}} = 9 \times 10^3 \text{ L of Ar in the room}$$

$$PV = nRT, \quad n = \frac{PV}{RT} = \frac{(1.0 \text{ atm}) (9 \times 10^3 \text{ L})}{(0.08206 \text{ L atm K}^{-1}\text{mol}^{-1}) (298 \text{ K})} = 4 \times 10^2 \text{ mol Ar}$$

$$4 \times 10^2 \text{ mol Ar} \times \frac{39.95 \text{ g}}{\text{mol}} = 2 \times 10^4 \text{ g Ar in the room}$$

$$4 \times 10^2 \text{ mol Ar} \times \frac{6.022 \times 10^{23} \text{ atoms}}{\text{mol}} = 2 \times 10^{26} \text{ atoms Ar in the room}$$

A 2 L breath contains: $2 \text{ L air} \times \dfrac{0.9 \text{ L Ar}}{100 \text{ L air}} = 2 \times 10^{-2} \text{ L Ar}$

$$n = \frac{PV}{RT} = \frac{(1.0 \text{ atm}) (2 \times 10^{-2} \text{ L})}{(0.08206 \text{ L atm K}^{-1}\text{mol}^{-1}) (298 \text{ K})} = 8 \times 10^{-4} \text{ mol Ar}$$

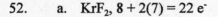

$$8 \times 10^{-4} \text{ mol Ar} \times \frac{6.022 \times 10^{23} \text{ atoms}}{\text{mol}} = 5 \times 10^{20} \text{ atoms of Ar in a 2 L breath}$$

Since Ar and Rn are both noble gases, then both species will be relatively unreactive. However, all nuclei of Rn are radioactive, unlike most nuclei of Ar. The radioactive decay products of Rn can cause biological damage when inhaled.

52.   a. KrF_2, $8 + 2(7) = 22$ e⁻   b. KrF_4, $8 + 4(7) = 36$ e⁻

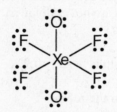

      linear; 180°; dsp³

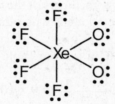

      square planar; 90°; d²sp³

   c. XeO_2F_2, $8 + 2(6) + 2(7) = 34$ e⁻

      All are: see-saw; ≈ 90° and ≈ 120°; dsp³

   d. XeO_2F_4, $8 + 2(6) + 4(7) = 48$ e⁻

      All are: octahedral; 90°; d²sp³

53. XeF_2 can react with oxygen to produce explosive xenon oxides and oxyfluorides and react with water to form HF as well.

Additional Exercises

54.   In order to form a π bond, the d and p orbitals must overlap "side to side" instead of "head to head" as in sigma bonds. A representation of the "side to side" overlap follows.

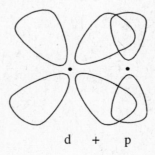

d   +   p

55.   a.   The Lewis structures for NNO and NON are (16 valence electrons each):

$$:N\!\!=\!\!N\!\!=\!\!\ddot{O}: \quad \longleftrightarrow \quad :N\!\!\equiv\!\!N\!\!-\!\!\ddot{\underset{..}{O}}: \quad \longleftrightarrow \quad :\ddot{N}\!\!-\!\!N\!\!\equiv\!\!O:$$

$$:\ddot{N}\!\!=\!\!O\!\!=\!\!\ddot{N}: \quad \longleftrightarrow \quad :N\!\!\equiv\!\!O\!\!-\!\!\ddot{\underset{..}{N}}: \quad \longleftrightarrow \quad :\ddot{\underset{..}{N}}\!\!-\!\!O\!\!\equiv\!\!N:$$

The NNO structure is correct. From the Lewis structures we would predict both NNO and NON to be linear. However, we would predict NNO to be polar and NON to be nonpolar. Since experiments show N_2O to be polar, then NNO is the correct structure.

b.   Formal charge = number of valence electrons of atoms - [(number of lone pair electrons) + 1/2 (number of shared electrons)].

$$:N\!\!=\!\!N\!\!=\!\!\ddot{O}: \quad \longleftrightarrow \quad :N\!\!\equiv\!\!N\!\!-\!\!\ddot{\underset{..}{O}}: \quad \longleftrightarrow \quad :\ddot{N}\!\!-\!\!N\!\!\equiv\!\!O:$$
$$\quad -1 \quad +1 \quad \ \ 0 \qquad\qquad \ \ 0 \quad +1 \quad -1 \qquad\qquad -2 \quad +1 \quad +1$$

The formal charges for the atoms in the various resonance structures appear below each atom. The central N is sp hybridized in all of the resonance structures. We can probably ignore the third resonance structure on the basis of the relatively large formal charges on the various atoms in N_2O as compared to the first two resonance structures.

c.   The sp hybrid orbitals on the center N overlap with atomic orbitals (or hybrid orbitals) on the other two atoms to form the two sigma bonds. The remaining two unhybridized p orbitals on the center N overlap with two p orbitals on the peripheral N to form the two π bonds.

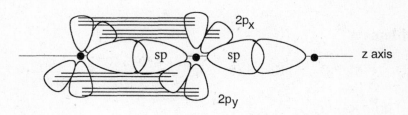

56.   For $NCl_3 \rightarrow NCl_2 + Cl$, only the N – Cl bond is broken. For $O=N-Cl \rightarrow NO + Cl$, the NO bond gets stronger (bond order increases from 2.0 to 2.5) when the N – Cl bond is broken. This makes ΔH for the reaction smaller than just the energy necessary to break the N – Cl bond.

57.   Xe has one more valence electron than I. Thus, the isoelectric species will have I plus one extra electron substituted for Xe, giving a species with a net minus one charge.

a. IO_4^- b. IO_3^- c. IF_2^- d. IF_4^- e. IF_6^- f. IOF_3^-

58.   Release of Sr is probably more harmful. Xe is chemically unreactive. Strontium is in the same family as calcium and could be absorbed and concentrated in the body in a fashion similar to Ca. This puts the radioactive Sr in the bones: red blood cells are produced in bone marrow. Xe would not be readily incorporated in the body.

The chemical properties determine where a radioactive material may be concentrated in the body or how easily it may be excreted. The length of time of exposure and what is exposed to radiation significantly affects the health hazard.

59. $1.0 \times 10^4 \text{ kg waste} \times \dfrac{3.0 \text{ kg NH}_4^+}{100 \text{ kg waste}} \times \dfrac{1000 \text{ g}}{\text{kg}} \times \dfrac{1 \text{ mol NH}_4^+}{18.04 \text{ g NH}_4^+} \times \dfrac{1 \text{ mol C}_5\text{H}_7\text{O}_2\text{N}}{55 \text{ mol NH}_4^+}$

$\times \dfrac{113.12 \text{ g C}_5\text{H}_7\text{O}_2\text{N}}{\text{mol C}_5\text{H}_7\text{O}_2\text{N}} = 3.4 \times 10^4 \text{ g tissue if all NH}_4^+ \text{ converted}$

Since only 95% of the NH_4^+ ions react:

mass of tissue = $(0.95)(3.4 \times 10^4 \text{ g}) = 3.2 \times 10^4$ g or 32 kg bacterial tissue

60.   The answers to the clues are:

(1) H<u>I</u> has the second highest boiling point; (2) H<u>F</u> is the weak hydrogen halide acid; (3) <u>He</u> was first discovered from the sun's emission spectrum; (4) Both Bi and Sb form MOCl precipitates. For a message that makes sense, <u>Bi</u> is the correct choice; (5) <u>Te</u> is a semiconductor; (6) <u>S</u> has both rhombic and monoclinic solid forms; (7) <u>Cl</u>$_2$ is a yellow-green gas and Cl$^-$ forms the indicated precipitates; (8) <u>O</u> is the most abundant element in and near the earth's crust; (9) <u>Se</u> appears to furnish some form of protection against cancer; (10) Kr forms compounds. The symbol in reverse order is <u>rk</u>; (11) <u>As</u> forms As$_4$ molecules; (12) <u>N</u>$_2$ is a major inert component of air and N is often found in fertilizers and explosives.

Filling in the blank spaces with the answers to the clues, the message is "If he bites, close ranks."

Challenge Problems

61. $Mg^{2+} + P_3O_{10}^{5-} \rightleftharpoons MgP_3O_{10}^{3-}$ pK = -8.60; $[Mg^{2+}]_0 = \dfrac{50. \times 10^{-3} \text{ g}}{\text{L}} \times \dfrac{1 \text{ mol}}{24.3 \text{ g}} = 2.1 \times 10^{-3} \, M$

$[P_3O_{10}^{5-}]_0 = \dfrac{40. \text{ g Na}_5\text{P}_3\text{O}_{10}}{\text{L}} \times \dfrac{1 \text{ mol}}{367.9 \text{ g}} = 0.11 \, M$

Assume the reaction goes to completion since K is large (K = $10^{8.60}$ = 4.0×10^8). Then solve the back equilibrium problem to determine the small amount of Mg^{2+} present.

$$Mg^{2+} \quad + \quad P_3O_{10}^{5-} \quad \rightleftharpoons \quad MgP_3O_{10}^{3-}$$

	Mg^{2+}	$P_3O_{10}^{5-}$	$MgP_3O_{10}^{3-}$	
Before	2.1×10^{-3} M	0.11 M	0	
Change	-2.1×10^{-3}	-2.1×10^{-3} $\rightarrow$	$+2.1 \times 10^{-3}$	React completely
After	0	0.11	2.1×10^{-3}	New initial

x mol/L $MgP_3O_{10}^{3-}$ dissociates to reach equilibrium

	Mg^{2+}	$P_3O_{10}^{5-}$	$MgP_3O_{10}^{3-}$
Change	$+x$	$+x$ $\quad\leftarrow$	$-x$
Equil.	x	$0.11 + x$	$2.1 \times 10^{-3} - x$

$$K = 4.0 \times 10^8 = \frac{[MgP_3O_{10}^{3-}]}{[Mg^{2+}][P_3O_{10}^{5-}]} = \frac{2.1 \times 10^{-3} - x}{x(0.11 + x)} \quad \text{(assume } x \ll 2.1 \times 10^{-3})$$

$$4.0 \times 10^8 \approx \frac{2.1 \times 10^{-3}}{x(0.11)}, \quad x = [Mg^{2+}] = 4.8 \times 10^{-11} \ M; \quad \text{Assumptions good.}$$

62. $N_2 + 3 H_2 \rightarrow 2 NH_3$

For sake of simplicity, assume 3.0 mol of N_2 and 3.0 mol H_2.

$$
\begin{array}{ccc}
N_2 & + \ 3 H_2 & \rightarrow \ 2 NH_3 \\
3.0 & 3.0 & 0 \\
-1.0 & -3.0 & +2.0 \\
\hline
2.0 & 0 & 2.0 \\
\end{array}
$$

Thus, we had 6 mol initially, and we end with 4 mol.

a. $P_{NH_3} = 0.50$ atm (NH_3 contributes 1/2 the moles of gas, and the total pressure remains constant at 1.0 atm.)

b. $\chi_{NH_3} = 0.50 = $ mol NH_3/total moles $= 2.0/4.0$

c. $V_i = 15.0$ L $n_i = 6x$; $V_f = $? $n_f = 4x$

$$PV = nRT \rightarrow \frac{V}{n} = \frac{RT}{P} \quad \frac{V_1}{n_1} = \frac{V_2}{n_2}; \quad \frac{15.0 \text{ L}}{6x} = \frac{V_f}{4x}; \quad V_f = 10.0 \text{ L}$$

63. $3 O_2(g) \rightleftharpoons 2 O_3(g); \quad \Delta H^\circ = 2(143) = 286 \text{ kJ}; \quad \Delta G^\circ = 2(163) = 326 \text{ kJ}$

$$\ln K_p = \frac{-\Delta G^\circ}{RT} = \frac{-326 \times 10^3 \text{ J}}{(8.3145 \text{ J K}^{-1} \text{ mol}^{-1})(298 \text{ K})} = -131.573, \quad K_p = e^{-131.573} = 7.22 \times 10^{-58}$$

Note: We carried extra significant figures for the K_p calculation.

We need the value of K at 230. K. From Section 10.11 of the text: $\ln K = \dfrac{-\Delta H^\circ}{RT} + \dfrac{\Delta S^\circ}{R}$

For two sets of K and T:

$$\ln K_1 = \frac{-\Delta H^\circ}{R}\left(\frac{1}{T_1}\right) + \frac{\Delta S^\circ}{R}; \quad \ln K_2 = \frac{-\Delta H^\circ}{R}\left(\frac{1}{T_2}\right) + \frac{\Delta S^\circ}{R}$$

Subtracting the first expression from the second:

$$\ln K_2 - \ln K_1 = \frac{\Delta H^\circ}{R}\left(\frac{1}{T_1} - \frac{1}{T_2}\right) \text{ or } \ln\frac{K_2}{K_1} = \frac{\Delta H^\circ}{R}\left(\frac{1}{T_1} - \frac{1}{T_2}\right)$$

Let $K_2 = 7.22 \times 10^{-58}$, $T_2 = 298$; $K_1 = K_{230}$, $T_1 = 230.$ K; $\Delta H° = 286 \times 10^3$ J

$$\ln \frac{7.22 \times 10^{-58}}{K_{230}} = \frac{286 \times 10^3}{8.3145} \left(\frac{1}{230.} - \frac{1}{298} \right) = 34.13 \qquad \text{(Carrying extra sig. figs.)}$$

$$\frac{7.22 \times 10^{-58}}{K_{230}} = e^{34.13} = 6.6 \times 10^{14}, \; K_{230} = 1.1 \times 10^{-72}$$

$$K_{230} = 1.1 \times 10^{-72} = \frac{P_{O_3}^2}{P_{O_2}^3} = \frac{P_{O_3}^2}{(1.0 \times 10^{-3} \text{ atm})^3}, \; P_{O_3} = 3.3 \times 10^{-41} \text{ atm}$$

The volume occupied by one molecule of ozone is:

$$V = \frac{nRT}{P} = \frac{(1/6.022 \times 10^{23} \text{ mol}) (0.08206 \text{ L atm mol}^{-1} \text{ K}^{-1}) (230. \text{ K})}{(3.3 \times 10^{-41} \text{ atm})}, \; V = 9.5 \times 10^{17} \text{ L}$$

Equilibrium is probably not maintained under these conditions. When only two ozone molecules are in a volume of 9.5×10^{17} L, the reaction is not at equilibrium. Under these conditions, $Q > K$ and the reaction shifts left. But with only 2 ozone molecules in this huge volume, it is extremely unlikely that they will collide with each other. At these conditions, the concentration of ozone is not large enough to maintain equilibrium.

64. $NH_3 + NH_3 \rightleftharpoons NH_4^+ + NH_2^-$, $K = [NH_4^+][NH_2^-] = 1.8 \times 10^{-12}$,

$[NH_4^+] = [NH_2^-] = 1.3 \times 10^{-6}$, $P(NH_4^+) = -\log (1.3 \times 10^{-6}) = 5.87$

This could also be written as:

$NH_3 \rightleftharpoons H^+ + NH_2^-$ (like $H_2O \rightleftharpoons H^+ + OH^-$)

Just like we abbreviate H_3O^+ with H^+, NH_4^+ is the abbreviation for H^+ in this world.

Thus $P(NH_4^+) = pH = 5.87$

65.   a. NO is the catalyst. NO is present in the first step of the mechanism on the reactant side, but it is not a reactant since it is regenerated in the second step and does not appear in the overall balanced equation.

        b. NO_2 is an intermediate. Intermediates also never appear in the overall balanced equation. In a mechanism, intermediates always appear first on the product side while catalysts always appear first on the reactant side.

        c. $k = A \exp(-E_a/RT)$; $\dfrac{k_{cat}}{k_{un}} = \dfrac{A \exp [-E_a(cat)/RT]}{A \exp [-E_a(un)/RT]} = \exp \left(\dfrac{E_a(un) - E_a(cat)}{RT} \right)$

$$\frac{k_{cat}}{k_{un}} = \exp\left(\frac{2100 \text{ J/mol}}{8.3145 \text{ J K}^{-1} \text{ mol}^{-1} \times 298 \text{ K}}\right) = e^{0.85} = 2.3$$

The catalyzed reaction is approximately 2.3 times faster than the uncatalyzed reaction at 25°C.

d. The mechanism for the chlorine catalyzed destruction of ozone is:

$$O_3 + Cl \rightarrow O_2 + ClO \quad \text{slow}$$
$$ClO + O \rightarrow O_2 + Cl \quad \text{fast}$$

$$\overline{\quad O_3 + O \rightarrow 2\,O_2 \quad}$$

e. Since the chlorine atom catalyzed reaction has a lower activation energy, then the Cl catalyzed rate is faster. Hence, Cl is a more effective catalyst. Using the activation energy, we can estimate the efficiency that Cl atoms destroy ozone as compared to NO molecules.

At 25°C: $\dfrac{k_{Cl}}{k_{NO}} = \exp\left(\dfrac{-E_a(Cl)}{RT} + \dfrac{E_a(NO)}{RT}\right) = \exp\left(\dfrac{(-2100 + 11{,}900) \text{ J/mol}}{(8.3145 \times 298) \text{ J/mol}}\right) = e^{3.96} = 52$

At 25°C, the Cl catalyzed reaction is roughly 52 times faster (more efficient) than the NO catalyzed reaction, assuming the frequency factor A is the same for each reaction and assuming similar rate laws.

66. $2\,SO_2 + O_2 \rightarrow 2\,SO_3$ or $SO_2 + 1/2\,O_2 \rightarrow SO_3$
             (all gases)

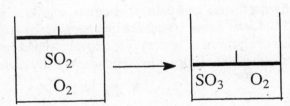

2.00 mol O_2

$d = \dfrac{mass}{vol}$; $d_1 = \dfrac{mass}{V_1}$; $d_2 = \dfrac{mass}{V_2}$ mass is conserved!

$$\frac{V_2}{V_1} = \frac{d_1}{d_2} = \frac{0.8000}{0.8471} = 0.9444$$

$$\frac{n_2\,(total)}{n_1\,(total)} = \frac{V_2}{V_1} = 0.9444 = \frac{n_{SO_3} + \left(2.00 - \dfrac{n_{SO_2}}{2}\right)}{n_{SO_2} + 2.00};\ n_{SO_3} = n_{SO_2}$$

Solving $n_{SO_2} = 0.250$ mol $= n_{SO_3}$, mass $SO_3 = (0.250 \text{ mol})(80.07 \text{ g/mol}) = 20.0$ g SO_3

CHAPTER TWENTY

TRANSITION METALS AND COORDINATION CHEMISTRY

Transition Metals

6. Transition metal ions lose the s electrons before the d electrons.

   a. Ti: $[Ar]4s^23d^2$

      Ti^{2+}: $[Ar]3d^2$

      Ti^{4+}: $[Ar]$ or $[Ne]3s^23p^6$

   b. Re: $[Xe]6s^24f^{14}5d^5$

      Re^{2+}: $[Xe]4f^{14}5d^5$

      Re^{3+}: $[Xe]4f^{14}5d^4$

   c. Ir: $[Xe]6s^24f^{14}5d^7$

      Ir^{2+}: $[Xe]4f^{14}5d^7$

      Ir^{3+}: $[Xe]4f^{14}5d^6$

7. Cr and Cu are exceptions to the normal filling order of electrons.

   a. Cr: $[Ar]4s^13d^5$

      Cr^{2+}: $[Ar]3d^4$

      Cr^{3+}: $[Ar]3d^3$

   b. Cu: $[Ar]4s^13d^{10}$

      Cu^+: $[Ar]3d^{10}$

      Cu^{2+}: $[Ar]3d^9$

   c. V: $[Ar]4s^23d^3$

      V^{2+}: $[Ar]3d^3$

      V^{3+}: $[Ar]3d^2$

8. Since transition metals form bonds that donate lone pairs of electrons, transition metals are Lewis acids (electron pair acceptors). The Lewis bases in coordination compounds are the ligands that must have at least one unshared pair of electrons. The coordinate covalent bond between the ligand and the transition metal just indicates that both electrons in the bond originally came from one of the atoms in the bond.

9. Most transition metals have unfilled d orbitals, which creates a large number of valence electrons that can be removed. Stable ions of the representative metals are determined by how many s and p valence electrons can be removed. In general, representative metals lose all of the s and p valence electrons to form their stable ions. Transition metals generally lose the s electron(s) to form +1 and +2 ions, but they can also lose some (or all) of the d electrons to form other oxidation states as well.

10. The lanthanide elements are located just before the 5d transition metals. The lanthanide contraction is the steady decrease in the atomic radii of the lanthanide elements when going from left to right across the periodic table. As a result of the lanthanide contraction, the sizes of the 4d and 5d elements are very similar (see Exercise 12.87). This leads to a greater similarity in the chemistry of the 4d and 5d elements in a given vertical group.

11.   a.   molybdenum(IV) sulfide; molybdenum(VI) oxide

         b. MoS_2, +4; MoO_3, +6; $(NH_4)_2Mo_2O_7$, +6; $(NH_4)_6Mo_7O_{24} \cdot 4\ H_2O$, +6

12.   a.   4 O atoms on faces × 1/2 O/face = 2 O atoms, 2 O atoms inside body, Total: 4 O atoms

            8 Ti atoms on corners × 1/8 Ti/corner + 1 Ti atom/body center = 2 Ti atoms

            Formula of the unit cell is Ti_2O_4. The empirical formula is TiO_2.

         b. +4 -2 0 0 +4 -1 +4 -2 +2 -2

            $2\ TiO_2 + 3\ C + 4\ Cl_2 \rightarrow 2\ TiCl_4 + CO_2 + 2\ CO$; Cl is reduced and C is oxidized. Cl_2 is the oxidizing agent and C is the reducing agent.

             +4 -1 0 +4 -2 0

            $TiCl_4 + O_2 \rightarrow TiO_2 + 2\ Cl_2$; O is reduced and Cl is oxidized. O_2 is the oxidizing agent and $TiCl_4$ is the reducing agent.

13. TiF_4: ionic compound containing Ti^{4+} ions and F^- ions. $TiCl_4$, $TiBr_4$, and TiI_4: covalent compounds containing discrete, tetrahedral TiX_4 molecules. As these covalent molecules get larger, the bp and mp increase because the London dispersion forces increase. TiF_4 has the highest bp since the interparticle forces are usually stronger in ionic compounds as compared to covalent compounds.

14. $CoCl_2(s) + 6\ H_2O(g) \rightleftharpoons CoCl_2 \cdot 6\ H_2O(s)$; If rain were imminent, there would be a lot of water vapor in the air causing the reaction to shift to the right. The indicator would take on the color of $CoCl_2 \cdot 6\ H_2O$, pink.

15. $H^+ + OH^- \rightarrow H_2O$; Sodium hydroxide (NaOH) will react with the H^+ on the product side of the reaction. This effectively removes H^+ from the equilibrium, which will shift the reaction to the right to produce more H^+ and CrO_4^{2-}. Since more CrO_4^{2-} is produced, the solution turns yellow.

Coordination Compounds

16. $Fe_2O_3(s) + 6\ H_2C_2O_4(aq) \rightarrow 2\ Fe(C_2O_4)_3^{3-}(aq) + 3\ H_2O(l) + 6\ H^+(aq)$; The oxalate anion forms a soluble complex ion with iron in rust (Fe_2O_3), which allows rust stains to be removed.

17.   a.   ligand: Species that donates a pair of electrons to form a covalent bond to a metal ion. Ligands act as Lewis bases (electron pair donors).

         b.   chelate: Ligand that can form more than one bond to a metal ion.

         c.   bidentate: Ligand that forms two bonds to a metal ion.

         d.   complex ion: Metal ion plus ligands.

18.   a.   hexaamminecobalt(II) chloride   b.   hexaaquacobalt(III) iodide

c. potassium tetrachloroplatinate(II)

d. potassium hexachloroplatinate(II)

e. pentaamminechlorocobalt(III) chloride

f. triamminetrinitrocobalt(III)

19. a. pentaamminechlororuthenium(III) ion

b. hexacyanoferrate(II) ion

c. tris(ethylenediamine)manganese(II) ion

d. pentaamminenitrocobalt(III) ion

20. a. pentaaquabromochromium(III) bromide

b. sodium hexacyanocobaltate(III)

c. bis(ethylenediamine)dinitroiron(III) chloride

d. tetraamminediiodoplatinum(IV) tetraiodoplatinate(II)

21. a. $K_2[CoCl_4]$

b. $[Pt(H_2O)(CO)_3]Br_2$

c. $Na_3[Fe(CN)_2(C_2O_4)_2]$

d. $[Cr(NH_3)_3Cl(NH_2CH_2CH_2NH_2)]I_2$

22. a. $FeCl_4^-$

b. $[Ru(NH_3)_5H_2O]^{3+}$

c. $[Cr(CO)_4(OH)_2]^+$

d. $[Pt(NH_3)Cl_3]^-$

23. $BaCl_2$ gives no precipitate so SO_4^{2-} must be in the coordination sphere. A precipitate with $AgNO_3$ means that the Cl^- is not in the coordination sphere. Since there are only four ammonia molecules in the coordination sphere, then the SO_4^{2-} must be acting as a bidentate ligand (assuming an octahedral complex ion). The structure is:

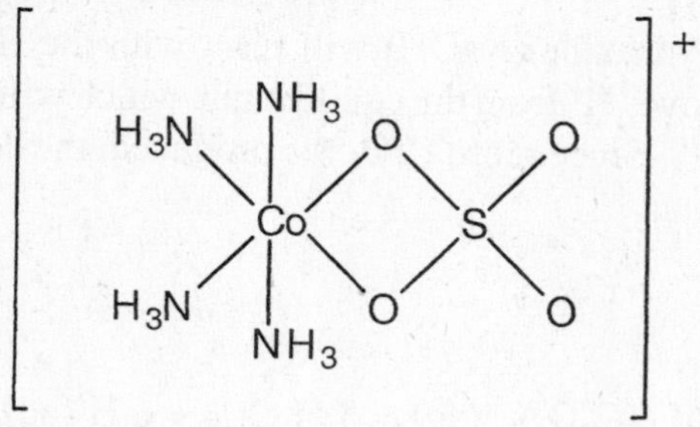

24. CN^- is a weak base so OH^- ions are present. When the acid H_2S is added, OH^- and CN^- ions are removed as H_2O and HCN. The two reactions are:

$Ni^{2+}(aq) + 2\ OH^-(aq) \rightarrow Ni(OH)_2(s)$; The precipitate is $Ni(OH)_2(s)$.

$Ni(OH)_2(s) + 4\ CN^-(aq) \rightarrow Ni(CN)_4^{2-}(aq) + 2\ OH^-(aq)$; $Ni(CN)_4^{2-}$ is a soluble species.

25. $Hg^{2+}(aq) + 2\ I^-(aq) \rightarrow HgI_2(s)$ (orange precipitate)

$HgI_2(s) + 2\ I^-(aq) \rightarrow HgI_4^{2-}(aq)$ (soluble complex ion)

26.   Test tube 1: added Cl^- reacts with Ag^+ to form a silver chloride precipitate. The net ionic equation is $Ag^+(aq) + Cl^-(aq) \rightarrow AgCl(s)$. Test tube 2: added NH_3 reacts with Ag^+ ions to form a soluble complex ion $Ag(NH_3)_2^+$. As this complex ion forms, Ag^+ is removed from solution, which causes the $AgCl(s)$ to dissolve. When enough NH_3 is added, all of the silver chloride precipitate will dissolve. The equation is $AgCl(s) + 2\ NH_3(aq) \rightarrow Ag(NH_3)_2^+(aq) + Cl^-(aq)$. Test tube 3: added H^+ reacts with the weak base NH_3 to form NH_4^+. As NH_3 is removed from the $Ag(NH_3)_2^+$ complex ion, Ag^+ ions are released to solution and can then react with Cl^- to reform $AgCl(s)$. The equations are $Ag(NH_3)_2^+(aq) + 2\ H^+(aq) \rightarrow Ag^+(aq) + 2\ NH_4^+(aq)$ and $Ag^+(aq) + Cl^-(aq) \rightarrow AgCl(s)$.

27.   a.   isomers: Species with the same formulas but different properties. See text for examples of the following types of isomers.

        b.   structural isomers: Isomers that have one or more bonds that are different.

        c.   stereoisomers: Isomers that contain the same bonds but differ in how the atoms are arranged in space.

        d.   coordination isomers: Structural isomers that differ in the atoms that make up the complex ion.

        e.   linkage isomers: Structural isomers that differ in how one or more ligands are attached to the transition metal.

        f.   geometric isomers: (cis - trans isomerism) Stereoisomers that differ in the positions of atoms with respect to a rigid ring, bond, or each other.

        g.   optical isomers: Stereoisomers that are nonsuperimposable mirror images of each other; that is, they are different in the same way that our left and right hands are different.

28.   a.   2; Forms bonds through the lone pairs on the two oxygen atoms.

        b.   3; Forms bonds through the lone pairs on the three nitrogen atoms.

        c.   4; Forms bonds through the two nitrogen atoms and the two oxygen atoms.

        d.   4; Forms bonds through the four nitrogen atoms.

29. **a.**

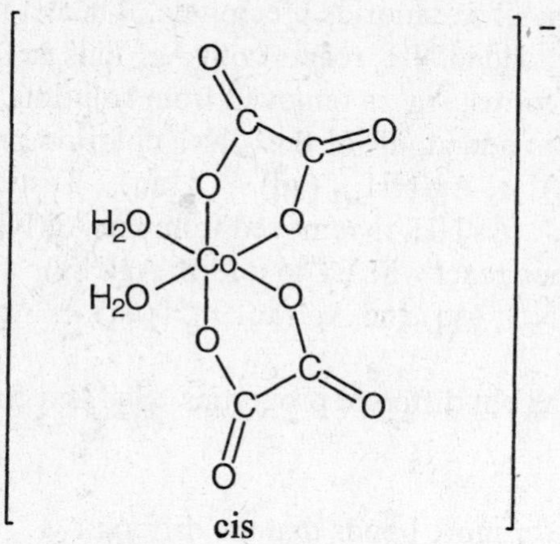

cis 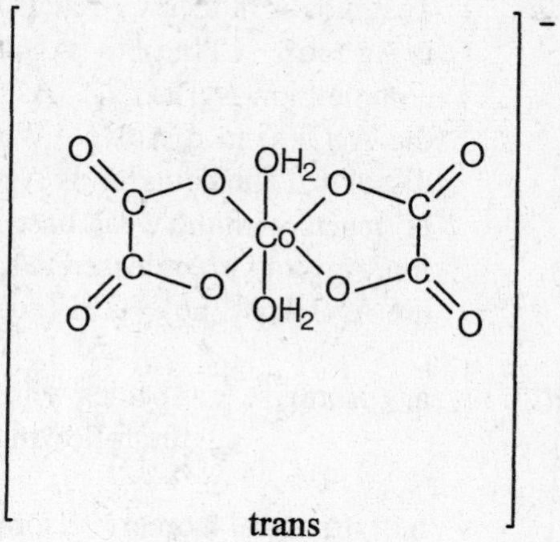   trans

Note: $C_2O_4{}^{2-}$ is a bidentate ligand. Bidentate ligands bond to the metal at two positions which are 90° apart from each other in octahedral complexes. Bidentate ligands do not bond to the metal at positions 180° apart.

b.

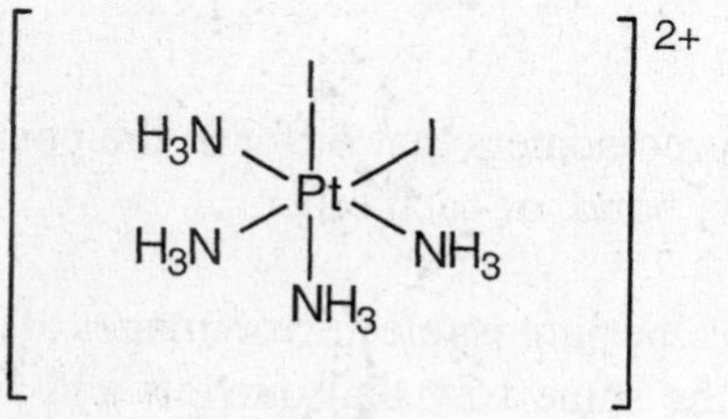

cis 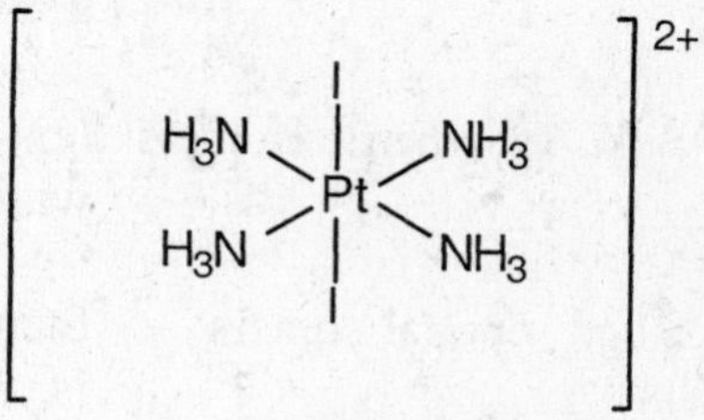   trans

c.

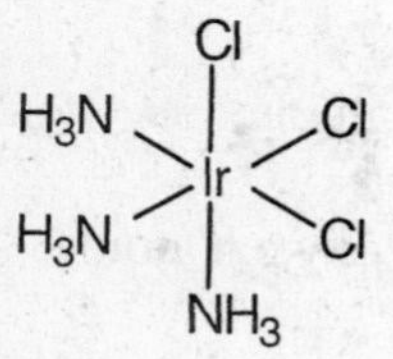

cis 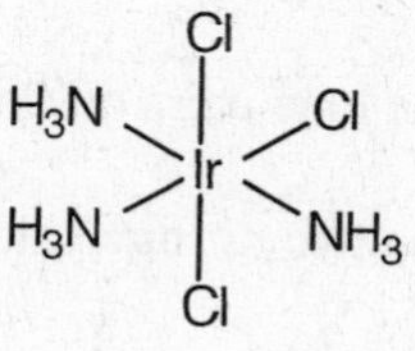   trans

d.

Note: N⌢N is an abbreviation for the bidentate ligand ethylenediamine ($NH_2CH_2CH_2NH_2$).

30.   a.   b.

c.   d.

e.

31.

M = transition metal ion

32.   monodentate   bidentate   bridging

33.   Linkage isomers differ in the way that the ligand bonds to the metal. SCN⁻ can bond through the sulfur or through the nitrogen atom. NO_2^- can bond through the nitrogen or through the oxygen atom. OCN⁻ can bond through the oxygen or through the nitrogen atom. N_3^-, $NH_2CH_2CH_2NH_2$ and I⁻ are not capable of linkage isomerism.

34.

35.   Similar to the molecules discussed in Figures 20.16 and 20.17 of the text, $Cr(acac)_3$ and cis-$Cr(acac)_2(H_2O)_2$ are optically active.   The mirror images of these two complexes are nonsuperimposable. There is a plane of symmetry in trans-$Cr(acac)_2(H_2O)_2$, so it is not optically active. A molecule with a plane of symmetry is never optically active as the mirror images are always superimposable. A plane of symmetry is a plane through a molecule where one side reflects on the other side of the molecule.

36. There are five geometrical isomers (labeled i-v). Only isomer v where the CN^-, Br^- and H_2O ligands are cis to each other is optically active. The nonsuperimposable mirror image is shown for isomer v.

optically   mirror   mirror image of v
active   (nonsuperimposable)

Bonding, Color, and Magnetism in Coordination Compounds

37. a. Ligand that will give complex ions with the maximum number of unpaired electrons.

b. Ligand that will give complex ions with the minimum number of unpaired electrons.

c. Complex with a minimum number of unpaired electrons (low-spin = strong-field).

d. Complex with a maximum number of unpaired electrons (high-spin = weak-field).

38. Cu^{2+}: $[Ar]3d^9$; Cu^+: $[Ar]3d^{10}$; Cu(II) is d^9 and Cu(I) is d^{10}. Color is a result of the electron transfer between split d orbitals. This cannot occur for the filled d orbitals in Cu(I). Cd^{2+}, like Cu^+, is also d^{10}. We would not expect $Cd(NH_3)_4Cl_2$ to be colored since the d orbitals are filled in this Cd^{2+} complex.

39. Sc^{3+} has no electrons in d orbitals. Ti^{3+} and V^{3+} have d electrons present. The color of transition metal complexes results from electron transfer between split d orbitals. If no d electrons are present, no electron transfer can occur and the compounds are not colored.

40. All these complex ions contain Co^{3+} bound to different ligands so the difference in d-orbital splitting for each complex ion is due to the difference in ligands. The spectrochemical series indicates that CN^- is a stronger field ligand than NH_3 which is a stronger field ligand than F^-. Therefore, $Co(CN)_6^{3-}$ will have the largest d-orbital splitting and will absorb the lowest wavelength electromagnetic radiation ($\lambda = 290$ nm) since energy and wavelength are inversely related ($\lambda = hc/E$). $Co(NH_3)_6^{3+}$ will absorb 440 nm electromagnetic radiation while CoF_6^{3-} will absorb the longest wavelength electromagnetic radiation ($\lambda = 770$ nm) since F^- is the weakest field ligand present.

41.   a. Fe^{2+}: $[Ar]3d^6$

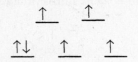

    ↑   ↑   ―――   ―――

  ↑↓ ↑ ↑   ↑↓ ↑↓ ↑↓

High spin, small Δ   Low spin, large Δ

b. Fe^{3+}: $[Ar]3d^5$ c. Ni^{2+}: $[Ar]3d^8$

   ↑   ↑   ↑   ↑

 ↑ ↑ ↑   ↑↓ ↑↓ ↑↓

High spin, small Δ

d. Zn^{2+}: $[Ar]3d^{10}$

   ↑↓   ↑↓

 ↑↓ ↑↓ ↑↓

e. Co^{2+}: $[Ar]3d^7$

   ↑   ↑   ↑   ―――

 ↑↓ ↑↓ ↑   ↑↓ ↑↓ ↑↓

High spin, small Δ   Low spin, large Δ

42. NH_3 and H_2O are neutral ligands so the oxidation states of the metals are Co^{3+} and Fe^{2+}. Both have six d electrons ($[Ar]3d^6$). To explain the magnetic properties, we must have a strong-field for $Co(NH_3)_6^{3+}$ and a weak-field for $Fe(H_2O)_6^{2+}$.

Co^{3+}: $[Ar]3d^6$ Fe^{2+}: $[Ar]3d^6$

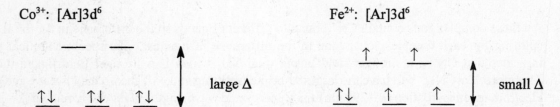

   ―――   ―――   ↑   ↑

                  large Δ   small Δ

 ↑↓ ↑↓ ↑↓   ↑↓ ↑ ↑

Only this splitting of d-orbitals gives a diamagnetic $Co(NH_3)_6^{3+}$ (no unpaired electrons) and a paramagnetic $Fe(H_2O)_6^{2+}$ (unpaired electrons present).

43.   To determine the crystal field diagrams, you need to determine the oxidation state of the transition metal which can only be determined if you know the charges of the ligands (see Table 20.13). The electron configurations and the crystal field diagrams follow.

a. Ru^{2+}: [Kr]$4d^6$, no unpaired e⁻   b. Ni^{2+}: [Ar]$3d^8$, 2 unpaired e⁻

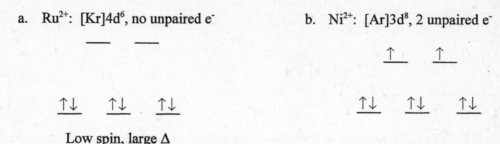

Low spin, large Δ

c. V^{3+}: [Ar]$3d^2$, 2 unpaired e⁻

        Note: Ni^{2+} must have 2 unpaired electrons, whether high-spin or low-spin, and V^{3+} must have 2 unpaired electrons, whether high-spin or low-spin.

44.   In both compounds, iron is in the +3 oxidation state with an electron configuration of [Ar]$3d^5$. Fe^{3+} complexes have one unpaired electron when a strong-field case and five unpaired electrons when a weak-field case. $Fe(CN)_6^{2-}$ is a strong-field case and $Fe(SCN)_6^{3-}$ is a weak-field case. Therefore, cyanide, CN⁻, is a stronger field ligand than thiocyanate, SCN⁻.

45.   From Table 20.16 of the text, the violet complex ion absorbs yellow-green light ($\lambda \sim 570$ nm), the yellow complex ion absorbs blue light ($\lambda \sim 450$ nm), and the green complex ion absorbs red light ($\lambda \sim 650$ nm). The spectrochemical series shows that NH_3 is a stronger-field ligand than H_2O which is a stronger-field ligand than Cl⁻. Therefore, $Cr(NH_3)_6^{3+}$ will have the largest d-orbital splitting and will absorb the lowest wavelength electromagnetic radiation ($\lambda \sim 450$ nm) since energy and wavelength are inversely related ($\lambda = hc/E$). Thus, the yellow solution contains the $Cr(NH_3)_6^{3+}$ complex ion. Similarly, we would expect the $Cr(H_2O)_4Cl_2^+$ complex ion to have the smallest d-orbital splitting since it contains the weakest-field ligands. The green solution with the longest wavelength of absorbed light contains the $Cr(H_2O)_4Cl_2^+$ complex ion. This leaves the violet solution, which contains the $Cr(H_2O)_6^{3+}$ complex ion. This makes sense as we would expect $Cr(H_2O)_6^{3+}$ to absorb light of a wavelength between that of $Cr(NH_3)_6^{3+}$ and $Cr(H_2O)_4Cl_2^+$.

46.   Octahedral Cr^{2+} complexes should be used. Cr^{2+}: [Ar]$3d^4$; High-spin (weak-field) Cr^{2+} complexes have 4 unpaired electrons and low-spin (strong-field) Cr^{2+} complexes have 2 unpaired electrons. Ni^{2+}: [Ar]$3d^8$; Octahedral Ni^{2+} complexes will always have 2 unpaired electrons, whether high or low-spin. Therefore, Ni^{2+} complexes cannot be used to distinguish weak from strong-field ligands by examining magnetic properties. Alternatively, the ligand field strengths can be measured using visible spectra. Either Cr^{2+} or Ni^{2+} complexes can be used for this method.

47. a. Ru(phen)$_3^{2+}$ exhibits optical isomerism [similar to Co(en)$_3^{3+}$ in Figure 20.16 of the text].

b. Ru^{2+}: [Kr]4d^6; Since there are no unpaired electrons, then Ru^{2+} is a strong-field (low-spin) case.

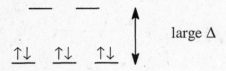

large Δ

48. Co^{2+}: [Ar]3d^7; The corresponding d-orbital splitting diagram for tetrahedral Co^{2+} complexes is:

$\uparrow$ $\uparrow$ $\uparrow$

$\uparrow\downarrow$ $\uparrow\downarrow$

All tetrahedral complexes are high spin since the d-orbital splitting is small. Ions with 2 or 7 d electrons should give the most stable tetrahedral complexes since they have the greatest number of electrons in the lower energy orbitals as compared to the number of electrons in the higher energy orbitals.

49. CoBr$_6^{4-}$ has an octahedral structure and CoBr$_4^{2-}$ has a tetrahedral structure (as do most Co^{2+} complexes with four ligands). Coordination complexes absorb electromagnetic radiation (EMR) of energy equal to the energy difference between the split d-orbitals. Since the tetra-hedral d-orbital splitting is less than one-half of the octahedral d-orbital splitting, then tetrahedral complexes will absorb lower energy EMR which corresponds to longer wavelength EMR (E = hc/λ). Therefore, CoBr$_6^{2-}$ will absorb EMR having a wavelength shorter than 3.4×10^{-6} m.

50. Pd is in the +2 oxidation state in PdCl$_4^{2-}$; Pd^{2+}: [Kr]4d^8. If PdCl$_4^{2-}$ were a tetrahedral complex, then it would have 2 unpaired electrons and would be paramagnetic (see diagram below). Instead, PdCl$_4^{2-}$ has a square planar molecular structure with a d-orbital splitting diagram shown below. Note that all electrons are paired in the square planar diagram which explains the diamagnetic properties of PdCl$_4^{2-}$.

                                                      $\underline{\quad}$

$\uparrow\downarrow$ $\uparrow$ $\uparrow$ $\uparrow\downarrow$

$\uparrow\downarrow$ $\uparrow\downarrow$ $\uparrow\downarrow$

                                     $\uparrow\downarrow$ $\uparrow\downarrow$

tetrahedral d^8 square planar d^8

Additional Exercises

51. $Ni(CO)_4$ is composed of 4 CO molecules and Ni. Thus, nickel has an oxidation state of zero.

52. CN^- and CO form much stronger complexes with Fe(II) than O_2. Thus, O_2 cannot be transported by hemoglobin in the presence of CN^- or CO.

53.   i. $0.0203 \text{ g } CrO_3 \times \dfrac{52.00 \text{ g Cr}}{100.0 \text{ g } CrO_3} = 0.0106 \text{ g Cr};$ $\% \text{ Cr} = \dfrac{0.0106 \text{ g}}{0.105 \text{ g}} \times 100 = 10.1\% \text{ Cr}$

   ii. $32.93 \text{ mL HCl} \times \dfrac{0.100 \text{ mmol HCl}}{\text{mL}} \times \dfrac{1 \text{ mmol } NH_3}{\text{mmol HCl}} \times \dfrac{17.03 \text{ mg } NH_3}{\text{mmol}} = 56.1 \text{ mg } NH_3$

   $\% \ NH_3 = \dfrac{56.1 \text{ mg}}{341 \text{ mg}} \times 100 = 16.5\% \ NH_3$

   iii. $73.53\% + 16.5\% + 10.1\% = 100.1\%$;   The compound must be composed of only Cr, NH_3, and I.

   Out of 100.00 of compound:

   $10.1 \text{ g Cr} \times \dfrac{1 \text{ mol}}{52.00 \text{ g}} = 0.194$ $\dfrac{0.194}{0.194} = 1.00$

   $16.5 \text{ g } NH_3 \times \dfrac{1 \text{ mol}}{17.03 \text{ g}} = 0.969$ $\dfrac{0.969}{0.194} = 4.99$

   $73.53 \text{ g I} \times \dfrac{1 \text{ mol}}{126.9 \text{ g}} = 0.5794$ $\dfrac{0.5794}{0.194} = 2.99$

   $Cr(NH_3)_5I_3$ is the empirical formula. Cr(III) forms octahedral complexes. So compound A is made of the octahedral $[Cr(NH_3)_5I]^{2+}$ complex ion and two I^- ions as counter ions; the formula is $[Cr(NH_3)_5I]I_2$. Lets check this proposed formula using the freezing point data.

   iv. $\Delta T_f = iK_f m$;   For $[Cr(NH_3)_5I]I_2$, $i = 3.0$ (assuming complete dissociation).

   $\text{molality} = m = \dfrac{0.601 \text{ g complex}}{1.000 \times 10^{-2} \text{ kg } H_2O} \times \dfrac{1 \text{ mol complex}}{517.9 \text{ g complex}} = 0.116 \text{ mol/kg}$

   $\Delta T_f = 3.0 \times 1.86°C \text{ kg/mol} \times 0.116 \text{ mol/kg} = 0.65°C$

   Since ΔT_f is close to the measured value, then this is consistent with the formula $[Cr(NH_3)_5I]I_2$.

54.   a.   Copper is both oxidized and reduced in this reaction, so yes this reaction is an oxidation-reduction reaction. The oxidation state of copper in $[Cu(NH_3)_4]Cl_2$ is +2, the oxidation state of copper in Cu is zero and the oxidation state of copper in $[Cu(NH_3)_4]Cl$ is +1.

b. Total mass of copper used:

$$10{,}000 \text{ boards} \times \frac{(8.0 \text{ cm} \times 16.0 \text{ cm} \times 0.060 \text{ cm})}{\text{board}} \times \frac{8.96 \text{ g}}{\text{cm}^3} = 6.9 \times 10^5 \text{ g Cu}$$

Amount of Cu to be recovered $= 0.80 \times 6.9 \times 10^5 \text{ g} = 5.5 \times 10^5 \text{ g Cu}$

$$5.5 \times 10^5 \text{ g Cu} \times \frac{1 \text{ mol Cu}}{63.55 \text{ g Cu}} \times \frac{1 \text{ mol } [Cu(NH_3)_4]Cl_2}{\text{mol Cu}} \times \frac{202.59 \text{ g } [Cu(NH_3)_4]Cl_2}{\text{mol } [Cu(NH_3)_4]Cl_2}$$

$$= 1.8 \times 10^6 \text{ g } [Cu(NH_3)_4]Cl_2$$

$$5.5 \times 10^5 \text{ g Cu} \times \frac{1 \text{ mol Cu}}{63.55 \text{ g Cu}} \times \frac{4 \text{ mol NH}_3}{\text{mol Cu}} \times \frac{17.03 \text{ g NH}_3}{\text{mol NH}_3} = 5.9 \times 10^5 \text{ g NH}_3$$

55.   M = metal ion

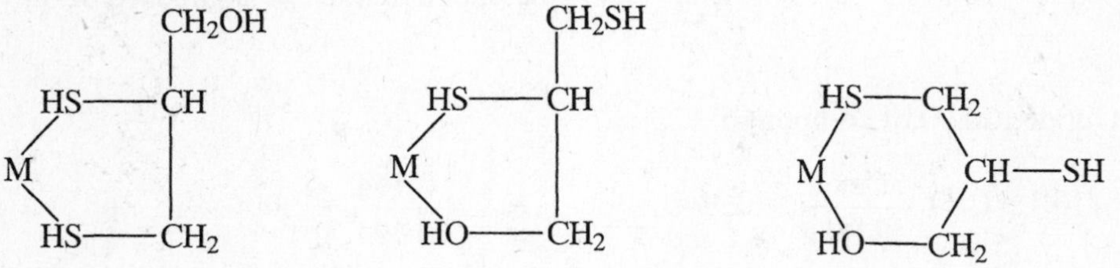

56.   a. The optical isomers of this compound are similar to the ones discussed in Figure 20.16 of the text. In the following structures, we omitted the 4 NH_3 ligands coordinated to the outside cobalt atoms.

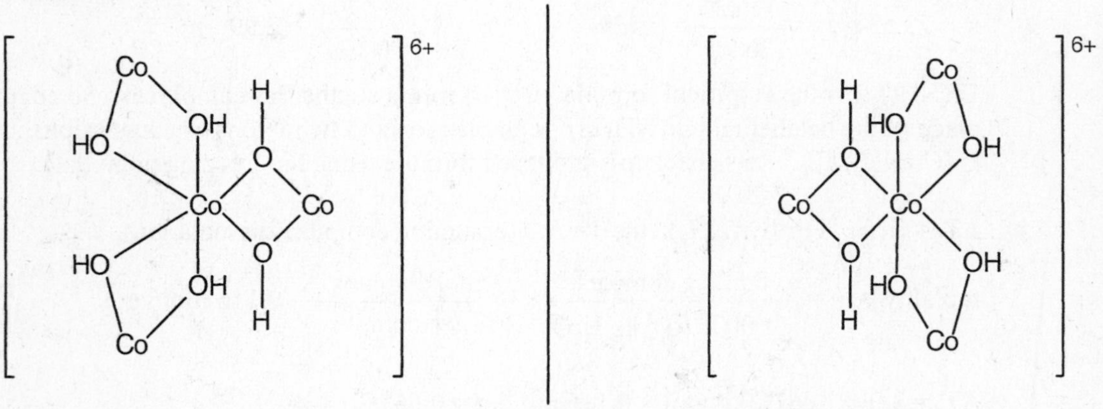

mirror

b. All are Co(III). The three "ligands" each contain 2 OH^- and 4 NH_3 groups. If each cobalt is in the +3 oxidation state, then each ligand has a +1 overall charge. The +3 charge from the three ligands along with the +3 charge of the central cobalt atom gives the overall complex a +6 charge. This is balanced by the -6 charge of the six Cl^- ions.

c. Co^{3+}: $[Ar]3d^6$; There are zero unpaired electrons if a low-spin (strong-field) case.

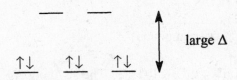

57.   No; In all three cases, six bonds are formed between Ni^{2+} and nitrogen, so ΔH values should be similar. $\Delta S°$ for formation of the complex ion is most negative for 6 NH_3 molecules reacting with a metal ion (7 independent species become 1). For penten reacting with a metal ion, 2 independent species become 1, so $\Delta S°$ is least negative for this reaction as compared to the other reactions. Thus, the chelate effect occurs because the more bonds a chelating agent can form to the metal, the more favorable $\Delta S°$ is for the formation of the complex ion and the larger the formation constant.

58. $CrCl_3 \cdot 6H_2O$ contains nine possible ligands; only six of which are used to form the octahedral complex ion. The three species not present in the complex ion will either be counter ions to balance the charge of the complex ion and/or waters of hydration. The number of counter ions for each compound can be determined from the silver chloride precipitate data and the number of waters of hydration can be determined from the dehydration data. In all experiments, the ligands in the complex ion do not react.

Compound I:

$$\text{mol } CrCl_3 \cdot 6H_2O = 0.27 \text{ g} \times \frac{1 \text{ mol}}{266.5} = 1.0 \times 10^{-3} \text{ mol } CrCl_3 \cdot 6H_2O$$

$$\text{mol waters of hydration} = 0.036 \text{ g } H_2O \times \frac{1 \text{ mol}}{18.02 \text{ g}} = 2.0 \times 10^{-3} \text{ mol } H_2O$$

$$\frac{\text{mol waters of hydration}}{\text{mol compound}} = \frac{2.0 \times 10^{-3} \text{ mol}}{1.0 \times 10^{-3} \text{ mol}} = 2.0$$

In compound I, two of the H_2O molecules are waters of hydration so the other four water molecules are present in the complex ion. Therefore, the formula for compound I must be $[Cr(H_2O)_4Cl_2]Cl \cdot 2H_2O$. Two of the Cl^- ions are present as ligands in the octahedral complex ion and one Cl^- ion is present as a counter ion. The AgCl precipitate data that refers to this compound is the one that produces 1430 mg AgCl:

$$\text{mol } Cl^- \text{ from compound I} = 0.1000 \text{ L} \times \frac{0.100 \text{ mol } [Cr(H_2O)_4Cl_2]Cl \cdot 2H_2O}{L}$$

$$\times \frac{1 \text{ mol } Cl^-}{\text{mol } [Cr(H_2O)_4Cl_2]Cl \cdot 2H_2O} = 0.0100 \text{ mol } Cl^-$$

$$\text{mass AgCl produced} = 0.0100 \text{ mol } Cl^- \times \frac{1 \text{ mol AgCl}}{\text{mol } Cl^-} \times \frac{143.4 \text{ g AgCl}}{\text{mol AgCl}} = 1.43 \text{ g} = 1430 \text{ mg AgCl}$$

Compound II:

$$\frac{\text{mol waters of hydration}}{\text{mol compound}} = \frac{0.018 \text{ g } H_2O \times \dfrac{1 \text{ mol}}{18.02 \text{ g}}}{1.0 \times 10^{-3} \text{ mol compound}} = 1.0$$

The formula for compound II must be $[Cr(H_2O)_5Cl]Cl_2 \cdot H_2O$. The 2870 mg AgCl precipitate data refers to this compound. For 0.0100 mol of compound II, 0.0200 mol Cl^- are present as counter ions:

$$\text{mass AgCl produced} = 0.0200 \text{ mol } Cl^- \times \frac{1 \text{ mol AgCl}}{\text{mol } Cl^-} \times \frac{143.4 \text{ g}}{\text{mol}} = 2.87 \text{ g} = 2870 \text{ mg AgCl}$$

Compound III:

This compound has no mass loss on dehydration so there are no waters of hydration present. The formula for compound III must be $[Cr(H_2O)_6]Cl_3$. 0.0100 mol of this compound produces 4300 mg of AgCl(s) when treated with $AgNO_3$.

$$0.0300 \text{ mol } Cl^- \times \frac{1 \text{ mol AgCl}}{\text{mol } Cl^-} \times \frac{143.4 \text{ g AgCl}}{\text{mol AgCl}} = 4.30 \text{ g} = 4.30 \times 10^3 \text{ mg AgCl}$$

The structural formulas for the compounds are:

Compound I

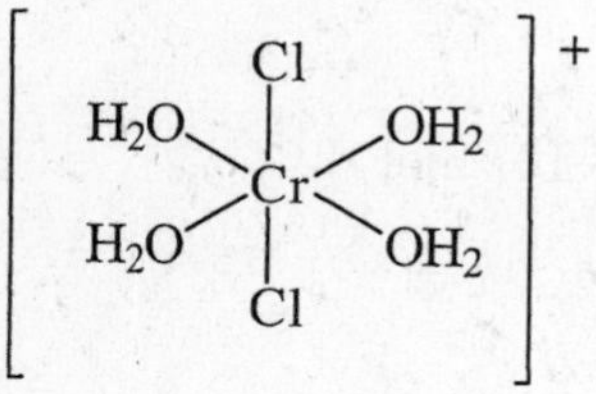

$Cl \bullet 2H_2O$ or

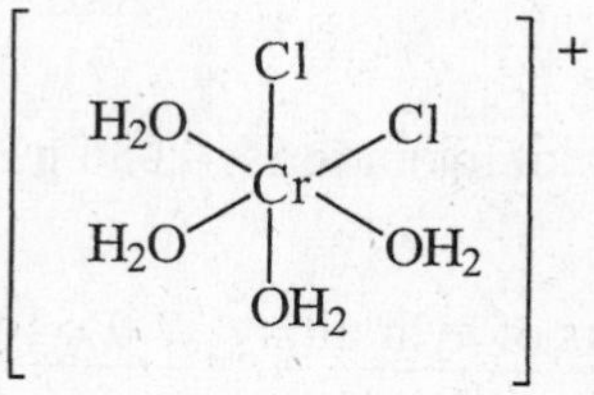

$Cl \bullet 2H_2O$

Compound II

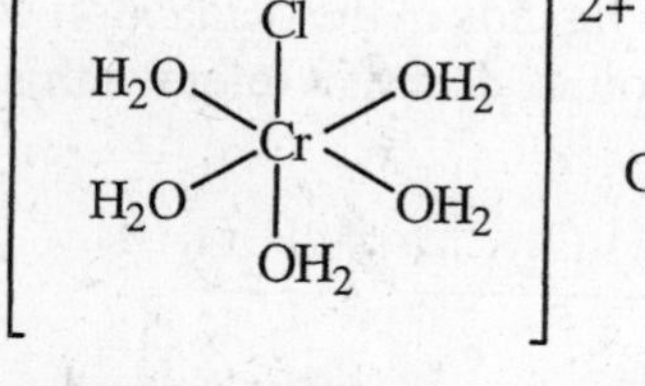

$Cl_2 \bullet H_2O$

Compound III

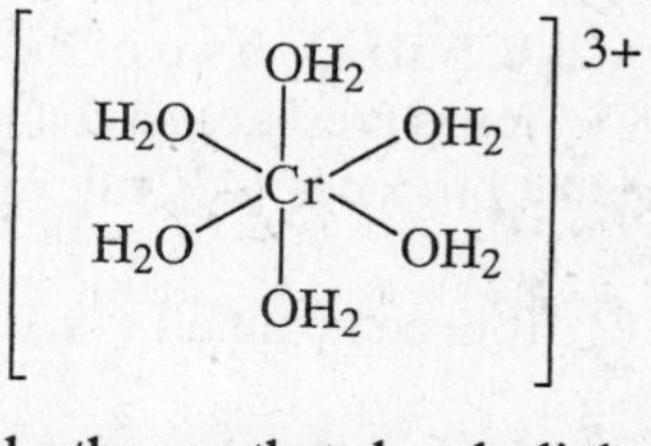

Cl_3

From Table 20.16 of the text, the violet compound will be the one that absorbs light with the shortest wavelength (highest energy). This should be compound III. H_2O is a stronger field ligand than Cl^-; compound III with the most coordinated H_2O molecules will have the largest d-orbital splitting and will absorb the higher energy light.

59. $\overset{II}{(H_2O)_5Cr} - Cl - \overset{III}{Co(NH_3)_5} \rightarrow \overset{III}{(H_2O)_5Cr} - Cl - \overset{II}{Co(NH_3)_5} \rightarrow Cr(H_2O)_5Cl^{2+} + Co(II)$ complex

Yes, this is consistent. After the oxidation, the ligands on Cr(III) won't exchange. Since Cl^- is in the coordination sphere, then it must have formed a bond to Cr(II) before the electron transfer occurred (as proposed through the formation of the intermediate).

60.   a.   Be(tfa)$_2$ exhibits optical isomerism. A representation for the tetrahedral optical isomers are:

mirror

Note: The dotted line indicates a bond pointing into the plane of the paper and the wedge indicates a bond pointing out of the plane of the paper.

   b.   Square planar Cu(tfa)$_2$ molecules exhibit geometric isomerism. In one geometric isomer, the CF$_3$ groups are cis to each other and in the other isomer, the CF$_3$ groups are trans.

cis   trans

61.   a. $Fe(H_2O)_6^{3+} + H_2O \rightleftharpoons Fe(H_2O)_5(OH)^{2+} + H_3O^+$

Initial	0.10 M	0	~0
Equil.	0.10 - x	x	x

$$K_a = \frac{[Fe(H_2O)_5(OH)^{2+}][H_3O^+]}{[Fe(H_2O)_6^{3+}]} = 6.0 \times 10^{-3} = \frac{x^2}{0.10 - x} \approx \frac{x^2}{0.10}$$

$x = 2.4 \times 10^{-2}$; Assumption is poor (x is 24% of 0.10). Using successive approximations:

$$\frac{x^2}{0.10 - 0.024} = 6.0 \times 10^{-3}, \; x = 0.021$$

$$\frac{x^2}{0.10 - 0.021} = 6.0 \times 10^{-3}, \; x = 0.022; \quad \frac{x^2}{0.10 - 0.022} = 6.0 \times 10^{-3}, \; x = 0.022$$

$$x = [H^+] = 0.022 \; M; \; pH = 1.66$$

b. Because of the lower charge, $Fe^{2+}(aq)$ will not be as strong an acid as $Fe^{3+}(aq)$. A solution of iron(II) nitrate will be less acidic (have a higher pH) than a solution with the same concentration of iron(III) nitrate.

62. We need to calculate the Pb^{2+} concentration in equilibrium with $EDTA^{4-}$. Since K is large for the formation of $PbEDTA^{2-}$, let the reaction go to completion; then solve an equilibrium problem to get the Pb^{2+} concentration.

$$Pb^{2+} \quad + \quad EDTA^{4-} \quad \rightleftharpoons \quad PbEDTA^{2-} \quad K = 1.1 \times 10^{18}$$

Before	0.010 M	0.050 M	0
	0.010 mol/L Pb^{2+} reacts completely (large K)		
Change	-0.010	-0.010 $\rightarrow$	+0.010	Reacts completely
After	0	0.040	0.010	New initial condition
	x mol/L $PbEDTA^{2-}$ dissociates to reach equilibrium		
Equil.	x	0.040 + x	0.010 - x

$$1.1 \times 10^{18} = \frac{(0.010 - x)}{(x)(0.040 + x)} \approx \frac{(0.010)}{x(0.040)}, \; x = [Pb^{2+}] = 2.3 \times 10^{-19} \; M \quad \text{Assumptions good.}$$

Now calculate the solubility quotient for $Pb(OH)_2$ to see if precipitation occurs. The concentration of OH^- is 0.10 M since we have a solution buffered at pH = 13.00.

$$Q = [Pb^{2+}]_o [OH^-]_o^2 = (2.3 \times 10^{-19})(0.10)^2 = 2.3 \times 10^{-21} < K_{sp} \; (1.2 \times 10^{-15})$$

$Pb(OH)_2(s)$ will not form since Q is less than K_{sp}.

63. a. In the lungs, there is a lot of O_2, and the equilibrium favors $Hb(O_2)_4$. In the cells, there is a deficiency of O_2, and the equilibrium favors HbH_4^{4+}.

b. CO_2 is a weak acid, $CO_2 + H_2O \rightleftharpoons HCO_3^- + H^+$. Removing CO_2 essentially decreases H^+. $Hb(O_2)_4$ is then favored, and O_2 is not released by hemoglobin in the cells. Breathing into a paper bag increases $[CO_2]$ in the blood, thus increasing $[H^+]$ which shifts the reaction left.

c. CO_2 builds up in the blood, and it becomes too acidic, driving the equilibrium to the left. Hemoglobin can't bind O_2 as strongly in the lungs. Bicarbonate ion acts as a base in water and neutralizes the excess acidity.

64. $HbO_2 \rightarrow Hb + O_2$ $\Delta G° = -(-70 \text{ kJ})$
       $Hb + CO \rightarrow HbCO$ $\Delta G° = -80 \text{ kJ}$

       _____

       $HbO_2 + CO \rightarrow HbCO + O_2$ $\Delta G° = -10 \text{ kJ}$

$$\Delta G° = -RT \ln K, \quad K = \exp\left(\frac{-\Delta G°}{RT}\right) = \exp\left(\frac{-(-10 \times 10^3 \text{ J})}{(8.3145 \text{ J/K} \cdot \text{mol})(298 \text{ kJ})}\right) = 60$$

Challenge Problems

65.

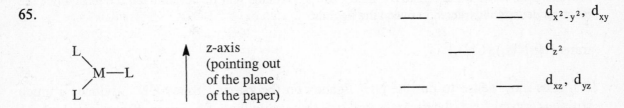

The $d_{x^2-y^2}$ and d_{xy} orbitals are in the plane of the three ligands and should be destabilized the most. The amount of destabilization should be about equal when all the possible interactions are considered. The d_{z^2} orbital has some electron density in the xy plane (the doughnut) and should be destabilized a lesser amount as compared to the $d_{x^2-y^2}$ and d_{xy} orbitals. The d_{xz} and d_{yz} orbitals have no electron density in the plane and should be lowest in energy.

66. $Ni^{2+} = d^8$

If A and B produced very similar crystal fields, the complex trans-$[NiA_2B_4]^{2+}$ would give an octahedral crystal field diagram:

       ↿ ↿
    ↿⇂ ↿⇂ ↿⇂

This is paramagnetic.

Thus A and B must produce different crystal fields. For example, if B produced a much stronger crystal field, the diagram would be similar to square planar:

       ‾
      ↿⇂
      ↿⇂
    ↿⇂ ↿⇂

This is diamagnetic.

67.

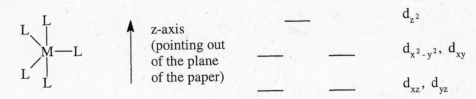

The d_{z^2} orbital will be destabilized much more than in the trigonal planar case (see Exercise 20.65). The d_{z^2} orbital has electron density on the z-axis directed at the two axial ligands. The $d_{x^2-y^2}$ and d_{xy} orbitals are in the plane of the three trigonal planar ligands and should be destabilized a lesser amount as compared to the d_{z^2} orbital; only a portion of the electron density in the $d_{x^2-y^2}$ and d_{xy} orbitals is directed at the ligands. The d_{xz} and d_{yz} orbitals will be destabilized the least since the electron density is directed between the ligands.

68.   trans-$[Ni(NH_3)_2(CN)_4]^{2-}$

It makes most sense to put the NH_3 ligands on the z-axis. Since CN^- produces a much stronger crystal field, the diagram will most resemble that of a square planar complex:

$$
\begin{array}{c}
NC \diagdown \quad \overset{NH_3}{|} \diagup CN^{\cdots y} \\
NC \diagup \overset{\displaystyle Ni}{\underset{\displaystyle |}{}} \diagdown CN \\
\underset{z}{\overset{NH_3}{}} \diagdown x
\end{array}
$$

$d_{x^2-y^2}$ —

d_{xy} ⥮

d_{z^2} ⥮

d_{xz} ⥮ ⥮ d_{yz}

69.   a.   Consider the following electrochemical cell:

$$Co^{3+} + e^- \rightarrow Co^{2+} \qquad\qquad E_c^\circ = 1.82 \text{ V}$$

$$Co(en)_3^{2+} \rightarrow Co(en)_3^{3+} + e^- \qquad -E_a^\circ = ?$$

$$\overline{Co^{3+} + Co(en)_3^{2+} \rightarrow Co^{2+} + Co(en)_3^{3+} \qquad E_{cell}^\circ = 1.82 - E_a^\circ}$$

The equilibrium constant for this overall reaction is:

$$Co^{3+} + 3 \text{ en} \rightarrow Co(en)_3^{3+} \qquad\qquad K_1 = 2.0 \times 10^{47}$$

$$Co(en)_3^{2+} \rightarrow Co^{2+} + 3 \text{ en} \qquad\qquad K_2 = 1/1.5 \times 10^{12}$$

$$\overline{Co^{3+} + Co(en)_3^{2+} \rightarrow Co(en)_3^{3+} + Co^{2+} \qquad K = K_1K_2 = \dfrac{2.0 \times 10^{47}}{1.5 \times 10^{12}} = 1.3 \times 10^{35}}$$

From the Nernst equation for the overall reaction:

$$E^{\circ}_{cell} = \frac{0.0591}{n} \log K = \frac{0.0591}{1} \log (1.3 \times 10^{35}), \ E^{\circ}_{cell} = 2.08 \ V$$

$$E^{\circ}_{cell} = 1.82 - E^{\circ}_{a} = 2.08 \ V, \ \ -E^{\circ}_{a} = 2.08 \ V - 1.82 \ V = 0.26 \ V \ \text{so} \ E^{\circ}_{c} = -0.26 \ V$$

b. The strongest oxidizing agent is the species most easily reduced and will have the most positive standard reduction potential. From the reduction potentials, Co^{3+} ($E^{\circ} = 1.82$ V) is a much stronger oxidizing agent than $Co(en)_3^{3+}$ ($E^{\circ} = -0.26$ V).

c. In aqueous solution, Co^{3+} forms the hydrated transition metal complex, $Co(H_2O)_6^{3+}$. In both complexes, $Co(H_2O)_6^{3+}$ and $Co(en)_3^{3+}$, cobalt exists as Co^{3+} which has 6 d electrons. Assuming a strong-field case for each complex ion, then the d-orbital splitting diagram for each is:

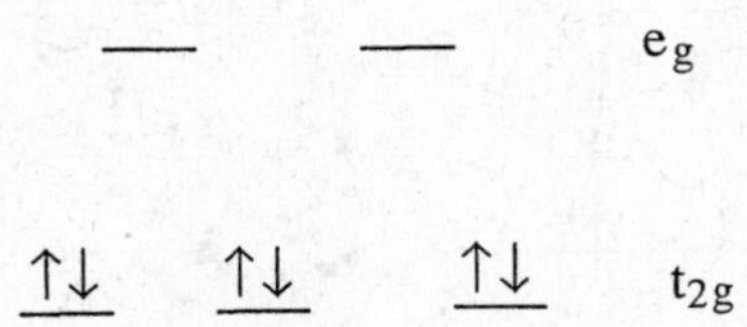

When each complex gains an electron, the electron enters the higher energy e_g orbitals. Since en is a stronger field ligand than H_2O, then the d-orbital splitting is larger for $Co(en)_3^{3+}$ and it takes more energy to add an electron to $Co(en)_3^{3+}$ than to $Co(H_2O)_6^{3+}$. Therefore, it is more favorable for $Co(H_2O)_6^{3+}$ to gain an electron than for $Co(en)_3^{3+}$ to gain an electron.

70. a.

b.

c) The only difference n the two diagrams involves the d_{xy}, d_{xz}, and d_{yz} orbitals. These are degenerate in MO (σ only) but not degenerate in the crystal field diagram. This difference can be involved in π bonding. One expects involvement of d_{xy} to be different from d_{xz} and d_{yz} because of the symmetry of the complex. This would remove the degeneracy of these orbitals in the MO picture.

71.   a. $AgBr(s) \rightleftharpoons Ag^+ + Br^-$ $K_{sp} = [Ag^+][Br^-] = 5.0 \times 10^{-13}$

Initial   s = solubility (mol/L)   0   0
Equil.   s   s

$K_{sp} = 5.0 \times 10^{-13} = s^2$, $s = 7.1 \times 10^{-7}$ mol/L

b. $AgBr(s) \rightleftharpoons Ag^+ + Br^-$ $K_{sp} = 5.0 \times 10^{-13}$
        $Ag^+ + 2 NH_3 \rightleftharpoons Ag(NH_3)_2^+$ $K_f = 1.7 \times 10^7$

$AgBr(s) + 2 NH_3(aq) \rightleftharpoons Ag(NH_3)_2^+(aq) + Br^-(aq)$ $K = K_{sp} \times K_f = 8.5 \times 10^{-6}$

                $AgBr(s) + 2 NH_3 \rightleftharpoons Ag(NH_3)_2^+ + Br^-$

Initial   3.0 M 0   0
        s mol/L of AgBr(s) dissolves to reach equilibrium = molar solubility
Equil.   3.0 - 2s   s   s

$K = \dfrac{[Ag(NH_3)_2^+][Br^-]}{[NH_3]^2} = \dfrac{s^2}{(3.0 - 2s)^2} = 8.5 \times 10^{-6} \approx \dfrac{s^2}{(3.0)^2}$, $s = 8.7 \times 10^{-3}$ mol/L

Assumption good.

c.   The presence of NH_3 increases the solubility of AgBr. Added NH_3 removes Ag^+ from solution by forming the complex ion $Ag(NH_3)_2^+$. As Ag^+ is removed, more AgBr(s) will dissolve to replenish the Ag^+ concentration.

d.   mass AgBr $= 0.2500 \text{ L} \times \dfrac{8.7 \times 10^{-3} \text{ mol AgBr}}{\text{L}} \times \dfrac{187.8 \text{ g AgBr}}{\text{mol AgBr}} = 0.41 \text{ g AgBr}$

e.   Added HNO_3 will have no effect on the AgBr(s) solubility in pure water. Neither H^+ nor NO_3^- react with Ag^+ or Br^- ions. Br^- is the conjugate base of the strong acid HBr, so it is a terrible base. Added H^+ will not react with Br^- to any great extent. However, added HNO_3 will reduce the solubility of AgBr(s) in the ammonia solution. NH_3 is a weak base ($K_b = 1.8 \times 10^{-5}$). Added H^+ will react with NH_3 to form NH_4^+. As NH_3 is removed, a smaller amount of the $Ag(NH_3)_2^+$ complex ion will form resulting in a smaller amount of AgBr(s) which will dissolve.

CHAPTER TWENTY-ONE

THE NUCLEUS: A CHEMIST'S VIEW

Radioactive Decay and Nuclear Transformations

1. All nuclear reactions must be charge balanced and mass balanced. To charge balance, balance the sum of the atomic numbers on each side of the reaction and to mass balance, balance the sum of the mass numbers on each side of the reaction.

   a. $^{51}_{24}Cr + ^{0}_{-1}e \rightarrow ^{51}_{23}V$

   b. $^{131}_{53}I \rightarrow ^{0}_{-1}e + ^{131}_{54}Xe$

   c. $^{32}_{15}P \rightarrow ^{0}_{-1}e + ^{32}_{16}S$

   d. $^{235}_{92}U \rightarrow ^{4}_{2}He + ^{231}_{90}Th$

2. a. $^{73}_{31}Ga \rightarrow ^{73}_{32}Ge + ^{0}_{-1}e$

   b. $^{192}_{78}Pt \rightarrow ^{188}_{76}Os + ^{4}_{2}He$

   c. $^{205}_{83}Bi \rightarrow ^{205}_{82}Pb + ^{0}_{+1}e$

   d. $^{241}_{96}Cm + ^{0}_{-1}e \rightarrow ^{241}_{95}Am$

3. a. $^{68}_{31}Ga + ^{0}_{-1}e \rightarrow ^{68}_{30}Zn$

   b. $^{62}_{29}Cu \rightarrow ^{0}_{+1}e + ^{62}_{28}Ni$

   c. $^{212}_{87}Fr \rightarrow ^{4}_{2}He + ^{208}_{85}At$

   d. $^{129}_{51}Sb \rightarrow ^{0}_{-1}e + ^{129}_{52}Te$

4. a. $^{241}_{95}Am \rightarrow ^{4}_{2}He + ^{237}_{93}Np$

   b. $^{241}_{95}Am \rightarrow 8 \ ^{4}_{2}He + 4 \ ^{0}_{-1}e + ^{209}_{83}Bi$; The final product is $^{209}_{83}Bi$.

   c. $^{241}_{95}Am \rightarrow ^{237}_{93}Np + \alpha \rightarrow ^{233}_{91}Pa + \alpha \rightarrow ^{233}_{92}U + \beta \rightarrow ^{229}_{90}Th + \alpha \rightarrow ^{225}_{88}Ra + \alpha$

   $^{213}_{84}Po + \beta \leftarrow ^{213}_{83}Bi + \alpha \leftarrow ^{217}_{85}At + \alpha \leftarrow ^{221}_{87}Fr + \alpha \leftarrow ^{225}_{89}Ac + \beta$

   $^{209}_{82}Pb + \alpha \rightarrow ^{209}_{83}Bi + \beta$

The intermediate radionuclides are:

$$^{237}_{93}\text{Np}, \ ^{233}_{91}\text{Pa}, \ ^{233}_{92}\text{U}, \ ^{229}_{90}\text{Th}, \ ^{225}_{88}\text{Ra}, \ ^{225}_{89}\text{Ac}, \ ^{221}_{87}\text{Fr}, \ ^{217}_{85}\text{At}, \ ^{213}_{83}\text{Bi}, \ ^{213}_{84}\text{Po}, \text{ and } ^{209}_{82}\text{Pb}.$$

5. $^{247}_{97}\text{Bk} \rightarrow \ ^{207}_{82}\text{Pb} + ? \ ^{4}_{2}\text{He} + ? \ ^{0}_{-1}\text{e};$ The change in mass number (247 - 207 = 40) is due exclusively to the alpha particles. A change in mass number of 40 requires 10 $^{4}_{2}$He particles to be produced. The atomic number only changes by 97 - 82 = 15. The 10 alpha particles change the atomic number by 20, so 5 $^{0}_{-1}$e (5 beta particles) are produced in the decay series of ^{247}Bk to ^{207}Pb.

6. $^{53}_{26}$Fe has too many protons. It will undergo either positron production, electron capture and/or alpha particle production. $^{59}_{26}$Fe has too many neutrons and will undergo beta particle production. (See Table 21.2 of the text.) The reactions are:

$$^{53}_{26}\text{Fe} \rightarrow \ ^{53}_{25}\text{Mn} + \ ^{0}_{+1}\text{e}; \ ^{53}_{26}\text{Fe} + \ ^{0}_{-1}\text{e} \rightarrow \ ^{53}_{25}\text{Mn}; \ ^{53}_{26}\text{Fe} \rightarrow \ ^{49}_{24}\text{Cr} + \ ^{4}_{2}\text{He}; \ ^{59}_{26}\text{Fe} \rightarrow \ ^{59}_{27}\text{Co} + \ ^{0}_{-1}\text{e}$$

7.   Reference Table 21.2 of the text for potential radioactive decay processes. ^{17}F and ^{18}F contain too many protons or too few neutrons. Electron capture or positron production are both possible decay mechanisms that increase the neutron to proton ratio. Alpha particle production also increases the neutron to proton ratio, but it is not likely for these light nuclei. ^{21}F contains too many neutrons or too few protons. Beta particle production lowers the neutron to proton ratio, so we expect ^{21}F to be a β-emitter.

8.   The most abundant isotope is generally the most stable isotope. The periodic table predicts that the most stable isotopes for Exercises a - d are ^{39}K, ^{56}Fe, ^{23}Na and ^{204}Tl. (Reference Table 21.2 of the text for potential decay processes.)

   a.   Unstable; ^{45}K has too many neutrons and will undergo beta particle production.

   b.   Stable

   c.   Unstable; ^{20}Na has too few neutrons and will most likely undergo electron capture or positron production. Alpha particle production makes too severe of a change to be a likely decay process for the relatively light ^{20}Na nuclei. Alpha particle production usually occurs for heavy nuclei.

   d.   Unstable; ^{194}Tl has too few neutrons and will undergo electron capture, positron production and/or alpha particle production.

9.   a. $^{249}_{98}\text{Cf} + \ ^{18}_{8}\text{O} \rightarrow \ ^{263}_{106}\text{Sg} + 4 \ ^{1}_{0}\text{n}$ b. $^{259}_{104}\text{Rf}; \ ^{263}_{106}\text{Sg} \rightarrow \ ^{4}_{2}\text{He} + \ ^{259}_{104}\text{Rf}$

10. a. $^{240}_{95}\text{Am} + \ ^{4}_{2}\text{He} \rightarrow \ ^{243}_{97}\text{Bk} + \ ^{1}_{0}\text{n}$ b. $^{238}_{92}\text{U} + \ ^{12}_{6}\text{C} \rightarrow \ ^{244}_{98}\text{Cf} + 6 \ ^{1}_{0}\text{n}$

c. $^{249}_{98}Cf + ^{15}_{7}N \rightarrow ^{260}_{105}Db + 4\,^{1}_{0}n$ d. $^{249}_{98}Cf + ^{10}_{5}B \rightarrow ^{257}_{103}Lr + 2\,^{1}_{0}n$

Kinetics of Radioactive Decay

11. $k = \dfrac{\ln 2}{t_{1/2}} = \dfrac{0.69315}{432.2\,yr} \times \dfrac{1\,yr}{365\,d} \times \dfrac{1\,d}{24\,h} \times \dfrac{1\,hr}{3600\,s} = 5.086 \times 10^{-11}\,s^{-1}$

Rate $= kN = 5.086 \times 10^{-11}\,s^{-1} \times 5.00\,g \times \dfrac{1\,mol}{241\,g} \times \dfrac{6.022 \times 10^{23}\,nuclei}{mol} = 6.35 \times 10^{11}$ decays/s

6.35×10^{11} alpha particles are emitted each second from a 5.00 g ^{241}Am sample.

12.   Kr-81 is most stable since it has the longest half-life while Kr-73 is hottest (least stable) since it has the shortest half-life.

12.5% of each isotope will remain after 3 half-lives:

100% $\xrightarrow{t_{1/2}}$ 50% $\xrightarrow{t_{1/2}}$ 25% $\xrightarrow{t_{1/2}}$ 12.5

For Kr-73: t = 3(27 s) = 81 s

For Kr-74: t = 3(11.5 min) = 34.5 min

For Kr-76: t = 3(14.8 h) = 44.4 h

For Kr-81: t = 3(2.1 × 10⁵ yr) = 6.3 × 10⁵ yr

13.   a. $k = \dfrac{\ln 2}{t_{1/2}} = \dfrac{0.6931}{12.8\,d} \times \dfrac{1\,d}{24\,h} \times \dfrac{1\,h}{3600\,s} = 6.27 \times 10^{-7}\,s^{-1}$

b.   Rate $= kN = 6.27 \times 10^{-7}\,s^{-1} \times \left(28.0 \times 10^{-3}\,g \times \dfrac{1\,mol}{64.0\,g} \times \dfrac{6.022 \times 10^{23}\,nuclei}{mol} \right)$

Rate $= 1.65 \times 10^{14}$ decays /s

c.   25% of the ^{64}Cu will remain after 2 half-lives (100% decays to 50% after one half-life which decays to 25% after a second half-life). Hence, 2(12.8 days) = 25.6 days is the time frame for the experiment.

14.   a. $0.0100\,Ci \times \dfrac{3.7 \times 10^{10}\,decays/s}{Ci} = 3.7 \times 10^{8}$ decays/s; $k = \dfrac{\ln 2}{t_{1/2}}$

Rate $= kN$, $\dfrac{3.7 \times 10^{8}\,decays}{s} = \left(\dfrac{0.6931}{2.87\,h} \times \dfrac{1\,h}{3600\,s} \right) \times N$, $N = 5.5 \times 10^{12}$ atoms of ^{38}S

$$5.5 \times 10^{12} \text{ atoms } {}^{38}S \times \frac{1 \text{ mol } {}^{38}S}{6.02 \times 10^{23} \text{ atoms}} \times \frac{1 \text{ mol } Na_2{}^{38}SO_4}{\text{mol } {}^{38}S} = 9.1 \times 10^{-12} \text{ mol } Na_2{}^{38}SO_4$$

$$9.1 \times 10^{-12} \text{ mol } Na_2{}^{38}SO_4 \times \frac{148.0 \text{ g } Na_2{}^{38}SO_4}{\text{mol } Na_2{}^{38}SO_4} = 1.3 \times 10^{-9} \text{ g} = 1.3 \text{ ng } Na_2{}^{38}SO_4$$

b. 99.99% decays, 0.01% left; $\ln\left(\frac{0.01}{100}\right) = -kt = \frac{-0.6931\,t}{2.87 \text{ h}}$, $t = 38.1 \text{ hours} \approx 40 \text{ hours}$

15. $t = 59.0 \text{ yr};\ k = \frac{\ln 2}{t_{1/2}};\ \ln\left(\frac{N}{N_o}\right) = -kt = \frac{-0.6931 \times 59.0 \text{ yr}}{28.8 \text{ yr}} = -1.42,\ \left(\frac{N}{N_o}\right) = e^{-1.42} = 0.242$

24.2% of the ${}^{90}Sr$ remains as of July 16, 2004.

16. $\ln(N/N_o) = -kt;\ N = 0.010\,N_o;\ t_{1/2} = (\ln 2)/k$

$\ln(0.010) = \frac{-(\ln 2)t}{t_{1/2}} = \frac{-0.693\,t}{8.1 \text{ d}}$, $t = 54 \text{ days}$

17. $175 \text{ mg } Na_3{}^{32}PO_4 \times \frac{32.0 \text{ mg } {}^{32}P}{165.0 \text{ mg } Na_3{}^{32}PO_4} = 33.9 \text{ mg } {}^{32}P;\ k = \frac{\ln 2}{t_{1/2}}$

$\ln\left(\frac{N}{N_o}\right) = -kt = \frac{-0.6931\,t}{t_{1/2}},\ \ln\left(\frac{m}{33.9 \text{ mg}}\right) = \frac{-0.6931\,(35.0 \text{ d})}{14.3 \text{ d}}$; Carrying extra sig. figs.:

$\ln(m) = -1.696 + 3.523 = 1.827,\ m = e^{1.827} = 6.22 \text{ mg } {}^{32}P$ remains

18.   The assumptions are that the ${}^{14}C$ level in the atmosphere is constant or that the ${}^{14}C$ level at the time the plant died can be calculated. A constant ${}^{14}C$ level is a poor assumption and accounting for variation is complicated. Another problem is that some of the material must be destroyed to determine the ${}^{14}C$ level.

19. $t_{1/2} = 5730 \text{ yr};\ k = (\ln 2)/t_{1/2};\ \ln(N/N_o) = -kt;\ \ln\frac{15.1}{15.3} = \frac{-(\ln 2)\,t}{5730 \text{ yr}}$, $t = 109 \text{ yr}$

No; From ${}^{14}C$ dating, the painting was produced (at the earliest) during the late 1800s.

20. $k = \frac{\ln 2}{t_{1/2}};\ \ln\left(\frac{N}{N_o}\right) = -kt = \frac{-0.6931\,t}{t_{1/2}},\ \ln\left(\frac{N}{15.3}\right) = \frac{-0.693\,(15,000 \text{ yr})}{5730 \text{ yr}} = -1.8$

$\frac{N}{15.3} = e^{-1.8} = 0.17,\ N = 15.3 \times 0.17 = 2.6 \text{ counts per minute per g of C}$

If we had 10. mg C, we would see:

$$10. \text{ mg} \times \frac{1 \text{ g}}{1000 \text{ mg}} \times \frac{2.6 \text{ counts}}{\text{min g}} = \frac{0.026 \text{ counts}}{\text{min}}$$

It would take roughly 40 min to see a single disintegration. This is too long to wait and the background radiation would probably be much greater than the ^{14}C activity. Thus, ^{14}C dating is not practical for very small samples.

21. $\ln\left(\dfrac{N}{N_o}\right) = -kt = \dfrac{-(\ln 2)\,t}{12.3\ \text{yr}},\quad \ln\left(\dfrac{0.17 \times N_o}{N_o}\right) = -5.64 \times 10^{-2}\,t,\ \ t = 31.4\ \text{yr}$

It takes 31.4 yr for the tritium to decay to 17% of the original amount. Hence, the watch stopped fluorescing enough to be read in 1975 (1944 + 31.4).

22. $\ln(N/N_o) = -kt;\ \ k = (\ln 2)/t_{1/2}\,;\ \ N = 0.001 \times N_o$

$\ln\left(\dfrac{0.001 \times N_o}{N_o}\right) = \dfrac{-(\ln 2)\,t}{24{,}100\ \text{yr}},\ \ \ln 0.001 = -2.88 \times 10^{-5}\,t,\ \ t = 2 \times 10^5\ \text{yr} = 200{,}000\ \text{yr}$

23.   Assuming 1.000 g ^{238}U present in a sample, then 0.688 g ^{206}Pb is present. Since 1 mol ^{206}Pb is produced per mol ^{238}U decayed, then:

$^{238}U\ \text{decayed} = 0.688\ \text{g Pb} \times \dfrac{1\ \text{mol Pb}}{206\ \text{g Pb}} \times \dfrac{1\ \text{mol U}}{\text{mol Pb}} \times \dfrac{238\ \text{g U}}{\text{mol U}} = 0.795\ \text{g}\ ^{238}U$

Original mass ^{238}U present = 1.000 g + 0.795 g = 1.795 g ^{238}U

$\ln\left(\dfrac{N}{N_o}\right) = -kt = \dfrac{-(\ln 2)\,t}{t_{1/2}},\quad \ln\left(\dfrac{1.000\ \text{g}}{1.795\ \text{g}}\right) = \dfrac{-0.693\,(t)}{4.5 \times 10^9\ \text{yr}},\ \ t = 3.8 \times 10^9\ \text{yr}$

24.   a.   The decay of ^{40}K is not the sole source of ^{40}Ca.

b.   Decay of ^{40}K is the sole source of ^{40}Ar and that no ^{40}Ar is lost over the years.

c. $\dfrac{0.95\ \text{g}\ ^{40}Ar}{1.00\ \text{g}\ ^{40}K}$ = current mass ratio

0.95 g of ^{40}K decayed to ^{40}Ar. 0.95 g of ^{40}K is only 10.7% of the total ^{40}K that decayed, or:

0.107 (m) = 0.95 g, m = 8.9 g = total mass of ^{40}K that decayed

Mass of ^{40}K when the rock was formed was 1.00 g + 8.9 g = 9.9 g.

$\ln\left(\dfrac{1.00\ \text{g}\ ^{40}K}{9.9\ \text{g}\ ^{40}K}\right) = -kt = \dfrac{-(\ln 2)\,t}{t_{1/2}} = \dfrac{-0.6931\,t}{1.27 \times 10^9\ \text{yr}},\ \ t = 4.2 \times 10^9\ \text{years old}$

d. If some ^{40}Ar escaped, then the measured ratio of ^{40}Ar/^{40}K would be less than it should be. We would calculate the age of the rocks to be less than it actually is.

Energy Changes in Nuclear Reactions

25. $\Delta E = \Delta mc^2$, $\Delta m = \dfrac{\Delta E}{c^2} = \dfrac{3.9 \times 10^{23} \text{ kg m}^2/\text{s}^2}{(3.00 \times 10^8 \text{ m/s})^2} = 4.3 \times 10^6$ kg

The sun loses 4.3×10^6 kg of mass each second. Note: $1 \text{ J} = 1 \text{ kg m}^2/\text{s}^2$

26. $\dfrac{1.8 \times 10^{14} \text{ kJ}}{\text{s}} \times \dfrac{1000 \text{ J}}{\text{kJ}} \times \dfrac{3600 \text{ s}}{\text{h}} \times \dfrac{24 \text{ h}}{\text{day}} = 1.6 \times 10^{22}$ J/day

$\Delta E = \Delta mc^2$, $\Delta m = \dfrac{\Delta E}{c^2} = \dfrac{1.6 \times 10^{22} \text{ J}}{(3.00 \times 10^8 \text{ m/s})^2} = 1.8 \times 10^5$ kg of solar material provides 1 day of
solar energy to the earth.

$1.6 \times 10^{22} \text{ J} \times \dfrac{1 \text{ kJ}}{1000 \text{ J}} \times \dfrac{1 \text{ g}}{32 \text{ kJ}} \times \dfrac{1 \text{ kg}}{1000 \text{ g}} = 5.0 \times 10^{14}$ kg of coal is needed to provide the same
amount of energy.

27. From the table at the back of the text, the mass of a proton = 1.00728 amu, the mass of a neutron = 1.00866 amu, and the mass of an electron = 5.486×10^{-4} amu.

Mass of nucleus = mass of atom - mass of electrons = 55.9349 - 26(0.0005486) = 55.9206 amu

$26\,^1_1\text{H} + 30\,^1_0\text{n} \rightarrow\,^{56}_{26}\text{Fe}$; $\Delta m = 55.9206 \text{ amu} - [26(1.00728) + 30(1.00866)] \text{ amu} = -0.5285$ amu

$\Delta E = \Delta mc^2 = -0.5285 \text{ amu} \times \dfrac{1.6605 \times 10^{-27} \text{ kg}}{\text{amu}} \times (2.9979 \times 10^8 \text{ m/s})^2 = -7.887 \times 10^{-11}$ J

$\dfrac{\text{binding energy}}{\text{nucleon}} = \dfrac{7.887 \times 10^{-11} \text{ J}}{56 \text{ nucleons}} = 1.408 \times 10^{-12}$ J/nucleon

28. For ^2_1H: mass defect = Δm = mass of ^2_1H nucleus - mass of proton - mass of neutron. The mass of the ^{2}H nucleus will equal the atomic mass of ^{2}H minus the mass of the electron in a ^{2}H atom. From the back of the text, the pertinent masses are: $m_e = 5.49 \times 10^{-4}$ amu, $m_p = 1.00728$ amu, $m_n = 1.00866$ amu.

$\Delta m = 2.01410 \text{ amu} - 0.000549 \text{ amu} - [1.00728 \text{ amu} + 1.00866 \text{ amu}] = -2.39 \times 10^{-3}$ amu

$\Delta E = \Delta mc^2 = -2.39 \times 10^{-3} \text{ amu} \times \dfrac{1.6605 \times 10^{-27} \text{ kg}}{\text{amu}} \times (2.998 \times 10^8 \text{ m/s})^2 = -3.57 \times 10^{-13}$ J

$\dfrac{\text{BE}}{\text{nucleon}} = \dfrac{3.57 \times 10^{-13} \text{ J}}{2 \text{ nucleons}} = 1.79 \times 10^{-13}$ J/nucleon

For $_1^3$H: $\Delta m = 3.01605 - 0.000549 - [1.00728 + 2(1.00866)] = -9.10 \times 10^{-3}$ amu

$$\Delta E = -9.10 \times 10^{-3} \text{ amu} \times \frac{1.6605 \times 10^{-27} \text{ kg}}{\text{amu}} \times (2.998 \times 10^8 \text{ m/s})^2 = -1.36 \times 10^{-12} \text{ J}$$

$$\frac{\text{BE}}{\text{nucleon}} = \frac{1.36 \times 10^{-12} \text{ J}}{3 \text{ nucleons}} = 4.53 \times 10^{-13} \text{ J/nucleon}$$

29.   Let m_e = mass of electron; For ^{12}C (6e, 6p, 6n): mass defect = Δm = mass of ^{12}C nucleus -[mass of 6 protons + mass of 6 neutrons]. Note: Atomic masses given include the mass of the electrons.

$\Delta m = 12.00000$ amu - 6 m_e - [6(1.00782 - m_e) + 6(1.00866)]; Mass of electrons cancel.

$\Delta m = 12.00000 - [6(1.00782) + 6(1.00866)] = -0.09888$ amu

$$\Delta E = \Delta mc^2 = -0.09888 \text{ amu} \times \frac{1.6605 \times 10^{-27} \text{ kg}}{\text{amu}} \times (2.9979 \times 10^8 \text{ m/s})^2 = -1.476 \times 10^{-11} \text{ J}$$

$$\frac{\text{BE}}{\text{nucleon}} = \frac{1.476 \times 10^{-11} \text{ J}}{12 \text{ nucleons}} = 1.230 \times 10^{-12} \text{ J/nucleon}$$

For ^{235}U (92e, 92p, 143n):

$\Delta m = 235.0439 - 92\, m_e - [92(1.00782 - m_e) + 143(1.00866)] = -1.9139$ amu

$$\Delta E = \Delta mc^2 = -1.9139 \text{ amu} \times \frac{1.66054 \times 10^{-27} \text{ kg}}{\text{amu}} \times (2.99792 \times 10^8 \text{ m/s})^2 = -2.8563 \times 10^{-10} \text{ J}$$

$$\frac{\text{BE}}{\text{nucleon}} = \frac{2.8563 \times 10^{-10} \text{ J}}{235 \text{ nucleons}} = 1.2154 \times 10^{-12} \text{ J/nucleon}$$

Since ^{26}Fe is the most stable know nucleus, then the binding energy per nucleon for ^{56}Fe (1.408 $\times$ 10^{-12} J/nucleon) will be larger than that of ^{12}C or ^{235}U (see Figure 21.9 of the text).

30. $\Delta m = -2(5.486 \times 10^{-4}$ amu) $= -1.097 \times 10^{-3}$ amu

$$\Delta E = \Delta mc^2 = -1.097 \times 10^{-3} \text{ amu} \times \frac{1.6605 \times 10^{-27} \text{ kg}}{\text{amu}} \times (2.9979 \times 10^8 \text{ m/s})^2 = -1.637 \times 10^{-13} \text{ J}$$

$E_{\text{photon}} = 1/2(1.637 \times 10^{-13}$ J) $= 8.185 \times 10^{-14}$ J $= hc/\lambda$

$$\lambda = \frac{hc}{E} = \frac{6.6261 \times 10^{-34} \text{ J s} \times 2.9979 \times 10^8 \text{ m/s}}{8.185 \times 10^{-14} \text{ J}} = 2.427 \times 10^{-12} \text{ m} = 2.427 \times 10^{-3} \text{ nm}$$

31. $_1^2$H + $_1^3$H $\rightarrow$ $_2^4$He + $_0^1$n; Mass of electrons cancel when determining Δm for this nuclear reaction.

$\Delta m = [4.00260 + 1.00866 - (2.01410 + 3.01605)]$ amu $= -1.889 \times 10^{-2}$ amu

For the production of one mol of $_2^4$He: $\Delta m = -1.889 \times 10^{-2}$ g $= -1.889 \times 10^{-5}$ kg

$\Delta E = \Delta mc^2 = -1.889 \times 10^{-5}$ kg $\times (2.9979 \times 10^8$ m/s$)^2 = -1.698 \times 10^{12}$ J/mol

For 1 nuclei of $_2^4$He:

$$\frac{-1.698 \times 10^{12} \text{ J}}{\text{mol}} \times \frac{1 \text{ mol}}{6.0221 \times 10^{23} \text{ nuclei}} = -2.820 \times 10^{-12} \text{ J/nuclei}$$

32. $_1^1$H $+$ $_1^1$H $\rightarrow$ $_1^2$H $+$ $_{+1}^0$e; $\Delta m = (2.01410$ amu $- m_e + m_e) - 2(1.00782$ amu $- m_e)$

$\Delta m = 2.01410 - 2(1.00782) + 2(0.000549) = -4.4 \times 10^{-4}$ amu for two protons reacting

When two mol of protons undergo fusion, $\Delta m = -4.4 \times 10^{-4}$ g.

$\Delta E = \Delta mc^2 = -4.4 \times 10^{-7}$ kg $\times (3.00 \times 10^8$ m/s$)^2 = -4.0 \times 10^{10}$ J

$$\frac{-4.0 \times 10^{10} \text{ J}}{2 \text{ mol protons}} \times \frac{1 \text{ mol}}{1.01 \text{ g}} = -2.0 \times 10^{10} \text{ J/g of hydrogen nuclei}$$

Detection, Uses, and Health Effects of Radiation

33.   The Geiger-Müller tube has a certain response time. After the gas in the tube ionizes to produce a "count," some time must elapse for the gas to return to an electrically neutral state. The response of the tube levels out because at high activities, radioactive particles are entering the tube faster than the tube can respond to them.

34.   Not all of the emitted radiation enters the Geiger-Müller tube. The fraction of radiation entering the tube must be constant for a meaningful measurement.

35.   Fission: Splitting of a heavy nucleus into two (or more) lighter nuclei.

      Fusion: Combining two light nuclei to form a heavier nucleus.

      The maximum binding energy per nucleon occurs at Fe. Nuclei smaller than Fe become more stable by fusing to form heavier nuclei closer in mass to Fe. Nuclei larger than Fe form more stable nuclei by splitting to form lighter nuclei closer in mass to Fe.

36.   For fusion reactions, a collision of sufficient energy must occur between two positively charged particles to initiate the reaction. This requires high temperatures. In fission, an electrically neutral neutron collides with the positively charged nucleus. This has a much lower activation energy.

37.   moderator: Slows the neutrons to increase the efficiency of the fission reaction.

      control rods: Absorbs neutrons to slow or halt the fission reaction.

38.   The temperatures of fusion reactions are so high that all physical containers would be destroyed. At these high temperatures most of the electrons are stripped from the atoms. A plasma of gaseous ions is formed which can be controlled by magnetic fields.

39.   Even though gamma rays penetrate human tissue very deeply, they are very small and cause only occasional ionization of biomolecules. Alpha particles, because they are much more massive, are very effective at causing ionization of biomolecules and produce a dense trail of damage once they get inside an organism.

40.   In order to sustain a nuclear chain reaction, the neutrons produced by the fission must be contained within the fissionable material so that they can go on to cause other fissions. The fissionable material must be closely packed together to ensure that neutrons are not lost to the outside. The critical mass is the mass of material in which exactly one neutron from each fission event causes another fission event so that the process sustains itself. A supercritical situation occurs when more than one neutron from each fission event causes another fission event. In this case, the process rapidly escalates and the heat build up causes a violent explosion.

41.   Magnetic fields are needed to contain fusion reactions. Superconductors allow the production of very strong magnetic fields by their ability to carry large electric currents. Stronger magnetic fields should be more capable of containing fusion reactions.

42.   No, coal fired power plants also pose risks. A partial list of risks are:

Coal	Nuclear
Air pollution	Radiation exposure to workers
Coal mine accidents	Disposal of wastes
Health risks to miners	Meltdown
(black lung disease)	Terrorists

43.   A nonradioactive substance can be put in equilibrium with a radioactive substance. The two materials can then be checked to see whether all the radioactivity remains in the original material or if it has been scrambled by the equilibrium.

44.   Water is produced in this reaction by removing an OH group from one substance and an H from the other substance. There are two ways to do this:

Since the water produced is not radioactive, then methyl acetate forms by the first reaction where all of the oxygen-18 ends up in methyl acetate.

45.   All evolved oxygen in O_2 comes from water and not from carbon dioxide.

46.   Release of Sr is probably more harmful. Xe is chemically unreactive. Strontium is in the same family as calcium and could be absorbed and concentrated in the body in a fashion similar to Ca. This puts the radioactive Sr in the bones: red blood cells are produced in bone marrow. Xe would not be readily incorporated into the body.

        The chemical properties determine where a radioactive material may be concentrated in the body or how easily it may be excreted. The length of time of exposure and what is exposed to radiation significantly affects the health hazard. (See exercise 21.47 for a specific example.)

47.   (i) and (ii) mean that Pu is not a significant threat outside the body. Our skin is sufficient to keep out the α particles. If Pu gets inside the body, it is easily oxidized to Pu^{4+} (iv), which is chemically similar to Fe^{3+} (iii). Thus, Pu^{4+} will concentrate in tissues where Fe^{3+} is found, including the bone marrow where red blood cells are produced. Once inside the body, α particles can cause considerable damage.

Additional Exercises

48.   Mass of nucleus = atomic mass - mass of electron = 2.01410 amu - 0.000549 amu = 2.01355 amu

$$u_{rms} = \left(\frac{3\,RT}{M} \right)^{1/2} = \left(\frac{3(8.3145\text{ J K}^{-1}\text{ mol}^{-1})\,(4 \times 10^7\text{ K})}{2.01355\text{ g (1 kg/1000 g)}} \right)^{1/2} = 7 \times 10^5 \text{ m/s}$$

$$KE_{avg} = \frac{1}{2}mu^2 = \frac{1}{2}\left(2.01355\text{ amu} \times \frac{1.66 \times 10^{-27}\text{ kg}}{\text{amu}} \right)(7 \times 10^5\text{ m/s})^2 = 8 \times 10^{-16}\text{ J}$$

49. $20{,}000 \text{ ton TNT} \times \dfrac{4 \times 10^9\text{ J}}{\text{ton TNT}} \times \dfrac{1\text{ mol }^{235}\text{U}}{2 \times 10^{13}\text{ J}} \times \dfrac{235\text{ g }^{235}\text{U}}{\text{mol }^{235}\text{U}} = 940\text{ g }^{235}\text{U} \approx 900\text{ g }^{235}\text{U}$

        This assumes that all of the ^{235}U undergoes fission.

50.   Characteristic frequencies of energies emitted in a nuclear reaction suggests that discrete energy levels exist in the nucleus. Extra stability of certain numbers of nucleons and the predominance of nuclei with even numbers of nucleons suggests that the nuclear structure might be described by using quantum numbers.

51.   The only product in the fast equilibrium step is assumed to be $N^{16}O^{18}O_2$, where N is the central atom. However, this is a reversible reaction where $N^{16}O^{18}O_2$ will decompose to NO and O_2. Since any two oxygen atoms can leave $N^{16}O^{18}O_2$ to form O_2, then we would expect (at equilibrium) 1/3 of the NO present in this fast equilibrium step to be $N^{16}O$ and 2/3 to be $N^{18}O$. In the second step (the slow step), the intermediate $N^{16}O^{18}O_2$ reacts with the scrambled NO to form the NO_2 product, where

N is the central atom in NO_2. Any one of the three oxygen atoms can be transferred from $N^{16}O\,^{18}O_2$ to NO when the NO_2 product is formed. The distribution of ^{18}O in the product can best be determined by forming a probability table.

	$N^{16}O$ (1/3)	$N^{18}O$ (2/3)
^{16}O (1/3) from $N^{16}O\,^{18}O_2$	$N^{16}O_2$ (1/9)	$N^{18}O^{16}O$ (2/9)
^{18}O (2/3) from $N^{16}O\,^{18}O_2$	$N^{16}O^{18}O$ (2/9)	$N^{18}O_2$ (4/9)

From the probability table, 1/9 of the NO_2 is $N^{16}O_2$, 4/9 of the NO_2 is $N^{18}O_2$ and 4/9 of the NO_2 is $N^{16}O^{18}O$ (2/9 + 2/9 = 4/9). Note: $N^{16}O^{18}O$ is the same as $N^{18}O^{16}O$. In addition, $N^{16}O\,^{18}O_2$ is not the only NO_3 intermediate formed; $N^{16}O_2\,^{18}O$ and $N^{18}O_3$ can also form in the fast equilibrium first step. However, the distribution of ^{18}O in the NO_2 product is the same as calculated above, even when these other NO_3 intermediates are considered.

52. For a "third-life", $\dfrac{N}{N_o} = \dfrac{1}{3}$, $t_{1/2} = \dfrac{0.6931}{k}$

$31.4 \text{ yr.} = \dfrac{0.6931}{k}$, $k = 2.21 \times 10^{-2}\ \text{yr}^{-1}$, $\ln\left(\dfrac{N}{N_o}\right) = -kt$, $\ln\left(\dfrac{1}{3}\right) = (-2.21 \times 10^{-2})\, t_{1/3}$

$t_{1/3} = 49.7$ yr

53. Assuming that the radionuclide is long lived enough such that no significant decay occurs during the time of the experiment, the total counts of radioactivity injected are:

$$0.10 \text{ mL} \times \dfrac{5.0 \times 10^3 \text{ cpm}}{\text{mL}} = 5.0 \times 10^2 \text{ cpm}$$

Assuming that the total activity is uniformly distributed only in the rats blood, the blood volume is:

$$V \times \dfrac{48 \text{ cpm}}{\text{mL}} = 5.0 \times 10^2 \text{ cpm},\ \ V = 10.4 \text{ mL} = 10.\ \text{mL}$$

54. a. ^{12}C; It takes part in the first step of the reaction but is regenerated in the last step. ^{12}C is not consumed so it is not a reactant.

b. ^{13}N, ^{13}C, ^{14}N, ^{15}O, and ^{15}N are the intermediates.

c. $4\,{}^{1}_{1}H \rightarrow {}^{4}_{2}He + 2\,{}^{0}_{+1}e$; $\Delta m = 4.00260$ amu $- 2\,m_e + 2\,m_e - [4(1.00782$ amu $- m_e)]$

$\Delta m = 4.00260 - 4(1.00782) + 4(0.000549) = -0.02648$ amu for 4 protons reacting

For 4 mol of protons, $\Delta m = -0.02648$ g and ΔE for the reaction is:

$$\Delta E = \Delta mc^2 = -2.648 \times 10^{-5}\ \text{kg} \times (2.9979 \times 10^8\ \text{m/s})^2 = -2.380 \times 10^{12}\ \text{J}$$

For 1 mol of protons reacting: $\dfrac{-2.380 \times 10^{12}\ \text{J}}{4\ \text{mol }{}^1\text{H}} = -5.950 \times 10^{11}$ J/mol ^{1}H

Challenge Problems

55.   mol I $= \dfrac{33\ \text{counts}}{\text{min}} \times \dfrac{1\ \text{mol I} \bullet \text{min}}{5.0 \times 10^{11}\ \text{counts}} = 6.6 \times 10^{-11}$ mol I

$[I^-] = \dfrac{6.6 \times 10^{-11}\ \text{mol I}^-}{0.150\ \text{L}} = 4.4 \times 10^{-10}$ mol/L

$$Hg_2I_2(s) \rightarrow Hg_2{}^{2+}(aq) \quad + \quad 2\ I^-(aq) \qquad K_{sp} = [Hg_2{}^{2+}][I^-]^2$$

Initial s = solubility (mol/L)   0   0

Equil. s $2s$

From the problem, $2s = 4.4 \times 10^{-10}$ mol/L, $s = 2.2 \times 10^{-10}$ mol/L

$K_{sp} = (s)(2s)^2 = (2.2 \times 10^{-10})(4.4 \times 10^{-10})^2 = 4.3 \times 10^{-29}$

56.   a. ${}^{238}_{92}U \rightarrow {}^{222}_{86}Rn + ?\ {}^{4}_{2}He + ?\ {}^{0}_{-1}e$; To account for the mass number change, 4 alpha

particles are needed.   To balance the number of protons, 2 beta particles are needed.

${}^{222}_{86}Rn \rightarrow {}^{4}_{2}He + {}^{218}_{84}Po$; Polonium-84 is produced when ^{222}Rn decays.

b.   Alpha particles cause significant ionization damage when inside a living organism. Since the half-life of ^{222}Rn is relatively short, a significant number of alpha particles will be produced when ^{222}Rn is present (even for a short period of time) in the lungs.

c. ${}^{222}_{86}Rn \rightarrow {}^{4}_{2}He + {}^{218}_{84}Po$; ${}^{218}_{84}Po \rightarrow {}^{4}_{2}He + {}^{214}_{82}Pb$; Polonium-218 is produced when radon-222 decays. ^{218}Po is a more potent alpha particle producer since it has a much shorter half-life than ^{222}Rn. In addition, ^{218}Po is a solid, so it can get trapped in the lung tissue once it is produced. Once trapped, the alpha particles produced from polonium-218 (with its very short half-life) can cause significant ionization damage.

d. Rate = kN;   rate $= \dfrac{4.0 \text{ pCi}}{L} \times \dfrac{1 \times 10^{-12} \text{ Ci}}{\text{pCi}} \times \dfrac{3.7 \times 10^{10} \text{ decays/sec}}{\text{Ci}} = 0.15$ decays/sec • L

$k = \dfrac{\ln 2}{t_{1/2}} = \dfrac{0.6931}{3.82 \text{ d}} \times \dfrac{1 \text{ d}}{24 \text{ hr}} \times \dfrac{1 \text{ hr}}{3600 \text{ s}} = 2.10 \times 10^{-6} \text{ s}^{-1}$

$N = \dfrac{\text{rate}}{k} \times \dfrac{0.15 \text{ decay/sec} \cdot L}{2.10 \times 10^{-6} \text{ s}^{-1}} = 7.1 \times 10^{4} \ ^{222}\text{Rn atoms/L}$

$\dfrac{7.1 \times 10^{4} \ ^{222}\text{Rn atoms}}{L} \times \dfrac{1 \text{ mol } ^{222}\text{Rn}}{6.02 \times 10^{23} \text{ atoms}} = 1.2 \times 10^{-19} \text{ mol } ^{222}\text{Rn/L}$

57. a. For a gas, $u_{avg} = \sqrt{8\,RT/\pi M}$ where M is the molar mass in kg. From the equation, the lighter the gas molecule, the faster the average velocity. Therefore, $^{235}\text{UF}_6$ will have the greater average velocity at a certain temperature since it is the lighter molecule.

b. From Graham's law (see Section 5.7 of the text):

$$\dfrac{\text{diffusion rate for } ^{235}\text{UF}_6}{\text{diffusion rate for } ^{238}\text{UF}_6} = \sqrt{\dfrac{M(^{238}\text{UF}_6)}{M(^{235}\text{UF}_6)}} = \sqrt{\dfrac{352.05 \text{ g/mol}}{349.03 \text{ g/mol}}} = 1.0043$$

Each diffusion step increases the $^{235}\text{UF}_6$ concentration by a factor of 1.0043. To determine the number of steps to get to the desired 3.00% ^{235}U, we use the following formula:

$$\dfrac{0.700 \ ^{235}\text{UF}_6}{99.3 \ ^{238}\text{UF}_6} \times (1.0043)^N = \dfrac{3.00 \ ^{235}\text{UF}_6}{97.0 \ ^{238}\text{UF}_6}$$

original ratio   final ratio

where N represents the number of steps required.

Solving (and carrying extra sig. figs.):

$(1.0043)^N = \dfrac{297.9}{67.9} = 4.387$,   N log 1.0043 = log 4.387

$N = \dfrac{0.6422}{1.863 \times 10^{-3}} = 345$ steps

Thus, 345 steps are required to obtain the desired enrichment.

c. $\dfrac{^{235}UF_6}{^{238}UF_6} \times (1.0043)^{100} = \dfrac{1526}{1.000 \times 10^5 - 1526}$, $\dfrac{^{235}UF_6}{^{238}UF_6} \times 1.5358 = \dfrac{1526}{98500}$

 original ratio   final ratio

$\dfrac{^{235}UF_6}{^{238}UF_6} = 1.01 \times 10^{-2} = \text{initial } ^{235}U \text{ to } ^{238}U \text{ atom ratio}$

58.   a.   From Table 11.1: $2\,H_2O + 2\,e^- \rightarrow H_2 + 2\,OH^-$ $E° = -0.83\,V$

$E°_{cell} = E°_{H_2O} - E°_{Zr} = -0.83\,V + 2.36\,V = 1.53\,V$

Yes, the reduction of H_2O to H_2 by Zr is spontaneous at standard conditions since $E°_{cell} > 0$.

   b. $(2\,H_2O + 2\,e^- \rightarrow H_2 + 2\,OH^-) \times 2$
        $Zr + 4\,OH^- \rightarrow ZrO_2 \bullet H_2O + H_2O + 4\,e^-$
        _____
        $3\,H_2O(l) + Zr(s) \rightarrow 2\,H_2(g) + ZrO_2 \bullet H_2O(s)$

   c. $\Delta G° = -nFE° = -(4\,\text{mol } e^-)(96{,}485\,\text{C/mol } e^-)(1.53\,\text{J/C}) = -5.90 \times 10^5\,J = -590.\,kJ$

$E = E° - \dfrac{0.0591}{n} \log Q$; At equilibrium, $E = 0$ and $Q = K$.

$E° = \dfrac{0.0591}{n} \log K$, $\log K = \dfrac{4(1.53)}{0.0591} = 104$, $K \approx 10^{104}$

   d. $1.00 \times 10^3\,\text{kg Zr} \times \dfrac{1000\,g}{kg} \times \dfrac{1\,\text{mol Zr}}{91.22\,\text{g Zr}} \times \dfrac{2\,\text{mol } H_2}{\text{mol Zr}} = 2.19 \times 10^4\,\text{mol } H_2$

$2.19 \times 10^4\,\text{mol } H_2 \times \dfrac{2.016\,\text{g } H_2}{\text{mol } H_2} = 4.42 \times 10^4\,\text{g } H_2$

$V = \dfrac{nRT}{P} = \dfrac{(2.19 \times 10^4\,\text{mol})(0.08206\,\text{L atm K}^{-1}\,\text{mol}^{-1})(1273\,K)}{1.0\,\text{atm}} = 2.3 \times 10^6\,\text{L } H_2$

   e.   Probably yes; Less radioactivity overall was released by venting the H_2 than what would have been released if the H_2 exploded inside the reactor (as happened at Chernobyl). Neither alternative is pleasant, but venting the radioactive hydrogen is the less unpleasant of the two alternatives.

CHAPTER TWENTY-TWO

ORGANIC CHEMISTRY

Hydrocarbons

1. A difficult task in this problem is recognizing different compounds from compounds that differ by rotations about one or more C–C bonds (called conformations). The best way to distinguish different compounds from conformations is to name them. Different name = different compound; same name = same compound so it is not an isomer, but instead, is a conformation.

a.

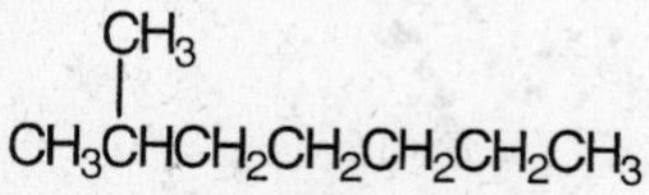

$$CH_3$$
$$CH_3CHCH_2CH_2CH_2CH_2CH_3$$

2-methylheptane

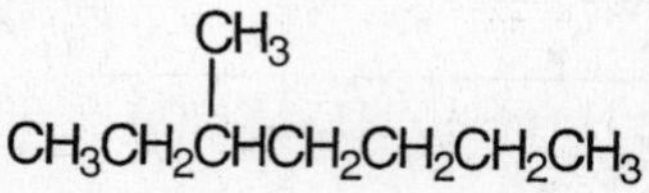

$$CH_3$$
$$CH_3CH_2CHCH_2CH_2CH_2CH_3$$

3-methylheptane

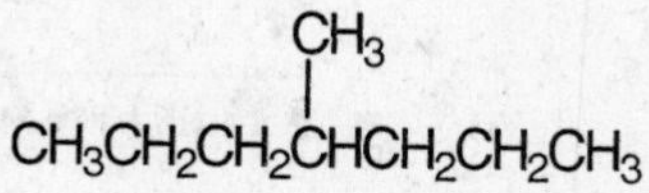

$$CH_3$$
$$CH_3CH_2CH_2CHCH_2CH_2CH_3$$

4-methylheptane

b.

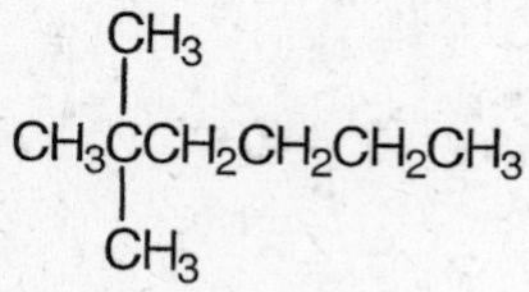

$$CH_3$$
$$CH_3CCH_2CH_2CH_2CH_3$$
$$CH_3$$

2,2-dimethylhexane

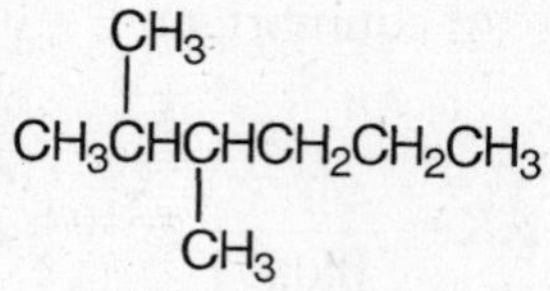

$$CH_3$$
$$CH_3CHCHCH_2CH_2CH_3$$
$$CH_3$$

2,3-dimethylhexane

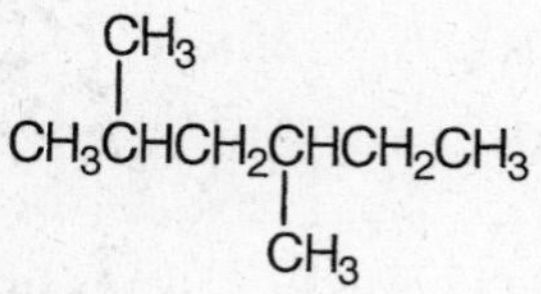

$$CH_3$$
$$CH_3CHCH_2CHCH_2CH_3$$
$$CH_3$$

2,4-dimethylhexane

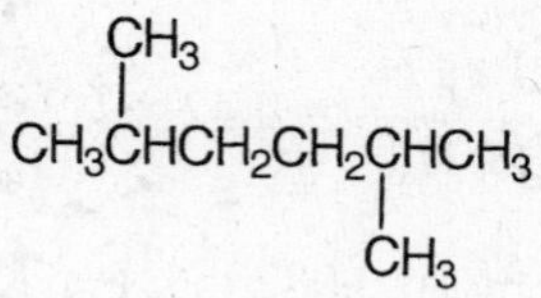

$$CH_3$$
$$CH_3CHCH_2CH_2CHCH_3$$
$$CH_3$$

2,5-dimethylhexane

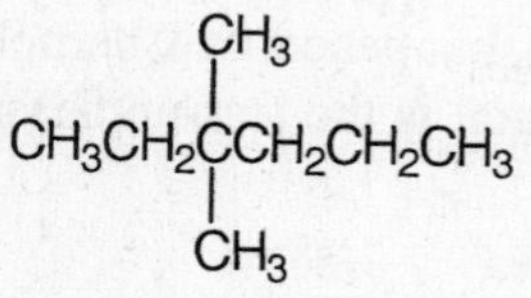

$$CH_3$$
$$CH_3CH_2CCH_2CH_2CH_3$$
$$CH_3$$

3,3-dimethylhexane

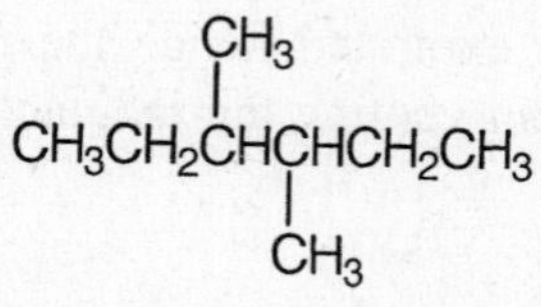

$$CH_3$$
$$CH_3CH_2CHCHCH_2CH_3$$
$$CH_3$$

3,4-dimethylhexane

$$CH_2CH_3$$
$$CH_3CH_2CHCH_2CH_2CH_3$$

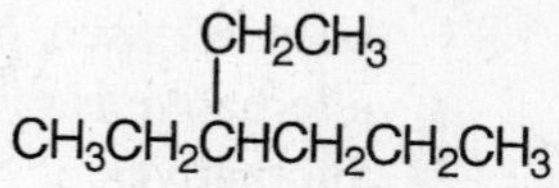

3-ethylhexane

656

c.

$$CH_3—\overset{\overset{\displaystyle CH_3}{|}}{\underset{\underset{\displaystyle CH_3}{|}}{C}}—\overset{\overset{\displaystyle CH_3}{|}}{CH}—CH_2—CH_3$$

2,2,3-trimethylpentane

$$CH_3—\overset{\overset{\displaystyle CH_3}{|}}{\underset{\underset{\displaystyle CH_3}{|}}{C}}—CH_2—\overset{\overset{\displaystyle CH_3}{|}}{CH}—CH_3$$

2,2,4-trimethylpentane

$$CH_3—\overset{\overset{\displaystyle CH_3}{|}}{CH}—\overset{\overset{\displaystyle CH_3}{|}}{\underset{\underset{\displaystyle CH_3}{|}}{C}}—CH_2—CH_3$$

2,3,3-trimethylpentane

$$CH_3—\overset{\overset{\displaystyle CH_3}{|}}{CH}—\overset{\overset{\displaystyle CH_3}{|}}{CH}—\overset{\overset{\displaystyle CH_3}{|}}{CH}—CH_3$$

2,3,4-trimethylpentane

$$CH_3—\overset{\overset{\displaystyle CH_3}{|}}{CH}—\overset{\overset{\displaystyle CH_2CH_3}{|}}{CH}—CH_2—CH_3$$

3-ethyl-2-methylpentane

$$CH_3—CH_2—\overset{\overset{\displaystyle CH_2CH_3}{|}}{\underset{\underset{\displaystyle CH_3}{|}}{C}}—CH_2—CH_3$$

3-ethyl-3-methylpentane

d.

$$CH_3—\overset{\overset{\displaystyle CH_3}{|}}{\underset{\underset{\displaystyle CH_3}{|}}{C}}—\overset{\overset{\displaystyle CH_3}{|}}{\underset{\underset{\displaystyle CH_3}{|}}{C}}—CH_3$$

2,2,3,3-tetramethylbutane

2.   There is only one consecutive chain of C-atoms in the molecule. They are not all in a true straight line since the bond angles at each carbon atom are the tetrahedral angles of 109.5°.

3.   London dispersion (LD) forces are the primary intermolecular forces exhibited by hydrocarbons. The strength of the LD forces depends on the surface area contact among neighboring molecules. As branching increases, there is less surface area contact among neighboring molecules, leading to weaker LD forces and lower boiling points.

4.   i.

$$CH_3–CH_2–CH_2–CH_2–CH_2–CH_3$$

hexane

ii.

$$CH_3—\overset{\overset{\displaystyle CH_3}{|}}{CH}—CH_2—CH_2—CH_3$$

2-methylpentane

iii.

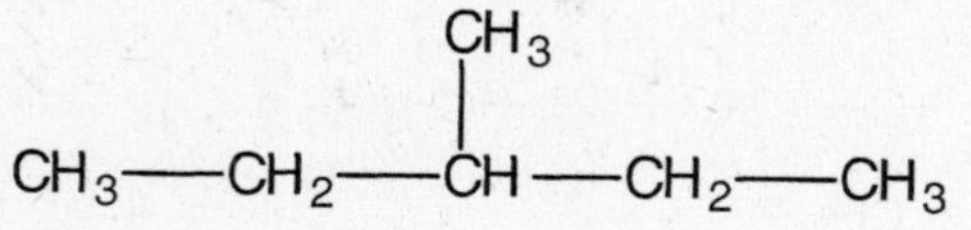

3-methylpentane

iv.

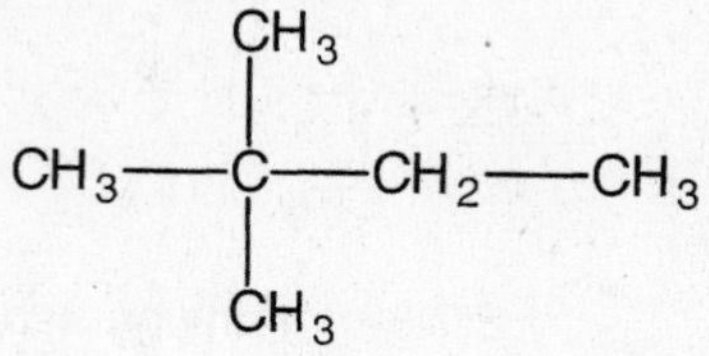

2,2-dimethylbutane

v.

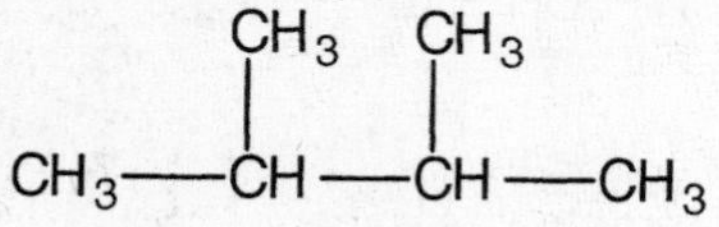

2,3-dimethylbutane

All other possibilities are identical to one of these five compounds.

5. a.

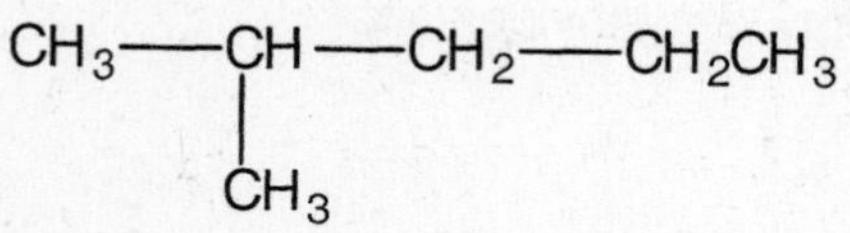

b.

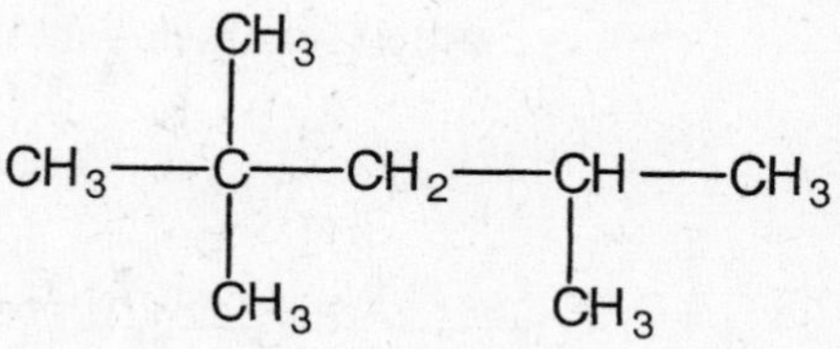

c.

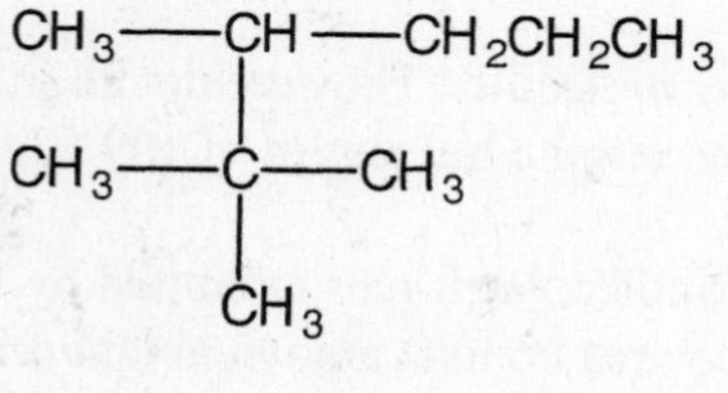

d. The longest chain is 6 carbons long.

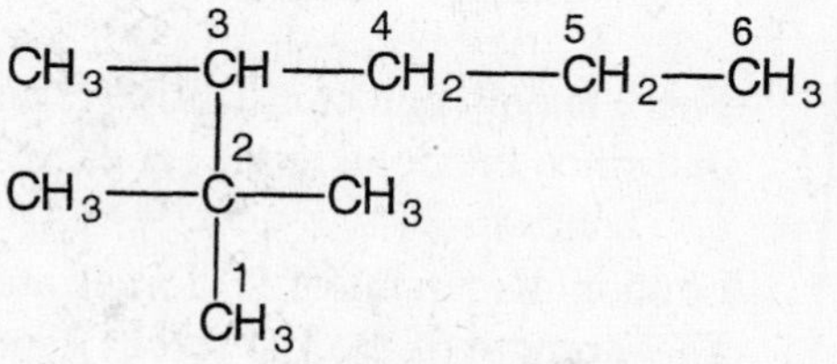

2,2,3-trimethylhexane

6.

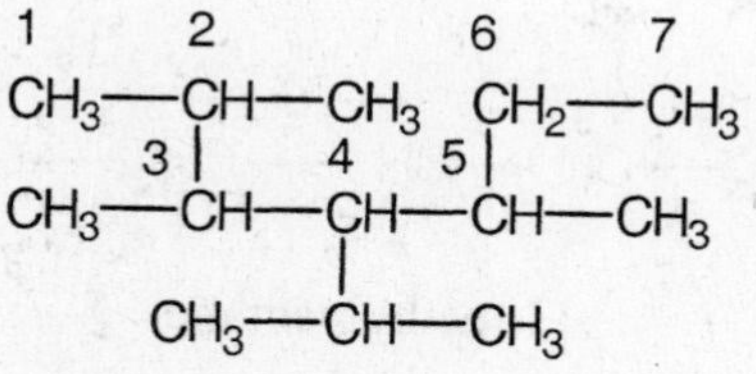

4-isopropyl-2,3,5-trimethylheptane

7. a. 2,2,4-trimethylhexane b. 5-methylnonane c. 2,2,4,4-tetramethylpentane

d. 3-ethyl-3-methyloctane

Note: For alkanes always identify the longest carbon chain for the base name first, then number the carbons to give the lowest overall numbers for the substituent groups.

8. The hydrogen atoms in ring compounds are commonly omitted. In organic compounds, carbon atoms satisfy the octet rule of electrons by forming four bonds to other atoms. Therefore, add C-H bonds to the carbon atoms in the ring in order to give each C atom four bonds. You can also determine the formula of these cycloalkanes by using the general formula C_nH_{2n}.

   a. isopropylcyclobutane; C_7H_{14}

   b. 1-tert-butyl-3-methylcyclopentane; $C_{10}H_{20}$

   c. 1,3-dimethyl-2-propylcyclohexane; $C_{11}H_{22}$

9. a. 1-butene

   b. 2-methyl-2-butene

   c. 2,5-dimethyl-3-heptene

   d. 2,3-dimethyl-1-pentene

   e. 1-ethyl-3-methylcyclopentene (double bond assumed between C_1 and C_2)

   f. 4-ethyl-3-methylcyclopentene   g. 4-methyl-2-pentyne

Note: Multiple bonds are assigned the lowest number possible.

10. a. $CH_3-CH_2-CH=CH-CH_2-CH_3$

   b. $CH_3-CH=CH-CH=CH-CH_2CH_3$

   c.
   $$CH_3-\underset{\underset{\displaystyle CH_3}{|}}{CH}-CH=CH-CH_2CH_2CH_2CH_3$$

   d.
   $$HC\equiv C-CH_2-\underset{\underset{\displaystyle CH_3}{|}}{CH}-CH_3$$

11. a. 1,3-dichlorobutane

   b. 1,1,1-trichlorobutane

   c. 2,3-dichloro-2,4-dimethylhexane

   d. 1,2-difluoroethane

   e. 3-iodo-1-butene

   f. 2-bromotoluene (or 1-bromo-2-methylbenzene)

   g. 1-bromo-2-methylcyclohexane

   h. 4-bromo-3-methylcyclohexene (double bond assumed between C_1 and C_2)

12. a.

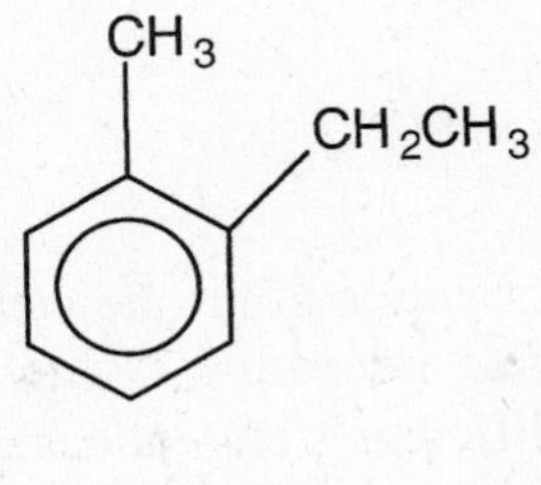

   b.

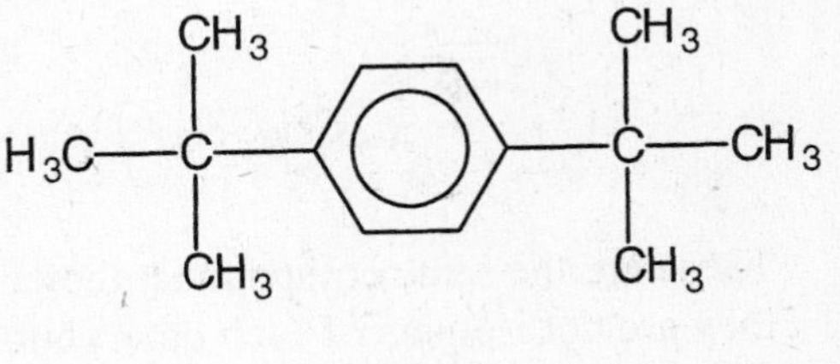

c.

CH_2CH_3

CH_2CH_3

d.

CH_2—CH=CH—CH_3

13.   isopropylbenzene or 2-phenylpropane

Isomerism

14.   resonance: All atoms are in the same position. Only the position of π electrons are different.

isomerism: Atoms are in different locations in space.

Isomers are distinctly different substances. Resonance is the use of more than one Lewis structure to describe the bonding in a single compound. Resonance structures are <u>not</u> isomers.

15.   structural isomers: Same formula but different bonding, either in the kinds of bonds present or the way in which the bonds connect atoms to each other.

geometrical isomers: Same formula and same bonds but differ in the arrangement of atoms in space about a rigid bond or ring.

16. CH_2Cl–CH_2Cl, 1-2-dichloroethane; There is free rotation about the C–C single bond which doesn't lead to different compounds. $CHCl$=$CHCl$, 1,2-dichloroethene; There is no rotation about the C=C double bond. This creates the cis and trans isomers which are different compounds.

17.   To exhibit cis-trans isomerism, a compound must first have restricted rotation about a carbon-carbon bond. This occurs in compounds with double bonds and ring compounds. Secondly, the compound must have two carbons in the restricted rotation environment that each have two different groups bonded. For example, the compound in 22.9a has a double bond, but the first carbon in the double bond has two H-atoms attached. This compound does not exhibit cis-trans isomerism. To see this, let's draw the potential cis-trans isomers:

H   H
  \   /
   C = C
  /   \
H CH_2CH_3

H CH_2CH_3
  \   /
   C = C
  /   \
H   H

These are the same compounds; they only differ by a simply rotation of the molecule. Therefore, they are not isomers of each other, but instead they are the same compound. The only compounds that fulfill the restricted rotation requirement **and** have two different groups attached to carbons in the restricted rotation are compounds c and f. The cis-trans isomerism for these follows.

c.

(structures)

CH₃—CH₂—CH(CH₃)—C(H)=C(H)—CH(CH₃)—CH₃   **cis**

CH₃—CH₂—CH(CH₃)—C(H)=C—(CH—CH₃ / CH₃ / H)   **trans**

f.

(ring structures)

cis   **trans**

────── = out of plane of paper; - - - - - = into plane of paper

18.   In Exercise 22.10, 3-hexene, 2,4-heptadiene, and 2-methyl-3-octene meet the requirements for cis-trans isomerism as outlined in Exercise 22.17. Only 4-methyl-1-pentyne does not exhibit cis-trans isomerism. Because of the triple bond in alkynes, the carbons with the restricted rotation only have one group bonded to them (not two groups as is a necessity for geometric isomerism). See the structure below.

$$H_3C—CH—CH_2—C{\equiv}C—H$$
$$\qquad\ \ |$$
$$\qquad\ \ CH_3$$

4-methyl-1-pentyne

19.   The cis isomer has the CH₃ groups on the same side of the ring. The trans isomer has the CH₃ groups on opposite sides of the ring.

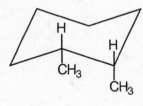

cis   trans

20.

a. H_3C $CH_2CH_2CH_3$ / $C=C$ / H H

b. H_3C H / $C=C$ / H CH_3

c. H_3C CH_2CH_3 / $C=C$ / Cl Cl

21. To help distinguish the different isomers, we will name them.

Cl CH_3 / $C=C$ / H H

cis-1-chloro-1-propene

H CH_3 / $C=C$ / Cl H

trans-1-chloro-1-propene

$CH_2=C-CH_3$ / Cl

2-chloro-1-propene

$CH_2=CH-CH_2$ / Cl

3-chloro-1-propene

Cl (triangle)

chlorocyclopropane

22.

F CH_2CH_3 / $C=C$ / H H

H CH_2CH_3 / $C=C$ / F H

F / $CH_2=CCH_2CH_3$

F / $CH_2=CHCHCH_3$

F / $CH_2=CHCH_2CH_2$

H_2CF CH_3 / $C=C$ / H H

F CH_3 / $C=C$ / H_3C H

H_3C CH_3 / $C=C$ / F H

H CH_3 / $C=C$ / H_2CF H

F CH_3 / $CH=CCH_3$

CH_3 / $CH_2=CCH_2$ / F

cis   trans

23. C_5H_{10} has the general formula for alkenes, C_nH_{2n}. To distinguish the different isomers from each other, we will name them. Each isomer must have a different name.

$$CH_2\!=\!CHCH_2CH_2CH_3$$

1-pentene

$$CH_3CH\!=\!CHCH_2CH_3$$

2-pentene

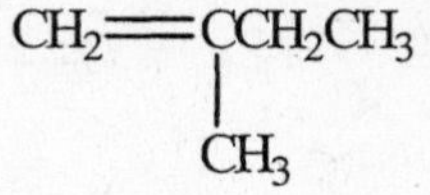

$$CH_2\!=\!CCH_2CH_3$$
$$\quad\;\; |$$
$$\quad\; CH_3$$

2-methyl-1-butene

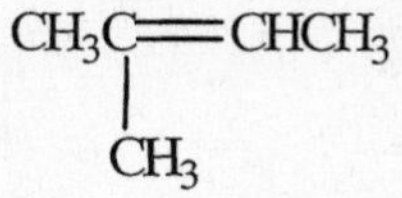

$$CH_3C\!=\!CHCH_3$$
$$\quad\; |$$
$$\quad CH_3$$

2-methyl-2-butene

$$CH_3CHCH\!=\!CH_2$$
$$\quad\; |$$
$$\quad CH_3$$

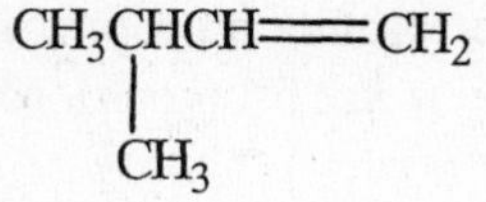

3-methyl-1-butene

Only 2-pentene exhibits cis-trans isomerism. The isomers are:

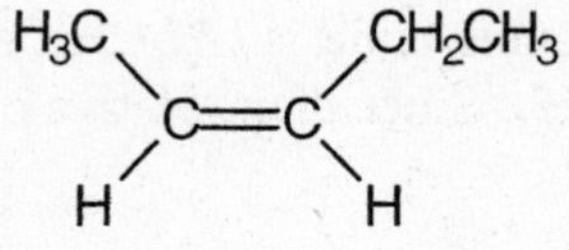

cis

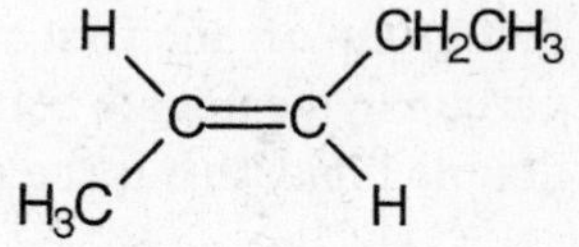

trans

The other isomers of C_5H_{10} do not contain carbons in the double bond that each contain two different groups attached.

24.

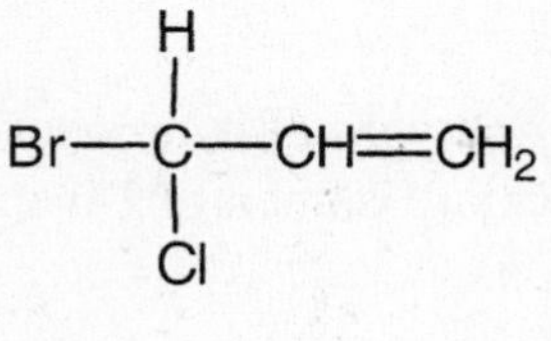

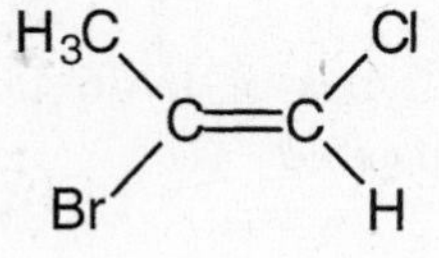

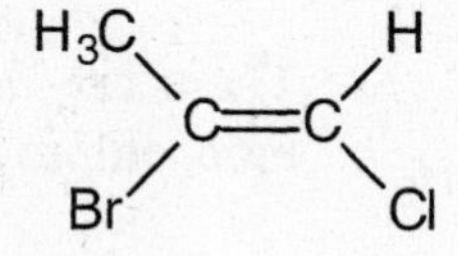

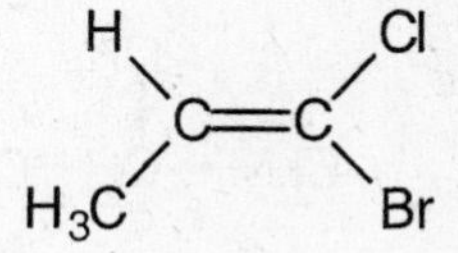

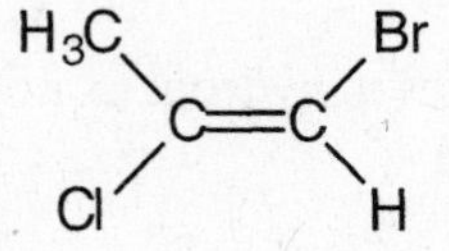

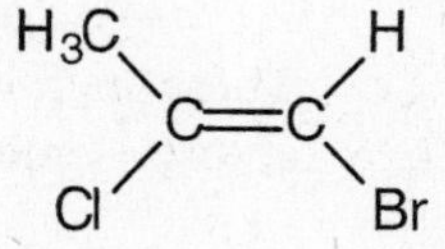

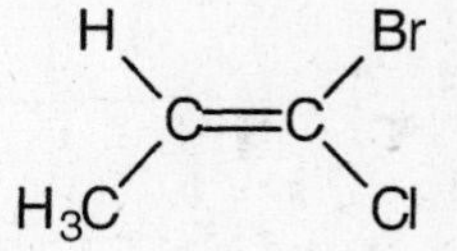

H_2CBr
$\underset{Cl}{\overset{}{C}}=CH_2$

$H_2CBr \quad Cl$
$\underset{H}{C}=\underset{H}{C}$

$H_2CBr \quad H$
$\underset{H}{C}=\underset{Cl}{C}$

H_2CCl
$\underset{Br}{\overset{}{C}}=CH_2$

$H_2CCl \quad Br$
$\underset{H}{C}=\underset{H}{C}$

$H_2CCl \quad H$
$\underset{H}{C}=\underset{Br}{C}$

Note: 1-bromo-1-chlorocyclopropane, cis-1-bromo-2-chlorocyclopropane and trans-1-bromo-2-chlorocyclopropane are the ring structures that are isomers of bromochloropropene. We did not include the ring structures in the answer since their base name is not bromochloropropene.

25.   a. cis-1-bromo-1-propene   b. cis-4-ethyl-3-methyl-3-heptene

        c. trans-1,4-diiodo-2-propyl-1-pentene

Note: In general, cis-trans designations refer to the relative positions of the largest groups. In compound b, the largest group off the first carbon in the double bond is CH_2CH_3, and the largest group off the second carbon in the double bond is $CH_2CH_2CH_3$. Since their relative placement is on the same side of the double bond, this is the cis isomer.

26.   a. $CH_3\overset{*}{-}CH_2\overset{*}{-}CH_2\overset{*}{-}CH_2-CH_3$ There are three different types of hydrogens in n-pentane (see asterisks). Thus there are three mono-chloro isomers of n-pentane (1-chloropentane, 2-chloropentane and 3-chloropentane).

        b. $CH_3\overset{*}{-}\underset{\underset{CH_3}{|}}{CH}\overset{*}{-}CH_2\overset{*}{-}CH_3^{*}$ There are four different types of hydrogens in 2-methylbutane, so four monochloro isomers of 2-methylbutane are possible.

        c. $CH_3\overset{*}{-}\underset{\underset{CH_3}{|}}{CH}\overset{*}{-}CH_2\overset{*}{-}\underset{\underset{CH_3}{|}}{CH}-CH_3$ There are three different types of hydrogens, so three monochloro isomers are possible.

        d. There are four different types of hydrogens, so four monochloro isomers are possible.

27.   a.

ortho   meta   para

b.   There are three trichlorobenzenes (1,2,3-trichlorobenzene, 1,2,4-trichlorobenzene and 1,3,5-trichlorobenzene).

c.   The meta isomer will be very difficult to synthesize.

d.   1,3,5-trichlorobenzene will be the most difficult to synthesize since all Cl groups are meta to each other in this compound.

28.

There are many possibilities for isomers. Any structure with four chlorines in any four of the numbered positions would be an isomer, i.e., 1,2,3,4-tetrachloro-dibenzo-p-dioxin is a possible isomer.

Functional Groups

29.   Reference Table 22.4 for the common functional groups.

a.   ketone   b.   aldehyde   c.   carboxylic acid   d.   amine

30.

a.

b.

c.

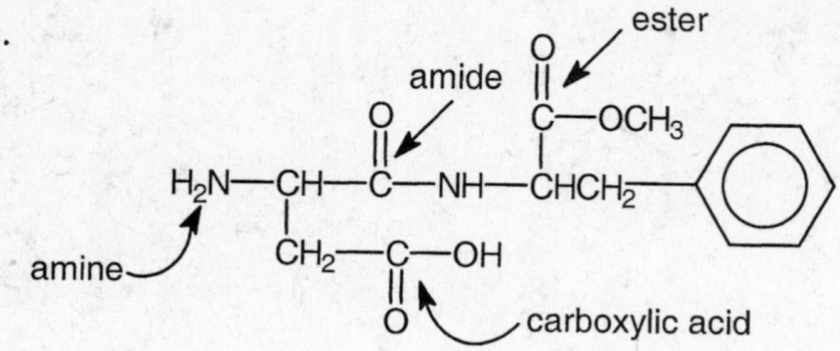

Note: the amide functional group $\left(\text{R}-\overset{\overset{\displaystyle O}{\|}}{\text{C}}-\overset{\overset{\displaystyle R'}{|}}{\text{N}}-\text{R''}\right)$ is mentioned in Section 22.6 of the text. We point it out for your information.

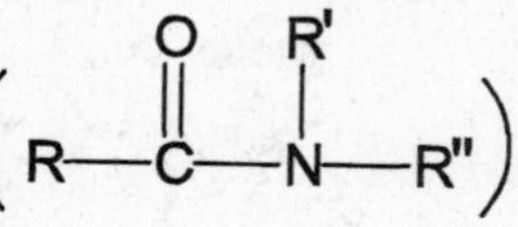

31.   a.

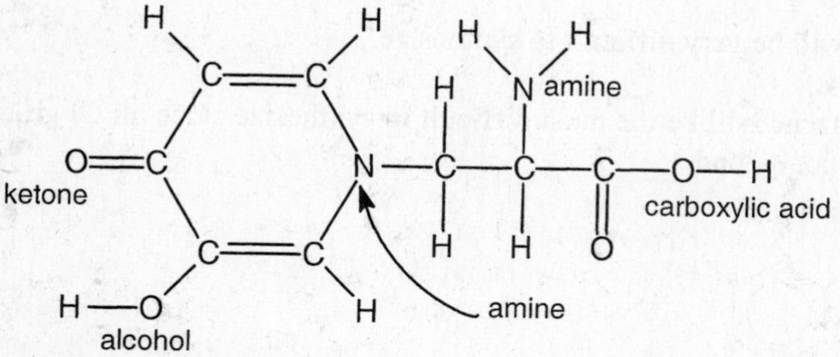

b.   5 carbons in ring and the carbon in $-CO_2H$: sp^2; the other two carbons: sp^3

c.   24 sigma bonds; 4 pi bonds

32.   Hydrogen atoms are usually omitted from ring structures. In organic compounds, the carbon atoms generally form four bonds. With this in mind, the following structure has the missing hydrogen atoms included in order to give each carbon atom the four bond requirement.

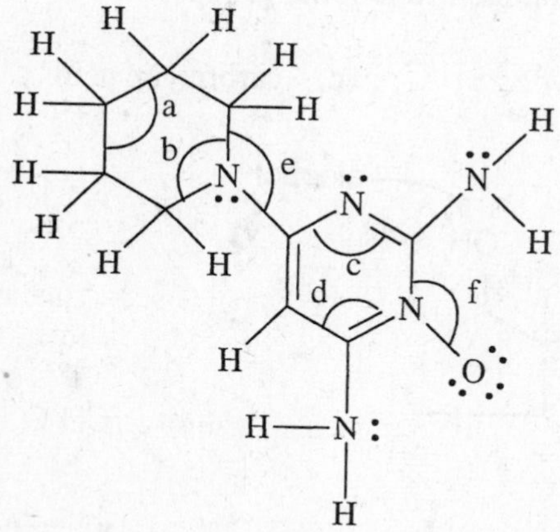

a.   Minoxidil would be more soluble in acidic solution. The nitrogens with lone pairs can be protonated, forming a water soluble cation.

b. The two nitrogen atoms in the ring with the double bonds are sp^2 hybridized. The other three N atoms are sp^3 hybridized.

c. The five carbon atoms in the ring with one nitrogen are all sp^3 hybridized. The four carbon atoms in the other ring with the double bonds are all sp^2 hybridized.

d. Angles a, b, and e $\approx 109.5°$; Angles c, d, and f $\approx 120°$

e. 31 sigma bonds

f. 3 pi bonds

33.   a. 3-chloro-1-butanol: Since the carbon containing the OH group is bonded to just 1 other carbon (1 R group), then this is a primary alcohol.

b. 3-methyl-3-hexanol; Since the carbon containing the OH group is bonded to three other carbons (3 R groups), then this is a tertrary alcohol

c. 2-methylcyclopentanol; Secondary alcohol (2 R groups bonded to carbon containing the OH group); Note: In ring compounds, the alcohol group is assumed to be bonded to C_1 so the number designation is commonly omitted for the alcohol group.

34.

a.

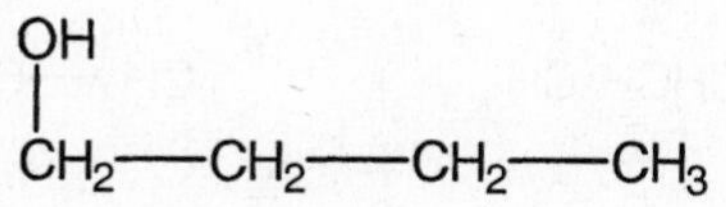

$$\overset{\overset{\displaystyle OH}{|}}{CH_2}-CH_2-CH_2-CH_3 \qquad\qquad \text{primary alcohol}$$

b.

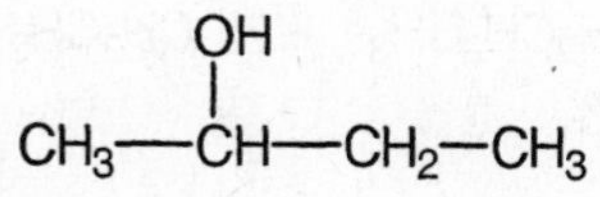

$$CH_3-\overset{\overset{\displaystyle OH}{|}}{CH}-CH_2-CH_3 \qquad\qquad \text{secondary alcohol}$$

c.

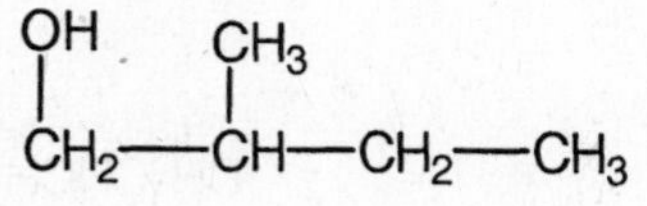

$$\overset{\overset{\displaystyle OH}{|}}{CH_2}-\overset{\overset{\displaystyle CH_3}{|}}{CH}-CH_2-CH_3 \qquad\qquad \text{primary alcohol}$$

d.

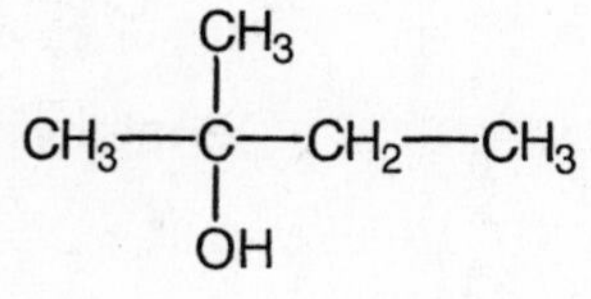

$$CH_3-\overset{\overset{\displaystyle CH_3}{|}}{\underset{\underset{\displaystyle OH}{|}}{C}}-CH_2-CH_3 \qquad\qquad \text{tertiary alcohol}$$

35.

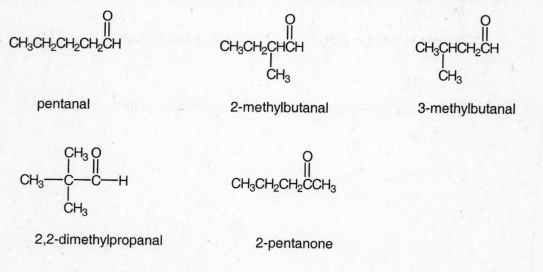

OH
CH₃CH₂CH₂CH₂CH₂

1-pentanol

OH
CH₃CH₂CH₂CHCH₃

2-pentanol

OH
CH₃CH₂CHCH₂CH₃

3-pentanol

OH
CH₃CH₂CHCH₂
            |
            CH₃

2-methyl-1-butanol

OH
CH₃CHCH₂CH₂
     |
     CH₃

3-methyl-1-butanol

OH
CH₃CH₂CCH₃
          |
          CH₃

2-methyl-2-butanol

OH
CH₃CHCHCH₃
     |
     CH₃

3-methyl-2-butanol

CH₃ OH
      | |
CH₃—C—CH₂
      |
      CH₃

2,2-dimethyl-1-propanol

There are six isomeric ethers with formula $C_5H_{12}O$. The structures follow.

CH₃—O—CH₂CH₂CH₂CH₃

CH₃
 |
CH₃—O—CHCH₂CH₃

CH₃
 |
CH₃—O—CH₂CHCH₃

CH₃
 |
CH₃—O—C—CH₃
 |
CH₃

CH₃CH₂—O—CH₂CH₂CH₃

CH₃
 |
CH₃CH₂—O—CH
 |
CH₃

36.   There are four aldehydes and three ketones with formula $C_5H_{10}O$. The structures follow.

O
‖
CH₃CH₂CH₂CH₂CH

pentanal

O
‖
CH₃CH₂CHCH
        |
        CH₃

2-methylbutanal

O
‖
CH₃CHCH₂CH
     |
     CH₃

3-methylbutanal

CH₃ O
 | ‖
CH₃—C—C—H
 |
CH₃

2,2-dimethylpropanal

O
‖
CH₃CH₂CH₂CCH₃

2-pentanone

$$CH_3CH_2\overset{\overset{\displaystyle O}{\|}}{C}CH_2CH_3$$

$$CH_3\overset{\overset{\displaystyle O}{\|}}{\underset{\underset{\displaystyle CH_3}{|}}{CH}}CCH_3$$

3-pentanone   3-methyl-2-butanone

37.   a. 4,5-dichloro-3-hexanone   b. 2,3-dimethylpentanal

      c. 3-methylbenzaldehyde or m-methylbenzaldehyde

38.   a. 4-chlorobenzoic acid or p-chlorobenzoic acid

      b. 3-ethyl-2-methylhexanoic acid

      c. methanoic acid (common name = formic acid)

39.
      a.   trans-2-butene:
$$\underset{H}{\overset{CH_3}{}}C=C\underset{CH_3}{\overset{H}{}}$$
, formula = C_4H_8

      or

      b.   propanoic acid: $CH_3CH_2\overset{\overset{\displaystyle O}{\|}}{C}-OH,$ formula = $C_3H_6O_2$

$$CH_3\overset{\overset{\displaystyle O}{\|}}{C}-O-CH_3$$ or $$H\overset{\overset{\displaystyle O}{\|}}{C}-O-CH_2CH_3$$

      c.   butanal: $CH_3CH_2CH_2\overset{\overset{\displaystyle O}{\|}}{C}H,$ formula = C_4H_8O

$$CH_3CH_2\overset{\overset{\displaystyle O}{\|}}{C}CH_3$$

d.　butylamine:　$CH_3CH_2CH_2CH_2NH_2$,　formula = $C_4H_{11}N$:

A secondary amine has two R groups bonded to N.

$$CH_3—\underset{\underset{CH_2CH_2CH_3}{|}}{N}—H \qquad \text{or} \qquad CH_3—\underset{\underset{CH_3CHCH_3}{|}}{N}—H \qquad \text{or} \qquad CH_3CH_2—\underset{\underset{CH_2CH_3}{|}}{N}—H$$

e.　A tertiary amine has three R groups bonded to N.　(See answer d for structure of butylamine.)

$$CH_3—\underset{\underset{CH_2CH_3}{|}}{N}—CH_3$$

f.　2-methyl-2-propanol:　$CH_3\underset{\underset{OH}{|}}{\overset{\overset{CH_3}{|}}{C}}CH_3$,　formula = $C_4H_{10}O$

$$CH_3—O—CH_2CH_2CH_3 \quad \text{or} \quad CH_3—O—\underset{\underset{CH_3}{|}}{\overset{\overset{CH_3}{|}}{CH}} \quad \text{or} \quad CH_3CH_2—O—CH_2CH_3$$

g.　A secondary alcohol has two R groups attached to the carbon bonded to the OH group. (See answer f for the structure of 2-methyl-2-propanol.)

$$CH_3\underset{\underset{OH}{|}}{\overset{\overset{OH}{|}}{CH}}CH_2CH_3$$

40.　$$\underset{13}{HC}\!\equiv\!\underset{12}{C}—\underset{11}{C}\!\equiv\!\underset{10}{C}—\underset{9}{CH}\!=\!\underset{8}{C}\!=\!\underset{7}{CH}—\underset{6}{CH}\!=\!\underset{5}{CH}—\underset{4}{CH}\!=\!\underset{3}{CH}—\underset{2}{CH_2}—\underset{1}{\overset{\overset{O}{\|}}{C}}—OH$$

Reactions of Organic Compounds

41.　substitution:　An atom or group is replaced by another atom or group.

e.g., H in benzene is replaced by Cl.　$C_6H_6 + Cl_2 \xrightarrow{\text{catalyst}} C_6H_5Cl + HCl$

addition:　Atoms or groups are added to a molecule.

e.g., Cl_2 adds to ethene.　$CH_2\!=\!CH_2 + Cl_2 \rightarrow CH_2Cl - CH_2Cl$

42.   a.   Only one monochlorination product can form (1-chloro-2,2-dimethylpropane) the other
           possibilities differ from this compound by a simple rotation so they are not different com-
           pounds.

$$CH_3-\overset{\overset{\displaystyle CH_3}{|}}{\underset{\underset{\displaystyle CH_3}{|}}{C}}-CH_2Cl$$

      b.   Three different monochlorination products are possible (ignoring cis-trans isomers).

      c.   Two different monochlorination products are possible (the other possibilities differ by a
           simple rotation of one of these two compounds).

43.

      a. $CH_3\overset{\overset{\displaystyle H}{|}}{C}H-\overset{\overset{\displaystyle H}{|}}{C}HCH_3$ b.

      c.   —Cl + HCl

      d. $C_4H_8(g) + 6\ O_2(g) \rightarrow 4\ CO_2(g) + 4\ H_2O(g)$

44.   a.   The two possible products for the addition of HOH to this alkene are:

           major product   minor product

We would get both products in this reaction. Using the rule given in the problem, the first compound listed is the major product. In the reactant, the terminal carbon has more hydrogens bonded to it (2 vs. 1) so H forms a bond to this carbon and OH forms a bond to the other carbon in the double bond for the major product. We will only list the major product for the remaining parts to this problem.

b.
$$CH_3CH_2\overset{\overset{\displaystyle Br}{|}}{C}H\text{—}\overset{\overset{\displaystyle H}{|}}{C}H_2$$

c.
$$CH_3CH_2\overset{\overset{\displaystyle Br}{|}}{\underset{\underset{\displaystyle Br}{|}}{C}}\text{—}\overset{\overset{\displaystyle H}{|}}{\underset{\underset{\displaystyle H}{|}}{C}H}$$

d.

（cyclopentane ring with CH$_3$, OH, and H substituents）

e.
$$CH_3CH_2\text{—}\overset{\overset{\displaystyle Cl}{|}}{\underset{\underset{\displaystyle CH_3}{|}}{C}}\text{—}\overset{\overset{\displaystyle H}{|}}{\underset{\underset{\displaystyle H}{|}}{C}}\text{—}CH_3$$

45.   Primary alcohols (a, d and f) are oxidized to aldehydes which can be oxidized further to carboxylic acids. Secondary alcohols (b, e and f) are oxidized to ketones, and tertiary alcohols (c and f) do not undergo this type of oxidation reaction. Note that compound f contains a primary, secondary and tertiary alcohol. For the primary alcohols (a, d and f), we listed both the aldehyde and the carboxylic acid as possible products.

a.
$$H\overset{\overset{\displaystyle O}{\|}}{\text{—}C}\text{—}CH_2\overset{}{\underset{\underset{\displaystyle CH_3}{|}}{C}}HCH_3 \quad + \quad HO\overset{\overset{\displaystyle O}{\|}}{\text{—}C}\text{—}CH_2\overset{}{\underset{\underset{\displaystyle CH_3}{|}}{C}}HCH_3$$

b.
$$CH_3\text{—}\overset{\overset{\displaystyle O}{\|}}{C}\text{—}\overset{}{\underset{\underset{\displaystyle CH_3}{|}}{C}}HCH_3$$

c.   No reaction

d.

（benzene ring）$\overset{\overset{\displaystyle O}{\|}}{C}$—H + （benzene ring）$\overset{\overset{\displaystyle O}{\|}}{C}$—OH

e.

（cyclohexanone ring with —CH$_3$ substituent）

f.

（cyclohexanone ring with OH, CH$_3$, and C—H aldehyde group） + （cyclohexanone ring with OH, CH$_3$, and C—OH carboxylic acid group）

46.   **a.**

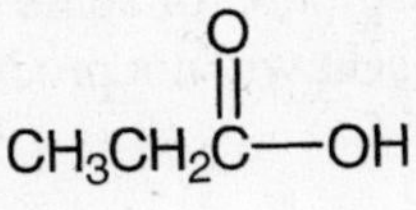

$$CH_3CH_2\overset{\displaystyle O}{\overset{\displaystyle \|}{C}}—OH$$

b.

$$CH_3CH_2\overset{\displaystyle CH_3}{\underset{\displaystyle CH_3}{CH}}—\overset{\displaystyle O}{\overset{\displaystyle \|}{C}}—OH$$

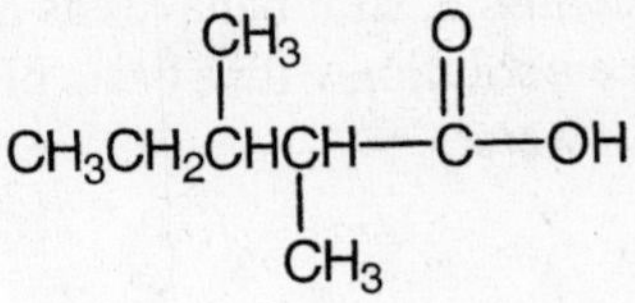

c.

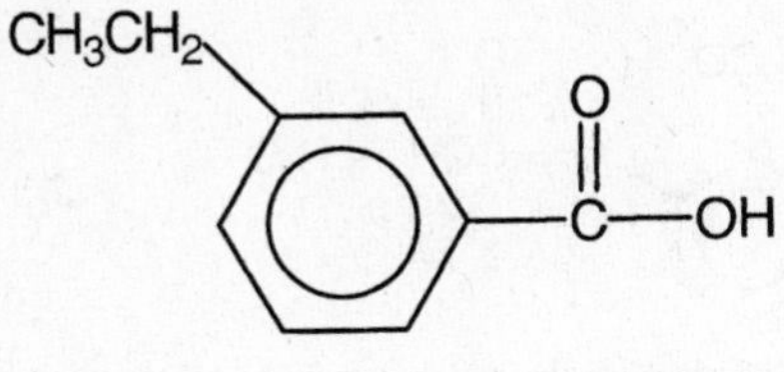

47.   **a.** $CH_3CH=CH_2 + Br_2 \rightarrow CH_3CHBrCH_2Br$ (Addition reaction of Br_2 with propene)

b.

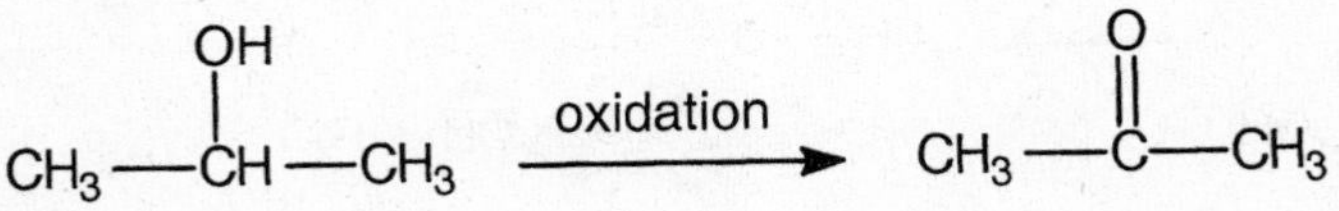

$$CH_3—\overset{\displaystyle OH}{\underset{\displaystyle |}{CH}}—CH_3 \xrightarrow{\text{oxidation}} CH_3—\overset{\displaystyle O}{\overset{\displaystyle \|}{C}}—CH_3$$

Oxidation of 2-propanol yields acetone (2-propanone).

c.

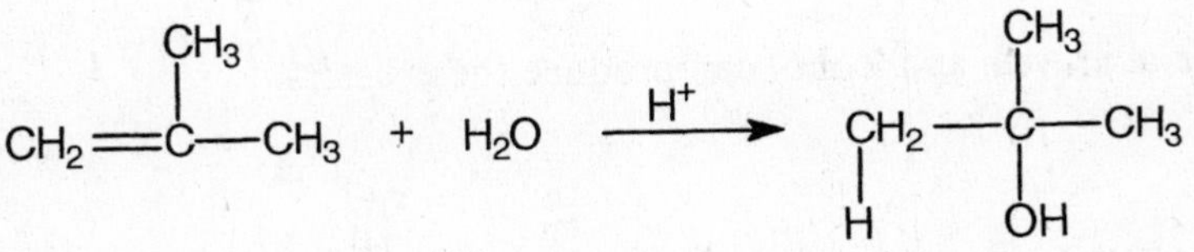

$$CH_2=\overset{\displaystyle CH_3}{\underset{\displaystyle |}{C}}—CH_3 + H_2O \xrightarrow{H^+} \overset{\displaystyle CH_3}{CH_2—\underset{\displaystyle |}{\overset{\displaystyle |}{C}}—CH_3}$$

Addition of H_2O to 2-methylpropene would yield tert-butyl alcohol (2-methyl-2-propanol) as the major product.

d. $CH_3CH_2CH_2OH \xrightarrow{KMnO_4} CH_3CH_2\overset{\displaystyle O}{\overset{\displaystyle \|}{C}}—OH$

Oxidation of 1-propanol would eventually yield propanoic acid. Propanal is produced first in this reaction and is then oxidized to propanoic acid.

48.   **a.** $CH_2=CHCH_2CH_3$ will react with Cl_2 without any catalyst present. $CH_3CH_2CH_2CH_3$ only reacts with Cl_2 when ultraviolet light is present.

b. $CH_3CH_2CH_2\overset{\displaystyle O}{\overset{\displaystyle \|}{C}}OH$ is an acid, so this compound should react positively with a base like $NaHCO_3$. The other compound is a ketone, which will not react with a base.

c. $CH_3CH_2CH_2OH$ can be oxidized with $KMnO_4$ to propanoic acid. 2-propanone (a ketone) will not react with $KMnO_4$.

d. $CH_3CH_2NH_2$ is an amine, so it behaves as a base in water. Dissolution of some of this base in water will produce a solution with a basic pH. The ether, CH_3OCH_3, will not produce a basic pH when dissolved in water.

49.

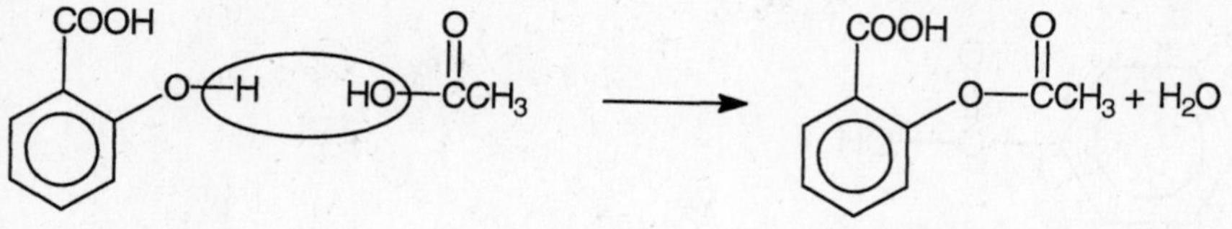

acetylsalicylic acid (aspirin)

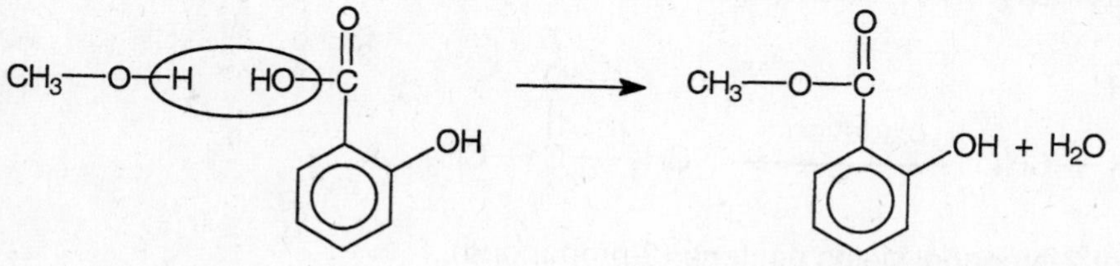

methyl salicylate

50. Reaction of a carboxylic acid with an alcohol can produce these esters.

a. $CH_3C(=O)—OH + HOCH_2(CH_2)_6CH_3 \longrightarrow CH_3C(=O)—O—CH_2(CH_2)_6CH_3 + H_2O$

ethanoic acid (acetic acid); octanol; n-octylacetate

b. $CH_3CH_2C(=O)—OH + HOCH_2(CH_2)_4CH_3 \longrightarrow CH_3CH_2C(=O)—O—CH_2(CH_2)_4CH_3 + H_2O$

propanoic acid; hexanol

Polymers

51. a. addition polymer: Polymer that forms by adding monomer units together (usually by reacting double bonds). Teflon, polyvinyl chloride and polyethylene are examples of addition polymers.

b. condensation polymer: Polymer that forms when two monomers combine by eliminating a small molecule (usually H_2O or HCl). Nylon and Dacron are examples of condensation polymers.

c. copolymer: Polymer formed from more than one type of monomer. Nylon and Dacron are also copolymers.

52.   a.   repeating unit:

$$\left(\!-CHF-CH_2\!-\right)_n$$ monomer: $CHF=CH_2$

b.   repeating unit:

$$\left(\!-OCH_2CH_2\overset{\overset{\displaystyle O}{\|}}{C}\!-\right)_n$$ monomer: $HO-CH_2CH_2-CO_2H$

c.   repeating unit:

$$\left(\!-\overset{\overset{\displaystyle H}{|}}{N}-CH_2CH_2-\overset{\overset{\displaystyle H}{|}}{N}-\overset{\overset{\displaystyle O}{\|}}{C}-CH_2CH_2-\overset{\overset{\displaystyle O}{\|}}{C}\!-\right)_n$$ copolymer of: $H_2NCH_2CH_2NH_2$
                                                                      and $HO_2CCH_2CH_2CO_2H$

d.   monomer: e.   monomer:

$CH_3-C=CH_2$ (with phenyl ring attached to C) $CH=CH$ (with phenyl ring and CH_3)

f.   copolymer of:

$HOCH_2-$(cyclohexane ring)$-CH_2OH$ and HO_2C-(benzene ring)$-CO_2H$

Addition polymers: a, d, and e; Condensation polymers: b, c and f; Copolymers: c and f

53.   The backbone of the polymer contains only carbon atoms, which indicates that Kel-F is an addition polymer. The smallest repeating unit of the polymer and the monomer used to produce this polymer are:

$$\left(\!-\overset{\overset{\displaystyle F}{|}}{\underset{\underset{\displaystyle Cl}{|}}{C}}-\overset{\overset{\displaystyle F}{|}}{\underset{\underset{\displaystyle F}{|}}{C}}\!-\right)_n$$ $$\overset{\overset{\displaystyle F}{|}}{\underset{\underset{\displaystyle Cl}{|}}{C}}=\overset{\overset{\displaystyle F}{|}}{\underset{\underset{\displaystyle F}{|}}{C}}$$

54.   The monomers for nitrile are $CH_2=CHCN$ (acrylonitrile) and $CH_2=CHCH=CH_2$ (butadiene). The structure of polymer nitrile is:

$$\left(\!-CH_2-\underset{\underset{\underset{\displaystyle N}{\displaystyle \parallel}}{\underset{\displaystyle C}{|}}}{CH}-CH_2-CH=CH-CH_2\!-\right)_n$$

55.   a.

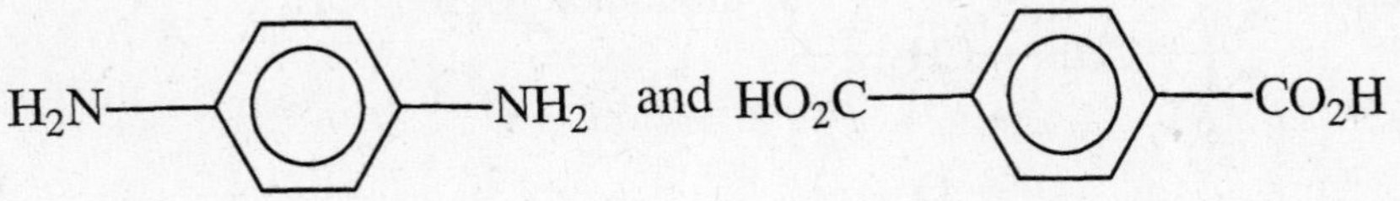

b.   Repeating unit:

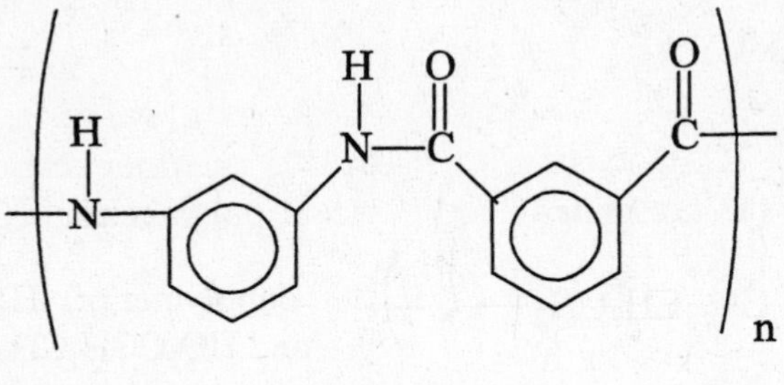

The two polymers differ in the substitution pattern on the benzene rings. The Kevlar chain is straighter and there is more efficient hydrogen bonding between Kevlar chains than between Nomex chains.

56.   This condensation polymer forms by elimination of water. The ester functional group repeats hence the term polyester.

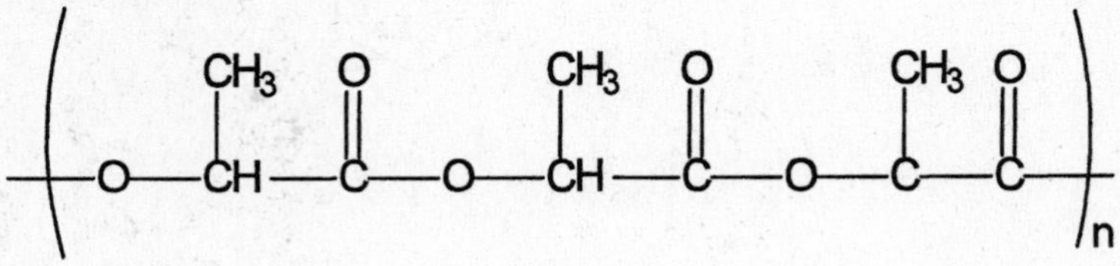

57.

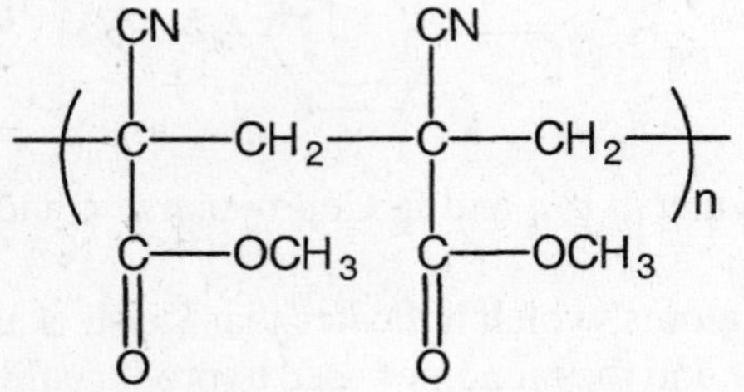

Super glue is an addition polymer formed by reaction of the $C\!=\!C$ bond in methyl cyanoacrylate.

58.   a.   2-methyl-1,3-butadiene

b.

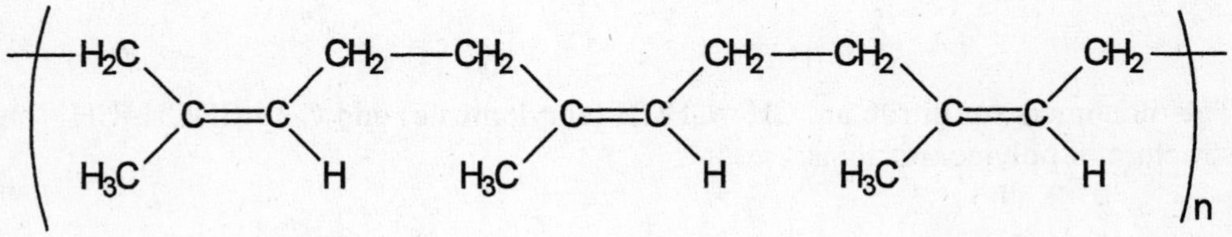

cis-polyisoprene (natural rubber)

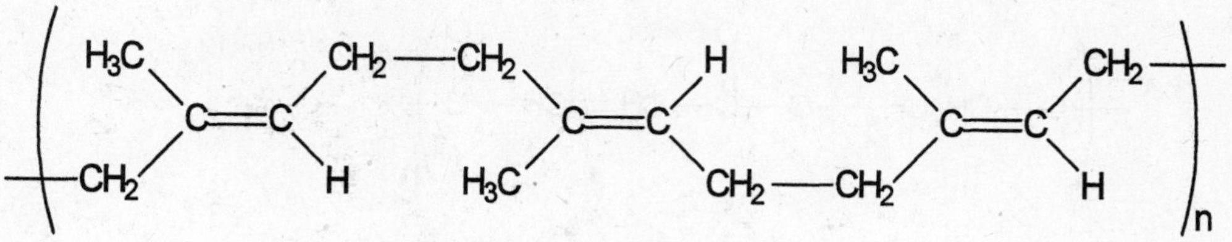

trans-polyisoprene (gutta percha)

59.   Divinylbenzene is a crosslinking agent. Divinylbenzene has two reactive double bonds which are both used when divinylbenzene inserts itself into two adjacent polymer chains. The chains cannot move past each other because the crosslinks bond adjacent polymer chains together making the polymer more rigid.

60.   This is a condensation polymer where two molecules of H_2O form when the monomers link together.

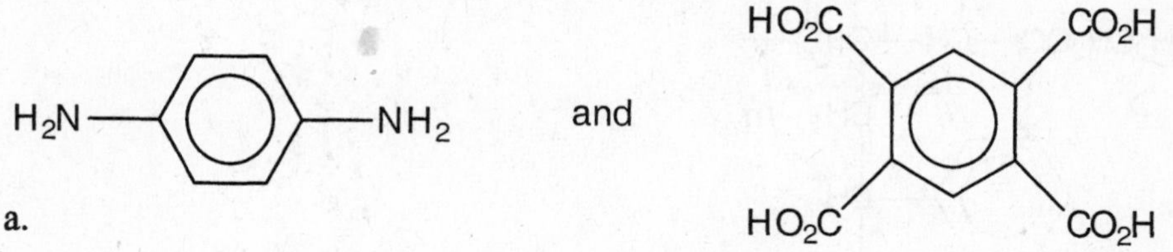

and

61.   a.

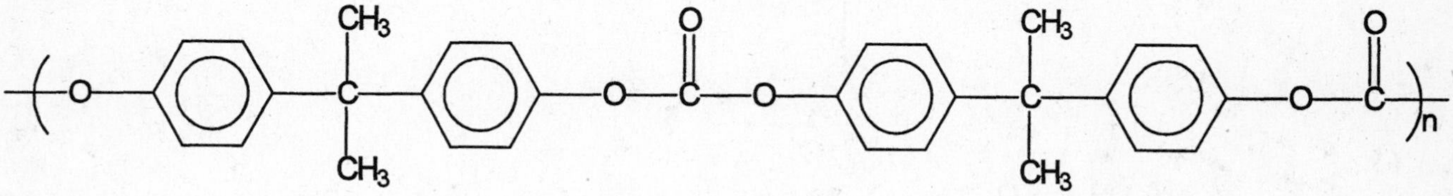

      b.   Condensation; HCl is eliminated when the polymer bonds form.

62.   Polyvinyl chloride contains some polar C–Cl bonds as compared to only relatively nonpolar C–H bonds in polyethylene. The stronger intermolecular forces would be found in polyvinyl chloride since there are dipole-dipole forces present in PVC that are not present in polyethylene.

63.   Polyacrylonitrile:

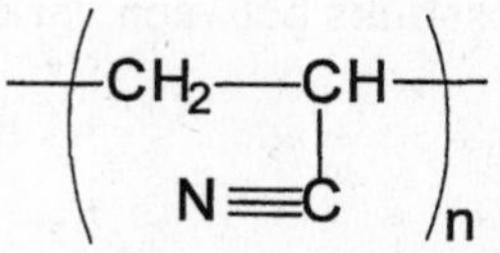

The CN triple bond is very strong and will not easily break in the combustion process. A likely combustion product is the toxic gas hydrogen cyanide, HCN(g).

64.   a.

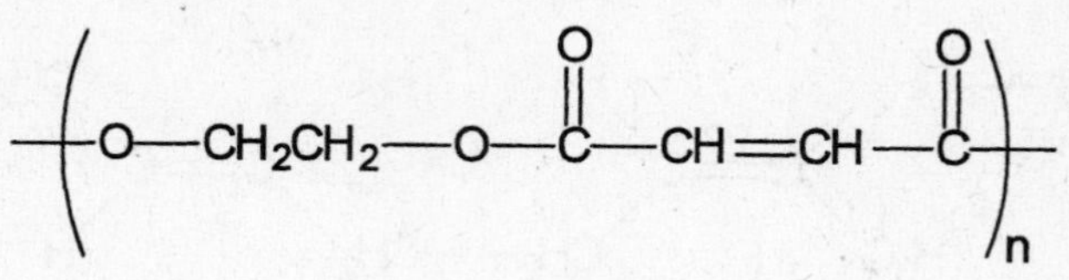

$$\left(-O-CH_2CH_2-O-\overset{\overset{\textstyle O}{\|}}{C}-CH=CH-\overset{\overset{\textstyle O}{\|}}{C}-\right)_n$$

b.

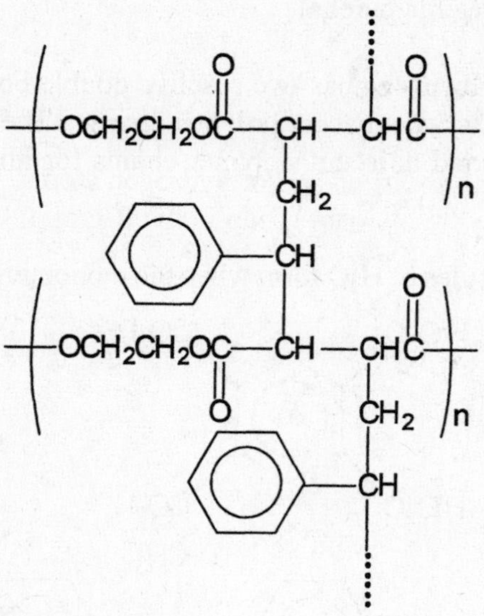

$$\left(-OCH_2CH_2O\overset{\overset{\textstyle O}{\|}}{C}-CH-\overset{\overset{\textstyle O}{\|}}{CHC}-\right)_n$$

(structure with CH_2 group connected to a benzene ring via CH)

$$\left(-OCH_2CH_2O\overset{}{C}-CH-\overset{\overset{\textstyle O}{\|}}{CHC}-\right)_n$$

(structure with CH_2 group connected to a benzene ring via CH)

65.

$$\left(-OCH_2\overset{\overset{\textstyle OH}{|}}{C}HCH_2O\overset{\overset{\textstyle O}{\|}}{C}-\bigcirc-\overset{\overset{\textstyle O}{\|}}{C}O\overset{\overset{\textstyle CH_2OH}{|}}{C}HCH_2O\overset{\overset{\textstyle O}{\|}}{C}-\bigcirc-\overset{\overset{\textstyle O}{\|}}{C}-\right)_n$$

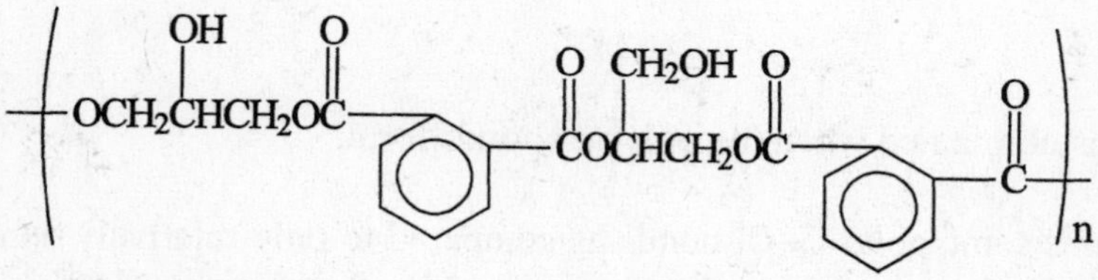

Two linkages are possible with glycerol. A possible repeating unit with both types of linkages is shown above. With either linkage, there are free OH groups on the polymer chains. These can react with the acid groups of phthalic acid to form crosslinks between various polymer chains.

Natural Polymers

66.   Primary: The amino acid sequence in the protein. Covalent bonds (peptide linkages) are the forces that link the various amino acids together in the primary structure.

Secondary: Includes structural features known as α-helix or pleated sheet. Both are maintained mostly through hydrogen bonding interactions.

Tertiary: The overall shape of a protein, long and narrow or globular. Maintained by hydrophobic and hydrophilic interactions, such as salt linkages, hydrogen bonds, disulfide linkages and dispersion forces.

67.   Denaturation changes the three-dimensional structure of a protein. Once the structure is affected, the function of the protein will also be affected.

68.   All amino acids can act as both a weak acid and a weak base; this is the requirement for a buffer. The weak acid is the carboxylic end of the amino acid and the weak base is the amine end of the amino acid.

69.   a.   Serine, tyrosine and threonine contain the -OH functional group in the R group.

       b.   Aspartic acid and glutamic acid contain the -COOH functional group in the R group.

       c.   An amine group has a nitrogen bonded to other carbon and/or hydrogen atoms. Histidine, lysine, arginine and tryptophan contain the amine functional group in the R group.

       d.   The amide functional group is:

$$R-\overset{\overset{\displaystyle O}{\|}}{C}-\overset{\overset{\displaystyle R'}{|}}{N}-R''$$

            This functional group is formed when individual amino acids bond together to form the peptide linkage. Glutamine and asparagine have the amide functional group in the R group.

70.   Crystalline amino acids exist as zwitterions, $^+H_3NCHRCOO^-$, which are held together by ionic forces. The ionic interparticle forces are strong. Before the temperature gets high enough to melt the solid, the amino acid decomposes.

71   a.   Aspartic acid and phenylalanine make up aspartame.

       b.   Aspartame contains the methyl ester of phenylalanine. This ester can hydrolyze to form methanol:

$$R-CO_2CH_3 + H_2O \rightleftharpoons RCO_2H + HOCH_3$$

72.

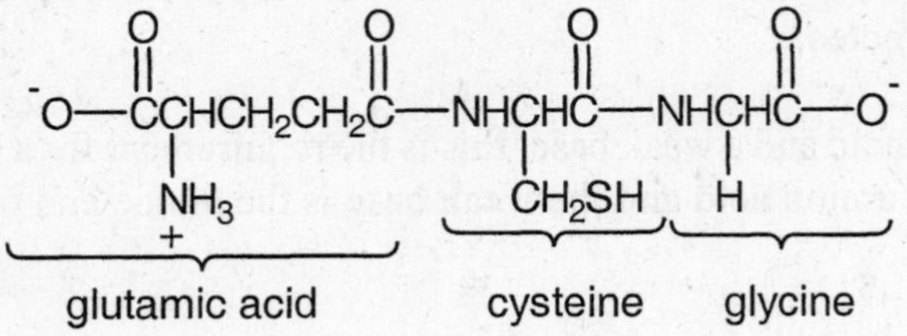

glutamic acid   cysteine   glycine

Glutamic acid, cysteine and glycine are the three amino acids in glutathione. Glutamic acid uses the -COOH functional group in the R group to bond to cysteine instead of the carboxylic acid group bonded to the α-carbon. The cysteine-glycine bond is the typical peptide linkage.

73.

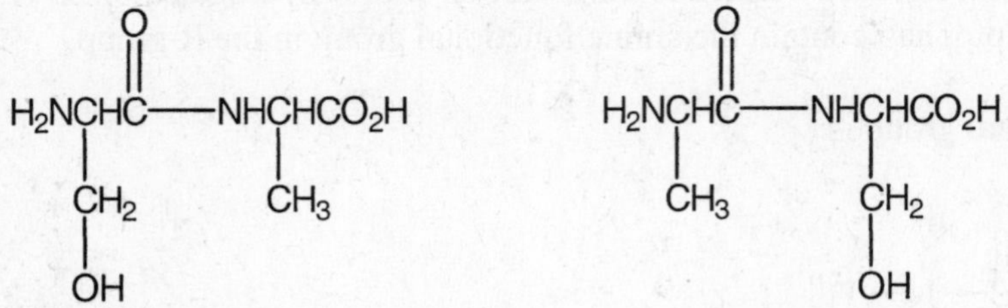

ser - ala   ala - ser

74.

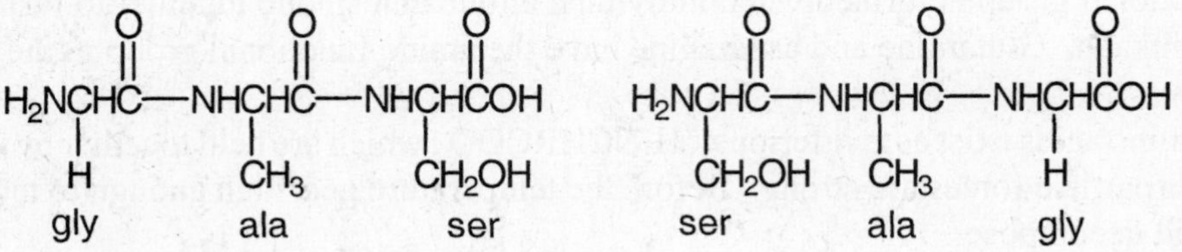

gly   ala   ser   ser   ala   gly

There are six possible tripeptides with gly, ala and ser. The other four tripeptides are gly-ser-ala, ser-gly-ala, ala-gly-ser and ala-ser-gly.

75. a. Six tetrapeptides are possible. From NH$_2$ to CO$_2$H end:

phe-phe-gly-gly, gly-gly-phe-phe, gly-phe-phe-gly,

phe-gly-gly-phe, phe-gly-phe-gly, gly-phe-gly-phe

b. Twelve tetrapeptides are possible. From NH$_2$ to CO$_2$H end:

phe-phe-gly-ala, phe-phe-ala-gly, phe-gly-phe-ala,

phe-gly-ala-phe, phe-ala-phe-gly, phe-ala-gly-phe,

gly-phe-phe-ala, gly-phe-ala-phe, gly-ala-phe-phe

ala-phe-phe-gly, ala-phe-gly-phe, ala-gly-phe-phe

76.   There are 5 possibilities for the first amino acid, 4 possibilities for the second amino acid, 3 possibilities for the third amino acid, 2 possibilities for the fourth amino acid and 1 possibility for the last amino acid. The number of possible sequences is:

$$5 \times 4 \times 3 \times 2 \times 1 = 5! = 120 \text{ different pentapeptides}$$

77.   a.   Covalent (forms a disulfide linkage)

        b.   Hydrogen bonding (need N-H or O-H bond in side chain)

        c.   Ionic (need NH_2 group on side chain of one amino acid with CO_2H group on side chain of the other amino acid)

        d.   London dispersion (need amino acids with nonpolar R groups)

78.   a.   Ionic: Need $-NH_2$ on side chain of one amino acid with CO_2H on side chain of the other amino acid. The possibilities are:.

             NH_2 on side chain = His, Lys or Arg; CO_2H on side chain = Asp or Glu

        b.   Hydrogen bonding: Need N–H or O–H bond in side chain. The hydrogen bonding interaction occurs between the X– H bond and a carbonyl group from any amino acid.

             $$X–H \cdots\cdots O = C \text{ (carbonyl group)}$$

             Ser Asn   Any amino acid
             Glu Thr
             Tyr Asp
             His Gln
             Arg Lys

        c.   Covalent: Cys – Cys (forms a disulfide linkage)

        d.   London dispersion: Need amino acids with nonpolar R groups. They are:

                Gly, Ala, Pro, Phe, Ile, Trp, Met, Leu and Val

        e.   Dipole-dipole: Need side chain with OH group. Tyr, Thr and Ser all could form this specific dipole-dipole force with each other since all contain an OH group in the side chain.

79.   Glutamic acid: $R = -CH_2CH_2CO_2H$; Valine: $R = -CH(CH_3)_2$; A polar side chain is replaced by a nonpolar side chain. This could affect the tertiary structure of hemoglobin and the ability of hemoglobin to bind oxygen.

80.   Alanine can be thought of as a diprotic acid. The first proton to leave comes from the carboxylic acid end with $K_a = 4.5 \times 10^{-3}$. The second proton to leave comes from the protonated amine end (K_a for $R–NH_3^+ = K_w/K_b = 1.0 \times 10^{-14}/7.4 \times 10^{-5} = 1.4 \times 10^{-10}$).

In 1.0 M H$^+$, both the carboxylic acid and the amine end will be protonated since H$^+$ is in excess. The protonated form of alanine is below. In 1.0 M OH$^-$, the dibasic form of alanine will be present since the excess OH$^-$ will remove all acidic protons from alanine. The dibasic form of alanine follows.

1.0 M H$^+$:

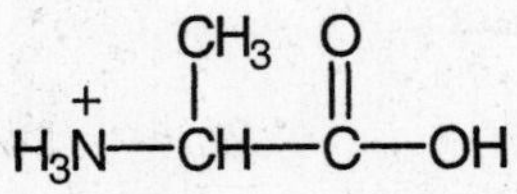

$$\overset{+}{H_3N}-\underset{\underset{CH_3}{|}}{CH}-\overset{\overset{O}{\|}}{C}-OH$$

protonated form

1.0 M OH$^-$:

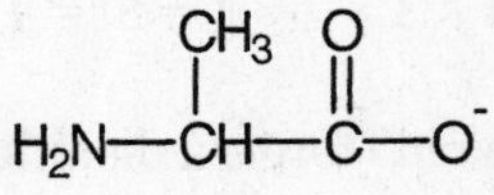

$$H_2N-\underset{\underset{CH_3}{|}}{CH}-\overset{\overset{O}{\|}}{C}-O^-$$

dibasic form

81.   Glutamic acid:

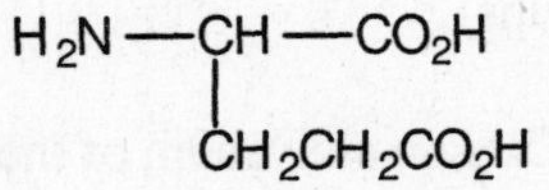

$$H_2N-\underset{\underset{CH_2CH_2CO_2H}{|}}{CH}-CO_2H$$

Monosodium glutamate:

$$H_2N-\underset{\underset{CH_2CH_2CO_2^-Na^+}{|}}{CH}-CO_2H$$

One of the two acidic protons in the carboxylic acid groups is lost to form MSG. Which proton is lost is impossible for you to predict.

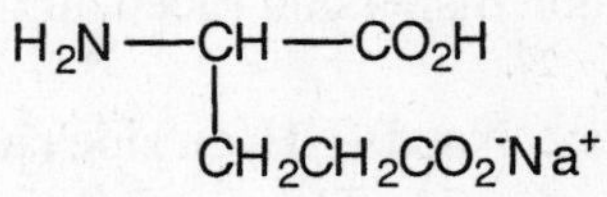

In MSG, the acidic proton from the carboxylic acid in the R group is lost, allowing formation of the ionic compound.

82.   Hydrogen bonding occurs between the -OH groups of starch and water molecules.

83.   See Figures 22.30 and 22.31 of the text for examples of the cyclization process.

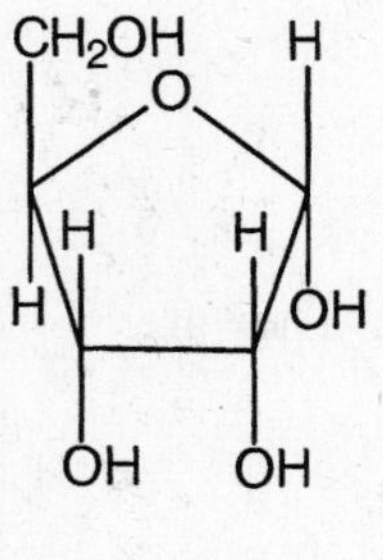

D-Ribose

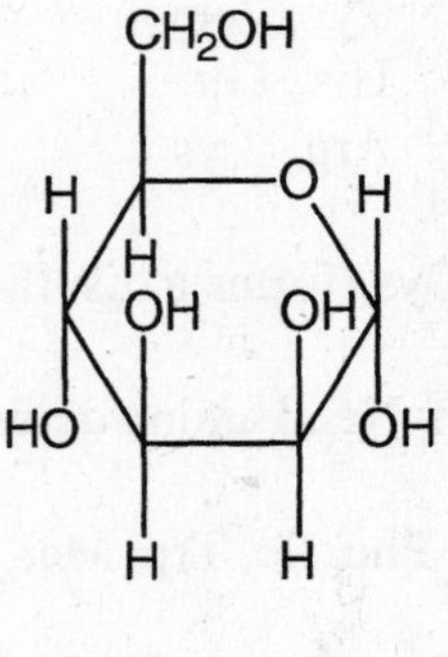

D-Mannose

84.   The chiral carbon atoms are marked with asterisks.

D-Ribose

D-Mannose

Note: A chiral carbon atom has four different substituent groups attached.

85.   The aldohexoses contain 6 carbons and the aldehyde functional group. Glucose, mannose and galactose are aldohexoses. Ribose and arabinose are aldopentoses since they contain 5 carbons with the aldehyde functional group. The ketohexose (6 carbons + ketone functional group) is fructose and the ketopentose (5 carbons + ketone functional group) is ribulose.

86.   This is an example of Le Chatelier's principle at work. For the equilibrium reactions between the various forms of glucose, reference Figure 22.31 of the text. The chemical tests involve reaction of the aldehyde group found only in the open-chain structure. As the aldehyde group is reacted, the equilibrium between the cyclic forms of glucose and the open-chain structure will shift to produce more of the open-chain structure. This process continues until either the glucose or the chemicals used in the tests run out.

87.   A disaccharide is a carbohydrate formed by bonding two monosaccharides (simple sugars) together. In sucrose, the simple sugars are glucose and fructose, and the bond formed between these two monosaccharides is called a glycoside linkage.

88.   Humans do not possess the necessary enzymes to break the β-glycosidic linkages found in cellulose. Cows, however, do possess the necessary enzymes to break down cellulose into the β-D-glucose monomers and, therefore, can derive nutrition from cellulose.

89.   The α and β forms of glucose differ in the orientation of a hydroxy group on one specific carbon in the cyclic forms (see Figure 22.31 of the text). Starch is a polymer composed of only α-D-glucose and cellulose is a polymer composed of only β-D-glucose.

90.   Optical isomers: The same formula and the same bonds, but the compounds are nonsuperimposable mirror images of each other. The key to identifying optical isomerism in organic compounds is to look for a tetrahedral carbon atom with four different substituents attached. When four different groups are bonded to a carbon atom, then a nonsuperimposable mirror image does exist.

91.   A chiral carbon has four different groups attached to it. A compound with a chiral carbon is optically active. Isoleucine and threonine contain more than the one chiral carbon atom (see asterisks).

isoleucine   threonine

92.   There is no chiral carbon atom in glycine since it contains no carbon atoms with four different groups bonded to it.

93.   Only one of the isomers is optically active. The chiral carbon in this optically active isomer is marked with an asterisk.

94.

The compound has four chiral carbon atoms (see asterisks). The fourth group bonded to the three chiral carbon atoms in the ring is a hydrogen atom.

95.   They all contain nitrogen atoms with lone pairs of electrons.

96.   DNA: Deoxyribose sugar; double stranded; Adenine, cytosine, guanine and thymine are the bases.

       RNA: Ribose sugar; single stranded; Adenine, cytosine, guanine and uracil are the bases.

       When the two strands of a DNA molecule are compared, it is found that a given base in one strand is always found paired with a particular base in the other strand. Because of the shapes and side atoms along the rings of the nitrogen bases, only certain pairs are able to approach and hydrogen bond with each other in the double helix. Adenine is always found paired with thymine; cytosine is always found paired with guanine. When a DNA helix unwinds for replication during cell division, only the appropriate complementary bases are able to approach and bond to the nitrogen bases of each strand.

For example, for a guanine-cytosine pair in the original DNA, when the two strands separate, only a new cytosine molecule can approach and bond to the original guanine, and only a new guanine molecule can approach and bond to the original cytosine.

97.   The complimentary base pairs in DNA are cytosine (C) and guanine (G), and thymine (T) and adenine (A). The complimentary sequence is: C-C-A-G-A-T-A-T-G

98.   For each letter, there are 4 choices: A, T, G, or C. Hence, the total number of codons is $4 \times 4 \times 4 = 64$.

99.   Uracil will hydrogen bond to adenine.

100. The tautomer could hydrogen bond to guanine, forming a G–T base pair instead of A–T.

101. Base pair:

RNA	DNA
A	T
G	C
C	G
U	A

a. Glu: CTT, CTC   Val: CAA, CAG, CAT, CAC

    Met: TAC   Trp: ACC

    Phe: AAA, AAG   Asp: CTA, CTG

b.   DNA sequence for trp-glu-phe-met:

ACC - CTT - AAA - TAC
or   or
CTC   AAG

c.   Due to glu and phe, there is a possibility of four different DNA sequences. They are:

ACC - CTT - AAA - TAC or ACC - CTC - AAA - TAC or

ACC - CTT - AAG - TAC or ACC - CTC - AAG - TAC

d . T—A—C—C—T—G—A—A—G
     ⏟   ⏟   ⏟
     met   asp   phe

e.   TAC - CTA - AAG; TAC - CTA - AAA; TAC - CTG - AAA

102.   In sickle cell anemia, glutamic acid is replaced by valine. DNA codons: Glu: CTT, CTC; Val: CAA, CAG, CAT, CAC; Replacing a T with an A in the code for Glu will code for Val.

CTT → CAT or CTC → CAC
Glu   Val   Glu   Val

103.   A deletion may change the entire code for a protein, thus giving an entirely different sequence of amino acids. A substitution will change only one single amino acid in a protein.

104.   The number of approximate base pairs in a DNA molecule is:

$$\frac{4.5 \times 10^9 \text{ g/mol}}{600 \text{ g/mol}} = 8 \times 10^6 \text{ base pairs}$$

The approximate number of complete turns in a DNA molecule is:

$$8 \times 10^6 \text{ base pairs} \times \frac{0.34 \text{ nm}}{\text{base pair}} \times \frac{1 \text{ turn}}{3.4 \text{ nm}} = 8 \times 10^5 \text{ turns}$$

Additional Exercises

105. $CH_3CH_2CH_2CH_2CH_2CH_2CH_2COOH + OH^- \rightarrow CH_3{-}(CH_2)_6{-}COO^- + H_2O$; Octanoic acid is more soluble in 1 M NaOH. Added OH^- will remove the acidic proton from octanoic acid, creating a charged species. As is the case with any substance with an overall charge, solubility in water increases. When morphine is reacted with H^+, the amine group is protonated creating a positive charge on morphine $(R_3N + H^+ \rightarrow R_3NH)$. By treating morphine with HCl, an ionic compound results that is more soluble in water and in the bloodstream than is the neutral covalent form of morphine.

106.

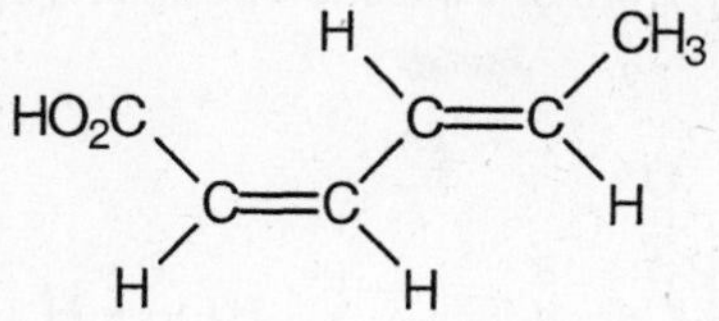

cis-2-trans-4-hexadienoic acid

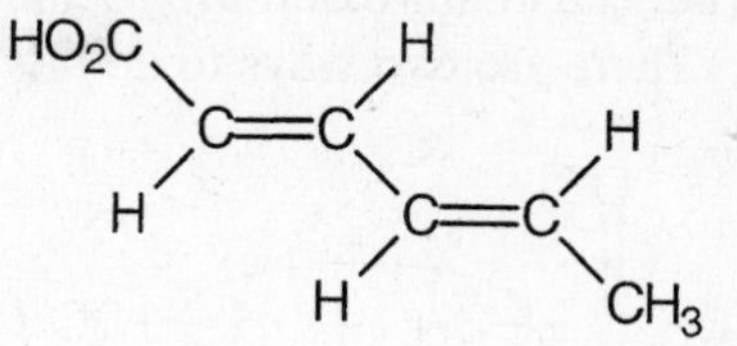

trans-2-trans-4-hexadienoic acid

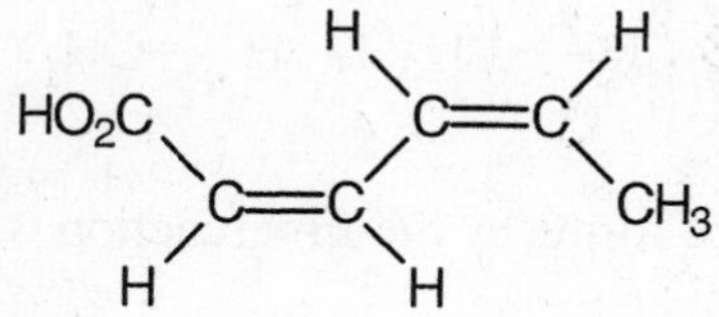

cis-2-cis-4-hexadienoic acid

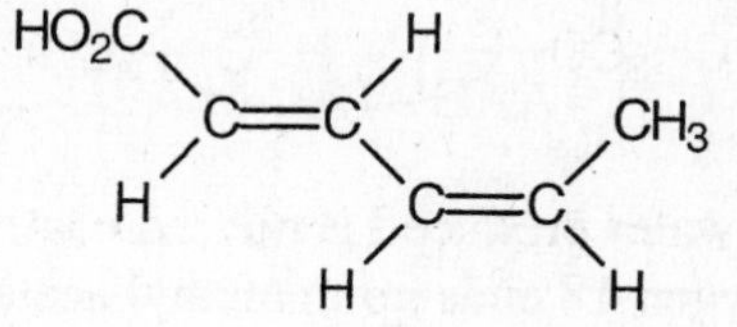

trans-2-cis-4-hexadienoic acid

107.

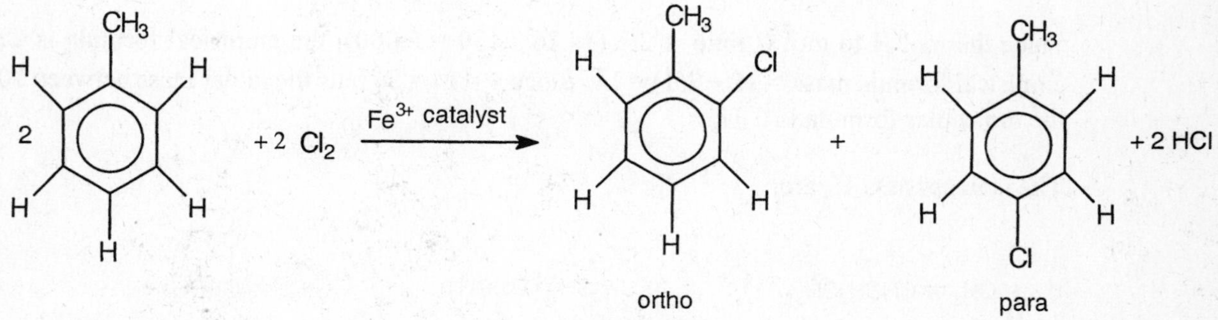

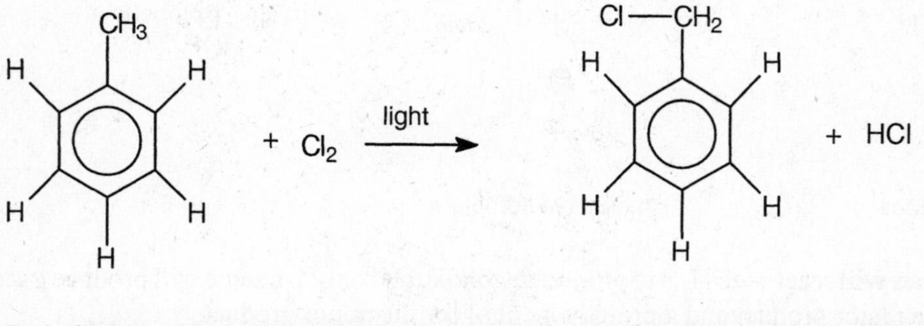

To substitute for the benzene ring hydrogens, an iron(III) catalyst must be present. Without this special iron catalyst, the benzene ring hydrogens are unreactive. To substitute for an alkane hydrogen, specific wavelengths of light must be present. For toluene, the light catalyzed reaction substitutes a chlorine for a hydrogen in the methyl group attached to the benzene ring.

108. Water is produced in this reaction by removing an OH group from one substance and H from the other substance. There are two ways to do this:

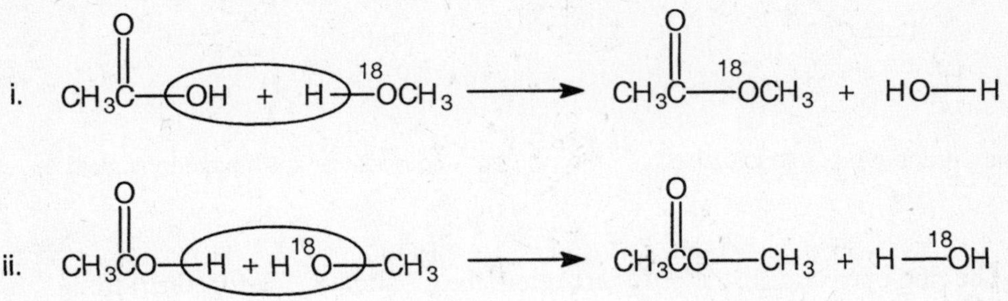

i.

ii.

Since the water produced is not radioactive, methyl acetate forms by the first reaction where all the oxygen-18 ends up in methyl acetate.

109. $85.63 \text{ g C} \times \dfrac{1 \text{ mol C}}{12.01 \text{ g C}} = 7.130 \text{ mol C}; \quad 14.37 \text{ g H} \times \dfrac{1 \text{ mol H}}{1.008 \text{ g H}} = 14.26 \text{ mol H}$

Since the mol H to mol C ratio is 2:1 ($14.26/7.130 = 2.000$), the empirical formula is CH_2. The empirical formula mass $\approx 12 + 2(1) = 14$. Since $4 \times 14 = 56$ puts the molar mass between 50 and 60, the molecular formula is C_4H_8.

The isomers of C_4H_8 are:

$CH_2\!=\!CHCH_2CH_3$

1-butene

$CH_3CH\!=\!CHCH_3$

2-butene

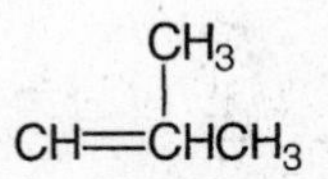

2-methyl-1-propene

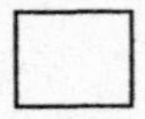

cyclobutane

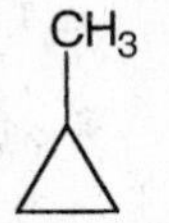

methylcyclopropane

Only the alkenes will react with H_2O to produce alcohols, and only 1-butene will produce a secondary alcohol for the major product and a primary alcohol for the minor product.

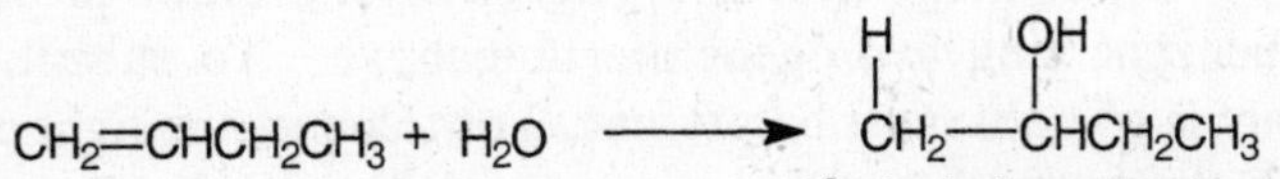

$CH_2\!=\!CHCH_2CH_3 + H_2O \longrightarrow$

$2°$ alcohol, major product

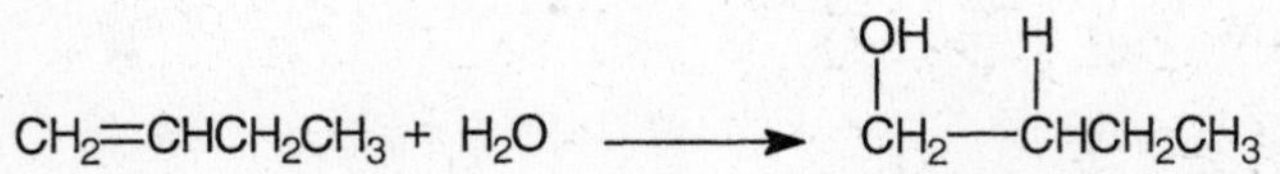

$CH_2\!=\!CHCH_2CH_3 + H_2O \longrightarrow$

$1°$ alcohol, minor product

2-butene will produce only a secondary alcohol when reacted with H_2O, and 2-methyl-1-propene will produce a tertiary alcohol as the major product and a primary alcohol as the minor product.

110.   At low temperatures, the polymer is coiled into balls. The forces between poly(lauryl metha-crylate) and oil molecules will be minimal and the effect on viscosity will be minimal. At higher temperatures, the chains of the polymer will unwind and become tangled with the oil molecules, increasing the viscosity of the oil. Thus, the presence of the polymer counteracts the temperature effect and the viscosity of the oil remains relatively constant.

111.   a.   The bond angles in the ring are about 60°. VSEPR predicts bond angles close to 109°. The bonding electrons are closer together than they prefer resulting is strong electron-electron repulsions. Thus, ethylene oxide is unstable (reactive).

        b.   The ring opens up during polymerization; the monomers link together through the formation of O–C bonds.

$$\left(\!-O—CH_2CH_2—O—CH_2CH_2—O—CH_2CH_2\!-\right)_{\!n}$$

112.

113.

114.   a.   The temperature of the rubber band increases when it is stretched.

        b.   Exothermic since heat is released.

        c.   As the chains are stretched, they line up more closely together resulting in stronger London dispersion forces between the chains. Heat is released as the strength of the intermolecular forces increases.

        d.   Stretching is not spontaneous so ΔG is positive. $\Delta G = \Delta H - T\Delta S$; Since ΔH is negative then ΔS must be negative in order to give a positive ΔG.

e.

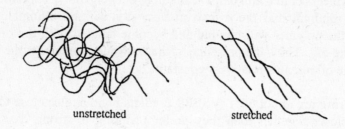

unstretched   stretched

The structure of the stretched polymer is more ordered (lower S).

115.   The structures, the types of intermolecular forces exerted and the boiling points for the compounds are:

$$CH_3CH_2CH_2\overset{\overset{\displaystyle O}{\|}}{C}OH$$

butanoic acid, 164°C
LD + dipole + H-bonding

$$CH_3CH_2CH_2CH_2CH_2OH$$

1-pentanol, 137°C
LD + H-bonding

$$CH_3CH_2CH_2CH_2\overset{\overset{\displaystyle O}{\|}}{C}H$$

pentanal, 103°C
LD + dipole

$$CH_3CH_2CH_2CH_2CH_2CH_3$$

n-hexane, 69°C
LD only

All these compounds have about the same molar mass. Therefore, the London dispersion (LD) forces in each are about the same. The other types of forces determine the boiling point order. Since butanoic acid and 1-pentanol both exhibit hydrogen bonding (H-bonding) interactions, then these two compounds will have the two highest boiling points. Butanoic acid has the highest boiling point since it exhibits H-bonding along with dipole-dipole forces due to the polar $C = O$ bond.

116.   a.

$$H_2N-CH_2-CO_2H + H_2N-CH_2-CO_2H \rightleftharpoons$$

$$H_2N-CH_2-\overset{\overset{\displaystyle O}{\|}}{C}-\underset{\underset{\displaystyle H}{|}}{N}-CH_2-CO_2H + H-O-H$$

Bonds broken: Bonds formed:

1 C – O (358 kJ/mol)   1 C – N (305 kJ/mol)
1 H – N (391 kJ/mol)   1 H – O (467 kJ/mol)

$\Delta H = 358 + 391 - (305 + 467) = -23$ kJ

b. ΔS for this process is negative (unfavorable) since order increases (disorder decreases).

c. ΔG = ΔH - TΔS; ΔG is positive because of the unfavorable entropy change. The reaction is not spontaneous.

117. ΔG = ΔH - TΔS; For the reaction, we break a P–O and O–H bond and form a P–O and O–H bond. Thus, ΔH ≈ 0. ΔS < 0, since 2 molecules are going to form one molecule (order increases). Thus, ΔG > 0 and the reaction is not spontaneous.

118   Both proteins and nucleic acids must form for life to exist. From the simple analysis, it looks as if life can't exist, an obviously incorrect assumption. A cell is not an isolated system. There is an external source of energy to drive the reactions. A photosynthetic plant uses sunlight and animals use the carbohydrates produced by plants as sources of energy. When all processes are combined, ΔS_{univ} must be greater than zero as is dictated by the second law of thermodynamics.

119. a. Even though this form of tartaric acid contains 2 chiral carbon atoms (see asterisks in the following structure), the mirror image of this form of tartaric acid is superimposable. Therefore, it is not optically active. One way to identify optical activity in molecules with two or more chiral carbon atoms is to look for a plane of symmetry in the molecule. If a molecule has a plane of symmetry, then it is never optically active. A plane of symmetry is a plane that bisects the molecule where one side exactly reflects on the other side.

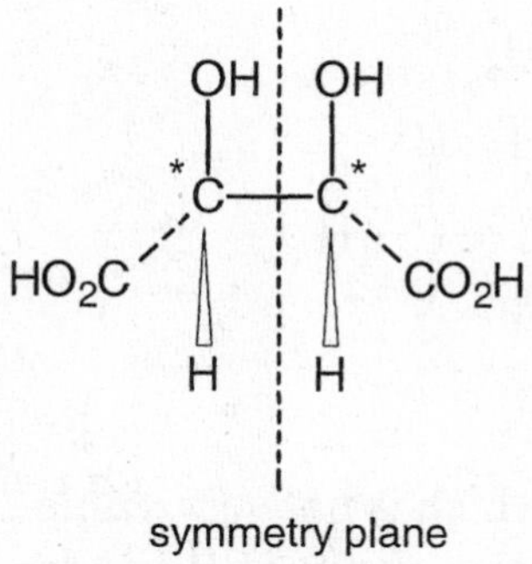

symmetry plane

b. The optically active forms of tartaric acid have no plane of symmetry. The structures of the optically active forms of tartaric acid are:

mirror

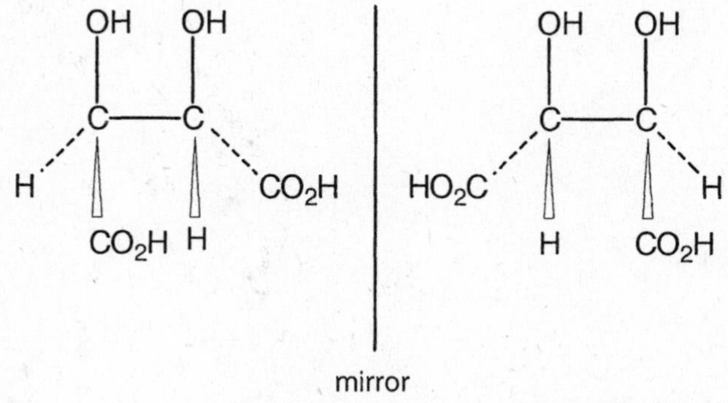

These two forms of tartaric acid are nonsuperimposable.

120. a. $^+H_3NCH_2COO^- + H_2O \rightleftharpoons H_2NCH_2CO_2^- + H_3O^+$

$$K_{eq} = K_a\,(-NH_3^+) = \frac{K_w}{K_b\,(-NH_2)} = \frac{1.0 \times 10^{-14}}{6.0 \times 10^{-5}} = 1.7 \times 10^{-10}$$

   b. $H_2NCH_2CO_2^- + H_2O \rightleftharpoons H_2NCH_2CO_2H + OH^-$

$$K_{eq} = K_b\,(-CO_2^-) = \frac{K_w}{K_a\,(-CO_2H)} = \frac{1.0 \times 10^{-14}}{4.3 \times 10^{-3}} = 2.3 \times 10^{-12}$$

   c. $^+H_3NCH_2CO_2H \rightleftharpoons 2\,H^+ + H_2NCH_2CO_2^-$

$$K_{eq} = K_a(-CO_2H) \times K_a(-NH_3^+) = (4.3 \times 10^{-3})(1.7 \times 10^{-10}) = 7.3 \times 10^{-13}$$

121.   For the reaction:

$$^+H_3NCH_2CO_2H \rightleftharpoons 2\,H^+ + H_2NCH_2CO_2^-   \quad K_{eq} = 7.3 \times 10^{-13} = K_a\,(-CO_2H) \times K_a\,(-NH_3^+)$$

$$7.3 \times 10^{-13} = \frac{[H^+]^2[H_2NCH_2CO_2^-]}{[^+H_3NCH_2CO_2H]} = [H^+]^2, \quad [H^+] = (7.3 \times 10^{-13})^{1/2}$$

$[H^+] = 8.5 \times 10^{-7}; \quad pH = -\log[H^+] = 6.07 = $ isoelectric point

122. B_2H_6 C_2H_6

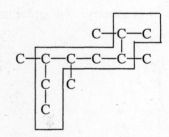

B_2H_6 has a 3-center bond, B-H-B, which is not very stable. The C-H and C-C bonds in C_2H_6 are much stronger and more stable than the B-H-B bonds.

123. a.

C—C—C
C—C—C—C—C—C
C C
C

2,3,5,6-tetramethyloctane

b.

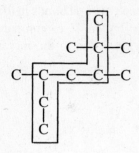

2,2,3,5-tetramethylheptane

c.

2,3,4-trimethylhexane

d.

3-methyl-1-pentyne

124.

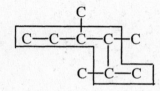

H—C—C—Ö—H   ethanol

H—C—Ö—C—H   dimethyl ether

H—C—C—Ö—H →^oxidation H—C—C—H →^oxidation H—C—C—OH

ethanal   ethanoic acid

125.   In nylon, hydrogen bonding interactions occur due to the presence of N–H bonds in the polymer. For a given polymer chain length, there are more N–H groups in Nylon-46 as compared to Nylon-6. Hence, Nylon-46 forms a stronger polymer compared to Nylon-6 due to the increased hydrogen bonding interactions.

Challenge Problems

126.   One of the resonance structures for benzene is:

To break $C_6H_6(g)$ into $C(g)$ and $H(g)$ requires the breaking of 6 C–H bonds, 3 C=C bonds and 3 C–C bonds:

$$C_6H_6(g) \rightarrow 6\ C(g) + 6\ H(g) \quad \Delta H = 6\ D_{C-H} + 3\ D_{C=C} + 3\ D_{C-C}$$

$$\Delta H = 6(413\ kJ) + 3(614\ kJ) + 3(347\ kJ) = 5361\ kJ$$

The question wants ΔH_f° for $C_6H_6(g)$ which is ΔH for the reaction:

$$6\ C(s) + 3\ H_2(g) \rightarrow C_6H_6(g) \quad \Delta H = \Delta H_{f,\ C_6H_6(g)}^\circ$$

To calculate ΔH for this reaction, we will use Hess's law along with the ΔH_f° value for $C(g)$ and the bond energy value for H_2 ($D_{H_2} = 432\ kJ/mol$).

$$
\begin{array}{ll}
6\ C(g) + 6\ H(g) \rightarrow C_6H_6(g) & \Delta H_1 = \text{-}5361\ kJ \\
6\ C(s) \rightarrow 6\ C(g) & \Delta H_2 = 6(717\ kJ) \\
3\ H_2(g) \rightarrow 6\ H(g) & \Delta H_3 = 3(432\ kJ) \\
\hline
6\ C(s) + 3\ H_2(g) \rightarrow C_6H_6(g) & \Delta H = \Delta H_1 + \Delta H_2 + \Delta H_3 = 237\ kJ;\quad \Delta H_{f,\ C_6H_6(g)}^\circ = 237\ kJ/mol
\end{array}
$$

The experimental ΔH_f° value for $C_6H_6(g)$ is more stable (lower in energy) by 154 kJ as compared to the ΔH_f° value calculated from bond energies (83 - 237 = -154 kJ). This extra stability is related to benzene's ability to exhibit resonance. Two equivalent Lewis structures can be drawn for benzene. The π bonding system implied by each Lewis structure consists of three localized π bonds. This is not correct as all C–C bonds in benzene are equivalent. We say the π electrons in benzene are delocalized over the entire surface of C_6H_6 (see Section 14.5 of the text). The large discrepancy between ΔH_f° values is due to the delocalized π electrons, whose effects were not accounted for in the calculated ΔH_f° value. The extra stability associated with benzene can be called resonance stabilization. In general, molecules that exhibit resonance are usually more stable than predicted using bond energies.

127.   a.   The three structural isomers of C_5H_{12} are:

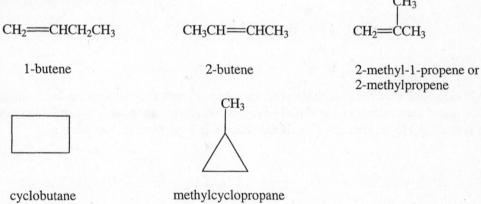

n-pentane will form three different monochlorination products: 1-chloropentane, 2-chloro-pentane and 3-chloropentane (the other possible monochlorination products differ by a simple rotation of the molecule; they are not different products from the ones listed).

2-2,dimethylpropane will only form one monochlorination product: 1-chloro-2,2-dimethyl-propane. 2-methylbutane is the isomer of C_5H_{12} that forms four different monochlorination products: 1-chloro-2-methylbutane, 2-chloro-2-methylbutane, 3-chloro-2-methylbutane (or we could name this compound as 2-chloro-3-methylbutane), and 1-chloro-3-methylbutane.

   b.   The isomers of C_4H_8 are:

$$CH_2{=\!=}CHCH_2CH_3 \qquad\qquad CH_3CH{=\!=}CHCH_3 \qquad\qquad CH_2{=\!=}\overset{\displaystyle CH_3}{\underset{\displaystyle |}{C}}CH_3$$

1-butene   2-butene   2-methyl-1-propene or
                                                                  2-methylpropene

cyclobutane   methylcyclopropane

The cyclic structures will not react with H_2O; only the alkenes will add H_2O to the double bond. From Exercise 22.44, the major product of the reaction of 1-butene and H_2O is 2-butanol (a 2° alcohol). 2-butanol is also the major (and only) product when 2-butene and H_2O react. 2-methylpropene forms 2-methyl-2-propanol as the major product when reacted with H_2O; this product is a tertiary alcohol. Therefore, the C_4H_8 isomer is 2-methylpropene.

$$CH_2{=\!=}\overset{\displaystyle CH_3}{\underset{\displaystyle |}{C}}{-\!-}CH_3 \;+\; HOH \;\longrightarrow\; CH_3{-\!-}\overset{\displaystyle CH_3}{\underset{\displaystyle \underset{\displaystyle OH}{|}}{C}}{-\!-}CH_3$$

2-methyl-2-propanol
(a 3° alcohol, 3 R
groups)

c. The structure of 1-chloro-1-methylcyclohexane is:

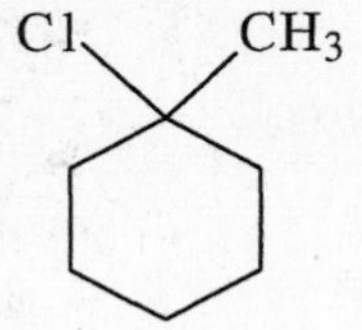

The addition reaction of HCl with an alkene is a likely choice for this reaction (see Exercise 22.44). The two isomers of C_7H_{12} that produce 1-chloro-1-methylcyclohexane as the major product are:

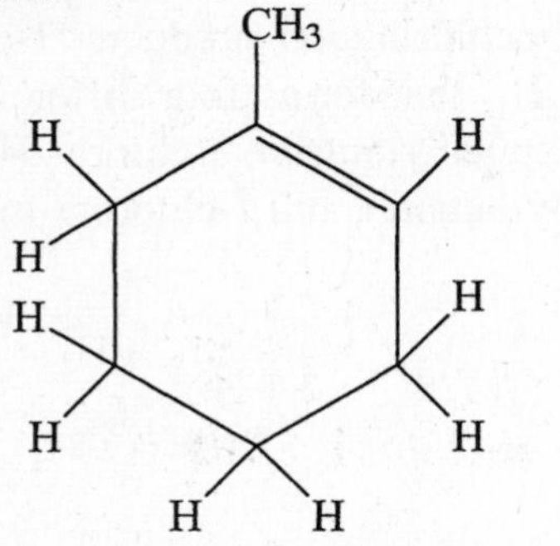

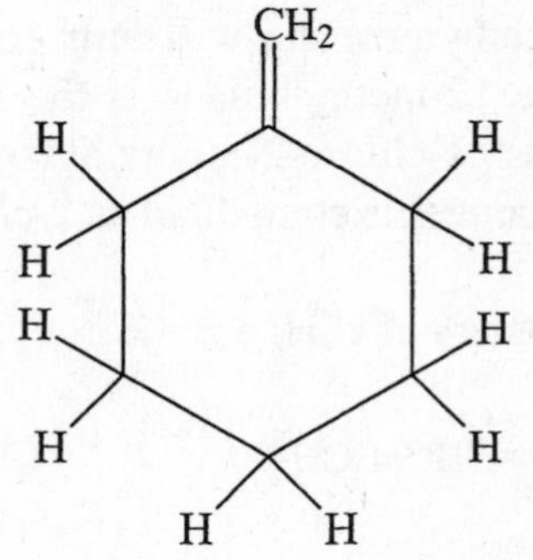

d. Working backwards, 2° alcohols produce ketones when they are oxidized (1° alcohols produce aldehydes, then carboxylic acids). The easiest way to produce the 2° alcohol from a hydrocarbon is to add H_2O to an alkene. The alkene reacted is 1-propene (or propene).

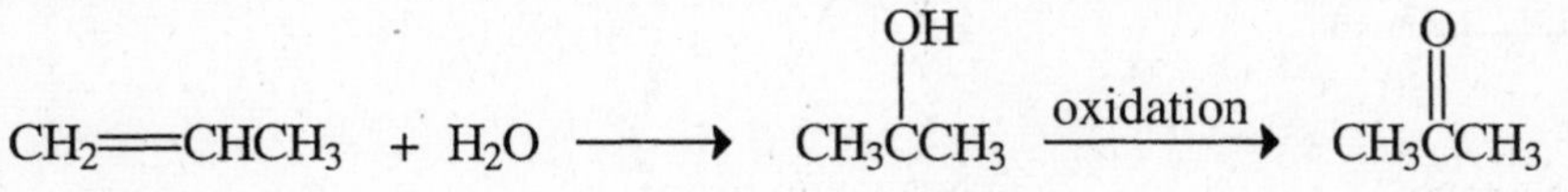

e. The $C_5H_{12}O$ formula has too many hydrogens to be anything other than an alcohol (or an unreactive ether). 1° alcohols are first oxidized to aldehydes, then to carboxylic acids. Therefore, we want a 1° alcohol. The 1° alcohols with formula $C_5H_{12}O$ are:

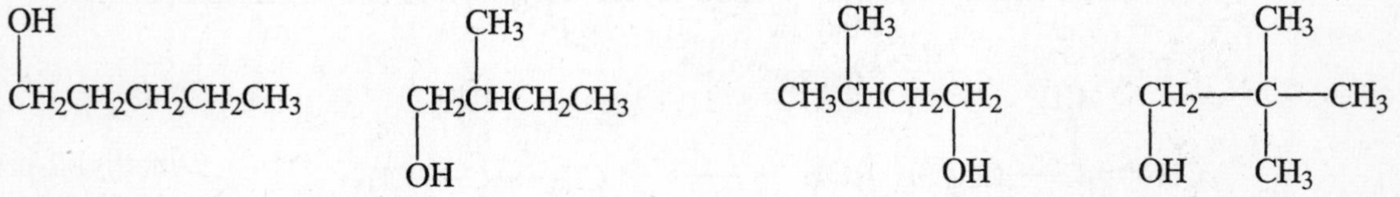

1-pentanol	2-methyl-1-butanol	3-methyl-1-butanol	2,2-dimethyl-1-propanol

There are other alcohols with formula $C_5H_{12}O$, but they are all 2° or 3° alcohols, which do not produce carboxylic acids when oxidized.

128.   a.

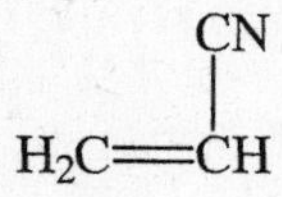

acrylonitrile 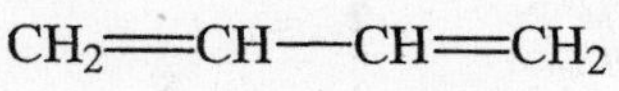   butadiene 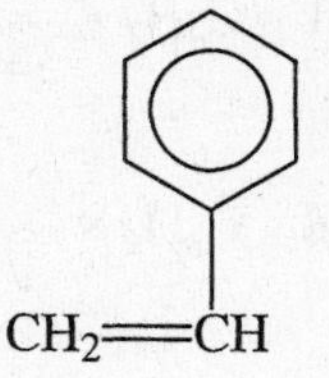   styrene

The structure of ABS plastic assuming a 1:1:1 mol ratio is:

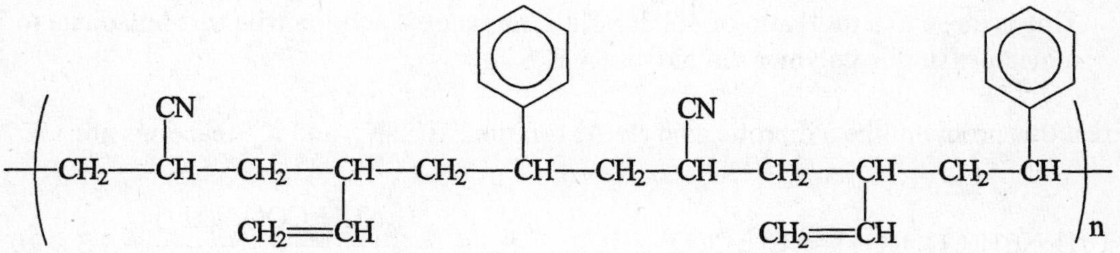

Note: Butadiene does not polymerize in a linear fashion in ABS plastic (unlike other butadiene polymers). There is no way for you to be able to predict this.

b.   Only acrylonitrile contains nitrogen. If we have 100.00 g of polymer:

$$8.80 \text{ g N} \times \frac{1 \text{ mol C}_3\text{H}_3\text{N}}{14.01 \text{ g N}} \times \frac{53.06 \text{ g C}_3\text{H}_3\text{N}}{1 \text{ mol C}_3\text{H}_3\text{N}} = 33.3 \text{ g C}_3\text{H}_3\text{N}$$

$$\% \text{ C}_3\text{H}_3\text{N} = \frac{33.3 \text{ g C}_3\text{H}_3\text{N}}{100.00 \text{ g polymer}} = 33.3\% \text{ C}_3\text{H}_3\text{N}$$

Br_2 adds to double bonds of alkenes (benzene's delocalized π bonds in the styrene monomer will not react with Br_2 unless a special catalyst is present). Only butadiene in the polymer has a reactive double bond. From the polymer structure in part a, butadiene will react in a 1:1 mol ratio with Br_2.

$$0.605 \text{ g Br}_2 \times \frac{1 \text{ mol Br}_2}{159.8 \text{ g Br}_2} \times \frac{1 \text{ mol C}_4\text{H}_6}{\text{mol Br}_2} \times \frac{54.09 \text{ g C}_4\text{H}_6}{\text{mol C}_4\text{H}_6} = 0.205 \text{ g C}_4\text{H}_6$$

$$\% \text{ C}_4\text{H}_6 = \frac{0.205 \text{ g}}{1.20 \text{ g}} \times 100 = 17.1\% \text{ C}_4\text{H}_6$$

$\% \text{ styrene (C}_8\text{H}_8) = 100.0 - 33.3 - 17.1 = 49.6\% \text{ C}_8\text{H}_8$.

c.   If we have 100.0 g of polymer:

$$33.3 \text{ g C}_3\text{H}_3\text{N} \times \frac{1 \text{ mol C}_3\text{H}_3\text{N}}{53.06 \text{ g}} = 0.628 \text{ mol C}_3\text{H}_3\text{N}$$

$$17.1 \text{ g } C_4H_6 \times \frac{1 \text{ mol } C_4H_6}{54.09 \text{ g } C_4H_6} = 0.316 \text{ mol } C_4H_6$$

$$49.6 \text{ g } C_8H_8 \times \frac{1 \text{ mol } C_8H_8}{104.14 \text{ g } C_8H_8} = 0.476 \text{ mol } C_8H_8$$

Dividing by 0.316:

$$\frac{0.628}{0.316} = 1.99; \quad \frac{0.316}{0.316} = 1.00; \quad \frac{0.476}{0.316} = 1.51$$

This is close to a mol ratio of 4:2:3.   Thus, there are 4 acrylonitrile to 2 butadiene to 3 styrene molecules in this polymer sample; or $(A_4B_2S_3)_n$.

129.   Treat this problem like a diprotic acid (H_2A) titration. The K_{a1} and K_{a2} reactions are:

$$H_3\overset{+}{N}CH_2COOH \rightleftharpoons H_3\overset{+}{N}CH_2COO^- + H^+ \qquad K_{a1} = \frac{[H_2\overset{+}{N}CH_2COO^-][H^+]}{[H_3\overset{+}{N}CH_2COOH]} = 4.3 \times 10^{-3}$$

$$H_3\overset{+}{N}CH_2COO^- \rightleftharpoons H_2NCH_2COO^- + H^+ \qquad K_{a2} = \frac{[H_2NCH_2COO^-][H^+]}{[H_3\overset{+}{N}CH_2COO^-]}$$

$$K_{a2} = \frac{K_w}{K_b} = \frac{1.0 \times 10^{-14}}{6.0 \times 10^{-5}} = 1.7 \times 10^{-10}$$

As OH^- is added, it reacts completely with the best acid present. From 0 - 50.0 mL of OH^- added, the reaction is:

$$H_3\overset{+}{N}CH_2COOH + OH^- \rightarrow H_3\overset{+}{N}CH_2COO^- + H_2O$$

At 50.0 mL OH^- added (the first equivalence point), all of the $H_3\overset{+}{N}CH_2COOH$ has been converted into $H_3\overset{+}{N}CH_2COO^-$. This is an amphoteric species. To determine the pH when an amphoteric species is the major species present, we use the formula pH = $(pK_{a1} + pK_{a2})/2$. From 50.1 - 100.0 mL of OH^- added, the reaction that occurs is:

$$H_3\overset{+}{N}CH_2COO^- + OH^- \rightarrow H_2NCH_2COO^- + H_2O$$

100.0 mL of OH^- added represents the second equivalence point where $H_2NCH_2COO^-$ is the major amino acid species present.

a.   25.0 mL of OH⁻ added represents the first halfway point to equivalence. Here, $[H_3\overset{+}{N}CH_2COOH]$ = $[H_3\overset{+}{N}CH_2COO^-]$. This is a buffer solution where $pH = pK_{a1}$. At 25.0 mL OH⁻ added:

$$pH = pK_{a1} = -\log 4.3 \times 10^{-3} = 2.37$$

50.0 mL of OH⁻ added represents the first equivalence point. Here, $H_3\overset{+}{N}CH_2COO^-$ is the major amino acid species present. This is amphoteric species. At 50.0 mL OH⁻ added:

$$pH = \frac{pK_{a1} + pK_{a2}}{2} = \frac{2.37 - \log 1.7 \times 10^{-10}}{2} = \frac{2.37 + 9.77}{2} = 6.07$$

75.0 mL of OH⁻ added represents the second halfway point to equivalence. Here, $[H_3\overset{+}{N}CH_2COO^-] = [H_2NCH_2COO^-]$ and $pH = pK_{a2}$. At 75.0 mL OH⁻ added:

$$pH = pK_{a2} = -\log 1.7 \times 10^{-10} = 9.77$$

b.

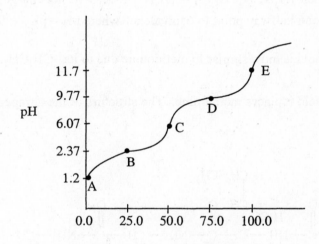

The major amino acid species present are:

      point A (0.0 mL OH⁻): $H_3\overset{+}{N}CH_2COOH$

      point B (25.0 mL OH⁻): $H_3\overset{+}{N}CH_2COOH$ and $H_3\overset{+}{N}CH_2COO^-$

      point C (50.0 mL OH⁻): $H_3\overset{+}{N}CH_2COO^-$

      point D (75.0 mL OH⁻): $H_3\overset{+}{N}CH_2COO^-$ and $H_2NCH_2COO^-$

      point E (100.0 mL OH⁻): $H_2NCH_2COO^-$

c. The various charged amino acid species are:

$H_3\overset{+}{N}CH_2COOH$ net charge = +1

$H_3\overset{+}{N}CH_2COO^-$ net charge = 0

$H_2NCH_2COO^-$ net charge = -1

The net charge is zero at the pH when the major amino acid species present is the $H_3\overset{+}{N}CH_2COO^-$ form; this happens at the first equivalence point in our titration problem. From part a, this occurs at pH = 6.07 (the isoelectric point).

d. The net charge is +1/2 when $[H_3\overset{+}{N}CH_2COOH] = [H_3\overset{+}{N}CH_2COO^-]$; net charge = (+1 + 0)/2 = +1/2. This occurs at the first half-way point to equivalence where pH = pK_{a1} = 2.37. The net charge is -1/2 when $[H_3\overset{+}{N}CH_2COO^-] = [H_3NCH_2COO^-]$; net charge = (0 - 1)/2 = -1/2. This occurs at the second halfway point to equivalence where pH = pK_{a2} = 9.77.

130.   a. The new amino acid is most similar to methionine due to its $-CH_2CH_2SCH_3$ R group.

b. The new amino acid replaces methionine. The structure of the tetrapeptide is:

c.   The chiral carbons are indicated with an asterisk.

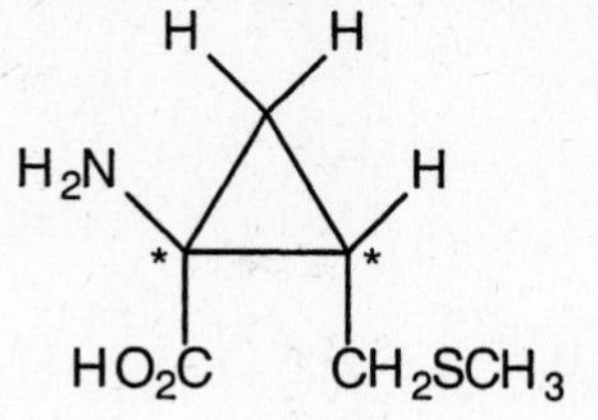

d.   Geometric isomers are possible because there are 2 carbons in the ring structure that each have two different groups bonded to them. The geometric isomers are:

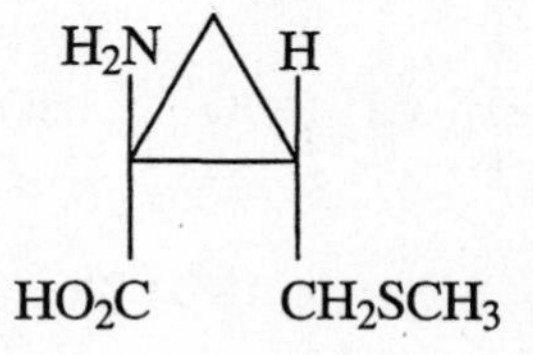

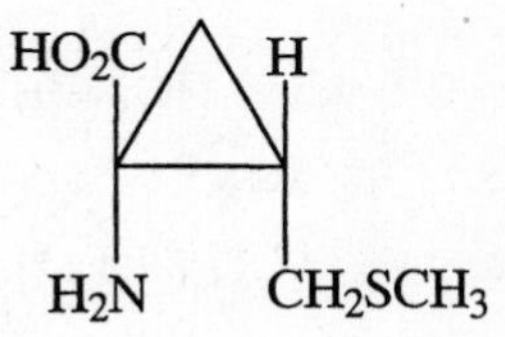

In the first structure, CO_2H and CH_2SCH_3 are on the same side of the ring plane; in the second structure, CO_2H and CH_2SCH_3 are on opposite sides of the ring plane.